Educational Psychology

Educational Psychology

Theory and Practice

SIXTH EDITION

Robert E. Slavin

Johns Hopkins University

ALLYN AND BACON

BOSTON • LONDON • TORONTO • SYDNEY • TOKYO • SINGAPORE

Vice President, Editor in Chief, Education: Paul A. Smith
Editorial Assistant: Jill Jeffrey
Senior Development Editor: Linda Bieze
Director of Education Programs: Ellen Mann Dolberg
Marketing Manager: Brad Parkins
Editorial-Production Administrator: Annette Joseph
Text Designer: Carol Somberg/Omegatype Typography, Inc.
Editorial-Production Service
and Electronic Composition: Omegatype Typography, Inc.
Photo Editor: Susan Duane
Composition and Prepress Buyer: Linda Cox
Manufacturing Buyer: Megan Cochran
Cover Administrator: Linda Knowles
Cover Designer: Studio Nine

Between the time Website information is gathered and then published, it is not unusual for some sites to have closed. Also, the transcription of URLs can result in unintended typographical errors. The publisher would appreciate notification where these occur so that they may be corrected in subsequent editions. Thank you.

Library of Congress Cataloging-in-Publication Data

Slavin, Robert E.
  Educational Psychology : theory and practice / Robert E. Slavin —
6th ed.
      p.   cm.
  Includes bibliographical references and indexes.
  ISBN 0-205-29270-4 (alk. paper)
  1. Educational psychology.   I. Title.
LB1051.S615   2000
370.15—dc21
                                        99-20561
                                        CIP

Printed in the United States of America
10 9 8 7 6 5 4 3 2 1   04 03 02 01 00 99

Text and photo credits continue on page 596, which constitutes a continuation of the copyright page.

BRIEF CONTENTS

1. Educational Psychology: A Foundation for Teaching   1

2. Theories of Development   26

3. Development during Childhood and Adolescence   66

4. Student Diversity   104

5. Behavioral Theories of Learning   138

6. Cognitive Theories of Learning: Basic Concepts   172

7. The Effective Lesson   216

8. Student-Centered and Constructivist Approaches to Instruction   252

9. Accommodating Instruction to Meet Individual Needs   288

10. Motivating Students to Learn   324

11. Effective Learning Environments   362

12. Learners with Exceptionalities   404

13. Assessing Student Learning   452

14. Standardized Tests and Grades   496

Gratis

99341

CONTENTS

Features   xv
Preface   xvii
About the Author   xxv

CHAPTER 1

Educational Psychology: A Foundation for Teaching   1

WHAT MAKES A GOOD TEACHER?   3
Knowing the Subject Matters (but So Does Teaching Skill)   4
Mastering the Teaching Skills   4
Can Good Teaching Be Taught?   5

TEACHERS IN ACTION: *How have educational psychology theory and research helped you in your teaching?*   6
The Intentional Teacher   7

THE INTENTIONAL TEACHER   *Guiding Questions to Help You Improve Teaching and Learning*   11

WHAT IS THE ROLE OF RESEARCH IN EDUCATIONAL PSYCHOLOGY?   11
Goals of Research in Educational Psychology   12
The Value of Research in Educational Psychology to the Teacher   12
Teaching As Decision Making   13

Theory *into* Practice: *Teaching As Decision Making*   14
Research + Common Sense = Effective Teaching   15
Research on Effective Programs   15
Impact of Research on Educational Practice   16

Theory *into* Practice: *How to Be an Intelligent Consumer of Educational Psychology Research*   16

WHAT RESEARCH METHODS ARE USED IN EDUCATIONAL PSYCHOLOGY?   18
Experiments   18
Correlational Studies   20

CASE TO CONSIDER: *Evaluating Curriculum in the Classroom: Some Research of Our Own*   22
Descriptive Research   23

CHAPTER 2

Theories of Development   26

WHAT ARE SOME VIEWS OF HUMAN DEVELOPMENT?   28
Aspects of Development   28
Issues of Development   29

HOW DID PIAGET VIEW COGNITIVE DEVELOPMENT?   30
How Development Occurs   30
Piaget's Stages of Development   32

HOW IS PIAGET'S WORK VIEWED TODAY?   40
Criticisms and Revisions of Piaget's Theory   40

Theory *into* Practice: *Educational Implications of Piaget's Theory*   41
Neo-Piagetian and Information-Processing Views of Development   42

HOW DID VYGOTSKY VIEW COGNITIVE DEVELOPMENT?   43
How Development Occurs   43

TEACHERS IN ACTION: *How has your knowledge of child development helped you to make instruction developmentally appropriate?*   44
Applications of Vygotskian Theory in Teaching   46

Theory *into* Practice: *Classroom Applications of Vygotsky's Theory*   47

HOW DID ERIKSON VIEW PERSONAL AND SOCIAL DEVELOPMENT?   48
Stages of Psychosocial Development   48
Implications and Criticisms of Erikson's Theory   51

WHAT ARE SOME THEORIES OF MORAL DEVELOPMENT?   52
Piaget's Theory of Moral Development   52
Kohlberg's Stages of Moral Reasoning   54

Theory *into* Practice: *Fostering Moral Development in the Classroom*   56
Criticisms of Kohlberg's Theory   57

THE INTENTIONAL TEACHER   *Using What You Know about Human Development to Improve Teaching and Learning*   58
Hoffman's Development of Moral Behavior   60

CASE TO CONSIDER: *Cheating and Moral Orientations*   61

CHAPTER 3

Development during Childhood and Adolescence   66

HOW DO CHILDREN DEVELOP DURING THE PRESCHOOL YEARS? 69

Physical Development in Early Childhood 70

Language Acquisition 71

CASE TO CONSIDER: *I CN SPL* 74

Bilingual Education 74

Theory *into* Practice: *Promoting Language Development in Young Children* 75

Socioemotional Development 76

WHAT KINDS OF EARLY CHILDHOOD EDUCATION PROGRAMS EXIST? 79

Day-Care Programs 79

Nursery Schools 79

Compensatory Preschool Programs 80

Early Intervention 80

Kindergarten Programs 81

Developmentally Appropriate Practice 81

TEACHERS IN ACTION: *How has your knowledge of child development helped you to make instruction developmentally appropriate?* 82

HOW DO CHILDREN DEVELOP DURING THE ELEMENTARY YEARS? 83

Physical Development during Middle Childhood 84

Cognitive Abilities 84

Socioemotional Development in Middle Childhood 84

Theory *into* Practice: *Applying Hoffman's Theories* 85

Theory *into* Practice: *Promoting the Development of Self-Esteem* 87

Theory *into* Practice: *Helping Children Develop Social Skills* 89

HOW DO CHILDREN DEVELOP DURING THE MIDDLE SCHOOL AND HIGH SCHOOL YEARS? 90

Physical Development during Adolescence 90

Cognitive Development 90

Characteristics of Hypothetical–Deductive Reasoning 91

Implications for Educational Practice 92

Socioemotional Development in Adolescence 93

Identity Development 93

Marcia's Four Identity Statuses 94

Self-Concept and Self-Esteem 94

Social Relationships 95

Emotional Development 96

Problems of Adolescence 96

THE INTENTIONAL TEACHER *Using What You Know about Early Childhood, Middle Childhood, and Adolescent Students to Improve Teaching and Learning* 98

Theory *into* Practice: *Providing Developmental Assets for Adolescents* 99

CHAPTER 4

Student Diversity   104

WHAT IS THE IMPACT OF CULTURE ON TEACHING AND LEARNING? 106

HOW DOES SOCIOECONOMIC STATUS AFFECT STUDENT ACHIEVEMENT? 107

The Role of Child-Rearing Practices 109

The Link between Income and Summer Learning 109

The Role of Schools As Middle-Class Institutions 109

School and Community Factors 110

CASE TO CONSIDER: *What Would You Do, Mrs. Brown?* 111

Is the Low Achievement of Children from Low-Income Groups Inevitable? 112

Implications for Teachers 112

HOW DO ETHNICITY AND RACE AFFECT STUDENTS' SCHOOL EXPERIENCES? 113

Racial and Ethnic Composition of the United States 113

Academic Achievement of Minority-Group Students 113

Why Have Minority-Group Students Lagged in Achievement? 115

Effects of School Desegregation 116

Theory *into* Practice: *Teaching in a Culturally Diverse School* 117

HOW DO LANGUAGE DIFFERENCES AND BILINGUAL PROGRAMS AFFECT STUDENT ACHIEVEMENT? 119

Bilingual Education 119

Effectiveness of Bilingual Programs 120

WHAT IS MULTICULTURAL EDUCATION? 122

Dimensions of Multicultural Education 122

HOW DO GENDER AND GENDER BIAS AFFECT STUDENTS' SCHOOL EXPERIENCES? 123

TEACHERS IN ACTION: *How do you foster social acceptance and multicultural awareness?* 124

Do Males and Females Think and Learn Differently? 125

Sex-Role Stereotyping and Gender Bias 126

Theory *into* Practice: *Avoiding Gender Bias in Teaching* 127

HOW DO STUDENTS DIFFER IN INTELLIGENCE AND LEARNING STYLES?   128

Definitions of Intelligence   129

Theory *into* Practice: *Multiple Intelligences*   130

Origins of Intelligence   131

THE INTENTIONAL TEACHER   *Using What You Know about Student Diversity to Improve Teaching and Learning*   132

Theories of Learning Styles   134

Aptitude–Treatment Interactions   134

CHAPTER 5

Behavioral Theories of Learning   138

WHAT IS LEARNING?   140

WHAT BEHAVIORAL LEARNING THEORIES HAVE EVOLVED?   142

Pavlov: Classical Conditioning   142

Thorndike: The Law of Effect   143

Skinner: Operant Conditioning   144

WHAT ARE SOME PRINCIPLES OF BEHAVIORAL LEARNING?   146

The Role of Consequences   146

Reinforcers   146

Theory *into* Practice: *Classroom Uses of Reinforcement*   148

Intrinsic and Extrinsic Reinforcers   149

Theory *into* Practice: *Practical Reinforcers*   149

Punishers   150

Immediacy of Consequences   151

Shaping   153

Extinction   153

Schedules of Reinforcement   155

Maintenance   157

The Role of Antecedents   158

CASE TO CONSIDER: *Kindergarten Is Big Business*   159

THE INTENTIONAL TEACHER   *Using What You Know about Behavioral Theories of Learning to Improve Teaching and Learning*   160

HOW HAS SOCIAL LEARNING THEORY CONTRIBUTED TO OUR UNDERSTANDING OF HUMAN LEARNING?   163

Bandura: Modeling and Observational Learning   163

Theory *into* Practice: *Observational Learning*   165

Meichenbaum's Model of Self-Regulated Learning   166

TEACHERS IN ACTION: *How have you applied behavioral and social learning theories in your teaching?*   168

Strengths and Limitations of Behavioral Learning Theories   169

CHAPTER 6

Cognitive Theories of Learning: Basic Concepts   172

WHAT IS AN INFORMATION-PROCESSING MODEL?   175

Sensory Register   175

Short-Term or Working Memory   177

Long-Term Memory   180

Factors That Enhance Long-Term Memory   183

Other Information-Processing Models   184

WHAT CAUSES PEOPLE TO REMEMBER OR FORGET?   187

Forgetting and Remembering   187

Theory *into* Practice: *Reducing Retroactive Inhibition*   188

Practice   192

TEACHERS IN ACTION: *What strategies have you used to help students process and retain new learning?*   193

HOW CAN MEMORY STRATEGIES BE TAUGHT?   194

Verbal Learning   194

Paired-Associate Learning   195

Serial and Free-Recall Learning   196

WHAT MAKES INFORMATION MEANINGFUL?   197

Theory *into* Practice: *Meaning versus Abstract Material*   198

Rote versus Meaningful Learning   199

Schema Theory   200

CASE TO CONSIDER: *Knowledge and Learning How to Learn*   201

HOW DO METACOGNITIVE SKILLS HELP STUDENTS LEARN?   203

WHAT STUDY STRATEGIES HELP STUDENTS LEARN?   204

Note-Taking   204

Underlining   205

Summarizing   205

Outlining and Mapping   205

The PQ4R Method   206

Theory *into* Practice: *Teaching the PQ4R Method*   206

HOW DO COGNITIVE TEACHING STRATEGIES HELP STUDENTS LEARN?   206

Making Learning Relevant and Activating Prior Knowledge   207

Organizing Information   209

THE INTENTIONAL TEACHER   *Using What You Know about Cognitive Theories of Learning to Improve Teaching and Learning*   210

CHAPTER 7

The Effective Lesson 216

WHAT IS DIRECT INSTRUCTION? 220

HOW IS A DIRECT INSTRUCTION LESSON TAUGHT? 221

State Learning Objectives 221

Theory *into* Practice: *Planning a Lesson* 221

Orient Students to the Lesson 222

Theory *into* Practice: *Communicating Objectives to Students* 225

Review Prerequisites 225

Present New Material 226

Conduct Learning Probes 228

Provide Independent Practice 232

Assess Performance and Provide Feedback 233

Provide Distributed Practice and Review 234

WHAT DOES RESEARCH ON DIRECT INSTRUCTION METHODS SUGGEST? 235

Advantages and Limitations of Direct Instruction 236

HOW DO STUDENTS LEARN AND TRANSFER CONCEPTS? 236

Concept Learning and Teaching 236

CASE TO CONSIDER: *How Can You Cover It All?* 237

Teaching for Transfer of Learning 238

HOW ARE DISCUSSIONS USED IN INSTRUCTION? 242

Subjective and Controversial Topics 242

Difficult and Novel Concepts 242

Affective Objectives 242

Whole-Class Discussions 243

TEACHERS IN ACTION: *What strategies have you applied to make direct instruction most effective?* 245

THE INTENTIONAL TEACHER *Using What You Know about Direct Instruction to Improve Teaching and Learning* 246

Small-Group Discussions 246

CHAPTER 8

Student-Centered and Constructivist Approaches to Instruction 252

WHAT IS THE CONSTRUCTIVIST VIEW OF LEARNING? 255

Historical Roots of Constructivism 256

Top-Down Processing 257

Cooperative Learning 259

Discovery Learning 259

Theory *into* Practice: *Discovery Learning in the Classroom* 260

Self-Regulated Learning 260

Scaffolding 261

APA's Learner-Centered Psychological Principles 262

Constructivist Methods in the Content Areas 263

CASE TO CONSIDER: *Teaching First-Graders to Regulate Their Learning* 265

Theory *into* Practice: *Introducing Reciprocal Teaching* 266

Research on Constructivist Methods 268

HOW IS COOPERATIVE LEARNING USED IN INSTRUCTION? 268

Cooperative Learning Methods 269

Theory *into* Practice: *Student Teams–Achievement Divisions (STAD)* 269

Theory *into* Practice: *Using Constructivist Methods to Help Students Develop Self-Understanding* 272

Research on Cooperative Learning 273

TEACHERS IN ACTION: *How have you applied student-centered or constructivist approaches in your teaching?* 275

HOW ARE PROBLEM-SOLVING AND THINKING SKILLS TAUGHT? 276

The Problem-Solving Process 276

Obstacles to Problem Solving 278

Teaching Creative Problem Solving 279

Teaching Thinking Skills 280

Critical Thinking 283

THE INTENTIONAL TEACHER *Using What You Know about Student-Centered and Constructivist Approaches to Improve Teaching and Learning* 284

CHAPTER 9

Accommodating Instruction to Meet Individual Needs 288

WHAT ARE ELEMENTS OF EFFECTIVE INSTRUCTION BEYOND A GOOD LESSON? 290

Carroll's Model of School Learning and QAIT 291

HOW ARE STUDENTS GROUPED TO ACCOMMODATE ACHIEVEMENT DIFFERENCES? 294

Between-Class Ability Grouping 295

Untracking 298

Regrouping for Reading and Mathematics 299

Nongraded (Cross-Age Grouping) Elementary Schools 299

Within-Class Ability Grouping 299

WHAT IS MASTERY LEARNING? 301

Forms of Mastery Learning 301

Theory *into* Practice: *Applying the Principles of Mastery Learning* 301

Research on Mastery Learning 303

WHAT ARE SOME WAYS OF INDIVIDUALIZING INSTRUCTION? 304

Peer Tutoring 304

Adult Tutoring 305

Theory *into* Practice: *Effectively Using Tutoring Methods to Meet Individual Needs* 306

Programmed Instruction 307

Computer-Based Instruction 307

TEACHERS IN ACTION: *What strategies have you used to meet students' individual needs for instruction?* 308

CASE TO CONSIDER: *Individualization and Computers: Two Perspectives* 312

THE INTENTIONAL TEACHER *Using What You Know about Accommodating Instruction to Meet Individual Needs* 314

WHAT EDUCATIONAL PROGRAMS EXIST FOR STUDENTS PLACED AT RISK? 316

Compensatory Education Programs 317

Early Intervention Programs 319

CHAPTER 10

Motivating Students to Learn 324

WHAT IS MOTIVATION? 327

WHAT ARE SOME THEORIES OF MOTIVATION? 328

Motivation and Behavioral Learning Theory 328

Motivation and Human Needs 329

Motivation and Attribution Theory 331

Theory *into* Practice: *Giving Students Motivating Feedback* 335

Motivation and Expectancy Theory 335

HOW CAN ACHIEVEMENT MOTIVATION BE ENHANCED? 337

Motivation and Goal Orientations 337

Learned Helplessness and Attribution Training 340

Theory *into* Practice: *Helping Students Overcome Learned Helplessness* 341

Teacher Expectations and Achievement 341

Anxiety and Achievement 343

HOW CAN TEACHERS INCREASE STUDENTS' MOTIVATION TO LEARN? 343

Intrinsic and Extrinsic Motivation 344

How Can Teachers Enhance Intrinsic Motivation? 346

TEACHERS IN ACTION: *How have you dealt with motivational challenges in your classroom?* 347

Principles for Providing Extrinsic Incentives to Learn 349

THE INTENTIONAL TEACHER *Using What You Know about Motivation to Improve Teaching and Learning* 350

HOW CAN TEACHERS REWARD PERFORMANCE, EFFORT, AND IMPROVEMENT? 353

Using Praise Effectively 353

Teaching Students to Praise Themselves 354

Using Grades As Incentives 355

Individual Learning Expectations 355

Theory *into* Practice: *Computing ILE Base Scores and Improvement Points* 355

Incentive Systems Based on Goal Structure 357

CASE TO CONSIDER: *Motivating a Reluctant Student* 358

CHAPTER 11

Effective Learning Environments 362

WHAT IS AN EFFECTIVE LEARNING ENVIRONMENT? 365

WHAT IS THE IMPACT OF TIME ON LEARNING? 366

Using Allocated Time for Instruction 367

Using Engaged Time Effectively 370

Can Time On-Task Be Too High? 375

Classroom Management in the Student-Centered Classroom 375

WHAT PRACTICES CONTRIBUTE TO EFFECTIVE CLASSROOM MANAGEMENT? 376

Starting Out the Year Right 376

Setting Class Rules 377

WHAT ARE SOME STRATEGIES FOR MANAGING ROUTINE MISBEHAVIOR? 378

CASE TO CONSIDER: *An Ounce of Prevention* 379

The Principle of Least Intervention 379

Prevention 380

Nonverbal Cues 380

Praising Behavior That Is Incompatible with Misbehavior 381

Praising Other Students 381

THE INTENTIONAL TEACHER *Using What You Know about Effective Learning Environments to Improve Teaching and Learning* 382

Verbal Reminders 382

Repeated Reminders 383

TEACHERS IN ACTION: *What classroom management techniques work best for you and your students?* 384

Applying Consequences 385

HOW IS APPLIED BEHAVIOR ANALYSIS USED TO MANAGE MORE SERIOUS BEHAVIOR PROBLEMS?   386

How Student Misbehavior Is Maintained   386

Principles of Applied Behavior Analysis   388

Applied Behavior Analysis Programs   392

Theory *into* Practice: *Using a Daily Report Card System*   393

Theory *into* Practice: *Establishing a Group Contingency Program*   395

Ethics of Behavioral Methods   396

HOW CAN SERIOUS BEHAVIOR PROBLEMS BE PREVENTED?   397

Identifying Causes of Misbehavior   397

Enforcing Rules and Practices   398

Enforcing School Attendance   398

Avoiding Tracking   398

Practicing Intervention   398

Requesting Family Involvement   399

Using Peer Mediation   399

Judiciously Applying Consequences   400

CHAPTER 12

Learners with Exceptionalities   404

WHO ARE LEARNERS WITH EXCEPTIONALITIES?   407

Types of Exceptionalities and the Numbers of Students Served   408

Students with Mental Retardation   410

Theory *into* Practice: *Teaching Adaptive Behavior Skills*   413

Students with Learning Disabilities   413

Theory *into* Practice: *Teaching Students with Learning Disabilities*   415

THE INTENTIONAL TEACHER   *Using What You Know about Learners with Exceptionalities to Improve Teaching and Learning*   418

Theory *into* Practice: *Students with ADHD: The Role of the Teacher*   418

Students with Communication Disorders   420

Students with Emotional and Behavioral Disorders   421

TEACHERS IN ACTION: *What rewarding experience have you had with a student with special needs?*   422

Students with Sensory, Physical, and Health Impairments   424

Students Who Are Gifted and Talented   427

WHAT IS SPECIAL EDUCATION?   429

Public Law 94–142 and IDEA   429

An Array of Special-Education Services   431

Theory *into* Practice: *Preparing IEPs*   438

WHAT ARE MAINSTREAMING AND INCLUSION?   440

Research on Mainstreaming and Inclusion   441

Adapting Instruction   443

Theory *into* Practice: *Adapting Instruction for Students with Special Needs*   443

Teaching Learning Strategies and Metacognitive Awareness   444

Prevention and Early Intervention   445

Computers and Students with Disabilities   445

CASE TO CONSIDER: *Exceptionalities: Barriers to Getting to Know Students*   446

Buddy Systems and Peer Tutoring   447

Special-Education Teams   448

Social Integration of Students with Disabilities   448

CHAPTER 13

Assessing Student Learning   452

WHAT ARE INSTRUCTIONAL OBJECTIVES AND HOW ARE THEY USED?   454

Planning Lesson Objectives   456

Theory *into* Practice: *Planning Courses, Units, and Lessons*   459

Linking Objectives and Assessment   461

Using Taxonomies of Instructional Objectives   462

Research on Instructional Objectives   464

WHY IS EVALUATION IMPORTANT?   465

Evaluation As Feedback   466

Evaluation As Information   466

Evaluation As Incentive   467

HOW IS STUDENT LEARNING EVALUATED?   468

Formative and Summative Evaluations   469

Norm-Referenced, Criterion-Referenced, and Authentic Evaluations   469

Matching Evaluation Strategies with Goals   469

CASE TO CONSIDER: *Making the Grade*   472

HOW ARE TESTS CONSTRUCTED?   472

Principles of Achievement Testing   473

Using a Table of Specifications   474

Writing Objective Test Items   476

Theory *into* Practice: *Writing Multiple-Choice Tests*   476

Writing and Evaluating Essay Tests   479

Writing and Evaluating Problem-Solving Items   481

Theory *into* Practice: *Evaluating Problem-Solving Items*   482

WHAT ARE PORTFOLIO AND PERFORMANCE
ASSESSMENTS? 483

Portfolio Assessment 484

Theory *into* Practice: *Using Portfolios in the Classroom* 486

TEACHERS IN ACTION: *What has been your experience with
alternatives to traditional forms of assessment?* 488

Performance Assessment 489

How Well Do Performance Assessments Work? 489

Scoring Rubrics for Performance Assessments 491

THE INTENTIONAL TEACHER *Using What You Know about
Assessing Student Learning to Improve Teaching and
Learning* 492

CHAPTER 14

Standardized Tests and Grades 496

WHAT ARE STANDARDIZED TESTS AND HOW ARE
THEY USED? 499

Selection and Placement 500

Diagnosis 501

Evaluation 501

School Improvement 501

Accountability 502

Theory *into* Practice: *Teaching Test-Taking Skills* 503

WHAT TYPES OF STANDARDIZED TESTS ARE GIVEN? 504

Aptitude Tests 505

Norm-Referenced Achievement Tests 507

Criterion-Referenced Achievement Tests 508

HOW ARE STANDARDIZED TESTS INTERPRETED? 509

Percentile Scores 510

Grade-Equivalent Scores 510

Standard Scores 511

Theory *into* Practice: *Interpreting Standardized Test
Scores* 514

WHAT ARE SOME ISSUES CONCERNING STANDARDIZED AND
CLASSROOM TESTING? 519

CASE TO CONSIDER: *The Great Testing Controversy* 520

Validity and Reliability 521

Test Bias 522

HOW ARE GRADES DETERMINED? 523

Establishing Grading Criteria 524

Assigning Letter Grades 524

TEACHERS IN ACTION: *What is the best way to prepare
students for standardized tests?* 525

THE INTENTIONAL TEACHER *Using What You Know about
Standardized Tests and Grading to Improve Teaching
and Learning* 526

Performance Grading 528

Other Alternative Grading Systems 528

Assigning Report Card Grades 530

REFERENCES 535

NAME INDEX 575

SUBJECT INDEX 587

FEATURES

CASE TO CONSIDER

Evaluating Curriculum in the Classroom: Some Research of Our Own   22

Cheating and Moral Orientations   61

I CN SPL   74

What Would You Do, Mrs. Brown?   111

Kindergarten Is Big Business   159

Knowledge and Learning How to Learn   201

How Can You Cover It All?   237

Teaching First-Graders to Regulate Their Learning   265

Individualization and Computers: Two Perspectives   312

Motivating a Reluctant Student   358

An Ounce of Prevention   379

Exceptionalities: Barriers to Getting to Know Students   446

Making the Grade   472

The Great Testing Controversy   520

THE INTENTIONAL TEACHER

Guiding Questions to Help You Improve Teaching and Learning   11

Using What You Know about Human Development to Improve Teaching and Learning   58

Using What You Know about Early Childhood, Middle Childhood, and Adolescent Students to Improve Teaching and Learning   98

Using What You Know about Student Diversity to Improve Teaching and Learning   132

Using What You Know about Behavioral Theories of Learning to Improve Teaching and Learning   160

Using What You Know about Cognitive Theories of Learning to Improve Teaching and Learning   210

Using What You Know about Direct Instruction to Improve Teaching and Learning   246

Using What You Know about Student-Centered and Constructivist Approaches to Improve Teaching and Learning   284

Using What You Know about Accommodating Instruction to Meet Individual Needs   314

Using What You Know about Motivation to Improve Teaching and Learning   350

Using What You Know about Effective Learning Environments to Improve Teaching and Learning   382

Using What You Know about Learners with Exceptionalities to Improve Teaching and Learning   418

Using What You Know about Assessing Student Learning to Improve Teaching and Learning   492

Using What You Know about Standardized Tests and Grading to Improve Teaching and Learning   526

TEACHERS IN ACTION

How have educational psychology theory and research helped you in your teaching?   6

How has your knowledge of child development helped you to make instruction developmentally appropriate?   44, 82

How do you foster social acceptance and multicultural awareness?   124

How have you applied behavioral and social learning theories in your teaching?   168

What strategies have you used to help students process and retain new learning?   193

What strategies have you applied to make direct instruction most effective?   245

How have you applied student-centered or constructivist approaches in your teaching?   275

What strategies have you used to meet students' individual needs for instruction?   308

How have you dealt with motivational challenges in your classroom?   347

What classroom management techniques work best for you and your students?   384

What rewarding experience have you had with a student with special needs?   422

What has been your experience with alternatives to traditional forms of assessment?   488

What is the best way to prepare students for standardized tests?   525

THEORY *into* PRACTICE

Teaching As Decision Making   14

How to Be an Intelligent Consumer of Educational Psychology Research   16

Educational Implications of Piaget's Theory   41

Classroom Applications of Vygotsky's Theory   47

Fostering Moral Development in the Classroom   56

Promoting Language Development in Young Children   75

Applying Hoffman's Theories   85

Promoting the Development of Self-Esteem   87

Helping Children Develop Social Skills   89

Providing Developmental Assets for Adolescents   99

Teaching in a Culturally Diverse School   117

Avoiding Gender Bias in Teaching   127

Multiple Intelligences   130

Classroom Uses of Reinforcement   148

Practical Reinforcers   149

Observational Learning   165

Reducing Retroactive Inhibition   188

Meaning versus Abstract Material   198

Teaching the PQ4R Method   206

Planning a Lesson   221

Communicating Objectives to Students   225

Discovery Learning in the Classroom   260

Introducing Reciprocal Teaching   266

Student Teams–Achievement Divisions (STAD)   269

Using Constructivist Methods to Help Students Develop Self-Understanding   272

Applying the Principles of Mastery Learning   301

Effectively Using Tutoring Methods to Meet Individual Needs   306

Giving Students Motivating Feedback   335

Helping Students Overcome Learned Helplessness   341

Computing ILE Base Scores and Improvement Points   355

Using a Daily Report Card System   393

Establishing a Group Contingency Program   395

Teaching Adaptive Behavior Skills   413

Teaching Students with Learning Disabilities   415

Students with ADHD: The Role of the Teacher   418

Preparing IEPs   438

Adapting Instruction for Students with Special Needs   443

Planning Courses, Units, and Lessons   459

Writing Multiple-Choice Tests   476

Evaluating Problem-Solving Items   482

Using Portfolios in the Classroom   486

Teaching Test-Taking Skills   503

Interpreting Standardized Test Scores   514

PREFACE

When I first set out to write *Educational Psychology: Theory and Practice,* I had a very clear purpose in mind. I wanted to give you, tomorrow's teachers, the intellectual grounding and practical strategies you will need to be effective instructors. Most of the textbooks published then, I felt, fell into one of two categories: stuffy or lightweight. The stuffy books were full of research but were ponderously written, losing the flavor of the classroom and containing few guides to practice. The lightweight texts were breezy and easy to read but lacked the dilemmas and intellectual issues brought out by research. They contained suggestions for practice of the "Try this!" variety, without considering evidence about the effectiveness of those strategies.

My objective was to write a text that

- presents information that is as complete and up to date as the most research-focused texts but is also readable, practical, and filled with examples and illustrations of key ideas.
- includes suggestions for practice based directly on classroom research (tempered by common sense) so that I can have confidence that when you try what I suggest, it will be likely to work.
- helps you transfer what you learn in educational psychology to your own teaching by making explicit the connection between theory and practice through numerous realistic examples. Even though I have been doing educational research since the mid-1970s, I find that I never really understand theories or concepts in education until someone gives me a compelling classroom example; and I believe that most of my colleagues (and certainly teacher education students) feel the same way. As a result, the words *for example* or similar ones appear hundreds of times in this text.
- appeals to readers; therefore, I have tried to write in such a way that you will almost hear students' voices and smell the lunch cooking in the school cafeteria as you read.

These have been my objectives in the sixth edition as well as in earlier editions. In addition, I have made changes throughout the text, adding new examples, refining language, and deleting dated or unessential material. I am meticulous about keeping the text up to date, so this edition has more than 1,800 reference citations, more than one-third of which are from 1995 or later. While some readers may not care much about citations, I want you and your professors to know what research supports the statements I've made and where to find additional information.

The field of educational psychology and the practice of education have changed a great deal in recent years, and I have tried to reflect these changes in this edition. Only a few years ago, direct instruction and related teacher effectiveness research were dominant in educational psychology. Then discovery learning, portfolio and performance assessments, and other humanistic strategies returned. Now, emphasis on "back to the basics" is returning, which requires teachers more than ever to plan outcomes and teach purposefully, qualities that I emphasize in this edition as *intentional teaching.* In the first and second editions of this text, I said that we shouldn't entirely discard discovery learning and humanistic methods despite the popularity, then, of direct instruction. In the next editions, I made just the opposite plea: that we shouldn't completely discard direct instruction despite the popularity of active, student-centered teaching and constructivist methods of instruction. With this edition, I continue to advocate a balanced approach to instruction. No matter what their philosophical orientations, experienced teachers know that they must be proficient in a wide range of methods and must use them with intentionality.

The sixth edition presents new research and practical applications of these and many other topics. Throughout, this edition reflects the "cognitive revolution" that is transforming educational psychology and teaching. The accompanying figure presents a concept map of the book's organization.

Given the developments since the mid-1970s—such as the Carnegie Foundation reports on secondary education and the teaching profession, the National Commission on Excellence in Education report *A Nation at Risk,* and the adoption of national educational goals such as Goals 2000—no one can deny that teachers matter or that teachers' behaviors have a profound impact on student achievement. To make that impact positive, teachers must have both a deep understanding of the powerful principles of psychology as they apply to education and a clear sense of how these principles can be applied. To that end, I have introduced the concept of "the intentional teacher," one who constantly reflects on his or her practices and makes instructional decisions based on a clear conception of how these practices affect students. Effective teaching is neither a bag of tricks nor a set of abstract principles; rather, it is intelligent application of well-understood principles to address practical needs. I hope this edition will help give you the intellectual and practical skills you need to do the most important job in the world—teaching.

HOW THIS BOOK IS ORGANIZED

The chapters in this book address three principal themes: students, learning, and teaching (see the Concept Map). Each chapter discusses important theories and includes many examples of how these theories apply to classroom teaching.

This book emphasizes the intelligent use of theory and research to improve instruction. The chapters on teaching occupy about one-third of the total pages in the book, and the other chapters all relate to the meaning of theories and research practice. Whenever possible, the guides in this book present specific programs and strategies that have been evaluated and found to be effective, not just suggestions for things to try.

NEW AND EXPANDED COVERAGE

Among the many topics that receive new or greater coverage in this edition are the impact of educational research on educational practice (Chapter 1); school and community factors that affect the achievement levels of children from low-income

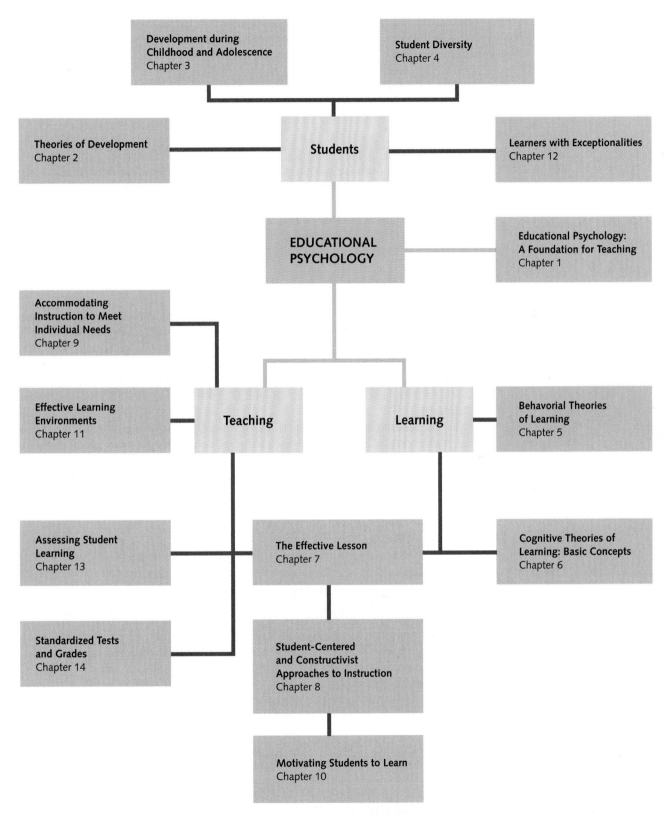

Concept Map: Text Organization in Relation to the Concept of Educational Psychology

groups (Chapter 4); research in techniques for increasing generalization of learned behavior (Chapter 5); automaticity in the information-processing model (Chapter 6); teaching problem-solving strategies (Chapter 8); use of the Internet and the World Wide Web to individualize instruction (Chapter 9); and recent laws, such as IDEA 97, that affect the education of students with disabilities (Chapter 12).

FEATURES

Each chapter of the text opens with a vignette depicting a real-life situation that educators encounter. Throughout the chapter narrative, I refer to the issues raised in the vignette. In addition, you have the opportunity to respond to the vignette in several related features, such as the **Using Your Experience** section that follows each vignette. This section provides critical and creative thinking questions and cooperative learning activities that allow you to work with the issues brought up in the vignette, activate your prior knowledge, and begin thinking about the ideas the chapter will explore.

The **Theory into Practice** sections in each chapter help you acquire and develop the tools you need to be a good teacher. These sections present specific strategies for applying information to the classroom. New Theory into Practice sections added to this edition address being an intelligent consumer of educational psychology research (Chapter 1), fostering moral development (Chapter 2), development of student self-esteem (Chapter 3), observational learning (Chapter 5), meaning versus abstract material (Chapter 6), and constructivist teaching methods (Chapter 8).

In the **Teachers in Action** sections, practicing master teachers contribute personal essays describing how they faced and met particular teaching challenges. In each chapter two teachers respond in depth to the same question, relating concepts in educational psychology to classroom practice. Their responses show the relevance of educational psychology theory and research, as well as the rich variety of teachers' reflective and problem-solving approaches. New voices make contributions to about one-fourth of the chapters in this edition; see, for example, Teachers in Action in Chapter 2.

The recurring **Case to Consider** feature presents a realistic dialogue among teachers and students or between teachers and parents, administrators, or specialists. The cases present authentic dilemmas or conflicts for you to discuss and resolve. Problem-solving questions guide you to develop proposed solutions through writing and role-playing. New Case to Consider features focus on early childhood language development (Chapter 3), teacher–parent communication (Chapter 4), applications of behavioral learning principles (Chapter 5), direct instruction (Chapter 7), and teaching students with exceptionalities (Chapter 12).

In addition, each chapter offers features to help you regulate your own learning: a chapter outline to guide your study objectives; **Self-Check** questions at the end of each main section to help you determine whether you have mastered your objectives; glossary and cross-referenced **Connections** annotations in the margins; a chapter **Summary** to help you review your reading; a list of **Key Terms** with page references at the end of each chapter; and a **Self-Assessment** quiz with multiple-choice, matching, and essay items. A **Study Guide**, available separately, rounds out the features to help you regulate your own learning. It includes Answer Feedback for the Self-Check items and Self-Assessments in the text, as well as concept maps, practice tests, and features to extend your learning.

THE INTENTIONAL TEACHER

One attribute seems to be a characteristic of all outstanding teachers: intentionality, or the ability to do things for a reason, purposefully. Intentional teachers constantly think about the outcomes they want for their students and how each decision they make moves students toward those outcomes. A key new feature in each chapter of this edition, **The Intentional Teacher** is designed to help you develop and apply a set of strategies to carry out your intentionality. It will help you internalize a set of questions that can aid you in planning, teaching, and revising your practice in intentional ways. In each chapter, you will consider answers to the following questions from a new vantage point grounded in chapter content, and you will find new examples at all grade levels and in all subject areas to illustrate those answers. The Intentional Teacher focuses your attention on these questions:

1. *What am I trying to accomplish?*—to help you keep your teaching goals in mind.
2. *What are my students' relevant experiences and needs?*—to assist you in keeping your students' needs in sight.
3. *What approaches and materials are available to help me challenge every student?*—to remind you to vary your methods so as to challenge all students.
4. *How will I know whether and when to change my strategy or modify my instruction?*—to remind you to be flexible in order to reach your goals.
5. *What information will I accept as evidence that my students and I are experiencing success?*—to help you reflect on your practice.

The Intentional Teacher will help you combine your increasing knowledge of principles of educational psychology, your growing experience with learners, and your creativity to make intentional instructional decisions that will help students become enthusiastic, effective learners.

ACKNOWLEDGMENTS

Andrea Guillaume of California State University–Fullerton deserves special thanks for her excellent work in developing and writing each chapter's Intentional Teacher section. Her contribution is truly appreciated. I also thank those who contributed material for other text features, including Theory into Practice, Case to Consider, Using Your Experience, and Teachers in Action. I especially thank Carole Grove, author of the Instructor's Resource Manual. Catherine McCartney, who wrote the Study Guide, Assessment Package, Practice Tests booklet, and online Study Guide, as well as revising the text's Self-Check features and Self-Assessments, also receives my special thanks.

Those who have responded to Allyn and Bacon's educational psychology survey deserve thanks for the valuable information they provided:

Linda Airey	Ripon College
Edna D. Butterfield	Freed–Hardeman University
Benita Chaum	California State University–Northridge
Glenna DeBrota	
George Ferrell	California State University–Northridge
Timothy M. Flynn	Fayetteville State University
Ellen Gagné	Catholic University
James Mahler	California Lutheran University
Nancy A. Maihoff	University of Charleston

Anastasia S. Marrone	Indiana University–Purdue University, Indianapolis
Joseph C. McCloskey	Gloucester County College
Joe Nichols	Indiana University–Purdue University, Fort Wayne
Scott A. Olsen	Truman State University
Mahadev Rathnam	George Washington University
Martha H. Rusnak	Lewis University
Sandra M. Stokes	University of Wisconsin–Green Bay
Bernice Stone	California State University–Fresno
Francine M. Tompkins	University of Wisconsin–Green Bay

I also wish to thank my many colleagues who served as reviewers and contributors for this edition. Reviewers' comments provided invaluable information that helped me revise and augment the text. Contributors' work has made the features and supplements to this text first-rate.

Douglas Beed	University of Montana
Elizabeth Conway	Texas School for the Deaf
Ruth Doyle	Casper College
Ellen D. Gagné	Catholic University
William J. Gehring	University of Michigan
Carole C. Grove	Bridgewater College
Andrea Guillaume	California State University–Fullerton
John Isch	Martin Luther College
Catherine E. McCartney	Bemidji State University
Rosemary Rosser	University of Arizona
Judith Speed	University of California, Davis
Pamela Tiedt	University of California, Berkeley
Francine M. Tompkins	University of Wisconsin–Green Bay
Dorlene Walker	University of Utah
Shawn L. Ward	LeMoyne College

My thanks also go to the authors of *Allyn and Bacon's Custom Cases in Education,* whose cases have been adapted for this work: June Isaacs Elia of Holy Names College, Linda K. Elksnin of The Citadel, Diane Birschbach, Susan P. Gurganus of the College of Charleston, J. Merrell Hansen of Brigham Young University, Joan Isenberg and the Case Writing Team of George Mason University and the Fairfax County Schools, and Arlisa Johnson.

I am also grateful to contributors to previous editions, such as Kathryn Wentzel, Curtis Bonk, Gordon Greenwood, Stacie Goffin, William Zangwill, Thomas Andre, and Sandra Damico. At Allyn and Bacon, my thanks go to Nancy Forsyth, Vice President and Editorial Director; Sean Wakely, former Vice President and Editor in Chief, Education; Paul A. Smith, Vice President and Editor in Chief, Education; and Linda Bieze, Senior Development Editor for the sixth edition. In particular, Linda Bieze put scores of hours into helping me with everything from reviewers to references to wording. In addition to planning and guiding the work of contributors, she coordinated all the print and multimedia supplements. I am also grateful to others on the Education Team at Allyn and Bacon and the freelancers who helped bring this edition to fruition: Annette Joseph, Editorial-Production Administrator; Mary Young, Production Coordinator; Jay Howland, Copyeditor; Ellen Mann Dolberg, Director of Education Programs; Brad Parkins, Marketing Manager; Linda Knowles, Cover Administrator; Laurie Frankenthaler, Permissions Researcher; Susan Duane, Photo Editor; and Jill Jeffrey, Editorial Assistant. In addition, I am grateful to Jada Fletcher and Catherine Hodgetts for their help with typing and references.

In addition, I thank the classroom teachers and education specialists from Alaska to the nation's capital who contributed illustrated essays for the Teachers in Action feature: Randall Amour, Margaret Ball, Suzanne Cary, Nicole DePalma Cobb, Elizabeth J. Conway, Gail C. Dawson, Linda J. Di Pasquale-Morello, Robert W. Fardy, Louis J. Gotlib, Chuck Greiner, Louise Gruppen, Gail C. Hartman, Elonda Hogue, Gemma Staub Hoskins, Mike Jones, Lynn Rylander Kaufman, Karen Kusayanagi, Nancy Letts, Rosa E. Lujan, Lynne McKee, Sandi McNeice, Lynne Larsen-Miller, Joyce Vining Morgan, Ricardo C. Morris, Vicki Olsen, M. Peach Robidoux, Benetta M. Skrundz, Gloria H. Thompson, and Richard C. Thorne Jr.

Finally, it is customary to acknowledge the long-suffering patience of one's spouse and children. In my case, this acknowledgment is especially appropriate. My wife, Nancy Madden, kept our classroom research going while I was in the throes of writing. Our children contributed to this work by providing examples for sections of Chapter 3. They also provided me with a sense of purpose for writing; I had to keep thinking about the kind of school experience I want for them as a way of making concrete my concern for the school experiences of all children.

This book was written while I was supported in part by grants from the Office of Educational Research and Improvement, U.S. Department of Education (No. OERI-R-117-R90002 and OERI-R-117-D40005). However, any opinions I have are mine alone and do not represent OERI positions or policy.

R. E. S.

ABOUT THE AUTHOR

Robert Slavin is Co-Director of the Center for Research on the Education of Students Placed at Risk, Johns Hopkins University, and Chairman of the Success for All Foundation. He received his Ph.D. in Social Relations from Johns Hopkins in 1975, and since that time he has authored more than 200 articles and book chapters on such topics as cooperative learning, ability grouping, school and classroom organization, desegregation, mainstreaming, and research review. Dr. Slavin is the author or coauthor of 15 books, including *Cooperative Learning, School and Classroom Organization, Effective Programs for Students at Risk, Preventing Early School Failure,* and *Every Child, Every School: Success for All.* In 1985 Dr. Slavin received the Raymond Cattell Early Career Award for Programmatic Research from the American Educational Research Association. In 1988 he received the Palmer O. Johnson Award for the best article in an AERA journal. In 1994 he received the Charles A. Dana Award, and in 1998 he received the James Bryant Conant Award from the Education Commission of the States. Dr. Slavin is pictured here with his daughter Becca.

Educational Psychology

Chapter 1

WHAT MAKES A GOOD TEACHER?

Knowing the Subject Matters (but So Does Teaching Skill)

Mastering the Teaching Skills

Can Good Teaching Be Taught?

The Intentional Teacher

WHAT IS THE ROLE OF RESEARCH IN EDUCATIONAL PSYCHOLOGY?

Goals of Research in Educational Psychology

The Value of Research in Educational Psychology to the Teacher

Teaching As Decision Making

Research + Common Sense = Effective Teaching

Research on Effective Programs

Impact of Research on Educational Practice

WHAT RESEARCH METHODS ARE USED IN EDUCATIONAL PSYCHOLOGY?

Experiments

Correlational Studies

Descriptive Research

Educational Psychology: A Foundation for Teaching

Ellen Mathis was baffled. She was a new teacher who had been trying to teach creative writing to her third-grade class, but

things were just not going the way she'd hoped. Her students were not producing very much, and what they did write was not very imaginative and was full of errors. For example, she had recently assigned a composition on "My Summer Vacation," and all that one of her students wrote was "On my summer vacation I got a dog and we went swimming and I got stinged by a bee."

Ellen wondered whether her kids were just not ready for writing and needed several months of work on such skills as capitalization, punctuation, and usage before she tried another writing assignment. One day, however, Ellen noticed some compositions in the hall outside of Leah Washington's class. Leah's third-graders were just like Ellen's, but their compositions were fabulous! The students wrote pages of interesting material on an astonishing array of topics.

At the end of the day, Ellen caught Leah in the hall. "How do you get your kids to write such great compositions?" she asked.

Leah explained how she first got her children writing on topics they cared about and then gradually introduced "mini-lessons" to help them become better authors. She had the students work in small groups and help one another plan compositions. Then the students critiqued one another's drafts, helped one another with editing, and finally "published" final versions.

"I'll tell you what," Leah offered. "I'll schedule my next writing class during your planning period. Come see what we're doing."

Ellen agreed. When the time came, she walked into Leah's class and was overwhelmed by what she saw. Children were writing everywhere—on the floor, in groups, at tables. Many were talking with partners. Leah was conferencing with individual children. Ellen looked over the children's shoulders and saw one student writing about her pets, another writing a gory story about Ninjas, and another writing about a dream. Marta Delgrado, a Mexican American child, was writing a funny story about her second-grade teacher's attempts to speak Spanish. One student, Melinda Navens, was even writing a very good story about her summer vacation!

After school, Ellen met with Leah. She was full of questions. "How did you get students to do all that writing? How can you manage all that noise and activity? How did you learn to do this?"

"I did go to a series of workshops on teaching writing," Leah said. "But if you think about it, everything I'm doing is basic educational psychology."

Ellen was amazed. "Educational psychology? I got an A in that course in college, but I don't see what it has to do with your writing program."

"Well, let's see," said Leah. "To begin with, I'm using a lot of motivational strategies I learned in ed psych. For instance, when I started my writing instruction this year, I read students some funny and intriguing stories written by other classes, to arouse their curiosity. I got them motivated by letting them write about whatever they wanted, and also by having 'writing celebrations' in which students read their finished compositions to the class for applause and comments. My educational psychology professor was always talking about adapting to students' needs. I do this by conferencing with students and helping them with the specific problems they're having. I first learned about cooperative learning in ed psych, and later on I took some workshops on it. I use cooperative learning groups to let students give each other immediate feedback on their writing, to let them model effective writing for each other, and to get them to encourage each other to write. The groups also solve a lot of my management problems by keeping each other on task and dealing with many classroom routines. I remember that we learned about evaluation in ed psych. I use a flexible form of evaluation. Everybody eventually gets an A on his or her composition, but only when it meets a high standard, which may take many drafts. I apply what we learned about child development just about every day. For example, I adapt to students' developmental levels and cultural styles by encouraging them to write about things that matter to them—if dinosaurs or video games are important right now, or if children are uncomfortable about being Muslim or Jewish at Christmas time, that's what they should write about!"

Ellen was impressed. She and Leah arranged to visit each other's classes a few more times to exchange ideas and observations, and in time, Ellen's writers began to be almost as good as Leah's. But what was particularly important to her was the idea that educational psychology could really be useful in her day-to-day teaching. She dragged out her old textbook and found that concepts that had seemed theoretical and abstract in ed psych class actually helped her think about problems of teaching.

Using Your EXPERIENCE

Creative Thinking Based on Leah's explanation of her writing instruction, work with one or more partners to brainstorm about what educational psychology is and what you will learn this semester. Guidelines: (1) the more ideas you generate, the better; (2) hitchhike on others' ideas as well as combining them; and (3) make no evaluation of these ideas at this time. Take this list out a few times during the semester and add to it as well as evaluate it.

What is **educational psychology?** An academic definition would perhaps say that educational psychology is the study of learners, learning, and teaching. However, for students who are or expect to be teachers, educational psychology is something more. It is the accumulated knowledge, wisdom, and seat-of-the-pants theory that every teacher should possess to intelligently solve the daily problems of teaching. Educational psychology cannot tell teachers what to do, but it can give them the principles to use in making a good decision. Consider the case of Ellen Mathis and Leah Washington. Nothing in this or any other educational psychology text will tell teachers exactly how to teach creative writing to a particular group of third-graders. However, Leah uses concepts of educational psychology to consider how she will teach writing, to interpret and solve problems she runs into, and to explain to Ellen what she is doing. Educational psychologists carry out research on the nature of students, principles of learning, and methods of teaching to give educators the information they need to think critically about their craft and to make teaching decisions that will work for their students.

WHAT MAKES A GOOD TEACHER?

What makes a good teacher? Is it warmth, humor, and caring about people? Is it planning, hard work, and self-discipline? What about leadership, enthusiasm, a contagious love of learning, and speaking ability? Most people would agree that all of these qualities are needed to make someone a good teacher, and they would certainly be correct. But these qualities are not enough.

educational psychology
The study of learning and teaching.

Knowing the Subject Matters (but So Does Teaching Skill)

There is an old joke that goes like this:

Question: What do you need to know to be able to teach a horse?
Answer: More than the horse!

This joke makes the obvious point that the first thing a teacher must have is some knowledge or skills that the learner does not have; teachers must know the subject matter they expect to teach. But if you think about teaching horses (or children), you will soon realize that although subject matter knowledge is necessary, it is not enough. A rancher may have a good idea of how a horse is supposed to act and what a horse is supposed to be able to do, but if he doesn't have the skills to make an untrained, scared, and unfriendly animal into a good saddle horse, he's going to end up with nothing but broken ribs and teeth marks for his troubles. Children are a little more forgiving than horses, but teaching them has this in common with teaching horses: Knowledge of how to transmit information and skills is at least as important as knowledge of the information and skills themselves. We have all had teachers (most often college professors, unfortunately) who were brilliant and thoroughly knowledgeable in their fields but who could not teach. Ellen Mathis may know as much as Leah Washington about what good writing should look like, but she has a lot to learn about how to get third-graders to write well.

For effective teaching, subject matter knowledge is not a question of being a walking encyclopedia. Effective teachers not only know their subjects, but they can also communicate their knowledge to students. The celebrated math teacher Jaime Escalante taught the concept of positive and negative numbers to students in a high school in a Los Angeles barrio by explaining that when you dig a hole, you might call the pile of dirt $+1$, the hole -1. What do you get when you put the dirt back in the hole? Zero. Escalante's ability to relate the abstract concept of positive and negative numbers to his students' experiences is one example of how the ability to communicate knowledge goes far beyond simply knowing it.

Mastering the Teaching Skills

The link between what the teacher wants students to learn and students' actual learning is called instruction, or **pedagogy.** Effective instruction is not a simple matter of one person with more knowledge transmitting that knowledge to another. If telling were teaching, this book would be unnecessary. Rather, effective instruction demands the use of many strategies.

For example, suppose Paula Ray wants to teach a lesson on statistics to a diverse class of fourth-graders. To do this, Paula must accomplish many things. She must make sure that the class is orderly and that students know what behavior is expected of them. She must find out whether students have the prerequisite skills; for example, students need to be able to add and divide to find averages. If any do not, Paula must find a way to teach students those skills. She must engage students in activities that lead them toward an understanding of statistics, such as having students roll dice, play cards, or collect data from experiments; and she must use teaching strategies that help students remember what they have been taught. The lessons should also take into account the intellectual and social characteristics of students in the fourth grade and the intellectual, social, and cultural characteristics of these particular students. Paula must make sure that students are interested in the lesson and are motivated to learn statistics. To see whether students are learn-

pedagogy
The study of teaching and learning with applications to the instructional process.

ing what is being taught, she may ask questions or use quizzes or have students demonstrate their understanding by setting up and interpreting experiments, and she must respond appropriately if these assessments show that students are having problems. After the series of lessons on statistics ends, Paula should review this topic from time to time to ensure that it is remembered.

These tasks—motivating students, managing the classroom, assessing prior knowledge, communicating ideas effectively, taking into account the characteristics of the learners, assessing learning outcomes, and reviewing information—must be attended to at all levels of education, in or out of schools. They apply as much to the training of astronauts as to the teaching of reading. How these tasks are accomplished, however, differs widely according to the ages of the students, the objectives of instruction, and other factors.

What makes a good teacher is the ability to carry out all the tasks involved in effective instruction (Reynolds, 1995). Warmth, enthusiasm, and caring are essential, as is subject matter knowledge. But it is the successful accomplishment of all the tasks of teaching that makes for instructional effectiveness.

Can Good Teaching Be Taught?

Some people think that good teachers are born that way. Outstanding teachers sometimes seem to have a magic, a charisma, that mere mortals could never hope to achieve. Yet research since the early 1970s has begun to identify the specific behaviors and skills that make up the "magic" teacher (Mayer, 1992). An outstanding teacher does nothing that any other teacher cannot also do—it is just a question of knowing the principles of effective teaching and how to apply them. Take one small example. In a high school history class, two students in the back of the class are whispering to each other—and they are not discussing the Treaty of Paris! The teacher slowly walks toward them without looking at them, continuing his lesson

CONNECTIONS

For more on effective instruction, see Chapter 7. Pedagogical strategies are also presented in Chapters 7 (p. 220), 8 (p. 276), and 9 (p. 304), as well as throughout the text in features entitled The Intentional Teacher.

What characteristics of good teaching might this expert teacher possess? What behaviors might distinguish this teacher's attitudes and practices from those of a novice?

TEACHERS IN ACTION

How have educational psychology theory and research helped you in your teaching?

Linda J. DiPasquale-Morello
Kindergarten Teacher
John C. Milanesi School
Buena, New Jersey

Educational psychology has played an important role from the beginning of my teaching career, for I began teaching as an eager 18-year-old in a parochial school. (The year was 1969 and they desperately needed staff members.) I started taking college courses two weeks after my high school graduation, because I knew I wanted to be a teacher! Day, evening, and extension courses at a local state college served me well during 1968 and 1969. Many of my courses were practical applications as well as educational theory and behavior courses.

During my first year of teaching, my application course work was useful, but many times I would refer to my educational psychology books for specific information (looking for the right terms to describe the actions that had taken place in my classroom that day). I continued to teach by day and study by night. I read about teaching strategies and used my class as a *case in study.* I constantly read, evaluated, and continued to search for more information that could help me and my students become the best team we could be. Many nights, I would try to understand the actions, behaviors, and practices of the school day from the perspective of educational psychology. I continued to read everything I could get my hands on regarding teaching practices and their application to students and learning development.

Education is not a field of "learn today . . . learn forever." Research is constantly changing what we know about how we learn. The latest information on early brain development, stemming from advanced scientific technology, would have had my Aunt Lil (a former kindergarten teacher for 40 years) in a tizzy. She believed her job was to teach the children social skills and how to get along with others. This is still very true for teachers; however, a much different approach is now recommended by early childhood specialists. Future teachers will need to become more aware of their students' needs, abilities, experiences, and backgrounds to formulate their plans for effective teaching in the twenty-first century.

As I now enter my 30th year in the field of education, I continue to find myself thinking about, searching for, and reading the latest information on the psychology of learning. Maybe the true mark of effective teachers is that *we must be lifelong learners before we can promote lifelong learning in the children we teach.*

Rosa E. Lujan
Bilingual Teacher, Grades 5–6
Ysieta Elementary School
El Paso, Texas

A few years ago, I was selected to participate in a national research project being implemented in my school district—a 5-year study of the effects of cooperative learning among Hispanic students using a program known as CIRC (Cooperative Integrated Reading and Composition). Educational researchers are working with teachers like me to develop a process for effective bilingual and second-language instruction through cooperative learning. My students and I have helped in piloting, giving feedback, and experimenting with assessments.

Originally, CIRC was developed to be used with monolingual English students, but this model is now being adapted to classrooms with large numbers of language-minority students. This adaptation has required extensive teacher and staff development so that I and other teachers could become researchers in our own classrooms. My involvement in this research has made me more analytical about what I observe in the classroom and more appreciative of the importance of educational psychology theory and research in what I do.

The greatest result, though, has been the increased self-esteem and achievement of my students. Even the most reluctant learner becomes actively involved in learning. Students know they are important, a part of the classroom *familia.* Academically, they are now reading and writing in two languages. As a professional, my commitment and excitement for teaching and learning is stronger. I'm on fire!

as he walks. The students stop whispering and pay attention. If you didn't know what to look for, you might miss this brief but critical interchange and believe that the teacher just has a way with students, a knack for keeping their attention. But the teacher is simply applying principles of classroom management that anyone could learn: Maintain momentum in the lesson, deal with behavior problems by using the mildest intervention that will work, and resolve minor problems before they become major ones. When Jaime Escalante gave the example of digging a hole to illustrate the concept of positive and negative numbers, he was also applying several important principles of educational psychology: Make abstract ideas concrete by using many examples, relate the content of instruction to the students' background, state rules, give examples, and then restate rules.

Can good teaching be taught? The answer is definitely yes. Good teaching has to be observed and practiced, but there are principles of good teaching that teachers need to know, which can then be applied in the classroom. The major components of effective instruction are summarized in Figure 1.1 on page 8.

The Intentional Teacher

There is no formula for good teaching, no seven steps to Teacher of the Year. Teaching involves planning and preparation, and then dozens of decisions every hour (Sabers, Cushing, & Berliner, 1991; Swanson, O'Connor, & Cooney, 1990). Yet one attribute seems to be characteristic of outstanding teachers: **intentionality.** Intentionality means doing things for a reason, on purpose. Intentional teachers are those who are constantly thinking about the outcomes they want for their students and about how each decision they make moves children toward those outcomes. Intentional teachers know that maximum learning does not happen by chance. Yes, children do learn in unplanned ways all the time, and many will learn from even the most chaotic lesson. But to really challenge students, to get their best efforts, to help them make conceptual leaps and organize and retain new knowledge, teachers need to be purposeful, thoughtful, and flexible, without ever losing sight of their goals for every child. In a word, they need to be intentional.

The idea that teachers should always do things for a reason seems obvious, and in principle it is. Yet in practice, it is difficult to constantly make certain that all students are engaged in activities that lead to an important outcome; and teachers very frequently fall into strategies that they themselves would recognize, on reflection, as being time fillers rather than instructionally essential activities. For example, an otherwise outstanding third-grade teacher once assigned seatwork to one of her reading groups. The children were given two sheets of paper with words in squares. Their task was to cut out the squares on one sheet and then paste them onto synonyms on the other. When all the words were pasted correctly, lines on the pasted squares would form an outline of a cat, which the children were then to color. Once the children pasted a few squares, the puzzle became clear, so they could paste the remainder without paying any attention to the words themselves. For almost an hour of precious class time, these children happily cut, pasted, and colored—not high-priority skills for third graders. The teacher would have said that the objective was for children to learn or practice synonyms, of course; but in fact the activity could not possibly have moved the children forward on that skill. Similarly, many teachers have one child laboriously work a problem on the chalkboard while the rest of the class has nothing important to do. Many secondary teachers spend most of the class period going over homework and classwork and end up doing very little teaching. Again, these may be excellent teachers in other

intentionality
Doing things for a purpose; teachers who use intentionality plan their actions based on the outcomes they want to achieve.

FIGURE 1.1 ● Components of Good Teaching

ways, but they sometimes lose sight of what they are trying to achieve and how they are going to achieve it.

Intentional teachers are constantly asking themselves whether each portion of their lesson is appropriate to students' background knowledge, skills, and needs; whether each activity or assignment is clearly related to a valued outcome; whether each instructional minute is used wisely and well. An intentional teacher trying to build students' synonym skills during follow-up time might have them work in pairs to master a set of synonyms in preparation for individual quizzes. An intentional

What does this teacher need to know about his students in order to be an intentional teacher? What strategies does he need to know how to use to help his students experience success?

teacher might have all children work a given problem while one works at the board, so that all can compare answers and strategies together. An intentional teacher might quickly give homework answers for students to check themselves, ask for a show of hands for correct answers, and then review and reteach only those exercises missed by many children. An intentional teacher uses a wide variety of instructional methods, experiences, assignments, and materials to be sure that children are achieving all sorts of cognitive objectives, from knowledge to application to creativity, and that at the same time children are learning important affective objectives, such as love of learning, respect for others, and personal responsibility.

The most important purpose of this book is to give tomorrow's teachers the intellectual grounding in research, theory, and practical wisdom they will need in order to become intentional, effective teachers. To plan and carry out effective lessons, discussions, projects, and other learning experiences, teachers need to know a great deal. Besides knowing their subjects, they need to understand the developmental levels and needs of their children. They need to understand how learning, memory, problem-solving skill, and creativity are acquired, and how to promote their acquisition. They need to know how to set objectives, organize activities designed to help students attain those objectives, and assess students' progress toward them. They need to know how to motivate children, how to use class time effectively, and how to respond to individual differences among students. Like Leah Washington, the teacher in the vignette that opened this chapter, intentional teachers are constantly combining their knowledge of principles of educational psychology, their experience, and their creativity to make instructional decisions and help children become enthusiastic and effective learners. They are continually experimenting with strategies to solve problems of instruction and then observing the results of their actions to see if they were effective (Schmuck, 1997).

This text highlights the ideas that are central to educational psychology and the research related to these ideas. It also presents many examples of how these ideas

These teachers are discussing the outcomes they want for their students and how their decisions will move children toward those outcomes. How can you become an intentional teacher?

apply in practice. The emphasis is on teaching methods that have been evaluated and found to be effective, not just theory or suggestions. The text is designed to help the reader develop **critical-thinking** skills for teaching: a logical and systematic approach to the many dilemmas that are found in practice and research. No text can provide all the right answers for teaching, but this one tries to pose the right questions and to engage the reader by presenting realistic alternatives and the concepts and research behind them.

Many studies have looked at the differences between expert and novice teachers and between more and less effective teachers. One theme comes through these studies: Expert teachers are critical thinkers (Anderson et al., 1995; Floden & Klinzing, 1990; Swanson et al., 1990). Teachers are constantly upgrading and examining their own teaching practices, reading and attending conferences to learn new ideas, and using their own students' responses to guide their instructional decisions (Sabers et al., 1991; Schmuck, 1997). There's an old saying to the effect that there are teachers with 20 years of experience and there are teachers with 1 year of experience 20 times. Teachers who get better each year are the ones who are open to new ideas and who look at their own teaching critically. Perhaps the most important goal of this book is to start the habit of informed reflection with tomorrow's expert teachers.

critical thinking
Evaluation of conclusions through logical and systematic examination of the problem, the evidence, and the solution.

SELF-CHECK

Reassess the chapter-opening vignette. In terms of the concepts introduced in this section, what qualities identify Leah Washington as an intentional teacher?

The Intentional Teacher

● Guiding Questions to Help You Improve Teaching and Learning

An intentional teacher is one who plans for success. An intentional teacher worries little about filling the minutes and thinks often about ensuring that each student is engaged in meaningful activities that result in important learning. An intentional teacher thinks about students in terms broader than cognitive growth; this teacher sees students as individuals who are also progressing physically, linguistically, morally, and socially—and the intentional teacher takes responsibility for fostering students' growth in each of these areas. The intentional teacher questions classroom practice to ensure that it is in line with appropriate goals, that it meets individuals' needs, and that it is equitable. The intentional teacher consistently gathers information about students' responses and learning and adjusts instruction based upon this information. The intentional teacher seeks to do even better tomorrow.

How will you begin your journey toward intentional expertise? How will you systematically plan, teach, and reflect in ways that enact your professional knowledge base and your understanding of specific students in the classroom context? What strategies can you use to ensure that you are sharpening your educational decisions so that they are flexible, responsive, and critical?

Intentional teachers ask questions. A generic set of questions can guide your journey by providing signposts to direct you as you consider the content of each chapter in this book. The following five generic questions can start you on your way.

Because intentional teachers *keep goals in mind,* you can ask yourself:

1 What am I trying to accomplish?

Because intentional teachers *consider their students' needs and backgrounds,* you can ask yourself:

2 What are my students' relevant experiences and needs?

Because intentional teachers *vary their methods, experiences, assignments, and materials* in their *aim to challenge students,* you can ask yourself:

3 What approaches and materials are available to help me challenge every student?

Because intentional teachers *are flexible in light of their goals,* you can ask yourself:

4 How will I know whether and when to change my strategy or modify my instruction?

Because intentional teachers *reflect,* you can ask yourself:

5 What information will I accept as evidence that my students and I are experiencing success?

Whether you will teach mathematics to high school students or the foundations of literacy to kindergarten students, these five questions can provide markers for you. They can point you toward intentional practice by reminding you to keep inquiring about your goals, your students, your actions, and evidence of your success.

The aim of this feature—The Intentional Teacher—is to enable you to internalize a set of questions that can help you plan, teach, and revise your practice in intentional ways. Each chapter allows you to revisit these essential questions from a new vantage point, to consider different aspects of your practice in light of the chapter's content. Because you'll be asked to think about these questions 13 more times, here they are once again as a set:

1. What am I trying to accomplish?
2. What are my students' relevant experiences and needs?
3. What approaches and materials are available to help me challenge every student?
4. How will I know whether and when to change my strategy or modify my instruction?
5. What information will I accept as evidence that my students and I are experiencing success?

In each chapter you will find specific answers to these questions, along with illustrative examples for different grade levels and subject areas. By considering questions such as these, you can become a teacher who does things on purpose—an intentional teacher.

WHAT IS THE ROLE OF RESEARCH IN EDUCATIONAL PSYCHOLOGY?

Teachers who are intentional, critical thinkers are likely to enter their classrooms equipped with knowledge about research in educational psychology. One problem educational psychologists face, in fact, is that almost everyone thinks he or she is an expert on their subject. Most adults have spent many years in schools watching what teachers do. Add to that a certain amount of knowledge of human nature, and *voila!* Everyone is an amateur educational psychologist. For this reason, professional educational psychologists are often accused of studying the obvious (Gage, 1991).

However, as we have painfully learned, the obvious is not always true. For example, most people assume that if students are assigned to classes according to their ability, the resulting narrower range of abilities in a class will let the teacher adapt the instruction to the specific needs of the students and thereby increase student achievement. This assumption turns out to be false. Many teachers believe that scolding students for misbehavior will improve student behavior. Many students will indeed respond to a scolding by behaving better, but for others, scolding may be a reward for misbehavior and will actually increase it. Some "obvious" truths even conflict with one another. For example, most people would agree that students learn better from a teacher's instruction than by working alone. This belief supports teacher-centered direct instructional strategies, in which a teacher actively works with the class as a whole. On the other hand, most people would also agree that students often need instruction tailored to their individual needs. This belief, also correct, would demand that teachers divide their time among individuals, or at least among groups of students with differing needs, which would result in some students' working independently while others received the teacher's attention. If schools could provide tutors for every student, there would be no conflict; direct instruction and individualization could coexist. In practice, however, classrooms typically have 20 or more students; as a result, more direct instruction (the first goal) almost always means less individualization (the second goal). The intentional teacher's task is to balance these competing goals according to the needs of particular students and situations.

Goals of Research in Educational Psychology

The goal of research in educational psychology is to carefully examine obvious as well as less than obvious questions, using objective methods to test ideas about the factors that contribute to learning (see Gage, 1994). The products of this research are principles, laws, and theories. A **principle** explains the relationship between factors, such as the effects of alternative grading systems on student motivation. Laws are simply principles that have been thoroughly tested and found to apply in a wide variety of situations. A **theory** is a set of related principles and laws that explains a broad aspect of learning, behavior, or another area of interest. Without theories the facts and principles that are discovered would be like disorganized specks on a canvas. Theories tie together these facts and principles to give us the big picture. However, the same facts and principles may be interpreted in different ways by different theorists. As in any science, progress in educational psychology is slow and uneven (see Carroll, 1993). A single study is rarely a breakthrough, but over time evidence accumulates on a subject and allows theorists to refine and extend their theories.

The Value of Research in Educational Psychology to the Teacher

It is probably true that the most important things teachers learn, they learn on the job—in internships, while student teaching, or during their first years in the classroom (Darling-Hammond, Gendler, & Wise, 1990). However, teachers make hundreds of decisions every day, and each decision has a theory behind it, whether or

CONNECTIONS

For more on ability grouping, see Chapter 9, page 294.

CONNECTIONS

For more on effectively handling misbehavior, see Chapter 5, page 150.

principle
Explanation of the relationship between factors, such as the effects of alternative grading systems on student motivation.

theory
A set of principles that explains and relates certain phenomena.

not the teacher is aware of it. The quality, accuracy, and usefulness of those theories are what ultimately determine the teacher's success (see, e.g., Doyle, 1990a). For example, one teacher may offer a prize to the student with the best attendance, on the theory that rewarding attendance will increase it. Another may reward the student whose attendance is most improved, on the theory that it is poor attenders who most need incentives to come to class. A third may not reward anyone for attendance but may try to increase attendance by teaching more interesting lessons. Which teacher's plan is most likely to succeed? This depends in large part on the ability of each teacher to understand the unique combination of factors that shape the character of his or her classroom and therefore to apply the most appropriate theory.

Teaching As Decision Making

The aim of educational psychology is to test the various theories that guide the actions of teachers and others involved in education. Here is another example of how a teacher might use educational psychology.

Mr. Harris teaches an eighth-grade social studies class. He has a problem with Tom, who frequently misbehaves. Today, Tom makes a paper airplane and flies it across the room when Mr. Harris turns his back, to the delight of the entire class.

What should Mr. Harris do?

As an intentional teacher, Mr. Harris considers a range of options for solving this problem, each of which comes from a theory about why Tom is misbehaving and what will motivate him to behave more appropriately.

Some actions Mr. Harris might take, and the theories on which they are based, are as follows:

Action	Theory
1. Reprimand Tom.	**1.** A reprimand is a form of punishment. Tom will behave to avoid punishment.
2. Ignore Tom.	**2.** Attention may be rewarding to Tom. Ignoring him would deprive him of this reward.
3. Send Tom to the office.	**3.** Being sent to the office is punishing. It also deprives Tom of the (apparent) support of his classmates.
4. Tell the class that it is everyone's responsibility to maintain a good learning environment and that if any student misbehaves, 5 minutes will be subtracted from recess.	**4.** Tom is misbehaving to get his classmates' attention. If the whole class loses out when he misbehaves, the class will keep him in line.
5. Explain to the class that Tom's behavior is interfering with lessons that all students need to know and that his behavior goes against the rules the class set for itself at the beginning of the year.	**5.** The class holds standards of behavior that conflict with both Tom's behavior in class and the class's reaction to it. By reminding the class of its own needs (to learn the lesson) and its own rules set at the beginning of the year, the teacher may make Tom see that the class does not really support his behavior.

Each of these actions is a common response to misbehavior. But which theory (and therefore which action) is correct?

The key may be in the fact that his classmates laugh when Tom misbehaves. This response is a clue that Tom is seeking their attention. If Mr. Harris scolds

Tom, this may increase Tom's status in the eyes of his peers and may reward his behavior. Ignoring misbehavior might be a good idea if a student were acting up to get the teacher's attention, but in this case it is apparently the class's attention that Tom is seeking. Sending Tom to the office does deprive him of his classmates' attention and therefore may be effective. But what if Tom is looking for a way to get out of class to avoid work? What if he struts out to confront the powers that be, to the obvious approval of his classmates? Making the entire class responsible for each student's behavior is likely to deprive Tom of his classmates' support and to improve his behavior; but some students may think that it is unfair to punish them for another student's misbehavior. Finally, reminding the class (and Tom) of its own interest in learning and its usual standards of behavior might work if the class does, in fact, value academic achievement and good behavior.

Research in education and psychology bears directly on the decision Mr. Harris must make. Developmental research indicates that as students enter adolescence, the peer group becomes all-important to them, and they try to establish their independence from adult control, often by flouting or ignoring rules. Basic research on behavioral learning theories shows that when a behavior is repeated many times, some reward must be encouraging the behavior, and that if the behavior is to be eliminated, the reward must first be identified and removed. This research would also suggest that Mr. Harris consider problems with the use of punishment (such as scolding) to stop undesirable behavior. Research on specific classroom management strategies has identified effective methods to use both to prevent a student like Tom from misbehaving in the first place and to deal with his misbehavior when it does occur. Finally, research on rule setting and classroom standards indicates that student participation in setting rules can help convince each student that the class as a whole values academic achievement and appropriate behavior, and that this belief can help keep individual students in line.

Armed with this information, Mr. Harris can choose a response to Tom's behavior that is based on an understanding of why Tom is doing what he is doing and what strategies are available to deal with the situation. He may or may not make the right choice; but because he knows several theories that could explain Tom's behavior, he will be able to observe the outcomes of his strategy and, if it is ineffective, to learn from that and try something else that will work. Research does not give Mr. Harris a specific solution; that requires his own experience and judgment. But research does give Mr. Harris basic concepts of human behavior to help him understand Tom's motivations and an array of proven methods that might solve the problem.

THEORY into Practice

Teaching As Decision Making

If there were no educational problems to solve, there would be no need for teachers to function as professionals. Professionals distinguish themselves from nonprofessionals in part by the fact that they must make decisions that influence the course of their work.

Educators must decide (1) how to recognize problems and issues, (2) how to consider situations from multiple perspectives, (3) how to call up relevant professional knowledge to formulate actions, (4) how to take the most appropriate action, and (5) how to judge the consequences.

Ms. O'Hara has a student named Shanika in her social studies class. Most of the time, Shanika is rather quiet and withdrawn. Her permanent record indicates considerable academic ability, but a casual observer would never know it. Ms. O'Hara asks herself the following questions:

1. What problems do I perceive in this situation? Is Shanika bored, tired, uninterested, or shy, or might her participation be inhibited by something I or others are doing or not doing? What theories of educational psychology might I consider?
2. I wonder what Shanika thinks about being in this class? Does she feel excluded? Does she care about the subject matter? Is she concerned about what I or others think about her lack of participation? Why or why not? What theories of motivation will help me make a decision?
3. What do I know from theory, research, and/or practice that might guide my actions to involve Shanika more directly in class activities?
4. What might I actually do in this situation to enhance Shanika's involvement?
5. How would I know if I were successful with Shanika?

CONNECTIONS

For more on multiculturalism, see Chapter 4.

If Ms. O'Hara asked and tried to answer these questions—not just in the case of Shanika, of course, but at other times as well—she would improve her chances to learn about her work from doing her work. John Dewey taught that the problems teachers face are the natural stimuli for reflective inquiry. The key is to accept the problems and to think productively about them.

Research + Common Sense = Effective Teaching

As the case of Mr. Harris illustrates, no theory, no research, no book can tell teachers what to do in a given situation. Making the right decisions depends on the context within which the problem arises, the objectives the teacher has in mind, and many other factors, all of which must be assessed in the light of educated common sense. For example, research in mathematics instruction usually finds that a rapid pace of instruction increases achievement (Good, Grouws, & Ebmeier, 1983). Yet a teacher may quite legitimately slow down and spend a lot of time on a concept that is particularly critical or may let students take time to discover a mathematical principle on their own. It is usually much more efficient (that is, it takes less time) to teach students skills or information directly than to let them make discoveries for themselves; but if the teacher wants students to gain a deeper understanding of a topic or to know how to find information or figure things out for themselves, then the research findings about pace can be temporarily shelved.

The point is that while research in educational psychology can sometimes be translated directly to the classroom, it is best to apply the principles with a hefty dose of common sense and a clear view of what is being taught to whom for what purpose.

Research on Effective Programs

Research in educational psychology not only provides evidence for principles of effective practice, but it also provides evidence about the effectiveness of particular programs or practices (Rhine, 1998). For example, in the vignette at the beginning of this chapter, Leah Washington was using a specific approach to creative writing instruction that has been extensively evaluated as a whole (Hillocks, 1984). In other words, there is evidence that, on average, children whose teachers are using such methods learn to write better than those whose teachers use more traditional approaches. There is evidence on the effectiveness of dozens of widely used programs, from methods in particular subjects to strategies for reforming entire schools (see, for example, Block, Everson, & Guskey, 1995; Ellis & Fouts, 1993; Slavin & Fashola, 1998). An intentional teacher should be aware of research on programs for his or her subject and grade level, and should seek out professional development opportunities to learn methods known to make a difference for children.

Impact of Research on Educational Practice

Many researchers and educators have bemoaned the limited impact of research in educational psychology on teachers' practices (see, for example, Hargreaves, 1996; Kennedy, 1997). Indeed, research in education has nowhere near as great an impact on practice as research in medicine or agriculture or engineering (Gage, 1994). Yet research in education does have a profound indirect impact on educational practice (Hattie & Marsh, 1996), even if teachers are not aware of it. It affects educational policies, professional development programs, and teaching materials. For example, the Tennessee class size study, which found important effects of class size in the early grades on student achievement, had a direct impact on state and federal proposals for class size reduction. Recent research on beginning reading (National Academy of Sciences, 1998) has begun to dramatically transform curriculum, instruction, and professional development for this subject. Research on the effects of career academies in high schools (Kemple, 1997) has led to a substantial increase in such programs. Research on two-way bilingual programs, in which children of different linguistic backgrounds learn both English and (usually) Spanish, has led to expansion of these programs (August & Hakuta, 1997).

It is important for educators to become intelligent consumers of research, not to take every finding or every expert's pronouncement as truth from Mount Olympus (Tanner, 1998). The following section briefly describes the methods of research that most often produce findings of use to educators.

THEORY *into* Practice

How to Be an Intelligent Consumer of Educational Psychology Research

Let's say you're in the market for a new car. Before laying out your hard-earned money, you'll probably review the findings from various consumer research reports. You may want to know something about how various cars have performed in crash tests, which cars have the best gas mileage, or what trade-in value a particular model has. Before embarking on this major investment, you want to feel as confident as you can about your decision. If you've been in this situation before, you probably remember that all of your research helped you make an informed decision.

Now that you are about to enter the profession of teaching, you will need to apply a similar consumer orientation in your decision making. As a teacher, you will be called upon to make hundreds of decisions each day. Your car-buying decision was influenced by a combination of sound research findings and common sense, and your decisions about teaching and learning should follow this same pattern. Teaching and learning are complex concepts subject to a wide variety of influences, so your knowledge of relevant research will serve to guide you into making informed choices.

How can knowing the simple formula *research + common sense = effective teaching* help you to be a more intelligent consumer of educational psychology research? The following recommendations show how you can put this formula into practice:

Be a consumer of relevant research. It's obvious you can't apply what you don't know. As a professional, you have a responsibility to maintain a working knowledge of relevant research. In addition to your course textbooks, which will be excellent resources for you in the future, you should become familiar with the professional journals in your field. You may want to review the following journals, which typically present research that has direct application for classroom practices: *Educational Psychologist, Journal of Educational Psychology,* and *American Educational Research Journal.* In addition, check out *Annual Editions: Educational Psychology,* a yearly publication that reprints articles from various professional journals. Also, don't overlook the value of networking with other teachers, face to face or via the Internet. The example of Ellen Mathis and Leah Washington is an excellent illustration of how collaboration can expand your research base.

Be an intentional teacher. While there is no recipe for the ingredients that make up a commonsense approach to teaching, the behaviors consistent with being an intentional teacher are about as close as we can get. Intentional teachers are thoughtful. Like Mr. Harris, they consider multiple perspectives on classroom situations. When they take action, they are purposeful and think about *why* they do what they do. Intentional teachers follow their actions with careful reflection, evaluating their actions to determine whether they have resulted in the desired outcomes. You probably learned about the "scientific method" sometime during high school. Intentional teachers employ such a method in their teaching. That is, they formulate a working hypothesis based on their observations and background knowledge, collect data to test their hypothesis, effectively organize and analyze the data, draw sound conclusions based on the data, and take a course of action based on their conclusions. For many experienced teachers, this cycle becomes automatic and internalized. When applied systematically, these practices can serve to validate research and theory and, as a result, increase a teacher's growing professional knowledge base.

Share your experiences. When you combine your knowledge of research with your professional common sense, you will find yourself engaged in more effective practices. As you and your students experience success, share your findings. Avenues for dissemination are endless. In addition to publishing articles in traditional sources such as professional journals and organizational newsletters, don't overlook the importance of preparing schoolwide in-service presentations, papers for state and national professional conferences, and presentations to school boards. In addition, the Internet offers various newsgroups where teachers engage in ongoing discussions about their work. One such group is the Appalachia Educational Laboratory listserv (aelaction). This listserv is a free, facilitated forum on the Internet. To subscribe, send an e-mail message to majordomo@ael.org. Leave the subject line blank and in the body of the message type "subscribe aelaction" and include your e-mail address. One day you may find yourself becoming a valued contributor to the field of educational psychology research, and future students and colleagues will be reading about you and your work!

In the opening scenario Leah Washington explains to Ellen Mathis that she uses basic educational psychology to get her students to write. From their discussions, create a list of research-based and commonsense strategies that an intentional teacher may use.

WHAT RESEARCH METHODS ARE USED IN EDUCATIONAL PSYCHOLOGY?

How do we know what we know in educational psychology? As in any scientific field, knowledge comes from many sources. Sometimes researchers study schools, teachers, or students as they are, and sometimes they create special programs, or **treatments,** and study their effects on one or more **variables** (anything that can have more than one value, such as age, sex, achievement level, or attitudes). The principal methods educational researchers use to learn about schools, teachers, students, and instruction (see Slavin, 1992) are *experiments, correlational studies,* and *descriptive research.* The following sections discuss these methods.

Experiments

In an **experiment,** researchers can create special treatments and analyze their effects. In one classic study, Lepper, Greene, and Nisbett (1973) set up an experimental situation in which children used felt-tipped markers to draw pictures. Children in the *experimental group* (the group that receives a treatment) were given a prize (a "good player award") for drawing pictures. Children in a *control group* received no prizes. At the end of the experiment, all students were allowed to choose among various activities, including drawing with felt-tipped markers. The children who had received the prizes chose to continue drawing with felt-tipped markers about half as frequently as did those who had not received prizes. This result was interpreted as showing that rewarding individuals for doing a task they already liked could reduce their interest in doing the task when they were no longer rewarded.

The Lepper study illustrates several important aspects of experiments. First, the children were randomly assigned to receive prizes or not. For example, the children's names might have been put on slips of paper that were dropped into a hat and then drawn at random for assignment to a "prize" or "no-prize" group. **Random assignment** ensured that the two groups were essentially equivalent before the experiment began. This equivalence is critical, because if we were not sure that the two groups were equal before the experiment, we would not be able to tell whether it was the prizes that made the difference in their subsequent behavior.

A second feature of this study that is characteristic of experiments is that everything other than the treatment itself (the prizes) was kept the same for the prize and no-prize groups. The children played in the same rooms with the same materials and with the same adults present. The researcher who gave the prize spent the same amount of time watching the no-prize children draw. Only the prize itself was different for the two groups. The goal was to be sure that it was the treatment, not some other factor, that explained the difference between the two groups.

treatment
A special program that is the subject of an experiment.

variable
Something that can have more than one value.

experiment
Procedure used to test the effect of a treatment.

random assignment
Selection by chance into different treatment groups; intended to ensure equivalence of the groups.

LABORATORY EXPERIMENTS ● The Lepper et al. (1973) study is an example of a **laboratory experiment.** Even though the experiment took place in a school building, the researchers created a highly artificial, structured setting that existed for a very brief period of time. The advantage of laboratory experiments is that they permit researchers to exert a very high degree of control over all the factors involved in the study. Such studies are high in **internal validity,** which is to say that we can confidently attribute any differences they find to the treatments themselves (rather than to other factors). The primary limitation of laboratory experiments is that they are typically so artificial and so brief that their results may have little relevance to real-life situations. For example, the Lepper et al. (1973) study, which was later repeated several times, was used to support a theory that rewards can diminish individuals' interest in an activity when the rewards are withdrawn. This theory served as the basis for attacks on the use of classroom rewards, such as grades and stars. However, later research in real classrooms using real rewards has generally failed to find such effects (see, e.g., Cameron & Pierce, 1994). This finding does not discredit the Lepper and colleagues (1973) study; it does show that theories based on artificial laboratory experiments cannot be assumed to apply to all situations in real life but must be tested in the real settings.

RANDOMIZED FIELD EXPERIMENTS ● Another kind of experiment that is often used in educational research is the **randomized field experiment,** in which instructional programs or other practical treatments are evaluated over relatively long periods in real classes under realistic conditions. For example, Pinnell, Lyons, DeFord, Bryk, and Seltzer (1994) compared four approaches to reading instruction for first-graders who were at risk for reading failure. One of these was Reading Recovery, a one-to-one tutoring model for at-risk first-graders that requires extensive training. In each of 10 schools, the 10 lowest-performing students were identified. Four were assigned at random to the **experimental group** using Reading Recovery, and 6 were assigned to a control group. **Control group** students continued to receive the reading program and remedial services they would have received anyway.

After 4 months (in February), all children were tested. Reading Recovery children scored significantly higher than control students on each of four measures. The following October, students were tested again, and Reading Recovery students still performed significantly higher than control students.

Note the similarities and differences between the Pinnell and colleagues (1994) randomized field experiment and the Lepper and colleagues (1973) laboratory experiment. Both used random assignment to make sure that the experimental and control groups were essentially equal at the start of the study. Both tried to make all factors except the treatment equal for the experimental and control groups, but the Pinnell and colleagues study was (by its very nature as a field experiment) less able to do this. For example, experimental and control students were taught by different teachers. Because many teachers were involved, this factor probably balanced out; but the fact remains that in a field setting, control is never as great as in a laboratory situation (see Pressley & Harris, 1994). On the other hand, the fact that the Pinnell and colleagues study took place over a long period of time in real classrooms means that its **external validity** (real-life validity) is far greater than that of the Lepper et al. study. That is, the results of the Pinnell et al. study have direct relevance to reading instruction for at-risk first-graders.

Both laboratory experiments and randomized field experiments make important contributions to the science of educational psychology. Laboratory experi-

laboratory experiment
Experiment in which conditions are highly controlled.

internal validity
The degree to which an experiment's results can be attributed to the treatment in question, not to other factors.

randomized field experiment
Experiment conducted under realistic conditions in which individuals are assigned by chance to receive different practical treatments or programs.

experimental group
Group that receives treatment during an experiment.

control group
Group that receives no special treatment during an experiment.

external validity
Degree to which results of an experiment can be applied to real-life situations.

ments are primarily important in researchers' efforts to build and test theories, whereas randomized field experiments are the acid test for evaluating practical programs or improvements in instruction. For example, the writing process method that Leah Washington was using has been evaluated many times in comparison to traditional methods and found to be highly effective (Hillocks, 1984). This finding is not a guarantee that this method will work in every situation, but it does give educators a good direction to follow to improve writing.

SINGLE-CASE EXPERIMENTS ● One type of experiment that is often used in educational research is the **single-case experiment** (see Franklin, Allison, & Gorman, 1997; Neuman & McCormick, 1995). In one typical form of this type of experiment, a single student's behavior may be observed for several days. Then a special program is begun, and the student's behavior under the new program is observed. Finally, the new program is withdrawn. If the student's behavior improves under the special program but the improvement disappears when the program is withdrawn, the implication is that the program has affected the student's behavior. Sometimes the "single case" can be several students, an entire class, or a school that is given the same treatment.

An example of a single-case experiment is a classic study by Barrish, Saunders, and Wolf (1969). In this study, a fourth-grade class was the single case. Observers recorded the percentage of time that at least one student in the class was talking out (talking without permission) during reading and math periods. After 10 days, a special program was introduced. The class was divided into two large teams, and whenever any student on a team misbehaved, the team was given a check mark. At the end of each day, the team with the fewer check marks (or both teams if both received fewer than five check marks) could take part in a 30-minute free period.

The results of this study are illustrated in Figure 1.2. Before the Good Behavior Game began (baseline), at least one student in the math class was talking out 96 percent of the time, and at least one student was out-of-seat without permission 82 percent of the time. When the game was begun in math, the class's behavior improved dramatically. When the game was withdrawn, the class's behavior got worse again but improved once more when the game was reintroduced. Note that when the game was introduced in reading class, the students' behaviors also improved. The fact that the program made a difference in both math and reading gives us even greater confidence that the Good Behavior Game is effective.

One important limitation of the single-case experiment is that it can be used only to study outcomes that can be measured frequently. For this reason, most single-case studies involve observable behaviors, such as talking out and being out-of-seat, which can be measured every day or many times per day.

Correlational Studies

Perhaps the most frequently used research method in educational psychology is the **correlational study.** In contrast to an experiment, in which the researcher deliberately changes one variable to see how this change will affect other variables, in correlational research the researcher studies variables as they are to see whether they are related. Variables can be positively correlated, negatively correlated, or uncorrelated. An example of a **positive correlation** is the relationship between reading achievement and mathematics achievement. In general, someone who is better than average in reading will also be better than average in math. Of course, some students who are good readers are not good in math, and vice versa; but on the av-

single-case experiment
Experiment that studies a treatment's effect on one person or one group by contrasting behavior before, during, and after application of the treatment.

correlational study
Research into the relationships between variables as they naturally occur.

positive correlation
Relationship in which high levels of one variable correspond to high levels of another.

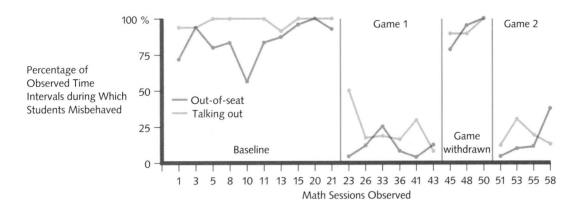

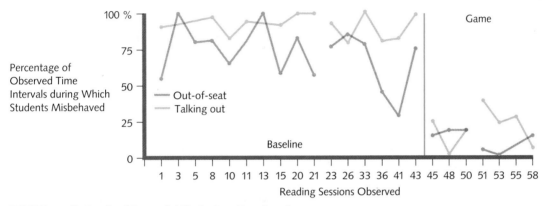

FIGURE 1.2 ● **Results of Successful Single-Case Experiments**
The effect of rewarding good behavior in fourth-grade math and reading classes is clear from these graphs. They show that misbehavior was high during the baseline period (before the Good Behavior Game was introduced) but fell during the game. For instance, in reading session 13, before the game was introduced, students were out of their seats during nearly 100 percent of the observed time intervals. In reading session 53, however, when the game was in use, the percentage of time intervals in which students were out-of-seat approached zero. In single-case experiments on treatments affecting behaviors that can be frequently measured, graphs like these can prove a treatment's effectiveness.

Adapted from H. H. Barrish, M. Saunders, and M. M. Wolf, "Good Behavior Game: Effects of Individual Contingencies for Group Consequences on Disruptive Behavior in a Classroom," *Journal of Applied Behavior Analysis, 2,* 1969, pp. 119–124. Reprinted by permission.

erage, skills in one academic area are positively correlated with skills in other academic areas: When one variable is high, the other tends also to be high. An example of a **negative correlation** is days absent and grades. The more days a student is absent, the lower his or her grades are likely to be; when one variable is high, the other tends to be low. With **uncorrelated variables,** in contrast, there is no correspondence between them. For example, student achievement in Poughkeepsie, New York, is probably completely unrelated to the level of student motivation in Portland, Oregon.

One classic example of correlational research is a study by Lahaderne (1968), who investigated the relationship between students' attentiveness in class and their achievement and IQ. She observed 125 students in four sixth-grade classes to see how much of the time students were paying attention (e.g., listening to the teacher and doing assigned work). She then correlated attentiveness with achievement in

negative correlation
Relationship in which high levels of one variable correspond to low levels of another.

uncorrelated variables
Variables for which there is no relationship between high/low levels of one and high/low levels of the other.

CASE TO CONSIDER

Evaluating Curriculum in the Classroom: Some Research of Our Own

Jane Spivak and Mike Brown are both teachers at the elementary level. Susan Esposito teaches in the district's high school. John Hammond coordinates the K through 12 math curriculum and teaches at the middle school. They serve on a districtwide committee to evaluate the current math program and choose a new one:

Jane: I like some of the new programs we've looked at. They incorporate problem-solving strategies even in first grade, and they encourage cooperative learning.

John: But do they teach the basic skills? I mean, we're still getting kids in the sixth grade who don't know their basic math facts.

Susan: I agree. But they definitely need more critical thinking about math at earlier ages if they are going to handle some of the expectations at the high school level.

Mike: I think these would work out great if you *started* the kids out with it in kindergarten, but how about the upper grades? Are you just going to switch them from the relatively traditional program we have now into one that is much more problem-solving oriented and less teacher directed?

John: OK, OK—another consideration is the expense of these programs, both in time and money to us and

the district. I think we all agree that the easiest thing would be to keep what we've got but that the students need more.

Susan: How about a pilot study? You know, purchase materials for one or two classes at selected grade levels and do a careful comparison. We can find out both the difficulties and the benefits, then make our decision. We've certainly done some research already—the workshops we've gone to, visits to other schools using the program. But how about some research of our own?

Jane: OK, but it will have to be well done, a matched control group class using the old program for each one piloting the new. We should compare how each class does at reaching the same set of objectives we've decided on for those grade levels.

Susan: I want some qualitative feedback from teachers too. Maybe some rating scales. We could send a questionnaire home to parents. . . .

PROBLEM SOLVING

1. What are the benefits of this type of curriculum evaluation?
2. Devise an outline of the proposed research to compare the two curricular approaches.
3. Extend the discussion with the system superintendent. He doesn't want to spend the time or money on research before choosing a curriculum. How will the teachers defend their need for personal research?

reading, arithmetic, and language and with students' IQs and attitudes toward school. The advantage of correlational studies is that they allow the researcher to study variables as they are, without creating artificial situations. Many important research questions can be studied only in correlational studies. For example, if we wanted to study the relationship between gender and math achievement, we could hardly randomly assign students to be boys or girls! Also, correlational studies let researchers study the interrelationships of many variables at the same time.

The principal disadvantage of correlational methods is that while they may tell us that two variables are related, they do not tell us what causes what. The Lahaderne study of attentiveness, achievement, and IQ raised the question: Does student attentiveness cause high achievement, or are high-ability, high-achieving students simply more attentive than other students? A correlational study cannot answer this question completely. However, correlational researchers do typically use statistical methods to try to determine what causes what. In Lahaderne's study, it would have been possible to find out whether among students with the same IQ, attentiveness was related to achievement. For example, given two students of average intelligence, will the one who is more attentive tend to achieve more? If not, then we may conclude that the relationship between attentiveness and achieve-

Explanation A

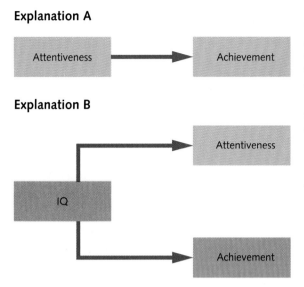

Explanation B

FIGURE 1.3 ● **Possible Explanations for Correlations among Attentiveness, Achievement, and IQ** Correlational studies can show that variables are related, but such studies cannot prove what causes what. In Lahaderne's (1968) study, for example, did the attentiveness of the students cause higher achievement scores (Explanation A), or did a third factor—intelligence—determine both attentiveness and performance on achievement tests (as diagrammed in Explanation B)? Both explanations are partially correct.

ment is simply the result of high-IQ students being more attentive and higher achieving than other students, not the result of any effect of attention on achievement.

Figure 1.3 illustrates two possible explanations for the correlation between attentiveness, achievement, and IQ. In Explanation A, attentiveness causes achievement. In Explanation B, both attentiveness and achievement are assumed to be caused by a third variable, IQ. Which is correct? Evidence from other research on this relationship suggests that both explanations are partially correct; that even when the effect of IQ is removed, student attentiveness is related to achievement.

Descriptive Research

Experimental and correlational research look for relationships between variables. However, some research in educational psychology simply seeks to describe something of interest. One type of **descriptive research** is a survey or interview. Another, called ethnography (Bogdan & Biklen, 1992), involves observation of a social setting (such as a classroom or school) over an extended period. For example, Jonathan Kozol (1991) wrote a descriptive study of life in well-funded and poorly funded schools that paints a devastating portrait of inequality in the U.S. educational system. Jeannie Oakes (1985) described teachers' practices in tracked and untracked middle schools. These and many other descriptive studies provide a much more complete story of what happens in schools and classrooms than could a study that boiled down the findings into cold, hard numbers. Descriptive research usually does not have the scientific objectivity of correlational or experimental research, but it makes up for this lack in richness of detail and interpretation (Bogdan & Biklen, 1992; Strauss & Corbin, 1990).

Developmental psychologists use descriptive research extensively to identify characteristics of children at different ages. The most important research in developmental psychology was done by the Swiss psychologist Jean Piaget (1952b), who began by carefully observing his own children. As a result of his observations, he developed a theory that describes the cognitive development of children from infancy through adolescence.

CONNECTIONS

For more on the use of descriptive research in developmental psychology, see Chapters 2 and 3.

descriptive research
Study aimed at identifying and gathering detailed information about something of interest.

SELF-CHECK

Construct a comparison chart with the columns headed Experimental, Correlational, and Descriptive. Enter information in the following five categories: goals of research, forms studies take, kinds of findings, advantages and disadvantages, and examples.

CHAPTER SUMMARY

WHAT MAKES A GOOD TEACHER?

Good teachers know their subject matter and have mastered pedagogical skills. They accomplish all the tasks involved in effective instruction with warmth, enthusiasm, and caring. They are intentional teachers, and they use principles of educational psychology in their decision making and teaching. They combine research and common sense.

WHAT IS THE ROLE OF RESEARCH IN EDUCATIONAL PSYCHOLOGY?

Educational psychology is the systematic study of learners, learning, and teaching. Research in educational psychology focuses on the processes by which information, skills, values, and attitudes are communicated between teachers and students in the classroom and on applications of the principles of psychology to instructional practices. Such research shapes educational policies, professional development programs, and teaching materials.

WHAT RESEARCH METHODS ARE USED IN EDUCATIONAL PSYCHOLOGY?

Experimental research involves testing particular educational programs or treatments. Random assignment of experimental subjects into groups before the testing helps to ensure that groups are equivalent and findings will be valid. An experimental group receiving the treatment is matched with a control group whose members do not receive treatment. Laboratory experiments are highly structured and short term. All the variables involved are strictly controlled. Randomized field experiments are less structured and take place over a long period of time under realistic conditions in which not all variables can be controlled. A single-case experiment involves observation of one student or group of students over a specified period before and after treatment. Correlational studies examine variables to see whether they are related. Variables can be positively correlated, negatively correlated, or uncorrelated. Correlational studies provide information about variables without manipulating them or creating artificial situations. However, they do not indicate the causes of relationships between variables. Descriptive research uses surveys, interviews, and/or observations to describe behavior in social settings.

KEY TERMS

control group 19	critical thinking 10
correlational study 20	descriptive research 23

educational psychology   3
experiment   18
experimental group   19
external validity   19
intentionality   7
internal validity   19
laboratory experiment   19
negative correlation   21
pedagogy   4

positive correlation   20
principle   12
random assignment   18
randomized field experiment   19
single-case experiment   20
theory   12
treatment   18
uncorrelated variables   21
variable   18

Self-Assessment

1. Write a paragraph that begins with the following topic sentence: Intentional teachers do things on purpose.

2. Define and provide an example of a principle, a law, and a theory.

3. Match the type of research listed with the advantage it offers.
   _____ laboratory experiment
   _____ randomized field experiment
   _____ single-case experiment

   a. has high internal validity and rigorous controls
   b. involves observation of one individual's behavior over time
   c. involves frequent assessments over time

4. Match the following types of experiments with the situations that illustrate each. (A research type may be used more than once or not at all.)
   _____ observing and noting how preschoolers play
   _____ recording the number of times a student misbehaves before, during, and after a special reinforcement program
   _____ determining the relationship between reading ability and math achievement
   _____ evaluating a new teaching technique for a short period of time under highly controlled conditions

   a. randomized field experiment
   b. descriptive research
   c. laboratory experiment
   d. correlational study

5. A teacher wants to know whether a new teaching strategy is more effective than the traditional one she uses in several 10th-grade composition classes.

   She selects two classes that are the same in ability, then uses the new approach in one class while continuing with the traditional approach in the other class. She then compares compositions written by each group. What type of research is the teacher conducting?

   a. experimental
   b. correlational
   c. descriptive

6. In a hypothetical schoolwide correlational study, the number of days a student was absent during a marking period was shown on the average to have a negative correlation with the student's class ranking from one marking period to the next. This negative correlation would mean that

   a. absenteeism causes lower class rankings.
   b. the study does not have internal validity.
   c. class rankings tend to rise as absenteeism decreases.
   d. class rank decreases absenteeism.

7. A type of descriptive research that involves observation in a social setting over an extended period of time is sometimes called

   a. a randomized field experiment.
   b. a correlational study.
   c. an ethnographic study.

8. Describe the relationship between subject matter knowledge and pedagogy.

9. Explain why teachers need knowledge of research on teaching as well as common sense.

10. Why do teachers need to study educational psychology?

Chapter 2

WHAT ARE SOME VIEWS OF HUMAN DEVELOPMENT?
Aspects of Development
Issues of Development

HOW DID PIAGET VIEW COGNITIVE DEVELOPMENT?
How Development Occurs
Piaget's Stages of Development

HOW IS PIAGET'S WORK VIEWED TODAY?
Criticisms and Revisions of Piaget's Theory
Neo-Piagetian and Information-Processing Views of Development

HOW DID VYGOTSKY VIEW COGNITIVE DEVELOPMENT?
How Development Occurs
Applications of Vygotskian Theory in Teaching

HOW DID ERIKSON VIEW PERSONAL AND SOCIAL DEVELOPMENT?
Stages of Psychosocial Development
Implications and Criticisms of Erikson's Theory

WHAT ARE SOME THEORIES OF MORAL DEVELOPMENT?
Piaget's Theory of Moral Development
Kohlberg's Stages of Moral Reasoning
Criticisms of Kohlberg's Theory
Hoffman's Development of Moral Behavior

Theories of Development

Each week, day, and hour, you will encounter students with differing individual needs based on their cognitive, physical, social, and moral development. An understanding of some documented stages in development that are important at various ages will help you to become a more effective teacher and a more skilled evaluator of productive learning environments. The following three scenarios cover distinct time periods and developmental dilemmas.

- In the first week of school, Mr. Jones tried to teach his first-graders how to behave in class. He said, "When I ask a question, I want you to raise your right hand, and I'll call on you. Can you all raise your right hands, as I am doing?" Thirty hands went up. All were left hands.

- Because her students were getting careless about handing in their homework, Ms. Lewis decided to lay down the law to her fourth-grade class. "Anyone who does not hand in all his or her homework this week will not be allowed to go on the field trip." It happened that one girl's mother became ill and was taken to the hospital that week. As a result of her family's confusion and concern, the girl failed to hand in one of her homework assignments. Ms. Lewis explained to the class that she would make an exception in this case because of the girl's mother's illness, but the class wouldn't hear of it. "Rules are rules," they said. "She didn't hand in her homework, so she can't go!"

• Ms. Quintera started her eighth-grade English class one day with an excited announcement: "Class, I wanted to tell you all that we have a poet in our midst. Frank wrote such a wonderful poem that I thought I'd read it to you all." Ms. Quintera read Frank's poem, which was indeed very good. However, she noticed that Frank was turning bright red and looking distinctly uncomfortable. A few of the other students in the class snickered. Later, Ms. Quintera asked Frank whether he would like to write another poem for a citywide poetry contest. He said he'd rather not, because he really didn't think he was that good; and besides, he didn't have the time.

Using Your EXPERIENCE

Critical Thinking   Why do you think Frank reacted the way he did? How could Ms. Quintera alter her approach so as to motivate Frank?

Critical Thinking   Compare and contrast these three scenarios. Explain which case(s) involved a behavioral, cognitive, social, moral, or physical development dilemma. Specify the dilemma.

WHAT ARE SOME VIEWS OF HUMAN DEVELOPMENT?

The term **development** refers to how and why people grow, adapt, and change over the course of their lifetimes. People grow, adapt, and change through physical development, personality development, socioemotional development, cognitive development (thinking), and language development. This chapter presents five major theories of human development that are widely accepted: Jean Piaget's theory of cognitive and moral development, Lev Vygotsky's theory of cognitive development, Erik Erikson's theory of personal and social development, and Lawrence Kohlberg's and Martin Hoffman's theories of moral development.

Aspects of Development

Children are not miniature adults. They think differently, they see the world differently, and they live by different moral and ethical principles than adults do. The three scenarios just presented illustrate a few of the many aspects of children's thinking that differ from those of adults. When Mr. Jones raised his right hand, his first-graders imitated his action without taking his perspective; they didn't realize that since he was facing them, his right hand would be to their left. The situation in Ms. Lewis's class illustrates a stage in children's moral development at which rules are rules and extenuating circumstances do not count. Ms. Quintera's praise of Frank's poem had an effect opposite to what she intended; but had she paused to consider the situation, she might have realized that highlighting Frank's achievement could cast him in the role of teacher's pet, a role that many students in early adolescence strongly resist.

development
Orderly and lasting growth, adaptation, and change over the course of a lifetime.

One of the first requirements of effective teaching is that the teacher understand how students think and how they view the world. Effective teaching strategies must take into account students' ages and stages of development. A bright fourth-grader might appear to be able to learn any kind of mathematics but in fact might not have the cognitive maturity or experience in mathematics to do the abstract thinking required for algebra. Similarly, Ms. Quintera's public recognition of Frank's poetry might have been quite appropriate if Frank had been three years younger or three years older.

Issues of Development

Two central issues have been debated for decades among developmental psychologists. One relates to the degree to which development is affected by experience, and the other to the question of whether development proceeds in stages.

NATURE–NURTURE CONTROVERSY ● Is development predetermined at birth, by heredity and biological factors, or is it affected by experience and other environmental factors? Today, most developmental psychologists (e.g., Berk, 1997; Elkind, 1994) believe that nature and nurture combine to influence development, biological factors playing a stronger role in some aspects of development, such as physical development, and environmental factors playing a stronger role in others, such as moral development.

CONTINUOUS AND DISCONTINUOUS THEORIES ● A second issue revolves around the notion of how change occurs. One perspective assumes that development occurs in a smooth progression as skills develop and experiences are provided by parents and the environment. This **continuous theory of development** would suggest that at a fairly early age, children are capable of thinking and acting like adults, given the proper experience and education.

A second perspective assumes that children progress through a set of predictable and invariant stages of development. In this case, change can be fairly abrupt as children advance to a new stage of development. All children are believed to acquire skills in the same sequence, although rates of progress differ from child to child. The abilities that children gain in each subsequent stage are not simply "more of the same"; at each stage, children develop qualitatively different understandings, abilities, and beliefs. Skipping stages is impossible, although at any given point the same child may exhibit behaviors characteristic of more than one stage (Epstein, 1990). In contrast to continuous theories, these **discontinuous theories of development** focus on inborn factors rather than environmental influences to explain change over time. Environmental conditions may have some influence on the pace of development, but the sequence of developmental steps is essentially fixed.

Some of the theories in this chapter emphasize discontinuous theories of development. Piaget, Vygotsky, Erikson, Kohlberg, and Hoffman all focus on different aspects of development. Nevertheless, all are stage theorists, because they share the belief that distinct stages of development can be identified and described. This agreement does not, however, extend to the particulars of their theories, which differ significantly in the numbers of stages and in their details. Also, each theorist focuses on different aspects of development (e.g., cognitive, socioemotional, personality, moral).

continuous theory of development
Theory based on the belief that human development progresses smoothly and gradually from infancy to adulthood.

discontinuous theories of development
Theories describing human development as occurring through a fixed sequence of distinct, predictable stages governed by inborn factors.

Today, most developmentalists acknowledge the role of both inborn factors and social experiences when explaining children's behavior (see Petrill & Thompson, 1993). Vygotsky's and Hoffman's theories rely on social interactions as well as predictable stages of growth to explain development.

SELF-CHECK

Begin a four-column comparison chart with the columns headed Piaget, Vygotsky, Erikson, and Kohlberg. Identify the theory that each proposed, the type of development involved, and whether the theory is continuous or discontinuous. After you finish reading the chapter, explain the three chapter-opening scenarios in terms of the theories and concepts presented in the chapter.

HOW DID PIAGET VIEW COGNITIVE DEVELOPMENT?

Jean Piaget, born in Switzerland in 1896, is the best-known child psychologist in the history of psychology (see Flavell, 1996). After receiving his doctorate in biology, he became more interested in psychology, basing his earliest theories on careful observation of his own three children. Piaget thought of himself as applying biological principles and methods to the study of human development, and many of the terms he introduced to psychology were drawn directly from biology.

Piaget explored both why and how mental abilities change over time. His explanation of developmental change assumes that the child is an active organism. For Piaget, development depends in large part on the child's manipulation of and active interaction with the environment. In Piaget's view, knowledge comes from action (see Ginsburg & Opper, 1988; Wadsworth, 1996). Piaget's theory of **cognitive development** proposes that a child's intellect, or cognitive abilities, progresses through four distinct stages. Each stage is characterized by the emergence of new abilities and ways of processing information.

How Development Occurs

SCHEMES ● Piaget believed that all children are born with an innate tendency to interact with and make sense of their environments. He referred to the basic ways of organizing and processing information as cognitive structures. Young children demonstrate patterns of behavior or thinking, called **schemes,** that older children and adults also use in dealing with objects in the world. We use schemes to find out about and act in the world; each scheme treats all objects and events in the same way. For example, most young infants will discover that one thing you can do with objects is bang them. When they do this, the object makes a noise, and they see the object hitting a surface. Their observations tell them something about the object. Babies also learn about objects by biting them, sucking on them, and throwing them. Each of these approaches to interacting with objects is a scheme. When babies encounter a new object, how are they to know what this object is all about? According to Piaget, they will use the schemes they have developed and will find out whether the object makes a loud or soft sound when banged, what it tastes like, whether it gives milk, and maybe whether it rolls or just goes thud when dropped (see Figure 2.1a).

---

cognitive development
Gradual, orderly changes by which mental processes become more complex and sophisticated.

CONNECTIONS
For information on schema theory (a topic related to schemes) in connection with information processing and memory, see Chapter 6, pages 182 and 200.

schemes
Mental patterns that guide behavior.

FIGURE 2.1 ● Schemes
Babies use patterns of behavior called *schemes* to learn about their world.

a. Banging is a favorite **scheme** used by babies to explore their world.

b. **Assimilation** occurs when they incorporate new objects into the scheme.

c. **Accommodation** occurs when a new object does not fit the existing scheme.

ASSIMILATION AND ACCOMMODATION ● According to Piaget, **adaptation** is the process of adjusting schemes in response to the environment by means of assimilation and accommodation. **Assimilation** is the process of understanding a new object or event in terms of an existing scheme. If you give young infants small objects that they have never seen before but that resemble familiar objects, they are likely to grasp them, bite them, and bang them. In other words, they will try to use existing schemes to learn about these unknown things (see Figure 2.1b). Similarly, a high school student may have a studying scheme that involves putting information on cards and memorizing the cards' contents. She may then try to apply this scheme to learn difficult concepts such as economics, for which this approach may not be effective.

Sometimes, however, old ways of dealing with the world simply don't work. When this happens, a child may modify an existing scheme in light of new information or experience, a process called **accommodation.** For example, if you give an egg to a baby who has a banging scheme for small objects, what will happen to the egg is obvious (Figure 2.1c). Less obvious, however, is what will happen to the baby's banging scheme. Because of the unexpected consequences of banging the egg, the baby might change the scheme. In the future the baby might bang some objects hard and others softly. The high school student who studies only by means of memorization may learn to use a different strategy to study economics, such as discussing difficult concepts with a friend.

The baby who banged the egg and the student who tried to memorize rather than comprehend had to deal with situations that could not be fully handled by existing schemes. This, in Piaget's theory, creates a state of disequilibrium, or an imbalance between what is understood and what is encountered. People naturally try to reduce such imbalances by focusing on the stimuli that cause the disequilibrium and developing new schemes or adapting old ones until equilibrium is restored. This process of restoring balance is called **equilibration.** According to Piaget, learning depends on this process. When equilibrium is upset, children have

adaptation
The process of adjusting schemes in response to the environment by means of assimilation and accommodation.

assimilation
Understanding new experiences in terms of existing schemes.

accommodation
Modifying existing schemes to fit new situations.

equilibration
The process of restoring balance between present understanding and new experiences.

the opportunity to grow and develop. Eventually, qualitatively new ways of thinking about the world emerge, and children advance to a new stage of development. Piaget believed that physical experiences and manipulation of the environment are critical for developmental change to occur. However, he also believed that social interaction with peers, especially arguments and discussions, helps to clarify thinking and, eventually, to make it more logical. Recent research has stressed the importance of confronting students with experiences or data that do not fit into their current theories of how the world works as a means of advancing their cognitive development (Chinn & Brewer, 1993).

Piaget's theory of development represents **constructivism,** a view of cognitive development as a process in which children actively build systems of meaning and understandings of reality through their experiences and interactions (see DeVries, 1997). In this view, children actively construct knowledge by continually assimilating and accommodating new information (Anderson, 1989). Applications of constructivist theories to education are discussed in Chapter 8.

Piaget's Stages of Development

Piaget divided the cognitive development of children and adolescents into four stages: sensorimotor, preoperational, concrete operational, and formal operational. He believed that all children pass through these stages in order and that no child can skip a stage, although different children pass through the stages at somewhat different rates (see de Ribaupierre & Rieben, 1995). The same individuals may perform tasks associated with different stages at the same time, particularly at points of transition into a new stage (Crain, 1985). Table 2.1 summarizes the ap-

constructivism
View of cognitive development that emphasizes the active role of learners in building their own understanding of reality.

TABLE 2.1

Piaget's Stages of Cognitive Development

People progress through four stages of cognitive development between birth and adulthood, according to Jean Piaget. Each stage is marked by the emergence of new intellectual abilities that allow people to understand the world in increasingly complex ways.

STAGE	APPROXIMATE AGES	MAJOR ACCOMPLISHMENTS
Sensorimotor	Birth to 2 years	Formation of concept of "object permanence" and gradual progression from reflexive behavior to goal-directed behavior.
Preoperational	2 to 7 years	Development of the ability to use symbols to represent objects in the world. Thinking remains egocentric and centered.
Concrete operational	7 to 11 years	Improvement in ability to think logically. New abilities include the use of operations that are reversible. Thinking is decentered, and problem solving is less restricted by egocentrism. Abstract thinking is not possible.
Formal operational	11 years to adulthood	Abstract and purely symbolic thinking possible. Problems can be solved through the use of systematic experimentation.

proximate ages at which children and adolescents pass through Piaget's four stages. It also shows the major accomplishments of each stage.

SENSORIMOTOR STAGE (BIRTH TO AGE 2) ● The earliest stage is called **sensorimotor,** because during this stage babies and young children explore their world by using their senses and their motor skills.

Piaget believed that all children are born with an innate tendency to interact with and make sense of their environments. Dramatic changes occur as infants progress through the sensorimotor period. Initially, all infants have inborn behaviors called **reflexes.** Touch a newborn's lips, and the baby will begin to suck; place your finger in the palm of an infant's hand, and the infant will grasp it. These and other behaviors are innate and are the building blocks from which the infant's first schemes form.

Infants soon learn to use these reflexes to produce more interesting and intentional patterns of behavior. This learning occurs initially through accident and then through more intentional trial-and-error efforts. According to Piaget, by the end of the sensorimotor stage, children have progressed from their earlier trial-and-error approach to a more planned approach to problem solving. For the first time they can mentally represent objects and events. What most of us would call "thinking" appears now. This is a major advance, because it means that the child can think through and plan behavior. For example, suppose a 2-year-old is in the kitchen watching his mother prepare dinner. If the child knows where the step stool is kept, he may ask to have it set up to afford a better view of the counter and a better chance for a nibble. The child did not stumble onto this solution accidentally. Instead, he thought about the problem, figured out a possible solution that used the step stool, tried out the solution mentally, and only then tried the solution in practice.

Another hallmark of the sensorimotor period is the development of a grasp of **object permanence.** Piaget argued that children must learn that objects are physically stable and exist even when the objects are not in the child's physical presence. For example, if you cover an infant's bottle with a towel, the child may not remove it, believing that the bottle is gone. By 2 years of age, children understand that objects exist even if they cannot be seen. When children develop this notion of object permanence, they have taken a step toward more advanced thinking. Once they realize that things exist out of sight, they can start using symbols to represent these things in their minds so that they can think about them.

PREOPERATIONAL STAGE (AGES 2 TO 7) ● Whereas infants can learn about and understand the world only by physically manipulating objects, preschoolers have greater ability to think about things and can use symbols to mentally represent objects. During the **preoperational stage,** children's language and concepts develop at an incredible rate. Yet much of their thinking remains surprisingly primitive. One of Piaget's earliest and most important discoveries was that young children lacked an understanding of the principle of **conservation.** For example, if you pour milk from a tall, narrow container into a shallow, wide one in the presence of a preoperational child, the child will firmly believe that the tall glass has more milk (see Figure 2.2). The child focuses on only one aspect (the height of the milk), ignoring all others, and cannot be convinced that the amount of milk is the same. Similarly, a preoperational child is likely to believe that a sandwich cut in four pieces is more sandwich or that a line of blocks that is spread out contains more blocks than a line that is compressed, even after being shown that the number of blocks is identical.

sensorimotor stage
Stage during which infants learn about their surroundings by using their senses and motor skills.

reflexes
Inborn, automatic responses to stimuli (e.g., eye blinking in response to bright light).

object permanence
The fact that an object exists even if it is out of sight.

preoperational stage
Stage at which children learn to represent things in the mind.

conservation
The concept that certain properties of an object (such as weight) remain the same regardless of changes in other properties (such as length).

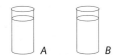

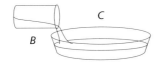

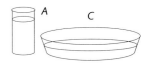

Step 1: The child agrees that containers *A* and *B* contain the same quantity of milk.

Step 2: The child observes the contents of container *B* poured into a third, different-shaped container, *C*.

Step 3: The child is then asked to compare the quantity of milk in containers *A* and *C*.

FIGURE 2.2 ● **The Task of Conservation**
A typical procedure for studying conservation of liquid quantity.
From Robert V. Kail and Rita Wicks-Nelson, *Developmental Psychology* (5th ed.), p. 190. Copyright © 1993. Reprinted by permission of Prentice Hall, Upper Saddle River, New Jersey.

centration
Paying attention to only one aspect of an object or situation.

reversibility
The ability to perform a mental operation and then reverse one's thinking to return to the starting point.

Several aspects of preoperational thinking help to explain the error on conservation tasks. One characteristic is **centration:** paying attention to only one aspect of a situation. In the example illustrated in Figure 2.2, children might have claimed that there was less milk after pouring because they centered on the height of the milk, ignoring its width. In Figure 2.3, children focus on the length of the line of blocks but ignore its density (or the actual number of blocks).

Preschoolers' thinking can also be characterized as being irreversible. **Reversibility** is a very important aspect of thinking, according to Piaget; it simply means the ability to change direction in one's thinking so that one can return to a starting point. As adults, for example, we know that if $7 + 5 = 12$, then $12 - 5 = 7$. If we add five things to seven things and then take the five things away (reverse what we've done), we are left with seven things. If preoperational children could think this way, then they could mentally reverse the process of pouring the milk and realize that if the milk were poured back into the tall beaker, its quantity would not change.

Another characteristic of the preoperational child's thinking is its focus on states. In the milk problem the milk was poured from one container to another.

How will this child likely respond to the Piagetian conservation task that she is attempting? What stage of development does she demonstrate? As a teacher, how might you help a young child discover errors caused by centration and irreversibility?

Which row has more blocks?

Situation A

Examiner's blocks

Child's blocks

The preoperational child is likely to say that the rows have the same number of blocks, because the rows are equal in length.

Situation B

Examiner's blocks

Child's blocks

The preoperational child may say that the examiner has fewer blocks, because that row is shorter.

FIGURE 2.3 ● Centration
Centration, or focusing on only one aspect of a situation, helps to explain some errors in perception that young children make.

From Barry Wadsworth, *Piaget for the Classroom Teacher,* 1978, p. 225, published by Longman Publishing Group. Adapted by permission of the author.

Preschoolers ignore this pouring process and focus only on the beginning state (milk in a tall glass) and end state (milk in a shallow dish). "It is as though [the child] were viewing a series of still pictures instead of the movie that the adult sees" (Phillips, 1975). You can understand how a preoccupation with states can interfere with a child's thinking if you imagine yourself presented with the milk problem and being asked to close your eyes while the milk is poured. Lacking the knowledge of what took place, you would be left with only your perception of the milk in the wide, shallow container and your memory of the milk in the tall, narrow glass. Unlike adults, the young preschooler forms concepts that vary in definition from situation to situation and are not always logical. How else can we explain the 2-year-old's ability to treat a stuffed animal as an inanimate object one minute and an animate object the next? Eventually, though, the child's concepts become more consistent and less private. Children become increasingly concerned that their definitions of things match other people's. But they still lack the ability to coordinate one concept with another. Consider the following conversation:

Adult: Sally, how many boys are in your play group?
Sally: Eight.
Adult: How many girls are in your play group?
Sally: Five.
Adult: Are there more boys or girls in your play group?
Sally: More boys.
Adult: Are there more boys or children in your play group?
Sally: More boys.
Adult: How do you know?
Sally: I just do!

Sally clearly understands the concepts of *boy, girl,* and even *more.* She also knows what children are. However, she lacks the ability to put these separate pieces of knowledge together to correctly answer the question comparing boys and children. She also cannot explain her answer, which is why Piaget used the term *intuitive* to describe her thinking.

Finally, preoperational children are **egocentric** in their thinking. Children at this stage believe that everyone sees the world exactly as they do. For example, Piaget and Inhelder (1956) seated children on one side of a display of three mountains and asked them to describe how the scene looked to a doll seated on the other

egocentric
Believing that everyone views the world as you do.

side. Children below the age of 6 or 7 described the doll's view as being identical to their own, even though it was apparent to adults that this could not be so. Preoperational children also interpret events entirely in reference to themselves. Owen, Froman, and Moscow (1981) cite a passage from A. A. Milne's *Winnie-the-Pooh* to illustrate the young child's egocentrism. Winnie-the-Pooh is sitting in the forest and hears a buzzing sound.

> That buzzing-noise means something. You don't get a buzzing-noise like that just buzzing and buzzing, without its meaning something. If there is a buzzing-noise, somebody's making a buzzing-noise, and the only reason for making a buzzing-noise that *I* know of is because you're a bee . . . and the only reason for being a bee that *I* know of is for making honey . . . and the only reason for making honey is so as *I* can eat it.

Of course, egocentrism does diminish gradually over time. Two-year-old Benjamin and his 4-year-old brother Jacob were driving with their father through dairy country, admiring the cows. "Why do farmers keep cows?" said their father. "So my [I] can look at them!" said Benjamin. "No," said his older and wiser brother. "The farmer likes to play with them." Benjamin's egocentrism is extreme; he believes that everything that happens in the world relates to him. Jacob, at 4, realizes that the farmer has his own needs but assumes that they are the same as his.

CONNECTIONS

For more on how to accommodate instruction to the developmental characteristics of children and adolescents, see Chapter 3, page 81.

CONCRETE OPERATIONAL STAGE (AGES 7 TO 11) ● Although the differences between the mental abilities of preoperational preschoolers and concrete operational elementary school students are dramatic, *concrete operational* children still do not think like adults. They are very much rooted in the world as it is and have difficulty with abstract thought. Flavell describes the concrete operational child as taking "an earthbound, concrete, practical-minded sort of problem-solving approach, one that persistently fixates on the perceptible and inferable reality right there in front of him. A theorist the elementary-school child is not" (1985, p. 103). The term **concrete operational stage** reflects this earthbound approach. The child at this stage can form concepts, see relationships, and solve problems, but only as long as they involve objects and situations that are familiar.

During the elementary school years, children's cognitive abilities undergo dramatic changes. Elementary school children no longer have difficulties with conservation problems, because they have acquired the concept of reversibility. For example, they can now see that the amount of milk in the short, wide container must be the same as that in the tall, narrow container, because if the milk were poured back in the tall container, it would be at the same level as before. The child is able to imagine the milk being poured back and can recognize the consequences—abilities that are not evident in the preoperational child.

concrete operational stage
Stage at which children develop the capacity for logical reasoning and understanding of conservation but can use these skills only in dealing with familiar situations.

inferred reality
The meaning of stimuli in the context of relevant information.

seriation
Arranging objects in sequential order according to one aspect, such as size, weight, or volume.

Another fundamental difference between preoperational and concrete operational children is that the younger child, who is in the preoperational stage, responds to perceived appearances, whereas the older, concrete operational child responds to *inferred reality*. Flavell (1986) demonstrated this concept by showing children a red car and then, while they were still watching, covering it with a filter that made it look black. When asked what color the car was, 3-year-olds responded "black," and 6-year-olds responded "red." The older, concrete operational child is able to respond to **inferred reality,** seeing things in the context of other meanings; preschoolers see what they see, with little ability to infer the meaning behind what they see.

One important task that children learn during the concrete operational stage is **seriation,** or arranging things in a logical progression; for example, lining up sticks from smallest to largest. To do this, they must be able to order or classify objects according to some criterion or dimension, in this case length. Once this ability is acquired, children can master a related skill known as **transitivity,** the ability to infer a relationship between two objects on the basis of knowledge of their respective relationships with a third object. For example, if you tell preoperational preschoolers that Tom is taller than Becky and that Becky is taller than Fred, they will not see that Tom is taller than Fred. Logical inferences such as this are not possible until the stage of concrete operations, during which school-age children develop the ability to make two mental transformations that require reversible thinking. The first of these is inversion ($+A$ is reversed by $-A$), and the second is reciprocity ($A < B$ is reciprocated by $B > A$). By the end of the concrete operational stage, children have the mental abilities to learn how to add, subtract, multiply, and divide; to place numbers in order by size; and to classify objects by any number of criteria. Children can think about what would happen if . . . , as long as the objects are in view (e.g., "what would happen if I pulled this spring and then let it go?"). Children can understand time and space well enough to draw a map from their home to school and are building an understanding of events in the past.

Children in the elementary grades also are moving from egocentric thought to decentered or objective thought. Decentered thought allows children to see that others can have different perceptions than they do. For example, children with decentered thought will be able to understand that different children may see different patterns in clouds. Children whose thought processes are decentered are able to learn that events may be governed by physical laws, such as the laws of gravity. A final ability that children acquire during the concrete operational stage is **class inclusion.** Recall the example of Sally, who was in the preoperational stage and believed that there were more boys than children in her play group. What Sally lacked was the ability to think simultaneously about the whole class (children) and the subordinate class (boys, girls). She could make comparisons within a class, as shown by her ability to compare one part (the boys) with another part (the girls). She also knew that boys and girls are both members of the larger class called *children.* What she could not do was make comparisons between classes. Concrete operational children, by contrast, have no trouble with this type of problem, because they have additional tools of thinking. First, they no longer exhibit irreversibility of thinking and can now re-create a relationship between a part and the whole. Second, concrete operational thought is decentered, so the child can now focus on two classes simultaneously. Third, the concrete operational child's thinking is no longer limited to reasoning about part-to-part relationships. Now part-to-whole relationships can be dealt with too. These changes do not happen all at the same time. Rather, they occur gradually during the concrete operational stage.

FORMAL OPERATIONAL STAGE (AGE 11 TO ADULTHOOD) ● Some time around the onset of puberty, children's thinking begins to develop into the form that is characteristic of adults. The preadolescent begins to be able to think abstractly and to see possibilities beyond the here and now. These abilities continue to develop into adulthood. With the **formal operational stage** thought comes the ability to deal with potential or hypothetical situations; the form is now separate from the content. Inhelder and Piaget (1958) described one task that will be approached differently by elementary school students in the concrete operational stage and by adolescents in the formal operational stage. The children and adolescents were given a pendulum consisting of a string with a weight at the end. They could change the length of the string, the amount of weight, the height from which the pendulum was released, and the force with which the pendulum was pushed. They were asked

transitivity
A skill learned during the concrete operational stage of cognitive development in which individuals can mentally arrange and compare objects.

class inclusion
A skill learned during the concrete operational stage of cognitive development in which individuals can think simultaneously about a whole class of objects and about relationships among its subordinate classes.

formal operational thought
Stage at which one can deal abstractly with hypothetical situations and can reason logically.

FIGURE 2.4 ● A Test of Problem-Solving Abilities
The pendulum problem uses a string, which can be shortened or lengthened, and a set of weights. When children in the concrete operational stage are asked what determines the speed of the pendulum's swing, they will tackle the problem less systematically than will adolescents who have entered the stage for formal operations. (The answer is that only the string's length affects the speed of the pendulum's swing.)

which of these factors influenced the speed at which the pendulum swings back and forth. Essentially, the task was to discover a principle of physics, which is that only the length of the string makes any difference in the speed of the pendulum (the shorter the string, the faster it swings). This experiment is illustrated in Figure 2.4. The adolescent who has reached the stage of formal operations is likely to proceed quite systematically, varying one factor at a time (e.g., leaving the string the same length and trying different weights). For example, in Inhelder and Piaget's (1958) experiment, one 15-year-old selected 100 grams with a long string and a medium-length string, then 20 grams with a long and a short string, and finally 200 grams with a long and a short string and concluded, "It's the length of the string that makes it go faster and slower; the weight doesn't play any role" (p. 75). In contrast, 10-year-olds (who can be assumed to be in the concrete operational stage) proceeded in a chaotic fashion, varying many factors at the same time and hanging onto preconceptions. One boy varied simultaneously the weight and the impetus (push); then the weight, the impetus, and the length; then the impetus, the weight, and the elevation; and so on. He first concluded, "It's by changing the weight and the push, certainly not the string."

"How do you know that the string has nothing to do with it?"

"Because it's the same string."

He had not varied its length in the last several trials; previously, he had varied it simultaneously with the impetus, thus complicating the account of the experiment (adapted from Inhelder and Piaget, 1958, p. 71).

The transitivity problem also illustrates the advances brought about by formal thought. Recall the concrete operational child who, when told that Tom was taller than Becky and Becky was taller than Fred, understood that Tom was taller than Fred. However, if the problem had been phrased in the following way, only an older child who had entered the formal operational stage would have solved it: "Becky is shorter than Tom, and Becky is taller than Fred. Who is the tallest of the three?" Here the younger concrete operational child, lost in the combinations of greater-than and less-than relationships, might reason that Becky and Tom are "short," Becky and Fred are "tall," and therefore Fred is the tallest, followed by Becky, and then Tom, who is the shortest. Adolescents in the formal operational stage may also get confused by the differing relationships in this problem, but they can imagine several different relationships between the heights of Becky, Tom, and Fred and can figure out the accuracy of each until they hit on the correct one. This example shows another ability of preadolescents and adolescents who have reached the formal operational stage: They can monitor, or think about, their own thinking.

Generating abstract relationships from available information and then comparing those abstract relationships to each other is a general skill underlying many tasks in which adolescents' competence leaps forward. Piaget (1952a) described a task in which students in the concrete operational stage were given a set of 10 proverbs and a set of statements that meant the same thing as the proverbs. They were asked to match each proverb to the equivalent statement. Again, concrete operational children can understand the task and choose answers. However, their answers are often incorrect because they often do not understand that a proverb describes a general principle. For example, asked to explain the proverb "Don't cry over spilled milk," a child might explain that once milk is spilled, there's nothing to cry about but might not see that the proverb has a broader meaning. Adolescents and adults have little difficulty with this type of task.

HYPOTHETICAL CONDITIONS ● Another ability that Piaget and others recognized in the young adolescent is the ability to reason about situations and conditions that have not been experienced. The adolescent can accept, for the sake of argument or discussion, conditions that are arbitrary, that are not known to exist, or even that are known to be contrary to fact. Adolescents are not bound to their own experiences of reality, so they can apply logic to any given set of conditions. One illustration of the ability to reason about hypothetical situations is found in formal debate, in which participants must be prepared to defend either side of an issue, regardless of their personal feelings or experience, and their defense is judged on its documentation and logical consistency. For a dramatic illustration of the difference between children and adolescents in the ability to suspend their own opinions, compare the reactions of fourth- and ninth-graders when you ask them to present an argument in favor of the proposition that schools should be in session 6 days a week, 48 weeks a year. The abilities that make up formal operational thought—thinking abstractly, testing hypotheses, and forming concepts that are independent of physical reality—are critical in the learning of higher-order skills. For example, learning algebra or abstract geometry requires the use of formal operational thought, as does understanding difficult concepts in science, social studies, and other subjects. According to Piaget, the formal operational stage brings cognitive development to a close. For Piaget, what began as a set of inborn reflexes has developed into the system of cognitive structures that makes human thought what it is. However, intellectual growth may continue to take place beyond adolescence. According to Piaget, the foundation has been laid, and no new structures need to develop; all that is needed is the addition of knowledge and the development of more complex schemes. However, some researchers (e.g., Byrnes, 1988; Commons, Richards, & Kuhn, 1982) have taken issue with Piaget's belief that the formal operational stage is the final one.

CONNECTIONS

For more on thinking about one's own thinking, or metacognition, see Chapter 6, page 203.

SELF-CHECK

Think of an original example from your own experience or observation for each of the following phenomena, as described by Piaget:

scheme   accommodation
assimilation   equilibration

Add Piaget's four stages of development to the comparison chart you started in the first Self-Check. Then classify the following phenomena or capabilities in terms of Piaget's stages. At what stage is each one achieved? Give an example of each.

inferred reality   reflexes   abstract thinking
object permanence egocentrism   use of symbols
centration   use of logic   reversibility
goal direction   conservation perceived appearances
reciprocity   inversion   classification

HOW IS PIAGET'S WORK VIEWED TODAY?

Piaget's theory revolutionized, and in many ways still dominates, the study of human development. However, some of his central principles have been questioned in more recent research, and modern descriptions of development have revised many of his views.

Criticisms and Revisions of Piaget's Theory

One important Piagetian principle is that development precedes learning. Piaget held that developmental stages were largely fixed and that such concepts as conservation could not be taught. However, research has established some cases in which Piagetian tasks can be taught to children at earlier developmental stages. For example, several researchers have found that young children can succeed on simpler forms of Piaget's tasks that require the same skills (Black, 1981; Donaldson, 1978; Kusaka, 1989). Gelman (1979) found that young children could solve the conservation problem involving the number of blocks in a row when the task was presented in a simpler way with simpler language. Boden (1980) found that the same formal operational task produced passing rates from 19 to 98 percent, depending on the complexities of the instructions (see also Nagy & Griffiths, 1982).

Similar kinds of research have also led to a reassessment of children's egocentricity. In simple, practical contexts, children demonstrated their ability to consider the point of view of others (Black, 1981; Damon, 1983). In addition, infants have been shown to demonstrate aspects of object permanence much earlier than Piaget predicted (Baillargeon, DeVos, & Graber, 1989; Baillargeon, Graber, DeVos, & Black, 1990).

The result of this research has been a recognition that children are more competent than Piaget originally thought, especially when their practical knowledge is being assessed. Gelman (1979) suggests that the cognitive abilities of preschoolers are more fragile than those of older children and therefore are evident only under certain conditions. Piaget (1964) responded to such demonstrations by arguing that the children must have been on the verge of the next developmental stage already—but the fact remains that some (though not all) of the Piagetian tasks can be taught to children well below the age at which they usually appear without instruction.

Another area in which Piaget's work has been criticized in recent years goes to the heart of his "stage" theory. Many researchers now doubt that there are broad stages of development affecting all types of cognitive tasks; instead, they argue that children's skills develop in different ways on different tasks and that their experience (including direct teaching in school or elsewhere) can have a strong influence on the pace of development (see Byrnes, 1988; Gelman & Baillargeon, 1983; Overton, 1984). The evidence is particularly strong that children can be taught to perform well on the Piagetian tasks assessing formal operations, such as the pendulum problems illustrated in Figure 2.4 (Greenbowe, Herron, Nurrenbern, Staver, & Ward, 1981). Clearly, experience matters. De Lisi and Staudt (1980), for example, found that college students were likely to show formal operational reasoning on tasks related to their majors but not on other tasks. Watch an intelligent adult learning to sail. Initially, he or she is likely to engage in a lot of concrete operational behavior, trying everything in a chaotic order, before systematically beginning to learn how to adjust the tiller and the sail to wind and direction (as in formal operational thought).

Educational Implications of Piaget's Theory

Piaget's theories have had a major impact on the theory and practice of education (Case, 1993). First, the theories focused attention on the idea of **developmentally appropriate education**—an education with environments, curriculum, materials, and instruction that are suitable for students in terms of their physical and cognitive abilities and their social and emotional needs (Elkind, 1989). In addition, several major approaches to curriculum and instruction are explicitly based on Piagetian theory (Berrueta-Clement, Schweinhart, Barnett, Epstein, & Weikart, 1984), and this theory has been influential in constructivist models of learning, which will be described in Chapter 8. Berk (1997) summarizes the main teaching implications drawn from Piaget as follows:

1. A focus on the process of children's thinking, not just its products. In addition to checking the correctness of children's answers, teachers must understand the processes children use to get to the answer. Appropriate learning experiences build on children's current level of cognitive functioning, and only when teachers appreciate children's methods of arriving at particular conclusions are they in a position to provide such experiences.

2. Recognition of the crucial role of children's self-initiated, active involvement in learning activities. In a Piagetian classroom the presentation of ready-made knowledge is deemphasized, and children are encouraged to discover for themselves through spontaneous interaction with the environment. Therefore, instead of teaching didactically, teachers provide a rich variety of activities that permit children to act directly on the physical world.

3. A deemphasis on practices aimed at making children adultlike in their thinking. Piaget referred to the question "How can we speed up development?" as "the American question." Among the many countries he visited, psychologists and educators in the United States seemed most interested in what techniques could be

THEORY *into* Practice

developmentally appropriate education
Instruction felt to be adapted to the current developmental status of children (rather than to their age alone).

used to accelerate children's progress through the stages. Piagetian-based educational programs accept his firm belief that premature teaching may be worse than no teaching at all, because it leads to superficial acceptance of adult formulas rather than true cognitive understanding (Johnson & Hooper, 1982).

4. Acceptance of individual differences in developmental progress. Piaget's theory assumes that all children go through the same developmental sequence but that they do so at different rates. Therefore, teachers must make a special effort to arrange classroom activities for individuals and small groups of children rather than for the total class group. In addition, because individual differences are expected, assessment of children's educational progress should be made in terms of each child's own previous course of development, not in terms of normative standards provided by the performances of same-age peers.

From Laura E. Berk, *Child Development* (2nd ed.), p. 244. Copyright © Allyn & Bacon. Reprinted by permission.

CONNECTIONS

For more on information processing, see Chapter 6, page 175.

Neo-Piagetian and Information-Processing Views of Development

Neo-Piagetian theories are recent modifications of Piaget's theory that attempt to overcome the theory's limitations and address problems its critics have identified. In particular, neo-Piagetians have demonstrated that children's abilities to operate at a particular stage depend a great deal on the specific tasks involved (Gelman & Brenneman, 1994); that training and experience, including social interactions, can accelerate children's development (DeVries, 1997; Flavell, Miller, & Miller, 1993); and that culture has an important impact on development (Gelman & Brenneman, 1994; Rogoff & Chavajay, 1995). One example of neo-Piagetian work on cognitive development is that of R. Case (1992), who believes, like Piaget, that children progress through developmental stages. These stages reflect the kinds of mental representations children can form and how information is processed. The stages proposed by Case are different from those described by Piaget in that ways of processing information become more complex but not necessarily different (Case, 1985). Unlike Piaget, Case believed that developmental change is based on a child's capacity to process and remember information. According to Case, this short-term memory capacity increases with physical maturity of the brain but also becomes more efficient with practice and instruction. Research in this direction could lead to a new conceptualization of developmental stages that accounts for the fact that cognitive development proceeds at different rates on different tasks (see Flavell et al., 1993; Gelman & Brenneman, 1994; Siegler, 1991).

Alternatives to Piagetian views of cognitive development include information-processing approaches (Siegler, 1991), based on the idea that people process information in a way similar to computers. Information-processing theorists tend to agree with Piaget's description of cognition but, unlike Piaget, believe that thinking skills can be directly taught. Siegler (1988, 1991) observes, for example, that children acquire increasingly powerful rules or procedures for solving problems and can be stimulated to discover deficiencies in their own logic and to apply new logical principles. That is, they can discern rules and assess their application. In this way, children develop greater capacity for abstract thought. The implications of the rule-assessment approach for education is that stimulating new methods of instruction may actually enhance children's thinking abilities (Sternberg, 1995).

SELF-CHECK

List four general teaching implications of Piagetian principles. Describe a teaching strategy that applies Piagetian concepts in the classroom. Summarize the arguments against Piaget's theory of cognitive development.

HOW DID VYGOTSKY VIEW COGNITIVE DEVELOPMENT?

Lev Semionovich Vygotsky was a Russian psychologist who was a contemporary of Piaget but died in 1934. His work was not widely read in English until the 1970s, however, and only since then have his theories become influential in North America. Vygotskian theory is now a powerful force in developmental psychology, and many of the critiques he made of the Piagetian perspective more than 60 years ago have come to the fore today (see Das, 1995; Karpov & Bransford, 1995; Kozulin & Presseisen, 1995).

Vygotsky's work is based on two key ideas. First, he proposed that intellectual development can be understood only in terms of the historical and cultural contexts children experience (van der Veer & Valsiner, 1991). Second, he believed that development depends on the **sign systems** that individuals grow up with (Ratner, 1991): the symbols that cultures create to help people think, communicate, and solve problems—for example, a culture's language, writing system, or counting system.

In contrast to Piaget, Vygotsky proposed that cognitive development is strongly linked to input from others. Like Piaget, however, Vygotsky believed that the acquisition of sign systems occurs in an invariant sequence of steps that is the same for all children (Daniels, 1995).

How Development Occurs

Recall that Piaget's theory suggests that development precedes learning. In other words, specific cognitive structures need to develop before certain types of learning can take place. Vygotsky's theory suggests that learning precedes development. For Vygotsky, learning involves the acquisition of signs by means of instruction and information from others. Development involves the child's internalizing these signs so as to be able to think and solve problems without the help of others. This ability is called **self-regulation.**

The first step in the development of self-regulation and independent thinking is learning that something has a meaning. For example, a baby learns that the process of reaching toward an object is interpreted by others as a signal that the infant wants the object. In the case of language acquisition, children learn to associate certain sounds with meaning. The second step in developing internal structures and self-regulation involves practice. The infant practices gestures that will get attention. The preschooler will enter into conversations with others to master language. The final step involves using signs to think and solve problems without the help of others. At this point, children become self-regulating, and the sign system has become internalized. The young child intentionally uses the "pointing" gesture to get others' attention. In language development, children begin to initiate conversations with themselves.

CONNECTIONS

For more on self-regulated learning, see Chapter 8, page 260.

sign systems
Symbols that cultures create to help people think, communicate, and solve problems.

self-regulation
The ability to think and solve problems without the help of others.

TEACHERS IN ACTION

How has your knowledge of child development helped you to make instruction developmentally appropriate?

Nicole DePalma Cobb and Sandi McNeice
Sterling Middle School
Quincy, Massachusetts

Vygotsky's research into cognitive development provides us as teachers with the essential tools we need to develop a curriculum appropriate for the many levels of learning and achievement we find among our students. Applying Vygotsky's principles, not just understanding them, is fundamental. We see ourselves as facilitators who observe the strengths and needs of specific students and then provide scaffolding appropriate to their levels of social and cognitive development to support their growth. The following example shows how we applied Vygotsky's principle of the zone of proximal development to help one of our eighth-grade students.

Casey was on the basketball team. When she went for a layup shot, she was all business. Her game was precise, and she always went for the win. She had entered the school year organized, disciplined, and motivated to achieve. Well liked by her classmates, Casey was elected Student Council president. She came from a supportive family and had the drive to succeed academically and socially. One of her strengths was her ability to communicate articulately. Casey always completed her schoolwork and homework. She was both tenacious about succeeding and open to receiving support.

Casey's reading and writing abilities, however, did not mirror her eighth-grade persona. As the year progressed, she began to show a lack of confidence. She couldn't readily participate aloud in Reading/Language Arts class, for she read in a monotone voice and lacked the ability to self-regulate. Also, she inconsistently used visual and structural strategies to edit her writing and correct her own reading. Because she couldn't detect her own errors, Casey's writing often did not make sense. When she began to prepare and give class speeches, showing her lack of self-corrective skills, she became embarrassed and angry.

Having identified Casey's strengths and needs, we created a non-threatening atmosphere at school that used her strengths—her discipline, drive, and commitment—as a springboard to accelerate her cognitive and social growth. With the support of her parents, we worked as a team to develop a curriculum that surrounded Casey with high-end learners, tutors, and mentors, both in school and at home. We used *peer grouping,* such as reading and writing partnerships; *literature circles,* which encouraged Casey to respond by talking and writing to learn; *conferencing with facilitators* so that, through constant reflection, she could learn problem-solving and self-assessment strategies; and *editing and peer editing* to help her detect her own writing errors. We also modeled leadership roles to encourage Casey to assume greater responsibility for leadership during Student Council meetings and other presentations, in and out of school.

Because we were able to work as a team and apply Vygotsky's concept of scaffolding, we could meet the needs of a student who was once unable to recognize, internalize, and process new information. When Casey left middle school, she entered high school with the ability to strategize on a higher level and to be an independent lifelong learner. Now when we see Casey on the basketball court, we see more than just a self-confident and self-reliant team player. We see a successful student.

Chuck Greiner
Psychology, Grades 11 and 12
James M. Bennett High School
Salisbury, Maryland

"What are we learning this for?" Those six dreaded words sounded to me like fingernails on a chalkboard. How can students sit in my class for weeks and ask such a silly question? But it is possible that it's not silly after all. The question speaks to our understanding of issues of development. When I fail to take students' development into consideration as I plan, it results in their frustration as well as my feeling that I have failed to reach them as I might have. I have found that lessons developed with students' cognitive, social, emotional, and even moral development in mind are far more rewarding for both students and me.

Incorporating knowledge of adolescent development into a lesson is as simple as phrasing a question at different levels (such as concrete and abstract) to give students an opportunity to work at their level, but also to move beyond and improve their critical thinking skills. Students who are analyzing things at a formal operational level are bored easily by rote memorization, while those who are not quite at the formal operational level feel intimidated by their peers' lofty responses. It is important to recognize these tendencies and plan accordingly.

Providing alternative methods of assessment is another way in which I can address developmental issues. Opportunities to use essays, as well as video and other forms of technology, to convey understanding can also benefit student learning. I require students to keep journals. These reflections on their own understanding of class notes, discussions, or events in their lives that relate to our studies allow me to further tailor my curriculum to meet the individual needs of students. Students often become aware of their own cognitive development (that is, they use metacognition) when they review their journal entries. Of course, these also allow me to assess students' understanding of the course material.

When students feel I understand them, we develop a connection, and teaching becomes an enriching experience. I have found that adjusting to and understanding the development of my students allows me to be a better teacher and my students to be more effective learners.

This preschooler's conversation with an older person will help her master language, an important step in the development of self-regulation. What steps has this child already taken, and what still lies ahead?

PRIVATE SPEECH ● **Private speech** is a mechanism that Vygotsky emphasized for turning shared knowledge into personal knowledge. Vygotsky proposed that children incorporate the speech of others and then use that speech to help themselves solve problems. Private speech is easy to see in young children, who frequently talk to themselves, especially when faced with difficult tasks (Berk & Garvin, 1984). Later, private speech becomes silent but is still very important. Studies have found that children who make extensive use of private speech learn complex tasks more effectively than do other children (Bivens & Berk, 1990).

THE ZONE OF PROXIMAL DEVELOPMENT ● Vygotsky's theory implies that cognitive development and the ability to use thought to control our own actions require first mastering cultural communication systems and then learning to use these systems to regulate our own thought processes. The most important contribution of Vygotsky's theory is an emphasis on the sociocultural nature of learning (Vygotsky, 1978; Wertsch, 1986). He believed that learning takes place when children are working within their **zone of proximal development.** Tasks within the zone of proximal development are ones that a child cannot yet do alone but could do with the assistance of more competent peers or adults. That is, the zone of proximal development describes tasks that a child has not yet learned but is capable of learning at a given time. Vygotsky further believed that higher mental functioning usually exists in conversation and collaboration among individuals before it exists within the individual.

SCAFFOLDING ● A key idea derived from Vygotsky's notion of social learning is that of **scaffolding** (Wood, Bruner, & Ross, 1976): the assistance provided by more competent peers or adults. Typically, scaffolding means providing a child with a great deal of support during the early stages of learning and then diminishing

private speech
Children's self-talk, which guides their thinking and action; eventually internalized as silent inner speech.

zone of proximal development
Level of development immediately above a person's present level.

scaffolding
Support for learning and problem solving; may include clues, reminders, encouragement, breaking the problem down into steps, providing an example, or anything else that allows the student to grow in independence as a learner.

CONNECTIONS
For more on scaffolding, see Chapter 8, page 261.

support and having the child take on increasing responsibility as soon as he or she is able (Rosenshine & Meister, 1992). Parents use scaffolding when they teach their children to play a new game or to tie their shoes (Plumert & Nichols-Whitehead, 1996). In fact, scaffolding is common whenever one-to-one instruction takes place. For example, in *Life on the Mississippi,* Mark Twain describes how he was taught to be a steamboat pilot. At first the experienced pilot talked him through every bend in the river, but gradually he was left to figure things out for himself, with the pilot there to intervene only if the boat was about to run aground.

Applications of Vygotskian Theory in Teaching

CONNECTIONS

For more on cooperative learning, see Chapter 8, pages 259 and 268.

CONNECTIONS

For more on reciprocal teaching, see Chapter 8, page 264.

Vygotsky's theories of education have two major implications. One is the desirability of setting up cooperative learning arrangements among groups of students with differing levels of ability. Tutoring by more competent peers would be most effective in promoting growth within the zone of proximal development (Forman & McPhail, 1989). Second, a Vygotskian approach to instruction emphasizes scaffolding, with students taking more and more responsibility for their own learning. For example, in reciprocal teaching, teachers lead small groups of students in asking questions about material they have read and gradually turn over responsibility for leading the discussion to the students (Palincsar, Brown, & Martin, 1987). Tharp and Gallimore (1988) emphasize scaffolding in an approach they call "assisted discovery," which calls for explicitly teaching students to use private speech to talk themselves through problem solving. (See Figure 2.5.)

FIGURE 2.5 ● Teaching Model Based on Vygotsky's Theory
In (a) the child performs a learned task; in (b) the child is assisted by a teacher or peer who interacts with the child to help him move into a new zone of proximal development (un-learned tasks at limits of learner's abilities) with a new learned task.

a. Learned task   **b.** Assisted learning at zone of proximal development

Classroom Applications of Vygotsky's Theory

THEORY *into* Practice

Vygotsky's concept of the zone of proximal development is based on the idea that development is defined both by what a child can do independently and by what the child can do when assisted by an adult or more competent peer (Daniels, 1995; Wertsch, 1991). Knowing both levels of Vygotsky's zone is useful for teachers, for these levels indicate where the child is at a given moment as well as where the child is going. The zone of proximal development has several implications for teaching in the classroom.

According to Vygotsky, for the curriculum to be developmentally appropriate, the teacher must plan activities that encompass not only what children are capable of doing on their own but what they can learn with the help of others (Karpov & Haywood, 1998).

Vygotsky's theory does not mean that anything can be taught to any child. Only instruction and activities that fall within the zone promote development. For example, if a child cannot identify the sounds in a word even after many prompts, the child may not benefit immediately from instruction in this skill. Practice of previously known skills and introduction of concepts that are too difficult and complex have little positive impact. Teachers can use information about both levels of Vygotsky's zone of proximal development in organizing classroom activities in the following ways:

- Instruction can be planned to provide practice in the zone of proximal development for individual children or for groups of children. For example, hints and prompts that helped children during the assessment could form the basis of instructional activities.
- Cooperative learning activities can be planned with groups of children at different levels who can help each other learn.
- Scaffolding (Wood, Bruner, & Ross, 1976) is a tactic for helping the child in his or her zone of proximal development in which the adult provides hints and prompts at different levels. In scaffolding, the adult does not simplify the task, but the role of the learner is simplified "through the graduated intervention of the teacher" (Greenfield, 1984, p. 119).

For example, a child might be shown pennies to represent each sound in a word (e.g., three pennies for the three sounds in *man*). When this word is mastered, the child might be asked to place a penny to show each sound in a word, and finally the child might identify the sounds without the pennies. When the adult provides the child with pennies, the adult provides a scaffold to help the child move from assisted to unassisted success at the task (Spector, 1992). In a high school laboratory science class, a teacher might provide scaffolding by first giving students detailed guides to carrying out experiments, then giving them brief outlines that they might use to structure experiments, and finally asking them to set up experiments entirely on their own.

SELF-CHECK

On your comparison chart of theorists, enter information comparing and contrasting the views of Piaget and Vygotsky on the nature of learning and the contexts in which learning takes place. Describe a teaching strategy that applies Vygotskian concepts in the classroom.

HOW DID ERIKSON VIEW PERSONAL AND SOCIAL DEVELOPMENT?

As children improve their cognitive skills, they are also developing self-concepts, ways of interacting with others, and attitudes toward the world. Understanding of these personal and social developments is critical to the teacher's ability to motivate, teach, and successfully interact with students at various ages. Like cognitive development, personal and social development is often described in terms of stages. We speak of the "terrible twos," not the "terrible ones" or "terrible threes"; and when someone is reacting in an unreasonable, selfish way, we accuse that person of "behaving like a two-year-old." The words *adolescent* and *teenager* are associated in our culture with rebelliousness, identity crises, hero worship, and sexual awakening. These associations reflect stages of development that we believe everyone goes through. This section focuses on a theory of personal and social development proposed by Erik Erikson, which is an adaptation of the developmental theories of the great psychiatrist Sigmund Freud. Erikson's work is often called a **psychosocial theory,** because it relates principles of psychological and social development.

Stages of Psychosocial Development

Like Piaget, Erikson had no formal training in psychology, but as a young man he was trained by Freud as a psychoanalyst. Erikson hypothesized that people pass through eight psychosocial stages in their lifetimes. At each stage, there are crises or critical issues to be resolved. Most people resolve each **psychosocial crisis** satisfactorily and put it behind them to take on new challenges, but some people do not completely resolve these crises and must continue to deal with them later in life (Miller, 1983). For example, many adults have yet to resolve the "identity crisis" of adolescence. Table 2.2 summarizes the eight stages of life according to Erikson's theory. Each is identified by the central crisis that must be resolved.

STAGE I: TRUST VERSUS MISTRUST (BIRTH TO 18 MONTHS) ● The goal of infancy is to develop a basic trust in the world. Erikson (1968, p. 96) defined basic trust as "an essential trustfulness of others as well as a fundamental sense of one's own trustworthiness." This crisis has a dual nature: Infants not only have their needs met, but they also help in meeting the mother's needs. The mother, or maternal figure, is usually the first important person in the child's world. She is the one who must satisfy the infant's need for food and affection. If the mother is inconsistent or rejecting, she becomes a source of frustration for the infant rather than a source of pleasure. The mother's behavior creates in the infant a sense of mistrust for his or her world that may persist throughout childhood and into adulthood.

STAGE II: AUTONOMY VERSUS DOUBT (18 MONTHS TO 3 YEARS) ● By the age of 2, most babies can walk and have learned enough about language to communicate with other people. Children in the "terrible twos" no longer want to depend totally

psychosocial theory
A set of principles that relates social environment to psychological development.

psychosocial crisis
The set of critical issues that individuals must address as they pass through each of the eight life stages, according to Erikson.

TABLE 2.2

Erikson's Stages of Personal and Social Development

As people grow, they face a series of psychosocial crises that shape personality, according to Erik Erikson. Each crisis focuses on a particular aspect of personality and involves the person's relationship with other people.

STAGE	APPROXIMATE AGES	PSYCHOSOCIAL CRISES	SIGNIFICANT RELATIONSHIPS	PSYCHOSOCIAL EMPHASIS
I	Birth to 18 months	Trust vs. mistrust	Maternal person	To get To give in return
II	18 months to 3 years	Autonomy vs. doubt	Parental persons	To hold on To let go
III	3 to 6 years	Initiative vs. guilt	Basic family	To make (= going after) To "make like" (= playing)
IV	6 to 12 years	Industry vs. inferiority	Neighborhood, school	To make things To make things together
V	12 to 18 years	Identity vs. role confusion	Peer groups and models of leadership	To be oneself (or not to be) To share being oneself
VI	Young adulthood	Intimacy vs. isolation	Partners in friendship, sex, competition, cooperation	To lose and find oneself in another
VII	Middle adulthood	Generativity vs. self-absorption	Divided labor and shared household	To take care of
VIII	Late adulthood	Integrity vs. despair	"Mankind," "My kind"	To be, through having been To face not being

Source: From *Childhood and Society* by Erik H. Erikson. Copyright 1950, © 1963 by W. W. Norton & Company, Inc. renewed © 1978, 1991 by Erik H. Erikson. Reprinted by permission of W. W. Norton & Company, Inc.

on others. Instead, they strive toward autonomy, or the ability to do things for themselves. The child's desires for power and independence often clash with the desires of the parent. Erikson believes that children at this stage have the dual desire to hold on and to let go. Parents who are flexible enough to permit their children to explore freely and do things for themselves, while at the same time providing an ever-present guiding hand, encourage the establishment of a sense of autonomy. Parents who are overly restrictive and harsh give their children a sense of powerlessness and incompetence, which can lead to shame and doubt in one's abilities.

STAGE III: INITIATIVE VERSUS GUILT (3 TO 6 YEARS) ● During this period, children's continually maturing motor and language skills permit them to be increasingly aggressive and vigorous in the exploration of both their social and their physical environment. Three-year-olds have a growing sense of initiative, which can be encouraged by parents, other family members, and other caregivers who permit children to run, jump, play, slide, and throw. "Being firmly convinced that he is a

According to Erikson, what specific psychosocial tasks are especially important for these adolescents to accomplish? As a teacher, how might you support each task?

person on his own, the child must now find out what kind of person he may become" (Erikson, 1968, p. 115). Parents who severely punish children's attempts at initiative will make the children feel guilty about their natural urges both during this stage and later in life.

STAGE IV: INDUSTRY VERSUS INFERIORITY (6 TO 12 YEARS) ● Entry into school brings with it a huge expansion in the child's social world. Teachers and peers take on increasing importance for the child, while the influence of parents decreases. Children now want to make things. Success brings with it a sense of industry, a good feeling about oneself and one's abilities. Failure creates a negative self-image, a sense of inadequacy that may hinder future learning. And "failure" need not be real; it may be merely an inability to measure up to one's own standards or those of parents, teachers, or brothers and sisters.

STAGE V: IDENTITY VERSUS ROLE CONFUSION (12 TO 18 YEARS) ● The question "Who am I?" becomes important during adolescence. To answer it, adolescents increasingly turn away from parents and toward peer groups. Erikson believed that during adolescence the individual's rapidly changing physiology, coupled with pressures to make decisions about future education and career, creates the need to question and redefine the psychosocial identity established during the earlier stages. Adolescence is a time of change. Teenagers experiment with various sexual, occupational, and educational roles as they try to find out who they are and who they can be. This new sense of self, or "ego identity," is not simply the sum of the prior identifications. Rather, it is a reassembly or "an alignment of the individual's basic drives (ego) with his or her endowment (resolutions of the previous crises) and his or her opportunities (needs, skills, goals, and demands of adolescence and approaching adulthood)" (Erikson, 1980, p. 94).

STAGE VI: INTIMACY VERSUS ISOLATION (YOUNG ADULTHOOD) ● Once young people know who they are and where they are going, the stage is set for the sharing of their life with another. The young adult is now ready to form a new relationship of trust and intimacy with another individual, a "partner in friendship, sex, competition, and cooperation." This relationship should enhance the identity of both partners without stifling the growth of either. The young adult who does not seek out such intimacy or whose repeated tries fail may retreat into isolation.

STAGE VII: GENERATIVITY VERSUS SELF-ABSORPTION (MIDDLE ADULTHOOD) ● Generativity is "the interest in establishing and guiding the next generation" (Erikson, 1980, p. 103). Typically, people attain generativity through raising their own children. However, the crisis of this stage can also be successfully resolved through other forms of productivity and creativity, such as teaching. During this stage, people should continue to grow; if they don't, a sense of "stagnation and interpersonal impoverishment" develops, leading to self-absorption or self-indulgence (Erikson, 1980, p. 103).

STAGE VIII: INTEGRITY VERSUS DESPAIR (LATE ADULTHOOD) ● In the final stage of psychosocial development, people look back over their lifetime and resolve their final identity crisis. Acceptance of accomplishments, failures, and ultimate limitations brings with it a sense of integrity, or wholeness; a realization that one's life has been one's own responsibility. The finality of death must also be faced and accepted. Despair can occur in those who regret the way they have led their lives or how their lives have turned out.

Implications and Criticisms of Erikson's Theory

As with Piaget's stages, not all people experience Erikson's crises to the same degree or at the same time. The age ranges stated here may represent the best times for a crisis to be resolved, but they are not the only possible times. For example, children who were born into chaotic homes that failed to give them adequate security may develop trust after being adopted or otherwise brought into a more stable environment. People whose negative school experiences gave them a sense of inferiority may find as they enter the work world that they can learn and that they do have valuable skills, a realization that may help them finally to resolve the industry versus inferiority crisis that others resolved in their elementary school years. Erikson's theory emphasizes the role of the environment, both in causing the crises and in determining how they will be resolved. The stages of personal and social development are played out in constant interactions with others and with society as a whole. During the first three stages the interactions are primarily with parents and other family members, but the school plays a central role for most children in Stage IV (industry versus inferiority) and Stage V (identity versus role confusion).

Erikson's theory describes the basic issues that people confront as they go through life. However, his theory has been criticized because it does not explain how or why individuals progress from one stage to another.

SELF-CHECK

Compare Erikson's eight stages of psychosocial development to Piaget's four stages of cognitive development on your comparison chart. Which of Erikson's stages pertain to preschool, elementary school, middle school, and secondary school students? Think of an example in which an individual experiences and then successfully resolves each psychosocial crisis that occurs before and during the school years. In each instance, give an example of how a parent or teacher might help a child resolve developmental crises in a positive way.

WHAT ARE SOME THEORIES OF MORAL DEVELOPMENT?

Society could not function without rules that tell people how to communicate with one another, how to avoid hurting others, and how to get along in life generally. If you are around children much, you may have noticed that they are often rigid about rules. Things are either right or wrong; there is no in-between. If you think back to your own years in junior high or high school, you may recall being shocked to find that people sometimes break rules on purpose and that the rules that apply to some people may not apply to others. These experiences probably changed your concept of rules. Your idea of laws may also have changed when you learned how they are made. People meet and debate and vote; the laws that are made one year can be changed the next. The more complexity you can see, the more you find exists. Just as children differ from adults in cognitive and personal development, they also differ in their moral reasoning. First we will look at the two stages of moral reasoning described by Piaget; then we will discuss related theories developed by Lawrence Kohlberg and Martin Hoffman. Piaget proposed that there is a relationship between the cognitive stages of development and the ability to reason about moral issues. Kohlberg believed that the development of the logical structures proposed by Piaget is necessary to, although not sufficient for, advances in the area of moral judgment and reasoning.

Piaget's Theory of Moral Development

Piaget's theory of cognitive development also included a theory about the development of moral reasoning. Piaget believed that cognitive structures and abilities develop first. Cognitive abilities then determine children's abilities to reason about social situations. As with cognitive abilities, Piaget proposed that moral development progresses in predictable stages, in this case from a very egocentric type of moral reasoning to one based on a system of justice based on cooperation and reciprocity. Table 2.3 summarizes Piaget's stages of moral development.

To understand children's moral reasoning, Piaget spent a great deal of time watching children play marbles and asking them about the rules of the game. The first thing he discovered was that before about the age of 6, children play by their own idiosyncratic rules. Piaget believed that very young children were incapable of interacting in cooperative ways and therefore unable to engage in moral reasoning.

Piaget found that by the age of 6, children acknowledged the existence of rules, though they were inconsistent in following them. Frequently, several children who were supposedly playing the same game were observed to be playing by different sets of rules. Children at this age also had no understanding that game rules are arbitrary and something that a group can decide by itself. Instead, they saw rules as being imposed by some higher authority and unchangeable.

Piaget (1964) labeled the first stage of moral development **heteronomous morality**; it has also been called the stage of "moral realism" or "morality of constraint." *Heteronomous* means being subject to rules imposed by others. During this period, young children are consistently faced with parents and other adults telling them what to do and what not to do. Violations of rules are believed to bring automatic punishment. Justice is seen as automatic, and people who are bad will even-

heteronomous morality
In Piaget's theory of moral development, stage at which children think that rules are unchangeable and that breaking them leads automatically to punishment.

TABLE 2.3

Piaget's Stages of Moral Development

As people develop their cognitive abilities, their understanding of moral problems also becomes more sophisticated. Young children are more rigid in their view of right and wrong than older children and adults tend to be.

HETERONOMOUS MORALITY (YOUNGER)	AUTONOMOUS MORALITY (OLDER)
Based on relations of constraint; for example, the complete acceptance by the child of adult prescriptions.	Based on relations of cooperation and mutual recognition of equality among autonomous individuals, as in relations between people who are equals.
Reflected in attitudes of *moral realism:* Rules are seen as inflexible requirements, external in origin and authority, not open to negotiation; and right is a matter of literal obedience to adults and rules.	Reflected in *rational* moral attitudes: Rules are viewed as products of mutual agreement, open to renegotiation, made legitimate by personal acceptance and common consent, and right is a matter of acting in accordance with the requirements of cooperation and mutual respect.
Badness is judged in terms of the objective form and consequences of actions; fairness is equated with the content of adult decisions; arbitrary and severe punishments are seen as fair.	Badness is viewed as relative to the actor's intentions; fairness is defined as equal treatment or taking account of individual needs; fairness of punishment is defined by appropriateness to the offense.
Punishment is seen as an automatic consequence of the offense, and justice is seen as inherent.	Punishment is seen as affected by human intention.

Source: Table from *Social and Personality Development* by Michael E. Lamb, p. 213, copyright © 1978 by Holt, Rinehart and Winston, reproduced by permission of the publisher.

tually be punished. At this stage, Piaget also described children as judging the morality of behavior on the basis of its consequences. Children at this stage judge behavior as bad if it results in negative consequences even if the actor's original intentions were good.

Piaget found that children did not conscientiously use and follow rules until the age of 10 or 12 years, when children are capable of formal operations. At this age, every child playing the game followed the same set of rules. Children understood that the rules existed to give the game direction and to minimize disputes between players. They understood that rules were something that everyone agreed on and that therefore, if everyone agreed to change them, they could be changed.

Piaget also observed that children at this age tend to base moral judgments on the intentions of the actor rather than the consequences of the actions. Children often engage in discussions of hypothetical circumstances that might affect rules. This second stage is labeled **autonomous morality** or "morality of cooperation." It arises as the child's social world expands to include more and more peers. By

autonomous morality
In Piaget's theory of moral development, stage at which a person understands that people make rules and that punishments are not automatic.

continually interacting and cooperating with other children, the child's ideas about rules and therefore morality begin to change. Rules are now what we make them to be. Punishment for transgressions is no longer automatic but must be administered with a consideration of the transgressor's intentions and extenuating circumstances.

According to Piaget, children progress from the stage of heteronomous morality to that of autonomous morality with the development of cognitive structures but also because of interactions with equal-status peers. He believed that resolving conflicts with peers weakened children's reliance on adult authority and heightened their awareness that rules are changeable and should exist only as the result of mutual consent.

Kohlberg's Stages of Moral Reasoning

Kohlberg's (1963, 1969) stage theory of moral reasoning is an elaboration and refinement of Piaget's. Like Piaget, Kohlberg studied how children (and adults) reason about rules that govern their behavior in certain situations. Kohlberg did not study children's game playing, but rather probed for their responses to a series of structured situations or **moral dilemmas.** His most famous one is the following:

> In Europe a woman was near death from cancer. One drug might save her, a form of radium that a druggist in the same town had recently discovered. The druggist was charging $2,000, ten times what the drug cost him to make. The sick woman's husband, Heinz, went to everyone he knew to borrow the money, but he could only get together about half of what it cost. He told the druggist that his wife was dying and asked him to sell it cheaper or let him pay later. But the druggist said "No." The husband got desperate and broke into the man's store to steal the drug for his wife. Should the husband have done that? Why? (Kohlberg, 1969, p. 379)

On the basis of the answers he received, Kohlberg proposed that people pass through a series of six stages of moral judgment or reasoning. Kohlberg's levels and stages are summarized in Table 2.4. He grouped these six stages into three levels: preconventional, conventional, and postconventional. These three levels are distinguished by how the child or adult defines what he or she perceives as correct or moral behavior. As with other stage theories, each stage is more sophisticated and more complex than the preceding one, and most individuals proceed through them in the same order (Colby & Kohlberg, 1984). Like Piaget, Kohlberg was concerned not so much with the direction of the child's answer as with the reasoning behind it. The ages at which children and adolescents go through the stages in Table 2.4 may vary considerably; in fact, the same individual may behave according to one stage at some times and according to another at other times. However, most children pass from the preconventional to the conventional level by the age of 9 (Kohlberg, 1969).

Stage 1, which is on the **preconventional level of morality,** is very similar in form and content to Piaget's stage of heteronomous morality. Children simply obey authority figures to avoid being punished. In Stage 2, children's own needs and desires become important, yet they are aware of the interests of other people. In a concrete sense they weigh the interests of all parties when making moral judgments, but they are still "looking out for number one." The **conventional level of morality** begins at Stage 3. Here morality is defined in terms of cooperation with peers, just as it was in Piaget's stage of autonomous morality. This is the stage at which children have an unquestioning belief in the Golden Rule (Hogan & Emler, 1978). Because of the decrease in egocentrism that accompanies concrete

moral dilemmas
In Kohlberg's theory of moral reasoning, hypothetical situations that require a person to consider values of right and wrong.

preconventional level of morality
Stages 1 and 2 in Kohlberg's model of moral reasoning, in which individuals make moral judgments in their own interests.

conventional level of morality
Stages 3 and 4 in Kohlberg's model of moral reasoning, in which individuals make moral judgments in consideration of others.

TABLE 2.4

Kohlberg's Stages of Moral Reasoning

When people consider moral dilemmas, it is their reasoning that is important, not their final decision, according to Lawrence Kohlberg. He theorized that people progress through three levels as they develop abilities of moral reasoning.

I. PRECONVENTIONAL LEVEL	II. CONVENTIONAL LEVEL	III. POSTCONVENTIONAL LEVEL
Rules are set down by others. **Stage 1: Punishment and Obedience Orientation.** Physical consequences of action determine its goodness or badness. **Stage 2: Instrumental Relativist Orientation.** What is right is whatever satisfies one's own needs and occasionally the needs of others. Elements of fairness and reciprocity are present, but they are mostly interpreted in a "you scratch my back, I'll scratch yours" fashion.	Individual adopts rules and will sometimes subordinate own needs to those of the group. Expectations of family, group, or nation seen as valuable in own right, regardless of immediate and obvious consequences. **Stage 3: "Good Boy–Good Girl" Orientation.** Good behavior is whatever pleases or helps others and is approved of by them. One earns approval by being "nice." **Stage 4: "Law and Order" Orientation.** Right is doing one's duty, showing respect for authority, and maintaining the given social order for its own sake.	People define own values in terms of ethical principles they have chosen to follow. **Stage 5: Social Contract Orientation.** What is right is defined in terms of general individual rights and in terms of standards that have been agreed on by the whole society. In contrast to Stage 4, laws are not "frozen"— they can be changed for the good of society. **Stage 6: Universal Ethical Principle Orientation.** What is right is defined by decision of conscience according to self-chosen ethical principles. These principles are abstract and ethical (such as the Golden Rule), not specific moral prescriptions (such as the Ten Commandments).

Source: From L. Kohlberg, "Stage and Sequence: The Cognitive–Developmental Approach to Socialization." In David A. Goslin (Ed.), *Handbook of Socialization Theory and Research,* pp. 347–380, 1969, published by Rand McNally, Chicago. Adapted by permission of David A. Goslin.

operations, children are cognitively capable of putting themselves in someone else's shoes. They can consider the feelings of others when making moral decisions. No longer do they simply do what will not get them punished (Stage 1) or what makes them feel good (Stage 2). At Stage 4, society's rules and laws replace those of the peer group. A desire for social approval no longer determines moral judgments. Laws are followed without question, and breaking the law can never be justified. Most adults are probably at this stage. Stage 5 signals entrance into the **postconventional level of morality.** This level of moral reasoning is probably attained by fewer than 25 percent of adults. Here there is a realization that the laws and values of a society are somewhat arbitrary and particular to that society (Hogan & Emler, 1978). Laws are seen as necessary to preserve the social order and to ensure the basic right of life and liberty. In Stage 6, one's ethical principles are self-chosen and based on abstract concepts such as justice and the equality and value of human rights. Laws that violate these principles can and should be

postconventional level of morality
Stages 5 and 6 in Kohlberg's model of moral reasoning, in which individuals make moral judgments in relation to abstract principles.

disobeyed because "justice is above the law." Later, Kohlberg (1978, 1984) specu-lated that Stage 6 is not really separate from Stage 5 and suggested that the two be combined.

Kohlberg (1969) believed that moral dilemmas can be used to advance a child's level of moral reasoning, but only one stage at a time. He theorized that the way in which children progress from one stage to the next is by interacting with others whose reasoning is one or, at most, two stages above their own. The implication for teaching is that teachers must first try to determine children's approximate stage of moral reasoning. They can do this by presenting the children with a dilemma, like the Heinz dilemma discussed earlier. Once a child's level of reasoning is es-tablished, other moral dilemmas can be discussed, and the teacher can challenge the child's reasoning with explanations from the next higher stage. After the child's reasoning advances to this stage, the teacher can advance again. All this must be done over an extended period of time, however. Teachers can help students pro-gress in moral reasoning by weaving discussions of justice and moral issues into their lessons, particularly in response to events that occur in the classroom (see Nucci, 1987). In addition, concern with moral development has led to the creation of curricula and teaching tools for affective education—that is, for fostering greater awareness of students' own and others' feelings, social responsibilities, and ethical choices.

Kohlberg found that his stages of moral reasoning ability occurred in the same order and at about the same ages in the United States, Mexico, Taiwan, and Turkey. Other research throughout the world has generally found the same sequence of stages (Snarey, 1985).

THEORY
into
Practice

Fostering Moral Development in the Classroom

The study of moral development is one of the oldest topics of interest to those cu-rious about human nature, but the implementation of moral education curricula has not taken place without controversy. Educators and families active in these en-deavors have grappled with the important distinction that theories deal with moral reasoning rather than with actual moral behavior. Successful programs have in-corporated values education at the global, local, and individual levels.

GLOBAL LEVEL–DISTRICTWIDE APPROACH

Many schools have chosen to institutionalize a global, inclusive approach to char-acter building with input from teachers, administrators, parents, and, at the higher grade levels, even students (see Kohlberg, 1980, and Lickona, 1992). Here, values education is found across the curriculum, implemented throughout the school building, and connected to the home. Such programs emphasize the individual cit-izen as a member of the social institution and advocate particular levels of moral behavior. They provide students with a framework of expected behavior; violations of these standards can then be addressed. At the elementary level, students receive guidelines and are invited to discuss violations and their consequences. In middle school and throughout the high school years, students are more involved in the cre-ation and maintenance of guidelines and even play a significant role in the decision making surrounding violations of the guidelines.

LOCAL LEVEL–CLASSROOM INSTRUCTION

At the more local level, the teacher may choose to capitalize on students' natural curiosity and may teach values and decision making through "What if . . . ?" discussions. The classroom is an ideal laboratory in which students can test hypothetical situations and potential consequences (see Mattox, 1975). Teachers must recognize the cognitive abilities of those in their class and maximize these abilities through problem-solving activities. Being an effective moral educator is no easy task. Teachers must reexamine their teaching role; they must be willing to create cognitive conflict in their classrooms and to stimulate social perspective taking in students (see Reimer, Paolitto, & Hersh, 1990).

INDIVIDUAL LEVEL–CONFLICT MANAGEMENT

The shootings in Jonesboro, Arkansas, and Edinboro, Pennsylvania, in the late 1990s clearly showed the most horrific face of school violence and drew attention to the overall problem of violence in schools. Families want schools to provide students with the necessary tools to mediate serious conflicts without violence, and teachers and administrators are evaluating or initiating conflict resolution programs in many schools (see Bodine, Crawford, & Schrumpf, 1994).

Children's conflicts and their understanding of conflict-related events are a critical context for the development of both their moral understanding and their behavior (see Killen, 1996). Although a great deal of attention is given to aggressive conflicts because of the nature of the consequences, nonaggressive conflicts are more pervasive across all age and grade levels. Many children's conflicts require them to coordinate both moral and personal elements. In peer–peer conflicts children explore the boundaries between their own legitimate personal needs and goals and the legitimate needs and goals of others.

Teachers are in a position to foster the necessary social skills to allow students to become autonomous and socially competent individuals. Through the use of cooperative learning, a teacher builds a collaborative atmosphere in the classroom. This collaboration is an opportunity for each student to demonstrate the social competence that helps the group reach equitable solutions while fostering personal success.

Through efforts like these to foster sound moral development, teachers play a tremendous role in preparing students to be good citizens in a world in which the potential for conflicts continues to increase.

Criticisms of Kohlberg's Theory

One limitation of Kohlberg's work is that it mostly involved boys (Aron, 1977). Some research on girls' moral reasoning finds patterns that are somewhat different from Kohlberg's. Whereas boys' moral reasoning revolves primarily around issues of justice, girls are more concerned about issues of caring and responsibility for others (Gibbs, Arnold, & Burkhart, 1984; Gilligan, 1982, 1985). Carol Gilligan has argued, for example, that males and females use different moral criteria: that male moral reasoning is focused on people's individual rights, whereas female moral reasoning is focused more on individuals' responsibilities for other people. This is why, she argues, females tend to suggest altruism and self-sacrifice rather than rights and rules as solutions to moral dilemmas (Gilligan, 1982). Kohlberg (Levine, Kohlberg, & Hewer, 1985) later revised his theory on the basis of these criticisms. However, most research has failed to find any male–female differences in moral maturity (Smetana, Killen, & Turiel, 1991; Thoma, 1986; Walker, 1989); nor is there convincing evidence that women are more caring, cooperative, or helpful than men (Eagley & Crowley, 1986).

CONNECTIONS
For more on gender issues in education, see Chapter 4, page 123.

The Intentional Teacher

● **Using What You Know about Human Development to Improve Teaching and Learning**

Intentional teachers use what they know about predictable patterns of moral, psychosocial, and cognitive development to make instructional decisions. They assess their students' functioning, and they provide instruction that addresses the broad range of stages of development they find in their students. They modify their instruction when they find that particular students need additional challenges or different opportunities. Thinking about student development—and watching for it in the classroom—helps intentional teachers foster growth for each student.

1 What am I trying to accomplish?

The goals teachers set need to be developmentally appropriate. Check prevalent theories of human development for general guidelines about what to expect from people who are your students' ages. Are your goals in line with what we know about human development?

When you plan your first-grade science program, you refer to Piaget's theory and recall that 6- and 7-year-olds have to struggle when asked to think about more than one variable at a time (centration). For that reason, your science program goals focus heavily upon students' active, open-ended exploration of their world and far less upon formal experimentation requiring the control of variables.

The goals teachers set need to foster students' development. Think about whether your goals encourage students to acquire knowledge *and* challenge students to progress developmentally.

As a middle school English teacher, you review your list of semester goals and verify that it includes not just an emphasis on a set of writing conventions but also a focus on students' moral development. You plan to include activities that challenge students to experience characters' emotional distress or to view good and bad from different characters' perspectives.

2 What are my students' relevant experiences and needs?

Teachers need to assess their own students' developmental functioning in light of their understanding of general expectations for student development.

When third-graders tease a younger student during recess, you seize the moment to assess their moral reasoning. You lead a class discussion about how the person being teased must feel. Based upon what you learn about your students' perspectives, you and your class devise a list of alternatives to teasing.

Students' backgrounds and experiences influence their development. Find out what prior experiences may have influenced your students' development. What experiences have students had with language? With concrete materials? With opportunities to experience success?

The teenagers in your classroom are struggling through Erikson's identity versus role confusion stage of psychosocial development. You lead a brainstorming session with your fifth-period world history class: Who are some role models throughout the ages? The session gives you the opportunity to assess your adolescents' experiences with a broad range of notable figures.

3 What approaches and materials are available to help me challenge every student?

A broad range of individual differences can be found in each classroom, and individual students exhibit inconsistencies between their

Another criticism of both Piaget's and Kohlberg's work is that young children can often reason about moral situations in more sophisticated ways than the stage theory would suggest (Rest, Edwards, & Thomas, 1997). For example, although young children often consider consequences to be more important than intentions when evaluating conduct (Olthof, Ferguson, & Luiten, 1989), under certain circumstances, children as young as 3 and 4 years of age use intentions to judge the behavior of others (Bussey, 1992). Six- to 10-year-olds at the stage of heteronomous morality have also been shown to make distinctions between rules that parents are justified in making and enforcing and rules that are under personal or peer jurisdiction (Laupa, 1991; Tisak & Tisak, 1990). Finally, Turiel (1983) has suggested that young children make a distinction between moral rules, such as not lying and stealing, that are based on principles of justice, and social-conventional

thinking and their behavior. How can you create a rich environment that includes a range of materials and experiences to meet a variety of needs and challenges students at all developmental levels?

> To teach your seventh-grade unit on environmental studies, you stock your classroom with a variety of print sources, including science magazines, newspapers, children's literature, and almanacs. You include maps, physical models, and real objects. You search out CD-ROM disks and Internet resources that students can select as they study the environment.

Opportunities for social interaction are important in children's development of language, thought, and moral reasoning. Consider how you can implement cooperative learning experiences as a regular element of your instruction.

> You make it a point to use partner strategies with your second-graders. For instance, during math, you encourage student pairs to check each other's work. During social studies, you direct them, "Tell your partner about a time when you had to share something even though you didn't want to." During science, you give partner groups two mirrors and ask them to determine whether together they can use the mirrors to see around a corner.

Teachers scaffold by providing varying levels of support until students can, figuratively, stand alone. Plan to provide support only as long as it is required. Remember that the kinds and levels of support you provide will vary by student and by task.

> As you teach sixth-graders to write haiku, you show and read aloud several examples. You ask students to find the similarities in the poems. Some students easily discern the pattern of each line consisting of a set number of syllables. You allow those students to begin composing. You invite a small group of students who need more support to the back of the room and provide additional instruction about the poem's format. Together you write a sample haiku, and then students return to their seats to write their own verses.

4 How will I know whether and when to change my strategy or modify my instruction?

Observe your students carefully to determine whether they are working within their zone of proximal development: Are they experiencing success with your current level of support? Provide more support for students who are working outside—above or below—their zone of proximal development.

> You review students' art portfolios and determine that your projects do not challenge certain students with well-honed artistic abilities. You search out additional resources and provide more challenging projects for this group.

5 What information will I accept as evidence that my students and I are experiencing success?

Your responsibility as a teacher includes more than cognitive growth. Use a variety of measures to assess moral and psychosocial growth as well.

> You ask sophomores to write brief analyses of current social issues, and you collect their paragraphs in folders. In spring, for each student, you pull a sampling of essays from several points in the year to examine evolving moral and social perspectives.

Whether it is incremental or whether it occurs in fits and starts, development takes time. Collect information that will allow you to look for long-term growth.

> In your metal shop class, you collect an early sample of each student's work and ask the students to evaluate their work by writing a paragraph on an index card. Near the end of the term, you collect another set of samples. Students are pleased to assess their progress over time and their growing ability to form smooth, sophisticated pieces.

rules, such as not wearing pajamas to school, that are based on social consensus and etiquette. Research has supported this view, demonstrating that children as young as 2½ to 3 years old make distinctions between moral and social-conventional rules.

The most important limitation of Kohlberg's theory is that it deals with moral reasoning rather than with actual behavior. Many individuals at different stages behave in the same way, and individuals at the same stage often behave in different ways (Walker, DeVries, & Trevethan, 1987). In a classic study of moral behavior, Hartshorne and May (1928) presented children of various ages with opportunities to cheat or steal when they thought they would not be caught. Very few children behaved honestly in every case, and very few behaved dishonestly in every case (see Newstead, Franklyn-Stokes, & Armstead, 1996). This study

What signs does this older child give that he has developed what Hoffman calls *empathic distress*? How well is a child this age able to put him- or herself in the crying child's situation, identify the source of distress, and find a solution to it?

showed that moral behavior does not conform to simple rules but is far more complex. Similarly, the link between children's moral reasoning and moral behavior may be quite weak (Blasi, 1983), although certain aspects of moral reasoning are related to social competence more strongly than others (Bear & Rys, 1995). Rest (1983) has argued that explanations of moral behavior must take into account moral reasoning but also the ability to interpret correctly what is happening in a social situation, the motivation to behave in a moral fashion, and the social skills necessary to actually carry out a moral plan of action.

Hoffman's Development of Moral Behavior

Martin Hoffman's theory of moral development (1993) complements the work of Piaget and Kohlberg by acknowledging the role of cognitive abilities and reasoning skills in explaining moral behavior. His theory differs from the stage theories of moral development by also considering the role of motivation and parenting practices. Hoffman argues that **empathic distress,** or experiencing the suffering of others, is a powerful motivator of moral choices and helping behavior. He also suggests that parental disciplinary practices can play a significant role in the development of moral behavior.

Hoffman's theory of empathic distress is similar to Piaget's and Kohlberg's in that he believes that cognitive abilities determine the kinds of empathic distress a child can experience and that as a consequence, empathic abilities develop in a stagelike fashion. Initially, infants experience global empathy when they react to others' distress as if it were their own. For example, after hearing another baby's cry, an infant will often seek out his or her own mother for comfort. According to Hoffman, between the ages of 2 and 6, children develop role-taking abilities that allow them to take the perspective of someone in distress. These abilities allow chil-

empathic distress
Experiencing the suffering of others.

CASE TO CONSIDER

Cheating and Moral Orientations

Ms. Jackson administered a unit test to students in her eighth-grade pre-algebra class. As the class began to take the test, however, she was summoned to the office for an urgent call. Rather than interrupt the activity flow, she quickly appointed Nichole, a high-achieving student who always finished tests early, to serve as classroom monitor during her absence. Ms. Jackson expected to be back in class in only a few minutes. She thought the students might not even notice she was gone. Unfortunately, Ms. Jackson was detained. As Nichole watched with growing alarm, Kirk and Martin began to discuss test items and compare answers. Gradually, other students became aware of their behavior.

Kirk: What did you get for number two? Mine doesn't look right.

Nichole: Shhhhh.

Martin: I got x equals four. But I can't do the first one.

Nichole and Sandy: Shhhhh.

Kirk: I think you have to divide everything by two.

Sandy: They're cheating! That's not fair!

Nichole: If you don't stop right now, I'll have to tell the teacher you were talking.

Martin: You better not. I'm not the only one. Look around. Vicki even has her book open.

Vicki: I'm not going to get a bad mark because of you guys cheating.

Kirk: So, if everyone does it then it's fair, right? We could all get good grades.

Dan: That's dumb. If everyone cheated, school would be a total joke. Teachers wouldn't know if we were learning anything. Grades would be worthless.

Carmen: Everybody, shhhh. We shouldn't go against the rules. Everybody knows you're not supposed to cheat.

Sandy: Yeah, Kirk, how can you look at yourself in the mirror? What would your father say, Martin?

Martin: Don't be so self-righteous. The main thing is not getting caught. It's getting caught that's dumb. If nobody's the wiser it doesn't matter, and if you're dumb enough to get caught, then you deserve whatever you get.

Sandy: Cheater! Cheater!

Vicki: I don't want to be a cheater. See, I closed my book. My mother would die if she thought I cheated. You're not going to tell, are you, Nichole?

Nichole: I want to do whatever is best for everyone.

Kirk: Well, I'm not doing detention over this.

Dan: We could all get detention over this, because it's wrong to cheat. Meanwhile, we've lost ten minutes, so if everyone would just shut up, maybe we'll be able to finish. This is a test!

When Ms. Jackson returned to class, she knew instantly that something had gone wrong. Nichole wore an embarrassed expression and quickly returned to her seat. Martin looked angry and had a paper balled up on his desk. Kirk looked shifty and scared. Vicki was gazing sadly out the window, and Sandy seemed to have some secret she desperately wanted to share. Only Dan was able to finish the test by the bell.

PROBLEM SOLVING

1. Analyze the differences in moral reasoning evident in the dialogue. How might Piaget have interpreted each speech in relation to stages of moral development? How might Kohlberg classify each speech in relation to stages of moral reasoning? How might Gilligan interpret the dialogue to support her view that males and females reason differently?

2. What should Ms. Jackson do to follow up on her suspicions? Assuming that she learned that cheating had taken place, how should she address cheating as a moral issue in a way that would help her students?

dren to put themselves in another's situation, to identify the source of distress, and then to find the most appropriate solution based on the distressed person's needs. By age 9, children develop a greater sensitivity to social conditions such as poverty that might also be a chronic source of distress. The resulting empathy is believed to promote prosocial activities aimed to benefit groups of people who are disadvantaged and in need of help. Hoffman considers the emotion of guilt to develop in similar ways. He believes that empathic distress combined with guilt is what motivates individuals to act on their moral principles.

SELF-CHECK

On your comparison chart, compare Piaget's two stages of moral development to Kohlberg's five stages of moral reasoning. By what ages do children seem capable of each level of thinking? Think of an original example of a moral dilemma, and show how different individuals' judgments would illustrate each of Kohlberg's stages.

CHAPTER SUMMARY

WHAT ARE SOME VIEWS OF HUMAN DEVELOPMENT?

Human development includes physical, cognitive, personal, social, and moral development. Most developmental psychologists believe nature and nurture combine to influence development. Continuous theories of development focus on social experiences that a child goes through, whereas discontinuous theories emphasize inborn factors rather than environmental influence. Development can be significantly affected by heredity, ability, exceptionality, personality, child rearing, culture, and the total environment. Jean Piaget and Lev Vygotsky proposed theories of cognitive development. Erik Erikson's theory of psychosocial development and Piaget's, Lawrence Kohlberg's, and Martin Hoffman's theories of moral development also describe important aspects of development.

HOW DID PIAGET VIEW COGNITIVE DEVELOPMENT?

Piaget postulated four stages of cognitive development through which people progress between birth and young adulthood. People adjust their schemes for dealing with the world through assimilation and accommodation. Piaget's developmental stages include the sensorimotor stage (birth to 2 years of age), the preoperational stage (2 to 7 years of age), and the concrete operational stage (ages 7 to 11). During the formal operational stage (age 11 to adulthood), young people develop the ability to deal with hypothetical situations and to monitor their own thinking.

HOW IS PIAGET'S WORK VIEWED TODAY?

Piaget's theory has been criticized for relying exclusively on broad, fixed, sequential stages through which all children progress and for underestimating children's abilities. In contrast, neo-Piagetian theories place greater emphasis on social and environmental influences on cognitive development. Nevertheless, Piaget's theory has important implications for education. Piagetian principles are embedded in the curriculum and in effective teaching practices, and Piaget-influenced concepts such as cognitive constructivism and developmentally appropriate instruction guide education reform.

HOW DID VYGOTSKY VIEW COGNITIVE DEVELOPMENT?

Vygotsky viewed cognitive development as an outgrowth of social development through interaction with others and the environment. Assisted learning takes place in children's zones of proximal development, where they can do new tasks that are within their capabilities only with a teacher's or peer's assistance. Children internalize learning, develop self-regulation, and solve problems through vocal or silent private speech. Teachers provide interactional contexts, such as cooperative learning groups, and scaffolding.

HOW DID ERIKSON VIEW PERSONAL AND SOCIAL DEVELOPMENT?

Erikson proposed eight stages of psychosocial development, each dominated by a particular psychosocial crisis precipitated through interaction with the social environment. In Stage I, trust versus mistrust, the goal is to develop a sense of trust through interaction with caretakers. In Stage II, autonomy versus doubt (18 months to age 3), children have a dual desire to hold on and to let go. In Stage III, initiative versus guilt (3 to 6 years of age), children elaborate their sense of self through exploration of the environment. Children enter school during Stage IV, industry versus inferiority (6 to 12 years of age), when academic success or failure is central. In Stage V, identity versus role confusion (12 to 18 years), adolescents turn from family to peer group and begin their searches for partners and careers. Adulthood brings Stage VI (intimacy versus isolation), Stage VII (generativity versus self-absorption), and Stage VIII (integrity versus despair).

WHAT ARE SOME THEORIES OF MORAL DEVELOPMENT?

According to Piaget, children develop heteronomous morality (obedience to authority through moral realism) by around age 6 and later advance to autonomous morality (rational morality based on moral principles). Kohlberg's five stages of moral reasoning reflect children's responses to moral dilemmas. In Stages 1 and 2 (the preconventional level), children obey rules set down by others while maximizing self-interest. In Stages 3 and 4 (the conventional level) the individual adopts rules, believes in law and order, and seeks the approval of others. In Stages 5 and 6 (the postconventional level), people define their own values in terms of abstract ethical principles they have chosen to follow.

Critics point out that Kohlberg's study was based only on male subjects. Studies suggest that there may be little connection between what children say and their actual moral behavior.

Hoffman's theory focuses on both the stagelike development of empathic distress and environmental input from parents in its explanation of moral behavior.

KEY TERMS

accommodation   31

adaptation   31

assimilation   31

autonomous morality   53

centration   34

class inclusion   37

cognitive development   30

concrete operational stage   36

conservation   33

constructivism   32

continuous theory of development   29

conventional level of morality   54

development   28

developmentally appropriate education   41

discontinuous theories of
development   29
egocentric   35
empathic distress   60
equilibration   31
formal operational stage   37
heteronomous morality   52
inferred reality   36
moral dilemmas   54
object permanence   33
postconventional level of
morality   55
preconventional level of morality   54
preoperational stage   33

private speech   45
psychosocial crisis   48
psychosocial theory   48
reflexes   33
reversibility   34
scaffolding   45
schemes   30
self-regulation   43
sensorimotor stage   33
seriation   36
sign systems   43
transitivity   37
zone of proximal development   45

Self-Assessment

1. Which of the following pairs of issues are central in developmental psychology?
   a. assimilation and accommodation
   b. nature versus nurture and continuous versus discontinuous development
   c. preconventional thinking and postconventional thinking
   d. zone of proximal development versus private speech and scaffolding

2. Match each stage of cognitive development with its definition.
   _____ sensorimotor
   _____ preoperational
   _____ concrete operational
   _____ formal operational

   a. Exploration of the environment occurs mostly through the use of the five senses and motor skills.
   b. Learners are capable of hypothetical, abstract thought and scientific reasoning.
   c. Learners make errors when attempting to solve conservation tasks because they center on one aspect of the problem.
   d. Inferable reality, seriation, and transitivity are cognitive skills possessed by these learners.

3. Write a brief paragraph explaining the difference between assimilation and accommodation.

4. Piaget's principles have been criticized because recent research demonstrates that
   a. many children go through cognitive stages in varying orders.
   b. cognitive tasks such as conservation cannot be taught unless the child is in the appropriate stage.
   c. the clarity of task instruction can significantly influence young children's performance on conservation tasks.
   d. children, on the average, are actually less competent than Piaget thought.

5. Vygotsky suggested that when children are capable of learning but have not yet learned, teachers should assist them by using any of the following methods except
   a. social interaction and private speech.
   b. assisted discovery and problem solving.
   c. perceived appearances.
   d. scaffolding.

6. A typical individual who is in Piaget's stage of concrete operations is, at the same time, in Erikson's stage of
   a. autonomy versus doubt.
   b. industry versus inferiority.
   c. intimacy versus isolation.
   d. generativity versus self-absorption.

7. The psychosocial stage associated with adolescence is
   a. identity versus role confusion.
   b. industry versus inferiority.
   c. intimacy versus isolation.
   d. integrity versus despair.

8. Match each level of Kohlberg's theory of moral development with its definition.
   _____ preconventional
   _____ conventional
   _____ postconventional

   a. Self-chosen ethical principles guide moral decision making.

   b. The self is of the greatest concern.
   c. Moral decisions are made to satisfy the needs of the group and to maintain the social order.

9. Describe Hoffman's theory of moral behavior and parenting. What is empathic distress?

10. Describe typical preoperational, concrete operational, and formal operational learners (i.e., learners who are developing as the theorists proposed); then add statements about their psychosocial and moral development.

Chapter 3

HOW DO CHILDREN DEVELOP DURING THE PRESCHOOL YEARS?

Physical Development in Early Childhood

Language Acquisition

Bilingual Education

Socioemotional Development

WHAT KINDS OF EARLY CHILDHOOD EDUCATION PROGRAMS EXIST?

Day-Care Programs

Nursery Schools

Compensatory Preschool Programs

Early Intervention

Kindergarten Programs

Developmentally Appropriate Practice

HOW DO CHILDREN DEVELOP DURING THE ELEMENTARY YEARS?

Physical Development during Middle Childhood

Cognitive Abilities

Socioemotional Development in Middle Childhood

HOW DO CHILDREN DEVELOP DURING THE MIDDLE SCHOOL AND HIGH SCHOOL YEARS?

Physical Development during Adolescence

Cognitive Development

Characteristics of Hypothetical–Deductive Reasoning

Implications for Educational Practice

Socioemotional Development in Adolescence

Identity Development

Marcia's Four Identity Statuses

Self-Concept and Self-Esteem

Social Relationships

Emotional Development

Problems of Adolescence

Development during Childhood and Adolescence

At Parren Elementary/Middle School, eighth-graders are encouraged to become tutors for first-graders. They help them with reading, math, and other subjects. As part of this program, Jake Stevens has been working for about a month with Billy Ames.

"Hey, shorty!" said Jake one day when he met Billy for a tutoring session.

"Hey, Jake!" As always, Billy was delighted to see his big buddy. But today his friendly greeting turned into a look of astonishment. "What have you got in your ear?"

"Haven't you ever seen an earring?"

"I thought those were just for girls."

Jake laughed. "Not like this one! Can you see it?"

Billy squinted at the earring and saw that it was in the shape of a small sword. "Awesome!"

"Besides," said Jake, "girls wear two earrings, guys only wear one. A lot of guys are wearing them."

"Didn't it hurt to get a hole in your ear?"

"A little, but I'm tough! Boy, was my mom mad though. I have to take my earring off before I go home, but I put it back on while I'm walking to school."

"But didn't your mom . . . ."

"Enough of that, squirt! You've got some heavy math to do. Let's get to it!"

The interaction between Jake and Billy illustrates the enormous differences between the world of the adolescent and that of the child. Jake, at 13, is a classic young teen. His idealism and down-deep commitment to the positive is shown in his volunteering to serve as a tutor and in the caring, responsible relationship he has established with Billy. At the same time, Jake is asserting his independence by having his ear pierced and wearing an earring, against his mother's wishes. This independence is strongly supported by his peer group, however, so it is really only a shift of dependence from parents and teachers toward peers. His main purpose in wearing an earring is to demonstrate conformity to the styles and norms of his peers rather than to those of adults. Yet Jake does still depend on his parents and other adults for advice and support when making decisions that he knows have serious consequences for his future, and he does take off his earring at home to avoid a really serious battle with his parents.

Billy lives in a different world. He can admire Jake's audacity, but he would never go so far. Billy's world has simpler rules. For one thing, boys are boys and girls are girls, so he is shocked by Jake's flouting of convention to wear something usually associated with females. He is equally shocked by Jake's willingness to directly disobey his mother. Billy may misbehave, but within much narrower limits. He knows that rules are rules, and he fully expects to be punished if he breaks them.

Using Your EXPERIENCE

Creative Thinking   Reflect on a tutoring or mentoring experience that was significant in your life. Then free-write for 3 to 4 minutes about everything you remember that happened. Share your experiences with two or three classmates.

Educators must know the principal theories of cognitive, social, and moral development presented in Chapter 2 so that they will understand how young people grow over time in each of these domains. However, teachers usually deal with children of a particular age or in a narrow age range. A preschool teacher needs to know what preschool children are like. Elementary teachers are concerned with middle childhood. Middle, junior high, and senior high school teachers are concerned with adolescence. This chapter presents the physical, social, and cognitive characteristics of students at each phase of development (see Elkind, 1994; Schickedanz, Schickedanz, Forsyth, & Forsyth, 1998). It discusses how the principles of development presented in Chapter 2 apply to children of various ages, and adds information on physical development, language development, and self-concept. Figure 3.1 identifies central themes or emphases in development during early childhood, middle childhood, and adolescence.

Early Childhood

Cognitive development
Language acquisition

Physical development
Large and small muscle skills

Socioemotional development
Prosocial behavior

FIGURE 3.1 ● Central Issues in Development during Early Childhood, Middle Childhood, and Adolescence These are some developmental concerns that are characteristically (but not exclusively) important during each of the three broad age levels discussed in this chapter.

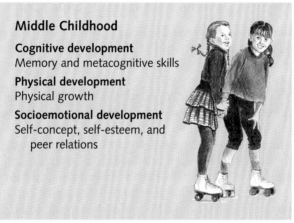

Middle Childhood

Cognitive development
Memory and metacognitive skills

Physical development
Physical growth

Socioemotional development
Self-concept, self-esteem, and peer relations

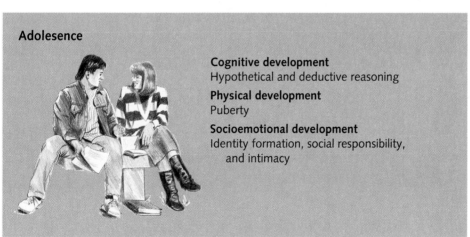

Adolesence

Cognitive development
Hypothetical and deductive reasoning

Physical development
Puberty

Socioemotional development
Identity formation, social responsibility, and intimacy

HOW DO CHILDREN DEVELOP DURING THE PRESCHOOL YEARS?

Children can be termed *preschoolers* when they are between 3 and 6 years of age. This is a time of rapid change in all areas of development. Children master most motor skills by the end of this period and can use their physical skills to achieve a wide range of goals. Cognitively, they start to develop an understanding of classes and relationships and absorb an enormous amount of information about their social and physical worlds. By the age of 6, children use almost completely mature speech, not only to express their wants and needs, but also to share their ideas and experiences. Socially, children learn appropriate behaviors and rules and become increasingly adept at interacting with other children.

As each of these aspects of development is discussed, keep in mind the complexity of development and how all facets of a child's growth are interrelated. Although physical, cognitive, and social development can be put in separate sections in a book, in real life they not only are intertwined but are also affected by the environment within which children grow up.

Physical Development in Early Childhood

Physical development describes the changes in the physical appearance of children as well as in their motor skills. During the preschool years the sequence in which all children develop motor skills is generally the same, though some children gain skills faster than others.

The major physical accomplishment for preschoolers is increased control over the large and small muscles. **Small muscle development,** sometimes called fine motor activity, relates to movements requiring precision and dexterity, such as buttoning a shirt or zipping a coat. **Large muscle development,** or gross motor activities, involves such movements as walking and running. Table 3.1 shows the ages at which most children acquire various motor skills.

By the end of the preschool period, most children can easily perform self-help tasks such as buckling, buttoning, snapping, and zipping. They can go up and down steps with alternating feet. They can perform fine motor activities such as cutting with scissors and using crayons to color a predefined area. They also begin learning to write letters and words. After 6 or 7 years of age, children gain few completely new basic skills; rather, the quality and complexity of their movements improve (Schickedanz et al., 1998).

small muscle development
Development of dexterity of the fine muscles of the hand.

large muscle development
Development of motor skills such as running or throwing, which involve the limbs and large muscles.

TABLE 3.1

Motor Development of Preschool Children

AGE	SKILLS
2-year-olds	Walk with wide stance and body sway. Can climb, push, pull, run, hang by both hands. Have little endurance. Reach for objects with two hands.
3-year-olds	Keep legs closer together when walking and running. Can run and move more smoothly. Reach for objects with one hand. Smear and daub paint; stack blocks.
4-year-olds	Can vary rhythm of running. Skip awkwardly; jump. Have greater strength, endurance, and coordination. Draw shapes and simple figures; make paintings; use blocks for buildings.
5-year-olds	Can walk a balance beam. Skip smoothly; stand on one foot. Can manage buttons and zippers; may tie shoelaces. Use utensils and tools correctly.

Language Acquisition

From birth to about 2 years of age, infants understand their world through their senses. Their knowledge is based on physical actions, and their understanding is restricted to events in the present or the immediate past. Only when children make the transition from the sensorimotor stage to the preoperational stage (at about age 2) and begin to talk and to use mental symbols can they use thoughts or concepts to understand their world. During the preoperational stage, however, their thoughts are still prelogical, tied to physical actions and the way things appear to them. Most children remain in the preoperational stage of cognitive development until they are 7 or 8 years old.

Children normally develop basic language skills before entering school. Language development involves both oral and written communication. Verbal abilities develop very early, and by age 3, children are already skillful talkers. By the end of the preschool years, children can use and understand an almost infinite number of sentences, can hold conversations, and know about written language (Anglin, 1993).

Although there are individual differences in the rates at which children acquire language abilities, the sequence of accomplishments is similar for all children. Around age 1, children produce one-word utterances such as "bye-bye" and "Mommy." These words typically represent objects and events that are important to the child. Over the course of the second year of life, children begin to combine words into two-word sentences (e.g., "More milk"). During the preschool years, children's vocabulary increases, along with their knowledge of the rules of spoken language. By the time they start school, children have mastered most of the grammatical rules of language, and their vocabulary consists of thousands of words.

ORAL LANGUAGE ● Development of oral language, or spoken language, requires not only learning words but also learning the rules of word and sentence construction. For example, children learn the rules for how to form plurals before they enter kindergarten. Berko (1985) showed preschoolers a picture of a made-up

What language acquisition knowledge and skills will these children likely have by the time they enter kindergarten? As a teacher, what general approaches to formal instruction in reading and writing might you use to build on their knowledge and skills?

bird, called a "Wug." She then showed them two such pictures and said, "Now there is another one. There are two of them. There are two _____." The children readily answered, "Wugs," showing that they could apply general rules for forming plurals to a new situation. In a similar fashion, children learn to add "-ed" and "-ing" to verbs. As they learn these rules, they initially overgeneralize them, saying "goed" instead of "went," for example, and "mouses" instead of "mice."

Interestingly, children often learn the correct forms of irregular verbs (such as "He broke the chair") and then replace them with incorrect but more rule-based constructions ("He breaked [or broked] the chair"). One 4-year-old said, "I flew my kite." He then thought for a moment and emphatically corrected himself, saying, "I flewed my kite!" These errors are a normal part of language development and should not be corrected (Fenson et al., 1994).

Just as they learn rules for forming words, children learn rules for sentences. Their first sentences usually contain just two words ("Want milk," "See birdie," "Jessie outside"), but they soon learn to form more complex sentences and to vary their tone of voice to indicate questions ("Where doggie go?") or to indicate emphasis ("Want cookie!"). Three-year-olds can usually express rather complex thoughts, even though their sentences may still lack such words as "a," "the," and "did." Later, children continually expand their ability to express and understand complex sentences. However, they still have difficulty with certain aspects of language throughout the preschool and early elementary school years. For example, Carol Chomsky (1969) showed children a doll that was blindfolded and asked, "Is the doll easy to see or hard to see?" Only 22 percent of 5-year-olds could respond correctly; not until age 9 could all her subjects respond appropriately to the question. Many students confuse such words as "ask" and "tell" and "teach" and "learn" well into the elementary grades.

Preschoolers often play with language or experiment with its patterns and rules (Garvey, 1990). This experimentation frequently involves changing sounds, patterns, and meanings. One 3-year-old was told by his exasperated parent, "You're impossible!" He replied, "No, I'm impopsicle!" The same child said that his baby brother, Benjamin, was a man because he was a "Benja-man." Children often rearrange word sounds to create new words, rhymes, and funny sentences. The popularity of finger plays, nonsense rhymes, and Dr. Seuss storybooks shows how young children enjoy playing with language.

Oral language development is heavily influenced by the amount and quality of talking parents do with their children. A study by Hart and Risley (1995) found that middle-class parents talked far more to their children than working-class or welfare parents, and that their children had substantially different numbers of words in their vocabularies. The amount of parent speech was as important as socioeconomic status; children of low-income parents who spoke to their children a great deal also had large vocabularies.

emergent literacy
Knowledge and skills relating to reading that children usually develop from experience with books and other print media before the beginning of formal reading instruction in school.

READING ● Learning to read in the early elementary grades is one of the most important of all developmental tasks, if only because in our society school success is so often equated with reading success. The process of learning to read can begin quite early if children are read to. Research on **emergent literacy,** or preschoolers' knowledge and skills related to reading (Glazer & Burke, 1994; Laminack, 1990; Sulzby & Teale, 1991), has shown that children may enter school with a great deal of knowledge about reading and that this knowledge contributes to success in formal reading instruction. For example, young children have often learned concepts of print such as that print is arranged from left to right, that spaces between words have meaning, and that books are read from front to back. Many preschoolers can "read" books from beginning to end by interpreting the pictures on each page. They understand about story plots and can often predict what will happen next in a simple story. They can recognize logos on familiar stores and products; for example, very young children often know that *M* is for *McDonald's*. Further, even if they have not been read to, children have developed complex language skills that are critical in reading. Children from families in which there are few literacy-related activities can learn concepts of print, plot, and other prereading concepts if they attend preschools or kindergartens that emphasize reading and discussing books in class (Purcell-Gates, McIntire, & Freppon, 1995; Whitehurst et al., 1994). Similarly, young children can be taught to hear specific sounds within words (a skill called phonemic awareness), and this contributes to later success in reading (Blachman, Ball, Black, & Tangel, 1994; Byrne & Fielding-Barnsley, 1995).

There is a long-standing debate about methods of teaching reading. Some educators favor direct teaching of phonics, whereas others oppose this. The term **whole language** (Goodman & Goodman, 1989) is used to refer to a broad range of teaching practices that attempt to move away from teaching reading as a set of discrete skills. Whole language emphasizes having students read whole stories and novels, newspaper articles, and other real materials. It emphasizes integrating reading with writing and writing for real audiences and purposes. Word attack skills (such as knowing how a silent *e* changes the sound of *a* in *can* and *cane*) may be taught in whole language classes, but usually only in the context of what students are reading.

Because whole language is not a single, well-specified practice, it is difficult to evaluate. Programs based on whole language principles do seem to be effective in kindergarten, but there is little evidence of any positive effects in first grade or beyond (Stahl & Miller, 1989). The problem is that many children need to be given a more systematic approach to learning phonics, a way to crack the reading code, at the same time that they need to learn that reading has meaning. Although debate on this topic still rages, most researchers (Adams, 1990; Ehri, 1991; Honig, 1996; Juel, 1991; Learning First Alliance, 1998; Vellutino, 1991) favor a balanced approach emphasizing real reading; integration of reading and writing; and systematic instruction in word attack skills, or phonics, in the context of meaningful materials.

WRITING ● Most children begin to grasp the fundamentals of writing during early childhood. Children as young as 3 years of age recognize differences between print and drawings. They gradually begin to discriminate the distinctive features of print, such as whether lines are straight or curved, open or closed, diagonal, horizontal, or vertical, and how they are oriented. But through the early elementary grades, many children continue to reverse letters such as *b* and *d* and *p* and *q* until they learn that the orientation of letters is an important characteristic (Temple, Nathan, Temple, & Burris, 1993). Letter reversal is not an indication of reading or writing problems if other development in these areas is normal. Children's writing follows a developmental sequence. It emerges out of early scribbles and at first is spread randomly across a page. This characteristic reflects an incomplete understanding of word boundaries as well as an inability to mentally create a line for placing letters. Children invent spellings by making judgments about English sounds and by relating the sounds they hear to the letters they know. In trying to represent what they hear, they typically use letter names rather than letter sounds; short vowels are frequently left out because they are not directly associated with letter names (Downing, Coughlin, & Rich, 1986). For example, one kindergartner labeled a picture of a dinosaur "DNSR." Many teachers encourage kindergartners

whole language
Educational philosophy that emphasizes the integration of reading, writing, and language and communication skills across the curriculum in the context of authentic or real-life materials, problems, and tasks.

CASE TO CONSIDER

I CN SPL

Brenda, a first-grade teacher at Clark Elementary School, had just finished her presentation on what the class was learning this year to her students' parents on Family Night. She asked if there were any questions. Jayann's mother, Joan, raised her hand, as did Steven's father, Bob.

Joan: You mentioned invented spelling. There seems to be a big controversy in our neighborhood about whether it works or not. I don't know if I understand why you're using it.

Bob: I don't either. That's not the way I was taught. I learned with phonics and I spell fine. I can't read the journals my son is bringing home. My neighbor's child is in Mrs. Williams's room. I saw her journal and I could read every word she wrote. They have a list of five words each week and Mrs. Williams makes sure every one of them is spelled correctly.

Brenda: Well, actually, invented spelling is a pretty natural way for kids to learn how to spell the words they use every day. I call it approximate spelling—you know, close but not exact. When I read through the kids' journals, I look for words I think they're ready to learn to spell. These are the words they'll want to learn because they're using them a lot.

Bob: Yeah, but close isn't really right. You know that phrase, "Close but no cigar." It seems to me that kids either learn to spell right or not.

Brenda: Let me give you an example of how the kids in our class are learning to spell. Every day, I ask the class to help me write a morning message on the chalkboard. Last week, the class was excited about a dog that had gotten into the building, so they chose, "A dog ran through our school this morning" as the message.

Several parents smiled and nodded, remembering how their children had still been talking about the dog in school at the end of the day.

Brenda: I write the sentence on the board as the students dictate it to me. As I call on the students, we review letter sounds, punctuation rules, and capitalization skills. Now why don't you be my class and dictate the message of the day to me, and I'll demonstrate how I teach it?

Most of the parents got into the role-playing and a lively interchange ensued. But Bob, Steven's father, didn't join in, so Brenda decided to "call" on him.

Brenda: Bob, this is how I try to get all the students involved at their own levels: What letter do you hear at the beginning of *dog*?

Bob (getting frustrated): But that's my son Steven's problem. He doesn't seem to hear the letter sounds the way the other kids do. How is he going to learn to spell correctly unless he is taught phonics?

Brenda took a deep breath. She understood that first-grade parents were usually anxious. Bob's statement would only heighten their anxiety. Some children, Steven among them, were indeed struggling. She wondered whether this approach was really working for them. She looked at Steven's parents and the parents of the other children who were having difficulty. They were all waiting to hear her answer.

PROBLEM SOLVING

1. Using what you know about language acquisition in children between the ages of 3 and 6, how would you explain the differences in spelling ability in Brenda's first-grade class?
2. Should Brenda be a firm believer in invented spelling? What other teaching strategies might she use to help students like Steven?
3. How should Brenda answer Bob's question about the way in which spelling is taught?

Adapted by permission from "I CN SPL" by Joan Isenberg and the Case Writing Team at George Mason University and Fairfax County Schools, from *Allyn & Bacon's Custom Cases in Education,* edited by Greta Morine-Dershimer and Joyce Huth Munro (1997).

and first-graders to write stories using invented spellings to help them learn reading as well as writing (Morrow, 1993).

Bilingual Education

It is projected that by the year 2020 there will be 50 million children in the United States whose primary language is not English (Garcia, 1994; General Accounting

Office, 1994a). An increasingly important issue in language acquisition, therefore, is how to teach these children when they enter U.S. schools. The debate centers on how best to teach these children: in their primary language (e.g., Spanish or Vietnamese); in English; or bilingually, in both English and their primary language. Many educators are opposed to primary language or bilingual education because they think that students will learn English more rapidly if they are exposed to it more often. Others oppose it because they believe that it will hinder assimilation into U.S. culture. Based on arguments of this type, California voters banned bilingual education in 1998. However, proponents of bilingual education cite evidence suggesting that instruction in both English and a student's primary language promotes the development of cognitive skills (including reading) and makes schooling a less threatening experience (Carter & Chatfield, 1986; E. E. Garcia, 1993); Krashen & Biber, 1988). Research on the effects of bilingual education finds it to be no worse than English-only instruction, but also not consistently better (August & Hakuta, 1997).

CONNECTIONS

For more on bilingual education, see Chapter 4, page 119.

Promoting Language Development in Young Children

THEORY *into* **Practice**

Many of the educational implications derived from research on children's language development transfer findings from two sources: parental behaviors that encourage oral language development and studies of young children who learn to read without formal classroom instruction. The most frequent recommendations include reading to children; surrounding them with books and other printed materials; making various writing materials available; encouraging reading and writing; and being responsive to children's questions about letters, words, and spellings (Schickedanz et al., 1998).

Computers can also contribute to language development or emergent literacy. For example, computers can help children of preschool age learn to discriminate and recognize letters. In one type of program, children see letters on the screen that they match with keyboard letters. Other programs with speech attachments allow the children to hear the sound of each letter they type. Children can also link words to pictures of objects. They can create a story by moving words into a scene, where they are transformed to images. In some computer programs children explore words and their meanings by constructing simple sentences and then observing an animated illustration of the sentence they have typed. Young children can also use word-processing programs by either typing or dictating words and phrases, which are put into print. Other computer programs pronounce words as the child types them and then read the child's sentence or story in a synthesized voice. Many well-known children's stories have been put on CD-ROMs. The story is told while animated figures on the screen dramatize the events. The text of the story also appears on the screen so that children can follow the words of the story as they listen.

Does any of this help children in reading or writing readiness? One study (Hess, 1987) found that when kindergarten children used computers, they improved their reading readiness scores significantly more than children who did not have computers. In addition, the study indicated positive effects of computers on the social and emotional climate of the classroom. Other studies (Adkins, 1989) have had mixed results. Whatever the research on computer use seems to say about helping children with emergent literacy, there is a caution. Computers can become a means to push academic learning further downward into early childhood, and many who are involved in early childhood education (see, for example, Hohmann, 1990) believe this is a wrong direction.

In addition to computer programs, teachers can use numerous props in the classroom, such as telephone books and office space in a dramatic play area (Neumann & Roskos, 1993). Classrooms can have writing centers with materials such as typewriters, magnetic letters, chalkboards, pencils, crayons, markers, and paper (Wasik, in press). Art activities also contribute to children's understanding of print. Children's recognition that their images can stand for something else helps them develop an understanding of abstractions, an understanding that is essential to comprehension of symbolic language (Eisner, 1982).

Teachers can encourage children's involvement with print by reading in small groups, having tutors read to children individually, and allowing children to choose books to read. Intimate reading experiences allow children to turn pages, pause to look at pictures or ask questions, and read along with an adult. These experiences cannot occur as easily if the teacher sits at the front of the room reading to a large group of children.

Predictable books such as *The Three Little Pigs* and *There Was an Old Lady Who Swallowed a Fly* allow beginning readers to rely on what they already know about language while learning sound–letter relationships. Stories are predictable if a child can remember what the author is going to say and how it will be stated. Repetitive structures, rhyme and rhythm, and a match between pictures and text increase predictability.

Children's understanding of language is enhanced when adults point out the important features of print (Dyson, 1984; Harste & Burke, 1980). Statements such as "We must start at the front, not at the back of the book"; "Move your finger; you're covering the words and I can't see to read them"; and "You have to point to each word as you say it, not to each letter, like this" help to clarify the reading process. Teachers can indicate features in print that are significant and can draw attention to patterns of letters, sounds, or phrases. These informal experiences also teach children the words that are related to written language, such as *letter, word,* and *a, b, c* (Morrow, 1993).

Socioemotional Development

A young child's social life evolves in relatively predictable ways. The social network grows from an intimate relationship with parents or other guardians to include other family members, nonrelated adults, and peers. Social interactions extend from home to neighborhood and from nursery school or other child-care arrangements to formal school. Erik Erikson's theory of personal and social development suggests that during early childhood, children must resolve the personality crisis of initiative versus guilt. The child's successful resolution of this stage results in a sense of initiative and ambition tempered by a reasonable understanding of the permissible. Early educators can encourage this resolution by giving children opportunities to take initiative, to be challenged, and to succeed.

peers
People who are equal in age or status.

PEER RELATIONSHIPS ● During the preschool years, **peers** (other children who are a child's equal) begin to play an increasingly important role in children's social and cognitive development (Garvey, 1990). Children's relations with their peers differ in several ways from their interactions with adults. Peer play allows children to interact with other individuals whose level of development is similar to their own. When peers have disputes among themselves, they must make concessions and must cooperate in resolving them if the play is to continue; unlike in adult–child disputes, in a peer dispute no one can claim to have ultimate authority. Peer conflicts also let children see that others have thoughts, feelings, and viewpoints that are different from their own. Conflicts also heighten children's sensitivity to the effects of their behavior on others. In this way, peer relationships help young children to overcome the egocentrism that Piaget described as being characteristic of preoperational thinking (Kutnick, 1988).

PROSOCIAL BEHAVIOR ● Research involving children who are socially rejected by their peers suggests that these children are likely to lack positive prosocial skills (Asher & Coie, 1990). **Prosocial behaviors** are voluntary actions toward others such as caring, sharing, comforting, and cooperation. Research on the roots of prosocial behavior has contributed to our knowledge of children's moral as well as social development. Several factors seem to be associated with the development of prosocial behaviors (Eisenberg & Mussen, 1989). These include the following:

- Parental disciplinary techniques that stress the consequences of the child's behavior for others and that are applied within a warm, responsive parent–child relationship (Hoffman, 1993).
- Contact with adults who indicate they expect concern for others, who let children know that aggressive solutions to problems are unacceptable, and who provide acceptable alternatives (Konig, 1995).
- Contact with adults who attribute positive characteristics to children when they do well ("What a helpful boy you are!") (Grusec & Goodnow, 1994).

PLAY ● Most of a preschooler's interactions with peers occur during play (Hughes, 1995). However, the degree to which play involves other children increases over the preschool years (Howes & Matheson, 1992). In a classic study of preschoolers, Mildred Parten (1932) identified four categories of play that reflect increasing levels of social interaction and sophistication. **Solitary play** is play that occurs alone, often with toys, and is independent of what other children are doing. **Parallel play** involves children engaged in the same activity side by side but with very little interaction or mutual influence. **Associative play** is much like parallel play but with increased levels of interaction in the form of sharing, turn-taking, and general interest in what others are doing. **Cooperative play** occurs when children join together to achieve a common goal, such as building a large castle with each child building a part of the structure. For example, Howes and Matheson (1992) followed a group of children for 3 years, observing their play when they were 1 to 2 years old and continuing until they were 3 to 4 years old. They found that children engage in more complex types of play as they grow older, advancing from simple forms of parallel play to complex pretend play in which children cooperate in planning and carrying out activities (Roopnarine et al., 1992; Verba, 1993).

Play is important for children because it exercises their linguistic, cognitive, and social skills and contributes to their general personality development (Christie & Wardle, 1992). Children use their minds when playing, because they are thinking and acting as if they were another person. When they make such a transformation,

prosocial behaviors
Actions that show respect and caring for others.

solitary play
Play that occurs alone.

parallel play
Play in which children engage in the same activity side by side but with very little interaction or mutual influence.

associative play
Play that is much like parallel play but with increased levels of interaction in the form of sharing, turn-taking, and general interest in what others are doing.

CONNECTIONS
For suggested cooperative learning activities, see Chapter 8, page 269.

cooperative play
Play in which children join together to achieve a common goal.

Are these children engaging in parallel, associative, or cooperative play? How might such play sessions benefit their development of prosocial behaviors and peer relations?

they are taking a step toward abstract thinking in that they are freeing their thoughts from a focus on concrete objects. Play is also associated with creativity, especially the ability to be less literal and more flexible in one's thinking (Garvey, 1990). Play has an important role in Vygotsky's theories of development, because it allows children to freely explore ways of thinking and acting that are above their current level of functioning. Vygotsky (1978) wrote, "In play a child is always above his average age, above his daily behavior; in play it is as though he were a head taller than himself" (p. 102).

CONNECTIONS

For more on Vygotsky, see Chapter 2, page 43.

Preschoolers' play appears to be influenced by a variety of factors. For instance, preschoolers' interactions with peers are related to how they interact with their parents (Ladd & Hart, 1992). Three-year-olds who have warm and nurturing relationships with parents are more likely to engage in social pretend play and resolve conflicts with peers than are children with less secure relationships with their parents (Howes & Rodning, 1992). Children also play better with familiar peers and same-sex peers (Ladd & Price, 1987). Providing age-appropriate toys and play activities can also support the development of play and peer interaction skills.

SELF-CHECK

Begin a comparison chart with the columns headed Early Childhood, Middle Childhood, and Adolescence. Enter information concerning early childhood in terms of the categories listed below.

relevant ages
relevant grade levels
Piagetian stage(s)
Eriksonian stage(s)
characteristics of behavior
examples of key social relationships

physical characteristics
examples of physical abilities
characteristics of language and thought
examples of cognitive abilities
sources of impact on development

WHAT KINDS OF EARLY CHILDHOOD EDUCATION PROGRAMS EXIST?

In almost all the countries of the world, children begin their formal schooling at about 6 years of age, a time when they have typically attained the cognitive and social skills they need for organized learning activities. However, there is much less agreement on what kind of schooling, if any, children younger than the age of 5 need. The kindergarten originated in Germany in the 1800s but did not gain widespread acceptance until the turn of the century. Since World War II, nursery schools and day-care programs have mushroomed as increasing numbers of women with children have entered the work force (Scarr, 1998). In the United States, half of all mothers of infants (less than a year old) and three-quarters of mothers of school-age children now work outside the home (Behrman, 1996). By contrast, only 32 percent of mothers with young children were working in 1970 (West, Hausken, & Collins, 1993). Group day-care programs exist for children from infancy on, and organized preschool and nursery school programs sometimes take children as young as 2. As programs for very young children have expanded, the quality of many children's experiences has become higher. Early childhood education has become a major focus of national policy (Carnegie Corporation of New York, 1994, 1996; Kagan & Neuman, 1998; National Education Goals Panel, 1997; Shore, 1998; Weikart, 1995).

Day-Care Programs

Day-care programs exist primarily to provide child-care services for working parents. They range from a baby-sitting arrangement in which one adult takes care of several children to organized preschool programs that differ little from nursery schools (General Accounting Office, 1995; Kagan & Cohen, 1997; Scarr, 1998). Research shows that the quality of early child care can have a lasting effect (Carnegie Corporation of New York, 1994; Peisner-Feinberg et al., 1998), especially for children from disadvantaged homes (Scarr, 1998).

Nursery Schools

The primary difference between day-care and nursery school programs is that nursery schools are more likely to provide a planned program designed to foster the social and cognitive development of young children. Most nursery schools are half-day programs, with two or three adults supervising a class of 15 to 20 children. Unlike day-care centers and Head Start programs (which are discussed in the following section), nursery schools most often serve middle-class families (General Accounting Office, 1995; West et al., 1993). A key concept in nursery school education is **readiness training:** students learn skills that are supposed to prepare them for formal instruction later, such as how to follow directions, stick to a task, cooperate with others, and display good manners. Children are also encouraged to grow emotionally and develop a positive self-concept and to improve their large and small muscle skills. The nursery school day usually consists of a variety of more and less structured activities, ranging from art projects to group discussion to unstructured indoor and outdoor play. These activities are often organized around themes. For example, a unit on animals might involve making drawings of animals, acting out animal behavior, hearing stories about animals, and taking a trip to the zoo.

readiness training
Instruction in the background skills and knowledge that prepare children for formal teaching later.

CONNECTIONS

For more on compensatory programs for students placed at risk, see Chapter 9, page 316.

Compensatory Preschool Programs

Perhaps the most important development in early childhood education since the mid-1960s has been the introduction of **compensatory preschool programs** for children from disadvantaged backgrounds. This development has become increasingly important in recent years as the number of children in poverty has grown (General Accounting Office, 1994a). A wide variety of programs were introduced as part of the overall federal Head Start program, begun in 1965. Head Start was part of President Lyndon Johnson's war on poverty, an attempt to break the cycle of poverty. The idea was to give disadvantaged children, who are (as a group) at risk for school failure (McLoyd, 1998; Stipek & Ryan, 1997), a chance to start their formal schooling with the same preacademic and social skills that middle-class children possess. Typically, Head Start includes early childhood education programs that are designed to increase school readiness. However, the program also includes medical and dental services for children, at least one hot meal per day, and social services for the parents.

Research on Head Start has generally found positive effects on children's readiness skills and on many other outcomes (Ramey & Ramey, 1998). The effects on academic readiness skills have been greatest for those Head Start programs that stress academic achievement (Stallings & Stipek, 1986). Research that followed disadvantaged children who participated in several such programs found that these students did better throughout their school years than did similar students who did not participate in the programs (Berrueta-Clement, Schweinhart, Barnett, Epstein, & Weikart, 1984). For example, 67 percent of the students in one program, the Perry Preschool, ultimately graduated from high school, compared with 49 percent of students in a control group who did not attend preschool (Schweinhart, Barnes, & Weikart, 1993). Effects of early childhood participation could still be detected at age 27 (Schweinhart & Weikart, 1998). However, preschool programs by themselves are much less effective than are preschool programs followed up by high-quality programs in the early elementary grades (Behrman, 1995; Fuerst & Petty, 1996; Ramey & Ramey, 1998; Reynolds, 1998; Reynolds & Temple, 1998). The research on compensatory early childhood education might seem to indicate that preschool programs are crucial for all students. However, many researchers (e.g., Nurss & Hodges, 1982) hypothesize that preschool programs are more critical for lower-class children than for middle-class children, because many of the experiences that preschools provide are typically present in middle-class homes but lacking in homes of lower socioeconomic status.

Despite research supporting the overall effectiveness of Head Start, questions have been raised about the current quality of Head Start programs (General Accounting Office, 1994b). Because research finds lasting effects only for high-quality intensive programs (Ramey & Ramey, 1998), improving the quality of Head Start programs is beginning to take precedence over increasing the numbers of children served in Head Start (Kagan & Neuman, 1998).

compensatory preschool programs
Programs that are designed to prepare disadvantaged children for entry into kindergarten and first grade.

early intervention programs
Compensatory preschool programs that target very young children at the greatest risk of school failure.

Early Intervention

Most compensatory preschool programs, including Head Start, have begun working with children and their parents when the children are 3 or 4 years of age. However, many researchers believe that earlier intervention is needed for children who are at the greatest risk for school failure (Carnegie Corporation of New York, 1994; Powell, 1995). Numerous **early intervention programs** have been developed to start with children as young as 6 months old. One was a program in an inner-city Milwaukee neighborhood for the children of mothers who had mental retardation. An intensive program of infant stimulation, high-quality preschool, and family services made it possible for the children to perform adequately through elementary school; nearly all of the children in a comparison group were assigned to special education programs (Garber, 1988). Several other early intervention programs have also had strong effects on students that have lasted beyond elementary school (Campbell & Ramey, 1995; Ramey & Ramey, 1998; Reynolds, 1998; Wasik & Karweit, 1994).

CONNECTIONS

For more on early intervention programs for students placed at risk, see Chapter 9, page 319.

Kindergarten Programs

Most students attend kindergarten the year before they enter first grade. However, only a minority of states require kindergarten attendance (Karweit, 1989b). The original purpose of kindergarten was to prepare students for formal instruction by encouraging development of their social skills, but in recent years this function has increasingly been taken on by nursery schools and preschool programs. The kindergarten has focused more and more on academics, emphasizing prereading and premathematical skills as well as behaviors that are appropriate in school (such as raising hands, lining up, and taking turns). In some school districts kindergarten programs are becoming similar to what first grades once were, a trend that most child development experts oppose (e.g., Bryant, Clifford, & Peisner, 1991; Elkind, 1981). One particularly distressing aspect of this trend is that many schools are failing students in kindergarten if they do not meet certain performance standards (Mantzicopoulos & Morrison, 1992). Research on holding students back in kindergarten has found that while it improves children's performance relative to their grademates in the short run, it is detrimental in the long run (Ellwein, Walsh, Eads, & Miller, 1991; Karweit & Wasik, 1994; Shepard & Smith, 1986). Many schools attempt to adjust to young students' different developmental stages by inserting an additional year between the beginning of kindergarten and the end of first grade for children who appear to be at risk. Different versions of the strategy are called junior kindergarten, transitional first grade, prefirst, and so on. Studies of these strategies have found few benefits in the long run (Karweit & Wasik, 1994).

Research on kindergarten indicates that attending a full- or half-day kindergarten program is beneficial for academic readiness and increases a child's achievement in the first and second grades but that these effects diminish or disappear by the third or fourth grade (Nurss & Hodges, 1982). Additional research has indicated that students of a lower socioeconomic status gain more from well-structured full-day kindergarten programs than from half-day programs (Karweit, 1989b, 1994b).

Developmentally Appropriate Practice

A concept that has become increasingly important in early childhood education is *developmentally appropriate practice*. This is instruction based on students' individual characteristics and needs, not their ages (Bowman, 1993; Elkind, 1989). The National Association for the Education of Young Children (NAEYC) (1989, p. 4) has described developmentally appropriate practice for students ages 5 through 8 as follows.

Each child is viewed as a unique person with an individual pattern and timing of growth. Curriculum and instruction are responsive to individual differences in ability and interests. Different levels of ability, development, and learning styles are

TEACHERS IN ACTION

How has your knowledge of child development helped you to make instruction developmentally appropriate?

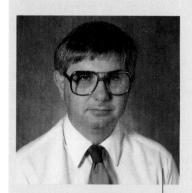

Randall Amour
Special Educator, Grades 6–12
Special Education Cooperative School
Columbus, Texas

As a language arts and English teacher of high school–aged students with specific learning disabilities, I need to be aware of students' cognitive abilities and language development. I need to be sensitive to the learning channels by which individual students learn best. For example, some students learn best if instructions are shown as well as told. Some learn best if learning is broken down into small tasks and presented as a skill-building hierarchical process. I also need to gear instruction so that each student clearly understands instructions and can successfully complete the assignments. Many modifications can help, including the use of oral tests, additional time, reduction in the number of problems or sentences, questions read to a student, or dictation received from a student who has difficulty writing. Students have combinations of capabilities and deficits that interact with one another to which teachers must respond. By using students' best modes of learning, we can maximize their success.

As a teacher of adolescents, I also need to know about their physical, social, moral, and emotional development. Adolescence is a time for experimentation with possible roles. Most students would be expected to have reached or approached the stage of formal operations. It is in the social and emotional areas that the turmoil of adolescence is most apparent. Knowledge of physical, cognitive, and socioemotional development enables teachers to accommodate instruction to individual needs and to help students take small steps toward greater competence, maturity, and freedom.

Gail C. Dawson
Art Teacher
John Muir Middle School
San Leandro, California

Curriculum is often developmentally inappropriate for students at the middle school level. There are problems with reading, mathematics, science—even art. Perspective drawing is a good example. Perspective drawing is based on a fixed, somewhat arbitrary point of view, with a set of inflexible rules. Some students understand the existence of viewpoints other than their own, while others struggle with the idea. For many, simultaneously thinking about another point of view and manipulating a set system of rules presents a significant cognitive challenge. Perspective drawing also requires an ability to measure. I have students who are unable to read or measure in standard units. Others sigh with indignation when we stop to examine the increments on rulers.

However, most students bring with them an intense desire to learn to draw realistically. That interest has allowed me to adapt the art curriculum and to teach perspective with good results. We begin with three-dimensional, concrete experiences before we attempt any drawing. Then, to get from three to two dimensions, I have students use a piece of glass as a "window on the world" and markers to trace what they see onto the glass. By the time we start drawing, they've had the opportunity to experience and to think about points of view, how we learn to read distance with our eyes, and how the real world translates to a two-dimensional surface.

Developmentally appropriate practice often requires adapting the curriculum to match and to challenge the students' abilities in relation to their cognitive development. In my experience the results are truly worth the effort.

expected, accepted, and used to design curriculum. Children are allowed to move at their own pace in acquiring important skills, including those of writing, reading, spelling, math, social studies, science, art, music, health, and physical activity. For example, it is accepted that not every child will learn how to read at age 6. Most will learn by age 7, but some will need intensive exposure to appropriate literacy experiences to learn to read by age 8 or 9.

One type of developmentally appropriate practice was developed by Maria Montessori (1870–1952). The goal of Montessori education is development of the individual. Montessori programs concentrate on developing general intellectual skills rather than particular subject-matter concepts. Montessori schools often use child-size school furniture and specially designed learning materials. Emphasis is on independent work by children under the guidance of a trained educator. Intellectual development is achieved through activities that are designed to help children organize, classify, seriate, and heighten their perceptual awareness. Equally important are physical, social, and emotional development, which are reflected in outdoor play, discussions of appropriate behavior on the playground, and respect for each individual's work and space in the classroom (Brewer, 1995).

The NAEYC and other advocates of developmentally appropriate practice recommend extensive use of projects, play, exploration, group work, learning centers, and the like, and a deemphasis on teacher-directed instruction, basal readers, phonics, and workbooks (Kostelnik, 1992).

Along with a renewed emphasis on developmentally appropriate practice has come the reemergence of an innovation of the 1960s, the nongraded primary or elementary school, in which students are assigned to multiage classes and are flexibly grouped for instruction across age lines (see Katz, Evangelou, & Hartman, 1991; Pavan, 1992). A review of studies of nongraded programs done in the 1960s and 1970s found that such programs could be beneficial for student achievement if they still emphasized whole-class instruction from the teacher. To the extent that they emphasized individualized instruction, learning centers, and other work done independently of the teacher, however, they became ineffective (Gutiérrez & Slavin, 1992).

SELF-CHECK

Describe a day-care center, a nursery school, compensatory preschool, and kindergarten. What do research findings suggest about the value of early intervention, compensatory preschool programs, and kindergarten retention? What is meant by developmentally appropriate practice?

HOW DO CHILDREN DEVELOP DURING THE ELEMENTARY YEARS?

Children entering the first grade are in a transitional period from the rapid growth of early childhood to a phase of more gradual development. Shifts in both mental and social development characterize the early school years. Several years later, when children reach the upper elementary grades, they are nearing the end of childhood and entering preadolescence. Children's success in school is particularly important during the early school years, as it is in the elementary grades that they largely define themselves as students (Carnegie Corporation of New York, 1996).

Physical Development during Middle Childhood

As children progress through the primary grades, their physical development slows in comparison with earlier childhood. Children change relatively little in size during the primary years. To picture the typical child in the primary grades, we must picture a child in good physical condition. Girls are slightly shorter and lighter than boys until around the age of 9, when height and weight are approximately equal for boys and girls. Muscular development is outdistanced by bone and skeletal development. This may cause the aches that are commonly known as growing pains. Also, the growing muscles need much exercise, and this need may contribute to the primary-grade child's inability to stay still for long. By the time children enter the primary grades, they have developed many of the basic motor skills they need for balance, running, jumping, and throwing. During the latter part of the fourth grade, many girls begin a major growth spurt that will not be completed until puberty. This spurt begins with the rapid growth of the arms and legs. At this point there is not an accompanying change in trunk size. The result is a gangly or all-arms-and-legs appearance. Because this bone growth occurs before the development of associated muscles and cartilage, children at this growth stage temporarily lose some coordination and strength.

By the start of the fifth grade, almost all girls have begun their growth spurt. In addition, muscle and cartilage growth of the limbs resumes in the earlier-maturing females, and they regain their strength and coordination. By the end of the fifth grade, girls are typically taller, heavier, and stronger than boys. Males are 12 to 18 months behind girls in development, so even early-maturing boys do not start their growth spurt until age 11. By the start of the sixth grade, therefore, most girls will be near the peak of their growth spurt, and all but the early-maturing boys will be continuing the slow, steady growth of late childhood. Girls will usually have started their menstrual period by age 13. For boys the end of preadolescence and the onset of early adolescence is measured by the first ejaculation, which occurs between the ages of 13 and 16.

Cognitive Abilities

Between the ages of 5 and 7, children's thought processes undergo significant changes (Ginsburg & Opper, 1988; Osborn & Osborn, 1983). This is a period of transition from the stage of preoperational thought to the stage of concrete operations. This change allows children to do mentally what was previously done physically and to mentally reverse the actions involved. Not all children make this transition at the same age, and no individual child changes from one stage to the next quickly. Children often use cognitive behaviors that are characteristic of two stages of development at the same time. As individuals advance from one stage to the next, the characteristics of the previous stage are maintained as the cognitive behaviors of the higher stage develop.

In addition to entering the concrete operational stage, elementary school–age children are rapidly developing memory and cognitive skills, including metacognitive skills—the ability to think about their own thinking and to learn how to learn.

CONNECTIONS
For more on the development of memory and metacognitive skills, see Chapter 6, pages 194 and 203.

Socioemotional Development in Middle Childhood

By the time children enter elementary school, they have developed skills for more complex thought, action, and social influence. Up to this point, children have been basically egocentric, and their world has been that of home, family, and possibly a nursery school or day-care center. The early primary grades will normally be spent working through Erikson's (1963) fourth stage, industry versus inferiority. Assuming that a child has developed trust during infancy, autonomy during the early years, and initiative during the preschool years, that child's experiences in the primary grades can contribute to his or her sense of industry and accomplishment. During this stage, children start trying to prove that they are "grown up"; in fact, this is often described as the I-can-do-it-myself stage. Work becomes possible. As children's powers of concentration grow, they can spend more time on chosen tasks, and they often take pleasure in completing projects. This stage also includes the growth of independent action, cooperation with groups, performing in socially acceptable ways, and a concern for fair play.

Hoffman believed that parents could have a strong influence on the development of children's moral behavior. In a study of seventh-graders and their parents, Hoffman and Saltzstein (1967) found that parents tend to use three approaches in disciplining their children:

1. **Power assertion:** Using physical force or punishment, depriving children of possessions or privileges, or threatening to take these actions. This technique takes advantage of parents' greater physical strength and control over resources and relies on the child's fear of punishment for its effects.
2. **Love withdrawal:** Expressing anger, disappointment, or disapproval in non-physical ways. This technique takes advantage of the child's emotional bond with parents and relies on the child's fear of abandonment and loss of approval for its effects.
3. **Induction:** Focusing on the reasons why certain behaviors are wrong and on the negative consequences of one's actions on the other person. This technique appeals to the child's affection or respect for the other person, stimulates feelings of empathic distress and guilt, and develops mature moral reasoning skills.

Hoffman and Saltzstein's early work and recent research by others (Crockenberg & Litman, 1990; Hart, DeWolf, Wozniak, & Burts, 1992; Kuczynski & Kochanska, 1990) have demonstrated that parents who use inductive techniques tend to have children who show more mature moral reasoning, emotional reactions, and behavior than do parents who use power-assertive techniques. Hoffman (1983) has also suggested, however, that the most powerful technique might be to use power-assertive or love-withdrawal techniques to get a child's initial attention and then use inductive reasoning to promote the appropriate emotional and cognitive reactions to the situation.

Applying Hoffman's Theories

THEORY
into
Practice

Hoffman's work focuses on the role of parents in promoting the development of moral behavior in children. However, his ideas about how to respond to children's misconduct have direct implications for teachers who want their students to behave in helpful and cooperative ways. In discussing specific strategies that foster children's social development, Katz and McClellan (1991) suggest the following to foster social understanding:

• Stimulate empathy by calling attention to how others feel (e.g., "Robin has been waiting a long time, and you know how it feels to wait").

- Alert children to the feelings and interests of others by calling attention to how they might help other children in need.
- Encourage positive interpretations of other children's behavior (e.g., translate comments about something that is "weird" into something that is "interesting").
- Help children to discover common ground by pointing out similar interests.

In successful interventions designed to promote prosocial and cooperative behavior, Solomon and his colleagues (Solomon, Watson, Delucchi, Schaps, & Battisch, 1988) have teachers use specific types of developmental discipline. Teachers are trained to use inductive reasoning, to engage students in mutual problem solving and decision making, and to set clear and reasonable standards for behavior. In addition, teachers are given instruction in how to emphasize and model prosocial values, to develop cooperative activities that will encourage children to think about and practice prosocial values, and to provide activities that involve perspective taking and role-playing to promote the development of social understanding.

SELF-CONCEPT AND SELF-ESTEEM ● Important areas of personal and social development for elementary school children are self-concept and self-esteem. These aspects of children's development will be strongly influenced by experiences at home, with peers, and at school. **Self-concept** includes the way in which we perceive our strengths, weaknesses, abilities, attitudes, and values. Its development begins at birth and is continually shaped by experience. **Self-esteem** refers to how we evaluate our skills and abilities.

As children progress through middle childhood, their ways of thinking become less concrete and more abstract. This trend is also evident in the development of their self-concepts (Selman, 1980). Preschoolers think about themselves in terms of their physical and material characteristics, including size, gender, and possessions. In contrast, by the early elementary school years, children begin to focus on more abstract, internal qualities such as intelligence and kindness when describing themselves. They can also make a distinction between their private or inner selves and their external, public selves. This becomes especially evident as they depend more on intentions and motives and less on objective behavior in their explanations of their own and others' actions (Selman, 1980).

During middle childhood, children also begin to evaluate themselves in comparison to others. A preschooler might describe herself by saying, "I like baseball," whereas several years later this same girl is likely to say, "I like baseball more than Sally does." Ruble, Eisenberg, and Higgins (1994) have suggested that younger children use **social comparison** primarily to learn about social norms and the appropriateness of certain types of conduct. As children get older, they also tend to use social comparison to evaluate and judge their own abilities (Borg, 1998).

The trend to use social comparison information to evaluate the self appears to correspond with developmental changes in academic self-esteem. Preschoolers and young children tend to evaluate themselves very positively, in ways that bear no relationship to their school performance or other objective factors (Cole, 1991). By second or third grade, however, children who are having difficulty in school tend to have poorer self-concepts (Harter, 1993; Marsh, 1989; Marsh, Craven, & Debus, 1991). This begins a declining spiral. Students who perform poorly in elementary school are at risk for developing poor academic self-concepts and subsequent poor

self-concept
A person's perception of his or her own strengths, weaknesses, abilities, attitudes, and values.

self-esteem
The value each of us places on our own characteristics, abilities, and behaviors.

social comparison
The process of comparing oneself to others to gather information and to evaluate and judge one's abilities, attitudes, and conduct.

performance in upper elementary and secondary school (Ma & Kishor, 1997; Marsh & Yeung, 1997).

The primary grades give many children their first chance to compare themselves with others and to work and play under the guidance of adults outside their family. These adults must provide experiences that let children succeed, feel good about themselves, and maintain their enthusiasm and creativity (Canfield & Siccone, 1995).

The key word regarding personal and social development is *acceptance*. The fact is, children do differ in their abilities; and no matter what teachers do, students will have figured out by the end of the elementary years (usually earlier) who is more able and who is less able. However, teachers can have a substantial impact on how students feel about these differences and on the value that low-achieving students place on learning even when they know they will never be class stars.

Promoting the Development of Self-Esteem

THEORY *into* Practice

Society and public institutions in the United States work on the premise that people, including students, are of equal worth. That is also the premise in a classroom. But believing students are of equal worth doesn't necessarily mean that they are equally competent. Some students are good in reading, others in math, others in sports, others in art.

Some classroom activities can give certain students the impression that they as individuals are of less value or worth than other students. Research findings indicate that inappropriate competition (Cohen, 1986) or inflexible ability groups within the classroom (MacIver, Reuman, & Main, 1995; Slavin, 1987c) may teach the wrong thing to students.

This kind of research can help teachers avoid practices that may discourage children. Other research, however, provides no support for the belief that specific programs or curriculums will develop a healthy self-esteem in students (Kohn, 1994). Nor is it clear that improving self-esteem results in greater school achievement (Scheirer & Kraut, 1979). In fact, at least one review (Stebbins et al., 1977) suggested that the reverse may be true: As a student grows more competent in school tasks, his or her self-esteem also improves. Lerner calls this "earned self-esteem" (1996).

Showing students their success can be an important part of maintaining a positive self-image. Rosenholtz and Simpson (1984) described the multidimensional classroom, in which teachers make it clear that there are many ways to succeed. Such teachers emphasize how much students are learning. For example, many teachers give students pretests before they begin an instructional unit and then show the class how much everyone gained by means of a posttest. Multidimensional teachers may stress the idea that different students have different skills. By valuing all these skills, the teacher can communicate the idea that there are many routes to success, rather than a single path (Cohen, 1984).

It is not necessary to lie and say that all students are equally good in reading or math (Beane, 1991; Damon, 1991). Teachers can, however, recognize progress rather than level of ability, focusing their praise on the student's effort and growing competence. As the student sees his or her success in school, a feeling of earned self-esteem will also result.

GROWING IMPORTANCE OF PEERS ● The influence of the child's family, which was the major force during the early childhood years, continues in importance as parents provide role models in terms of attitudes and behaviors. In addition, relationships with brothers and sisters affect relationships with peers, and routines from home either are reinforced or must be overcome in school. However, the peer group takes on added importance. Speaking of the child's entrance into the world outside the family, Ira Gordon noted the importance of peers:

> If all the world's the stage that Shakespeare claimed, children and adolescents are playing primarily to an audience of their peers. Their peers sit in the front rows and the box seats; parents and teachers are now relegated to the back rows and the balcony. (Gordon, 1975, p. 166)

In the lower elementary grades, peer groups usually consist of same-sex children who are around the same age. This preference may be due to the variety of abilities and interests among young children. By the sixth grade, however, students often form groups that include both boys and girls. Whatever the composition of peer groups, they let children compare their abilities and skills to those of others. Members of peer groups also teach one another about their different worlds. Children learn through this sharing of attitudes and values how to sort out and form their own attitudes and values.

FRIENDSHIPS IN MIDDLE CHILDHOOD ● During middle childhood, children's conceptions of friendship also mature. Friendship is the central social relationship between peers during childhood, and it undergoes a series of changes before adulthood. Using as their basis Piaget's developmental stages and children's changing abilities to consider the perspective of others, Selman (1981; Selman & Selman, 1979) described how children's understanding of friendship changes over the years. Between the ages of 3 and 7, children usually view friends as momentary playmates. Children of this age might come home from school exclaiming, "I made a new friend today! Jamie shared her doll with me," or "Bill's not my friend anymore 'cause he wouldn't play blocks with me." These comments reveal the child's view of friendship as a temporary relationship based on a certain situation rather than on shared interests or beliefs. As children enter middle childhood, friendships become more stable and reciprocal. At this age, friends are often described in terms of personal traits ("My friend Mary is nice"), and friendships are based on mutual support, caring, loyalty, and mutual give-and-take.

Friendships are important to children for several reasons (Hartup, 1989, 1992). During the elementary school years, friends are companions to have fun and do things with. They also serve as important emotional resources by providing children with a sense of security in new situations and when family or other problems arise. Friends are also cognitive resources when they teach or model specific intellectual skills. Social norms for conduct, social interaction skills, and how to resolve conflicts successfully are also learned within the context of friendships.

PEER ACCEPTANCE ● One of the most understood and perhaps important aspects of peer relations in middle childhood is peer acceptance, or status within the peer group (McCallum & Bracken, 1993). *Popular* children are those who are named most often by their peers as being someone they like and least often as someone they dislike. In contrast, *rejected* children are those who are named most often by their peers as being someone they dislike and least often as someone they like. Children are also classified as being *neglected;* these children are neither frequently named as someone who is liked nor frequently named as someone who is disliked. *Controversial* children are frequently named as someone who is liked but also frequently named as someone who is disliked. *Average* children are those who are named as being liked and disliked with moderate frequency.

In a review of the research on peer acceptance, Hatzichriston and Hopf (1996) conclude that children who are not well accepted or are rejected by their peers in elementary school are at high risk. These children are more likely to drop out of school, engage in delinquent behavior, and have emotional and psychological problems in adolescence and adulthood than are their peers who are more accepted (see also Kupersmidt & Coie, 1990; Morrison & Masten, 1991). Some rejected children tend to be highly aggressive; others tend to be very passive and withdrawn. Children who are rejected, aggressive, and withdrawn seem to be at highest risk for difficulties (Hymel, Bowker, & Woody, 1993).

Many characteristics seem to be related to peer acceptance, including physical attractiveness (Kennedy, 1990) and cognitive abilities (Wentzel, 1991). Studies have also linked behavioral styles to peer acceptance (see Coie, Dodge, & Kupersmidt, 1990). Well-accepted and popular children tend to be cooperative, helpful, and caring and are rarely disruptive or aggressive. Children who are disliked by their peers tend to be highly aggressive and to lack prosocial and conflict resolution skills. Neglected and controversial children display less distinct behavioral styles and often change status over short periods of time (Newcomb & Bukowski, 1984).

Helping Children Develop Social Skills

Because peer acceptance is such a strong predictor of current and long-term adjustment, many intervention techniques have been designed to improve the social skills and levels of acceptance of unpopular and rejected children. Common approaches involve the following:

THEORY
into
Practice

- **Reinforcement of appropriate social behavior:** Adults can systematically reinforce prosocial skills such as helping and sharing and can ignore antisocial behavior such as fighting and verbal aggression. Reinforcement techniques will be most successful if a teacher or other adult uses them with an entire group of children. This allows the child who lacks skills to observe others being reinforced for positive behavior, and it draws the attention of the peer group to the target child's positive rather than negative actions (Price & Dodge, 1989).
- **Modeling:** Children who observe models learning positive social interaction skills show significant improvement in their own skills (Asher, Renshaw, & Hymel, 1982).
- **Coaching:** This strategy involves a sequence of steps that include demonstrating positive social skills, explaining why these skills are important, providing opportunities for practice, and giving follow-up feedback (Mize & Ladd, 1990a, 1990b).

CONNECTIONS

For more on systematically reinforcing prosocial skills, see Chapter 5, page 148.

The effectiveness of any intervention is likely to depend largely on the involvement of the rejected child's peers and classroom teachers. If peers and teachers notice positive changes in behavior, they are more likely to change their opinions of and accept the child than if interventions are conducted in isolation (Olweus, 1994; Price & Dodge, 1989; White & Kistner, 1992).

SELF-CHECK

Continue the comparison chart you began earlier, adding information in each category for middle childhood.

HOW DO CHILDREN DEVELOP DURING THE MIDDLE SCHOOL AND HIGH SCHOOL YEARS?

The adolescent period of development begins with puberty. The pubertal period, or early adolescence, is a time of rapid physical and intellectual development. Middle adolescence is a more stable period of adjustment to and integration of the changes of early adolescence. Later adolescence is marked by the transition into the responsibilities, choices, and opportunities of adulthood (Wigfield, Eccles, & Pintrich, 1996). In this section we will review the major changes that occur as the child becomes an adolescent, and we will examine how adolescent development affects teaching, curriculum, and school structure.

Physical Development during Adolescence

Puberty is a series of physiological changes that render the immature organism capable of reproduction. Nearly every organ and system of the body is affected by these changes. The prepubertal child and the postpubertal adolescent are different in outward appearance because of changes in stature and proportion and the development of primary and secondary sex features (Tanner, 1991).

Table 3.2 summarizes the typical sequence of physical development in adolescence. Although the sequence of events at puberty is generally the same for each person, the timing and the rate at which they occur vary widely. The average female typically begins pubertal changes 1½ to 2 years earlier than the average male. In each sex, however, the range of normal onset ages is approximately 6 years. Like the onset, the rate of changes also varies widely. Some people take only 18 to 24 months to go through the pubertal changes to reproductive maturity; others may require 6 years to pass through the same stage. These differences mean that some individuals may be completely mature before others the same age have even begun puberty. The age of maximum diversity is 13 for males and about 11 for females. The comparisons that children make among themselves, as well as the tendency to hold maturity in high regard, can be a problem for the less mature. On the other hand, the first to mature are also likely to experience temporary discomfort because they stand out from the less mature majority.

Cognitive Development

As the rest of the body changes at puberty, the brain and its functions also change. Just as the timing of pubertal changes varies widely across individuals, so does the timing of intellectual changes. One indication of this is that scores on intelligence tests obtained over several years from the same individual fluctuate most during the period from 12 to 15 years of age. Some researchers refer to an "intellectual growth spurt" at this age (Andrich & Styles, 1994). In Piaget's theory of cognitive development, adolescence is the stage of transition from the use of concrete operations

puberty
Developmental stage at which a person becomes capable of reproduction.

TABLE 3.2

Average Age and Age Range of Major Pubertal Changes in North American Girls and Boys

GIRLS	AVERAGE	RANGE	BOYS	AVERAGE	RANGE
Breasts begin to bud	10.0	(8–13)	Testes begin to enlarge	11.5	(9.5–13.5)
Height spurt begins	10.0	(8–13)	Pubic hair appears	12.0	(10–15)
Pubic hair appears	10.5	(8–14)	Penis begins to enlarge	12.0	(10.5–14.5)
Peak of strength spurt	11.6	(9.5–14)	Height spurt begins	12.5	(10.5–16)
Peak of height spurt	11.7	(10–13.5)	Spermarche (first ejaculation) occurs	13.0	(12–16)
Menarche (first menstruation) occurs	12.8	(10.5–15.5)	Peak of height spurt	14.0	(12.5–15.5)
Adult stature reached	13.0	(10–16)	Facial hair begins to grow	14.0	(12.5–15.5)
Breast growth completed	14.0	(10–16)	Voice begins to deepen	14.0	(12.5–15.5)
Pubic hair growth completed	14.5	(14–15)	Penis growth completed	14.5	(12.5–16)
			Peak of strength spurt	15.3	(13–17)
			Adult stature reached	15.5	(13.5–17.5)
			Pubic hair growth completed	15.5	(14–17)

Source: From Laura E. Berk, *Infants, Children, and Adolescents* (2nd ed.). Copyright © 1996 by Allyn & Bacon. Reprinted by permission. Sources: Malina & Bouchard, 1991; Tanner, 1990.

to the application of formal operations in reasoning. Adolescents begin to be aware of the limitations of their thinking. They wrestle with concepts that are removed from their own experience. Inhelder and Piaget (1958) acknowledge that brain changes at puberty may be necessary for the cognitive advances of adolescence. However, they assert that experience with complex problems, the demands of formal instruction, and exchange and contradiction of ideas with peers are also necessary for formal operational reasoning to develop. Adolescents who reach this stage (not all do) have attained an adult level of reasoning.

CONNECTIONS
For more on Piaget's theories on cognitive development in adolescence, see Chapter 2, page 37.

Characteristics of Hypothetical–Deductive Reasoning

Hypothetical–deductive reasoning is one of the characteristics that marks the development of formal operational thinking, which emerges by the time children are about 12 years old (Atwater, 1996; Flavell et al., 1993). Before formal operations, thought is concrete operational in nature. The differences between these two stages of thinking are listed in Table 3.3. Piaget found that the use of formal operations depended on the learner's familiarity with a given subject area. When students were familiar with a subject, they were more likely to use formal operations. When they were unfamiliar with a subject, students proceeded more slowly, tended to use concrete reasoning patterns, and used self-regulation sparingly. Later research has confirmed Piaget's observation that use of formal operational thought differs according to tasks, background knowledge, and individual differences (Cobb, 1995). Not all adolescents develop formal operational thinking, but there is evidence that adolescents who have not reached this level can be taught to solve problems requiring this level of thinking (Vasta & Liben, 1996).

TABLE 3.3

Comparing Concrete and Formal Operations

PERSON NOT CAPABLE OF HYPOTHETICAL–DEDUCTIVE REASONING (CONCRETE OPERATIONAL THINKER)	PERSON CAPABLE OF HYPOTHETICAL–DEDUCTIVE REASONING (FORMAL OPERATIONAL THINKER)
Can form limited hypotheses; reasons with reference to actions, objects, and properties that are familiar or that can be experienced.	Can form multiple hypotheses, has combinatorial logic, reasons with concrete and formal abstract concepts and relationships; reasons about intangible properties and theories.
May memorize prominent words, phrases, formulas, and procedures but will apply them with little understanding of the abstract meaning or principles underlying them.	Can understand the abstract meaning and principles underlying formal concepts, relationships, and theories.
Has problems reasoning logically about ideas that are contrary to fact or personal beliefs, or that are arbitrary.	Can argue logically about ideas that are contrary to fact or personal belief or that are arbitrary; can reason on the basis of testimonials.
Needs step-by-step instructions when planning a lengthy, complex procedure.	Can plan a lengthy, complex procedure given a set of conditions, goals, and resources.
Is unaware of inconsistencies and contradictions within own thinking.	Is aware and critical of own reasoning; can reflect on problem-solving process and verify conclusions by checking sources, using other known information, or seeking a solution from another perspective.

Implications for Educational Practice

Consider the following general guidelines:

1. When introducing new information, particularly information involving abstract concepts and theories, allow students enough time to absorb the ideas and to use formal thought patterns. Begin with more familiar examples, and encourage students to apply hypothetical–deductive reasoning.
2. Students who have not yet attained formal operational thought may need more support for planning complex tasks. Pairing children who can plan with those who need support is one way of handling the situation.
3. Encourage students to state principles and ideas in their own words and to search for the meaning behind abstract ideas and theories.
4. Incorporate a variety of activities that promote the use of hypothetical deductive thinking. The following are some examples:

   • Have students write a paper that requires a debate between arguments pro and con and a discussion of the evidence that supports the two perspectives. For younger students you might want to pair children or groups and have one child or group write from one perspective and the other from another perspective.
   • Have students discuss each other's ideas, purposefully picking specific opposing positions. Debates and mock trials are two ways in which this can be done.
   • Develop cooperative activities that require substantial planning and organization. Have students work in groups composed of children with different levels of planning and organizing skills. For children who are still at the con-

crete operational level, provide an outline of what to think about as the planning process proceeds.

- Develop activities in which facts come from different testimonials that may be contradictory, such as television commercials. For example, use commercials in which Brand X claims to be the best-selling domestic car and to have more features than other cars and Brand Y claims that its cars are the highest rated and have higher levels of owner satisfaction. Have the students discuss and weigh the evidence from these different sources.
- Have students critique their own work. Ask students to generate a list of ways in which one could look for flaws in thinking or other sources that might be used to verify results.

What part of adolescent socioemotional developments is depicted here? As a teacher, how will the socioemotional needs of your students affect your teaching?

Socioemotional Development in Adolescence

In adolescence, children undergo significant changes in their social and emotional lives as well. Partly as a result of their changing physical and cognitive structures, children in the upper elementary grades seek to be more grown up. They want their parents to treat them differently, even though many parents are unwilling to see them differently. They also report that though they believe that their parents love them, they do not think their parents understand them. For both boys and girls in the upper elementary grades, membership in groups tends to promote feelings of self-worth. Not being accepted can bring serious emotional problems. Herein lies the major cause of the preadolescent's changing relationship with parents. It is not that preadolescents care less about their parents. It is just that their friends are more important than ever. This need for acceptance by peers helps to explain why preadolescents often dress alike (Baumeister & Leary, 1995). The story of Jake Stevens's earring at the beginning of this chapter illustrates how young adolescents express their belongingness with other peer group members through distinctive dress or behavior.

The middle school years often also bring changes in the relationship between children and their teachers. In primary school, children easily accept and depend on teachers. During the upper elementary years, this relationship becomes more complex. Sometimes students will tell teachers personal information they would not tell their parents. Some preadolescents even choose teachers as role models. At the same time, however, some preteens talk back to teachers in ways they would never have considered several years earlier, and some openly challenge teachers.

Identity Development

One of the first signs of early adolescence is the appearance of **reflectivity,** the tendency to think about what is going on in one's own mind and to study oneself. Adolescents begin to look more closely at themselves and to define themselves differently. They start to realize that there are differences between what they think and feel and how they behave. Using the developing intellectual skills that permit them to consider possibilities, adolescents are prone to be dissatisfied with themselves. They critique their personal characteristics, compare themselves to others, and try to change the way they are.

Adolescents may also ponder whether other people see and think about the world in the same way they do (Phelan, Yu, & Davidson, 1994). They become more aware of their separateness from other people and of their uniqueness. They learn that other people cannot fully know what they think and feel. The issue of who and what one

reflectivity
The tendency to analyze oneself and one's own thoughts.

"really" is dominates personality development in adolescence. According to Erikson, the stage is set during adolescence for a major concern with one's identity.

Marcia's Four Identity Statuses

On the basis of Erikson's work, James Marcia (1991) identified four identity statuses from in-depth interviews with adolescents. The statuses reflect the degree to which adolescents have made firm commitments to religious and political values as well as to a future occupation. These are as follows:

1. **Foreclosure:** Individuals in a state of **foreclosure** have never experienced an identity crisis. Rather, they have prematurely established an identity on the basis of their parents' choices rather than their own. They have made occupational and ideological commitments, but these commitments reflect more an assessment of what their parents or authority figures could do than an autonomous process of self-assessment. Foreclosure indicates a kind of "pseudo-identity" that generally is too fixed and rigid to serve as a foundation for meeting life's future crises.
2. **Identity diffusion:** Adolescents experiencing **identity diffusion** have found neither an occupational direction nor an ideological commitment of any kind, and they have made little progress toward these ends. They may have experienced an identity crisis, but if so, they were unable to resolve it.
3. **Moratorium:** Adolescents in a state of **moratorium** are those who have begun to experiment with occupational and ideological choices but have not yet made definitive commitments to either. These individuals are directly in the midst of an identity crisis and are currently examining alternate life choices.
4. **Identity achievement: Identity achievement** signifies a state of identity consolidation in which adolescents have made their own conscious, clear-cut decisions about occupation and ideology. The individual is convinced that these decisions were autonomously and freely made, and that they reflect his or her true nature and deep inner commitments.

By late adolescence (18 to 22 years of age), most individuals have developed a status of identity achievement. However, adolescents' emotional development seems to be linked to their identity status. For instance, levels of anxiety tend to be highest for adolescents in moratorium and lowest for those in foreclosure (Marcia, 1991). Self-esteem also varies, with adolescents in identity achievement and moratorium reporting the highest levels and those in foreclosure and identity diffusion reporting the lowest levels (Marcia, 1991; Wallace-Broscious, Serafica & Osipow, 1994).

In general, adolescents need to experiment and remain flexible if they are successfully to find their own identity. By trying out ways to be, then testing and modifying them, the adolescent can pick the characteristics that are most comfortable and drop the others. To do this, the adolescent must have the self-confidence to experiment and to declare an experiment over; to vary behavior; and to drop characteristics that don't fit, even if the characteristics are supported by others. It helps to have a stable and accepting set of parents, teachers, and peers who will respond positively to one's experimentation.

Self-Concept and Self-Esteem

Self-concept and self-esteem also change as children enter and go through adolescence. The shift toward more abstract portrayals that began in middle childhood

foreclosure
An adolescent's premature establishment of an identity based on parental choices, not on his or her own.

identity diffusion
Inability to develop a clear direction or sense of self.

moratorium
Experimentation with occupational and ideological choices without definite commitment.

identity achievement
A state of consolidation reflecting conscious, clear-cut decisions concerning occupation and ideology.

continues, and adolescents' self-descriptions often include personal traits (friendly, obnoxious), emotions (depressed, psyched), and personal beliefs (liberal, conservative) (Damon & Hart, 1988). In addition, the self-concept becomes more differentiated. Susan Harter's work has identified eight distinct aspects of adolescent concept: scholastic competence, job competence, athletic competence, physical appearance, social acceptance, close friendships, romantic appeal, and conduct (Harter, 1990). Marsh (1993) identified five distinct self-concepts; academic verbal, academic mathematic, parent relations, same-sex, and opposite sex.

Self-esteem also undergoes fluctuations and changes during adolescence. Self-esteem is lowest as children enter middle school or junior high school and with the onset of puberty (Simmons & Blyth, 1987). Early-maturing girls and students who make the transition into junior high at or before seventh grade tend to suffer the most dramatic and long-lasting decreases in self-esteem. In general, adolescent girls have lower self-esteem than do boys (Marsh, 1993; Simmons & Blyth, 1987). Global self-esteem or feelings of self-worth appear to be influenced most strongly by physical appearance and then by social acceptance from peers.

Social Relationships

FRIENDSHIPS ● As children enter adolescence, changes in the nature of friendships also take place. In general, the amount of time spent with friends increases dramatically; adolescents spend more time with their peers than they do with family members or by themselves. In fact, in contrast to their Japanese and Russian counterparts, who spend 2 to 3 hours a week with friends, American teenagers spend an average of 20 hours a week with their friends outside of school (Czikszentmihalyi & Larson, 1984). Adolescents who have satisfying and harmonious friendships also report higher levels of self-esteem, are less lonely, have more mature social skills, and do better in school than do adolescents who lack supportive friendships (Savin-Williams & Berndt, 1990).

During adolescence the capacity for mutual understanding and the knowledge that others are unique individuals with feelings of their own also contribute to a dramatic increase in self-disclosure, intimacy, and loyalty among friends. As early adolescents strive to establish personal identities that are independent of those of their parents, they also look increasingly to their peers for security and social support. Whereas elementary school–aged children look to parents for such support, by seventh grade same-sex friends are perceived to be as supportive as parents, and by tenth grade they are perceived to be the primary source of social support (Furman & Buhrmester, 1992).

RELATIONSHIPS WITH PEERS ● In addition to their close friends, most adolescents also place high value on the larger peer group as a source of ideas and values as well as companionship and entertainment.

The nature of peer relationships in adolescence has been characterized in terms of social status and peer crowds. Social status, or levels of acceptance by peers, is studied with respect to the same status groups that are identified in middle childhood. As with elementary school–aged children, popular and well-accepted adolescents tend to display positive conflict resolution and academic skills, prosocial behavior, and leadership qualities, whereas rejected and low-accepted children tend to display aggressive and antisocial behavior and low levels of academic performance (Parkhurst & Asher, 1992; Wentzel, 1991; Wentzel & Erdley, 1993). These socially rejected children appear to be at great risk for later academic and social problems (Parker & Asher, 1987). Wentzel and Asher (1995) found, however, that rejected middle school children who were socially submissive did not display the same school-related problems as their rejected aggressive counterparts. These findings suggest that peer rejection and negative behavior together place these children at risk.

Peer relationships in adolescence have also been studied in terms of cliques and crowds with whom adolescents associate (Brown, 1990). A clique is a fairly small, intimate group that is defined by the common interests, activities, and friends of its members. In contrast, a crowd is a larger group defined by its reputation. Allegiance to a clique or crowd is common during adolescence but not necessarily long-term or stable. Although the pressure to conform can be very powerful within these groups, only adolescents who are highly motivated to belong appear to be influenced by these norms in significant ways (Brown, 1990).

Emotional Development

Most adolescents experience emotional conflicts at some point. This is hardly surprising, since they are going through rapid and dramatic changes in body image, expected roles, and peer relationships. The transitions from elementary to middle school or junior high and then on to high school can also be quite stressful (Harter, Whitesell, & Kowalski, 1992; Hirsch & Radkin, 1987). For most adolescents, emotional distress is temporary and is successfully handled, but for some the stresses lead to delinquency, drug abuse, or suicide attempts (Matheny, Aycock, & McCarthy, 1993; O'Neil, 1991; Range, 1993).

Emotional problems related to the physical, cognitive, and social development of upper elementary school–aged children are common. Though preadolescents are generally happy and optimistic, they also have many fears, such as fear of not being accepted into a peer group, not having a best friend, being punished by their parents, having their parents get a divorce, or not doing well in school.

Other emotions of this age group include anger (and fear of being unable to control it), guilt, frustration, and jealousy. Preadolescents need help in realizing that these emotions and fears are a natural part of growing up. Adults must let them talk about these emotions and fears, even if they seem unrealistic to an adult. Feelings of guilt often arise when there is a conflict between children's actions (based on values of the peer group) and their parents' values. Anger is a common emotion at this age and is displayed with more intensity than many of the other emotions. Just as they often tell their preadolescents that they should not be afraid, parents often tell them that they should not get angry. Unfortunately, this is an unrealistic expectation, even for adults.

Problems of Adolescence

Adolescence can be a time of great risk for many, as teenagers are now able, for the first time, to engage in behaviors or make decisions that can have long-term negative consequences (Dryfoos, 1998; National Research Council, 1995).

CONNECTIONS

For more on emotional disorders, see Chapter 12, page 421.

EMOTIONAL DISORDERS ● Secondary school teachers should be sensitive to the stresses that adolescents face and should realize that emotional disturbances are common. They should understand that depressed, hopeless, or unaccountably angry behavior can be a clue that the adolescent needs help, and they should try to put such students in touch with school counselors or other psychologically trained adults.

What are some of the problems of adolescent students that you might encounter as a teacher? How would you respond to these problems?

DROPPING OUT ● Dropping out of secondary school can put adolescents at considerable risk, as dropouts condemn themselves to low-level occupations, unemployment, and poverty. Of course, the factors that lead to dropping out begin early in students' school careers; school failure, retention (staying back), assignment to special education, and poor attendance all predict dropout (Garnier, Stein, & Jacobs, 1997). Dropout rates have generally been declining, especially among African American students, whose dropout rate is now almost the same as that for whites. For Latino students, however, dropout rates remain very high (Secada et al., 1998). Dropout among at-risk students can be greatly reduced by programs that give these students individual attention, high-status roles, and assistance with academic deficits (Fashola & Slavin, 1998).

DRUG AND ALCOHOL ABUSE ● Substance use continues to be widespread among adolescents (U.S. Department of Health and Human Services, 1994). Ninety percent of high school seniors drink alcohol, and one in three has tried marijuana (Atwater, 1996).

DELINQUENCY ● One of the most dangerous problems of adolescence is the beginning of serious delinquency. The problem is far more common among males than among females (U.S. Department of Justice, 1992). Delinquents are usually low achievers who have been given little reason to believe that they can succeed by following the path laid out for them by the school. Delinquency in adolescence is overwhelmingly a group phenomenon; most delinquent acts are done in groups or with the active support of a delinquent subgroup (Downs & Rose, 1991; Windle, 1994).

RISK OF PREGNANCY ● Pregnancy and childbirth are serious problems among all groups of female adolescents but particularly among those from lower-income homes (Coley & Chase-Lansdale, 1998; Scott-Jones, 1993). Just as adolescent males

CONNECTIONS

To learn about prevention of delinquency, see Chapter 11, page 397.

The Intentional Teacher

Using What You Know about Early Childhood, Middle Childhood, and Adolescent Students to Improve Teaching and Learning

Intentional teachers realize that students in their early years, in middle childhood, and in adolescence face different challenges as they develop physically, cognitively, and socially. Such teachers compose student goals that account for different levels of development and address students as individuals who are developing in many ways at once. Intentional teachers provide learning opportunities that foster students' resolution of developmental issues and push them forward in each area of growth. Finally, intentional teachers modify their instruction when they find that particular students need additional—or different—support in their growth toward independence.

1 What am I trying to accomplish?

Teachers need to build understanding of the issues that typically arise at their students' age levels, and they need to develop understanding of the stress that can be involved as students move from one level to the next. Check to see that your goals reflect a general understanding of student issues.

> As a high school teacher, you build into your long-term plans activities that capitalize on the important influence of the peer culture. Examples include allowing students to study content through connections to topical interests like fashion, music, and sports.

Teachers' goals should match the kinds of issues that students face at different stages in their school careers, during early childhood, middle childhood, and adolescence.

> As a kindergarten teacher, you realize that young children are working to refine large muscle and small muscle control. You request playground equipment that will foster agility and classroom materials such as clay and toys that lace to encourage dexterity.

2 What are my students' relevant experiences and needs?

Instruction is most appropriate when it addresses students' current functioning. Use a variety of formal and informal measures to gather information about your students' linguistic, physical, and cognitive development.

> As a preschool teacher, you check for students' concepts about print: Can they identify the front of a book? Do they track from left to right?

> As a middle school teacher, you use informal conversation and academic materials to assess your new student's English language skills. You converse with other professionals to determine the most effective mode of instruction for your student.

> As your eighth-graders cut out magazine pictures to create collages, you listen for hints that they are becoming increasingly reflective about their inner lives, a sign that marks adolescent thinking.

Students' relationships with peers change over time. Assess students' peer interactions so that you can encourage prosocial behavior.

> You observe your kindergartners during their free time, taking notes about the different forms of play you observe.

> You listen to your sixth-graders' lunch table conversations, asking yourself: "Do my students compare themselves to their peers in order to evaluate themselves?" You make a mental note to help them make appropriate comparisons.

---

often engage in delinquent behavior to try to establish their independence from adult control, adolescent females often engage in sex, and in many cases have children, to force the world to see them as adults. Because early childbearing makes it difficult for adolescent females to continue their schooling or get jobs, it is a primary cause of the continuation of the cycle of poverty into which many adolescent mothers were themselves born (Hoffman, Foster, & Furstenberg, 1993). Of course, the other side of teen pregnancy is teen fatherhood. Teen fathers also suffer behavioral and academic problems in school (Hanson, Morrison, & Ginsburg, 1989).

RISK OF AIDS ● Compounding the traditional risks of early sexual activity is the rise in AIDS and other sexually transmitted diseases (Kalichman, 1996). AIDS is still very rare during the adolescent years, but it is increasing among individuals in their 20s. Because full-blown AIDS can take 10 years to appear, the assumption is that unprotected sex, needle sharing, and other high-risk behavior among teens

3 **What approaches and materials are available to help me challenge every student?**

Classroom environments may be most likely to allow for development if they include a rich variety of materials that can foster social, linguistic, physical, and academic development.

In your first-grade classroom, you include a puppet center and a storytelling area to encourage oral language development.

In your fourth-grade classroom, you build a sense of community and acceptance that welcomes all students, no matter their differences. You use classroom meetings, in which students are encouraged to share openly, to help build this accepting attitude.

In your chemistry class, you provide opportunities for students to explore their more finely differentiated self-concepts by investigating chemistry's role in many different realms of our lives.

4 **How will I know whether and when to change my strategy or modify my instruction?**

Proponents of developmentally appropriate practice urge teachers to treat each student as an individual with a unique pattern of growth.

You assess your materials to verify that they will enable first-graders with wide-ranging abilities to succeed. You add more books, writing materials, and construction materials.

It is important to check not just your plans and materials, but students' reactions to those plans and materials as well. Are your activities moving students forward?

You review your first-graders' portfolios to trace their growth in fine motor control, in self-concept, and in academic mastery. You watch for patterns that emerge throughout the class and use that information to adjust learning opportunities.

You review your lesson plans for your trigonometry class to ensure that they provide opportunities for social interaction and formal problem solving, activities that help adolescents move into Piaget's stage of formal operations.

Teachers need to collect information about student learning that allows for a long-term, broad view of students' emotional, physical, and social growth. Be certain to collect information from a variety of formal and informal sources.

You watch your fifth-graders during recess to assess their ability to play together and resolve conflict. You take note of students who behave aggressively and formulate a plan to encourage prosocial behavior for those students.

When your first-period U.S. history students talk in small groups, you tune in to one student whose language suggests that she may need help with the emotional stress that often accompanies adolescence.

5 **What information will I accept as evidence that my students and I are experiencing success?**

Assess the information you have gathered from different sources over time. Does it suggest that students are growing in each important area of human development?

You ask your third-graders to write in their journals about their friends, and you use their entries to help you determine whether students are developing friendships that can provide social and cognitive resources for them.

Provide opportunities for students to self-assess.

You hold a class discussion, addressing such questions as "What can you do better now than at the beginning of the year?" "What would you still like to improve?" "How can I help?"

---

is what is causing the AIDS epidemic among young adults (Hein, 1993). The appearance of AIDS has made the need for early, explicit sex education critical, potentially a life-or-death matter. However, knowledge alone is not enough (Woodring, 1995); sexually active adolescents must have access to condoms and realistic, psychologically sophisticated inducements to use them (Aronson, 1995).

Providing Developmental Assets for Adolescents

G. Stanley Hall, an early American psychologist who studied child development, called adolescence a time of storm and stress. Whether or not that is an accurate description of all teenagers, many contemporary writers (e.g., Dryfoos, 1990) believe young people in the United States are at risk because of the choices they make. Such a view of at-risk behaviors can result in a "deficit-thinking" approach

THEORY
into
Practice

to helping teenagers. That is, our society declares "war" on teenage pregnancy, school dropout rates, drug and alcohol abuse, gangs, and violence. As Goleman (1995) noted, however, such programs often come too late and do too little. In a deficit approach we try to stop adolescents from doing risky things, but adolescents don't always listen.

A different approach to helping teenagers live in responsible ways has been suggested by Benson (1997) and his associates. Using results from surveys of more than a quarter million public school students across the country, Benson has identified what he calls "developmental assets": characteristics of the teenager and of the environment in which he or she lives that can promote healthy development. Among the 40 assets Benson has identified, for example, are family support, parental involvement in schooling, community service (one hour or more a week by the young person), a family that provides clear boundaries for the young person, parents and teachers who hold high expectations for the young person, and a feeling of self-control over "things that happen to me."

Communities can use a survey instrument developed by Benson to determine the percentage of assets that the youth in those communities hold. Research on the value of these assets indicates that they can protect youth from engaging in at-risk behaviors, can enhance or promote positive developmental outcomes, and can help youth weather or bounce back from adversity.

The downside of Benson's research: His findings indicate that the average student in 6th through 12th grade experiences only about half of the 40 assets. According to Benson's studies, however, communities can provide the developmental assets that youth need by calling on all resources of the community—families, schools, youth organizations, religious organizations, local government, health care systems, and businesses—to cooperate in this effort.

SELF-CHECK

Add information about adolescence in the last column of your comparison chart, using the same categories as before. Reread the vignette at the beginning of this chapter, and explain the interaction between Jake and Billy in terms of what you have learned about child development.

CHAPTER SUMMARY

HOW DO CHILDREN DEVELOP DURING THE PRESCHOOL YEARS?

Physically, young children develop strength and coordination of the large muscles first and then of the small muscles (as in cutting with scissors or writing). Cognitive abilities corresponding to Piaget's sensorimotor and preoperational stages also include the acquisition of language. Oral language is usually acquired by age 3 and includes the development of vocabulary, grammatical rules, and conventions of discourse. The foundations of reading and writing are usually acquired before formal schooling begins.

Socioemotional development in early childhood can be partly described in terms of Erikson's initiative versus guilt stage. Peer relationships help children overcome the egocentrism that Piaget described as characteristic of preoperational thinking. Prosocial behavior includes caring, sharing, comforting, and cooperation. Parten identified four categories of play—solitary, parallel, associative, and cooperative—that reflect increasing levels of social interaction and sophistication. Play exercises children's linguistic, cognitive, social, and creative skills.

WHAT KINDS OF EARLY CHILDHOOD EDUCATION PROGRAMS EXIST?

Economic and social factors have led to an increasing demand for early childhood education programs, including day-care centers, nursery schools, compensatory preschool programs, and kindergartens. Research findings have tended to support trends toward early intervention, school-readiness training, continuation of compensatory programs in the early elementary grades, targeting of students who are at risk, and avoidance of the potential drawbacks of kindergarten retention. Developmentally appropriate practice, instruction based on individuals' characteristics and needs rather than on age, has become increasingly important.

HOW DO CHILDREN DEVELOP DURING THE ELEMENTARY YEARS?

Between the ages of 5 and 7, children have slower growth but greater health and skill. They think in ways described in Piaget's theory as the concrete operational stage. Children in the upper elementary grades move from egocentric thought to more decentered thought. At 9 to 12 years of age, children can use logical, reversible thought, can reason abstractly, and can have insight into causal and interpersonal relationships.

Hoffman's work on parenting styles suggests that parents who use inductive rather than power-assertive techniques tend to be more effective in promoting prosocial and moral behavior in children.

In middle childhood, children may be seen as resolving Erikson's industry versus inferiority psychosocial crisis. School becomes a major influence on development, a place where the child develops a public self, builds social skills, and establishes self-esteem on the basis of academic and nonacademic competencies. In preadolescence, between ages 9 and 12, conformity in peer relations, mixed-sex peer groupings, and challenges to adult authority become more important.

HOW DO CHILDREN DEVELOP DURING THE MIDDLE SCHOOL AND HIGH SCHOOL YEARS?

Puberty is a series of major physiological changes leading to the ability to reproduce. Significant differences exist in the age of onset of puberty, and both early maturers and late maturers may experience difficulties. Adolescents develop reflectivity and greater metacognitive skills, such as those described in Piaget's formal operations: combinatorial problem solving and hypothetical reasoning.

Adolescents may be seen as resolving Erikson's identity versus role confusion psychosocial crisis. They pay attention to how other people view them, search the past, experiment with roles, act on feelings and beliefs, and gradually seek greater autonomy and intimacy in peer relations. Identity foreclosure occurs when the individual chooses a role prematurely, but by late adolescence, most individuals have developed a state of identity achievement. Many factors, such as dropping out, substance abuse, and AIDS, place adolescents at risk.

KEY TERMS

associative play   77

compensatory preschool programs   80

cooperative play   77

early intervention programs   80

emergent literacy   72

foreclosure   94

identity achievement   94

identity diffusion   94

large muscle development   70

moratorium   94

parallel play   77

peers   76

prosocial behaviors   77

puberty   90

readiness training   79

reflectivity   93

self-concept   86

self-esteem   86

small muscle development   70

social comparison   86

solitary play   77

whole language   73

Self-Assessment

1. A major accomplishment for preschoolers is
   a. increased control over the large and small muscles.
   b. hypothetical thought.
   c. deductive thinking.
   d. puberty.

2. Which of the following statements about play is false?
   a. Psychologists today generally agree that play is overemphasized in kindergarten and detracts from academics.
   b. Parallel play occurs when children do not interact purposefully with each other to create shared experiences.
   c. Sociodramatic play follows pretend play in the developmental sequence.
   d. Because play is spontaneous and nonreflective, it appears to stimulate creativity.

3. Participation in compensatory preschool programs has been found to
   a. benefit middle-class children more than lower-class children.
   b. increase disadvantaged children's readiness for kindergarten and first grade.
   c. have stronger effects on long-term achievement than on initial achievement.

   d. be of little benefit to children under the age of two.

4. Which of the following cognitive abilities do children usually have when they enter first grade?
   a. They understand abstract concepts.
   b. They know an almost infinite variety of sentences.
   c. They use systematic approaches to solving problems.
   d. They concentrate for long periods of time.

5. During the elementary years, children in middle childhood typically develop all of the following characteristics except
   a. decentered thought.
   b. preoperational thought.
   c. group conformity.
   d. fear of not having a best friend.

6. Which of the following attributes is characteristic of children during the elementary years?
   a. Peers become important.
   b. Reflectivity appears.
   c. Identity issues are central.
   d. Emotional conflicts are experienced.

7. Adolescents who have never experienced an identity crisis because they have prematurely established an identity based on their parents' values and beliefs are in Marcia's
   a. identity diffusion status.
   b. foreclosure status.
   c. moratorium status.
   d. identity achievement status.

8. Predictors of dropping out of school include all of the following except
   a. assignment to special education classes.
   b. poor attendance.
   c. retention.
   d. assistance with academic deficits.

9. Match each developmental challenge that follows with the period of development in which it is most likely to first occur.

_____ identity diffusion
_____ friendship
_____ prosocial behavior
_____ intimacy
_____ oral language
_____ sociodramatic play
_____ conflict management

   a. early childhood
   b. middle childhood and preadolescence
   c. adolescence

10. Develop an outline for an essay that would begin with the following thesis statement: "Child development has important implications for classroom instruction at each grade level."

Chapter 4

WHAT IS THE IMPACT OF CULTURE ON TEACHING AND LEARNING?

HOW DOES SOCIOECONOMIC STATUS AFFECT STUDENT ACHIEVEMENT?
The Role of Child-Rearing Practices
The Link between Income and Summer Learning
The Role of Schools As Middle-Class Institutions
School and Community Factors
Is the Low Achievement of Children from Low-Income Groups Inevitable?
Implications for Teachers

HOW DO ETHNICITY AND RACE AFFECT STUDENTS' SCHOOL EXPERIENCES?
Racial and Ethnic Composition of the United States
Academic Achievement of Minority-Group Students
Why Have Minority-Group Students Lagged in Achievement?
Effects of School Desegregation

HOW DO LANGUAGE DIFFERENCES AND BILINGUAL PROGRAMS AFFECT STUDENT ACHIEVEMENT?
Bilingual Education
Effectiveness of Bilingual Programs

WHAT IS MULTICULTURAL EDUCATION?
Dimensions of Multicultural Education

HOW DO GENDER AND GENDER BIAS AFFECT STUDENTS' SCHOOL EXPERIENCES?
Do Males and Females Think and Learn Differently?
Sex-Role Stereotyping and Gender Bias

HOW DO STUDENTS DIFFER IN INTELLIGENCE AND LEARNING STYLES?
Definitions of Intelligence
Origins of Intelligence
Theories of Learning Styles
Aptitude–Treatment Interactions

Student Diversity

Marva Vance and John Rossi are first-year teachers at Emma Lazarus Elementary School. It's November, and Marva and John are meeting over coffee to discuss the event dreaded by many a first-year teacher: the upcoming Thanksgiving pageant.

"This is driving me crazy!" Marva starts. "Our classes are like the United Nations. How are we supposed to cast a Thanksgiving pageant? I have three Navajo children. Should I cast them as Indians, or would they be offended? My Vietnamese kids have probably never seen a turkey, and the idea of eating a big bird like that must be revolting to them. I wonder how meaningful this will be to my African Americans. I remember when I was in a Thanksgiving pageant and our teacher had us black students be stagehands because she said there weren't any black Pilgrims! Besides, what am I going to do about a narrator? Jose says he wants to be narrator, but his English isn't too good. Lakesha would be good, but she's often out for gifted class and would miss some rehearsals. I've also been worrying about the hunters. Should they all be boys? Wouldn't it be stereotyping if the boys were hunters and the girls were cooks? What about Mark? He's in a wheelchair. Should I let him be a hunter?"

John sighs and looks into his coffee. "I know what you're talking about. I just let my kids sign up for each part in the pageant. The boys signed up as hunters, the girls as cooks, the Indians as Indians. Maybe it's too late for us to do anything about stereotyping when the kids have already bought into their roles. Where I went to school, everyone was white, and no one questioned the idea that hunters were boys and cooks were girls. How did everything get so complicated?"

Using Your EXPERIENCE

Critical Thinking Spend 4 or 5 minutes writing a plausible ending to the vignette. What did Marva Vance end up doing, and what were the results? Besides the cultural differences, how might she have addressed different students' intellectual and learning strengths in the pageant?

Cooperative Learning In small groups of four students, role-play Marva and John's situation. Then discuss the issues they are raising. After 6 minutes, report your group's conclusions to the class.

Students differ. They differ in performance level, learning rate, and learning style. They differ in ethnicity, culture, social class, and home language. They differ in gender. Some have disabilities, and some are gifted or talented in one or more areas. These and other differences can have important implications for instruction, curriculum, and school policies and practices. Marva and John are concerned with student diversity as it relates to the Thanksgiving pageants they are planning, but diversity and its meaning for education are important issues every day, not just on Thanksgiving. This chapter discusses some of the most important ways in which students differ and some of the ways in which teachers can accept, accommodate, and celebrate student diversity in their daily teaching. However, diversity is such an important theme that almost every chapter in this book touches on this issue. Teachers are more than instructors of students. Together with their students they are builders of tomorrow's society. A critical part of every teacher's role is to ensure that the equal opportunity that we hold to be central to our nationhood is translated into equal opportunity in day-to-day life in the classroom. This chapter was written with this goal in mind.

WHAT IS THE IMPACT OF CULTURE ON TEACHING AND LEARNING?

If you have ever traveled to a foreign country, you noticed differences in behaviors, attitudes, dress, language, and food. In fact, part of the fun of traveling is in discovering these differences in **culture,** which refers to the shared norms, traditions, behaviors, language, and perceptions of a group (Erickson, 1997). Though we usually think of cultural differences as being mostly national differences, there is probably as much cultural diversity within the United States as between the United States and other industrialized nations. The life of a middle-class family in the United States or Canada is probably more like that of a middle-class family in Italy, Ireland, or Israel than it is like that of a low-income family living a mile away. Yet while we value cultural differences between nations, we are often less tolerant of differences within our own society. Our tendency is to value the characteristics of mainstream, high-status groups and devalue those of other groups.

By the time children enter school, they have absorbed many aspects of the culture in which they were raised, such as language, beliefs, attitudes, ways of behaving, and food preferences. More accurately, most children are affected by several cultures, in that most are members of many overlapping groups. The cultural background of an individual child is affected by his or her ethnicity, social class, religion,

culture
The language, attitudes, ways of behaving, and other aspects of life that characterize a group of people.

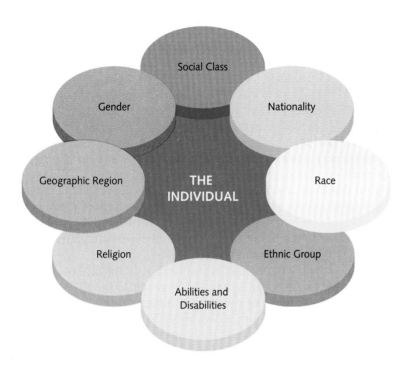

FIGURE 4.1 ● Cultural Diversity and Individual Identity
Reprinted with permission of the author and publisher from James A. Banks, *Multiethnic Education: Theory and Practice* (3rd ed.), 1993, p. 89. Boston: Allyn & Bacon.

home language, gender, and other group identities and experiences (see Figure 4.1). Many of the behaviors that are associated with being brought up in a particular culture have important consequences for classroom instruction. For example, schools expect children to speak standard English. This is easy for students from homes in which standard English is spoken but difficult for those whose families speak other languages or significantly divergent dialects of English. Schools also expect students to be highly verbal, to spend most of their time working independently, and to compete with other students for grades and recognition. However, many cultures in our society place a higher value on cooperation and peer orientation than on independence and competitiveness (Boykin, 1994a, 1994b). Because the culture of the school reflects mainstream middle-class values (Grossman, 1995), and because most teachers are from middle-class backgrounds, the child from a different culture is often at a disadvantage. Understanding students' backgrounds is critical for effectively teaching both academic material and the behaviors and expectations of the school.

SELF-CHECK

List as many components of culture as you can think of, and then hypothesize about the impact of each one on teaching and learning.

HOW DOES SOCIOECONOMIC STATUS AFFECT STUDENT ACHIEVEMENT?

One important way in which students differ from one another is in social class. Even in small rural towns in which almost everyone is the same in ethnicity and religion, the children of the town's bankers, doctors, and teachers probably have a different upbringing from that experienced by the children of most farmhands or domestic workers.

Sociologists define social class, or **socioeconomic status (SES),** in terms of an individual's income, occupation, education, and prestige in society. These factors tend to go together, so SES is most often measured as a combination of the individual's income and years of education, because these are most easily quantified.

Levine and Levine (1996) divide the American socioeconomic class structure into five groups: upper (3 percent), upper middle (22 percent), lower middle (34 percent), upper working (28 percent), and lower working (13 percent). Within the lower working class they distinguish a very impoverished subgroup, the urban underclass, that has particularly severe difficulties in terms of unemployment, crime, and social disorganization (Danziger, Sandefur, & Weinberg, 1994; Miller & Ferroggiaro, 1995). In this book the term *middle-class* is used to refer to families whose wage earners are in occupations requiring significant education, *working-class* to those who have relatively stable occupations not requiring higher education, and *lower-class* to those in the urban or rural underclass who are chronically unemployed and often living on government assistance.

However, social class indicates more than level of income and education. Along with social class goes a pervasive set of behaviors, expectations, and attitudes, which intersect with and are affected by other cultural factors. Students' social-class origins are likely to have a profound effect on attitudes and behaviors in school. Students from working-class or lower-class backgrounds are less likely than middle-class students to enter school knowing how to count, to name letters, to cut with scissors, or to name colors. They are less likely to perform well in school than are children from middle-class homes (Knapp & Woolverton, 1995; Levine & Levine, 1996; Mullis, Dossey, Foertsch, Jones, & Gentile, 1991). Of course, these differences are true only on the average; many working-class and lower-class parents do an outstanding job of supporting their children's success in school, and many working-class and lower-class children achieve at a very high level. Social class cuts across categories of race and ethnicity. Although it is true that Latino and African American families are lower in social class on the average than are white families, there is substantial overlap; the majority of all low-income families in the United States are white, and there are many middle-class minority families (U.S. Department of Education, 1991). Definitions of social class are based on such factors as income, occupation, and education, never on race or ethnicity.

Table 4.1 shows the reading performance of 4th-, 8th-, and 12th-graders on the 1994 National Assessment of Educational Progress (Campbell, Donahue, Reese, & Phillips, 1996). Note that children of more educated parents (a key component of social class) consistently scored higher than children of less educated parents.

TABLE 4.1

NAEP Reading Scores by Parents' Education

PARENTS' EDUCATION	GRADE 4	GRADE 8	GRADE 12
Graduated college	224	270	298
Some education after high school	223	266	289
Graduated high school	207	252	277
Did not finish high school	188	238	266

socioeconomic status (SES)
A measure of prestige within a social group that is most often based on income and education.

Source: Adapted from Campbell, Donahue, Reese, & Phillips, 1996.

The Role of Child-Rearing Practices

Much research has focused on the differences in child-rearing practices between the average middle-class family and the average working-class or lower-class family. Many children from low-income families receive an upbringing that is less consistent with what they will be expected to do in school than that of middle-class children. By the time they enter school, middle-class children are likely to be good at following directions, explaining and understanding reasons, and comprehending and using complex language, while working-class or lower-class children may have less experience in all these areas (Clark & Ramsey, 1992; Slaughter & Epps, 1994).

Another important difference between middle-class and lower-class families is in the kinds of activities parents tend to do with their children. Middle-class parents are likely to express high expectations for their children and to reward them for intellectual development. They are likely to provide good models for language use, to talk and read to their children frequently, and to encourage reading and other learning activities. They are particularly apt to provide all sorts of learning materials for children at home, such as books, encyclopedias, records, puzzles, and, increasingly, computers. These parents are also likely to expose their children to learning experiences outside the home, such as museums, concerts, and zoos. Middle-class parents are likely to expect and demand high achievement from their children; working-class and lower-class parents are more likely to demand good behavior and obedience (Knapp & Woolverton, 1995; Metz, 1990).

The Link between Income and Summer Learning

One very interesting study underscored the link between social class and school achievement. This study found that students from families of different social class backgrounds achieved quite similarly during the school year. However, over the summer, students from low-income families lost much of the achievement they had gained, while those in wealthier families gained in achievement level (Heyns, 1978). In fact, in only 3 summer months, the lowest-income group of students lost more than half of the word knowledge they had gained in the fifth grade, while the wealthiest gained one-third more during the summer over their school-year gains (Heyns, 1978). Many later studies confirmed this observation: middle-class children gain in achievement over the summer, while children in low-income families (regardless of ethnicity) tend to lose ground (Cooper, Lindsay, Nye, & Greathouse, 1998; Entwisle & Alexander, 1992).

What these data suggest is that home environment influences not only academic readiness for school but also the level of achievement throughout students' careers in school. Middle-class children are more likely to be engaged in school-like activities during the summer and to have available more school-like materials. Working-class and lower-class children may be receiving less academically relevant stimulation at home and are more likely to be forgetting what they learned in school (Thompson, Entwisle, Alexander, & Sundius, 1992).

The Role of Schools As Middle-Class Institutions

Students from backgrounds other than the mainstream middle class have difficulties in school in part because their upbringing emphasizes different behaviors from those valued in school. The problem is that the school overwhelmingly represents the values and expectations of the middle class. Two of these values are individuality and future time orientation (see Boykin, 1994a). Most U.S. class-rooms operate on the assumption that children should do their own work. Helping others is often defined as cheating. Students are expected to compete for grades, for the teacher's attention and praise, and for other rewards. Competition and individual work are values that are instilled early on in most middle-class homes. However, students from lower-class white families (Pepitone, 1985) and from many other ethnic backgrounds (Boykin, 1994a) are less willing to compete and are more interested in cooperating with their peers than are middle-class European Americans. These students have often learned from an early age to rely on their communities, friends, and family, and have always also helped and been helped by others. Not surprisingly, students who are most oriented toward cooperation with others learn best in cooperation with others, whereas those who prefer to compete learn best in competition with others (Kagan, Zahn, Widaman, Schwartzwald, & Tyrrell, 1985). Because of the mismatch between the cooperative orientation of many lower-class and minority-group children and the competitive orientation of the school, Kagan and colleagues (1985) have argued that there is a structural bias in traditional classrooms that works against these children. Kagan recommends that teachers use cooperative learning strategies at least part of the time with these students so that they receive instruction that is consistent with their cultural orientations.

CONNECTIONS

For more on cooperative learning strategies, see Chapter 8, page 268.

Schools are geared to reward behavior "sometime in the future." That future may be the end of the day but is more likely the end of the week, the end of the grading period, or even the end of the school year. Therefore, success in school requires the ability to forgo present gratification for the sake of a future reward. Middle-class children are likely to have learned not only to work for a delayed reward but also to plan their own actions so that they accomplish tasks on schedule. Schools demand this type of behavior all the time. An example is a social studies project that is assigned on Monday and due on Friday. Working-class and lower-class families, who are often concerned with day-to-day survival, may not provide as much support for their children in making and following through on long-term plans. Their children may therefore have difficulty pacing their work so as to complete projects when required. However, all students can learn to manage their time and to develop and carry out plans if they are given many opportunities to do so and are taught strategies for making effective use of their time and organizing their work.

School and Community Factors

Often, children from low-income families are placed at risk by the characteristics of the communities they live in and the schools they attend. For example, school funding in most areas of the United States is correlated with social class; middle-class children are likely to attend schools with greater resources, better-paid (and therefore better-qualified) teachers, and other advantages (Darling-Hammond, 1995). On top of these differences, schools serving low-income neighborhoods may have to spend much more on security, on services for children having difficulties, and on many other needs, leaving even less for regular education (Kozol, 1991; Persell, 1997). This lack of resources can significantly affect student achievement (Greenwald, Hedges, & Laine, 1996). In very impoverished neighborhoods, crime, a lack of positive role models, inadequate social and health services, and other factors can create an environment that undermines children's motivation, achievement, and mental health (Behrman, 1997; Black & Krishnakumar, 1998; Vernez,

CASE TO CONSIDER

What Would You Do, Mrs. Brown?

Fluent in both Spanish and English, Elizabeth Montgomery had changed careers in her mid-thirties to become a bilingual elementary teacher. After earning a Master of Education degree with honors and successfully completing her student teaching, Elizabeth was hired to teach a fourth-grade Spanish bilingual class at a large elementary school in a working- and lower-class urban community. Of the 30 students in her class, 26 are Latino, 2 are African American, and 2 are European American.

LaShonda Brown is one of the African American students in Ms. Montgomery's class. After school she is startlingly sweet and often confides pleasant facts about her home life, but she is amazingly recalcitrant during class time. She often comes to school late and usually responds with "I ain't doin' that shit" to even the smallest request. In class she sits limply during assignments, makes farting noises during reading (which delights her classmates no end), and refuses to participate in her math group. She seems both angry and dependent. By the fifth week of class, Ms. Montgomery has decided to call LaShonda's mother but plans to describe LaShonda's behavior as depression rather than anger.

Ms. Montgomery: Mrs. Brown, I'm concerned about LaShonda. She doesn't participate in class and seems especially dependent. Could she be depressed about something?

Mrs. Brown: Ms. Montgomery, that girl certainly isn't depressed because even though I'm raising her alone, I work very hard to buy her everything she wants and to make her happy. I'll admit that she's way too dependent, you might even say spoiled, but she isn't depressed.

Ms. Montgomery: Well, perhaps when you come to our class open house next week, we can talk some more about how to help LaShonda participate more in class.

During the open house, Ms. Montgomery shows Mrs. Brown and the other parents around the classroom, discusses the bilingual approach she is using, and also tells them about a sex education unit that is planned for later in the term. The meeting is pleasant, but there is no opportunity to talk with Mrs. Brown alone about LaShonda, whose behavior is now prompting Ms. Montgomery to send her out of the classroom for small periods so her acting out does not get reinforced by her classmates.

Later that week, Ms. Montgomery receives a letter from Mrs. Brown that says, "It's too bad you are so concerned with sex education but can't be bothered to really teach my girl. It seems you prefer the Mexican American children in your class over the black children."

Stunned, Ms. Montgomery shows the letter to the vice-principal, an African American woman with whom LaShonda has rapport. Vice-Principal Johnson suggests inviting Mrs. Brown to a meeting with her and Ms. Montgomery in her office.

Vice-Principal Johnson: Mrs. Brown, I'm so glad you could come in to talk with us about your concerns about LaShonda's class.

Mrs. Brown: Well, I don't mean any disrespect, but I think a white woman from the ritzy suburbs, who calls me up telling me my LaShonda is "depressed" and who teaches things like sex education to fourth-graders, may not be the best teacher for my daughter.

Ms. Montgomery: What would *you* do, Mrs. Brown, if LaShonda came into the room in the morning and said "shit" first thing, refused to participate or do her work, and then refused to join the group for extra math help?

Mrs. Brown: She does *that*?

Ms. Montgomery: Every day.

Mrs. Brown: You've never told me this. I can't deal with her if you don't tell me what's going on. I wish you would have told me earlier.

PROBLEM SOLVING

1. Discuss how socioeconomics, child-rearing practices, and the middle-class values of school may each be a factor in LaShonda's behavior in class.

2. If you were Ms. Montgomery, what would you have done differently with LaShonda and her mother?

3. Role-play the continuing discussion among Vice-Principal Johnson, Ms. Montgomery, and Mrs. Brown. What would you say, as one of these three participants, to bring a more positive and cooperative conclusion to the meeting?

Adapted by permission from "What Would You Do, Mrs. Brown?" by June Isaacs Elia, Professor of Education at Holy Names College, Oakland, California, from *Allyn & Bacon's Custom Cases in Education,* edited by Greta Morine-Dershimer, Paul Eggen, and Donald Kauchak (1997).

1998). These factors do not doom children to failure; many children succeed despite the odds (Garbarino, 1997; Wandersman & Nation, 1998). But such factors do make success much more difficult.

Is the Low Achievement of Children from Low-Income Groups Inevitable?

Schools can do a great deal to enable children from low-income families to succeed in school (Slavin, 1997/98). For example, intensive interventions have been designed to help develop children's cognitive skills early in life and to help their parents do a better job of preparing them for school. Studies of these programs have shown long-term positive effects for children growing up in very impoverished families, especially when the programs are continued into the early elementary grades (Ramey & Ramey, 1998; Reynolds, 1998). Reading Recovery (Lyons, Pinnell, & DeFord, 1993) and other tutoring programs for first-graders have shown substantial effects on the reading achievement of at-risk children (Wasik & Slavin, 1993). Success for All (Slavin et al., 1996), which combines effective instructional programs, tutoring, and family support services, has demonstrated substantial and lasting impacts on the achievement of children in high-poverty schools. Significant reductions in class size have been found to be particularly beneficial to children in high-poverty schools (Achilles, Finn, & Bain, 1997/98). These and other programs and practices demonstrate that low achievement by lower-class children is not inevitable. Achievement can be greatly improved by use of strategies that are expensive, but are readily available to schools.

Implications for Teachers

Children enter school with varying degrees of preparation for the school behaviors that lead to success. Their behaviors, attitudes, and values also vary. However, the mere fact that some children initially do not know what is expected of them and have fewer entry-level skills than others does not mean that they are destined for academic failure. Although there is a modest positive correlation between social class and achievement, it should not be assumed that this relationship holds for all children from lower-SES families. There are many exceptions. Working-class and lower-class families can provide home environments that are supportive of their children's success in school. Autobiographies of people who have overcome poverty (e.g., Comer, 1990) often refer to the influence of strong parents with high standards who expected nothing less than the best from their children and did what they could to help them achieve. While educators need to be aware of the problems encountered by many lower-class pupils, they also need to avoid converting this knowledge into stereotypes. In fact, there is evidence that middle-class teachers often have low expectations for working-class and lower-class students (Persell, 1997) and that these low expectations can become a self-fulfilling prophecy, causing students to perform less well than they could have (Alexander, Entwisle, & Thompson, 1987).

SELF-CHECK

Summarize the U.S. social class structure. Identify four or more factors related to social class that affect teaching and learning. Give an example of each factor.

HOW DO ETHNICITY AND RACE AFFECT STUDENTS' SCHOOL EXPERIENCES?

A major determinant of the culture in which students will grow up is their ethnic origin. An **ethnic group** is one in which individuals have a shared sense of identity, usually because of a common place of origin (such as Swedish, Polish, or Greek Americans), religion (such as Jewish or Catholic Americans), or race (such as African or Asian Americans). Note that **ethnicity** is not the same as race; **race** refers only to physical characteristics, such as skin color. Ethnic groups usually share a common culture, which may not be true of all people of a given race. African Americans who are recent immigrants from Nigeria or Jamaica, for example, are from ethnic backgrounds that are quite different from that of African Americans whose families have been in the United States for many generations, even if they are of the same race.

Most European Americans identify with one or more European ethnic groups, such as Polish, Italian, Irish, Greek, or German. Identification with these groups may affect a family's traditions, holidays, food preferences, and, to some extent, outlook on the world. However, white ethnic groups have been largely absorbed into mainstream U.S. society, so the differences among them have few implications for education (Alba, 1990).

The situation is quite different for other ethnic groups. In particular, African Americans (Frederick D. Patterson Research Institute, 1997), Latinos (Secada et al., 1998), and Native Americans (Deyhle & Swisher, 1995) have yet to be fully accepted into mainstream U.S. society and have not yet attained the economic success or security that the white ethnic groups have achieved (Carter & Goodwin, 1994). Students from these ethnic groups face special problems in school and have been the focus of two of the most emotional issues in U.S. education since the mid-1960s: desegregation and bilingual education. The following sections discuss the situation of students of different ethnic backgrounds in schools today.

Racial and Ethnic Composition of the United States

The people who make up the United States have always come from many ethnic backgrounds, but every year the proportion of nonwhites and Latinos is increasing. Table 4.2 shows U.S. Census Bureau projections of the percentages of the U.S. population under the age of 25 according to ethnicity. Note that the proportion of non-Latino whites is expected to continue to decline; as recently as 1970, 83.3 percent of all Americans were in this category. In contrast, the proportions of Latinos and "Other" (mostly Asians) will grow dramatically by 2010. The Latino population under the age of 25 may be as much as 40 percent higher in 2010 than in 1990, and the "Other" group may grow by 33 percent. There may be 14 percent more African Americans under the age of 25, and almost 7 percent fewer whites in absolute terms. These trends, which are due to immigration patterns and differences in birth rates, have profound implications for U.S. education. Our nation is becoming far more ethnically diverse.

Academic Achievement of Minority-Group Students

If **minority-group** students achieved at the same level as European Americans, there would probably be little concern about ethnic-group differences in U.S.

ethnic group
A group within a larger society that sees itself as having a common history, social and cultural heritage, and traditions, often based on race, religion, language, or national identity.

ethnicity
A history, culture, and sense of identity shared by a group of people.

race
Visible genetic characteristics of individuals that cause them to be seen as members of the same broad group (e.g., African, Asian, Caucasian)

minority group
An ethnic or racial group that is a minority within a broader population.

TABLE 4.2

Actual and Projected Percentages of the U.S. Population, Birth to Age 24, by Race/Ethnicity

RACE/ETHNICITY	1990	1995	2000	2010
European American	70.7	69.0	67.4	64.2
Latino	10.5	11.5	12.4	14.2
African American	15.5	15.9	16.4	17.3
Other	3.3	3.6	3.8	4.3
Total	100.0	100.0	100.0	100.0

Source: Adapted from U.S. Department of Education, 1991.

schools. Unfortunately, they don't. On virtually every test of academic achievement, African American, Latino, and Native American students score significantly lower than their European American classmates.

Table 4.3 shows reading scores on the 1994 National Assessment of Educational Progress (NAEP) according to students' race or ethnicity. African American, Latino, and Native American children scored significantly lower than non-Latino white or Asian American children at all grade levels. These differences correspond closely with differences among the groups in average socioeconomic status, which themselves translate into achievement differences (recall Table 4.1).

One recent development in the academic performance of minority-group students is heartening: The achievement gap between them and European Americans is narrowing. For example, African American and Latino students are gaining more rapidly than whites on Scholastic Assessment Tests (SATs). On the SAT verbal test, for instance, whites' scores declined by 9 points from 1976 to 1992, while African Americans' scores increased by 20 points. The white–minority achievement gap is also declining on the National Assessment of Educational Progress (NAEP). Figure 4.2 shows the change in white–minority achievement differences

TABLE 4.3

NAEP Reading Scores by Race/Ethnicity

RACE/ETHNICITY	GRADE 4	GRADE 8	GRADE 12
White	224	268	294
African American	187	237	265
Latino	191	240	270
Asian American	232	273	280
Pacific Islander	219	259	280
Native American	201	251	275

Source: Adapted from Campbell, Donahue et al., 1996.

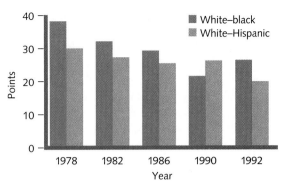

FIGURE 4.2 ● White–Minority Difference in Math Achievement of 17-Year-Olds
From *The Condition of Education,* National Center for Education Statistics, 1994, p. VI.

for 17-year-olds in math from 1978 to 1992. Similar trends are being seen in most subjects and at most age levels. Gains have been particularly dramatic for the lowest-achieving minority-group children (Carroll, 1987). But although African American and Latino students are gaining in achievement more rapidly than whites, they still have a long way to go; the gap between whites and members of minority groups remains wide (Mullis et al., 1991).

Why Have Minority-Group Students Lagged in Achievement?

Why do many minority-group students score so far below European Americans on achievement tests? The most important reason is that in our society, African Americans, Latinos (particularly Mexican Americans and Puerto Ricans), and Native Americans tend to occupy the lowest rungs of the socioeconomic ladder. Consequently, many families in these groups are unable to provide their children with the stimulation and academic preparation that are typical of a middle-class upbringing (Halle, Kurtz-Coster, & Mahoney, 1997). Again, there are many exceptions; nevertheless, these broad patterns largely explain the average differences (Portes, 1996). Chronic unemployment, underemployment, and employment in very low-wage jobs, which are endemic in many minority communities, have a negative effect on family life, including contributing to high numbers of single-parent families in minority-group communities (U.S. Department of Education, 1991).

Another important disadvantage that many minority-group students face is academically inferior, overcrowded urban schools (Gay, 1997; Kozol, 1991; Miller-Lachman & Taylor, 1995). Middle-class and many working-class families of all ethnicities throughout the United States buy their way out of center-city schools by moving to the suburbs or sending their children to private or parochial schools, leaving the public schools to serve people who lack the resources to afford alternatives. The remaining children, who are disproportionately members of ethnic minorities, are likely to attend the lowest-quality, worst-funded schools in the country (Darling-Hammond, 1995).

Often, minority-group students perform poorly because the instruction they receive is inconsistent with their cultural background (Boykin, 1994b; Fordham, 1996; Henry & Pepper, 1990; Latham, 1997a; Ogbu, 1994; Vasquez, 1993). Academic excellence itself may be seen as inconsistent with acceptance in a student's own community; for example, Ogbu (1992), Boykin (1986), Cross (1995), and others have noted the tendency of many African American students to accuse their peers of "acting white" if they strive to achieve. In contrast, many Asian American parents strongly stress academic excellence as an expectation, and as a result many (though not all) Asian subgroups do very well in school (Lee, 1996; Okagaki & Frensch, 1998). African Americans (Boykin, 1994a), Native Americans (Henry & Pepper, 1990), and Mexican Americans (Losey, 1995) generally prefer to work in collaboration with others and perform better in cooperative settings than in traditional competitive ones. Lack of respect for students' home languages and dialects can also lead to a diminishing of commitment to school (Delpit, 1995). Low expectations for minority-group students can contribute to their low achievement (Delpit, 1995; Nieto, 1997; Ogbu, 1994). This is especially true if, as often happens, low expectations lead well-meaning teachers or administrators to place minority-group students disproportionately in low-ability groups or tracks (see Braddock, Dawkins, & Wilson, 1995) or in special education (Heward & Cavanaugh, 1997). Interestingly, though African American students often suffer from the low expectations of teachers and others, their expectations for themselves and their academic self-concepts tend to be at least as high as those of their white classmates (Graham, 1994).

These students' low achievement may well be a temporary problem. Within a few decades, as minority groups increasingly achieve economic security and enter the middle class, their children's achievement will probably come to resemble that of other groups. In the 1920s it was widely believed that immigrants from southern and eastern Europe (such as Italians, Greeks, Poles, and Jews) were hopelessly backward and perhaps retarded (Oakes & Lipton, 1994), yet the children and grandchildren of these immigrants now achieve as well as the descendants of the Pilgrims. However, we cannot afford to wait a few decades. The school is one institution that can break the cycle of poverty, by giving children from impoverished backgrounds the opportunity to succeed (see Banks, 1993; Gordon, 1991).

CONNECTIONS ▶

To learn about motivational factors that affect some minority-group students and low achievers, including the role of teacher expectations and the phenomenon of learned helplessness, see Chapter 10, pages 340 and 341.

Effects of School Desegregation

Before 1954, black, white, and often Latino students were legally required to attend separate schools in 20 states and the District of Columbia, and segregated schools were common in the remaining states. Minority-group students were often bused miles away from their nearest public school to separate schools. The doctrine of separate but equal education was upheld in several Supreme Court decisions. In 1954, however, the Supreme Court struck down this practice in the landmark *Brown v. Board of Education of Topeka* case on the grounds that separate education was inherently unequal (White, 1994). *Brown v. Board of Education* did away with legal segregation, but it was many years before large numbers of racially different students were attending school together. In the 1970s a series of Supreme Court decisions found that the continued segregation of many schools throughout the United States was due to past discriminatory practices, such as drawing neighborhood boundary lines deliberately to separate schools along racial lines. These decisions forced local school districts to desegregate their schools by any means necessary (Kantor & Lowe, 1995).

Many districts were given specific standards for the proportions of minority-group students who could be assigned to any particular school. For example, a district in which 45 percent of the students were African American might be required to have an enrollment of 35 to 55 percent African Americans in its schools. To achieve desegregation, some school districts simply changed school attendance areas; others created special magnet schools (such as schools for the performing arts, for talented and gifted students, or for special vocational preparation) to induce students to attend schools outside their own neighborhoods. However, in many large, urban districts, segregation of neighborhoods is so extensive that districts must bus students to achieve racially balanced schools. School desegregation was supposed to increase the academic achievement of low-income minority-group students by giving them opportunities to interact with more middle-class, achievement-oriented peers. All too often, however, the schools to which students are bused are no better than the segregated schools they left behind, and the outflow of middle-class families from urban areas (which was well under way before busing began) often means that lower-class African American or Latino students are integrated with similarly lower-class whites (Trent, 1997). Also, it is important to note that because of residential segregation and opposition to busing, most minority students still attend schools in which there are few, if any, whites; and in many areas segregation is once again on the increase (Orfield, 1994). Support for busing to achieve integration has greatly diminished among African American and Latino parents (Shujaa, 1996), and in fact there is a small movement toward the deliberate creation of Afrocentric academies in some urban areas.

The overall effect of desegregation on the academic achievement of minority students has been small, though positive. However, when desegregation begins in elementary school, particularly when it involves busing minority-group children to high-quality schools with substantially middle-class student bodies, desegregation can have a significant effect on the achievement of minority-group students (Schofield, 1995b; Trent, 1997; Wells, 1995). This effect is thought to result not from sitting next to whites but rather from attending a better school. One important outcome of desegregation is that African American and Latino students who attend desegregated schools are more likely to attend desegregated colleges, to work in integrated settings, and to attain higher incomes than their peers who attend segregated schools (Schofield, 1995b; Wells & Crain, 1994).

Teaching in a Culturally Diverse School

Following are some recommendations for promoting social harmony and equal opportunity among students in racially and ethnically diverse classrooms and schools (see also J. A. Banks, 1997b; Cheng & Soudack, 1994; Gay, 1997; Grossman, 1995; Nieto, 1997).

- Use fairness and balance in dealing with students. Students should never have any justification for believing that "people like me [whites, African Americans, Latinos, Vietnamese] don't get a fair chance" (McIntyre, 1992).
- Use instructional materials that show all ethnic groups in equally positive and nonstereotyped roles (J. Garcia, 1993).
- Choose texts and instructional materials carefully to make sure minority groups are not underrepresented or misrepresented. Themes should be nonbiased, and minority-group individuals should appear in nonstereotyped high-status roles (J. A. Banks, 1995c, 1997b).
- Supplement textbooks with authentic material from different cultures taken from newspapers, magazines, and other media of the culture (Florida State Department of Education, 1990).
- Use community resources: representatives of various cultures talking to classes; actors portraying characters or events; and musicians or dance groups, such as salsa bands or bagpipe units, performing (Florida State Department of Education, 1990).

THEORY
into
Practice

- Avoid communicating bias, but discuss racial or ethnic relations openly rather than trying to pretend there are no differences (Grant & Sleeter, 1997; Schofield, 1997).

- Let students know that racial or ethnic bias, including slurs, taunts, and jokes, will not be tolerated in the classroom or in the school. Institute consequences to enforce this standard.

- Help all students to value their own and others' cultural heritages and contributions to history and civilization. At the same time, avoid trivializing or stereotyping cultures merely in terms of ethnic foods and holidays (Boutte & McCormick, 1993; Karp, 1998). Because the United States is becoming a mosaic rather than a melting pot (Janzen, 1994), students need more than ever to value diversity and to acquire a more substantive knowledge and appreciation of other ways of life (see J. A. Banks, 1995a; Grossman, 1995; Hu-Dehart, 1993).

- Decorate classrooms, hallways, and the library/media center with murals, bulletin boards, posters, artifacts, and other materials that are representative of the students in the class or school or of the other cultures being studied (Florida State Department of Education, 1990).

- Avoid resegregation. Tracking, or between-class ability grouping, tends to segregate high and low achievers; and because of historical and economic factors, minority-group students tend to be overrepresented in the ranks of low achievers. For this and other reasons, tracking should be avoided (Braddock & Slavin, 1992; Schofield, 1995a; Slavin, 1995b).

- Be sure that assignments are not offensive or frustrating to students of cultural minorities. For example, asking students to write about their Christmas experiences is inappropriate for non-Christian students (Florida State Department of Education, 1990).

- Provide structure for intergroup interaction. Proximity alone does not lead to social harmony among racially and ethnically different groups (Schofield, 1997). Students need opportunities to know one another as individuals and to work together toward common goals (Slavin, 1995a; Tamura, 1996). For example, students who participate in integrated sports and extracurricular activities are more likely than other students to have friends who are ethnically or racially different from themselves (Braddock, Dawkins, & Wilson, 1995; Slavin, 1995b).

- Use cooperative learning, which has been shown to improve relations across racial and ethnic lines (Schofield, 1995a; Slavin, 1995a). The positive effects of cooperative learning experiences often outlast the teams or groups themselves and may extend to relationships outside of school. Cooperative learning contributes to both achievement and social harmony (Johnson & Johnson, 1998; Slavin, 1995a) and can increase the participation of minority children (Cohen & Lotan, 1995).

SELF-CHECK

Define the terms *race, ethnic group,* and *minority group.* List cultural, social, economic, and historical factors that help to account for achievement differences among students. Assess the effectiveness of school desegregation.

HOW DO LANGUAGE DIFFERENCES AND BILINGUAL PROGRAMS AFFECT STUDENT ACHIEVEMENT?

As recently as the early 1980s, only 13.3 percent of all U.S. children aged 5 to 14 were from families in which the primary language spoken was not English. This segment of the school-age population is increasing rapidly, however. Projections forecast that by 2026, 25 percent of all students will come from homes in which the primary language is not English (Garcia, 1994; General Accounting Office, 1994). Most of these students' families speak Spanish, and they are located primarily in the Southwest and in the New York City, Miami, and Chicago areas (Arias, 1986; Garcia, 1992). However, many students speak any of dozens of Asian, African, or European languages. The term **language minority** is used for all such students, and **limited English proficient (LEP)** and *English language learners (ELL)* are terms used for the much smaller number who have not yet attained an adequate level of English to succeed in an English-only program. These students are learning **English as a second language (ESL)** and may attend ESL classes in their schools.

Students with limited English proficiency present a dilemma to the educational system (Ovando, 1997; Rothstein, 1998). Clearly, those who have limited proficiency in English need to learn English to function effectively in U.S. society. However, until they are proficient in English, should they be taught math or social studies in their first language or in English? Should they be taught to read in their first language? These questions are not just pedagogical; they have political and cultural significance that has provoked emotional debate. One issue is that many Latino parents want their children to be instructed in the Spanish language and culture to maintain their group identity and pride (Cline, 1998; E. E. Garcia, 1993). Other parents whose language is neither English nor Spanish often feel the same way. Many educators and others who are concerned with the problem believe that the students should be fully integrated into U.S. society and fear that bilingualism and biculturalism will be detrimental to our country's melting pot tradition (see Suhor, 1989).

Bilingual Education

The term **bilingual education** refers to programs for students who are acquiring English that teach the students in their first language part of the time while English is being learned. The rationale for bilingual education was given by the U.S. Commission on Civil Rights (1975):

> Lack of English proficiency is the major reason for language minority students' academic failure. Bilingual education is intended to ensure that students do not fall behind in subject matter content while they are learning English, as they would likely do in an all-English program, since limited English proficiency will no longer impede their academic progress.

Bilingual programs vary enormously in content and quality (Faltis & Hudelson, 1998). At a minimum they include instruction in ESL for students with limited English proficiency. Typically, bilingual programs offer some instruction in Spanish. (By far, the largest number of bilingual programs in the United States are in Spanish, so the examples in this section all refer to Spanish. However, the same general principles apply to bilingual programs in other languages.) The programs differ in the degree to which Latino culture is taught to all students (Darder,

language minority
In the United States, native speakers of any language other than English.

limited English proficient (LEP)
Possessing limited mastery of English.

English as a second language (ESL)
Subject taught in English classes and programs for students who are not native speakers of English.

bilingual education
Instructional program for students who speak little or no English in which some instruction is provided in the native language.

According to research, students such as these in a bilingual program will ultimately achieve in English as well as or better than their peers who are taught only in English. Why do you think this is true?

Torres, & Gutierrez, 1997). Also, a few bilingual programs teach Spanish to all students, whether or not their primary language is Spanish (Gersten & Woodward, 1995; Jimenez, García, & Pearson, 1995). Programs in which students from different language backgrounds learn one another's languages are called two-way bilingual programs, or double immersion (Christian, 1996; Stipek, Ryan, & Alarcon, 1998; Thomas & Collier, 1998). Two-way bilingual programs are expanding as parents of English-dominant students are realizing the importance of bilingualism in an increasingly multilingual world (Christian, Montone, Lindholm, & Carranza, 1997).

Most bilingual programs are transitional programs designed to support students in Spanish until they can make it in the regular classroom in English. Today, for example, many bilingual programs begin teaching students with limited English proficiency in their primary language in kindergarten but move them to English-only classes by the end of the second or third grade. However, in a small proportion of schools, students continue to receive some instruction in their primary language until the sixth grade. Students may receive anywhere from 30 minutes to several hours of instruction per week in their primary language, but at least half of their instruction will be in English from the very beginning (Faltis & Hudelson, 1998; Garcia, 1992; Gersten, Baker, & Marks, 1998).

Effectiveness of Bilingual Programs

Reviews of research focusing on the best-designed studies of good-quality bilingual programs have found that children in bilingual programs ultimately achieve in English as well as or better than children taught only in English (Hakuta & McLaughlin, 1996; August & Hakuta, 1997; Willig, 1985; Wong-Fillmore & Valadez, 1986). Researchers have rarely found bilingual programs to be harmful to students in their English development, and bilingual instruction has a clear positive impact on their reading performance in their first language. Bilingual education can also increase students' self-esteem (Wright & Taylor, 1995). But more research on this important topic is needed to identify the types of programs that are most likely to improve the achievement of language-minority students (see Lam, 1992).

Increasingly, research on bilingual education is focusing on the identification of effective forms of instruction for language-minority students rather than on the question of which is the best language of instruction (Fashola, Slavin, Calderón, & Durán, 1996; Goldenberg, 1996; Secada et al., 1998). Cooperative learning programs have been particularly effective both in improving the outcomes of Spanish reading instruction and in helping bilingual students make a successful transition to English-only instruction in the upper elementary grades (Calderón, 1994; Calderón, Tinajero, & Hertz-Lazarowitz, 1992; Durán, 1994). In particular, a program called Success for All, which combines cooperative learning with one-to-one tutorial for primary-grades students, family support services, and other elements, has had positive effects on the Spanish and English reading of children in bilingual programs (Dianda & Flaherty, 1995; Slavin & Madden, 1998).

Bilingualism itself has not been found to interfere with performance in either language. In fact, Canadian studies have found bilingualism to increase achievement in areas other than the language studied (Cummins, 1998). This evidence has been cited as a reason to promote bilingual education for all students. The United States is one of the few countries in the world in which most students graduate from high school knowing only their own language (Hakuta & McLaughlin, 1996).

Bilingual education has many problems, however. One is the lack of teachers who are themselves completely bilingual. This is a particular problem for bilingual education in the languages of the most recent immigrants, such as those from Southeast Asia. A second problem is the difficulty of the transition from the bilingual program to the English-only mainstream program. Third, the goals of bilingual education sometimes conflict with those of desegregation by removing language-minority students from classes containing European American or African American students. Despite all these problems, the alternative to bilingual education—leaving students in the regular class with no support or with part-time instruction in English as a second language (sometimes known as the sink-or-swim approach)—has not been found to be beneficial for students' English language development and risks allowing the language-minority child to fail in school. For example, language-minority children are sometimes assigned to special education because of academic difficulties that are in fact due to lack of proficiency in English (Council of Chief State School Officers, 1990).

Recently, there has been a movement to abandon bilingual education in favor of English-only instruction. In California, which has the largest number of language-minority students in the United States, a referendum called Proposition 227 was passed in 1998 (Schnaiberg, 1998). It mandates a maximum of one year for students with limited English proficiency to receive intensive assistance in learning English. After that, children are expected to be in mainstream classes. This legislation has reduced but not eliminated bilingual education in California, as parents may still apply for waivers to have their children taught in their first language. However, Proposition 227 has had a chilling effect on bilingual education, particularly because of the margin of voter approval (61 percent in favor) and because of the fact that many Latino voters (about 37 percent) also voted in favor of the proposition.

SELF-CHECK

Define *language minority* and *bilingual education*. Make a chart comparing the many forms bilingual programs can take. According to research, which approaches to bilingual education are most effective? Which are least effective?

WHAT IS MULTICULTURAL EDUCATION?

In recent years, multicultural education has become a much-discussed topic in U.S. education. Definitions of **multicultural education** vary broadly. The simplest definitions emphasize including non-European perspectives in the curriculum; for example, the works of African, Latino, and Native American authors in English curricula, teaching about Columbus from the point of view of Native Americans, and teaching more about the cultures and contributions of non-Western societies (Hilliard, 1991/92). J. A. Banks (1993) defines multicultural education more broadly. He sees the term as encompassing all policies and practices schools might use to improve educational outcomes not only for students of different ethnic, social class, and religious backgrounds, but also for students of different genders and exceptionalities (e.g., children who have mental retardation, hearing loss, or vision loss or who are gifted). J. A. Banks (1993) summarizes this definition as follows:

> Multicultural education is an idea stating that all students, regardless of the groups to which they belong, such as those related to gender, ethnicity, race, culture, social class, religion, or exceptionality, should experience educational equality in the schools. (p. 25)

Dimensions of Multicultural Education

Banks (1995b) discusses five key dimensions of multicultural education (see Figure 4.3).

Content integration is teachers' use of examples, data, and information from a variety of cultures. This is what most people think of as multicultural education: teaching about different cultures and about contributions made by individuals from diverse cultures, inclusion in the curriculum of works by minority-group members and women, and the like (see Siccone, 1995; Sleeter, 1995).

Knowledge construction refers to teachers helping children "understand how knowledge is created and how it is influenced by the racial, ethnic, and social-class positions of individuals and groups" (Banks, 1995b, p. 4). For example, students might be asked to write a history of the early colonization of America from the perspectives of Indians or African Americans to learn how the knowledge we take as given is in fact influenced by our own origins and points of view (see Cortés, 1995; Gordon, 1995).

Prejudice reduction is a critical goal of multicultural education. Prejudice reduction involves both development of positive relationships among students of different ethnic backgrounds (Schofield, 1995a; Slavin, 1995b) and development of more democratic and tolerant attitudes toward others (Banks, 1995c).

The term **equity pedagogy** refers to the use of teaching techniques that facilitate the academic success of students from different ethnic and social class groups. For example, there is evidence that members of some ethnic groups, especially Mexican Americans and African Americans, learn best with active and cooperative methods (Boykin, 1994a, 1994b; Kagan et al., 1985; Losey, 1995).

An **empowering school culture** is one in which school organization and practices are conducive to the academic and emotional growth of all students. A school with such a culture might, for example, eliminate tracking or ability grouping, increase inclusion (and reduce labeling) of students with special needs, try to keep all students on a path leading to higher education, and consistently show high

---

multicultural education
Education that teaches the value of cultural diversity.

content integration
Teachers' use of examples, data, and other information from a variety of cultures.

knowledge construction
Helping students understand how the knowledge we take in is influenced by our origins and points of view.

prejudice reduction
A critical goal of multicultural education; involves development of positive relationships and tolerant attitudes among students of different backgrounds.

equity pedagogy
Teaching techniques that facilitate the academic success of students from different ethnic and social class groups.

empowering school culture
A school culture in which the institution's organization and practices are conducive to the academic and emotional growth of all students.

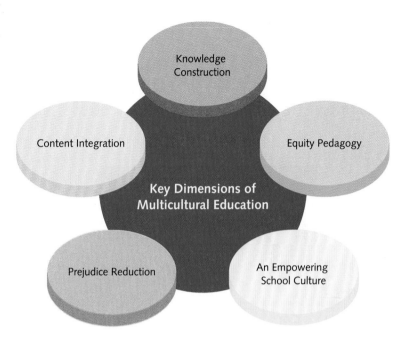

FIGURE 4.3 ● Five Key Dimensions of Multicultural Education
From James A. Banks, "Historical Development, Dimensions, and Practice." Reprinted with the permission of Macmillan General Reference USA, a division of Ahsuog, Inc., from *Handbook of Research on Multicultural Education* by James A. Banks, Editor in Chief, Cherry A. McGee Banks, Associate Editor. Copyright © 1995 by Simon & Schuster Macmillan.

expectations. An excellent example of an empowering school culture is the AVID project (Swanson, Mehan, & Hubbard, 1995), which places at-risk minority-group students in college preparatory classes and provides them with tutors and other assistance to help them succeed in a demanding curriculum.

The first step in multicultural education is for teachers, administrators, and other school staff to learn about the cultures from which their children come and to carefully examine all the policies, practices, and curricula used in the school to identify any areas of possible bias (e.g., teaching only about European and European American culture or history). Books by J. A. Banks (1994), Banks and Banks (1995), Baruth and Manning (1992), Hernandez (1990), and Siccone (1995) are good places to start. These and other books identify some of the characteristics of various cultures and teaching strategies and materials that are appropriate to each. Multicultural education should pervade all aspects of school life (Sleeter, 1995).

SELF-CHECK

Define *multicultural education*. List the five key dimensions of multicultural education. Give an example of each. Reread the vignette at the beginning of this chapter. How should Marva and John proceed? How might multicultural education help the two teachers to resolve their concerns about the Thanksgiving pageant?

HOW DO GENDER AND GENDER BIAS AFFECT STUDENTS' SCHOOL EXPERIENCES?

A child's sex is a visible, permanent attribute. Cross-cultural research indicates that gender roles are among the first that individuals learn and that all societies treat males differently from females. Therefore, gender-role or sex-role behavior is

TEACHERS IN ACTION

How do you foster social acceptance and multicultural awareness?

Ricardo C. Morris
Teacher, Grades 9–12
Hixson High School
Chattanooga, Tennessee

It was the Friday afternoon pep rally. Sometimes the students get a little overenthusiastic. In the past they have thrown toilet paper. But this rally took a different turn. Our school is like any other school. We have our in crowd and our out crowd—all of whom stay within their own little groups. During the pep rally, the black students separated themselves by all sitting in one area of the gym. The problem started when some white students brought out a Confederate flag. A group of black students began to confront the students with the flag. Thanks to a quick-thinking assistant principal, the trouble was quickly averted. Needless to say, tension at the school was at an all-time high.

In my English classes I took advantage of an opportunity not only to teach literature but also to attempt to ease the racial tension that existed. We began reading *Roll of Thunder, Hear My Cry,* by Mildred Taylor. I felt it would be appropriate because racism of the 1930s is shown through the segregation of the schools, stores, and churches. Before we read, we had a discussion of discrimination. I tried to avoid focusing on black and white but discussed other targets of discrimination, such as women, overweight people, shy people, short people, smart people, non-English-speaking people, and people with labels. I asked whether students discriminated against people in these groups or were members of the groups themselves. Answers varied, but by the end of the discussion the students agreed that any type of discrimination is wrong.

As an educator, I feel a need to shape not only the minds of youth but also the character. Educators have a responsibility to help stop discrimination.

Vicki Olsen
English Instructor
Bemidji High School
Bemidji, Minnesota

Nestled between three of the largest Ojibwe reservations in Minnesota, my high school has come full circle in recognizing its cultural diversity. We have a multicultural Awareness Club, a Native American Club, and other groups in the school that promote diversity. But what pulls us together? Classroom teachers still handle history and literature with kid gloves. How does one introduce a Native American story? When this question was posed to Jim Bedeau, a White Earth Ojibwe, he said, "Why do you have to say, 'This is an Indian story'? Why not say, 'This is a story about a little girl who . . . '? Don't teach separation. If nothing in the story connects for you, you don't need it."

Searching for unity in diversity is my goal in an assignment I designed for one of my English classes. After a lesson on aspects of culture all humans share, the class forms two groups to generate hypothetical cultures that include these universal elements. Each group creates artifacts that represent or illustrate the culture and buries these artifacts somewhere in the country. Then each group goes on an archaeological dig to recover the other group's artifacts and use them to interpret that fantasy culture. This requires creative cooperation and bridges cultural barriers in the classroom, since all students must think about constructing new cultures.

Jim Bedeau and other Ojibwes believe that everyone is born in balance. It is only as people face decisions that this delicate balance is continually maintained or destroyed. "We are born with love," Bedeau says, "and we learn to hate." With this culture project, students learn the fragility of this balance, and I can only hope they will carry that understanding with them when they walk out of the classroom.

learned behavior. However, the range of roles occupied by males and females across cultures is broad. What is considered natural behavior for each gender is based more on cultural belief than on biological necessity. Nevertheless, the extent to which biological differences and gender socialization affect behavioral patterns and achievement is still a much-debated topic. The consensus of a large body of research is that no matter what the inherent biological differences, many of the observed differences between males and females can be clearly linked to differences in early socialization experiences (Feingold, 1992; Grossman & Grossman, 1994).

Do Males and Females Think and Learn Differently?

The question of gender differences in intelligence or academic achievement has been debated for centuries, and the issue has taken on particular importance since the early 1970s. The most important thing to keep in mind about this debate is that no responsible researcher has ever claimed that any male–female differences on any measure of intellectual ability are large in comparison to the amount of variability within each sex. In other words, even in areas in which true gender differences are suspected, these differences are so small and so variable that they have few practical consequences (Fennema, Carpenter, Jacobs, Franke, & Levi, 1998; Sadker, Sadker, & Long, 1997). Far more important are differences caused by cultural expectations and norms. For example, 12th-grade girls score significantly lower than boys on the quantitative section of the Scholastic Assessment Test (SAT) (Gallagher & De Lisi, 1994) and on Advanced Placement tests in these subjects (Stumpf & Stanley, 1996). There may be a biological basis for such a difference, but none has been proven (see Feingold, 1992; Friedman, 1995). The most important cause is that females in our society are discouraged from studying mathematics and therefore take many fewer math courses than males do. In fact, as females have begun to take more math courses over the past two decades, the gender gap on the SAT and

How does this photo depict changes in U.S. culture about appropriate gender roles? What are some other examples of these changes? What impact will these changes likely have on you as a teacher?

on other measures has been steadily diminishing (Maple & Stage, 1991; Murphy, 1994; National Center for Education Statistics, 1997).

Bearing these cautions in mind, note that studies generally find that males score higher than females on tests of general knowledge, mechanical reasoning, and mental rotations; females score higher on language measures and on attention and planning tasks (Warrick & Naglieri, 1993). There are no male–female differences in general verbal ability, arithmetic skills, abstract reasoning, spatial visualization, or memory span (Fennema et al., 1998; Friedman, 1995; Halpern, 1994). There is an interesting argument about variability of performance in certain areas. For example, Feingold (1992) has argued that males are more variable than females in quantitative reasoning—that is, that there are more very high-achieving males and more very low-achieving males than there are females in either category. Studies of students who are extremely gifted in mathematics consistently find a substantially higher number of males than females in this category (e.g., Mills, Ablard, & Stumpf, 1993). However, there is still a lively debate about the idea that males are more variable than females in intellectual abilities (Hedges & Friedman, 1993; Noddings, 1992; Tavris, 1992).

In school grades, females start out with an advantage over males and maintain this advantage into high school. Even in math and science, in which females score somewhat lower on tests, females still get better grades in class (Sadker, Sadker, & Steindam, 1989). Despite this, high school males tend to overestimate their skills in language and math (as measured by standardized tests), while females underestimate their skills (Bornholt, Goodnow, & Cooney, 1994). In elementary school, males are much more likely than females to have reading problems (Smith, 1994) and are much more likely to have learning disabilities or emotional disorders (Smith & Luckasson, 1995).

Sex-Role Stereotyping and Gender Bias

If there are so few genetically based differences between males and females, why do so many behavioral differences exist? These behavioral differences originate from different experiences, including reinforcement by adults for different types of behavior.

Male and female babies have traditionally been treated differently from the time they are born. The wrapping of the infant in either a pink or a blue blanket symbolizes the variations in experience that typically greet the child from birth onward. In early studies, adults described boy or girl babies wrapped in blue blankets as being more active than the same babies wrapped in pink. Other masculine traits were also ascribed to those wrapped in blue (Baxter, 1994). Although gender bias awareness has begun to have some impact on child-rearing practices, children do begin to make gender distinctions and have gender preferences by around the age of 3 or 4. Thus, children enter school having been socialized into appropriate gender-role behavior for their age in relation to community expectations (Eisenberg, Martin, & Fabes, 1996). Differences in approved gender roles between boys and girls tend to be much stronger in low SES families than in high SES families (Flanagan, 1993).

sex-role behavior
Socially approved behavior associated with one gender as opposed to the other.

Early socialization into this kind of approved **sex-role behavior** continues throughout life. Schools contribute to this socialization. Though interactions between socialization experiences and achievement are complex and it is difficult to make generalizations, schools differentiate between the sexes in a number of ways. In general, males receive more attention from their teachers than females do (Bailey, 1993). Males receive more disapproval and blame from their teachers than females do; but they also engage in more interactions with their teachers in such areas as approval, instruction giving, and being listened to (Bailey, 1993; Sadker & Sadker, 1994). Teachers tend to punish females more promptly and explicitly for aggressive behavior than they do males. Torrance (1986) found that the creative behavior of males was rewarded by teachers three times as often as that of females. Other differentiations are subtle, as when girls are directed to the house corner while boys are provided with blocks or when boys are given the drums to play in music class and girls are given the triangles.

Avoiding Gender Bias in Teaching

THEORY *into* **Practice**

"In my science class the teacher never calls on me, and I feel like I don't exist. The other night I had a dream that I vanished" (Sadker & Sadker, 1994). Unfortunately, the girl who complained of being ignored by her teacher is not alone. According to a national study undertaken by the American Association of University Women (1992), schools shortchange female students in a variety of ways, from ignoring instances of sexual harassment to interacting less frequently with females than with males and less frequently with African American females than with white females. Teachers tend to choose boys, boost the self-esteem of their male students, and select literature with male protagonists (Smith, Greenlaw, & Scott, 1987). The contributions and experiences of girls and women are still often ignored in textbooks, curricula, and standardized tests (Tetreault, 1997).

Teachers, usually without being aware of it, exhibit **gender bias** in classroom teaching in three principal ways: reinforcing gender stereotypes, maintaining sex separation, and treating males and females differently as students (see Grossman & Grossman, 1994; Horgan, 1995; Keating, 1994; Klein & Ortman, 1994; Laird, 1995; Sadker, Sadker, Fox, & Salata, 1994). These inequities can have negative consequences for boys as well as girls (Bailey, 1995).

Avoiding stereotypes. Teachers should avoid promoting sexual stereotypes. For example, they can assign jobs in the classroom without regard to gender, avoiding automatically appointing males as group leader and females as secretary, and can ask both males and females to help in physical activities. Teachers should also refrain from stating stereotypes, such as "Boys don't cry" and "Girls don't fight," and should avoid such terms as *tomboy*. Teachers should encourage students who show an interest in activities and careers that do not correspond to cultural stereotypes, such as a female who likes math and science (Sadker, Sadker, & Long, 1997).

Promoting integration. One factor that leads to gender stereotyping is the tendency for boys and girls (particularly in elementary school) to have few friends of the other sex and to engage mostly in activities with members of their own sex. Teachers sometimes encourage this by having boys and girls line up separately, assigning them to sex-segregated tables, and organizing separate sports activities for males and females. As a result, interaction between boys and girls in schools is less frequent than between students of the same sex (Lockheed, 1984). However, in classes in which cross-sex collaboration is encouraged, children have less stereotyped views of the abilities of males and females (Klein, 1994).

Treating females and males equally. Too often, teachers do not treat males and females equally. Observational studies of classroom interactions have found that teachers interact more with boys than with girls and ask boys more questions, especially more abstract questions (Sadker et al., 1997). In one study, researchers

gender bias
Stereotyped views and differential treatment of males and females, often favoring one gender over the other.

showed teachers videotapes of classroom scenes and asked them whether boys or girls participated more. Most teachers responded that the girls talked more, even though in fact the boys participated more than the girls by a ratio of 3 to 1 (Sadker et al., 1997). The researchers interpreted this finding as indicating that teachers expect females to participate less and thus see low rates of participation as normal. Teachers must be careful to allow all students equal opportunities to participate in class, to take leadership roles, and to engage in all kinds of activities (Horgan, 1995; Klein, 1994).

SELF-CHECK

Use research findings to support the view that cultural expectations concerning gender outweigh any actual differences as determinants of student achievement. Give specific examples of gender bias commonly found in classrooms. What can teachers do to avoid gender bias?

HOW DO STUDENTS DIFFER IN INTELLIGENCE AND LEARNING STYLES?

Intelligence is one of those words that everyone thinks they understand until you ask them to define it. At one level, **intelligence** can be defined as a general aptitude for learning or an ability to acquire and use knowledge or skills. However, even experts on this topic do not agree in their definitions; in a survey of 24 experts by Sternberg and Detterman (1986), definitions varied widely. A consensus definition expressed by Snyderman and Rothman (1987) is that intelligence is the ability to deal with abstractions, to solve problems, and to learn.

The biggest problem comes when we ask whether there is such a thing as general aptitude (Snow, 1992; Sternberg, 1996). Many people are terrific at calculus but couldn't write a good essay or paint a good picture if their lives depended on it. Some people can walk into a room full of strangers and immediately figure out the relationships and feelings among them; others may never learn this skill. Clearly, individuals vary in their aptitude for learning any specific type of knowledge or skill taught in a specific way. A hundred students attending a lecture on a topic they knew nothing about beforehand will all walk away with different amounts and kinds of learning, and aptitude for that particular content and that particular teaching method is one important factor in explaining these differences. The student who learned the most from the lecture would be likely also to learn very well from other lectures on similar topics. But would this student also learn the most if the lecture were on a different topic or if the same material were presented through hands-on experiences or in small groups?

The concept of intelligence has been discussed since before the time of the ancient Greeks, but the scientific study of this topic really began with the work of Alfred Binet, who devised the first measure of intelligence in 1904. The French government asked Binet to find a way to identify children who were likely to need special help in their schooling. His measure assessed a broad range of skills and performances but produced a single score, called **intelligence quotient (IQ),** which was set up so that the average French child would have an IQ of 100.

intelligence
General aptitude for learning, often measured by the ability to deal with abstractions and to solve problems.

intelligence quotient (IQ)
An intelligence test score that for people of average intelligence should be near 100.

CONNECTIONS
For more on the measurement of IQ, see Chapter 14, page 505.

Definitions of Intelligence

Binet's work greatly advanced the science of intelligence assessment, but it also began to establish the idea that intelligence was a single thing—that there were "smart" people who could be expected to do well in a broad range of learning situations. Ever since Binet, debate has raged about this issue. In 1927 Charles Spearman claimed that while there were, of course, variations in a person's abilities from task to task, there was a general intelligence factor, or "g," that existed across all learning situations. Is there really one intelligence, as Spearman suggested, or are there many distinct intelligences?

The evidence in favor of "g" is that abilities are correlated with each other. Individuals who are good at learning one thing are likely, on the average, to be good at learning other things. The correlations are consistent enough for us to say that there are not a thousand completely separate intelligences, but they are not nearly consistent enough to allow us to say that there is only one general intelligence (Gustafsson, 1994; Lohman, 1989). In recent years, much of the debate about intelligence has focused on deciding how many distinct types of intelligence there are and describing each. For example, Sternberg (1990; 1997) describes 3 types of intellectual ability: intelligence, wisdom, and creativity. Guilford (1988) proposes 180 types of intelligence: 6 types of mental operations (e.g., thinking, memory, and creativity) times 5 types of content (e.g., visual, auditory, and verbal content) times 6 types of products (e.g., relations and implications). Gardner and Hatch (1989) describe 8 **multiple intelligences.** These are listed and defined in Table 4.4.

> **multiple intelligences**
> In Gardner's theory of intelligence, a person's eight separate abilities: logical/mathematical, linguistic, musical, naturalist, spatial, bodily/kinesthetic, interpersonal, and intrapersonal.

TABLE 4.4

The Eight Intelligences

INTELLIGENCE	END STATES	CORE COMPONENTS
Logical/mathematical	Scientist, mathematician	Sensitivity to, and capacity to discern, logical or numerical patterns; ability to handle long chains of reasoning
Linguistic	Poet, journalist	Sensitivity to the sounds, rhythms, and meanings of words; sensitivity to the different functions of language
Musical	Composer, violinist	Abilities to produce and appreciate rhythm, pitch, and timbre; appreciation of the forms of musical expressiveness
Naturalist	Naturalist, botanist, hunter	Sensitivity to natural objects, like plants and animals; making fine sensory discriminations
Spatial	Navigator, sculptor	Capacities to perceive the visual–spatial world accurately and to perform transformations on one's initial perceptions
Bodily/kinesthetic	Dancer, athlete	Abilities to control one's body movements and to handle objects skillfully
Interpersonal	Therapist, salesperson	Capacities to discern and respond appropriately to the moods, temperaments, motivations, and desires of other people
Intrapersonal	Person with detailed, accurate self-knowledge	Access to one's own feelings and the ability to discriminate among them and draw on them to guide behavior; knowledge of one's own strengths, weaknesses, desires, and intelligences

Source: From H. Gardner and T. Hatch, "Multiple Intelligences Go to School," *Educational Researcher,* *18*(8), p. 6. Copyright © 1989 by the American Educational Research Association. Adapted by permission of the publisher and the authors.

The precise number of intelligences is not important for educators. What is important is the idea that good or poor performance in one area in no way guarantees similar performance in another. Teachers must avoid thinking about children as smart or not smart, since there are many ways to be smart. Unfortunately, schools have traditionally recognized only a narrow set of performances, creating a neat hierarchy of students primarily in terms of what Gardner calls linguistic and logical/ mathematical skills (only two of his eight intelligences). If schools want all children to be smart, they must use a broader range of activities and reward a broader range of performances than they have in the past.

THEORY *into* **Practice**

Multiple Intelligences

Gardner's theory of multiple intelligences implies that concepts should be taught in a variety of ways that call on many types of intelligence (Campbell, Campbell, & Dickinson, 1996; Hatch, 1997; Krechevsky, Hoer, & Gardner, 1995). To illustrate this, Armstrong (1994) gives the following example of eight ways to teach Boyle's Law to secondary students.

- Students are provided with a verbal definition of Boyle's Law: "For a fixed mass and temperature of gas, the pressure is inversely proportional to the volume." They discuss the definition. [Linguistic]
- Students are given a formula that describes Boyle's Law: $P \times V = K$. They solve specific problems connected to it. [Logical/mathematical]
- Students are given a metaphor or visual image for Boyle's Law: "Imagine that you have a boil on your hand that you start to squeeze. As you squeeze it, the pressure builds. The more you squeeze, the higher the pressure, until the boil finally bursts and pus spurts out all over your hand!" [Spatial]
- Students do the following experiment: They breathe air into their mouths so that their cheeks puff up slightly. Then they put all the air into one side of their mouth (less volume) and indicate whether pressure goes up or down (it goes up); then they're asked to release the air in both sides of their mouth (more volume) and asked to indicate whether pressure has gone up or down (it goes down). [Bodily/kinesthetic]
- Students rhythmically repeat the following musical mnemonic: [Musical]
  When the volume goes down
  The pressure goes up
  The blood starts to boil
  And a scream erupts
  "I need more space
  Or I'm going to frown"
  The volume goes up
  And the pressure goes down
- Students become "molecules" of air in a "container" (a clearly defined corner of the classroom). They move at a constant rate (temperature) and cannot leave the container (constant mass). Gradually, the size of the container is reduced as two volunteers holding a piece of yarn representing one side of the container start moving it in on the "molecules." The smaller the space, the more pressure (i.e., bumping into each other) is observed; the greater the space, the less pressure is observed. [Interpersonal, bodily/kinesthetic]
- Students do lab experiments that measure air pressure in sealed containers and chart pressure against volume [Logical/mathematical, bodily/kinesthetic]

According to Gardner's theory of multiple intelligences, which of the eight intelligences might these students use to learn? As a teacher, how would you vary your lessons to address student differences in learning style?

- Students are asked about times in their lives when they were "under pressure": "Did you feel like you had a lot of space?" (Typical answer: lots of pressure/not much space.) Then students are asked about times when they felt little pressure (little pressure/lots of space). Students' experiences are related to Boyle's Law. [Intrapersonal]

Few lessons will contain parts that correspond to all types of intelligence, but a key recommendation of multiple-intelligence theory for the classroom is that teachers seek to include a variety of presentation modes in each lesson to expand the number of students who are likely to succeed (Campbell, Campbell, & Dickinson, 1996; Gardner, 1995).

Origins of Intelligence

The origins of intelligence have been debated for decades. Some psychologists (such as Herrnstein & Murray, 1994; Jensen, 1980) hold that intelligence is overwhelmingly a product of heredity—that children's intelligence is largely determined by that of their parents and is set the day they are conceived. Others (such as Gordon & Bhattacharyya, 1994; Plomin, 1989; Rifkin, 1998) just as vehemently hold that intelligence is shaped mostly by factors in a person's social environment, such as the amount a child is read to and talked to. Most investigators agree that both heredity and environment play an important part in intelligence (Scarr & McCartney, 1983; Schiff, Duyme, Dumaret, & Tomkiewicz, 1982). It is clear that children of high-achieving parents are, on the average, more likely to be high achievers themselves, but this is due as much to the home environment created by high-achieving parents as to genetics (Turkheimer, 1994). French studies of children of low-SES parents adopted into high-SES families find strong positive effects on the children's IQs compared to nonadopted children raised in low-SES families (Capron & Duyme, 1991; Schiff & Lewontin, 1986). One important piece of evidence in favor of the environmental view is that schooling itself clearly affects IQ

The Intentional Teacher

● **Using What You Know about Student Diversity to Improve Teaching and Learning**

Intentional teachers view student diversity as a rich resource. They learn about their students' home lives, cultures, languages, and strengths, and they value each student as an individual. Intentional teachers examine data from their classrooms and question their own practices, guarding against the possibility that their perspectives may inadvertently limit students' success. Intentional teachers use what they know about their own practices and their particular students to improve the quality of education for all.

1 What am I trying to accomplish?

Teachers need to examine the influence of their own cultural perspectives on the expectations they hold for students. Ask yourself, "Do my goals reflect only the values of the middle class?"

> You curb your impulse to give stickers to the first five of your third-graders who earn 100 percent on their multiplication facts, deciding that your appreciation of individual competition may not be shared by all.

Many educators feel that educational goals should reflect, at least to some extent, the community within which children are educated. Ask yourself, "How can I revise my goals to better reflect the needs, values, and interests of my students and their families?"

> You begin your current issues class with an informal discussion about what students would like to learn and about students' definitions of success.

Teachers also need to examine their goals to ensure that they encourage success for all students. No matter your grade level, you may ask:

> How can I revise my goals to address students' different strengths?

Are my expectations for students equally high, with no variation for students' gender or socioeconomic status?

Is there an achievement gap for minority-group students in my setting? How can my goals help to close that achievement gap?

2 What are my students' relevant experiences and needs?

Intentional teachers learn about their students and draw on information about the students' home lives and community resources to plan their instruction. What is your understanding of students' cultures and community? You may want to gather information related to such questions as:

> What are the values of the home regarding, for example, intellectual achievement? Obedience?

> What is the overall quality of the school? Is the school safe? Is it focused on academic success? An important social force in the community?

The home experience can serve as a resource that enhances school experiences. Ask yourself, "What experiences and strengths have my students gathered outside of school that can foster their learning?"

> Although you provide instruction in English, you look for ways to value students' home language, reinforcing the idea that knowing two languages is an asset.

> You carefully observe your seventh-graders' "street smarts," which help them adjust easily to different conditions, and you remind yourself to draw from those "smarts" as you teach students to interact in academic and workplace settings.

---

scores. A review by Ceci (1991) found that the experience of being in school has a strong and systematic impact on IQ. For example, studies of Dutch children who entered school late because of World War II showed significant declines in IQ as a result, although their IQs increased when they finally entered school. A study of the children of mothers with mental retardation in inner-city Milwaukee (Garber, 1988) found that a program of infant stimulation and high-quality preschool could raise children's IQs substantially, and these gains were maintained at least through the end of elementary school. Studies of the Abecedarian program, which combined infant stimulation, child enrichment, and parent assistance, also found lasting effects of early instruction on IQ (Campbell & Ramey, 1994, 1995). This and other evidence supports the idea that IQ is not a fixed, unchangeable attribute of individuals but can change as individuals respond to changes in their environment (Cardellichio & Field, 1997; Lohman, 1993). Further, some evidence indicates that

3 What approaches and materials are available to help me challenge every student?

Tapping into students' prior knowledge helps students connect new information meaningfully to their own experiences.

> You and your sixth-graders construct a chart to display what they already know about the solar system. You plan your science unit to build on their previous knowledge.

Traditional schooling practices tend to reinforce patterns of inequity found in the larger society. Modify your practices to make knowledge accessible to each student.

> You vary grouping structures in your life science class so that students work in whole-class, individual, and flexible small groups over the semester.

> You employ principles of sheltered instruction, which makes grade-level content accessible to all, for your English literature students. For example, you provide graphic organizers of the literature. You teach just a small number of concepts, but you emphasize conceptual understanding. You bring in real examples of the items described in your readings.

> In your fourth-grade Gold Rush unit, you include a variety of ways for students to build and display their knowledge. Some examples include map reading, listening to historic recreations of important events, and simulation activities that teach the unit's concepts.

Teachers can assist students in mastering skills that will help them succeed in mainstream culture.

> To help students learn to manage their time and pace themselves in long-term assignments, you provide daily check-off sheets and a weekly reporting format for their semester reports.

Effective teachers work as part of an educational team. Draw upon the strengths that can come from teachers' and parents' working together.

You survey parents about relevant summer projects. To help students maintain academic gains, you help them acquire library cards and suggest books for them to read over vacation. You give them each a journal and invite them—and their parents!—to write to you.

4 How will I know whether and when to change my strategy or modify my instruction?

When students feel accepted, they are more likely to voice their questions and uncertainties. Create an atmosphere that encourages risk taking and a sense of community.

> Your sixth-graders stare at you blankly through your lesson on subtracting fractions with unlike denominators. The next day, you return and share your analysis of where your lesson went wrong, laughing at the lesson's shortcomings and thereby modeling the willingness to admit and learn from a mistake.

Frequently invite students to provide feedback on your teaching.

> You invite students in your physics classes to assess your teaching through a variety of measures such as journal writings, "report cards," and informal discussions.

5 What information will I accept as evidence that my students and I are experiencing success?

Collect information on your teaching to ensure that your practices are equitable. An observer may gather information, or you may tape your teaching for later analysis. Key questions may include:

> Do I give equal time to interacting with males and females?

> Do I praise and admonish students for the same types of behaviors, no matter their group?

> To the extent appropriate, do I use the classroom as a forum for students to question mainstream perspectives and existing conditions? To encourage social improvement?

IQ can be directly changed by programs designed for this purpose (Adams, 1989; Feuerstein & Kozulin, 1995; Lohman, 1995; Prawat, 1991).

Intelligence, whether general or specific, is only one of many factors that influence the amount children are likely to learn in a given lesson or course. It is probably much less important than prior knowledge (the amount the student knew about the course beforehand), motivation, and the quality and nature of instruction. Intelligence does become important at the extremes, as it is a critical issue in identifying students who have mental retardation or those who are gifted; but in the middle range, where most students fall, other factors are more important. IQ testing has very frequently been misused in education, especially when it has been used to assign students inappropriately to special education or to tracks or ability groups (Hilliard, 1994). Actual performance is far more important than IQ and is more directly susceptible to being influenced by teachers and schools.

CONNECTIONS

For a description of studies indicating that IQ can be directly changed by certain programs, see Chapter 8, page 280.

Are these science students more likely to have a field-dependent or a field-independent learning style?

Theories of Learning Styles

Just as students have different personalities, they also have different ways of learning. For example, think about how you learn the names of people you meet. Do you learn a name better if you see it written down? If so, you may be a visual learner, one who learns best by seeing or reading. If you learn a name better by hearing it, you may be an auditory learner. Of course, we all learn in many ways, but some of us learn better in some ways than in others (Hodgin & Wooliscroft, 1997; McCarthy, 1997). Students with learning disabilities may have great difficulty learning in one way even if they have no trouble learning in another.

There are several other differences in **learning styles** that educational psychologists have studied. One has to do with **field dependence** versus **field independence** (Kogan, 1994). Field-dependent individuals tend to see patterns as a whole and have difficulty separating out specific aspects of a situation or pattern; field-independent people are more able to see the parts that make up a large pattern. Field-dependent people tend to be more oriented toward people and social relationships than are field-independent people; for example, they tend to be better at recalling such social information as conversations and relationships, to work best in groups, and to prefer such subjects as history and literature. Field-independent people are more likely to do well with numbers, science, and problem-solving tasks (Wapner & Demick, 1991; Witkin & Goodenough, 1981).

Students may also vary in preferences for different learning environments or conditions. For example, Dunn and Dunn (1987) found that students differ in preferences about such things as the amount of lighting, hard or soft seating, quiet or noisy surroundings, and working alone or with peers. These differences can predict to some extent which learning environments will be most effective for each child.

Aptitude–Treatment Interactions

Given the well-documented differences in learning styles and preferences, it would seem logical that different styles of teaching would have different impacts on different learners; yet this commonsense proposition has been difficult to demonstrate conclusively. Studies that have attempted to match teaching styles to learning styles have

---

CONNECTIONS

For more on students with learning disabilities, see Chapter 12, page 413.

---

learning styles
Orientations for approaching learning tasks and processing information in certain ways.

field dependence
Cognitive style in which patterns are perceived as a whole.

field independence
Cognitive style in which separate parts of a pattern are perceived and analyzed.

only inconsistently found any benefits for learning (Knight, Halpin, & Halpin, 1992; Snow, 1992). However, the search for such **aptitude–treatment interaction** goes on, and a few studies have found positive effects for programs that adapt instruction to an individual's learning style (Dunn, Beaudrey, & Klavas, 1989; Wilkerson & White, 1988).

SELF-CHECK

Define *intelligence*. Discuss present-day understanding of intelligence from a historical perspective. Define *learning styles* and describe traits of field-dependent and field-independent learners.

CHAPTER SUMMARY

WHAT IS THE IMPACT OF CULTURE ON TEACHING AND LEARNING?

Culture profoundly affects teaching and learning. Many aspects of culture contribute to the learner's identity and self-concept and affect the learner's beliefs and values, attitudes and expectations, social relations, language use, and other behaviors.

HOW DOES SOCIOECONOMIC STATUS AFFECT STUDENT ACHIEVEMENT?

Socioeconomic status—based on income, occupation, education, and social prestige—can profoundly influence the learner's attitudes toward school, background knowledge, school readiness, and academic achievement. Working-class and low-income families experience stress that contributes to child-rearing practices, communication patterns, and lowered expectations that may handicap children when they enter school. Low-SES students often learn a normative culture that is different from the middle-class culture of the school, which demands independence, competitiveness, and goal-setting. However, low achievement is not the inevitable result of low socioeconomic status.

HOW DO ETHNICITY AND RACE AFFECT STUDENTS' SCHOOL EXPERIENCES?

Minority-group populations are growing dramatically as diversity in the United States increases. Students who are members of certain minority groups—self-defined by race, religion, ethnicity, origins, history, language, and culture, such as African Americans, Native Americans, and Latinos—tend to have lower scores than those of European Americans on standardized tests of academic achievement. The lower scores correlate with lower socioeconomic status and reflect in part a legacy of discrimination against minority groups and consequent poverty. School desegregation, long intended as a solution to educational inequities due to race and social class, has had mixed benefits. Continuing issues include delivering fairness and equal opportunity, fostering racial harmony, and preventing segregation.

HOW DO LANGUAGE DIFFERENCES AND BILINGUAL PROGRAMS AFFECT STUDENT ACHIEVEMENT?

Bilingual education addresses problems of students who have limited proficiency in English and for whom English is a second language. Research suggests that bilingual

aptitude–treatment interaction
Interaction of individual differences in learning with particular teaching methods.

education has clear benefits for students. Difficulties include the shortage of bilingual teachers, inadequate transition programs for students entering English-only classes, and conflict between the goals of bilingualism and those of desegregation. Recent legislation, notably in California, has had a chilling effect on bilingual education.

WHAT IS MULTICULTURAL EDUCATION?

Multicultural education is no single program but a philosophy—with instructional and curriculum recommendations—calling for the celebration of cultural diversity and the promotion of educational equity and social harmony in the schools. Multicultural education includes content integration, knowledge construction, prejudice reduction, equity pedagogy, and an empowering school culture.

HOW DO GENDER AND GENDER BIAS AFFECT STUDENTS' SCHOOL EXPERIENCES?

Many observed differences between males and females are clearly linked to differences in early socialization, when children learn sex-role behaviors regarded as appropriate. Ongoing research shows very few genetically based gender differences in thinking and abilities. However, gender bias in the classroom, including subtle teacher behaviors toward male and female students and curriculum materials that contain sex-role stereotypes, has clearly affected student choices and achievement. One outcome is a gender gap in mathematics and science, though this gap has decreased steadily.

HOW DO STUDENTS DIFFER IN INTELLIGENCE AND LEARNING STYLES?

Students differ in their ability to deal with abstractions, to solve problems, and to learn. They also differ in any number of specific intelligences, so accurate estimations of intelligence should probably rely on broader performances than traditional IQ tests allow. Therefore teachers should not base their expectations of students on IQ test scores. Binet, Spearman, Sternberg, Guilford, and Gardner have contributed to theories and measures of intelligence. Both heredity and environment determine intelligence. Research shows that home environments, schooling, and life experiences can profoundly influence IQ.

Students differ in their prior learning and in their cognitive learning styles. Field-dependent people tend to see patterns as a whole and do better with people and social relationships. Field-independent people are more likely to see parts that make up a large pattern and do better with subjects such as science. Individual preferences in learning environments and conditions also affect student achievement.

KEY TERMS

aptitude–treatment interaction   135

bilingual education   119

content integration   122

culture   106

empowering school culture   122

English as a second language (ESL)   119

equity pedagogy   122

ethnicity   113

ethnic group   113

field dependence   134

field independence   134

gender bias   127

intelligence   128

intelligence quotient (IQ)   128

knowledge construction   122

language minority   119

learning styles   134

limited English proficient (LEP)   119

minority group   113

multicultural education   122

multiple intelligences   129

prejudice reduction   122

race   113

sex-role behavior   126

socioeconomic status (SES)   108

Self-Assessment

1. All of the following are defined as indicators of socioeconomic status except
   a. occupation.
   b. race.
   c. income.
   d. education.

2. Which of the following terms refers to families whose wage earners are in occupations that are relatively stable but do not require significant higher education?
   a. upper class
   b. working class
   c. lower class
   d. middle class

3. The socioeconomic status of various racial and ethnic groups and the groups' scores on standardized tests appear to be
   a. positively correlated.
   b. negatively correlated.
   c. unrelated.

4. What are some specific ways in which cultural differences influence the ways students approach learning tasks?

5. By 2026, what percentage of U.S. students will come from homes in which the primary language is not English?
   a. 60
   b. 45
   c. 25
   d. 10

6. Recent referendums about bilingual education in states such as California show that there has been a movement to

   a. increase the amount of tax dollars spent on bilingual education.
   b. abandon bilingual education in favor of English-only instruction.
   c. require all teachers to be proficient in at least two languages.
   d. require all students to be bilingual.

7. In a short essay, explain how multicultural education might have been implemented to address the goals of educational and social equality in your own school experience.

8. Studies report all of the following findings except
   a. Males score higher than females on tests of general knowledge.
   b. Females score higher than males on language measures.
   c. Females show more variability in overall academic performance than males.
   d. SAT math scores for females are improving.

9. Which of the following statements about gender bias is accurate?
   a. Children begin to make gender distinctions after they enter first grade.
   b. Males receive more disapproval and blame from teachers than females.
   c. Creativity is rewarded by teachers for females but not for males.
   d. Females receive more attention from teachers than males.

10. Give several definitions of *intelligence*.

Chapter 5

WHAT IS LEARNING?

WHAT BEHAVIORAL LEARNING THEORIES HAVE EVOLVED?
Pavlov: Classical Conditioning
Thorndike: The Law of Effect
Skinner: Operant Conditioning

WHAT ARE SOME PRINCIPLES OF BEHAVIORAL LEARNING?
The Role of Consequences
Reinforcers
Intrinsic and Extrinsic Reinforcers
Punishers
Immediacy of Consequences
Shaping
Extinction
Schedules of Reinforcement
Maintenance
The Role of Antecedents

HOW HAS SOCIAL LEARNING THEORY CONTRIBUTED TO OUR UNDERSTANDING OF HUMAN LEARNING?
Bandura: Modeling and Observational Learning
Meichenbaum's Model of Self-Regulated Learning
Strengths and Limitations of Behavioral Learning Theories

Behavioral Theories of Learning

Julia Esteban, first-grade teacher at Tanner Elementary School, was trying to teach her students appropriate classroom behavior.

"Children," she said one day, "we are having a problem in this class that I'd like to discuss with you. Whenever I ask a question, many of you shout out your answers instead of raising your hand and waiting to be called on. Can anyone tell me what you should do when I ask the class a question?" Rebecca's hand shot into the air. "I know, I know!" she said. "Raise your hand and wait quietly!"

Ms. Esteban sighed to herself. She tried to ignore Rebecca, who was doing exactly what she had just been told not to do, but Rebecca was the only student with her hand up, and the longer she delayed, the more frantically Rebecca waved her hand and shouted her answer.

"All right, Rebecca. What are you supposed to do?"

"We're supposed to raise our hands and wait quietly for you to call on us."

"If you know the rule, why were you shouting out your answer before I called on you?"

"I guess I forgot."

"All right. Can anyone remind the class of our rule about talking out of turn?" Four children raised their hands and shouted together.

"One at a time!"

"Take turns!"

"Don't talk when someone else is talking!"

Ms. Esteban called for order. "You kids are going to drive me crazy!" she said. "Didn't we just talk about how to raise your hands and wait for me to call on you?"

"But Ms. Esteban," said Stephen without even raising his hand. "You called on Rebecca and she wasn't quiet!"

Using Your EXPERIENCE

Critical and Creative Thinking   Reflect on what Ms. Esteban might do differently in this situation to accomplish her goal.

Cooperative Learning   Discuss with another student what went wrong here. Also discuss similar ways in which you have seen inappropriate behavior reinforced in the past. Share some of these anecdotes with the class.

Children are excellent learners. What they learn, however, may not always be what we intend to teach. Ms. Esteban is trying to teach students how to behave in class, but by paying attention to Rebecca's outburst, she is actually teaching them the opposite of what she intends. Rebecca craves her teacher's attention, so being called on (even in an exasperated tone of voice) rewards her for calling out her answer. Not only does Ms. Esteban's response increase the chances that Rebecca will call out answers again, but Rebecca now serves as a model for her classmates' own calling out. What Ms. Esteban says is less important than her actual response to her students' behaviors.

The purpose of this chapter is to define learning and then to present **behavioral learning theories,** explanations for learning that emphasize observable behaviors. Behavioral theories focus on the ways in which pleasurable or unpleasant consequences of behavior change individuals' behavior over time and ways in which individuals model their behavior on that of others. Later chapters present **cognitive learning theories,** which emphasize unobservable mental processes that people use to learn and remember new information or skills. Behavioral learning theorists try to discover principles of behavior that apply to all living beings. Cognitive theorists are concerned exclusively with human learning. Actually, however, the boundaries between behavioral and cognitive learning theories have become increasingly indistinct in recent years as each school of thought has incorporated the findings of the other.

behavioral learning theories
Explanations of learning that emphasize observable changes in behavior.

cognitive learning theories
Explanations of learning that focus on mental processes.

WHAT IS LEARNING?

What is learning? This seems like a simple question until you begin to think about it. Consider the following four examples. Are they instances of learning?

1. A young child takes her first steps.
2. An adolescent male feels a strong attraction to certain females.

3. A child feels anxious when he sees the doctor coming with a needle.

4. Long after learning how to multiply, a girl realizes on her own that another way to multiply by 5 is to divide by 2 and multiply by 10 (e.g., 428 × 5 can be figured as follows: $428/2 = 214 \times 10 = 2140$).

Learning is usually defined as a change in an individual caused by experience (see Mazur, 1990). Changes caused by development (such as growing taller) are not instances of learning. Neither are characteristics of individuals that are present at birth (such as reflexes and responses to hunger or pain). However, humans do so much learning from the day of their birth (and some say earlier) that learning and development are inseparably linked. Learning to walk (example 1 above) is mostly a developmental progression but also depends on experience with crawling and other activities. The adolescent sex drive (example 2) is not learned, but learning shapes individuals' choices of desirable partners.

A child's anxiety on seeing a doctor with a needle (example 3) is definitely learned behavior. The child has learned to associate the needle with pain, and his body reacts emotionally when he sees the needle. This reaction may be unconscious or involuntary, but it is learned nonetheless.

The fourth example, the girl's insight into the multiplication shortcut, is an instance of internally generated learning, better known as thinking. Some theorists would not call this learning, because it was not caused by the environment. But it might be considered a case of delayed learning, in which deliberate instruction in multiplication plus years of experience with numbers plus mental effort on the part of the girl produced an insight.

Learning takes place in many ways. Sometimes it is intentional, as when students acquire information presented in a classroom or when they look something up in the encyclopedia. Sometimes it is unintentional, as in the case of the child's reaction to the needle. All sorts of learning are going on all the time. As you are reading this chapter, you are learning something about learning. However, you are also learning that educational psychology is interesting or dull, useful or useless. Without knowing it, you are probably learning about where on the page certain pieces of information are to be found. You may be learning to associate the content of this chapter with unimportant aspects of your surroundings as you read it, such as the smell of books in a library or the temperature of the room in which you are reading. The content of this chapter, the placement of words on the page, and the smells, sounds, and temperature of your surroundings are all **stimuli.** Your senses are usually wide open to all sorts of stimuli, or environmental events or conditions, but you are consciously aware of only a fraction of them at any one time.

The problem educators face is not how to get students to learn; students are already engaged in learning every waking moment. Rather, it is how to help students learn particular information, skills, and concepts that will be useful in adult life. How do we present students with the right stimuli on which to focus their attention and mental effort so that they will acquire important skills? That is the central problem of instruction.

SELF-CHECK

List examples of learning. As you read, identify your examples in terms of the kind of learning that is taking place, and add new examples.

learning
A change in an individual that results from experience.

stimuli
Environmental conditions that activate the senses; the singular is *stimulus.*

WHAT BEHAVIORAL LEARNING THEORIES HAVE EVOLVED?

The systematic study of learning is relatively new. Not until the late nineteenth century was learning studied in a scientific manner. Using techniques borrowed from the physical sciences, researchers began conducting experiments to understand how people and animals learn. Two of the most important early researchers were Ivan Pavlov and Edward Thorndike. Among later researchers, B. F. Skinner was important for his studies of the relationship between behavior and consequences.

Pavlov: Classical Conditioning

In the late 1800s and early 1900s, Pavlov and his colleagues studied the digestive process in dogs. During the research, the scientists noticed changes in the timing and rate of salivation of these animals. Pavlov observed that if meat powder was placed in or near the mouth of a hungry dog, the dog would salivate. Because the meat powder provoked this response automatically, without any prior training or conditioning, the meat powder is referred to as an **unconditioned stimulus.** Similarly, because salivation occurred automatically in the presence of meat, also without the need for any training or experience, this response of salivating is referred to as an **unconditioned response.**

Whereas the meat will produce salivation without any previous experience or training, other stimuli, such as a bell, will not produce salivation. Because these stimuli have no effect on the response in question, they are referred to as **neutral stimuli.** Pavlov's experiments showed that if a previously neutral stimulus is paired with an unconditioned stimulus, the neutral stimulus becomes a **conditioned stimulus** and gains the power to prompt a response similar to that produced by the unconditioned stimulus. In other words, after the bell and the meat are presented together, the ringing of the bell alone causes the dog to salivate. This process is referred to as **classical conditioning.** A diagram of Pavlov's theory is shown in Figure 5.1, and a drawing of his apparatus is shown in Figure 5.2.

1. **Before training:** Presenting an unconditioned stimulus (meat) produces unconditioned response (salivation); presenting a neutral stimulus (bell) does not produce any salivation.
2. **During training:** The bell is rung when the meat is presented. The formerly neutral stimulus (the bell) becomes a conditioned stimulus.
3. **After training:** Presenting a conditioned stimulus (ringing the bell) produces a **conditioned response** (salivation).

In experiments such as these, Pavlov and his colleagues showed how learning could affect what were once thought to be involuntary, reflexive behaviors, such as salivating.

Pavlov's emphasis on observation and careful measurement and his systematic exploration of several aspects of learning helped to advance the scientific study of learning. Pavlov also left other behavioral theorists with significant mysteries, such as the process by which neutral stimuli take on meaning. Although his findings have few applications to classroom instruction, they can help a teacher understand many situations, such as when a child's anxiety about being among strangers gradually develops into a debilitating fear of coming to school.

unconditioned stimulus
A stimulus that naturally evokes a particular response.

unconditioned response
A behavior that is prompted automatically by a stimulus.

neutral stimuli
Stimuli that have no effect on a particular response.

conditioned stimulus
A previously neutral stimulus that evokes a particular response after having been paired with an unconditioned stimulus.

classical conditioning
The process of repeatedly associating a previously neutral stimulus with an unconditioned stimulus in order to evoke a conditioned response.

conditioned response
The response that comes to be elicited by a previously neutral stimulus as a result of the stimulus's repeated pairing with an unconditioned stimulus.

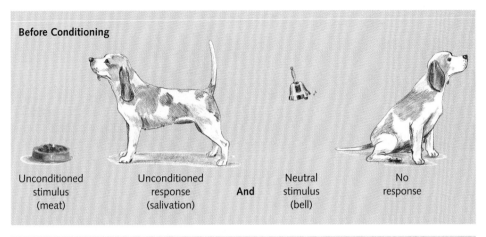

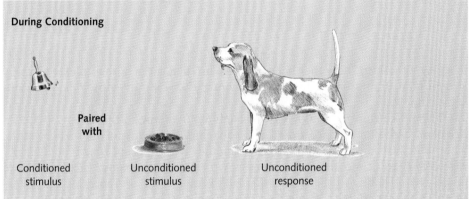

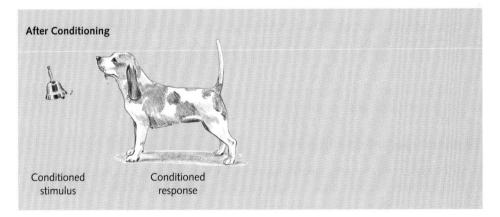

FIGURE 5.1 ● Classical Conditioning
In classical conditioning, a neutral stimulus (such as a bell) that at first prompts no response becomes paired with an unconditioned stimulus (such as meat) and gains the power of that stimulus to cause a response (such as salivation).

Thorndike: The Law of Effect

Pavlov's work inspired researchers in the United States such as E. L. Thorndike (Hilgard & Bower, 1966). Thorndike, like many of the early behavioral learning theorists, linked behavior to physical reflexes. In his early work he also viewed most behavior as a response to stimuli in the environment. This view that stimuli can prompt responses was the forerunner of what became known as stimulus–response (S–R) theory. Early learning theorists noted that certain reflexes, such as the knee jerking upward when it is tapped, occur without processing by the brain.

FIGURE 5.2 ● Apparatus Used in Classical Conditioning Experiments
The apparatus that Pavlov used in his classical conditioning experiments included a harness to hold a dog quiet and a tube attached to the dog's salivary gland to measure salivation.

They hypothesized that other behavior was also determined in a reflexive way by stimuli that are present in the environment rather than by conscious or unconscious thoughts.

Thorndike went beyond Pavlov by showing that stimuli that occurred after a behavior had an influence on future behaviors. In many of his experiments, Thorndike placed cats in boxes from which they had to escape to get food. He observed that over time, the cats learned how to get out of the box more and more quickly by repeating the behaviors that led to escape and not repeating the behaviors that were ineffective. From these experiments, Thorndike developed his Law of Effect.

Thorndike's **Law of Effect** states that if an act is followed by a satisfying change in the environment, the likelihood that the act will be repeated in similar situations increases. However, if a behavior is followed by an unsatisfying change in the environment, the chances that the behavior will be repeated decrease. Thus, Thorndike showed that the consequences of one's present behavior play a crucial role in determining one's future behavior.

Law of Effect
Thorndike's law stating that an act that is followed by a favorable effect is more likely to be repeated in similar situations; an act that is followed by an unfavorable effect is less likely to be repeated.

operant conditioning
The use of pleasant or unpleasant consequences to control the occurrence of behavior.

Skinner: Operant Conditioning

Some human behaviors are clearly prompted by specific stimuli. Just like Pavlov's dogs, we salivate when we are hungry and see appetizing food. We also lend credibility to Thorndike's early emphasis on reflexive behavior when we learn things—such as how to ride a bicycle—so well that the brain seems to respond reflexively. However, B. F. Skinner proposed that reflexive behavior accounts for only a small proportion of all actions. Skinner proposed another class of behavior, which he labeled *operant* behaviors because they operate on the environment in the apparent absence of any unconditioned stimuli, such as food. Like Thorndike's, Skinner's work focused on the relation between behavior and its consequences. For example, if an individual's behavior is immediately followed by pleasurable consequences, the individual will engage in that behavior more frequently. The use of pleasant and unpleasant consequences to change behavior is often referred to as **operant conditioning.**

How does this Skinner box work? What type of conditioning is the rat undergoing? How does that type of conditioning take place, and how is it different from the type of conditioning Pavlov studied?

Skinner's work focused on placing subjects in controlled situations and observing the changes in their behavior produced by systematic changes in the consequences of their behavior (see Iversen, 1992). Skinner is famous for his development and use of a device that is commonly referred to as the **Skinner box.** Skinner boxes contain a very simple apparatus for studying the behavior of animals, usually rats and pigeons. A Skinner box for rats would consist of a bar that is easy for the rat to press, a food dispenser that could give the rat a pellet of food, and a water dispenser. The rat could not see or hear anything outside of the box, so all stimuli would be controlled by the experimenter.

In some of the earliest experiments involving Skinner boxes, the apparatus was first set up so that if the rat happened to press the bar, it would receive a food pellet. After a few accidental bar presses, the rat would start pressing the bar frequently, receiving a pellet each time. The food reward had conditioned the rat's behavior, strengthening bar pressing and weakening all other behaviors (such as wandering around the box). At this point, the experimenter might do any of several things. The electronics controlling the bar and food dispenser might be set up so that several bar presses were now required to obtain food, or so that some bar presses produced food but others did not, or so that bar presses no longer produced food. In each case the rat's behavior would be recorded. One important advantage of the Skinner box is that it allows for careful scientific study of behavior in a controlled environment (Delprato & Midgley, 1992). Anyone with the same equipment can repeat Skinner's experiments.

SELF-CHECK

Develop a chart to compare the contributions of Pavlov, Thorndike, and Skinner to our understanding of learning. Label the chart headings Name of Theorist, Name of Theory, Main Concepts, and Research Conducted. Give examples of how the research findings can be applied to classroom learning.

Skinner box
An apparatus developed by B. F. Skinner for observing animal behavior in experiments in operant conditioning.

WHAT ARE SOME PRINCIPLES OF BEHAVIORAL LEARNING?

Principles of behavioral learning include the role of consequences, reinforcers, punishers, immediacy of consequences, shaping, extinction, schedules of reinforcement, maintenance, and the role of antecedents. Each of these principles will be discussed in the sections that follow.

The Role of Consequences

Skinner's pioneering work with rats and pigeons established a set of principles of behavior that have been supported in hundreds of studies involving humans as well as animals. Perhaps the most important principle of behavioral learning theories is that behavior changes according to its immediate **consequences.** Pleasurable consequences strengthen behavior; unpleasant consequences weaken it. In other words, pleasurable consequences increase the frequency with which an individual engages in a behavior, whereas unpleasant consequences reduce the frequency of a behavior. If students enjoy reading books, they will probably read more often. If they find stories boring or are unable to concentrate, they may read less often, choosing other activities instead. Pleasurable consequences are called *reinforcers;* unpleasant consequences are called *punishers.*

Reinforcers

A **reinforcer** is defined as any consequence that strengthens (that is, increases the frequency of) a behavior. Note that the effectiveness of the reinforcer must be demonstrated. We cannot assume that a particular consequence is a reinforcer until we have evidence that it strengthens behavior for a particular individual. For example, candy might generally be considered a reinforcer for young children, but after a big meal a child might not find candy pleasurable, and some children do not like candy at all. A teacher who says, "I reinforced him with praise for staying in his seat during math time, but it didn't work," may be misusing the term *reinforced* if there is no evidence that praise is in fact a reinforcer for this particular student. No reward can be assumed to be a reinforcer for everyone under all conditions.

PRIMARY AND SECONDARY REINFORCERS ● Reinforcers fall into two broad categories: primary and secondary. **Primary reinforcers** satisfy basic human needs. Some examples are food, water, security, warmth, and sex. **Secondary reinforcers** are reinforcers that acquire their value by being associated with primary reinforcers or other well-established secondary reinforcers. For example, money has no value to a young child until the child learns that money can be used to buy things that are themselves primary or secondary reinforcers. Grades have little value to students unless their parents notice and value good grades, and parents' praise is of value because it is associated with love, warmth, security, and other reinforcers. Money and grades are examples of secondary reinforcers because they have no value in themselves but have been associated with primary reinforcers or with other well-established secondary reinforcers. There are three basic categories of secondary reinforcers. One is social reinforcers, such as praise, smiles, hugs, or attention. When Ms. Esteban recognized Rebecca, she was inadvertently giving Rebecca a social reinforcer: her own attention. Other types of secondary rein-

---

consequences
Pleasant or unpleasant conditions that follow behaviors and affect the frequency of future behaviors.

reinforcer
A pleasurable consequence that maintains or increases a behavior.

primary reinforcer
Food, water, or other consequence that satisfies a basic need.

secondary reinforcer
A consequence that people learn to value through its association with a primary reinforcer.

These students have completed their work and now get to care for the class pet. What kind of consequences are they experiencing? What is being reinforced?

forcers are activity reinforcers (such as access to toys, games, or fun activities) and token (or symbolic) reinforcers (such as money, grades, stars, or points that individuals can exchange for other reinforcers).

POSITIVE AND NEGATIVE REINFORCERS ● Most often, reinforcers that are used in schools are things given to students. These are called **positive reinforcers** and include praise, grades, and stars. However, another way to strengthen a behavior is to have the behavior's consequence be an escape from an unpleasant situation or a way of preventing something unpleasant from occurring. For example, a parent might release a student from doing the dishes if the student completes his or her homework. If doing the dishes is seen as an unpleasant task, release from it will be reinforcing. Reinforcers that are escapes from unpleasant situations are called **negative reinforcers.**

This term is often misinterpreted to mean punishment, as in "I negatively reinforced him for being late by having him stay in during recess" (Cipani, 1995). One way to avoid this error in terminology is to remember that reinforcers (whether positive or negative) strengthen behavior, whereas punishment is designed to weaken behavior. (See Table 5.1.)

THE PREMACK PRINCIPLE ● One important principle of behavior is that we can promote less-desired (low-strength) activities by linking them to more-desired activities. In other words, access to something desirable is made contingent on doing something less desirable. For example, a teacher might say, "As soon as you finish your work, you may go outside" or "Clean up your art project, and then I will read you a story." These are examples of the Premack Principle (Premack, 1965). The **Premack Principle** is sometimes called "Grandma's Rule" from the age-old statement "Eat your vegetables, and then you may play." Teachers can use the Premack Principle by alternating more enjoyable activities with less enjoyable ones and

positive reinforcer
Pleasurable consequence given to strengthen behavior.

negative reinforcer
Release from an unpleasant situation, given to strengthen behavior.

Premack Principle
Rule stating that enjoyable activities can be used to reinforce participation in less enjoyable activities.

TABLE 5.1

Consequences in Behavioral Learning

STRENGTHENS BEHAVIOR	DISCOURAGES BEHAVIOR
Positive Reinforcement	**No Reinforcement**
Example: Rewarding or praising	*Example:* Ignoring
Negative Reinforcement	**Removal Punishment**
Example: Excusing from an undesirable task or situation	*Example:* Forbidding a desirable task or situation
	Presentation Punishment
	Example: Imposing an undesirable task or situation

making participation in the enjoyable activities depend on successful completion of the less enjoyable ones. For example, in elementary school it may be a good idea to schedule music, which most students consider an enjoyable activity, after completion of a difficult subject so that students will know that if they fool around in the difficult subject, they will be using up part of their desired music time.

THEORY *into* Practice

CONNECTIONS

For more on reinforcing desirable behaviors, see page 153 on Shaping.

CONNECTIONS

For more on helping students recognize the behaviors you want, see page 158 on Discrimination.

Classroom Uses of Reinforcement

The behavioral learning principle most useful for classroom practice is also the simplest: Reinforce behaviors you wish to see repeated. This principle may seem obvious, but in practice it is not as easy as it appears. For example, some teachers take the attitude that reinforcement is unnecessary, reasoning, "Why should I reinforce them? They're just doing what they're supposed to do!"

The main guidelines for the use of reinforcement to increase desired behavior in the classroom are as follows (see Wielkiewicz, 1995):

1. *Decide what behaviors you want from students, and reinforce these behaviors when they occur. For example, praise or reward good work. Do not praise or reward work that is not up to students' capabilities.* As students begin a new task, they will need to be reinforced at every step along the way. Close approximations of what you hope to accomplish as a final product must receive positive feedback. Break down new behaviors (classroom assignments) into smaller parts and provide adequate rewards along the way.

2. *Tell students what behaviors you want; also, when they exhibit the desired behaviors and you reinforce them, tell them why.* Present students with a rubric that itemizes the criteria you will use when evaluating their work and include the point value for each criterion. Students then will be able to discriminate their own strengths and weaknesses from the feedback they receive from you.

3. *Reinforce appropriate behavior as soon as possible after it occurs. Delayed reinforcement is less effective than immediate reinforcement.* When you are grading an assignment, present feedback to the students as soon as possible. It is important that students know how they are doing in class, so don't delay with their grades. When constructing an assignment, you should always consider the grading scheme that you will use and how long it will take you to provide the intended feedback.

CONNECTIONS

For more on immediate reinforcement, see page 151 on Immediacy of Consequences.

Intrinsic and Extrinsic Reinforcers

Often, the most important reinforcer that maintains behavior is the pleasure inherent in engaging in the behavior. For example, most people have a hobby that they work on for extended periods without any reward. People like to draw, read, sing, play games, hike, or swim for no reason other than the fun of doing it. Reinforcers of this type are called **intrinsic reinforcers,** and people can be described as being intrinsically motivated to engage in a given activity. Intrinsic reinforcers are contrasted with **extrinsic reinforcers,** praise or rewards given to motivate people to engage in a behavior that they might not engage in without it. There is some evidence that reinforcing children for certain behaviors they would have done anyway can undermine long-term intrinsic motivation (Kohn, 1993; Sethi, Drake, Dialdin, & Lepper, 1995). Research on this topic finds that the undermining effect of extrinsic reinforcers occurs only in a limited set of circumstances, in which rewards are provided to children for engaging in an activity without any standard of performance, and only if the activity is one that children would have done on their own without any reward (Cameron & Pierce, 1994, 1996). Verbal praise and other types of feedback are extrinsic reinforcers that have been found to increase, not decrease, intrinsic interest. What this research suggests for practice is that teachers should be cautious about giving tangible reinforcers to children for activities they would have done on their own. However, for most school tasks, there is no basis for concern that use of extrinsic reinforcers will undermine intrinsic motivation.

CONNECTIONS

For more on intrinsic and extrinsic motivation, see Chapter 10, page 344.

Practical Reinforcers

Anything that children like can be an effective reinforcer, but there are obvious practical limitations on what should be used in classrooms. One general principle of positive reinforcement is that it is best to use the least elaborate or tangible reinforcer that will work. In other words, if praise or self-reinforcement will work, don't use certificates. If certificates will work, don't use small toys. If small toys will work, don't use food. However, do not hesitate to use whatever practical reinforcer is necessary to motivate children to do important things. In particular, try all possible reinforcement strategies before even thinking of punishment (described below). A few categories of reinforcers and examples of each appear here (also see Alberto & Troutman, 1995; Martin & Pear, 1996; Schloss & Smith, 1998; Wielkiewicz, 1995). These are arranged from least tangible to most tangible.

SELF-REINFORCEMENT

Students may be taught to praise themselves, give themselves a mental pat on the back, check off progress on a form, give themselves a short break, or otherwise reinforce themselves for completing a task or staying out of trouble.

PRAISE

Phrases such as "Good job," "Way to go," "I knew you could do it," and other verbal praise can be effective, but the same message can often be delivered with a smile,

intrinsic reinforcers
Behaviors that a person enjoys engaging in for their own sake, without any other reward.

extrinsic reinforcers
Praise or rewards given to motivate people to engage in behavior that they might not engage in without them.

a wink, a thumbs-up signal, or a pat on the back. In cooperative learning and peer tutoring, students can be encouraged to praise each other for appropriate behavior.

ATTENTION

The attention of a valued adult or peer can be a very effective reinforcer for many children. Listening, nodding, or moving closer may provide a child with the positive attention he or she is seeking. For outstanding performance or for meeting goals over a longer time period, students might be allowed a special time to visit with the custodian, help in the office, or take a walk with the principal.

GRADES AND RECOGNITION

Grades and recognition (e.g., certificates of accomplishment) can be effective both in giving students positive feedback on their efforts and in communicating progress to parents, who are likely to reinforce good reports themselves. Public displays of good work, notes from the principal, and other honors can have the same effect. Quiz scores, behavior ratings, and other feedback given frequently can be more effective than report card grades given for months of work.

HOME-BASED REINFORCEMENT

CONNECTIONS

For more on working with parents to reinforce behavior, see Chapter 11, page 393.

Parents can be explicitly included in a reinforcement system. Teachers can work out with parents an arrangement in which parents give their children special privileges at home if the children meet well-specified standards of behavior or performance.

PRIVILEGES

Children can earn free time, access to special equipment (e.g., soccer balls), or special roles (such as running errands or distributing papers). Children or groups who behaved well can simply be allowed to line up first for recess or dismissal or to have other small privileges.

ACTIVITY REINFORCERS

CONNECTIONS

For more on the use of activity reinforcers, see Chapter 11, pages 389 and 394.

On the basis of achieving preestablished standards, students can earn free time, videos, games, or access to other fun activities. Activity reinforcers lend themselves particularly well to group contingencies, in which a whole class can earn free time or special activities if the whole class achieves a standard.

TANGIBLE REINFORCERS

Children may earn points for achievement or good behavior that they can exchange for small toys, erasers, pencils, marbles, comic books, stickers, and so on.

FOOD

Raisins, fruit, peanuts, or other healthy snacks can be used as reinforcers.

Punishers

punishment
Unpleasant consequences used to weaken behavior.

Consequences that weaken behavior are called *punishers.* Note that there is the same catch in the definition of **punishment** as in the definition of reinforcement: If an apparently unpleasant consequence does not reduce the frequency of the behavior it follows, it is not necessarily a punisher. For example, some students like being sent to the principal's office or out to the hall, because it releases them from the classroom, which they see as an unpleasant situation (Pfiffer, Rosen, & O'Leary, 1985). Some students like to be scolded, because it gains them the teacher's attention and perhaps enhances their status among their peers. As with reinforcers, the effectiveness of a punisher cannot be assumed but must be demonstrated.

PRESENTATION AND REMOVAL PUNISHMENT ● Punishment can take two primary forms. **Presentation punishment** is the use of unpleasant consequences, or **aversive stimuli,** as when a student is asked to write "I will not talk in class" 100 times or is scolded or criticized.

TIME OUT ● One frequently used form of punishment in classrooms is **time out,** in which a student who misbehaves is required to sit in the corner or in the hall for several minutes. Teachers often use time out when they believe that the attention of other students is serving to reinforce misbehavior; time out deprives the miscreant of this reinforcer and so constitutes a form of **removal punishment.** The use of time out as a consequence for misbehavior has generally been found to reduce the misbehavior (Costenbader & Rending-Brown, 1995).

For example, White and Bailey (1990) evaluated use of a sit-and-watch consequence for physical education classes. Children who misbehaved were told what they had done wrong and were given a 3-minute sand timer and asked to sit and watch until the sand ran out. The program was first tried in an alternative class for fourth- and fifth-graders with serious behavior problems. Figure 5.3 summarizes the findings. After a baseline of up to 343 disruptive behaviors in 10 minutes was observed, a behavioral checklist program was tried, in which teachers rated each child's behavior and sent poorly behaved children to the office or deprived them of a free period. This reduced misbehavior but did not eliminate it. However, when the sit-and-watch procedure was introduced, misbehavior virtually disappeared. The same sit-and-watch method was used in a regular fourth-grade physical education class, and the results were similar.

The topic of if, when, and how to punish has been a source of considerable controversy among behavioral learning theorists. Some have claimed that the effects of punishment are only temporary, that punishment produces aggression, and that punishment causes individuals to avoid settings in which it is used (Bates, 1987). Even behavioral learning theorists who do support the use of punishment agree that it should be resorted to only when reinforcement for appropriate behavior has been tried and has failed; that when punishment is necessary, it should take the mildest possible form; and that punishment should always be used as part of a careful plan, never inconsistently or out of frustration. Physical punishment in schools (such as spanking) is illegal in most places and is almost universally opposed by behavioral learning theorists on ethical as well as scientific grounds (see Jenson, Sloane, & Young, 1988).

Immediacy of Consequences

One very important principle of behavioral learning theories is that consequences that follow behaviors closely in time affect behavior far more than delayed consequences do. If we waited a few minutes to give a rat in a Skinner box its food pellet after it pressed a bar, the rat would take a long time to learn the connection between bar pressing and food; because by the time the food arrived, the rat might be doing something other than bar pressing. A smaller reinforcer that is given immediately generally has a much larger effect than does a large reinforcer that is given later (Kulik & Kulik, 1988). This concept explains much about human behavior. It suggests, for example, why people find it so difficult to give up smoking or overeating. Even though the benefits of giving up smoking or losing weight are substantial and well known, the small but immediate reinforcement of just one cigarette or one doughnut often overcomes the behavioral effect of the large but delayed reinforcers.

presentation punishment
An aversive stimulus following a behavior, used to decrease the chances that the behavior will occur again.

aversive stimulus
An unpleasant consequence that a person tries to avoid or escape.

time out
Procedure of removing a student from a situation in which misbehavior was being reinforced.

removal punishment
Withdrawal of a pleasant consequence that is reinforcing a behavior; designed to decrease the chances that the behavior will recur.

FIGURE 5.3 ● Reducing Disruptive Behavior with Sit-and-Watch
Number of disruptive behaviors per 10-minute observation period.

From A. G. White and J. S. Bailey, "Reducing Disruptive Behaviors of Elementary Physical Education Students with Sit and Watch," *Journal of Applied Behavior Analysis, 3,* 1990, p. 357. Adapted by permission.

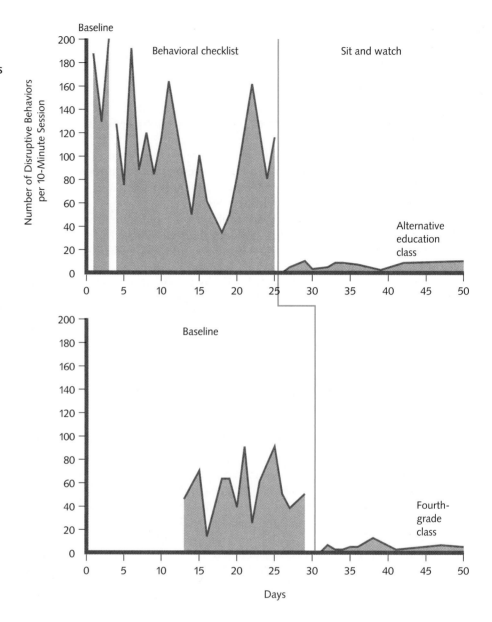

In the classroom the principle of immediacy of consequences is also very important. Particularly for younger students, praise for a job well done that is given immediately can be a stronger reinforcer than a good grade given much later.

Immediate feedback serves at least two purposes. First, it makes clear the connection between behavior and consequence. Second, it increases the informational value of the feedback. In practice, few classroom teachers can provide individual feedback immediately to all their students. However, the same results can be obtained by giving students answers right after they complete their work. In dealing with misbehavior, teachers can apply the principle of immediacy of consequences by responding immediately and positively when students are not misbehaving—in effect, by catching them in the act of being good!

Shaping

Immediacy of reinforcement is important to teaching, but so is the decision as to what to reinforce. Should a kindergarten teacher withhold reinforcement until a child can recite the entire alphabet? Certainly not. It would be better to praise children for recognizing one letter, then for recognizing several, and finally for learning all 26 letters. Should a music teacher withhold reinforcement until a young student has played a piano piece flawlessly? Or should the teacher praise the first halting run-through? Most students need reinforcement along the way. When teachers guide students toward goals by reinforcing the many steps that lead to success, they are using a technique called *shaping*.

The term **shaping** is used in behavioral learning theories to refer to the teaching of new skills or behaviors by reinforcing learners for approaching the desired final behavior. For example, in teaching children to tie their shoelaces, we would not simply show them how it is done and then wait to reinforce them until they do the whole job themselves. Rather, we would first reinforce them for tying the first knot, then for making the loops, and so on, until they can do the entire task. In this way we would be shaping the children's behavior by reinforcing all those steps that lead toward the final goal.

Shaping is an important tool in classroom instruction. Let's say we want students to be able to write paragraphs with a topic sentence, three supporting details, and a concluding sentence. This task has many parts: being able to recognize and then produce topic sentences, supporting details, and concluding sentences; being able to write complete sentences using capitalization, punctuation, and grammar correctly; and being able to spell. If a teacher taught a lesson on all these skills, asked students to write paragraphs, and then scored them on content, grammar, punctuation, and spelling, most students would fail and would probably learn little from the exercise.

Instead, the teacher might teach the skills step by step, gradually shaping the final skill. Students might be taught how to write first topic sentences, then supporting details, then concluding sentences. Early on, they might be held responsible only for paragraph content. Later, the requirement for reinforcement might be increased to include grammar and punctuation. Finally, spelling might be added as a criterion for success. At each stage, students would have a good chance to be reinforced, because the criterion for reinforcement would be within their grasp. The principle here is that students should be reinforced for behaviors that are within their current capabilities but that also stretch them toward new skills.

Extinction

By definition, reinforcers strengthen behavior. But what happens when reinforcers are withdrawn? Eventually, the behavior will be weakened, and ultimately, it will disappear. This process is called **extinction** of a previously learned behavior.

Extinction is rarely a smooth process. When reinforcers are withdrawn, individuals often increase their rate of behavior for a while. For example, think of a door that you've used as a shortcut to somewhere you go frequently. Imagine that one day the door will not open. You may push even harder for a while, shake the door, turn the handle both ways, perhaps even kick the door. You are likely to feel frustrated and angry. However, after a short time you will realize that the door is locked and go away. If the door is permanently locked (without your knowing it), you may try it a few times over the next few days, then perhaps once after a month; only eventually will you give up on it.

shaping
The teaching of a new skill or behavior by means of reinforcement for small steps toward the desired goal.

extinction
The weakening and eventual elimination of a learned behavior as reinforcement is withdrawn.

How can a teacher foster extinction of a previously learned behavior, such as calling out in class, and shape a desired behavior, such as raising one's hand in class, as this girl does?

Your behavior when confronted by the locked door is a classic extinction pattern. Behavior intensifies when the reinforcer is first withdrawn, then rapidly weakens until the behavior disappears. The behavior may return after much time has passed. For example, you may try the door again a year later to see whether it is still locked. If it is, you will probably leave it alone for a longer time, but probably not forever.

The characteristic **extinction burst,** the increase in levels of a behavior in the early stages of extinction, has important consequences for classroom management. For example, imagine that you have decided to extinguish a child's inappropriate calling out of answers (instead of raising his hand to be recognized) by ignoring him until he raises his hand quietly. At first, ignoring the child is likely to *increase* his calling-out behavior, a classic extinction burst. You might then mistakenly conclude that ignoring isn't working, when in fact continuing to ignore inappropriate call-outs is exactly the right strategy if you keep it up (Schloss & Smith, 1998). Worse, you might finally decide to give in and recognize the child after his third or fourth call-out. This would teach the child the worst possible message: that calling out works eventually if you keep doing it. This would probably result in an increase in the very behavior you were trying to reduce, as children learn that "if at first you don't succeed, try, try again" (O'Leary, 1995). This was the case in the vignette presented at the beginning of this chapter. Ms. Esteban at first ignored Rebecca's calling out, so Rebecca called out even louder. Then she called on Rebecca, unintentionally communicating to her that only loud and persistent calling out would be reinforced!

extinction burst
The increase in levels of a behavior in the early stages of extinction.

Extinction of a previously learned behavior can be hastened when some stimulus or cue informs the individual that behaviors that were once reinforced will no longer be reinforced. In the case of the locked door, a sign saying, "Door permanently locked—use other entrance" would have greatly reduced the number of times you tried the door before giving up on it. Call-outs would be reduced much more quickly if the teacher told the class, "I will no longer respond to anyone unless they are silent and are raising their hand," and then ignored all other attempts to get her attention.

Schedules of Reinforcement

The effects of reinforcement on behavior depend on many factors, one of the most important of which is the **schedule of reinforcement.** This term refers to the frequency with which reinforcers are given, the amount of time that elapses between opportunities for reinforcement, and the predictability of reinforcement.

FIXED RATIO (FR) ● One common schedule of reinforcement is the **fixed-ratio (FR) schedule,** in which a reinforcer is given after a fixed number of behaviors. For example, a teacher might say, "As soon as you finish ten problems, you may go outside." Regardless of the amount of time it takes, students are reinforced as soon as they finish 10 problems. This is an example of an FR10 schedule (10 behaviors for one reinforcer). One common form of a fixed-ratio schedule is one in which each behavior is reinforced. This is called continuous reinforcement (CRF), though it could just as well be called FR1, because one behavior is required for reinforcement. Putting money in a soda machine is (usually) an example of continuous reinforcement, because one behavior (inserting coins) results in one reinforcer (a soda). Giving correct answers in class is also usually continuously reinforced. The student gives a good answer, and the teacher says, "Right! Good answer!"

One important process in instruction is gradually increasing reinforcement ratios. Early in a sequence of lessons, it may be necessary to reinforce students for every correct answer, such as a single math problem. However, this is inefficient in the long run. As soon as students are answering math problems correctly, it may be possible to reinforce every 5 problems (FR5), every 10 (FR10), and so on. Thinning out the reinforcement schedule in this way makes the student more able to work independently without reinforcement and makes the behavior more resistant to extinction. Ultimately, students may be asked to do entire projects on their own, receiving no reinforcement until the project is completed. As adults, we often take on tasks that take years to complete and years to pay off. (Writing an educational psychology text is one such task!)

Fixed-ratio schedules are effective in motivating individuals to do a great deal of work—especially if the fixed ratio starts with continuous reinforcement (FR1) to get the individual going and then moves to high requirements for reinforcement. One reason that high requirements for reinforcement produce higher levels of behavior than low requirements is that reinforcing too frequently can make the value of the reinforcer wear off. Students who were praised for every math problem would soon grow tired of being praised, and the reinforcer might lose its value.

VARIABLE RATIO (VR) ● A **variable-ratio (VR) schedule** of reinforcement is one in which the number of behaviors required for reinforcement is unpredictable, although it is certain that the behaviors will eventually be reinforced. For example,

schedule of reinforcement
The frequency and predictability of reinforcement.

fixed-ratio (FR) schedule
Reinforcement schedule in which desired behavior is rewarded following a fixed number of behaviors.

variable-ratio (VR) schedule
Reinforcement schedule in which desired behavior is rewarded following an unpredictable number of behaviors.

a slot machine is a variable-ratio reinforcer. It may pay off after 1 pull one time and after 200 the next, and there is no way to predict which pull will win. In the classroom a variable-ratio schedule exists when students raise their hands to answer questions. They never know when they will be reinforced by being able to give the correct answer, but they may expect to be called on about 1 time in 30 in a class of 30. This would be called a VR30 schedule, because, on the average, 30 behaviors are required for one reinforcer. Variable-ratio schedules tend to produce high and stable rates of behavior. In fact, almost all gambling games involve VR schedules, and so they can be quite literally addicting. Similarly, use of frequent random checks of student work can help to addict students to steady, careful work.

Variable-ratio schedules are highly resistant to extinction. Even after behaviors are no longer being reinforced, people may not give up working for a long time. Because they have learned that it may take a lot of work to be rewarded, they keep on working in the mistaken belief that the next effort might just pay off.

FIXED INTERVAL (FI) ● In **fixed-interval schedules,** reinforcement is available only at certain periodic times. The final examination is a classic example of a fixed-interval schedule. Fixed-interval schedules create an interesting pattern of behavior. The individual may do very little until just before reinforcement is available, then put forth a burst of effort as the time for reinforcement approaches. This pattern can be demonstrated with rats and pigeons on fixed-interval schedules, but it is even more apparent in students who cram at the last minute before a test or who write their monthly book reports the night before they are due. These characteristics of fixed-interval schedules suggest that frequent short quizzes may be better than infrequent major exams for encouraging students to give their best effort all the time rather than putting in all-nighters before the exam (Crooks, 1988).

VARIABLE INTERVAL (VI) ● In a **variable-interval schedule,** reinforcement is available at some times but not at others, and we have no idea when a behavior will be reinforced. An example of this is a teacher making spot checks of students who are doing assignments in class. Students are reinforced if they are working well at the particular moment the teacher comes by. Since they cannot predict when the teacher will check them, students must be doing good work all the time. People may obey traffic laws out of respect for the law and civic responsibility, but it also helps that the police randomly check drivers' compliance with the law. Troopers hide on overpasses or behind hills so that they can get a random sampling of drivers' behavior. If they were always in plain sight, they would be a signal to drive carefully, so the necessity for driving carefully at other times would be reduced.

fixed-interval schedule
Reinforcement schedule in which desired behavior is rewarded following a constant amount of time.

variable-interval schedule
Reinforcement schedule in which desired behavior is rewarded following an unpredictable amount of time.

Like variable-ratio schedules, variable-interval schedules are very effective for maintaining a high rate of behavior and are highly resistant to extinction. For example, let's say a teacher has a policy of having students hand in their seatwork every day. Rather than checking every paper, the teacher pulls three papers at random and gives these students extra credit if their seatwork was done well. This variable-interval schedule would probably motivate students to do their seatwork carefully. If the teacher secretly stopped spot-checking halfway through the year, the students might never know it, figuring that their own paper just hadn't been pulled to be checked rather than realizing that reinforcement was no longer available for anyone.

Table 5.2 defines and gives additional examples of schedules of reinforcement.

TABLE 5.2

Schedules of Reinforcement

Specific response patterns during reinforcement and extinction characterize each of the four types of schedules.

SCHEDULE	DEFINITION	RESPONSE PATTERNS	
		During Reinforcement	During Extinction
Fixed ratio	Constant number of behaviors required for reinforcement	Steady response rate; pause after reinforcement	Rapid drop in response rate after required number of responses passes without reinforcement
Variable ratio	Variable number of behaviors required for reinforcement	Steady, high response rate	Response rate stays high, then drops off
Fixed interval	Constant amount of time passes before reinforcement is available	Uneven rate, with rapid acceleration at the end of each interval	Rapid drop in response rate after interval passes with no reinforcement
Variable interval	Variable amount of time passes before reinforcement is available	Steady, high response rate	Slow decrease in response rate

Maintenance

The principle of extinction holds that when reinforcement for a previously learned behavior is withdrawn, the behavior fades away. Does this mean that teachers must reinforce students' behaviors indefinitely or they will disappear?

Not necessarily. For rats in a Skinner box, the withdrawal of reinforcement for bar pressing will inevitably lead to extinction of bar pressing. However, humans live in a much more complex world. Our world is full of natural reinforcers for most of the skills and behaviors that we learn in school. For example, students may initially require frequent reinforcement for behaviors that lead to reading. However, once they can read, they have a skill that unlocks the entire world of written language, a world that is highly reinforcing to most students. After a certain point, reinforcement for reading may no longer be necessary, because the content of reading material itself maintains the behavior. Similarly, poorly behaved students may need careful, systematic reinforcement for doing schoolwork. After a while, however, they will find out that doing schoolwork pays off in grades, in parental approval, in ability to understand what is going on in class, and in knowledge. These natural reinforcers for doing schoolwork were always available, but the students could not experience them until their schoolwork was improved by more systematic means.

This kind of **maintenance** of behavior also occurs with behaviors that do not need to be reinforced because they are intrinsically reinforcing, which is to say that engaging in these behaviors is pleasurable in itself. For example, many children love to draw, to figure out problems, or to learn about things even if they are never reinforced for doing so. Many of us even complete books of crossword puzzles or other problem-solving activities, even though after we have completed them, no one will ever check our work.

maintenance
Continuation (of behavior).

The concept of resistance to extinction, discussed earlier (in the section on schedules of reinforcement), is central to an understanding of maintenance of learned behavior. As was noted earlier, when new behaviors are being introduced, reinforcement for correct responses should be frequent and predictable. However, once the behaviors are established, reinforcement for correct responses should become less frequent and less predictable. The reason for this is that variable schedules of reinforcement and schedules of reinforcement that require many behaviors before reinforcement is given are much more resistant to extinction than are fixed schedules or easy ones. For example, if a teacher praises a student every time the student does a math problem but then stops praising, the student may stop doing math problems. In contrast, if the teacher gradually increases the number of math problems a student must do to be praised and praises the student at random intervals (a variable-ratio schedule), then the student is likely to continue to do math problems for a long time with little or no reinforcement from the teacher.

The Role of Antecedents

We have seen that the consequences of behavior strongly influence behavior. Yet it is not only what follows a behavior that has influence. The stimuli that precede a behavior also play an important role.

CUEING ● **Antecedent stimuli,** events that precede a behavior, are also known as **cues,** because they inform us what behavior will be reinforced and/or what behavior will be punished. Cues come in many forms and give us hints as to when we should change our behavior and when we should not. For example, during a math session, most teachers will reinforce students who are working on problems. However, after the teacher has announced that math is over and it is time for lunch, the consequences change. The ability to behave one way in the presence of one stimulus—"It's math time"—and a different way in the presence of another stimulus—"It's time for lunch"—is known as stimulus discrimination.

DISCRIMINATION ● When is the best time to ask your boss for a raise? When the company is doing well, the boss looks happy, and you have just done something especially good? Or when the company has just gotten a poor earnings report, the boss is glowering, and you have just made a costly error? Obviously, the first situation is more likely to lead to success. You know this because you have learned to discriminate between good and bad times to ask your boss to do something for you. **Discrimination** is the use of cues, signals, or information to know when behavior is likely to be reinforced. The company's financial condition, the boss's mood, and your recent performance are discriminative stimuli with regard to the chances that your request for a raise will be successful. For students to learn discrimination, they must have feedback on the correctness or incorrectness of their responses. Studies of discrimination learning have generally found that students need to know when their responses are incorrect as well as correct.

Learning is largely a matter of mastering more and more complex discriminations. For example, all letters, numbers, words, and mathematical symbols are discriminative stimuli. A young child learns to discriminate between the letters *b* and *d*. An older student learns the distinction between the words *effective* and *efficient*. An educational psychology student learns to discriminate *negative reinforcement* from *punishment*. A teacher learns to discriminate facial and verbal cues indicating that students are bored or interested by a lecture.

antecedent stimuli
Events that precede behaviors.

cues
Signals as to what behavior(s) will be reinforced or punished.

discrimination
Perception of and response to differences in stimuli.

CASE TO CONSIDER

Kindergarten Is Big Business

Sam, a boy with a talkative and bubbly personality, has just entered Mrs. Roberts's kindergarten class at Elliott Elementary School. Sam has had a complicated medical history since birth, culminating a year ago in back surgery to correct spinal scoliosis, followed by many months in a full-body cast. Last year, after the surgery, Sam was in Diana's preschool class at Elliott, where, after a rough start, he made good academic and social progress. Now, however, after two weeks of school, Mrs. Roberts is afraid that Sam doesn't have the maturity to be in kindergarten yet. She meets with Diana and Sam's mother, Janet, to discuss her concerns.

Mrs. Roberts: Thank you both for taking the time to meet with me this afternoon. I'm concerned because Sam is starting to exhibit some of the same behaviors he showed at the beginning of his preschool year with you, Diana.

Diana: Sam certainly demonstrated separation anxiety when he began preschool. I remember the tantrums he would throw when Janet dropped him off for school. Then he would complain that he felt sick, begin to cry, and even make himself throw up so he could go home.

Janet: Sam became overly dependent on me when he had his back surgery and was in the body cast. But Diana and I worked out a plan that seemed to help Sam get over his problems last year.

Mrs. Roberts: Well, it appears that Sam is having what psychologists call an extinction burst of that behavior now that he's started kindergarten. I was at my wits' end yesterday, Janet, when I had to call you for the second time this week to pick Sam up because he had had a thirty-minute tantrum and made himself sick. Diana, tell me again how you helped Sam last year.

Diana: Sure. Janet and I talked about Sam's overdependence on adults and how that could negatively affect his academic progress. We also talked about his need to develop better social skills with his classmates so that he didn't always need to be the center of attention.

Janet: I told Diana how I thought my dad was reinforcing Sam's dependence. Whenever I picked Sam up from preschool because he was "sick," I'd have to take him to work with me. I work for my dad, who has a small business in town. Sam would sit in the reception area while I worked, and Dad's customers would give him their undivided attention, because Sam would just turn on the charm.

Diana: Janet and I decided that whenever Sam left school "sick," Janet would ask her father and the customers not to give Sam any attention. Instead, she would tell Sam to rest in a side room until she could take him home and put him to bed.

Janet: Sam got "sick" several more times, but once he realized that Dad, the customers—and me, too—weren't going to give him any attention at the store, he didn't play sick anymore.

Diana: Meanwhile, at school, I had made Sam and one of his classmates the "Attendance Helpers" who took the absence report to the school secretary every day. I rotated Sam's partner often so that he could form one-on-one relationships with several classmates. And Mrs. Thompson's third-grade class developed a buddy system to help Sam interact with teachers and children in more appropriate ways.

Janet: By winter, Sam had made friends with several children in his class.

Diana: And everyone enjoyed being with him since he didn't demand center stage anymore.

Mrs. Roberts: It's been a big help to hear about all you did for Sam last year. It seems like you did all the right things to help him get over his separation anxiety and to get along better with his peers. I guess I'll just have to try the same techniques again to help him adjust to kindergarten. Janet, I hope you'll support me in this.

Janet: Oh, yes, Mrs. Roberts. I really want Sam to have a good year in kindergarten.

PROBLEM SOLVING

1. Do you think that Mrs. Roberts is correct in saying that Sam is showing an extinction burst in the way he is behaving in kindergarten? Why or why not?
2. How effective do you think it will be to repeat in kindergarten the plan Diana used to extinguish Sam's behavior in preschool?
3. If you were Mrs. Roberts, what, if anything, would you do to reinforce Sam's behavior as it improves? What type of schedule of reinforcement would you use?

Adapted by permission from "Kindergarten Is Big Business" by Linda K. Elksnin, Professor of Education at The Citadel; Diane Birschbach, a teacher of preschoolers with special needs; and Susan P. Gurganus, Associate Professor of Special Education at the College of Charleston, from *Allyn & Bacon's Custom Cases in Education,* edited by Greta Morine-Dershimer, Daniel Hallahan, and James Kauffman (1997).

The Intentional Teacher

● Using What You Know about Behavioral Theories of Learning to Improve Teaching and Learning

Intentional teachers think about their vision of education and use theory and empirical research to help them achieve that vision. Intentional teachers have a clear sense of how they want students to behave. They consider behavioral learning theories as one set of tools that can help them support positive changes in students' behavior and, to a limited extent, their learning. Intentional teachers make effective use of behaviorist theories, and they modify their actions in light of evidence related to the success of their efforts.

1 What am I trying to accomplish?

Your vision of education probably includes the goal of student self-direction. If so, consider teaching cognitive behavior modification and self-regulation.

As your fifth-graders work in spirited groups, writing television commercials, you briefly interrupt their work to ask a few questions: "Are you on task?" "Have you said at least one nice thing about someone else's idea?" The questions help students check their own behavior.

Before the school year begins, develop a discipline plan that supports appropriate behavior through a variety of reinforcers and seeks to extinguish negative behaviors. In developing your plan, consider four key questions.

You ask yourself, "What social, activity, and token reinforcers will be most effective?"

"What are my plans for extinguishing undesirable behaviors?"

"What (if any) punishments are appropriate for my plan?"

"According to what schedule will I provide reinforcement?"

Each day rehearse your use of your plan, revising it as appropriate for particular groups of students, so that you can apply the plan consistently, systematically, and without emotion.

Before your noisy sixth period begins, you rehearse: "I will recognize only those who make an appropriate bid for the floor. No matter what. I will ignore attention-seeking behaviors. I will use praise to reinforce on-task behavior." You smile and greet students at the door.

2 What are my students' relevant experiences and needs?

Reinforcers and punishers vary in their effectiveness for individuals. Determine what kinds of reinforcers are effective for particular students.

You hand out a survey to your fifth-graders early in the year. The survey asks open-ended questions such as: "If you had time to do any activity at all in the classroom, what would you do?" and "It bothers me when teachers . . . ." The survey also includes a closed-ended rating form for a variety of social, token, and activity reinforcers. You include the high-rated reinforcers in your discipline program.

Reinforcers are most effective when they immediately follow the desired behavior. Provide immediate feedback so that students have knowledge of the results of their efforts and learn to link each behavior to its consequence.

Your kindergartners are working hard on forming the lower-case letter *b*. You provide white boards and ask students to hold up their boards when they've written *b*. You are able to provide feedback on each student's *b* quickly, praising and redirecting as necessary. Students get feedback that is meaningful at a time when they can most easily connect it to their efforts.

Applying the concept of discriminative stimuli to classroom instruction and management is easy: Teachers should tell students what behaviors will be reinforced. In theory, a teacher could wait until students did something worthwhile and then reinforce it, but this would be incredibly inefficient. Rather, teachers should give students messages that say, in effect, "To be reinforced (e.g., with praise, grades, or stars), these are the things you must do." In this way, teachers can avoid having students spend time and effort on the wrong activities. If students know that what they are doing will pay off, they will usually work hard.

GENERALIZATION ● If students learn to stay in their seats and do careful work in math class, will their behavior also improve in science class? If students can subtract 3 apples from 7 apples, can they also subtract 3 oranges from 7 oranges? If students

3 What approaches and materials are available to help me challenge every student?

Use reinforcers and punishers to help students connect their choices with consequences.

> When two students shoot rubber bands during geoboard time in math, they are removed from the group to sit and watch. They learn that the consequence of their choice to shoot rubber bands is that they cannot engage in the rewarding experience of using geoboards.

Use behavior theory principles to enhance your instruction.

> You break down complex skills and performances into smaller bits so that you can shape behavior and learning gradually.

> You model behaviors before you expect students to perform them.

> You teach students to discriminate and to generalize among examples and settings by suggesting the relevant characteristics and information to look for. Then you provide feedback on their responses. For instance, in teaching second-graders about mammals, you provide 40 large pictures of animals, pointing out characteristics of the mammals. Then students sort the pictures into mammals and nonmammals, and you praise them for their accuracy.

> You increase the likelihood of students' generalizing (transferring) their learning to new situations by using real-life applications and many examples from different contexts. For instance, after studying a variety of graphs with your fifth-graders, you prepare a bulletin board. You invite students to fill it with examples of graphs from newspapers, advertisements, and other print sources.

4 How will I know whether and when to change my strategy or modify my instruction?

Gather information on whether and when to change your instruction by watching the perceptible effects on students. Also, assess the effects of the strategies on your own attitude and performance.

As you explain fractions to your third-graders, you do quick visual sweeps of the classroom, taking note of nonverbal hints from the students as to whether they are actively engaged in the ideas. Later, you pull aside a small group of students who seemed frustrated during the lesson and provide additional instruction.

When reinforcers stop having the desired effect, it is time to change reinforcers.

> Your seventh-graders were initially very enthusiastic about the team points that added up to popcorn parties. Lately, though, you notice the team points seem to have no effect on students' behavior. You open a discussion: "Are you tired of popcorn?" You and the class decide to allow winning teams to select their reward from a longer list of reinforcers.

5 What information will I accept as evidence that my students and I are experiencing success?

Look back to your vision of education and your hopes for how students will behave. Use data about student behavior to assess the class's progress toward those goals.

> You tape-record your English literature class. To analyze the tape, you tally the number of times students interrupt or make off-task remarks, and you take note of how students respond in positive ways to the comments and ideas of their peers.

Use informal observational data and other forms of student feedback to discern students' reaction to your discipline plan and instruction.

> You sit and watch while second-graders work in groups on their social studies projects. You assess not only whether students are following the class rules but also whether and how they are solving their own problems.

can interpret symbolism used by Shakespeare, can they also interpret symbolism used in African folk tales? These are all questions of **generalization,** or transfer of behaviors learned under one set of conditions to other situations. Generalization cannot be taken for granted. Usually, when a classroom management program is successfully introduced in one setting, students' behaviors do not automatically improve in other settings. Instead, students learn to discriminate among settings. Even young children readily learn what is encouraged and what is forbidden in kindergarten, at home, and at various friends' houses. Their behavior may be quite different in each setting, according to the different rules and expectations.

For generalization to occur, it usually must be planned for. A successful classroom management program used in social studies class may be transferred to English class to ensure generalization to that setting. Students may need to study

generalization
Carryover of behaviors, skills, or concepts from one setting or task to another.

the use of symbolism by many authors in many cultures before they acquire the skill to interpret symbolism in general.

Obviously, generalization is most likely to occur across similar settings or across similar concepts. A new behavior is more likely to generalize from reading class to social studies class than to recess or home settings. However, even in the most similar-appearing settings, generalizations may not occur. For example, many students will demonstrate complete mastery of spelling or language mechanics and then fail to apply this knowledge to their own compositions. Teachers should not assume that because students can do something under one set of circumstances, they can also do it under a different set of circumstances.

TECHNIQUES FOR INCREASING GENERALIZATION ● Schloss and Smith (1998) describe 11 techniques for increasing the chances that a behavior learned in one setting, such as a given class, will generalize to other settings, such as other classes or, more importantly, real-life applications (also see Haring & Liberty, 1990). Some of these strategies involve teaching in a way that makes generalization easier. For example, arithmetic lessons involving money will probably transfer better to real life if they involve manipulating real or simulated coins and bills than if they involve only problems on paper. Another teaching strategy known to contribute to generalization is using many examples from different contexts. For example, students are more likely to be able to transfer the concept of supply and demand to new areas if they learn examples relating to prices for groceries, prices for natural resources, values of collectibles (such as Beanie Babies), and wages for common and rare skills than if they learn only about grocery pricing. An obvious strategy for increasing generalization is "on-the-job training": teaching a given skill in the actual environment in which it will be used, or in a simulation of such an environment.

Teaching arithmetic involving money and values will probably transfer better to real life if instruction involves real-life examples, like this "Allowance" game. How else might these students' teacher increase generalization of these behaviors to other settings?

After initial instruction has taken place, there are many ways to increase generalization. One is to repeat instruction in a variety of settings. For example, after teaching students to use a given test-taking strategy in mathematics, such as "skip difficult problems and go back to them after answering the easy ones," a teacher might give students the opportunity to use this same strategy on a science test, a grammar test, and a health test. Another after-teaching technique is to help students make the link between a new skill and natural reinforcers in the environment so as to maintain that skill. For example, when children are learning to read, they can be given a regular homework assignment to read books or magazines that are of high interest to them, even if those materials are not "good literature." Initially, new reading skills may be better maintained by comic books than by *Caddie Woodlawn,* because for some children the comic books tie their new skill more immediately to the pleasure of reading, making generalization to nonschool settings more likely. Finally, a teacher can increase generalization by directly reinforcing generalization—for example, by praising a student who connects a new idea to a different context or uses a skill in a new application.

SELF-CHECK

List principles of behavioral learning and think of a specific classroom example illustrating each one. Then classify the items in your list in a concept map organized around the headings Consequence, Reinforcement, Punishment, and Antecedent.

HOW HAS SOCIAL LEARNING THEORY CONTRIBUTED TO OUR UNDERSTANDING OF HUMAN LEARNING?

Social learning theory is a major outgrowth of the behavioral learning theory tradition. Developed by Albert Bandura, **social learning theory** accepts most of the principles of behavioral theories but focuses to a much greater degree on the effects of cues on behavior and on internal mental processes, emphasizing the effects of thought on action and action on thought (Bandura, 1986).

Bandura: Modeling and Observational Learning

Bandura noted that the Skinnerian emphasis on the effects of the consequences of behavior largely ignored the phenomena of **modeling**—the imitation of others' behavior—and of vicarious experience—learning from others' successes or failures. He felt that much of human learning is not shaped by its consequences but is more efficiently learned directly from a model (Bandura, 1986). The physical education teacher demonstrates jumping jacks, and students imitate. Bandura calls this *no-trial learning,* because students do not have to go through a shaping process but can reproduce the correct response immediately.

Bandura's (1986) analysis of **observational learning** involves four phases: the attentional, retention, reproduction, and motivational phases.

1. **Attentional phase:** The first phase in observational learning is paying attention to a model. In general, students pay attention to role models who are attractive, successful, interesting, and popular. This is why so many students

social learning theory
Learning theory that emphasizes not only reinforcement but also the effects of cues on thought and of thought on action.

modeling
Imitation of others' behavior.

observational learning
Learning by observation and imitation of others.

CONNECTIONS
For the relation of social learning theory to Vygotskian and neo-Piagetian views of development, see Chapter 2, pages 42 and 43.

CONNECTIONS
For the relation of social learning theory to social construction of meaning, see Chapter 8, page 256.

copy the dress, hairstyle, and mannerisms of pop culture stars. In the classroom the teacher gains the students' attention by presenting clear and interesting cues, by using novelty or surprise, and by motivating students to pay attention.

2. **Retention phase:** Once teachers have students' attention, it is time to model the behavior they want students to imitate and then give students a chance to practice or rehearse. For example, a teacher might show how to write a script *A*. Then students would imitate the teacher's model by trying to write *A*s themselves.

3. **Reproduction:** During the reproduction phase, students try to match their behavior to the model's. In the classroom the assessment of student learning takes place during this phase. For example, after seeing the script *A* modeled and practicing it several times, can the student reproduce the letter so that it looks like the teacher's model?

4. **Motivational phase:** The final stage in the observational learning process is motivation. Students will imitate a model because they believe that doing so will increase their own chances to be reinforced. In the classroom the motivational phase of observational learning often entails praise or grades given for matching the teacher's model. Students pay attention to the model, practice it, and reproduce it because they have learned that this is what the teacher likes and they want to please the teacher.

VICARIOUS LEARNING ● Although most observational learning is motivated by an expectation that correctly imitating the model will lead to reinforcement, it is also important to note that people learn by seeing others reinforced or punished for engaging in certain behaviors (Bandura, 1986). This is why magazine distributors always include happy winners in their advertisements to induce people to enter promotional contests. We may consciously know that our chances of winning are one in several million, but seeing others so handsomely reinforced makes us want to imitate their contest-entering behavior.

Classroom teachers use the principle of **vicarious learning** all the time. When one student is fooling around, teachers often single out others who are working well and reinforce them for doing a good job. The misbehaving student sees that working is reinforced and (it is hoped) gets back to work. This technique was systematically studied by Broden, Hall, Dunlap, & Clark (1970). Two disruptive second-graders, Edwin and Greg, sat next to each other. After a baseline period, the teacher began to notice and praise Edwin whenever he was paying attention and doing his classwork. Edwin's behavior improved markedly under this condition. Of greater interest, however, is that Greg's behavior also improved, even though no specific reinforcement for appropriate behavior was directed toward him. Apparently, Greg learned from Edwin's experience. In the case of Ms. Esteban and Rebecca at the opening of this chapter, other students saw Rebecca get Ms. Esteban's attention by calling out answers, so they modeled their behavior on Rebecca's.

One of the classic experiments in social learning theory is a study done by Bandura (1965). Children were shown one of three films. In all three, an adult modeled aggressive behavior. In one film the model was severely punished. In another the model was praised and given treats. In a third the model was given no consequences. After viewing one of the films, the children were observed playing with toys. The children who had seen the model punished engaged in significantly fewer aggressive acts in their own play than did the children who had seen the model rewarded or had viewed the no-consequences film.

vicarious learning

Learning based on observation of the consequences of others' behavior.

Observational Learning

Have you ever tried to teach someone to tie his or her shoes? Imagine explaining this task to someone without the use of a model or imitation! Such a simple task, and one that many of us take for granted, can be quite a milestone for a kindergartner. Learning to tie our shoes is certainly a prime example of how observational learning works.

Acquiring new skills by observing the behaviors of others is a common part of everyday life. In many situations children watch others talking and acting, and they witness the consequences of those activities as well. Such observations provide models that teach children strategies to use at other times and places.

Although the major focus of research on observational learning has been on specific behaviors, studies have also shown that attitudes, too, may be acquired through observation (Miller, 1993). Teachers and parents alike are concerned with the models emulated by children. The value of these models goes beyond the specific abilities they possess and includes the attitudes they represent. In the classroom the teacher must be certain to exemplify a standard of behavior consistent with the expectations he or she has for the students. For instance, if promptness and politeness are characteristics the teacher wants to foster in the students, then the teacher must be certain to demonstrate those traits.

In cooperative learning groups, the success of the group may depend on the models present in that group. Peers have a strong influence on the behaviors of the individual. When teachers place students in groups, it may be just as important to include students who possess a high motivation for learning in a group as it is to include students with strong math skills. The attitudes and behaviors that accompany high motivation will be imitated by fellow students.

SELF-REGULATED LEARNING ● Another important concept in social learning theory is **self-regulation** (Pressley, 1995; Winne, 1995; Zimmerman, 1995). Bandura (1977) hypothesized that people observe their own behavior, judge it against their own standards, and reinforce or punish themselves. We have all had the experience of knowing we've done a job well and mentally patting ourselves on the back, regardless of what others have said. Similarly, we all know when we've done less than our best. To make these judgments, we have to have expectations for our own performance. One student might be delighted to get 90 percent correct on a test, while another might be quite disappointed.

Students can be taught to use self-regulation strategies, and they can be reminded to do so in a variety of contexts so that self-regulation becomes a habit. For example, students might be asked to set goals for the amount of time they expect to study each evening and to record whether or not they meet their goals. Children who are studying multiplication facts might be asked to time themselves on how quickly and accurately they can complete a 50-item facts test and then to try to beat their own record. Students might be asked to grade their own essays in terms of content, mechanics, and organization, and to see whether they can match the teacher's ratings. Each of these strategies puts students in control of their own learning goals, and each is likely to build a general strategy of setting and meeting personal goals and personal standards (Butler & Winne, 1995).

As with any skill, self-regulated learning skills are likely to remain limited to one situation or context unless they are applied in many contexts. For example,

CONNECTIONS
For more on self-regulated learning, see Chapter 8, page 260.

self-regulation
Rewarding or punishing one's own behavior.

children who learn to set study goals for themselves when working alone may not transfer these skills to situations in which they are working in groups or in the presence of a teacher (Alexander, 1995; Corno, 1995; Zimmerman, 1995), although they can readily learn to make these generalizations if they are taught or reminded to do so. Similarly, children may not transfer self-regulated learning strategies from English to math, or even from computations to problem solving (Boekaerts, 1995). For this reason, students need many opportunities to use goal-setting and self-evaluation strategies in a variety of contexts, to monitor and celebrate their progress, and to understand how, when, and why they should self-regulate (Pressley, 1995).

Meichenbaum's Model of Self-Regulated Learning

Students can be taught to monitor and regulate their own behavior. Self-regulated learning strategies of this kind are often called **cognitive behavior modification** (see Harris, 1990; Manning, 1991). For example, Meichenbaum (1977) developed a strategy in which students are trained to say to themselves, "What is my problem? What is my plan? Am I using my plan? How did I do?" This strategy has also been used to reduce disruptive behavior of students at many grade levels (Webber, Scheuermann, McCall, & Coleman, 1993; Workman & Katz, 1995). Manning (1988) taught disruptive third-graders self-statements to help them remember appropriate behavior and to reinforce it for themselves. As one instance, for appropriate hand-raising, students were taught to say to themselves while raising their hands, "If I scream out the answer, others will be disturbed. I will raise my hand and wait my turn. Good for me. See, I can wait!" (Manning, 1988, p. 197). Similar strategies have been successfully applied to helping students monitor their own achievement. For example, poor readers have been taught to ask themselves questions as they read and to summarize paragraphs to make sure they comprehend text (Bornstein, 1985).

The steps involved in self-instruction are described by Meichenbaum (1977) as follows:

1. An adult model performs a task while talking to self out loud (cognitive modeling).
2. The child performs the same task under the direction of the model's instructions (overt, external guidance).
3. The child performs the task while instructing self aloud (overt self-guidance).
4. The child whispers the instructions to self as he or she goes through the task (faded, overt self-guidance).
5. The child performs the task while guiding his or her performance via private speech (covert self-instruction). (p. 32)

Note the similarity of Meichenbaum's self-regulated learning strategy to the Vygotskian approach to scaffolded instruction described in Chapter 2. Both approaches emphasize modeling private speech and gradually moving from teacher-controlled to student-controlled behaviors, with the students using private speech to talk themselves through their tasks. Encouraging self-regulated learning is a means of teaching students to think about their own thinking. Self-regulated learning strategies not only have been found to improve performance on the task students were taught, but also have generalized to other tasks (Harris, 1990; Harris & Pressley, 1992).

One example of a way to help children engage in self-regulated learning is providing students, when assigning a long or complex task, with a form for monitor-

cognitive behavior modification
Procedures based on both behavioral and cognitive principles for changing one's own behavior by means of self-talk and self-instruction.

ing their progress. For example, a teacher might assign students to write a report on the life of Martin Luther King Jr. Students might be given the following self-monitoring checklist:

Task Completion Form

Located material on Martin Luther King Jr. in the library.

Read and took notes on material.

Wrote first draft of report.

Checked draft for sense.

Checked draft for mechanics:

    Spelling

    Grammar

    Punctuation

Composed final draft typed or neatly handwritten.

The idea behind this form is that breaking down a complex task into smaller pieces encourages students to feel that they are making progress toward their larger goal. Checking off each step allows them to give themselves a mental pat on the back that reinforces their efforts (see Jenson et al., 1988). Along similar lines, Trammel, Schloss, and Alper (1994) found that having children with learning disabilities keep records and make graphs of their homework completion significantly increased the amount of homework they did (also see DiGangi, Maag, & Rutherford, 1991; Lloyd, Landrum, & Hallahan, 1991).

SELF-REINFORCEMENT ● Drabman, Spitalnik, and O'Leary (1973) designed and evaluated a procedure to teach students to regulate their own behavior. They asked teachers to rate student behaviors each day and reinforce students when they earned high ratings. Then they changed the program: They asked students to guess what rating the teacher had given them. The students were reinforced for guessing correctly. Finally, the reinforcers were gradually removed. The students' behavior improved under the reinforcement and guessing conditions, and it remained at its improved level long after the program was ended. The authors explained that students who were taught to match the teacher's ratings developed their own standards for appropriate behavior and reinforced themselves for meeting those standards.

Information about one's own behavior has often been found to change behavior (Rosenbaum & Drabman, 1982), even when that information is self-provided. For example, researchers have increased on-task behavior by having children mark down every few minutes whether or not they have been studying in the last few minutes (Maag, Rutherford, & DiGangi, 1992; Webber et al., 1993). When coupled with self-reinforcement, self-observation often has important effects on student behavior (Jenson et al., 1988). Many of us use this principle in studying, saying to ourselves that we will not take a break for lunch until we have finished reading a certain amount of material.

Students who feel confident in their ability to use metacognitive and self-motivational behaviors are likely to be high in self-efficacy—the belief that one's own efforts (rather than luck or other people or other external or uncontrollable factors) determine one's success or failure. Self-efficacy beliefs are perhaps the most important factor (after ability) in determining students' success in school (Bandura, 1993; Corno & Kanfer, 1993; Zimmerman & Bandura, 1994).

CONNECTIONS

For more on self-efficacy beliefs and student success, see Chapter 10, pages 333 and 334.

TEACHERS IN ACTION

How have you applied behavioral and social learning theories in your teaching?

Gemma Staub Hoskins
Teacher, Grade 5
Jarrettsville Elementary School
Jarrettsville, Maryland

I have used behavioral and social learning theories with mainstreamed students with special needs. My experience with many children suffering the pain of family dysfunction has led me to see the school as a reenacted family setting. For students whose early years are marked by abuse, alcohol, and neglect, development and behavior are anything but normal.

In working with one such child recently, I saw immediately that this 10-year-old boy, new to my school, had had little or no exposure to language models, social skills, experiential stimulation, or appropriate work habits. Surprisingly, this fifth-grader did not qualify for remedial services in any academic areas and so would remain in the regular classroom throughout the day. To begin the work of filling in the blatant gaps in this child's development, an informal teacher-assistance team was created, made up of the guidance counselor, the pupil personnel worker, a special-education teacher, and an administrator, to design a learning and behavior management plan.

Three broad goals were identified as desirable outcomes: cooperating in a group, working independently for at least 15 minutes, and following directions. We decided that an efficient way to shape appropriate behavior would be to use some primary needs not sufficiently met for this child in the past. Food, for example, was an extremely effective behavior modifier. We established his involvement in his management program by having him draw up a list of favorite foods, which he could "purchase" from a snack box with points he earned by following his plan.

Benetta M. Skrundz
Learning Disabilities Teacher
Franklin Elementary School
East Chicago, Indiana

Identifying reinforcers can be tricky. For instance, I had one 9-year-old boy in my class who was extremely disruptive on a daily basis. He would shove and hit other children, poke them with scissors and pencils, throw food. He was continually speaking out and out-of-seat. Separating him from other children didn't help, because the minute I turned my attention from him, he would slam down a book or tear up a classmate's paper.

Initially, I set up a behavior modification program that rewarded Artie at 5-minute intervals for proper school behavior. A pattern quickly emerged in which he would have a good day, followed by 2 days when I could not find a way to reward him. During good days, Artie was a totally different child. He would be helpful toward classmates. He'd raise his hand and answer appropriately. He also showed his true academic ability on these days. Soon, however, I noticed Artie having more bad days. After he received a 1-day suspension, his mother returned him to school, and that's when I learned for the first time about Artie's older brother. The brother, who had by then dropped out of school, was the only consistent male figure in his life, and Artie looked up to him. Whenever Artie brought home a good report, his brother would ridicule him. When his brother found out about the suspension, he praised Artie and spent more time with him as a reward, taking him out to lunch.

At school, those of us who had daily contact with Artie decided to spend more time talking with him about setting positive goals for himself. Repeatedly, we stressed pride and trust. It took a while, and there were setbacks, but Artie's behavior and academic performance began to improve. By the end of the year, everyone noticed his improved behavior and he earned his way onto the Good Citizens Wall.

Strengths and Limitations of Behavioral Learning Theories

The basic principles of behavioral learning theories are as firmly established as any in psychology and have been demonstrated under many different conditions. These principles are useful for explaining much of human behavior; they are even more useful in changing behavior.

It is important to recognize, however, that behavioral learning theories are limited in scope. With the exception of social learning theorists, behavioral learning theorists focus almost exclusively on observable behavior. This is one reason that so many of the examples presented in this chapter involve the management of behavior (see Wielkiewicz, 1995; Wolfgang, 1995). Less visible learning processes, such as concept formation, learning from text, problem solving, and thinking, are difficult to observe directly and have therefore been studied less often by behavioral learning theorists. These processes fall more into the domain of cognitive learning. Social learning theory, which is a direct outgrowth of behavioral learning theories, helps to bridge the gap between the behavioral and cognitive perspectives.

Behavioral and cognitive theories of learning are often posed as competing, opposite models. There are indeed specific areas in which these theories take contradictory positions. However, it is more accurate to see them as complementary rather than competitive—that is, as tackling different problems.

SELF-CHECK

Extend the comparison chart you began earlier by adding the contributions of social learning theorists as represented by Bandura and Meichenbaum.

CHAPTER SUMMARY

WHAT IS LEARNING?

Learning involves the acquisition of abilities that are not innate. Learning depends on experience, including feedback from the environment.

WHAT BEHAVIORAL LEARNING THEORIES HAVE EVOLVED?

Early research into learning studied the effects of stimuli on reflexive behaviors. Ivan Pavlov contributed the idea of classical conditioning, in which neutral stimuli can acquire the capacity to evoke behavioral responses through their association with unconditioned stimuli that trigger reflexes. E. L. Thorndike developed the Law of Effect, emphasizing the role of the consequences of present behavior in determining future behavior. B. F. Skinner continued the study of the relationship between behavior and consequences. He described operant conditioning, in which reinforcers and punishers shape behavior.

WHAT ARE SOME PRINCIPLES OF BEHAVIORAL LEARNING?

Reinforcers increase the frequency of a behavior, and punishers decrease its frequency. Reinforcement can be primary or secondary, positive or negative. Intrinsic reinforcers are rewards inherent in a behavior itself. Extrinsic reinforcers are praise or rewards. Punishment involves weakening behavior by either introducing aversive consequences or removing reinforcers. The Premack Principle states that a way to increase less-enjoyed activities is to link them to more-enjoyed activities.

Shaping through timely feedback on each step of a task is an effective teaching practice based on behavioral learning theory. Extinction is the weakening and gradual disappearance of behavior as reinforcement is withdrawn.

Schedules of reinforcement are used to increase the probability, frequency, or persistence of desired behavior. Reinforcement schedules may be based on ratios or intervals and may be fixed or variable.

Antecedent stimuli serve as cues indicating which behaviors will be reinforced or punished. Discrimination involves using cues to detect differences between stimulus situations, whereas generalization involves responding to similarities between stimuli. Generalization is transfer or carryover of behaviors learned under one set of conditions to other situations.

HOW HAS SOCIAL LEARNING THEORY CONTRIBUTED TO OUR UNDERSTANDING OF HUMAN LEARNING?

Social learning theory is based on a recognition of the importance of observational learning and self-regulated learning. Bandura noted that learning through modeling—directly or vicariously—involves four phases: paying attention, retaining the modeled behavior, reproducing the behavior, and being motivated to repeat the behavior. Bandura proposed that students should be taught to have expectations for their own performances and to reinforce themselves. Meichenbaum proposed steps for self-regulated learning that represent a form of cognitive behavior modification.

Behavioral learning theories are central to the application of educational psychology in classroom management, discipline, motivation, instructional models, and other areas. Behavioral learning theories are limited in scope, however, in that they describe only observable behavior that can be directly measured.

KEY TERMS

antecedent stimuli   158

aversive stimulus   151

behavioral learning theories   140

classical conditioning   142

cognitive behavior modification   166

cognitive learning theories   140

conditioned response   142

conditioned stimulus   142

consequences   146

cues   158

discrimination   158

extinction   153

extinction burst   154

extrinsic reinforcers   149

fixed-interval schedule   156

fixed-ratio (FR) schedule   155

generalization   161

intrinsic reinforcers   149

Law of Effect   144

learning   141

maintenance   157

modeling   163

negative reinforcer   147

neutral stimuli   142

observational learning   163

operant conditioning   144

positive reinforcer   147

Premack Principle   147

presentation punishment   151

primary reinforcer   146

punishment   150

reinforcer   146

removal punishment 151

schedule of reinforcement 155

secondary reinforcer 146

self-regulation 165

shaping 153

Skinner box 145

social learning theory 163

stimuli (stimulus) 141

time out 151

unconditioned response 142

unconditioned stimulus 142

variable-interval schedule 156

variable-ratio (VR) schedule 155

vicarious learning 164

Self-Assessment

1. Which of the following most clearly represents an example of learning?
   a. Moving one's hand away from a hot object.
   b. Being startled by a loud noise.
   c. Feeling thirsty after exercising.
   d. Having test anxiety.

2. Match the following theories or laws of learning with the theorist most closely associated with each.
   _____ classical conditioning
   _____ law of effect
   _____ operant conditioning
   _____ social learning
   a. Albert Bandura
   b. Edward Thorndike
   c. Ivan Pavlov
   d. B. F. Skinner

3. An example of a primary reinforcer is
   a. safety or security.
   b. a good grade in school.
   c. money.
   d. praise.

4. What is the Premack Principle? Give two classroom examples.

5. A teacher praises a student for completing a homework assignment with 100 percent accuracy. If the student continues to turn in exceptional assignments, the praise most likely served as a
   a. positive reinforcer.
   b. presentation punisher.
   c. removal punisher.
   d. negative reinforcer.

6. Attention, retention, reproduction, and motivation are four phases of
   a. observational learning.
   b. shaping.
   c. classical conditioning.
   d. reinforcement.

7. Meichenbaum's model for cognitive behavior modification involves all of the following concepts except
   a. self-regulated learning.
   b. private speech.
   c. vicarious learning.
   d. modeling.

8. Which of the following is a limitation of behavioral learning theories?
   a. They compete against cognitive theories of learning.
   b. They attempt to describe learning directly.
   c. They limit the study of learning to observable behaviors.
   d. They rely on faulty research studies to explain learning.

9. Does punishment—for example, reprimands or lost privileges—work well with children? What are some negative effects of punishment? What, according to Skinner, is the best way to deal with good and bad behaviors of students?

10. Explain the difference between classical conditioning and operant conditioning.

Chapter 6

WHAT IS AN INFORMATION-PROCESSING MODEL?
Sensory Register
Short-Term or Working Memory
Long-Term Memory
Factors That Enhance Long-Term Memory
Other Information-Processing Models

WHAT CAUSES PEOPLE TO REMEMBER OR FORGET?
Forgetting and Remembering
Practice

HOW CAN MEMORY STRATEGIES BE TAUGHT?
Verbal Learning
Paired-Associate Learning
Serial and Free-Recall Learning

WHAT MAKES INFORMATION MEANINGFUL?
Rote versus Meaningful Learning
Schema Theory

HOW DO METACOGNITIVE SKILLS HELP STUDENTS LEARN?

WHAT STUDY STRATEGIES HELP STUDENTS LEARN?
Note-Taking
Underlining
Summarizing
Outlining and Mapping
The PQ4R Method

HOW DO COGNITIVE TEACHING STRATEGIES HELP STUDENTS LEARN?
Making Learning Relevant and Activating Prior Knowledge
Organizing Information

Cognitive Theories of Learning: Basic Concepts

Verona Bishop's biology class was doing a unit on human learning. At the start of one lesson, Ms. Bishop did an experiment with her students. For 3 seconds, using an overhead projector, she flashed a diagram of a model of information processing identical to the one in Figure 6.1. Then she asked students to recall what they noticed. Some mentioned that they saw yellow boxes and blue arrows. Some saw the words *memory* and *forgotten* and inferred that the figure had something to do with learning. One student even saw the word *learning,* though it wasn't in the figure.

"Come now," said Ms. Bishop. "You noticed a lot more than that! You just may not have noticed what you noticed. For example, what did you smell?"

The whole class laughed. They all recalled smelling the broccoli cooking in the cafeteria. The students caught on to the idea and began to recall all the other details they had noticed that had nothing to do with the diagram: the sounds of a truck going by, details of the classroom and the people in it, and so on.

After this discussion, Ms. Bishop said, "Isn't the brain amazing? In only three seconds you received an enormous amount of information. You didn't even know you were noticing the smell of the broccoli until I reminded you about it, but it was in your mind just the same. Also, in only three seconds your mind was already starting to make sense of the information in the figure. Cheryl thought she saw the word *learning,* which wasn't there at all. But her mind leaped to that word because she saw words like *memory* that relate to learning.

"Now imagine that you could keep in your mind forever everything that occurred in the three seconds you looked at the diagram: the arrows, the boxes, the words, the truck, the broccoli—everything. In fact, imagine that you could keep everything that ever entered your mind. What would that be like?"

"You'd be a genius!" ventured Samphan.

"You'd go crazy!" countered Jamal.

"I think Jamal is closer to the truth," said Ms. Bishop. "If your mind filled up with all this useless junk, you'd be a blithering idiot! One of the most important things we're going to learn about learning is that it is an active process of focusing in on important information, screening out unimportant information, and using what is already in our minds to decide which is which."

Ms. Bishop turned on the overhead projector again.

"When we study this diagram in more detail, you'll use what you already know about learning, memory, forgetting, and diagrams to make sense of it. I hope you'll always remember the main ideas it's trying to show you. You'll soon forget that the arrows are blue and the boxes are yellow, and even the smell of the broccoli will fade from your memory, but the parts of this diagram that make sense to you and answer questions you care about may stay in your memory your whole life!"

Using Your EXPERIENCE

Cooperative Learning   Jot down two or three ways in which you try to memorize lists and study new concepts. Share with other students a strategy that you use to learn information better.

Cooperative Learning   What is your picture of learning, memory, and forgetting? After drafting your own picture, meet with four or five classmates to compose a summary illustration or diagram of human memory and cognition based on your individual ideas. After 10 minutes, share with the class.

The human mind is a meaning maker. From the first microsecond you see, hear, taste, or feel something, you start a process of deciding what it is, how it relates to what you already know, and whether it is important to keep in your mind or should be discarded. This whole process may take place consciously, unconsciously, or both. This chapter describes how information is received and processed in the mind, how memory and forgetting work, and how teachers can help students understand and remember critical information, skills, and ideas. This chapter also presents cognitive theories of learning, theories that relate to processes that go on within the minds of learners, and means of helping students use their minds more effectively to learn, remember, and use knowledge.

WHAT IS AN INFORMATION-PROCESSING MODEL?

Information constantly enters our minds through our senses. Most of this information is almost immediately discarded, and we may never even be aware of much of it. Some is held in our memories for a short time and then forgotten. For example, we may remember the seat number on a baseball ticket until we find our seats, at which point we will forget the number. However, some information is retained much longer, perhaps for the rest of our lives. What is the process by which information is absorbed, and how can teachers take advantage of this process to help students retain critical information and skills? These are questions that have been addressed by cognitive learning theorists and that have led to **information-processing theory,** the dominant theory of learning and memory since the mid-1970s.

Research on human memory (see, e.g., Anderson, 1995; Atkinson & Shiffrin, 1968; Ericsson & Kintsch, 1995; Massaro & Cowan, 1993) has helped learning theorists to describe the process by which information is remembered (or forgotten). This process, usually referred to as the Atkinson–Shiffrin model of information processing, is illustrated in Figure 6.1.

Sensory Register

The first component of the memory system that incoming information meets is the sensory register, shown at the left of Figure 6.1. **Sensory registers** receive large amounts of information from the senses (sight, hearing, touch, smell, taste) and

information-processing theory
Cognitive theory of learning that describes the processing, storage, and retrieval of knowledge in the mind.

sensory register
Component of the memory system in which information is received and held for very short periods of time.

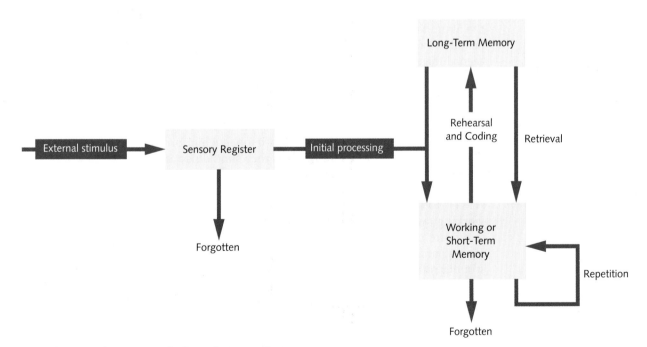

FIGURE 6.1 ● The Sequence of Information Processing
Information that is to be remembered must first reach a person's senses, then be attended to and transferred from the sensory register to the working memory, then be processed again for transfer to long-term memory.
From Charles G. Morris, *Psychology: An Introduction* (8th ed.), p. 233. Copyright © 1993. Adapted by permission of Prentice Hall, Upper Saddle River, New Jersey.

FIGURE 6.2 ● Display Used in Sensory Register Experiments
This is a typical display used by G. A. Sperling to detect the existence and limits of the sensory register. People who were shown the display for an instant and then asked to recall a specific row were usually able to do so. However, they were not able to recall all 12 letters.

From G. A. Sperling, "The Information Available in Brief Visual Presentations," *Psychological Monographs, 74*, 1960, American Psychological Association.

hold it for a very short time, no more than a couple of seconds. If nothing happens to information held in the sensory registers, it is rapidly lost.

Ingenious experiments have been used to detect the sensory registers. A person might be shown a display like that in Figure 6.2 for a very short period of time, say 50 milliseconds. The person is usually able to report seeing 3, 4, or 5 of the letters but not all 12 of them. In a classic early experiment, Sperling (1960) presented a display like Figure 6.2 to people. After the display disappeared, he signaled viewers to try to recall the top, middle, or bottom row. He found that people could recall any one row almost perfectly. Therefore they must have seen all the letters in the 50 milliseconds and retained them for a short period of time. However, when people tried to recall all 12 letters, the time it took them to do so apparently exceeded the amount of time the letters lasted in their sensory registers, so they lost some of the letters.

The existence of sensory registers has two important educational implications. First, people must pay attention to information if they are to retain it. Second, it takes time to bring all the information seen in a moment into consciousness. For example, if students are bombarded with too much information at once and are not told which aspects of the information they should pay attention to, they may have difficulty learning any of the information at all.

PERCEPTION ● When the senses receive stimuli, the mind immediately begins working on some of them. Therefore the sensory images of which we are conscious are not exactly the same as what we saw, heard, or felt; they are what our senses perceived. **Perception** of stimuli is not as straightforward as reception of stimuli; rather, it involves mental interpretation and is influenced by our mental state, past experience, knowledge, motivations, and many other factors.

First, we perceive different stimuli according to rules that have nothing to do with the inherent characteristics of the stimuli. If you are sitting in a building, for example, you may not pay much attention to, or even hear, a fire engine's siren. If you are driving a car, you pay a great deal more attention. If you are standing outside a burning building waiting for the fire fighters to arrive, you pay even more attention. Second, we do not perceive stimuli as we see or sense them but as we know (or assume) they really are. From across a room, a book on a bookshelf looks like a

perception
A person's interpretation of stimuli.

thin strip of paper, but we infer that it is a rectangular form with many pages. You may see the edge of a table and mentally infer the entire table.

ATTENTION ● When teachers say to students, "Pay attention" or "Lend me your ears," they are using the words *pay* and *lend* appropriately (Kinchla, 1992). Like money, **attention** is a limited resource. When a teacher asks students to spend their limited attention capacity on whatever the teacher is saying, students must give up actively attending to other stimuli, shifting their priorities so that other stimuli are screened out. For example, when people listen intently to an interesting speaker, they are unaware of minor body sensations (such as itches or hunger) and other sounds or sights. An experienced speaker knows that when the audience looks restless, its attention is no longer focused on the lecture but may be turning toward considerations of lunch or other activities; it is time to recapture the listeners' attention.

GAINING ATTENTION ● How can teachers focus students' attention on the lesson at hand, and in particular on the most important aspects of what is being taught?

There are several ways to gain students' attention, all of which go under the general heading of arousing student interest. One way is to use cues that indicate "This is important." Some teachers raise or lower their voices to signal that they are about to impart critical information. Others use gestures, repetition, or body position to communicate the same message.

Another way to gain attention is to increase the emotional content of material. Some publications accomplish this by choosing very emotional words. This is probably why newspaper headlines say "Senate Kills Mass Transit Proposal" rather than "Senate Votes Against Mass Transit Proposal." Olson and Pau (1966) found that use of such emotionally charged words helps students to retain information better than more neutral synonyms do.

Unusual, inconsistent, or surprising stimuli also attract attention. For example, science teachers often introduce lessons with a demonstration or magic trick to engage student curiosity.

Finally, informing students that what follows is important to them will catch their attention. For example, teachers can ensure attention by telling students, "This will be on tomorrow's test." Of course, learners make their own decisions about what is important, and they learn more of what they think is important than of other material because they pay more attention to it. Students can be taught to identify what is important in texts and then to devote more attention to those aspects. This increases their comprehension (R. E. Reynolds, 1992).

Short-Term or Working Memory

Information that a person perceives and pays attention to is transferred to the second component of the memory system: the **short-term memory** (Squire, Knowlton, & Musen, 1993). Short-term memory is a storage system that can hold a limited amount of information for a few seconds. It is the part of memory in which information that is currently being thought about is stored. The thoughts we are conscious of having at any given moment are being held in our short-term memory. When we stop thinking about something, it disappears from our short-term memory. Another term for short-term memory is **working memory** (Anderson, 1995; Ericsson & Kintsch, 1995). This term emphasizes that the most important

attention
Active focus on certain stimuli to the exclusion of others.

short-term or **working memory**
The component of memory in which limited amounts of information can be stored for a few seconds.

aspect of short-term memory is not its duration, but the fact that it is active. Working memory is where the mind operates on information, organizes it for storage or discarding, and connects it to other information.

As depicted in Figure 6.1, information may enter working memory from sensory registers or from the third basic component of the memory system: long-term memory. Often, both things happen at the same time. When you see a robin, your sensory register transfers the image of the robin to your working memory. Meanwhile, you may (unconsciously) search your long-term memory for information about birds so that you can identify this particular one as a robin. Along with that recognition may come a lot of other information about robins, memories of past experiences with robins, or feelings about robins—all of which were stored in long-term memory but are brought into consciousness (working memory) by your mental processing of the sight of the robin.

One way to hold information in working memory is to think about it or say it over and over. You have probably used this strategy to remember a phone number for a short time. This process of maintaining an item in working memory by repetition is called **rehearsal** (Baddeley, 1990). Rehearsal is important in learning because the longer an item remains in working memory, the greater the chance that it will be transferred to long-term memory. Without rehearsal, items will probably not stay in working memory for more than about 30 seconds. Because working memory has a limited capacity, information can also be lost from it by being forced out by other information. You have probably had the experience of looking up a telephone number, being interrupted briefly, and finding that you had forgotten the number.

Teachers must allocate time for rehearsal during classroom lessons. Teaching too much information too rapidly is likely to be ineffective, because unless students are given time to mentally rehearse each new piece of information, later information is likely to drive it out of their working memories. When teachers stop a lesson to ask students whether they have any questions, they are also giving students a few moments to think over and mentally rehearse what they have just learned. This helps students to process information in working memory and thereby to establish it in long-term memory. This mental work is critical when students are learning new, difficult material.

WORKING MEMORY CAPACITY ● Working memory is believed to have a capacity of five to nine bits of information (Miller, 1956). That is, we can think about only five to nine distinct things at a time. However, any particular bit may itself contain a great deal of information. For example, think how difficult it would be to memorize the following shopping list:

flour	orange juice	pepper	mustard
soda pop	parsley	cake	butter
relish	mayonnaise	oregano	canned tomatoes
potatoes	milk	lettuce	syrup
hamburger	hot dogs	eggs	onions
tomato paste	apples	spaghetti	buns

rehearsal
Mental repetition of information, which can improve its retention.

This list has too many bits of information to remember easily. All 24 food items would not fit into working memory in random order. However, you could easily memorize the list by organizing it according to familiar patterns. As shown in Table 6.1, you might mentally create three separate memory files: breakfast, lunch, and dinner. In each, you expect to find food and beverages; in the lunch and din-

TABLE 6.1

Example of Organization of Information to Facilitate Memory

A 24-item shopping list that would be very hard to remember in a random order can be organized into a smaller number of familiar categories, making the list easier to recall.

BREAKFAST	LUNCH	DINNER
Pancakes:	Hot Dogs:	Spaghetti:
• Flour	• Hot dogs	• Spaghetti
• Milk	• Buns	• Onions
• Eggs	• Relish	• Hamburger
• Butter	• Mustard	• Canned tomatoes
• Syrup	Potato Salad:	• Tomato paste
Beverage: Orange juice	• Potatoes	• Oregano
	• Mayonnaise	• Pepper
	• Parsley	Salad:
	Beverage: Soda pop	• Lettuce
	Dessert: Apple	Beverage: Milk
		Dessert: Cake

ner files, you expect to find dessert as well. You can then think through the recipes for each item on the menus. In this way, you can recall what you have to buy and need maintain only a few bits of information in your working memory. When you enter the store, you are thinking, "I need food for breakfast, lunch, and dinner." First, you bring the breakfast file out of your long-term memory. It contains food (pancakes) and beverage (orange juice). You might think through how you make pancakes step by step and buy each ingredient, plus orange juice as a beverage. When you have done this, you can discard breakfast from your working memory and replace it with the lunch file and then the dinner file, going through the same processes. Note that all you did was to replace 24 little bits of information with three big bits that you could then separate into their components.

Working memory can be thought of as a bottleneck through which information from the environment reaches long-term memory. The limited capacity of working memory is one aspect of information processing that has important implications for the design and practice of instruction (Sweller, van Merrienboer & Paas, 1998). For example, you cannot present students with many ideas at once unless the ideas are so well organized and well connected to information already in the students' long-term memories that their working memories (with assistance from their long-term memories) can accommodate them, as in the case of the shopping list just discussed. Other instructional implications of the nature of working memory appear throughout this and the following chapters.

INDIVIDUAL DIFFERENCES IN WORKING MEMORY ● Individuals differ, of course, in the capacity of their working memories to accomplish a given learning task. One of the main factors in enhancing this capacity is background knowledge. The more a person knows about something, the better able the person is to organize and absorb new information (Engle, Nations, & Cantor, 1990; Kuhara-Kojima & Hatano, 1991). However, prior knowledge is not the only factor. Individuals also differ in their abilities to organize information and can be taught to consciously use strategies for making more efficient use of their working memory capacity (Levin & Levin, 1990; Peverly, 1991; Pressley & Harris, 1990). Strategies of this kind are discussed later in this chapter.

Long-Term Memory

long-term memory
The components of memory in which large amounts of information can be stored for long periods of time.

Long-term memory is that part of our memory system where we keep information for long periods of time. Long-term memory is thought to be a very large-capacity, very long-term memory store. In fact, many theorists believe that we may never forget information in long-term memory; rather, we may just lose the ability to find the information within our memory. For this reason, some theorists use the term *permanent memory* (Byrnes, 1996). We do not live long enough to fill up our long-term memory. The differences among sensory registers, working memory, and long-term memory are summarized in Table 6.2.

Ericsson and Kintsch (1995) hypothesize that people store not only information but also learning strategies in long-term memory for easy access. This capacity, which Ericsson and Kintsch call long-term working memory, accounts for the

TABLE 6.2

Differences Among the Three Components of Memory

The three basic components of memory differ in function, capacity, and organization.

FEATURE	SENSORY REGISTERS	WORKING OR SHORT-TERM MEMORY	LONG-TERM MEMORY
Entry of information	Preattentive	Requires attention	Rehearsal
Maintenance of information	Not possible	Continued attention Rehearsal	Repetition Organization
Format of information	Literal copy of input	Phonemic Probably visual Possibly semantic	Largely semantic Some auditory and visual
Capacity	Large	Small	No known limit
Information loss	Decay	Displacement Possibly decay	Possibly no loss Loss of accessibility by interference
Trace duration	¼ to 2 seconds	Up to 30 seconds	Minutes to years
Retrieval	Readout	Probably automatic Items in consciousness Temporal/phonemic cues	Retrieval cues Possibly search process

Source: From F. I. M. Craik and R. S. Lockhart, "Level of Processing," *Journal of Verbal Learning and Verbal Behavior,* 1972, pp. 671–684. Adapted by permission of Academic Press.

extraordinary skills of experts (such as medical diagnosticians) who must match current information with a vast array of patterns held in their long-term memories.

Theorists divide long-term memory into at least three parts: episodic memory, semantic memory, and procedural memory (Squire et al., 1993; Tulving, 1993). **Episodic memory** is our memory of personal experiences, a mental movie of things we saw or heard. When you remember what you had for dinner last night or what happened at your high school prom, you are recalling information stored in your long-term episodic memory. Long-term **semantic memory** contains the facts and generalized information that we know; concepts, principles, or rules and how to use them; and our problem-solving skills and learning strategies. Most things that are learned in class lessons are retained in semantic memory. **Procedural memory** refers to "knowing how" in contrast to "knowing that" (Solso, 1998). The abilities to drive, type, and ride a bicycle are examples of skills that are retained in procedural memory.

Episodic, semantic, and procedural memory store and organize information in different ways. Information in episodic memory is stored in the form of images that are organized on the basis of when and where events happened. Information in semantic memory is organized in the form of networks of ideas. Information in procedural memory is stored as a complex of stimulus–response pairings (Anderson, 1995). Recent brain studies (e.g., Byrnes & Fox, 1998; Tulving, Kapur, Craik, Moscovitch, & Houle, 1994) have suggested that operations relating to each of these types of long-term memory take place in different parts of the brain. Let's examine in detail what we mean by these three kinds of memory.

EPISODIC MEMORY ● Episodic memory contains images of experiences organized by when and where they happened (Tulving, 1993). For example, answer this question: In the house in which you lived as a child, when you entered your bedroom, was the head of your bed to the right, left, away from, or pointed toward you? If you are like most people, you answered this question by imagining the bedroom and seeing where the head of the bed was. Now consider this question: What did you do on the night of your senior prom or dance? Most people answer this question by imagining themselves back on that night and describing the events. Finally, suppose you are asked to recall the names of your high school classmates. One psychologist asked graduate students to come to a specific place for 1 hour a day and try to remember the names. Over the course of a month, the students continued to recall new names. Interestingly, they used space and time cues, which are associated with episodic memory, to imagine incidents that allowed them to recall the names. For example, they might recall the day their social studies teacher came to school dressed as an Arctic explorer and then mentally scan the faces of the students who were there.

These demonstrations indicate that images are important in episodic memory and that cues related to space and time help us to retrieve information from this part of memory. You have probably taken an exam and said to yourself, "I should know this answer. I remember reading this section. It was right on the bottom left corner of the page with the diagram in the upper right."

Episodic memories are often difficult to retrieve, because most episodes in our lives are repeated so often that later episodes get mixed up in memory with earlier ones, unless something happens during the episode to make it especially memorable. For example, few people remember what they had for lunch a week ago, much less years ago. However, there is a phenomenon called **flashbulb memory** in which the occurrence of an important event fixes mainly visual and auditory mem-

episodic memory
A part of long-term memory that stores images of our personal experiences.

semantic memory
A part of long-term memory that stores facts and general knowledge.

procedural memory
A part of long-term memory that stores information about how to do things.

flashbulb memory
Important events that are fixed mainly in visual and auditory memory.

ories in a person's mind. For example, people who happened to be eating lunch at the moment they heard about Princess Diana's death or the *Challenger* disaster, or at the moment when they were first kissed or received a proposal of marriage, may well remember that particular meal (and other trivial aspects of the setting) forever. The reason for this is that the unforgettable event of that moment gives us access to the episodic (space and time) memories relating to what would usually be forgotten details.

Martin (1993) has speculated that educators could improve retention of concepts and information by explicitly creating memorable events involving visual or auditory images. For example, uses of projects, plays, simulations, and other forms of active learning could give students vivid images that they could remember and then use to retrieve other information presented at about the same time. In support of this idea, there is much evidence that pictures illustrating text help children to remember the text even when the pictures are no longer presented (Small, Lovett, & Scher, 1993). The pictures presumably tie the semantic information to the child's episodic memory, making the information easier to retrieve.

SEMANTIC MEMORY ● Semantic (or declarative) memory is organized in a very different way. It is mentally organized in networks of connected ideas or relationships called **schemata** (singular: *schema*) (Anderson, 1995; Flavell et al., 1993; Voss & Wiley, 1995). Recall that Piaget introduced the word *scheme* to describe a cognitive framework that individuals use to organize their perceptions and experiences. Cognitive processing theorists similarly use the terms *schema* and *schemata* to describe networks of concepts that individuals have in their memories that enable them to understand and incorporate new information. A schema is like an outline, with different concepts or ideas grouped under larger categories. Various aspects of schemata may be related by series of propositions, or relationships. For example, Figure 6.3 illustrates a simplified schema for the concept "bison," showing how this concept is related to other concepts in memory.

In the figure, the concept "bison" is linked to several other concepts. These may be linked to still more concepts (such as "How did Plains Indians hunt bison?") and to broader categories or concepts (such as "How have conservationists saved many species from extinction?"). Schema theory (Anderson, 1995) holds that we gain access to information held in our semantic long-term memory by mentally following paths like those illustrated in Figure 6.3. For example, you might have deep in your memory the idea that the Spanish introduction of the horse to North America revolutionized how the Plains Indians hunted bison. To get to that bit of information, you might start thinking about characteristics of bison, then think about how Plains Indians hunted bison on horseback, then recall (or imagine) how they hunted bison before they had horses. Many pathways can be used to get at the same bit of information. In fact, the more pathways you have leading to a piece of information and the better established those pathways are, the better access you will have to information in long-term semantic memory (Solso, 1998). The problem of long-term memory is not that information is lost but that our access to information is lost.

One clear implication of schema theory is that new information that fits into a well-developed schema is retained far more readily than is information that does not fit into a schema. Schema theory will be covered in more detail later in this chapter.

PROCEDURAL MEMORY ● Procedural memory is the ability to recall how to do something, especially a physical task. This type of memory is apparently stored in

CONNECTIONS

For more on the concept of schemes, see Chapter 2, page 30.

schemata
Mental networks of related concepts that influence understanding of new information; the singular is *schema*.

FIGURE 6.3 ● Schema for the Concept "Bison"
Information in long-term semantic memory is organized in networks of related ideas. The concept "bison," for example, falls under the more general concepts "mammals" and "animals" and is related to many other ideas that help to differentiate it from other concepts in memory.

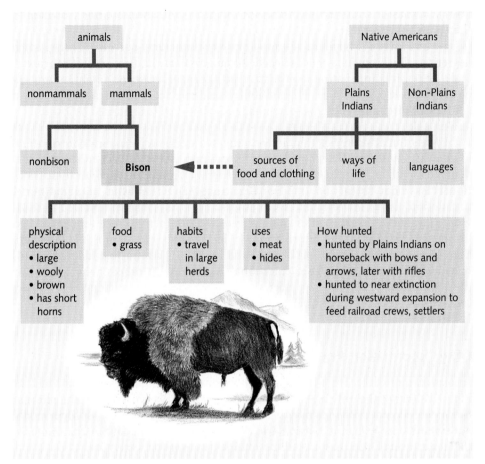

a series of stimulus–response pairings. For example, even if you have not ridden a bicycle for a long time, as soon as you get on one, the stimuli begin to evoke responses. When the bike leans to the left (a stimulus), you "instinctively" shift your weight to the right to maintain balance (a response). Other examples of procedural memory include handwriting, typing, and running skills. Neurological studies show that procedural memories are stored in a different part of the brain than are semantic and episodic memories; procedural memories are stored in the cerebellum, whereas semantic and episodic memories are stored in the cerebral cortex (Byrnes & Fox, 1998).

Factors That Enhance Long-Term Memory

Contrary to popular belief, people retain a large portion of what they learn in school. Semb and Ellis (1994), in reviewing research on this topic, note that laboratory studies of retention of nonsense words and other artificial material greatly underestimate the degree to which information and skills learned in school can be retained. Long-term retention of information that is learned in school varies a great deal according to the type of information. For example, concepts are retained much longer than names (Conway, Cohen, & Stanhope, 1991). In general, retention drops rapidly in the first few weeks after instruction but then levels off (Bahrick & Hall,

1991). Whatever students have retained about 12 to 24 weeks after instruction, they may retain forever.

Several factors contribute to long-term retention. One, not surprisingly, is the degree to which students had learned the material in the first place (Bahrick & Hall, 1991). It is interesting to note that the effects of ability on retention are unclear (Semb & Ellis, 1994). Higher-ability students score better at the end of a course but often lose the same percentage of what they had learned as low-ability students do.

Instructional strategies that actively involve students in lessons contribute to long-term retention. For example, MacKenzie and White (1982) contrasted students in eighth and ninth grades learning geography under three conditions: traditional classroom instruction, traditional instruction plus fieldwork, and traditional instruction plus fieldwork plus active processing of information involved in fieldwork. Twelve weeks later (after summer vacation), the active processing group had lost only 10 percent of the information, while the other two groups had lost more than 40 percent. Similarly, Specht and Sandling (1991) contrasted undergraduates who learned accounting from traditional lectures with others who learned it through role-playing. After 6 weeks, the traditionally taught students lost 54 percent of their problem-solving performance, whereas the role-playing group lost only 13 percent.

Other Information-Processing Models

Atkinson and Shiffrin's (1968) model of information processing outlined in Figure 6.1 is not the only one accepted by cognitive psychologists. Several alternative models do not challenge the basic assumptions of the Atkinson–Shiffrin model but elaborate aspects of it, particularly aspects relating to the factors that increase the chances that information will be retained in long-term memory. These alternative theories are as follows.

LEVELS-OF-PROCESSING THEORY ● One widely accepted model of information processing is called **levels-of-processing theory** (Craik, 1979; Craik & Lockhart, 1972), which holds that people subject stimuli to different levels of mental processing and retain only the information that has been subjected to the most thorough processing. For example, you might perceive a tree but pay little attention to it. This is the lowest level of processing, and you are unlikely to remember the tree. Second, you might give the tree a name, such as *tree* or *oak*. Once named, the tree is somewhat more likely to be remembered. The highest level of processing, however, is giving meaning to the tree. For example, you might remember having climbed the tree or having commented on the tree's unusual shape, or you might have wondered whether the tree would fall on your house if it were struck by lightning. According to levels-of-processing theory, the more you attend to the details of a stimulus, the more mental processing you must do with a stimulus and the more likely you are to remember it. This was illustrated in a study by Bower and Karlin (1974), who had Stanford undergraduates look at yearbook pictures from Yale. Some of the students were told to classify the pictures as "male" or "female," and some were told to classify them as "very honest" or "less honest." The students who had to categorize the faces as very honest or less honest remembered them far better than did those who merely categorized them as male or female. Presumably, the honesty raters had to do a much higher level of mental processing with the pictures than did the gender raters, and for this reason they

levels-of-processing theory

Explanation of memory that links recall of a stimulus with the amount of mental processing it receives.

remembered the faces better. Similarly, students who were asked to rate a series of words as pleasant or unpleasant recalled over 60 percent more of the words than did students who were asked only to count the letters or identify words with *e* in them (Hyde & Jenkins, 1969).

DUAL CODE THEORY ● A concept that is related to levels-of-processing theory is Paivio's **dual code theory of memory,** which hypothesizes that information is retained in long-term memory in two forms: visual and verbal (corresponding to episodic and semantic memory, respectively) (Clark & Paivio, 1991; Mayer & Moreno, 1998; Sadoski, Goetz, & Fritz, 1993). This theory predicts that information represented both visually and verbally is recalled better than information represented only one way. For example, you remember a face better if you also know a name, and you remember a name better if you can connect it to a face (Mayer & Anderson, 1991).

TRANSFER-APPROPRIATE PROCESSING THEORY ● Levels-of-processing theory has been modified and extended by the work of Bransford and his associates (Bransford et al., 1982). These researchers noted that memory depended not on depth of processing alone but also on the way in which information was learned and then tested. In a classic study by Morris, Bransford, and Franks (1977), students were given two types of sentences, involving either the meaning of words (e.g., "Does a dog have ears?") or rhymes (e.g., "Does *dog* rhyme with *log?*"). As predicted by level-of-processing theory, students could recall more words whose meaning they had to consider than words for which they had to focus only on rhymes—a lower level of processing. Yet when the memory test used rhymes, students recalled

> **dual code theory of memory**
> Theory suggesting that information coded both visually and verbally is remembered better than information coded in only one of those two ways.

According to levels-of-processing theory, the more these boys attend to the details of a stimulus, the more mental processing they will do with it and the more likely they are to remember it. How well will these boys remember this tree?

more of the words they had learned through rhymes, something not predicted by levels-of-processing theory. Similarly, Godden and Baddeley (1975) had divers learn a list of words under water and another list on land. When tested under water, they recalled more of the words they learned under water; but on land the opposite was the case! These and other demonstrations of the degree to which learning is limited to the context in which it took place led Bransford (1979) to propose a **transfer-appropriate processing theory,** which holds that the strength and durability of memory depend not only on the depth of processing, but also on the similarity between the conditions under which the material was learned and those under which it is called for. This distinction has great importance for instruction; for example, it helps to explain why so many students can recall and apply rules of grammar and punctuation on a multiple-choice or fill-in-the-blank test (a format similar to that in which they learned these skills) but can be unable to recall or apply the same skills in their own writing.

PARALLEL DISTRIBUTED PROCESSING MODEL ● The Atkinson–Shiffrin model of learning emphasized in this chapter is felt by many modern researchers to be a bit too simplistic in proposing a sequence of steps by which information is processed. Lewandowsky and Murdock (1989) have described a **parallel distributed processing model** based on the idea that information is processed simultaneously in the three parts of the memory system, each part operating on the same information at the same time. For example, when reading this paragraph, you are not looking at individual letters, forming them into words and meanings, and then working with them in short-term memory to file them in long-term memory. Instead, you are immediately using information in your long-term memory to interpret the words and meanings. Even at the first stages of perception, what you see is heavily influenced by what you expect to see, which means that your long-term memory is operating at the same time as your sensory register and short-term memory.

CONNECTIONIST MODELS ● A major alternative to the Atkinson–Shiffrin model has been taking shape in recent years. This model, called *connectionism* (Rumelhart & McClelland, 1986), is closely associated with parallel distributed processing theories. It emphasizes the idea that knowledge is stored in the brain in a network of connections, not in a system of rules or in storage of individual bits of information. In this view, experience leads to learning by strengthening certain connections, often at the expense of others. For example, a little boy may learn the concept "dog" by seeing many quite different-looking animals and hearing them referred to as dogs (Rumelhart & McClelland, 1986). Each time the child sees a new dog, connections are strengthened between the concept "dog" and attributes that are common to dogs, while false connections, caused by unique characteristics of particular dogs, are weakened. Let's say the boy's family has a poodle, and he therefore believes that dogs bark, wag their tails, and have curly hair. As he meets more dogs, the "bark" and "wag" connections are strengthened and the "curly hair" connection is weakened by experience. Other dog attributes are also strengthened, until the child can readily identify any dog, even if he has never seen that breed of dog before. Similarly, a young girl may confidently and correctly use the word *went*, because she hears it frequently and finds it very useful in her own speech. However, over time she experiences a different pattern: past tenses in English are usually formed by the addition of *-ed*. The connection "past tense = *-ed*" is strengthened by experience and may even become stronger than the existing "past tense of go = *went*"

transfer-appropriate processing theory
A theory that proposes that memory is stronger and lasts longer when the conditions of performance are similar to those under which learning occurred.

parallel distributed processing model
A model based on the idea that information is processed simultaneously in the sensory register, working memory, and long-term memory.

connection; as a result, the child may start using the word *goed.* But as the network of connections becomes more complex and the child sees that *goed* does not match other people's usage, she is able to maintain both connections, "past tense of go = *went*" and "past tense = *-ed,*" and to apply them appropriately. Note that even though the child's behavior becomes rulelike, no explicit teaching or learning of rules is assumed. Instead, through direct experience the child strengthens connections that work and weakens ones that do not (Bereiter, 1991; Driscoll, 1994; Iran–Nejad, Marsh, & Clements, 1992; Schneider & Graham, 1992).

Connectionist models are consistent with current research on the brain, which has established that information is not held in any one location but is distributed in many locations and connected by intricate neural pathways (Hendry & King, 1994; Solso, 1998). However, the implications of connectionism for teaching and learning are not clear. A straightforward application would be to place a greater emphasis on experience-based teaching and to deemphasize the teaching of rules (such as grammar or arithmetic rules); but researchers in this tradition (e.g., Bereiter, 1991; Schneider & Graham, 1992) are careful to note that the connectionist model does have a place for rule-based teaching.

CONNECTIONS

For more on language acquisition during the preschool years, see Chapter 3, page 71.

SELF-CHECK

Draw a diagram representing the Atkinson–Shiffrin information-processing model that includes the following terms: sensory register, attention, short-term (working) memory, rehearsal, repetition, coding, long-term (permanent) memory, and retrieval. Using one specific example, explain how information is processed in memory.

WHAT CAUSES PEOPLE TO REMEMBER OR FORGET?

Why do we remember some things and forget others? Why can we sometimes remember trivial things that happened years ago but not important things that happened yesterday? Most forgetting occurs because information in working memory was never transferred to long-term memory. However, it can also occur because we have lost our ability to recall information that is in long-term memory.

Forgetting and Remembering

Over the years, researchers have identified several factors that make it easier or harder to remember information.

INTERFERENCE ● One important reason people forget is **interference** (Anderson, 1995). Interference happens when information gets mixed up with, or pushed aside by, other information. One form of interference occurs when people are prevented from mentally rehearsing newly learned information. In one classic experiment, Peterson and Peterson (1959) gave subjects a simple task: the memorization of sets of three nonsense letters (such as FQB). The subjects were then immediately asked to count backward by 3s from a three-digit number (e.g., 287, 284, 281, etc.) for up to 18 seconds. At the end of that time the subjects were asked to recall the letters. They had forgotten far more of them than had subjects who had learned the letters and then simply waited for 18 seconds to repeat them. The

connectionist models
Theories proposing that knowledge is stored in the brain in a network of connections, not in systems of rules or in individual bits of information.

interference
Inhibition of recall of certain information by the presence of other information in memory.

What kind of memory strategy is illustrated here? According to research on memory and forgetting, what factors will determine how well these students remember the information?

reason for this is that the subjects who were told to count backward were deprived of the opportunity to rehearse the letters mentally to establish them in their working memories. As was noted earlier in this chapter, teachers must take into account the limited capacity of working memory by allowing students time to absorb or practice (that is, mentally rehearse) new information before giving them additional instruction.

RETROACTIVE INHIBITION ● Another form of interference is called **retroactive inhibition.** This occurs when previously learned information is lost because it is mixed up with new and somewhat similar information. For example, young students may have no trouble recognizing the letter *b* until they are taught the letter *d.* Because these letters are similar, students often confuse them. Learning the letter *d* thus interferes with the previously learned recognition of *b.* In the same way, a traveler may know how to get around in a particular airport but then lose that skill to some extent after visiting many similar airports.

Of all the reasons for forgetting, retroactive inhibition is probably the most important. This phenomenon explains, for example, why we have trouble remembering frequently repeated episodes, such as what we had for dinner a week ago. Last night's dinner will be forgotten because memories of dinners that come after it will interfere, unless something remarkable happens to clearly distinguish last night's dinner from the dinners that will follow.

retroactive inhibition
Decreased ability to recall previously learned information, caused by learning of new information.

THEORY *into* Practice ●

Reducing Retroactive Inhibition

There are two ways to reduce retroactive inhibition. The first is by not teaching similar and confusing concepts too closely in time. The second is to use different methods to teach similar concepts. The first way to reduce retroactive inhibition implies that one of several confusing or similar concepts should be taught thoroughly before the next is introduced. For example, students should be completely able to recognize the letter *b* before the letter *d* is introduced. If these letters are introduced at close to the same time, learning of one may inhibit learning of the other. When the new letter is introduced, the teacher must carefully point out the differences between *b* and *d,* and students must practice discriminating between the two until they can unerringly say which is which. As another example, consider the following lists of Spanish and English word pairs:

A	B
llevar—to carry	*perro*—dog
llorar—to cry	*gato*—cat
llamar—to call	*caballo*—horse

List B is much easier to learn. The similarities among the Spanish words in list A (they all are verbs, start with *ll*, end with *ar,* and have the same number of letters and syllables) make them very difficult to tell apart. The English words in list A are also somewhat difficult to discriminate among, because all are verbs that start with a *c.* In contrast, the words in list B are easy to discriminate from one another. Because of the problem of retroactive inhibition, presenting all the word pairs in list A in the same lesson would be a poor instructional strategy. Students would be likely to confuse the three Spanish words because of their similar spellings. Rather, students should be completely familiar with one word pair before the next is introduced.

Another way to reduce retroactive inhibition is to use different methods to teach similar concepts or to vary other aspects of instruction for each concept. For example, Andre (1973) had students study two descriptions of African tribes. For some students the two passages were organized and printed in the same way. For others the second passage was organized differently from the first and printed on different-colored paper. Students who were given the second procedure showed less confusion between the two passages on a later test. Researchers also found that when students were asked to memorize two lists, those who used the same memorization strategy for both forgot more than did those who used a different strategy for each (Andre, Anderson, & Watts, 1976). These and other research findings imply that teachers can help students to retain information and avoid confusion by varying their presentation strategies for different material. For example, a teacher might teach about Spain by using lectures and discussion, about France by using group projects, and about Italy by using films. This would help students avoid confusing information about one country with information about the others.

Most things that are forgotten were never firmly learned in the first place. The best way to ensure long-term retention of material taught in school is to make certain that students have mastered the essential features of the material. This means assessing students' understanding frequently and reteaching if it turns out that students have not achieved adequate levels of understanding.

PROACTIVE INHIBITION ● **Proactive inhibition** occurs when learning one set of information interferes with learning later information. A classic case is that of a North American learning to drive on the left side of the road in England. It may be easier for a North American nondriver to learn to drive in England than for an experienced North American driver, because the latter has so thoroughly learned to stay to the right—a potentially fatal error in England.

proactive inhibition
Decreased ability to learn new information, caused by interference from existing knowledge.

TABLE 6.3

Retroactive and Proactive Inhibition and Facilitation

Summary of the effects on memory of retroactive and proactive inhibition and facilitation.

EFFECT ON LEARNING	EFFECT ON MEMORY	
	Inhibition (Negative)	Facilitation (Positive)
Later learning affects earlier learning	Retroactive inhibition (*Example:* Learning *d* interferes with learning *b.*)	Retroactive facilitation (*Example:* Learning to teach math helps with previously learned math skills.)
Earlier learning affects later learning	Proactive inhibition (*Example:* Learning to drive in the U.S. interferes with learning to drive in the U.K.)	Proactive facilitation (*Example:* Learning Spanish helps with later learning of Italian.)

FACILITATION ● It should also be noted that learning one thing can often *help* a person learn similar information. For example, learning Spanish first may help an English-speaking student learn Italian, a similar language. This would be a case of **proactive facilitation.** Learning a second language can also help with an already established language. It is often the case, for example, that English-speaking students find that the study of Latin helps them understand their native language better. This would be **retroactive facilitation.**

For another example, consider teaching. We often have the experience that learning to teach a subject helps us understand the subject better. Because later learning (e.g., learning to teach addition of fractions) increases our understanding of previously learned information (addition of fractions), this is a prime example of retroactive facilitation. Table 6.3 summarizes the relationships among retroactive and proactive inhibition and facilitation.

PRIMACY AND RECENCY EFFECTS ● One of the oldest findings in educational psychology is that when people are given a list of words to learn and then tested immediately afterward, they tend to learn the first few and last few items much better than those in the middle of the list (Stigler, 1978). The tendency to learn the first things presented is called the **primacy effect;** the tendency to learn the last things is called the **recency effect.** The most common explanation for the primacy effect is that we pay more attention and devote more mental effort to items presented first. As was noted earlier in this chapter, mental rehearsal is important in establishing new information in long-term memory. Usually, much more mental rehearsal is devoted to the first items presented than to later items (Anderson, 1995). Recency effects, in contrast, are due in large part to the fact that little or no other information intervenes between the final items and the test (Greene, 1986).

Teachers should consider primacy and recency effects. These effects imply that information taught at the beginning or the end of the period is more likely to be retained than other information. To take advantage of this, teachers might organize their lessons to put the most essential new concepts early in the lesson and then to

proactive facilitation
Increased ability to learn new information due to the presence of previously acquired information.

retroactive facilitation
Increased comprehension of previously learned information due to the acquisition of new information.

primacy effect
The tendency for items at the beginning of a list to be recalled more easily than other items.

recency effect
The tendency for items at the end of a list to be recalled more easily than other items.

summarize at the end. Many teachers take roll, collect lunch money, check homework, and do other noninstructional activities at the beginning of the period. However, it is probably a better idea to postpone these activities, to start the period right away with important concepts and only toward the end of the period deal with necessary administrative tasks.

AUTOMATICITY ● Information or skills may exist in long-term memory, but may take so much time or so much mental effort to retrieve that they are of limited value when speed of access is essential. The classic case of this is reading. A child may be able to sound out every word on a page, but if he or she does so very slowly and laboriously, the child will lose comprehension and will be unlikely to read for pleasure (Adams, 1990). For reading and for other skills in which speed and limited mental effort are necessary, existence in long-term memory is not enough. **Automaticity** is required; that is, a level of rapidity and ease such that a task or skill involves little or no mental effort. Breathing is a classic case of automaticity, as it requires no mental effort at all. For a proficient reader reading simple material, decoding requires almost no mental effort. Recent neurological studies show that the brain becomes more efficient as a person becomes a skilled reader (Eden et al., 1996). A beginning reader with serious learning disabilities uses both auditory and visual parts of the brain during reading, trying laboriously to sound out new words. In contrast, a skilled reader uses only a small, well-defined portion of the brain relating to visual processing.

Automaticity is primarily gained through practice far beyond the amount needed to establish information or skills in long-term memory. A soccer player knows after 10 minutes of instruction how to kick a ball, but the player practices

automaticity
A level of rapidity and ease such that tasks can be performed or skills utilized with little mental effort.

By practicing scales far beyond the amount needed to establish the skills in his long-term memory, this young musician gains automaticity. How will this benefit him?

this skill thousands of times until it becomes automatic. A chess player quickly learns the rules of chess but spends a lifetime learning to quickly recognize patterns that suggest winning moves. Bloom (1986), who studied the role of automaticity in the performances of gifted pianists, mathematicians, athletes, and others, called automaticity "the hands and feet of genius."

Practice

The most common method for committing information to memory is also the most mundane: practice. Does practice make perfect?

Practice is important at several stages of learning. As was noted earlier in this chapter, information received in working memory must be mentally rehearsed if it is to be retained for more than a few seconds. The information in working memory must usually be practiced until it is established in long-term memory.

MASSED AND DISTRIBUTED PRACTICE ● Is it better to practice newly learned information intensively until it is thoroughly learned, a technique called **massed practice**? Or is it more effective to practice a little each day over a period of time—**distributed practice**? Massed practice allows for faster initial learning; but for most kinds of learning, distributed practice is better for retention, even over short time periods. This is especially true of factual learning (Dempster, 1989); cramming factual information the night before a test may get you through that test, but the information probably won't be well integrated into your long-term memory. Long-term retention of all kinds of information and skills is greatly enhanced by distributed practice. This is the primary purpose of homework: to provide practice on newly learned skills over an extended period of time to increase the chances that the skills will be retained.

PART LEARNING ● It is very difficult for most people to learn a long list all at once. Rather, it is easier to break the list down into smaller lists. This strategy is called **part learning.** Its effectiveness explains why teachers teaching multiplication facts, for example, first have students master the 2s table, then the 3s, and so on. Note that this strategy helps to reduce retroactive inhibition, as the earlier partial lists are thoroughly learned before the next partial list is introduced.

OVERLEARNING ● As was noted earlier, one of the most important factors governing long-term retention of information or skills is how well they were learned in the first place. If students practice just long enough to learn something and then do no more, they are likely to forget much of what they have learned. However, if they continue to practice beyond the point at which they can recall the answers, retention will increase. This strategy is called **overlearning.** In an early experiment, Krueger (1929) had students learn a list of words until they could recite the list with no errors. Then some students were asked to engage in overlearning, to keep practicing the list for an amount of time equal to the time it took them to learn the list originally. Four days after the experiment, these students retained six times as many words as were retained by the students who did not engage in overlearning. By the 28th day, the nonoverlearning group had forgotten all the words, while the overlearning group still remembered a few.

Overlearning has only a few important applications in instructional practice. It is useful for drilling information that must be accurately recalled for a long time but has little meaning. The prime example of a learning task that is suitable for

massed practice
Technique in which facts or skills to be learned are repeated many times over a concentrated period of time.

distributed practice
Technique in which items to be learned are repeated at intervals over a period of time.

part learning
Strategy for mastering new material by learning it one part or subskill at a time.

overlearning
A method of improving retention by continuing to practice new knowledge or behaviors after mastery is achieved.

TEACHERS IN ACTION

What strategies have you used to help students process and retain new learning?

Lynn Rylander Kaufman
Bess Streeter Aldrich School
Omaha, Nebraska

Learning is natural: it beckons, captivates, and enchants. But education is planned: It enlightens, develops, and empowers. As a teacher, I synthesize learning and education so students can construct their own understanding of the world. Often, they process information and retain what they've learned through hands-on learning experiences.

One morning, a large python snakeskin was brought to the first-grade class. After the students were finished looking at the snakeskin, I quickly pulled out books on reptiles from our class library. Then I found snakeskins in our science boxes. The sixth grade had a live bull snake, so I borrowed it for a real hands-on experience. Learning was intense and energizing. At dismissal time I overheard Kristine say, "We learned *too* much today!" Her classmate, Emily, immediately countered, "Oh, no! It is always okay to learn too much; it's never okay to learn nothing!"

Another hands-on experience in my class took place in the fall as we studied pumpkins. I intentionally left one by the chalkboard. A week later, when a student noticed gray fuzz and black ooze, eager young scientists rushed to see the rotting pumpkin. Disgust and curiosity were followed by questions. For two weeks we observed the pumpkin slowly disappear. With subsequent research we discovered we were watching the pumpkin *decompose*.

Students continued learning about decomposing a month later when we buried the class turtle, Alex. Thiago asked if Alex would decompose like our pumpkin. I matter-of-factly answered, "Yes, Thiago, all living things decompose." He paused, looked at me in astonishment, and asked loudly, "Am I going to decompose?"

My goal is to design learning with power to create deep understanding. Teachers must construct possibilities and seize opportunities to connect learning with the potency of real life.

Gail C. Hartman
Teacher
Edison Elementary School
Hobbs, New Mexico

Retention improves if the concept lesson itself is memorable. Geography concepts were particularly challenging to my third-graders. I gave what I thought was a good lesson. The results of the first short quiz, however, showed me that I had not been successful. During recess duty the next day, I noticed groups of children playing four-square, and I suddenly got the idea of using those squares to teach the concepts of north, south, east, and west.

After recess, my class was thrilled with the idea of returning to the playground. With a piece of chalk, I had a child draw a large compass rose next to the four-square. This analogy worked perfectly. We were able to establish that the horizontal center line of the four-square was equivalent to the equator on the compass rose and that the vertical center line was equivalent to the prime meridian. We marked each quadrant (NE, NW, SE, and SW), and then the children took turns standing in various quadrants while the other children called out the location. After every child had demonstrated competence, I drew lines subdividing the quadrants, representing degrees of latitude and longitude. I had the children number the horizontal lines and give a letter value to the vertical lines. Then each child chose a spot to stand on where two lines intersected and had to describe the geographical coordinates. Evaluating the students' understanding was easy. Each child took a turn directing another child to a particular spot and was the judge as to whether or not that child was successful. This activity gave each child a lot of experience using geography concepts. They also used their bodies as well as their minds to learn, and they were learning in a memorable context.

overlearning is memorization of multiplication facts, which students should be able to recall automatically and without error. Overlearning of multiplication facts is often accomplished by the regular use of speed drills, mental arithmetic (e.g., "Class: What is four times seven minus three divided by five times nine?"), or games. Spelling lists may also be overlearned, particularly for frequently missed words that do not follow regular spelling rules.

ENACTMENT ● Everyone knows that we learn by doing. It turns out that research on **enactment** supports this commonsense conclusion. That is, in learning how to perform tasks of many kinds, individuals learn much better if they are asked to enact the tasks (to physically carry them out) than if they simply read the instructions or watch a teacher enact the task (Cohen, 1989). For example, students learn much more from a lesson on drawing geometric solids (such as cubes and spheres) if they have an opportunity to draw some rather than just watching the teacher do so.

SELF-CHECK

Reread the vignette at the beginning of this chapter on Ms. Bishop's memory experiment. Why did her students remember some things but not others? How might the different kinds of practice enhance the students' learning in this case?

HOW CAN MEMORY STRATEGIES BE TAUGHT?

Many of the things that students learn in school are facts that must be remembered. These form the framework on which more complex concepts depend. Factual material must be learned as efficiently and effectively as possible to leave time and mental energy for meaningful learning, such as problem-solving, conceptual, and creative activities. If students can memorize the routine things more efficiently, they can free their minds for tasks that involve understanding and reasoning. Some learning involves memorization of facts or of arbitrary associations between terms. For example, *pomme,* the French word for *apple,* is an arbitrary term associated with an object. The capital of Iowa could just as well have been called *Iowapolis* as *Des Moines.* Similarly, the figure 2 is an arbitrary representation of the concept "two." Students often learn things as facts before they understand them as concepts or skills. For instance, students may learn the formula for the volume of a cylinder as an arbitrary fact long before they understand why the formula is what it is.

Verbal Learning

In many studies psychologists have examined **verbal learning,** or how students learn verbal materials, in laboratory settings (Raaijmakers & Shiffrin, 1992). For example, students might be asked to learn lists of words or nonsense syllables. Three types of verbal learning tasks that are typically seen in the classroom have been identified and studied extensively: the paired-associate learning task, the serial learning task, and the free-recall learning task.

1. **Paired-associate learning** involves learning to respond with one member of a pair when given the other member of the pair. Usually there is a list of pairs

enactment
A learning process in which individuals physically carry out tasks.

verbal learning
Learning of words (or facts expressed in words).

paired-associate learning
Learning of items in linked pairs so that when one member of a pair is presented, the other can be recalled.

to be memorized. In typical experiments, the pairs are arbitrary. Educational examples of paired-associate tasks include learning the states' capitals, the names and dates of Civil War battles, the addition and multiplication tables, the atomic weights of the elements, and the spelling of words.

2. **Serial learning** involves learning a list of terms in a particular order. Memorization of the notes on the musical staff, the Pledge of Allegiance, the elements in atomic weight order, and poetry and songs are serial learning tasks. Serial learning tasks occur less often in classroom instruction than paired-associate tasks do.

3. **Free-recall learning** tasks also involve memorizing a list, but not in a special order. Recalling the names of the 50 states, types of reinforcement, kinds of poetic feet, and the organ systems in the body are examples of free-recall tasks.

The following sections describe these three verbal learning tasks in more detail.

Paired-Associate Learning

In paired-associate learning, the student must associate a response with each stimulus. For example, the student is given a picture of a bone (the stimulus) and must respond *tibia,* or is given the symbol *Au* and must respond *gold.* One important aspect of the learning of paired associates is the degree of familiarity the student already has with the stimuli and the responses. For example, it would be far easier to learn to associate foreign words with English words, such as *dog—chien* (French) or *dog—perro* (Spanish) than to learn to associate two foreign words, such as *chien—perro.*

IMAGERY ● Many powerful memory techniques are based on forming mental images to help remember associations. For example, the French word for fencing is *l'escrime,* pronounced "le scream." It is easy to remember this association (*fencing—l'escrime*) by forming a mental picture of a fencer screaming while being skewered by an opponent, as illustrated in Figure 6.4.

One ancient method of enhancing memory by use of **imagery** is the creation of stories to weave together information (Egan, 1989). For example, images from Greek myths and other sources have long been used to help people recall the constellations.

serial learning
Memorization of a series of items in a particular order.

free-recall learning
Learning of a list of items in any order.

imagery
Mental visualization of images to improve memory.

FIGURE 6.4 ● Example of the Use of Images to Aid Recall
An English-speaking student learning French can easily remember that the French word for fencing is *l'escrime* by linking it to the English word *scream* and picturing a fencer screaming.

KEYWORD MNEMONICS ● One of the most extensively studied methods of using imagery and **mnemonics** (memory devices) to help paired-associate learning is the **keyword method,** which was originally developed for teaching foreign language vocabulary but was later applied to many other areas (Hall, 1991; Pressley, 1991). The example used earlier of employing vivid imagery to recall the French word *l'escrime* is an illustration of the keyword method. In that case, the keyword was *scream.* It is called a keyword because it evokes the connection between the word *l'escrime* and the mental picture. The Russian word for building, *zdanie,* pronounced "zdawn'-yeh," might be recalled by using the keyword *dawn* and imagining the sun coming up behind a building with an onion dome on top. Atkinson and Raugh (1975) used this method to teach students a list of 120 Russian words over a 3-day period. Other students were given English translations of the Russian words and allowed to study as they wished. At the end of the experiment, the students who used the keyword method recalled 72 percent of the words, while the other students recalled only 46 percent. This result has been repeated dozens of times, using a wide variety of languages (Pressley, Levin, & Delaney, 1982), with students from preschoolers to adults. However, young children seem to require pictures of the mental images they are meant to form, while older children (starting in upper elementary school) learn equally well making their own mental images (Pressley & Levin, 1978).

The images that are used in the keyword method work best if they are vivid and active, preferably involving interaction. For example, the German word for room, *zimmer* (pronounced "tsimmer"), might be associated with the keyword *simmer.* The German word would probably be better recalled by using an image of a distressed person in a bed immersed in a huge, steaming cauldron of water in a large bedroom than by using an image of a small pot of water simmering in the corner of a bedroom. The drama, action, and bizarreness of the first image make it memorable; the second is too commonplace to be easily recalled.

Although most research on mnemonic learning strategies has focused on learning foreign language vocabulary, several studies have demonstrated that the same methods can be used for other information, including names of state capitals and English vocabulary words (Levin, Shriberg, Miller, McCormick, & Levin, 1980; Miller, Levin, & Pressley, 1980), reading comprehension (Peters, Levin, McGivern, & Pressley, 1985), biographical information (McCormick & Levin, 1984), and science facts and concepts (Atkinson, Levin, & Atkinson, 1998). A review of many studies involving various mnemonic strategies found substantial positive effects, on average (Hattie, Bibbs, & Purdie, 1996). However, it should be noted that most of the research done on the use of mnemonic strategies has taken place under rather artificial, laboratorylike conditions, using materials that are thought to be especially appropriate for these strategies. Evaluations of actual classroom applications of these strategies show more mixed results (Pressley & Levin, 1983), and there are questions about the long-term retention of material learned by means of keywords (Carney & Levin, 1998; Wang & Thomas, 1995). Although the strategies have been relatively successful for teaching foreign language vocabulary (especially nouns) to elementary school students, they have yet to show success in helping students actually speak foreign languages better.

mnemonics
Devices or strategies for aiding the memory.

keyword method
A strategy for improving memory by using images to link pairs of items.

Serial and Free-Recall Learning

Serial learning is learning facts in a particular order. Learning the events on a timeline, learning the order of operations in long division, and learning the relative hardnesses of minerals are examples of serial learning. Free-recall learning is learning a list of items that need not be remembered in order, such as the names of the nine Supreme Court justices.

LOCI METHOD ● A mnemonic device for serial learning that was used by the ancient Greeks employs imagery associated with a list of locations (see Anderson, 1990). In the **loci method** the student thinks of a very familiar set of locations, such as rooms in his or her own house, and then imagines each item on the list to be remembered in one specific location. Vivid or bizarre imagery is used to place the item in the location. Once the connections between the item and the room or other location are established, the learner can recall each place and its contents in order. The same locations can be mentally cleared and used to memorize a different list. However, they should always be used in the same order to ensure that all items on the list were remembered.

PEGWORD METHOD ● Another imagery method useful for serial learning is called the **pegword method** (Krinsky & Krinsky, 1996). To use this mnemonic, the student might memorize a list of pegwords that rhyme with the numbers 1 to 10. To use this method, the student creates mental images relating to items on the list to be learned with particular pegwords. For example, in learning the order of the first 10 U.S. presidents, you might picture George Washington eating a bun (1) with his wooden teeth, John Adams tying his shoe (2), Thomas Jefferson hanging by his knees from a branch of a tree (3), and so on.

INITIAL-LETTER STRATEGIES ● One memory strategy that involves a reorganization of information is taking initial letters of a list to be memorized and making a more easily remembered word or phrase. For example, many trigonometry classes have learned about the imaginary SOH CAH TOA tribe, whose letters help us recall that sine = opposite/hypotenuse; cosine = adjacent/hypotenuse; tangent = opposite/adjacent. Many such **initial-letter strategies** exist for remembering the relative distances of the planets from the sun. The planets, in order, are Mercury, Venus, Earth, Mars, Jupiter, Saturn, Uranus, Neptune, and Pluto. Students are taught a sentence in which the first letters of the words are the first letters of the planets in order, such as "My very educated monkey just served us nine pizzas."

In a similar fashion, acronyms help people remember the names of organizations. Initial-letter strategies may also help students remember procedural knowledge, such as steps in a process.

SELF-CHECK

Draw a diagram of the memory strategies associated with paired-associate learning, serial learning, and free-recall learning.

WHAT MAKES INFORMATION MEANINGFUL?

Consider the following sentences:

1. Enso flrs hmen matn snoi teha erso iakt siae otin tnes esna nrae.
2. Easier that nonsense information to makes than sense is learn.
3. Information that makes sense is easier to learn than nonsense.

loci method
A strategy for remembering lists by picturing items in familiar locations.

pegword method
A strategy for memorization in which images are used to link lists of facts to a familiar set of words or numbers.

initial-letter strategies
Strategies for learning in which initial letters of items to be memorized are made into a more easily remembered word or phrase.

Which sentence is easiest to learn and remember? Obviously, sentence 3. All three sentences have the same letters, and sentences 2 and 3 have the same words. Yet to learn sentence 1, you would have to memorize 52 separate letters, and to learn sentence 2, you would have to learn 10 separate words. Sentence 3 is easiest because to learn it you need only learn one concept, a concept that readily fits your common sense and prior knowledge about how learning takes place. You know the individual words, you know the grammar that connects them, and you already have in your mind a vast store of information, experiences, and thoughts about the same topic. For these reasons, sentence 3 slides smoothly into your understanding.

The message in sentence 3 is what this chapter is all about. Most human learning, particularly school learning, involves making sense out of information, sorting it in our minds until it fits in a neat and orderly way, and using old information to help assimilate new learning. We have limited ability to recall rote information—how many telephone numbers can you remember for a month? However, we can retain meaningful information far more easily. Recall that most of the mnemonic strategies discussed in the previous section involve adding artificial meaning to arbitrary associations in order to take advantage of the much greater ease of learning meaningful information.

The message in sentence 3 has profound implications for instruction. One of the teacher's most important tasks is to make information meaningful to students by presenting it in a clear, organized way; by relating it to information already in students' minds; and by making sure that students have truly understood the concepts being taught and can apply them to new situations.

THEORY into Practice

Meaning versus Abstract Material

The issue of meaningfulness, or the relevance of material, has become a major focus of Piaget's theory of the development of logical reasoning (Piaget & Garcia, 1986). Most of our everyday thinking about the world is represented in the logical form of the conditional, "If . . . then. . . ." For young thinkers, this is often presented in the form of a promise such as, "If you finish all your dinner, then you can have some dessert!" Piaget proposed that this form of expression is a major characteristic of adolescent and adult thinking.

One application of the conditional is in scientific thought, where it appears in the form of hypotheses. Students in science class may struggle with a hypothesis expressed in abstract terms, but if we replace the abstract content with meaningful materials, student performance will improve (Ward & Overton, 1990). The relation between antecedent and consequent clauses in a conditional proposition is one of implication. That is, in a conditional proposition the antecedent implies the consequent; if the antecedent is true, then the consequent is true. Scientists look for some identifiable relation, linkage, or relevance between the antecedent and consequent.

For example, the conditional "If the moon is made of blue cheese, then the oceans are full of water," is a true conditional expressing material implication, but it lacks relevance and therefore is difficult to understand.

Conditional Proposition with Material Implication

If the moon is made of blue cheese,   then the oceans are full of water.

Antecedent ◄—————— no relevance —————► *Consequent*

Now consider the conditional "If he is a bachelor, then he is unmarried."

Conditional Proposition

If he is a bachelor,   then he is unmarried.

Antecedent ◄——————— definitional relevance ———————► *Consequent*

This conditional is a genuine implication because of definitional relevance: an unmarried man *is* a bachelor. Relevance relations can be defined according to criteria such as definition, convention, or causality. However, better than telling students the type of relevance relation is to allow individual students to judge for themselves the degree of meaning between the clauses of a hypothesis. When students are allowed to express their hypotheses about subject matter, they will be more motivated to explore the topic than if the material is given to them as established fact.

Another application of meaning and relevance is found in domain-specific learning. Students are more likely to perform at their highest levels of reasoning ability if the task is related to their specialty area rather than outside their area (DeLisi & Staudt, 1980). Many college students perform better in courses within their major, for example, than in general education courses.

If we can make the material relevant, then we will succeed!

Rote versus Meaningful Learning

Ausubel (1963) discussed the distinction between rote learning and meaningful learning. **Rote learning** refers to the memorization of facts or associations, such as the multiplication tables, the chemical symbols for the elements, words in foreign languages, or the names of bones and muscles in the human body. Much of rote learning involves associations that are essentially arbitrary. For example, the chemical symbol for gold *(Au)* could just as well have been *Go* or *Gd*. In contrast, **meaningful learning** is not arbitrary, and it relates to information or concepts learners already have. For example, if we learn that silver is an excellent conductor of electricity, this information relates to our existing information about silver and about electrical conductivity. Further, the association between "silver" and "electrical conductivity" is not arbitrary. Silver really is an excellent conductor, and while we could state the same principle in many ways or in any language, the meaning of the statement "Silver is an excellent conductor of electricity" could not be arbitrarily changed.

rote learning
Memorization of facts or associations that may be essentially arbitrary.

meaningful learning
Mental processing of new information that relates to previously learned knowledge.

USES OF ROTE LEARNING ● We sometimes get the impression that rote learning is "bad" and meaningful learning is "good." This is not necessarily true. For example, when the doctor tells us we have a fractured tibia, we hope that the doctor has mastered the rote association between the word *tibia* and the leg bone it names. The mastery of foreign language vocabulary is an important case of rote learning. However, rote learning has gotten a bad name in education because it is overused. We can all remember being taught to parrot facts that were supposed to be meaningful but that we were forced to learn as rote, meaningless information.

William James, in a book called *Talks to Teachers on Psychology* (1912), gave an excellent example of this kind of false learning:

> A friend of mine, visiting a school, was asked to examine a young class in geography. Glancing at the book, she said: "Suppose you should dig a hole in the ground, hundreds of feet deep, how should you find it at the bottom—warmer or colder than on top?" None of the class replying, the teacher said: "I'm sure they know, but I think you don't ask the question quite rightly. Let me try." So, taking the book, she asked: "In what condition is the interior of the globe?" and received the immediate answer from half the class at once. "The interior of the globe is in a condition of igneous fusion." (p. 150)

Clearly, the students had memorized the information without learning its meaning. The information was useless to them because it did not tie in with other information they had.

INERT KNOWLEDGE ● The "igneous fusion" information that students had memorized in the class James's friend visited is an example of what Bransford, Burns, Delclos, and Vye (1986) call **inert knowledge.** This is knowledge that could and should be applicable to a wide range of situations but is applied only to a restricted set of circumstances. Usually, inert knowledge consists of information or skills learned in school that we cannot apply in life. For example, you may know people who could pass an advanced French test but would be unable to communicate in Paris, or who can solve volume problems in math class but have no idea how much sand to order to fill a sandbox. Many problems in life arise not from a lack of knowledge but from an inability to use the knowledge we already have.

An interesting experiment by Perfetto, Bransford, and Franks (1983) illustrates the concept of inert knowledge. In the experiment, college students were given problems such as the following: "Uriah Fuller, the famous Israeli superpsychic, can tell you the score of any baseball game before the game starts. What is his secret?"

Before seeing the problems, some of the students were given a list of sentences to memorize that were clearly useful in solving the problems; among the sentences was "Before it starts, the score of any game is 0 to 0." Students who were told to use the sentences in their memories as clues performed much better on the problem-solving task than did other students, but students who memorized the clues but were not told to use them did no better than students who never saw the clues. What this experiment tells us is that having information in your memory does not guarantee that you can bring it out and use it when appropriate. Rather, you need to know how and when to use the information you have.

Teachers can help students learn information in a way that will make it useful as well as meaningful to them. Effective teaching requires an understanding of how to make information accessible to students so that they can connect it to other information and apply it outside of the classroom.

Schema Theory

As was noted earlier, meaningful information is stored in long-term memory in networks of connected facts or concepts called schemata. Recall the representation of the concept "bison" presented in Figure 6.3, showing how this one concept was linked to a wide range of other concepts. The most important principle of **schema theory** is that information that fits into an existing schema is more easily understood, learned, and retained than information that does not fit into an existing schema (Anderson & Bower, 1983). The sentence "Bison calves can run soon after they are born" is an example of information that will be easily incorporated into

inert knowledge
Learned information that could be applied to a wide range of situations but whose use is limited to restricted, often artificial applications.

schema theory
Theory stating that information is stored in long-term memory in schemata (networks of connected facts and concepts), which provide a structure for making sense of new information.

CASE TO CONSIDER

Knowledge and Learning How to Learn

Two 11th-grade U.S. history teachers, Helen Baker and George Kowalski, are talking in George's classroom after school. Helen has taught for 7 years and George for 21 years at Garfield High School, home of the current state high school basketball champions. Both teachers are members of the Social Studies Department's curriculum committee, which is in the process of revising the U.S. history course.

Helen: It really is wonderful, the kind of school spirit we have here at G.H.S.

George: Well, having won the state basketball championship twice in the last five years hasn't hurt any! Do you realize we were among the top four teams each of the last ten years except 1991 and 1994?

Helen (smiling): You're very good with facts like that, George. And speaking of facts, I wanted to talk to you about our disagreement about the curriculum revision. I thought that if you and I could work out our differences, maybe the committee would get out of the stalemate we're in.

George: Well, Helen, as I see it, you contend that students first need to master the facts of U.S. history before they can move on to higher-order thinking like problem solving and working with abstract concepts. My view is just the reverse. For generations we've taught students facts, and they forget them right after the test is over. That's because we don't ask them to use the facts in higher-order thought. To me, that's the only way you can learn to think abstractly and solve problems.

Helen: But, George, trying to think abstractly and solve problems must be based on knowledge. Otherwise, problem solving is a pointless exercise—it amounts to a sharing of ignorance among the uninformed.

George: But I don't think that's as pointless as the other extreme—sticking to lecture and discussion and objective tests on key names, dates, terms, and events!

Helen: I know you use a lot of small-group and independent study work and give essay-type tests. I heard some students talking about how your questions really blew their minds. I think one was "What would the United States be like today if the South had won the Civil War?"

George (chuckling): Yes, that stirred them up a bit!

Helen: But, George, believe it or not, I've asked my students to write on that question from time to time when we're on the Civil War, and their answers were terrible—totally devoid of facts. The kids just wrote their opinions.

George: That's my point, Helen! Students have to learn how to use facts—and practice organizing and incorporating them into answers. Basketball players look terrible the first time they try a slam-dunk. But after they learn the technique, it's easy!

Helen: I think where we really disagree is on strategy. I maintain that learning the facts is the first step and higher-order thinking follows. You begin by posing problems and questions and hope that the kids will learn the facts to answer the questions. That seems like throwing kids into a lake and asking them to swim.

George: Sure, the facts and fundamentals are important, but in my experience, kids just forget them. But if you compel kids to determine and then use the facts, they'll remember them long after the test. I'll bet some of the things they learn in my course are still with them when they're adults.

Helen: Well, George, I just can't see how we are going to reconcile our two positions. Can you?

PROBLEM SOLVING

1. How do Helen's and George's positions differ on the nature of information processing, memory, and forgetting? What are the merits and drawbacks of each approach?
2. If you were settling the argument between Helen and George, what advice would you give them on the basis of information in this chapter?
3. Extend the dialogue with a third character who brings a problem-solving approach to the impasse.

your "bison" schema, because you know that (1) bison rely on speed to escape from predators and (2) more familiar animals (such as horses) that also rely on speed have babies that can run very early. Without all this prior knowledge, "Bison calves can run soon after they are born" would be more difficult to assimilate mentally and more easily forgotten.

FIGURE 6.5 ● Example of a Knowledge Structure Arranged As a Hierarchy
A person who understands the place of a particular animal (Rex) within the animal kingdom might have that information arranged in memory as shown here.

From J. M. Royer and R. S. Feldman, *Educational Psychology: Applications and Theory,* p. 255. Copyright 1984 by McGraw-Hill, Inc. Reproduced with permission of The McGraw-Hill Companies.

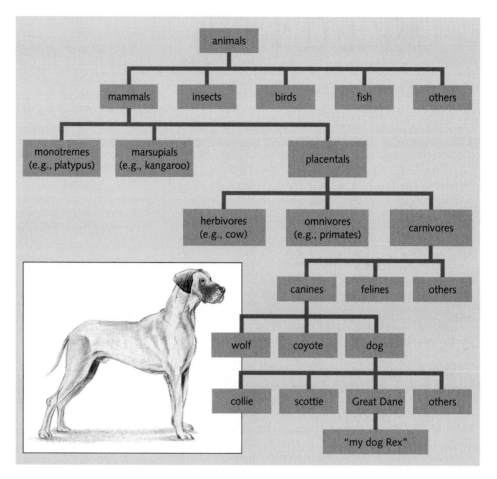

HIERARCHIES OF KNOWLEDGE ● It is thought that most well-developed schemata are organized in hierarchies similar to outlines, with specific information grouped under general categories, which are grouped under still more general categories. This is illustrated in Figure 6.5. Note that in moving from the top to the bottom of the figure, you are going from general (animals) to specific ("my dog Rex"). The concepts in Figure 6.5 are well anchored in the schema. Any new information relating to this schema will probably be learned and incorporated into the schema much more readily than would information relating to less established schemata or rote learning that does not attach to any schema.

One important insight of schema theory is that meaningful learning requires the active involvement of the learner, who has a host of prior experiences and knowledge to bring to understanding and incorporating new information (Alexander, 1992). What you learn from any experience depends in large part on the schema you apply to the experience.

THE IMPORTANCE OF BACKGROUND KNOWLEDGE ● One of the most important determinants of how much you can learn about something is how much you already know about it (Alexander, Kulikowich, & Jetton, 1994, 1995; Schneider, 1993). A study in Japan by Kuhara-Kojima and Hatano (1991) illustrated this clearly. College students were taught information about baseball and music. Those who knew a great deal about baseball but not about music learned much more about baseball; the converse was true of those who knew a lot about music and little about baseball. In fact, background knowledge was much more important than general learning ability in predicting how much the students would learn. Learners who know a great deal about a subject have more well-developed schemata for incorporating new knowledge. Not surprisingly, interest in a given subject contributes to background knowledge in it, as well as depth of understanding and willingness to use background knowledge to solve new problems (Tobias, 1994). However, learners often do not spontaneously use their prior knowledge to help them learn new material. Teachers must link new learning to students' existing background knowledge (Fennema, Franke, Carpenter, & Cary, 1993; Pressley et al., 1992; Spires & Donley, 1998).

SELF-CHECK

Explain the difference between rote and meaningful learning, the role of schemes in learning, and the importance of prior knowledge in learning. Create a chart showing examples of rote learning and meaningful learning.

HOW DO METACOGNITIVE SKILLS HELP STUDENTS LEARN?

The term **metacognition** means knowledge about one's own learning (Flavell, 1985; Garner & Alexander, 1989) or about how to learn. Thinking skills and study skills are examples of **metacognitive skills.** Students can be taught strategies for assessing their own understanding, figuring out how much time they will need to study something, and choosing an effective plan of attack to study or solve problems (Schraw & Moshman, 1995). For example, in reading this book, you are bound to come across a paragraph that you don't understand on first reading. What do you do? Perhaps you reread the paragraph more slowly. Perhaps you look for other clues, such as pictures, graphs, or glossary terms to help you understand. Perhaps you read farther back in the chapter to see whether your difficulty arose because you did not fully understand something that came earlier. These are all examples of metacognitive skills; you have learned how to know when you are not understanding and how to correct yourself (Zimmerman & Schunk, 1989). Another metacognitive strategy is the ability to predict what is likely to happen or to tell what is sensible and what is not. For example, when you first read the word *modeling* in Chapter 5, you knew right away that this did not refer to building models of ships or airplanes, because you knew that meaning would not fit in the context of this book.

While most students do gradually develop adequate metacognitive skills, some do not. Teaching metacognitive strategies to students can lead to a marked improvement in their achievement (Alexander, Graham, & Harris, 1998; Hattie et al., 1996). Students can learn to think about their own thinking processes and apply specific learning strategies to think themselves through difficult tasks (Butler & Winn, 1995; Pressley, Harris, & Marks, 1992; Pressley et al., 1990). **Self-questioning strategies** are particularly effective. In self-questioning, students look for common elements in a given type of task and ask themselves questions about these elements. For example, many researchers (e.g., Dimino, Gersten, Carnine, & Blake, 1990; Stevens, Madden, Slavin, & Farnish, 1987) have taught students to

metacognition
Knowledge about one's own learning or about how to learn ("thinking about thinking").

metacognitive skills
Methods for learning, studying, or solving problems.

CONNECTIONS

The term *modeling* is discussed in Chapter 5, page 163, in relation to Bandura's social learning theory.

self-questioning strategies
Learning strategies that call upon students to ask themselves *who, what, where,* and *how* questions as they read material.

look for characters, settings, problems, and problem solutions in stories. Instructors start with specific questions and then let students find these critical elements on their own. Paris, Cross, and Lipson (1984) and King (1992) found that students comprehended better if they were taught to ask themselves *who, what, where,* and *how* questions as they read. Englert, Raphael, Anderson, Anthony, and Stevens (1991) gave students planning sheets to help them plan creative writing. Among the questions students were taught to ask themselves were: For whom am I writing? What is being explained? What are the steps? Essentially, students are taught to talk themselves through the activities they are engaged in, asking themselves or each other the questions a teacher would ask. Students have been successfully taught to talk themselves through mathematics problem solving (Cardelle-Elawar, 1990), spelling (Block & Peskowitz, 1990), creative writing (Zellermayer, Salomon, Globerson, & Givon, 1991), reading (Chin, 1998; Kucan & Beck, 1997), and many other subjects (see Chan, Burtis, Scardamalia, & Bereiter, 1992; Guthrie, Bennett, & Weber, 1991; McInerney & McInerney, 1998).

SELF-CHECK

Define *metacognition* and explain how self-questions promote learning.

WHAT STUDY STRATEGIES HELP STUDENTS LEARN?

How are you reading this book? Are you underlining or highlighting key sentences? Are you taking notes or summarizing? Are you discussing the main ideas with a classmate? Are you putting the book under your pillow at night and hoping the information will somehow seep into your mind? Students have used these and many other strategies ever since the invention of reading, and such strategies have been studied almost as long. Even Aristotle wrote on the topic. Yet educational psychologists are still debating which study strategies are most effective (see Mayer, 1996; Pressley, Yokoi, van Meter, van Etten, & Freebern, 1997).

Research on effective study strategies is confusing at best. Few forms of studying are found to be always effective, and fewer still are never effective. Clearly, the value of study strategies depends on their specifics and on the uses to which they are put (Thomas & Rohwer, 1986). Research on the most common study strategies is summarized in the following sections.

Note-Taking

A common study strategy that is used both in reading and in learning from lectures is **note-taking.** Note-taking can be effective for certain types of material, because it can require mental processing of main ideas, as one makes decisions about what to write. However, the effects of note-taking have been found to be inconsistent. Positive effects are most likely when note-taking is used for complex conceptual material in which the critical task is to identify the main ideas (Anderson & Armbruster, 1984; Rickards, Fajen, Sullivan, & Gillespie, 1997). Also, note-taking that requires some mental processing is more effective than simply writing down what was read (Kiewra, 1991; Kiewra et al., 1991). For example, Bretzing and Kulhavy

note-taking
A study strategy that requires decisions about what to write.

(1981) found that writing paraphrase notes (stating the main ideas in different words) and taking notes in preparation to teach others the material were effective note-taking strategies, because they required a high degree of mental processing of the information.

One apparently effective means of increasing the value of students' note-taking is for the teacher to provide skeletal notes before a lecture or reading, giving students categories to direct their own note-taking. Several studies have found that this practice, combined with student note-taking and review, increases student learning (Kiewra, 1991).

Underlining

Perhaps the most common study strategy is underlining or highlighting. Yet despite the widespread use of this method, research on underlining generally finds few benefits (Anderson & Armbruster, 1984; Gaddy, 1998; Snowman, 1984). The problem is that most students fail to make decisions about what material is most critical and simply underline too much. When students are asked to underline the one sentence in each paragraph that is most important, they do retain more, probably because deciding which is the most important sentence requires a higher level of processing (Snowman, 1984).

Summarizing

Summarizing involves writing brief statements that represent the main ideas of the information being read. The effectiveness of this strategy depends on how it is used (Hidi & Anderson, 1986; King, 1991). One effective way is to have students write one-sentence summaries after reading each paragraph (Wittrock, 1991). Another is to have students prepare summaries that are intended to help others learn the material—partly because this activity forces the summarizer to be brief and to consider seriously what is important and what is not (Brown, Bransford, Ferrara, & Campione, 1983). However, it is important to note that several studies have found no effects of summarization, and the conditions under which this strategy increases comprehension or retention of written material are not well understood (Anderson & Armbruster, 1984; Wittrock, 1991; Wittrock & Alesandrini, 1990).

Outlining and Mapping

A related family of study strategies requires the student to represent the material studied in skeletal form. These strategies include outlining, networking, and mapping. **Outlining** presents the main points of the material in a hierarchical format, with each detail organized under a higher-level category. In networking and **mapping,** students identify main ideas and then diagram connections between them (Hyerle, 1995; Robinson & Skinner, 1996). For example, the schematic representation of the concept "bison" shown in Figure 6.3 might have been produced by students themselves as a network to summarize factual material about bison and their importance to Plains Indians (see Clark, 1990; Rafoth, Leal, & De Fabo, 1993).

Research on outlining, networking, and mapping is limited and inconsistent but generally finds that these methods are helpful as study aids (Anderson & Armbruster, 1984; Katayama & Robinson, 1998; Robinson & Kiewra, 1995).

summarizing
Writing brief statements that represent the main idea of the information being read.

outlining
Representing the main points of material in hierarchical format.

mapping
Diagramming main ideas and the connections between them.

The PQ4R Method

One of the best-known study techniques for helping students understand and remember what they read is a procedure called the **PQ4R method** (Thomas & Robinson, 1972), which is based on an earlier version known as SQ3R, developed by F. P. Robinson (1961). The acronym stands for *preview, question, read, reflect, recite, and review.*

Research has shown the effectiveness of the PQ4R method for older children (Adams, Carnine, & Gersten, 1982), and the reasons seem clear. Following the PQ4R procedure focuses students on the meaningful organization of information and involves students in other effective strategies, such as question generation, elaboration, and distributed practice (opportunities to review information over a period of time) (Anderson, 1990).

THEORY
into
Practice

Teaching the PQ4R Method

Explain and model the steps of the PQ4R method for your older students, using the following guidelines:

1. **Preview:** Survey or scan the material quickly to get an idea of the general organization and major topics and subtopics. Pay attention to headings and subheadings, and identify what you will be reading about and studying.
2. **Question:** Ask yourself questions about the material as you read it. Use headings to invent questions using the *wh* words: *who, what, why, where.*
3. **Read:** Read the material. Do not take extensive written notes. Try to answer the questions that you posed while reading.
4. **Reflect on the material:** Try to understand and make meaningful the presented information by (1) relating it to things you already know, (2) relating the subtopics in the text to primary concepts or principles, (3) trying to resolve contradictions within the presented information, and (4) trying to use the material to solve problems suggested by the material.
5. **Recite:** Practice remembering the information by stating points out loud and asking and answering questions. You may use headings, highlighted words, and notes on major ideas to generate those questions.
6. **Review:** In the final step, actively review the material, focusing on asking yourself questions; reread the material only when you are not sure of the answers.

SELF-CHECK

Make a list of all the study strategies listed in this section. Provide a plan showing how each strategy is taught.

HOW DO COGNITIVE TEACHING STRATEGIES HELP STUDENTS LEARN?

PQ4R method
A study strategy that has students preview, question, read, reflect, recite, and review material.

In *Alice's Adventures in Wonderland* the White Rabbit is unsure how to give his evidence in the trial of the Knave of Hearts. The King of Hearts gives him a bit of advice: "Begin at the beginning . . . and go on until you come to the end: then stop."

This teacher is giving students an advance organizer to help them activate their prior knowledge before an assignment. With what types of materials and in what situations do advance organizers work best?

The "King of Hearts method" is a common means of delivering lectures, especially at the secondary and college levels. However, teachers can do more to help their students understand lessons. They can prepare students to learn new material by reminding them of what they already know, they can use questions, and they can help students link and recall new information. Many aspects of effective lesson presentation are covered in Chapter 7; but the following sections discuss practices derived from cognitive psychology that can help students understand, recall, and apply essential information, concepts, and skills.

CONNECTIONS

See, for example, "How Is a Direct Instruction Lesson Taught?" in Chapter 7, page 221.

Making Learning Relevant and Activating Prior Knowledge

Read the following passage:

> With the hocked gems financing him our hero bravely defied all scornful laughter that tried to prevent his scheme. Your eyes deceive he had said. An egg, not a table, correctly typifies this unexplored planet. Now three sturdy sisters sought proof. Forging along, sometimes through calm vastness, yet more often through turbulent peaks and valleys, days became weeks as many doubters spread fearful rumors about the edge. At last, from nowhere, welcome winged creatures appeared signifying momentous success. (Dooling & Lachman, 1971, p. 217)

Now read the paragraph again with the following information: The passage is about Christopher Columbus. Before you knew what the passage was about, it probably made little sense to you. You could understand the words and grammar and could probably infer that the story involved a voyage of discovery. However, once you learned that the story was about Columbus, you could bring all your prior knowledge about Columbus to bear on comprehending the paragraph, so that seemingly obscure references made sense. The "hocked gems" (Queen Isabella's jewelry), the egg (the shape of the earth), the three sturdy sisters (the *Niña, Pinta,* and *Santa Maria),* and the winged creatures (birds) become comprehensible when you know what the story is about.

In terms of schema theory, advance information that the story concerns Columbus activates your schema relating to Columbus. You are ready to receive and incorporate information relating to Columbus, to Isabella and Ferdinand, and to the ships. It is as though you had a filing cabinet with a drawer labeled "Columbus." When you know you are about to hear about Columbus, you mentally open the drawer, which contains files marked "Isabella," "ships," and "scoffers and doubters." You are now ready to file new information in the proper places. If you learned that the *Santa Maria* was wrecked in a storm, you would mentally file that information in the "ships" file. If you learned that most of the educated world agreed with Columbus that the earth was round, you would file that information in the "scoffers and doubters" file. The file drawer analogy is not completely appropriate, however, because the files of a schema are all logically connected with one another. Also, you are actively using the information in your files to interpret and organize the new information.

ADVANCE ORGANIZERS ● David Ausubel (1963) developed a method called **advance organizers** to orient students to material they were about to learn and to help them recall related information that could assist them in incorporating the new information. An advance organizer is an initial statement about a subject to be learned that provides a structure for the new information and relates it to information students already possess. For example, in one study (Ausubel & Youssef, 1963) college students were assigned to read a passage on Buddhism. Before reading the passage, some students were given an advance organizer comparing Buddhism to Christianity, while others read an unrelated passage. The students who were given the advance organizer retained much more of the material than did the other students. Ausubel and Youssef maintained that the reason for this was that the advance organizer activated most students' knowledge of Christianity, and the students were able to use that knowledge to incorporate information about a less familiar religion.

Many studies have established that advance organizers increase students' understanding of certain kinds of material (see, e.g., Corkill, 1992; Schwartz, Ellsworth, Graham, & Knight, 1998). Advance organizers seem to be most useful for teaching content with a well-organized structure that may not be immediately apparent to students. However, they have not generally been found to help students learn factual information that does not lend itself to a clear organization or subjects that consist of a large number of separate topics (Ausubel, 1978; Corkill, 1992). In addition, methods designed to activate prior knowledge, such as advance organizers, can be counterproductive if the prior knowledge is weak or lacking (Alvermann et al., 1985). If students know little about Christianity, relating Buddhism to Christianity may confuse rather than help them.

The use of advance organizers is a valuable strategy in its own right, but research on advance organizers also illustrates a broader principle that is extremely important: Activating prior knowledge enhances understanding and retention (Pressley, Wood, et al., 1992). Strategies other than advance organizers draw on this same principle. For example, having students discuss what they already know about a topic before they learn it (Pressley, Tannenbaum, McDaniel, & Wood, 1990) and having them make predictions about material to be learned (Fielding, Anderson, & Pearson, 1990) are additional ways to encourage students to make conscious use of prior knowledge.

advance organizers
Activities and techniques that orient students to the material before reading or class presentation.

ANALOGIES ● Like advance organizers, use of explanatory analogies (comparisons or parallels) can contribute to an understanding of the lessons or the text. For example, a teacher could introduce a lesson on the human body's disease-fighting mechanisms by telling students to imagine a battle and to consider it as an analogy for the body's fight against infection. Similarly, a teacher could preface a lesson on termite societies by asking students to think of the hierarchy of citizens within a kingdom, using that as an analogy for such insect societies. **Analogies** can help students learn new information by relating it to concepts they already know (McDaniel & Dannelly, 1996; Zook, 1991).

One interesting study (Halpern, Hansen, & Riefer, 1990) found that analogies work best when they are most different from the process being explained. For example, college students' learning about the lymph system was aided more by an analogy of the movement of water through a sponge than by one involving the movement of blood through veins. What this probably illustrates is that it is more important that analogies be thoroughly familiar to the learner than that they relate in any direct way to the concepts being taught.

ELABORATION ● Cognitive psychologists use the term **elaboration** to refer to the process of thinking about material to be learned in a way that connects the material to information or ideas that are already in the learner's mind (Ayaduray & Jacobs, 1997). As an example of the importance of elaboration, Stein, Littlefield, Bransford, and Persampieri (1984) conducted a series of experiments in which students were given lists of phrases to learn, such as "The gray-haired man carried the bottle." Some students were given the same phrases embedded in a more elaborate sentence, such as "The gray-haired man carried the bottle of hair dye." These latter students recalled the phrases much better than did those who did not receive the elaboration, because the additional words tied the phrase to a well-developed schema that was already in the students' minds. The connection between *gray-haired man* and *bottle* is arbitrary until we give it meaning by linking these words with the *hair dye* idea.

Teachers can apply this principle—that elaborated information is easier to understand and remember—to helping students comprehend lessons. Students may be asked to think of connections between ideas or to relate new concepts to their own lives. For example, it might help students to understand the U.S. annexation of Texas and California if they consider these events from the perspective of Mexicans or if they compare the events to a situation in which a friend borrows a bicycle and then decides not to give it back. In discussing a story or novel, a teacher might ask students from time to time to stop and visualize what is happening or what's about to happen as a means of helping them to elaborate their understanding of the material. Elaboration can be taught as a skill to help students comprehend what they read (Weinstein, Ridley, Dahl, & Weber, 1988/89).

Organizing Information

Recall the shopping list discarded earlier in this chapter. When the list was presented in random order, it was very difficult to memorize, partly because it contained too many items to be held in working memory all at once. However, when the list was organized in a logical way, it was meaningful and therefore easy to learn and remember. The specific foods were grouped according to familiar recipes (e.g., flour, eggs, and milk were grouped under "pancakes"); and the recipes and other foods were grouped under "breakfast," "lunch," and "dinner."

Material that is well organized is much easier to learn and remember than material that is poorly organized (Durso & Coggins, 1991). Hierarchical organization, in which specific issues are grouped under more general topics, seems particularly

analogies
Images, concepts, or narratives that compare new information to information students already understand.

elaboration
The process of connecting new material to information or ideas already in the learner's mind.

The Intentional Teacher

● Using What You Know about Cognitive Theories of Learning to Improve Teaching and Learning

Intentional teachers know how information is received, processed, and stored in memory. Intentional teachers demonstrate that teaching is more than telling; they help students connect new information with what they already know and encourage students to apply information in other contexts. Incorporating research findings about cognition into the classroom allows intentional teachers to help students build lasting and meaningful understandings.

1 What am I trying to accomplish?

Meaningful information tends to be remembered best. Review your goals and objectives to ensure that you plan for meaningful learning.

> Before teaching your unit on the human body, you review your plans: "Three days spent on memorizing the bones of the body? Hmm . . . ." You reconsider this goal, remembering that meaningful learning encourages personal relevance and deeper processing. You revise the goal to include a smaller number of bones to be learned, but in richer ways. You plan to bring in X rays and animal bones to enrich learning.

Rote learning and meaningful learning are both appropriate in the school setting. Think about *which* belongs *where* in your instructional program.

> You review your long-term goals for your first-grade reading program and find that you have included many opportunities for students to have meaningful interactions with print. You notice, though, that you have excluded rote learning of key words that can help students read with fluency. You revise your plans to include sight word mastery through flash cards.

2 What are my students' relevant experiences and needs?

The more students know about a subject, the better they can organize and absorb new information. Find out what your students already know about the topics you study.

In your history class, you begin a unit on World War II by spending a period charting what students already know about the war. You add student responses to a diagram like the one below:

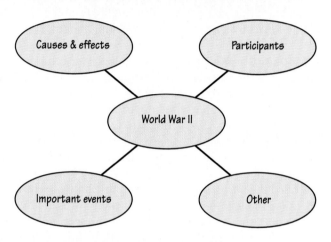

Schema theory suggests that new information is added to existing networks of connected ideas. Help students fit new knowledge into their existing networks.

> In your art lesson on perspective, you relate new information to what students already know: "We've been studying the use of line in art. Think about some different ways you've seen artists use line to communicate a message." After listening to students' responses, you state, "Today we'll use line in a new way: to capture three dimensions on a two-dimensional surface—paper." You show examples and begin.

helpful for student understanding (Van Patten, Chao, & Reigeluth, 1986). For example, in a classic study by Bower, Clark, Lesgold, and Winzenz (1969), one group of students was taught 112 words relating to minerals in random order. Another group was taught the same words, but in a definite order. Figure 6.6 shows the hierarchy within which the words were organized. The students were taught the words at levels 1 and 2 in the first of four sessions; those at levels 1, 2, and 3 in the second session; and those at levels 1 through 4 in the third and fourth sessions. The students in this second group recalled an average of 100 words, in comparison to

3 What approaches and materials are available to help me challenge every student?

Careful organization of information ensures that students can better access long-term memory and accommodate new ideas in short-term memory. Organize your lessons so that main points are clear and information is chunked (grouped) into useful categories.

> You review your social studies lesson on communities for your third-graders and double-check that you have just a few key ideas to present: goods, services, and interdependence. You group related ideas and plan to present the information according to these categories.

Active processing and rehearsal increase the chances that information will move from short-term to long-term memory and be retained in long-term memory. Build time into your plans for students to apply and practice new information.

> You keep a note card before you in your religions class: "Remember to have students process!" After presenting a few key concepts, you pause to have students act on the material. You use a variety of strategies: teacher questions, student questions, drawings, and directions such as "Tell your neighbor one important thing about Hinduism" or "Think about a recent instance when you heard the idea of revealed truth discussed outside of this class."

Emotion and personal meaning and relevance can help students process information deeply so that they remember better. Begin your lesson in ways that capture student interest, and provide instruction that focuses on developing understanding beyond surface-level features.

> You begin a lesson on density by displaying two cans of soda in an aquarium: One sinks, but the other floats! The students' curiosity is piqued and they actively engage themselves in discovering the rule that allows for the cans' behavior. At the lesson's close, you create a powerful visual image of an immense iceberg floating in the chilling sea. You ask students to explain, using their new understanding of density, why the iceberg floats despite its vast size.

4 How will I know whether and when to change my strategy or modify my instruction?

Check your instruction to ensure that you are providing opportunities for students to process information, to connect new information with what they already know, and to organize it in useful ways. Revise your instruction when you find that it falls short.

> Your university supervisor comes to observe your lesson on problem solving in mathematics. You ask him to assess how well your lesson (a) makes use of students' prior experiences with problem solving; (b) teaches them to organize information to solve problems efficiently; and (c) encourages students to reflect on their thinking and to revise and check their work. You incorporate your supervisor's suggestions into a follow-up lesson.

5 What information will I accept as evidence that my students and I are experiencing success?

Students need to demonstrate different kinds of understanding: rote learning, meaningful learning, and the ability to use information in new contexts. Give them tasks that allow you to check for different uses of knowledge: Are they forgetting? Are they transferring? Are they applying? Adjust your instruction based upon your results.

> As teacher of the advanced German class, you assess students' recall of vocabulary terms, their ability to describe rules and structures of the language, and their ability to communicate in German. You find that students have good recall of vocabulary but struggle with forming messages in German, so you plan for opportunities for them to speak in German in realistic contexts . . . like the Hoffbrau Haus!

Students demonstrate success when they show they can control their own learning. Check to see that students use self-questioning strategies and metacognition to assess their own learning.

> Before you hand your fourth-graders a reading passage on reptiles, you prompt them to ask themselves questions as they read, and you suggest they record their findings. After they complete the passage, you ask them which sections of text were difficult and what they do when they encounter difficult text. Their answers tell you that your students are on their way toward actively monitoring their own learning.

only 65 for the group that received the random presentation—demonstrating the effectiveness of a coherent, organized presentation. In teaching complex concepts, not only is it necessary that material be well organized; it is also important that the organizing framework itself be made clear to students (Kallison, 1986; Shimmerlik, 1978). For example, in teaching about the minerals shown in Figure 6.6, the teacher might refer frequently to the framework and mark transitions from one part of it to another, as follows:

"Recall that alloys are combinations of two or more metals."

FIGURE 6.6 ● **The Hierarchical Structure for Minerals**

From G. H. Bower, M. C. Clark, A. M. Lesgold, and D. Winzenz, "Hierarchical Retrieval Schemes in Recall of Categorized Word Lists," *Journal of Verbal Learning and Verbal Behavior, 8,* 1969, pp. 323–343. Reprinted by permission of Academic Press.

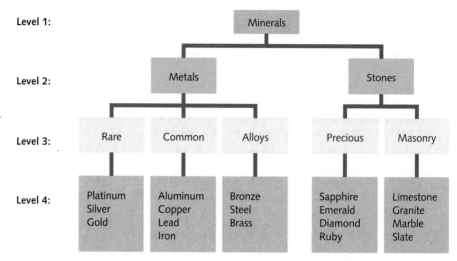

"Now that we've covered rare and common metals and alloys, let's move on to the second category of minerals: stones."

USING QUESTIONING TECHNIQUES ● One strategy that helps students learn from written texts, lectures, and other sources of information is the insertion of questions requiring students to stop from time to time to assess their own understanding of what the text or teacher is saying (Crooks, 1988; Pressley, Tannenbaum, et al., 1990). Presenting questions before the introduction of the instructional material can also help students learn material related to the questions (Hamaker, 1986; Hamilton, 1985), as can having students generate their own questions (Rosenshine, Meister, & Chapman, 1996).

USING CONCEPTUAL MODELS ● Another means that teachers can use to help students comprehend complex topics is the introduction of conceptual models, or diagrams showing how elements of a process relate to one another. Figure 6.1, which illustrates information processing, is a classic example of a conceptual model. Use of such models organizes and integrates information. Examples of topics that lend themselves to use of conceptual models are electricity, mechanics, computer programming, and the processes by which laws are passed. When models are part of a lesson, not only do students learn more, but they are also better able to apply their learning to creatively solve problems (see Hiebert, Wearne, & Taber, 1991; Mayer & Gallini, 1990; Winn, 1991). Knowledge maps, a variation on conceptual models, can be used to teach a wider variety of content. A knowledge map graphically shows the main concepts of a topic of study and the links between them. Giving students knowledge maps after a lesson has been shown to increase their retention of the lesson's content (Hall & O'Donnell, 1992; Hall, Sidio-Hall, & Saling, 1995).

SELF-CHECK

Compare cognitive teaching strategies that help students to elicit prior knowledge with cognitive teaching strategies that assist the learner in organizing new learned information. Give an example of how each strategy can be used in the classroom.

CHAPTER SUMMARY

WHAT IS AN INFORMATION-PROCESSING MODEL?

The three major components of memory are the sensory register, short-term or working memory, and long-term memory. The sensory registers are very short-term memories linked to the senses. Information that is received by the senses but not attended to will be quickly forgotten. Once information is received, it is processed by the mind in accord with our experiences and mental states. This activity is called *perception.*

Short-term or working memory is a storage system that holds five to nine bits of information at any one time. Information enters working memory from both the sensory register and the long-term memory. Rehearsal is the process of repeating information in order to hold it in working memory.

Long-term memory is the part of the memory system in which a large amount of information is stored for an indefinite time period. Cognitive theories of learning stress the importance of helping students relate information being learned to existing information in long-term memory.

The three parts of long-term memory are episodic memory, which stores our memories of personal experiences; semantic memory, which stores facts and generalized knowledge in the form of schemata; and procedural memory, which stores knowledge of how to do things. Schemata are networks of related ideas that guide our understanding and action. Information that fits into a well-developed schema is easier to learn than information that cannot be so accommodated. Levels-of-processing theory suggests that learners will remember only the things that they process. Students are processing information when they manipulate it, look at it from different perspectives, and analyze it. Dual code theory further suggests the importance of using both visual and verbal coding to learn bits of information. Other elaborations of the information-processing model are transfer-appropriate processing, parallel distributed processing, and connectionist models.

WHAT CAUSES PEOPLE TO REMEMBER OR FORGET?

Interference theory helps explain why people forget. It suggests that students can forget information when it gets mixed up with, or pushed aside by, other information. Interference theory states that two situations cause forgetting: retroactive inhibition, when learning a second task makes a person forget something that was learned previously, and proactive inhibition, when learning one thing interferes with the retention of things learned later. The primacy and recency effects state that people remember best information that is presented first and last in a series. Automaticy is gained by practicing information or skills far beyond the amount needed to establish them in long-term memory so that using such skills requires little or no mental effort. Practice strengthens associations of newly learned information in memory. Distributed practice, which involves practicing parts of a task over a period of time, is usually more effective than massed practice. Part learning, overlearning, and enactment also help students to remember information.

HOW CAN MEMORY STRATEGIES BE TAUGHT?

Teachers can help students remember facts by presenting lessons in an organized way and by teaching students to use memory strategies called *mnemonics.* Three types of verbal learning are paired-associate learning, serial learning, and free-recall learning. Paired-associate learning is learning to respond with one member of a pair when given the other member. Students can improve their learning of paired associates by using imagery techniques such as the keyword method. Serial learning involves recalling a list of items in a specified order. Free-recall learning involves recalling the list in any order. Helpful strategies are the loci method, the pegword method, rhyming, and initial-letter strategies.

WHAT MAKES INFORMATION MEANINGFUL?

Information that makes sense and has significance to students is more meaningful than inert knowledge and information learned by rote. According to schema theory, individuals' meaningful knowledge is constructed of networks and hierarchies of schemata.

HOW DO METACOGNITIVE SKILLS HELP STUDENTS LEARN?

Metacognition helps students learn by thinking about, controlling, and effectively using their own thinking processes.

WHAT STUDY STRATEGIES HELP STUDENTS LEARN?

Note-taking, selective directed underlining, summarizing, outlining, and mapping can effectively promote learning. The PQ4R method is an example of a strategy that focuses on the meaningful organization of information.

HOW DO COGNITIVE TEACHING STRATEGIES HELP STUDENTS LEARN?

Advance organizers help students process new information by activating background knowledge. Analogies, information elaboration, organizational schemes, questioning techniques, and conceptual models are other examples of teaching strategies that are based on cognitive learning theories.

KEY TERMS

advance organizers　208

analogies　209

attention　177

automaticity　191

connectionist models　187

distributed practice　192

dual code theory of memory　185

elaboration　209

enactment　194

episodic memory　181

flashbulb memory　181

free-recall learning　195

imagery　195

inert knowledge　200

information-processing theory　175

initial-letter strategies　197

interference　187

keyword method　196

levels-of-processing theory　184

loci method　197

long-term memory　180

mapping　205

massed practice　192

meaningful learning　199

metacognition　203

metacognitive skills　203

mnemonics　196

note-taking　204

outlining　205

overlearning　192

paired-associate learning   194

parallel distributed processing model   186

part learning   192

pegword method   197

perception   176

PQ4R method   206

primacy effect   190

proactive facilitation   190

proactive inhibition   189

procedural memory   181

recency effect   190

rehearsal   178

retroactive facilitation   190

retroactive inhibition   188

rote learning   199

schemata   182

schema theory   200

self-questioning strategies   203

semantic memory   181

sensory register   175

serial learning   195

short-term memory   177

summarizing   205

transfer-appropriate processing theory   186

verbal learning   194

working memory   177

Self-Assessment

1. Sperling's study involving the recall of 12 letters projected briefly on a screen illustrates the limitations of which of the following memory areas?
   a. long-term memory
   b. short-term or working memory
   c. external environment
   d. sensory register

2. Match each of the following types of memory with its definition.
   a. procedural memory
   b. episodic memory
   c. semantic memory

   _____ part of long-term memory that stores images of personal experiences.
   _____ mental networks of related concepts associated with understanding new information
   _____ type of memory associated with automaticity

3. Which of the following teaching strategies would be least effective in reducing retroactive inhibition?
   a. Be consistent in the methods used when teaching similar concepts.
   b. Teach one concept thoroughly before introducing the next one.
   c. Use mnemonic devices to point out differences in concepts.
   d. Teach concepts at different times, such as in separate class periods.

4. Provide an example of how someone develops automaticity.

5. Match each type of verbal learning skill with its example.
   a. free-recall learning
   b. paired-associate learning
   c. serial learning

   _____ learning U.S. states and capitals
   _____ memorizing the order of planets
   _____ learning about major organs of the body

6. Give several examples of mnemonics.

7. Which of the following study strategies is associated with note-taking?
   a. outlining and mapping
   b. PQ4R method
   c. loci method
   d. pegword method

8. What is the name given to the prelearning activities and techniques that orient students to new material?
   a. the PQ4R method
   b. metacognition
   c. advance organizers
   d. keyword method

9. Give three examples of how a teacher can make learning relevant to students by activating prior knowledge.

10. How does organizing information enhance learning?

Chapter 7

WHAT IS DIRECT INSTRUCTION?

HOW IS A DIRECT INSTRUCTION LESSON TAUGHT?
State Learning Objectives
Orient Students to the Lesson
Review Prerequisites
Present New Material
Conduct Learning Probes
Provide Independent Practice
Assess Performance and Provide Feedback
Provide Distributed Practice and Review

WHAT DOES RESEARCH ON DIRECT INSTRUCTION METHODS SUGGEST?
Advantages and Limitations of Direct Instruction

HOW DO STUDENTS LEARN AND TRANSFER CONCEPTS?
Concept Learning and Teaching
Teaching for Transfer of Learning

HOW ARE DISCUSSIONS USED IN INSTRUCTION?
Subjective and Controversial Topics
Difficult and Novel Concepts
Affective Objectives
Whole-Class Discussions
Small-Group Discussions

The Effective Lesson

Ms. Logan's eighth-grade physical science class is a happy mess. Students are working in small groups at lab stations, filling all sorts of bottles with water and then tapping them to see how various factors affect the sound. One group has set up a line of identical bottles and put different amounts of water in each one so that tapping the bottles in sequence makes a crude musical scale. "The amount of water in the bottle is all that matters," one group member tells Ms. Logan, and her groupmates nod in agreement. Another group has an odd assortment of bottles and has carefully measured the same amount of water into each. "It's the shape and thickness of the bottles that make the difference," says one group member. Other groups are working more chaotically, filling and tapping large and small, narrow and wide, and thick and thin bottles with different amounts of water. Their theories are wild and varied.

After a half hour of experimentation, Ms. Logan calls the class together and asks group members to describe what they did and what they concluded. Students loudly uphold their group's point of view. "It's the amount of water!" "It's the height of the bottles!" "It's the thickness of the bottles!" "No, it's their shape!" "It's how hard you tap the bottles!" Ms. Logan moderates the conversation but lets students confront each other's ideas and give their own arguments.

The next day, Ms. Logan teaches a lesson on sound. She explains how sound causes waves in the air and how the waves cause the eardrum to vibrate, transmitting sound information to the brain. She has two students come to the front of the class with a Slinky and uses the Slinky to illustrate how sound waves travel.

She asks many questions of students, both to see whether they are understanding and to get them to take the next mental step. She then explains how sound waves in a tube become lower in pitch the longer the tube is. To illustrate this, she plays a flute and a piccolo. Light bulbs are starting to click on in the students' minds, and Ms. Logan can tell from the responses to her questions that the students are starting to get the idea. At the end of the period, Ms. Logan lets the students get back into their groups to discuss what they have learned and to try to apply their new knowledge to the bottle problem.

When the students come into class on the third day of the sound lesson, they are buzzing with excitement. They rush to their lab stations and start filling and tapping bottles to test out the theories they came up with the day before. Ms. Logan walks among the groups, listening in on their conversations. "It's not the amount of water, it's the amount of air," she hears one student say. "It's not the bottle; it's the air," says a student in another group. She helps one group that is still floundering to get on track. Finally, Ms. Logan calls the class together to discuss their findings and conclusions. Representatives of some of the groups demonstrate the experiments they used to show how it was the amount of air in each bottle that determined the sound.

"How could we make one elegant demonstration that it's only the amount of air that controls the sound?" asks Ms. Logan.

The students buzz among themselves and then assemble all their bottles into one experiment. They make one line of identical bottles with different amounts of water. Then to show that it is the air, not the water, that matters, they put the same amount of water in bottles of different sizes. Sure enough, in each case, the more air space left in the bottle, the lower the sound.

Ms. Logan ends the period with a homework assignment: to read a chapter on sound in a textbook. She tells the students that they will have an opportunity to work in their groups to make certain that every group member understands everything in the sound lesson, and then there will be a quiz in which students will have to show individually that they can apply their new knowledge. She reminds them that their groups can be "superteams" only if everyone knows the material.

The bell rings, and the students pour into the hallway, still talking excitedly about what they have learned. Some groupmates promise to call each other that evening to prepare for the group study the next day. Ms. Logan watches them file out. She's exhausted, but she knows that this group of students will never forget the lessons they've learned about sound, about experiments, and, most important, about their ability to use their minds to figure out difficult concepts.

Creative Thinking   Write the phrase *Effective Lesson* in the middle of a sheet of paper and circle it. Brainstorm all of the types of instructional approaches you can think of that make an effective lesson. Now list the types of instructional approaches that Ms. Logan uses.

Critical Thinking   How does Ms. Logan motivate the students? What strategies does she use to encourage retention of the material?

The lesson is where education takes place. All other aspects of schooling, from buildings to buses to administration, are designed to support teachers in delivering effective lessons; they do not educate in themselves. Most teachers spend most of their class time teaching lessons. The typical elementary or secondary school teacher may teach 800 to 1,000 class lessons each year!

Conducting effective lessons is at the heart of the teacher's craft. Some aspects of lesson presentation have to be learned on the job; good teachers get better at it every year. Yet educational psychologists have studied the elements that go into effective lessons, and we know a great deal that is useful in day-to-day teaching at every grade level and in every subject (Good & Brophy, 1989; Porter & Brophy, 1988). This chapter and the four that follow it present the principal findings of this research and translate them into ways of thinking about the practical demands of everyday teaching.

As Ms. Logan's lesson illustrates, effective lessons use many teaching methods. In four periods on one topic, she used discovery, direct instruction, discussion, cooperative learning, and other techniques. These methods are often posed as different philosophies, and the ideological wars over which is best go on incessantly (see, e.g., Berg & Clough, 1990/91; Hunter, 1990/91). Yet few experienced teachers would deny that teachers must be able to use all of them and must know when to use each. Traditionally, teachers have probably used too much direct instruction and not enough discovery or cooperative learning. Yet there are times when discovery learning is inefficient or when students are not likely to discover the right principles. I once visited a teacher who was using an exciting, inquiry-oriented approach to science that tried to teach entirely through discovery. "What do you do if students discover the wrong principles?" I asked the teacher. She looked around carefully and then beckoned me over to a quiet corner. "I *teach* them," she whispered in a conspiratorial tone.

This chapter focuses on the strategies that teachers use to transmit information to students in ways that are most likely to help students understand, incorporate, and use new concepts and skills. Chapter 8 focuses on student-centered methods, in which students play an active role in structuring learning for themselves and for each other. However, the teaching strategies presented in these two chapters should be seen not as representing two sharply conflicting philosophies of education, but as complementary approaches to be used at different times for different purposes.

WHAT IS DIRECT INSTRUCTION?

There are times when the most effective and efficient way to teach students is for the teacher to present information, skills, or concepts in a direct fashion. The term **direct instruction** is used to describe lessons in which the teacher transmits information directly to students, structuring class time to reach a clearly defined set of objectives as efficiently as possible. Direct instruction is particularly appropriate for teaching a well-defined body of information or skills that all students must master. It is less appropriate when deep conceptual change is an objective or when exploration, discovery, and open-ended objectives are the object of instruction. Also, direct instruction relates more obviously to declarative knowledge ("knowing what") than to procedural knowledge ("knowing how").

An enormous amount of research was done in the 1970s and 1980s to discover the elements of effective direct instruction lessons. Different authors describe these elements differently (see, e.g., Evertson, Emmer, Clements, Sanford, & Worsham, 1994; Gagné & Briggs, 1979; Good et al., 1983; Hunter, 1995; Rosenshine & Stevens, 1986). There is general agreement among researchers and teachers as to the sequence of events that characterize effective direct instruction lessons. First, students are brought up to date on any skills they might need for today's lesson (e.g., the teacher might briefly review yesterday's lesson if today's is a continuation) and are told what they are going to learn. Then the teacher devotes most of the lesson time to teaching the skills or information, giving students opportunities to practice the skills or express the information, and questioning or quizzing students to determine whether or not they are learning the objectives.

A brief description of the parts of a direct instruction lesson follows. The next section of this chapter will cover each part in detail.

1. **State learning objectives and orient students to the lesson:** Tell students what they will be learning and what performance will be expected of them. Whet students' appetites for the lesson by informing them how interesting, important, or personally relevant it will be to them.
2. **Review prerequisites:** Go over any skills or concepts students need in order to understand today's lesson.
3. **Present new material:** Teach the lesson, presenting information, giving examples, demonstrating concepts, and so on.
4. **Conduct learning probes:** Pose questions to students to assess their level of understanding and correct their misconceptions.
5. **Provide independent practice:** Give students an opportunity to practice new skills or use new information on their own.
6. **Assess performance and provide feedback:** Review independent practice work or give a quiz. Give feedback on correct answers, and reteach skills if necessary.
7. **Provide distributed practice and review:** Assign homework to provide distributed practice on the new material. In later lessons, review material and provide practice opportunities to increase the chances that students will remember what they learned and will be able to apply it in different circumstances.

direct instruction
Approach to teaching in which the teacher transmits information directly to the students; lessons are goal-oriented and structured by the teacher.

SELF-CHECK

List the sequence of steps that characterize a direct instruction lesson.

HOW IS A DIRECT INSTRUCTION LESSON TAUGHT?

The general lesson structure takes vastly different forms in different subject areas and at different grade levels. Teachers of older students may take several days for each step of the process, ending with a formal test or quiz. Teachers of younger students may go through the entire cycle in a class period, using informal assessments at the end. Two quite different lessons are presented in Tables 7.1 and 7.2 to illustrate how direct instruction would be applied to different subjects and grade levels. The first lesson, "Subtraction with Renaming," is an example of the first of a series of lessons directed at a basic math skill. In contrast, the second lesson, "The Origins of World War II," is an example of a lesson directed at higher-order understanding of critical events in history and their causes and interrelationships. Note that the first lesson (Table 7.1) proceeds step by step and emphasizes frequent learning probes and independent practice to help students thoroughly learn the concepts being taught, whereas the second lesson (Table 7.2) is characterized by an alternation between new information, discussion, and questions to assess comprehension of major concepts.

The sequence of activities outlined in these two lessons flows along a logical path, from arousing student interest to presenting new information to allowing students to practice their new knowledge or skills to assessment. This orderly progression is essential to direct instruction lessons at any grade level and in any subject, although the various components and how they are implemented would, of course, look different for different subjects and grades.

State Learning Objectives

The first step in presenting a lesson is planning it in such a way that the reasons for teaching and learning the lesson are clear. What do you want students to know or be able to do at the end of the lesson? Setting out objectives at the beginning of the lesson is an essential step in providing a framework into which information, instructional materials, and learning activities will fit.

Planning a Lesson

The first step of a lesson, stating learning objectives or outcomes, represents a condensation of much advance **lesson planning.** As a teacher planning a lesson, you will need, at the least, to answer the following questions:

1. What will students know or be able to do after the lesson? What will be the outcomes of their learning? How will you know when and how well students have achieved these learning outcomes or objectives?
2. What information, activities, and experiences will you provide to help students acquire the knowledge and skills they need in order to attain the learning outcomes? How much time will be needed? How will you use in-class and out-of-class time? How will seatwork and homework assignments help students to achieve the learning objectives?
3. What books and materials will you use to present the lesson, and what is their availability? When will you preview or test all the materials and create guidelines

---

lesson planning
Procedure that includes stating learning objectives such as what the students should know or be able to do after the lesson; what information, activities, and experiences the teacher will provide; how much time will be needed to reach the objective; what books, materials, and media support the teacher will provide; and what instructional method(s) and participation structures will be used.

CONNECTIONS
For more on lesson planning, see Chapter 13, page 456.

THEORY
into
Practice

for students' responses to them? Are all materials accurate, pedagogically sound, fair to different cultures, and appropriate in content and grade level?

4. How many different methods of teaching will you incorporate? For example, will you combine reading, lecture, role-playing, videotape viewing, a demonstration, and a writing assignment?

5. What participation structures will you use: whole-group or small-group discussions, cooperative learning groups, ability groups, individual assignments? What learning tasks will groups and individuals perform? How will you organize, monitor, and evaluate groups?

Orient Students to the Lesson

One important task at the beginning of a lesson is to establish a positive **mental set,** or attitude of readiness, in students: "I'm ready to get down to work. I'm eager to learn the important information or skills the teacher is about to present, and I have a rough idea of what we will be learning." This mental set can be established in many ways. First, it is important to expect students to be on time to class and to start the lesson immediately when the period begins (Evertson et al., 1994). This establishes a sense of seriousness of purpose that is lost in a ragged start. Second, it is important to arouse students' curiosity or interest in the lesson they are about to learn. This was done in the first sample lesson (Table 7.1) by introducing subtraction with renaming as a skill that would be necessary in connection with counting cupcakes for a class party, a situation of some reality and interest to young students. In the second sample lesson (Table 7.2) the teacher advertised the importance of the lesson on the basis that understanding the origins and events of World War II would help students understand events today, and made the lesson personally relevant to students by having them think of a relative who fought in World War II or was deeply affected by it. In the chapter-opening vignette, Ms. Logan whetted students' curiosity about sound by giving them an opportunity to experiment with it before the formal lesson.

A lesson on genetics might be introduced as follows:

> Did you ever wonder why tall parents have taller-than-average children and red-haired children usually have at least one red-haired parent? Think of your own family. If your father and mother are both taller than average, then you will probably be taller than average. Well, today we are going to have a lesson on the science called genetics, in which we will learn how characteristics of parents are passed on to their children.

This introduction might be expected to grab students' interest because it makes the subject personally relevant.

Humor or drama can also establish a positive mental set. One teacher occasionally used a top hat and a wand to capture student interest by "magically" transforming adjectives into adverbs (e.g., *sad* into *sadly*). Popular and instructionally effective children's television programs use this kind of device constantly to get young children's attention and hold their interest in basic skills. Finally, it is important in starting a lesson to give students a road map of where the lesson is going and what they will know at the end. Stating lesson objectives clearly has generally been found to enhance student achievement of those objectives (Melton, 1978). Giving students an outline of the lesson may also help them to incorporate new information (Kiewra, 1985).

mental set
Students' attitude of readiness to begin a lesson.

TABLE 7.1

Sample Lesson for Basic Math: Subtraction with Renaming

LESSON PART	TEACHER PRESENTATION
1. State learning objective and orient students to lesson.	"There are 32 students in this class. Let's say we were going to have a party, and I was going to get one cupcake for each student in the class. But five of you said you didn't like cupcakes. How many cupcakes would I need to get for the students who do like cupcakes? Let's set up the problem on the chalkboard the way we have before, and mark the tens and ones . . . " tens ones 3 2 Students − 5 Don't like cupcakes "All right, let's subtract: 2 take away 5 is . . . *hey!* We can't do that! Five is more than 2, so how can we take 5 away from 2? We can't! "In this lesson we are going to learn how to subtract when we don't have enough ones. By the end of this lesson, you will be able to show how to rename tens as ones so that you can subtract."
2. Review prerequisites.	"Let's review subtraction when we have enough ones." Put on the chalkboard and have students solve: 47 56 89 − 3 − 23 − 8 How many tens are in 23? _____ How many ones are in 30? _____ Give answers, discuss all items missed by many students.
3A. Present new material (first subskill).	Hand out 5 bundles of 10 popsicle sticks each and 10 individual sticks to each student. Using an overhead projector, explain how to use sticks to show 13, 27, 30. Have students show each number at their own desks. Walk around to check.
4A. Conduct learning probes (first subskill).	Have students show 23 using their sticks. Check desks. Then have students show 40. Check desks. Continue until all students have the idea.
3B. Present new material (second subskill).	Using an overhead projector, explain how to use sticks to show 6 minus 2 and 8 minus 5. Then show 13 and try to take away 5. Ask for suggestions on how this could be done. Show that by removing the rubber band from the tens bundle, we have a total of 13 ones and can remove 5. Have students show this at their desks.
4B. Conduct learning probes (second subskill).	Have students show 12 (check) and then take away 4 by breaking apart the ten bundle. Then have students show 17 and take away 9. Continue until all students have the idea.
3C. Present new material (third subskill).	Give students worksheets showing tens bundles and single units. Explain how to show renaming by crossing out a bundle of ten and rewriting it as 10 units and then subtracting by crossing out units.
4C. Conduct learning probes (third subskill).	Have students do the first items on the worksheet one at a time until all students have the idea.
5. Provide independent practice.	Have students continue, completing the worksheet on their own.
6. Assess performance and provide feedback.	Show correct answers to worksheet items on overhead projector. Have students mark their own papers. Ask how many got item 1, item 2, etc., and discuss all items missed by more than a few students. Have students hand in papers.
7. Provide distributed practice and review.	Hand out homework, and explain how it is to be done. Review lesson content at start of following lesson and in later lessons.

TABLE 7.2

Sample Lesson for History: The Origins of World War II

LESSON PART	TEACHER PRESENTATION
1. State learning objective and orient students to lesson.	"Today we will begin to discuss the origins and causes of World War II—perhaps the most important event in the twentieth century. The political situation of the world today—the map of Europe, the political predominance of the United States, the problems of the Eastern European countries formerly under Soviet domination, even the problems of the Middle East—all can be traced to the rise of Hitler and the bloody struggle that followed. I'm sure many of you have relatives who fought in the war or whose lives were deeply affected by it. Raise your hand if a relative or someone you know well fought in World War II." • "Germany today is peaceful and prosperous. How could a man like Hitler have come to power? To understand this, we must first understand what Germany was like in the years following its defeat in World War I and why an unemployed Austrian painter could come to lead one of the largest countries in Europe." • "By the end of this lesson you will understand the conditions in Germany that led up to the rise of Hitler, the reasons he was successful, and the major events of his rise to power."
2. Review prerequisites.	Have students recall from the previous lesson: • The humiliating provisions of the Treaty of Versailles —Reparations —Demilitarization of the Ruhr —Loss of territory and colonies • The lack of experience with democracy in Germany
3. Present new material.	Discuss with students: • Conditions in Germany before the rise of Hitler —Failure of the Weimar Republic —Economic problems, inflation, and severe impact of the U.S. Depression —Belief that Germany lost World War I because of betrayal by politicians —Fear of Communism • Events in Hitler's rise to power —Organization of National Socialist (Nazi) Party —Beer-Hall Putsch and Hitler's imprisonment —*Mein Kampf* —Organization of Brown Shirts (S.A.) —Election and appointment as chancellor
4. Conduct learning probes.	Questions to students throughout lesson should assess student comprehension of the main points.
5. Provide independent practice.	Have students independently write three reasons why the situation in Germany in the 1920s and early 1930s might have been favorable to Hitler's rise, and have students be prepared to defend their answers.
6. Assess performance and provide feedback.	Call on randomly selected students to read and justify their reasons for Hitler's success. Discuss well-justified and poorly justified reasons. Have students hand in papers.
7. Provide distributed practice and review.	Review lesson content at start of next lesson and in later lessons.

Communicating Objectives to Students

THEORY *into* Practice

Teacher education programs include training in creating lesson plans, beginning with a consideration of instructional objectives and learning outcomes. Sharing lesson plans with students is a good idea, because research suggests that knowledge of objectives can lead to improvements in student achievement. Practical suggestions follow for sharing lesson objectives with students.

1. The objectives you communicate to students should be broad enough to encompass everything the lesson will teach. Research suggests that giving students too narrow a set of objectives may lead them to devalue or ignore other meaningful aspects of a lesson. In addition, broad objectives provide greater flexibility for adapting instruction as needed once the lesson is under way.
2. The objectives you communicate should be specific enough in content to make clear to students what the outcomes of their learning will be—what they will know and be able to do and how they will use their new knowledge and skills.
3. Consider stating objectives both orally and in writing and repeating them during the lesson to remind students why they are learning. Teachers often use verbal and written outlines or summaries of objectives. Providing demonstrations or models of learning products or outcomes is also effective. Examples of outcomes, along with the steps or skills involved, help students to see the organization of the lesson and what it will take to complete the lesson objectives.
4. Consider using questioning techniques to elicit from students their own statements of objectives or outcomes. Their input will likely both reflect and inform your lesson plan. Some teachers ask students to express their ideas for meeting objectives or demonstrating outcomes, because research suggests that students who have a stake in the lesson plan and a sense of control over their learning will be more motivated to learn.

Review Prerequisites

CONNECTIONS
For more about the importance of activating students' prior knowledge, see Chapter 6, page 207.

The next major task in a lesson is to be sure that students have mastered prerequisite skills and to link information that is already in their minds to the information you are about to present. If today's lesson is a continuation of yesterday's and you are reasonably sure that students understood yesterday's lesson, then the review may just remind them about the earlier lesson and ask a few quick questions before beginning the new one. For instance, you might say, "Yesterday we learned how to add the suffix *-ed* to a word ending in *y*. Who will tell us how this is done?"

As today's lesson—adding other suffixes to words ending in *y*—is a direct continuation of yesterday's, this brief reminder is adequate. However, if a new skill or concept is being introduced and depends on skills learned much earlier, then more elaborate discussion and assessment of prerequisite skills may be needed.

Sometimes it is necessary to assess students on prerequisite skills before starting a lesson. In the first sample lesson (Table 7.1), the teacher briefly quizzed students on subtraction without renaming and numeration skills in preparation for a lesson on subtraction with renaming. If students had shown poor understanding of either prerequisite skill, the teacher would have reviewed those skills before going on to the new lesson.

CONNECTIONS
See page 208 in Chapter 6 for a definition of advance organizers.

Another reason to review prerequisites is to provide advance organizers. As defined in Chapter 6, advance organizers are introductory statements by the teacher that remind students of what they already know and give them a framework for understanding the new material to be presented. In the second sample lesson (Table 7.2), the teacher set the stage for the new content (Hitler's rise to power) by reviewing the economic, political, and social conditions in Germany that made Hitler's success possible.

Present New Material

Here begins the main body of the lesson, the point at which the teacher presents new information or skills.

CONNECTIONS
See page 209 in Chapter 6 for a discussion of retention of well-organized information.

LESSON STRUCTURE ● Lessons should be logically organized. Recall from Chapter 6 that information that has a clear, well-organized structure is retained better than less clearly presented information (Fuchs et al., 1997). A lesson on the legislative branch of the U.S. government might be presented as follows:

The Legislative Branch of the Federal Government (First Lesson)

I. Functions and nature of the legislative branch (Congress)
   A. Passes laws
   B. Approves money for executive branch
   C. Has two houses—House of Representatives and Senate

II. House of Representatives
   A. Designed to be closest to the people—representatives elected to 2-year terms—proportional representation
   B. Responsible for originating money bills

III. Senate
   A. Designed to give greater continuity to legislative branch—senators elected to 6-year terms—each state has two senators
   B. Approves appointments and treaties made by executive branch

This would be a beginning lesson; subsequent lessons would present how laws are introduced and passed, checks and balances on legislative power, and so on. The lesson has a clear organization that should be pointed out to students. For example, you might pause at the beginning of the second topic and say, "Now we are going to learn about the lower house of Congress, the House of Representatives." The purpose of this is to help students form a mental outline that will help them remember the material. A clearly laid out structure and transitional statements about the structure of the lesson have been found to increase student understanding (Kallison, 1986). A study by Woodward (1994) found that students learned more about earth science if the material was organized in a causal structure (*A* causes *B*) than if the material was organized according to topics.

LESSON EMPHASIS ● In addition to making clear the organization of a lesson by noting when the next subtopic is being introduced, instructionally effective teachers give clear indications about the most important elements of the lesson by saying, for example, "It is particularly important to note that . . . " (Maddox & Hoole, 1975). Important points should be repeated and brought back into the lesson whenever appropriate. For example, in teaching about the presidential veto in the lesson on the legislative branch of government, it might be good to say:

> Here again, we see the operation of the system of checks and balances we discussed earlier. The executive can veto legislation passed by the Congress, which in turn can withhold funds for actions of the executive. Remember, understanding how this system of checks and balances works is critical to an understanding of how the U.S. government works.

The idea here is to emphasize one of the central concepts of the U.S. government—the system of checks and balances among the executive, legislative, and judicial branches—by bringing it up whenever possible and by labeling it as important.

One carefully controlled experiment found that teachers who used the lesson presentation strategies outlined in this section were more successful than other teachers in increasing student achievement (Clark et al., 1979). The researchers studied the effectiveness of teachers who reviewed main ideas, stated objectives at the beginning of the lesson, outlined lesson content, signaled transitions between parts of the lesson, indicated important points in the lesson, and summarized the parts of the lesson as the lesson proceeded. These teachers' students learned more than did students whose teachers did not do these things.

LESSON CLARITY ● One consistent feature of effective lessons is clarity—the use of direct, simple, and well-organized language to present concepts (Land, 1987; McCaleb & White, 1980; Smith & Land, 1981). Wandering off into digressions or irrelevant topics or otherwise interrupting the flow of the lesson detracts from clarity. Clear presentations avoid the use of vague terms that do not add to the meaning of the lesson, such as the italicized words in the following sentence (from Smith & Land, 1981): "*Maybe* before we get to *probably* the main idea of the lesson, you should review a few prerequisite concepts."

EXPLANATIONS ● Effective teachers have also been found to use many explanations and explanatory words (such as *because, in order to,* and *consequently*) and frequently to use a pattern of **rule–example–rule** when presenting new concepts (Van Patten et al., 1986). For example:

> Matter may change forms, but it is never destroyed. If I were to burn a piece of paper, it would appear that the paper was gone, but in fact it would have been combined with oxygen atoms from the air and changed to a gas (mostly carbon dioxide) and ash. If I could count the atoms in the paper plus the atoms from the air before and after I burned the paper, we could see that the matter involved did not disappear, but merely changed forms.

Note that the rule was stated ("Matter . . . is never destroyed"), an example was given, and the rule was restated in the explanation of how the example illustrates the rule. Also note that a rule–example–rule sequence was used in this book to illustrate the rule–example–rule pattern!

DEMONSTRATIONS, MODELS, AND ILLUSTRATIONS ● Cognitive theorists emphasize the importance of students' seeing and, when appropriate, having hands-on experience with concepts and skills. Visual representations are maintained in long-term memory far more readily than is information that is only heard (Hiebert et al., 1991; Mayer & Gallini, 1990). Showing, rather than just telling, is particularly essential for children who are acquiring English (August & Hakuta, 1997). Recall how Ms. Logan gave her students both hands-on experience (filling and tapping

rule–example–rule
Pattern of teaching concepts by presenting a rule or definition, giving examples, and then showing how examples illustrate the rule.

bottles) and a visual analogy (the Slinky representing sound waves) to give the students clear and lasting images of the main principles of sound. Visual media (e.g., video, film, and slides) can be especially effective in providing visual information (Kozma, 1991).

CONNECTIONS

For more on the importance of attention in learning, see Chapter 6, page 177.

MAINTAINING ATTENTION ● Straight, dry lectures can be boring, and bored students soon stop paying attention to even the most carefully crafted lesson. For this reason it is important to introduce variety, activity, or humor to enliven the lecture and maintain student attention. For example, the use of humor has been found to increase student achievement (Ziv, 1988), and illustrating a lecture with easily understood graphics can help to hold students' attention. On the other hand, too much variation in mode of presentation can hurt achievement if it distracts students from the lesson content (Wyckoff, 1973). Several studies have established that students learn more from lessons that are presented with enthusiasm and expressiveness than from dry lectures (Abrami, Leventhal, & Perry, 1982; Crocker & Brooker, 1986). In one sense, teaching is performing, and it appears that some of the qualities we would look for in a performer are also those that increase teachers' effectiveness (see Timpson & Tobin, 1982).

CONTENT COVERAGE AND PACING ● One of the most important factors in effective teaching is the amount of content covered. In general, students of teachers who cover more material learn more than other students do (e.g., Barr, 1987; Barr & Dreeben, 1983). This does not necessarily mean that teachers should teach faster; obviously, there is such a thing as going too fast and leaving students behind. Yet research on instructional pace does imply that most teachers could increase their pace of instruction (Good et al., 1983), as long as degree of understanding is not sacrificed. In addition to increasing content coverage, a relatively rapid pace of instruction can help with classroom management.

CONNECTIONS

For more on the impact of time on learning, see Chapter 11, page 366.

Conduct Learning Probes

Imagine an archer who shoots arrows at a target but never finds out how close to the bull's-eye the arrows fall. The archer wouldn't be very accurate to begin with and would certainly never improve in accuracy. Similarly, effective teaching requires that teachers be constantly aware of the effects of their instruction. All too often, teachers mistakenly believe that if they have covered a topic well and students appear to be paying attention, then their instruction has been successful. Students often believe that if they have listened intently to an interesting lecture, they know the material presented. Yet this may not be true. If teachers do not regularly probe students' understanding of the material being presented, students may be left with serious misunderstandings or gaps in knowledge.

The term **learning probe** refers to a variety of ways of asking for brief student responses to lesson content. Learning probes give the teacher feedback on students' levels of understanding and allow students to try out their understanding of a new idea to find out whether they have it right. Learning probes can take the form of questions to the class, as in the sample lesson on World War II presented in Table 7.2, or brief written or physical demonstrations of understanding, as in the sample subtraction lesson in Table 7.1.

learning probe
A method, such as questioning, that helps teachers find out whether students understand a lesson.

CHECKS FOR UNDERSTANDING ● Whether the response to the learning probe is written, physical, or oral, the purpose of the probe is checking for understanding

This teacher is checking for understanding. Why is this step important? What decision will he make as part of this step? What steps come before this one?

(Rosenshine & Stevens, 1986). That is, the learning probe is used not so much to teach or to provide practice as to find out whether students have understood what they just heard. Teachers use the probes to set their pace of instruction. If students are having trouble, teachers must slow down and repeat explanations. If all students show understanding, the teacher can move on to new topics. The following interchange shows how a teacher might use learning probes to uncover student strengths and misunderstandings and then adjust instruction accordingly. The teacher, Mr. Swift, has written several sentences containing conversation on an overhead projector transparency, and students are learning the correct use of commas and quotation marks.

Mr. Swift: Now we are ready to punctuate some conversation. Everyone get out a sheet of paper and copy this sentence, adding punctuation where needed: Take the criminal downstairs Tom said condescendingly. Is everyone ready? . . . Carl, how did you punctuate the sentence?

Carl: Quote take the criminal downstairs quote comma Tom said condescendingly period.

Mr. Swift: Close, but you made the most common error people make with quotation marks. Maria, what did you write?

Maria: I think I made the same mistake Carl did, but I understand now. It should be: Quote take the criminal downstairs comma quote Tom said condescendingly period.

Mr. Swift: Good. How many got this right the first time? (Half of class raises hands.) Okay, I see we still have some problems with this one. Remember, commas and periods go inside the quotation mark. I know that sometimes this doesn't make much sense, but if English always made sense, a lot of English teachers would be out of work! Think of quotation marks as wrappers for conversation, and the conversation, punctuation and all, goes inside the wrapper. Let's all try another. Drive carefully Tom said recklessly. Samphan?

Samphan: Quote drive carefully comma quote Tom said recklessly period.

Mr. Swift: Great! How many got it? (All but one or two raise hands.) Wonderful, I think you're all with me. The quotation marks "wrap up" the conversation, including its punctuation. Now let's all try one that's a little harder: I wonder Tom said quizzically whether quotation marks will be on the test.

This interchange contains several features worth noting. First, Mr. Swift had all students work out the punctuation, called on individuals for answers, and then asked all students whether they got the right answers. This is preferable to asking only one or two students to work (say, on the chalkboard) while the others watch, thus wasting the time of most of the class. When all students have to figure out the punctuation and no one knows on whom Mr. Swift will call, all students actively participate and test their own knowledge, and Mr. Swift gets a quick reading on the level of understanding of the class as a whole.

Note also that when Mr. Swift found that half the class missed the first item, he took time to reteach the skill students were having trouble with, using a different explanation from the one he had used in his first presentation. By giving students the mental image of quotation marks as wrappers, he helped them to remember the order of punctuation in conversation. When almost all students got the second item, he moved to the next step, because the class had apparently mastered the first one.

Finally, note that Mr. Swift had plenty of sentences prepared on the overhead projector, so he did not have to use class time to write out sentences. Learning probes should always be brief and should not be allowed to destroy the tempo of the lesson. By being prepared with sentences for learning probes, Mr. Swift was able to maintain student involvement and interest. In fact, he might have done even better if he had given students photocopies with unpunctuated sentences on them to reduce the time used in copying the sentences.

QUESTIONS ● Questions to students in the course of the lesson serve many purposes (Carlsen, 1991; Ramsey, Gabbard, Clawson, Lee, & Henson, 1993). Questions may be used as Socrates used them, to prompt students to take the next mental step; for example, "Now that we've learned that heating a gas makes it expand, what do you suppose would happen if we cool a gas?"(Tredway, 1995). Questions may also be used to encourage students to think further about information they learned previously or to get a discussion started; for example, "We've learned that if we boil water, it becomes water vapor. Now, water vapor is a colorless, odorless, invisible gas. In that case, why do you suppose we can see steam coming out of a tea kettle?" With guidance, a class discussion would eventually arrive at the answer, which is that the water vapor recondenses when it hits the relatively cool air and that what is visible in steam is water droplets, not vapor. It is often helpful to have students generate their own questions, either for themselves or for each other (King, 1992).

Finally, questions can be used as learning probes. In fact, any question is to some degree a learning probe, in that the quality of response will indicate to the teacher how well students are learning the lesson. Research on the frequency of questions indicates that teachers who ask more questions related to the lesson at hand are more instructionally effective than are those who ask relatively few questions (Dunkin & Biddle, 1974; Gall et al., 1978; Stallings & Kaskowitz, 1974). A study by Perry, Vanderstoep, and Yu (1993) found that Asian teachers asked more conceptual questions of first-graders than did U.S. teachers. This might be one reason Asian students' math achievement is higher than that of U.S. students. At all levels of schooling it is probable that factual questions will help with factual skills (Clark et al., 1979) and questions that encourage students to think about concepts will help with conceptual skills (Fagan, Hassler, & Szabo, 1981; Gall, 1984; Redfield & Rousseau, 1981).

A great deal of evidence indicates that students gain from generating their own questions (Foos, Mora, & Tkacz, 1994; Rosenshine, Meister, & Chapman, 1996; Wittrock, 1991), especially questions that relate to students' existing background knowledge about a topic they are studying (King, 1994).

WAIT TIME ● One issue related to questioning that has received much research attention is **wait time,** the length of time the teacher waits for a student to answer a question before giving the answer or going on to another student. Research has found that teachers tend to give up too rapidly on students whom they perceive to be low achievers, a practice that tells those students that the teacher expects little from them (Rowe, 1974; Tobin & Capie, 1982).

Teachers who wait approximately 3 seconds after asking a student a question obtain better learning results than do those who give up more rapidly (Tobin, 1986). Furthermore, following up with students who do not respond has been associated with higher achievement (Anderson, Evertson, & Brophy, 1979; Brophy & Evertson, 1974; Larrivee, 1985). Waiting for students to respond or staying with them when they do not communicates positive expectations for them (Brophy & Good, 1974). On the other hand, there is such a thing as waiting too long. A study by Duell (1994) found that a wait time as long as 6 seconds had a small negative effect on the achievement of university students.

CALLING ORDER ● In classroom questioning, **calling order** is a concern. Calling on volunteers is perhaps the most common method, but this allows some students to avoid participating in the lesson by keeping their hands down (Brophy & Evertson, 1974).

Research findings are inconclusive concerning how students should be called on. Common sense would suggest that when the question is a problem to be worked (as in math), all students should work the problem before any individual is called on. When questions are not problems to be worked, it is probably best to pose the question to the class as a whole and then ask a randomly chosen student (not necessarily a volunteer) to answer. Some teachers even carry around a class list on a clipboard and check off the students called on to make sure that all get frequent chances to respond. One teacher put her students' names on cards, shuffled them before class, and randomly selected cards to decide which student to call on. This system worked well until one student found the cards after class and removed his name from the deck!

In conducting learning probes, it may be especially important to ask questions of students who usually perform above, at, and below the class average to be sure that all students understand the lesson.

CHORAL RESPONSE ● Researchers generally favor the frequent use of **choral responses** when there is only one possible correct answer (Becker & Carnine, 1980; Hunter, 1982; Rosenshine & Stevens, 1986). For example, the teacher might say, "Class, in the words listed on the board [*write, wring, wrong*], what sound does the *wr* make?" To which the class responds together, "Rrrr!" Similarly, when appropriate, all students can be asked to use hand signals to indicate true or false, to hold up a certain number of fingers to indicate an answer in math, or to write a short answer on a small chalkboard and hold it up on cue (Hunter, 1982). This type of all-pupil

wait time
Length of time that a teacher waits for a student to answer a question.

calling order
The order in which students are called on by the teacher to answer questions during the course of a lesson.

choral responses
Responses to questions made by an entire class in unison.

response has been found to have a positive effect on student learning (McKenzie, 1979; McKenzie & Henry, 1979). In the subtraction with renaming example used earlier in this chapter, recall that all students worked with popsicle sticks at their desks, and the teacher walked around to check their work. The purpose of these all-student responses is to give students many opportunities to respond and to give the teacher information on the entire class's level of knowledge and confidence.

Provide Independent Practice

The term **independent practice** refers to work students do in class on their own to practice or express newly learned skills or knowledge. For example, after hearing a lesson on solving equations in algebra, students need an opportunity to work several equations on their own without interruptions, both to crystallize their new knowledge and to help the teacher assess their knowledge. Practice is an essential step in the process of transferring new information in working memory to long-term memory.

Independent practice is most critical when students are learning skills, such as mathematics, reading, grammar, composition, map interpretation, or a foreign language. Students can no more learn arithmetic, writing, or Spanish without practicing them than they could learn to ride a bicycle from lectures alone. By contrast, independent practice is less necessary for certain concept lessons, such as the lesson on the origins of World War II outlined in Table 7.2 or a science lesson on the concept of magnetic attraction. In lessons of this kind, independent practice can be used to let students rehearse knowledge or concepts on their own, as was done in the World War II lesson, but rehearsal is not as central to this type of lesson as practice of skills is to a subtraction lesson.

SEATWORK ● Research on **seatwork,** or in-class independent practice, suggests that seatwork is typically both overused and misused (Anderson, 1985; Brophy & Good, 1986). Several researchers have found that student time spent receiving instruction directly from the teacher is more productive than time spent in seatwork (Brophy & Evertson, 1974; Evertson, Emmer, & Brophy, 1980; Good & Grouws, 1977). For example, Evertson and colleagues (1980) found that the most effective seventh- and eighth-grade math teachers in their study spent about 16 minutes on lecture–demonstration and 19 minutes on seatwork, while the least effective teachers spent less than 7 minutes on lecture–demonstration and about 25 minutes on seatwork. Yet studies of elementary mathematics and reading classes find students spending 50 to 70 percent of their class time doing seatwork (Fisher et al., 1978; Rosenshine, 1980). Anderson, Brubaker, Alleman-Brooks, and Duffy (1985) have noted that time spent on seatwork is often wasted for students who lack the motivation, reading skills, or self-organization skills to work well on their own. Many students simply give up when they run into difficulties. Others fill out worksheets with little care for correctness, apparently interpreting the task as finishing the paper rather than learning the material.

EFFECTIVE USE OF INDEPENDENT PRACTICE TIME ● A set of recommendations for effective use of independent practice time, derived from the work of Anderson (1985), Evertson and colleagues (1994), and Good and colleagues (1983), follows.

1. Do not assign independent practice until you are sure students can do it. This is probably the most important principle. Independent practice is practice, not instruction, and the students should be able to do most of the items they are as-

CONNECTIONS

For more on working memory and long-term memory, see Chapter 6, pages 177 and 180.

independent practice
Component of instruction in which students work by themselves to demonstrate and rehearse new knowledge.

seatwork
Work that students are assigned to do independently during class.

signed to do on their own (Brophy & Good, 1986). In cognitive terms, practice serves as rehearsal for transferring information from working memory to long-term memory. For this to work, the information must first be established in students' working memories.

A high success rate on independent practice work can be accomplished in two ways. First, assignments should be clear and self-explanatory and should cover content on which all students can succeed. Second, students should rarely be given independent practice worksheets until they have indicated in learning probes that they can handle the material. For example, a teacher might use the first items of a worksheet as learning probes, assigning them one at a time and discussing each one after students have attempted it until it is clear that all or almost all students have the right idea.

2. Keep independent practice assignments short. There is rarely a justification for long independent practice assignments. About 10 minutes of work is adequate for most objectives, but this is far less than what most teachers assign (Rosenshine, 1980). Massed practice (e.g., many items at one sitting) has a limited effect on retention. Students are more likely to profit from relatively brief independent practice in class supplemented by distributed practice such as homework (Dempster, 1989; Krug, Davis, & Glover, 1990).

3. Give clear instructions. In the lower grades it may be necessary to ask students to read aloud or paraphrase the instructions to be sure that they have understood them.

4. Get students started, and then avoid interruptions. When students start on their independent practice work, circulate among them to be sure that everyone is under way before attending to the problems of individual students or other tasks. Once students have begun, avoid interrupting them.

5. Monitor independent work. It is important to monitor independent work (see Medley, 1979); for example, by walking around the class while students are doing their assignment. This helps to keep students working and makes the teacher easily available for questions. Teachers can also look in on students who may be struggling, to give them additional assistance.

6. Collect independent work and include it in student grades. A major problem with seatwork as it is often used is that students see no reason to do their best on it because it has little or no bearing on their grades. Students should usually know that their seatwork will be collected and will count toward their grade. To this end, it is a good idea to save a few minutes at the end of each class period to briefly read answers to assigned questions and allow students to check their own papers or exchange papers with partners. Then students may pass in their papers for spot checking and recording. This procedure gives students immediate feedback on their seatwork and relieves the teacher of having to check all papers every day. Make this checking time brief to avoid taking time from instruction.

Assess Performance and Provide Feedback

Every lesson should contain an assessment of the degree to which students have mastered the objectives set for the lesson. The teacher may do this assessment informally by questioning students, may use independent work as an assessment, or may give a separate quiz. One way or another, however, the effectiveness of the lesson should be assessed, and the results of the assessment should be given to students as soon as possible (Brophy & Evertson, 1976; Gage, 1978). Students need to know when they are right and when they are wrong if they are to use feedback to improve their performance (see Meyer, 1987). In addition to assessing the results of each lesson, teachers need to test students from time to time on their learning of larger units of information. In general, more frequent testing results in greater achievement than does less frequent testing, but any testing is much more effective than none at all (Bangert-Drowns, Kulik, & Kulik, 1986). Feedback to students is important, but feedback to teachers on student performance is probably even more important. If students are learning everything they are taught, it may be possible to pick up the pace of instruction. On the other hand, if assessment reveals serious misunderstandings, the lesson can be retaught or other steps can be taken to get students back on track. If some students mastered the lesson and some did not, it may be appropriate to give more instruction just to the students who need it.

Provide Distributed Practice and Review

Retention of many kinds of knowledge is increased by practice or review spaced out over time (Dempster, 1989). This has several implications for teaching. First, it implies that reviewing and recapitulating important information from earlier lessons enhances learning (Nuthall, 1987). Review of important material at long intervals (e.g., monthly) is particularly important to maintain previous skills. In addition, it is important to assign homework in most subjects and at most grade levels. Homework gives students a chance to practice skills learned in one setting and at one time (school) in another setting at a different time (home). Research on homework finds that it generally does increase achievement, particularly if it is checked and comments on it are given to students (Cooper et al., 1998; Keith, Reimers, Fehrmann, Pottebaum, & Aubey, 1986). However, the effects of homework are not as clear in elementary schools as they are at the secondary level (Cooper, 1989; Corno, 1996).

For a self-evaluation to assess how effective your instruction is, see Figure 7.1.

FIGURE 7.1 ● Teacher Self-Evaluation: How Effective Is Your Instruction?
From Mary Alice Gunter, Thomas H. Estes, and Jan Schwab, *Instruction: A Models Approach* (2nd ed.), p. 92. Copyright © 1995 by Allyn & Bacon. Reprinted by permission.

If students do not seem to be learning the material you are teaching, ask yourself the following questions:

- [ ] Did the students have the required background to learn the new set of skills or material?
- [ ] Were the steps in the learning process broken into sufficiently small steps?
- [ ] Was each step learned before a new step was introduced?
- [ ] Were the learning objectives and the directions stated clearly?
- [ ] Was the content organized logically, and were the examples and demonstrations effective?
- [ ] Were sufficient questions asked to determine if the class understood what was being taught?
- [ ] Was there enough guided practice? Were all the students involved in the practice, and were errors corrected quickly?
- [ ] Was there independent practice of the skill or learning? Was this independent practice checked carefully to determine if the students were performing without error?
- [ ] Was there periodic review and opportunities for practice of the new learning?

SELF-CHECK

What is the purpose of each step of a direct instruction model? List strategies and provide examples for each of the seven steps.

WHAT DOES RESEARCH ON DIRECT INSTRUCTION METHODS SUGGEST?

Most of the principles of direct instruction discussed in this chapter have been derived from **process–product studies,** in which observers recorded the teaching practices of teachers whose students consistently achieved at a high level. These principles have been assembled into specific direct instruction programs and evaluated in field experiments; that is, other teachers have been trained in the methods used by successful teachers, and their students' achievement has been compared to that of students whose teachers did not receive the training.

Many studies have found a correlation between student achievement and teachers' use of strategies associated with direct instruction (e.g., Gage & Needels, 1989; Weinert & Helmke, 1995). However, experimental studies that compare the achievement of students whose teachers have been trained in specific direct instruction strategies to that of students whose teachers have not received this training have shown more mixed results. In a study of a direct instruction math approach called the Missouri Mathematics Program (MMP), Good and Grouws (1979) found that fourth-graders whose teachers used the MMP methods learned considerably more than did students whose teachers were not trained in MMP. Later evaluations of the MMP found smaller positive effects (Good et al., 1983; Slavin & Karweit, 1985).

Evaluations of another direct instruction model, Madeline Hunter's (1982, 1995) Mastery Teaching program, have not generally found that the students of teachers trained in the model have learned more than other students (Mandeville, 1992; Mandeville & Rivers, 1991; Slavin, 1986). A study of explicit teaching, a form of direct instruction, found that this method made no difference in reading achievement of low achievers unless the method was supplemented by peer tutoring (Simmons, Fuchs, Fuchs, Mathes, & Hodge, 1995). More successful have been direct instruction models that place a greater emphasis on building teachers' classroom management skills (e.g., Evertson, Weade, Green, & Crawford, 1985) and models that improve teachers' use of reading groups (Anderson et al., 1979).

Studies of DISTAR, a direct instruction program built around specific teaching materials and structured methods, have found strong positive effects of this approach in elementary schools, particularly with low achievers and at-risk students (Adams & Engelmann, 1996; Carnine, Grosen, & Silbert, 1995). One study (Meyer, 1984) followed the progress of students from an inner-city Brooklyn, New York, neighborhood who had been in DISTAR classes in first through third grades and found that these students were considerably more likely to graduate from high school than were students in a similar Brooklyn school who had not been taught with DISTAR. Other studies have also found long-term effects of this approach (Gersten & Carnine, 1984; Gersten & Keating, 1987; Meyer, Gersten, & Gutkin, 1983).

Although the research on direct instruction models has had mixed conclusions, most researchers agree that the main elements of these models are essential minimum

process–product studies
Research approach in which the teaching practices of effective teachers are recorded through classroom observation.

skills that all teachers should have (see, e.g., Gage & Needels, 1989). In fact, most of the recommendations from direct instruction research are so commonsensical that they seem obvious. A study by Wong (1995), however, found that the *opposites* of some direct instruction principles also seemed obvious to teachers and university students. When studies find no differences between teachers trained in the models and other teachers, it is often because both groups of teachers already had most of the direct instruction skills before the training took place (see Slavin, 1986).

Advantages and Limitations of Direct Instruction

It is clear that direct instruction methods can improve the teaching of certain basic skills, but it is equally clear that much is yet to be learned about how and for what purposes they should be used. The prescriptions derived from studies of effective teachers cannot be applied uncritically in the classroom and expected to make a substantial difference in student achievement. Structured, systematic instructional programs based on these prescriptions can markedly improve student achievement in basic skills, but it is important to remember that the research on direct instruction has focused mostly on basic reading and mathematics, mostly in the elementary grades. For other subjects and at other grade levels we have less of a basis for believing that direct instruction methods will improve student learning.

SELF-CHECK

List three variants of direct instruction. What does research suggest about the effectiveness of each?

HOW DO STUDENTS LEARN AND TRANSFER CONCEPTS?

A very large proportion of all lessons focus on teaching concepts (see Klausmeier, 1992). A **concept** is an abstract idea that is generalized from specific examples. For example, a red ball, a red pencil, and a red chair all illustrate the simple concept "red." A green book is not an instance of the concept "red." If you were shown the red ball, pencil, and chair and asked to say what they have in common, you would produce the concept "red objects." If the green book were also included, you would have to fall back on the much broader concept "objects."

Of course, many concepts are far more complex and less well defined than the concept "red." For example, the concept "justice" is one that people may spend a lifetime trying to understand. This book is engaged primarily in teaching concepts; in fact, at this very moment you are reading about the concept "concept"!

Concept Learning and Teaching

Concepts are generally learned in one of two ways. Most concepts that we learn outside of school we learn by observation. For example, a child learns the concept "car" by hearing certain vehicles referred to as "cars." Initially, the child might include pickup trucks or motorcycles under the concept "car"; but as time goes on, the concept is refined until the child can clearly differentiate "car" from "noncar." Similarly, the child learns the more difficult concepts "naughty," "clean," and "fun" by observation and experience.

concept
An abstract idea that is generalized from specific examples.

CASE TO CONSIDER

How Can You Cover It All?

Mr. Benson has been teaching secondary social studies for several years. When he was a student, he had one remarkable history teacher who made the subject come alive for him and inspired him to become a teacher. When he received his assignment to teach world history in a high school, he thought that nothing could be better. But over the years he has come to realize that there is just too much to cover in the course, and he is growing frustrated. Today, he is attending a conference sponsored by the state social studies curriculum adoption committee. In a roundtable discussion with other high school teachers and a professor from a local state university, Mr. Benson learns that he is not alone.

Mr. Benson: My textbook has forty-three chapters, and there are only thirty-six weeks in the school year, so I'm behind before I even start. I teach every lesson in an organized way: On Mondays, we review what we studied last week and I orient the class to this week's subject matter and learning objectives. On Tuesdays and Wednesdays, I present the new material and question students along the way to be sure they understand the main points. On Thursdays, I have the students work on independent projects, such as papers, debates, or media projects related to the week's material. On Fridays, I give the class a quiz, and we discuss the answers to the quiz, as well as remaining issues from the chapter.

Ms. Gleason: And you're trying to pack all of world history into this routine? How do your students handle it?

Mr. Benson: I'm starting to get a lot of remarks like, "I have other classes that I have to read for, too" and "I can't remember all this stuff." And I'm just not able to make history exciting for them, like it was for me as a student.

Mr. Lasser: We just can't teach everything. There is too much to learn. Entire college courses are devoted to single units or topics that we are expected to cover within a week or two.

Mr. Benson: But what can we leave out? I know that with state curriculum exams coming up this semester, we'll get the usual criticism afterwards that the students just don't know the facts of history.

Mr. Smith: Is it more important that they know the current and up-to-date historical events than the ancient ones? I know I never get as far as the middle twentieth century, so how many kids really have a good understanding of World War II, the Korean War, or the Vietnam conflict?

Professor Forsyth: At our university, in our social studies methods courses, we're emphasizing "real history"—telling students specific stories that make history come alive. For instance, a lesson can focus on the civil rights movement in one southern community, and students can read some of the legal papers written by Thurgood Marshall about the movement. It's not just coverage of the subject that is important. Real history occurs when one gets a microscope and just looks at one single, small event until it is understood. Then the individual owns it.

Mr. Benson: That's what makes me love history, but if I were to have my students study something in depth and look at historical instances that enrich, I'd have even less time to teach. I have lesson plans to cover, a resource file that's too thick and never gets used, and ideas for cooperative learning activities and critical thinking questions that I never have time to include. How can I cover it all?

PROBLEM SOLVING

1. Evaluate Mr. Benson's use of direct instruction as he describes it. What are the strengths of his approach? What might be its limitations?
2. How can Mr. Benson incorporate Professor Forsyth's "real history" approach into his teaching? What difference do you think this would make in his students' comprehension and appreciation of the subject matter? What difference could it make in their curriculum exam scores?
3. How can Mr. Benson and his colleagues cover it all? Or should they attempt to do so? Discuss your thoughts with your classmates.

Adapted by permission from "Breadth versus Depth: Curricular Conflicts in a Secondary Classroom" by J. Merrell Hansen, Professor of Education at Brigham Young University, from *Allyn & Bacon's Custom Cases in Education,* edited by Greta Morine-Dershimer, Paul Eggen, and Donald Kauchak (1996).

Other concepts are typically learned by definition. For example, it is very difficult to learn the concepts "aunt" or "uncle" by observation alone. One could observe hundreds of "aunts" and "nonaunts" without deriving a clear concept of "aunt." In this case the concept is best learned by definition: To be an aunt, one must be a female whose brother or sister (or brother- or sister-in-law) has children. With this definition, instances and noninstances of "aunt" can be readily differentiated.

DEFINITIONS ● Just as concepts can be learned in two ways, they can be taught in two ways. Students may be given instances and noninstances of a concept and later asked to derive or infer a definition. Or students may be given a definition and then asked to identify instances and noninstances. Some concepts lend themselves to the example–definition approach. For most concepts that are taught in school, it makes most sense to state a definition, present several instances (and noninstances, if appropriate), and then restate the definition, showing how the instances typify the definition. Use of this rule–example–rule pattern has been found to be characteristic of instructionally effective teachers. For example, the concept "learning" might be defined as "a change in an individual caused by experience." Instances might include learning of skills, of information, of behaviors, and of emotions. Noninstances might include maturational changes, such as changes in behaviors or emotions caused by the onset of puberty. Finally, the definition might be restated and discussed in light of the instances and noninstances.

EXAMPLES ● Teaching concepts involves extensive and skillful use of examples. Tennyson and Park (1980, p. 59) suggest that teachers follow three rules when presenting examples of concepts:

1. Order the examples from easy to difficult.
2. Select examples that differ from one another.
3. Compare and contrast examples and nonexamples.

Consider the concept "mammal." Easy examples are dogs, cats, and humans, and nonexamples are insects, reptiles, and fish. No problem so far. But what about dolphins? Bats? Snakes that bear live young? Kangaroos? Each of these is a more difficult example or nonexample of the concept "mammal"; it challenges the simplistic belief, based on experience, that terrestrial animals that bear live young are mammals and that fish, birds, and other egg-layers are not. The easy examples (dogs versus fish) establish the concept in general, but the more difficult examples (snakes versus whales) test the true boundaries of the concept. Students should thoroughly understand simple examples before tackling the odd cases.

Teaching for Transfer of Learning

Students often get so wrapped up in preparing for tests, and teachers in preparing students to take tests, that both forget what the primary purpose of school is: to give students the skills and knowledge necessary for them to function effectively as adults. If a student can fill in blanks on a language arts test but cannot write a clear letter to a friend or a prospective employer, or can multiply with decimals and percents on a math test but cannot figure sales tax, then that student's education has been sadly misdirected. Yet all too frequently, students who do very well in school or on tests are unable to transfer their knowledge or skills to real-life situations.

transfer of learning
The application of knowledge acquired in one situation to new situations.

REAL-LIFE LEARNING ● **Transfer of learning** from one situation to another depends on the degree to which the information or skills were learned in the original situation and on the degree of similarity between the situation in which the skill or concept was learned and the situation to which it is to be applied (Phye, 1992; Pressley & Yokoi, 1994; Price & Driscoll, 1997; Smagorinsky & Smith, 1992).

These students are viewing a picture they have studied in an art museum. As a teacher, how will you ensure that your students are able to transfer what they have learned in the classroom to real-life situations?

These principles, known since the beginning of the twentieth century, have important implications for teaching. We cannot simply assume that students will be able to transfer their school learning to practical situations, so we must teach them to use skills in situations like those they are likely to encounter in real life or in other situations to which we expect learning to transfer. Students must be given specific instruction in how to use their skills and information to solve problems and be exposed to a variety of problem-solving experiences if they are to be able to apply much of what they learned in school.

The most important thing to know about transfer of learning is that it cannot be assumed. Just because a student has mastered a skill or concept in one setting or circumstance, there is no guarantee whatsoever that the student will be able to apply this skill or concept to a new setting, even if the setting seems (at least to the teacher) to be very similar (Mayer & Wittrock, 1996). Classic examples are people who score well on tests of grammar and punctuation but cannot apply these skills in their own compositions (Smagorinsky & Smith, 1992) and people who can solve all sorts of math problems in school but do not apply their math knowledge in real life. As an example of this, Lave (1988) describes a man in a weight-loss program who was faced with the problem of measuring out a serving of cottage cheese that was three-quarters of the usual two-thirds cup allowance. The man, who had passed college calculus, measured out two-thirds of a cup of cottage cheese, dumped it out in a circle on a cutting board, marked a cross on it, and scooped away one quadrant. It never occurred to him to multiply $\frac{2}{3} \times \frac{3}{4} = \frac{1}{2}$, an operation that almost any sixth-grader could do on paper (but few could apply in a practical situation).

LEARNING IN CONTEXT ● If transfer of learning depends in large part on similarity between the situation in which information is learned and that in which it is applied, then how can we teach in the school setting so that students will be able to apply their knowledge in the very different setting of real life?

One important principle of transfer is that the ability to apply knowledge in new circumstances depends in part on the variety of circumstances in which we have learned or practiced the information or skill (Salomon & Perkins, 1989). For example, a few weeks' experience as a parking attendant, driving all sorts of cars, would probably be better than years of experience driving one kind of car for enabling a person to drive a completely new and different car (at least in a parking lot!).

In teaching concepts, one way to increase the chance that the concepts will be appropriately applied to new situations is to give examples from a range of situations. A set of classic experiments by Nitsch (1977) illustrated this principle. Students were given definitions of words and were then presented with examples to illustrate the concepts. Some were given several examples in the same context; others received examples from mixed contexts. For example, *minge* is a cowboy word meaning "to gang up on." The examples are shown in Table 7.3.

Students who were given only the same-context examples were able to identify additional examples in the same context but were less successful in applying the concepts to new contexts. By contrast, the students who learned with the varied-context examples had some difficulties in learning the concept at first but, once they did, were able to apply it to new situations. The best strategy was a hybrid in which students were given the same-context examples first and then the varied-context examples.

There are many other ways to increase the probability that information or skills learned in one context will transfer to other contexts, particularly to real-life applications. For example, simulations can be used to approximate real-life conditions, as when secondary students prepare for job interviews by acting out inter-

TABLE 7.3

Teaching of Concepts

Research demonstrates that to teach a new concept, teachers should first present examples of the concept used in similar contexts and then offer examples in widely different contexts. This approach promotes the students' abilities to transfer the concept to new situations. The example here comes from a classic study in which students learned new concepts from the traditional culture of cowboys.

Concept to be taught: *Minge*
Definition: To gang up on a person or thing.

SAME-CONTEXT EXAMPLES	VARIED-CONTEXT EXAMPLES
The three riders decided to converge on the cow.	The band of sailors angrily denounced the captain and threatened a mutiny.
Four people took part in branding the horse.	A group in the audience booed the inept magician's act.
They circled the wolf so it would not escape.	The junk dealer was helpless to defend himself from the three thieves.
All six cowboys fought against the rustler.	All six cowboys fought against the rustler.

Source: From John D. Bransford, *Human Cognition,* Wadsworth Publishing, 1979. (Adapted from an unpublished doctoral thesis entitled *Structuring Decontextualized Forms of Knowledge* by Nitsch, 1977.) Reprinted by permission of John D. Bransford.

views with teachers or peers pretending to be interviewers. Teachers can also facilitate transfer by introducing skills learned in one setting into a new setting. For example, a history teacher might do well to find out what writing or grammar skills are being taught in English classes and then remind students to use these same skills in history essays.

TRANSFER VERSUS INITIAL LEARNING ● The tricky aspect of teaching for transfer is that some of the most effective procedures for enhancing transfer are exactly the opposite of those for initial learning. As the Nitsch (1977) study illustrated, teaching a concept in many different contexts was confusing to students if it was done at the beginning of a sequence of instruction, but it enhanced transfer if it was done after students understood the concept in one setting. The implications of this principle for teaching are extremely important. In introducing a new concept, it is important to use similar examples until the concept is well understood and only then to use diverse examples that still demonstrate the essential aspects of the concept.

As one example of this, consider a series of lessons on evolution. In introducing the concept, it would first be important to use clear examples of how animals evolved in ways that increased their chances of survival in their environments, using such examples as the evolution of flippers in seals or the evolution of humps in camels. Then evolution in plants (e.g., evolution of a waxy skin on desert plants) might be presented, somewhat broadening the concept. The evolution of social behaviors (such as cooperation in lions, baboons, and humans) might then be discussed; finally, phenomena that resemble the evolutionary process (such as the modification of businesses in response to selective pressures of free-market economies) might be explored. The idea here is first to establish the idea of evolution in one clear context (animals) and then to gradually broaden the concept until students can see how processes in quite different contexts demonstrate the principles of selective adaptation. If the lessons had begun with a mixed discussion of animals, plants, societies, and businesses, it would have been too confusing. If they had never moved beyond the evolution of animals, the concept would not have had much chance of transferring to different contexts. After learning about the concept of evolution in many different contexts, students are much more likely to be able to distinguish scientific and metaphorical uses and apply the concept to a completely new context, such as the evolution of art in response to changes in society.

It is important in teaching for transfer not only to provide many examples, but also to point out in each example how the essential features of the concept are reflected (Kosonen & Winne, 1995). In the evolution lessons the central process might be explained as it applied to each particular case. The development of cooperation among lions, for instance, shows how a social trait evolved because groups of lions that cooperated were better able than others to catch game, to survive, and to ensure that their offspring would survive. Pointing out the essential elements in each example helps students apply a concept to new instances they have never encountered (Perkins & Salomon, 1988).

SELF-CHECK

Describe how you would use the following approaches to teach students: a rule–example–rule approach and an examples and nonexamples approach.

HOW ARE DISCUSSIONS USED IN INSTRUCTION?

Discussions are used as part of instruction for many reasons (see Gall, 1987), as detailed in the sections below.

Subjective and Controversial Topics

In many subjects there are questions that do not have simple answers. There may be one right answer to an algebra problem or one right way to conjugate a German verb, but is there one right set of factors that explains what caused the Civil War? How were Shakespeare's writings influenced by the politics of his day? Should genetic engineering be banned as a danger to world health? These and many other questions have no clear-cut answers, so it is important for students to discuss and understand these issues instead of simply receiving and rehearsing information or skills. Such subjects as history, government, economics, literature, art, and music include many issues that lend themselves to discussion and multiple and diverse explanations. Discussing controversial issues has been found to increase knowledge about the issues as well as to encourage deeper understanding of the various sides of an issue (Johnson & Johnson, 1994).

Difficult and Novel Concepts

In addition to subjective and controversial subjects, discussions are useful for topics that do contain single right answers but which involve difficult concepts that force students to see something in a different way. For example, a science teacher could simply give a lesson on buoyancy and specific gravity. However, since this lesson would challenge a simplistic view of why things float ("Things float because they are light"), students might understand buoyancy and specific gravity better if they were given an opportunity to make and defend their own theories about why things float and if they were confronted with such questions as "If things float because they are light, then why does a battleship float?" and "If you threw some things in a lake, they would sink part way but not to the bottom. Why would they stop sinking?" In searching together for theories to explain these phenomena, students might gain an appreciation for the meaning of buoyancy and specific gravity that a lecture could not provide.

Affective Objectives

Another situation calling for use of discussions is one in which affective objectives (objectives that are concerned with student attitudes and values) are of particular importance. For example, a course on civics or government contains much information to be taught about how our government works but also involves important values to be transmitted, such as civic duty and patriotism. A teacher could teach "six reasons why it is important to vote," but the real objective here is not to teach reasons for voting, but rather to instill respect for the democratic process and a commitment to register and vote when the time comes. Similarly, a discussion of peer pressure might be directed at giving students the skills and the willingness to say no when classmates pressure them to engage in illegal, unhealthy, or undesirable behaviors. A long tradition of research in social psychology has established that group discussion, particularly when group members must publicly commit themselves, is far more effective at changing individuals' attitudes and behaviors than is even the most persuasive lecture (see Lewin, 1947).

Whole-Class Discussions

Discussions take two principal forms. In one, the entire class discusses an issue, with the teacher as moderator (Tredway, 1995). In the other, students form small groups (usually with four to six students in each group) to discuss a topic, and the teacher moves from group to group, aiding the discussion.

What differentiates a **whole-class discussion** from a usual lesson is that in discussions the teacher plays a less dominant role. Teachers may guide the discussion and help the class avoid dead ends, but the ideas should be drawn from the students. The following vignette (from Joyce & Weil, 1986, pp. 55–56) illustrates an inquiry-oriented discussion led (but not dominated) by a teacher:

> One morning, as Mrs. Harrison's fourth-grade students are settling down to their arithmetic workbooks, she calls their attention. As they raise their eyes toward her, a light bulb directly over Mrs. Harrison's desk blows out, and the room darkens.
> "What happened?" asks one child.
> "Can't you see, dopey?" remarks another. "The light bulb blew out."
> "Yeah," inquires another, "but what does that mean?"
> "Just that. We have all seen a lot of light bulbs blow out, but what does that really mean? What happens?" their teacher prods.
> Mrs. Harrison unscrews the light bulb and holds it up. The children gather around and she passes it among them. After she receives it back, she says, "Well, why don't you see if you can develop a hypothesis about what happened?"
> "What's inside the glass?" asks one of the children.
> "Is there a gas inside?" asks another.
> "No," says Mrs. Harrison. The children look at one another in puzzlement. Finally, one asks, "Is it a vacuum?"
> "Yes," nods Mrs. Harrison.
> "Is it a complete vacuum?" someone inquires.
> "Almost," replies Mrs. Harrison.
> "Is the little wire made of metal?"
> "Yes," she agrees.

By asking questions such as these, the children gradually identify the materials that make up the lightbulb and the process that caused it to burn out. Finally, they begin to venture hypotheses about what happened. After they have thought up four or five of these, they search through reference books or the Internet in an effort to verify them. Students may also engage with other classes far away, using e-mail or chat room connections on a given topic.

EXPLORING POINTS OF VIEW ● In contrast to the lightbulb example, the following vignette describes a situation in which a teacher does not have a specific principle or concept in mind, but rather wants students to explore and develop their own ideas about a topic, using information they have recently learned:

Ms. Wilson: In the past few weeks we've been learning about the events leading up to the American Revolution. Of course, since we are all Americans, we tend to take the side of the revolutionaries. We use the term *Patriots* to describe them; King George probably used a less favorable term. Yet many of the colonists were Loyalists, and at times, the Loyalists outnumbered the

whole-class discussion
A discussion among all the students in the class with the teacher as moderator.

Patriots. Let's think about how Loyalists would have argued against the idea of independence from Britain.

Beth: I think they'd say King George was a good king.

Vinnie: But what about all the things he did to the colonists?

Ms. Wilson: Give some examples.

Vinnie: Like the Intolerable Acts. The colonists had to put up British soldiers in their own houses, and they closed Boston Harbor.

Tanya: But those were to punish the colonists for the Boston Tea Party. The Loyalists would say that the Patriots caused all the trouble in the first place.

Ms. Wilson: Good point.

Frank: I think the Loyalists would say, "You may not like everything he does, but King George is still our king."

Richard: The Loyalists probably thought the Sons of Liberty were a bunch of hoods.

Ms. Wilson: Well, I wouldn't put it quite that way, but I think you're right. What did they do that makes you think that?

Ramon: They destroyed things and harassed the Loyalists and the British troops. Like they called them names and threw things at them.

Ms. Wilson: How do you think Loyalists would feel about the Boston Massacre?

Beth: They'd say those creeps got what they deserved. They'd think that it was Sam Adams's fault for getting everyone all stirred up.

Ms. Wilson: Let's think about it another way. We live in California. Our nation's capital, Washington, is 3,000 miles away. We have to pay all kinds of taxes, and a lot of those taxes go to help people in Boston or Baltimore rather than people here. Many of the things our government does make people in California mad. We've got plenty of food, and we can make just about anything we want to right here. Why don't we have a California Revolution and have our own country?

Sara: But we're part of America!

Tanya: We can't do that! The army would come and put down the revolution!

Ms. Wilson: Don't you think that the Loyalists thought some of the same things?

Vinnie: But we can vote and they couldn't.

Ramon: Right. Taxation without representation!

Beth: I'll bet a lot of Loyalists thought the British would win the war and it would be better to stay on the side of the winners.

In this discussion the teacher was not looking for any particular facts about the American Revolution, but rather was trying to get students to use the information they had learned previously to discuss issues from a different perspective. Ms. Wilson let the students determine the direction of the discussion to a substantial degree. Her main tasks were to keep the discussion rolling, to get students to use specifics to defend their positions, to ensure that many students participated, and to help the students avoid dead ends or unproductive avenues.

INFORMATION BEFORE DISCUSSION ● Before beginning a discussion, it is important to make sure that students have an adequate knowledge base. There is nothing so dreary as a discussion in which the participants don't know much about the topic. The lightbulb discussion would have been less fruitful if students had not

TEACHERS IN ACTION

Joyce Vining Morgan
Russian Teacher, Grades 7–12
Exeter Area Junior and
Senior High School
Exeter, New Hampshire

What strategies have you applied to make direct instruction most effective?

M. Peach Robidoux
The Art Institute of Philadelphia
Philadelphia, Pennsylvania

Over and over, the same lament: "I just don't get it!" The cause for concern is Russian grammar, especially the case endings. But sometimes it's any kind of grammatical analysis that stymies students.

How to help students get a feel for grammar use? Add something touchable, see-able to abstract textbook approaches. *Play* with the concepts. So I made a set of Russian grammar Tinkertoys: wooden spheres for verbs, colored in blues and greens to reflect tense and aspect; cubes for nouns, each colored to show gender and each side daubed in one of six warm hues to indicate case; octagons, colored like the nouns, were adjectives, which have to match the nouns in gender, number, and case; adverbs were small gray spheres with one end cut off; prepositions were flat wooden circles, colored by the case each required; and so forth. Then we played.

Students began to distinguish parts of speech by perceiving the activity of verbs, the stolidity of nouns. We colored sentences as we wrote them to see whether the parts fit together to make the meaning intended, especially since Russian doesn't use English-style word order as a clue to meaning. I rewrote Russian grammar rules into color sequences and Tinkertoy constructs.

Now we discuss the yellow accusative direct object case and the dark green imperfective past verb. I present traditional grammar rules together with the grammar Tinkertoys and the color analysis, so that several learning styles are served at once, and all the students learn together.

Some teachers see themselves as captains of the classroom, commanding respect and hard work, showing students the way. I show students that I am devoting time to them because I have a passion for the subject, the learning process, and student success. I make that evident every day that I teach.

Working with my students to make decisions and learn is very important. It is equally important to remain flexible to meet the needs of students. There are many techniques I use in direct instruction that help students to learn. For example, when I introduce a unit on "magical realism," I ask students if they have ever had something inexplicable happen to them. After students relate ghost stories and strange sightings, I tell them my ghost story and explain how these stories relate to the idea of magical realism. Then we come up with the objectives for our study of magical realism.

When I give an assignment to students, I also do the work. I read my response aloud to the students after they have read theirs. I ask students why they thought the assignment was given and how it relates to our objectives. By doing this, the classroom turns into a think tank. Students see their work as valuable and relevant, not just busywork.

I give students control of their own learning by encouraging them to express their opinions about assignments—what went well, what went wrong, and how the assignment could improve to reflect our objectives more accurately. My students provide frank, insightful answers.

If a lesson is not going well, I adapt it to suit the students' needs. At times, I give students the freedom to revise an assignment to fit their needs. For example, I'll allow students to devise their own essay question or experiment.

The Intentional Teacher

● **Using What You Know about Direct Instruction to Improve Teaching and Learning**

Intentional teachers select their instructional strategies with purpose. They understand the benefits and shortcomings of the strategies they select, and they choose strategies based upon their students, the content, and the context.

Intentional teachers capitalize upon their power as directors of learning by using the components of effective instruction. They take responsibility for presenting clear lessons that carefully lead students toward mastery of objectives. They use their time well by providing a quick instructional pace, by checking for student understanding frequently, and by providing for meaningful practice in which students learn to transfer information and skills to new settings. Intentional teachers relish their roles as instructional leaders.

1 What am I trying to accomplish?

Effective instruction requires careful preparation, which begins with teachers' thoughtful selection and phrasing of learning objectives. Think in specific terms about what content students are to master, and plan your lesson to focus directly on those objectives.

> You begin planning a series of lessons on spiders for your second-graders with the goal: "Students will learn about spiders' bodies and behaviors." From that goal, you develop specific objectives that will frame your lessons. You list your first objective: "Students will point to, label, and describe at least three features of a spider's anatomy."

Stating the objective and purpose for a lesson helps students prepare mentally for the information that follows. Begin your lessons with a clear declaration of *what* and *why* students are to learn.

> You begin a lesson with your seventh-grade earth science students: "Take a look at the two rocks here on my table." After students observe and comment briefly, you state, "By the time you leave today, you'll be able to state how each of these rocks was formed. That's important information, because it can give us some clues about the conditions of the earth far back in time. It helps us solve the earth's puzzles!"

2 What are my students' relevant experiences and needs?

Intentional teachers use preassessments to ensure that their objectives and instruction are appropriate for students' needs.

> Before teaching a unit on the metric system to your fourth-graders, you give a 10-item pretest to determine their current knowledge of metrics. One sample question is: "Which unit would you use to measure how long something is: liter, meter, gram?"

Effective lessons include a review of prerequisite skills. Briefly review previous learnings that students will need in the current lesson.

> You introduce the next assignment, a persuasive speech, to students in your public speaking class. You remind students that the skills they learned from earlier speeches—organization, clarity, poise, and effective use of gestures—will be especially important for persuasive speeches.

3 What approaches and materials are available to help me challenge every student?

Effective instruction maintains a high degree of student attention. Visual input is especially important for students who are acquiring

---

already had a concept of a vacuum and of air as a gas. The American Revolution discussion depended on students' knowledge of the main events preceding the Revolution. A discussion can sometimes be used before instruction as a means of generating interest in a topic, but at some point students must be given information. In the chapter-opening vignette, for example, Ms. Logan let students discuss and experiment not only before presenting a formal lesson but also after the lesson, when they had more information.

small-group discussion
A discussion among four to six students in a group working independently of a teacher.

Small-Group Discussions

In a **small-group discussion,** students work in four- to six-member groups to discuss a particular topic. Because small-group discussions require that students work independently of the teacher most of the time, young or poorly organized students

English. Pace lessons rapidly (without sacrificing student understanding), and use humor, novelty, and variety to support the lesson focus.

You and your third-graders are working on descriptive writing. Rather than rely upon mental images, you bring in an assortment of odd kitchen utensils and toolbox treasures. Students pass items around, conjecturing about their uses. The objects' novelty enhances students' written descriptions.

Students need time to process information. Use wait time after you ask a question, and follow through with students who do not express understanding.

You pose a question to your literature students: "What emotion do you suppose our main character was experiencing at this point?" Instead of calling on the first student to raise a hand, you say: "I see three hands up. I think I'll wait for more." After a few seconds, many hands are in the air, and you select three or four students to share their responses.

4 How will I know whether and when to change my strategy or modify my instruction?

During direct instruction, teachers conduct many learning probes. Check for understanding frequently, and modify your instruction based upon results.

In geometry work with kindergartners, you arrange students in small groups and give each group a set of large shapes. You ask: "Please hold up a shape that has four corners. Please hold up a shape that reminds you of a stop sign. Please hold up the shape that has the fewest number of sides." You note that students struggle with your last prompt but easily responded to the first two, and you make a note to provide additional work on problem solving and vocabulary terms like *least, most, more,* and *fewer.*

Active participation devices allow teachers to assess *all* of their students' understandings. Use strategies that provide feedback on every student's progress.

After working on different spellings of the long *a* sound (as in *made*), you distribute individual chalkboards, chalk, and erasers. You recite a few words. Students silently write the words on their boards and then raise the boards for you to check. You quickly—and silently—assess each student's mastery of spelling patterns. You make a list of students who require further instruction.

Students need frequent feedback. Include an assessment segment—formal or informal—in each of your lessons, and use frequent testing to provide feedback.

You make it a point to close each lesson with a brief assessment of students' mastery of the objective. Today you close your physics class with the clear point/fuzzy point strategy: Students record anonymously on 3-by-5-inch cards one point that was clear from today's class and one point that remains fuzzy. They leave the cards in a basket near the door.

5 What information will I accept as evidence that my students and I are experiencing success?

Students demonstrate success when they transfer knowledge from one context to another. Do not assume that students can transfer; check for it.

You teach your mathematics students to use the memory key on their calculators and assess their mastery at the lesson's close. You make a note in your plan book to double-check students' transfer of their knowledge of the memory key by circulating and observing them as they solve problems in which the memory key would be helpful.

need a great deal of preparation and, in fact, may not be able to benefit from them at all. However, most students at or above the fourth-grade level can profit from small-group discussions.

Like any discussion, most small-group discussions should follow the presentation of information through teacher-directed lessons, books, or films. When students know something about a subject, they may start to work in their groups, pulling desks together if necessary to talk and hear one another more easily.

Each group should have a leader appointed by the teacher. Leaders should be responsible, well-organized students but should not always be the highest-achieving students. Groups may all discuss the same topic, or each may discuss a different subtopic of a larger topic that the whole class is studying. For example, in a unit on the Great Depression, one group might focus on causes of the Depression, another on the collapse of the banking system, a third on the social consequences of the

These students are involved in a small-group discussion. What does research tell us about the effectiveness of small-group discussions?

Depression, and a fourth on the New Deal. Each group should be given a series of questions to be answered on the topic to be discussed. For example, if the topic were the collapse of the banking system, the questions might be the following:

1. What was the connection between the stock market crash of 1929 and the failures of so many banks?
2. What caused savers to lose confidence in the banks?
3. Why did the banks not have enough funds to pay savers who wished to withdraw their money?
4. Why is a widespread run on banks unlikely today?

The leader's role in each discussion group is to make sure that the group stays on the topic and questions assigned to it and to ensure that all group members participate. A group secretary may be appointed to write down the group's ideas. At the end of the discussion the group members may prepare a report on their activities or conclusions to be presented to the rest of the class.

Research on small-group discussions indicates that these activities can increase student achievement more than traditional lessons if the students are well prepared to work in small groups and if the group task is well organized (Sharan et al., 1984; Sharan & Shachar, 1988). Also, some research suggests that small-group discussions have greater effects on student achievement if students are encouraged to engage in controversy rather than to seek a consensus (Johnson & Johnson, 1994).

SELF-CHECK

Create a two-column chart comparing whole-class discussion and small-group discussion. Use the following categories for your chart: appropriate uses, prerequisites, benefits, and limitations.

CHAPTER SUMMARY

WHAT IS DIRECT INSTRUCTION?

Direct instruction is a teaching approach that emphasizes teacher control of most classroom events and the presentation of structured lessons. Direct instruction programs call for active teaching; clear lesson organization; step-by-step progression between subtopics; and the use of many examples, demonstrations, and visual prompts.

HOW IS A DIRECT INSTRUCTION LESSON TAUGHT?

The first part of a lesson is stating learning objectives and orienting students to the lesson. The principal task is to establish both a mental set, so that students are ready to work and learn, and a "road map," so that students know where the lesson is going.

Part two of a lesson is to review prerequisites or pretest to ensure that students have mastered required knowledge and skills. The review may function as an advance organizer for the lesson.

Part three involves presenting the new material in an organized way, providing explanations and demonstrations, and maintaining attention.

Part four, conducting learning probes, elicits students' responses to lesson content. This practice gives teachers feedback and lets students test their ideas. Questioning techniques are important, including the uses of wait time and calling order.

Part five of a lesson is independent practice, or seatwork, in which students apply their new skill. Research shows that independent practice should be given as short assignments with clear instructions and no interruptions, and that it should be given only when students can do the assignments. Teachers should monitor work, collect it, and include it in assessments.

Part six is to assess performance and provide feedback. Every lesson should include an assessment of student mastery of the lesson objectives.

Part seven is to provide distributed practice, or homework, and review. Information is retained better when practice is spaced out over a period of time.

WHAT DOES RESEARCH ON DIRECT INSTRUCTION METHODS SUGGEST?

Research does not support clear superiority of instruction methods such as the Missouri Mathematics Program or Madeline Hunter's Mastery Teaching program over other direct instruction methods. One instruction program, DISTAR, proved to be successful for teaching reading and mathematics to low achievers and at-risk students.

HOW DO STUDENTS LEARN AND TRANSFER CONCEPTS?

Students learn concepts through observation and definition. Concepts are taught through examples and nonexamples and through the rule–example–rule approach, in which teachers first state a definition, then give examples, and finally restate the definition. Easy examples should be given before hard ones, and teachers should compare and contrast examples given. Students transfer their learning to similar situations and must be taught to transfer concepts to different contexts and real-life situations.

HOW ARE DISCUSSIONS USED IN INSTRUCTION?

In whole-group discussion the teacher plays a less dominant role than in a regular lesson. Students need an adequate knowledge base before beginning a discussion. In small-group discussion, each group should have a leader and a specific focus.

KEY TERMS

calling order   231
choral responses   231
concept   236
direct instruction   220
independent practice   232
learning probe   228
lesson planning   221
mental set   222

process–product studies   235
rule–example–rule   227
seatwork   232
small-group discussion   246
transfer of learning   238
wait time   231
whole-class discussion   243

Self-Assessment

1. Which of the following strategies does not belong in a direct instruction lesson?
   a. Provide immediate feedback.
   b. Allow students to control the learning activities.
   c. Set clear and meaningful learning goals.
   d. Monitor student progress.

2. The seven steps in a direct instruction lesson are listed below in alphabetical order. Rearrange the steps in the proper order.
   a. Assess performance and provide feedback.
   b. Conduct learning probes.
   c. Present new material.
   d. Provide distributed practice and review.
   e. Provide independent practice.
   f. Review prerequisites.
   g. State learning objectives and orient students to lesson.

3. Teacher demonstrations take place during which step of a direct instruction lesson?
   a. Present new material.
   b. Provide independent practice.
   c. Assess performance and provide feedback.
   d. Review prerequisites.

4. List three strategies that make independent practice time effective.

5. Direct instruction methods work best in all of the following contexts except
   a. teaching basic skills.
   b. elementary reading.
   c. teaching low achievers.
   d. teaching critical thinking skills.

6. List several advantages and several limitations of direct instruction.

7. Which of the following conclusions is supported by research?
   a. Give low achievers as much time to respond as high achievers.
   b. Call on another if a student does not answer quickly.
   c. Call on volunteers rather than selecting students randomly.
   d. Call on a student, then ask a question.

8. Which of the following best illustrates transfer of learning?
   a. Students who study carefully do well on a quiz.

b. Students use their knowledge in one subject to solve problems in another.

c. Students rehearse after memorizing.

d. Students correctly identify an example of a concept being taught.

9. All of the following are appropriate for whole-class and small-group discussions except

a. subjective and controversial issues.

b. difficult and novel concepts.

c. affective topics.

d. questions with simple answers.

10. How would you address the following situations in a whole-class discussion?

a. a student who never makes a comment

b. a student who talks too much

c. a student who argues

d. a student who interrupts

Chapter 8

WHAT IS THE CONSTRUCTIVIST VIEW OF LEARNING?
Historical Roots of Constructivism
Top-Down Processing
Cooperative Learning
Discovery Learning
Self-Regulated Learning
Scaffolding
APA's Learner-Centered Psychological Principles
Constructivist Methods in the Content Areas
Research on Constructivist Methods

HOW IS COOPERATIVE LEARNING USED IN INSTRUCTION?
Cooperative Learning Methods
Research on Cooperative Learning

HOW ARE PROBLEM-SOLVING AND THINKING SKILLS TAUGHT?
The Problem-Solving Process
Obstacles to Problem Solving
Teaching Creative Problem Solving
Teaching Thinking Skills
Critical Thinking

Student-Centered and Constructivist Approaches to Instruction

"You'll all recall," began Mr. Dunbar, "how last week we figured out how to compute the area of a circle and the volume of a cube.

Today you're going to have a chance to discover how to compute the volume of a cylinder. This time, you're really going to be on your own. At each of your lab stations you have five unmarked cylinders of different sizes. You also have a metric ruler and a calculator, and you may use water from your sink. The most important resources you'll have to use, however, are your minds and your partners. Remember, at the end of this activity, everyone in every group must be able to explain not only the formula for volume of a cylinder, but also precisely how you derived it. Any questions? You may begin!"

The students in Mr. Dunbar's middle school math/science class got right to work. They were seated around lab tables in groups of four. One of the groups, the Master Minds, started off by filling all its cylinders with water.

"OK," said Miguel, "we've filled all of our cylinders. What do we do next?"

"Let's measure them," suggested Margarite. She took the ruler and asked Dave to write down her measurements.

"The water in this little one is 36 millimeters high and ... just a sec ... 42 millimeters across the bottom."

"So what?" asked Yolanda. "We can't figure out the volume this way. Let's do a little thinking before we start measuring everything."

"Yolanda's right," said Dave. "We'd better work out a plan."

"I know," said Miguel, "let's make a hypo, hypotha, what's it called?"

"Hypothesis," said Yolanda. "Yeah! Let's guess what we think the solution is."

"Remember how Mr. Dunbar reminded us about the area of a circle and the volume of a cube? I'll bet that's an important clue."

"You're right, Miguel," said Mr. Dunbar, who happened to be passing by. "But what are you guys going to do with that information?"

The Master Minds were quiet for a few moments. "Let's try figuring out the area of the bottom of one of these cylinders," ventured Dave. "Remember that Margarite said the bottom of the little one was 42 millimeters? Give me the calculator . . . now how do we get the area?"

Yolanda said, "I think it was pi times the radius squared."

"That sounds right. So 42 squared. . . ."

"Not 42; 21 squared," interrupted Margarite. "If the diameter is 42, the radius is 21."

"OK, OK, I would have remembered. Now, 21 squared is . . . 441, and pi is about 3.14, so my handy dandy calculator says . . . 13,847."

"Can't be," said Miguel. "Four hundred times three is twelve hundred, so 441 times 3.14 can't be thirteen thousand. I think you did something wrong."

"Let me do it again . . . 441 times 3.14 . . . you're right. Now it's about 1,385."

"So what?" said Yolanda.

"That doesn't tell us how to figure the volume!"

Margarite jumped in excitedly. "Just hang on for a minute, Yolanda. Now, I think we should multiply the area of the bottom by the height of the water."

"But why?" asked Miguel.

"Well," said Margarite, "when we did the volume of a cube, we multiplied length times width times height. Length times width is the area of the bottom. I'll bet we could do the same with a cylinder!"

"The girl's brilliant!" said Miguel. "Sounds good to me. But how could we prove it?"

"I've got an idea," said Yolanda. She emptied the water out of all the cylinders and filled the smallest one to the top. "This is my idea. We don't know what the volume of this cylinder is, but we do know that it's always the same. If we pour the same amounts of water into all four cylinders and use our formula, it should always come out to the same amount!"

"Let's try it!" said Miguel. He poured the water from the small cylinder into a larger one, refilled it, and poured it into another of a different shape.

The Master Minds measured the bases and the heights of the water in their cylinders, wrote down the measurements, and tried out their formula. Sure enough, their formula always gave the same answer for the same volume of water. In great excitement they called Mr. Dunbar to come see what they were doing. Mr. Dunbar asked each of the students to explain what they had done.

"Terrific!" he said. "Not only did you figure out a solution, but everyone in the group participated and understood what you did. Now I'd like you to help me out. I've got a couple of groups that are really stumped. Do you suppose you could help them? Don't give them the answer, but help them get on track. How about Yolanda and Miguel helping with the Brainiacs, and Dave and Margarite help with the Dream Team. OK? Thanks!"

Using Your EXPERIENCE

Cooperative Learning and Critical Thinking   After reading this case, randomly select or appoint a four- to eight-member panel of "experts" on constructivism who sit in front of the class to explain why this method of teaching worked so well for Mr. Dunbar in his middle school math/science classroom. (Students might want to volunteer for the panel.) Members of the audience can ask questions once each panelist has spoken.

Critical Thinking   Reflect on Mr. Dunbar's teaching style. How would you characterize it (e.g., Piagetian, Vygotskian, discovery, other)? How does he frame the task and interact with students? His addressing of students' prior learning and questioning are critical from a constructivist point of view. Why?

Learning is much more than memory. For students to really understand and be able to apply knowledge, they must work to solve problems, to discover things for themselves, to wrestle with ideas. Mr. Dunbar could have told his students that the formula for the volume of a cylinder is pr^2h. With practice the students would have been able to feed numbers into this formula and grind out correct answers. But how much would it have meant to them, and how well could they have applied the ideas behind the formula to other problems? The task of education is not to pour information into students' heads, but to engage students' minds with powerful and useful concepts. The focus of this chapter is on ways of doing this.

WHAT IS THE CONSTRUCTIVIST VIEW OF LEARNING?

One of the most important principles of educational psychology is that teachers cannot simply give students knowledge. Students must construct knowledge in

constructivist theories of learning
Theories that state that learners must individually discover and transform complex information, checking new information against old rules and revising rules when they no longer work.

their own minds. The teacher can facilitate this process by teaching in ways that make information meaningful and relevant to students, by giving students opportunities to discover or apply ideas themselves, and by teaching students to be aware of and consciously use their own strategies for learning. Teachers can give students ladders that lead to higher understanding, yet the students themselves must climb these ladders.

A revolution is taking place in educational psychology. This revolution goes by many names, but the name that is most frequently used is **constructivist theories of learning.** The essence of constructivist theory is the idea that learners must individually discover and transform complex information if they are to make it their own (Brooks & Brooks, 1993; Brown, Collins, & Duguid, 1989; Leinhardt, 1993; Steffe & Gale, 1995). Constructivist theory sees learners as constantly checking new information against old rules and then revising rules when they no longer work. This view has profound implications for teaching, as it suggests a far more active role for students in their own learning than is typical in many classrooms. Because of the emphasis on students as active learners, constructivist strategies are often called *student-centered instruction*. In a student-centered classroom the teacher becomes the "guide on the side" instead of the "sage on the stage," helping students to discover their own meaning instead of lecturing and controlling all classroom activities.

CONNECTIONS
The work of Piaget and of Vygotsky is discussed on pages 30–48 of Chapter 2.

Historical Roots of Constructivism

The constructivist revolution has deep roots in the history of education. It draws heavily on the work of Piaget and Vygotsky (recall Chapter 2), both of whom emphasized that cognitive change takes place only when previous conceptions go through a process of disequilibration in light of new information. Piaget and Vygotsky also emphasized the social nature of learning, and both suggested the use of mixed-ability learning groups to promote conceptual change.

SOCIAL LEARNING ● Modern constructivist thought draws most heavily on Vygotsky's theories (see John-Steiner & Mahn, 1996; Karpov & Bransford, 1995), which have been used to support classroom instructional methods that emphasize cooperative learning, project-based learning, and discovery. Four key principles derived from Vygotsky's ideas have played an important role. First is his emphasis on the social nature of learning (Hickey, 1997; O'Connor, 1998; Salomon & Perkins, 1998). Children learn, he proposed, through joint interactions with adults and more capable peers. On cooperative projects, like the one in Mr. Dunbar's class, children are exposed to their peers' thinking processes; this method not only makes the learning outcome available to all students, but also makes other students' thinking processes available to all. Vygotsky noted that successful problem solvers talk themselves through difficult problems. In cooperative groups, children can hear this inner speech out loud and can learn how successful problem solvers are thinking through their approaches.

CONNECTIONS
For more on the zone of proximal development, see Chapter 2, page 45.

ZONE OF PROXIMAL DEVELOPMENT ● A second key concept is the idea that children learn best the concepts that are in their zone of proximal development. As discussed in Chapter 2, children are working within their zone of proximal development when they are engaged in tasks that they could not do alone but can do with the assistance of peers or adults. For example, if a child could not find the median of a set of numbers by himself but could do so with some assistance from his teacher, then finding medians is probably in his zone of proximal development. When children are working together, each child is likely to have a peer performing on a given task at a slightly higher cognitive level, exactly within the child's zone of proximal development.

COGNITIVE APPRENTICESHIP ● Another concept derived from Vygotsky's emphases both on the social nature of learning and on the zone of proximal development is **cognitive apprenticeship** (Gardner, 1991; Greeno, Collins, & Resnick, 1996). This term refers to the process by which a learner gradually acquires expertise through interaction with an expert, either an adult or an older or more advanced peer. In many occupations, new workers learn their jobs through a process of apprenticeship, in which a new worker works closely with an expert, who provides a model, gives feedback to the less experienced worker, and gradually socializes the new worker into the norms and behaviors of the profession. Student teaching is a form of apprenticeship. Constructivist theorists suggest that teachers transfer this long-standing and highly effective model of teaching and learning to day-to-day activities in classrooms, both by engaging students in complex tasks and helping them through these tasks (as a master electrician would help an apprentice rewire a house) (Newmann & Wehlage, 1993) and by engaging students in heterogeneous, cooperative learning groups in which more advanced students help less advanced ones through complex tasks.

MEDIATED LEARNING ● Finally, Vygotsky's emphasis on scaffolding, or *mediated learning* (Kozulin & Presseisen, 1995), is important in modern constructivist thought. Current interpretations of Vygotsky's ideas emphasize the idea that students should be given complex, difficult, realistic tasks and then be given enough help to achieve these tasks (rather than being taught little bits of knowledge that are expected someday to build up to complex tasks). This principle is used to support the classroom use of projects, simulations, explorations in the community, writing for real audiences, and other authentic tasks. The term *situated learning* (Prawat, 1992) is used to describe learning that takes place in real-life, authentic tasks.

Top-Down Processing

Constructivist approaches to teaching emphasize top-down rather than bottom-up instruction. The term *top-down* means that students begin with complex problems to solve and then work out or discover (with the teacher's guidance) the basic skills required. For example, students might be asked to write compositions and only later learn about spelling, grammar, and punctuation. This top-down processing approach is contrasted with the traditional bottom-up strategy, in which basic skills are gradually built into more complex skills. In top-down teaching, the tasks students begin with are complex, complete, and authentic, meaning that they are not parts or simplifications of the tasks that students are ultimately expected to perform but are the actual tasks. As one instance of a constructivist approach to mathematics teaching, consider an example from Lampert (1986). The traditional, bottom-up approach to teaching the multiplication of two-digit numbers by one-digit numbers (e.g., $4 \times 12 = 48$) is to teach students a step-by-step procedure to get the right answer. Only after students have mastered this basic skill are they given simple application problems, such as "Sondra saw some pencils that cost 12 cents each. How much money would she need to buy four of them?"

cognitive apprenticeship
The process by which a learner gradually acquires expertise through interaction with an expert, either an adult or an older or more advanced peer.

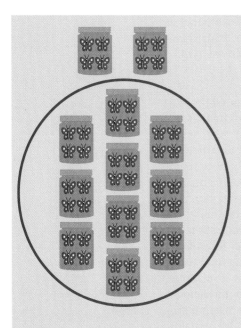

Teacher: Can anyone give me a story that could go with this multiplication . . . 12 × 4?

Student 1: There were 12 jars, and each had 4 butterflies in it.

Teacher: And if I did this multiplication and found the answer, what would I know about those jars and butterflies?

Student 1: You'd know you had that many butterflies altogether.

Teacher: Okay, here are the jars. [*Draws a picture to represent the jars of butterflies—see diagram.*] Now, it will be easier for us to count how many butterflies there are altogether if we think of the jars in groups. And, as usual, the mathematician's favorite number for thinking about groups is?

Student 2: 10

Teacher: Each of these 10 jars has 4 butterflies in it. [*Draws a loop around 10 jars.*]

Teacher: Suppose I erase my circle and go back to looking at the 12 jars again all together: Is there any other way I could group them to make it easier for us to count all the butterflies?

Student 3: You could do 6 and 6.

Teacher: Now, how many do I have in this group?

Student 4: 24

Teacher: How did you figure that out?

Student 4: 8 and 8 and 8. [*He puts the 6 jars together into 3 pairs, intuitively finding a grouping that made the figuring easier for him.*]

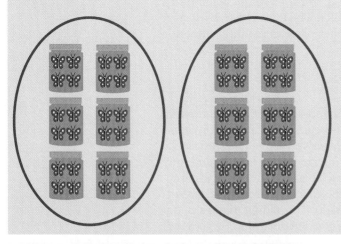

Teacher: That's 3 × 8. It's also 6 × 4. Now how many are in this group?

Student 3: 24. It's the same. They both have 6 jars.

Teacher: And how many are there altogether?

Student 5: 24 and 24 is 48.

Teacher: Do we get the same number of butterflies as before? Why?

Student 5: Yeah, because we have the same number of jars and they still have 4 butterflies in each.

FIGURE 8.1 ● Mathematical Stories for Teaching Multiplication
From Magdalene Lampert, "Knowing, Doing and Teaching Multiplication," *Cognition and Instruction, 3,* 1986, pp. 305–342. Reprinted by permission of Lawrence Erlbaum Associates, Inc.

The constructivist approach works in exactly the opposite order, beginning with problems (often proposed by the students themselves) and then helping students figure out how to do the operations. Lampert's example of this appears in Figure 8.1.

For example, in the chapter-opening vignette, Mr. Dunbar used cooperative groups to help students derive a formula for the volume of a cylinder. Recall how the Master Minds bounced ideas off of each other, tried out and discarded false leads, and ultimately came up with a solution and a way to prove that their solution was correct. None of the students could have solved the problem alone, so the group work was helpful in arriving at a solution. More important, the experience of hearing others' ideas, trying out and receiving immediate feedback on proposed solutions, and arguing about different ways to proceed gave the Master Minds the cognitive scaffolding that Vygotsky, Bruner, and other constructivists hold to be essential to higher-order learning (Brooks & Brooks, 1993).

Cooperative Learning

Constructivist approaches to teaching typically make extensive use of cooperative learning, on the theory that students will more easily discover and comprehend difficult concepts if they can talk with each other about the problems. Again, the emphasis on the social nature of learning and the use of groups of peers to model appropriate ways of thinking and expose and challenge each other's misconceptions are key elements of Piaget's and Vygotsky's conceptions of cognitive change (Pontecorvo, 1993). Cooperative learning methods are described in more detail later in this chapter.

Discovery Learning

Discovery learning is an important component of modern constructivist approaches that has a long history in education innovation. In **discovery learning** (Wilcox 1993), students are encouraged to learn largely on their own through active involvement with concepts and principles, and teachers encourage students to

discovery learning
A constructivist approach to teaching in which students are encouraged to discover principles for themselves.

These students are encouraged to learn on their own. What are some of the advantages of discovery learning?

have experiences and conduct experiments that permit them to discover principles for themselves. Bruner (1966), an advocate of discovery learning, put it this way: "We teach a subject not to produce little living libraries on that subject, but rather to get a student to think . . . for himself, to consider matters as an historian does, to take part in the process of knowledge-getting. Knowing is a process, not a product" (1966, p. 72).

Discovery learning has applications in many subjects. For example, some science museums have a series of cylinders of different sizes and weights, some hollow and some solid. Students are encouraged to race the cylinders down a ramp. By careful experimentation the students can discover the underlying principles that determine the cylinders' speed.

Discovery learning has several advantages. It arouses students' curiosity, motivating them to continue to work until they find answers. Students also learn independent problem-solving and critical-thinking skills, because they must analyze and manipulate information.

THEORY *into* Practice

Discovery Learning in the Classroom

Teachers who subscribe to Bruner's fundamental goal of making students self-sufficient should encourage independence from the very beginning of the child's school career. But how can you help students gain independence? Perhaps the most appropriate answer from the discovery perspective is to let the students follow their natural interests in achieving competence and satisfying their curiosity. You should encourage students to solve problems on their own or in groups instead of teaching them the answers. Students often benefit more from being able to see and do things than from hearing lectures. You can help students understand difficult concepts by using demonstrations and pictures.

Learning should be flexible and exploratory. If students appear to be struggling with a concept, allow them time to try to solve the problem on their own before providing the solution.

Teachers must also consider the students' attitudes toward learning. According to Bruner, school should arouse children's curiosity, minimize the risk of failure, and be as relevant for the student as possible.

Here are some additional suggestions based on the discovery approach to teaching:

1. Encourage informed guessing by asking leading questions.
2. Use a variety of materials and games.
3. Let students satisfy their curiosity even if they pursue ideas that are not directly related to the lesson.
4. Use plenty of examples that contrast the subject matter to related topics.

self-regulated learners
Students who have knowledge of effective learning strategies and how and when to use them.

Self-Regulated Learning

A key concept of constructivist theories of learning is a vision of the ideal student as a self-regulated learner (Weinstein & McCombs, 1995). **Self-regulated learners** are ones who have knowledge of effective learning strategies and how and when to use them (Bandura, 1991; Howard-Rose & Winne, 1993; Schunk & Zimmerman, 1997; Winne, 1997). For example, they know how to break complex problems into simpler steps or to test out alternative solutions; they know how and when to skim and how and when to read for deep understanding; and they know how to write to persuade and how to write to inform. Further, self-regulated learners are motivated by learning itself, not only by grades or others' approval (Boekaerts, 1995; Corno, 1992; Schunk, 1995), and they are able to stick to a long-term task until it is done. When students have both effective learning strategies and the motivation and persistence to apply these strategies until a job is done to their satisfaction, then they are likely to be effective learners (Williams, 1995; Zimmerman, 1995) and to have a lifelong motivation to learn (Corno & Kanfer, 1993).

CONNECTIONS

For more on the motivational aspects of self-regulated learning, see Chapter 10, page 354.

Scaffolding

CONNECTIONS

For more on scaffolding, see Chapter 2, page 45.

As was noted in Chapter 2, scaffolding is a practice based on Vygotsky's concept of assisted learning. According to Vygotsky, higher mental functions, including the ability to direct memory and attention in a purposeful way and to think in symbols, are mediated behaviors. Mediated externally by culture, these and other behaviors become internalized in the learner's mind as psychological tools. In assisted learning, or **mediated learning,** the teacher is the cultural agent who guides instruction so that students will master and internalize the skills that permit higher cognitive functioning. The ability to internalize cultural tools relates to the learner's age or stage of cognitive development. Once acquired, however, internal mediators allow greater self-mediated learning.

In practical terms, scaffolding may include giving students more structure at the beginning of a set of lessons and gradually turning responsibility over to them to operate on their own (Palincsar, 1986; Rosenshine & Meister, 1992, 1994). For example, students can be taught to generate their own questions about material they are reading. Early on, the teacher may suggest the questions, modeling the kinds of questions students might ask, but students later take over the question-generating task. For another example of scaffolding, see Figure 8.2.

Research has measured parents' use of scaffolding while helping fifth-graders with math homework. Researchers measured the degree to which adults shifted their level of intervention to fit the child's zone of proximal development. When the child is having difficulty, the adult who stays within this region increases his or her directiveness just enough to provide support but not so much as to take over the

mediated learning
Assisted learning; an approach in which the teacher guides instruction by means of scaffolding to help students master and internalize the skills that permit higher cognitive functioning.

Early in the scaffolding process, the teacher may provide more structure and then gradually turn responsibility over to the student. As a teacher, how would you use scaffolding to be most effective?

FIGURE 8.2 ● Scaffolding
From Laura E. Berk, *Infants, Children, and Adolescents* (2nd ed.), p. 328. Copyright © 1996 by Allyn & Bacon. Reprinted by permission.

Here is a brief example of an adult scaffolding a young child's efforts to put a difficult puzzle together.

Jason: I can't get this one in. *(Tries to insert a piece in the wrong place)*

Adult: Which piece might go down here? *(Points to the bottom of the puzzle)*

Jason: His shoes. *(Looks for a piece resembling the clown's shoes but tries the wrong one)*

Adult: Well, what piece looks like this shape? *(Points again to the bottom of the puzzle)*

Jason: The brown one. *(Tries it and it fits; then attempts another piece and looks at the adult)*

Adult: There you have it! Now try turning that piece just a little. *(Gestures to show him)*

Jason: There! *(Puts in several more, commenting to himself, "Now a green piece to match," "Turn it [meaning the puzzle piece]," as the adult watches)*

task, then reduces directiveness when the child begins to succeed. Findings revealed that use of this principle predicted gains in children's learning of mathematics. A later section in this chapter describes reciprocal teaching, a method that uses scaffolding in just this way. Scaffolding is closely related to cognitive apprenticeship; experts working with apprentices typically engage them in complex tasks and then give them decreasing amounts of advice and guidance over time.

APA's Learner-Centered Psychological Principles

In 1992 the American Psychological Association's Task Force on Psychology in Education published a document called *Learner-Centered Psychological Principles: Guidelines for School Redesign and Reform* (American Psychological Association, 1992, 1997; see also Alexander & Murphy, 1994). Revised in 1997, this publication presents a consensus view of principles of learning and motivation among prominent educational psychologists primarily working within the constructivist tradition. Table 8.1 shows the APA's 14 principles.

The Learner-Centered Psychological Principles paint a picture of the learner as actively seeking knowledge, reinterpreting information and experience for himself or herself, motivated by the quest for knowledge itself (rather than by grades or other rewards), working with others to socially construct meaning, and aware of his or her own learning strategies and capable of applying them to new problems or circumstances.

TABLE 8.1

Learner-Centered Psychological Principles: Cognitive and Metacognitive Factors

PRINCIPLE	EXPLANATION
Principle 1 Nature of the learning process	The learning of complex subject matter is most effective when it is an intentional process of constructing meaning from information and experience.
Principle 2 Goals of the learning process	The successful learner, over time and with support and instructional guidance, can create meaningful, coherent representations of knowledge.
Principle 3 Construction of knowledge	The successful learner can link new information with existing knowledge in meaningful ways.
Principle 4 Strategic thinking	The successful learner can create and use a repertoire of thinking and reasoning strategies to achieve complex learning goals.
Principle 5 Thinking about thinking	Higher-order strategies for selecting and monitoring mental operations facilitate creative and critical thinking.
Principle 6 Context of learning	Learning is influenced by environmental factors, including culture, technology, and instructional practices.
Principle 7 Motivational and emotional influences on learning	What and how much is learned is influenced by the learner's motivation. Motivation to learn, in turn, is influenced by the individual's emotional states, beliefs, interests and goals, and habits of thinking.
Principle 8 Intrinsic motivation to learn	The learner's creativity, higher-order thinking, and natural curiosity all contribute to motivation to learn. Intrinsic motivation is stimulated by tasks that are of optimal novelty and difficulty, are relevant to personal interests, and provide for personal choice and control.
Principle 9 Effects of motivation on effort	Acquisition of complex knowledge and skills requires extended learner effort and guided practice. Without learners' motivation to learn, the willingness to exert this effort is unlikely without coercion.
Principle 10 Developmental influences on learning	As individuals develop, there are different opportunities and constraints for learning. Learning is most effective when differential development within and across physical, intellectual, emotional, and social domains is taken into account.
Principle 11 Social influences on learning	Learning is influenced by social interactions, interpersonal relations, and communication with others.
Principle 12 Individual differences in learning	Learners have different strategies, approaches, and capabilities for learning that are a function of prior experience and heredity.
Principle 13 Learning and diversity	Learning is most effective when differences in learners' linguistic, cultural, and social backgrounds are taken into account.
Principle 14 Standards and assessment	Setting appropriately high and challenging standards and assessing the learner as well as learning process—including diagnostic, process, and outcome assessment—are integral parts of the learning process.

From American Psychological Association, *Learner-centered psychological principles: A framework for school redesign and reform,* pp. 4–7. Copyright 1997 by the American Psychological Association. Adapted by permission.

Constructivist Methods in the Content Areas

Constructivist and student-centered methods have come to dominate current thinking in all areas of curriculum. The following sections describe constructivist approaches in reading and mathematics.

Teacher: The title of this story is "Genius with Feathers." Let's have some predictions. I will begin by guessing that this story will be about birds that are very smart. Why do I say that?

First student: Because a genius is someone very smart.

Second student: Because they have feathers.

Teacher: That's right. Birds are the only animals that have feathers. Let's predict now the kind of information you might read about very smart birds.

Third student: What kinds of birds?

Teacher: Good question. What kinds would you guess are very smart?

Third student: Parrots or blue jays.

First student: A cockatoo.

Teacher: What other information would you want to know? *[No response from students]*

Teacher: I would like to know what these birds do that is so smart. Any ideas?

Second student: Some birds talk.

Fourth student: They can fly.

Teacher: That's an interesting one. As smart as people are, they can't fly. Well, let's read this first section now and see how many of our predictions were right. I will be the teacher for this section. *(All read the section silently.)*

Teacher: Who is the genius with feathers?

First student: Crows.

Teacher: That's right. We were correct in our prediction that this story would be about birds, but we didn't correctly guess which kind of bird, did we? My summary of the first section would be that it describes the clever things that crows do, which make them seem quite intelligent.

Let's read on. Who will be the teacher for this section? Jim?

Jim: How do crows communicate with one another?

Teacher: Good question! You picked right up on our prediction that this is about the way crows communicate. Whom do you choose to answer your question?

Jim: Barbara.

Barbara: Crows have built-in radar and a relay system.

Jim: That's a good part of it. That answer I wanted was how they relay the messages from one crow to the other crow.

Teacher: Summarize now.

Jim: This is about how crows have developed a system of communication.

Teacher: That's right. The paragraph goes on to give examples of how they use pitch and changes in interval, but these are supporting details. The main idea is that crows communicate through a relay system, Jim?

Jim: It says in this section that crows can use their communication system to play tricks, so I predict the next section will say something about the tricks crows play. I would like Sue to be the next teacher.

Teacher: Excellent prediction. The last sentence of a paragraph often suggests what the next paragraph will be about. Good, Jim.

FIGURE 8.3 ● Example of a Reciprocal Teaching Lesson
From Anne Marie Palinscar, "The Role of Dialogue in Providing Scaffolded Instruction," *Educational Psychologist, 21,* 1986, pp. 73–98. Adapted by permission of Lawrence Erlbaum Associates, Inc.

reciprocal teaching
A small-group teaching method based on principles of question generation; through instruction and modeling, teachers foster metacognitive skills primarily to improve the reading performance of students who have poor comprehension.

RECIPROCAL TEACHING IN READING ● One well-researched example of a constructivist approach based on principles of question generation is **reciprocal teaching** (Palincsar & Brown, 1984). This approach, designed primarily to help low achievers in elementary and middle schools learn reading comprehension, involves the teacher working with small groups of students. Initially, the teacher models questions students might ask as they read, but students are soon appointed to act as "teacher" to generate questions for each other. Figure 8.3 presents an example of reciprocal teaching in use. Note in the example how the teacher directs the conversation about crows at first but then turns the responsibility over to Jim (who is about to turn it over to another student as the example ends). The teacher is modeling the behaviors she wants the students to be able to do on their own and then changes her role to that of facilitator and organizer as the students begin to

CASE TO CONSIDER

Teaching First-Graders to Regulate Their Learning

Mrs. Evertson has just finished reading *Clifford's Birthday Party* with her first-grade class. This week the students are doing activities related to the story. Mrs. Evertson describes the activities and explains that students should select three from the sheet to complete that morning. Activities include writing a story about Clifford, arranging word cards into sentences from the story, and writing a letter to Clifford about his birthday. Students move from center to center working on the activities. Thirty minutes before lunch, Mrs. Evertson asks the students to join her on the rug.

Mrs. Evertson: We had a lot of different activities this morning, and I wanted to know how you did. Were you successful?

Jessica: I didn't get all three of my activities done.

Mrs. Evertson: Could someone help Jessica by telling her how you planned your activities so that you finished them?

José: I kept working and if my friends talked to me too much, I took my work to another place in the room.

Crystal: I asked my friend to help me spell some of the words so I could write the story about Clifford. I got to use big words!

Mrs. Evertson: I see. José knew that he had to watch out and not get distracted so he could focus on his reading. Crystal knew that she should try to spell the words, but that friends can really help us learn new things. Those are good ideas to help us concentrate. Here is another question: Some of you were working with words from the book; you were putting them together so that they were just like the sentences in the story. How did you do that?

Susanna: First, I took out the word that started with a capital letter because I knew it would be the first word.

Mrs. Evertson: You thought about the beginning of the sentence. Did you think about the end, too?

Susanna: Yes, it had a period.

Juwan: I read all the words and kept changing them till they made sense.

Mrs. Evertson: Did you know all the words in the sentence, Tamika?

Tamika: No, I sounded one out. It started with *cl.* I knew *clap,* and I used that to figure out *close.*

Mrs. Evertson: So I hear that some people used the capital letters and punctuation as clues; some kept asking if the words made sense, and some used the letters they already knew to help them sound out new words. Those are all good strategies. You all knew that the sentence was supposed to make sense, just like the story, and you used different ways to do that. Before we go to lunch, I would like to check to see how many students marked off the activities they completed today. [Only three quarters of the students raise their hands.] Do that now. One way you could remember is to make a small mark by each activity you are choosing. Then, before you move on to the next center, mark it off in the box. Any other ideas?

Pasqual: I remember the work I did, and that helps me remember at the end.

Mrs. Evertson: Yes, when you remember the Clifford story you wrote, you can find that on your activity sheet and check it off. Tomorrow, I hope everyone will try some of these good ideas to help them think about how they do their work.

PROBLEM SOLVING

1. Some instructional techniques that teachers can use to help students develop self-regulation include modeling, pointing out successful performance, giving feedback for improvement, providing instructions, asking questions, and providing cognitive structures (e.g., identifying the theme of a story as "heroes" or reminding students to use strategies). Find some examples of these strategies in the dialogue above, critique their effectiveness, and change two to be more effective.

2. Could you characterize this instruction as metacognitive? Why or why not?

3. Imagine that Jessica has just announced that she didn't complete her three activities or that she didn't know how to write the letter to Clifford. Rewrite or role-play the dialogue from that point on using different approaches to help her understand and solve her problem.

generate the actual questions. Research on reciprocal teaching has generally found this strategy to increase the achievement of low achievers (Alfassi, 1998; Carter, 1997; Lysynchuk, Pressley, & Vye, 1990; Palincsar & Brown, 1984; Rosenshine & Meister, 1994).

THEORY
into
Practice

Introducing Reciprocal Teaching

In introducing reciprocal teaching to students, you might begin as follows: "For the coming weeks we will be working together to improve your ability to understand what you read. Sometimes we are so busy figuring out what the words are that we fail to pay much attention to what the words and sentences mean. We will be learning a way to pay more attention to what we are reading. I will teach you to do the following activities as you read:

1. To think of important questions that might be asked about what is being read and to be sure that you can answer those questions.
2. To summarize the most important information that you have read.
3. To predict what the author might discuss next in the passage.
4. To point out when something is unclear in the passage or doesn't make sense and then to see if we can make sense of it.

"These activities will help you keep your attention on what you are reading and make sure that you are understanding it.

"The way in which you will learn these four activities is by taking turns in the role of teacher during our reading group sessions. When I am the teacher, I will show you how I read carefully by telling you the questions I made up while reading, by summarizing the most important information I read, and by predicting what I think the author might discuss next. I will also tell you if I found anything I read to be unclear or confusing and how I made sense out of it.

"When you are the teacher, you will first ask the rest of us the questions you made up while reading. You will tell us if our answers are correct. You will summarize the most important information you learned while reading. You will also tell us if you found anything in the passage to be confusing. Several times throughout the story you will also be asked to predict what you think might be discussed next in the passage. When you are the teacher, the rest of us will answer your questions and comment on your summary.

"These are activities that we hope you will learn and use, not only when you are here in reading class, but whenever you want to understand and remember what you are reading—for example, in social studies, science, or history."

Daily Procedures

1. Pass out the passage for the day.
2. Explain that you will be the teacher for the first segment.
3. Instruct the students to read silently whatever portion of the passage you determine is appropriate. At the beginning, it will probably be easiest to work paragraph by paragraph.
4. When everyone has completed the first segment, model the following:

   - "The question that I thought a teacher might ask is _____ _____."

   - Have the students answer your question. They may refer to the text if necessary. "I would summarize the important information in this paragraph in the following way: _____ _____."

   - "From the title of the passage, I would predict that the author will discuss _____."

   - If appropriate, "When I read this part, I found the following to be unclear _____."

5. Invite the students to make comments regarding your teaching and the passage. For example:

- "Was there more important information?"
- "Does anyone have more to add to my prediction?"
- "Did anyone find something else confusing?"

6. Assign the next segment to be read silently. Choose a student to act as teacher for this segment. Begin with students who are more verbal and who you think will have less difficulty with the activities.

7. Coach the student teacher through the activities as necessary. Encourage the other students to participate in the dialogue, but always give the student teacher for that segment the opportunity to go first and lead the dialogue. Be sure to give the student teacher plenty of feedback and praise for his or her participation.

8. As the training days go by, try to remove yourself more and more from the dialogue so that the student teacher initiates the activities himself or herself and other students provide feedback. Your role will continue to be monitoring, keeping students on track, and helping them over obstacles. Throughout the training, however, continue to take your turn as teacher, modeling at least once a session.

CONSTRUCTIVIST APPROACHES TO MATHEMATICS TEACHING IN THE PRIMARY GRADES ●
Carpenter and colleagues (1994) described four approaches to early mathematics instruction for the early elementary grades. In all four, students work together in small groups; teachers pose problems and then circulate among groups to facilitate the discussion of strategies, join students in asking questions about strategies they have proposed, and occasionally offer alternative strategies when students appear to be stuck. In Supporting Ten-Structured Thinking (STST) (Fuson, 1992), children use base-10 blocks to invent procedures for adding and subtracting large numbers. Conceptually Based Instruction (CBI) (Hiebert & Wearne, 1993) makes extensive use of physical, pictorial, verbal, and symbolic presentations of mathematical ideas and gives students opportunities to solve complex problems using these representations and to contrast different representations of the same concepts. Similarly, the Problem Centered Mathematics Project (PCMP) (Murray, Olivier, & Human, 1992) leads children through stages, from modeling with counters to solving more abstract problems without counters. Cognitively Guided Instruction (CGI) (Carpenter & Fennema, 1992; Fennema, Franke, Carpenter, & Carey, 1993), unlike STST and CBI, does not have a specific curriculum or recommended set of activities but provides extensive professional development for teachers of primary mathematics, focusing on principles similar to those used in the other programs. There is good evidence that this program increases student achievement not only on measures related to higher-level thinking in mathematics, which is the program's focus, but also on computational skills (Carpenter & Fennema, 1992; Carpenter, Fennema, Peterson, Chiang, & Loef, 1989).

In these and other constructivist approaches to mathematics, the emphasis is on beginning with real problems for students to solve intuitively and letting students use their existing knowledge of the world to solve problems any way they can (Hiebert et al., 1996; Schifter, 1996). The problem and solutions in Figure 8.1 illustrate this approach. Only at the end of the process, when students have achieved a firm conceptual understanding, are they taught formal, abstract representations of the mathematical processes they have been working with (see Clements & Battista, 1990).

CONSTRUCTIVIST APPROACHES IN SCIENCE ● Discovery, group work, and conceptual change have long been emphasized in science education, so it is not surprising that many elementary and secondary science educators have embraced constructivist ideas. In this subject, constructivism translates into an emphasis on hands-on, investigative laboratory activities (Bainer & Wright, 1998; Cobb, 1994; White & Frederiksen, 1998); identifying misconceptions and using experimental approaches to correct these misconceptions (Hand & Treagust, 1991; Sandoval, 1995); and cooperative learning (Pea, 1993; Wheatley, 1991).

Research on Constructivist Methods

Research comparing constructivist and traditional approaches to instruction is often difficult to interpret, because constructivist methods are usually intended to produce outcomes that are qualitatively different from those of traditional methods. For example, it is obvious that acquisition of skills and basic information must be balanced against constructivist approaches (Airasian & Walsh, 1997; Harris & Graham, 1996). But what is the appropriate balance, for which objectives (Harris & Alexander, 1998; von Glaserfeld, 1996)? Also, much of the research on constructivist methods is descriptive rather than comparative. However, there are studies showing positive effects of constructivist approaches on traditional achievement measures in mathematics (e.g., Carpenter & Fennema, 1992), science (e.g., Neale, Smith, & Johnson, 1990), reading (e.g., Duffy & Roehler, 1986), and writing (e.g., Bereiter & Scardamalia, 1987). Furthermore, a study by Knapp (1995) found a correlation between use of more constructivist approaches and achievement gains in high-poverty schools. Still, much more research is needed to establish the conditions under which constructivist approaches are effective for enhancing student achievement.

SELF-CHECK

Write a short essay explaining how each of the following terms is related to constructivist theory: (1) cooperative learning; (2) discovery learning; (3) self-regulated learning.

HOW IS COOPERATIVE LEARNING USED IN INSTRUCTION?

In **cooperative learning** instructional methods, students work together in small groups to help each other learn. Many quite different approaches to cooperative learning exist. Most involve students in four-member, mixed-ability groups (e.g., Slavin, 1994a), but some methods use dyads (e.g., Dansereau, 1985; Fantuzzo, Polite, & Grayson, 1990; Maheady, Harper, & Mallette, 1991), and some use varying group sizes (e.g., Cohen, 1986; Johnson & Johnson, 1994; Kagan, 1992; Sharan & Sharan, 1992). Typically, students are assigned to cooperative groups and stay together as a group for many weeks or months. They are usually taught specific skills that will help them work well together, such as active listening, giving good explanations, avoiding putdowns, and including other people.

Cooperative learning activities can play many roles in lessons (Webb & Palincsar, 1996). Recall the chapter-opening vignette in Chapter 7: Ms. Logan used cooperative learning for three distinct purposes. At first, students worked as dis-

cooperative learning
Instructional approaches in which students work in small mixed-ability groups.

covery groups, helping each other figure out how water in bottles could tell them about principles of sound. After the formal lesson, students worked as discussion groups. Finally, students had an opportunity to work together to make sure that all group members had learned everything in the lesson in preparation for a quiz, working in a group study format. In the vignette at the beginning of this chapter, Mr. Dunbar used cooperative groups to solve a complex problem.

Cooperative Learning Methods

Many quite different cooperative learning methods have been developed and researched. The most extensively evaluated cooperative learning methods are described in the following sections.

STUDENT TEAMS–ACHIEVEMENT DIVISIONS (STAD) ● In **Student Teams–Achievement Divisions (STAD)** (Slavin, 1994a), students are assigned to four-member learning teams that are mixed in performance level, gender, and ethnicity. The teacher presents a lesson, and then students work within their teams to make sure that all team members have mastered the lesson. Finally, all students take individual quizzes on the material, at which time they may not help one another.

Students' quiz scores are compared to their own past averages, and points are awarded on the basis of the degree to which students meet or exceed their own earlier performance. These points are then summed to form team scores, and teams that meet certain criteria may earn certificates or other rewards. In a related method called Teams–Games–Tournaments (TGT), students play games with members of other teams to add points to their team scores.

STAD and TGT have been used in a wide variety of subjects, from mathematics to language arts to social studies, and have been used from second grade through college. The STAD method is most appropriate for teaching well-defined objectives with single right answers, such as mathematical computations and applications, language usage and mechanics, geography and map skills, and science facts and concepts. However, it can easily be adapted for use with less well-defined objectives by incorporating more open-ended assessments, such as essays or performances. STAD is described in more detail in the next Theory into Practice.

> **CONNECTIONS**
>
> To learn about the benefits of cooperative learning methods in promoting harmony in culturally diverse classrooms, see Chapter 4, page 117.

> **Student Teams–Achievement Divisions (STAD)**
>
> A cooperative learning method for mixed-ability groupings involving team recognition and group responsibility for individual learning.

Student Teams–Achievement Divisions (STAD)

THEORY *into* Practice

An effective cooperative learning method is called Student Teams–Achievement Divisions, or STAD (Slavin, 1994a, 1995a). STAD consists of a regular cycle of teaching, cooperative study in mixed-ability teams, and quizzes, with recognition or other rewards provided to teams whose members most exceed their own past records.

STAD consists of a regular cycle of instructional activities, as follows:

- **Teach:** Present the lesson.
- **Team study:** Students work on worksheets in their teams to master the material.
- **Test:** Students take individual quizzes or other assessments (such as essays or performances).
- **Team recognition:** Team scores are computed on the basis of team members' improvement scores, and certificates, a class newsletter, or a bulletin board recognizes high-scoring teams.

The following steps describe how to introduce students to STAD:

1. Assign students to teams of four or five members each. Four are preferable; make five-member teams only if the class is not divisible by four. To assign the students, rank them from top to bottom on some measure of academic performance (e.g., past grades, test scores) and divide the ranked list into quarters, placing any extra students in the middle quarters. Then put one student from each quarter on each team, making sure that the teams are well balanced in gender and ethnicity. Extra (middle) students may become fifth members of teams.

2. Make a worksheet and a short quiz for the lesson you plan to teach. During team study (one or two class periods) the team members' tasks are to master the material you presented in your lesson and to help their teammates master the material. Students have worksheets or other study materials that they can use to practice the skill being taught and to assess themselves and their teammates.

3. When you introduce STAD to your class, read off team assignments.

- Have teammates move their desks together or move to team tables, and allow students about 10 minutes to decide on a team name.
- Hand out worksheets or other study materials (two of each per team).
- Suggest that students on each team work in pairs or threes. If they are working problems (as in math), each student in a pair or threesome should work the problem and then check with his or her partner(s). If anyone missed a question, that student's teammates have a responsibility to explain it. If students are working on short-answer questions, they may quiz each other, with partners taking turns holding the answer sheet or attempting to answer the questions.
- Emphasize to students that they are not finished studying until they are sure that all their teammates will make 100 percent on the quiz.
- Make sure that students understand that the worksheets are for studying—not for filling out and handing in. That is why it is important for students to have the answer sheets to check themselves and their teammates as they study.
- Have students explain answers to one another instead of just checking each other against the answer sheet.
- When students have questions, have them ask a teammate before asking you.
- While students are working in teams, circulate through the class, praising teams that are working well and sitting in with each team to hear how the members are doing.

4. Distribute the quiz or other assessment, and give students adequate time to complete it. Do not let students work together on the quiz; at this point they must show what they have learned as individuals. Have students move their desks apart if this is possible. Either allow students to exchange papers with members of other teams or collect the quizzes to score after class.

CONNECTIONS

For more on the ILE system, see Chapter 10, page 355.

5. Figure individual and team scores. Team scores in STAD are based on team members' improvements over their own past records. As soon as possible after each quiz, you should compute individual improvement scores (using the ILE system described in Chapter 10) and team scores, and write a class newsletter (or prepare a class bulletin board) to announce the team scores. If at all possible, the announcement of team scores should be made in the first period after the quiz. This makes the connection between doing well and receiving recognition clear to students, increasing their motivation to do their best. Compute team scores by adding up the improvement points earned by the team members and dividing the sum by the number of team members who are present on the day of the quiz.

6. Recognize team accomplishments. As soon as you have calculated points for each student and figured team scores, you should provide some sort of recognition to any teams that averaged 20 improvement points or more. You might give certificates to team members or prepare a bulletin board display. It is important to help students value team success. Your own enthusiasm about team scores will help. If you give more than one quiz in a week, combine the quiz results into a single weekly score. After 5 or 6 weeks of STAD, reassign students to new teams. This allows students to work with other classmates and keeps the program fresh.

COOPERATIVE INTEGRATED READING AND COMPOSITION (CIRC) ● **Cooperative Integrated Reading and Composition (CIRC)** (Stevens & Slavin, 1995a) is a comprehensive program for teaching reading and writing in the upper elementary grades. Students work in four-member cooperative learning teams. They engage in a series of activities with one another, including reading to one another, making predictions about how narrative stories will come out, summarizing stories to one another, writing responses to stories, and practicing spelling, decoding, and vocabulary. They also work together to master main idea and other comprehension skills. During language arts periods, students engage in writing drafts, revising and editing one another's work, and preparing for publication of team books. Three studies of the CIRC program have found positive effects on students' reading skills, including improved scores on standardized reading and language tests (Stevens et al., 1987; Stevens & Slavin, 1991, 1995a).

JIGSAW ● In **Jigsaw** (Aronson, Blaney, Stephen, Sikes, & Snapp, 1978), students are assigned to six-member teams to work on academic material that has been broken down into sections. For example, a biography might be divided into early life, first accomplishments, major setbacks, later life, and impact on history. Each team member reads his or her section. Next, members of different teams who have studied the same sections meet in expert groups to discuss their sections. Then the students return to their teams and take turns teaching their teammates about their sections. Since the only way students can learn sections other than their own is to listen carefully to their teammates, they are motivated to support and show interest in one another's work. In a modification of this approach called Jigsaw II (Slavin, 1994a), students work in four- or five-member teams as in STAD. Instead of each student being assigned a unique section, all students read a common text, such as a book chapter, a short story, or a biography. However, each student receives a topic on which to become an expert. Students with the same topics meet in expert groups to discuss them, after which they return to their teams to teach what they have learned to their teammates. The students take individual quizzes, which result in team scores, as in STAD.

LEARNING TOGETHER ● **Learning Together,** a model of cooperative learning developed by David Johnson and Roger Johnson (1994), involves students working in four- or five-member heterogeneous groups on assignments. The groups hand in a single completed assignment and receive praise and rewards based on the group product. This method emphasizes team-building activities before students begin working together and regular discussions within groups about how well they are working together.

Cooperative Integrated Reading and Composition (CIRC)
A comprehensive program for teaching reading and writing in the upper elementary grades; students work in four-member cooperative learning teams.

Jigsaw
A cooperative learning model in which students are assigned to six-member teams to work on academic material that has been broken down into sections for each member.

Learning Together
A cooperative learning model in which students in four- or five-member heterogeneous groups work together on assignments.

GROUP INVESTIGATION ● **Group Investigation** (Sharan & Sharan, 1992) is a general classroom organization plan in which students work in small groups using cooperative inquiry, group discussion, and cooperative planning and projects. In this method, students form their own two- to six-member groups. After choosing subtopics from a unit that the entire class is studying, the groups break their subtopics into individual tasks and carry out the activities that are necessary to prepare group reports. Each group then makes a presentation or display to communicate its findings to the entire class.

COOPERATIVE SCRIPTING ● Many students find it helpful to get together with classmates to discuss material they have read or heard in class. A formalization of this age-old practice has been researched by Dansereau (1985) and his colleagues. In it, students work in pairs and take turns summarizing sections of the material for one another. While one student summarizes, the other listens and corrects any errors or omissions. Then the two students switch roles, continuing in this way until they have covered all the material to be learned. A series of studies of this **cooperative scripting** method has consistently found that students who study this way learn and retain far more than students who summarize on their own or who simply read the material (Newbern, Dansereau, Patterson, & Wallace, 1994). It is interesting that while both participants in the cooperative pairs gain from the activity, the larger gains are seen in the sections that students teach to their partners rather than in those for which they serve as listeners (Spurlin, Dansereau, Larson, & Brooks, 1984). More recent studies of various forms of peer tutoring find similar results (Fuchs & Fuchs, 1997; King, 1997, 1998).

THEORY *into* Practice

Using Constructivist Methods to Help Students Develop Self-Understanding

In the constructivist perspective, the individual constructs knowledge through interactions with the environment (Murphy & Rhéaume, 1997). Theorists in this field suggest that instead of emphasizing rote memorization, teachers should be "guides" and students should be "sense makers" (Mayer, 1996). Each person learns in a different manner, and we all learn and use strategies that help us retain information. Furthermore, when students are grouped together, they have an opportunity to learn from one another as well as from their environment. When you give students opportunities to learn concepts in a manner that is applicable to their daily lives, they are more likely to be able to use that knowledge or the acquired skill in the future. Students learn to mentor others as well as to work with peers in solving complex problems. These opportunities allow students to apply newly acquired knowledge firsthand. While the students are working together to learn new concepts, the teacher is a coordinator, facilitator, resource adviser, coach, or tutor (Gergen, 1995).

Many employers today say that flexibility, willingness to cooperate and work as a team member, and amenability to learning new skills are most desirable in an employee (Michigan Department of Education, 1998). To prepare students for this new kind of work environment, teachers are throwing out the old principles and beginning to use more manipulatives and experiential learning. They are taking more field trips and helping students learn how to manipulate information using complex critical thinking skills. Students have opportunities to gain more self-confidence and self-esteem in the process. This is important because, as the theory states, students tend to retain information that is applicable to their lives or that is taught in a way that allows them to have control over how they learn information (Rogers & Freiburg, 1994).

Group Investigation
A cooperative learning model in which students work in small groups using cooperative inquiry, group discussion, and cooperative planning and projects, and then make presentations to the whole class on their findings.

cooperative scripting
A study method in which students work in pairs and take turns orally summarizing sections of material to be learned.

At the Texas School for the Deaf in Austin, first-year high school students complete a unit called Self-Understanding. Instead of following the traditional practice of giving them definitions to memorize, the instructor lists vocabulary words such as "physical characteristics" on the board and then asks the students to describe themselves. As the students offer information, the teacher categorizes each fact or item, such as brown hair or blue eyes, under one of the vocabulary words. When the class has contributed about five items under each vocabulary-word heading, the teacher breaks the students into small groups to define the vocabulary words. This encourages the students to suggest definitions that they will remember. The groups then share the information, and most of the time the students come very close to the dictionary definition of each word. If they do not, the teacher provides some clues or hints that will lead them to an acceptable definition.

Throughout the unit, the students are divided into groups. They measure their heights, guess their weights, describe one another, and draw pictures together. Another activity is their Positive Statement Book. Each student must write something positive about each other pupil in the class. When they are finished, the students put all their writings together in books. Each student then has a book with several pages of positive statements about him- or herself.

The culminating activity is a ME book. Each student gathers everything he or she has done in the unit, meticulously types or prints it out onto final-copy pages, and then presents it to the class. The class as a whole grades the presentations of the others, as well as assessing themselves individually. This assessment activity, which stresses teamwork and cooperation, allows each student to appreciate the time and effort others have expended on their presentations, because of the fact that everyone is required to accomplish the same task. The students learn about one another and about themselves in an interesting and hands-on way.

Research on Cooperative Learning

Cooperative learning methods fall into two broad categories. One category might be called *group study methods* (Slavin, 1996b), in which students primarily work together to help one another master a relatively well-defined body of information or skills—what Cohen (1994b) calls "well-structured problems." The other category is often called *project-based learning* or *active learning* (Stern, 1996). Project-based learning methods involve students working in groups to create a report, experiment, mural, or other product (Webb & Palinscar, 1996). Project-based learning methods such as those described by Blumenfeld, Marx, Soloway, and Krajcik (1996); Cohen (1994a), Palincsar, Anderson, and David (1993); and Sharan and Sharan (1992) focus on ill-structured problems, which typically have less of a clear expected outcome or instructional objective. Methods of this kind are often referred to as collaborative learning methods (Webb & Palinscar, 1996).

Most research comparing cooperative learning to traditional teaching methods has evaluated group study methods such as STAD, Jigsaw II, CIRC, and Johnson's methods. More than 100 studies have compared achievement of students in such methods to that of students in traditional classrooms over periods of at least 4 weeks (Slavin, 1995a). The results have consistently favored cooperative learning as long as two essential conditions are met. First, some kind of recognition or small reward must be provided to groups that do well so that group members can see that it is in their interest to help their groupmates learn (O'Donnell, 1996). Second, there must be individual accountability. That is, the success of the group must depend on the individual learning of all group members, not on a single group product. For example, groups might be evaluated on the basis of the average of their members' scores on individual quizzes or essays (as in STAD), or students might be individually responsible for a unique portion of a group task (as in Group Investigation). Without this individual accountability there is a danger that one student may do the work of the others, or that some students may be shut out of group interaction because they are thought to have little to contribute (O'Donnell & O'Kelly, 1994; Slavin, 1995a).

Studies of cooperative learning methods that incorporate group goals and individual accountability show substantial positive effects on the achievement of students in grades 2 through 12 in all subjects and in all types of schools (Slavin, 1995a). Effects are similar for all grade levels and for all types of content, from basic skills to problem solving (Qin, Johnson, & Johnson, 1995). Although cooperative learning methods are usually used for only a portion of a student's school day and school year, a recent study found that students in schools that used a variety of cooperative learning methods in almost all subjects for a 2-year period achieved significantly better than did students in traditionally organized schools (Stevens & Slavin, 1995b). These effects were particularly positive for the highest achievers (compared to equally high achievers in the control group) and for the special-education students. Other studies have found equal effects of cooperative learning for high, average, and low achievers and for boys and girls (Slavin, 1995a). There is some evidence that these methods are particularly effective for African American and Latino students, but this trend is not consistent (Slavin, 1995b).

In addition to group goals and individual accountability, a few classroom practices can contribute to the effectiveness of cooperative learning. For example, students in cooperative groups who are taught communication and helping skills (Webb & Farrivar, 1994) or are taught metacognitive learning strategies (Fantuzzo, King, & Heller, 1992; Hoek, Terwel, & van den Eeden, 1997) learn more than do students in usual cooperative groups. A great deal of research has shown that students who give extensive explanations to others learn more in cooperative groups than do those who give or receive short answers or no answers (Nattiv, 1994; Webb, 1992; Webb, Trooper, & Fall, 1995).

There is less research on the effects of project-based forms of cooperative learning focused on ill-structured problems; but the studies that do exist show equally favorable results of cooperative methods designed for such problems (Blumenfeld et al., 1996; Lazarowitz, 1995; Thousand & Villa, 1994). In particular, a study by Sharan and Shachar (1988) found substantial positive effects of the Group Investigation method on higher-order objectives in language and literature, and studies by Cohen (1994a) have shown that the more consistently teachers implement her Complex Instruction program, the better children achieve.

In addition to boosting achievement, cooperative learning methods have had positive effects on such outcomes as improved intergroup relations (Slavin, 1995b), self-esteem, attitudes toward school, and acceptance of children with special educational needs (Schmuck & Schmuck, 1997; Shulman, Lotan, & Whitcomb, 1998; Slavin, 1995a).

CONNECTIONS

For more on how cooperative learning methods benefit the social integration of students with special education needs in the general education classroom, see Chapter 12, page 448.

SELF-CHECK

Explain how each of the following cooperative learning methods can be used in the classroom: (1) Jigsaw; (2) Learning Together; (3) Group Investigation; (4) cooperative scripting.

TEACHERS IN ACTION

How have you applied student-centered or constructivist approaches in your teaching?

Suzanne Cary
Mendenhall River Community School
Juneau, Alaska

Final countdown: 10, 9, 8, 7, 6, 5, 4, . . . "Wait a second!" Before a space shuttle safely and successfully blasts off and completes an actual mission in space, it's important to realize that teams of experts have spent hours preparing for this culminating event. As a result of attending International Space Camp and being exposed to the importance of teams of scientists working together prior to and during an actual mission, I thought, What better way to apply cooperative learning and inquiry-based learning to young children than through the exciting framework of space science?

In the first few days of our interdisciplinary unit on space science, my primary students learn about rockets, rocket design, and designers, and they focus on the astronaut's role in space flight. However, few students indicate an understanding of the team element required for a successful space shuttle flight. To focus the student on this aspect, I read the book *Space Camp,* by Anne Baird. It is a wonderful illustration of the roles played not only by astronauts but also by mission control ground crews. Through the book, boys and girls experience the excitement, challenges, and importance of every team member. Both boys and girls are portrayed in equally difficult and demanding roles. Sally Ride's significant role as the first American woman in space is explored through posters, biography, and the books she has contributed to.

As a team, students design cardboard instrument panels that are placed on a table arranged to simulate mission control. Other teams create mission patches to symbolize their particular mission. In reader's theater style, students dictate a mission script and, after a few days of practice, assemble for the actual launch. Using launch portions of the video *The Dream Is Alive,* students don their earphones, speak their lines, begin the countdown, and watch the video screen as the shuttle lifts off the launch pad. Everyone wants to be an astronaut! More important, everyone values the shared responsibility involved in real teamwork.

Robert W. Fardy
Concord Public Schools
Concord, Massachusetts

"Remember, it's LABORatory, not labORATORY." I remember seeing that sign in a science classroom many years ago. The message was clear: Science class is about working, not talking! In my experience, however, first as an elementary school teacher and later as a science curriculum specialist, I have seen the powerful role that student-to-student discourse plays in children's conceptual development of science content and in their understanding of how scientists work. Cooperative learning science experiences provide opportunities for student-to-student discussions that can be used as an assessment of the students' prior knowledge and alternative conceptions in order to guide the kind of instruction that will lead to conceptual change.

At the beginning of a second-grade unit on plant growth and development, I often ask the class to generate a list of things that plants need. Earlier, I had observed that whole-class brainstorming often resulted in a rather predictable and limited list of examples, such as *rain, sun, soil,* and *air,* and I wondered about all the unspoken student ideas that were never shared. However, when I changed the instructional environment and asked the second-graders to generate a list of plant needs by using cooperative learning strategies such as Teammates Consult and Round Table, the results were dramatically different. First, many more student ideas were expressed, and examples such as *time, oxygen, carbon dioxide, care,* and *space* were included. Second, some responses, such as *bees to pollinate the flowers* and *worms to enrich the soil,* reflected a qualitatively different level of student thinking and indicated the students' knowledge about such concepts as the interdependence of organisms. Through classroom discourse, the students learned that inquiry-based science involves cooperation, collaboration, and communication; and I realized that in science class, it's *both* "LABORatory and labORATORY!"

HOW ARE PROBLEM-SOLVING AND THINKING SKILLS TAUGHT?

Students cannot be said to have learned anything useful unless they have the ability to use information and skills to solve problems. For example, a student might be quite good at adding, subtracting, and multiplying but have little idea of how to solve this problem: "Sylvia bought four hamburgers at $1.25 each, two orders of french fries at 65 cents, and three large sodas at 75 cents. How much change did she get from a 10-dollar bill?"

Sylvia's situation is not an unusual one in real life, and the computations involved are not difficult. However, many students (and even some otherwise competent adults) would have difficulty solving this problem. The difficulty of most applications problems in mathematics lies not in the computations but in knowing how to set the problem up so that it can be solved. **Problem solving** is a skill that can be taught and learned (Bransford & Stein, 1993; Martinez, 1998; Mayer & Wittrock, 1996).

The Problem-Solving Process

GENERAL PROBLEM-SOLVING STRATEGIES ● Students can be taught several well-researched strategies to use in solving problems (see, for example, Derry, 1991; Gallini, 1991; Tishman, Perkins, & Jay, 1995). Bransford and Stein (1993) developed and evaluated a five-step strategy called IDEAL:

I   Identify problems and opportunities
D   Define goals and represent the problem
E   Explore possible strategies
A   Anticipate outcomes and act
L   Look back and learn

IDEAL and similar strategies begin with careful consideration of what problem needs to be solved, what resources and information are available, and how the problem can be represented (e.g., in a drawing, outline, or flowchart) and then broken into steps that lead to a solution. For example, the first step is to identify the goal and figure out how to proceed. Newell and Simon (1972) suggest that the problem solver repeatedly ask, "What is the difference between where I am now and where I want to be? What can I do to reduce that difference?" In solving Sylvia's problem, the goal is to find out how much change she will receive from a 10-dollar bill after buying food and drinks. We might then break the problem into substeps, each with its own subgoal:

1. Figure how much Sylvia spent on hamburgers.
2. Figure how much Sylvia spent on french fries.
3. Figure how much Sylvia spent on sodas.
4. Figure how much Sylvia spent in total.
5. Figure how much change Sylvia gets from $10.00.

MEANS–ENDS ANALYSIS ● Deciding what the problem is and what needs to be done involves a **means–ends analysis.** Learning to solve problems requires a great deal of practice with different kinds of problems that demand thought. All too often, textbooks in mathematics and other subjects that include many prob-

problem solving
The application of knowledge and skills to achieve certain goals.

means–ends analysis
A problem-solving technique that encourages identifying the goal (ends) to be attained, the current situation, and what needs to be done (means) to reduce the difference between the two conditions.

What steps should these students take to successfully solve the problem?

lems fail to present problems that will make students think. For example, they might give students a set of word problems whose solutions require the multiplication of two numbers. Students soon learn that they can solve such problems by looking for any two numbers and multiplying them. In real life, however, problems do not line themselves up neatly in categories. We might hear, "Joe Smith got a 5 percent raise last week, which amounted to $1,200." If we want to figure out how much Joe was making before his raise, the hard part is not doing the calculation, but knowing what calculation is called for. In real life this problem would not be on a page titled "Dividing by Percents." The more different kinds of problems students learn to solve, and the more they have to think to solve the problems, the greater the chance that, when faced with real-life problems, students will be able to transfer their skills or knowledge to the new situation.

EXTRACTING RELEVANT INFORMATION ● Realistic problems are rarely neat and tidy. Imagine that Sylvia's problem had been as follows:

> Sylvia walked into the fast-food restaurant at 6:18 with three friends. Between them, they bought four hamburgers at $1.25 each, two orders of french fries at 65 cents, and three large sodas at 75 cents. Onion rings were on sale for 55 cents. Sylvia's mother told her to be in by 9:00, but she was already 25 minutes late by the time she and her friends left the restaurant. Sylvia drove the 3 miles home at an average of 30 miles per hour. How long was Sylvia in the restaurant?

The first part of this task is to clear away all the extraneous information to get to the important facts. The means–ends analysis suggests that only time information is relevant, so all the money transactions and the speed of Sylvia's car can be ignored. Careful reading of the problem reveals that Sylvia left the restaurant at 9:25. This and her arrival time of 6:18 are all that matters for solving the problem. Once we know what is relevant and what is not, the solution is easy.

REPRESENTING THE PROBLEM ● For many kinds of problems, graphic representation may be an effective means of finding a solution. Adams (1974) provides a story that illustrates this:

> A Buddhist monk has to make a pilgrimage and stay overnight in a temple that is at the top of a high mountain. The road spirals around and around the mountain. The monk begins walking up the mountain at sunrise. He walks all day long and finally reaches the top at about sunset. He stays all night in the temple and performs his devotions. At sunrise the next day the monk begins walking down the mountain. It takes him much less time than walking up, and he is at the bottom shortly after noon. The question is: Is there a point on the road when he was coming down that he passed at the same time of day when he was coming up the mountain?

This can seem to be a difficult problem because people begin to reason in a variety of ways as they think about the man going up and down. Adams points out one representation that makes the problem easy: Suppose there were two monks, one leaving the top at sunrise and one starting up at sunrise. Would they meet? Of course they would.

In addition to drawings, there are many other ways of representing problems. Students may be taught to make diagrams, flowcharts, outlines, and other means of summarizing and depicting the critical components of a problem (Katayama & Robinson, 1998; Robinson & Kiewra, 1995).

Obstacles to Problem Solving

Sometimes we fail to see the answer to a problem because we cannot free ourselves from familiar knowledge and assumptions. For example, Maier (1930) gave students the following problem:

> Two strings are hanging from the ceiling. The strings are of such a length and distance apart that you cannot reach one string while holding onto the other. You have a scissors, a paper clip, a pencil, and a piece of chewing gum in your pocket. Your task is, using just those materials, to tie the strings together.

Many of Maier's students were stumped because they did not consider that the scissors could be used for something besides cutting. To solve the problem, they had to use the scissors as a weight with which to make a pendulum to swing one of the strings toward the other. The problem would have been easier to solve if the word "scissors" had been replaced by "fishing weight," since that object's function is more like that of a pendulum weight. This blocking of a new use of an object by its common use is called **functional fixedness.** For example, Duncker (1945) gave students a box, candles, tacks, and matches. In some cases the candles, tacks, and matches were in the box; in others they weren't. The task was to attach a candle to the wall in such a way that it could be lighted. The solution was to tack to the wall the box, on which the candle could stand. Duncker found that when the other objects were in the box, a setup that emphasized the box's container function, students were less likely to use the box as a candle stand. Other researchers found that when the instructions mentioned the box among the materials to be used, the subjects were more likely to solve the problem. This finding suggests that people erect a mental boundary against using objects that are not mentioned in the instructions to a problem.

Emotional factors can also contribute to blocks in problem solving. People who do well on tests of creative problem solving seem to be less afraid of making mistakes and appearing foolish than do those who do poorly. Successful problem solvers also seem to treat problem-solving situations more playfully (Benjafield, 1992). This implies that a relaxed, fun atmosphere may be important in teaching

functional fixedness
A block to solving problems that is caused by an inability to see new uses for familiar objects or ideas.

problem solving. Students should certainly be encouraged to try different solutions and not be criticized for taking a wrong turn.

Teaching Creative Problem Solving

Most of the problems students encounter in school may require careful reading and some thought, but little creativity. However, many of the problems we face in life are not so cut-and-dried. The scissors-and-string problem discussed earlier is of this type. Life is full of situations that call for creative problem solving, as in figuring out how to change or end a relationship without hurt feelings or how to repair a machine with a bent paper clip (Sternberg, 1995).

The following sections describe a strategy for teaching creative problem solving (Beyer, 1997; Frederiksen, 1984a).

INCUBATION ● Creative problem solving is quite different from the analytical, step-by-step process that was used to solve Sylvia's problems. In creative problem solving, one important principle is to avoid rushing to a solution; instead, it is useful to pause and reflect on the problem and think through, or incubate, several alternative solutions before choosing a course of action. Consider the following simple problem:

> Roger baked an apple pie in his oven in three quarters of an hour. How long would it take him to bake three apple pies?

Many students would rush to multiply 45 minutes by 3. However, if they took some time to reflect, most would realize that baking three pies in the same oven would actually take about the same amount of time as baking one pie! In teaching this process, teachers must avoid putting time pressures on students. Instead of speed, they should value ingenuity and careful thought.

SUSPENSION OF JUDGMENT ● In creative problem solving, students should be encouraged to suspend judgment, to consider all possibilities before trying out a solution. One specific method based on this principle is called *brainstorming* (Osborn, 1963), in which two or more individuals suggest as many solutions to a problem as they can think of, no matter how seemingly ridiculous. Only after they have thought of as many ideas as possible is any idea evaluated as a possible solution. The point of brainstorming is to avoid focusing on one solution too early and perhaps ignoring better ways to proceed.

APPROPRIATE CLIMATES ● Creative problem solving is enhanced by a relaxed, even playful environment (Wallach & Kogan, 1965). Perhaps even more important, students who are engaging in creative problem solving must feel that their ideas will be accepted. Establishing an appropriate climate is an important step.

ANALYSIS ● One method of creative problem solving that is often suggested is to analyze and juxtapose major characteristics or specific elements of a problem (Lesgold, 1988). For example, the scissors-and-string problem mentioned earlier might have been solved by listing characteristics of the strings (one of which might have been that they are too light to be swung together) and of the scissors (one of which is that they have weight). Careful analysis of the situation might help solve the following problem:

> A tennis tournament was set up with a series of rounds. The winner of each match advanced to the next round. If there were an odd number of players in a round, one

player (chosen at random) would advance automatically to the next round. In a tournament with 147 players, how many matches would take place before a single winner would be declared?

We might solve this problem the hard way, making diagrams of the various matches. However, careful analysis of the situation would reveal that each match would produce exactly one loser. Therefore it would take 146 matches to produce 146 losers (and one winner).

THINKING SKILLS ● Teach the underlying cognitive abilities. Students can be taught specific strategies for approaching creative problem solving, such as (see Beyer, 1988) the following:

- Thinking of unusual ideas
- Generating many ideas
- Planning
- Mapping the possibilities
- Assembling the facts
- Getting the problem clearly in mind

FEEDBACK ● Provide practice with feedback. Perhaps the most effective way to teach problem solving is to provide students with a great deal of practice on a wide variety of problem types, giving feedback not only on the correctness of their solutions but also on the process by which they arrived at the solutions (Swanson, 1990). The role of practice with feedback in solving complex problems cannot be overemphasized. Mr. Dunbar's students, in the chapter-opening vignette, could not have arrived at the solution to their problem if they had not had months of practice and feedback on simpler problems.

Teaching Thinking Skills

One of the oldest dreams in education is that there might be some way to make students smarter—not just more knowledgeable or skillful but actually better able to learn new information of all kinds. Perhaps someday someone will come up with a "smart pill" that will have this effect; but in the meantime, several groups of researchers have been developing and evaluating instructional programs that are designed to increase students' general thinking skills.

The most widely known and extensively researched of several thinking-skills programs that are currently in use was developed by an Israeli educator, Reuven Feuerstein (1980). In this program, called **Instrumental Enrichment,** students work through a series of paper-and-pencil exercises that are intended to build such intellectual skills as categorization, comparison, orientation in space, and numerical progressions. Figure 8.4 shows one example of an activity designed to increase analytic perception. The Instrumental Enrichment treatment is meant to be administered for 3 to 5 hours per week over a period of at least 2 years, usually to underachieving or learning-disabled adolescents. Studies of this duration have found that the program has positive effects on tests of aptitude, such as IQ tests, but generally not on achievement (Savell, Twohig, & Rachford, 1986; Sternberg & Bhana, 1986). Less intensive interventions, particularly those involving fewer than 80 hours of instruction, have rarely been successful. In one study done in Israel (Feuerstein et al., 1981) and one in Venezuela (Ruiz, 1985), positive effects of Instrumental Enrichment on aptitude test scores were still found 2 years after the

Instrumental Enrichment
A thinking skills program in which students work through a series of paper-and-pencil exercises that are designed to develop various intellectual abilities.

program ended. Many reviewers of the research on Instrumental Enrichment have suggested that this method is simply teaching students how to take IQ tests rather than teaching them anything of real value (Sternberg & Bhana, 1986). Many of the exercises, such as the one reproduced in Figure 8.4, are, in fact, quite similar to items that are used in nonverbal IQ tests. A similar pattern of results has been found for many other thinking-skills programs (Adams, 1989). In fact, researchers have now begun to question whether there are broadly applicable thinking skills; the evidence points more toward the existence of teachable thinking skills in specific domains, such as math problem solving or reading comprehension (Perkins & Salomon, 1989). In fact, researchers have combined teaching of thinking skills with instruction in specific content areas, and results of these combined models are more encouraging (Adams, 1989; Bellanca, 1998; Derry & Murphy, 1986; Prawat, 1991).

Another approach to the teaching of thinking skills is to incorporate them in daily lessons and classroom experiences—to create a "culture of thinking" (Perkins, Jay, & Tishman, 1993). As an example of integrating thinking skills into daily lessons, Tishman, Perkins, and Jay (1995) describe an impromptu discussion in a class that has been taught a generic strategy for problem solving. This strategy is built around a four-step process (state, search, evaluate, and elaborate) that is

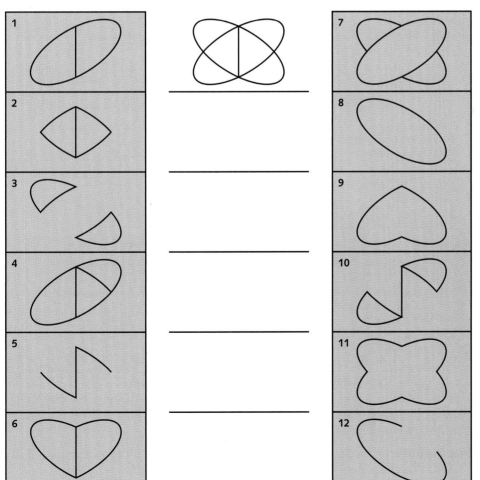

FIGURE 8.4 ● Examples from Analytic Perception
Look at the three columns at the right. For each drawing in the left column, there is a drawing in the right column that completes it to make the form shown in the middle column. Write the number of the form in the right column needed to complete the form in the first column. The student must select the appropriate drawing from the right to complete the one on the left to obtain a figure identical to the model in the middle column on this page. The task requires representation, internalization and labeling of the model, definition of the missing parts, systematic work, and comparison to the model for self-criticism.

From Reuven Feuerstein, "Instrumental Enrichment: A Selected Sample of Material for Review Purposes." Jerusalem: The Hadassah-Wizo-Canada Research Institute, May 1973, p. 5. Reprinted by permission of the author.

TABLE 8.2

Thinking Skills: Build a Strategy

STRATEGY BUILDING BLOCKS

WHEN . . .	STRATEGY STEP	TACTICS
When you need to be clear about what you're doing or where you're going . . .	**State . . .** either the problem, the situation, or your goal(s).	Identify the different dimensions of the situation. Identify the parts of the situation you will focus on. State precisely what you want to change or what you want your outcome to be. Be specific!
When you need to think broadly about something . . .	**Search . . .** for ideas, options, possibilities, purposes, features, assumptions, causes, effects, questions, dimensions, hypotheses, facts, or interpretations.	Brainstorm. Look for different kinds of ideas. Look at things from different points of view. Look for hidden ideas. Build on other people's ideas. Use categories to help you search.
When you need to assess, rate, or decide something . . .	**Evaluate . . .** options, plans, ideas, theories, or objects.	Look for lots of reasons. Consider the immediate and long-term consequences. List all the pros and cons, paying attention to both. Try to be objective; avoid bias. Use your imagination: How will it affect others?
When you need to think about the details of something . . .	**Elaborate . . .** possibilities, plans, options, hypotheses, or ideas.	Make a detailed plan: Say what will happen at each step. Visualize what it will look/feel/seem like *in detail*. Ask yourself: What resources will be used? How will it happen? Who will be affected? How long will it take? Think about the different parts. Draw a picture or write a description; imagine *telling* someone about it.

Source: From Shari Tishman, David N. Perkins, and Eileen Jay, *The Thinking Classroom.* Copyright © 1995 by Allyn & Bacon. Reprinted by permission.

summarized in Table 8.2. In Tishman and her colleagues' example, Ms. Mandly's sixth-graders discuss why plants in terrariums the class planted a month earlier are starting to die and what they might do about it. The class learned the steps summarized in Table 8.2 and has a poster identical to the table posted in the classroom. The discussion goes as follows:

Ms. Mandly: Let's take a look at the poster. How can we build a strategy to deal with this situation? Which building blocks can we use?

Rory: We should use the search step, to search for a solution to the problem.

Marc: Yeah, but we're not even exactly sure what the problem is. We don't know if the plants in the terrarium are wilted because they have too much water or too little.

Ms. Mandly: Are you suggesting we also need a state step, Marc?

Marc *(after a moment of looking at the poster):* Yes. In two ways: I think we need to state the problem and we need to state our goal.

Ms. Mandly: That sounds reasonable. Any other building blocks we can use?

Marc: Yeah, that might not be enough. What if you take care of a terrarium, and it still wilts? Other people in your group will want to know what went wrong.

Ms. Mandly: It sounds like we have two goals here. One, decide how to care for the terrarium. And two, make a plan for keeping track of the terrarium's care.

After more discussion, students agree on exactly what outcomes they want and move to the "search" step. Looking at the search tactics, they decide to brainstorm lots of different possible solutions. Ms. Mandly keeps track of their ideas on the blackboard and occasionally reminds them to keep in mind some key tactics: to look for hidden ideas and to look for different kinds of ideas. Some of the ideas students come up with are the following:

1. Have a sign-up list.
2. Let the teacher decide who should water.
3. Have one person volunteer to do it all.
4. Make a rotating schedule for each group.
5. Make a rotating schedule, plus have weekly group meetings to discuss progress.

After students review (evaluate) their brainstormed list, they unanimously agree that option 5—rotating schedule plus weekly meetings—is best.

They then go on to step 4: elaborate, and make a plan. They design a rotation schedule for each terrarium group, and with Ms. Mandly's help they pick a time for weekly group meetings. Working through the elaborate step, they invent a detailed checklist for the designated weekly waterer, to help track factors that might contribute to the terrarium's health, such as how much water has been given, the date of watering, the temperature of the classroom, and so on (Tishman et al., 1995).

In the course of discussing the terrarium problem, the students are learning a broadly applicable strategy for approaching and solving complex problems. By calling on this and other strategies frequently as they are appropriate in a classroom context, Ms. Mandly not only gives students useful strategies but also communicates the idea that strategy use is a normal and expected part of daily life.

Critical Thinking

One key objective of schooling is enhancing students' abilities to think critically, to make rational decisions about what to do or what to believe (Marzano, 1995). Examples of **critical thinking** include identifying misleading advertisements, weighing competing evidence, and identifying assumptions or fallacies in arguments. As with any other objective, learning to think critically requires practice; students can be given many dilemmas, logical and illogical arguments, valid and misleading advertisements, and so on (Halpern, 1995). Effective teaching of critical thinking depends on setting a classroom tone that encourages the acceptance of divergent perspectives and free discussion. There should be an emphasis on giving reasons for opinions rather than only giving correct answers. Skills in critical thinking are best acquired in relation to topics with which students are familiar. For example, students will learn more from a unit evaluating Nazi propaganda if they know

critical thinking
The ability to make rational decisions about what to do or what to believe.

The Intentional Teacher

● **Using What You Know about Student-Centered and Constructivist Approaches to Improve Teaching and Learning**

Intentional teachers keep sight of one of the overarching goals of education: to foster students' ability to solve real, complex problems. Intentional teachers work toward this lofty goal by ensuring that schooling provides more than a series of lectures and discrete workbook exercises. Intentional teachers furnish opportunities for students to build their own knowledge, to work with others in discovering important ideas, and to attack challenging issues.

1 What am I trying to accomplish?

Intentional teachers build in regular opportunities for students to approach complex, difficult, realistic tasks. Check your goals and curriculum: Where and how often do you encourage students to construct knowledge through student-centered approaches?

You review your yearlong planning chart for mathematics and realize that if you follow your chart, your third-graders will have only rare opportunities to use mathematics in realistic contexts. You revise your plans to include regular opportunities for students to study and use mathematics in realistic settings. For example, you plan for the class to develop, administer, analyze, and act upon a schoolwide survey about a current issue, the purchase of playground equipment.

Intentional teachers think about the balance between direct, teacher-centered instructional approaches and constructivist, student-centered approaches. Select your teaching strategies based upon your goals for students, and realize that a balance of both kinds of approaches may be best for promoting a variety of learning outcomes.

You feel pressed to cover a great deal of information in your U.S. government class; as a result, you find yourself lecturing almost daily. Then you recall that your major goal is to help your students become citizens who make informed decisions about complicated issues. Therefore, you review your plan book to ensure that you are using discovery approaches regularly. You begin with a discovery lesson the very next day by distributing nickels and asking students to draw inferences about the culture that created them.

2 What are my students' relevant experiences and needs?

Background knowledge affects students' ability to build meaning and solve problems. Gather baseline assessment information on students' social and problem-solving behaviors.

In September you provide to each of your fifth-grade student groups a few paper clips, scissors, and three sheets of paper. You ask groups to build the tallest freestanding tower they can using these materials. As students work, you circulate and take notes on students' work: *(a)* Do they entertain a variety of ideas before they begin? *(b)* Do they attempt to listen and learn from each other? *(c)* Do they persist? *(d)* How do they resolve conflict? *(e)* Do they use what they know about constructions in real life?

3 What approaches and materials are available to help me challenge every student?

Intentional teachers make use of top-down processing by beginning instruction with holistic problems or issues and moving to analysis of their parts. Begin your lessons with real problems within the context of a supportive atmosphere.

Instead of beginning your fourth-period math class with a statement, "Today we'll study combinatorial mathematics," you begin with a question: "If there are five flavors of fruity candies

a great deal about the history of Nazi Germany and the culture of the 1930s and 1940s. Perhaps most important, the goal of teaching critical thinking is to create a critical spirit, which encourages students to question what they hear and to examine their own thinking for logical inconsistencies or fallacies (Norris, 1985).

Beyer (1988) identified 10 critical-thinking skills that students might use in judging the validity of claims or arguments, understanding advertisements, and so on:

1. Distinguishing between verifiable facts and value claims
2. Distinguishing relevant from irrelevant information, claims, or reasons
3. Determining the factual accuracy of a statement
4. Determining the credibility of a source
5. Identifying ambiguous claims or arguments
6. Identifying unstated assumptions
7. Detecting bias

in this bag, how many flavor combinations can I create?" You make a list of students' initial responses: "A million!" "Fifty!" "Seventeen!" Then you pass out bags of candy and allow students to get to work on the problem.

Intentional teachers teach strategies for problem solving. Examples include drawing pictures, acting out situations, and making diagrams. Model a variety of problem-solving strategies, using them as scaffolds to keep students working within their zone of proximal development.

Your fourth-period class, still working on the candy combination problem, is stymied. You praise their approach thus far, taking special note of their willingness to take risks. Then you suggest that they try a charting strategy to work on a single part of the problem: How many combinations of *just two* flavors are there? You and your class devise the chart below, quickly finding patterns and discovering that there are 10 flavor combinations of two candies. Students discern that they simply need to make similar charts for 3-, 4-, and 5-flavor combinations to arrive at their answer.

Flavor 1	1-1 (1-2 1-3 1-4 1-5) (symbols represent flavor 1 with flavors 2, 3, 4, and 5)
Flavor 2	2-1 2-2 (2-3 2-4 2-5)
Flavor 3	3-1 3-2 3-3 (3-4 3-5)
Flavor 4	4-1 4-2 4-3 4-4 (4-5)
Flavor 5	5-1 5-2 5-3 5-4 5-5

4 How will I know whether and when to change my strategy or modify my instruction?

Intentional teachers modify instruction based upon evidence of student learning. Collect ongoing information related to students' ef-

forts to build meaning. Check for appropriate attitudes, cognitive processing, and social problem-solving behaviors.

As students work on a cooperative art project, you watch them. What does their nonverbal behavior tell you about how well they are working with peers? How willing are they to take risks? When you see that students are unwilling to accept peers' ideas, you stop the lesson and provide instruction on working well with others: "When someone gives a new idea, wait before you say no. Think for twenty seconds about how that idea may work. Watch, I'll pretend I'm in your group and you tell me a new idea. . . ."

5 What information will I accept as evidence that my students and I are experiencing success?

Assess your instruction using multiple measures.

To examine your efforts to provide student-centered instruction, you select three measures. First, you review your plan book, checking to see how many realistic opportunities you have provided in the last week. Second, you audiotape yourself teaching and analyze the kinds of questions and prompts you use. Finally, you ask students for feedback on your teaching: You give a survey with questions like this one: "The teacher _____(never/sometimes/often/always) gives us opportunities to figure things out on our own."

Students' products provide information about success. Examine students' work for evidence of sense-making, of critical thinking, and of creativity.

You've just collected a stack of essays on students' analysis of a current environmental issue: destruction of the rain forests. You begin your assessment by listing two questions to help you focus on students' knowledge construction: *(a)* How well do students marshal factual details to support their position? *(b)* What evidence is there of creative, inventive thinking?

8. Identifying logical fallacies
9. Recognizing logical inconsistencies in a line of reasoning
10. Determining the strength of an argument or claim (p. 57)

Beyer notes that this is not a sequence of steps but rather a list of possible ways in which a student might approach information to evaluate whether or not it is true or sensible. The key task in teaching critical thinking to students is to help them learn not only how to use each of these strategies but also how to tell when each is appropriate.

SELF-CHECK

Describe the problem-solving process. Give an example of an obstacle to problem solving.

CHAPTER SUMMARY

WHAT IS THE CONSTRUCTIVIST VIEW OF LEARNING?

Constructivists believe that knowing is a process and that learners must individually and actively discover and transform complex information to make it their own. Constructivist approaches emphasize top-down processing, in which students begin with complex problems or tasks and discover the basic knowledge and skills needed to solve the problems or perform the tasks. Constructivist approaches also emphasize cooperative learning, questioning or inquiry strategies, and other metacognitive skills.

Discovery learning and scaffolding are constructivist learning methods based on cognitive learning theories. Bruner's discovery learning highlights students' active self-learning, curiosity, and creative problem solving. Scaffolding, based on Vygotsky's views, calls for teacher assistance to students at critical points in their learning.

HOW IS COOPERATIVE LEARNING USED IN INSTRUCTION?

In cooperative learning, small groups of students work together to help one another learn. Cooperative learning groups are used in discovery learning, discussion, and study for assessment. Cooperative learning programs such as Student Teams–Achievement Divisions (STAD) are successful because they reward both group and individual effort and improvement and because groups are responsible for the individual learning of each group member.

HOW ARE PROBLEM-SOLVING AND THINKING SKILLS TAUGHT?

Problem-solving skills are taught through a series of steps, including, for example, means–ends analysis and problem representation. Creative problem solving requires incubation time, suspension of judgment, conducive climates, problem analysis, the application of thinking skills, and feedback. Thinking skills include, for example, planning, classifying, divergent thinking, identifying assumptions, identifying misleading information, and generating questions. Thinking skills can be taught through programs such as Instrumental Enrichment; creating a culture of thinking in the classroom is another useful technique.

KEY TERMS

cognitive apprenticeship   257

constructivist theories of learning   256

Cooperative Integrated Reading and Composition (CIRC)   271

cooperative learning   268

cooperative scripting   272

critical thinking   283

discovery learning   259

functional fixedness   278

Group Investigation   272

Instrumental Enrichment   280

Jigsaw   271

Learning Together   271

means–ends analysis   276

mediated learning   261

problem solving   276

reciprocal teaching   264

self-regulated learners   260

Student Teams–Achievement Divisions (STAD)   269

Self-Assessment

1. Constructivism has its roots in the works of
   a. Piaget and Vygotsky.
   b. behaviorists.
   c. moral development theorists.
   d. Albert Bandura.

2. In assisted or mediated learning, the teacher
   a. lets students explore topics to further their learning.
   b. presents information in a structured lesson.
   c. guides instruction so that students acquire learning tools.
   d. gives instruction in basic skills.

3. All of the following strategies reflect a constructivist view of learning except
   a. self-regulated learning.
   b. cooperative learning.
   c. bottom-up processing.
   d. discovery learning.

4. Define scaffolding and give an example of how it is used in the classroom.

5. Research suggests that cooperative learning programs are effective under all of the following conditions except when
   a. the group receives rewards or recognition for achievement.
   b. the groups are mixed in terms of race, ethnicity, gender, and special needs.
   c. the success of the group depends on the individual learning of each group member.
   d. the students are grouped by ability.

6. Match the cooperative learning method with its definition.
   a. Jigsaw
   b. Learning Together
   c. Group Investigation

_____ Groups work together, then hand in a single completed assignment.

_____ Groups choose subtopics from a unit that the entire class is studying, then present to others.

_____ Groups work on academic material that is broken down into sections.

7. What does the research on cooperative learning say about its effectiveness?
   a. No significant difference is seen between cooperative learning and traditional teaching approaches.
   b. Only the Jigsaw method of cooperative learning shows significant differences in achievement over traditional learning methods.
   c. The results of studies consistently show that, with rewards and individual accountability, cooperative learning strategies are superior to traditional teaching methods.

8. Describe an example of discovery learning. What is the teacher's role in a discovery lesson? What strengths and limitations exist with discovery learning?

9. Problem solving may require all of the following skills except
   a. critical thinking.
   b. incubation.
   c. functional fixedness.
   d. brainstorming.

10. How can teachers improve students' problem-solving abilities?

Chapter 9

WHAT ARE ELEMENTS OF EFFECTIVE INSTRUCTION BEYOND A GOOD LESSON?
Carroll's Model of School Learning and QAIT

HOW ARE STUDENTS GROUPED TO ACCOMMODATE ACHIEVEMENT DIFFERENCES?
Between-Class Ability Grouping
Untracking
Regrouping for Reading and Mathematics
Nongraded (Cross-Age Grouping) Elementary Schools
Within-Class Ability Grouping

WHAT IS MASTERY LEARNING?
Forms of Mastery Learning
Research on Mastery Learning

WHAT ARE SOME WAYS OF INDIVIDUALIZING INSTRUCTION?
Peer Tutoring
Adult Tutoring
Programmed Instruction
Computer-Based Instruction

WHAT EDUCATIONAL PROGRAMS EXIST FOR STUDENTS PLACED AT RISK?
Compensatory Education Programs
Early Intervention Programs

Accommodating Instruction to Meet Individual Needs

Mr. Arbuthnot is in fine form. He is presenting a lesson on long division to his fourth-grade class and feels that he's never been so clear, so interesting, and so well organized. When he asks questions, several students raise their hands; when he calls on them, they always know the answers. "Arbuthnot, old boy," he says to himself, "I think you're really getting to these kids!"

At the end of the period he passes out a short quiz to see how well his students have learned the long-division lesson. When the papers are scored, he finds to his shock and disappointment that only about a third of the class got every problem right. Another third missed every problem; the remaining students fell somewhere in between. "What went wrong?" he thinks. "Well, no matter, I'll set the situation right in tomorrow's lesson."

The next day, Mr. Arbuthnot is even better prepared, uses vivid examples and diagrams to show how to do long division, and gives an active, exciting lesson. Even more hands than before go up when he asks questions, and the answers are usually correct. However, some of the students are beginning to look bored, particularly those who got perfect papers on the quiz and those who got none right.

Toward the end of the period he gives another brief quiz. The scores are better this time, but there is still a group of students who got none of the problems correct. He is crestfallen. "I had them in the palm of my hand," he thinks. "How could they fail to learn?"

To try to find out what went wrong, Mr. Arbuthnot goes over the quiz papers of the students who missed all the problems. He immediately sees a pattern. By the second lesson, almost all students were proceeding correctly in setting up the long-division problems. However, some were making consistent errors in subtraction. Others had apparently forgotten their multiplication facts. Their problems were not with division at all; the students simply lacked the prerequisite skills.

"Well," thinks Mr. Arbuthnot, "at least I was doing great with some of the kids." It occurs to him that one of the students who got a perfect paper after the first lesson might be able to give him an idea about how to teach the others better. He asks Teresa how she grasped long division so quickly.

"It was easy," she says. "We learned long division last year!"

Using Your EXPERIENCE

Critical Thinking List all of the ways in which Mr. Arbuthnot could be more effective in addressing student individual differences. Then list all of the ways in which he is effective in addressing student needs.

Cooperative Learning Work with a group of four or five classmates. Pass a sheet of paper around the group, and ask each member to write down an idea to help Mr. Arbuthnot become more effective in addressing students' needs. After one idea is added, the sheet is passed to the next person in the group, who adds an idea and passes the sheet and so on. Share some of these ideas with the class.

WHAT ARE ELEMENTS OF EFFECTIVE INSTRUCTION BEYOND A GOOD LESSON?

As Mr. Arbuthnot learned to his chagrin, effective instruction takes a lot more than effective lectures. He gave a great lesson on long division, yet it was appropriate for only some of his students, those who had the needed prerequisites but had not already learned long division. To make his lesson effective for all of his students, he needed to adapt it to meet their diverse needs. Furthermore, the best lesson in the world won't work if students are not motivated to learn it or if inadequate time is allotted to allow all students to learn.

If the quality of lectures were all that mattered in effective instruction, we could probably find the best lecturers in the world, videotape their lessons, and show the tapes to students. If you think about why videotaped lessons would not work very well, you will realize how much more is involved in effective instruction than simply giving good lectures. First, the video teacher would have no idea of what students already knew. A particular lesson might be too advanced or too easy for a particular group of students. Second, some students might be learning the lesson quite well while others were missing key concepts and falling behind. The video teacher would have no way of knowing which students needed additional help and, in any case, would have no way of providing it. There would be no way to question students to find out whether they were getting the main points and then to reteach any concept they had missed. Third, the video teacher would have no way of motivating students to pay attention to the lesson or to really try to learn it. If students failed to pay attention or misbehaved, the video teacher could not do anything about it. Finally, the video teacher would never know at the end of a lesson whether students had actually learned the main concepts or skills.

This analysis of video teaching illustrates why teachers must be concerned with many elements of instruction in addition to the presentation of information. Teachers must know how to adapt their instruction to the students' levels of knowledge. They must motivate students to learn, manage student behavior, group students for instruction, and assess the students' learning.

To help make sense of all these elements of effective instruction, educational psychologists have proposed models of effective instruction. These models explain the critical features of high-quality lessons and how they relate to one another to enhance learning.

Carroll's Model of School Learning and QAIT

One of the most influential articles ever published in the field of educational psychology was a paper by John Carroll entitled "A Model of School Learning" (1963, 1989). In it he describes teaching in terms of the management of time, resources, and activities to ensure student learning. Carroll proposed that learning is a function of (1) time actually spent on learning and (2) time needed to learn. That is, learning is greater the more time students spend on learning in relation to the amount of time they need to learn. Time needed is a product of aptitude and ability to learn; time actually spent depends on clock time available for learning, quality of instruction, and student perseverance.

Slavin (1987d) described a model focusing on the alterable elements of Carroll's model, those that the teacher or school can directly change. It is called the **QAIT model** (quality, appropriateness, incentive, time) of effective instruction.

1. **Quality of instruction:** The degree to which presentation of information or skills helps students easily learn the material. Quality of instruction is largely a product of the quality of the curriculum and of the lesson presentation itself.
2. **Appropriate levels of instruction:** The degree to which the teacher makes sure that students are ready to learn a new lesson (that is, have the necessary skills and knowledge to learn it) but have not already learned the lesson. In other words, the level of instruction is appropriate when a lesson is neither too difficult nor too easy for students.
3. **Incentive:** The degree to which the teacher makes sure that students are motivated to work on instructional tasks and to learn the material being presented.
4. **Time:** The degree to which students are given enough time to learn the material being taught.

For instruction to be effective, each of these four elements must be adequate. No matter how high the quality of instruction, students will not learn a lesson if they lack the necessary prior skills or information, if they lack the motivation, or if they lack the time they need to learn the lesson. On the other hand, if the quality of instruction is low, then it makes no difference how much students already know, how motivated they are, or how much time they have. Figure 9.1 illustrates the relationship among the elements in the QAIT model.

QAIT model
A model of effective instruction that focuses on elements teachers can directly control: quality, appropriateness, incentive, and time.

FIGURE 9.1 ● **The QAIT Model**
Each of the elements of the QAIT model is like a link in a chain, and the chain is only as strong as the weakest link.

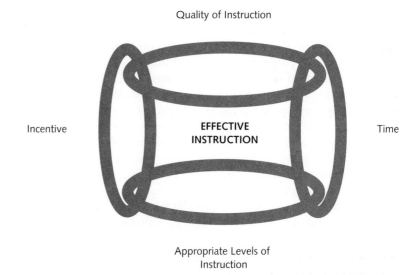

Quality of Instruction

Incentive

EFFECTIVE INSTRUCTION

Time

Appropriate Levels of Instruction

QUALITY OF INSTRUCTION ● Quality of instruction refers to the set of activities most people first think of when they think of teaching: lecturing, calling on students, discussing, helping students with seatwork, and so on. When instruction is high in quality, the information presented makes sense to students, is interesting to them, and is easy to remember and apply.

The most important aspect of quality of instruction is the degree to which the lesson makes sense to students. To ensure that lessons make sense, teachers must present material in an orderly, organized way. They need to relate new information to what students already know. They need to use examples, demonstrations, pictures, and diagrams to make ideas vivid for students. They may use such cognitive strategies as advance organizers and memory strategies. Sometimes a concept will not make sense to students until they discover it or experience it themselves or until they discuss it with others.

Another important aspect of quality of instruction is the degree to which the teacher monitors how well students are learning and adapts the pace of instruction so that it is neither too fast nor too slow. For example, teachers should ask questions frequently to determine how much students have grasped. If the answers show that students are keeping up with the lesson, the teacher might move along a little more rapidly. But if students' answers show that they are having trouble keeping up, the teacher might review parts of the lesson and slow down the pace.

APPROPRIATE LEVELS OF INSTRUCTION ● Perhaps the most difficult problem of classroom organization is dealing with the fact that students come into class with different levels of prior knowledge, skills, and motivation, and with different learning rates (Corno, 1995). This was Mr. Arbuthnot's main dilemma. Student diversity requires teachers to provide appropriate levels of instruction. Teaching a class of 30 students (or even a class of 10) is fundamentally different from one-to-one tutoring because of the inevitability of student-to-student differences that affect the success of instruction. Teachers can always be sure that if they teach one lesson to the whole class, some students will learn the material much more quickly than others. In fact, some students may not learn the lesson at all; they may lack important prerequisite skills or may not be given adequate time (because to give them enough time would waste too much of the time of students who learn rapidly). Recognition of these instructionally important differences leads many teachers to search for ways of individualizing instruction, adapting instruction to meet students' different needs, or grouping students according to their abilities.

However, some of these solutions create problems of their own that may be more serious than the ones they are meant to solve. For example, a teacher may give all students materials that are appropriate to their individual needs and allow students to work at their own rates. This solves the problem of providing appropriate levels of instruction but creates serious new problems of managing the activities of 20 or 30 students doing 20 or 30 different things. A teacher may group students by ability (e.g., Redbirds, Bluebirds, and Yellowbirds) so that each group will have a relatively narrow range of abilities. However, this creates problems, too, because when the teacher is working with the Redbirds, the Bluebirds and Yellowbirds must work without supervision or help. Effective ways of adapting instruction to meet student needs are discussed later in this chapter.

INCENTIVE ● Thomas Edison once wrote that "genius is one per cent inspiration and ninety-nine per cent perspiration." The same could probably be said of learning. Learning is work. This is not to say that learning isn't or can't be fun or stimulating—far from it. But it is true that students must exert themselves to pay attention, to conscientiously perform the tasks required of them, and to study; and students must somehow be motivated to do these things. This incentive, or motivation, may come from characteristics of the tasks themselves (e.g., the interest value of the material being learned), from characteristics of students (such as their curiosity or positive orientation toward learning), or from rewards provided by the teacher or the school (such as grades and certificates).

If students want to know something, they will be motivated to exert the necessary effort to learn it. This is why there are students who can rattle off the names, batting averages, number of home runs, and all sorts of other information about every player of the Chicago Cubs but can't name the 50 states or perform basic multiplication. To such students, baseball facts have great interest value, so they are willing to invest a great deal of effort to master them. Some information is naturally interesting to some or all students, but teachers can do much to create interest in a topic by arousing students' curiosity or by showing how knowledge gained in school can be useful outside of school. For example, baseball fans may be much more interested in learning about computing proportions if they are convinced that this information is necessary for computing batting averages.

However, not every subject can be made fascinating to all students at all times. Most students need some kind of recognition or reward if they are to exert maximum effort to learn skills or concepts that may seem unimportant at the moment but will be critical for later learning. For this reason, schools use praise, feedback, grades, certificates, stars, prizes, and other rewards to increase student motivation.

CONNECTIONS

The rewards and general principles of motivation are discussed throughout Chapter 10.

TIME ● The final element of the QAIT model is time. Instruction takes time. More time spent teaching something does not necessarily mean more learning, but if instructional quality, appropriateness of instruction, and incentive are all high, then more time on instruction will pay off in greater learning. The amount of time that is available for learning depends largely on two factors. The first is the amount of time that the teacher (1) schedules for instruction and (2) actually uses to teach. The other is the amount of time students pay attention to the lesson. Both kinds of time are affected by classroom management and discipline strategies. If students are well behaved, are well motivated, and have a sense of purpose and direction and if teachers are well prepared and well organized, then there is plenty of time for students to learn whatever teachers want to teach. However, many factors, such as interruptions, behavior problems, and poor transitions between activities, eat away at the time available for learning (see Karweit, 1989c).

CONNECTIONS

Principles of classroom management and discipline are discussed throughout Chapter 11.

SELF-CHECK

Draw a diagram showing the significance of and interrelationships among the following terms: (1) strong incentive; (2) appropriate levels of instruction; (3) high quality of curriculum; (4) high quality of lesson presentation; (5) effective instruction; and (6) optimal use of time.

HOW ARE STUDENTS GROUPED TO ACCOMMODATE ACHIEVEMENT DIFFERENCES?

CONNECTIONS

To learn more about student differences in general intelligence, specific aptitudes, and abilities and learning styles, see Chapter 4, page 128.

From the day they walk into school, students differ in their knowledge, skills, motivations, and predispositions toward what is about to be taught. Some students are already reading when they enter kindergarten; others need much time and support to learn to read well. A teacher starting a new lesson can usually assume that some students already know a great deal about the lesson's content, some know less but will master the content early on, and some may not be able to master the content at all within the time provided (see Biemiller, 1993). Some have the prerequisite skills and knowledge they need in order to learn the lesson, while others do not. This was Mr. Arbuthnot's problem: Some of his students were not ready to learn long division, while others had already learned it before he began. Some of his students lacked basic multiplication and subtraction skills that are crucial for long division. Others already knew long division before he began his lesson, and many probably learned it during the first lesson and did not need the second. If Mr. Arbuthnot stops to review multiplication and division, he will be wasting the time of the better-prepared students. If he sets his pace of instruction according to the needs of his more able students, those with learning problems will never catch up. How can Mr. Arbuthnot teach a lesson that will work for all of his students, who are performing within the normal range but differ in prior knowledge, skills, and learning rates?

Accommodating instruction to student differences is one of the most fundamental problems of education and often leads to politically and emotionally charged policies (Loveless, 1998). For example, most countries outside of North America attempt to deal with the problem of student differences, or student heterogeneity, by testing children at around 10 to 12 years of age and assigning them to different types of schools, only one of which is meant to prepare students for higher education. These systems have long been under attack and are changing in some countries (such as the United Kingdom) but remain in others (such as Germany). In the United States a similar function is carried out by assignment of students to college preparatory, general, and vocational **tracks.** Tracking, in which students are assigned to a specified curriculum sequence within which they take all their academic courses, has rapidly diminished in the 1980s and 1990s. Today, most secondary schools place students in ability-grouped classes separately by subject area; a student may be in a high-level math class but in a middle- or low-level English class

tracks
Curriculum sequences to which students of specified achievement or ability level are assigned.

(Loveless, 1998). Many secondary schools allow students, in consultation with counselors, to choose the level of each class, perhaps changing levels if a course turns out to be too difficult or too easy. All of these strategies, which result in students' attending classes that are more or less homogeneous in performance level, are called **between-class ability grouping** (Slavin, 1991). This is the predominant form of ability grouping in middle, junior high, and high schools and is sometimes used in elementary schools. Another common means of accommodating instruction to student differences in elementary schools is **within-class ability grouping,** as in the use of reading groups (Bluebirds, Redbirds, Yellowbirds) that divide students according to their reading performance (Lou et al., 1996). The problem of accommodating student differences is so important that many educators have suggested that instruction be completely individualized so that students can work independently at their own rates. This point of view has led to the creation of individualized instructional programs and computer-based instruction.

Each of the many ways of accommodating students' differences has its own benefits, but each introduces its own problems, which sometimes outweigh the benefits. This chapter discusses the research on various means of accommodating classroom instruction to student differences. Some student differences can be easily accommodated. For example, teachers can often accommodate different learning styles by, for example, augmenting oral presentations with visual cues—perhaps writing on the chalkboard or showing pictures and diagrams to emphasize important concepts. A teacher can accommodate other differences in learning style by varying classroom activities, as in alternating active and quiet tasks or individual and group work. Teachers can sometimes work with students on an individual basis and adapt instruction to their learning styles—for example, by reminding impulsive students to take their time or by teaching overly reflective students strategies for skipping over items with which they are having problems so that they can complete tests on time.

Differences in prior knowledge and learning rates are more difficult to deal with. Sometimes the best way to deal with these differences is to ignore them: to teach the whole class at a single pace, perhaps offering additional help to low-achieving students and giving extra enrichment activities to students who tend to finish assignments rapidly. Appropriate use of cooperative learning methods, in which students of different performance levels can help each other, can be an effective means of helping all children learn (Slavin, 1995a). Some subjects lend themselves more than others to a single pace of instruction for all (Slavin, 1993a). For example, it is probably less important to accommodate student achievement differences in social studies, science, and English than in mathematics, reading, and foreign languages. This is because in the latter subjects, skills build directly on one another, so teaching at one pace to a heterogeneous class may do a disservice to both low and high achievers; low achievers may fail because they lack prerequisite skills, and high achievers may become bored at what is for them a slow pace of instruction. This was the case in Mr. Arbuthnot's mathematics class.

The following sections discuss strategies for accommodating student achievement differences.

Between-Class Ability Grouping

Probably the most common means of dealing with instructionally important differences is to assign students to classes according to their abilities. This between-class ability grouping may take many forms. In high schools there may be college preparatory and general tracks that divide students on the basis of measured ability.

between-class ability grouping
The practice of grouping students in separate classes according to ability level.

within-class ability grouping
A system of accommodating student differences by dividing a class of students into two or more ability groups for instruction in certain subjects.

In some junior high and middle schools, students are assigned to one class by general ability, and they then stay with that class, moving from teacher to teacher. For example, the highest-performing seventh-graders might be assigned to class 7–1, middle-performing students to 7–5, and low-performing students to 7–12. In other junior high and middle schools (and in many high schools), students are grouped separately by ability for each subject, so a student might be in a high-performing math class and an average-performing science class (Slavin, 1993b). In high schools this is accomplished by course placements. For example, some ninth-graders take Algebra I, while others who do not qualify for Algebra I take general mathematics. Elementary schools use a wide range of strategies for grouping students, including many of the patterns that are used in secondary schools. Often, students in elementary schools will be assigned to a mixed-ability class for homeroom, social studies, and science but regrouped by ability for reading and math. Elementary schools are less likely than secondary schools to use ability grouping between classes but more likely to use ability grouping within classes, especially in reading (McPartland, Coldiron, & Braddock, 1987). At any level, however, provision of separate special-education programs for students with serious learning problems is one form of between-class ability grouping, as is provision of separate programs for academically gifted and talented students.

CONNECTIONS

Programs for students who are gifted and who have special needs are discussed in Chapter 12, pages 428 and 429.

RESEARCH ON BETWEEN-CLASS ABILITY GROUPING ● Despite the widespread use of between-class ability grouping, research on this strategy does not support its use. Researchers have found that although ability grouping may have slight benefits for students who are assigned to high-track classes, these benefits are balanced by losses for students who are assigned to low-track classes (Argys, Rees, & Brewer, 1995; Oakes & Wells, 1998; Pallas, Entwistle, Alexander, & Stluka, 1994; Slavin, 1987b, 1990).

Why is between-class ability grouping so ineffective? Several researchers have explored this question. The primary purpose of ability grouping is to reduce the range of student performance levels that teachers must deal with so that they can adapt instruction to the needs of a well-defined group. However, grouping is often done on the basis of standardized test scores or other measures of general ability rather than according to performance in a particular subject. As a result, the reduction in the range of differences that are actually important for a specific class may be too small to make much difference (Oakes, 1995). Furthermore, concentrating low-achieving students in low-track classes seems to be harmful because it exposes them to too few positive role models (Page, 1991). Then, too, many teachers do not like to teach such classes and may subtly (or not so subtly) communicate low expectations for students in them (Weinstein, 1996). Studies find that teachers actually do not make many adaptations to the needs of students in low-ability groups (Ross, Smith, Lohr, & McNelis, 1994). Several studies have found that the quality of instruction is lower in low-track classes than in middle- or high-track classes. For example, teachers of low-track classes are less enthusiastic, are less organized, and teach more facts and fewer concepts than do teachers of high-track classes (Gamoran, Nystrand, Berends, & LePore, 1995; Muskin, 1990; Oakes, 1995; Raudenbush, Rowan, & Cheong, 1993). Instruction in mixed-ability, untracked classes more closely resembles that in high- and middle-track classes than that in low-track classes (Goodlad, 1983; Oakes, 1985). Perhaps the most damaging effect of tracking is its stigmatizing effect on students who are assigned to the low tracks; the message these students get is that academic success is not within their capabilities (Oakes & Guiton, 1995; Page, 1991). Schafer and Olexa (1971) interviewed one non-college-prep girl who said that she carried her general-track books upside down to avoid being humiliated while walking down the hall. One student described in an interview how he felt when he went to junior high school and found out that he was in the basic track:

> I felt good when I was with my [elementary] class, but when they went and separated us—that changed us. That changed our ideas, our thinking, the way we thought about each other, and turned us to enemies toward each other—because they said I was dumb and they were smart.
>
> When you first go to junior high school you do feel something inside—it's like a ego. You have been from elementary to junior high, you feel great inside . . . you get this shirt that says Brown Junior High . . . and you are proud of that shirt. But then you go up there and the teacher says—"Well, so and so, you're in the basic section, you can't go with the other kids." The devil with the whole thing—you lose—something in you—like it goes out of you. (Schafer and Olexa, 1971, pp. 62–63)

Students in lower-track classes are far more likely than other students to become delinquent and truant and drop out of school (Goodlad, 1983; Oakes, 1985; Rosenbaum, 1980). These problems are certainly due in part to the fact that students in low-track classes are low in academic performance to begin with. However, this is probably not the whole story. For example, students who are assigned to the low track in junior high school experience a rapid loss of self-esteem (Goodlad, 1983), as the preceding interview illustrates. Slavin and Karweit (1982) found that fifth- and sixth-graders in urban elementary schools were absent about 8 percent of the time. When these same students entered the tracked junior high school, absenteeism rose almost immediately to 26 percent, and the truancy was concentrated among students assigned to the bottom-track classes. The change happened too rapidly to be attributed entirely to characteristics of students. Something about the organization of the junior high school apparently convinced a substantial number of students that school was no longer a rewarding place to be.

Some of these students are reading well above grade level, whereas others are still only learning to read. As a teacher, how might you accommodate instruction to their different abilities? What are the advantages and disadvantages of such strategies as between-class and within-class ability groupings?

One of the most insidious aspects of tracking is that it often creates low-track classes that are composed predominantly of students from lower socioeconomic backgrounds and from minority groups, while upper-track classes are more often composed of children from higher socioeconomic levels (Braddock & Dawkins, 1993; Dornbusch, 1994). There is evidence that this difference is due in part to discrimination (intended or not) against African American and Latino students (Hoffer & Nelson, 1993). Even if it were not, the creation of groupings that are associated with social class and race is impossible to justify in light of the lack of evidence that such groupings are educationally necessary.

Although individual teachers can rarely set policies on between-class ability grouping, it is useful for all educators to know that research does not support this practice at any grade level, and tracking should be avoided whenever possible. This does not mean that all forms of between-class grouping should be abandoned, however. For example, there is probably some justification for acceleration programs, such as offering Algebra I to mathematically talented seventh-graders or offering advanced placement classes in high school (e.g., Swiatek & Benbow, 1991). Also, some between-class grouping is bound to occur in secondary schools, because some students choose to take advanced courses and others do not. However, the idea that having high, middle, and low sections of the same course can help student achievement has not been supported by research. Mixed-ability classes can be successful at all grade levels, particularly if other, more effective means of accommodating student differences are used. These include within-class ability grouping, tutoring for low achievers, and certain individualized instruction programs that are described in this chapter, as well as cooperative learning strategies.

Untracking

There has been a movement in recent years to challenge the use of between-class ability grouping at all levels. Influential groups such as the National Governors' Association (1993) and the Carnegie Corporation of New York (1989) have recommended moving away from traditional ability grouping practices, and a number of guides to untracking and examples of successful untracking have been published (e.g., Bellanca & Swartz, 1993; Cusik, 1993; MacIver, Reumann, & Main, 1995; Marsh & Raywid, 1994; Oakes, Quartz, Gong, Guiton, & Lipton, 1993; Oxley, 1994; Pool & Page, 1995; Wheelock, 1992). **Untracking** recommendations focus on having students in mixed-ability groups and holding them to high standards but providing many ways for them to reach those standards, including extra assistance for students who are having difficulties keeping up (Corno, 1995). Use of appropriate forms of cooperative learning and project-based learning has often been recommended as a means of opening up more avenues to high performance for all children (Cohen, 1992; George, 1992; Pool & Page, 1995). Yet the road to untracking is far from easy, especially in middle schools and high schools. In particular, untracking often runs into serious opposition from the parents of high achievers. Oakes and colleagues (1993) and Wells, Hirshberg, Lipton, & Oakes (1995) have pointed out that untracking requires changes in thinking about children's potentials, not only changes in school or classroom practices. Teachers, parents, and students themselves, these researchers claim, must come to see the goal of schooling as success for every child, not as sorting students into categories, if untracking is to take hold (Hubbard & Mehan, 1997). This change in perceptions is difficult to bring about; perhaps as a result, the move toward untracking is going slowly at the secondary level.

CONNECTIONS

Cooperative learning strategies are described in Chapter 8, page 269.

CONNECTIONS

Various forms of cooperative and project-based learning are described in Chapter 8, page 269.

untracking

A focus on having students in mixed-ability groups and holding them to high standards but providing many ways for students to reach those standards.

Regrouping for Reading and Mathematics

Another form of ability grouping that is often used in the elementary grades is **regrouping.** In regrouping plans, students are in mixed-ability classes most of the day but are assigned to reading and/or math classes on the basis of their performance in these subjects. For example, at 9:30 A.M. the fourth-graders in a school may move to different teachers so that they can receive reading instruction that is appropriate to their reading levels. One form of regrouping for reading, the **Joplin Plan,** regroups students across grade lines. For example, a reading class at the fourth-grade, first-semester reading level may contain third-, fourth-, and fifth-graders.

One major advantage of regrouping over all-day ability grouping is that in regrouping plans the students spend most of the day in a mixed-ability class. Thus low achievers are not separated out as a class and stigmatized. Perhaps for these reasons, regrouping plans, especially the Joplin Plan, have generally been found to increase student achievement (Gutierrez & Slavin, 1992; Slavin, 1987b).

Nongraded (Cross-Age Grouping) Elementary Schools

A form of grouping that was popular in the 1960s and early 1970s that is returning in various forms today is nongraded organization, or cross-age grouping (Fogarty, 1993; Pavan, 1992). **Nongraded programs** (or *cross-age grouping programs*) combine children of different ages in the same classes. Most often, students aged 5 to 7 or 6 to 8 may be mixed in a nongraded primary program. Students work across age lines but are often flexibly grouped for some instruction according to their needs and performance levels (Kasten & Lolli, 1998). A review of research on the nongraded programs of the 1960s and 1970s found that these programs had a positive effect on achievement when they focused on flexible grouping for instruction but were less effective when they had a strong focus on individualized instruction (Gutiérrez & Slavin, 1992). In essence, the nongraded elementary school ultimately became the open classroom, which emphasized individualized learning activities and deemphasized teacher instruction. Research on the open classroom similarly failed to find achievement benefits (Giaconia & Hedges, 1982). There has been little research on today's application of the nongraded primary program (see Pavan, 1992), but one study did find achievement benefits for a nongraded school (Tanner & Decotis, 1994).

Sometimes cross-grade grouping is used out of necessity, because there are too few children at a given grade level to make up a whole class. Such combination classes (e.g., grades 3–4 or 5–6) have not been found to enhance student achievement and may even be harmful (Mason & Burns, 1997; Veenman, 1995, 1997).

Within-Class Ability Grouping

Another way to adapt instruction to differences in student performance levels is to group students within classes, as is typical in elementary school reading classes. For example, a third-grade teacher might have the Rockets group using a 3–1 (third-grade, first-semester) text, the Stars group using a 3–2 (third-grade, second-semester) text, and the Planets group using a 4–1 (fourth-grade, first-semester) text.

Within-class ability grouping is far more common in elementary schools than in secondary schools (McPartland et al., 1987), and it is very common in elementary reading classes. Surveys of principals have found that more than 90 percent of elementary reading teachers use multiple reading groups (Puma et al., 1997),

regrouping
A method of ability grouping in which students in mixed-ability classes are assigned to reading or math classes on the basis of their performance levels.

Joplin Plan
A regrouping method in which students are grouped across grade lines for reading instruction.

nongraded programs
Programs, generally at the primary level, that combine children of different ages in the same class. Also called *cross-age grouping programs.*

whereas only 15 to 18 percent of elementary math teachers do so (Good, Mulryan, & McCaslin, 1992; Mason, 1995). Within-class ability grouping is rare in subjects other than reading or mathematics. In reading, teachers typically have each group working at a different point in a series of reading texts and allow each group to proceed at its own pace. Teachers who group in math may use different texts with the different groups or, more often, allow groups to proceed at their own rates in the same book, so the higher-performing group will cover more material than the lower-performing group. In many math classes the teacher teaches one lesson to the whole class and then meets with two or more ability groups during times when students are doing seatwork to reinforce skills or provide enrichment as needed.

RESEARCH ON WITHIN-CLASS ABILITY GROUPING ● Research on the achievement effects of within-class ability grouping has taken place almost exclusively in elementary mathematics classes. The reason is that researchers want to look at teaching situations in which some teachers use within-class ability grouping and others do not, and this is typically true only in elementary math. Until recently, almost all elementary reading teachers used reading groups, whereas in elementary subjects other than math, and in secondary classes, very few teachers did. Most studies that have evaluated within-class ability grouping methods in math (in which the different groups proceed at different paces on different materials) have found that students in the ability-grouped classes learned more than did students in classes that did not use grouping (Slavin, 1987b). Students of high, average, and low achievement levels seem to benefit equally from within-class ability grouping (Lou et al., 1996). One study by Mason and Good (1993) found that teachers who flexibly grouped and regrouped students according to their needs had better math achievement outcomes than did those who used permanent within-class groups.

The research suggests that small numbers of ability groups are better than large numbers (Slavin & Karweit, 1984). Smaller numbers of groups have the advantage of allowing more direct instruction from the teacher and using less seatwork time and transition time. With three groups this rises to two thirds of class time.

Teachers who try to teach more than three reading or math groups may also have problems with classroom management. Dividing the class into more than three groups does not decrease the magnitude or range of differences within each group enough to offset these problems (see Hiebert, 1983).

It is important to note that the research finding benefits of within-class grouping in elementary mathematics was mostly done many years ago with traditional teaching methods that were intended primarily to teach computation rather than problem solving. As mathematics moves toward use of constructivist approaches that are more directed at problem solving, discovery, and cooperative learning, within-class grouping may become unnecessary (Good et al., 1992). The main point to be drawn from research on within-class ability grouping is not that it is desirable but that if some form of grouping is thought to be necessary, grouping within the class is preferable to grouping between classes. Beyond its more favorable achievement outcomes, within-class grouping can be more flexible and less stigmatizing and occupies a much smaller portion of the school day than between-class grouping does (Rowan & Miracle, 1983).

SELF-CHECK

Describe the two major types of ability grouping. Give examples of their appropriate use. What does the research literature say about the effectiveness of ability grouping?

WHAT IS MASTERY LEARNING?

One means of adapting instruction to the needs of diverse students is called **mastery learning** (Guskey, 1995). The basic idea behind mastery learning is to make sure that all or almost all students have learned a particular skill to a preestablished level of mastery before moving on to the next skill.

Mastery learning was first proposed as a solution to the problem of individual differences by Benjamin Bloom (1976), who based his recommendations in part on the earlier work of John Carroll (1963). As was discussed earlier in this chapter, Carroll had suggested that school learning was related to the amount of time needed to learn what was being taught and the amount of time spent on instruction.

One implication of Carroll's model is that if time spent is the same for all students and all students receive the same kind of instruction, then differences in student achievement will primarily reflect differences in student aptitude. However, in 1968, Bloom proposed that rather than providing all students with the same amount of instructional time and allowing learning to differ, perhaps we should require that all or almost all students reach a certain level of achievement by allowing time to differ. That is, Bloom suggested that we give students as much time and instruction as they need to bring them all to a reasonable level of learning. If some students appear to be in danger of not learning, then they should be given additional instruction until they do learn.

The assumption underlying mastery learning is that almost every student can learn the essential skills in a curriculum. This assumption is both communicated to the students and acted on by the teacher, whose job it is to provide the instruction necessary to make the expectation come true.

Forms of Mastery Learning

The problem inherent in any mastery learning strategy is how to provide the additional instructional time to students who need it. In some of the research on mastery learning, this additional instruction was given outside of regular class time, such as after school or during recess. Students who failed to meet a preestablished **mastery criterion** (such as 90 percent correct on a quiz) following a lesson were given this extra **corrective instruction** until they could earn a 90 percent score on a similar quiz. Research on mastery learning programs that provide corrective instruction in addition to regular class time has generally found achievement gains, particularly for low achievers (Bloom, 1984; Kulik, Kulik, & Bangert-Drowns, 1990; Slavin, 1987c).

Forms of mastery learning that require additional instructional time are not easily applicable to elementary or secondary education, in which amounts of time available are relatively fixed. For example, it is possible to have students stay after school to receive corrective instruction for a few weeks, but this would be difficult to arrange over the long haul. Also, there is some question whether the additional time required for corrective instruction in mastery learning might not be better spent in covering more material.

> **mastery learning**
> A system of instruction that seeks to enable all students to achieve instructional objectives by allowing learning time to vary as needed.
>
> **mastery criterion**
> A standard that students must meet to be considered proficient in a skill.
>
> **corrective instruction**
> Educational activities given to students who initially fail to master an objective; designed to increase the number of students who master educational objectives.

Applying the Principles of Mastery Learning

There's a classic Rolling Stones song called "Time Is on My Side." There probably couldn't be a less appropriate theme song for teachers. Yet because a significant element of mastery learning is the varying of time to meet individual needs, we cannot discuss the application of this approach without addressing realistic strategies for working within the time constraints of today's classrooms.

THEORY *into* Practice

The basic assumption of mastery learning is that almost all students can learn the essential knowledge and skills within a curriculum when the learning is broken into its component parts and presented sequentially. To implement this approach effectively, teachers must meet several challenges.

The first challenge is to find the time to engage in effective planning prior to instruction. Whether you use whole-group or individualized direct instruction, you will need to analyze thoroughly the content to be learned. This analysis will require you to divide the content and/or skills into small units that you can present sequentially using sound teaching strategies (such as clearly stated objectives, appropriate modeling, multiple opportunities for practice, feedback and correction, and so on).

Before beginning actual instruction, you will need to assess your students. The data you obtain will help you determine where in the sequence of the curriculum your instruction should begin. This assessment is a critical aspect of the mastery learning process, and it will take time to develop and administer the assessment and analyze the data. However, because preinstructional assessment allows you to be more efficient and effective in your instruction, you should view the time spent as "cost-effective." Quality assessment will allow you to link your instructional activities to individual student need.

While you are involved in actual instructional activities, another challenge you will face is how to address the variations in student learning. For students who quickly grasp concepts, you will need to promote learning by developing relevant enrichment opportunities. This extension of basic concepts will allow these students to remain engaged in appropriate higher-level learning activities while simultaneously allowing you to extend the learning opportunities of the students who need more time to master the basics.

To increase the effectiveness of the instructional process and subsequent student learning, you should engage in ongoing **formative evaluations:** frequent assessments of student learning that will enable you to adjust your instruction to meet the individual needs of your students. This assessment process can be most useful if it is authentic (that is, related to real-world situations) and is a natural part of the teaching/learning process.

As students in your classroom progress through the learning sequence, you may find your **summative evaluations,** or final evaluations on each objective, reveal that some learners still have not reached a mastery level of the basic knowledge/skills within the time frame you have provided. In these cases, you will likely need to develop creative ways for reteaching, presenting alternative learning opportunities, and/or extending practice. Strategies such as those already mentioned in the text (e.g., after-school corrective instruction, peer or cross-age tutoring, or use of paraprofessionals) can help students achieve mastery of the essentials.

Initially, this process will seem time-consuming. However, working with your grade-level or discipline-area colleagues can be productive: This collaborative approach will allow you to "divide and conquer" the curriculum. Because a mastery learning approach can be labor and time intensive, you will want to be selective in its application. Identifying the key aspects of the curriculum to which mastery learning is most relevant and limiting the use of this approach to situations where prerequisite knowledge/skills are *essential* for future learning will enhance your ability to apply mastery learning principles effectively. You and your students will feel you've made a wise investment of time and energy when the payoff is increased achievement for all.

formative evaluations
Evaluations designed to determine whether additional instruction is needed.

summative evaluations
Final evaluations of students' achievement of an objective.

One form of mastery learning varies the instructional time given to students with different needs by providing corrective instruction to students who need it while allowing those who do not need it to do enrichment work. For example, a high school earth science teacher might teach a lesson on volcanoes and earthquakes. At the end of the lesson, students would be quizzed. Those who scored less than 80 percent would receive corrective instruction on concepts they had problems with, while the remaining students would do **enrichment activities,** such as finding out about the San Francisco earthquake or the Mount Vesuvius eruption that buried Pompeii.

Research on Mastery Learning

Research on the earliest conceptualization of mastery learning is much less clear than research on later-developed forms of this approach (see Ellis & Fouts, 1993; Slavin, 1987c). Studies of at least 4 weeks' duration in which instructional time was the same for mastery and nonmastery classes generally found either no differences in effectiveness or small and short-lived differences favoring the mastery groups. Some of the most promising forms of mastery learning are ones that combine this approach with cooperative learning, in which students work together to help each other learn in the first place and then help groupmates who need corrective instruction (Guskey, 1990; Mevarech & Kramarski, 1997).

The practical implications of research on mastery learning are only partially clear. First, if the staff time is available to provide corrective instruction in addition to regular classroom instruction, the effects of mastery learning on achievement can be quite positive. Second, any form of mastery learning can help teachers become clearer about their objectives, routinely assess student progress, and modify their instruction according to how well students are learning—all elements of effective instruction. Third, when high levels of mastery are needed to form a basis for later learning, mastery learning appears to be particularly appropriate. For example, many mathematics skills are fundamental for later learning, and these skills might profitably be taught through a mastery approach. Similarly, basic reading skills, map or chart interpretation, essential vocabulary and grammar in foreign languages, and elements of the periodic table lend themselves to mastery learning.

However, the central problem of mastery learning is that it involves a tradeoff between the amount of content that can be covered and the degree to which students master each concept (Slavin, 1987c). The time needed to bring all or almost all students to a preestablished level of mastery must come from somewhere. If corrective instruction is provided during regular class time, it must reduce content coverage. And, as was noted in Chapter 7, content coverage is one of the most important predictors of achievement gain (Cooley & Leinhardt, 1980). This is not at all to say that mastery learning should be used only when additional time for corrective instruction is available; it is merely to emphasize that teachers should be aware of the trade-off involved and make decisions accordingly.

enrichment activities
Assignments or activities designed to broaden or deepen the knowledge of students who master classroom lessons quickly.

CONNECTIONS
For more on the relation between content coverage and achievement gain, see Chapter 7, page 228.

SELF-CHECK

Define *mastery learning*. What are its underlying philosophy and assumptions? In what context is mastery learning appropriate? Explain formative assessment, summative assessment, and corrective instruction.

WHAT ARE SOME WAYS OF INDIVIDUALIZING INSTRUCTION?

The problem of providing all students with appropriate levels of instruction could be completely solved if schools could simply assign each student his or her own teacher. Not surprisingly, studies of one adult–one student tutoring find substantial positive effects of tutoring on student achievement (Wasik & Slavin, 1993). One major reason for the effectiveness of tutoring is that the tutor can provide **individualized instruction,** tailoring instruction precisely to a student's needs. If the student learns quickly, the tutor can move to other tasks; if not, the tutor can figure out what the problem is, try another explanation, or just spend more time on the task.

There are situations in which tutoring by adults is feasible and necessary. Peer tutors (usually older students working with younger ones) can also be very effective. In addition, educational innovators have long tried to simulate the one-to-one teaching situation by individualizing instruction with programmed instruction or computer-based instruction. All of these strategies are discussed in the following sections.

Peer Tutoring

Students can help one another learn. In **peer tutoring,** one student teaches another. There are two principal types of peer tutoring: **cross-age tutoring,** in which the tutor is several years older than the student being taught, and same-age peer tutoring, in which a student tutors a classmate. Cross-age tutoring is recommended by researchers more often than same-age tutoring—partly because of the obvious fact that older students are more likely to know the material, and partly because students may accept an older student as a tutor but resent having a classmate appointed to tutor them (Topping & Ehly, 1998). Sometimes peer tutoring is used with students who need special assistance, in which case a few older students might work with a few younger students. Other tutoring schemes have involved, for example, entire fifth-grade classes tutoring entire second-grade classes. In these cases, half of the younger students may be sent to the older students' classroom while half of the older students go to the younger students' classroom. Otherwise, peer tutoring may take place in the cafeteria, the library, or another school facility.

Peer tutoring among students of the same age can be easier to arrange and has also been found to be very effective (e.g., King, 1997; Simmons, Fuchs, Fuchs, Mathes, & Hodge, 1995). Among classmates of the same age and performance level, reciprocal peer tutoring, in which students take turns as tutors and tutees, can be both practical and effective (Fantuzzo, King, & Heller, 1992).

Adequate training and monitoring of tutors are essential (Jenkins & Jenkins, 1987). Tutors who have been taught specific tutoring strategies produce much better results than do those who have not had such training (Fuchs, Fuchs, Bentz, Phillips, & Hamlett, 1994; Merrill, Reiser, Merrill, & Landes, 1995). Also, involving parents in support of a tutoring program enhances its effectiveness (Fantuzzo, Davis, & Ginsburg, 1995).

RESEARCH ON PEER TUTORING ● Research evaluating the effects of peer tutoring on student achievement has generally found that this strategy increases the achievement of both tutees and tutors (Fantuzzo et al., 1992; King, Staffieni, &

individualized instruction
Instruction tailored to particular students' needs, in which each student works at his or her own level and rate.

peer tutoring
Tutoring of one student by another.

cross-age tutoring
Tutoring of a younger student by an older one.

What type of tutoring is taking place in this picture? What other means of individualizing instruction are available to you as a teacher?

Adelgais, 1998; Rekrut, 1992; Simmons et al., 1995). In fact, some studies have found greater achievement gains for tutors than for tutees (Rekrut, 1992), and peer tutoring is sometimes used as much to improve the achievement of low-achieving older students as to improve that of the students being tutored (Top & Osguthorpe, 1987). As many teachers have noted, the best way to learn something thoroughly is to teach it to someone else. High achievers who tutor other students usually enjoy and value this activity (Thorkildsen, 1993).

Adult Tutoring

One-to-one adult-to-child tutoring is one of the most effective instructional strategies known, and it essentially solves the problem of appropriate levels of instruction. The principal drawback to this method is its cost. However, it is often possible, on a small scale, to provide adult tutors for students who are having problems learning in the regular class setting. For example, adult volunteers such as parents, college students, or senior citizens are often willing to tutor students (Morris, Shaw, & Perney, 1990). Volunteer tutors who are well supervised and who use well-structured materials can have a positive effect on children's reading performance (Wasik, in press). Tutoring is an excellent use of school aides; some school districts hire large numbers of paraprofessional aides precisely for this purpose. In fact, classroom aides often have little impact on student achievement unless they are doing one-to-one tutoring (see Slavin, 1994b).

There are some circumstances in which the high costs of one-to-one tutoring can be justified. One of these is that of first-graders who are having difficulties learning to read. Failing to learn to read in the lower grades of elementary school is so detrimental to later school achievement that an investment in tutors who can prevent reading failure is worthwhile. A one-to-one tutoring program, Reading Recovery, uses highly trained, certified teachers to work with first-graders who are at risk for failing to learn to read. Research on this strategy has found that students who received tutoring in first grade read significantly better than comparable students (Pinnell, 1989; Pinnell, Lyons, DeFord, Bryk, & Seltzer, 1994). Another effective program, Success for All, makes extensive use of one-to-one tutoring for at-risk first-graders (Slavin et al., 1996). Reading Recovery and Success for All are discussed later in this chapter. Other one-to-one tutoring programs for at-risk first-graders have also found substantial positive effects (see Wasik & Slavin, 1993).

THEORY into Practice

Effectively Using Tutoring Methods to Meet Individual Needs

Peer tutoring is an effective way to improve learning for both the tutee and the tutor, and no one doubts the value of this strategy for meeting individual needs within a classroom. However, it takes more than simply pairing off students to make peer tutoring result in improved learning.

Although you are likely to use informal tutoring practices in your classroom every day (e.g., asking one student to help another student with a problem), establishing a formalized tutoring program requires more involved planning. The following strategies can help you create and sustain an effective program within your classroom. As with most initiatives, if you can work with your building administrator and other teachers to establish a schoolwide tutoring program, you will be able to serve the needs of all students more successfully.

To establish a tutoring program, recognize that specific skills need to be developed in both the tutors and tutees. Whether the tutors are same-age peers, older students, or even adults, use care in selecting tutors. It is always wise to begin with volunteers. Consider not only the knowledge base of the tutors (i.e., their proven proficiency with the subject matter) but also their ability to convey their knowledge clearly.

Typically, training will be minimal and will include basic instruction in modeling, prompting responses from tutees, using corrective feedback and praise/reinforcement, alternating teaching methods and materials (i.e., using multisensory methods), and recording and reporting progress. If this is a schoolwide initiative, classroom teachers or even parents or paraprofessionals can train students who will tutor as part of an extracurricular service activity.

Students receiving tutoring need to be clear about their role in this process. It would be counterproductive to force any student into a tutorial relationship. Therefore, initially select only students who express a willingness to work with a tutor. Steadily make tutoring a part of the natural learning activities within a classroom or an entire school. In this collaborative model, every student at some point in time will have the opportunity to be both tutor and tutee. Even students with less knowledge and skills may be able to find peers or younger students with whom they can work. Many students with special education needs have gained confidence and improved their own abilities by working with younger students.

During the training process help all students to understand that the tutor represents the teacher and therefore should be respected accordingly. In addition, tutees and tutors must understand that the goal of the activity is to have each tutee reach a clear understanding of the concepts, not merely complete an assignment. To make this clear, you may want to use various role-playing activities during the training process. Demonstrate appropriate and inappropriate forms of instruction, feedback, reinforcement, and so on; then allow the participants to practice under supervised conditions. Corrective feedback within this controlled environment will allow you to feel more confident as the tutor–tutee pairs work together without your direct supervision.

Whether you decide to begin this process solely within your own classroom or to develop a schoolwide tutorial program, keep these issues in mind:

1. Tutors need to be trained in specific instructional practices.
2. Tutors and tutees need to have a clear understanding of their roles and expectations.
3. Tutors and tutees need to receive supervision and feedback about their work, particularly during the early stages of the tutoring process.
4. Teachers need to work with the tutors to create effective and efficient ways of recording and reporting the progress of the sessions.

Programmed Instruction

The term **programmed instruction** refers to individualized instruction methods in which students work on self-instructional materials at their own levels and rates (see Fletcher, 1992). For example, in one math class, some students might be working on division, others on fractions, others on decimals, and still others on measurement or geometry, all at the same time. The materials that students use are meant to be self-instructional, which means that the students are expected to learn (at least in large part) from the materials, rather than principally from the teacher. For this reason, programmed instruction materials typically break skills down into small subskills so that students may go step by step with little chance of making an error at each step. The materials give frequent and immediate feedback so that students can check the correctness of their work.

Despite great expectations and considerable investments, the programmed instruction techniques that were developed in the 1960s and 1970s generally failed to show any achievement benefits. The results vary somewhat by subject, but with few exceptions, such as programs that combine individualized with cooperative methods (see Slavin, 1985), programmed instruction methods have not lived up to expectations. Partly as a result of these disappointing findings and partly because of the expense and difficulty of using programmed instruction, this strategy is seldom used today as a primary approach to instruction. However, similar approaches are quite common in computer-based instruction, which will be discussed below.

Computer-Based Instruction

One means of individualizing instruction that has been receiving a great deal of attention in recent years is **computer-based instruction (CBI).** The decreasing cost and increasing availability of microcomputers in schools have led researchers as well as teachers to become more interested in CBI. As of the 1995–96 school year, there were 4.4 million computers in U.S. elementary schools. A typical school owns 21 to 50 computers, and 98 percent have at least one (Educational Testing Service, 1996). There is approximately one computer for every 10 students, with a higher ratio in high schools than in middle or elementary schools.

The idea behind computer-based instruction is to use the computer as a tutor to present information, give students practice, assess their level of understanding, and provide additional instruction if needed. In theory, a well-designed CBI program is

programmed instruction
Structured lessons that students can work on individually, at their own paces.

computer-based instruction (CBI)
Individualized instruction that is administered by computer.

TEACHERS IN ACTION

Elizabeth J. Conway
High School Instructor
Texas School for the Deaf
Austin, Texas

What strategies have you used to meet students' individual needs for instruction?

Karen Kusayanagi
Fourth-Grade Teacher
Jean Hayman Elementary School
Lake Elsinore, California

As a reading and language instructor for deaf and hard-of-hearing high school students, I use a multitude of strategies simultaneously to facilitate learning. Every student has a different learning style, so my job is to find out what works best for each. At the beginning of the year, I plan learning opportunities during which I can observe each student in order to determine which style works for each one.

Among the strategies I use in my lessons are nongraded activities, mastery learning, word walls, picture dictionaries, and various other vocabulary development opportunities. As a team, our department has developed a curriculum that we feel works best with the individual students that we serve. We have also developed an Outcomes Test and End of Course Exams that each student must pass in order to move to the next level. This is an excellent way to evaluate our own teaching and curriculum.

In addition to each unit exam and the Outcomes Test, I use a variety of hands-on activities. I do not give students grades on these activities, but I do expect certain outcomes from each activity. The students and I do the planning together, they help one another prepare, and then we do the activity. One of our favorite activities was a project that involved reading recipes and measuring ingredients. The students decided to cook something, so together we found recipes and bought the ingredients. Then I helped the students form groups, and each one prepared one of the recipes, which involved lots of cooperation. Each group had a student who could read well, and he or she helped those who were having trouble.

The most important thing to remember as a teacher is to vary your strategies continually. Do not get stuck repeating the same thing merely because it is easy for you or because you already have it prepared. Too many teachers use worksheets and other paperwork to keep the classroom busy, often losing the students' enthusiasm in the process. Students' learning experiences should be positive and productive, and this calls for high-quality work from you as well as from them.

I feel that within-class ability grouping is essential to a good learning environment. To group my students for language arts, initially I use an informal reading assessment from a published whole-language series. I also examine each student's performance within the instructional setting. I then group each child, starting out with one group for "average" and one for "above average" and subdividing further as necessary. My day usually includes 30 minutes of whole-class instruction in spelling and grammar and then a longer period of small-group literature instruction. Moving to small groups is a little tricky. While one group is reading a new chapter or working on a project, I read, reteach grammar and spelling skills, and so on with the other group. The average/low average group always receives more time, because those students need more reinforcement and have greater difficulty working independently. Within my two large groups, I regroup the students every day into dyads, triads, girls and boys, all students wearing tennis shoes, all not wearing tennis shoes—anything clever. The kids love it and it helps keep the same kids from being together all the time. In addition, I love to use cooperative learning groups, especially for report writing and group projects.

Cooperative learning groups work best when the responsibility for cooperating is placed on the students themselves. They realize that they are a team and that if one person does not do his or her job, the rest of their team suffers. The children learn so much more from each other and from discovering things together that I feel cooperative learning should be a part of the day in every classroom.

nearly perfect at providing appropriate levels of instruction; it can analyze students' responses immediately to determine whether to spend more time on a particular topic or skill. The computer can be quite effective in presenting ideas, using pictures or diagrams to reinforce concepts. For many students the computer seems to have a motivating quality of its own so that they work longer and harder when using the computer than they would on comparable paper-and-pencil tasks. Many CBI programs stress drill and practice exercises; others teach students facts and concepts; others engage students in complex problem solving or discovery learning. Whatever their differences, CBI programs generally share the following characteristics: (1) using a structured curriculum; (2) letting students work at their own pace; (3) giving students controlled, frequent feedback and reinforcement; and (4) measuring performance quickly and giving students information on their performance.

TYPES OF COMPUTER APPLICATIONS IN THE CLASSROOM ● Computers are used for a variety of purposes in classrooms. See Figure 9.2 for a breakdown of how K–12 teachers use computers. A discussion of the most common classroom applications follows (see Geisert & Futrell, 1995; Hooper & Rieber, 1995; Provenzo, Brett, & McCloskey, 1998).

1. Drill and practice: One of the most common applications of microcomputers in education is to provide students with **drill and practice** on skills or knowledge. For example, many software programs provide students with practice on math facts or computations, geography, history facts, or science. Computer experts often frown on drill and practice programs as "electronic page turning," and the programs are generally less than exciting. They typically replace independent seatwork and do have several major advantages over seatwork, including immediate feedback; record keeping; and, in many cases, appealing graphics and variations in pace or level of items depending on the student's responses. Drill and practice programs should not be expected to teach; rather, they can reinforce skills or knowledge that students have learned elsewhere.

2. Tutorial programs: More sophisticated than drill and practice programs, **tutorial programs** are intended to teach new material. See Figure 9.3 for a sample of a tutorial program. The best tutorial programs come close to mimicking a patient human tutor. Increasingly, tutorial programs use speech and graphics to engage students' attention and present new information. Typically, students are asked many questions, and the program branches in different directions depending on the answers, reexplaining if the student makes mistakes or moving on if a student responds correctly. Very sophisticated tutorial programs that simulate the behaviors of expert

CONNECTIONS

To learn about the use of computers for students with disabilities, see Chapter 12, page 445.

drill and practice
Application of computer technology to provide students with practice of skills and knowledge.

tutorial programs
Computer programs that teach new material, varying their content and pace according to the student's responses.

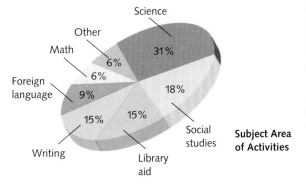

Science 31%
Other 6%
Math 6%
Foreign language 9%
Writing 15%
Library aid 15%
Social studies 18%

Subject Area of Activities

FIGURE 9.2 ● **How K–12 Teachers Use Computers**
From Jon Peha, "How K–12 Teachers Are Using Computer Networks," *Educational Leadership, 53*(2), October 1995, p. 21. Copyright © 1995 by ASCD. All rights reserved. Used by permission of the Association for Supervision and Curriculum Development.

FIGURE 9.3 ● **A Sample Tutorial Program**
Discovering Music by Voyetra Technologies presents a
complete introduction to the world of music.
(Courtesy of Voyetra Technologies.)

human tutors are being developed and applied in a variety of settings (Schofield, Eurich-Fuller, & Britt, 1994; Snow & Swanson, 1992).

3. Instructional games: Most children are first introduced to computers through video games, and many educators (and parents) have wondered whether the same intensity, motivation, and perseverance that they see in children playing Nintendo could be brought to the classroom. Many instructional games have been designed; most are simple extrapolations of drill and practice designs into a game format, but some are more creative. For example, the enormously popular program *Where in the World Is Carmen Sandiego?* is designed to teach geography by engaging children in tracking a gang of criminals through various countries.

4. Simulation software: Simulation software involves students in a simulation of some sort of reality. Students operate within a simulated environment and, by doing so, learn about that environment from the inside. For example, one of the earliest simulations, *Oregon Trail,* gives students limited allocations of food, water, money, horses, and other resources, and students must use these resources wisely to successfully move their wagon trains to the West. Other popular simulations let children build their own civilizations, build new forms of life, and so on. Simulations are engaging, fun, and creative, but there is little evidence that they improve achievement compared to traditional teaching methods (Geisert & Futrell, 1995; Woodward,

simulation software
Computer programs that model real-life phenomena to promote problem-solving abilities and motivate interest in the areas concerned.

Students can imagine what life was really like in this simulation program of the Old West. Oregon Trail II includes realistic images, video, digitized speech, and original music. (Courtesy of MECC.)

Carnine, & Gersten, 1988). The photo on page 310 shows students using a simulation program.

5. Word processing software: One of the fastest-growing educational applications of microcomputers is **word processing** or desktop publishing. Increasingly, students are asked to write compositions on classroom computers. A key advantage of word processing over paper-and-pencil composition is that word processing facilitates revision. Spell checkers and other utilities help students to worry less about mechanics and focus on the meaning and organization of their compositions. As writing instruction has moved toward an emphasis on a process of revision and editing, this capability has become very important. Word processing is probably the best-researched application of computers to instruction. Studies of word processing show that students who use computers write more, revise more, and take greater pride in their writing than do paper-and-pencil writers (Cochran-Smith, 1991; Russell, 1991). Writing quality tends to be somewhat better when students have access to word processors (Bangert-Drowns, 1993), and students often learn communication skills that generalize beyond the computer (Roblyer, Castine, & King, 1988). Of course, word processing itself has become an essential skill in a vast range of occupations, so teaching students to use word-processing programs (e.g., in high school business courses) has obvious value.

6. Spreadsheets and databases: As with word processing, use of spreadsheets and databases is an extension to education of software that adults use widely. Spreadsheets are used to organize and compute data. Typically, they can convert raw data into graphs, charts, and other data summaries so that students can easily organize information and see the effects of different variables on outcomes. For example, a student could enter data for the number of tadpoles caught in each of five ponds at three times. By assigning a formula to a given column, the student could customize the spreadsheet program to total the numbers for each pond and each time. Changing any number would automatically change row and column totals. The spreadsheet program could then show the data in raw, numeric form or convert the data into a graph. Teachers use spreadsheets in gradebook, scheduling, and other programs, and students are increasingly using them to record data from science experiments and to reinforce mathematics skills.

Databases are more powerful than spreadsheets. A database is a computer program that keeps a lot of information to be referred to later on and sometimes manipulated.

There are two types of databases. The first type is an all-information database. An example is information that is available on CD-ROMs, such as encyclopedias, or information that is available in libraries. The other type consists of databases that are used as worksheets. In this case the database is used to program and store information, then portions of the information are stored and used in analyses and computations.

7. CD-ROM: CD-ROM (*ROM* stands for *read-only memory*) databases provide information including pictures, music, and sometimes video. Students can learn to search CD-ROM databases such as encyclopedias, road maps, catalogs, and so on to find information for a variety of instructional purposes. Databases of this type can be particularly important in project-based learning, because they may put a great deal of information into easy reach for open-ended reports and other projects. Access to CD-ROM technology is growing rapidly; in 1995–96, 54 percent of schools had this capability (ETS, 1996).

8. Hypertext and hypermedia: Hypertext programs are incorporated with many CD-ROM databases. In these programs, students can search a database (such

word processing
A computer application for writing compositions that lends itself to revising and editing.

CD-ROM
A computer database designed for read-only memory that provides massive amounts of information, including pictures and audio; can be of particular importance to students doing projects and research activities.

CONNECTIONS
For more on project-based learning, see Chapter 8, page 273.

CASE TO CONSIDER

Individualization and Computers: Two Perspectives

Liz Stephens and Mark Monroe teach sections of ninth- and tenth-grade English at Middleton High School. This year they have six new computer systems and a quiet laser printer in the back of each of their classrooms.

Liz: I haven't settled on specific uses for my computers yet. Have you?

Mark: I think so. My ninth-grade classes are all over the place when it comes to basic writing skills. I'm going to use an integrated learning system in my class to individualize the lessons.

Liz: How does the ILS you're thinking about work?

Mark: The ILS the district bought a few years ago has well over two hundred short lessons on topics we cover in our composition classes. After taking the diagnostic pretest, my students will sit down at the computer, and the ILS program will bring up a lesson they need. When they finish the lesson, the ILS will test them on that material and prescribe remedial work if needed. It's great!

Liz: I thought about doing something like that, but I wonder whether students will get bored. Most of the lessons require students to read a paragraph or two, answer a multiple-choice question, read a little more, and answer another question.

Mark: Some of the stuff is boring, but I don't see any way to make a lesson on semicolons as exciting as a Boyz II Men concert.

Liz: Actually, I'm leaning in another direction. I posted a message on one of the America Online electronic forums for teachers, and several answered my message. Quite a few are using computers for problem-based learning.

Mark: I'm not familiar with that approach. How does it work?

Liz: The teacher, or the students, pose a question or problem. It might be "Are the topics that interest teenagers different from country to country or the same?" Then collaborative groups of students use the computers to search for information they need. Some might use encyclopedias on CD-ROM or post a message on an electronic service that teens in other countries read. They might also use computers to organize the data they collect and to create a report on their conclusions.

Mark: I guess they would have a lot of fun doing that, but how would that teach them the basics?

Liz: As they needed those basics, I might teach little mini-lessons or direct them to writing helper programs that they can pop up on the computer screen while they're writing.

PROBLEM SOLVING

1. Mark and Liz seem to take fundamentally different approaches to teaching. Which approaches to individualization would Mark be likely to prefer? Which approaches would appeal to Liz? Why would they prefer different approaches?

2. Are there times when it would be more appropriate to use computers to support direct instruction? Student-centered instruction? Does it depend on the type or difficulty level of content? On differences in students? On characteristics of the teacher?

3. What problems would you expect Liz to encounter if she implemented her plan? What problems would Mark encounter? How could they overcome the problems?

---

as an encyclopedia) by clicking on a word or picture. This leads the student to related or more detailed information on a specific portion of the text. Hypermedia can similarly provide pictures, music, video footage, or other information to illuminate and extend the information on a CD-ROM database (Bortnick, 1995; Carver, Lehrer, Connell, & Erikson, 1992; Bortnick, 1995).

9. Videodisc: Interactive **videodisc** programs make available enormous resources, including videos, films, still pictures, and music. These can be valuable in student projects, explorations, and reports. Students can use videodiscs to create multimedia reports that combine audio, video, music, and pictures. One innovative application of videodisc technology is the Jasper series, developed and researched at Vanderbilt University (Cognition and Technology Group at Vanderbilt, 1992). In this program, students are shown videos in which a character, Jasper Woodbury, faces a series of

videodisc
Interactive computer technology; may include videos, films, still pictures, and music.

challenges that require applications of mathematics and thinking skills. Students must solve the problems Jasper faces before they see his solution. In addition to working with computers, students work in cooperative groups on off-line activities that are related to the stories. Evaluations found that in comparison to matched controls, students in classes that used the Jasper program performed similarly in math computations and concepts but better in word problems and planning.

10. Integrated learning systems: Early in the microcomputer revolution, schools typically assembled hardware and software from many sources, often with little coordination. Today, schools are increasingly purchasing **integrated learning systems:** entire packages of hardware and software, including most of the types of software described above. Integrated learning systems provide many terminals that are linked to each other and to computers that teachers use to monitor individual student work. Becker (1992) reviewed research on the effectiveness of commercial integrated learning systems and found positive but small effects on student achievement.

11. Computer programming: A popular notion is that learning computer programming (learning to "teach the computer" rather than being taught by it) will increase children's achievement and ability to solve problems. Programming has also been promoted as a virtual synonym for the term *computer literacy.* Much of the research on teaching computer programming to elementary students has focused on the computer language Logo, which was designed to be accessible to young children. Children draw on the computer's display screen by directing the movements of a graphic "turtle," a small triangular point that can move around the screen in response to messages that the programmer sends to it. Seymour Papert (1980), one of the creators of Logo and a leading supporter of the use of computer programming to expand children's intellectual power, has argued that students who learn Logo will gain in general thinking skills; others have made similar arguments for the teaching of other computer languages. Research is unclear on the degree to which this is true. When learning of computer programming has effects on thinking skills or other cognitive skills (such as mathematics), the effects are generally restricted to the problem-solving skills that are most similar to those involved in the programming itself (Blume, 1984; Palumbo, 1990).

12. Internet. Perhaps the fastest-growing technology applications in U.S. schools involve the **Internet** (Lev & Lev, 1999). A survey in fall 1996 found that 64 percent of schools had Internet access, and by 2000 Internet access is expected to be almost universal (ETS, 1996). The Internet gives schools access to vast stores of information, including databases on every imaginable subject, libraries throughout the world, and other specialized information (Levin & Thurston, 1996; Mehlinger, 1995; Peha, 1995; Scardamalia & Bereiter, 1996). The Internet can also enable students to communicate with students in other schools, including those far away; through this capability students can create international projects, carry out cooperative projects with schools elsewhere (Bradsher & Hagan, 1995; Brownlee-Conyers & Kraber, 1996), and so on. Schools have set up their own pages on the **World Wide Web,** a menu-driven format for accessing databases (Monahan & Tomko, 1996), and have created their own "virtual museums" or encyclopedias by collecting and synthesizing information from many sources.

There is little research on the achievement outcomes of Internet involvement (Levin & Thurston, 1996), and many critics argue that the Internet is a costly frill that can allow corporate interests to further penetrate schools (Frazier, 1995; Noble, 1996). There are also serious concerns about how to limit children's access to pornography or other inappropriate materials that can be found on the Web. Yet

integrated learning systems
Commercially developed comprehensive, multipurpose packages of interlinked hardware and instructional software.

Internet
A large and growing telecommunications network of computers around the world that communicate electronically via modems and telephone lines.

World Wide Web
A menu-driven format for accessing databases on the Internet that includes multimedia such as photos, audio recordings, and video clips.

The Intentional Teacher

● **Using What You Know about Accommodating Instruction to Meet Individual Needs**

Intentional teachers use students, not textbooks, as the starting point for planning and providing instruction. They expect students to have varied areas of strength and struggle, and they plan instruction that meets the needs of individual students. Intentional teachers monitor student progress carefully and use resources beyond the classroom to meet the needs of students placed at risk. Intentional teachers expect to continue learning and mastering new strategies that encourage all students to succeed.

1 What am I trying to accomplish?

Clarity of goals can be particularly important when students are at many instructional levels. Think about whether one set of goals is appropriate for all of your learners.

> You meet your first-grade class on the first day of school and find that it includes students who begin the year as readers and students who are just mastering concepts about print. You double-check the goals you wrote for your literacy program to ensure that the goals are both reasonable and challenging for all students.

Intentional teachers think about instructional quality in terms of many components. As you plan and assess your lessons, analyze the extent to which they focus upon providing high-quality, appropriate instruction; student motivation; and appropriate use of classroom time (this chapter's QAIT).

> You review a videotape of yourself teaching and are pleased to see that student levels of enthusiasm and engagement are high during most parts of the lesson. However, you note with dismay that you spent nearly 20 minutes of the 50-minute period handling routines and interruptions. You resolve to try a few management strategies that will allow you and your students to use instructional time to fuller advantage.

2 What are my students' relevant experiences and needs?

All students—even kindergartners—bring a range of experiences and achievements to the classroom. Check students' prerequisite knowledge through strategies like informal discussion, student drawings, and pretests. Then decide whether and how your instruction in specific instances should be modified to reflect differences in students' experiences.

> As a middle school math/science teacher with 60 students at two grade levels, you discover that students display a wide range of reading achievement. These reading differences have little bearing on your mathematics instruction, but you modify your science instruction carefully to accommodate students' diverse reading abilities. You arrange for a variety of print materials and for peer tutoring, and you devise skeleton outlines to guide students' reading.

3 What approaches and materials are available to help me challenge every student?

Skilled teachers use a variety of approaches and resources to accommodate student differences. When you find relevant student differences, consider a wide variety of strategies that can help you meet needs. Examples include mastery learning, grouping strategies, tutoring, and computer-based instruction.

> One third of your sixth-graders are working substantially above your grade-level mathematics curriculum, but more than half

---

This student is using instructional software to learn. What does research say about the advantages and disadvantages of computer-based instruction? Are certain types of computer-based instruction more effective?

it seems that the Internet is here to stay, at least as a tool to supplement libraries with a broad range of information.

RESEARCH ON COMPUTER-BASED INSTRUCTION ● Can computers teach? Most reviews of research on the effects of computer-based instruction conclude that computer-based instruction has small to moderate-sized positive effects on achievement (Atkinson, 1984; Kulik & Kulik, 1991; Niemiec & Walberg, 1985; Roblyer et al., 1988). As was noted earlier, there is also evidence favoring specific applications of CBI, especially word processing (Bangert-Drowns, 1993; Russell, 1991).

CBI is often effective when it is used in addition to regular classroom instruction; it has smaller and less consistent achievement effects when it entirely replaces classroom instruction. Some reviewers have argued that when the content of instruction is carefully controlled, computers are no more effective than other instructional methods (Clark, 1985). For example, one study, which randomly assigned students to use CBI or traditional methods to learn mathematics, found that some CBI methods enhanced learning, whereas some were less effective than the traditional teaching methods (Becker, 1990b). Researchers today generally agree that

are wrestling with most concepts and skills. Over coffee, you and an experienced colleague discuss your options. You consider four strategies that may work: (1) combining your students with his for peer tutoring; (2) spending a portion of each period in mastery learning, in which you and your colleague would divide students into levels of particular skills; (3) calling in volunteer tutors from a local senior center; (4) arranging for tutorial and drill and practice work in mathematics at your school's computer lab. You make a tentative plan to use tutoring strategies and call the computer lab director for scheduling.

Effective teachers use grouping practices that are supported by research. Think about alternatives to between-class ability grouping. Consider options such as regrouping, within-class grouping, and cross-age grouping.

You ask the principal of your high school to put you on a faculty meeting agenda to discuss alternatives to your school's traditional tracks for college preparation, basic, and remedial courses. You share an overview of the research on ability grouping and share some descriptions of schools that have engaged in untracking. A group of teachers is enthusiastic about pursuing the topic, and the principal assigns your group to lead future study efforts.

4 How will I know whether and when to change my strategy or modify my instruction?

Effective teachers use a variety of ongoing assessments to monitor how well students are learning, and they use this information to adapt their instruction to accommodate individual needs. Assess student progress frequently and be prepared to modify future lessons based on your findings.

You use semiweekly journal entries and weekly objective quizzes to check student progress in your biology class. To students who demonstrate that they have quickly mastered objectives, you provide enrichment opportunities to study the content through Web sites, software packages, readings, and investigations. For students who need additional scaffolding, you provide more intensive instruction. You take care, though, not to supplant your regular program with opportunities for enrichment and reinforcement.

Intentional teachers advocate for their students beyond the regular instructional program. Search out resources for students placed at risk. Determine whether and how your students can gain access to compensatory education programs (for instance, Title I) and early intervention programs.

You are thrilled to obtain a first-grade position at the school where you did your student teaching. During your first weeks there, you ask about projects and programs that are available through your site and district.

5 What information will I accept as evidence that my students and I are experiencing success?

Assumptions that accommodations are uniformly effective may prove faulty. Gather data to determine the extent to which your accommodations are having desired effects. Check effects on attitude and self-esteem as well as achievement.

This semester you have implemented a within-class ability grouping system for mathematics. Before winter break, you compare pre- and postgrouping test results, and you survey students about their perceptions of their own abilities and of your instruction.

Students' attitudinal profiles and achievement are frequently inconsistent both across and within subject areas. Check your instructional modifications to ensure that they accommodate different areas of strength for individual students.

You check student records to compare various areas of achievement, and you ask students to tell you about their most and least favorite areas of study.

the computer itself is not magic; what matters is the curriculum, instruction, and social context surrounding the use of the computer (Cochran-Smith, 1991; Cognition and Technology Group at Vanderbilt, 1996; Fletcher-Flinn & Gravatt, 1995; Means, Olson, & Singh, 1995; Salomon, Perkins, & Globerson, 1991). Asking whether computers enhance learning is like asking whether chalkboards enhance learning. In either case it depends on how they are used.

Leaving aside issues of effectiveness, it is clear that students do not all have the same access to computers. Middle-class children are considerably more likely than children of a lower socioeconomic status to have access to computers (ETS, 1996). Within schools, boys tend to spend much more time on computers than girls do (Laboratory of Comparative Human Cognition, 1989; Sutton, 1991). To the extent that computers become increasingly effective and important in providing state-of-the-art instruction, these inequities must be addressed.

Use of computers and research on CBI are developing so rapidly that it is difficult to anticipate what the future will bring (see Committee for Economic Development, 1995; Mehlinger, 1995). However, at this time, computers are rarely being used to provide basic instruction. In secondary schools they are used primarily to teach programming and word processing, and in elementary schools they are used chiefly for enrichment. Many schools that originally bought computers for CBI have ended up using them to teach computer programming or "computer literacy"—giving students hands-on experience with the computer but not depending on it to achieve major instructional objectives (Becker, 1990a). The majority of teachers still feel uncomfortable with computers and poorly prepared to use them (Office of Technology Assessment, 1995). Several decades into the "computer revolution," there is still a long way to go before computers fundamentally change the practice of education.

SELF-CHECK

Describe appropriate ways of individualizing instruction (e.g., peer and adult tutoring, programmed instruction, and computer-based instruction). Explain how drill and practice, tutorials, instructional games, and simulations can be used in classrooms. What does the research literature say about the use of the Internet in classrooms?

WHAT EDUCATIONAL PROGRAMS EXIST FOR STUDENTS PLACED AT RISK?

Any child can succeed in school. Any child can fail. The difference between success and failure depends primarily on what the school, the parents, community agencies, and the child himself or herself do to create conditions that are favorable for learning. Before school entry we cannot predict very well which individual children will succeed or fail, but there are factors in a child's background that make success or failure more likely (on the average). For example, students who come from impoverished or single-parent homes, those who have marked developmental delays, or those who exhibit aggressive or withdrawn behavior are more likely to experience problems in school than are other students (Kellam & Werthamer-Larsson, 1986; Silver & Hagin, 1990; Spivak, Marcus, & Swift, 1986). These children are often referred to as **students at risk** (Barr & Parrett, 1995; Manning & Baruth, 1995). The term *at risk* is borrowed from medicine, in which it has long been used to describe individuals who do not have a given disease but are more likely than average to develop it. For example, a heavy smoker or a person with a family history of cancer might be at risk for lung cancer, even though not all heavy smokers or people with family histories of cancer actually get the disease. High blood pressure is a known risk factor for heart attacks, even though most people with high blood pressure do not have heart attacks. Similarly, a given child from an impoverished home may do well in school; but 100 such children are likely to perform significantly worse, on the average, than 100 children from middle-class homes (Rossi & Stringfield, 1995).

Recently, the term *at risk* has often been replaced by the term *placed at risk* (Boykin, 1996). This term emphasizes the fact that it is often an inadequate response to a child's needs by school, family, or community that places the child at risk. For example, a child who could have succeeded in reading if he had been given appropriate instruction, a reading tutor, or eyeglasses could be said to be placed at risk by lack of these services.

Before children enter school, the most predictive risk factors relate to their socioeconomic status and family structure. After they begin school, however, such risk factors as poor reading performance, grade repetition, and poor behavior be-

students at risk
Students who are subject to school failure because of their own characteristics and/or because of inadequate responses to their needs by school, family, or community.

CONNECTIONS ▶

For more on factors such as poverty and limited English proficiency that may place students at risk of school failure, see Chapter 4, pages 107 and 119.

come more important predictors of later school problems (such as dropping out) than family background factors (Ensminger & Slusarcick, 1992).

Educational programs for students who are at risk fall into three major categories: compensatory education, early intervention programs, and special education. **Compensatory education** is the term used for programs designed to prevent or remediate learning problems among students who are from low-income families or who attend schools in low-income communities. Some intervention programs target at-risk infants and toddlers to prevent possible later need for remediation. Other intervention programs are aimed at keeping children in school. Compensatory and early intervention programs are discussed in the following sections. Special education, discussed in Chapter 12, is designed to serve children who have more serious learning problems as well as children with physical or psychological problems.

Compensatory Education Programs

Compensatory education programs are designed to overcome the problems associated with being brought up in low-income communities. Compensatory education supplements the education of students from disadvantaged backgrounds who are experiencing trouble in school or who are thought to be in danger of having school problems. Two such programs, Head Start and Follow Through, are designed to give disadvantaged preschool and primary school children the skills they need for a good start in school. These programs were discussed in Chapter 3. However, the largest compensatory education program, and the one that is most likely to affect regular classroom teachers, is called **Title I** (formerly Chapter 1), a federally funded program that gives schools money to provide extra services for students from low-income families who are having trouble in school.

More than 90 percent of all school districts, 70 percent of elementary schools, and 30 percent of middle schools and high schools provide Title I services (U.S. Department of Education, 1993). In addition, many states supplement Title I with their own compensatory education programs.

Title I is not merely a transfer of money from the federal government to local school districts. According to the federal guidelines, these funds must be used to "supplement, not supplant" local educational efforts. This means that most school districts cannot use the money to reduce class size for all students or increase teachers' salaries; the funds must go directly toward increasing the academic achievement of low achievers in schools that serve many disadvantaged students. The exception is that schools that serve very disadvantaged neighborhoods—neighborhoods in which at least 50 percent of the students qualify for a free lunch—can use Title I money to improve the school as a whole.

TITLE I PROGRAMS ● Title I programs can take many forms. Most often, a special Title I teacher provides remedial help to students who are experiencing difficulties in reading and, in many cases, in other subjects as well (Puma, Jones, Rock, & Fernandez, 1993). Programs of this type are called **pull-out programs,** because the students are pulled out of their general education classes to take part in the programs.

Pull-out programs have been criticized for many years. One major problem with pull-out programs is that often the regular teacher and the Title I teacher do not coordinate their efforts, so the very students who need the most consistent and structured instruction may have to deal with two completely different approaches (Allington & McGill-Franzen, 1989; Johnston, Allington, & Afflerbach, 1985; Meyers, Gelzheiser, Yelich, & Gallagher, 1990). One study found that half of a group

CONNECTIONS
To learn about factors such as problems of childhood and adolescence that may place students at risk of school failure, see Chapter 3, pages 89 and 96.

CONNECTIONS
Special education is discussed in detail in Chapter 12.

compensatory education
Programs designed to prevent or remediate learning problems among students from lower socioeconomic status communities.

Title I
Compensatory programs reauthorized under Title I of the Improving America's Schools Act (IASA) in 1994; formerly known as Chapter 1.

pull-out programs
Compensatory education programs in which students are placed in separate classes for remediation.

of Title I teachers could not even name the reading text series that their students were using in the general education class; two thirds could not name the specific book (Johnston et al., 1985). Johnston and colleagues (1985) argue that Title I programs must be directed at ensuring the success of students in the general education classroom and should therefore be closely coordinated with the general education teacher's instructional activities. For example, if a student is having trouble in the general education class with finding the main ideas of paragraphs, the Title I teacher should be working on main ideas, perhaps using the same instructional materials that the classroom teacher is using.

Some school districts are avoiding the problems of pull-out programs by having the Title I teacher or aide work as a team teacher in the general education reading classroom (see Harpring, 1985). This way, two teachers can give reading lessons to two groups of students at the same time, a strategy that avoids some of the problems of within-class ability grouping. Team teaching can also increase the levels of communication and collaboration between the general education classroom teacher and the Title I teacher. However, such in-class models of Title I services have not been found to be any more effective than pull-out programs (Anderson & Pellicer, 1990; Archambault, 1989).

Many other innovative programs have been found to accelerate the achievement gains of disadvantaged students. Among these are tutoring programs; continuous-progress programs, in which students are frequently assessed and regrouped as they proceed through a sequence of skills; and other structured instructional programs that have clear objectives and frequent assessments of students' attainment of these objectives (see Slavin & Madden, 1987; Slavin, Madden, & Karweit, 1989). The most effective approaches, however, are ones that prevent students from ever having academic difficulties in the first place (Hamburg, 1992; Slavin, Karweit, & Wasik, 1994). These include high-quality preschool and kindergarten programs (Berrueta-Clement et al., 1984; Reynolds, 1991) and one-to-one tutoring for first-graders who are just beginning to have reading problems (Pinnell, 1990; Wasik & Slavin, 1993).

RESEARCH ON THE EFFECTS OF TITLE I ● Two major nationwide studies of the achievement effects of the programs offered under Title I have been carried out. The first, called the Sustaining Effects Study (Carter, 1984), found that Title I students did achieve better in reading and math than did similar low-achieving students who did not receive Title I services, but that these effects were not large enough to enable Title I students to close the gap with students performing at the national average. The greatest gains were for first-graders; the benefits of Title I participation for students in fourth grade and above were slight.

The most recent study of the effects of the compensatory services funded under Title I, called *Prospects,* also compared elementary and middle school children receiving compensatory education services both to similar at-risk children not receiving services and to children who were never at risk. *Prospects* did not find any achievement benefits for children who received Title I services (Puma, Jones, Rock, & Fernandes, 1993). A more detailed analysis by Borman, D'Agostino, Wong, and Hedges (1998) found similarly disappointing outcomes, although there were some positive effects for children who were less disadvantaged and for those who received services during some years but not others. The most disadvantaged, lowest-achieving students were not narrowing their achievement gap with advanced peers.

While the *Prospects* data did not find overall positive effects of receiving compensatory services, results were positive in some situations. One particularly influential factor was the degree to which Title I services were closely coordinated with other school services (Borman, 1997; D'Agostino, Borman, Hedges, & Wong,

1998). In other words, schools that closely integrated remedial or instructional Title I services with the school's main instructional program, and especially schools that used Title I dollars to enhance instruction for all students in schoolwide projects, obtained the best outcomes. This kind of integration contrasts with the traditional practice of sending low-achieving students to remedial classes where instruction is poorly coordinated with that in the classes they are leaving.

Although it is possible that the national studies are too far from actual schools to show subtle effects (Borman & D'Agostino, 1996), no one familiar with the data would argue that Title I impacts are large. This is not a surprising conclusion, given that for most students Title I means no more than a 30-minute daily remedial session (Stringfield et al., 1997).

Research on effective practices in compensatory pull-out classes finds that, in general, practices that are effective in regular classes are also effective in pull-out classes. For example, more instructional time, more time on task, and other indicators of effective classroom management are important predictors of achievement gain in compensatory program classes (Crawford, 1989; Stein, Leinhardt, & Bickel, 1989). A large study of programs for students from high-poverty areas (Knapp, 1995; Knapp, Shields, & Turnbull, 1995) found that students in schools that emphasized instruction for deep understanding and meaning achieved significantly better than did students whose teachers emphasized drill and practice. Another large study, by Stringfield and colleagues (1997), evaluated a range of programs that are used in high-poverty schools. Two programs were particularly effective. One was the School Development Program designed by Yale psychiatrist James Comer (1988). The Comer model emphasizes building connections with parents and communities and organizing school staff to create engaging, effective instruction (Ramirez-Smith, 1995). The other effective method identified by Stringfield and colleagues (1997) was Success for All, which is discussed in the following section. These and other findings have led Title I policy-makers increasingly to favor schoolwide programs in which Title I funds are used to improve instruction for all children in the school (Wong, Sunderman, & Lee, 1995). In particular, Title I schools are being encouraged to adopt proven, comprehensive reform models for the entire school (see Slavin & Fashola, 1998).

Early Intervention Programs

Traditionally, Title I and other compensatory education programs have overwhelmingly emphasized remediation. They typically provide services to children only after the children have already fallen behind. Such children may also end up in special education or may be retained. All of the remedial strategies have shown little evidence of effectiveness. In fact, there is evidence that providing such services only after children have failed can be very detrimental to student achievement, motivation, and other outcomes (e.g., Roderick, 1994; Shepard & Smith, 1989). Recently, increasing emphasis has been placed on prevention and **early intervention** rather than remediation in serving children placed at risk of school failure (see Powell, 1995; Slavin et al., 1994). For example, the findings of long-term benefits of preschool for low-income children (Schweinhart, Barnes, & Weikart, 1993) have led to a dramatic expansion of prekindergarten programs for 4-year-olds.

Programs that emphasize infant stimulation, parent training, and other services for children from birth to age 5 also have been found to have long-term effects on at-risk students' school success. An example is the Carolina Abecedarian program (Campbell & Ramey, 1994), which found long-term achievement effects of an intensive program for children from low-income homes who received services from

CONNECTIONS

For more on prevention and early intervention, see Chapter 12, page 445.

early intervention
Programs that target at-risk infants and toddlers to prevent possible later need for remediation.

infancy through school entry. Other programs have had similar effects (Garber, 1988; Wasik & Karweit, 1994). In addition to such preventive programs, there is evidence that early intervention can keep children from falling behind in the early grades.

For example, a program called **Reading Recovery** (Lyons, Pinnell, & DeFord, 1993; Pinnell, DeFord, & Lyons, 1988) provides one-to-one tutoring from specially trained teachers to first-graders who are not reading adequately. This program is able to bring nearly all at-risk children to adequate levels of performance and can have long-lasting positive effects. Reading Recovery is used in more than 9,000 U.S. elementary schools. The cost-effectiveness of Reading Recovery and its long-term effects have been somewhat controversial (Hiebert, 1996; Pinnell, Lyons, & Jones, 1996; Shanahan, 1998). Although there is little disagreement that Reading Recovery has a positive effect on the reading success of at-risk first-graders (see, e.g., Lyons et al., 1993; Pinnell et al., 1994), there are conflicting findings concerning maintenance of these gains beyond first grade and concerning the question of whether positive effects for small numbers of first-graders represent the best use of limited funds for an entire age group of children.

In addition to Reading Recovery, several other programs have successfully used certified teachers, paraprofessionals, and even well-trained and well-supervised volunteers to improve the reading achievement of first-graders (Wasik, in press; Wasik & Slavin, 1993).

Success for All (Slavin, Madden, Dolan, & Wasik, 1996) is a comprehensive approach to prevention and early intervention in elementary schools that serve disadvantaged students. This program provides research-based reading programs for preschool, kindergarten, and grades 1 through 5; one-to-one tutoring for first-graders who need it; family support services; and other changes in instruction, curriculum, and school organization designed to ensure that students do not fall behind in the early grades. Longitudinal studies of Success for All have shown that students in this program read substantially better than do students in matched control schools throughout the elementary grades, and that they are far less likely to be assigned to special education or to fail a grade (see Madden, Slavin, Karweit, Dolan, & Wasik, 1993; Slavin et al., 1996). In 1998–99 Success for All was used in more than 1,100 Title I schools. An Australian program that also used a combina-

Reading Recovery
A program in which specially trained teachers provide one-to-one tutoring to first-graders who are not reading adequately.

Success for All
A comprehensive approach to prevention and early intervention for preschool, kindergarten, and grades 1 through 5, with one-to-one tutoring, family support services, and changes in instruction designed to prevent students from falling behind.

Early intervention programs can keep children from falling behind in the early grades. How do such programs differ from traditional compensatory programs?

tion of curricular reform, one-to-one tutoring (Reading Recovery), family support, and other elements showed significant effects on first-graders' reading performance (Crévola & Hill, 1998).

Research on Success for All, Reading Recovery, the Carolina Abecedarian program, and other preventive strategies shows that at-risk children can succeed if we are willing to give them high-quality instruction and intensive services early in their school careers (Slavin, 1997/98). Early intervention also ensures that children who do turn out to need long-term services are identified early—and that those whose problems can be solved early on are not needlessly assigned to special education (see Vellutino et al., 1996).

SELF-CHECK

Define *at risk* and *placed at risk*. What conditions place students at risk? Give examples of compensatory education programs and early intervention programs.

CHAPTER SUMMARY

WHAT ARE ELEMENTS OF EFFECTIVE INSTRUCTION BEYOND A GOOD LESSON?

Teachers must know how to adapt instruction to students' level of knowledge. According to Carroll's model of school learning, effectiveness of instruction depends on time needed (a function of student aptitude and ability to understand instruction) and time actually spent learning (which depends on time available, quality of instruction, and student perseverance).

Slavin's QAIT model of effective instruction identifies four elements that are subject to the teacher's direct control: quality of instruction, appropriate level of instruction, incentive, and amount of time. The model proposes that instruction that is deficient in any of these elements will be ineffective.

HOW ARE STUDENTS GROUPED TO ACCOMMODATE ACHIEVEMENT DIFFERENCES?

Many schools manage student differences in ability and academic achievement through between-class ability grouping, tracking, or regrouping into separate classes for particular subjects during part of a school day. However, research shows that within-class groupings are more effective, especially in reading and math, and are clearly preferable to groupings that segregate or stigmatize low achievers. Untracking recommends students be in mixed-ability groups. The students are held to high standards and are provided with assistance to reach those goals. Nongraded elementary schools combine children of different ages in the same classroom. Students are flexibly grouped according to their needs and performance levels.

WHAT IS MASTERY LEARNING?

Mastery learning is based on the idea that all or almost all students should have mastered a particular skill before proceeding to the next skill. Amounts of instructional time should vary so that all students have as much time as they need to attain the targeted knowledge and skills. Mastery learning takes a variety of forms, all of which involve formative and summative evaluations, corrective instruction, and enrichment activities. Mastery learning is generally effective in teaching basic skills but may reduce coverage of content.

WHAT ARE SOME WAYS OF INDIVIDUALIZING INSTRUCTION?

Peer and adult tutoring, programmed instruction, and computer-based instruction (CBI) are all methods for individualizing instruction. Research shows clear benefits of cross-age peer tutoring.

WHAT EDUCATIONAL PROGRAMS EXIST FOR STUDENTS PLACED AT RISK?

Students who are at risk are any students who are likely to fail academically for any reason stemming from the student or from the student's environment. Reasons are diverse and may include poverty.

Educational programs for students who are at risk include compensatory education, early intervention programs, and special education. Federally funded compensatory education programs include, for example, Head Start, which aims to help preschool-age children from low-income backgrounds achieve school readiness, and Title I, which mandates extra services to low-achieving students in schools that have many low-income students. Extra services may include pull-out programs, tutoring programs, and continuous-progress programs. Research is mixed regarding the effectiveness of compensatory education programs.

Research also supports the effectiveness of many prevention and intervention programs, such as Reading Recovery and Success for All, which provide extra services before children who are at risk fall behind.

KEY TERMS

between-class ability grouping   295
CD-ROM   311
compensatory education   317
computer-based instruction (CBI)   307
corrective instruction   301
cross-age tutoring   304
drill and practice   309
early intervention   319
enrichment activities   303
formative evaluations   302
individualized instruction   304
integrated learning systems   313
Internet   313
Joplin Plan   299
mastery criterion   301
mastery learning   301
nongraded programs (cross-age grouping programs)   299

peer tutoring   304
programmed instruction   307
pull-out programs   317
QAIT model   291
Reading Recovery   320
regrouping   299
simulation software   310
students at risk   316
Success for All   320
summative evaluations   302
Title I   317
tracks   294
tutorial programs   309
untracking   298
videodisc   312
within-class ability grouping   295
word processing   311
World Wide Web   313

Self-Assessment

1. The QAIT model of effective instruction includes which of the following components?
   a. quality of instruction, appropriate levels of instruction, incentive, time
   b. quantity of knowledge, assessment of learning, instructional time, teaching effectiveness
   c. quality of curriculum, affective outcomes, inclusion, tutoring
   d. question, assess, intervene, teach

2. Match each of the following elements from Carroll's model of school learning with its example.
   a. aptitude
   b. understanding of instruction
   c. perseverance
   d. opportunity
   e. quality of instruction

   _____ Students have prerequisite skills.
   _____ The teacher sets aside extra class time to present a lesson.
   _____ Students are eager to study until the skills are mastered.
   _____ Students show great ability to learn.
   _____ The lesson is presented in such a way that students learn quickly.

3. Which of the following statements represents a basic assumption of mastery learning?
   a. Levels of achievement vary while learning time is constant.
   b. Achievement level and learning time are flexible.
   c. Achievement level and learning time are fixed.
   d. Learning time varies while level of achievement is constant.

4. All of the following examples are central features of mastery learning except
   a. norm-referenced tests that compare students with each other.
   b. formative quizzes that provide feedback on students' progress.
   c. summative exams that assess performance at the conclusion of a lesson.
   d. corrective instruction that is given when mastery is not achieved.

5. Placing students in mixed-ability groups and holding them to high standards while providing a variety of instructional approaches is called
   a. compensatory education.
   b. remediation.
   c. individualized instruction.
   d. untracking.

6. Describe the differences between within-class and between-class ability grouping.

7. Which of the following statements about peer tutoring is accurate?
   a. Peer tutoring is an ineffective strategy for teaching secondary-level students.
   b. Peer tutoring increases the achievement of both the tutees and tutors.
   c. Peer tutoring yields greater achievement gains for tutees than for tutors.
   d. Peer tutoring is an ineffective strategy for teaching elementary-level students.

8. Individualized instruction in which students work on self-instructional materials at their own levels and rates is called
   a. early intervention.
   b. programmed instruction.
   c. cooperative learning.
   d. ability grouping.

9. Which of the following statements about the use of the Internet in classrooms is accurate?
   a. Most research studies show that the Internet is a powerful and cost-efficient learning tool.
   b. The Internet limits students' abilities to communicate with others.
   c. There is little research on the achievement outcomes of Internet involvement.
   d. Research demonstrates that the Internet decreases a student's achievement level.

10. Educational programs for students at risk that prevent or remediate learning problems and target students from poor or disadvantaged backgrounds include all of the following except
    a. compensatory education.
    b. special education.
    c. Title I.
    d. intervention programs.

Chapter 10

WHAT IS MOTIVATION?

WHAT ARE SOME THEORIES OF MOTIVATION?
Motivation and Behavioral Learning Theory
Motivation and Human Needs
Motivation and Attribution Theory
Motivation and Expectancy Theory

HOW CAN ACHIEVEMENT MOTIVATION BE ENHANCED?
Motivation and Goal Orientations
Learned Helplessness and Attribution Training
Teacher Expectations and Achievement
Anxiety and Achievement

HOW CAN TEACHERS INCREASE STUDENTS' MOTIVATION TO LEARN?
Intrinsic and Extrinsic Motivation
How Can Teachers Enhance Intrinsic Motivation?
Principles for Providing Extrinsic Incentives to Learn

HOW CAN TEACHERS REWARD PERFORMANCE, EFFORT, AND IMPROVEMENT?
Using Praise Effectively
Teaching Students to Praise Themselves
Using Grades As Incentives
Individual Learning Expectations
Incentive Systems Based on Goal Structure

Motivating Students to Learn

The students in Cal Lewis's 10th-grade U.S. history class were all in their seats before the bell rang, eagerly awaiting the start of the period. But Mr. Lewis himself was nowhere to be seen. Two minutes after the bell, in he walked dressed as George Washington, complete with an eighteenth-century costume and powdered wig, and carrying a gavel. He gravely took his seat, rapped the gavel, and said, "I now call to order this meeting of the Constitutional Convention."

The students had been preparing for this day for weeks. Each of them represented one of the 13 original states. In groups of two and three, they had been studying all about their states, the colonial era, the American Revolution, and the United States under the Articles of Confederation. Two days earlier, Mr. Lewis had given each group secret instructions from their "governor" on the key interests of their state. For example, the New Jersey and Delaware delegations were to insist that small states be adequately represented in the government, whereas New York and Virginia were to demand strict representation by population.

In preparing for the debate, each delegation had to make certain that any member of the delegation could represent the delegation's views. To ensure this, Mr. Lewis had assigned each student a number from one to three at random. When a delegation asked to be recognized, he would call out a number, and the student with that number would respond for the group.

Mr. Lewis, staying in character as George Washington, gave a speech on the importance of the task they were undertaking and then opened the floor for debate. First, he recognized the delegation from Georgia, represented by Beth Andrews. Beth was a shy girl, but she had been well prepared by her fellow delegates and knew that they were rooting for her.

"The great state of Georgia wishes to raise the question of a Bill of Rights. We have experienced the tyranny of government, and we demand that the people have a guarantee of their liberties!"

Beth went on to propose elements of the Bill of Rights that her delegation had drawn up. While she was talking, Mr. Lewis was rating her presentation on historical accuracy, appropriateness to the real interests of her state, organization, and delivery. He would use these ratings in evaluating each delegation at the end of each class period. The debate went on. The North Carolina delegates argued in favor of the right of states to expand to the West; the New Jersey delegation wanted western territories made into new states. Wealthy Massachusetts wanted taxes to remain in the states where they were collected; poor Delaware wanted national taxes. Between debates, the delegates had an opportunity to do some "horse trading," promising to vote for proposals important to other states in exchange for votes on issues important to them. At the end of the week, the class voted on 10 key issues. After the votes were taken and the bell rang, the students poured into the hall still arguing about issues of taxation, representation, powers of the executive, and so on.

After school, Rikki Ingram, another social studies teacher, dropped into Mr. Lewis's classroom. "I see you're doing your Constitutional Convention again this year. It looks great, but how can you cover all of U.S. history if you spend a month on just the Constitution?"

Cal smiled. "Don't you remember how boring high school social studies was?" he said. "It sure was for me. I know I'm sacrificing some coverage to do this unit, but look how motivated these kids are!" He picked up a huge sheaf of notes and position papers written by the South Carolina delegation. "These kids are working their tails off, and they're learning that history is fun and useful. They'll remember this material for the rest of their lives!"

Using Your EXPERIENCE

Critical Thinking   Rikki Ingram seems concerned that Mr. Lewis's class is not covering the material well enough. What do you think are the advantages, disadvantages, and interesting or unclear aspects of Mr. Lewis's teaching strategy?

Cooperative Learning   With another student, relate stories of a social studies or other high school teacher who tried methods similar to Mr. Lewis's method of teaching. As a pair, retell your stories to a student from another pair.

Motivation is one of the most important ingredients of effective instruction. Students who want to learn can learn just about anything. But how can teachers ensure that every student wants to learn and will put in the effort needed to learn complex material?

Mr. Lewis knows the value of motivation, so he has structured a unit that taps many aspects of motivation. By having students work in groups and be evaluated on the basis of presentations made by randomly selected group members, he has created a situation in which students are encouraging each other to excel. Social motivation of this kind is very powerful, especially for adolescents. Mr. Lewis is rating students' presentations according to clear, comprehensive standards and giving them feedback each day. He is tying an important period in history to students' daily lives by having them take an active role in debating and trading votes. All of these strategies are designed not just to make history fun but to give students many sources of motivation to learn and remember the history they have studied. Mr. Lewis is right. The students will probably never forget their experience in his class and are likely to approach new information about revolutionary history and the Constitution with enthusiasm throughout their lives.

This chapter presents the many ways in which teachers can enhance students' desire to learn academic material and the theories and research behind each method.

WHAT IS MOTIVATION?

One of the most critical components of learning, motivation is also one of the most difficult to measure. What makes a student want to learn? The willingness to put effort into learning is a product of many factors, ranging from the student's personality and abilities to characteristics of particular learning tasks, incentives for learning, settings, and teacher behaviors.

All students are motivated. The question is: Motivated to do what? Some students are motivated more to socialize or watch television than to do schoolwork. The educator's job is not to increase motivation per se but to discover, prompt, and sustain students' motivations to learn, and to engage in activities that lead to learning. Imagine that Cal Lewis had come to class in eighteenth-century costume but had not structured tasks and evaluations to induce students to study U.S. history. The students might have been amused and interested, but we cannot assume that they would have been motivated to do the work necessary to learn the material.

Psychologists define **motivation** as an internal process that activates, guides, and maintains behavior over time (Baron, 1998; Schunk, 1990). In plain language, motivation is what gets you going, keeps you going, and determines where you're trying to go.

Motivation may vary in both intensity and direction. Two students may be motivated to play video games, but one of them may be more strongly motivated to do so than the other. Or one student may be strongly motivated to play video games, and the other may be equally strongly motivated to play football. Gage and Berliner (1984) liken motivation to the engine (intensity) and steering wheel (direction) of a car. Actually, though, the intensity and direction of motivations are often difficult to separate. The intensity of a motivation to engage in one activity may depend in large part on the intensity and direction of motivations to engage in alternative activities. If someone has only enough time and money to go to the movies or to play

motivation
The influence of needs and desires on the intensity and direction of behavior.

video games, motivation to engage in one of these activities is strongly influenced by the intensity of motivation to engage in the other. Motivation is not only important in getting students to engage in academic activities. It is also important in determining how much students will learn from the activities they perform or the information to which they are exposed. Students who are motivated to learn something use higher cognitive processes in learning about it and absorb and retain more from it (Alexander & Jetton, 1996; Graham & Golan, 1991; Harp & Mayer, 1997). An important task for teachers is planning how they will support student motivation.

Motivation to do something can come about in many ways. Motivation can be a personality characteristic; individuals may have lasting, stable interests in participating in such broad categories of activities as academics, sports, or social activities. Motivation may come from intrinsic characteristics of a task: By making U.S. history fun, social, active, and engaging, Cal Lewis made students eager to learn it. Motivation may also come from sources extrinsic to the task, as when Cal Lewis rated students' performances in the Constitutional Convention simulation.

SELF-CHECK

Explain how motivation has intensity and direction.

WHAT ARE SOME THEORIES OF MOTIVATION?

The first half of this chapter presents contemporary theories of motivation, which seek to explain why people are motivated to do what they do. The second half discusses the classroom use of incentives for learning and presents strategies for increasing students' motivations to learn and to do schoolwork.

Motivation and Behavioral Learning Theory

CONNECTIONS

For more on reinforcement of behaviors, see Chapter 5, page 146.

The concept of motivation is closely tied to the principle that behaviors that have been reinforced in the past are more likely to be repeated than are behaviors that have not been reinforced or that have been punished. In fact, rather than using the concept of motivation, a behavioral theorist might focus on the degree to which students learn to do schoolwork to obtain desired outcomes (see Bandura, 1986; Wielkiewicz, 1995).

Why do some students persist in the face of failure while others give up? Why do some students work to please the teacher, others to make good grades, and still others out of interest in the material they are learning? Why do some students achieve far more than would be predicted on the basis of their ability and some achieve far less? Examination of reinforcement histories and schedules of reinforcement might provide answers to such questions, but it is usually easier to speak in terms of motivations to satisfy various needs.

REWARDS AND REINFORCEMENT ● One reason that reinforcement history is an inadequate explanation for motivation is that human motivation is highly complex and context-bound. With very hungry animals we can predict that food will be an effective reinforcer. With humans, even hungry ones, we can't be sure what will be a reinforcer and what will not, because the reinforcing value of most potential reinforcers is largely determined by personal or situational factors. As an example of this, think about the value of $50 for an hour's light work. Most of us would view $50 as a powerful reinforcer, more than adequate to get us to do a few hours of light work. But consider these four situations:

1. Mr. Scrooge offers Bill $60 to paint his fence. Bill thinks this is more than enough for the job, so he does his best work. However, when he is done, Mr. Scrooge says, "I don't think you did sixty dollars' worth of work. Here's fifty."
2. Now consider the same situation, except that Mr. Scrooge originally offers Bill $40 and, when Bill is finished, praises him for an excellent job and gives him $50.
3. Dave and Barbara meet at a party, like each other immediately, and after the party take a long walk in the moonlight. When they get to Barbara's house, Dave says, "Barbara, I enjoyed spending time with you. Here's fifty dollars I'd like you to have."
4. Marta's aunt offers her $50 to teach little Pepa how to play baseball next Saturday. However, if Marta agrees to do so, she will miss her chance to try out for the school baseball team.

In situations 1, 3, and 4, $50 is not a good reinforcer at all. In situation 1, Bill's expectations have been raised and then dashed by Mr. Scrooge. Even though the amount of monetary reward is the same in situation 2, this situation is much more likely to make Bill want to paint Mr. Scrooge's fence again, because in this case his reward exceeds his expectation. In situation 3, Dave's offer of $50 is insulting and would certainly not increase Barbara's interest in going out with him in the future. In situation 4, although Marta's aunt's offer would seem generous to Marta under most circumstances, it is insufficient reinforcement this particular Saturday, because it interferes with a more highly valued activity.

DETERMINING THE VALUE OF AN INCENTIVE ● These situations illustrate an important point: The motivational value of an incentive cannot be assumed, because it may depend on many factors (Chance, 1992; Strong, Silver, & Robinson, 1995). When teachers say, "I want you all to be sure to hand in your book reports on time, because they will count toward your grade," the teachers may be assuming that grades are effective incentives for most students. However, some students may not care about grades, perhaps because their parents don't or because they have a history of failure in school and have decided that grades are unimportant. If a teacher says to a student, "Good work! I knew you could do it if you tried!" this might be motivating to a student who had just completed a task he thought was difficult but punishing to one who thought the task was easy (because the teacher's praise implied that he had to work especially hard to complete the task). As in the case of Bill and Mr. Scrooge, students' expectations for rewards determine the motivational value of any particular reward. And it is often difficult to determine students' motivations from their behavior, because many different motivations can influence behavior. Sometimes one type of motivation clearly determines behavior; at other times, several motivations are influential.

Motivation and Human Needs

Whereas behavioral learning theorists (e.g., Bandura, 1986; Skinner, 1953) speak in terms of motivation to obtain reinforcers and avoid punishers, other theorists (e.g., Maslow, 1954) prefer the concept of motivation to satisfy needs. Some basic needs that we all must satisfy are those for food, shelter, love, and maintenance of positive self-esteem. People differ in the degree of importance they attach to each of these needs. Some need constant reaffirmation that they are loved or appreciated;

others have greater needs for physical comfort and security. Also, the same person has different needs at different times; a drink of water would be much more appreciated after a four-mile run than after a four-course meal.

MASLOW'S HIERARCHY OF NEEDS ● Given that people have many needs, which will they try to satisfy at any given moment? To predict this, Maslow (1954) proposed a hierarchy of needs, which is illustrated in Figure 10.1. In Maslow's theory, needs that are lower in this hierarchy must be at least partially satisfied before a person will try to satisfy higher-level needs. For example, a hungry person or someone who is in physical danger will be less concerned about maintaining a positive self-image than about obtaining food or safety; but once that person is no longer hungry or afraid, self-esteem needs may become paramount. One critical concept that Maslow introduced is the distinction between deficiency needs and growth needs. **Deficiency needs** (physiological, safety, love, and esteem) are those that are critical to physical and psychological well-being; these needs must be satisfied, but once they are, a person's motivation to satisfy them diminishes. In contrast, **growth needs,** such as the need to know and understand things, to appreciate beauty, or to grow and develop in appreciation of others, can never be satisfied completely. In fact, the more people are able to meet their need to know and understand the world around them, the greater their motivation may become to learn still more.

SELF-ACTUALIZATION ● Maslow's theory includes the concept of desire for **self-actualization,** which he defines as "the desire to become everything that one is capable of becoming" (Maslow, 1954, p. 92). Self-actualization is characterized by

deficiency needs
Basic requirements for physical and psychological well-being as identified by Maslow.

growth needs
Needs for knowing, appreciating, and understanding, which people try to satisfy after their basic needs are met.

self-actualization
A person's ability to develop his or her full potential.

FIGURE 10.1 ● Maslow's Hierarchy of Needs
Maslow identifies two types of needs: deficiency needs and growth needs. People are motivated to satisfy needs at the bottom of the hierarchy before seeking to satisfy those at the top.

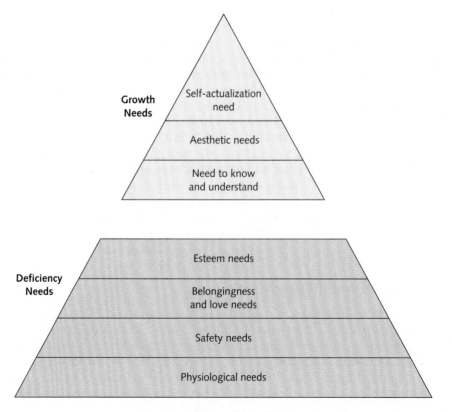

acceptance of self and others, spontaneity, openness, relatively deep but democratic relationships with others, creativity, humor, and independence—in essence, psychological health. Maslow places striving for self-actualization at the top of his hierarchy of needs, implying that achievement of this most important need depends on the satisfaction of all other needs. The difficulty of accomplishing this is recognized by Maslow (1968), who estimated that fewer than 1 percent of adults achieve self-actualization.

According to Maslow's theory, what needs are these children meeting? What other needs will they have to fulfill before they will be ready to put energy into learning?

IMPLICATIONS OF MASLOW'S THEORY FOR EDUCATION ● The importance of Maslow's theory for education is in the relationship between deficiency needs and growth needs. Obviously, students who are very hungry or in physical danger will have little psychological energy to put into learning. Schools and government agencies recognize that if students' basic needs are not met, learning will suffer. They have responded by providing free breakfast and lunch programs. The most important deficiency needs, however, may be those for love and self-esteem. Students who do not feel that they are loved and that they are capable are unlikely to have a strong motivation to achieve the higher-level growth objectives, such as the search for knowledge and understanding for their own sake or the creativity and openness to new ideas that are characteristic of the self-actualizing person. A student who is unsure of his or her lovableness or capability will tend to make the safe choice: Go with the crowd, study for the test without interest in learning the ideas, write a predictable but uncreative essay, and so on. A teacher who can put students at ease and make them feel accepted and respected as individuals is more likely (in Maslow's view) to help them become eager to learn for the sake of learning and willing to risk being creative and open to new ideas. If students are to become self-directed learners, they must believe that the teacher will respond fairly and consistently to them and that they will not be ridiculed or punished for honest errors.

CONNECTIONS

Motivational factors affecting the academic performance of students who are at risk of school failure are discussed in Chapter 9, page 316.

Motivation and Attribution Theory

Teresa usually gets good grades but receives a D on a certain quiz. The mark is inconsistent with her self-image and causes her discomfort. To resolve this discomfort, Teresa may decide to work harder to make certain that she never gets such a low grade again. On the other hand, she may try to rationalize her low grade: "The questions were tricky. I wasn't feeling well. The teacher didn't tell us the quiz was coming. I wasn't really trying. It was too hot." These excuses may help Teresa account for one D—but suppose she gets several poor grades in a row. Now she may decide that she never did like this subject anyway or that the teacher shows favoritism to the boys in the class or is a hard grader. All of these changes in opinions and excuses are directed at avoiding an unpleasant pairing of inconsistent ideas: "I am a good student" and "I am doing poorly in this class, and it is my own fault."

Teresa is struggling to find a reason for her poor grades that does not require her to change her perception of herself as a good student. She attributes her poor performance to her teacher, to the subject matter, or to other students—external factors over which she has no control. Or, if she acknowledges that her poor performance is her own fault, she decides that it must be a short-term lapse due to a momentary (but reversible) lack of motivation or attention regarding this unit of instruction.

Attribution theory (see, e.g., Graham, 1991; Graham & Weiner, 1996; Weiner, 1992, 1994) seeks to understand just such explanations and excuses, particularly when applied to success or failure (wherein lies the theory's greatest importance for education, in which success and failure are recurrent themes). Weiner (1992,

attribution theory
A theory of motivation that focuses on how people explain the causes of their own successes and failures.

1994) suggests that most explanations for success or failure have three character-istics. The first is whether the cause is seen as internal (within the person) or ex-ternal. The second is whether it is seen as stable or unstable. The third is whether it is perceived as controllable or not. A central assumption of attribution theory is that people will attempt to maintain a positive self-image (Thompson, Davidson, & Barber, 1995). Therefore, when they do well in an activity, they are likely to at-tribute their success to their own efforts or abilities; but when they do poorly, they will believe that their failure is due to factors over which they had no control (Vispoel & Austin, 1995). It has been demonstrated that if groups of people are given a task and then told that they either failed or succeeded (even though all, in fact, were equally successful), those who are told that they failed will say that their failure was due to bad luck, whereas those who are told that they succeeded will attribute their success to skill and intelligence (Forsyth, 1986).

Attributions for others' behavior are also important. For example, students are more likely to respond to a classmate's request for help if they believe that the class-mate needs help because of a temporary uncontrollable factor (such as getting hurt in a basketball game) than if they believe that help is needed because of a control-lable factor (such as failure to study) (Juvonen & Weiner, 1993).

ATTRIBUTIONS FOR SUCCESS AND FAILURE ● Attribution theory deals primarily with four explanations for success and failure in achievement situations: ability, effort, task difficulty, and luck. Ability and effort attributions are internal to the individual; task difficulty and luck attributions are external. Ability is taken to be a relatively stable, unalterable state; effort can be altered. Similarly, task difficulty is essentially a stable characteristic, whereas luck is unstable and unpredictable. These four attributions and representative explanations for success and failure are presented in Table 10.1.

TABLE 10.1

Attributions for Success and Failure

Attribution theory describes and suggests the implications of people's explanations of their successes and failures.

ATTRIBUTION	STABILITY	
	Stable	Unstable
Internal	*Ability*	*Effort*
Success:	"I'm smart."	"I tried hard."
Failure:	"I'm stupid."	"I didn't really try."
External	*Task Difficulty*	*Luck*
Success:	"It was easy."	"I lucked out."
Failure:	"It was too hard."	"I had bad luck."

Source: From Bernard Weiner, "A Theory of Motivation for Some Classroom Experiences," *Journal of Educational Psychology, 71,* pp. 3–25. Copyright © 1979 by the American Psychological Association. Adapted by permission.

Winners may attribute their success to effort, hard training, and a positive attitude. Losers may attribute failure to bad luck, poor adjudication, or (secretly) to personal inferiority. How would attribution theory and the concept of locus of control explain this situation, and what does this have to do with you as a teacher?

Table 10.1 shows how students may seek to explain success and failure differently. When students succeed, they would like to believe that it was because they are smart (an internal, stable attribution), not because they were lucky or because the task was easy or even because they tried hard (because "trying hard" says little about their likelihood of success in the future). In contrast, students who fail would like to believe that they had bad luck (an external, unstable attribution), which allows for the possibility of succeeding next time (Marsh, 1986; Weiner, 1994). Of course, over time, these attributions may be difficult to maintain. As we illustrated in the case of Teresa, a student who gets one bad grade is likely to blame it on bad luck or some other external, unstable cause. After several bad grades, though, an unstable attribution becomes difficult to maintain; no one can be unlucky on tests week after week. Therefore, a student like Teresa may switch to a stable but still external attribution. For example, she may decide that the course is too difficult or make some other stable, external attribution that lets her avoid making a stable, internal attribution that would shatter her self-esteem: "I failed because I don't have the ability." She may even reduce her level of effort so that she can maintain the idea that she could succeed if she really wanted to (Jagacinski & Nicholls, 1990).

LOCUS OF CONTROL AND SELF-EFFICACY ● One concept that is central to attribution theory is **locus of control** (Rotter, 1954). The word *locus* means *location*. A person with an internal locus of control is one who believes that success or failure is due to his or her own efforts or abilities. Someone with an *external locus of control* is more likely to believe that other factors, such as luck, task difficulty, or other people's actions, cause success or failure. Internal locus of control is often called self-efficacy, the belief that one's behavior makes a difference (Bandura, 1997; Pajares, 1996; Schunk, 1991; Zimmerman, 1998). Locus of control or self-efficacy can be very important in explaining a student's school performance. For example, several researchers have found that students who are high in internal

CONNECTIONS

Attributions for success or failure that are related to the socioemotional factors of self-esteem and peer relations are discussed in Chapter 3, pages 76, 86–89, and 94–95.

locus of control
A personality trait that concerns whether people attribute responsibility for their own failure or success to internal or external factors.

locus of control have better grades and test scores than do students of the same intelligence who are low in internal locus of control (Schunk, 1991; Shell, Colvin, & Bruning, 1995). Studies have found locus of control to be the second most important predictor of a student's academic achievement (after ability) (e.g., Pajares & Miller, 1994; Randhawa, Beamer, & Lundberg, 1993; Zimmerman & Bandura, 1994; Zimmerman, Bandura, & Martinez-Pons, 1992). The reason is easy to see. Students who believe that success in school is due to luck, the teacher's whims, or other external factors are unlikely to work hard. In contrast, students who believe that success and failure are due primarily to their own efforts can be expected to work hard (provided, of course, that they want to succeed). In reality, success in a particular class is a product of both students' efforts and abilities (internal factors) and luck, task difficulty, and teacher behaviors (external factors). But the most successful students will tend to overestimate the degree to which their own behavior produces success and failure. Some experiments have shown that even in situations in which success and failure are completely due to luck, students who are high in internal locus of control will believe that it was their efforts that made them succeed or fail (see Weiner, 1992). (See Figure 10.2.)

It is important to note that locus of control can change and depends somewhat on the specific activity or situation. One difficulty in studying the effects of locus of control on achievement is that achievement has a strong effect on locus of control (Weiner, 1992). For example, the same student might have an internal locus of control in academics (because of high academic ability) but an external locus of control in sports (because of low athletic ability). If this student discovered some unsuspected skill in a new sport, he or she might develop an internal locus of control in that sport (but probably still not in other sports).

IMPLICATIONS OF ATTRIBUTIONS AND SELF-EFFICACY FOR EDUCATION ● In the classroom, students receive constant information concerning their level of performance on academic tasks, either relative to others or relative to some norm of acceptabil-

FIGURE 10.2 ● **Items from the Intellectual Achievement Responsibility Questionnaire**
From V. C. Crandall, W. Katkovsky, and V. J. Crandall, "Children's Beliefs in Their Own Control of Reinforcement in Intellectual–Academic Achievement Situations," *Child Development, 36,* 1965, pp. 91–109. © The Society for Research in Child Development, Inc. Reprinted by permission.

1. If a teacher passes you to the next grade, would it probably be
   a. because she liked you, or
   b. because of the work you did? [*internal*]

2. When you do well on a test at school, is it more likely to be
   a. because you studied for it, or [*internal*]
   b. because the test was especially easy?

3. When you have trouble understanding something in school, is it usually
   a. because the teacher didn't explain it clearly, or
   b. because you didn't listen carefully? [*internal*]

4. Suppose your parents say you are doing well in school. Is it likely to happen
   a. because your school work is good, or [*internal*]
   b. because they are in a good mood?

5. Suppose you don't do as well as usual in a subject in school. Would this probably happen
   a. because you weren't as careful as usual, or [*internal*]
   b. because somebody bothered you and kept you from working?

ity. This feedback ultimately influences students' self-perceptions (Bandura, 1997; Pintrich & Blumenfeld, 1985). Attribution theory is important in helping teachers understand how students may interpret and use feedback on their academic performance and in suggesting to teachers how they might give feedback that has the greatest motivational value (see Ames, 1992; Graham, 1997).

THEORY
into
Practice

Giving Students Motivating Feedback

Students who believe that their past failures on tasks were due to lack of ability are unlikely to expect to succeed in similar tasks and are therefore unlikely to exert much effort (Ethington, 1991). Obviously, the belief that you will fail can be self-fulfilling. Students who believe that they will fail may be poorly motivated to do academic work, and this may in turn cause them to fail. Therefore, the most damaging idea a teacher can communicate to a student is that the student is "hopelessly stupid."

Few teachers would say such a thing directly to a student, but the idea can be communicated just as effectively in several other ways. One is to use a competitive grading system (e.g., grading on the curve) and to make grades public and relative student rankings important. This practice may make small differences in achievement level seem large, and students who receive the poorest grades may decide that they can never learn.

Alternatively, a teacher who deemphasizes grades and relative rankings but expresses the (almost always correct) expectation that *all* students in the class *can* learn is likely to help students see that their chances of success depend on their efforts—an internal but alterable attribution that lets students anticipate success in the future if they do their best (Ames & Ames, 1984).

A stable, internal attribution for success ("I succeed because I am smart") is also a poor motivator; able students, too, need to believe that it is their effort, not their ability, that leads to academic success. Teachers who emphasize the amount of effort as the cause of success as well as failure and who reward effort rather than ability are more likely to motivate all their students to do their best than are teachers who emphasize ability alone (Hunter & Barker, 1989; Resnick, 1998).

Some formal means of rewarding students for effort rather than ability are the use of individualized instruction, in which the basis of success is progress at the student's own level; the inclusion of effort as a component of grading or as a separate grade; and the use of rewards for improvement (described later in this chapter).

CONNECTIONS
For more on individualized instruction, see Chapter 9, page 304.

CONNECTIONS
For more on grading student effort, see Chapter 13, page 470.

expectancy theory
A theory of motivation based on the belief that people's efforts to achieve depend on their expectations of reward.

expectancy–valence model
A theory that relates the probability and the incentive value of success to motivation.

Motivation and Expectancy Theory

Expectancy theory is a theory of motivation based on the belief that people's efforts to achieve depend on their expectations of reward. Working within the framework of expectancy theory, Edwards (1954) and later Atkinson (1964) developed theories of motivation based on the following formula:

Motivation (M) = Perceived probability of success (Ps) × Incentive value of success (Is).

The formula is called an expectancy model, or **expectancy–valence model,** because it largely depends on the person's expectations of reward (see Feather,

1982; Locke & Latham, 1990). What this theory implies is that people's motivation to achieve something depends on the product of their estimation of their chance of success (perceived probability of success, *Ps*) and the value they place on success (incentive value of success, *Is*). For example, if Mark says, "I think I can make the honor roll if I try, and it is very important to me to make the honor roll," then he will probably work hard to make the honor roll. However, one very important aspect of the $M = Ps \times Is$ formula is that it is multiplicative, meaning that if people believe that their probability of success is zero or if they do not value success, then their motivation will be zero. If Mark would like very much to make the honor roll but believes that he hasn't a prayer of doing so, he will be unmotivated. If his chances are actually good but he doesn't care about making the honor roll, he will also be unmotivated. Wigfield (1995) found that students' beliefs that they were capable and their valuing of academic success were, taken together, more important than their actual ability in predicting their achievement.

Atkinson (1964) added an important aspect to expectancy theory in pointing out that under certain circumstances an overly high probability of success can be detrimental to motivation. If Mark is very able, it may be so easy for him to make the honor roll that he need not do his best. Atkinson (1958) explained this by arguing that there is a relationship between probability of success and incentive value of success such that success in an easy task is not as valued as is success in a difficult task. Therefore motivation should be at a maximum at moderate levels of probability of success. For example, two evenly matched tennis players will probably play their hardest. Unevenly matched players will not play as hard; the poor player may want very much to win but will have too low a probability of success to try very hard, and the better player will not value winning enough to exert his or her best effort. Confirming Atkinson's theory, more recent research has shown that a person's motivation increases as task difficulty increases up to a point at which the person decides that success is very unlikely or that the goal isn't worth the effort (Brehm & Self, 1989). This and other research findings indicate that moderate to difficult (but not impossible) tasks are better than easy ones for learning and motivation (Clifford, 1990).

IMPLICATIONS OF EXPECTANCY THEORY FOR EDUCATION ● The most important implication of expectancy theory is the commonsense proposition that tasks for students should be neither too easy nor too difficult. If some students believe that they are likely to get an A no matter what they do, then their motivation will not be at a maximum. Similarly, if some students feel certain to fail no matter what they do, their motivation will be minimal. Therefore grading systems should be set up so that earning an A is difficult (but possible) for as many students as feasible and so that earning a low grade is possible for students who exert little effort. Success must be within the reach, but not the easy reach, of all students.

SELF-CHECK

Organize the information from this section into a chart that includes the following headings: Behavioral Learning Theory, Human Needs Theory, Attribution Theory, and Expectancy Theory. For each one, define the underlying concept; identify any key experiments; and briefly describe and illustrate how the model works. Identify applications and implications for classroom teachers of each of the theories.

HOW CAN ACHIEVEMENT MOTIVATION BE ENHANCED?

One of the most important types of motivation for educational psychology is **achievement motivation** (McClelland & Atkinson, 1948), or the generalized tendency to strive for success and to choose goal-oriented, success/failure activities. For example, French (1956) found that given a choice of work partners for a complex task, achievement-motivated students tend to choose a partner who is good at the task, whereas affiliation-motivated students (who express needs for love and acceptance) are more likely to choose a friendly partner. Even after they experience failure, achievement-motivated students will persist longer at a task than will students who are less high in achievement motivation and will attribute their failures to lack of effort (an internal but alterable condition) rather than to external factors such as task difficulty or luck. In short, achievement-motivated students want and expect to succeed; when they fail, they redouble their efforts until they do succeed (see Weiner, 1992).

Not surprisingly, students who are high in achievement motivation tend to succeed at school tasks (Stipek, 1993). However, it is unclear which causes which: Does high achievement motivation lead to success in school, or does success in school (due to ability or other factors) lead to high achievement motivation? Actually, each contributes to the other; success breeds the desire for more success, which in turn breeds success (Wigfield, Eccles, & Rodriguez, 1998). In contrast, students who do not experience success in achievement settings will tend to lose the motivation to succeed in such settings and will turn their interest elsewhere (perhaps to social activities, sports, or even delinquent activities in which they may succeed). Achievement motivation tends to diminish over the school years, but it is unclear whether this trend is due to the nature of children or to the nature of middle and high schools (Eccles et al., 1993; Maehr & Anderman, 1993).

Motivation and Goal Orientations

Some students are motivationally oriented toward **learning goals** (also called task or **mastery goals**); others are oriented toward **performance goals** (Ames, 1992; Dweck, 1986; Köller & Baumert, 1997; Pintrich, Marx, & Boyle, 1993). Students with learning goals see the purpose of schooling as gaining competence in the skills being taught, whereas students with performance goals primarily seek to gain positive judgments of their competence (and avoid negative judgments). Students who are striving toward learning goals are likely to take difficult courses and to seek challenges; students with performance goals focus on getting good grades, take easy courses, and avoid challenging situations.

LEARNING VERSUS PERFORMANCE GOALS ● Students with learning goals and those with performance goals do not differ in overall intelligence, but their classroom performance can differ markedly. When they run into obstacles, performance-oriented students tend to become discouraged, and their performance is seriously hampered. In contrast, when learning-oriented students encounter obstacles, they tend to keep trying, and their motivation and performance may actually increase (Dweck, 1986; Schunk, 1996). Learning-oriented students are more likely to use metacognitive or self-regulated learning strategies (Greene & Miller, 1996; Pintrich, Marx, & Boyle, 1993). Performance-oriented students who perceive their

achievement motivation
The desire to experience success and to participate in activities in which success depends on personal effort and abilities.

learning goals
The goals of students who are motivated primarily by desire for knowledge acquisition and self-improvement. Also called *mastery goals*.

performance goals
The goals of students who are motivated primarily by a desire to gain recognition from others and to earn good grades.

abilities to be low are likely to fall into a pattern of helplessness, for they believe that they have little chance of earning good grades. Learning-oriented students who perceive their ability to be low do not feel this way; they are concerned with how much they themselves can learn, without regard for the performance of others (Fuchs et al., 1997; Kaplan & Midgley, 1997; Thorkildsen & Nicholls, 1998). Unfortunately, there is evidence that over their years in school, students tend to shift from learning or mastery goals to performance goals (Meece, Miller, & Ferron, 1995). Urdan and Maehr (1995) suggested a third goal orientation—social goals. That is, some students achieve to please the teacher, their parents, or their peers. (Wentzel & Wigfield, 1998).

The most important implication of research on learning goals versus performance goals is that teachers should try to convince students that learning rather than grades is the purpose of academic work. This can be done by emphasizing the interest value and practical importance of material students are studying and by deemphasizing grades and other rewards. For example, a teacher might say, "Today we're going to learn about events deep in the earth that cause the fiery eruptions of volcanoes!" rather than "Today we're going to learn about volcanoes. Pay attention so that you can do well on tomorrow's test." In particular, use of highly competitive grading or incentive systems should be avoided. When students perceive that there is only one standard of success in the classroom and that only a few people can achieve it, those who perceive their ability to be low will be likely to give up in advance (Ames, 1992). Table 10.2 (from Ames & Archer, 1988) summarizes the differences between the achievement goals of students with mastery (learning) goals and those of students with performance goals. Studies indicate that the types of tasks that are used in classrooms have a strong influence on students' adoption of learning goals. Use of tasks that are challenging, meaningful, and related to real life are more likely to lead to learning goals than are other tasks (Ames, 1992; Blumenfeld, 1992; Meece, 1991). Table 10.3 (from Maehr & Anderman, 1993) summarizes strategies that teachers can use to promote learning or task goals among students.

TABLE 10.2

Achievement Goal Analysis of Classroom Climate

CLIMATE DIMENSIONS	MASTERY GOAL	PERFORMANCE GOAL
Success defined as . . .	Improvement, progress	High grades, high normative performance
Value placed on . . .	Effort/learning	Normatively high ability
Reasons for satisfaction . . .	Working hard, challenge	Doing better than others
Teacher oriented toward . . .	How students are learning	How students are performing
View of errors/mistakes . . .	Part of learning	Anxiety eliciting
Focus of attention . . .	Process of learning	Own performance relative to others'
Reasons for effort . . .	Learning something new	High grades, performing better than others
Evaluation criteria . . .	Absolute progress	Normative

Source: From C. Ames and J. Archer, "Achievement Goals in the Classroom," *Journal of Educational Psychology, 80,* p. 261. Copyright © 1988 by the American Psychological Association. Reprinted by permission.

TABLE 10.3

School and Teacher Policies That Are Likely to Promote Learning or Task Goals

AREA	OBJECTIVES	EXAMPLES OF POSSIBLE STRATEGIES
Task	Enhance intrinsic attractiveness of learning tasks. Make learning meaningful.	Encourage instruction that relates to students' backgrounds and experience. Avoid payment (monetary or other) for attendance, grades, or achievement. Foster goal setting and self-regulation. Use extraclassroom programs that make learning experiences relevant.
Autonomy/ Responsibility	Provide optimal freedom for students to make choices and take responsibility.	Give alternatives in making assignments. Ask for student comments on school life—and take them seriously. Encourage instructional programs that encourage students to take initiatives and evaluate their own learning. Establish leadership opportunities for *all* students.
Recognition	Provide opportunities for *all* students to be recognized for learning. Recognize *progress* in goal attainment. Recognize challenge seeking and innovation.	Foster personal-best awards. Reduce emphasis on honor rolls. Recognize and publicize a wide range of school-related activities of students.
Resources	Encourage the development and maintenance of strategies that enhance task–goal emphases.	Underwrite action taken by staff that is in accord with a task–goal emphasis.
Grouping	Build an environment of acceptance and appreciation of all students. Broaden the range of social interaction, particularly of at-risk students. Enhance social skills development.	Provide opportunities for cooperative learning, problem solving, and decision making. Allow time and opportunity for peer interaction. Foster the development of subgroups (teams, schools within schools, etc.) within which significant interaction can occur. Encourage multiple group membership to increase range of peer interaction. Eliminate ability-grouped classes.
Evaluation	Grading and reporting processes. Practices associated with use of standardized tests. Definition of goals and standards.	Reduce emphasis on social comparisons of achievement by minimizing public reference to normative evaluation standards (e.g., grades, test scores). Establish policies and procedures that give students opportunities to improve their performance (e.g., study skills, classes). Establish grading/reporting practices that portray student progress in learning. Encourage student participation in the evaluation process.
Time	Allow the learning task and student needs to dictate scheduling. Provide opportunities for extended and significant student involvement in learning tasks.	Allow students to *progress at their own rate* whenever possible. Encourage flexibility in the scheduling of learning experiences. Give teachers greater control over time usage through, for example, block scheduling.

Source: From M. L. Maehr and E. M. Anderman, "Reinventing Schools for Early Adolescents," *The Elementary School Journal, 93*(5), 1993, pp. 593–610. Published by The University of Chicago Press. Adapted by permission.

SEEKING SUCCESS VERSUS AVOIDING FAILURE ● Atkinson (1964), extending McClelland's work on achievement motivation, noted that individuals may be motivated to achieve in either of two ways: to seek success or to avoid failure. He found that some people were more motivated to avoid failure than to seek success (failure avoiders), whereas others were more motivated to seek success than to avoid failure (success seekers). Success seekers' motivation is increased after a failure, as they intensify their efforts to succeed. Failure avoiders decrease their efforts after a failure (Weiner, 1986).

One very important characteristic of failure avoiders is that they tend to choose either very easy or very difficult tasks. For example, Atkinson and Litwin (1960) found that in a ring toss game, failure avoiders would choose to stand very near the target or very far away, and success seekers would choose an intermediate distance. They hypothesized that failure avoiders preferred either easy tasks (on which failure was unlikely) or such difficult tasks that no one would blame them if they failed.

Understanding that it is common for failure avoiders to choose impossibly difficult or ridiculously easy tasks for themselves is very important for the teacher. For example, a poor reader might choose to write a book report on *War and Peace* but then, when told that was too difficult, might choose a simple children's book. Such students are not being devious but are simply doing their best to maintain a positive self-image.

Learned Helplessness and Attribution Training

An extreme form of the motive to avoid failure is called **learned helplessness,** which is a perception that no matter what one does, one is doomed to failure or ineffectuality: "Nothing I do matters" (Maier, Seligman, & Solomon, 1969). In academic settings, learned helplessness can be related to an internal, stable explanation for failure: "I fail because I'm stupid, and that means I will always fail" (Diener & Dweck, 1978; Dweck, 1975).

Learned helplessness can arise from a child's upbringing (Hokoda & Fincham, 1995) but also from inconsistent, unpredictable use of rewards and punishments by teachers—a pattern that may lead students to believe that there is little they can do to be successful. Teachers can prevent or alleviate learned helplessness by giving students opportunities for success in small steps; immediate feedback; and, most important, consistent expectations and follow-through (see Alderman, 1990). Focusing on learning goals rather than on performance goals (see the previous section) can reduce helplessness, because all students can attain learning goals to one degree or another (Dweck, 1986).

CHANGES IN ACHIEVEMENT MOTIVATION ● Motivation-related personality characteristics can be altered. They are altered in the natural course of things when something happens to change a student's environment, as when students who have vocational but not academic skills move from a comprehensive high school in which they were doing poorly to a technical preparation program in which they find success. Such students may break out of a long-standing pattern of external locus of control and low achievement motivation because of their newfound success experience. Late bloomers, students who have difficulty in their earlier school years but take off in their later years, may also experience lasting changes in motivation-related personality characteristics, as may students who are initially successful in school but who later experience difficulty keeping up. However, achievement motivation and attributions can also be changed directly by special programs designed for this purpose.

learned helplessness
The expectation, based on experience, that one's actions will ultimately lead to failure.

Several studies have found that learned helplessness in the face of repeated failure can be modified by an attribution training program that emphasizes lack of effort, rather than lack of ability, as the cause of poor performance (Forsterling, 1985; McCombs, 1984). For example, Schunk (1982, 1983) found that students who received statements attributing their past successes and failures to effort performed better than did students who received no feedback.

Helping Students Overcome Learned Helplessness

THEORY *into* Practice

The concept of learned helplessness derives from the theory that students may become academic failures through a conditioning process based on negative feedback from teachers, school experiences, peers, and students themselves. Numerous studies show that when students consistently fail, they eventually give up. They become conditioned to helplessness (Seligman, 1975).

Teachers at both the elementary and secondary levels can help to counter this syndrome in a variety of ways, including attribution training, goal restructuring, self-esteem programs, success-guaranteed approaches, and positive feedback systems. The following general principles are helpful for all students, especially students who have shown a tendency to accept failure.

1. Accentuate the positive. Get to know the student's strengths, then use these as building blocks. Every student has something she or he does well. But be careful that the strength is authentic; don't make up a strength. For example, a student may like to talk a lot but write poorly. Have the student complete assignments by talking rather than writing. As confidence is restored, slowly introduce writing.

2. Eliminate the negative. Do not play down a student's weaknesses. Deal with them directly but tactfully. In the above example, talk to the student about problems with writing. Then have the student develop a plan to improve on the writing. Discuss the plan, and together make up a contract about how the plan will be completed.

3. Go from the familiar to the new, using advance organizers or guided discovery. Some students have difficulties with concepts, skills, or ideas with which they are not familiar. Also, students relate better to lessons that are linked to their own experiences. For example, a high school math teacher might begin a lesson with a math problem that students might face in the real world, such as calculating the sales tax when purchasing a CD player. Further, the teacher can ask students to bring to class math problems they have encountered outside of school. The whole class can become involved in solving a student's math problem.

4. Create challenges in which students actively create problems and solve them using their own knowledge and skills.

Teacher Expectations and Achievement

On the first day of class, Mr. Erhard called roll. Soon he got to a name that looked familiar. "Wayne Clements?"

"Here!"

"Do you have a brother named Victor?"

"Yes."

"I remember Victor. He was a terror. I'm going to keep my eye on you!"

As he neared the end of the roll, Mr. Erhard saw that several boys were starting to whisper to one another in the back of the room. "Wayne! I asked the class to remain silent while I read the roll. Didn't you hear me? I knew I'd have to watch out for you!"

This dialogue illustrates how teachers can establish expectations for their students and how these expectations can be self-fulfilling. Mr. Erhard doesn't know it, but Wayne is generally a well-behaved, conscientious student, quite unlike his older brother, Victor. However, because of his experience with Victor, Mr. Erhard expects that he will have trouble with Wayne. When he sees several boys whispering, it is Wayne he singles out for blame, confirming for himself that Wayne is a troublemaker. After a few episodes of this treatment, we can expect Wayne to begin playing the role Mr. Erhard has assigned to him.

Research on teachers' expectations for their students has generally found that students do (to some degree) live up to the expectations that their teachers have for them (Good, 1987). In one study, Rosenthal and Jacobson (1968) tested elementary school students and then picked out a few in each class that they told the teachers were late bloomers who should do well this year. In fact, these students were chosen at random and were of the same ability as their classmates. At the end of the year, when the students were tested again, those who had falsely been identified as late bloomers were found to have learned more than their classmates in the first and second grades, though this effect was not seen in grades 3 to 6. The teachers expected more from these students and transmitted those expectations. The Rosenthal and Jacobson study has been severely criticized (see Elashoff & Snow, 1971); but later evidence has generally supported the idea that teachers' expectations can affect students' behaviors (Jussim & Eccles, 1995; Wigfield & Harold, 1992), particularly in the younger grades and when teachers know relatively little about their students' actual achievement levels (Raudenbush, 1984). Further, there is evidence that students in schools whose teachers have high expectations achieve more than those in other schools (Marks, Doane, & Secada, 1998).

HOW TEACHERS COMMUNICATE POSITIVE EXPECTATIONS ● It is important for teachers to communicate to their students the expectation that they can learn (see Babad, 1993). Obviously, it is a bad idea to state the contrary—that a particular student cannot learn—and few teachers would explicitly do so. There are several implicit ways in which teachers can communicate positive expectations of their students (or avoid negative ones).

1. Wait for students to respond. Rowe (1974) and others have noted that teachers wait longer for answers from students for whom they have high expectations than from other students. Longer wait times may communicate high expectations and increase student achievement (Tobin, 1987).

2. Avoid unnecessary achievement distinctions among students. Assessment results and grades should be a private matter between students and their teacher, not public information. Reading and math groups may be instructionally necessary in some classrooms, but teachers should avoid establishing a rigid hierarchy of groups, should treat the groups equally and respectfully, and should be prepared to move a student out of one group and into another when appropriate (see Gamoran, 1984; Rosenholtz & Simpson, 1984). Students usually know who is good in school and who is not, but teachers can still successfully communicate the expectation that all students, not just the most able ones, are capable of learning (Weinstein, Madison, & Kuklinski, 1995).

3. Treat all students equally. Call on students at all achievement levels equally often, and spend equal amounts of time with them. In particular, guard against

CONNECTIONS

For more on grouping students, see Chapter 9, page 294.

bias. Research finds that teachers often unwittingly hold lower expectations for certain categories of students, such as minority-group students (Baron, Tom, & Cooper, 1985) or females (Kahle & Meece, 1993; Sadker & Sadker, 1985).

Anxiety and Achievement

Anxiety is a constant companion of education. Every student feels some anxiety at some time while in school; but for certain students, anxiety seriously inhibits learning or performance, particularly on tests (Everson, Smodlaka, & Tobias, 1994; Wigfield & Eccles, 1990).

The main source of anxiety in school is the fear of failure and, with it, loss of self-esteem (Hill & Wigfield, 1984). Low achievers are particularly likely to feel anxious in school, but they are by no means the only ones. We all know very able, high-achieving students who are also very anxious, maybe even terrified to be less than perfect at any school task.

Anxiety can block school performance in several ways (Naveh-Benjamin, 1991; Skaalvik, 1997). Anxious students may have difficulty learning in the first place; they may have difficulty using or transferring knowledge they do have; and they may have difficulty demonstrating their knowledge on tests (Bandalos, Yates, & Thorndike-Christ, 1995). Anxious students are likely to be overly self-conscious in performance settings, a feeling that distracts attention from the task at hand (Tobias, 1992).

One particularly common form of debilitating anxiety is math anxiety. Many students (and adults) simply freeze up when given math problems, particularly word problems. (Everson, Tobias, Hartman, & Gourgey, 1993).

Teachers can apply many strategies to reduce the negative impact of anxiety on learning and performance. Clearly, creating a classroom climate that is accepting, comfortable, and noncompetitive helps. Giving students opportunities to correct errors or improve their work before handing it in also helps anxious children, as does providing clear, unambiguous instructions (Wigfield & Eccles, 1989). In testing situations, teachers can do many things to help anxious students to do their best. They can avoid time pressure, giving students plenty of time to complete a test and check their work. Tests that begin with easy problems and only gradually introduce more difficult ones are better for anxious students, and tests with standard, simple answer formats help such students. Test-anxious children can be trained in test-taking skills and relaxation techniques, and these can have a positive impact on their test performance (Spielberger & Vagg, 1995).

> **CONNECTIONS**
>
> Programs designed to train test-anxious children in test-taking skills are discussed in Chapter 14, page 503.

SELF-CHECK

Define *achievement motivation*. How do students differ in their approaches to academic success or failure? How can attribution training and changes in teacher expectations affect students' motivation and performance?

HOW CAN TEACHERS INCREASE STUDENTS' MOTIVATION TO LEARN?

Learning takes work. Euclid, a Greek mathematician who lived around 300 B.C. and wrote the first geometry textbook, was asked by his king whether there were any shortcuts the king could use to learn geometry, as he was a very busy man. "I'm sorry," Euclid replied, "but there is no royal road to geometry." The same is true of every other subject: Students get out of any course of study only what they put into it.

The remainder of this chapter discusses the means by which students can be motivated to exert the effort learning requires. First, the issue of intrinsic motivation—the motivational value of the content itself—is presented. Extrinsic motivation—the use of praise, feedback, and incentives to motivate students to do their best—is then discussed.

Also in this section are specific strategies for enhancing student motivation and suggestions for solving motivational problems that are common in classrooms, including reward-for-improvement incentive systems.

Intrinsic and Extrinsic Motivation

Sometimes a course of study is so fascinating and useful to students that they are willing to do the work required to learn the material with no incentive other than the interest level of the material itself. For example, many students would gladly take auto mechanics or photography courses and work hard in them, even if the courses offered no credit or grades. For these students the favorite subject itself has enough **intrinsic incentive** value to motivate them to learn. Other students love to learn about particular topics such as insects, dinosaurs, or famous people in history and need little encouragement or reward to do so (Gottfried, 1990; Renninger, Hidi, & Krapp, 1992).

However, much of what must be learned in school is not inherently interesting or useful to most students in the short run. Students receive about 900 hours of instruction every year, and intrinsic interest alone will not keep them enthusiastically working day in and day out. In particular, students' intrinsic motivation

intrinsic incentive

An aspect of an activity that people enjoy and therefore find motivating.

This student is performing a task that has intrinsic value to her. How is her motivation affected? As a teacher, how could you maintain or extend her motivation? How could you present the same task to another student for whom the task does *not* have intrinsic value?

generally declines from early elementary school through secondary school (Sethi, Drake, Dialdin, & Lepper, 1995). For this reason, schools apply a variety of **extrinsic incentives,** rewards for learning that are not inherent in the material being learned. Extrinsic rewards may range from praise to grades to recognition to prizes or other rewards.

In the vignette at the beginning of this chapter, Cal Lewis tried to enhance both intrinsic and extrinsic motivation. His simulation of the Constitutional Convention was intended to arouse students' intrinsic interest in the subject, and his ratings of students' presentations and his feedback at the end of each period were intended to provide extrinsic motivation.

LEPPER'S EXPERIMENT ON THE IMPACT OF REWARDS ON MOTIVATION ● An important question in research on motivation concerns whether or not the providing of extrinsic rewards diminishes intrinsic interest in an activity. In a classic experiment exploring this topic, Lepper and colleagues (1973) gave preschoolers an opportunity to draw with felt-tip markers, which many of them did quite enthusiastically. Then the researchers randomly divided the children into three groups: One group was told that its members would receive a reward for drawing a picture for a visitor (a Good Player Award), one was given the same reward as a surprise (not dependent on the children's drawing), and one received no reward. Over the next 4 days, observers recorded the children's free-play activities. Children who had received a reward for drawing spent about half as much time drawing with felt-tip markers as did those who had received the surprise reward and those who had gotten no reward. The authors suggested that promising extrinsic rewards for an activity that is intrinsically interesting may undermine intrinsic interest by inducing children to expect a reward for doing what they had previously done for nothing. In a later study (Greene & Lepper, 1974), it was found that just telling children that they would be watched (through a one-way mirror) had an undermining effect similar to that of a promised reward.

DO REWARDS DESTROY INTRINSIC MOTIVATION? ● In understanding the results of these studies, it is important to recall the conditions of the research. The students who were chosen for the studies were ones who showed an intrinsic interest in using marking pens; those who did not were excluded from the experiments. Also, drawing with felt-tip pens does not resemble most school tasks. Many children love to draw at home; but few, even those who are most interested in school subjects, would independently study grammar and punctuation, work math problems, or learn the valences of chemical elements. Further, many of our most creative and self-motivated scientists were heavily reinforced as students with grades, science fair prizes, and scholarships for doing science; and virtually all successful artists have been reinforced at some point for engaging in artistic activities. This reinforcement certainly did not undermine the activities' intrinsic interest. Research on older students doing more school-like tasks has generally failed to replicate the results of the Lepper and colleagues (1973) experiment (Cameron & Pierce, 1994, 1996; Eisenberger & Cameron, 1998). In fact, the use of rewards more often increases intrinsic motivation, especially when rewards are contingent on the quality of performance rather than on mere participation in an activity (Deci & Ryan, 1985, 1987; Lepper, 1983), when the rewards are seen as recognition of competence (Rosenfield, Folger, & Adelman, 1980), when the task in question is not very interesting (Morgan, 1984), or when the rewards are social (e.g., praise) rather than material (Cameron & Pierce, 1994; Chance, 1992; Miller & Hom, 1990; Ryan & Stiller, 1991).

extrinsic incentive
A reward that is external to the activity, such as recognition or a good grade.

The research on the effects of extrinsic rewards on intrinsic motivation does counsel caution in the use of material rewards for intrinsically interesting tasks (See Kohn, 1996; Lepper, 1998; Lepper, Keavney, & Drake, 1996; Ryan & Deci, 1996). Teachers should attempt to make everything they teach as intrinsically interesting as possible and should avoid handing out material rewards when they are unnecessary, but teachers should not refrain from using extrinsic rewards when they are needed (Lepper, 1983). Often, extrinsic rewards may be necessary to get students started in a learning activity but may be phased out as students come to enjoy the activity and succeed at it (Stipek, 1993).

How Can Teachers Enhance Intrinsic Motivation?

Classroom instruction should enhance intrinsic motivation as much as possible. This means that teachers must try to get their students interested in the material they are presenting and then present it in an appealing way that both satisfies and increases students' curiosity about the material itself. A discussion of some means of doing this follows (see also Maehr & Meyer, 1997; Malone & Lepper, 1988; Schultz & Switzky, 1990; Stipek, 1996, 1998).

CONNECTIONS

The importance of student interest in creative problem solving and other constructivist approaches is discussed in Chapter 8, page 279.

AROUSING INTEREST ● It is important to convince students of the importance and interest level of the material that is about to be presented, to show (if possible) how the knowledge to be gained will be useful to students (Zahorik, 1996). For example, intrinsic motivation to learn a lesson on percents might be increased by introducing the lesson as follows:

> Today we will begin a lesson on percents. Percents are important in our daily lives. For example, when you buy something at the store and a salesperson figures the sales tax, he or she is using percents. When we leave a tip for a waiter or waitress, we use percents. We often hear in the news things like "Prices rose seven percent last year." In a few years, many of you will have summer jobs, and if they involve handling money, you'll probably be using percents all the time.

Introducing lessons with examples relating the material to students' cultures can be particularly effective. For example, in introducing astronomy, a teacher could say, "Thousands of years ago, the Maya of Central America had calendars that accurately predicted the movement of the moon and stars for centuries into the future. How could they do this? Today we will learn about how planets, moons, and stars move in predictable paths."

The purpose of these statements is to arouse student curiosity about the lesson to come, thereby enhancing intrinsic motivation to learn the material. Another way to enhance students' intrinsic interest is to give them some choice about what they will study or how they will study it (Cordova & Lepper, 1996; Stipek, 1998).

CONNECTIONS

The lesson referred to is described in Table 7.1 in Chapter 7, page 223.

MAINTAINING CURIOSITY ● A skillful teacher uses a variety of means to further arouse or maintain curiosity in the course of the lesson. Science teachers, for instance, often use demonstrations that surprise or baffle students and induce them to want to understand why. A floating dime makes students curious about the surface tension of liquids. "Burning" a dollar bill covered with an alcohol-water solution (without harming the dollar bill) certainly increases curiosity about the heat of combustion. Less dramatically, the lesson on subtraction with renaming described in Chapter 7 got students comfortable with subtracting such numbers as 47 – 3 and 56 – 23 but then stumped them with 13 – 5. Students were shocked out of a comfortable routine and forced to look at the problem in a new way.

TEACHERS IN ACTION

How have you dealt with motivational challenges in your classroom?

Nancy Letts
Teacher of Gifted and Talented
Post Road School
White Plains, New York

A motivational challenge I was concerned with was the lower levels of participation and achievement of my middle school female students. I had observed that the female students in my classes were more silent than the males, raised their hands less often, and shunned competitive situations. I assumed that socialized sex-role stereotypes played an important role in silencing girls' voices, but I also considered the possibility that I was a source of the problem. Did I really treat boys and girls equally in my classes? At the same time, was I sensitive to the possibility that boys and girls might learn differently?

Using information from educational research and books, such as *Women's Ways of Knowing* by Belenky, Clinchy, Goldberger, and Tarule, I developed a series of weekly Socratic Seminars in which I altered my role as a teacher in a way that invited greater participation. I became a facilitator whose task was to ask questions rather than to tell information. During the debriefing sessions that followed, the girls were quick to explain how they felt freer to disagree with their friends. They heard a variety of opinions with no right or wrong answers as long as each premise could be supported. They were talking about serious ideas, and this made them feel that their opinions matter. Mutual respect among all the participants, who represented diversity in ethnicity as well as in gender, pointed to the value of finding learning models that let all students choose to speak and be heard.

Gloria H. Thompson
Science Teacher
Taft Junior High School
Washington, D.C.

Violet was an academically unmotivated seventh-grader. She was not "ready to learn." I followed the expected protocol. Each stage began with great expectations and promises but resulted in few sustained positive changes in behavior or work habits. I knew that I had to use strategies that would let Violet buy into the plan.

I decided to try an Adopt-A-Student approach. Violet was delighted that I wanted to be her In-School Mom. I invited her to meet with me after school. This setting provided the groundwork for establishing positive rapport. I was able to use the strategies that had failed earlier, because we were developing a trust that had not been there before. I readministered a learning styles inventory and found that Violet would benefit most from active, hands-on, real-life learning. I also conducted a life-space interview and discovered how frightened Violet had been about entering junior high school and the negative perception she had of herself. Violet seemed to suffer from learned helplessness and had low self-esteem. In our after-school informal sessions, Violet gained confidence in her ability to complete tasks successfully, have positive interactions, and reflect on her classroom responsibilities and roles. She was finally ready to learn. This readiness transferred to her classwork, where she was given resources that matched her learning style preferences.

As her confidence grew, Violet blossomed. I have used the Adopt-A-Student approach with students through the years and have found that it helps to discover motivating factors for low achievers, students with low self-esteem, and students who resist school structures and distrust authority figures.

Berlyne (1965) discusses the concept of *epistemic curiosity*—behavior aimed at acquiring knowledge to master and understand the environment. He hypothesizes that epistemic curiosity results from conceptual conflict, as when new information seems to contradict earlier understandings. Berlyne suggests the deliberate use of surprise, doubt, perplexity, bafflement, and contradiction as means of arousing epistemic curiosity. Two examples he gives are teaching about how plants use chlorophyll to carry out photosynthesis and then introducing the problem of fungi, which do not need sunlight; and teaching about latitude and longitude and then asking students how they would estimate their location in the middle of the desert.

USING A VARIETY OF INTERESTING PRESENTATION MODES ● The intrinsic motivation to learn something is enhanced by the use of interesting materials (Shirey & Reynolds, 1988), as well as by variety in mode of presentation. For example, teachers can maintain student interest in a subject by alternating use of films, guest speakers, demonstrations, and so on, although the use of each resource must be carefully planned to be sure it focuses on the course objectives and complements the other activities. Use of computers can enhance most students' intrinsic motivation to learn (Lepper, 1985).

CONNECTIONS

The importance of student interest in lesson content and presentation is discussed in Chapter 7, page 227.

One excellent means of increasing interest in a subject is to use games or simulations. A simulation, or role play, is an exercise in which students take on roles and engage in activities appropriate to those roles. Cal Lewis used simulation to teach students about the Constitutional Convention. Programs exist that simulate many aspects of government; for example, students may take roles as legislators who must negotiate and trade votes to satisfy their constituents' interests or as economic actors (farmers, producers, consumers) who run a minieconomy. Creative teachers have long used simulations that they designed themselves. For example, teachers can have students write their own newspaper; design, manufacture, and market a product; or set up and run a bank.

The advantage of simulations is that they allow students to learn about a subject from the inside. Although research on use of simulations (see Greenblat, 1982; VanSickle, 1986) finds that they are generally little or no more effective than traditional instruction for teaching facts and concepts, studies do consistently find that simulations increase students' interest, motivation, and affective learning (Dukes & Seidner, 1978). They certainly impart a different affective knowledge of a subject.

Nonsimulation games can also increase motivation to learn a given subject. The spelling bee is a popular example of a nonsimulation game. Teams–Games–Tournament, or TGT (Slavin, 1995a), uses games that can be adapted to any subject. Team games are usually better than individual games; they provide an opportunity for teammates to help one another and avoid one problem of individual games, which is that more able students may consistently win. If all students are put on mixed-ability teams, all have a good chance of success (see Slavin, 1995a).

HELPING STUDENTS SET THEIR OWN GOALS ● One fundamental principle of motivation is that people work harder for goals that they themselves set than for goals set for them by others. For example, a student might set a minimum number of books she expects to read at home or a score she expects to attain on an upcoming quiz. At the next goal-setting conference the teacher would discuss student attainment of (or failure to attain) goals and set new goals for the following week. During these meetings the teacher might help students learn to set ambitious but realistic goals and would praise them for setting and then achieving their goals.

Principles for Providing Extrinsic Incentives to Learn

Teachers must always try to enhance students' intrinsic motivation to learn academic materials, but they must at the same time be concerned about extrinsic incentives for learning (Brophy, 1987). Not every subject is intrinsically interesting to all students, and students must be motivated to do the hard work necessary to master difficult subjects. The following sections discuss a variety of incentives that can help motivate students to learn academic material.

EXPRESSING CLEAR EXPECTATIONS ● Students need to know exactly what they are supposed to do, how they will be evaluated, and what the consequences of success will be. Often, students' failures on particular tasks stem from confusion about what they are being asked to do (see Anderson, Brubaker, Alleman-Brooks, & Duffy, 1985; Brophy, 1982). Communicating clear expectations is important. For example, a teacher might introduce a writing assignment as follows:

> Today, I'd like you all to write a composition about what Thomas Jefferson would think of government in the United States today. I expect your compositions to be about two pages long, and I want them to compare and contrast the plan of government laid out by the nation's founders with the way government actually operates today. Your compositions will be graded on the basis of your ability to describe similarities and differences between the structure and function of the U.S. government in Thomas Jefferson's time and today, as well as on the originality and clarity of your writing. This will be an important part of your six weeks' grade, so I expect you to do your best!

Note that the teacher is clear about what students are to write, how much material is expected, how the work will be evaluated, and how important the work will be for the students' grades. This clarity assures students that efforts directed at writing a good composition will pay off—in this case, in terms of grades. If the teacher had just said, "I'd like you all to write a composition about what Thomas Jefferson would think about government in the United States today," students might write the wrong thing, write too much or too little, or perhaps emphasize the if-Jefferson-were-alive-today aspect of the assignment rather than the comparative-government aspect. They would be unsure how much importance the teacher intended to place on the mechanics of the composition as compared to its content. Finally, they would have no way of knowing how their efforts would pay off, lacking any indication of how much emphasis the teacher would give to the compositions in computing grades.

A study by Graham, MacArthur, and Schwartz (1995) shows the importance of specificity. Low-achieving fifth- and sixth-graders were asked to revise compositions either to "make [your paper] better" or to "add at least three things that will add information to your paper." The students with the more specific instructions wrote higher-quality, longer revisions because they had a clearer idea of exactly what was being asked of them.

PROVIDING CLEAR FEEDBACK ● The word **feedback** means information on the results of one's efforts. The term has been used throughout this book to refer both to information students receive on their performance and to information teachers obtain on the effects of their instruction. Feedback can serve as an incentive. Research on feedback has found that provision of information on the results of one's actions can be an adequate reward in some circumstances (Gibbons, Duffin, Robertson, & Thompson, 1998). However, to be an effective motivator, feedback must be clear and specific and must be given close in time to performance (Kulik

CONNECTIONS
Feedback is also discussed in Chapter 7, page 233.

feedback
Information on the results of one's efforts.

The Intentional Teacher

● Using What You Know about Motivation to Improve Teaching and Learning

Intentional teachers know that, although students may be motivated by different things and to varying degrees, every student *is* motivated. Intentional teachers understand that many elements of motivation can be influenced by the teacher, and they capitalize on their ability to unearth and direct student motivation. They provide instruction that helps students find meaning in learning and take pride in their own accomplishments.

◼ What am I trying to accomplish?

Intentional teachers plan how they will support student motivation. Think about how you will discover and sustain students' drive to participate in learning.

You commit to using principles of motivation in your long- and short-term planning. You review major findings on motivation and jot down some guiding ideas on an index card that you clip to your plan book:

Motivation: Checkpoints for Planning

✓ Count on <u>different drives</u> for different students and different situations. Watch and ask: What motivates?

✓ Build on <u>student interests</u>. Emphasize meaning and relevance. Ask: What s the connection to real life?

✓ Remember Goldilocks! Lessons need to be <u>just right</u> (not too easy, not too difficult). Ask: How will I vary task difficulty if necessary?

✓ Plan a grading system that <u>rewards effort</u> and enhances motivation.

✓ <u>Ongoing strategy</u>: Say things to help students link their success with their effort. (Not I <u>got</u>.... Instead: I <u>earned</u>....)

◼ What are my students' relevant experiences and needs?

Motivation varies by student, situation, and domain. Determine your students' current motivation.

You gather information about your sixth-graders' motivation from a variety of sources. For instance, you observe the students during informal conversations and during instruction. You ask them to write journal entries on prompts such as "What accounts for your score on this test?" You analyze their answers and your observations to gather information about three areas of motivation: 1. Where do students seem to be functioning in terms of Maslow's hierarchy of needs? Are their basic physiological needs met? 2. Do students seem to be seeking success or avoiding failure? 3. Do students use internal or external causal attributions? Stable or unstable? Controllable or uncontrollable?

◼ What approaches and materials are available to help me challenge every student?

For motivation to be high, students need to perceive that with effort, success is possible. Provide tasks that require effort but allow students to see that success is within reach.

You check your grade book at the end of the first marking period and find that some of your earth science students have earned D's and F's across the board but that others have a string of apparently easy A's. You begin your quest to improve instruction by meeting with students individually. You ask how they earned their grades and what they expect to earn in the future. Based on your conversations, you develop research projects at the students' correct level of difficulty and devise careful

---

& Kulik, 1988). This is important for all students, but especially for young ones. For example, praise for a job well done should specify what the student did well:

- "Good work! I like the way you used the guide words in the dictionary to find the words on your worksheet."
- "I like that answer. It shows you've been thinking about what I've been saying about freedom and responsibility."
- "This is an excellent essay. It started with a statement of the argument you were going to make and then supported the argument with relevant information. I also like the care you took with punctuation and word usage."

Specific feedback is both informative and motivational (Kulhavy & Stock, 1989). It tells students what they did right, so that they will know what to do in the future, and helps give them an effort-based attribution for success ("You suc-

contracts so that students who have yet to achieve see that success is possible.

Some students display a performance orientation instead of the more useful learning orientation. Help students shift their focus from completion to mastery by emphasizing the practical importance of content. Deemphasize grades and rewards.

The students in your honors English class seem overly concerned with their scores on essays and the grading curve. You employ portfolio assessment and require students to analyze their growth over time. Students grade themselves on improvement rather than on how their work compares to that of their peers.

When students experience inconsistent, unpredictable use of rewards and punishments, they may not link their behavior to consequences and may conclude that nothing they do matters. Help students unlearn learned helplessness by teaching them to link failure to lack of effort—not lack of ability.

When you return tests on state history, Pat glances at his grade and tells you, "I don't care about that D. That's all I ever get. D is my middle name!" You take him aside, remind him of the many areas in which he does succeed, and ask him about how he prepared for the test. Finally, you help him pinpoint the concepts on the exam he has mastered and those with which he is still struggling. Pat returns to his seat with a shrug, a slight smile, and a more realistic appraisal of his efforts and abilities.

Praise needs to be used effectively. Be certain that your praise is sincere, specific, and contingent upon students' behavior.

You observe the teacher next door and hear him say something like "Super job! You're terrific" to each child who ventures an answer. You vow to reserve your praise for good performance, to focus on the behavior and not the student, and to be specific in what constitutes a good performance: "Jamal, look at the way

you blended those two colors. That really adds depth to the painting. It looks real!"

4 How will I know whether and when to change my strategy or modify my instruction?

Students need to develop accurate attributions for their success. Observe your students to note whether they perceive that their effort contributes to their learning. Intervene when students' attributions are inaccurate. Step up your efforts to help students set goals, take responsibility for their progress, and evaluate their work.

At the beginning of the second semester, you have students reflect on their first semester's work and set new learning goals. Together you devise a grading system that rewards performance, effort, and improvement.

5 What information will I accept as evidence that my students and I are experiencing success?

Maslow asserts that the goal for psychological health is self-actualization. Review your instruction and students' learning to determine the extent to which you and the students are meeting the broad span of their needs and reaching full potential.

You ask your peer coach to observe artifacts from your classroom and to observe you for a morning to help you analyze your use of principles of motivation. You ask her to examine a brief list of questions: What evidence is there that (1) the environment is safe and comfortable and encourages students to take risks? (2) instruction is meaningful and lively? (3) students are active participants in analyzing their growth and setting plans? Her data collection fuels a rich conversation about your progress in motivation.

ceeded because you worked hard"). In contrast, if students are praised or receive a good grade without any explanation, they are unlikely to learn from the feedback what to do next time to be successful and may form an ability attribution ("I succeeded because I'm smart") or an external attribution ("I must have succeeded because the teacher likes me, the task was easy, or I lucked out"). As was noted earlier in this chapter, effort attributions are most conducive to continuing motivation. Similarly, feedback about mistakes or failures can add to motivation if it focuses only on the performance itself (not on students' general abilities) and if it is alternated with success feedback (see Clifford, 1984, 1990).

PROVIDING IMMEDIATE FEEDBACK ● Immediacy of feedback is also very important (Kulik & Kulik, 1988). If students complete a project on Monday and don't receive any feedback on it until Friday, the informational and motivational value of the feedback will be diminished. First, if they made errors, they may continue all week making similar errors on related material that might have been averted by feedback on the performance. Second, a long delay between behavior and consequence confuses the relationship between the two. Young students, especially, may have little idea why they received a particular grade if the performance on which the grade is based occurred several days earlier.

PROVIDING FREQUENT FEEDBACK ● Feedback should be delivered frequently to students to maintain their best efforts. For example, it is unrealistic to expect most students to work hard for 6 or 9 weeks in hope of improving their grade unless they receive frequent feedback. Research in the behavioral learning theory tradition has established that no matter how powerful a reward is, it may have little impact on behavior if it is given infrequently; small, frequent rewards are more effective incentives than are large, infrequent ones. Research on frequency of testing has generally found that it is a good idea to give frequent brief quizzes to assess student progress rather than infrequent long tests (Dempster, 1991). Research also points up the importance of asking many questions in class so that students can gain information about their own level of understanding and can receive reinforcement (praise, recognition) for paying attention to lessons.

INCREASING THE VALUE AND AVAILABILITY OF EXTRINSIC MOTIVATORS ● Expectancy theories of motivation, discussed earlier in this chapter, hold that motivation is a product of the value an individual attaches to success and the individual's estimate of the likelihood of success (see Atkinson & Birch, 1978). One implication of this is that students must value incentives that are used to motivate them. Some students are not particularly interested in teacher praise or grades but may value notes sent home to their parents, a little extra recess time, or a special privilege in the classroom.

CONNECTIONS

For more on student portfolios, see Chapter 13, page 483.

Another implication of expectancy theory is that although all students must have a chance to be rewarded if they do their best, no student should have an easy time achieving the maximum reward. This principle is violated by traditional grading practices, because some students find it easy to earn A's and B's, whereas others believe that they have little chance of academic success no matter what they do. In this circumstance, neither high achievers nor low achievers are likely to exert their best efforts. This is one reason that it is important to reward students for effort, for doing better than they have done in the past, or for making progress, rather than only for getting a high score. For example, students can build a portfolio of compositions, projects, reports, or other work and can then see how their work is improving over time. Not all students are equally capable of achieving high scores; but all are equally capable of exerting effort, exceeding their own past record, or making progress, so these are often better, more equally available criteria for reward.

SELF-CHECK

Make a list of intrinsic and extrinsic motivators as well as specific strategies that teachers can use to enhance motivation in their classrooms. Then reread the chapter-opening vignette. Identify each event in Mr. Lewis's lesson in terms of the strategies you have listed.

Praise is effective as a classroom motivator when it is contingent, specific, and credible. As a teacher, how will you use praise to motivate your students?

HOW CAN TEACHERS REWARD PERFORMANCE, EFFORT, AND IMPROVEMENT?

As has been noted many times in this chapter, incentive systems that are used in the classroom should focus on student effort, not ability. A principal means of rewarding students for putting forth their best efforts is to reward effort directly by praising students for their efforts or, as is done in many schools, by giving a separate effort grade or rating along with the usual performance grade or including effort as an important part of students' grades.

Using Praise Effectively

Praise serves many purposes in classroom instruction but is primarily used to reinforce appropriate behaviors and to give feedback to students on what they are doing right. Overall, it is a good idea to use praise frequently, especially with young children and in classrooms with many low-achieving students (Brophy, 1981; Evans, 1996). However, what is more important than the amount of praise given is the way it is given (Nafpaktitis, Mayer, & Butterworth, 1985). Praise is effective as a classroom motivator to the extent that it is contingent, specific, and credible. **Contingent praise** depends on student performance of well-defined behaviors. For example, if a teacher says, "I'd like you all to open your books to page ninety-two and work problems one to ten," then praise will be given only to the students who follow directions. Praise should be given only for right answers and appropriate behaviors.

Specificity means that the teacher praises students for specific behaviors, not for general "goodness." For example, a teacher might say, "Susan, I'm glad you

CONNECTIONS

For more on the use of praise as a reinforcer, see Chapter 11, page 381.

contingent praise
Praise that is effective because it refers directly to specific task performances.

TABLE 10.4

Guidelines for Effective Praise

If used properly, praise can be an effective motivator in classroom situations.

EFFECTIVE PRAISE

1. Is delivered contingently.
2. Specifies the particulars of the accomplishment.
3. Shows spontaneity, variety, and other signs of credibility; suggests clear attention to the student's accomplishment.
4. Rewards attainment of specified performance criteria (which can include effort criteria, however).
5. Provides information to students about their competence or the value of their accomplishments.
6. Orients students toward better appreciation of their own task-related behavior and thinking about problem solving.
7. Uses students' own prior accomplishments as the context for describing present accomplishments.
8. Is given in recognition of noteworthy effort or success at difficult tasks (for *this* student).
9. Attributes success to effort and ability, implying that similar successes can be expected in the future.
10. Focuses students' attention on their own task-relevant behavior.
11. Fosters appreciation of, and desirable attributions about, task-relevant behavior after the process is completed.

Source: From Jere Brophy, "Teacher Praise," *Review of Educational Research, 51,* p. 26. Copyright © 1981 by the American Educational Research Association. Adapted by permission of the publisher.

followed my directions to start work on your composition," rather than "Susan, you're doing great!"

When praise is *credible,* it is given sincerely for good work. Brophy (1981) notes that when praising low-achieving or disruptive students for good work, teachers often contradict their words with tone, posture, or other nonverbal cues. Brophy's (1981) list of guidelines for effective praise appears in Table 10.4.

In addition to contingency, specificity, and credibility, Brophy's list includes several particularly important principles that reinforce topics discussed earlier in this chapter. For example, guidelines 7 and 8 emphasize that praise should be given for good performance relative to a student's usual level of performance. That is, students who usually do well should not be praised for a merely average performance, but students who usually do less well should be praised when they do better. This relates to the principle of accessibility of reward discussed earlier in this chapter; rewards should be neither too easy nor too difficult for students to obtain.

Teaching Students to Praise Themselves

CONNECTIONS

For more on self-regulated learning, see Chapter 5, page 166.

There is increasing evidence that students can learn to praise themselves and that this increases their academic success. For example, children can learn to mentally give themselves a pat on the back when they finish a task or to stop at regular intervals to notice how much they have done (Corno & Kanfer, 1993; Ross, Rolheiser, & Hogaboam-Gray, 1998). This strategy is a key component of self-regulated learning.

Using Grades As Incentives

CONNECTIONS

Principles and procedures of grading are discussed in Chapter 14, page 523.

The grading systems that most schools use serve three quite different functions at the same time: evaluation, feedback, and incentive. This mix of functions makes grades less than ideal for each function. For example, because grades are based largely on ability rather than on effort, they are less than ideal for motivating students to exert maximum effort, as was noted earlier in this chapter. Also, grades are given too infrequently to be very useful as either feedback or incentives for young children who cannot see the connection between today's work and a grade to be received in 6 weeks. Grades are effective as incentives for older students, however. Experiments comparing graded and ungraded college classes (e.g., Gold, Reilly, Silberman, & Lehr, 1971) find substantially higher performance in the graded classes. Grades work as incentives in part because they increase the value of other rewards given closer in time to the behaviors they reinforce. For example, when students get stars on their papers, they may value them in part because the stars are an indication that their grades in that subject may also be good. The accessibility problem of grades—the fact that good grades are too easy for some students but too difficult for others—may be partially diminished by the use of grading systems that have many levels. For example, low-performing students may feel rewarded if they simply pass or if they get a C, while their high-performing classmates may not be satisfied unless they get an A. Also, one major reason that students value grades is that their parents value them, and parents are particularly likely to praise their children for improvements in their grades. Even though good grades are not equally attainable by all students, improved grades certainly are, except by straight A students.

Individual Learning Expectations

Another way of providing incentives to learn is to recognize students' improvement over their own past record. The advantage of an improvement score is that it is quantifiable and does not rely as heavily on teachers' subjective judgments as an effort rating does. All but the highest-performing students are capable of improvement, and high-performing students can be rewarded for perfect papers, which should be well within their reach.

Slavin (1980; Beady, Slavin, & Fennessey, 1981) developed and evaluated a method of rewarding students for improvement called **Individual Learning Expectations (ILE).** The idea behind ILE is to recognize students for doing better than they have done in the past, for steadily increasing in performance until they are producing excellent work all the time. In this way, all students have an opportunity to earn recognition for academic work simply by doing their best. It was found that use of ILE significantly increased student achievement in comparison with classes that used traditional grading systems.

Individual Learning Expectations (ILE)
An incentive method that rewards students for improvement relative to past achievement.

Computing ILE Base Scores and Improvement Points

Students should take at least one short quiz per week in any subject in which the Individual Learning Expectations method is being used. Ten items are usually enough. Quizzes should be scored in class immediately after being given; students exchange papers, then the teacher reads the answers. Let students see their own papers, discuss any frequently missed items, then pass their papers in.

THEORY
into
Practice

INITIAL BASE SCORES

Base scores represent students' average scores on past quizzes. If you are starting ILE at the beginning of the year, assign initial base scores according to students' grades in the same subjects the preceding year.

Computing Initial Base Scores

Last Year's Grade	Initial Base Score
A	90
A– or B +	85
B	80
B– or C +	75
C	70
C– or D +	65
F	60

If your school uses percentages rather than grades, you may use last year's average as this year's base score. If you are starting to use ILE after you have given some quizzes in your class, use the average percent correct on those quizzes to compute an initial base score.

IMPROVEMENT POINTS

Every time you give a quiz, compare students' quiz scores with their base scores, and give students improvement points as shown in the following chart:

Computing improvement points

Quiz Score	Improvement Points	Comments
5 or more points below base score	0	"You can do better!"
4 points below to 4 points above base score	1	"About average for you—but you can do better."
5 to 9 points above base score	2	"Better than your average—good work."
10 or more points above base score or perfect score (regardless of base score)	3	"Super! Much better than average!"

Note that improvement points are given in relation to past performance. A student who averaged 75 on previous quizzes and gets an 80 would get the same number of improvement points (2) as a student who averaged 90 and gets a 95 this week. However, there is no danger of students topping out with too high a base score, since all students get the maximum score (3 improvement points) if they get a perfect paper, regardless of their base score.

FEEDBACK TO STUDENTS

Improvement points should be marked on students' quizzes and returned to them as soon as possible. In addition, every 2 weeks, students' improvement scores should be averaged for all quizzes given during that period. Then attractive certificates or other small rewards should be given to students who have averaged at least 2 improvement points. The first time you do this, also send home a note to parents explaining what the certificates are for. Parents are the key to the success of ILE. If they value reports of their children's improvement and if the teacher emphasizes progress and improvement, then students will value improvement too.

RECOMPUTING BASE SCORES

At the end of each marking period, average the percent correct scores on each quiz with the past average, and compute a new base score (drop any fraction when you divide). For example, let's say Zoe's past average was 84 and her quiz scores were 90, 95, and 90. You would compute her new base score as follows:

	84	Old base score
+	90	Quiz 1 score (2 improvement points)
+	95	Quiz 2 score (3 improvement points)
+	90	Quiz 3 score (2 improvement points)

359/4 = 89¾ = (drop fraction) 89 = new base score

In other words, because Zoe's quiz scores were all above her base score (84), her base score increases to 89. Next time, it will be somewhat harder for her to earn improvement points.

IMPROVEMENT POINTS AND GRADES

When you give grades, also report average improvement points for the marking period. In general, high improvement points should be reflected in higher grades. For example, a student who averaged 2 or more improvement points might increase from a C to a B or from a B to an A. Again, communication to students (and their parents) that effort and improvement are important is critical in making the improvement point system effective.

Incentive Systems Based on Goal Structure

One aspect of classroom incentive systems that has received considerable research attention in recent years is the **goal structure** of the classroom. This term refers to the degree to which students are in cooperation or competition with one another. If students are in competition, any student's success means another's failure. For example, if the teacher establishes a policy that only one quarter of the class can get an A, then students are in competition, because if any student gets an A, this means that another cannot get an A. Just the opposite is true of cooperation. If a group of four students is doing a laboratory exercise together, they will all succeed or fail together. If one student works hard, this increases the others' chances of success. A third goal structure is individualization, in which one individual's success or failure has no consequences for others. For example, if the teacher said, "I will give an A to all students who average at least 90 percent on all quizzes given this marking period," then the students would be under an individualized goal structure, because the success of any one student would have no consequences for the success of his or her classmates (see Johnson & Johnson, 1987).

COMPETITIVE GOAL STRUCTURES ● Competitive goal structures have been criticized for discouraging students from helping one another learn (Johnson & Johnson, 1987), for tending to set up a pecking order in the classroom (Ames, 1986), and for establishing a situation in which low achievers have little chance of success (Slavin, 1995a). Coleman (1961) noted that an individual student's success in sports is strongly supported by other students because the sports hero brings glory to the team and the school, but that students do not encourage one another's academic achievements because in the competitive academic system, achievement brings success only to the individual.

goal structure
The degree to which students are placed in competitive or cooperative relationships in earning classroom rewards.

CASE TO CONSIDER

Motivating a Reluctant Student

Written by Dr. Gordon E. Greenwood, University of Florida

Carl Rosatti, a fourth-grade teacher with 10 years' experience, talks in his classroom after school to Ruth Duncan about Ruth's son Jeremy.

Carl: I appreciate your taking time to come down today.
Ruth: Oh, I was glad to come. I must say, though, it's tricky. My husband and I run a store, and it's a 24-hour-a-day job. Anyway, how is Jeremy doing?
Carl: I'm sure you've noticed from his report cards that Jeremy has not been reaching our minimum goals for him in several areas, especially math. He seems to have trouble applying himself in class. His attention wanders. Also, he doesn't always turn in his homework. What happens to the work I send home with him?
Ruth: Well, he certainly doesn't seem to sit down and dig into it on his own. I see some books come home, but when I ask him about what he's supposed to do, he says it's nothing.
Carl: Hmm. I'd like to see that attitude change. Good work motivation develops early, and Jeremy needs to get a good start.

In math period the next day, the class is working on adding two-digit numbers with renaming. Carl sets up a store activity with Pete and a reluctant Jeremy.

Carl: OK, my desk is the counter, and these empty pencil boxes are new Lego kits, right? Each one has a price label. And you each have plenty of *Monopoly* money. So—may I help you, sir?
Pete: Well, I'll take these two: $17 and $26.
Carl: Fine. Now, unfortunately, my cash register is broken, sir, so I need you to add up what you owe me. Here, use the blackboard.
Pete (working): Seven and six makes thirteen, put down the three . . . $33? No, wait. I think I forgot something. We did this yesterday on that worksheet, right? Don't tell me, let me try again. $43!
Carl: Correct. And a good job of sticking with the problem, Pete. Here you are, sir, enjoy your purchases. Now, sir, what can I do for you?

Jeremy: Nothing. I don't want to do this.
Carl: Hey, Jeremy, this isn't hard. You made a good start on these kinds of problems when I worked with you yesterday, remember?
Jeremy: Maybe, but I still don't get it. It's not my fault, Mr. Rosatti. I just can't do it. I hate math.
Carl: Well, let me ask you, what do you like?
Jeremy: Like? I like riding my bike. I like helping my dad in his store.
Carl: You help in the store? That's excellent. What do you do to help?
Jeremy: I don't know. Sometimes I just hang around. Or I arrange the displays. Sometimes I tell Dad if we're out of something, or I show people where things are.
Carl: How about helping out with money? Do you put on price tags or work the cash register?
Jeremy: No, Mr. Rosatti! I couldn't do any of that! I can't do math.
Carl: Well, you just put your finger on the whole point. You need to learn to add and subtract here in school. Then you'll be able to have a lot more responsibility and do a lot of interesting things that you like to do.
Jeremy: I don't care. I'll learn math soon enough, I guess. Anyway, my mom and dad wouldn't ever let me use the cash register. They don't care about me doing math. Anyway, I could do most of those problems if I tried, I bet.
Carl: You might be right about that. So how about trying?
Jeremy: Yeah, maybe sometime, Mr. Rosatti.

PROBLEM SOLVING

1. How can Carl help motivate Jeremy to learn? Is it possible for one person to motivate another, or is motivation something inside a person? How can Carl encourage intrinsic motivation while using extrinsic motivation?
2. Drawing on what you know about the situation, develop a problem-solving approach for getting Jeremy motivated. How will you involve Jeremy's parents?
3. Model your problem-solving approach by extending the dialogue in writing or role play to the next day.

SELF-CHECK

Explain how rewards, praise, grades, ILE scores, individualized goal structures, and cooperative goal structures can be used appropriately as incentives to enhance students' motivation to learn.

CHAPTER SUMMARY

WHAT IS MOTIVATION?

Motivation is an internal process that activates, guides, and maintains behavior over time. There are different kinds, intensities, aims, and directions of motivation. Motivation to learn is critically important to students and teachers.

WHAT ARE SOME THEORIES OF MOTIVATION?

In behavioral learning theory (Skinner and others), motivation is a consequence of reinforcement. However, the value of a reinforcer depends on many factors, and the strength of motivation may be different in different students.

In Maslow's human needs theory, which is based on a hierarchy of needs, people must satisfy their lower-level (deficiency) needs before they will be motivated to try to satisfy their higher-level (growth) needs. Maslow's concept of the need for self-actualization, the highest need, is defined as the desire to become everything one is capable of becoming.

Attribution theory seeks to understand people's explanations for their success or failure. A central assumption is that people will attempt to maintain a positive self-image; so when good things happen, people attribute them to their own abilities, whereas they tend to attribute negative events to factors beyond their control. Locus of control may be internal (success or failure is due to personal effort or ability) or external (success or failure is due to luck or task difficulty). Expectancy theory holds that a person's motivation to achieve something depends on the product of that person's estimation of his or her chance of success and the value he or she places on success. Motivation should be at a maximum at moderate levels of probability of success. An important educational implication is that learning tasks should be neither too easy nor too difficult.

HOW CAN ACHIEVEMENT MOTIVATION BE ENHANCED?

Teachers can emphasize learning goals and positive or empowering attributions. Students with learning goals see the purpose of school as gaining knowledge and competence; these students tend to have higher motivation to learn than do students with the performance goals of positive judgments and good grades. Teachers can use special programs such as attribution training to help students out of learned helplessness, in which students feel that they are doomed to fail despite their actions. Teachers' expectations significantly affect students' motivation and achievement. Teachers can communicate positive expectations that students can learn and can take steps to reduce anxiety.

HOW CAN TEACHERS INCREASE STUDENTS' MOTIVATION TO LEARN?

An incentive is a reinforcer that people can expect to receive if they perform a specific behavior. Intrinsic incentives are aspects of certain tasks that in themselves have enough value to motivate students to do the tasks on their own. Extrinsic incentives include grades, gold stars, and other rewards. Teachers can enhance intrinsic motivation by arousing students' interest, maintaining curiosity, using a variety of presentation modes, and letting students set their own goals. Ways to offer extrinsic incentives include stating clear expectations; giving clear, immediate, and frequent feedback; and increasing the value and availability of rewards.

HOW CAN TEACHERS REWARD PERFORMANCE, EFFORT, AND IMPROVEMENT?

Classroom rewards include praise, which is most effective when it is contingent, specific, and credible. Feedback and grades can serve as incentives. A general method of rewarding effort is to recognize students' improvement over their own past records. The Individual Learning Expectations (ILE) system, for example, is based on the principle of recognizing individual students who show improvement over their own past performance. ILE uses quizzes, initial base scores, improvement points, feedback, certificates, and recomputations of base scores in addition to grades. Teachers can also use cooperative learning methods that emphasize cooperative goal structures over competitive goal structures and reward effort and improvement.

KEY TERMS

achievement motivation   337
attribution theory   331
contingent praise   353
deficiency needs   330
expectancy theory   335
expectancy–valence model   335
extrinsic incentives   345
feedback   349
goal structure   357
growth needs   330

Individual Learning Expectations (ILE)   355
intrinsic incentive   344
learned helplessness   340
learning goals   337
locus of control   333
mastery goals   337
motivation   327
performance goals   337
self-actualization   330

Self-Assessment

1. Rearrange the following needs from Maslow's hierarchy in the proper order.
   a. aesthetic
   b. belongingness and love
   c. need to know and understand
   d. physiological
   e. safety
   f. self-actualization
   g. self-esteem

2. Match each theory of motivation with its definition.
   a. expectancy theory

   b. behavioral theory
   c. attribution theory

   _____ A theory of motivation closely tied to the principle that behaviors that have been reinforced are likely to be repeated.
   _____ An explanation of motivation that focuses on how people explain the causes of their own successes and failures.
   _____ A theory that motivation is determined by the perceived probability and the incentive value of success.

3. How would Skinner's explanation of a student's incentive to obtain good grades differ from Maslow's explanation?

4. A student with an internal locus of control is likely to attribute a high test score to
   a. the test being easy.
   b. favored treatment from the teacher.
   c. careful studying.
   d. good luck.

5. Teachers who want their students to work harder regardless of ability level or task difficulty are trying to develop attributions that fall in which one of the following categories?
   a. internal–stable
   b. internal–unstable
   c. external–stable
   d. external–unstable

6. A student who tends to choose either very easy or very hard tasks may be
   a. seeking success.
   b. avoiding failure.
   c. risking learned helplessness.
   d. choosing an internal locus of control.

7. Which behavior is characteristic of students who are oriented toward learning goals?
   a. taking a challenging course
   b. trying to make the honor roll
   c. trying to get recognition from a teacher
   d. becoming discouraged in the face of obstacles

8. The main idea underlying the Individual Learning Expectations (ILE) model is
   a. a pass–fail grading system.
   b. an ungraded evaluation.
   c. grading on the basis of improvement.
   d. criterion-referenced grading.

9. Match each of the following goal structures with its description.
   a. competitive
   b. cooperative
   c. individualized

   _____ All succeed or all fail.
   _____ One person's success or failure has no influence on another's fate.
   _____ Some will succeed and others will fail.

10. What are the advantages and disadvantages of being graded on improvement?

Chapter 11

WHAT IS AN EFFECTIVE LEARNING ENVIRONMENT?

WHAT IS THE IMPACT OF TIME ON LEARNING?
Using Allocated Time for Instruction
Using Engaged Time Effectively
Can Time On-Task Be Too High?
Classroom Management in the Student-Centered Classroom

WHAT PRACTICES CONTRIBUTE TO EFFECTIVE CLASSROOM MANAGEMENT?
Starting Out the Year Right
Setting Class Rules

WHAT ARE SOME STRATEGIES FOR MANAGING ROUTINE MISBEHAVIOR?
The Principle of Least Intervention
Prevention
Nonverbal Cues
Praising Behavior That Is Incompatible with Misbehavior
Praising Other Students
Verbal Reminders
Repeated Reminders
Applying Consequences

HOW IS APPLIED BEHAVIOR ANALYSIS USED TO MANAGE MORE SERIOUS BEHAVIOR PROBLEMS?
How Student Misbehavior Is Maintained
Principles of Applied Behavior Analysis
Applied Behavior Analysis Programs
Ethics of Behavioral Methods

HOW CAN SERIOUS BEHAVIOR PROBLEMS BE PREVENTED?
Identifying Causes of Misbehavior
Enforcing Rules and Practices
Enforcing School Attendance
Avoiding Tracking
Practicing Intervention
Requesting Family Involvement
Using Peer Mediation
Judiciously Applying Consequences

Effective Learning Environments

The bell rang outside of Julia Cavalho's tenth-grade English class. The sound was still echoing in the hall when Ms. Cavalho started her lesson. "Today," she began, "you will become thieves. Worse than thieves. Thieves steal only your money or your property. You—" (she looked around the class and paused for emphasis) "—will steal something far more valuable. You will steal an author's style. An author builds his or her style, word by word, sentence by sentence, over many years. Stealing an author's style is like stealing a house someone built by hand. It's despicable, but you're going to do it."

During her speech the students sat in rapt attention. Two students, Mark and Gloria, slunk in late. Mark made a funny "Oops, I'm late" face and did an exaggerated tiptoe to his desk. Ms. Cavalho ignored both of them, as did the class. She continued her lesson.

"To whom are you going to do this dirty deed? Papa Hemingway, of course. Hemingway of the short, punchy sentence. Hemingway of the almost excessive attention to physical detail. You've read *The Old Man and the Sea.* You've read parts of *The Sun Also Rises* and *For Whom the Bell Tolls.*"

While Ms. Cavalho talked, Mark made an exaggerated show of getting out his books. He whispered to a neighboring student. Without stopping her lesson, Ms. Cavalho moved near Mark. He stopped whispering and paid attention.

"Today you will *become* Hemingway. You will steal his words, his pace, his meter, his similes, his metaphors, and put them to work in your own story."

Ms. Cavalho had students review elements of Hemingway's style, which the class had studied before.

"Everyone think for a moment. How would Hemingway describe an old woman going up the stairs at the end of a long day's work? Mai, what do you think?"

Mai gave her short description of the old woman.

"Sounds great to me. I like your use of very short sentences and physical description. Any other ideas? Kevin?"

Ms. Cavalho let several students give Hemingway-style descriptions, using them as opportunities to reinforce her main points.

"In a moment," she said, "you're going to get your chance to become Ernest Hemingway. As usual, you'll be working in your writing response groups. Before we start, however, let's go over our rules about effective group work. Who can tell me what they are?"

The students volunteered several rules: respect others, explain your ideas, be sure everyone participates, stand up for your opinion, keep voices low.

"All right," said Ms. Cavalho. "When I say begin, I'd like you to move your desks together and start planning your compositions. Ready? Begin."

The students moved their desks together smoothly and quickly and got right to work. During the transition, Ms. Cavalho called Mark and Gloria to her desk to discuss their lateness. Gloria had a good excuse, but Mark was developing a pattern of lateness and disruptiveness.

"Mark," said Ms. Cavalho, "I'm concerned about your lateness and your behavior in class. I've spoken to some of your other teachers, and they say you're behaving even worse in their classes than you do in mine. Please come here after school, and we'll see if we can come up with a solution to this problem."

Mark returned to his group and got to work. Ms. Cavalho circulated among the groups, giving encouragement to students who were working well. When she saw two girls who were goofing off, she moved close to them and put her hand on one girl's shoulder while looking at the plan for her composition. "Good start," she said. "Let's see how far you can get with this by the end of the period."

The students worked in a controlled but excited way through the end of the period, thoroughly enjoying "stealing" from Hemingway. The classroom sounded like a beehive with busy, involved students sharing ideas, reading drafts to each other, and editing each other's compositions.

At the end of the day, Mark returned to Ms. Cavalho's classroom.

"Mark," she said, "we need to do something about your lateness and your clowning in class. How would you suggest that we solve this problem?"

"Gloria was late, too," Mark protested.

"We're not talking about Gloria. We're talking about you. You are responsible for your own behavior."

"OK, OK, I promise I'll be on time."

"That's not good enough. We've had this conversation before. We need a different plan this time. I know you can succeed in this class, but you're making it hard on yourself as well as disrupting your classmates.

"Let's try an experiment," Ms. Cavalho went on. "Each day, I'd like you to rate your own behavior. I'll do the same. If we both agree at the end of each week that you've been on time and appropriately behaved, fine. If not, I'll need to call your parents and see whether we can make another plan. Are you willing to give it a try?"

"OK, I guess so."

"Great. I'm expecting to see a new Mark starting tomorrow. I know you won't let me down!"

Using Your EXPERIENCE

Critical Thinking   What methods of classroom management does Ms. Cavalho use? What potential problems is she preventing?

Creative Thinking   Suppose Mark continues to be late for class. Plan a conference with his parents. What are the goals? How will they be implemented?

Critical and Creative Thinking   Analyze two variables, grade level and classroom management strategies, in a matrix. Using Ms. Cavalho's classroom as a starter, create this matrix with grade level on the horizontal (e.g., elementary, middle, and high school), and then brainstorm classroom management strategies down the vertical column. Finally, check off which management strategies are influential at different grade levels.

WHAT IS AN EFFECTIVE LEARNING ENVIRONMENT?

Providing an effective learning environment includes strategies that teachers use to create a positive, productive classroom experience. Often called **classroom management,** strategies for providing effective learning environments include not only preventing and responding to misbehavior but also, more important, using class time well, creating an atmosphere that is conducive to interest and inquiry, and permitting activities that engage students' minds and imaginations. A class with no behavior problems can by no means be assumed to be a well-managed class.

The most effective approaches to classroom management are those discussed in Chapters 6 through 10. Students who are participating in well-structured activities that engage their interests, who are highly motivated to learn, and who are working on tasks that are challenging yet within their capabilities rarely pose any serious management problems. The vignette involving Ms. Cavalho illustrates this.

classroom management
Methods used to organize classroom activities, instruction, physical structure, and other features to make effective use of time, to create a happy and productive learning environment, and to minimize behavior problems and other disruptions.

She has a well-managed class not because she behaves like a drill sergeant, but because she teaches interesting lessons, engages students' imaginations and energies, makes efficient use of time, and communicates a sense of purpose, high expectations, and contagious enthusiasm. However, even a well-managed class is sure to contain individual students who will misbehave. While Ms. Cavalho's focus is on preventing behavior problems, she is also ready to intervene when necessary to see that students' behaviors are within acceptable limits. For some students a glance, physical proximity, or a hand on the shoulder are enough. For others, consequences may be necessary. Even in these cases, Ms. Cavalho does not let behavior issues disrupt her lesson or her students' learning activities.

This chapter focuses on the creation of effective learning environments (also known as classroom management) and on discipline. Creating an effective learning environment involves organizing classroom activities, instruction, and the physical classroom to provide for effective use of time, to create a happy, productive learning environment, and to minimize behavior problems and disruptions. **Discipline** refers to methods used to prevent behavior problems or to respond to existing behavior problems so as to reduce their occurrence in the future.

There is no magic or charisma that makes a teacher an effective classroom manager. Setting up an effective learning environment is a matter of knowing a set of techniques that any teacher can learn and apply. This chapter takes an approach to classroom management and discipline that emphasizes prevention of misbehavior, on the theory that effective instruction itself is the best means of avoiding discipline problems. In the past, creating an effective learning environment has often been seen as a matter of dealing with individual student misbehaviors. Current thinking emphasizes management of the class as a whole in such a way as to make individual misbehaviors rare (Evertson & Harris, 1993). Teachers who present interesting, well-organized lessons, who use incentives for learning effectively, who accommodate their instruction to students' levels of preparation, and who plan and manage their own time effectively will have few discipline problems to deal with. Still, every teacher, no matter how effective, will encounter discipline problems sometimes, and this chapter also presents means of handling these problems when they arise.

SELF-CHECK

What elements contribute to an effective learning environment? Make a list of discipline problems that you might encounter as a teacher. How might these problems be prevented or handled?

WHAT IS THE IMPACT OF TIME ON LEARNING?

discipline
Methods used to prevent behavior problems from occurring or to respond to behavior problems so as to reduce their occurrence in the future.

Obviously, if no time is spent teaching a subject, students will not learn it. However, within the usual range of time allocated to instruction, how much difference does time make? This has been a focus of considerable research (see Adelman, Haslam, & Pringle, 1996; National Education Commission on Time and Learning, 1994). Although it is clear that more time spent in instruction has a positive impact on student achievement, the effects of additional time are often modest or inconsistent (Gijselaers & Schmidt, 1995; Karweit, 1989c). In particular, the typical differences in lengths of school days and school years among different districts have only a minor impact on student achievement (see Karweit, 1981;

Walberg, 1988). What seems to be more important is how time is used in class. **Engaged time,** or **time on-task,** the number of minutes actually spent learning, is the time measure that is most frequently found to contribute to learning (e.g., Adelman, Haslam, & Pringle, 1996; Karweit & Slavin, 1981). In other words, the most important aspect of time is the one that is under the direct control of the teacher: the organization and use of time in the classroom. (Jones & Jones, 1998).

Using Allocated Time for Instruction

Time is a limited resource in schools. A typical school is in session about 6 hours a day for 180 days each year. Time for educational activities can be expanded by means of homework assignments or (for some students) summer school, but the total time available for instruction is essentially set. Out of these 6 hours (or so) must come time for teaching a variety of subjects plus time for lunch, recess, and physical education; transitions between classes; announcements; and so on. In a 40- to 60-minute period in a particular subject, many quite different factors reduce the time available for instruction. Figure 11.1 illustrates how time scheduled for mathematics instruction in 12 second- to fifth-grade classes observed by Karweit and Slavin (1981) was whittled away.

The classes that Karweit and Slavin (1981) observed were in schools in and around a rural Maryland town. Overall, the classes were well organized and businesslike, with dedicated and hardworking teachers. Students were generally well behaved and respectful of authority. However, even in these very good schools, the average student spent only 60 percent of the time scheduled for mathematics instruction actually learning mathematics. First of all, about 20 class days were lost to such activities as standardized testing, school events, field trips, and teacher absences. On days when instruction was given, class time was lost because of late starts and noninstructional activities such as discussions of upcoming events, announcements, passing out of materials, and disciplining of students. Finally, even when math was being taught, many students were not actually engaged in the instructional activity. Some were daydreaming during lecture or seatwork times,

engaged time
Time students spend actually learning; same as time on-task.

time on-task
Time students spend actively engaged in learning the task at hand.

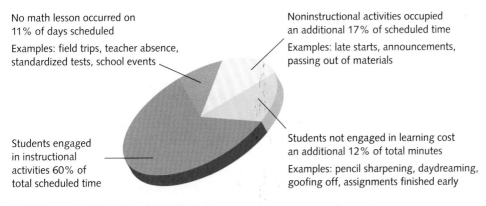

No math lesson occurred on 11% of days scheduled
Examples: field trips, teacher absence, standardized tests, school events

Noninstructional activities occupied an additional 17% of scheduled time
Examples: late starts, announcements, passing out of materials

Students engaged in instructional activities 60% of total scheduled time

Students not engaged in learning cost an additional 12% of total minutes
Examples: pencil sharpening, daydreaming, goofing off, assignments finished early

FIGURE 11.1 ● Where Does the Time Go?
Observations of elementary school mathematics classes showed that the time students actually spend learning in class is only about 60 percent of the time allocated for instruction. Based on data from N. L. Karweit and R. E. Slavin, "Measurement and Modeling Choices in Studies of Time and Learning," *American Educational Research Journal, 18*(2). Copyright © 1981 by the American Educational Research Association. Adapted by permission of the publisher.

goofing off, or sharpening pencils; others had nothing to do, either because they were finished with their assigned work or because they had not yet been assigned a task. The 60 percent figure estimated by Karweit and Slavin is, if anything, an overestimate. In a much larger study, Weinstein and Mignano (1993) found that elementary school students spent only about one-third of their time engaged in learning tasks.

A term for available instructional time is **allocated time:** the time during which students have an opportunity to learn. When the teacher is lecturing, students can learn by paying attention. When students have written assignments or other tasks, they can learn by doing them. A discussion follows of some common ways in which allocated time can be maximized (see Jones & Jones, 1995).

PREVENTING LOST TIME ● One way in which much instructional time disappears is through losses of entire days or periods. Many of these losses are inevitable because of such things as standardized testing days and snow days, and we certainly would not want to abolish important field trips or school assemblies just to get in a few more periods of instruction. However, frequent losses of instructional periods interrupt the flow of instruction and can ultimately deprive students of sufficient time to master the curriculum.

Making good use of all classroom time is less a matter of squeezing out a few more minutes or hours of instruction each year than of communicating to students that learning is an important business that is worth their time and effort. If a teacher finds excuses not to teach, students may learn that learning is not a serious enterprise. In studying an outstandingly effective inner-city Baltimore elementary school, Salganik (1980) described a third-grade teacher who took her class to the school library, which she found locked. She sent a student for the key, and while the class waited, the teacher whispered to her students, "Let's work on our doubles. Nine plus nine? Six plus six?" The class whispered the answers back in unison. Did a couple of minutes working on addition facts increase the students'

allocated time

Time during which students have the opportunity to learn.

This teacher's time for instruction is limited by the amount of time taken up in dealing with routine management concerns. As a teacher, how will you prevent loss of instruction time?

achievement? Of course not. But it probably did help to develop a perception that school is for learning, not for marking time.

PREVENTING LATE STARTS AND EARLY FINISHES ● A surprising amount of allocated instructional time is lost because the teacher does not start teaching at the beginning of the period. This can be a particular problem in self-contained elementary classes, in which there are no bells or fixed schedules to structure the period. It is also a problem in departmentalized secondary schools, where teachers may spend a long time dealing with late students or other problems before starting the lesson. A crisp, on-time start to a lesson is important for setting a purposive tone to instruction. If students know that a teacher does not start on time, they may be lackadaisical about getting to class on time; this attitude makes future on-time starts increasingly difficult. In Ms. Cavalho's class, students know that if they are late, they will miss something interesting, fun, and important. As a result, almost all of them are in class and ready to learn when the bell rings.

Teachers can also shortchange students if they stop teaching before the end of the period. This is less damaging than a ragged or late start but is still worth avoiding by planning more instruction than you think you'll need, in case you finish the lesson early (Evertson, 1982).

PREVENTING INTERRUPTIONS ● One important cause of lost allocated time for instruction is interruptions. Interruptions may be externally imposed, such as announcements or the need to sign forms sent from the principal's office; or they may be caused by teachers or students themselves. Interruptions not only directly cut into the time for instruction; they also break the momentum of the lesson, which reduces students' attention to the task at hand.

Avoiding interruptions takes planning. For example, some teachers put a "Do not disturb—learning in progress!" sign on the door to inform would-be interrupters to come back later. One teacher wore a special hat during small-group lessons to remind her other second-graders not to interrupt her during that time. Rather than signing forms or dealing with other "administrivia" at once, some teachers keep a box where students and others can put any forms and then deal with them after the lesson is over.

Anything the teacher can postpone doing until after a lesson should be postponed. For example, if the teacher has started a lesson and a student walks in late, the teacher should go on with the lesson and deal with the tardiness issue later.

HANDLING ROUTINE PROCEDURES ● Some teachers spend too much time on simple classroom routines. For example, some elementary teachers spend many minutes getting students ready for lunch or dismissal because they call students by name, one at a time. This is unnecessary. Early in the school year, many teachers establish a routine that only when the entire table (or row) is quiet and ready to go are students called to line up. Lining up for lunch then takes seconds, not minutes.

Other procedures must also become routine for students. They must know, for example, when they may go to the washroom or sharpen a pencil and not ask to do these things at other times. A teacher may collect papers by having students pass them to the front or to the left or by having table monitors collect the table's papers. Distribution of materials must also be planned for. Exactly how these tasks are done is less important than that students know clearly what they are to do. Many teachers assign regular classroom helpers to take care of distribution and collection of papers, taking messages to the office, erasing the blackboard, and other routine tasks that are annoying interruptions for teachers but that students love to do. Teachers should use student power as much as possible.

MINIMIZING TIME SPENT ON DISCIPLINE ● Methods of disciplining students are discussed at length later in this chapter. However, one aspect of disciplining should be mentioned at this point. Whenever possible—which is almost always— disciplinary statements or actions should not interrupt the flow of the lesson. A sharp glance, silently moving close to an offending student, or a hand signal, such as putting finger to lips to remind a student to be silent, are usually effective for the kind of minor behavior problems that teachers must constantly deal with, and they allow the lesson to proceed without interruption. For example, Ms. Cavalho could have interrupted her lesson to scold Mark and Gloria, but that would have wasted time and disrupted the concentration and focus of the whole class. If students need talking to about discipline problems, the time to do it is after the lesson or after school, not in the middle of a lesson. If Diana and Martin are talking during a quiet reading time instead of working, it would be better to say, "Diana and Martin, see me at three o'clock," than to launch into an on-the-spot speech about the importance of being on-task during seatwork times.

Using Engaged Time Effectively

CONNECTIONS

For more information about the importance of time use and time management in effective teaching, see Chapter 9, page 293.

Engaged time (or time on-task) is the time individual students actually spend doing assigned work. Allocated time and engaged time differ in that allocated time refers to the opportunity for the entire class to engage in learning activities, whereas engaged time may be different for each student, depending on a student's attentiveness and willingness to work. Strategies for maximizing student time on-task are discussed in the following sections. Several studies have found teacher training programs based on principles presented in the following sections to increase student engagement and, in some cases, learning (Evertson, 1989; Evertson & Harris, 1993; Jones & Jones, 1998).

CONNECTIONS

For more information about arousing student interest and focusing student attention, see Chapter 7, page 228, and Chapter 6, page 177.

TEACHING ENGAGING LESSONS ● The best way to increase students' time on-task is to teach lessons that are so interesting, engaging, and relevant to students' interests that students will pay attention and eagerly do what is asked of them. Part of this strategy calls for the teacher to emphasize active, rapidly paced instruction with varied modes of presentation and frequent opportunities for student participation and to deemphasize independent seatwork, especially unsupervised seatwork (as in follow-up time in elementary reading classes). Research has consistently shown that student engagement is much higher when the teacher is teaching than during individual seatwork (Evertson & Harris, 1992). Giving students many opportunities to participate actively in lessons is also associated with greater learning (Finn & Cox, 1992), and engaged time is much higher in well-structured cooperative learning programs than in independent seatwork (Slavin, 1990).

CONNECTIONS

For more information about active learning, see Chapter 8, page 273.

MAINTAINING MOMENTUM ● Maintaining momentum during a lesson is a key to keeping task engagement high. *Momentum* refers to the avoidance of interruptions or slowdowns (Kounin, 1970). In a class that maintains good momentum, students always have something to do and, once started working, are not interrupted. Anyone who has tried to write a term paper only to be interrupted by telephone calls, knocks on the door, and other disturbances knows that these interruptions cause much more damage to concentration and progress than the amount of time they take.

Kounin (1970) gives the following example of teacher-caused slowdowns and interruptions:

> The teacher is just starting a reading group at the reading circle while the rest of the children are engaged in seatwork with workbooks. She sat in front of the reading group and asked, "All right, who can tell me the name of our next chapter?" Before a child was called on to answer, she looked toward the children at seatwork, saying: "Let's wait until the people in Group Two are settled and working." (Actually most were writing in their workbooks.) She then looked at John, who was in the seatwork group, naggingly asking, "Did you find your pencil?" John answered something which was inaudible. The teacher got up from her seat, saying, "I'd like to know what you did with it." Pause for about two seconds. "Did you eat it?" Another pause. "What happened to it? What color was it? You can't do your work without it." The teacher then went to her desk to get a pencil to give to John, saying, "I'll get you a pencil. Make sure the pencil is here tomorrow morning. And don't tell me you lost that one too. And make it a new one, and see that it's sharpened." (p. 104)

This teacher destroyed the momentum of a reading lesson by spending more than a minute dealing with a child in the seatwork group who did not have a pencil. Of course, during this interchange, the entire class—both the reading group and the seatwork group—were off-task; but what is worse, they required much more time to get resettled and back to work after the incident. Just as a lesson was getting under way and students were ready to listen, the teacher broke this chain of activities with a completely unnecessary reprimand for a behavior that could easily have been ignored.

Kounin found momentum to be strongly related to total time on-task, and Brophy and Evertson (1976) and Anderson, Evertson, and Brophy (1979) found momentum to be related to student achievement. It is significant that some of the features of effective lessons described in Chapter 7 are largely directed at maintaining momentum. For example, in one model of direct instruction (Good et al., 1983), the teacher has students try a few problems under his or her watchful eye ("controlled practice") before letting them start their seatwork, to make sure that the flow from lesson to seatwork is not interrupted by student questions and problems.

MAINTAINING SMOOTHNESS OF INSTRUCTION ● *Smoothness* is another term Kounin (1970) uses to refer to continued focus on a meaningful sequence of instruction. Smooth instruction avoids jumping without transitions from topic to topic or from the lesson to other activities, which produces "jarring breaks in the activity flow" (Kounin, 1970, p. 97). For example:

> The teacher was conducting a recitation with a subgroup. She was walking towards a child who was reciting when she passed by the fish bowl. She suddenly stopped walking toward the boy, and stopped at the fish bowl, saying: "Oh my, I forgot to feed the fish!" She then got some fish food from a nearby shelf and started to feed the fish, saying: "My, see how hungry it is." She then turned to a girl, saying: "See, Margaret, you forgot to feed the fish. You can see how hungry it is. See how quickly it comes up to eat." (Kounin, 1970, pp. 98–99)

This example illustrates how smoothness and momentum are related. The teacher jumped from her lesson to housekeeping to (unnecessary) disciplining, interrupting one student's recitation and making it virtually impossible for the other students to focus on the lesson. As with momentum, smoothness was found to be strongly associated with student time on-task (Kounin, 1970) and achievement (Anderson et al., 1979; Brophy & Evertson, 1976).

MANAGING TRANSITIONS ● Transitions are changes from one activity to another; for example, from lecture to seatwork, from subject to subject, or from lesson to lunch. Elementary school classes have been found to have an average of 31 major transitions a day, occupying 15 percent of class time (Burns, 1984). Transitions are the seams of class management at which classroom order is most likely to come apart; Anderson and colleagues (1979) and Evertson, Emmer, and Brophy (1980) found that teachers' efficiency at managing transitions between activities was positively related to their students' achievement.

Following are three rules for the management of transitions:

1. When making a transition, the teacher should give a clear signal to which the students have been taught to respond. For example, in the elementary grades, some teachers use a bell to indicate to students that they should immediately be quiet and listen to instructions.

2. Before the transition is made, students must be certain about what they are to do when the signal is given. For example, a teacher might say, "When I say 'Go,' I want you all to put your books away and get out the compositions you started yesterday. Is everyone ready? All right, go!" When giving instructions to students to begin independent seatwork, the teacher can help them get started with the activity before letting them work independently, as in the following example:

> **Teacher:** Today we are going to find guide words for different pages in the dictionary. Everyone should have a ditto sheet with the words on it and a dictionary. Class, hold up your ditto sheet. [They do.] Now hold up your dictionary. [They do.] Good. Now turn to page eighty-two. [The teacher walks around to see that everyone does so.] Look at the top of the page, and put your finger on the first guide word. [The teacher walks around to check on this.] Class, what is the first guide word?
>
> **Class:** Carrot!
>
> **Teacher:** Good. The first guide word is carrot. Now look to the right on the same page. Class, what word do you see there?
>
> **Class:** Carve!
>
> **Teacher:** Right. The guide words are carrot and carve. Now turn to page five hundred fifty-five and find the guide words. [Students do this.] Class, what is the first guide word on page five hundred fifty-five?
>
> **Class:** Scheme!
>
> **Teacher:** Class, what is the second guide word?
>
> **Class:** Scissors!
>
> **Teacher:** Great! Now do the first problem on your assignment sheet by yourselves, and then check with a partner to see if you agree.

The teacher will then check whether all or almost all students have the first item correct before telling them to complete the worksheet. The idea, of course, is to make sure that students know exactly what they are to do before they start doing it.

3. Make transitions all at once. Students should be trained to make transitions as a group, rather than one student at a time (Charles, 1989). The teacher should usually give directions to the class as a whole or to well-defined groups: "Class, I want you all to put away your laboratory materials and prepare for dismissal as quickly and quietly as you can. . . . I see that Table Three is quiet and ready. Table Three, please line up quietly. Table Six, line up. Table One . . . Table Four. Everyone else may line up quietly. Let's go!"

MAINTAINING GROUP FOCUS DURING LESSONS ● *Maintaining group focus* means using classroom organization strategies and questioning techniques that ensure that all students in the class stay involved in the lesson, even when only one student is called on by the teacher. Two principal components of Kounin's concept of maintaining group focus were found to be significantly related to students' on-task behavior: accountability and group alerting.

Kounin (1970) uses the term **accountability** to mean "the degree to which the teacher holds the children accountable and responsible for their task performances during recitation sessions" (p. 119). Examples of tactics for increasing accountability are using choral responses, having all students hold up their work so the teacher can see it, circulating among the students to see what they are doing, and drawing other children into the performance of one child (e.g., "I want you all to watch what Suzanne is doing so you can tell me whether you agree or disagree with her answer"). Ms. Cavalho increased involvement and accountability by having *all* students prepare a Hemingway-like description and only then asking for a few of them to be read.

The idea behind these tactics is to maintain the involvement of all students in all parts of the lesson. A study of third- and fourth-graders found that students raised their hands an average of once every 6 minutes and gave an answer only once every 15 minutes, with some students hardly ever participating (Potter, 1977). This is not enough participation to ensure student attention. Teachers should be concerned not only about drawing all students into class activities but also about avoiding activities that relegate most students to the role of spectator for long periods. For example, a very common teaching error is to have one or two students work out a lengthy problem on the chalkboard or read an extended passage while the rest of the class has nothing to do. Such methods waste the time of much of the class, break the momentum of the lesson, and leave the door open for misbehavior (Gump, 1982).

Group alerting refers to questioning strategies that are designed to keep all students on their toes during a lecture or discussion. One example of group alerting is creating suspense before calling on a student by saying, "Given triangle *ABC*, if we know the measures of sides *A* and *B* and of angle *AB*, what else can we find out about the triangle? . . . [Pause] . . . Maria?" Note that this keeps the whole class thinking until Maria's name is called. The opposite effect would have been created by saying, "Maria, given triangle *ABC* . . . ," because only Maria would have been alerted. Calling on students in a random order is another example of group alerting, as is letting students know that they may be asked questions about the preceding reciter's answers. For example, the teacher might follow up Maria's answer with "What is the name of the postulate that Maria used? . . . Ralph?"

MAINTAINING GROUP FOCUS DURING SEATWORK ● During times when students are doing seatwork and the teacher is available to work with them, it is important to monitor the seatwork activities and to informally check individual students' work. That is, the teacher should circulate among the students' desks to see how they are doing. This allows the teacher to identify any problems students are having before they waste seatwork time practicing errors or giving up in frustration. If students are engaged in cooperative group work, students can check each other's work, but the teacher still needs to check frequently with each group to see that the students are on the right track.

Seatwork times provide excellent opportunities for providing individual help to students who are struggling to keep up with the class, but teachers should resist the temptation to work too long with an individual student. Interactions with

accountability
The degree to which people are held responsible for their task performances or decision outcomes.

group alerting
Questioning strategies that encourage all students to pay attention during lectures and discussions.

students during seatwork should be as brief as possible, because if the teacher gets tied down with any one student, the rest of the class may drift off-task or run into problems of their own (Doyle, 1984).

WITHITNESS ● **Withitness** is another term coined by Kounin (1970). It describes teachers' actions that indicate awareness of students' behavior at all times. Kounin calls this awareness "having eyes in the back of one's head." Teachers who are with-it can respond immediately to student misbehavior and know who started what. Teachers who lack withitness can make the error of scolding the wrong student, as in the following instance:

> Lucy and John, who were sitting at the same table as Jane, started to whisper. Robert watched this, and he too got into the act. Then Jane giggled and said something to John. Then Mary leaned over and whispered to Jane. At this point, the teacher said, "Mary and Jane, stop that!" (adapted from Kounin, 1970, p. 80)

By responding only to Mary and Jane, who were the last to get involved in the whispering and giggling incident, the teacher indicated that she did not know what was going on. A single incident of this kind may make little difference, but after many such incidents, students recognize the teacher's tendency to respond inappropriately to their behavior.

Another example of a lack of withitness is responding too late to a sequence of misbehavior. Lucy and John's whispering could have been easily nipped in the bud, perhaps with just a glance or a finger to the lips. By the time the whispering had escalated to giggling and spread to several students, a full stop in the lesson was needed to rectify the situation.

A major component of withitness is scanning the class frequently and establishing eye contact with individual students. Several studies have found that more effective classroom managers frequently scan the classroom visually, to monitor the pace of activity as well as individual students' behaviors (Brooks, 1985; Emmer, Evertson, & Anderson, 1980; Evertson & Emmer, 1982). Effective classroom managers have the ability to interpret and act on the mood of the class as a whole. They notice when students are beginning to fidget or are otherwise showing signs of flagging attention, and they act on this information to change activities to recapture student engagement (Carter, Cushing, Sabers, Stein, & Berliner, 1988).

OVERLAPPING ● **Overlapping** refers to the teacher's ability to attend to interruptions or behavior problems while continuing a lesson or other instructional activity. For example, one teacher was teaching a lesson on reading comprehension when he saw a student looking at a book that was unrelated to the lesson. Without interrupting his lesson, the teacher walked over to the student, took her book, closed it, and put it on her desk, all while continuing to speak to the class. This took care of the student's misbehavior without slowing the momentum of the lesson; the rest of the class hardly noticed that the event occurred. Similarly, Ms. Cavalho squelched a whispering incident just by moving closer to the whispering students while continuing her lesson.

Another example of a teacher doing a good job of overlapping is as follows:

> The teacher is at the reading circle and Lucy is reading aloud while standing. Johnny, who was doing seatwork at his desk, walks up toward the teacher, holding his workbook. The teacher glances at Johnny, then looks back at Lucy, nodding at Lucy, as Lucy continues to read aloud. The teacher remains seated and takes Johnny's workbook. She turns to Lucy, saying, "That was a hard word, Lucy, and you pronounced

withitness
The degree to which the teacher is aware of and responsive to student behavior at all times.

overlapping
A teacher's ability to respond to behavior problems without interrupting a classroom lesson.

it right." She checks about three more answers to Johnny's book saying, "That's fine, you can go ahead and do the next page now," and resumes looking at the reading book as Lucy continues reading. (Kounin, 1970, p. 84)

Johnny's interruption of the reading group might have been avoided altogether by a good classroom manager, who would have assigned enough work to keep all students productively busy during reading circle time and given clear instructions on what they were to do when they finished their seatwork. For example, Johnny's work could have been checked by a partner or teammate. However, interruptions are sometimes unavoidable, and the ability to keep the main activity going while handling them is strongly related to overall classroom order (Copeland, 1983; Kounin, 1970) and to achievement (Anderson et al., 1979; Brophy & Evertson, 1976).

Can Time On-Task Be Too High?

A class that is rarely on-task is certainly not a well-managed class. However, it is possible to go too far in the other direction, emphasizing time on-task to the exclusion of all other considerations (Weade & Evertson, 1988). For example, in a study of time on-task in elementary mathematics, one teacher's class was found to be engaged essentially 100 percent of the time. The teacher accomplished this by walking up and down the rows of desks looking for the slightest flicker of inattention. This class learned very little math over the course of the year. An overemphasis on engaged time rather than on engaging instruction can produce what Bloome, Puro, and Theodorou (1989) call **mock participation,** in which students appear to be on-task but are not really engaged in learning.

Several studies have found that increasing time on-task in classes in which students were already reasonably well behaved did not increase student achievement (Blackadar & Nachtigal, 1986; Slavin, 1986; Stallings & Krasavage, 1986). An overemphasis on time on-task can be detrimental to learning in several ways. For example, complex tasks involving creativity and uncertainty tend to produce lower levels of time on-task than do simple cut-and-dried tasks (Doyle & Carter, 1984; Evertson & Randolph, 1995). Yet it would clearly be a poor instructional strategy to avoid complex or uncertain tasks just to keep time on-task high. Maintaining classroom order is an important goal of teaching, but it is only one of many (see Evertson & Randolph, 1995; Slavin, 1987a).

Classroom Management in the Student-Centered Classroom

It is important to note that most research on classroom management has taken place in traditionally organized classrooms, in which students have few choices as to what they do and few interactions with each other. In more student-centered classrooms, children are likely to be spending much of their time working with each other, doing open-ended projects, writing, and experimenting. Evertson and Randolph (1995) have discussed the shift that must take place in thinking about classroom management for such classrooms. Clearly, classroom management is more participatory in a student-centered classroom, with students centrally involved in setting standards of behavior. Equally clearly, the type of behavior to be expected will be different. It is impossible to imagine a student-centered classroom that is silent, for example. Yet in other respects the requirements for managing student-centered classrooms are not so different from those for managing traditional ones. Rules are still needed and must be consistently communicated to students and consistently enforced (Freiberg, Stein, & Huang, 1995). If students in student-centered classrooms

mock participation
Situation in which students appear to be on-task but are not engaged in learning.

are deeply involved and motivated by the variety, activity, and social nature of classroom activities, then disciplinary actions will be less necessary (Rogers & Freiberg, 1994). Inevitably, however, certain students' misbehavior will disrupt others' learning, and the teacher must have strategies to help students live up to norms that all members of the class have agreed to.

The following sections describe strategies for preventing misbehavior in any classroom context and responding effectively to misbehavior when it does occur.

SELF-CHECK

Review the vignette at the beginning of the chapter. Identify all the ways in which time was used in Ms. Cavalho's class, including allocated time and engaged time. List ways in which allocated time and engaged time can be maximized. Give specific examples to show how a teacher might exhibit withitness and overlapping.

WHAT PRACTICES CONTRIBUTE TO EFFECTIVE CLASSROOM MANAGEMENT?

Research has consistently shown that basic commonsense planning and groundwork go a long way toward preventing discipline problems from ever developing. Simple measures include starting the year properly, arranging the classroom for effective instruction, setting class rules and procedures, and making expectations of conduct clear to students.

Different grade levels and student groups present different management concerns. For instance, with younger students, teachers need to be concerned about socializing students to the norms and behaviors that are expected in school (Evertson, Emmer, Clements, Sanford, & Worsham, 1994). Programs focusing on establishing consistent, schoolwide behavior expectations and on building positive relationships and school success through the use of cooperative learning have been effective in improving the behavior of elementary school children (Freiberg et al., 1995; O'Donnell, Hawkins, Catalano, Abbott, & Day, 1995).

In middle school and high school, students can grasp the principles that underlie rules and procedures and can rationally agree to observe them (Emmer, Evertson, Clements, & Worsham, 1994). At the same time, some adolescents resist authority and place greater importance on peer norms. Aggressive behavior, truancy, and delinquency also increase as students enter adolescence (Tierno, 1993). In the upper grades, departmentalization, tracking, and class promotion may become management issues, especially with students who have established patterns of learned helplessness or academic failure. Teachers of older students need to be more concerned with motivating them toward more self-regulation in observing rules and procedures and in learning the course material. Programs that increase the clarity of rules, consistency of rule enforcement, and frequency of communication with the home have been very effective in improving adolescents' behavior (Gottfredson, Gottfredson, & Hybl, 1993).

Starting Out the Year Right

Emmer and colleagues (1980) and Evertson and Emmer (1982) studied teachers' actions at the beginning of the school year and correlated them with students' behaviors later in the year. They found that the first days of school were critical in establishing classroom order. They compared teachers whose classes were mostly on-task over the course of the school year with teachers whose classes were less consistently on-task and found that the better classroom managers engaged in certain activities during the first days of school significantly more often than did the less effective managers. A list of six characteristics of effective classroom managers follows:

1. More effective managers had a clear, specific plan for introducing students to classroom rules and procedures and spent as many days as necessary carrying out their plan until students knew how to line up, ask for help, and so on.
2. More effective managers worked with the whole class initially (even if they planned to group students later). They were involved with the whole class at all times, rarely leaving any students without something to do or without supervision. For example, more effective managers seldom worked with an individual student unless the rest of the class was productively occupied (Doyle, 1984; Sanford & Evertson, 1981).
3. More effective managers spent extra time during the first days of school introducing procedures and discussing class rules (often encouraging students to suggest rules themselves). These teachers usually reminded students of class rules every day for at least the first week of school (Weinstein & Mignano, 1993).
4. More effective managers taught students specific procedures. For example, some had students practice lining up quickly and quietly; others taught students to respond to a signal, such as a bell, a flick of the light switch, or a call for attention.
5. As first activities, more effective managers used simple, enjoyable tasks. Materials for the first lessons were well prepared, clearly presented, and varied. These teachers asked students to get right to work on the first day of school and then gave them instructions on procedures gradually, to avoid overloading them with too much information at a time.
6. More effective managers responded immediately to stop any misbehavior.

Setting Class Rules

One of the first management-related tasks at the start of the year is setting class rules. Three principles govern this process. First, class rules should be few in number. Second, they should make sense and be seen as fair by students. Third, they should be clearly explained and deliberately taught to students (Brooks, 1985; Doyle, 1990b). A major purpose of clearly explaining general class rules is to give a moral authority for specific procedures (Freiberg, 1996). For example, all students will understand and support a rule such as "Respect others' property." This simple rule can be invoked to cover such obvious misbehaviors as stealing or destroying materials but also gives a reason for putting materials away, cleaning up litter, and refraining from marking up textbooks. Students may be asked to help set the rules, or they may be given a set of rules and asked to give examples of these rules. Class discussions give students a feeling of participation in setting rational rules that everyone can live by (Kauffman & Burbach, 1997). When the class as a whole has agreed on a set of rules, offenders know that they are transgressing community norms, not the teacher's arbitrary regulations. One all-purpose set of class rules follows:

1. **Be courteous to others.** This rule forbids interrupting others or speaking out of turn, teasing or laughing at others, fighting, and so on.
2. **Respect others' property.**

3. **Be on-task.** This includes listening when the teacher or other students are talking, working on seatwork, continuing to work during any interruptions, staying in one's seat, being at one's seat and ready to work when the bell rings, and following directions.

4. **Raise hands to be recognized.** This is a rule against calling out or getting out of one's seat for assistance without permission.

SELF-CHECK

For the grade level you plan to teach, construct a classroom layout and a "To Do" list for starting the academic year in a way that will minimize behavior problems.

WHAT ARE SOME STRATEGIES FOR MANAGING ROUTINE MISBEHAVIOR?

The preceding sections of this chapter discussed means of organizing classroom activities to maximize time for instruction and minimize time for such minor disturbances as students talking out of turn, getting out of their seats without permission, and not paying attention. Provision of interesting lessons, efficient use of class time, and careful structuring of instructional activities will prevent most such minor behavior problems—and many more serious ones as well. For example, Kounin (1970) found that teacher behaviors that were associated with high time on-task were also associated with fewer serious behavior problems. Time off-task can lead to more serious problems; many behavior problems arise because students are frustrated or bored in school. Instructional programs that actively involve students and provide all of them with opportunities for success may prevent such problems.

However, effective lessons and good use of class time are not the only means of preventing or dealing with inappropriate behavior. Besides structuring classes to reduce the frequency of behavior problems, teachers must have strategies for dealing with behavior problems when they do occur (see Cairns, 1987).

The great majority of behavior problems with which a teacher must deal are relatively minor disruptions, such as talking out of turn, getting up without permission, failing to follow class rules or procedures, and inattention—nothing really serious, but behaviors that must be minimized for learning to occur. Before considering disciplinary strategies, it is important to reflect on their purpose. Students should learn much more in school than the "Three Rs." They should learn that they are competent learners and that learning is enjoyable and satisfying. A classroom environment that is warm, supportive, and accepting fosters these attitudes. Furthermore, there is a strong link between attentive, nondisruptive behavior and student achievement (Finn, Pannozzo, & Voelkl, 1995; Wentzel, 1993).

A healthy classroom environment cannot be created if students do not respect teachers or teachers do not respect students. Though teachers should involve students in setting class rules and take student needs or input into account in organizing the classroom, teachers are ultimately the leaders who establish and enforce rules that students must live by. These class rules and procedures should become second nature to students. Teachers who have not established their authority in the classroom are likely to spend much too much time dealing with behavior problems or yelling at students to be instructionally effective. Furthermore, the clearer the structure and routine procedures in the classroom, the more freedom the teacher

CASE TO CONSIDER

An Ounce of Prevention

Althea Johnson, a third-grade teacher, is standing in front of her new class on the second day of school.

Althea: OK, class. I want to spend a few minutes talking with you about class rules. Let's start by listing some on the board. Please raise your hands if you have a rule you'd like to suggest and wait until I call on you.

In a few minutes Althea has written the following on the board under the heading "Rules":

- Do not talk in class.
- Do not run in the hallways.
- Do not put gum under your desk.
- Do not throw spitballs (or paper airplanes).
- Do not draw on your desk.
- Do not fight.
- Do not come late without a note from home.
- Do not yell in class.
- Do raise your hand to be called on.
- Do not bring radios to school.
- Do not pass notes to your friends.
- Do not write in your books.

Althea: Does everyone think these rules are fair? Hands? [Hands go up.] OK, that's a good start. But I see two problems. First, this is a long list to remember. And second, most of them start with "Do not." I'd like to try to group these as a few rules that tell us what we should do.

Her students offer ideas, and eventually the board shows the following rules, each with several examples underneath:

1. Respect the rights of others.
2. Respect other people's property.
3. Be courteous to others.
4. Be on-task.
5. Raise your hand to be called on.

Althea: OK, we've all agreed that these rules are fair. But if somebody does forget and breaks a rule, what should happen? What should the consequences be? Clare?

Clare: You go to the principal's office.

Althea: Yes, that's one consequence. Let's list more.

As before, Althea lists the students' suggestions under the heading "Consequences":

- Go to the principal's office.
- Sit in the corner for half an hour.
- Miss recess.
- Stay after school.
- Get a letter sent home to your parents.

Althea: Who has a suggestion for making people want to keep the rules in the first place, not break them? A kind of reward? Mimi? Clare?

Mimi: Getting gold stars?

Clare: We could all get an extra recess if the whole class was good all day.

Billy (interrupting)**:** We could all just stay home!

Althea: Billy, we've all agreed to raise hands and to be courteous. So are you trying to give the class an example of how not to behave?

Billy: Sorry, Mrs. Johnson.

Althea: OK, now I want everyone to copy down our basic rules and think about them. We'll talk a little more about rewards and consequences tomorrow.

PROBLEM SOLVING

1. Do you agree with Althea that third-graders should be involved in setting class rules? How might a teacher of younger or older children approach the same task?
2. For the grade level you plan to teach, develop a problem-prevention plan of action for the first week of school. Model your plan by extending the dialogue with another character; for example, have Althea talk with a novice teacher.

can allow students (Mackenzie, 1997). The following sections discuss strategies for dealing with typical discipline problems (see Bacon, 1993; Hill, 1993; McDaniel, 1993; Schloss & Smith, 1994; Wielkiewicz, 1995).

The Principle of Least Intervention

In dealing with routine classroom behavior problems, the most important principle is that a teacher should correct misbehaviors by using the simplest intervention that will work (Wolfgang, 1995). Many studies have found that the amount of time spent disciplining students is negatively related to student achievement (Crocker

TABLE 11.1

Principle of Least Intervention

STEP	PROCEDURE	EXAMPLE
1	Prevention	Teacher displays enthusiasm, varies activities, keeps students interested.
2	Nonverbal cues	Tanya turns in paper late: teacher frowns.
3	Praise of correct behavior that is incompatible with misbehavior	"Tanya, I hear you completed your science fair project on time for the judging. That's great!"
4	Praise for other students	"I see most of you turned your papers in on time today. I really appreciate that."
5	Verbal reminders	"Tanya, please turn in your next paper on time."
6	Repeated reminders	"Tanya, it's important to turn your paper in on time."
7	Consequences	Tanya spends 10 minutes after class starting on the next paper assignment.

& Brooker, 1986; Evertson et al., 1980). The teacher's main goal in dealing with routine misbehavior is to do so in a way that both is effective and avoids unnecessarily disrupting the lesson (Evertson & Harris, 1992; Jones & Jones, 1995). If at all possible, the lesson must go on while any behavior problems are dealt with. A continuum of strategies for dealing with minor misbehaviors, from least disruptive to most, is listed in Table 11.1 and discussed in the following sections.

Prevention

The easiest behavior problems to deal with are those that never occur in the first place. As was illustrated earlier in this chapter, teachers can prevent behavior problems by presenting interesting and lively lessons, making class rules and procedures clear, keeping students busy on meaningful tasks, and using other effective techniques of basic classroom management (Doyle, 1990b; Jones & Jones, 1995). Ms. Cavalho's class is an excellent example of this. Her students rarely misbehave because they are interested and engaged.

Varying the content of lessons, using a variety of materials and approaches, displaying humor and enthusiasm, and using cooperative learning or project-based learning can all reduce boredom-caused behavior problems. A teacher can avert frustration caused by material that is too difficult or assignments that are unrealistically long by breaking assignments into smaller steps and doing a better job of preparing students to work on their own. Fatigue can be reduced if short breaks are allowed, activities are varied, and difficult subjects are scheduled in the morning, when students are fresh.

nonverbal cues
Eye contact, gestures, physical proximity, or touching a teacher uses to communicate without interrupting verbal discourse.

Nonverbal Cues

Teachers can eliminate much routine classroom misbehavior without breaking the momentum of the lesson by the use of simple **nonverbal cues** (Woolfolk & Brooks,

1985). Making eye contact with a misbehaving student may be enough to stop misbehavior. For example, if two students are whispering, the teacher might simply catch the eye of one or both of them. Moving close to a student who is misbehaving also usually alerts the student to shape up. If these techniques fail, a light hand on the student's shoulder is likely to be effective (although touch should be used cautiously with adolescents, who may be sensitive about being touched). These nonverbal strategies all clearly convey the same message: "I see what you are doing and don't like it. Please get back to work." The advantage of communicating this message nonverbally is that the lesson need not be interrupted. In contrast, verbal reprimands can cause a ripple effect; many students stop working while one is being reprimanded (Kounin, 1970). Instead of interrupting the flow of concentration for many to deal with the behavior of one, nonverbal cues usually have an effect only on the student who is misbehaving, as was illustrated earlier in this chapter by the example of the teacher who continued his lesson while silently closing and putting away a book one student was reading. That student was the only one in the class who paid much attention to the whole episode.

Praising Behavior That Is Incompatible with Misbehavior

Praise can be a powerful motivator for many students. One strategy for reducing misbehavior in class is to make sure to praise students for behaviors that are incompatible with the misbehavior you want to reduce. That is, catch students in the act of doing right. For example, if students often get out of their seats without permission, praise them on the occasions when they do get to work right away.

Praising Other Students

It is often possible to get one student to behave by praising others for behaving. For example, if Polly is goofing off, the teacher might say, "I'm glad to see so many students working so well—Jake is doing a good job, Carol is doing well, José and

This teacher is praising these students for behavior that is incompatible with previous misbehavior. As a teacher, what types of routine misbehaviors do you expect to encounter? How would you catch students in the act of good behavior?

The Intentional Teacher

● **Using What You Know about Effective Learning Environments to Improve Teaching and Learning**

Intentional teachers are authorities in their classrooms who take responsibility for managing time, activities, and behaviors. At the core of their success as classroom managers is high-interest, meaningful instruction. Intentional teachers use instructional time to its fullest by structuring a positive, consistent environment with reasonable rules and time-saving procedures. They implement a range of responses to misbehavior. Intentional teachers' actions reflect their understanding that effective learning environments result from careful planning and vigilant monitoring.

1 What am I trying to accomplish?

Students learn best when they are productively engaged in instruction. Develop a management plan that aims to prevent misbehavior.

Before the school year begins, you sit down at the computer and list some of the strategies that you can employ to help your second-graders make good choices about their behavior. At the top of your list you type in bold: **Provide instruction that taps students' curiosity and creativity!** Next you list two key terms and brief reminders about actions that can help to prevent misbehavior:

Fairness--Show genuine concern for the students and consider their perspectives! Apply consequences consistently and without emotion.

Withitness--remember to monitor all corners of the room! Keep my eyes on the students!

Research indicates that some teachers lose half—or more—of their instructional time. Make a plan to use your students' time well, and guard your instructional minutes carefully.

During this, your second year of teaching middle school, you commit to teach bell-to-bell, beginning your math lessons with an opener—usually a practice exercise or a brain teaser—that is on the overhead projector as students arrive, and closing the lessons with just a brief period of independent work during which you monitor students' progress carefully.

2 What are my students' relevant experiences and needs?

Bored or frustrated students may find greater rewards in avoiding schoolwork than in completing it. Provide instruction that engages students' curiosity and attends to the various preparation levels students bring to the classroom.

You notice that a small cluster of students has been unruly during the beginning of your unit on computation with decimals. You do a task analysis of the concepts and skills required in the unit and find that this small group of students is missing some prerequisite skills: Namely, they have not yet committed basic math facts to memory. So that students can succeed with decimal computations, you allow them to use their fact tables. At the same time, you arrange for peer tutoring for your students to master basic operations.

Teachers' expectations for student behavior should vary with the age and maturity of the students. Develop reasonable and challenging expectations that are appropriate for the social, cognitive, and physical states of individuals at your students' ages.

You review Chapters 2 and 3 of this text to refresh your memory about child development. Based upon your review, you pro-

---

Michelle are working nicely. . . ." When Polly finally does get to work, the teacher should praise her too, without dwelling on her past inattention: "I see James and Walter and Polly doing a good job."

Verbal Reminders

If a nonverbal cue is impossible or ineffective, a simple verbal reminder may help to bring a student into line. The reminder should be given immediately after the student misbehaves; delayed reminders are usually ineffective. If possible, the reminder should state what students are supposed to be doing rather than dwelling on what they are doing wrong. For example, it is better to say, "John, please attend to your own work" than, "John, stop copying off of Alfredo's paper." Stating the reminder positively communicates more positive expectations for future behavior

vide frequent shifts in activities for your kindergartners, alternating quiet activities with periods of greater movement.

3 **What approaches and materials are available to help me challenge every student?**

Effective managers start the year by teaching and reinforcing classroom rules and procedures. Spend time during the first days of school teaching students your expectations for behavior.

> Nervous about your first year teaching high school, you interview a few experienced colleagues about their first-day-of-school plans. From their suggestions, you develop a plan to (1) devise a set of classroom rules through class discussion, (2) develop consequences for instances when students choose to violate or ignore those rules, and (3) teach the students procedures for submitting homework, collecting work for an absent peer, and working effectively in small groups.

Different kinds of misbehavior require different levels of intervention. Develop a range of responses to misbehavior, beginning with the lowest level of intensity. When students exhibit serious misbehaviors, consider the motivations for their behavior, and respond in ways that take into account the individual and the problem.

> You address most misbehavior through low-level interventions like nonverbal cues, physical proximity, and hints. A few students, though, demonstrate persistent misbehavior. You develop behavior modification contracts for these few students. Their parents are supportive, and together you implement home-based reinforcement programs like the withdrawal of television privileges and added time at students' favorite activities.

4 **How will I know whether and when to change my strategy or modify my instruction?**

Collect ongoing information about your use of allocated and engaged time. Ask yourself whether you are devoting enough time to each subject and whether students are engaged in experiences that result in meaningful learning.

> You review your use of time by, first, examining your schedule to determine whether allocated time is appropriate. Then, for a week, you track start and end times for each of your lessons to determine where minutes may be lost. You ask your peer coach to observe your lessons to ensure that they allow for active participation and that they flow quickly and well. Finally, you examine students' work to assess the degree to which students demonstrate that their on-task behavior has resulted in significant learning.

Teachers need to review students' responses to their efforts to redirect behavior. Consider changing strategies when misbehavior persists or when you are spending too much time correcting it.

> When you overhear some of your eighth-graders bragging about being members of your Three O'Clock Club (after-school detention), you are forced to reconsider its effectiveness as a punishment.

5 **What information will I accept as evidence that my students and I are experiencing success?**

Take frequent "temperature readings" of the climate of your classroom environment. Gather information from several sources to determine that your strategies are efficient and productive and that students are happy and learning.

> You take the opportunity to reflect on the climate of your classroom community. You ask students to write an anonymous journal entry on their perceptions of how class is going. You ask, in particular, about whether they feel they have enough say in what happens in the classroom. You take a few minutes to write a similar journal entry from your perspective. After searching for patterns in the entries, you spend one class period on a classroom meeting to set new goals.

than does a negative statement (see Good & Brophy, 1984). Also, the reminder should focus on the behavior, not on the student. Although a particular student behavior may be intolerable, the student himself or herself is always accepted and welcome in the classroom.

Repeated Reminders

Most often a nonverbal cue, reinforcement of other students, or a simple reminder will be enough to end minor misbehavior. However, sometimes students test the teacher's resolve by failing to do what has been asked of them or by arguing or giving excuses. This testing will diminish over time if students learn that teachers mean what they say and will use appropriate measures to enforce an orderly, productive classroom environment.

TEACHERS IN ACTION

What classroom management techniques work best for you and your students?

Louise Gruppen
Music Teacher
Bates Elementary School
Dexter, Michigan

In my third- and fourth- grade music classroom, I strive to achieve an atmosphere of acceptance, respect, and responsibility. We hold a discussion at the beginning of the year, comparing our music class to a sports team. Students share their ideas of what makes a successful team: working together, helping each other, everyone trying to do his or her best. I explain how the same concepts apply to our classroom. We have three general rules: Respect others, respect yourself, and respect property. Each general rule includes several specific rules. For instance, under "Respect others," we list "Actively listen" and "Make only helpful and kind comments." Periodically, students fill out self-evaluation sheets that correspond with our rules. They decide how well they have done on each rule. Throughout the year, whenever an individual disrupts the class, he or she is asked to fill out a self-evaluation, including an explanation of how he or she will change the problem behavior.

The class also works on monthly goals such as "Everyone participating" or "Working together as a team." At the end of the month, the class votes on whether the goal has been met. If not, it stays on the board for another month. In addition, after three sessions of very good listening and cooperation, I reward classes with a chance to choose their seats for one class period.

I believe it is vital that students learn that they are responsible for their behavior and also for their learning. I tell them that when they don't do their best, they cheat themselves of opportunities to learn. Music class provides many opportunities for cooperation and participation, such as group singing and listening activities, playing instruments, and dancing. Each person needs to contribute his or her part. When everyone works hard, the results are wonderful, and the students experience the reward of a job well done.

Mike Jones
Advanced History Teacher
Athens Middle School
Athens, Alabama

I think that many components combine to make a positive classroom environment. Mutual respect among the students and from the teacher to each student is absolutely necessary. Fairness is another critical component. Responsibility and active participation are crucial as well. Sometimes students do not realize that they are the ones most responsible for their own learning. They often want the teacher to somehow learn the material for them. I explain to my classes that this can never happen. If they are to learn, they must put forth the effort to do so. The one ingredient that has been most helpful to me, however, has been humor.

In my classroom we laugh a lot. We look for *things* that we can laugh at, but we never laugh at people. We laugh at the mistakes we all make from time to time, but we separate the mistake from the person making the mistake. Students in my classroom know that they can take chances with an answer or an opinion and that they won't be attacked when their offering disagrees with the opinions of the majority. They are relaxed and at ease. As a history teacher, I do not want my students parroting my opinions. I want them to look at the facts, think them over, then form their own opinions. We then discuss the various viewpoints, apply the appropriate facts, season well with laws of logic, and decide which options are most likely to be relevant to the case at hand. My students are soon transformed from passive observers of life into active participants who will stand up for their viewpoint until the evidence indicates otherwise. In short, I treat them like responsible young people whose opinions matter and whose ideas I deem valuable. Before long, they begin to see themselves in the same light.

When a student refuses to comply with a simple reminder, one strategy to attempt first is a repetition of the reminder, ignoring any irrelevant excuse or argument. Canter and Canter (1992), in a program called **Assertive Discipline,** call this strategy the *broken record*. Teachers should decide what they want the student to do, state this clearly to the student (statement of want), and then repeat it until the student complies. An example of the broken record from Canter and Canter (1976) follows:

Teacher: "Craig, I want you to start your project now." (Statement of want)
Craig: "I will as soon as I finish my game. Just a few more minutes."
Teacher (firmly): "Craig, I understand, but I want you to start your project now." (Broken record)
Craig: "You never give me enough time with the games."
Teacher (calmly, firmly): "That's not the point. I want you to start your project now."
Craig: "I don't like doing my project."
Teacher (firmly): "I understand, but I want you to start your project."
Craig: "Wow, you really mean it. I'll get to work." (p. 80)

This teacher avoided a lengthy argument with a student by simply repeating the request. When Craig said, "You never give me enough time with the games," and "I don't like doing my project," he was not inviting a serious discussion but was simply procrastinating and testing the teacher's resolve. Rather than going off on a tangent with him, the teacher calmly restated the request, turning aside his excuses with "That's not the point . . . " and "I understand, but. . . ." Of course, if Craig had had a legitimate issue to discuss or a valid complaint, the teacher would have dealt with it; but all too often students' arguments or excuses are nothing more than a means of drawing out an interaction with the teacher to avoid getting down to work. Recall how Ms. Cavalho refused to be drawn into a discussion of Gloria's lateness when it was Mark's behavior that was at issue.

Applying Consequences

When all previous steps have been ineffective in getting the student to comply with a clearly stated and reasonable request, the final step is to pose a choice to the student: Either comply or suffer the consequences (Tierno, 1993). Examples of consequences are sending the student out of class, making the student miss a few minutes of recess or some other privilege, having the student stay after school, and calling the student's parents. A consequence for not complying with the teacher's request should be mildly unpleasant, short in duration, and applied as soon as possible after the behavior occurs. Certainty is far more important than severity; students must know that consequences follow misbehavior as night follows day. One disadvantage of using severe or long-lasting punishment (e.g., no recess for a week) is that it can create resentment in the student and a defiant attitude. Also, it may be difficult to follow through on severe or long-lasting consequences. Mild but certain consequences communicate, "I cannot tolerate that sort of behavior, but I care about you and want you to rejoin the class as soon as you are ready."

Before presenting a student with a consequence for noncompliance, teachers must be absolutely certain that they can and will follow through if necessary. When a teacher says, "You may choose to get to work right away, or you may choose to spend 5 minutes of your recess doing your work here," the teacher must be certain that someone will be available to monitor the student in the classroom during recess. Vague or empty threats ("You stop that or I'll make you wish you had!" or "You get to work or I'll have you suspended for a month!") are worse than useless.

Assertive Discipline
Method of giving a clear, firm, unhostile response to student misbehavior.

If teachers are not prepared to follow through with consequences, students will learn to shrug them off.

After a consequence has been applied, the teacher should avoid referring to the incident. For example, when the student returns from a 10-minute exclusion from class, the teacher should accept him or her back without any sarcasm or recriminations. The student now deserves a fresh start.

SELF-CHECK

List the sequence of strategies that are used for managing routine misbehavior according to the principle of least intervention. In each case, how does the strategy work? How would you identify examples of these strategies in student–teacher dialogues? Reread the vignette at the beginning of this chapter. How did Ms. Cavalho manage her students' misbehavior?

HOW IS APPLIED BEHAVIOR ANALYSIS USED TO MANAGE MORE SERIOUS BEHAVIOR PROBLEMS?

The previous section discussed how to deal with behaviors that might be appropriate on the playing field but are out of line in the classroom. There are other behaviors that are not appropriate anywhere. These include fighting, stealing, destruction of property, and gross disrespect for teachers or other school staff. These are far less common than routine classroom misbehavior but far more serious. Behavioral learning theories, described in Chapter 5, have direct application to classroom management. Simply put, behavioral learning theories hold that behaviors that are not reinforced or are punished will diminish in frequency. The following sections present **applied behavior analysis,** an analysis of classroom behavior in terms of behavioral concepts, and give specific strategies for preventing and dealing with misbehavior (see Martin & Pear, 1992).

How Student Misbehavior Is Maintained

A basic principle of behavioral learning theories is that if any behavior persists over time, it is being maintained by some reinforcer. To reduce misbehavior in the classroom, we must understand which reinforcers maintain misbehavior in the first place.

The most common reinforcer for classroom misbehavior is attention—from the teacher, the peer group, or both. Students receiving one-to-one tutoring rarely misbehave, both because they already have the undivided attention of an adult and because no classmates are present to attend to any negative behavior. In the typical classroom, however, students have to go out of their way to get the teacher's personal attention, and they have an audience of peers who may encourage or applaud their misdeeds.

applied behavior analysis
The application of behavioral learning principles to understanding and changing behavior.

TEACHER'S ATTENTION ● Sometimes students misbehave because they want the teacher's attention, even if it is negative. This is a more common reason for misbehavior than many teachers think. A puzzled teacher might say, "I don't know what is wrong with Nathan. I have to stay with him all day to keep him working! Sometimes I get exasperated and yell at him. My words fall off him like water off a duck's back. He even smiles when I'm scolding him!"

When students appear to misbehave to gain the teacher's attention, the solution is relatively easy: Pay attention to these students when they are doing well, and ignore them (as much as possible) when they misbehave. When ignoring their actions is impossible, imposing time out (e.g., sending these students to a quiet corner or to the principal's office) may be effective.

PEERS' ATTENTION ● Another very common reason that students misbehave is to get the attention and approval of their peers. The classic instance of this is the class clown, who is obviously performing for the amusement of his or her classmates. However, many other forms of misbehavior are motivated primarily by peer attention and approval—in fact, few students completely disregard the potential impact of their behavior on their classmates. For example, students who refuse to do what the teacher has asked are consciously or unconsciously weighing the effect of their defiance on their standing among their classmates.

Even preschoolers and early elementary school students may misbehave to gain peer attention, but beginning around the third grade (and especially during the middle school/junior high school years), it is particularly likely that student misbehavior is linked to peer attention and support. As students enter adolescence, the peer group takes on extreme importance, and peer norms begin to favor independence from authority. When older children and teenagers engage in serious delinquent acts (such as vandalism, theft, and assault), they are usually supported by a delinquent peer group.

Strategies for reducing peer-supported misbehavior are quite different from those for dealing with misbehavior that is meant to capture the teacher's attention. Ignoring misbehavior will be ineffective if the misbehavior is reinforced by peers. For example, if a student is balancing a book on his or her head and the class is laughing, the behavior can hardly be ignored, because it will continue as long as the class is interested (and will encourage others to behave likewise). Further, scolding may only attract more attention from classmates or, worse, enhance the student's standing among peers. Similarly, if two students are whispering or talking to each other, they are reinforcing each other for misbehaving, and ignoring their behavior will only encourage more of it.

There are two primary responses to peer-supported misbehavior. One is to remove the offender from the classroom to deprive him or her of peer attention. Another is to use **group contingencies,** strategies in which the entire class (or groups of students within the class) is rewarded on the basis of everyone's behavior. Under group contingencies, all students benefit from their classmates' good behavior, so peer support for misbehavior is removed. Group contingencies and other behavior management strategies for peer-supported misbehavior are described in more detail in the following sections.

RELEASE FROM UNPLEASANT STATES OR ACTIVITIES ● A third important reinforcer for misbehavior is release from boredom, frustration, fatigue, or unpleasant activities. As was explained in Chapter 5, escaping or avoiding an unpleasant stimulus is a reinforcer. Some students see much of what happens in school as unpleasant, boring, frustrating, or tiring. This is particularly true of students who experience repeated failure in school. But even the most able and motivated students feel bored or frustrated at times. Students often misbehave just to escape from unpleasant activities. This can be clearly seen with students who frequently ask permission to get a drink of water, go to the washroom, or sharpen their pencils. Such students are more likely to make these requests during independent

CONNECTIONS
For more information about behavioral theory, see Chapter 5, page 146.

group contingencies
Class rewards that depend on the behavior of all students.

seatwork than during cooperative learning activities or even a lecture, because seatwork can be frustrating or anxiety-provoking for students who have little confidence in their academic abilities. More serious misbehaviors can also be partially or completely motivated by a desire for release from boredom, frustration, or fatigue. A student may misbehave just to stir things up. Sometimes students misbehave precisely so that they will be sent out of the classroom. Obviously, sending such a student to the hall or the principal's office can be counterproductive.

The best solution for misbehaviors arising from boredom, frustration, or fatigue is prevention. Students rarely misbehave during interesting, varied, engaging lessons. Actively involving students in lessons can head off misbehaviors due to boredom or fatigue. Use of cooperative learning methods or other means of involving students in an active way can be helpful. A teacher can prevent frustration by using materials that ensure a high success rate for all, by making sure that all students are challenged but none are overwhelmed. Changing instruction and assessments to help students succeed can be an effective means of resolving frustration-related behavior problems.

Principles of Applied Behavior Analysis

The behavior management strategies outlined earlier (e.g., nonverbal cues, reminders, mild but certain punishment) might be described as informal applications of behavioral learning theories. These practices, plus the prevention of misbehavior by the use of efficient class management and engaging lessons, will be sufficient to create a good learning environment in most classrooms.

However, more systematic methods are sometimes needed. In classrooms in which most students are well-behaved but a few have persistent behavior problems, individual behavior management strategies can be effective. In classrooms in which many students have behavior problems, particularly when there is peer support for misbehavior, whole-class strategies or group contingencies may be needed. Such strategies are most often required when many low-achieving or poorly motivated students are put in one class, as often happens in special-education classes and in schools that use tracking or other between-class ability grouping methods.

Setting up and using any applied behavior analysis program requires following a series of steps that proceeds from the observation of the behavior through program implementation to program evaluation (see Schloss & Smith, 1994). The steps listed here are, to a greater or lesser extent, part of all applied behavior analysis programs:

1. Identify target behavior(s) and reinforcer(s).
2. Establish a baseline for the target behavior.
3. Choose a reinforcer and criteria for reinforcement.
4. If necessary, choose a punisher and criteria for punishment.
5. Observe behavior during program implementation, and compare it to baseline.
6. When the behavior management program is working, reduce the frequency of reinforcement.

Individual behavior management strategies are useful for coping with individual students who have persistent behavior problems in school. **Behavior modification** is a systematic application of antecedents and consequences to change behavior (McDaniel, 1993).

IDENTIFY TARGET BEHAVIORS AND REINFORCERS ● The first step in implementing a behavior management program is to observe the misbehaving student to identify

CONNECTIONS
For more information about the problems of tracking, see Chapter 9, pages 294–298.

behavior modification
Systematic application of antecedents and consequences to change behavior.

one or a small number of behaviors to target first and to see what reinforcers maintain the behavior(s). Another purpose of this observation is to establish a baseline against which to compare improvements. A structured individual behavior management program should aim to change only one behavior or a small set of closely related behaviors. Tackling too many behaviors at a time risks failure with all of them, because the student may not clearly see what he or she must do to be reinforced.

The first behavior targeted should be one that is serious; is easy to observe; and, most important, occurs frequently. For example, if a child gets into fights in the playground every few days but gets out of his or her seat without permission several times per hour, you might start with the out-of-seat behavior and deal with the fighting later. Ironically, the more frequent and persistent a behavior, the easier it is to extinguish. This is because positive or negative consequences can be applied frequently, making the connection between behavior and consequence clear to the student.

In observing a student, try to determine what reinforcer(s) are maintaining the target behavior. If a student misbehaves with others (e.g., talks without permission, swears, or teases) or if a student's misbehavior usually attracts the attention of others (e.g., clowning), then you might conclude that the behavior is peer-supported. If the behavior does not attract much peer attention but always requires teacher attention (e.g., getting out of seat without permission), then you might conclude that the behavior is supported by your own attention.

ESTABLISH BASELINE BEHAVIOR ● Observe the student to see how often the target behavior occurs. Before you do this, you will need to clearly define exactly what constitutes the behavior. For example, if the target behavior is "bothering classmates," you will have to decide what specific behaviors constitute "bothering" (perhaps teasing, interrupting, and taking materials).

SELECT REINFORCERS AND CRITERIA FOR REINFORCEMENT ● Typical classroom reinforcers include praise, privileges, and tangible rewards. Praise is especially effective for students who misbehave to get the teacher's attention. It is often a good idea to start a behavior management program by using praise for appropriate behavior to see whether this is sufficient. However, be prepared to use stronger reinforcers if praise is not enough (see McDaniel, 1993; Schloss & Smith, 1994).

In addition to praise, many teachers find it useful to give students stars, "smilies," or other small rewards when students behave appropriately. Some teachers use a rubber stamp to mark students' papers with a symbol indicating good work. These small rewards make the teacher's praise more concrete and visible and let students take their work home and receive praise from their parents. Figure 11.2 provides suggestions for social reinforcers and preferred activities to encourage positive behavior.

SELECT PUNISHERS AND CRITERIA FOR PUNISHMENT, IF NECESSARY ● Behavioral learning theories strongly favor the use of reinforcers for appropriate behavior rather than punishers for inappropriate behavior. The reasons for this are practical as well as ethical. Punishment often creates resentment; so even if it solves one problem, it may create others (see Skinner, 1968). Even if punishment would work as well as reinforcement, it should be avoided because it is not conducive to the creation of a happy, healthy classroom environment (Webber & Scheuermann, 1993). Punishment of one kind or another is necessary in some circumstances, and it

Social Reinforcers

Praising Words and Phrases

"That's clever."

"Good thinking."

"That shows a great deal of work."

"You really pay attention."

"You should show this to your father."

"That was very kind of you."

"I'm pleased with that."

"Keep up the good work."

"I appreciate your help."

"Now you've got the hang of it."

"That's an interesting point."

"You make it look easy."

"I like the way you got started on your homework."

Nearness

Walking together

Sitting together

Eating lunch together

Playing games with the student

Working after school together

Physical Contact

Touching

Hugging

Shaking hands

Holding hands

Expressions

Smiling

Winking

Nodding up and down

Looking interested

Laughing

Preferred Activities

Going first

Running errands

Getting to sit where he or she wants to

Telling a joke to the class

Having a party

Doing artwork related to studies

Choosing the game for recess

Earning an extra or longer recess

Helping the teacher

Visiting another class

Playing a short game: connect the dots, tic-tac-toe

Taking a class pet home for the weekend

Being team captain

Seeing a movie

Playing with a magnet or other science equipment

Reading with a friend

Getting free time in the library

Being asked what he or she would like to do

Planning a class trip or project

FIGURE 11.2 ● **Social Reinforcers and Preferred Activities**

From Vernon F. Jones and Louise S. Jones, *Comprehensive Classroom Management* (4th ed.), p. 363. Copyright © 1995 by Allyn & Bacon. Adapted by permission.

should be used without qualms when reinforcement strategies are impossible or ineffective. However, a program of punishment for misbehavior (e.g., depriving a student of privileges, never physical punishment) should always be the last option considered, never the first. A punisher is any unpleasant stimulus that an individual will try to avoid. Common punishers used in schools are reprimands, being sent out of class or to the principal's office, and detention or missed recess. Corporal punishment (e.g., spanking) is illegal in some states and districts (see Sulzer-Azaroff & Mayer, 1986) and highly restricted in others, though the practice still exists (Rose, 1984). Corporal punishment should never be used in schools. It is neither a necessary nor an effective response to misbehavior in school (see Gregory, 1995).

O'Leary and O'Leary (1972) list seven principles for the effective and humane use of punishment:

1. Use punishment sparingly.
2. Make it clear to the child why he or she is being punished.
3. Provide the child with an alternative means of obtaining some positive reinforcement.
4. Reinforce the child for behaviors that are incompatible with those you wish to weaken (e.g., if you punish for being off-task, also reinforce for being on-task).
5. Never use physical punishment.
6. Never punish when you are in a very angry or emotional state.
7. Punish when a behavior starts rather than when it ends.

One effective punisher is called **time out.** The teacher tells a misbehaving student to go to a separate part of the classroom, the hall, the principal's or vice principal's office, or another teacher's class. If possible, the place where the student is sent should be uninteresting and out of view of classmates. One advantage of time-out procedures is that they remove the student from the attention of his or her classmates. Therefore, time out may be especially effective for students whose misbehavior is motivated primarily by peer attention. The sit-and-watch procedure

> **time out**
> Removal of a student from a situation in which misbehavior was reinforced.

> **CONNECTIONS**
> For more information about sit-and-watch as a punishment for misbehavior, see Chapter 5, page 151 and Figure 5.3.

This student is in time out. In what contexts can time out be appropriate and effective? What ethical guidelines do you need to follow when considering behavior modification strategies?

described in Chapter 5 is a good example of the use of time out. Students who misbehaved in a physical education class were given a sand timer and asked to sit and watch for 3 minutes. This consequence, applied immediately and consistently, soon virtually eliminated misbehavior (White & Bailey, 1990).

Teachers should assign time outs infrequently. When they do assign them, they should do so calmly and surely. The student is to go straight to the time-out area and stay there until the prescribed time is up. Time-out assignments should be brief; about 5 minutes is usually adequate. However, timing should begin only after the student settles down; if the student yells or argues, that time should not count. During time out, no one should speak to the student. Teachers should not scold the student during time out. Students should be told why they are being given time out but should not otherwise be lectured. If the principal's office is used, the principal should be asked not to speak to the student.

REDUCE THE FREQUENCY OF REINFORCEMENT ● Once a reinforcement program has been in operation for a while and the student's behavior has improved and stabilized at a new level, the frequency of reinforcement can be reduced. Initially, reinforcers might be applied to every instance of appropriate behavior; as time goes on, every other instance, then every several instances, might be reinforced. Reducing the frequency of reinforcement helps to maintain the new behaviors over the long run and aids in extending the behaviors to other settings.

Applied Behavior Analysis Programs

Home-based reinforcement strategies and daily report card programs are examples of applied behavioral analysis involving individual students. A group contingency program is an example of an applied behavioral analysis in which the whole class is involved.

HOME-BASED REINFORCEMENT ● Some of the most practical and effective classroom management methods are **home-based reinforcement strategies** (see Barth, 1979). Teachers give students a daily or weekly report card to take home, and parents are instructed to provide special privileges or rewards to students on the basis of these teacher reports. Home-based reinforcement is not a new idea; a museum in Vermont displays weekly report cards from the 1860s.

Home-based reinforcement has several advantages over other, equally effective behavior management strategies. First, parents can give much more potent rewards and privileges than schools can. For example, parents control access to such activities as television, trips to the store, and going out with friends. Parents also know what their own children like and can therefore provide more individualized privileges than the school can. Second, home-based reinforcement gives parents frequent good news about their children. Parents of disruptive children usually hear from the school only when their child has done something wrong. This is bad for parent–school relations and leads to much blame and finger-pointing. Third, home-based reinforcement is easy to administer. The teacher can involve any adults who deal with the child (other teachers, bus drivers, playground or lunch monitors) in the program by having the student carry a daily report card all day. Finally, over time, daily report cards can be replaced by weekly report cards and then biweekly report cards without loss in effectiveness, until the school's usual 6- or 9-week report cards can be used.

home-based reinforcement strategies Behavior modification strategies in which a student's school behavior is reported to parents, who supply rewards.

STUDENT Homer H.	DAILY REPORT CARD		DATE March 21
PERIOD	BEHAVIOR	SCHOOLWORK	TEACHER
Reading	1 2 ③ 4	1 ② 3 4	Ms. Casa
Math	1 2 3 ④	1 2 3 ④	Ms. Casa
Lunch	1 2 ③ 4		Mr. Mason
Recess	1 2 ③ 4		Ms. Hauser
Language	1 2 3 ④	1 2 3 ④	Ms. Casa
Science/Soc. Stud.	1 2 ③ 4	1 2 ③ 4	Ms. Casa
	1 = Poor 2 = Fair 3 = Good 4 = Excellent	1 = Assignments not completed 2 = Assignments completed poorly 3 = Assignments completed adequately 4 = Assignments completed—excellent!	
Total rating 33	😊	Score needed 30	

FIGURE 11.3 ● Example of a Daily Report Card
Teachers who use a home-based reinforcement program must set up a daily report card so that a student's work and behavior can be assessed and reported to the student's parents. From E. Dougherty and A. Dougherty, "The Daily Report Card," *Psychology in the Schools, 14,* pp. 191–195. Copyright 1977 Clinical Psychology Publishing Co., Inc., Brandon, Vermont. Reprinted by permission.

DAILY REPORT CARDS ● Figure 11.3 presents a daily report card for Homer Heath, an elementary school student. His teacher, Ms. Casa, rated his behavior and schoolwork at the end of each academic period, and she arranged to have the lunch monitor and the recess monitor rate his behavior when Homer was with them. Homer was responsible for carrying his report card with him at all times and for making sure that it was marked and initialed at the end of each period. Whenever he made at least 30 points, his parents agreed to give him a special privilege: His father was to read him an extra story before bedtime and let him stay up 15 minutes longer than usual. Whenever he forgot to bring home his report card, his parents were to assume that he did not meet the criterion. If Homer had been a junior or senior high school student or if he had been in a departmentalized elementary school (where he changed classes for each subject), he would have carried his report card to every class, and each teacher would have marked it. Obviously, this approach requires some coordination among teachers, but the effort is certainly worthwhile if the daily report card dramatically reduces a student's misbehaviors and increases his or her academic output, as it has in dozens of studies evaluating this method (Barth, 1979).

Using a Daily Report Card System

Steps for setting up and implementing a daily report card system are as follows:

1. Decide which behaviors to include in the daily report card. Choose a behavior or set of behaviors on which the daily report card is to be based. Devise a rating scheme for each behavior, and construct a standard report card form. Your daily report card might be more or less elaborate than the one in Figure 11.3. For example, you might break behavior down into more precise categories, such as getting along with others, staying on-task, and following class rules.

THEORY
into
Practice

2. Explain the program to parents. Home-based reinforcement programs depend on parent participation, so it is critical to inform parents about the program and to obtain their cooperation. Parents should be told what the daily report card means and should be asked to reward their children whenever they bring home a good report card. In presenting the program to parents, teachers should explain what parents might do to reward their children. Communications with parents should be brief, positive, and informal and should generate a feeling that "we're going to solve this together." The program should focus on rewarding good behavior rather than punishing bad behavior. Examples of rewards parents might use at home (adapted from Walker & Shea, 1980) follow:

- Special activities with a parent (e.g., reading, flying a kite, building a model, shopping, playing a game, going to the zoo)
- Special foods
- Baking cookies or cooking
- Operating equipment that is usually reserved for adults (e.g., the dishwasher or vacuum cleaner)
- Access to special games, toys, or equipment
- Small rewards (such as coloring books, paper, comic books, erasers, or stickers)
- Additional play time, television time, and the like
- Having a friend spend the night
- Later bedtime or curfew

Parents should be encouraged to choose rewards that they can give every day (that is, nothing too expensive or difficult).

The best rewards are ones that build closeness between parent and child, such as doing special activities together. Many children who have behavior problems in school also have them at home and may have less than ideal relationships with their parents. Home-based reinforcement programs provide an opportunity for parents to show their love for their child at a time when the child has something to be proud of. A special time with Dad can be especially valuable as a reward for good behavior in school and for building the father–son or father–daughter relationship.

3. When behavior improves, reduce the frequency of the report. When home-based reinforcement works, it often works dramatically. Once the student's behavior has improved and has stabilized, it is time to decrease the frequency of the reports to parents. Report cards might then be issued only weekly (for larger but less frequent rewards). As was noted in Chapter 5, the best way to ensure maintenance is to thin out the reinforcement schedule—that is, to increase the interval between reinforcers.

group contingency program
A program in which rewards or punishments are given to a class as a whole for adhering to or violating rules of conduct.

GROUP CONTINGENCY PROGRAMS ● A **group contingency program** is a reinforcement system in which an entire group is rewarded on the basis of the behavior of the group members. Teachers have always used group contingencies, as in "We'll go to lunch as soon as all students have put their work away and are quiet." When the teacher says this, any one student can cause the entire class to be late to lunch. Or the teacher might say, "If the class averages at least ninety on tomorrow's quiz, then you'll all be excused from homework for the rest of the week." This group contingency will depend on the average performance of all group members rather than on any single student's performance.

One important advantage of group contingencies is that they are relatively easy to administer. Most often, the whole class is either rewarded or not rewarded, so the teacher need not do one thing with some students and something else with others. For example, suppose a teacher says, "If the whole class follows the class rules this morning, we will have five extra minutes of recess." If the class does earn the extra recess, they all get it together; the teacher does not have to arrange to have some students stay out longer while others are called inside.

The theory behind group contingencies is that when a group is rewarded on the basis of its members' behavior, the group members will encourage one another to do whatever helps the group gain the reward (Slavin, 1990). Group contingencies can turn the same peer pressure that often supports misbehaviors to pressure opposing misbehavior. When the class can earn extra recess only if all students are well behaved all morning, no one is liable to find it funny when Joan balances a book on her head or Quinn speaks disrespectfully to the teacher.

Group contingencies have been used successfully in many forms and for many purposes. Barrish and colleagues (1969) divided a fourth-grade class into two teams during math period. When the teacher saw any member of a team disobeying class rules, the whole team received a check mark on the chalkboard. If a team had five or fewer check marks at the end of the period, all team members would take part in a free-time activity at the end of the day. If both teams got more than five check marks, the one that got fewer would receive the free time. A recent study also found positive effects of the good behavior game on the behavior of first-graders (Dolan et al., 1993).

Establishing a Group Contingency Program

THEORY *into* **Practice**

As was noted earlier, a group contingency behavior management program can be as simple as the statement "Class, if you are all in your seats, on-task, and quiet this morning, you may have 5 extra minutes of recess." However, a little more structure than this can increase the effectiveness of the group contingency.

1. Decide which behaviors will be reinforced. As in any whole-class behavior modification program, the first step in setting up a group contingency is to establish a set of class rules.

2. Set up a developmentally appropriate point system. There are essentially three ways to implement a group contingency behavior management program. One is simply to rate class behavior each period or during each activity. That is, an elementary school class might receive 0 to 5 points during each individual instructional period such as reading, language arts, and math. A secondary school class might receive one overall rating each period or separate ratings for behavior and completed assignments. The class would then be rewarded each day or week if they exceeded a preestablished number of points.

Another way to set up a group contingency program is to rate the class at various times during the day. For example, you might set a timer to ring on the average of once every 10 minutes (but varying randomly from 1 to 20 minutes). If the whole class is conforming to class rules when the timer rings, then the class earns a point. The same program can be used without the timer if the teacher gives the class a point every 10 minutes or so if all students are conforming to class rules. Canter and Canter (1992) suggest that teachers use a bag of marbles and a jar, putting a marble into the jar from time to time whenever the class is following rules. Each marble would be worth 30 seconds of extra recess. In secondary schools, where extra recess is not possible, each marble might represent 30 seconds of break time held at the end of the period on Friday.

3. Consider deducting points for serious misbehavior. The group contingency reward system by itself should help to improve student behavior. However, it may still be necessary to react to occasional serious misbehavior. For example, you might deduct 10 points for any instance of fighting or of serious disrespect for the teacher. When points must be deducted, do not negotiate with students about it. Just deduct them, explaining why they must be deducted and reminding students that they may earn them back if they follow class rules.

4. When behavior improves, reduce the frequency of the points and reinforcers. Initially, the group contingency should be applied every day. When the class's behavior improves and stabilizes at a new level for about a week, you may change to giving rewards once a week. Ultimately, the class may graduate from the point-and-reward system entirely, though feedback and praise based on class behavior should continue.

5. Combine group and individual contingencies if necessary. The use of group contingencies need not rule out individual contingencies for students who need them. For example, students who continue to have problems in a class using a group contingency might still receive daily or weekly report cards to take home to their parents.

Ethics of Behavioral Methods

The behavior analysis strategies described in this chapter are powerful. Properly applied, they will usually bring the behavior of even the most disruptive students to manageable levels. However, there is a danger that teachers may use such techniques to overcontrol students. They may be so concerned about getting students to sit down, stay quiet, and look productive that they lose sight of the fact that school is for learning, not for social control. Winett and Winkler (1972) wrote an article entitled "Current Behavior Modification in the Classroom: Be Still, Be Quiet, Be Docile," in which they warned that behavior modification–based classroom management systems are being misused if teachers mistakenly believe that a quiet class is a learning class. This point parallels the basic premise of the QAIT model of effective instruction presented in Chapter 9. Behavior management systems can increase time for learning; but unless the quality of instruction, appropriate levels of instruction, and incentives for learning are also adequate, the additional time may be wasted (see Canter, 1989; Emmer & Aussiker, 1990).

CONNECTIONS

For more information about the QAIT model, see Chapter 9, page 291.

Some people object to applied behavior analysis on the basis that it constitutes bribing students to do what they ought to do anyway or that it is mind control. However, all classrooms use rewards and punishers (such as grades, praise, scolding, suspension). Applied behavior analysis strategies simply use these rewards in a more systematic way and avoid punishers as much as possible.

Applied behavior analysis methods should be used only when it is clear that preventive or informal methods of improving classroom management are not enough to create a positive environment for learning. It is unethical to overapply these methods, but it may be equally unethical to fail to apply them when they could avert serious problems. For example, it may be unethical to refer a child to special education or to suspend, expel, or retain a child on the basis of a pattern of behavior problems before using positive behavior management methods long enough to see whether they can resolve the problem without more draconian measures.

SELF-CHECK

Explain how applied behavior analysis is used in the classroom. Describe the appropriate and ethical use of praise, home-based reinforcement, punishment, daily report cards, and group contingencies.

HOW CAN SERIOUS BEHAVIOR PROBLEMS BE PREVENTED?

Everyone misbehaves. There is hardly a person on earth who has not at some time done something he or she knew to be wrong or even illegal. However, some people's misbehavior is far more frequent and/or serious than others', and students in this category cause their teachers and school administrators (not to mention their parents and themselves) a disproportionate amount of trouble and concern.

Serious behavior problems are not evenly distributed among students or schools. Most students who are identified as having severe behavior problems are male; from 3 to 8 times as many boys as girls are estimated to have serious conduct problems (Binder, 1988; Lowry, Sleet, Duncan, Powell, & Kolbe, 1995). Serious delinquency is far more common among students from impoverished backgrounds, particularly in urban locations. Students with poor family relationships are also much more likely than other students to become involved in serious misbehavior and delinquency, as are students who are low in achievement and those who have attendance problems (see Gottlieb, Alter, & Gottlieb, 1991; Kauffman, 1989).

The school has an important role to play in preventing or managing serious misbehavior and delinquency, but the student and the school are only one part of the story. Delinquent behavior often involves the police, courts, and social service agencies, as well as students' parents and peers. However, there are some guidelines for prevention of delinquency and serious misbehaviors.

Identifying Causes of Misbehavior

Even though some types of students are more prone to misbehavior than others, these characteristics do not cause misbehavior. Some students misbehave because they perceive that the rewards for misbehavior outweigh the rewards for good behavior. For example, students who do not experience success in school may perceive that the potential rewards for hard work and good behavior are small, so they turn to other sources of rewards. Some put their energies into sports, others into social activities. Some, particularly those who are failing in many different domains, find their niche in groups that hold norms that devalue achievement and other prosocial behavior. This can all happen very early, as soon as some students realize that they are unlikely to do well in school or to receive much support at home, from peers, or from the school itself for their academic efforts. Over time, students who fail in school and get into minor behavior difficulties may fall in with a delinquent subgroup and begin to engage in serious delinquent or even criminal behavior. The role of the delinquent peer group in maintaining delinquent behavior cannot be overstated. Delinquent acts among adolescents and preadolescents are usually done in groups and are supported by antisocial peer norms (Kauffman, 1989; Parks, 1995).

Enforcing Rules and Practices

Expectations that students will conform to school rules must be consistently expressed. For example, graffiti or other vandalism must be repaired at once so that other students do not get the idea that misbehavior is common or accepted.

Enforcing School Attendance

Truancy and delinquency are strongly related; when students are out of school, they are often in the community making trouble. There are many effective means of reducing truancy (Haslinger, Kelly, & O'Lara, 1996). Brooks (1975) had high school students with serious attendance problems carry cards to be signed by their teachers at the end of each period they attended. Students received a ticket for each period attended, plus bonus tickets for good behavior in class and for going 5 days without missing a class. The tickets were used in a drawing for a variety of prizes. Before the program began, the target students were absent 60 percent of all school days. During the program, absences dropped to 19 percent of school days. Over the same period, truancy among other students with attendance problems who were not in the program increased from 59 percent to 79 percent.

Barber and Kagey (1977) markedly increased attendance in an entire elementary school by making full participation in once-a-month parties depend on student attendance. Several activities were provided during the parties, and students could earn access to some or all of them according to the number of days they attended class.

Fiordaliso, Lordeman, Filipczak, and Friedman (1977) increased attendance among chronically truant junior high school students by having the school call their parents whenever the students were present several days in a row. The number of days before calling depended on how severe the student's truancy had been. Parents of the most truant students, who had been absent 6 or more days per month, were called after the student attended for only 3 consecutive days.

Avoiding Tracking

Tracking (between-class ability grouping) should be avoided if possible (see Chapter 9). Low-track classes are ideal breeding grounds for antisocial delinquent peer groups (Howard, 1978). Similarly, behavioral and academic problems should be dealt with in the context of the regular class as much as possible, rather than in separate special-education classes (Madden & Slavin, 1983b; Safer, 1982).

Practicing Intervention

Classroom management strategies should be used to reduce inappropriate behavior before it escalates into delinquency. Improving students' behavior and success in school can prevent delinquency. For example, Hawkins, Doueck, and Lishner (1988) used preventive classroom management methods such as those emphasized in this chapter along with interactive teaching and cooperative learning to help low-achieving seventh-graders. In comparison with control-group students, the students who were involved in the program were suspended and expelled less often, had better attitudes toward school, and were more likely to expect to complete high school. Use of applied behavior analysis programs for misbehavior in class can also contribute to the prevention of delinquency. Group contingencies can be especially effective with predelinquent students, because this strategy can deprive students of peer support for misbehavior.

Requesting Family Involvement

Involve the student's home in any response to serious misbehavior. When misbehavior occurs, parents should be notified. If misbehavior persists, parents should be involved in establishing a program, such as a home-based reinforcement program, to coordinate home and school responses to misbehavior.

Using Peer Mediation

Students can be trained to serve as peer mediators, particularly to resolve conflicts between fellow students. Students who are having problems with other students may be asked to take these problems to peer mediators rather than to adults for resolution, and the peer mediators themselves may actively look for interpersonal problems among their classmates and offer help when they occur. Peer mediators have been found to be effective in resolving a variety of interpersonal problems, from insults and perceptions of unfairness among students to stealing to physical aggression (Araki, 1990; Hanson, 1994; Johnson & Johnson, 1996; Johnson, Johnson, Dudley, Ward, & Magnuson, 1995). However, peer mediators need to be carefully trained and monitored if they are to be effective (Latham, 1997a). Figure 11.4 shows a guide for peer mediators used in one conflict management program.

These students are demonstrating peer mediation as a way to resolve a conflict. As a teacher, how would you advise student mediators to handle conflicts with a group of students?

1. Introduce yourselves: "Hi, my name is _____. I'm conflict manager and this is my partner _____."

2. Ask the parties: "Do you want to solve the problem with us or with a teacher?" If necessary, move to a quiet place to solve the problem.

3. Explain to the parties: "First you have to agree to four rules":
   a. Agree to solve the problem.
   b. No name-calling.
   c. Do not interrupt.
   d. Tell the truth.

4. Conflict Manager #1 asks Person #1: "What happened? How do you feel?" Conflict Manager #1 repeats what Person #1 said, using active listening: "So, what you're saying is . . ."

5. Conflict Manager #2 asks Person #2: "What happened? How do you feel?" Conflict Manager #2 repeats what Person #2 said, using active listening: "So, what you're saying is . . ."

6. Ask Person #1: "Do you have a solution?" Ask Person #2: "Do you agree with the solution?" If no: "Do you have another solution?" and so on until disputants have reached a solution agreeable to both of them.

7. Have disputants tell each other what they have just agreed to: "So will you tell each other what you've just agreed to?"

8. Congratulate them both: "Thank you for working so hard to solve your problem. Congratulations."

9. Fill out Conflict Manager Report Form.

FIGURE 11.4 ● Peer Conflict Management
From Classroom Law Project, 6318 S.W. Corbett, Portland, OR 97201. Adapted by permission.

Judiciously Applying Consequences

Avoid the use of suspension (or expulsion) as punishment for all but the most serious misbehavior (see Chobot & Garibaldi, 1982). Suspension often exacerbates truancy problems, both because it makes students fall behind in their work and because it gives them experience in the use of time out of school. In-school suspension, detention, and other penalties are more effective.

When students misbehave, they should be punished; but when punishment is applied, it should be brief. Being sent to a time-out area or detention room is a common punishment and is effective for most students. Loss of privileges may be used. However, whatever punishment is used should not last too long. It is better to make a student miss two days of football practice than to throw him off the team, in part because once the student is off the team, the school may have little else of value to offer or withhold. Every child has within himself or herself the capacity for good behavior as well as for misbehavior. The school must be the ally of the good in each child at the same time that it is the enemy of misbehavior. Overly harsh penalties or penalties that do not allow the student to reenter the classroom on an equal footing with others risk pushing students into the antisocial, delinquent subculture. When a student has paid his or her debt by losing privileges, experiencing detention, or whatever the punishment may be, he or she must be fully reaccepted as a member of the class.

SELF-CHECK

Describe how you would prevent serious discipline problems. Develop and defend a plan for preventing serious discipline problems.

CHAPTER SUMMARY

WHAT IS AN EFFECTIVE LEARNING ENVIRONMENT?

Creating effective learning environments involves strategies that teachers use to maintain appropriate behavior and respond to misbehavior in the classroom. Keeping students interested and engaged and showing enthusiasm are important in preventing misbehavior. Creating an effective learning environment is a matter of knowing a set of techniques that teachers can learn and apply.

WHAT IS THE IMPACT OF TIME ON LEARNING?

Methods of maximizing allocated time include preventing late starts and early finishes, preventing interruptions, handling routine procedures smoothly and quickly, minimizing time spent on discipline, and using engaged time effectively. Engaged time, or time on-task, is the time individual students spend actually doing assigned work. Teachers can maximize engaged time by teaching engaging lessons, maintaining momentum, maintaining smoothness of instruction, managing transitions, maintaining group focus, practicing withitness, and overlapping. In a student-centered classroom, classroom management is more participatory, with students involved in setting standards of behavior; yet rules are still needed and must be consistently communicated and enforced.

WHAT PRACTICES CONTRIBUTE TO EFFECTIVE CLASSROOM MANAGEMENT?

Practices that contribute to effective classroom management include starting the year properly and developing rules and procedures. Class rules and procedures should be explicitly presented to students and applied promptly and fairly.

WHAT ARE SOME STRATEGIES FOR MANAGING ROUTINE MISBEHAVIOR?

One principle of classroom discipline is good management of routine misbehavior. The principle of least intervention means using the simplest methods that will work. There is a continuum of strategies from least to most disruptive: prevention of misbehavior; nonverbal cues such as eye contact, which can stop a minor misbehavior; praise of incompatible, correct behavior; praise of other students who are behaving; simple verbal reminders given immediately after students misbehave; repetition of verbal reminders; and application of consequences when students refuse to comply. For serious behavior problems, swift and certain consequences must be applied. A call to the student's parents can be effective.

HOW IS APPLIED BEHAVIOR ANALYSIS USED TO MANAGE MORE SERIOUS BEHAVIOR PROBLEMS?

The most common reinforcer for both routine and serious misbehavior is attention from teacher or peers. When the student misbehaves to get the teacher's attention, one effective strategy is to pay attention to correct behavior while ignoring misbehavior as much as possible; scolding often acts as a reinforcer of misbehavior.

Individual behavior management strategies are useful for students with persistent behavior problems in school. After establishing baseline behavior, the teacher selects reinforcers such as verbal praise or small, tangible rewards, and punishers such as time outs (removing a child from a situation that reinforces misbehavior). The teacher also establishes criteria for applying reinforcement and punishment.

Home-based reinforcement strategies may involve giving students daily or weekly report cards to take home and instructing parents to provide rewards on the basis of these reports. The steps to setting up such a program include deciding on behaviors to use for the daily report card and explaining the program to parents.

Group contingency programs are those in which an entire group is rewarded on the basis of the behavior of the group members.

One objection to behavior management techniques is that they can be used to overcontrol students. Behavior management strategies should always emphasize praise and reinforcement, reserving punishment as a last resort.

HOW CAN SERIOUS BEHAVIOR PROBLEMS BE PREVENTED?

There are few sure methods of preventing delinquency, but some general principles include clearly expressing and consistently enforcing classroom rules, reducing truancy however possible, avoiding the use of between-class ability grouping, using preventive classroom management strategies, involving parents in any response to serious misbehavior, using peer mediation, avoiding the use of suspension, applying only brief punishment, and reintegrating students after punishment.

KEY TERMS

accountability   373

allocated time   368

applied behavior analysis   386

Assertive Discipline   385

behavior modification   388

classroom management   365

discipline   366

engaged time   367

group alerting   373

group contingencies   387

group contingency program   394

home-based reinforcement strategies   392

mock participation   375

nonverbal cues   380

overlapping   374

time on-task   367

time out   391

withitness   374

Self-Assessment

1. Which of the following refers to methods used to prevent behavior problems and disruptions?
   a. management
   b. discipline
   c. learning environment
   d. instruction

2. According to research, which of the following strategies would be most likely to increase student achievement?
   a. Increase allocated time for instruction by 10 percent above what is normal.
   b. Increase engaged time to 100 percent of the allocated classroom time.
   c. Increase engaged time by 10 percent above what is normal.
   d. Decrease allocated time by late starts and early finishes.

3. Engaged time is synonymous with
   a. time on-task.
   b. allocated time.
   c. momentum.
   d. overlapping.

4. Match each of the following terms with its definition.
   a. accountability
   b. group alerting
   c. withitness
   d. overlapping

   _____ monitoring the behavior of all students and responding when necessary
   _____ using questioning strategies that hold the attention of all students
   _____ maintaining the flow of instruction in spite of small interruptions
   _____ involving all students in all parts of a lecture or discussion

5. All of the following statements about class rules are accurate except
   a. Class rules should be few in number.
   b. Class rules should be seen as fair by students.
   c. Class rules should be clearly explained and deliberately taught to students.
   d. Class rules should be created by the teacher and the students together.

6. According to the principle of least intervention, in what order should the following management methods be used in dealing with discipline problems?
   a. prevention
   b. consequences
   c. nonverbal cues
   d. verbal reminders
   e. praising appropriate behaviors

7. Sequence the following steps of a behavior management program in the order in which they should be used.
   a. Select and use reinforcers and, if necessary, punishers.
   b. Establish a baseline for the targeted behavior.
   c. Phase out reinforcement.
   d. Identify the target behavior and its reinforcer(s).

8. Daily report cards, group contingency programs, home-based reinforcement programs, and individual behavior management programs are all based on
   a. assertive discipline practices.
   b. delinquency prevention.
   c. behavioral learning theory.
   d. the principle of least intervention.

9. Discuss ethical considerations in the use of individual and group behavior management programs.

10. Explain how you would prevent the following misbehaviors: speaking out of turn, teasing, physical fighting.

Chapter 12

WHO ARE LEARNERS WITH EXCEPTIONALITIES?

Types of Exceptionalities and the Numbers of Students Served

Students with Mental Retardation

Students with Learning Disabilities

Students with Communication Disorders

Students with Emotional and Behavioral Disorders

Students with Sensory, Physical, and Health Impairments

Students Who Are Gifted and Talented

WHAT IS SPECIAL EDUCATION?

Public Law 94–142 and IDEA

An Array of Special-Education Services

WHAT ARE MAINSTREAMING AND INCLUSION?

Research on Mainstreaming and Inclusion

Adapting Instruction

Teaching Learning Strategies and Metacognitive Awareness

Prevention and Early Intervention

Computers and Students with Disabilities

Buddy Systems and Peer Tutoring

Special-Education Teams

Social Integration of Students with Disabilities

Learners with Exceptionalities

Elaine Wagner, assistant principal at Pleasant-ville Elementary School, came in to work one day and was stopped by the school secretary.

"Good morning," the secretary said. "There's a Helen Ross here to see you. She is interested in enrolling her children. She's waiting in your office. Looks nervous—I gave her some coffee and settled her down."

"Thanks, Beth," said Ms. Wagner. She went into her office and introduced herself to Ms. Ross.

"I appreciate your seeing me," said Ms. Ross. "We're planning to move to Pleas-antville next fall, and I wanted to look at the schools before we move. We have one child, Tommy, going into second grade, and Annie is going into kindergarten. I'm really concerned about Tommy. In the school he's in now, he's not doing very well. It's spring, and he's hardly reading at all. His teacher says he might have a learning disability, and the school wants to put him in special education. I don't like that idea. He's a normal, happy kid at home, and it would crush him to find out he's 'different,' but I want to do what's best for him. I guess the main thing I want to see is what you do for kids like Tommy."

"Well," said Ms. Wagner, "the most important thing I can tell you about our school is that our philosophy is that every child can learn, and it is our job to find out how to reach each one. I can't tell you exactly what we'd do with Tommy, of course, since I don't know him, but I can assure you of a few things. First, we'll attend to his reading problem right away. We believe in prevention and early in-tervention. If Tommy is having serious reading problems, we'll probably arrange to give him one-to-one tutoring so that he can catch up quickly with the other second-graders. Second, we'll try to keep him in his regular classroom if we possibly can. If he needs special-education services, he'll get them, but in this school we try everything to solve a child's learning problems before we refer him or her for testing that might lead to special-education placement. Even if Tommy does qualify for special education, we'll structure his program so that he is with his regular class as much as possible. We will develop an individualized education plan for him. Finally, I want to assure you that you will be very much involved in all decisions that have to do with Tommy and that we'll talk with you frequently about his progress and ask for your help at home to make sure that Tommy is doing well."

"Ms. Wagner, that all sounds great. But how can you give Tommy the help he needs and still let him stay in his regular class?"

"Why don't I take you to see some of our classes in operation right now?" said Ms. Wagner. "I think you'll see what I mean."

Ms. Wagner led the way through the brightly lit corridors lined with student projects, artwork, and compositions. She turned in at Mr. Esposito's second-grade class. There, she and Ms. Ross were met by a happy, excited buzz of activity. The children were working in small groups, measuring each other's heights and the lengths of fingers and feet. Some children were trying to figure out how to measure the distance around each other's heads. Another teacher, Ms. Park, was working with some of the groups.

Ms. Wagner and Ms. Ross stepped back into the hall. "What I wanted to show you," said Ms. Wagner, "is how we integrate our students with special needs into the general education classroom. Could you tell which students were special-needs students?"

"No," admitted Ms. Ross.

"That's what we hope to create—a classroom in which children with special needs are so well integrated that you can't pick them out. Ms. Park is the special-education teacher for the younger grades, and she teams with Mr. Esposito during math and reading periods to serve all of the second-graders who need special services. Ms. Park will help any child who is having difficulty, not just students with special needs, since a large part of her job is to prevent students from ever needing special education. Sometimes she'll work with individual kids or small groups that need help. She often teaches skills children will be learning in advance, so they will be better prepared in class. For example, she might have gone over measurement with some of the kids before this lesson so that they'd have a leg up on the concept."

Ms. Wagner led the way to the music room. She pointed through a window at a teacher working with one child. "What you see there is a tutor working with a first-grader who is having difficulty in reading. If your Tommy were here, this is what we might be doing with him. We try to do anything we can to keep kids from falling behind in the first place so that they can stay out of special education and progress along with their classmates."

Ms. Wagner showed Ms. Ross all over the school. In one class a child with a visual impairment was reading text from a computer that had inch-high letters. In another they saw a child with Down syndrome working in a cooperative learning group on a science project. In a third classroom a child in a wheelchair was leading a class discussion.

Ms. Ross was fascinated.

"I had no idea a school could be like this. I'm so excited that we're moving to Pleasantville. This looks like the perfect school for both of my children. I only wish we could have moved here two years ago!"

Using Your EXPERIENCE

Cooperative Learning   In groups of five, discuss Tommy Ross and students like him. One person assumes the role of Ms. Wagner; one is his future homeroom teacher, Mr. Esposito; one is Ms. Ross; one is the special-education teacher, Ms. Park; and one is the special-education director for the district. Discuss how Tommy will be screened for a potential learning disability in reading, and list some strategies that his teachers might use if, in fact, he does have a learning disability.

Cooperative Learning   Divide groups of four classmates into pairs. The pairs interview a partner about what a learning disability in reading might look like (i.e., how a reading disability might be identified) and what a teacher might do to address this situation. The two interviewers share what they have learned within their group. Roles are then reversed. The two new interviewers tell their group what they have learned about reading disabilities.

Pleasantville Elementary School is organized around two key ideas: that all children can learn, and that it is the school's responsibility to find ways to meet each child's needs in the general education classroom to the maximum extent possible. Pleasantville Elementary is organized to identify children's strengths as well as their problems and to provide the best program it can for each child. Every school has children with exceptionalities who can do well in school when they are given the specific supports they need to learn. This chapter describes children with exceptionalities and programs that are designed to help them achieve their full potential.

WHO ARE LEARNERS WITH EXCEPTIONALITIES?

In one sense, every child is exceptional. No two children are exactly alike in their ways of learning and behaving, in their activities and preferences, in their skills and motivations. All students would benefit from programs uniquely tailored to their individual needs.

However, schools cannot practically meet the precise needs of every student. For the sake of efficiency, students are grouped into classes and given common instructional experiences designed to provide the greatest benefit to the largest number at a moderate cost. This system works reasonably well for the great majority of students. However, some students do not fit easily into this mold. Some students have physical or sensory disabilities, such as hearing or vision loss or orthopedic disabilities, that restrict their ability to participate in the general education classroom program without special assistance. Other students have mental retardation, emotional disorders, or learning disabilities that make it difficult for them to learn in the general education classroom without assistance. Finally, some students have such outstanding talents that the general education classroom teacher is unable to meet their unique needs without help.

To receive special-education services, a student must have one of a small number of categories of disabilities or disorders. These general labels, such as "learning disabled," "mentally retarded," or "orthopedically disabled," cover a wide diversity of problems. Categories evolve over time. For example, many children who would previously have been called students with mild retardation are now identified as students with learning disabilities.

Labels tend to stick, making change difficult, and the labels themselves can become handicaps for the student. Education professionals must avoid using labels in a way that unintentionally stigmatizes students, dehumanizes them, segregates them socially from their peers, or encourages discrimination against them in any form (Trent, Artiles, & Englert, 1998). Teachers of learners with exceptionalities need to be sensitive to the political and social dimensions of these students' differences (Heward & Cavanaugh, 1997). The term **learners with exceptionalities** may be used to describe any individuals whose physical, mental, or behavioral performance is so different from the norm—either higher or lower—that additional services are need to meet the individuals' needs.

The terms *disability* and *handicap* are not interchangeable. A **disability** is a functional limitation a person has that interferes with the person's physical or cognitive abilities. A **handicap** is a condition imposed on a person with disabilities by society, the physical environment, or the person's attitude. For example, a student who uses a wheelchair is handicapped by a lack of access ramps. *Handicap* is therefore not a synonym for *disability* (Hallahan & Kauffman, 1997).

Even though labels are neither exact nor unchanging and may be harmful in some situations, they are a useful shorthand for educators to use to indicate the type and extent of a student's exceptionalities—as long as the limitations of the labels are taken into consideration. The following sections discuss characteristics of students with the types of exceptionalities that are most commonly seen in schools.

Types of Exceptionalities and the Numbers of Students Served

Some exceptionalities, such as loss of vision and hearing, are relatively easy to define and measure. Others, such as mental retardation, learning disabilities, and emotional disorders, are much harder to define, and their definitions have evolved over time. In fact, recent decades have seen dramatic changes in these categories (Keogh & MacMillan, 1996). Since the mid-1970s, the numbers of children in categories of disabilities that are most easily defined, such as physical impairments, have remained fairly stable. However, the number of students categorized as learning disabled has steadily increased, and the use of the category "mentally retarded" has diminished. This trend, illustrated in Figure 12.1, continues today (see U.S. Department of Education, 1996).

learners with exceptionalities
Any individuals whose physical, mental, or behavioral performance is so different from the norm—either higher or lower—that additional services are needed to meet the individuals' needs.

disability
The limitation of a function, such as cognitive processing or physical or sensory abilities.

handicap
A condition imposed on a person with disabilities by society, the physical environment, or the person's attitude.

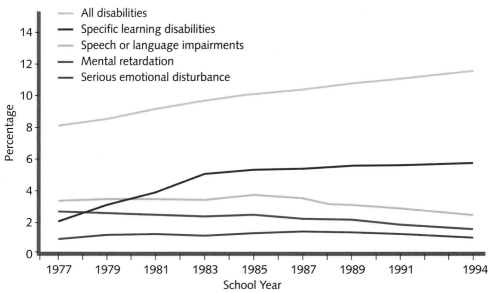

FIGURE 12.1 ● Number of Children with Disabilities Served by Federal Programs As a Percentage of Total Public K–12 Enrollment: School Years Ending 1977–1994
Includes students served under Chapter 1 of the Education Consolidation and Improvement Act (ECIA) and under Part B of the Individuals with Disabilities Education Act (IDEA). Prior to the 1987–88 school year, preschool students were included in the counts by disabling condition. Beginning in the 1987–88 school year, states were no longer required to report preschool students (0–5 years) with disabilities by disabling condition. From U.S. Department of Education, Office of Special Education and Rehabilitative Services, *Annual Report to Congress on the Implementation of the Individuals with Disabilities Education Act,* various years; and National Center for Education Statistics, *Digest of Education Statistics, 1995.*

Figure 12.2 shows the percentages of all students, ages 6 to 17, receiving special-education services in 1994–1995. There are several important pieces of information in this figure. First, notice that the overall percentage of students receiving special education was about 10 percent; that is, 1 out of 10 students ages 6 to 17

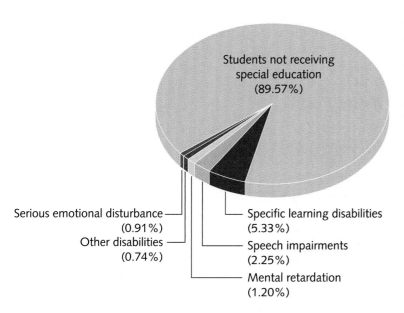

FIGURE 12.2 ● Disabilities of Students Ages 6 to 17 Receiving Special Education As a Percentage of All Students Ages 6 to 17: School Year 1994–1995
From U.S. Department of Education, *Eighteenth Annual Report to Congress on the Implementation of the Individuals with Disabilities in Education Act,* 1996.

TABLE 12.1

Disabilities among Students Ages 6 through 21: Numbers and Percentages, School Year 1994–1995

DISABILITY	NUMBER	PERCENTAGE
Specific learning disabilities	2,513,977	51.1
Speech or language impairments	1,023,665	20.8
Mental retardation	570,855	11.6
Serious emotional disturbance	428,168	8.7
Other health impairments	106,509	2.2
Multiple disabilities	89,646	1.8
Hearing impairments	65,568	1.3
Orthopedic impairments	60,604	1.2
Visual impairments	24,877	0.5
Autism	22,780	0.5
Traumatic brain injury	7,188	0.1
Deaf–blindness	1,331	0.0
All disabilities	4,915,168	100.0

Source: Adapted from U.S. Department of Education, Office of Special Education Programs, Data Analysis System (DANS), 1996.

was categorized as exceptional. Of these, the largest proportion were categorized as having specific learning disabilities (5.3 percent of all students) or speech disabilities (2.25 percent). Table 12.1 shows the percentages of students ages 6 to 21 with various disabilities in 1994–95 (U.S. Department of Education, 1996). Specific learning disabilities (51.1 percent of all students with disabilities), speech and language impairments (20.8 percent), mental retardation (11.6 percent), and serious emotional disturbance (8.7 percent) are far more common than physical or sensory disabilities. In a class of 30 a teacher might, on the average, have one or two students with learning disabilities and one with a speech impairment. In contrast, only about 1 class in 40 is likely to have a student who has hearing or vision loss or a physical disability.

Students with Mental Retardation

Approximately 1.2 percent of all students ages 6 to 17 have mental retardation (U.S. Department of Education, 1996). There are several definitions of **mental retardation.** In 1992 the American Association on Mental Retardation (AAMR) defined mental retardation as follows:

mental retardation
A condition, usually present at birth, that results in below-average intellectual skills and poor adaptive behavior.

> Mental retardation refers to substantial limitations in present functioning. It is characterized by significantly subaverage intellectual function, existing concurrently with related limitations in two or more of the following applicable adaptive skill areas: communication, self-care, home living, social skills, community use, self-direction, health and safety, functional academics, leisure and work. Mental retardation manifests before age 18. (Luckasson et al., 1992, p. 1)

This definition means that people with mental retardation have low scores on tests of intelligence and also show difficulty in maintaining the standards of personal independence and social responsibility that would be expected for their age and cultural group (Luckasson et al., 1992; MacLean, 1996). In addition, these impairments in intelligence and adaptive behavior become apparent some time between conception and age 18.

CAUSES OF MENTAL RETARDATION ● Among the many causes of mental retardation are genetic inheritance; chromosomal abnormalities, such as Down syndrome; diseases passed between mother and fetus in utero, such as rubella (German measles) and syphilis; fetal chemical dependency syndromes caused by a mother's abuse of alcohol or cocaine during pregnancy; birth accidents that result in oxygen deprivation; childhood diseases and accidents, such as encephalitis and head trauma; and toxic contamination from the environment, such as lead poisoning.

INTELLIGENCE QUOTIENT (IQ) ● To understand how severity of impairment in children with mental retardation is classified, it is first important to recall the concept of IQ, or **intelligence quotient,** derived from scores on standardized tests (see Dennis & Tapsfield, 1996; McArdle & Woodcock, 1998). Figure 12.3 illustrates a theoretical distribution of IQs among all students on the Stanford–Binet Intelligence Scale, which has a mean of 100 and a standard deviation of 15. Notice that the IQ scores form a bell-shaped curve, called a **normal curve.** That is, the greatest number of scores fall near the mean, with fewer scores extending above and below the mean. Students with IQs above 70 are generally regarded as being in the normal range. Slightly more than 2 percent of students have IQs below this range.

Consistent with AAMR recommendations, education professionals do not use IQs alone to determine the severity of cognitive impairment. They take into account a student's school and home performance, scores on other tests, and the student's cultural background. IQ tests have been criticized for cultural bias. Critics also claim that schools have misused IQ scores to discriminate against certain groups or to group students inappropriately for instruction or special education services (Hilliard, 1992).

CONNECTIONS
For more on IQ, see Chapter 4, page 128.

CONNECTIONS
For more about IQ testing, see Chapter 14, page 505.

CONNECTIONS
For a definition of standard deviation, see Chapter 14, page 512.

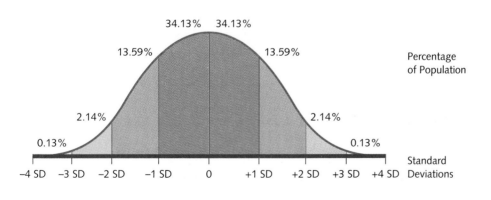

FIGURE 12.3 ● Distribution of Intelligence Test Scores
The distribution of intelligence test scores resembles a bell-shaped curve, called a normal curve.

intelligence quotient (IQ)
An intelligence test score that should be near 100 for people of average intelligence.

normal curve
A bell-shaped symmetrical distribution of scores in which most scores fall near the mean, with progressively fewer occurring as the distance from the mean increases.

CLASSIFICATIONS OF MENTAL RETARDATION ● In the past, individuals with mental retardation have been categorized according to their IQ scores. For example, the 1983 AAMR manual listed four degrees of severity of mental retardation in terms of ranges of IQ, including mild retardation (IQs 50–55 to 70–75), moderate retardation (IQs 35–40 to 50–55), severe retardation (IQs 20–25 to 35–40), and profound retardation (IQs below 20–25) (Luckasson et al., 1992). This categorization is still widely used. In an older classification system, students with mild retardation, typically with IQs between 55 and 70, are regarded as "educable" (EMR); that is, able to learn basic academic skills up to a fifth-grade level. Students with moderate retardation (IQs 40–55) are classified as "trainable" (TMR); that is, able to learn independent self-care and job skills for sheltered workshops (MacMillan & Forness, 1992). Children with IQs below 50 are often termed "custodial" and usually receive out-of-school services. This classification system has been challenged by some professionals who believe that the emphasis in present-day special education is that all people can learn and that education and training cannot be clearly differentiated (Smith & Luckasson, 1995). However, some school districts use this or a similar simplified system of classification (MacLean, 1996).

Current AAMR definitions emphasize the capabilities of individuals with mental retardation in two main areas—intellectual functioning and adaptive skills—and categorize individuals on the basis of the supports they need (Smith, 1998). Table 12.2 defines four categories of services people with mental retardation may need and gives examples of these services.

However the categories are defined, children with mild retardation, who need intermittent or limited support, are rarely identified before school entry (Luck-

TABLE 12.2

Definitions and Examples of Intensities of Supports, 1992

TYPE OF SUPPORT	DEFINITION AND EXAMPLES
Intermittent	Supports on an as needed basis. Characterized by episodic nature, person not always needing the support(s), or short-term supports needed during the life-span transitions (e.g., job loss or an acute medical crisis). Intermittent supports may be high or low intensity when provided.
Limited	An intensity of supports characterized by consistency over time, time-limited but not of an intermittent nature, may require fewer staff members and less cost than more intense levels of support (e.g., time-limited employment training or transitional supports during the school to adult period).
Extensive	Supports characterized by regular involvement (e.g., daily) in at least some environments (such as work at home) and not time-limited (e.g., long-term support and long-term home living support).
Pervasive	Supports characterized by their constancy, high intensity; provided across environments; potential life-sustaining nature. Pervasive supports typically involve more staff members and intrusiveness than do extensive or time-limited supports.

Source: From R. Luckasson, D. Coulter, E. Polloway, S. Reiss, R. Schalock, M. Snell, D. Spitalnik, and J. Stark, *Mental Retardation: Definitions, Classification, and Systems of Supports,* p. 26. Copyright 1992 by American Association on Mental Retardation. Reprinted by permission.

asson, Schalock, Snell, & Spitalnik, 1996). Approximately 89 percent of children with mental retardation have mild mental retardation (U.S. Department of Education, 1994).

There is increasing evidence that as many as 50 percent of all cases of mental retardation could have been prevented by improving prenatal care; ensuring proper nutrition; preventing accidents, diseases, and ingestions of poisons (such as lead paint) among children; and providing children with safe, supportive, and stimulating environments in early childhood (Smith & Luckasson, 1995). Studies of intensive early intervention programs emphasizing infant stimulation, effective preschool programs, parent support programs, and other services have shown lasting impacts on the performance of children who are at risk for mental retardation (Bradley et al., 1994; Campbell & Ramey, 1994; Garber, 1988; Noonan & McCormick, 1993; Ramey et al., 1992). Even children with more pervasive mental retardation benefit substantially from intensive prevention programs in their early childhood years (Casto & Mastropieri, 1986).

The following Theory into Practice section suggests ways in which general education classroom teachers can help students who have mental retardation to acquire adaptive behavior skills. Specific ways of modifying instruction for students with special needs are discussed later in this chapter.

Teaching Adaptive Behavior Skills

THEORY *into* **Practice**

Instructional objectives for helping students who have mental retardation to acquire adaptive behavior skills are not very different from those that are valuable for all students. Every student needs to cope with the demands of school, develop interpersonal relationships, develop language skills, grow emotionally, and take care of personal needs. Teachers can help students by directly instructing or supporting students in the following areas (see Hardman, Drew, Egan, & Wolf, 1996):

1. **Coping with the demands of school:** Attending to learning tasks, organizing work, following directions, managing time, and asking questions.
2. **Developing interpersonal relationships:** Learning to work cooperatively with others, responding to social cues in the environment, using socially acceptable language, responding appropriately to teacher directions and cues, and enhancing social awareness.
3. **Developing language skills:** Understanding directions, communicating needs and wants, expressing ideas, listening attentively, and using appropriate voice modulation and inflection.
4. **Socioemotional development:** Seeking out social participation and interaction (decreasing social withdrawal) and being motivated to work (decreasing work avoidance, tardiness, and idleness).
5. **Personal care:** Practicing appropriate personal hygiene, dressing independently, taking care of personal property, and moving successfully from one location to another.

Students with Learning Disabilities

Learning disabilities are not a single condition but a wide variety of specific disabilities that are presumed to stem from some dysfunction of the brain or central

learning disabilities (LD)
Disorders that impede academic progress of people who are not mentally retarded or emotionally disturbed.

nervous system. The following definition is adapted from the National Joint Committee on Learning Disabilities (1988, p. 1):

> Learning disabilities is a general term for a diverse group of disorders characterized by significant difficulties in the acquisition and use of listening, speaking, reading, writing, reasoning, or computing. These disorders stem from the individual and may occur across the life span. Problems in self-regulatory behaviors, social perception, and social interaction may exist with learning disabilities but do not by themselves constitute a learning disability. Learning disabilities may occur with other handicapping conditions but are not the result of those conditions.

Older definitions of learning disability included specific reference to dyslexia, a severely impaired ability to read; dysgraphia, an impaired ability to write; and dyscalculia, an impaired ability to learn mathematics. The source of these conditions in brain dysfunction can seldom be proved, however, and these terms must be used with caution (Smith & Luckasson, 1995).

IDENTIFYING STUDENTS WITH LEARNING DISABILITIES ● Different interpretations of the many definitions of *learning disability* have led state and local school districts to vary widely in their eligibility requirements and provisions for students with learning disabilities (Mercer, King-Sears, & Mercer, 1990; Reynolds, 1992; Spear-Swerling & Sternberg, 1998). The increasing numbers of students identified as having learning disabilities (recall Figure 12.1) have contributed to the confusion. In 1992–1993, for example, 57.1 percent of all children with disabilities were identified as having specific learning disabilities (U.S. Department of Education, 1994). The increasing numbers of students in this category are due to a shift in its definition, not to a change in the total number of children at risk.

Education professionals have the task of distinguishing students with learning disabilites from students who are nondisabled low achievers and students with mild mental retardation (Smith, 1998). In some school districts a student who falls more than two grade levels behind expectations and has an IQ in the normal range is likely to be called learning disabled. Some characteristics of students with learning disabilities follow:

- Normal intelligence or even giftedness
- Discrepancy between intelligence and performance
- Delays in achievement
- Attention deficit or high distractibility
- Hyperactivity or impulsiveness
- Poor motor coordination and spatial relation ability
- Difficulty solving problems
- Perceptual anomalies, such as reversing letters, words, or numbers
- Difficulty with self-motivated, self-regulated activities
- Overreliance on teacher and peers for assignments
- Specific disorders of memory, thinking, or language
- Immature social skills
- Disorganized approach to learning

Definitions of learning disabilities have historically required that there be a serious discrepancy between actual performance and the performance that might have been predicted on the basis of one or more tests of cognitive functioning, such as an IQ test (Frankenberger & Fronzaglio, 1991). In practice, many children are identified as having a learning disability as a result of having substantial differences between some subscales of an IQ test and others or between one ability test and another. This emphasis on discrepancies has increasingly come under attack in recent years, however. For example, Fletcher and colleagues (1994) studied children ages 7.5 to 9.5 who were failing in reading. Some of these children had major discrepancies between their IQs and their performance; others had (low) IQ scores consistent with their poor performance. On an extensive battery of assessments, the discrepant and "nondiscrepant" children were nearly identical. In either case, what they lacked were skills that were closely related to reading. Many other studies (e.g., Francis, Shaywitz, Shaywitz, Stuebing, & Fletcher, 1996; Metsala, Stanovich, & Brown, 1998; Stanovich, Siegel, & Gottard, 1997) have found the same result. These studies have undermined the idea that there is a sharp-edged definition of learning disabilities as distinct from low achievement.

The studies also point to a very different emphasis for prevention and treatment. There has been a long tradition of searching for exotic treatments for learning disabilities, from engaging children in activities to increase their hand–eye coordination to placing colored filters over reading material to experimenting with children's diets. Such treatments are based on the assumption that there is something qualitatively different about the brains of children with learning disabilities. Yet very few such children show any evidence of neurological dysfunction. Exotic treatments may work with some children, but for the great majority of children with learning disabilities, effective prevention and treatment focuses far more directly on the problems that brought the child to the attention of the special education system—most often reading problems, which are involved in more than 90 percent of referrals for students with possible learning disabilities (Kavale & Reese, 1992; Slavin, 1996a).

CHARACTERISTICS OF STUDENTS WITH LEARNING DISABILITIES ● On the average, students with learning disabilities tend to have lower self-esteem than do nondisabled students (Bear, Klever, & Proctor, 1991; Gresham & MacMillan, 1997). However, as was mentioned previously, on most social dimensions, children with learning disabilities resemble other low achievers (Larrivee & Horne, 1991; Sater & French, 1989). Boys are more likely than girls to be labeled as learning disabled. African Americans, Latinos, and children from families in which the head of household has not attended college tend to be overrepresented in special education classes, while female students are underrepresented (Heward & Cavanaugh, 1997). There is a great deal of concern about the overidentification of boys and minority students in special education (Meyer, Harry, & Sapon-Shevin, 1997).

Teaching Students with Learning Disabilities

There are many types of learning disabilities, and issues in teaching students with learning disabilities differ by age level. However, a few broad principles apply across many circumstances. In general, effective teaching for students with learning disabilities uses the same strategies that are effective with other students, except that there may be less margin for error. In other words, a student with learning disabilities is less likely than other students to learn from poor instruction. General concepts of effective teaching for students with learning disabilities include these (see Lerner, 1997; Smith, 1998):

1. *Emphasize prevention.* Many of the learning deficits that cause a child to be categorized as having learning disabilities can be prevented. For example, high-quality early childhood programs and primary-grades teaching significantly reduce the number of children identified with learning disabilities (Slavin, 1996a). One-to-one tutoring for first-graders struggling with reading can be particularly effective in preventing reading disabilities (Lyons et al., 1993; Slavin et al., 1996; Wasik & Slavin, 1993). Use of early reading strategies emphasizing phonics, beneficial to most children, is essential to a large proportion of children at risk for reading disabilities (Moats & Lyon, 1993). Clearly, the easiest learning disabilities to deal with are those that never appear in the first place.

2. *Teach learning-to-learn skills.* Many students with learning disabilities lack good strategies for studying, test-taking, and so on. These skills can be taught. Many studies have shown that students with learning disabilities who are directly taught study strategies and other cognitive strategies perform significantly better in school (Deshler, Ellis, & Lenz, 1996).

3. *Give frequent feedback.* Students with learning disabilities are less likely than other students to be able to work productively for long periods of time with little or no feedback. They do better in situations in which they get frequent feedback on their efforts, particularly feedback about how they have improved or how they have worked hard to achieve something. For example, children with learning disabilities are likely to do better with brief, concrete assignments that are immediately scored than with long-term assignments. If long-term projects or reports are assigned, the students should have many intermediate goals and should get feedback on each (see Deshler et al., 1996).

4. *Use teaching strategies that engage students actively in lessons.* Students with learning disabilities are particularly unlikely to learn from long lectures. They tend to do best when they are actively involved. This implies that teachers who have such students in their classes should make extensive use of hands-on projects, cooperative learning, and other active learning methods, although it is important that these activities be well-structured and have clear goals and roles (see Putnam, 1998a; Slavin, 1995a).

5. *Use effective classroom management methods.* Because of their difficulties with information processing and language, many students with learning disabilities experience a great deal of frustration in school and respond by engaging in minor (or major) misbehavior. Effective classroom management methods can greatly reduce this misbehavior, especially strategies that emphasize prevention. For example, students with learning disabilities are likely to respond well to a rapid pace of instruction with much variety and many opportunities to participate and respond successfully (Rivera & Smith, 1997).

6. *Coordinate supplementary services with classroom instruction.* Many students with learning disabilities will need some sort of supplementary services, such as small-group tutorials, resource teachers, one-to-one tutoring, or computer-assisted instruction. Whatever these services are, they should be closely aligned with the instruction being given in academic classes. For example, if a student is working on *Treasure Island* in class, a tutor should also work on *Treasure Island*. If a student's math class is working on fractions, so should the resource teacher. Of course, there are times when supplementary services cannot be coordinated fully with classroom instruction, as when a student needs work on study strategies or prerequisite skills. However, every effort should be made to create as much linkage as possible so that the student can see an immediate learning payoff for his or her efforts in the supplementary program. The students having the greatest difficulties in learning should not have to balance two completely different kinds of teaching on different topics.

ATTENTION DEFICIT DISORDER ● Students with specific learning disabilities often also have behavioral problems. They may be unable to control their behavior, for example, and have difficulty remaining still and paying attention (Aleman, 1990). Attention deficits become a particularly serious problem as students get beyond the second grade (McKinney & Speece, 1986). Such children may be labeled impulsive or hyperactive and are sometimes treated with behavior-control drugs. A general term used in connection with children who have difficulty focusing their attention long enough or well enough to learn is **attention deficit disorder (ADD).** Distinguishing attention deficit disorder from learning disabilities and from behavioral disorders or misbehavior is a continuing challenge, especially since students with learning disabilities often have attentional and emotional and behavioral problems as well. In fact, there is so much uncertainty in the definition of ADD that Goodman and Poillion (1992) suggest that it should stand for "any dysfunction or difficulty." (Also see Armstrong, 1995, 1996.)

ATTENTION DEFICIT HYPERACTIVITY DISORDER ● Students with **attention deficit hyperactivity disorder (ADHD)** have difficulties maintaining attention because of a limited ability to concentrate. ADHD includes impulsive actions and hyperactive behavior. These characteristics differentiate students with ADHD from students with learning disabilities, who have attention deficits for other unknown reasons (American Psychiatric Association, 1994). Children with attention deficit disorders do not qualify for special education unless they also have some other disability condition that is defined in the law (Aleman, 1990). As with ADD, there is much debate about whether ADHD exists as a distinct diagnostic category (Pellegrini & Horvat, 1995). Prevalence estimates for ADHD suggest that 3 to 5 percent of all children may have the disorder. Research indicates that males with ADHD outnumber females in ratios varying from 4:1 to 9:1 (American Psychiatric Association, 1994; Parker, 1990).

attention deficit disorder (ADD)
A person's inability to concentrate long enough or well enough to learn.

attention deficit hyperactivity disorder (ADHD)
A disorder characterized by difficulties maintaining attention because of a limited ability to concentrate; includes impulsive actions and hyperactive behavior.

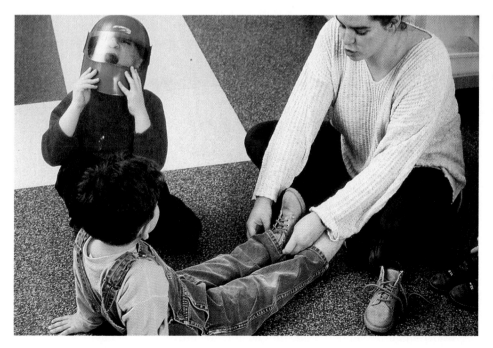

Students with attention deficit hyperactivity disorder (ADHD) may need more support in the classroom. As a teacher, what support services would you recommend be provided for students in your class who have learning disabilities?

The Intentional Teacher

● Using What You Know about Learners with Exceptionalities to Improve Teaching and Learning

Intentional teachers relish their responsibility to reach each of their students. They create inclusive environments and commit to fostering learning for all students. Intentional teachers serve as members of professional teams in order to collaborate to meet the needs of students with special needs.

■ What am I trying to accomplish?

Think about the goals you have devised for student learning. Consider the extent to which each of those goals is appropriate for learners with special needs. Work with other professionals to develop formal goal statements; for example, Individualized Education Programs that shape appropriate goals and instruction for your students with special needs.

When Michael and Renée, two students with learning disabilities in reading, struggle with the text for your history class, you consult with the special-education teacher. He reviews the students' IEPs with you, noting that reading comprehension is a goal for both students this year. Together you converse about possible adjustments to your course goals for Michael and Renée, and you discuss appropriate instructional modifications.

Consider your goals for your own professional development. Where in your professional development plans do you seek to gain additional knowledge and skills for working with students with a broad range of physical, cognitive, and social abilities?

When Sasha, a student with autism, is placed in your preschool class, you commit to learning all you can about meeting Sasha's educational needs. You conduct an online search of the litera-ture, and you order a book to enhance your knowledge base. You chat with Sasha's parents, who give you additional insights about strategies they have found to be successful.

■ What are my students' relevant experiences and needs?

Identification of students' special educational needs may begin before students enter formal schooling. When students with documented special needs are assigned to your class, talk with students (as appropriate), their parents, and professionals about students' preferences and past successes. Review past records as appropriate.

When Angela, a junior who is visually impaired, joins your earth science class, you set up an informal conference with Angela, her parents, and the resource teacher. They provide you with information about strategies that help Angela, especially in a science laboratory course, and she talks openly about her likes and her pet peeves. They also refer you to one of your colleagues who was particularly successful last year at providing a supportive environment without dwelling too much on Angela's vision.

Students may have special needs that have not yet been identified. Observe carefully for signs that students need extra support.

You notice that Sheila, who sits in the back row, often looks out the window or looks puzzled during your lessons. Noticing some differences in her enunciation, you suspect a hearing impairment and refer her for testing. In the meantime, you move her to the front row and provide visual input to support your direct instruction.

THEORY into Practice ●

Students with ADHD: The Role of the Teacher

Attention deficit hyperactivity disorder (ADHD) is usually associated with inattention, impulsivity, and hyperactivity. Educational implications of ADHD are that students may have significant academic, behavior, and social problems stemming from the inability to pay attention. Specific suggestions for the general education classroom teacher who has students with ADHD include the following (see Fachin, 1996; Smith, 1998):

- Make sure students understand all classroom rules and procedures.
- Consider carefully the seating arrangements of students with ADHD to prevent distractions and to keep these students in proximity to the teacher.
- Adhere to the principles of effective classroom management.
- Understand that certain behaviors, although not desirable, are not meant to be noncompliant—students may not be able to control their behaviors.
- Allow students who are hyperactive to have opportunities to be active.

3 What approaches and materials are available to help me challenge every student?

Teachers need to create a physical and intellectual environment that makes important ideas accessible to all. How will you reach each student?

You review your classroom environment and your curriculum to determine the extent to which it provides a balance of structure and choice, a variety of instructional materials and strategies, and opportunities for students to help each other.

Teachers need to create a social environment that fosters acceptance for every student. Think about how you will encourage students to accept and help each others as individuals.

Before Jarred, a student with cerebral palsy, is placed in your sixth-grade classroom, you and the students hold a classroom meeting to discuss ways to welcome a new student. You also talk about areas in which classmates have helped each other this year and the idea that you all have benefited by working with each other because of your varied strengths. When you hand out a "job application" for the position of "buddy" to new students, there is stiff competition as several students clamor to be Jarred's buddy.

Instruction should meet individual needs. Select from a variety of strategies to modify your instruction when you find that it does not challenge each student.

A few of your middle schoolers are struggling, despite your attempts to provide relevant and engaging instruction. You reread your notes on instructional modifications such as individualized instruction, cooperative learning, computers, and peer tutoring. You choose peer tutoring to capitalize on your students' social tendencies. You train three peer tutors in learning strategies and work out a schedule so that peer tutors and tutees can meet during class for 20 minutes three times per week.

4 How will I know whether and when to change my strategy or modify my instruction?

Teachers need to use information from a variety of sources to determine success for students with special needs. What evidence do you have that students maintain positive self-concepts? That their classmates' self-concepts are similarly enriched? That students are learning? Collect information that allows you to determine whether students are progressing on an individual basis.

You meet for a midyear review of Patrick's Individualized Education Program. To the review you bring anecdotal notes that you collected as students demonstrated their capacity to care about and help each other. You share vignettes of Patrick's sense of humor and impressive knowledge of dinosaurs. You show his portfolio, which demonstrates marked growth in his letter recognition and drawings. You commit to providing more intensive work in mathematics, though, because he shows less growth in shape and number recognition.

5 What information will I accept as evidence that my students and I are experiencing success?

Collaborate with parents and special-education professionals in order to analyze the learning environment, instruction, and learning outcomes.

The classroom and special-education teachers at your site plan an in-service development day to work on integrating services more closely. During the in-service, you develop a checklist that can be used for an initial screening of the inclusivity of classrooms. Eager to get started, special-education teachers buddy up with classroom teachers, and you make plans to visit each other's classes in the next week.

- Refrain from implementing a behavior management system that is predicated mostly on the use of punishment or threats.
- Group students with ADHD wisely, taking into consideration the purpose of the group and the other students who will be members of the group.
- Prepare students for all types of transitions that occur in the school day (in and out of the room, between activities, etc.).
- Teach students to manage their own behaviors—this includes self-monitoring, self-evaluation, self-reinforcement, and self-instruction.
- Maintain ongoing communication with the students' homes by using daily report cards or other instruments to convey information.
- Use homework assignment books with these students.
- Collaborate with special-education personnel to develop behavioral and instructional plans for dealing with attention problems.

Students with Communication Disorders

One of the most common disabilities is communication disorders: problems with speech and language. About 1 in every 40 students has a communication disorder serious enough to warrant speech therapy or other special education services.

Although the terms *speech* and *language* are often used interchangeably, they are not the same. Language is the communication of ideas using symbols and includes written language, sign language, gesture, and other modes of communication in addition to oral speech. Speech refers to the formation and sequencing of sounds. It is quite possible to have a speech disorder without a language disorder or to have a language disorder without a speech disorder.

STUDENTS WITH SPEECH DISORDERS ● There are many kinds of **speech disorders.** The most common are articulation (or phonological) disorders, such as omissions, distortions, or substitutions of sounds. For example, some students have difficulty pronouncing *r*'s, saying "sowee" for "sorry." Others have lisps, substituting *th* for *s,* saying "thnake" for "snake."

Misarticulated words are common and developmentally normal for many children in kindergarten and first grade but drop off rapidly through the school years. Moderate and extreme deviations in articulation diminish over the school years, with or without speech therapy. For this reason, speech therapists often decide not to work with a child who has a mild articulation problem. However, speech therapy is called for if a student cannot be understood or if the problem is causing the student psychological or social difficulties (such as being teased).

A less common but often more troublesome speech disorder is stuttering, the "abnormal timing of speech sound initiation" (Shames & Ramig, 1994; Van Riper & Erickson, 1996). Everyone stutters sometimes, but children with a serious problem stutter to a degree that impairs their ability to communicate. Stutterers may prolong sounds ("wwwwwe wwwwwent to the store"), or they may have difficulty making any sound at times. It is often particular sounds or words or situations that give stutterers difficulties. Unfortunately, anxiety increases stuttering, creating a vicious circle: When stutterers are afraid of stuttering, their fear makes them stutter.

With or without therapy, stuttering usually disappears by early adolescence. However, as in the case of articulation problems, speech therapy is often prescribed for stuttering because of the psychological and social problems it causes youngsters.

Speech disorders of all kinds are diagnosed by and treated by speech pathologists or speech therapists. The classroom teacher's role is less important here than with the mental disabilities. However, the classroom teacher does have one crucial role to play: displaying acceptance of students with speech disorders. Most speech disorders will eventually resolve themselves. The lasting damage is more often psychological than phonological; students with speech disorders often are subjected to a great deal of teasing and social rejection. Teachers can model acceptance of the child with speech disorders in several ways. First, teachers should be patient with students who are stuttering or have trouble producing words, never finishing a student's sentence or allowing others to do so. Second, teachers should avoid putting students who have speech problems into high-pressure situations that require quick verbal responses. Third, teachers should refrain from correcting students' articulation in class.

STUDENTS WITH LANGUAGE DISORDERS ● **Language disorders** are impairments of the ability to understand language or to express ideas in one's native language

---

speech disorders
Oral articulation problems, occurring most frequently among children in the early elementary school grades.

language disorders
Impairments in one's ability to understand language or to express ideas in one's native language.

(Owens, 1995). Problems due to limited English-speaking proficiency (LEP) for students whose first language is not English are not considered language disorders.

Difficulties in understanding language (receptive language disorders) or in communicating (expressive language disorders) may result from such physical problems as hearing or speech impairment. If not, they are likely to indicate mental retardation or learning disabilities. Many students from disadvantaged backgrounds come to school with what appear to be receptive or expressive language disorders but that in fact result from a lack of experience with standard English (Battle, 1996; Langdon & Cheng, 1992). Preschool programs that are rich in verbal experience and direct instruction in the fundamentals of standard English have been found to be effective in overcoming language problems that are characteristic of children from disadvantaged homes.

CONNECTIONS
Problems due to limited English proficiency are discussed in Chapter 4, page 119.

CONNECTIONS
For more on preschool programs that help overcome problems of children from disadvantaged homes, see Chapter 3, page 80.

Students with Emotional and Behavioral Disorders

All students are likely to have emotional problems at some point in their school career; but about 1 percent have such serious, long-lasting, and pervasive emotional or psychiatric disorders that they require special education. As in the case of learning disabilities, students with serious emotional and behavioral disorders are far more likely to be boys than girls, by a ratio of more than 3 to 1 (U.S. Department of Education, 1994).

Students with **emotional and behavioral disorders** have been defined as ones whose educational performance is adversely affected over a long period of time to a marked degree by any of the following conditions:

1. An inability to learn that cannot be explained by intellectual, sensory, or health factors
2. An inability to build or maintain satisfactory interpersonal relationships with peers and teachers
3. Inappropriate types of behavior or feelings under normal circumstances
4. A general, pervasive mood of unhappiness or depression
5. A tendency to develop physical symptoms, pains, or fears associated with personal or school problems

CAUSES OF EMOTIONAL AND BEHAVIORAL DISORDERS ● Serious and long-term emotional and behavioral disorders may be the result of numerous potential causal factors in the makeup and development of an individual (Lewis & Sullivan, 1996). Neurological functioning, psychological processes, a history of maladaptations, self-concept, and lack of social acceptance all play a role (Hardman, Drew, & Winston-Egan, 1996). Some of the same factors, including family dysfunction, also play a role in short-term disturbances that may temporarily affect a child's school performance.

Many factors that affect families may disrupt a student's sense of security and self-worth for a period of time. Changes in the family structure, for example, may leave a child depressed, angry, insecure, defensive, and lonely, especially in the case of divorce, relocation to a new community, the addition of a younger sibling, the addition of a new stepparent, or the death or serious illness of a family member.

One problem in identifying serious emotional and behavioral disorders is that the term covers a wide range of behaviors, from aggression or hyperactivity to withdrawal or inability to make friends (Epstein & Cullinan, 1992) to anxiety and phobias (King & Ollendick, 1989). Also, children with emotional disorders quite

emotional and behavioral disorders
Exceptionalities characterized by problems with learning, interpersonal relationships, and control of feelings and behavior.

TEACHERS IN ACTION

What rewarding experience have you had with a student with special needs?

Lynne McKee
School Psychologist
Indiana University of Pennsylvania
Indiana, Pennsylvania

As the coordinator of services for students with exceptionalities, I have assisted teachers in mainstreaming children with a variety of disabling conditions into the classroom setting. One child I remember very well is Roberta, an alert, bright-eyed little girl who had been diagnosed as having apraxia—a condition in which receptive language is normal but there is little or no expressive language.

When Roberta first entered the preschool program, other children often initiated conversation with her and could not understand why she was unable to respond. Roberta's teacher and I explained that we all have things we do really well and things that are hard for us to do. The children gave examples of personal strengths and weaknesses, which included recognizing letters of the alphabet, riding two-wheelers, and tying shoes. The teacher explained that one thing Roberta could not do very well was talk. The children accepted this without difficulty. Roberta's teacher and I worked on deemphasizing Roberta's weaknesses and emphasizing her strengths. As a calendar helper, for example, Roberta naturally showed classmates how she communicated through the use of gestures. With a minimum of adult intervention, her classmates quickly accepted her as a regular member of the class.

Roberta's teacher and I developed an Individualized Preschool Plan, along with staff from the local Intermediate Unit, Roberta's mother, and the consulting preschool special-education teacher. Roberta's interaction skills developed nicely, and she entered public school. Today, Roberta continues to be in a mainstreamed classroom. She relates well to both adults and children and continues to progress academically.

Lynne Larsen-Miller
Silver Mesa Elementary School
Sandy, Utah

Chad bursts into my room waving a general sixth-grade science test. "Mrs. Miller, you owe me another candy bar. It's a 96 percent today!" Chad is a student with severe learning disabilities. His reading level is only at second grade, yet with help he is successful in his regular sixth-grade academic areas. Chad compensates for his disabilities through the use of strategic interventions.

When I began at Silver Mesa several years ago, I inherited a program in which the emphasis was to "cure" students with disabilities, as if they were sick. Children's weaknesses were the only consideration in curriculum planning. A student like Chad was given a list of sight words to read and then returned to the classroom to fail. I knew there had to be a way to emphasize students' strengths. With added skills, students could manage their own learning successfully.

Strategic instruction became the bridge to independence for many of my students. There isn't an hour of our day when students aren't going about the task of either acquiring or applying these skills. Using strategies for reading comprehension, writing paragraphs, test-taking, note-taking, and problem solving are common. The acquisition of strategy skills becomes intertwined with the curriculum. For example, an endangered animal report was required in a creative writing class. Students used their reading comprehension strategies to skim and scan texts to find the facts they needed. Next, they used their note-taking skills to complete an outline.

As I use the strategic approach to teaching, I have found that students create appropriate products independently. They become reinforced, which initiates the continued effort necessary to produce success. Students with a disability can compensate by using their strengths to compete in the general education classroom.

frequently have other disabilities, such as learning disabilities or mental retardation, and it is often hard to tell whether an emotional problem is causing the diminished academic performance or school failure is causing the emotional problem.

Procedures that are used to identify children with serious emotional disturbances include observation, behavior rating scales and inventories, and psychological testing. Observation is the most direct method and requires the least amount of interference on the teacher's part (Taylor, 1984). However, although observation can help to document the behavior under question, a trained professional's judgment is required as to the amount, frequency, or degree of behavior that must be present for a student to be characterized as "disturbed" or "disordered."

Behavior rating scales used by teachers provide a measure of behavior characteristics. For example, a behavior rating scale might include a series of items (descriptions such as "is hostile and aggressive toward peers") grouped according to various categories of behavior (such as "withdrawn," "immature," "aggressive"). This information compares the behavior of one student with that of others and profiles the student's behavioral difficulties (see Achenbach & McConaughy, 1987; Walker et al., 1988).

CHARACTERISTICS OF STUDENTS WITH EMOTIONAL AND BEHAVIORAL DISORDERS ●

Scores of characteristics are associated with emotional and behavioral disorders (Kauffman, 1997). The important issue is the degree of the behavior problem. Virtually any behavior that is exhibited excessively over a long period of time might be considered an indication of emotional disturbance. However, most students who have been identified as having emotional and behavioral disorders share some general characteristics. These include poor academic achievement, poor interpersonal relationships, and poor self-esteem (Lewis & Sullivan, 1996). Quay and Werry (1986) noted four general categories: conduct disorder, anxiety–withdrawal, immaturity, and socialized–aggressive disorder. For example, children with **conduct disorders** are frequently characterized as disobedient, distractible, selfish, jealous, destructive, impertinent, resistive, and disruptive. Quay and Werry noted that the first three of these categories represent behaviors that are maladaptive or sources of personal distress. However, socialized–aggressive behavior, which relates to frequent aggression against others, seems to be tied more to poor home conditions that model or reward aggressive behavior and may therefore be adaptive (though certainly not healthy or appropriate). The inclusion of conduct disorders in classifications of emotional and behavioral disorders is controversial. By law, students with conduct disorders must have some other recognized disability or disorder to receive special-education services.

STUDENTS EXHIBITING AGGRESSIVE BEHAVIOR ●

Students with conduct disorders and socialized–aggressive behaviors may frequently fight, steal, destroy property, and refuse to obey teachers (Ruhl & Hughes, 1985). These students tend to be disliked by their peers, their teachers, and sometimes their parents. They typically do not respond to punishment or threats, though they may be skilled at avoiding punishment. Aggressive children not only pose a threat to the school and to their peers, but also put themselves in grave danger. Aggressive children, particularly boys, often develop serious emotional problems later in life, have difficulty holding jobs, and become involved in criminal behavior (Loeber & Stouthamer-Loeber, 1998).

The most effective treatments for students exhibiting aggressive behavior are well-structured, consistently applied behavior management programs (see Flannery, 1997).

conduct disorders
Socioemotional and behavioral disorders that are indicated in individuals who, for example, are chronically disobedient or disruptive.

CONNECTIONS
Behavior management programs for students exhibiting aggressive behavior are described in Chapter 11, page 388.

STUDENTS WITH WITHDRAWN AND IMMATURE BEHAVIOR ● Children who are withdrawn, immature, low in self-esteem, or depressed typically have few friends or may play with children much younger than themselves. They may have elaborate fantasies or daydreams and either very poor or grandiose self-images. Some may be overly anxious about their health and may feel genuinely ill when under stress. Some students exhibit school phobia, refusing to attend school or running away from school.

Unlike children who are aggressive, who may appear quite normal when they are not being aggressive, children who are withdrawn and immature often appear odd or awkward at all times. They almost always suffer from a lack of social skills.

STUDENTS WITH HYPERACTIVITY ● As was mentioned in the discussion of learning disabilities, one very common emotional and behavioral problem is **hyperactivity,** an inability to sit still or to concentrate for any length of time. Children who are hyperactive exhibit excessive restlessness and short attention spans. Hyperactivity is particularly common among students with learning disabilities and is seen much more frequently in boys than in girls. It is most prevalent among elementary school students (O'Leary, 1980).

Children with hyperactivity are usually impulsive, acting before they think or without regard for the situation they are in, and they find it hard to sit still (Shaywitz & Shaywitz, 1988). Students who are diagnosed as hyperactive are often given a stimulant medication, such as Ritalin. More than a million children take Ritalin, and this number has been rising in recent years (Smelter, Rasch, Fleming, Nazos, & Baranowski, 1996). These drugs usually do make some hyperactive children more manageable and may improve their academic performance (DuPaul, Barkley, & McMurray, 1991; Gadow, 1986; Ottenbacher & Cooper, 1983). They can also have side effects, such as insomnia, weight loss, and blood pressure changes (Gadow, 1986; Hersen, 1986).

STUDENTS WITH AUTISM ● In 1990, autism became a formal category of disability. The U.S. Department of Education (1991) defined **autism** as a developmental disability that significantly affects social interaction and verbal and nonverbal communication. It is usually evident before the age of 3 and has an adverse affect on educational performance. Children with autism are typically extremely withdrawn and have such severe difficulties with language that they may be entirely mute. They may engage in self-stimulation activities such as rocking, twirling objects, or flapping their hands. However, they may have normal or even outstanding abilities in certain areas. For unknown reasons, autism is far more prevalent among boys than among girls (Friend & Bursuck, 1999). It is thought to be caused by some sort of brain damage or other brain dysfunction, although this is not clear (Matson, 1994). There are promising treatments for autism, including methods of teaching people with autism to build relationships with others (Christof & Kane, 1991; Koegel & Koegel, 1995) and teaching them alternative means of communicating (Biklen, 1990).

Students with Sensory, Physical, and Health Impairments

Sensory impairments are problems with the ability to see or hear or otherwise receive information through the body's senses. Physical disorders include conditions such as cerebral palsy, spina bifida, spinal cord injury, and muscular dystrophy. Health disorders include, for example, acquired immune deficiency syndrome

hyperactivity
A condition characterized by extreme restlessness and by a short attention span relative to that of peers.

autism
A category of disability that significantly affects social interaction, verbal and nonverbal communication, and educational performance.

sensory impairments
Problems with the ability to receive information through the body's senses.

(AIDS); seizure disorders; diabetes; cystic fibrosis; sickle-cell anemia (in African American students); and bodily damage from chemical addictions, child abuse, or attempted suicide (Hardman et al., 1996).

vision loss
Degree of uncorrectable inability to see well.

STUDENTS WITH VISION LOSS ● Most students' visual problems are correctable by glasses or other type of corrective lenses. A **vision loss** is considered a disability only if it is not correctable. It is estimated that approximately 1 out of every 1,000 children has a visual disability. Individuals with such disabilities are usually re-ferred to as blind or visually impaired. A legally blind child is one whose vision is judged to be 20/200 or worse in the better eye even with correction or whose field of vision is significantly narrower than that of a person with normal vision. Partially sighted persons, according to this classification system, are those whose vision is between 20/70 and 20/200 in the better eye with correction (Rogow, 1988).

It is a misconception to assume that individuals who are legally blind have no sight. More than 80 percent of students who are legally blind can read large- or regular-print books (Levin, 1996). This implies that many students with vision loss can be taught by means of a modification of usual teaching materials. Hallahan and Kauffman (1991) offered an educational definition of visual im-pairment that depends on the amount of adaptation required in the school setting. They suggested that "the blind are those who are so severely impaired that they must be taught to read by Braille, while the partially sighted can read print even though they need to use magnifying devices or books with large print."

Classroom teachers should be aware of the signs that indicate that a child is having a vision problem. Undoubtedly, children who have difficulty seeing also have difficulty in many areas of learning, because classroom lessons typically use a tremendous amount of visual material. Several possible signs of vision loss in-clude the following: (1) Child often tilts head; (2) child rubs eyes often; (3) child's

The students in this class who are deaf use sign language to participate in class work. As a classroom teacher, how can you accommodate students with dif-ferent degrees of hearing loss who may be in your class?

eyes are red, inflamed, or crusty or water excessively; (4) child has difficulty reading small print or can't discriminate letters; (5) child complains of dizziness or headaches after a reading assignment (Smith & Luckasson, 1995). If you notice any of these problems, you should refer the student for appropriate vision screening.

STUDENTS WITH HEARING LOSS ● **Hearing loss** ranges from complete deafness to problems that can be alleviated with a hearing aid. The appropriate classification of an individual with hearing loss depends on the measures required to compensate for the problem. Simply having a student sit at the front of the classroom may be enough to compensate for a mild hearing loss. Many children can communicate adequately by listening to your voice and watching your lips. Others may need a hearing aid, and those with more severe problems will need to use a nonverbal form of communication such as sign language (see Stewart, 1992). Following are several suggestions to keep in mind:

1. Seat children with hearing problems in the front of the room, slightly off center toward the windows. This will allow them to see your face in the best light.
2. If the hearing problem is predominantly in one ear, students should sit in a front corner seat so that their better ear is toward you.
3. Speak at the student's eye level whenever possible.
4. Give important information and instructions while facing the class. Avoid talking while facing the chalkboard.
5. Do not use exaggerated lip movements when speaking.
6. Learn how to assist a child who has a hearing aid.

STUDENTS WITH CEREBRAL PALSY ● **Cerebral palsy** is a motor impairment caused by brain damage. The damage can be produced by any number of factors that result in oxygen deprivation, such as poisoning, cerebral bleeding, or direct injury. The damage usually occurs before, during, or shortly after birth and causes some degree of paralysis, weakness, or incoordination (United Cerebral Palsy Association, 1993). Cerebral palsy is not contagious, nor does it get progressively worse. Not all individuals with cerebral palsy have mental retardation. The damage to the brain is in the motor area and may not be associated with damage to other areas of the brain. Children with cerebral palsy may have average intelligence.

The severity of cerebral palsy varies tremendously. Some people have virtually no voluntary control over any of their movements; others have a motor problem that is barely discernible. In the more severe cases there is great difficulty in speaking. Obviously, the degree of severity affects the amount of adaptation that is necessary in the classroom. Increasingly sophisticated adaptive equipment, particularly in the area of communication, is now available to allow students with cerebral palsy to participate in the general education classroom as well as special-education classes.

hearing loss
Degree of deafness; uncorrectable inability to hear well.

cerebral palsy
A disorder in the ability to control movements that is caused by damage to the motor area of the brain.

seizure disorders
Forms of epilepsy.

STUDENTS WITH SEIZURE DISORDERS ● **Seizure disorders,** or forms of epilepsy, are conditions in which individuals have recurrent seizures caused by an abnormal amount of electrical discharge in the brain. Witnessing a seizure can be a frightening experience for an unknowledgeable observer.

There are several types of seizures that a child may experience. One type, tonic–clonic, affects the whole brain and results in a major seizure characterized by loss of consciousness, rigidity, shaking, and jerking. Before a seizure a child may experience an aura, a peculiar sensation in which certain sounds are heard, odors are smelled, or images are seen. Experiencing an identifiable aura often gives the child enough time to lie down. Immediately after the seizure, a deep sleep may follow. The most violent part of a tonic–clonic seizure lasts about 3 to 4 minutes; during this period, care must be taken that children do not hurt themselves by biting their lips or tongues or involuntarily striking furniture or other objects. If you know that a child in your class is prone to having seizures, discuss this with the class so that the students won't be surprised. The important thing is for everyone to remain calm.

A clonic, or absence, seizure is less severe but occurs more frequently. In this type of seizure the student experiences a brief lapse of consciousness. During this short interval (usually about 5 to 15 seconds), the student may look blank and stare, and the eyelids may flutter. Clonic seizures often go unnoticed or are misinterpreted as a short attention span or a behavior problem.

Between seizures, children with epilepsy usually show no signs of disability, and new medications and surgical methods have allowed most seizure disorders to be partially or completely controlled (Freeman, Vining, & Pillas, 1991).

STUDENTS WITH TRAUMATIC BRAIN INJURY ● The term **traumatic brain injury (TBI)** refers to direct injuries to the brain, such as a tearing of nerve fibers, bruising of the brain tissues against the skull, brain stem trauma, or swelling. Nearly 5 million children experience head injuries every year (Rosman, 1994). The prevalence of brain injuries increases dramatically between the ages of 15 and 19. This increase is attributable to factors that include contact sports, greater use of automobiles, more frequent use of racing and mountain bikes, and injuries sustained from firearms (Menkes & Till, 1990). Students with TBI may take longer to process information. Shorter assignments and more time to complete tasks are helpful. Concentration and memory can be problematic. Strategies need to be taught to compensate for poor memory and retrieval problems.

Students Who Are Gifted and Talented

Who are the gifted and talented? Almost all children, according to their parents; and in fact many students do have outstanding talents or skills in some area. **Giftedness** was once defined almost entirely in terms of superior IQ or demonstrated ability, such as outstanding performance in mathematics or chess, but the definition now encompasses students with superior abilities in a wide range of activities, including the arts (Reid & Romanoff, 1997). High IQ is still considered part of the definition of gifted and talented, and most students who are so categorized have IQs above 130. However, some groups are underidentified as gifted and talented, including females, students with disabilities, underachievers, and students who are members of racial or ethnic minority groups (Ford, 1996; Smith & Luckasson, 1995; Subotnik, 1997).

The 1978 Gifted and Talented Act stated that

the gifted and talented are children . . . who are identified . . . as possessing demonstrated or potential abilities that give evidence of high performance capabilities in areas such as intellectual, creative, specific academic or leadership ability or in the performing or visual arts and to by reason thereof require services or activities not ordinarily provided by the school (Public Law 95–561, Section 902).

This definition is meant to include students who possess extraordinary capabilities in any number of activities, not just in those areas that are part of the school curriculum. According to these rather vague criteria (see Gallagher, 1992), somewhere between 3 and 5 percent of all students are "gifted and talented" (Mitchell

traumatic brain injury (TBI)
Direct injury to the brain, such as a tearing of nerve fibers, bruising of the brain tissues against the skull, brain stem trauma, or swelling.

giftedness
Exceptional intellectual ability, creativity, or talent.

& Erickson, 1980). However, the percentage of students identified as gifted and talented varies from less than 1 percent in North Dakota to almost 10 percent in New Jersey (National Center for Education Statistics, 1988). This does not mean that New Jersey's students are especially talented; rather, it indicates the vast differences in defining and identifying the gifted and talented in different states.

CHARACTERISTICS OF GIFTED AND TALENTED STUDENTS ● Intellectually gifted children typically have strong motivation. They also are academically superior; usually learn to read early; and, in general, do excellent work in most school areas (Gallagher, 1992). One of the most important studies of the gifted, begun by Lewis Terman in 1926, followed 1,528 individuals who had IQs over 140 as children. Terman's research exploded the myth that high-IQ individuals were brainy but physically and socially inept. In fact, Terman found that children with outstanding IQs were larger, stronger, and better coordinated than other children and became better adjusted and more emotionally stable adults (Terman & Oden, 1959). Gifted students also have high self-concepts (Hoge & Renzulli, 1993), although they can suffer from perfectionism (Parker, 1997).

EDUCATION OF GIFTED STUDENTS ● How to educate gifted students is a matter of debate (see Gallagher, 1995; Torrance, 1986). Some programs for gifted and talented children involve special secondary schools for students who are gifted in science or in the arts. Some programs are special classes for high achievers in regular schools. One debate in this area concerns acceleration versus enrichment. Advocates of acceleration (e.g., Pendarvis & Howley, 1996; Van Tassel-Baska, 1989) argue that gifted students should be encouraged to move through the school curriculum rapidly, perhaps skipping grades and going to college at an early age. Others (e.g., Feldhusen, 1996; Gallagher, 1992; Renzulli & Reis, 1997) maintain that rather than merely moving students through school more rapidly, programs for the gifted should engage them in more creative and problem-solving activities.

Research on the gifted provides more support (in terms of student achievement gains) for acceleration than for enrichment (Kulik & Kulik, 1997; Swiatek & Benbow, 1991). However, this may be because the outcomes of enrichment, such as creativity or problem-solving skills, are difficult to measure. **Acceleration programs** for the gifted often involve the teaching of advanced mathematics to students at early ages, as in Stanley's Study of Mathematically Precocious Youth (SMPY) program. This program had a stated goal of getting mathematically talented seventh- and eighth-graders from algebra I through second-year college mathematics (calculus III, linear algebra, and differential equations) in as short a time as possible (see Stanley & Benbow, 1986). A variation on the acceleration theme is a technique called *curriculum compacting,* in which teachers may skip over portions of the curriculum that the very able students do not need (Reis & Purcell, 1993).

Enrichment programs take many forms. Many successful enrichment programs have involved self-directed or independent study (Parke, 1983; Reiss & Cellerino, 1983). Others have provided gifted students with adult mentors (Nash, Borman, & Colson, 1980). Renzulli (1994) suggests an emphasis on three types of activities: general exploratory activities, such as projects that allow students to find out about topics on their own; group training activities, such as games and simulations to promote creativity and problem-solving skills; and individual and small-group investigations of real problems, such as writing books or newspapers, interviewing elderly people to write oral histories, and conducting geological or archaeological investigations.

acceleration programs
Rapid promotion through advanced studies for students who are gifted or talented.

enrichment programs
Programs in which assignments or activities are designed to broaden or deepen the knowledge of students who master classroom lessons quickly.

One problem with enrichment programs for the gifted and talented is simply stated: Most of the activities that are suggested for gifted and talented students would benefit all students. In recognition of this, many schools are now infusing activities that are characteristic of enrichment programs into the curriculum for all students, thereby meeting the needs of gifted and talented students without physically separating them from their peers (see Maker, 1993). Examples of such activities include increased use of projects, experiments, independent study, and cooperative learning.

SELF-CHECK

Define *learners with exceptionalities* and distinguish between *disability* and *handicap*. Give examples of each and explain why labeling has limitations. Then define and describe the characteristics of each of the following concepts: mental retardation, giftedness, physical disability, vision loss, hearing loss, learning disability, emotional/behavioral disorder, communication disorder, speech disorder, language disorder, autism, traumatic brain injury.

WHAT IS SPECIAL EDUCATION?

Special education is any program provided for children with disabilities instead of, or in addition to, the general education classroom program. The practice of special education has changed dramatically in recent years and is still evolving. Federal legislation has been critical in setting standards for special-education services administered by states and local districts.

Public Law 94–142 and IDEA

As recently as the mid-1960s, education of children with exceptionalities was quite different from what it is today. Many "handicapped" students received no special services at all. Those who did get special services usually attended separate schools or institutions for people with mental retardation, emotional disturbances, or vision or hearing loss. In the late 1960s the special-education system came under attack (see, e.g., Christoplos & Renz, 1969; Dunn, 1968; Semmel, Gerber, & MacMillan, 1994). Critics argued that people who had serious disabilities were too often shut away in state institutions with inadequate educational services or were left at home with no services at all and that mildly disabled children (particularly those with mild mental retardation) were being isolated in special programs that failed to teach them the skills they needed to function in society. Four million of the eight million disabled students of school age were not in school.

As a result, in 1975, Congress passed **Public Law 94–142,** the Education for the Handicapped Act. P.L. 94–142, as it is commonly called, profoundly affected both special and general education throughout the United States. It prescribed the services that all disabled children must receive and gave the children and their parents legal rights that they had not previously possessed. A basic tenet of P.L. 94–142 was that every disabled child is entitled to special education appropriate to the child's needs at public expense. This means, for example, that school districts or states must provide special education to children who are severely retarded or disabled.

P.L. 94–142 was extended beyond its original focus in two major pieces of legislation. In 1986, Public Law 99–457 extended the entitlement to free, appropriate

special education
Programs that address the needs of students with mental, emotional, or physical disabilities.

Public Law 94–142
Federal law enacted in 1975 requiring provision of special education services to eligible students.

According to Public Law 94–142 and related legislation, what entitlements do children with disabilities have?

Individuals with Disabilities Education Act (IDEA)

P.L. 101–476, a federal law enacted in 1990 that changed the name of P.L. 94–142 and broadened services to adolescents with disabilities.

IDEA 97

Public Law 105–17, enacted in 1997 to reauthorize IDEA (P.L. 101–476) and add provisions for greater parental and classroom teacher involvement in the education of students with special needs.

least restrictive environment

Provision in IDEA that requires students with disabilities to be educated with nondisabled peers to the maximum extent appropriate.

mainstreaming

The temporal, instructional, and social integration of eligible children with exceptionalities with peers without exceptionalities based on an ongoing, individually determined educational planning and programming process.

education to children ages 3 to 5. It also added programs for seriously disabled infants and toddlers. Public Law 101–476, which passed in 1990, changed the name of the special-education law to the **Individuals with Disabilities Education Act (IDEA),** required that schools plan for the transition of adolescents with disabilities into further education or employment starting at age 16, and replaced the term *handicapped children* with the term *children with disabilities.*

In 1997, Public Law 105–17, the Individuals with Disabilities Education Act Amendments of 1997, or **IDEA 97,** was passed to reauthorize and strengthen the original act (National Information Center for Children and Youth with Disabilities, 1998). Among the goals of this law are raising educational expectations for children with disabilities, increasing the role of parents in the education of their children with disabilities, assuring that regular classroom teachers are involved in planning for and assessment of these children, including students with disabilities in local and state assessments, and supporting professional development for all who educate children with disabilities (U.S. Department of Education, 1998).

LEAST RESTRICTIVE ENVIRONMENT ● The provision of IDEA that is of greatest importance to general education classroom teachers is that students with disabilities must be assigned to the **least restrictive environment** that is appropriate to their needs. This provision gives a legal basis for the practice of **mainstreaming,** or "the temporal, instructional, and social integration of eligible exceptional children with normal peers based on an ongoing, individually determined educational planning and programming process" (Kaufman, Gottlieb, Agard, & Kukic, 1975, pp. 40–41). This means that general education classroom teachers are likely to have in their classes students with mild disabilities (such as learning disabilities, mild mental retardation, physical disabilities, or speech problems) who may leave class for special instruction part of the day. It also means that classes for students with more serious disabilities are likely to be located in general education school facilities and that these students will probably attend some activities with their nondisabled peers.

INDIVIDUALIZED EDUCATION PROGRAM (IEP) ● Another important requirement of IDEA is that every student with a disability must have an **Individualized Education Program (IEP)** that guides the services the student receives. The IEP describes a student's problems and delineates a specific course of action to address these problems. Generally, it is prepared by a special services committee composed of school professionals such as special-education teachers, special-education supervisors, school psychologists, the principal, counselors, and/or classroom teachers. Special services teams go by different names in different states; for example, they may be called child study teams or appraisal and review teams. The student's parent must consent to the IEP. The idea behind the use of IEPs is to give everyone concerned with the education of a child with a disability an opportunity to help formulate the child's instructional program. The requirement that a parent sign the IEP is designed to ensure parental awareness of and approval of what the school proposes to do for the child. A parent may hold the school accountable if the child does not receive the promised services.

The law requires that evaluations of students for possible placement in special-education programs be done by qualified professionals. Although general education classroom and special-education teachers will typically be involved in the evaluation process, teachers are not generally allowed to give the psychological tests (such as IQ tests) that are used for placement decisions.

IDEA gives children with disabilities and their parents legal safeguards with regard to special-education placement and programs. For example, if parents believe that a child has been diagnosed incorrectly or assigned to the wrong program or if they are unsatisfied with the services a child is receiving, they may bring a grievance against the school district. Also, the law specifies that parents be notified about all placement decisions, conferences, and changes in program.

For children with special needs who are under the age of 3, a specialized plan focusing on the child and his or her family is typically prepared. This is called an Individualized Family Service Plan (IFSP). At the other end of the education system, an Individualized Transition Plan (ITP) is often written for adolescents with special needs before their 17th birthday. The ITP anticipates the student's needs as he or she makes the transition from school to work and to adult life.

An Array of Special-Education Services

An important aspect of an IEP is a special-education program that is appropriate to the student's needs. Every school district offers children with special needs an array of services intended to be flexible enough to meet the unique needs of all. In practice, these services are often organized as a continuum going from least to most restrictive, as follows:

1. Direct or indirect consultation and support for general education teacher
2. Special education up to 1 hour per day
3. Special education 1 to 3 hours per day; resource program
4. Special education more than 3 hours per day; self-contained special education
5. Special day school
6. Special residential school
7. Home/hospital

In general, students with more severe disabilities receive more restrictive services than do those with less severe disabilities. For example, a student with severe mental retardation is unlikely to be placed in a general education classroom during academic periods, whereas a student with a speech problem or a mild learning

Individualized Education Program (IEP)
A program tailored to the needs of a learner with exceptionalities.

TABLE 12.3

Percentage of Students with Disabilities Ages 6 through 21 Served in Different Educational Environments, by Disability: School Year 1993–1994

	EDUCATIONAL ENVIRONMENTS*					
DISABILITY	GENERAL EDUCATION CLASS	RESOURCE ROOM	SEPARATE CLASS	SEPARATE SCHOOL	RESIDENTIAL FACILITY	HOMEBOUND/ HOSPITAL
Specific learning disabilities	39.3	41.0	18.8	0.6	0.1	0.1
Speech or language impairments	87.5	7.6	4.5	0.3	0.04	0.05
Mental retardation	8.6	26.1	57.0	7.0	0.7	0.5
Serious emotional disturbances	20.5	25.8	35.3	13.4	3.2	1.8
Multiple disabilities	9.1	19.8	44.1	21.8	3.2	2.0
Hearing impairments	30.6	20.0	30.6	7.0	11.6	0.2
Orthopedic impairments	37.4	20.7	33.3	5.3	0.5	2.9
Other health impairments	40.0	27.0	21.3	1.8	0.4	9.4
Visual impairments	45.2	21.3	18.3	4.1	10.6	0.5
Autism	9.6	8.1	54.5	23.4	3.9	0.5
Traumatic brain injury	22.3	23.5	30.2	18.3	2.6	3.0
Deaf–blindness	7.7	8.0	34.6	24.3	23.2	2.2
All disabilities	43.4	29.4	22.7	3.1	0.7	0.6

*Data for students placed in public and private separate schools and in public and private residential facilities have been combined for presentation in this table.

Source: Adapted from U.S. Department of Education, Office of Special Education Programs, Data Analysis System (DANS), 1996.

disability is likely to be in a general education classroom for most or all of the school day. However, severity of disability is not the sole criterion for placement; also considered is the appropriateness of the various settings for an individual student's needs. For example, a student in a wheelchair with a severe orthopedic disability but no learning problems could easily attend and profit from general education classes, whereas a student with a hearing deficit might not.

Table 12.3 shows the percentages of students with disabilities who receive special-education services in various settings. Note that with the exception of students who have physical or sensory disabilities, few students received special education outside of the school building. The great majority of students who have learning disabilities or speech impairments attend general education classes part or most of the day, usually supplemented by 1 or more hours per day in a special-education resource room. This is also true for the majority of students with physical disabilities and almost half of all students with emotional disorders. Most other students with special needs attend special classes located in their school buildings. The continuum of services available to students with disabilities, from least to most restrictive, is described in the following sections.

GENERAL EDUCATION CLASSROOM PLACEMENT ● The needs of many students with disabilities can be met in the general education classroom with little or no outside assistance. For example, students who have mild vision or hearing loss may simply be seated near the front of the room. Students with mild to moderate learning disabilities may have their needs met in the general education classroom if the teacher uses strategies for accommodating instruction to student differences. For example, the use of instructional aides, tutors, or parent volunteers can allow exceptional students to remain in the general education classroom. Classroom teachers can often adapt their instruction to make it easier for students to succeed. For example, one teacher noticed that a student with perceptual problems was having difficulties with arithmetic because he could not line up his numbers. She solved the problem by giving him graph paper to work on.

Research generally shows that the most effective strategies for dealing with students who have learning and behavior problems are those used in the general education classroom (Lloyd, Singh, & Repp, 1991). Special-education options should usually be explored only after serious efforts have been made to meet students' needs in the general education classroom (see Putnam, 1998b; Smith, Polloway, Patton, & Dowdy, 1998).

COLLABORATION WITH CONSULTING TEACHERS AND OTHER PROFESSIONALS ● In **collaboration,** several professionals work cooperatively to provide educational services. Students with disabilities who are included in the general education classroom benefit from professionals such as the consulting resource room teacher, school psychologist, speech and language specialists, and other professionals who collaborate with the general education teacher to develop and implement appropriate educational experiences for the students. Many school districts provide classroom teachers with consultants to help them adapt their instruction to the needs of students with disabilities. Consulting teachers typically are trained in special education as well as general education. They may come into the classroom to observe the behavior of a student, but most often they suggest solutions to the general education teacher rather than working directly with students (Warger & Pugach, 1996). Research finds that well-designed consulting models can be effective in assisting teachers to maintain students with mild disabilities, particularly those with learning disabilities, in the general education classroom (Fuchs & Fuchs, 1989; Rosenfield & Gravois, 1996).

For some types of disabilities, itinerant (traveling) teachers may provide special services to students a few times a week. This pattern of service is typical of programs for students with speech and language disorders.

RESOURCE ROOM PLACEMENT ● Many students with disabilities are assigned to general education classes for most of their school day but participate in resource programs at other times. Most often, resource programs focus on teaching reading, language arts, mathematics, and occasionally other subjects. A resource room program usually involves a small number of students working with a special-education teacher. Ideally, the resource teacher meets regularly with the classroom teacher to coordinate programs for students and to suggest ways in which the general education classroom teacher can adapt instruction when the students are in the general education class (Larrivee, Semmel, & Gerber, 1997).

Sometimes resource teachers work in the general education classroom. For example, a resource teacher might work with one reading group while the general education classroom teacher works with another. This arrangement avoids pulling students out of class—which is both inefficient (because of the transition time required) and potentially demeaning, because the students are excluded from class

CONNECTIONS
Strategies for accommodating instruction to student differences are discussed in Chapter 9, page 304.

collaboration
Process in which professionals work cooperatively to provide educational services.

for some period of time. Team teaching involving general education and special-education teachers also enhances communication between the teachers (Hardin & McNelis, 1996).

SPECIAL-EDUCATION CLASS PLACEMENT WITH PART-TIME MAINSTREAMING ● Many students with disabilities are assigned to special classes taught by a special-education teacher but are mainstreamed with nondisabled students part of the school day. These students join other students most often for music, art, and physical education; somewhat less often for social studies, science, and mathematics; and least often for reading. One important difference between this category of special services and the resource room model is that in the resource room, the student's primary placement is in the general education class; the classroom teacher is the homeroom teacher and generally takes responsibility for the student's program, with the resource teacher providing extra support. In the case of a student who is assigned to special education and is mainstreamed part of the day, the situation is reversed. The special-education teacher serves as the homeroom teacher and takes primary responsibility.

SELF-CONTAINED SPECIAL EDUCATION ● A self-contained special-education program is a class located in a school separately from the general education instructional program. Until the mainstreaming movement began in the early 1970s, this (along with separate schools for retarded and disabled children) was the typical placement for students with disabilities. Students in self-contained programs are taught by special-education teachers and have relatively few contacts with the general education instructional program.

Some students attend separate, special day schools. These are typically students with severe disabilities, such as severe retardation or physical disabilities, or students whose presence might be disruptive to the general education school, such as those with serious emotional disturbances. In addition, small numbers of students with disabilities attend special residential schools for students with profound disabilities who require special treatment.

OTHER SPECIAL SERVICES ● In addition to the placements just described, students with exceptionalities may need other special services. For example, school psychologists are often involved in the process of diagnosing students with disabilities and sometimes participate in the preparation of IEPs. In addition, they may counsel the student or consult with the teacher about behavioral and learning problems. Speech and language therapists generally work with students on a one-to-one basis, though they may provide some small-group instruction for students with similar problems. These therapists also consult with teachers about ways to address student difficulties. Physical and occupational therapists treat motor difficulties under the direction of a physician. Students who have physical disabilities may see a physical or occupational therapist whose treatment focuses on the development of large and small muscle skills.

School social workers and pupil personnel workers serve as a major link between the school and the family and are likely to become involved when problems at home are affecting students' school performance or behavior.

For students with disabilities who are unable to attend school because of a lengthy illness or complications related to a disability, instruction is often provided at home or in the hospital. Such instruction is designed to maintain and continue a student's academic progress. Homebound instruction is intended for short periods of time.

Classroom teachers have important roles in the education of children with disabilities. They are important in referring students to receive special services, in participating in the assessment of students, and in preparing and implementing IEPs. The Theory into Practice section on page 438 describes the process by which classroom teachers seek special-education services for students (see Hallahan & Kauffman, 1997; Smith, 1998).

In Figure 12.4 a flowchart shows how the IEP process operates. Figure 12.5 is an example of an IEP

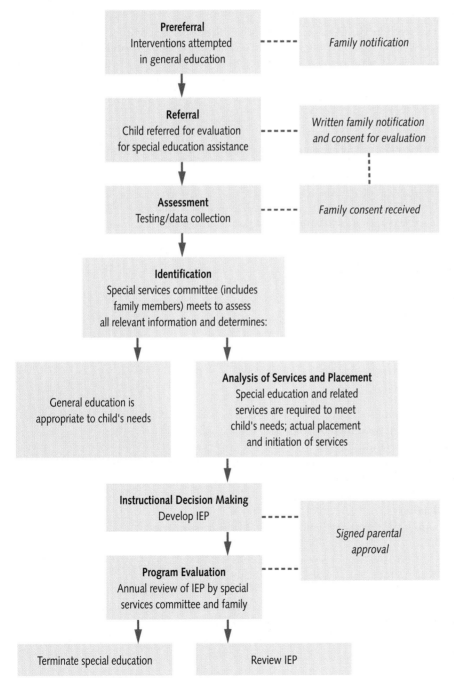

FIGURE 12.4 ● Flowchart for the Individualized Education Program Process
From Diane Pedrotty Rivera and Deborah Deutsch Smith, *Teaching Students with Learning and Behavior Problems* (3rd ed.), p. 52. Copyright © 1997 by Allyn & Bacon. Reprinted by permission.

Prereferral
Interventions attempted in general education

Family notification

Referral
Child referred for evaluation for special education assistance

Written family notification and consent for evaluation

Assessment
Testing/data collection

Family consent received

Identification
Special services committee (includes family members) meets to assess all relevant information and determines:

General education is appropriate to child's needs

Analysis of Services and Placement
Special education and related services are required to meet child's needs; actual placement and initiation of services

Instructional Decision Making
Develop IEP

Signed parental approval

Program Evaluation
Annual review of IEP by special services committee and family

Terminate special education

Review IEP

Quentinburg Public Schools—Special Education Department

Individualized Education Program

Student Name: Jillian Carol

School: Jefferson Elementary

Primary lang.: Home-English Student-English

Program start date: 8/28/00

Date of Birth: 4/2/90

Grade: 5

Date of meeting: 8/28/00

Review date: 8/28/01

Services required

General Education	Full-time participation with support from paraprofessional or special education teacher at least three hours weekly
Resources	Incidental as needed
Self-Contained	Speech/language therapy for language development
Related Services	40 minutes/week
Other	

Justification for Placement (include justification for any time spent not in general education): Student's needs indicate that learning can appropriately take place in the general education classroom with appropriate supports provided. Supports will include adapted materials as well as adult assistance up to three hours per week. Incidental time noted in the resource room is intended to pre-serve the option of one-to-one assistance on specific goals and objectives as needed, as determined by the teachers.

Tests Used

Intellectual	WISC-III (Full Scale IQ = 64)
Educational	Woodcock Reading, Keymath
Behavioral	NA
Speech/language	
Other	
Vision	Within normal limits
Hearing	Within normal limits

Strengths (present level of functioning)

Jillian enjoys talking with peers and adults.

Jillian is polite and well-mannered.

Jillian generally responds appropriately to directions.

Jillian likes to tell stories she creates.

Weaknesses (present level of functioning)

1. Below grade level in word identification (3.1) and reading comprehension (3.2)
2. Below grade level in vocabulary usage (2.1)
3. Below grade level in math computation and problem solving (1.6)

FIGURE 12.5 ● Sample Individualized Education Program

From Marilyn Friend and William D. Bursuck, *Including Students with Special Needs: A Practical Guide for Classroom Teachers* (2nd ed.), p. 55–56. Copyright © 1999 by Allyn & Bacon. Reprinted by permission.

Annual Goal: Jillian will improve her reading skills to approximately a 3.9 level.

> *STO 1:* Jillian will read from a 3rd grade reader at 80 words per minute with fewer than 3 errors per minute.

> *STO 2:* Jillian will answer with 80% accuracy comprehension questions about reading passages at a third-grade level.

> **Evaluation:** Oral performance **Person(s):** Special education teacher

Annual Goal: Jillian will use vocabulary at approximately a 3.0 level

> *STO 1:* Jillian will tell a story using vocabulary from third grade reading materials.

> *STO 2:* Jillian will use 3rd grade vocabulary when talking about her out-of-school activities.

> *STO 3:* Jillian will learn at least 40 vocabulary words by using a word bank.

> **Evaluation:** Oral performance, checklist **Person(s):** Special education teacher
> Classroom teacher

Annual Goal: Jillian will compute and problem solve at approximately a 2.5 level

> *STO 1:* Jillian will write answers to basic addition and subtraction facts with 100% accuracy.

> *STO 2:* Jillian will accurately compute two-digit addition and subtraction problems without regrouping with 90% accuracy.

> *STO 3:* Jillian will correctly solve word problems written at her reading level and at approximately a 2.5 difficulty level with 90% accuracy.

> **Evaluation:** Written performance **Person(s):** Special education teacher
> Classroom teacher

Team Signatures

LEA Representative	Eva Kim
Parent	Julia Carol
Special Education Teacher	Vera Delaney
General Education Teacher	
Psychologist	Nadine Showalter
Counselor	
Speech/Language Therapist	Ed Briggs
Other	
Other	

FIGURE 12.5 *(Continued)*

THEORY *into* Practice ●

Preparing IEPs

INITIAL REFERRAL

The process of preparing an Individualized Education Program begins when a student is referred for assessment. Referrals for special-education assessment can be made by parents, physicians, principals, or teachers. Classroom teachers most often initiate referrals for children with suspected learning disabilities, mental retardation, speech impairment, or emotional disturbance. Most other disabilities are diagnosed before students enter school. In most schools, initial referrals are made to the building principal, who contacts the relevant school district staff.

SCREENING AND ASSESSMENT

As soon as the student is referred for assessment, an initial determination is made to accept or reject the referral. In practice, almost all referrals are accepted. The evaluation and placement team may look at the student's school records and interview classroom teachers and others who know the student. If the team members decide to accept the referral, they must obtain parental permission to do a comprehensive assessment.

Members of the special services team include professionals designated by the school district plus the parents of the referred student and, if appropriate, the referred student. If the referral has to do with learning or emotional problems, a school psychologist or guidance counselor will usually be involved. If the referral has to do with speech or language problems, a speech pathologist or speech teacher will typically serve on the team. The building principal usually chairs the team but may designate a special-education teacher or other professional to do so.

The referred student is then given tests to assess strengths and weaknesses. For learning and emotional problems, these tests are usually given by a school psychologist. Specific achievement tests (such as reading or mathematics assessments) are often given by special-education or reading teachers. Parents must give permission for any specialized assessments. Increasingly, portfolios of student work, teacher evaluations, and other information collected over extended time periods are becoming important parts of the assessment process (Gomez, Grave, & Block, 1991).

If appropriate, the school may try a prereferral intervention before deciding on placement in special education (see Mamlin & Harris, 1998; Rosenfield & Gravois, 1996). For example, a child having serious reading problems might be given a tutor for a period of time before being determined to have a reading disability. For a child with a behavior problem, a home-based reinforcement program or other behavior management program might be set up. If these interventions worked, then the child might not be assigned to special education but could be served within the general education program. Even if a child does need special education services, the prereferral intervention is likely to provide important information about the kind of services most likely to work.

CONNECTIONS

For more on home-based reinforcement strategies, see Chapter 11, page 392.

WRITING THE IEP

When the comprehensive assessment is complete, the special services team members meet to consider the best placement for the student. If they determine that special education is necessary, they will prepare an IEP. Usually, the special-education teacher and/or the classroom teacher prepares the IEP. The student's parent(s) must sign a consent form regarding the placement decision, and in many school districts a parent must also sign the IEP. This means that parents can (and in some cases do) refuse to have their children placed in special-education programs. At a minimum, the IEP must contain the following information (see Odle & Galtelli, 1980, p. 248):

1. Statements indicating the child's present level of performance. These typically include the results of specific tests as well as descriptions of classroom functioning. Behavior rating checklists, work samples, or other observation forms may be used to clarify a student's strengths and weaknesses.

2. Goals indicating anticipated progress during the year. For example, a student might have goals of reading at a fourth-grade level as measured by a standardized test, of improving classroom behavior so that disciplinary referrals are reduced to zero, or of completing a bricklaying course in a vocational education program.

3. Intermediate (shorter-term) instructional objectives. A student who is having difficulties in reading might be given a short-term objective (STO) of completing a certain number of individualized reading comprehension units per month, or a student with emotional and behavior problems might be expected to get along with peers better and avoid fights.

4. A statement of the specific special-education and related services to be provided as well as the extent to which the student will participate in general education programs. The IEP might specify, for example, that a student would receive two 30-minute sessions with a speech therapist each week. An IEP for a student with a learning disability might specify 45 minutes per day of instruction from a resource teacher in reading plus consultation between the resource teacher and the classroom teacher on ways to adapt instruction in the general education classroom. A student with mental retardation might be assigned to a self-contained special-education class, but the IEP might specify that the student participate in the general physical education program. The IEP would specify any adaptations necessary to accommodate students in the general education class, such as wheelchair ramps, large-type books, or cassette tapes.

5. The projected date for the initiation of services and the anticipated duration of services. Once the IEP has been written, the student must receive services within a reasonable time period. Students may not be put on a waiting list; the school district must provide or contract for the indicated services.

6. Evaluation criteria and procedures for measuring progress toward goals on at least an annual basis. The IEP should specify a strategy for remediating the student's deficits. In particular, the IEP should state what objectives the student is to achieve and how those objectives are to be attained and measured. It is critical to direct special-education services toward a well-specified set of learning or behavior objectives rather than simply deciding that a student falls into some category and therefore should receive some service. Ideally, special education for students with mild disabilities should be a short-term, intensive treatment to give students the skills needed in a general education classroom. All too often, a student who is assigned to special education remains there indefinitely, even after the problem for which the student was initially referred has been remediated.

IEPs must be updated at least once a year. The updating provides an opportunity for the team to change programs that are not working or to reduce or terminate special-education services when the student no longer needs them.

SELF-CHECK

Define *special education*. Trace the history of federal laws—P.L. 94–142, P.L. 99–457, P.L. 101–476, and P.L. 105–17—that regulate the education of students with special needs. Define *least restrictive environment* and describe the educational environments in which students with special needs are placed. What other types of services are available? List the minimum information that an Individualized Education Program (IEP) must contain; then list the steps you would take to prepare one.

WHAT ARE MAINSTREAMING AND INCLUSION?

The least restrictive environment clause of P.L. 94–142 revolutionized the practice of special education as well as general education. As has already been noted, it requires that exceptional students be assigned to the least restrictive environment that is appropriate to their needs. Refer to Figure 12.6 for definitions of least restrictive environment, mainstreaming, and inclusion. This provision has resulted in greatly increased contact between students with disabilities and students without disabilities. In general, students with all types of disabilities have moved one or two notches up the continuum of special-education services. Students who were once placed in special schools are now generally put in separate classrooms in general education schools. Students who were once placed in separate classrooms in general education schools, particularly students with mild retardation and learning disabilities, are now most often assigned to general education classes for most of their instruction. A growing movement for **full inclusion** calls for including all children in general education classes, with appropriate assistance (see Gartner & Lipsky, 1987; Porter & Stone, 1998; Sailor, 1991).

full inclusion
Arrangement whereby students who have disabilities or are at risk receive all their instruction in a general education setting; support services are brought to the student.

FIGURE 12.6 ●
Terminology: From Mainstreaming to Inclusive Education

Mainstreaming means:

"the temporal, instructional, and social integration of eligible exceptional children with normal peers based on an ongoing, individually determined educational planning and programming process" (Kaufman et al., 1975, pp. 40–41).

Least restrictive environment means:

the provision in Public Law 94–142 (renamed the Individuals with Disabilities Education Act, or IDEA) that requires students with disabilities to be educated to the maximum extent appropriate with their nondisabled peers.

Inclusive education means:

"that students attend their home school with their age and grade peers. It requires that the proportion of students labeled for special services is relatively uniform for all of the schools within a particular district. . . . Included students are not isolated into special classes or wings within the school" (National Association of State Boards of Education, 1992, p. 12).

Full inclusion means that

students who are disabled or at risk receive all their instruction in a general education setting; support services come to the student.

Partial inclusion means that

students receive most of their instruction in general education settings, but the student may be pulled out to another instructional setting when such a setting is deemed appropriate to the student's individual needs.

This student with physical impairments is in a full inclusion program. According to research, how effective are full inclusion and mainstreaming compared to other approaches? As a teacher, how might you foster this girl's social acceptance by peers?

Proponents of full inclusion argue that pull-out programs discourage effective partnerships between general and special educators in implementing IEPs and that students in pull-out programs are stigmatized when they are segregated from other students. These proponents suggest that special-education teachers or aides team with classroom teachers and provide services in the general education classroom (Farlow, 1996; Giangreco, 1996; Jakupcak, 1998). Opponents of full inclusion argue that general education classroom teachers lack appropriate training and materials and are already overburdened with large class sizes and inadequate support services, and they worry that children with special needs may not receive necessary services (CASE, 1993; Kauffman, Lloyd, Baker, & Riedel, 1995; National Education Association, 1992; Shanker, 1994/1995; Turnbull, 1991).

Many (perhaps most) classroom teachers have students with disabilities, who are usually receiving some type of special educational services part of the day. Most of these mainstreamed students are categorized as having learning disabilities, speech impairments, mild retardation, or emotional disorders. High-quality inclusion models can improve the achievement and self-confidence of these students. Inclusion also allows students with disabilities to interact with peers and to learn conventional behavior. However, mainstreaming also creates challenges. When mainstreamed students are performing below the level of the rest of the class, some teachers struggle to adapt instruction to the mainstreamed students' needs—and to cope with the often negative attitudes of the nondisabled students toward their classmates with disabilities (McLeskey & Waldron, 1996), which may defeat attempts at social integration. Unfortunately, some classroom teachers are uncomfortable about having students with disabilities in their classes, and many feel poorly prepared to accommodate these students' needs (Schumm & Vaughn, 1992; Semmel, Abernathy, Butera, & Lesar, 1991). Inclusion provides an opportunity for more effective services but is by no means a guarantee that better services will actually be provided (see Fuchs & Fuchs, 1995).

Research on Mainstreaming and Inclusion

Research on mainstreaming has focused on students with learning disabilities, mild retardation, and mild emotional disorders, whose deficits can be termed "mild academic disabilities" (Manset & Semmel, 1997). Several studies have compared students with mild academic disabilities in special-education classes to those in general education classes. When the general education teacher uses an instructional method that is designed to accommodate a wide range of student abilities, students with mild disabilities generally learn much better in the general education classroom than in special-education classes. One classic study on this topic was done by Calhoun and Elliott (1977), who compared students with mild mental retardation and emotional disorders in general education classes with students with the same disabilities in special-education classes. General education classes as well as special-education classes used the same individualized materials, and teachers (trained in special education) were rotated across classes to ensure that the only difference between the general and special programs was the presence of nondisabled classmates. The results of the Calhoun and Elliott (1977) study, depicted in Figure 12.7, suggest the superiority of general education class placement.

Research on programs for general education classrooms that contain students with learning disabilities indicates that one successful strategy is to use individualized instructional programs. For example, the Cooperative Integrated Reading and Composition (CIRC) program described in Chapter 8 has been found to improve the achievement of mainstreamed students with learning disabilities, in comparison to mainstreamed students in traditionally organized classes (Slavin, Madden, & Leavey, 1984a, 1984b; Stevens & Slavin, 1995a).

Improving the social acceptance of students with academic disabilities is a critical task of inclusion. One consistently effective means of doing this is to involve the students in cooperative learning teams with their nondisabled classmates (Nevin, 1998). For example, a study of Student Teams–Achievement Divisions (STAD) in classes containing students with learning disabilities found that STAD reduced the social rejection of the students with learning disabilities while significantly increasing their achievement (Madden & Slavin, 1983a). Other cooperative learning programs have found similar effects on the social acceptance of students with mild academic disabilities (Slavin et al., 1984b; Slavin & Stevens, 1991; Stevens & Slavin, 1995a).

A key element in effective mainstreaming is maintaining close coordination between classroom and special teachers. Studies of pull-out programs for students with learning disabilities often find that special-education teachers have little knowledge of the school's general education curriculum and do little to integrate their instruction with it (Allington & McGill-Franzen, 1989). An experiment by

CONNECTIONS

Cooperative Integrated Reading and Composition (CIRC) is discussed in Chapter 8, page 271.

CONNECTIONS

For more on STAD, see Chapter 8, page 269.

FIGURE 12.7 ●
Achievement of Students in General Education and Special-Education Classes
In a classic study, placement in general education classes rather than special-education classes resulted in higher achievement levels over 3 years for students who are emotionally disturbed (ED) and educable mentally retarded (EMR). From N. A. Madden and R. E. Slavin, "Mainstreaming Students with Mild Handicaps," *Review of Educational Research, 53*(4), 1983, p. 525. Copyright 1983 by the American Educational Research Association. Reprinted by permission of the publisher. Based on data from G. Calhoun and R. Elliott, "Self-Concept and Academic Achievement of Educable Retarded and Emotionally Disturbed," *Exceptional Children, 44,* pp. 379–380. Copyright 1977 by The Council for Exceptional Children. Reprinted with permission.

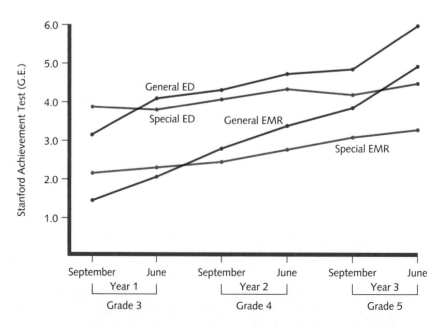

Fuchs, Fuchs, and Fernstrom (1993) showed how coordination could improve student performance and accomplish full integration of all students with learning disabilities into general education classes over a period of time. In this study, children in pull-out math programs were given frequent curriculum-based measures assessing their progress relative to the school's math program. Special-education teachers examined the requirements for success in the general education class and prepared children specifically to succeed in that setting. As the children reached a criterion level of skills in math, they were transitioned into the general education class and then followed up to ensure that they were succeeding there. Over the course of a school year, all 21 students involved in the study were successfully transitioned to full-time general education class placement and learned significantly more than matched control students did.

There is very little research on the outcomes of full inclusion programs that integrate children who generally would not have been integrated in traditional mainstreaming models. There are descriptions of outstanding full inclusion programs (e.g., Mahony, 1997; Raison, Hanson, Hall, & Reynolds, 1995; Van Dyke, Stallings, & Colley, 1995) and of apparently successful statewide inclusion policies in Vermont (Thousand & Villa, 1995) and in Pennsylvania (Kovaleski, Tucker, & Stevens, 1996), but there have also been reports of full inclusion disasters (e.g., Baines, Baines, & Masterson, 1994). Research comparing inclusive and special-education programs finds few differences (e.g., Baker, Wang, & Walberg, 1994/1995; Fuchs & Fuchs, 1995; Hunt & Goetz, 1997; Manset & Semmel, 1997; Zigmond, Jenkins, Fuchs, Deno, & Fuchs, 1995). However, the goals of including students with even the most profound disabilities in general education classrooms are difficult to measure (see McLeskey & Waldron, 1995; Zigmond et al., 1995). Full inclusion is a goal worth striving toward with care, caution, and flexibility. Research in this area is under way and should produce better information about the conditions under which full inclusion works best.

Adapting Instruction

Teacher behaviors that are associated with effective teaching for mainstreamed students are essentially the same as those that improve achievement for all students (Leinhardt & Bickel, 1989). Nevertheless, although good classroom instruction for most students with learning disabilities is similar to good instruction for nondisabled students (Larrivee, 1985; Leinhardt & Bickel, 1989), some adaptations in instructional strategies will help teachers to better meet the needs of students with disabilities. Whether they use individualized instruction, cooperative learning, or other means of accommodating student differences, teachers need to know how to adapt lessons to address students' needs. When students have difficulty with instruction or materials in learning situations, the recommendation is frequently to adapt or modify the instruction or the materials (see Burnette, 1987). The particular adaptation that is required depends on the student's needs and could be anything from format adaptation to the rewriting of textbook materials (Allen, Clark, Gallagher, & Scofield, 1982). The following Theory into Practice describes three common types of adaptations for accommodating mainstreamed students.

Adapting Instruction for Students with Special Needs

FORMAT ADAPTATIONS FOR WRITTEN ASSIGNMENTS

Teachers can change the format in which a task is presented without changing the actual task. Such a change may be needed for a variety of reasons: (1) An assignment is too long; (2) the spacing on the page is too close to allow the student to focus on

THEORY
into
Practice

individual items; (3) the directions for the task are insufficient or confusing; or (4) the models or examples for the task are either absent, misleading, or insufficient. The critical concept here is that while task and response remain the same, the teacher makes adaptations in the way the material is presented.

Occasionally, the directions for a task or assignment must be simplified. For example, you might substitute in a set of directions the word *circle* for *draw a ring around*. You could also teach students the words that are commonly found in directions (Cohen & de Bettencourt, 1983). By teaching students how to understand such words, you will help them to be more independent learners. Models or examples presented with a task may also be changed to more closely resemble the task.

CONTENT ADAPTATIONS

In some instances, students may require an adaptation in the content being presented, such as when so much new information is presented that the student cannot process it quickly or when the student lacks a prerequisite skill or concept necessary to complete a task.

One way to adapt the amount of content being presented is to isolate each concept (Bos & Vaughn, 1994) and require mastery of each concept as a separate unit before teaching the next concept. Although this type of adaptation involves smaller units of material, the same content will be covered in the end.

Adaptations that are required because students lack essential prerequisites may be as simple as explaining vocabulary or concepts before teaching a lesson. More complex adaptations are required when students lack prerequisite skills or concepts that cannot be explained easily or when students do not have a skill they need to learn the lesson. For example, if the math lesson involves solving word problems that require the division of three-digit numerals and a student has not yet learned how to divide three-digit numerals, this skill will have to be taught before the student can address the word problems.

ADAPTATIONS IN MODES OF COMMUNICATION

Some students require adaptations in either the way in which they receive information or the way in which they demonstrate their knowledge of specific information. Many students cannot learn information when their only means of getting it is through reading but can learn if the information is made available in other forms. Be creative in considering the possibilities. You might have students watch a demonstration, filmstrip, film, videotape, television program, computer program, or play. Or you might have them listen to an audiotape, lecture/discussion, or debate.

A different type of adaptation may be required if a student cannot respond as the task directs. If a student has a writing problem, for example, you might ask the student to tell you about the concept in a private conversation and record the student's response on a tape recorder, or ask the student to present an oral report to the class. Or you might let the student represent the knowledge by drawing a picture or diagram or by constructing a model or diorama.

Teaching Learning Strategies and Metacognitive Awareness

Many students do poorly in school because they have failed to learn how to learn. Programs that are directed at helping students learn such strategies as note-taking, summarization, and memorization methods have been very successful with children and adolescents who have learning disabilities (Mastropieri & Scruggs, 1992; Schumaker & Deshler, 1992). Reciprocal teaching, a method for helping nondisabled students learn metacognitive strategies for reading, has also been successful with adolescents with learning disabilities (Palincsar, 1987).

Prevention and Early Intervention

The debate over inclusion versus special education for children with learning problems revolves around concerns about children whose academic performance is far below that of their agemates. However, many of these children could have succeeded in school in the first place if they had had effective prevention and early intervention programs. Slavin (1996a) proposed a policy of "neverstreaming," which avoids the mainstreaming/special-education dilemma by focusing attention on intensive early intervention that is capable of bringing at-risk learners to performance levels high enough to remove any need for special-education services.

There is strong evidence that a substantial portion of students who are now in the special-education system could have been kept out of it if they had had effective early intervention. Studies of high-quality early childhood programs such as the Perry Preschool (Berrueta-Clement et al., 1984), the Abecedarian Project (Ramey & Ramey, 1992), and the Milwaukee Project (Garber, 1988) all showed substantial reductions in special-education placements for students with learning disabilities and mild mental retardation. Programs that provide one-to-one tutoring to first-graders who are struggling in reading have also shown reductions in the need for special-education services for students with learning disabilities (Lyons, 1989; Silver & Hagin, 1990). Success for All, which combines effective early childhood programs, curriculum reform, and one-to-one tutoring, has reduced special-education placement by more than half (Slavin et al., 1992, 1994, 1996; Smith, Ross, & Casey, 1994) and has substantially increased the reading achievement of children who have already been identified as needing special-education services (Ross, Smith, Casey, & Slavin, 1995; Smith et al., 1994). These and other findings suggest that the number of children who need special-education services could be greatly reduced if prevention and early intervention programs were more widely applied.

CONNECTIONS
For more on the Success for All approach, see Chapter 9, page 320.

Computers and Students with Disabilities

Computers provide opportunities for individualized instruction for students with disabilities. The use of computers to help children with exceptionalities has four major advantages (Latham, 1997c; Lewis, 1993). First, computers can help to individualize instruction in terms of method of delivery, type and frequency of reinforcement, rate of presentation, and level of instruction. Second, computers can give immediate corrective feedback and emphasize the active role of the child in learning (Ryba, Selby, & Nolan, 1995). Third, computers can hold the attention of children who are easily distractible. Fourth, computer instruction is motivating and patient. For students with physical disabilities, computers may permit greater ease in learning and communicating information.

CONNECTIONS
For more on computer-based instruction, see Chapter 9, page 307.

Children in special-education programs seem to like learning from computers. Poorly motivated students have become more enthusiastic about their studies. They feel more in control because they are being taught in a context that is positive, reinforcing, and nonthreatening. However, findings as to the actual learning benefits of computer-assisted instruction for students with disabilities have been inconsistent (Carnine, 1989; Malouf, Wizer, Pilato, & Grogan, 1990).

One valuable approach using computers is to provide children who are academically disabled with activities in which they can explore, construct, and communicate. Word processors serve this purpose (Messerer & Lerner, 1989), and other

CASE TO CONSIDER

Exceptionalities: Barriers to Getting to Know Students

Arlisa is 2 weeks into her teaching associateship practicum in Ms. Runson's kindergarten class at Central Elementary School. Kwan, a student with special needs who receives help from Amanda, the special-education resource teacher, has surprised Arlisa with an uncharacteristic outburst, screaming at her when she asked him a question and then moving into a corner with his back toward her. Later in the day, Arlisa, Ms. Runson, and Amanda discuss Kwan's situation.

Ms. Runson: Arlisa, don't be disheartened about the way Kwan acted today. This is a common episode for him.

Arlisa: I'm not disheartened, but I don't think I understand the nature of Kwan's special needs, so I don't know what to do in situations like this one.

Amanda: Kwan is very intelligent for his age—he reads very well already—but he has socializing problems.

Ms. Runson: Often, Kwan won't talk to me, either. When he acts like that, just leave him alone until he comes around.

Arlisa: I don't think it's that Kwan won't talk. Earlier this week on the playground, several other kindergarten boys were chasing him and Mary. Kwan was yelling at the boys to leave Mary alone. I stopped the boys and then asked Kwan what had happened. Kwan tried to yell at me, so I took the moment to try to help him with his communication. I encouraged him to calm down and speak to me, rather than yelling, to tell me what was wrong. Eventually, he calmed down enough to shout at me about what had happened, but his shouting seemed more out of frustration with the boys than intentional. I called the boys back, we talked, and the issue was resolved. Kwan and Mary left to play together.

Ms. Runson: I'm surprised, Arlisa, that Kwan listened to you and actually tried to talk! And Kwan hasn't chosen a classmate to play with since the first day of school. Maybe you should capitalize on Kwan's willingness to listen to you.

Amanda: I agree, Arlisa. When we work one-on-one, Kwan has told me that his classmates are too loud on the bus and at circle time. I've scheduled him for a hearing test, but meanwhile I've gotten him a pair of ear plugs to wear on the bus. The driver says this seems to calm him down.

Arlisa: Amanda, what strategies can I use to get Kwan to talk to me, instead of shouting or sulking?

Amanda: Well, he seems to sulk when we ask him to make a decision before he's ready to, like when you ask him what he wants to do during choosing time. You should tell him it's okay, and that he should speak to you when he has decided what he wants to do. Then move on to the other children. When he shouts at you, or when he simply points at what he wants, remind him to *tell* you what he needs or wants. Remind him that it is hard to listen to him when he shouts.

Ms. Runson: He often starts sulking or has an outburst when another child comes to take his or her turn at the computer he has been using. I think that giving him a time limit on the computers will encourage him to play with the other children.

Amanda: That's a good idea, Ms. Runson. And I can work with Kwan and a few other children on additional computer activities during my scheduled time with him to reinforce those ideas.

Arlisa: Isn't there something we can do to build on his strengths, like his reading abilities?

Amanda: That's another good idea. I could start writing responses to him on sticky notes and putting them on his shirt. Then, when he rejoins the entire class, both of you could ask him to read the sticky notes to you. This will reinforce his good reading abilities while also encouraging him to talk.

Arlisa: Do you really think these strategies will help Kwan?

Ms. Runson: We'll try them and see. Amanda and I are still talking with Kwan's parents, diagnosing his needs, and putting together an IEP for him. Then we'll have a better idea of how to help him.

PROBLEM SOLVING

1. List the special needs that Kwan seems to demonstrate. What additional instructional adaptations might you suggest to help Kwan succeed in kindergarten?

2. Evaluate the level of collaboration demonstrated among the three teachers. If you were Ms. Runson, the classroom teacher, how would you capitalize on the support offered by Amanda, the special education teacher? If you were Amanda, how would you propose additional accommodations that Ms. Runson and Arlisa could make for Kwan?

3. Kwan's exceptionalities have not been clearly diagnosed yet, but how has his labeling as a child with special needs already served as a barrier during the first 2 weeks of kindergarten? How can the three teachers work to remove this barrier?

Adapted from "Student Diversity: Barriers to Getting to Know Our Students" by Arlisa Johnson, a graduate of the University of Virginia with a Master's of Teaching and K–8 certification, from *Allyn & Bacon's Custom Cases in Education,* edited by Greta Morine-Dershimer, Paul Eggen, and Donald Kauchak (1997).

programs have been specifically designed for children with disabilities. For example, hypertext programs (Higgins & Boone, 1990) allow children to obtain additional information, explanations, or vocabulary for text they are reading. Videodisc instruction combines video, slides, and instruction in ways that can engage a broad range of learners (Woodward & Gersten, 1992). Refer to Figure 12.8 for examples of computers and other technology for students with disabilities.

Buddy Systems and Peer Tutoring

One way to help meet the needs of students with disabilities in the general education classroom is to provide these students with assistance from nondisabled classmates, using either a buddy system for noninstructional needs or peer tutoring to help with learning problems.

A student who volunteers to be a special-education student's buddy can help that student cope with the routine tasks of classroom life. For example, a buddy can guide a student with vision loss, help a student who is academically disabled to understand directions, or deliver cues or prompts as needed in some classes. In middle school and high school settings, a buddy can take notes for a student with hearing loss or learning disabilities by making photocopies of his or her own notes. The buddy can also ensure that the student with a disability has located the correct textbook page during a lesson and has the materials necessary for a class. The buddy's primary responsibility is to help the student with special needs adjust to the general education classroom, to answer questions, and to provide direction for

FIGURE 12.8 ● Adaptive Technology for Students with Disabilities
From Michael L. Hardman, Clifford J. Drew, M. Winston Egan, and B. Wolf, *Human Exceptionality* (5th ed.). Copyright © 1996 by Allyn & Bacon. Adapted by permission.

Students with Learning Disabilities
Hypertext

A development similar to computer-based instruction is called *hypertext.* Hypertext programs provide further explanation of material in textbooks, such as definitions of difficult vocabulary, the addition of maps, and more discussion of concepts.

Videodisc Instruction

Videodisc instruction provides visual and auditory presentations. Students watch presentations and are guided through instruction. This also frees the teacher to work individually with students while the videodisc is in use.

Word Processing Programs

Some word processing programs give instant feedback on possible spelling errors and cue the user with a beep or a flash on the screen. One such program, Write: OutLoud, reads back a sentence or a word so that the user can hear whether what was written is what was intended.

Students with Communication Disorders
Alternative and Augmentative Communication Devices

Alternative and augmentative communication devices can be either high-tech (such as speech talkers), or low-tech (such as communication boards). One example of a speech talker is called the Dynavox. It is touch-activated and creates verbal speech. Information can be programmed into it, and students can complete class presentations with picture cues and verbal messages to present to the class. Communication boards help people who are unable to speak. The person points to pictures or words that have been placed on the board. More high-tech devices can convert a typed message into voice or print, even allowing for selection of the voice qualities.

activities. Use of this resource allows the general education classroom teacher to address more important questions related to instructional activities.

Another way of helping students within the general education classroom is to use peer tutoring (Fantuzzo, King, & Heller, 1992; Scruggs & Richter, 1986). Teachers who use peers to tutor in their classroom should ensure that these tutors are carefully trained. This means that the peer tutor must be taught how to provide assistance by modeling and explaining, how to give specific positive and corrective feedback, and when to allow the student to work alone. Peer tutors and tutees may both benefit: the special-education student by acquiring academic concepts and the tutor by gaining a better acceptance and understanding of students with disabilities. Sometimes, older students with disabilities tutor younger ones; this generally benefits both students (Osguthorpe & Scruggs, 1986; Top & Osguthorpe, 1987).

CONNECTIONS

For more on peer tutoring, see Chapter 9, page 304.

Special-Education Teams

When a student with disabilities is integrated into the general education classroom, the classroom teacher often works with one or more special educators to ensure the student's successful integration (Bauwens, Hourcade, & Friend, 1989; Walter-Thomas, 1997; Warger & Pugach, 1996). The classroom teacher may participate in conferences with special-education personnel, the special-education personnel may at times be present in the classroom, or the classroom teacher may consult with a special educator at regular intervals. Whatever the arrangement, the classroom teacher and the special educator(s) must recognize that each has expertise that is crucial to the student's success. The classroom teacher is the expert on classroom organization and operation on a day-to-day basis, the curriculum of the classroom, and the expectations placed on students for performance. The special educator is the expert on the characteristics of a particular group of students with disabilities, the learning and behavioral strengths and deficits of the mainstreamed student, and instructional techniques for a particular kind of disability. All this information is important to the successful integration of students, which is why communication between the general education and special-education teachers is so necessary (Allington & Johnston, 1989; Leinhardt & Bickel, 1989).

Communication should begin before students are placed in the general education classroom and should continue throughout the placement. Both teachers must have up-to-date information about the student's performance in each setting to plan and coordinate an effective program. Only then can instruction targeted to improving the student's performance in the general education classroom be designed and presented. In addition, generalization of skills and behaviors from one setting to the other will be enhanced (see Fuchs, Fuchs, Bahr, Fernstrom, & Stecker, 1990).

CONNECTIONS

For more on teaching adaptive skills to help students in their socioemotional development, see Chapter 3, page 89.

Social Integration of Students with Disabilities

Placement of students in the general education classroom is only one part of their integration into that environment. These students must be integrated socially as well as instructionally. The classroom teacher plays a critical role in this process. Much has been written about the effects of teacher expectations on student achievement and behavior. In the case of students with disabilities, the teacher's attitude toward these students is important not only for teacher–student interactions but also as a model for the nondisabled students in the classroom. The research on attitudes toward individuals with disabilities provides several strategies that might be useful to the general education classroom teacher who wants to promote successful social integration by influencing the attitudes of nondisabled students. One strategy is to use

CONNECTIONS

For more on the effects of teacher expectations on student achievement and behavior, see Chapter 10, page 341.

Consider these tips for including secondary students in the general education classroom:

Secondary Students with Learning Disabilities

1. Specifically teach self-recording strategies such as asking, "Was I paying attention?"
2. Relate new material to knowledge that the student with learning disabilities already has, drawing specific implications from familiar information.
3. Teach the use of external memory enhancers (e.g., lists and note-taking).
4. Encourage the use of other devices to improve class performance (e.g., tape recorders).

Secondary Students with Emotional or Behavioral Disorders

1. Create positive relationships within your classroom through the use of cooperative learning teams and group-oriented assignments.
2. Use all students in creating standards for conduct as well as consequences for positive and negative behaviors.
3. Focus your efforts on developing a positive relationship with the student with behavior disorders by greeting him or her regularly, informally talking with him or her at appropriate times, attending to improvement in his or her performance, and becoming aware of his or her interests.
4. Work closely with the members of the teacher assistance team to be aware of teacher behaviors that may adversely or positively affect students' performance.
5. Realize that changes in behavior often occur very gradually, with periods of regression and sometimes tumult.

FIGURE 12.9 ● **Including Secondary Students with Disabilities in the General Education Classroom**
From Michael L. Hardman, Clifford J. Drew, and M. Winston Egan, *Human Exceptionality* (5th ed.). Copyright © 1996 by Allyn & Bacon. Adapted by permission.

cooperative learning methods (Nevin, 1998; Slavin & Stevens, 1991; Stevens & Slavin, 1995a). Social skills training has been found to improve the social acceptance of children with disabilities (Gresham, 1981). For practical ways to include secondary students with disabilities in the general education classroom, see Figure 12.9.

SELF-CHECK

Define *mainstreaming* and *inclusion.* Discuss research findings on the effectiveness of mainstreaming and full inclusion approaches. Describe the most effective strategies for accommodating instruction for mainstreamed students. How do computers, buddy systems, peer tutoring, special-education teams, and social integration approaches assist students with special needs?

CHAPTER SUMMARY

WHO ARE LEARNERS WITH EXCEPTIONALITIES?

Learners with exceptionalities are students who have special educational needs in relation to societal or school norms. An inability to perform appropriate academic tasks for any reason inherent in the learner makes that learner exceptional. A handicap is a condition or barrier imposed by the environment or the self; a disability is a functional limitation that interferes with a person's mental, physical, or sensory abilities. Classification systems for learners with exceptionalities are often arbitrary and debated, and the use of labels may lead to inappropriate treatment or damage students' self-concepts.

About 10 percent of students in the United States receive special education. Examples of learners with exceptionalities are students with mental retardation, specific learning disabilities, speech or language disorders, emotional disorders, behavioral disorders, vision or hearing loss, cerebral palsy, or seizure disorders.

Students who are gifted and talented are also regarded as exceptional and may be eligible for special accelerated or enrichment programs. Clearly identifying learners with exceptionalities and accommodating instruction to meet their needs are continual challenges.

WHAT IS SPECIAL EDUCATION?

Special-education programs serve children with disabilities instead of, or in addition to, the general education classroom program.

Public Law 94–142 (1975), which was amended by P.L. 99–457 (1986) to include preschool children and seriously disabled infants and is now called the Individuals with Disabilities Education Act (IDEA) according to P.L. 101–476 (1990), mandates that every child with a disability is entitled to appropriate special education at public expense. Strengthened by P.L. 105–17 (1997), IDEA calls for greater involvement of parents and classroom teachers in the education of children with disabilities. The least restrictive environment clause means that students with special needs must be mainstreamed into general education classes as much as possible. A requirement of IDEA is that every student with a disability must have an Individualized Education Program (IEP). The idea behind the use of IEPs is to give everyone concerned with the education of a child with a disability an opportunity to help formulate the child's instruction program. An array of services is available for exceptional students, including support for the general education teacher, special education for part of the day in a resource room, special education for more than 3 hours per day in a special-education classroom, special day schools, special residential schools, and home/hospitals.

WHAT ARE MAINSTREAMING AND INCLUSION?

Mainstreaming means placing students with special needs in general education classrooms for at least part of the time. Full inclusion of all children in general education classes with appropriate assistance is a widely held goal. Research has shown that mainstreaming is effective in raising many students' performance levels, especially when cooperative learning, buddy systems, peer tutoring, computer instruction, modifications in lesson presentation, and training in social skills are a regular part of classroom learning. Research has also shown that some disabilities, especially reading disabilities, can be prevented through programs of prevention and early intervention.

KEY TERMS

acceleration programs   428

attention deficit disorder (ADD)   417

attention deficit hyperactivity disorder (ADHD)   417

autism   424

cerebral palsy   426

collaboration   433

conduct disorders   423

disability   408

emotional and behavioral disorders   421

enrichment programs   428

full inclusion   440

giftedness   427

handicap   408

hearing loss   426

hyperactivity   424

Individualized Education Program (IEP)   431

Individuals with Disabilities Education Act (IDEA)   430

IDEA 97   430

intelligence quotient (IQ)   411

language disorders   420

learners with exceptionalities   408

learning disabilities (LD)   413

least restrictive environment   430

mainstreaming   430

mental retardation   410

normal curve   411

Public Law 94–142   429

seizure disorders   426

sensory impairments   424

special education   429

speech disorders   420

traumatic brain injury (TBI)   427

vision loss   425

Self-Assessment

1. Explain the difference between a handicap and a disability.

2. Approximately what percentage of all students ages 6 to 17 have mental retardation?
   a. 1.2 percent
   b. 5.8 percent
   c. 8.3 percent
   d. 10.1 percent

3. Match each of the following descriptions with its exceptionality type.
   a. emotional disorders
   b. language disorders
   c. learning disabilities
   d. speech disorders

   _____ difficulties with expressive and receptive communications
   _____ below what an IQ would predict
   _____ omissions, distortions, and substitutions of sounds
   _____ anxiety, phobias, aggression, or acute shyness

4. Problems with the ability to see or hear or otherwise receive information are labeled
   a. sensory impairments.
   b. learning disabilities.
   c. attention deficit disorders.
   d. emotional and behavioral disorders.

5. List two common options for adapting educational programs to the needs of students who are gifted and talented.

6. Match the federal law regarding the education of students with special needs with its description.
   a. P.L. 101–476
   b. P.L. 94–142
   c. P.L. 99–457
   d. P.L. 105–17

   _____ This federal law, enacted in 1975, requires that special services be provided to all students in need.
   _____ This federal law, enacted in 1986, extends free, appropriate education to children ages 3 to 5.
   _____ This federal law, enacted in 1990, requires schools to plan for the transition of adolescents with disabilities into future education or employment.
   _____ This federal law, enacted in 1997, increases parental and classroom teacher involvement in the education of students with disabilities.

7. Rank the following special education placements in order from environments that are least restrictive (1) to most restrictive (4).
   resource room
   part-time mainstreaming into general education classroom
   self-contained special-education classroom
   general education classroom

8. List the steps for developing an Individualized Education Program.

9. What problems or benefits may occur when students with special needs are included in the general education classroom?

10. In some areas of the country, minority group students account for two-thirds of the enrollment in classes for students with mental disabilities. What are some reasons for this overrepresentation?

Chapter 13

WHAT ARE INSTRUCTIONAL OBJECTIVES AND HOW ARE THEY USED?
Planning Lesson Objectives
Linking Objectives and Assessment
Using Taxonomies of Instructional Objectives
Research on Instructional Objectives

WHY IS EVALUATION IMPORTANT?
Evaluation As Feedback
Evaluation As Information
Evaluation As Incentive

HOW IS STUDENT LEARNING EVALUATED?
Formative and Summative Evaluations
Norm-Referenced, Criterion-Referenced, and Authentic Evaluations
Matching Evaluation Strategies with Goals

HOW ARE TESTS CONSTRUCTED?
Principles of Achievement Testing
Using a Table of Specifications
Writing Objective Test Items
Writing and Evaluating Essay Tests
Writing and Evaluating Problem-Solving Items

WHAT ARE PORTFOLIO AND PERFORMANCE ASSESSMENTS?
Portfolio Assessment
Performance Assessment
How Well Do Performance Assessments Work?
Scoring Rubrics for Performance Assessments

Assessing Student Learning

Mr. Sullivan was having a great time teaching about the Civil War, and his 11th-grade U.S. history class was having fun too. Mr. Sullivan was relating all kinds of anecdotes about the war. He described a battle fought in the nude (a group of Confederates was caught fording a river), the time Stonewall Jackson lost a battle because he took a nap in the middle of it, and several stories about women who disguised their gender to fight as soldiers. He told the story of a Confederate raid (from Canada) on a Vermont bank. He passed around real Minié balls and grapeshot. In fact, Mr. Sullivan had gone on for weeks about the battles, the songs, and the personalities and foibles of the generals. Finally, after an interesting math activity in which students had to figure out how much Confederate money they would need to buy a loaf of bread, Mr. Sullivan had students put away all their materials to take a test.

The students were shocked. The only question was: What were the main causes, events, and consequences of the Civil War?

Mr. Sullivan's lessons are fun. They are engaging. They use varied presentation modes. They integrate skills from other disciplines. They are clearly accomplishing one important objective of social studies: building enjoyment of the topic. However, as engaging as Mr. Sullivan's lessons are, there is little correspondence between what he is teaching and what he is testing. He and his students are on a happy trip, but where are they going?

Using Your EXPERIENCE

Cooperative Learning   In a group of four or five students, draw a value line from 1 to 100, with 1 representing poor teaching and 100 representing great teaching. Take turns marking where you would place Mr. Sullivan on this scale. Let each person explain his or her rating. Now review the ratings and change them as appropriate. Discuss better ways in which Mr. Sullivan might assess his students.

Critical Thinking   Write questions that Mr. Sullivan might be able to use in testing his Civil War unit that address the following levels of student thinking: recalling information, applying principles or abstractions, and analysis. Note that these are some of the levels of Bloom's taxonomy of educational objectives, which is discussed in this chapter.

This chapter discusses two important and closely linked topics: objectives and evaluation. The most important idea in the chapter is that teachers must have objectives, a plan for what students should know and be able to do at the end of a course of study; their lessons must be designed to accomplish these objectives; and their evaluation of students must tell them which objectives each student has actually mastered and can do by the end of the course (Mabry & Stake, 1994). Put another way, every teacher should have a clear idea of where the class is going, how it will get there, and how to know whether it has arrived.

WHAT ARE INSTRUCTIONAL OBJECTIVES AND HOW ARE THEY USED?

What do you want your students to know or be able to do at the end of today's lesson? What should they know at the end of a series of lessons on a particular subject? What should they know at the end of the course? Knowing the answers to these questions is one of the most important prerequisites for high-quality instruction. A teacher is like a wilderness guide with a troop of tenderfeet. If the teacher does not have a map or a plan for getting the group where it needs to go, the whole group will surely be lost. Mr. Sullivan's students are having a lot of fun, but because their teacher has no plan for how his lessons will give them essential concepts relating to the Civil War, they will be unlikely to learn these concepts.

Setting out objectives at the beginning of a course is an essential step in providing a framework into which individual lessons will fit. Without such a framework it is easy to wander off the track, to spend too much time on topics that are not central to the course. One high school biology teacher spent most of the year teaching biochemistry; her students knew all about the chemical makeup of DNA, red blood cells, chlorophyll, and starch but little about zoology, botany, anatomy, or other topics that are usually central to high school biology. Then in late May the teacher panicked, because she realized that the class had to do a series of laboratory exercises before the end of the year. On successive days they dissected a frog, an eye, a brain, and a pig fetus! Needless to say, the students learned little from those hurried labs and little about biology in general. This teacher did not have a master plan but was deciding week by week (or perhaps day by day) what to teach, thereby losing sight of the big picture—the scope of knowledge that is generally agreed to be important for a high school student to learn in biology class. Few teachers follow a plan rigidly once they make it, but the process of making it is still very helpful (Clark & Peterson, 1986).

An **instructional objective,** sometimes called a *behavioral objective,* is a statement of skills or concepts that students are expected to know at the end of some period of instruction. Typically, an instructional objective is stated in such a way as to make clear how the objective will be measured (see Mager, 1975). Some examples of instructional objectives are the following:

- Given 100 division facts (such as 27 divided by 3), students will give correct answers to all 100 in 3 minutes.
- When asked, students will name at least five functions that characterize all living organisms (respiration, reproduction, etc.).
- In an essay, students will be able to compare and contrast the artistic styles of van Gogh and Gauguin.
- Given the statement "Resolved: The United States should not have entered World War I," students will be able to argue persuasively either for or against the proposition.

Note that even though these objectives vary enormously in the type of learning involved and in the ability levels they address, they have several things in common. Mager (1975), whose work began the behavioral objectives movement, described objectives as having three parts: performance, conditions, and criteria. Explanations and examples are given in Table 13.1.

instructional objective
A statement of skills or concepts that students should master after a given period of instruction.

CONNECTIONS
For more on lesson planning and lesson objectives as components of effective instruction, see Chapter 7, page 221.

TABLE 13.1

Parts of a Behavioral Objectives Statement

	PERFORMANCE	CONDITIONS	CRITERION
Definition	An objective always says what a learner is expected to do.	An objective always describes the conditions under which the performance is to occur.	Whenever possible, an objective describes the criterion of acceptable performance.
Question Answered	What should the learner be able to do?	Under what conditions do you want the learner to be able to do it?	How well must it be done?
Example	Correctly use adjectives and adverbs.	Given 10 sentences with missing modifiers, . . .	. . . the student will correctly choose an adjective or adverb in at least 9 of the 10 sentences.

Planning Lesson Objectives

In practice, the skeleton of a behavioral objective is condition–performance–criterion. First, state the conditions under which learning will be assessed, as in the following:

- Given a 10-item test, students will be able to . . .
- In an essay the student will be able to . . .
- Using a compass and protractor, the student will be able to . . .

The second part of an objective is usually an action verb that indicates what students will be able to do; for example (from Gronlund, 1991):

- Write
- Distinguish between
- Identify
- Match

Finally, a behavioral objective generally states a criterion for success, such as the following:

- . . . all 100 multiplication facts in 3 minutes.
- . . . at least five of the nations that sent explorers to the New World.

Sometimes a criterion for success cannot be specified as the number correct. Even so, success should be specified as clearly as possible, as in the following:

- The student will write a two-page essay describing the social situation of women as portrayed in *A Doll's House.*
- The student will think of at least six possible uses for an eggbeater other than beating eggs.

WRITING SPECIFIC OBJECTIVES ● Instructional objectives must be adapted to the subject matter being taught (Hamilton, 1985). When students must learn well-defined skills or information with a single right answer, specific instructional objectives should be written as follows:

- Given 10 problems involving addition of two fractions with like denominators, students will solve at least 9 correctly.
- Given 10 sentences lacking verbs, students will correctly choose verbs that agree in number in at least 8 sentences. Examples: My cat and I _____ birthdays in May. (has, have) Each of us _____ to go to college. (want, wants)
- Given a 4-meter rope attached to the ceiling, students will be able to climb to the top in less than 20 seconds.

Some material, of course, does not lend itself to such specific instructional objectives, and it would be a mistake in such cases to adhere to objectives that have numerical criteria (TenBrink, 1986). For example, the following objective could be written:

- The student will list at least five similarities and five differences between the situation of immigrants to the United States in the early 1900s and that of immigrants today.

However, this objective asks for lists, which might not demonstrate any real understanding of the topic. A less specific but more meaningful objective might be the following:

- In an essay the student will compare and contrast the situation of immigrants to the United States in the early 1900s and that of immigrants today.

This general instructional objective would allow students more flexibility in expressing their understanding of the topic and would promote comprehension rather than memorization of lists of similarities and differences.

WRITING CLEAR OBJECTIVES ● Instructional objectives should be specific enough to be meaningful. For example, an objective concerning immigrants might be written as follows:

- Students will develop a full appreciation for the diversity of peoples who have contributed to the development of U.S. society.

This sounds nice, but what does "full appreciation" mean? Such an objective neither helps the teacher prepare lessons nor helps students understand what is to be taught and how they will be assessed. Mager (1975, p. 20) lists more slippery and less slippery words used to describe instructional objectives:

Words Open to Many Interpretations	Words Open to Fewer Interpretations
to know	to write
to understand	to recite
to appreciate	to identify
to fully appreciate	to sort
to grasp the significance	to solve
to enjoy	to construct

PERFORMING A TASK ANALYSIS ● In planning lessons, it is important to consider the skills required in the tasks to be taught or assigned. For example, a teacher might ask students to use the school library to write a brief report on a topic of interest. The task seems straightforward enough, but consider the separate skills involved:

- Knowing alphabetical order
- Using the card catalog to find books on a subject
- Using a book index to find information on a topic
- Getting the main idea from expository material
- Planning or outlining a brief report
- Writing expository paragraphs
- Knowing language mechanics skills (such as capitalization, punctuation, and usage)

These skills could themselves be broken down into subskills, all the way back to letter recognition and handwriting. The teacher must be aware of the subskills involved in any learning task to be certain that students know what they need to know to succeed. Before assigning the library report task, the teacher would need to be sure that students knew how to use the card catalog and book indexes, among other things, and could comprehend and write expository material. The teacher might teach or review these skills before sending students to the library.

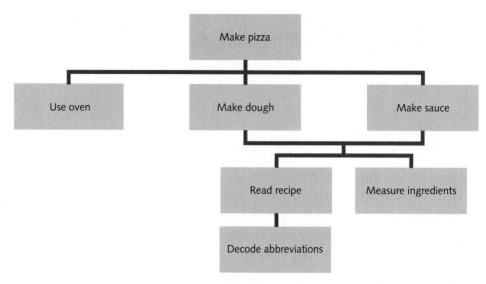

FIGURE 13.1 ● Example of a Task Analysis
Before students can practice the main skill (making pizza), they must be able to use an oven, make dough,
and make sauce. These skills must all be learned before the main skill can be mastered. They are independent of one another and can be learned in any order. Before making dough or making sauce, students must
be able to read a recipe and measure ingredients. Finally, to read a recipe the learner first has to learn how
to decode abbreviations. From Robert F. Mager, *Preparing Instructional Objectives,* p. 100. Copyright © 1984
by Lake Publishing Company, Belmont, CA 94002. Adapted by permission.

Similarly, in teaching a new skill, it is important to consider all the subskills
that go into it. Think of all the separate steps involved in long division, in writing
chemical formulas, or in identifying topic sentences and supporting details. For
that matter, consider the skills that go into making a pizza, as illustrated in
Figure 13.1.

This process of breaking tasks or objectives down into their simpler components is called **task analysis** (see Gagné, 1977; Gardner, 1985). In planning a lesson, a three-step process for task analysis may be used:

1. **Identify prerequisite skills.** What should students already know before you
   teach the lesson? For example, for a lesson on long division, students must
   know their subtraction, multiplication, and division facts and must be able to
   subtract and multiply with renaming.
2. **Identify component skills.** In the actual lesson, what subskills must students
   be taught before they can learn to achieve the larger objective? To return to the
   long-division example, students will need to learn estimating, dividing, multiplying, subtracting, checking, bringing down the next digit, and then repeating
   the process. Each of these steps must be planned for, taught, and assessed during the lesson.
3. **Plan how component skills will be assembled into the final skill.** The final step in task analysis is to assemble the subskills back into the complete process being taught. For example, students may be able to estimate, to divide, and
   to multiply, but this does not necessarily mean that they can do long division.
   The subskills must be integrated into a complete process that students can understand and practice.

task analysis
Breaking tasks down into fundamental subskills.

This student is giving an oral report. How might you use task analysis to plan your lesson objectives? How would you guide your students in assessing one another's performances?

BACKWARD PLANNING ● Just as lesson objectives are more than the sum of specific task objectives, the objectives of a course of study are more than the sum of specific lesson objectives. For this reason it makes sense to start by writing broad objectives for the course as a whole, then objectives for large units, and only then specific behavioral objectives (see Gronlund, 1991). This is known as **backward planning.** For example, Mr. Sullivan would have done well to have identified the objective of his Civil War unit as follows: "Students will understand the major causes, events, and consequences of the Civil War." Then he might have written more detailed objectives relating to causes, events, and consequences. A detailed example of the backward planning process is illustrated in Table 13.2 and described in the next Theory into Practice.

Up to now, this chapter has focused on planning of instruction according to specific instructional objectives. But how does this fit into the larger task of planning an entire course?

backward planning
Planning instruction by first setting long-range goals, then setting unit objectives, and finally planning daily lessons.

Planning Courses, Units, and Lessons

THEORY
into
Practice

In planning a course, it is important for a teacher to set long-term, middle-term, and short-term objectives before starting to teach (Brown, 1988; Shavelson, 1987). Before the students arrive for the first day of class, the teacher needs to have a general plan of what will be covered all year, a more specific plan for what will be in the first unit, and a very specific plan for the content of the first lessons (as shown in Table 13.2).

Table 13.2 implies a backward planning process. First the course objectives are established. Then unit objectives are designated. Finally, specific lessons are planned. The course objectives list all the topics to be covered during the year. The teacher might divide the number of weeks in the school year by the number of major topics to figure what each will require. More or less time could be reserved for any particular topic, as long as adequate time is allowed for the others. A whole semester could be spent on any one of the topics in Table 13.2, but this would be inappropriate in a survey course on life science. The teacher must make hard choices before the first day of class about how much time to spend on each topic to avoid spending too much time on early topics and not having enough time left to do a good job with later ones. Some history teachers always seem to find themselves still

TABLE 13.2

Example of Objectives for a Course in Life Science

Teachers can allocate instructional time for a course by (a) deciding what topics to cover during the year or semester, (b) deciding how many weeks to spend on each topic, (c) choosing units within each topic, (d) deciding how many days to spend on each, and (e) deciding what each day's lesson should be.

COURSE OBJECTIVES (WEEKS ALLOCATED)	UNIT OBJECTIVES (DAYS ALLOCATED)	LESSONS
Scientific Method 3	Observation and measurement 4	Lesson 1 Questions Observations
Characteristics of living things 3	Prediction and control 2	
Cells 3	Data 3	Lesson 2 Checking observation with measurement
Photosynthesis 3	Experiments 3	
Respiration 3	Problem solving 3	Lesson 3 Measurement of length
Human systems 4		
Reproduction 4		
Environment 3		Lesson 4 Measurement of mass Measurement of volume
Adaptation 4		
Relationships 3		
Balance 3		

Source: Objectives adapted from Wong, Bernstein, and Shevick, *Life Science* (2nd ed.), 1978.

on World War I in mid-May and have to compress most of the twentieth century into a couple of weeks!

Table 13.2 shows approximate allocations of weeks to each of the topics to be covered. These are just rough estimates to be modified as time goes on.

UNIT OBJECTIVES AND UNIT TESTS

After course objectives have been laid out, the next task is to establish objectives for the first unit and to estimate the number of class periods to spend on each objective. It is a good idea to write a unit test as part of the planning process. Writing a test in advance helps you to focus on the important issues to be covered. For example, in a 4-week unit on the Civil War you might decide that the most important things students should learn are the causes of the war, a few major points about the military campaigns, the importance of the Emancipation Proclamation, Lincoln's assassination, and the history of the Reconstruction period. These topics would be central to the unit test on the Civil War. Writing this test would put into proper perspective the importance of the various issues that should be covered.

The test that you prepare as part of your course planning may not be exactly the test that you give at the end of the unit. You may decide to change, add, or delete items to reflect the content you actually covered. But this does not diminish the importance of having decided in advance exactly what objectives you wanted to achieve and how you were going to assess them.

Many textbooks provide unit tests and objectives, making your task easier. However, even if you have ready-made objectives and tests, it is still important to review their content and change them as necessary to match what you expect to teach.

If you prepare unit tests from scratch, use the guide to test construction presented later in this chapter. Be sure that the test items cover the various objectives in proportion to their importance to the course as a whole (that is, that the more important objectives are covered by more items), and include items that assess higher-level thinking as well as factual knowledge.

LESSON PLANS AND LESSON ASSESSMENTS

The final step in backward planning is to plan daily lessons. Table 13.2 shows how a given unit objective might be broken down into daily lessons. The next step is to plan the content of each lesson. A lesson plan consists of an objective; a plan for presenting information; a plan for giving students practice (if appropriate); a plan for assessing student understanding; and, if necessary, a plan for reteaching students (or whole classes) if their understanding is inadequate.

Linking Objectives and Assessment

Because instructional objectives are stated in terms of how they will be measured, it is clear that objectives are closely linked to **assessment.** An assessment is any measure of the degree to which students have learned the objectives set out for them. Most assessments in schools are tests or quizzes, or informal verbal assessments such as questions in class. However, students can also show their learning by writing an essay, painting a picture, doing a car tune-up, or baking a pineapple upside-down cake.

One critical principle of assessment is that assessments and objectives must be clearly linked. Students learn some proportion of what they are taught; the greater the overlap between what was taught and what is tested, the better students will score on the test and the more accurately any need for additional instruction can be determined (Cooley & Leinhardt, 1980). Teaching should be closely linked to instructional objectives, and both should clearly relate to assessment. If any objective is worth teaching, it is worth testing, and vice versa. This idea was illustrated by Mager as follows:

> During class periods of a seventh grade algebra course, a teacher provided a good deal of skillful guidance in the solution of simple equations. . . . When it came time for an examination, however, the test items consisted mainly of word problems, and the students did rather poorly. The teacher's justification for this "sleight of test" was that the students didn't "really understand" algebra if they could not solve word problems. Perhaps the teacher was right. But the skill of solving equations is considerably different from the skill of solving word problems; if he wanted his students to learn how to solve word problems, he should have taught them how to do so. (Mager, 1975, p. 82)

Mager's algebra teacher really had one objective in mind (solving word problems) but taught according to another (solving equations). If he had coordinated his objectives, his teaching, and his assessment, he and his students would have been a lot happier, and the students would have had a much better opportunity to learn to solve algebra word problems.

assessment
A measure of the degree to which instructional objectives have been attained.

One way to specify objectives for a course is to actually prepare test questions before the course begins (see Gronlund, 1991). This allows the teacher to write general **teaching objectives** (clear statements of what students are expected to learn through instruction) and then to clarify them with very specific **learning objectives** (specific behaviors students are expected to exhibit at the end of a series of lessons), as in the following examples:

Teaching Objective	Specific Learning Objective (Test Questions)
a. Ability to subtract three-digit numbers renaming once or twice	**a1.** $\begin{array}{r} 237 \\ -184 \end{array}$ **a2.** $\begin{array}{r} 412 \\ -298 \end{array}$ **a3.** $\begin{array}{r} 596 \\ -448 \end{array}$
b. Understanding of use of language to set mood in Edgar Allan Poe's "The Raven"	**b1.** How does Poe reinforce the mood of "The Raven" after setting it in the first stanza?
c. Ability to identify the chemical formulas for common substances	Write the chemical formulas for the following: **c1.** Water _____ **c2.** Carbon dioxide _____ **c3.** Coal _____ **c4.** Table salt _____

Using Taxonomies of Instructional Objectives

CONNECTIONS

For information on thinking skills and critical thinking, see Chapter 8, page 280.

In writing objectives and assessments, it is important to consider different skills and different levels of understanding. For example, in a science lesson on insects for second-graders, you might want to impart both information (the names of various insects) and an attitude (the importance of insects to the ecosystem). In other subjects you might try to convey facts and concepts that differ by type. For example, in teaching a lesson on topic sentences in reading, you might have students first repeat a definition of *topic sentence,* then identify topic sentences in paragraphs, and finally write their own topic sentences for original paragraphs. Each of these activities demonstrates a different kind of understanding of the concept "topic sentence," and this concept has not been adequately taught if students can do only one of these activities. These various lesson goals can be classified by type and degree of complexity. A taxonomy, or system of classification, helps a teacher to categorize instructional activities.

BLOOM'S TAXONOMY ● In 1956, Benjamin Bloom and some fellow researchers published a **taxonomy of educational objectives** that has been extremely influential in the research and practice of education ever since. Bloom and his colleagues categorized objectives from simple to complex or from factual to conceptual. The key elements of what is commonly called Bloom's taxonomy (Anderson & Sosniak, 1994; Bloom, Englehart, Furst, Hill, & Krathwohl, 1956; Kreitzer & Madaus, 1994) for the cognitive domain are (from simple to complex):

teaching objectives
Clear statements of what students are intended to learn through instruction.

learning objectives
Specific behaviors that students are expected to exhibit at the end of a series of lessons.

taxonomy of educational objectives
Bloom's ordering of objectives from simple learning tasks to more complex ones.

1. **Knowledge (recalling information):** The lowest level of objectives in Bloom's hierarchy, knowledge refers to objectives such as memorizing math facts or formulas, scientific principles, or verb conjugations.

2. **Comprehension (translating, interpreting, or extrapolating information):** Comprehension objectives require that students show an understanding of information as well as the ability to use it. Examples are interpreting the meaning

of a diagram, graph, or parable; inferring the principle underlying a science experiment; and predicting what might happen next in a story.

3. Application (using principles or abstractions to solve novel or real-life problems): Application objectives require students to use knowledge or principles to solve practical problems. Examples include using geometric principles to figure out how many gallons of water to put into a swimming pool of given dimensions and using knowledge of the relationship between temperature and pressure to explain why a balloon is larger on a hot day than on a cold day.

4. Analysis (breaking down complex information or ideas into simpler parts to understand how the parts relate or are organized): Analysis objectives involve having students see the underlying structure of complex information or ideas. Examples of analysis objectives are contrasting schooling in the United States with education in Japan, understanding how the functions of the carburetor and distributor are related in an automobile engine, and identifying the main idea of a short story.

5. Synthesis (creation of something that did not exist before): Synthesis objectives involve using skills to create completely new products. Examples include writing a composition, deriving a mathematical rule, designing a science experiment to solve a problem, and making up a new sentence in a foreign language.

6. Evaluation (judging something against a given standard): Evaluation objectives require making value judgments against some criterion or standard. For example, students might be asked to compare the strengths and weaknesses of two home computers in terms of flexibility, power, and available software.

Because Bloom's taxonomy is organized from simple to complex, some people interpret it as a ranking of objectives from trivial (knowledge) to important (synthesis, evaluation). However, this is not the intent of the taxonomy. Different levels of objectives are appropriate for different purposes and for students at different stages of development.

The primary importance of Bloom's taxonomy is in its reminder that we want students to have many levels of skills. All too often, teachers focus on measurable knowledge and comprehension objectives and forget that students cannot be considered proficient in many skills until they can apply or synthesize those skills. On the other side of the coin, some teachers fail to make certain that students are well rooted in the basics before heading off into higher-order objectives.

USING A BEHAVIOR CONTENT MATRIX ● One way to be sure that your objectives cover many levels is to write a **behavior content matrix** (Gage & Berliner, 1984). This is simply a chart that shows how a particular concept or skill will be taught and assessed at different cognitive levels. Examples of objectives in a behavior content matrix appear in Table 13.3. Note that for each topic, objectives are listed for some but not all levels of Bloom's taxonomy. Some topics do not lend themselves to some levels of the taxonomy, and there is no reason that every level should be covered for every topic. However, using a behavior content matrix in setting objectives forces you to consider objectives above the knowledge and comprehension levels.

AFFECTIVE OBJECTIVES ● Learning facts and skills is not the only important goal of instruction. Sometimes the feelings that students have about a subject or about their own skills are at least as important as how much information they learn.

behavior content matrix
A chart that classifies lesson objectives according to cognitive level.

TABLE 13.3

Examples of Objectives in a Behavior Content Matrix

A behavior content matrix can remind teachers to develop instructional objectives that address skills at various cognitive levels.

TYPE OF OBJECTIVE	EXAMPLE 1: THE AREA OF A CIRCLE	EXAMPLE 2: MAIN IDEA OF A STORY	EXAMPLE 3: THE COLONIZATION OF AFRICA
Knowledge	Give the formula for area of a circle.	Define *main idea*.	Make a time line showing how Europeans divided Africa into colonies.
Comprehension		Give examples of ways to find the main idea of a story.	Interpret a map of Africa showing its colonization by European nations.
Application	Apply the formula for area of a circle to real-life problems.		
Analysis		Identify the main idea of a story.	Contrast the goals and methods used in colonizing Africa by the different European nations.
Synthesis	Use knowledge about the areas of circles and volumes of cubes to derive a formula for the volume of a cylinder.	Write a new story based on the main idea of the story read.	Write an essay on the European colonization of Africa from the perspective of a Bantu chief.
Evaluation		Evaluate the story.	

Instructional goals related to attitudes and values are called **affective objectives.** Many people would argue that a principal purpose of a U.S. history or civics course is to promote values of patriotism and civic responsibility, and one purpose of any mathematics course is to give students confidence in their ability to use mathematics. In planning instruction, it is important to consider affective as well as cognitive objectives. Love of learning, confidence in learning, and development of prosocial, cooperative attitudes are among the most important objectives teachers should have for their students.

Research on Instructional Objectives

Three principal reasons are given for writing instructional objectives. One is that this exercise helps to organize the teacher's planning. As Mager (1975) puts it, if you're not sure where you're going, you're liable to end up someplace else and not even know it. Another is that establishing instructional objectives helps to guide evaluation. Finally, it is hypothesized that development of instructional objectives improves student achievement.

Although it would be a mistake to overplan or to adhere rigidly to an inflexible plan (see Shavelson, 1987), most experienced teachers create, use, and value objectives and assessments that are planned in advance (Brown, 1988; Clark & Yinger, 1986).

affective objectives
Objectives that have to do with student attitudes and values.

It is important to make sure that instructional objectives that are communicated to students are broad enough to encompass everything the lesson or course is supposed to teach. There is some danger that giving students too narrow a set of objectives may focus them on some information to the exclusion of other facts and concepts (Klauer, 1984).

Perhaps the most convincing support for the establishment of clear instructional objectives is indirect. Cooley and Leinhardt (1980) found that the strongest single factor predicting student reading and math scores was the degree to which students were actually taught the skills that were tested. This implies that instruction is effective to the degree to which objectives, teaching, and assessment are coordinated with one another. Specification of clear instructional objectives is the first step in ensuring that classroom instruction is directed toward giving students critical skills, those that are important enough to test.

SELF-CHECK

Practice writing instructional objectives, perform a task analysis, and use backward planning to create a unit of study. Develop a behavior content matrix with one cognitive and one affective objective.

WHY IS EVALUATION IMPORTANT?

Evaluation refers to all the means used in schools to formally measure student performance. These include quizzes and tests, written evaluations, and grades. Student evaluation usually focuses on academic achievement, but many schools also evaluate behaviors and attitudes. Many elementary schools provide descriptions of students' behavior (such as "follows directions," "listens attentively," "works with others," "uses time wisely"). In upper elementary, middle, and high school the prevalence of behavior reports diminishes successively, but even many high schools rate students on such criteria as "works up to ability," "is prepared," and "is responsible" (Chansky, 1975).

Why do we use tests and grades? We use them because, one way or another, we must periodically check students' learning. Tests and grades tell teachers, students, and parents how students are doing in school. Teachers can use tests to determine whether their instruction was effective and to find out which students need additional help. Students can use tests to find out whether their studying strategies are paying off. Parents need grades to learn how their children are doing in school; grades serve as the one consistent form of communication between school and home. Schools sometimes need grades and tests to make student placements. States and school districts need tests to evaluate schools and, in some cases, teachers. Ultimately, colleges use grades and standardized test scores to decide whom to admit. We must therefore evaluate student learning; few would argue otherwise. Research on the use of tests finds that students learn more in courses that use tests than in those that do not (Dempster, 1991).

Student evaluations serve six primary purposes:

1. Feedback to students
2. Feedback to teachers
3. Information to parents
4. Information for selection and certification

evaluation
Measurement of student performance in academic and, sometimes, other areas; used to determine appropriate teaching strategies.

5. Information for accountability

6. Incentives to increase student effort

CONNECTIONS

For more on feedback as a component of effective teaching, see Chapter 7, page 233.

Evaluation As Feedback

Imagine that a store owner tried several strategies to increase business—first advertising in the newspaper, then sending fliers to homes near the store, and finally holding a sale. However, suppose that after trying each strategy, the store owner failed to record and compare the store's revenue. Without taking stock this way, the owner would learn little about the effectiveness of any of the strategies and might well be wasting time and money. The same is true of teachers and students. They need to know as soon as possible whether their investments of time and energy in a given activity are paying off by increasing learning.

FEEDBACK FOR STUDENTS ● Like the store owner, students need to know the results of their efforts (Bangert-Drowns, Kulik, Kulik, & Morgan, 1991; Munk & Bursuck, 1998). Regular evaluation gives them feedback on their strengths and weaknesses. For example, suppose a teacher had students write compositions and then gave back written evaluations. Some students might find out that they needed to work more on content, others on the use of modifiers, still others on language mechanics. This information would help students to improve their writing much more than would a grade with no explanation.

To be useful as feedback, evaluations should be as specific as possible. For example, Cross and Cross (1980–1981) found that students who received written feedback in addition to letter grades were more likely than other students to believe that their efforts, rather than luck or other external factors, determined their success in school.

FEEDBACK TO TEACHERS ● One of the most important (and often overlooked) functions of evaluating student learning is to provide feedback to teachers on the effectiveness of their instruction. Teachers cannot expect to be optimally effective if they do not know whether students have grasped the main points of their lessons. Asking questions in class and observing students as they work gives the teacher some idea of how well students have learned; but in many subjects brief, frequent quizzes are necessary to provide more detailed indications of students' progress.

Evaluation As Information

A report card is called a report card because it reports information on student progress. This reporting function of evaluation is important for several reasons.

INFORMATION TO PARENTS ● First, routine school evaluations of many kinds (test scores, stars, and certificates as well as report card grades) keep parents informed about their children's schoolwork. For example, if a student's grades are dropping, the parents may know why and may be able to help the student get back on track. Second, grades and other evaluations set up informal home-based reinforcement systems. Recall from Chapter 11 that many studies have found that reporting regularly to parents when students do good work and asking parents to reinforce good reports improves student behavior and achievement (Barth, 1979). Without much prompting, most parents naturally reinforce their children for bringing home good grades, thereby making grades important and effective as incentives (Natriello & Dornbusch, 1984).

INFORMATION FOR SELECTION ● Some sociologists see the sorting of students into societal roles as a primary purpose of schools: If schools do not actually determine who will be a butcher, a baker, or a candlestick maker, they do substantially influence who will be a laborer, a skilled worker, a white-collar worker, or a professional. This sorting function takes place gradually over years of schooling. In the early grades, students are sorted into reading groups and, in many cases, into tracks that may remain stable over many years (Slavin, 1987c, 1990). Tracking becomes more widespread and systematic by junior high or middle school, when students begin to be selected into different courses (McPartland, Coldiron, & Braddock, 1987). For example, some ninth-graders are allowed to take Algebra I while others take prealgebra or general mathematics. In high school, students are often steered toward college preparatory, general, or vocational tracks or toward advanced, basic, or remedial levels of particular courses; and of course a major sorting takes place when students are accepted into various colleges and training programs. Throughout the school years, some students are selected into special-education or gifted programs or into other special programs with limited enrollments.

Closely related to selection is certification, a use of tests to qualify students for promotion or for access to various occupations. For example, many states and local districts have minimum competency tests that students must pass to advance from grade to grade or to graduate from high school. Bar exams for lawyers, board examinations for medical students, and tests for teachers such as the National Teachers' Examination are examples of certification tests that control access to professions.

INFORMATION FOR ACCOUNTABILITY ● Often, evaluations of students serve as data for the evaluation of teachers, schools, districts, or even states. Most states have statewide testing programs that allow the states to rank every school in terms of student performance. Even in those that do not, school districts often use these tests for similar purposes. These test scores are also often used in evaluations of principals, teachers, and superintendents. Consequently, these tests are taken very seriously.

Evaluation As Incentive

One important use of evaluations is to motivate students to give their best efforts. In essence, high grades, stars, and prizes are given as rewards for good work. Students value grades and prizes primarily because their parents value them. Some high school students also value grades because they are important for getting into selective colleges.

Natriello and Dornbusch (1984) and Natriello (1989) have suggested criteria that must be satisfied if evaluations are to increase student effort (see also Crooks, 1988). An adaptation of their criteria follows.

1. Important evaluations: Evaluations are effective to the degree that they are important to students. For example, grades will be less effective as incentives for students whose parents pay little attention to their grades. They will be more effective for students who are planning to go to competitive colleges (which require

CONNECTIONS
For information on using grades as incentives, see Chapter 10, page 355.

high grades for admission). Natriello and Dornbusch (1984) state that evaluations will be important to students to the degree that they are seen as central to the students' attainment of valued objectives and influential in attaining those objectives.

2. **Soundly based evaluations:** Evaluations must be closely related to a student's actual performance. Students must believe that evaluations are fair, objective measures of their performance. To the degree that students believe that they can outfox the system and get away with shoddy efforts or that the system is rigged against them, evaluations will have little impact on the students' efforts. Students should have every opportunity to show what they really know on tests. Reducing test anxiety, a serious problem for many students (Hembree, 1988; Hill & Wigfield, 1984; Zeidner, 1995; Zohar, 1998), is one way to increase the soundness of evaluations. Teachers can do this by giving plenty of time for tests, by reducing pressure, and by closely linking tests to course content.

3. **Consistent standards:** Evaluations will be effective to the degree that students perceive them to be equal for all students. For example, if students believe that some of their classmates are evaluated more leniently than others, this will reduce the effectiveness of the evaluation system.

4. **Clear criteria:** The criteria for success must be clear to students; in other words, students should know precisely what they must do to obtain a good grade or other positive evaluation (Munk & Bursuck, 1998).

5. **Reliable interpretations of evaluations:** Appropriate interpretations must be made clear. Students often interpret evaluations (and their own efforts) in light of social contexts. For example, some students may believe that doing any homework at all shows a high level of effort when their classmates are doing none, or that a C is a good grade when many of their classmates are failing.

6. **Frequent evaluations:** There is evidence that the more frequently evaluations take place, the more students generally achieve (Crooks, 1988; Kulik & Kulik, 1988). Frequent, brief quizzes are better than infrequent, long tests. Quizzes require that students pay attention all the time rather than cram for the occasional exam; they give students more timely feedback; and they provide recognition for hard work closer in time to when the work was done.

7. **Challenging evaluations:** Evaluations should be challenging for all students but impossible for none. This can be done by evaluating students according to their improvement over their own past performance, a strategy that has been found to increase their achievement. Evaluation systems should be set up to encourage students always to be reaching for success, just as runners set goals for finishing a mile a little bit faster than their previous best time.

CONNECTIONS
For more on evaluating students by their improvement over their own past performance, see Chapter 10, page 355.

SELF-CHECK

List the six primary purposes for evaluating student learning. Give an example of each purpose.

HOW IS STUDENT LEARNING EVALUATED?

Evaluation strategies that are effective for any one purpose may be ineffective for other purposes. To understand how evaluations can be used most effectively in classroom instruction, it is important to know the differences between formative and summative evaluation and between norm-referenced and criterion-referenced evaluation.

Formative and Summative Evaluations

The distinction between formative and summative evaluations was explained in the discussion of mastery learning in Chapter 9, but this distinction also applies to a broader range of evaluation issues. Essentially, a *formative evaluation* asks, "How are you doing?" A *summative evaluation* asks, "How did you do?" Formative, or diagnostic, tests are given to discover strengths and weaknesses in learning and to make midcourse corrections in pace or content of instruction. Formative evaluation is useful to the degree that it is informative, closely tied to the curriculum being taught, timely, and frequent. For example, frequent quizzes that are given and scored immediately after specific lessons might serve as formative evaluations, providing feedback to help both teachers and students improve students' learning.

In contrast, summative evaluation refers to final tests of student knowledge. Summative evaluation may or may not be frequent, but it must be reliable and (in general) should allow for comparisons among students. Summative evaluations should also be closely tied to formative evaluations and to course objectives.

Norm-Referenced, Criterion-Referenced, and Authentic Evaluations

Norm-referenced evaluations focus on comparisons of a student's scores with those of other students. Within a classroom, grades usually give us an idea of how a student has performed in comparison with classmates. A student may also have a grade-level or school rank; and in standardized testing, student scores may be compared with those of a nationally representative norm group.

Criterion-referenced evaluations focus on assessing students' mastery of specific skills, regardless of how other students did on the same skills. Criterion-referenced evaluations are closely tied to the curriculum being taught and to the lesson or course objectives. Table 13.4 compares the principal features and purposes of criterion-referenced and norm-referenced testing (see also Popham, 1995; Shepard, 1989a).

Formative evaluation is almost always criterion-referenced. In formative testing, we want to know, for example, who is having trouble with Newton's laws of thermodynamics, not which student is 1st, 15th, or 30th in the class in physics knowledge. Summative testing, in contrast, may be either criterion-referenced or norm-referenced. Even if it is criterion-referenced, however, we usually want to know on a summative test how each student did in comparison with other students. In recent years there has been a movement toward innovative forms of testing, called **authentic assessment,** that focus more on what students can actually do (Herman, Aschbacher, & Winters, 1992; Newmann, Secada, & Wehlage, 1995; Tittle, 1991; Wolf, Bixby, Glenn, & Gardner, 1991). Authentic assessments, including student portfolios and performance assessments, are discussed later in this chapter.

Matching Evaluation Strategies with Goals

Considering all the factors discussed up to this point, what is the best strategy for evaluating students? The first answer is that there is no one best strategy. The best means of accomplishing any one objective of evaluation may be inappropriate for

CONNECTIONS
For the discussion of mastery learning, see Chapter 9, page 301.

CONNECTIONS
For more on standardized testing, see Chapter 14.

norm-referenced evaluations
Assessments that compare the performance of one student against the performance of others.

criterion-referenced evaluations
Assessments that rate how thoroughly students have mastered specific skills or areas of knowledge.

authentic assessment
Measurement of important abilities using procedures that simulate the application of these abilities to real-life situations.

TABLE 13.4

Comparison of Two Approaches to Achievement Testing

Norm-referenced tests and criterion-referenced tests serve different purposes and have different features.

FEATURE	NORM-REFERENCED TESTING	CRITERION-REFERENCED TESTING
Principal use	Survey testing	Mastery testing
Major emphasis	Measures individual differences in achievement	Describes tasks students can perform
Interpretation of results	Compares performance to that of other individuals	Compares performance to a clearly specified achievement domain
Content coverage	Typically covers a broad area of achievement	Typically focuses on a limited set of learning tasks
Nature of test plan	Table of specifications is commonly used	Detailed domain specifications are favored
Item selection procedures	Items selected to provide maximum discrimination among individuals (to obtain high score variability); easy items typically eliminated from the test	Includes all items needed to adequately describe performance; no attempt is made to alter item difficulty or to eliminate easy items to increase score variability
Performance standards	Level of performance determined by *relative* position in some known group (e.g., student ranks fifth in a group of 20)	Level of performance commonly determined by *absolute* standards (e.g., student demonstrates mastery by defining 90 percent of the technical terms)

Source: Adapted from Norman E. Gronlund, *How to Make Achievement Tests and Assessments* (5th ed.). Copyright © 1993 by Allyn & Bacon. Reprinted by permission.

other objectives. Therefore, teachers must choose different types of evaluation for different purposes. At a minimum, two types of evaluation should be used: one directed at providing incentive and feedback and the other directed at ranking individual students relative to the larger group.

EVALUATION FOR INCENTIVE AND FEEDBACK ● Traditional grades are often inadequate as incentives to encourage students to give their best efforts and as feedback to teachers and students. The principal problem is that grades are given too infrequently, are too far removed in time from student performance, and are poorly tied to specific student behaviors. Recall from Chapter 5 that the effectiveness of reinforcers and of feedback diminishes rapidly if there is much delay between behavior and consequences. By the same token, research has found that achievement is higher in classrooms where students receive immediate feedback on their quizzes than in classrooms where feedback is delayed (Crooks, 1988; Kulik & Kulik, 1988).

Another reason that grades are less than ideal as incentives is that they are usually based on comparative standards. In effect, it is relatively easy for high-ability students to achieve A's and B's but very difficult for low achievers to do so. As a result, some high achievers do less work than they are capable of doing, and some low achievers give up. As was noted in Chapter 10, a reward that is too easy or too difficult to attain, or that is felt to be a result of ability rather than of effort, is a poor motivator (Atkinson & Birch, 1978; Weiner, 1989).

CONNECTIONS

Rewards and motivation are discussed in Chapter 5, page 146.

CONNECTIONS

For more on what rewards make poor motivators, see Chapter 10, page 349.

For these reasons, traditional grades should be supplemented by evaluations that are better designed for incentive and feedback. For example, teachers might give daily quizzes of 5 or 10 items that are scored in class immediately after completion, or they might have students write daily "mini-essays" on a topic the class is studying. These give both students and teachers the information they need to adjust their teaching and learning strategies and to rectify any deficiencies revealed by the evaluations. If teachers make quiz results important by having them count toward course grades or by giving students with perfect papers special recognition or certificates, then quiz scores also serve as effective incentives, rewarding effective studying behavior soon after it occurs. Use of the Individual Learning Expectations (ILE) strategy by itself or as part of Student Teams–Achievement Divisions (STAD) adds the element of measuring students against their own past achievement. The emphasis is on improvement through increased effort rather than on high scores attained largely through ability or prior knowledge.

EVALUATION FOR GROUP COMPARISON ● There are times when teachers do need to know how well students are doing in comparison to others. This information is important to give parents and students themselves a realistic picture of student performance. For example, students who have outstanding skills in science ought to know that they are exceptional, not only in the context of their class or school, but also in a broader state or national context. In general, students need to form accurate perceptions of their strengths and weaknesses to guide their decisions about their futures.

Comparative evaluations are traditionally provided by grades and by standardized tests. Unlike incentive/feedback evaluations, comparative evaluations need not be conducted frequently. Rather, the emphasis in comparative evaluations must be on fair, unbiased, reliable assessment of student performance. Comparative evaluations should assess what students can do and nothing else. Student grades should be based primarily on demonstrated knowledge of the course content, not on politeness, good behavior, neatness, or punctuality; because the purpose of a grade is to give an accurate assessment of student performance, not to reward or punish students for their behavior. However, grades are imperfect as comparative evaluators, because many teachers consider subjective factors when assigning grades. One solution in secondary schools is for teachers in a given department to get together to write departmental exams for each course. For example, a high school science department might decide on common objectives for all chemistry classes and then make up common unit tests or final tests. This would ensure that students in all classes were evaluated according to the same criteria.

Comparative evaluations and other summative assessments of student performance must be firmly based on the objectives established at the beginning of the course and must be consistent with the formative incentive/feedback evaluations. No teacher wants a situation in which students do well on week-to-week assessments but then fail the summative evaluations because there is a lack of correspondence between the two forms of evaluation. For example, if the summative test uses essay questions to assess higher-order skills, then similar essay questions should be used all along as formative tests.

> **CONNECTIONS**
> For more on the Individual Learning Expectations (ILE) strategy, see Chapter 10, page 355.

> **CONNECTIONS**
> For more on Student Teams–Achievement Divisions, see Chapter 8, page 269.

> **CONNECTIONS**
> For more on grades and standardized tests, see Chapter 14.

SELF-CHECK

Construct a four-square matrix comparing formative and summative testing on one axis and norm-referenced and criterion-referenced testing on the other axis. In each square, write a brief description of optimal conditions for using each combination.

CASE TO CONSIDER

Making the Grade

Written by Gordon E. Greenwood, University of Florida

Rachel Greenberg is a beginning social studies teacher in a large urban high school. In preparation for a social studies department meeting, she talks with Toni Sue Garrick in the teachers' lounge.

Rachel: Toni, do you have a minute to tell me about the school's grading policy?

Toni Sue: Sure. Where do you want to begin?

Rachel: Well, we do have a policy, I assume?

Toni Sue: I guess you could say so. If you look on the report cards, you'll notice that 94 to 100 is an A, 88 to 94 is a B, and so forth. Anything below 70 is failing.

Rachel: What if no one gets in the 94 to 100 range?

Toni Sue: Then either you don't give any A's, if you think the test was fair, or you adjust the scale by adding on points to every student's score. There's no rigid policy, but if you give too many A's and B's, that could become a problem.

Rachel: How many are too many?

Toni Sue: Well, certainly there should be more B's than A's and more C's than either A's or B's. You try to approximate the normal bell-shaped curve in a general, flexible way. It all depends on the students' ability level. In an advanced placement history course, I seldom give D's or F's. In the sophomore-level world history course, however, the number of D's and F's fairly closely approximates the number of A's and B's.

Rachel: What if a teacher puts a mastery learning plan into effect, and it works so well that everyone achieves at practically 100 percent? What happens to the bell-shaped curve then?

Toni Sue: Well, that happened a few years back. One young teacher did give almost all A's and B's. It came to light when the students began comparing grades at report card time. Some other teachers and parents were quite upset. The administration smoothed things over with the parents and other teachers. As for the young teacher, he's at another school now. I hear he's doing a fine job.

Rachel: Oh. Well, another question: In my history classes I plan to emphasize individual and small-group projects. I am interested in cooperative learning approaches with mixed-ability groups.

Toni Sue: Group projects are nice, but grading them can be very subjective and hard to defend. I'd go easy on that.

Rachel: So you'd recommend objective tests, not essay tests?

Toni Sue: Right. Good objective tests are hard to write, but they're worth it because students and parents have a hard time arguing grading bias, favoritism, or subjectivity when you give objective tests. Also, I figure that objective tests help prepare the kids to succeed on standardized achievement tests.

Rachel: I see what you mean, but I try to keep outcomes in mind—overall objectives like verbal information, intellectual skills, cognitive strategies, and so on. But teaching for those outcomes may not always leave time for teaching to objective tests. What if some of my students get D's and F's? I'm a little afraid of some of the parents.

Toni Sue: I think communication is the key. If the students—and their parents—think you're fair, you'll have few problems. Spell out very clearly what you expect and what the grading procedures are. After all, our society was founded on competition. Our kids have to learn how to deal with failure as well as success. And parents should understand that too.

Rachel: Thanks, Toni Sue! I don't know if I altogether agree with you about the value of failure, but I really appreciate your support.

PROBLEM SOLVING

1. Do you agree with the advice Rachel received? Why or why not? For the grade level you plan to teach, what departmentwide evaluation strategy would you propose for your subject area?

2. If you were on a committee to evaluate and revise this school's evaluation and grading policies and procedures, what would you recommend and why?

3. Extend the dialogue to express an evaluation approach that would work best for the way Rachel wants to teach.

HOW ARE TESTS CONSTRUCTED?

Once you know the concept domains to be assessed in a test of student learning, it is time to write test items. From 5 to 15 percent of all class time is used in written testing (Dorr-Bremme & Herman, 1986; Haertel, 1986). Writing good achievement tests is therefore a critical skill for effective teaching. This section presents some basic principles of achievement testing and practical tools for test construction. Achievement testing is taken up again in Chapter 14 in relation to standardized tests.

Principles of Achievement Testing

Gronlund (1991) listed six principles to keep in mind in preparing achievement tests:

1. Achievement tests should measure clearly defined learning objectives that are in harmony with instructional objectives. Perhaps the most important principle of achievement testing is that the tests should correspond with the course objectives and with the instruction that is actually provided (Fuchs, Fuchs, Hamlett, & Stecker, 1991; Linn, 1983). An achievement test should never be a surprise for students; rather, it should assess the students' grasp of the most important concepts or skills the lesson or course is supposed to teach. Further, assessments should tap the true objectives of the course, not easy-to-measure substitutes. For example, a course on twentieth-century art should probably use a test in which students are asked to discuss or to compare artworks, not to match artists with their paintings (see Frederiksen, 1984).

2. Achievement tests should measure a representative sample of the learning tasks included in the instruction. With rare exceptions (such as multiplication facts), achievement tests do not assess every skill or fact students are supposed to have learned. Rather, they sample from among all the learning objectives. If students do not know in advance what questions will be on a test, then they must study the entire course content to do well. However, the test items must be representative of all the objectives and content that were covered. For example, if an English literature course spent 8 weeks on Shakespeare and 2 weeks on other Elizabethan authors, the test should have about 4 times as many items relating to Shakespeare as to the others. Items that are chosen to represent a particular objective must be central to that objective. There is no place in achievement testing for tricky or obscure questions. For example, a unit test on the American Revolution should ask questions relating to the causes, principal events, and outcomes of that struggle, not who rowed George Washington across the Delaware. (Answer: John Glover and his Marblehead Marines.)

3. Achievement tests should include the types of test items that are most appropriate for measuring the desired learning outcomes. Items on achievement tests should correspond as closely as possible to the ultimate instructional objectives. For example, in mathematics problem solving, our goal is to enable students to solve problems like the ones they will encounter outside of school. Multiple-choice items may be inappropriate for this kind of exam, because in real life we are rarely presented with four options as possible solutions to a problem.

4. Achievement tests should fit the particular uses that will be made of the results. Each type of achievement test has its own requirements. For example, a test that is used for diagnosis would focus on particular skills with which students might need help. A diagnostic test of elementary arithmetic might contain items on subtraction involving zeros in the minuend (e.g., 307 minus 127), a skill with which many students have trouble. In contrast, a test that is used to predict future performance might assess a student's general abilities and breadth of knowledge. Formative tests should be very closely tied to material that has recently been presented, whereas summative tests should survey broader areas of knowledge or skills.

CONNECTIONS

For more on achievement testing in relation to standardized tests, see Chapter 14, page 507.

CONNECTIONS

For more on the characteristics and uses of standardized achievement tests, see Chapter 14, page 499.

CONNECTIONS

For more on the reliability of achievement tests, see Chapter 14, page 521.

5. Achievement tests should be as reliable as possible and should be interpreted with caution. A test is *reliable* to the degree that students who were tested a second time would fall in the same rank order. In general, writers of achievement tests increase reliability by using relatively large numbers of items and by using few items that almost all students get right or that almost all students miss (Hopkins, 1998). The use of clearly written items that focus directly on the objectives that are actually taught also enhances test reliability. Still, no matter how rigorously reliability is built into a test, there will always be some error of measurement. Students have good and bad days or may be lucky or unlucky guessers. Some students are test-wise and usually test well; others are text-anxious and test far below their actual knowledge or potential. Therefore no single test score should be viewed with excessive confidence. Any test score is only an approximation of a student's true knowledge or skills and should be interpreted as such.

6. Achievement tests should improve learning. Achievement tests of all kinds, particularly formative tests, provide important information on students' learning progress. Achievement testing should be seen as part of the instructional process and should be used to improve instruction and guide student learning (Foos & Fisher, 1988). This means that achievement test results should be clearly communicated to students soon after the test is taken; in the case of formative testing, students should be given the results immediately. Teachers should use the results of formative and summative tests to guide instruction, to locate strong and weak points in students' understandings, and to set an appropriate pace of instruction. Including review items on each test (and telling students that you will do so) provides distributed practice of course content, an important aid in learning and retaining knowledge (Dempster, 1991).

Using a Table of Specifications

Gronlund's (1991) first principle—that achievement tests should measure well-specified objectives—is an important guide to the content of any achievement test. The first step in the test development process is to decide which concept domains the test will measure and how many test items will be allocated to each concept. Gronlund (1991) and Bloom, Hastings, and Madaus (1971) suggest that for each instructional unit teachers make up a **table of specifications** listing the various objectives taught and different levels of understanding to be assessed. The levels of understanding may correspond to Bloom's taxonomy of educational objectives (Bloom et al., 1956). Bloom and colleagues (1971) suggest classifying test items for each objective according to six categories, as shown in Table 13.5, a table of specifications for a chemistry unit.

The table of specifications varies for each type of course and is nearly identical to behavior content matrixes, discussed earlier in this chapter. This is as it should be; a behavior content matrix is used to lay out objectives for a course, and the table of specifications tests those objectives.

Once you have written items corresponding to your table of specifications, look over the test in its entirety and evaluate it against the following standards:

1. Do the items emphasize the same things you emphasized in day-to-day instruction? (Recall how Mr. Sullivan, in the chapter-opening vignette, ignored this commonsense rule.)

2. Has an important area of content or any objective been overlooked or underemphasized?

table of specifications

A list of instructional objectives and expected levels of understanding that guides test development.

TABLE 13.5

Table of Specifications for a Chemistry Unit

This table of specifications classifies test items (circled numbers) and objectives according to six categories ranging from knowledge of terms to ability to apply knowledge.

A. KNOWLEDGE OF TERMS	B. KNOWLEDGE OF FACTS	C. KNOWLEDGE OF RULES AND PRINCIPLES	D. SKILL IN USING PROCESSES AND PROCEDURES	E. ABILITY TO MAKE TRANSLATIONS	F. ABILITY TO MAKE APPLICATIONS
Atom ①		Boyle's law ⑫			
Molecule ②		Properties of a gas ⑬		Substance into diagram ㉒	
Element ③		Atomic theory ⑯			Writing and solving equations to fit experimental situations
Compound ④	Diatomic gases ⑪	Chemical formula ⑲		Compound into formula ㉑	㉘
Diatomic ⑤					㉓
Chemical formula ⑥		Avogadro's hypothesis ⑭			㉔
Avogadro's number ⑦		Gay-Lussac's law ⑮			㉕
Mole ⑧		Grams to moles ⑱			㉖
Atomic weight ⑨		Molecular weight ⑰	Molecular weight ⑳		㉗
Molecular weight ⑩					㉙

Source: From B. S. Bloom, J. T. Hastings, and G. F. Madaus, *Handbook on Formative and Summative Evaluation of Student Learning,* p. 121. Copyright 1971 by McGraw-Hill, Inc. Reproduced with permission of The McGraw-Hill Companies.

3. Does the test cover all levels of instructional objectives included in the lessons?
4. Does the language of the items correspond to the language and reading level you used in the lessons?
5. Is there a reasonable balance between what the items measure and the amount of time that will be required for students to develop a response?
6. Did you write model answers or essential component outlines for the short essay items? Does the weighting of each item reflect its relative value among all the other items?

Evaluation that is restricted to information acquired from paper-and-pencil tests provides only certain kinds of information about students' progress in school. Other sources and strategies for appraisal of student work must be used, including checklists, interviews, classroom simulations, role-playing activities, and anecdotal records. To do this systematically, you may keep a journal or log to record concise and cogent evaluative information on each student throughout the school year.

Writing Objective Test Items

Tests that can be evaluated in terms of the number of items that are correct or incorrect—without the need for interpretation—are referred to as objective tests. Multiple-choice, true-false, fill-in, and matching items are the most common forms. This section discusses these types of test items and their advantages and disadvantages.

MULTIPLE-CHOICE ITEMS ● Considered by some educators to be the most useful and flexible of all test forms (Ebel & Frisbie, 1991; Gronlund, 1991; Haladyna, 1997), **multiple-choice items** can be used in tests for most school subjects. The basic form of the multiple-choice item is a **stem** followed by choices, or alternatives. The stem may be a question or a partial statement that is completed by one of several choices. No truly optimum number of choices exists, but four or five are most common—one correct response and others that are referred to as **distractors.**

Here are two types of multiple-choice items, one with a question stem and the other with a completion stem:

1. What color results from the mixture of equal parts of yellow and blue paint?
   a. red
   b. green [*correct choice*]
   c. gray
   d. black
2. The actual election of the U.S. president to office is done by
   a. all registered voters.
   b. the Supreme Court.
   c. the Electoral College. [*correct choice*]
   d. our Congressional representatives.

When writing a multiple-choice item, keep two goals in mind. First, a knowledgeable student should be able to choose the correct answer and not be distracted by the wrong alternatives. Second, you should minimize the chance that a student who is ignorant of the subject matter can guess the correct answer. To achieve this, the distractors (the wrong choices) must look plausible to the uninformed; their wording and form must not identify them readily as bad answers. Hence, one of the tasks in writing a good multiple-choice item is to identify two or three plausible, but not tricky, distractors.

---

multiple-choice items
Test items that usually consist of a stem followed by choices or alternatives.

stem
A question or partial statement in a test item that is completed by one of several choices.

distractors
Incorrect responses that are offered as alternative answers to a multiple-choice question.

Writing Multiple-Choice Tests

Here are some guidelines for constructing multiple-choice items (see Haladyna, 1997):

1. Make the stem sufficiently specific to stand on its own without qualification. In other words, the stem should contain enough information to set the context for the concepts in it. At the same time, the stem should not be too wordy; a test is not the place to incorporate instruction that should have been given in the lessons. Here is an example of a stem for which insufficient context has been established:

   Applied behavior analysis is
   a. punishment.
   b. classical conditioning.

    c. self-actualization.
    d. reinforcement contingencies.

An improved version of this stem is as follows:

    Which of the following alternatives best characterizes the modern classroom use of
    applied behavior analysis?
    a. punishment
    b. classical conditioning
    c. self-actualization
    d. reinforcement contingencies [*correct choice*]

2. Do not put too much information into the stem or require too much reading.
Avoid complicated sentences unless the purpose of the item is to measure a student's ability to deal with new information or to interpret a paragraph.

3. The stem and every choice in the list of potential answers ought to fit grammatically. In addition, phrases or words that would commonly begin each of the alternatives should be part of the stem. It is also a sound idea to have the same grammatical form (say, a verb) at the beginning of each choice. For example:

    The task of statistics is to
    a. make the social sciences as respectable as the physical sciences.
    b. reduce large masses of data to an interpretable form. [*correct choice*]
    c. predict human behavior.
    d. make the investigation of human beings more precise and rigorous.

4. Take special care in using no-exception words such as "never," "all," "none,"
and "always." In multiple-choice items these words often give clues to the test-wise
but concept-ignorant student. However, by including these no-exception words in
correct choices, it is possible to discriminate knowledgeable from ignorant students.
Hill (1977) notes that such qualifying words as *often, sometimes, seldom, usually,
typically, generally,* and *ordinarily* are most often found in correct responses (or responses that are true) and, along with the no-exception words, should be avoided
whenever possible.

5. Avoid making the correct choice either the longest or shortest of the alternatives
(usually the longest, because absolutely correct answers often require qualification
and precision).

6. Be cautious in using "none of the above" as an alternative, because it too often
reduces the possible correct choices to one or two items. Here is an example illustrating how a student may know very little and get the correct answer. By knowing that only one of the choices is incorrect, a student will reduce the number of
plausible choices from four to two:

    Research suited to investigating the effects of a new instructional program on
    mathematics achievement is
    a. historical.
    b. experimental. [*correct choice*]
    c. correlational.
    d. all of the above.

The student who knows that "historical" is not a good choice also knows that *d*
must be incorrect, and the answer must be *b* or *c.*

7. After a test, discuss the items with students, and note their interpretations of
the wording of the items. Students often interpret certain phrases quite differently

from the way the teacher intended. Such feedback will help you revise items for the next test, as well as informing you about students' understandings.

8. Do not include a choice that is transparently absurd. All choices should seem plausible to a student who has not studied or otherwise become familiar with the subject.

Besides these guidelines for writing multiple-choice items, here are some suggestions about format:

- List the choices vertically rather than side by side.
- Use letters rather than numerals to label the choices, especially on scientific and mathematical tests.
- Use word structures that make the stem agree with the choices according to acceptable grammatical practice. For example, a completion-type stem would require that each of the choices begin with a lowercase letter (unless it begins with a proper noun).
- Avoid overusing one letter position as the correct choice; instead, correct choices should appear in random letter positions.

TRUE–FALSE ITEMS ● **True–false items** can be seen as one form of multiple choice. They are most useful when a comparison of two alternatives is called for, as in the following: "True or false: Controversy over the use of behavioral objectives in goal setting is caused more by differences in terminology than by real differences in philosophies. [*False*]"

The main drawback of true–false items is that students have a 50 percent chance of guessing correctly. For this reason, multiple-choice or other formats are generally preferable.

FILL-IN-THE-BLANK ITEMS ● When there is only one possible correct answer, the best item format is completion, or "fill in the blank," as in the following examples:

1. The largest city in Germany is _____ .
2. What is 15% of $198.00? _____
3. The measure of electric resistance is the _____ .

The advantage of these **completion items** is that they can reduce the element of test-wiseness to near zero. For example, compare the following items:

1. The capital of Maine is _____ .
2. The capital of Maine is
   a. Sacramento.
   b. Augusta.
   c. Juneau.
   d. Boston.

A student who has no idea what the capital of Maine is could pick Augusta from the list in item 2 because it is easy to rule out the other three cities. In item 1, however, the student has to know the answer. Completion items are especially useful in mathematics, in which use of multiple choice may help to give the answer away or reward guessing. For example:

$$4037$$
$$- 159$$

a. 4196
b. 4122

true–false items
A form of multiple-choice test items, most useful when a comparison of two alternatives is called for.

completion items
Fill-in-the-blank test items.

c. 3878 [*correct answer*]
d. 3978

If students subtract and get an answer other than any of those listed, they know that they have to keep trying. In some cases they can narrow the alternatives by estimating rather than knowing how to compute the answer.

It is critical to avoid ambiguity in completion items. In some subject areas this can be difficult, because two or more answers will reasonably fit a fragment that does not specify the context. Here are two examples:

1. The Battle of Hastings was in _____. [Date or place?]
2. "H_2O" represents _____. [Water or two parts hydrogen and one part oxygen?]

MATCHING ITEMS ● **Matching items** are commonly presented in the form of two lists, say *A* and *B*. For each item in list *A,* the student has to select one item in list *B.* The basis for choosing must be clearly explained in the directions. Matching items can be used to cover a large amount of content; that is, a large number of concepts should appear in the two lists. The primary cognitive skill that matching exercises test is recall.

Writing and Evaluating Essay Tests

Short essay questions allow students to respond in their own words. The most common form for a **short essay item** includes a question for the student to answer. The answer may range from a sentence or two to a page of, say, 100 to 150 words.

The essay form can elicit a wide variety of responses, from giving definitions of terms to comparing and contrasting important concepts or events. These items are especially suited for assessing students' ability to analyze, synthesize, and evaluate. Hence teachers may use them to appraise students' progress in organizing data and applying concepts at the highest levels of instructional objectives. Of course, these items depend heavily on writing skills and the ability to phrase ideas, so exclusive use of essays may cause the teacher to underestimate the knowledge and effort of a student who has learned the material but is a poor writer.

One of the crucial mistakes teachers make in writing essay items is failing to specify clearly the approximate detail required in the response and its expected length. Stating how much weight an item has relative to the entire test is generally not sufficient to tell students how much detail must be incorporated in a response. Here's an illustration of this point:

Bad Essay Item
Discuss Canadian politics.

Improvement
In a 400-word essay, identify at least three ways in which the Canadian prime minister and the U.S. president differ in their obligations to their respective constituencies.

A short essay item, like all test items, should be linked directly to instructional objectives taught in the lessons. Consequently, the short essay item should contain specific information that students are to address. Some teachers seem reluctant to name the particulars that they wish the student to discuss, as if they believe that recalling a word or phrase in the instructions is giving away too much information. But if recall of a name is what you are attempting to measure, then use other, more suitable forms of test items.

matching items
Test items that are presented in two lists, each item in one list matching one or more items in the other list.

short essay item
A test question the answer to which may range from a sentence or two to a page of 100 to 150 words.

Short essay items have a number of advantages in addition to letting students state ideas in their own words. Essay items are not susceptible to correct guesses. They can be used to measure creative abilities, such as writing talent or imagination in constructing hypothetical events. Short essay items may require students to combine several concepts in their response.

On the negative side is the problem of reliability in scoring essay responses. Some studies demonstrate that independent marking of the same essay response by several teachers results in appraisals ranging from excellent to a failing grade. This gross difference in evaluations indicates a wide range of marking criteria and standards among teachers of similar backgrounds.

A second drawback of essay items is that essay responses take considerable time to evaluate. The time you might have saved by writing one essay item instead of several other kinds of items must be paid back in grading the essays.

Here are some additional suggestions for writing short essay items:

1. Match items with the instructional objectives.
2. Write a response to the item before you give the test to estimate the time students will need to respond. About 4 times the teacher's time is a fair estimate.
3. Do not use such general directives in an item as "discuss," "give your opinion about . . . ," "tell all you know about. . . ." Rather, carefully choose specific response verbs such as "compare," "contrast," "identify," "list and define," and "explain the difference."

After writing a short essay item—and clearly specifying the content that is to be included in the response—you must have a clear idea of how you will mark various elements of a student's response. Of course, you want to use the same standards and criteria for all students' responses to that item. The first step is to write

These students and their teacher are going over the answers to short essay test items. How can this activity help both the students and their teacher learn more from this essay test?

a model response or a detailed outline of the essential elements students are being directed to include in their responses. You will compare students' responses to this model. If you intend to use evaluative comments but no letter grades, your outline or model will serve as a guide for pointing out to students the omissions and errors in their responses, as well as the good points of their answers. If you are using letter grades to mark the essays, you will compare elements of students' responses with the contents of your model and give suitable credit to responses that match the relative weights of elements in the model.

If possible, you should ask a colleague to assess the validity of the elements and their weights in your model response. Going a bit farther and having the colleague apply the model criteria to one or more student responses could increase the reliability of your marking.

One issue relating to essay tests is whether and how much to count grammar, spelling, and other technical features. If you do count these, give students separate grades in content and in mechanics so that they will know the basis on which their work was evaluated.

Writing and Evaluating Problem-Solving Items

CONNECTIONS
For more on problem solving, see Chapter 8, page 276.

In many subjects, such as mathematics and the physical and social sciences, instructional objectives include the development of skills in problem solving, so it is important to assess students' performance in solving problems (Haladyna, 1997). A **problem-solving assessment** requires students to organize, select, and apply complex procedures that have at least several important steps or components. It is important to appraise the students' work in each of these steps or components.

Here are a seventh-grade-level mathematical problem and a seventh-grader's response to it. In the discussion of evaluating problem solving to follow, the essential components are described in specific terms, but they can be applied to all disciplines.

Problem

Suppose two gamblers are playing a game in which the loser must pay an amount equal to what the other gambler has at the time. If Player A won the first and third games, and Player B won the second game, and they finished the three games with $12 each, with how much money did each begin the first game?

A student's response:

After game	A had	B had
3	$12.00	$12.00
2	6.00	18.00
1	15.00	9.00
In the beginning	$7.50	$16.50

When I started with Game 1, I guessed and guessed, but I couldn't make it come out to 12 and 12.

Then I decided to start at Game 3 and work backwards. It worked!

How will you objectively evaluate such a response? As in evaluating short essay items, you should begin your preparation for appraising problem-solving responses by writing either a model response or, perhaps more practically, an outline of the essential components or procedures that are involved in problem solving. As with essays, problem-solving responses may take several different yet valid approaches. The outline must be flexible enough to accommodate all valid possibilities.

problem-solving assessment
Test that calls for organizing, selecting, and applying complex procedures that have at least several important steps or components.

THEORY *into* Practice •

Evaluating Problem-Solving Items

Problem solving involves several important components that fit most disciplines. These include understanding the problem to be solved, attacking the problem systematically, and arriving at a reasonable answer. Following is a detailed checklist of elements common to most problem solving that can guide your weighting of elements in your evaluation of a student's problem-solving abilities.

Problem-Solving Evaluation Elements

1. Problem organization
   a. Representation by table, graph, chart, etc. _____
   b. Representation fits the problem. _____
   c. Global understanding of the problem. _____
2. Procedures (mathematical: trial-and-error, working backwards, experimental process, empirical induction)
   a. A viable procedure was attempted. _____
   b. Procedure was carried to a final solution. _____
   c. Computation (if any) was correct. _____
3. Solution (mathematical: a table, number, figure, graph, etc.)
   a. Answer was reasonable. _____
   b. Answer was checked. _____
   c. Answer was correct. _____
4. Logic specific to the detail or application of the given information was sound. _____

If you wish to give partial credit for an answer that contains correct elements or want to inform students about the value of their responses, you must devise ways to do this consistently. The following points offer some guidance:

1. Write model responses before giving partial credit for such work as essay writing, mathematical problem solving, laboratory assignments, or any work that you evaluate according to the quality of its various stages.
2. Tell students in sufficient detail the meaning of the grades you give to communicate the value of the work.

The following examples illustrate outlines of exemplary student work from mathematics and social studies or literature.

From Mathematics

Students are given the following problem:

In a single-elimination tennis tournament, 40 players are to play for the singles championship. Determine how many matches must be played.

Evaluation

a. Evidence that the student understood the problem, demonstrated by depiction of the problem with a graph, table, chart, equation, etc. (*3 points*)
b. Use of a method for solving the problem that had potential for yielding a correct solution—for example, systematic trial and error, empirical induction, elimination, working backwards. (*5 points*)
c. Arrival at a correct solution. (*3 points*)

The three components in the evaluation were assigned points according to the weight the teacher judged each to be worth in the context of the course of study and the purpose of the test. Teachers can give full credit for a correct answer even if all the work is not shown in the response, provided that they know that students can do the work in their heads.

From Social Studies or Literature

Students are asked to respond with a 100-word essay to the following item:

Compare and contrast the development of Inuit and Navajo tools on the basis of the climates in which these two peoples live.

Evaluation

a. The response gives evidence of specific and accurate recall of the climates in which the Inuit and Navajos live (*1point*) and of Inuit and Navajo tools. (*1 point*)

b. The essay develops with continuity of thought and logic. (*3 points*)

c. An accurate rationale is provided for the use of the various tools in the respective climates. (*3 points*)

d. An analysis comparing and contrasting the similarities and differences between the two groups and their tool development is given. (*8 points*)

e. The response concludes with a summary and closure. (*1 point*)

These two examples should suggest ways to evaluate items in other subject areas as well. Giving partial credit for much of the work students do certainly results in a more complete evaluation of student progress than does marking the work merely right or wrong. The examples show how to organize objective assessments for evaluating work that does not lend itself to the simple forms of multiple-choice, true–false, completion, and matching items. Points do not have to be used to evaluate components of the responses. In many situations, some kind of evaluative descriptors might be more meaningful. Evaluative descriptors are statements describing strong and weak features of a response to an item, a question, or a project. In the mathematics example a teacher's evaluative descriptor for item *a* might read, "You have drawn an excellent chart showing that you understand the meaning of the problem, and that is very good, but it seems you were careless when you entered several important numbers in your chart."

SELF-CHECK

Write a variety of test items, including multiple choice, true–false, completion, matching, short essay, and problem-solving questions.

WHAT ARE PORTFOLIO AND PERFORMANCE ASSESSMENTS?

After two decades of criticism of standardized testing (see Marzano & Costa, 1988), critics have finally succeeded in proposing, developing, and implementing alternative assessment systems that are designed to avoid the problems of typical multiple-choice tests. The key idea behind the new tests or testing alternatives is that students should be asked to document their learning or demonstrate that they

FIGURE 13.2 ● Assessment Criteria for a Science Concept Map

Sample assessment criteria for visual concept maps or mindmaps might consist of the following: a clear, central focus; an adequate number of key concepts, ideas; appropriate detail; pertinent examples; accurate relationships among data; and neatness, clarity, and legibility. From Linda Campbell, Bruce Campbell, and Dee Dickinson, *Teaching and Learning Through Multiple Intelligences.* Copyright © 1996 by Allyn & Bacon. Reprinted by permission.

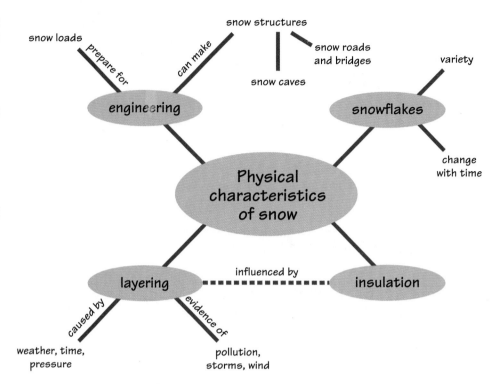

can actually do something real with the information and skills they have learned in school (Newmann et al., 1995). For example, students might be asked to keep a portfolio, design a method of measuring wind speed, draw a scale model of a racing car, or write something for a real audience. Such tests are referred to as *authentic assessments* or *performance assessments* (Herman et al., 1992; Wiggins, 1989). In reading, for example, the authentic assessment movement has led to the development of tests in which students are asked to read and interpret longer sections and show their metacognitive awareness of reading strategies (Roeber & Dutcher, 1989; Valencia, Pearson, Peters, & Wixson, 1989). In science, authentic assessments might involve having students set up and carry out an experiment. In writing, students might be asked to write real letters or newspaper articles. In math, students might solve complex realistic problems that require insight and creativity. Authentic tests are also likely to require students to integrate knowledge from different domains; for example, to use algebra in the context of a science experiment and write up the results.

See Figure 13.2 for assessment criteria for a science concept map.

Portfolio Assessment

One popular form of assessment is called **portfolio assessment:** the collection and evaluation of samples of student work over an extended period (Hambleton, 1996; Herbert & Schultz, 1995). Teachers may collect student compositions, projects, and other evidence of higher-order functioning and use this evidence to evaluate student progress over time. For example, many teachers maintain portfolios of student writings that show the development of a composition from first draft to final product, journal entries, book reports, artwork, computer printouts, or papers showing development in problem solving (Arter, 1991; Shaklee, Barbour, Ambrose,

portfolio assessment

Assessment of a collection of the student's work in an area showing growth, self-reflection, and achievement.

& Hansford, 1997; Wolf et al., 1991). Portfolios are increasingly being maintained in computers, to supplement paper files (Wiedmer, 1998). Refer to Figure 13.3 for sample criteria for evaluating student writing portfolios.

Portfolio assessment has important uses when teachers want to evaluate students for reports to parents or other within-school purposes. However, innovators have also proposed that portfolio assessment be used as part of assessments for school accountability. This use is more controversial (Herbert, 1998; Taylor, 1994), as a student's product can be greatly influenced by his or her teacher's or classmates' input (Gearhart & Herman, 1995). Also, evidence about the reliability of

Continua of Descriptors		
Strong Performance ⟵	⟶	**Needs Improvement**
Versatility		
Wide variety of reading and writing across genre	Some variety	Little or no variety
		Collection shows little breadth or depth
Process		
Samples reveal discoveries or pivotal learning experiences	Process illustrated in inflexible or mechanistic ways	Minimal use of process to reflect on achievements
Response		
Engaged with story	Personal reflection but focus is narrow	Brief retelling of isolated events
Discusses key issues		
Evidence of critical questioning		
Self-Evaluations		
Multidimensional	Developing insights	Single focus, global in nature
Wide variety of observations	Some specifics noted	
Establishing meaningful goals	Limited goal setting	Goal setting too broad or nonexistent
Notes improvement	Vague idea of improvement	
Individual Pieces		
Strong control of a variety of elements: organization, cohesion, surface features, etc.	Growing command evidenced; some flaws, but major ideas clear	Needs to improve: sophistication of ideas, text features, and surface features
Problem Solving		
Wrestles with problems using various resources	Uses limited resources	Seems helpless
Enjoys problem solving and learning new ways	Wants quick fix	Frustrated by problems
Purposefulness/Uses		
Uses reading and writing to satisfy various goals including sharing with others	Uses reading and writing to meet others' goals	Apathetic, resistant

FIGURE 13.3 ● Sample of Criteria for Evaluating Students' Writing Ability through Portfolio Assessment
From Cathy Collins Block, *Teaching the Language Arts: Expanding Thinking through Student Centered Instruction.* Copyright © 1993 by Allyn & Bacon. Reprinted by permission.

These students are putting together portfolios of their work for their teacher to use as an evaluative tool. What are some ways of implementing portfolio assessment?

portfolio assessment is largely disappointing; in particular, different raters can give very different ratings of the same portfolios (Cheung, 1995; Herman & Winters, 1994; Koretz, Stecher, & Deibert, 1993). However, portfolio assessments may be used in combination with other on-demand assessments that students take in a structured testing setting, and a few states are currently implementing just such a combined system (Baker & Niemi, 1996).

THEORY into Practice

Using Portfolios in the Classroom

PLANNING AND ORGANIZATION

- Develop an overall flexible plan for student portfolios (See Shaklee et al., 1997). What purposes will the portfolios serve? What items will be required? When and how will they be obtained? What criteria will be applied for reflection and evaluation?
- Plan sufficient time for students to prepare and discuss portfolio items. Portfolio assessments take more time and thought than correcting paper-and-pencil tests does.
- Begin with one aspect of student learning and achievement, and gradually include others as you and the students learn about portfolio procedures. The writing process, for instance, is particularly well suited to documentation through portfolios.
- Choose items to be included in portfolios that will show developing proficiency on important goals and objectives. Items that address multiple objectives help to make portfolio assessments more efficient.
- Collect at least two types of items: required indicators (Arter, 1990) or core items (Meisels & Steele, 1991) and optional work samples. Required or core indicators are items collected for every child that will show how each child is progressing. Optional work samples show individual students' unique approaches, interests, and strengths.

- Place a list of goals and objectives in the front of each portfolio, along with a list of required indicators and a place for recording optional items, so that you and the students can keep track of contents.

IMPLEMENTATION

- In order to save time, to ensure that portfolio items are representative of children's work, and to increase authenticity, embed the development of portfolio items into ongoing classroom activities.
- Give students responsibility for preparing, selecting, evaluating, and filing portfolio items and keeping portfolios up to date. Young children will need guidance with this.
- For selected portfolio items, model reflection and self-assessment for students to help them become aware of the processes they used, what they learned and have yet to learn, and what they may need to do differently next time.
- Be selective. A portfolio is not a haphazard collection of work samples, audiotapes, pictures, and other products. It is a thoughtful selection of items that exemplify children's learning. Random inclusion of items quickly becomes overwhelming.
- Use information in portfolios to place children on a sequence of developing skills. For example, Wiggins (1994) presented a developmental spelling sequence that was used in a performance assessment program in a New Jersey district. This appears in Figure 13.4.
- Analyze portfolio items for insight into students' knowledge and skills. As you do this, you will understand more of the students' strengths and needs, thinking processes, preconceptions, misconceptions, error patterns, and developmental benchmarks (Athanases, 1994).
- Use portfolio information to document and celebrate students' learning, to share with parents and other school personnel, and to improve and target classroom instruction. If portfolios are not linked to improving instruction, they are not working.

FIGURE 13.4 ● Scoring Guidelines for Spelling
This figure is from the South Brunswick, New Jersey, schools. Adapted from Grant Wiggins, "Toward Better Report Cards," *Educational Leadership, 52*(2), 1994, pp. 28–37. © Center on Learning, Assessment, and School Structure. Reprinted by permission of the author.

Look at the child's spelling list. Were most of the spellings *Precommunicative, Semiphonetic, Phonetic, Transitional,* or *Correct?* This is the child's probable developmental level. You might feel that a child truly falls between two of the categories, but try to select just one category per child.

1. **Precommunicative** spellers are in the "babbling" stage of spelling. Children use letters for writing words but the letters are strung together randomly. The letters in precommunicative spelling do correspond to sounds.

2. **Semiphonetic** spellers know that letters represent sounds. They often abbreviate spellings to represent initial and/or final sounds. Example: E = eagle; A = eighty.

3. **Phonetic** spellers spell words the way they sound. The speller perceives and represents all of the phonemes in a word, though spellings may be unconventional. Example: EGL = eagle; ATE = eighty.

4. **Transitional** spellers think about how words appear visually; a visual memory of spelling patterns is apparent. Spellings exhibit conventions of English orthography, such as vowels in every syllable, correctly spelled inflection endings, and frequent English letter sequences. Example: EGUL = eagle; EIGHTEE = eighty.

5. **Correct** spellers develop over years of word study and writing. Correct spelling can be categorized by instruction levels; for example, correct spelling for a body of words that can be spelled by the average fourth-grader would be fourth-grade-level correct spelling.

TEACHERS IN ACTION

What has been your experience with alternatives to traditional forms of assessment?

Margaret Ball
Teacher of English
Stratford High School
Stratford, Wisconsin

When a teacher stops feeling tied down to traditional pencil-and-paper tests, he or she discovers a whole new approach to teaching and evaluating students' actual mastery of skills. I follow these steps:

1. Identify the concepts I want to test for mastery. I use a multisensory approach when presenting the concepts to ensure that one method or another will capture each student's attention.
2. Examine each concept and the methods used to present it to determine further what I want to test for mastery.
3. Develop variations of tests for different classes and situations.

When developing tests, I also ask myself the following questions: Would conventional methods measure mastery best? Am I being flexible? What is a unique method I could use? Is it practical? Could it be modified to work? How do my learners learn best? What motivates them? Do I have hands-on materials to use in testing? Is it possible to test in a multisensory way? How can I modify assessment to meet individual needs? A multisensory approach helps all students acknowledge responsibility for their learning. After a story about Helen Keller I invited the Educational Interpreter at our school to help me present sign language as an alternative way of communicating. We chose a popular song and taught the students to sign that song with the music. Then we presented our "sign-song" to other classes. The experience and actual mastery of the sign-song was evaluation in itself, and I was able to award each student a grade based on participation. It is important to change students' ways of thinking about testing, to constantly reevaluate approaches to classroom measurement and evaluation.

Elonda Hogue
First-Grade Teacher
Cordley Elementary School
Lawrence, Kansas

I began many years ago keeping folders of student work that displayed each child's progress. Daily notes were added to the folder with information about each student's performance or behavior for the day. Since I don't keep numerical grades on a "learning first-grader," I couldn't always rely on my memory at grade-card time. This meant that the folders were invaluable.

As the years have passed, the evaluation folders have developed to include even more information. This year's folders I made specifically with parents in mind. The folders allow me to present to parents their child's specific growth during any grading period. I have also included student ownership in the folders this year. Weekly, each child gets to choose what he or she thinks is the best work to be included in the folder. Any paper that a child considers better than a previous paper can be substituted. This has worked very well. My students are aware of improvement. They try hard to make each piece of work better than the last. We've been collecting artwork, math projects, writing samples, oral readings on tape, photos, and anecdotes. Folders reveal whatever level of achievement a child is capable of accomplishing. Daily and weekly work shows continual learning.

Also, I send these folders on to second grade so that teacher can trace each student's growth. Children who lack specific skills will have the advantage of showing next year's teacher what they've actually accomplished, and that teacher will know exactly where to begin instruction. This assessment process is motivating to students, nonambiguous to parents, and practical to teachers.

Performance Assessment

Tests that involve actual demonstrations of knowledge or skills in real life are called **performance assessments** (Feuer & Fulton, 1993; Hambleton, 1996). For example, ninth-graders might be asked to conduct an oral history project, reading about a significant recent event and then interviewing the individuals involved. The quality of the oral histories, done over a period of weeks, would indicate the degree of the students' mastery of the social studies concepts involved (Wiggins, 1989). Wiggins (1993b) also describes assessments used in the last 2 weeks of school in which students must apply everything they have learned all year to analyze a sludge that mixes a variety of solids and liquids. Some schools are requiring elaborate "exhibitions," such as projects developed over many months, as demonstrations of competence (Sills-Briegel, Fisk, & Dunlop, 1996). More time-limited performance assessments might ask students to set up experiments, respond to extended text, write in various genres, or solve realistic math problems (Egeland, 1996).

A model for performance assessment is the doctoral thesis, an extended project required for Ph.D. candidates that is intended to show not only what students know, but also what they can do (Archibald & Newmann, 1988). Driver's tests, tests for pilots' licenses, and performance tests in medicine are also common examples of performance assessments (Swanson, Norman, & Linn, 1995).

How Well Do Performance Assessments Work?

One of the most important criticisms of traditional standardized testing is that it can focus teachers on teaching a narrow range of skills that happen to be on the test (see Shepard, 1989b; Slavin & Madden, 1991). How might performance assessments be better? At least in theory, it should be possible to create tests that would require such a broad understanding of subject matter that the test would be worth teaching to. Wiggins (1989, p. 41) puts it this way: "We should 'teach to the test.' The catch is to design and then teach to . . . tests so that practicing for and taking the tests actually enhances rather than impedes education."

For example, consider the performance test in science shown in Figure 13.5. Imagine that you know that your students will have to conduct an experiment to solve a problem like the one posed in the figure (but not that exact problem). The only way to teach to such a test will be to expose students to a broad range of information about electricity, experimentation, and problem-solving strategies (see Shepard, 1995).

Several states, including Vermont, Connecticut, Kentucky, and Maryland, are now using performance assessments in their state assessment programs (Baker & Niemi, 1996; Firestone, Mayrowetz, & Fairman, 1998). These programs are causing controversy (see, for example, Cizek, 1991; Wiggins, 1991) but appear to be generally accepted by educators and the public once their bugs are worked out (Kane & Khattri, 1995). Performance assessments are far more expensive than traditional multiple-choice measures, but most experts and policy makers are coming to agree that the investment is worthwhile if it produces markedly better tests and therefore leads to better teaching and learning (Bridge, Compton-Hall, & Cantrell, 1998; Stiggins, 1995; Wiggins, 1996, 1998). Beyond all the practical problems and expense of administering and scoring performance tests, it is not yet clear whether the new tests will solve all the problems of standardized testing (Cizek, 1993; Messick, 1994; Moss, 1992; Shepard, 1993b; Worthen & Spandel, 1993). For example, Shavelson, Baxter, and Pine (1992) studied performance assessments in science (Figure 14.8 in Chapter 14

performance assessments
Assessments of students' ability to perform tasks in real-life contexts, not just to show knowledge.

FIGURE 13.5 ● **Example of a Performance Assessment Activity**

From R. J. Shavelson, G. P. Baxter, and J. Pine, "Performance Assessments: Political Rhetoric and Measurement Reality," *Educational Researcher, 21*(2), p. 23. Copyright 1992 by the American Educational Research Association. Reprinted by permission of the publisher.

Find out what is in the six mystery boxes *A, B, C, D, E,* and *F.* They have five different things inside, shown below. Two of the boxes will have the same thing. All of the others will have something different inside.

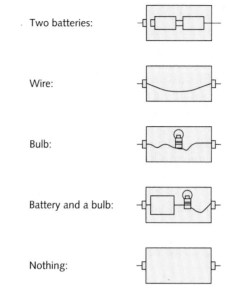

Two batteries:

Wire:

Bulb:

Battery and a bulb:

Nothing:

For each box, connect it in a circuit to help you figure out what is inside. You can use the bulbs, batteries, and wires any way you like.

is taken from their study). They found that student performance on such assessments could be reliably rated, but different performance assessments produced very different patterns of scores, and student scores were still related more closely to student aptitude than to what students were actually taught (see also Educational

This student's performance is being evaluated by his teacher and his classmates. What are the advantages and disadvantages of using a performance or group activity as a method for evaluating students?

Testing Service, 1995; Linn, 1994; Supovitz & Brennan, 1997). Further, the hope that performance assessments would show smaller differences between students of different ethnic backgrounds has not generally been realized (Klein et al., 1997).

Scoring Rubrics for Performance Assessments

Performance assessments are typically scored according to rubrics that specify in advance the type of performance that is expected for each rating (Goodrich, 1996). Figure 13.4 illustrated a very general rubric for spelling. However, rubrics can be written for individual tasks. Figure 13.6 shows one rubric (from Taylor, 1994) that was developed for an essay on character development in stories students have read.

Planning for performance assessments takes time, and avoiding the pitfalls of subjectivity in rating performances takes practice (Popham, 1997). However, a few well-thought-out, well-written items for a performance assessment could serve as a summative evaluation, for example, for all or most of your educational objectives for an entire unit.

FIGURE 13.6 ● Sample Scoring Rubric: Targeted Performance, Performance Criteria, and a Description of Performances at Different Score Points

From Catherine Taylor, "Assessment for Measurement or Standards," *American Educational Research Journal, 31*(2), pp. 231–262. Copyright 1994 by the American Educational Research Association. Reprinted by permission of the publisher.

Performance
Essay on Character Development in Literature

Performance Criteria
- Character is identified.
- At least three aspects of the character's development during the course of the story are described.
- Appropriate support for each character aspect is given using excerpts from the story.
- Character's contribution to the story's plot is described.
- At least three excerpts from the story are given as support for writer's ideas about the character's contribution to the story.
- Text references used for support are appropriate.

Scoring Rubric

4 points	Essay is complete, thorough, and insightful in describing the character's development and contribution to the story. Adequate support is given to encourage us to consider the writer's point of view. All excerpts from the text enhance our understanding of the writer's view of the character.
3 points	Essay is complete in describing the character's development and contribution to the story. Adequate support is given to encourage us to consider the writer's point of view. Most excerpts from the text enhance our understanding of the writer's view of the character.
2 points	Essay is complete in its description of either the character's development *or* the character's contribution to the story. Some support is given to help us consider the writer's point of view. Most excerpts from the text enhance our understanding of the writer's view of the character for the element described.
1 point	Essay is mostly complete in its description of either the character's development or the character's contribution to the story. Support is given for the writer's point of view, but it is not always convincing. Few excerpts from the text enhance our understanding of the writer's view of the character for the element described.
0 points	The written essay was not completed, is significantly lacking in performance of all criteria, or is off-task.

The Intentional Teacher

● **Using What You Know about Assessing Student Learning to Improve Teaching and Learning**

Intentional teachers assess student learning in ways that align with both their goals and their instruction. They use assessment results to adjust their instruction, and they use assessments to provide important feedback to students, families, and communities. Intentional teachers know that no one measure is ideal for every circumstance, and they implement a range of assessments that fit their purposes and circumstances.

1 What am I trying to accomplish?

One cardinal rule of assessing learning is that tests should be tied directly to learning goals and to instruction. Specify in advance what students are to learn. Design instruction to help students learn those things, and then assess their learning in relation to the specified goals.

> You plan your physical education unit on volleyball by writing three goals: Students will (1) develop an understanding of the rules of the game; (2) demonstrate fundamental skills such as setting, spiking, and serving; and (3) apply their knowledge and skills in the context of a real game. Specifying these three goals helps you streamline your planning and suggests appropriate assessments. You develop a paper-and-pencil test for the first goal and performance assessments for the last two.

The variety and range of objectives to which teachers should teach is large. Write objectives in different domains (for example, cognitive and affective) and at different levels of specificity (for example, long-term goals and lesson objectives, and goals for different levels of understanding according to Bloom's taxonomy).

> You begin your year-long planning by examining your state's and district's expected outcomes for fourth grade. Then you spread out the teacher's editions of your five texts, flipping each open to the scope and sequence chart that specifies content and learning objectives. This process allows you to examine and

evaluate the variety and levels of understanding set by your curricular materials.

2 What are my students' relevant experiences and needs?

Formative assessments allow teachers to discover their students' experiences, preferences, and needs. Use frequent formative assessments to gather information about students' attitudes and prior knowledge.

> To begin your unit on geology, you conduct interviews with small groups. You display a variety of rocks and minerals and listen as students converse about the rocks. Your notes document students' enthusiasm for the topic and their extensive out-of-class experiences studying rocks. You use this information to create a more sophisticated unit than you might have if students had no prior knowledge of rocks and minerals.

Students' levels of preparation may affect their performance on tests and other measures. Check to see that your measures truly assess the objective you intend to assess.

> A cluster of students who typically are highly successful in solving the challenging word problems you present in mathematics each week score surprisingly low on the problem-solving items of a school-based achievement test. When you review the items, you wonder whether students' reading ability—and not their problem-solving abilities—accounted for their low scores. To test your hunch, you read similar problems aloud to the students. They solve the problems accurately.

3 What approaches and materials are available to help me challenge every student?

Assessments should be challenging for all but impossible for none. Use assessments that are fair measures of the objectives and not of

SELF-CHECK

Make a list of items that might be included in a portfolio. Create rubrics for a specific performance.

CHAPTER SUMMARY

WHAT ARE INSTRUCTIONAL OBJECTIVES AND HOW ARE THEY USED?

Research supports the use of instructional, or behavioral, objectives, which are clear statements about what students should know and be able to do at the end of a lesson, unit, or course. These statements also specify the conditions of perfor-

general aptitude. Check that your assessments are applied consistently to all students.

You write weekly quizzes with a general format in mind: You put recall-level items first, reasoning that they provide immediate success for all or most students in demonstrating knowledge. Subsequent items test higher levels of understanding and stretch even the best-prepared students to apply content to new situations.

Different assessment formats are appropriate for different purposes. Use assessments that will provide you with varied kinds of information related to important objectives in their context.

You prepare a grid as you plan to assess learning for the semester. In the far-left column you list your goals. Along the top you list the variety of strategies you'll employ for assessment. Then you place check marks or brief phrases in the boxes that seem most appropriate for assessing each goal. This grid allows you to ensure that you are collecting appropriate and varied information about student learning.

Assessment Measures

Learning Goals	Norm-referenced or criterion-referenced measure? (N or C)	Multiple-choice, essay, or other paper–pencil test	Portfolio	Performance-based assessment	Other
Students will demonstrate social skills . . .	C [list of skills]			Informal observation and completion of checklist	Playground behavior commendation slips

4 How will I know whether and when to change my strategy or modify my instruction?

Assessment equals feedback. Use information from assessments to adjust your instruction and future assessments.

In reviewing your students' writing portfolios, you discern some trends that offer strong guidance for your instruction. For instance, students' reflections indicate that they seem to find particular meaning in writing autobiographical pieces and less relevance in other forms of writing. You build on their interests in autobiography by including prewriting experiences that tap into students' life experiences, no matter what the genre.

Evaluations need to be important to students if they are to serve as incentives for effort. If it appears that evaluations do not matter to students, determine whether students perceive the objectives as important and the assessments as fair, consistent, and driven by clear criteria.

As you assign a shelf-building project in your woodworking class, you display a set of samples of varying quality. You ask students to brainstorm the qualities of a well-made shelf. You also discuss the real-life consequences of poorly constructed shelves, with students laughing at the imagined disasters that accompany shoddy work. You develop a scoring rubric based on student-generated criteria and distribute it as students begin their work.

5 What information will I accept as evidence that my students and I are experiencing success?

Successful assessments are valid and reliable for the setting. Check the validity and reliability of your measures with the help of students and peers.

After writing a summative exam for your unit on oceanography, you hand the exam to a peer and ask her to assess whether the questions appropriately emphasize particular sections of content. When students complete the exam, you ask them to turn over their test papers and evaluate the exam for fairness. You invite them to write the things they know from the unit that were *not* assessed in your test.

mance and the criteria for assessment. In lesson planning, task analysis contributes to the formulation of objectives, and backward planning facilitates the development of specific objectives from general objectives in a course of study. Objectives are closely linked with assessment. Bloom's taxonomy of educational objectives classifies educational objectives from simple to complex, including knowledge, comprehension, application, analysis, synthesis, and evaluation. A behavior content matrix helps to ensure that objectives cover many levels.

WHY IS EVALUATION IMPORTANT?

Formal measures of student performance or learning are important as feedback for students and teachers, as information for parents, as information for selection and certification, as information for assessing school accountability, and as incentives for increasing student effort.

HOW IS STUDENT LEARNING EVALUATED?

Strategies for evaluation include formative evaluation; summative evaluation; norm-referenced evaluation, in which a student's scores are compared with other students' scores; and criterion-referenced evaluation, in which students' scores are compared to a standard of mastery. Students are evaluated through tests or performances. The appropriate method of evaluation is based on the goal of evaluation. For example, if the goal of testing is to find out whether students have mastered a key concept in a lesson, a criterion-referenced formative quiz or a performance would be the most appropriate.

HOW ARE TESTS CONSTRUCTED?

Tests are constructed to elicit evidence of student learning in relation to the instructional objectives. Achievement tests should be constructed in keeping with six principles: They should (1) measure clearly defined learning objectives, (2) measure a representative sample of the learning tasks included in instruction, (3) include the types of test items most appropriate for measuring the desired learning outcomes, (4) fit the uses that will be made of the results, (5) be as reliable as possible and be interpreted with caution, and (6) improve learning. A table of specifications helps in the planning of tests that correspond to instructional objectives. Types of test items include multiple-choice, true–false, completion, matching, short essay, and problem-solving items. Each type of test item has optimal uses, advantages, and disadvantages. For example, if you want to learn how students think about, analyze, synthesize, or evaluate some aspect of course content, a short essay test might be most appropriate, provided that you have time to administer it and evaluate students' responses.

WHAT ARE PORTFOLIO AND PERFORMANCE ASSESSMENTS?

Portfolio assessment and performance assessment avoid the negative aspects of pencil-and-paper multiple-choice tests by requiring students to demonstrate their learning through work samples or direct real-world applications. Performance assessments are usually scored according to rubrics that specify in advance the type of performance expected.

KEY TERMS

affective objectives   464

assessment   461

authentic assessment   469

backward planning   459

behavior content matrix   463

completion items   478

criterion-referenced evaluations   469

distractors   476

evaluation   465

instructional objective   455

learning objectives   462

matching items   479

multiple-choice items   476

norm-referenced evaluations   469

performance assessments   489

portfolio assessment   484

problem-solving assessment   481
short essay item   479
stem   476
table of specifications   474
task analysis   458

taxonomy of educational
objectives   462
teaching objectives   462
true–false items   478

Self-Assessment

1. A statement of concepts or skills that students are expected to know or be able to do at the end of some period of instruction is called a(n)
   a. table of specifications.
   b. content matrix.
   c. instructional objective.
   d. taxonomy.

2. For the following objective, label the condition, performance, and criterion: "Given a map of the United States, students will locate all of the state capitals."

3. A student is shown a model of a space shuttle and asked to explain what its different components are and how they interact. What type of learning is most clearly being emphasized?

4. What is the term used for the chart showing how a concept or skill will be taught at different cognitive levels in relation to an instructional objective?
   a. task analysis
   b. backward planning
   c. behavior content matrix
   d. table of specifications

5. List six reasons why evaluation is important.

6. According to Gronlund's principles of achievement testing, tests should
   a. include all instructional content.
   b. include all item types.

c. be free from the confines of instructional objectives.
   d. fit the particular uses that will be made of the results.

7. Match each of the following types of evaluations with its description.
   a. formative
   b. summative

   _____ follows conclusion of instructional unit
   _____ given during instruction; can guide lesson presentation

8. Giving feedback to parents on student performance is part of a teacher's job. What type of grading orientation—norm-referenced or criterion-referenced—would be best understood by parents? How might the choice of approach vary depending on grade level?

9. The purpose of devising a table of specifications in testing is to
   a. indicate the types of learning to be assessed for different instructional objectives.
   b. measure a student's performance against a specified standard.
   c. make comparisons among students.
   d. identify conditions of mastery.

10. In a typical portfolio, both subjective and objective measurements are included. Are these equally valid and useful in educational decision making?

Chapter 14

WHAT ARE STANDARDIZED TESTS AND HOW ARE THEY USED?
Selection and Placement
Diagnosis
Evaluation
School Improvement
Accountability

WHAT TYPES OF STANDARDIZED TESTS ARE GIVEN?
Aptitude Tests
Norm-Referenced Achievement Tests
Criterion-Referenced Achievement Tests

HOW ARE STANDARDIZED TESTS INTERPRETED?
Percentile Scores
Grade-Equivalent Scores
Standard Scores

WHAT ARE SOME ISSUES CONCERNING STANDARDIZED AND CLASSROOM TESTING?
Validity and Reliability
Test Bias

HOW ARE GRADES DETERMINED?
Establishing Grading Criteria
Assigning Letter Grades
Performance Grading
Other Alternative Grading Systems
Assigning Report Card Grades

Standardized Tests and Grades

Jennifer Tranh is a fifth-grade teacher at Lincoln Elementary School. Recently she met with the parents of one of her students, Anita McKay.

"Hello, Mr. and Mrs. McKay," said Ms. Tranh when Anita's parents arrived. "I'm so glad you could come. Please take a seat, and we'll start right in. First, I wanted to tell you what a delight it is to have Anita in my class. She is always so cheerful, so willing to help others. Her work is coming along very well in most subjects, although there are a few areas I'm a bit concerned about. Before I start, though, do you have any questions for me?"

Mr. and Mrs. McKay explained to Ms. Tranh that they thought Anita was having a good year and that they were eager to hear how she was doing.

"All right. First of all, I know you've seen the results of Anita's California Achievement Tests. We call those 'CATs' for short. Most parents don't understand these test scores, so I'll try to explain them to you. First, let's look at math. As you know, Anita has always been a good math student, and her scores and grades reflect this. She got an A on her last report card and a percentile score of 90 on math computations. That means that she scored better than 90 percent of all fifth-graders in the country. She did almost as well on math concepts and applications—her score is in the 85th percentile."

"What does this 'grade equivalent' mean?" asked Mrs. McKay.

"That's a score that's supposed to tell how a child is achieving in relation to his or her grade level. For example, Anita's grade equivalent of 6.9 means that she is scoring more than a year ahead of the fifth-grade level."

"Does this mean she could skip sixth-grade math?" asked Mr. McKay.

Ms. Tranh laughed. "I'm afraid not. It's hard to explain, but a grade equivalent score of 6.9 is supposed to be what a student at the end of sixth grade would score on a fifth-grade test. It doesn't mean that Anita already knows all the sixth-grade material. Besides, we take all of this testing information with a grain of salt. We rely much more on day-to-day performance and classroom tests to tell how students are doing. In this case the standardized CAT scores are pretty consistent with what we see Anita doing in class. But let me show you another example that shows less consistency. I'm sure you noticed that even though Anita's reading grades have been pretty good, her scores in reading comprehension were much lower than her scores in most other areas. She got a percentile score of only 30. This is almost a year below grade level. I think Anita is a pretty good reader, so I was surprised. I gave her another test, the Gray Oral Reading Test. This test is given one-on-one, so it gives you a much better indication of how well students are reading. On the Gray, Anita scored at grade level. This score is more indicative of where I see her reading in class, so I'm not concerned about her in this area.

"On the other hand, there is a concern I have about Anita that is not reflected in her standardized tests. She scored near the 70th percentile in both language mechanics and language expression. This might make you think Anita's doing great in language arts, and she is doing well in many ways. However, I'm concerned about Anita's writing. I keep a portfolio of student writing over the course of the year. This is Anita's here. She's showing some development in writing, but I think she could do a lot better. As you can see, her spelling, punctuation, and grammar are excellent, but her stories are very short, factual, and stilted. As you know, we don't give grades in writing. We use a rating form that shows the student's development toward proficient writing. Based on her portfolio I rated her at proficient, but to go to advanced, I'd like to see her write more and really let her imagination loose. She tells great stories orally, but I think she's so concerned about making a mistake in mechanics that she writes very conservatively. On vacation you might encourage her to write a journal or to do other writing wherever it makes sense."

"But if her standardized test scores are good in language," said Mrs. McKay, "doesn't that mean that she's doing well?"

"Test scores tell us some things, but not everything," said Ms. Tranh. "The CAT is good on simple things such as math computations and language mechanics, but it is not so good at telling us what children can actually do. That's why I keep portfolios of student work in writing, in math problem solving, and in science. I want to see how children are really developing in their ability to apply their skills to doing real things and solving real problems. In fact, now that we've gone over Anita's grades and standardized tests, let's look at her portfolios, and I think you'll get a much better idea of what she's doing here in school."

Using Your EXPERIENCE

Cooperative Learning and Creative Thinking   Act out this parent–teacher conference about test scores. Have volunteers for the roles of Mrs. McKay, Mr. McKay, and Ms. Tranh. One volunteer can act as moderator to clarify any miscommunications and to keep the conference moving.

Critical Thinking   What do you know from reading this case? What do you still want to know? And what did you learn here? Has Ms. Tranh told us everything we need to know about Anita's standardized test scores and portfolio assessments in writing, math, and science?

Jennifer Tranh's conversation with the McKays illustrates some of the uses and limitations of grades and standardized tests. The CATs and the Gray Oral Reading Test give Ms. Tranh information that does relate Anita's performance in some areas to national norms, and Anita's grades give Ms. Tranh some idea of how Anita is doing relative to her classmates; but neither standardized tests nor grades provide the detail or comprehensiveness reflected in portfolios of Anita's work and other observations of Anita's performance. Taken together, the cautiously interpreted standardized tests, the grades, the portfolios of Anita's work, and other classroom assessments provide a good picture of Anita's performance.

WHAT ARE STANDARDIZED TESTS AND HOW ARE THEY USED?

Do you remember taking SATs, ACTs, or other college entrance examinations? Did you ever wonder how those tests were constructed, what the scores meant, and the degree to which your scores represented what you really knew or could really do? The SATs and other college entrance examinations are examples of **standardized tests.** Unlike the teacher-made tests discussed in Chapter 13, a standardized test is typically given to thousands of students who are similar to those for whom the test is designed. This allows the test publisher to establish norms, or standards, to which any individual score can be compared. For example, if a representative national sample of fourth-graders had an average score of 37 items correct on a 50-item standardized test, then we might say that fourth-graders who score above 37 are "above national norms" on this test and those who score below 37 are "below national norms."

standardized tests
Tests that are usually commercially prepared for nationwide use and designed to provide accurate and meaningful information on students' performance relative to that of others at their age or grade levels.

Traditional standardized tests are under attack throughout the United States and Canada, and entirely new forms of broad-scale tests are being developed and used. However, standardized tests of many kinds continue to be used for a wide range of purposes at all levels of education. This chapter discusses how and why standardized tests are used and how scores on these tests can be interpreted and applied to important educational decisions. It also includes information on criticisms of standardized testing and on alternatives that are being developed, debated, and applied.

Standardized tests are usually used to offer a yardstick against which to compare individuals or groups of students that teacher-made tests cannot provide. For example, suppose a child's parents ask a teacher how their daughter is doing in math. The teacher says, "Fine, she got a score of 81 percent on our latest math test." For some purposes this information would be adequate. But for others the parents might want to know much more. How does 81 percent compare to the scores of other students in this class? How about other students in the school, the district, the state, or the whole country? In some contexts the score of 81 percent might help to qualify the girl for a special program for the mathematically gifted; in others it might suggest the need for remedial instruction. Also, suppose the teacher found that the class averaged 85 percent correct on the math test. How is this class doing compared to other math classes or to students nationwide? A teacher-made test cannot yield this information.

Standardized tests are typically carefully constructed to provide accurate information about students' levels of performance. Most often, curriculum experts establish what students at a particular age should know about a subject or should be able to do. Then questions are written to assess the various skills or information students are expected to possess. The questions are tried out on various groups of students. Items that almost all students get right or almost all miss are usually dropped, as are items that students find unclear or confusing. Patterns of scores are carefully examined. If students who score well on most items do no better than lower-scoring students on a particular item, that item will probably be dropped.

Eventually, a final test will be developed and given to a large selected group of students from all over the country. Attempts are usually made to ensure that this group resembles the larger population of students who will ultimately use the test. For example, a test of geometry for eleventh-graders might be given to a sampling of eleventh-graders in urban, rural, and suburban locations; in different regions of the country; in private as well as public schools; and to students with different levels of preparation in mathematics. This step establishes the **norms** for the test, which provide an indication of how an average student will score (Hopkins, 1998). Finally, a testing manual is prepared, explaining how the test is to be given, scored, and interpreted. This particular standardized test is now ready for general use. The test development process creates tests whose scores have meaning outside of the confines of a particular classroom or school. These scores are used in a variety of ways. Explanations of some of the most important functions of standardized testing follow (see Glaser & Silver, 1994).

norms
Standards that are derived from the a test scores of a sample of people who are similar to those who will take the test and that can be used to interpret scores of future test takers.

Selection and Placement

Standardized tests are often used to select students for entry or placement in specific programs. For example, the SAT (Scholastic Assessment Test) or ACT (American College Testing Program) that you probably took in high school was used to help your college admissions board decide whether to accept you as a student.

Similarly, admission to special programs for gifted and talented students might depend on standardized test scores. Standardized tests might also be used, along with other information, to help educators decide whether to place students in special-education programs or to assign students to tracks or ability groups. For example, high schools may use standardized tests in deciding which students to place or counsel into college preparatory, general, or vocational programs. Elementary schools may use them to place students in reading groups. Standardized tests are sometimes used to determine eligibility for grade-to-grade promotion, graduation from high school, or entry into an occupation.

CONNECTIONS

For discussions of between- and within-class ability grouping, see Chapter 9, pages 295 and 299.

Diagnosis

Standardized tests are often used to diagnose individual students' learning problems or strengths. For example, a student who is performing poorly in school might be given a battery of tests to determine whether he or she has a learning disability or is mentally retarded. At the same time the testing might identify specific deficits that need remediation. Teachers frequently employ diagnostic tests of reading skills, such as the Gray Oral Reading Test that Ms. Tranh used, to identify a student's particular reading problem. For example, a diagnostic test might indicate that a student's decoding skills are fine but that his or her reading comprehension is poor; or that a student has good computation skills but lacks problem-solving skills. Sophisticated assessments can now help teachers determine students' cognitive styles and the depth of their understanding of complex concepts (Carver, Lehrer, Connell, & Erickson, 1992; Nichols, 1994).

Evaluation

Perhaps the most common use of standardized testing is to evaluate students' progress and teachers' and schools' effectiveness. For example, parents often want to know how their children are doing in comparison with what is expected of children at their grade level. Of course, standardized test scores are meaningful as evaluation only if teachers use them along with other information, such as students' actual performance in school and in other contexts, as Ms. Tranh did. Many students who score poorly on standardized tests excel in school, college, or occupations; either they have trouble taking tests or they have important skills that are not measured by such tests.

School Improvement

Standardized tests can contribute to improving the schooling process. The results of some standardized tests provide information about appropriate student placement and diagnostic information that is important in remediation. In addition, achievement tests can guide curriculum development and revision when areas of weakness appear (see Hopkins, 1998). Standardized tests can play a role in guidance and counseling as well. This is true not only for achievement and aptitude testing but also for more specialized types of measures, such as vocational interest inventories and other psychological scales that are used in the counseling of students.

Standardized tests also have some administrative uses. Schools often turn to academic achievement tests to evaluate the relative success of competing educational programs or strategies. For example, if a teacher or school tries out an innovative teaching strategy, tests can help reveal whether it was more successful than previous methods. Districtwide test results often serve as a yardstick by which citizens can judge the success of their local schools. Tests can also contribute to accountability by indicating the relative teaching strengths and weaknesses of the school's faculty. However, educating students is a complex process, and standardized tests provide only a small portion of the information that is necessary for evaluating teachers, programs, or schools.

Accountability

A growing trend since the mid-1970s has been the effort to hold teachers and schools accountable for what students learn. Most states and school districts have implemented regular standardized testing programs and publish the results on a school-by-school basis (see Baker & Niemi, 1996; Kirst, 1990). Not surprisingly, principals and other administrators watch these scores the way business owners watch their profit sheets. Many states and districts issue school report cards listing such data as test scores, attendance, retentions, and suspensions; these may be reported in newspapers or otherwise publicized (Gorney, 1994). In many districts the scores of each teacher's students are made available to the school administration and may be used in decisions about hiring, firing, promotion, and transfer.

Many states and districts have established **minimum competency tests** that students must pass either to graduate from high school or to be promoted from grade to grade (see Bishop, 1998; Chaney, Burgdorf, & Atash, 1997; Griffin, 1996). These are typically criterion-referenced tests that focus on important skills students are expected to have mastered. School districts that use minimum competency tests also usually establish special remedial programs—often during the summer—to help students pass the tests and qualify for promotion or graduation.

The accountability movement stems in part from the public's loss of confidence in education. Legislators (among others), upset by examples of students graduating from high school unable to read or compute, have demanded that schools establish higher standards and that students achieve them.

The accountability movement has its critics, however (Taylor, 1994; Worthen & Spandel, 1993). Many argue that minimum competency testing focuses schools on minimums rather than maximums. Others are concerned that schools will teach only what is tested, emphasizing reading and mathematics at the expense of, for instance, science and social studies (Shepard, 1995), and emphasizing easily measured objectives (such as punctuation) over more important hard-to-measure objectives (such as composition). Many educators point out that accountability assessments fail to take into account differences among students. A school or classroom may test low because the students are from disadvantaged backgrounds rather than because they were given poor instruction. High-stakes testing can lead schools and districts to adopt policies that artificially inflate scores, such as assigning more children to special education, categorizing more students as limited English proficient, or retaining more students (Allington & McGill-Franzen, 1992).

Regardless of these criticisms, the demand for accountability is here to stay. One advantage of accountability is that it does increase the pressure on schools and teachers to pay attention to students who might otherwise fall through the cracks and to help those who need help the most. Another advantage is that accountability encourages schools to search out improved instructional methods and guarantees routine evaluation of any innovations schools try. For example, one principal had several teachers using an effective reading program. A new teacher said that she didn't like the program and preferred to use her own.

minimum competency tests

Criterion-referenced tests that focus on important skills students are expected to have mastered to qualify for promotion or graduation.

"Fine," the principal said. "If your program produces as much gain as ours, more power to you." As it turned out, the teacher's program did not increase reading scores as much as the principal's, so the teacher dropped her method and used the principal's. The standardized tests of reading skills gave the principal and the teacher a standard against which to evaluate their programs, so (presumably) the school ended up with the better program. One study found slightly higher performance in schools that had minimum competency tests for eighth- and eleventh-graders, but not in schools that had such tests for fourth-graders (Winfield, 1990).

CONNECTIONS

For more on teaching test-taking skills in the context of teaching metacognitive awareness and study skills, see Chapter 6, page 203.

Teaching Test-Taking Skills

As standardized testing has taken on increasing importance in the evaluation of students, teachers, and schools, so too has the preparation of students to take these tests. Of course, the best way to prepare students for tests is to do a good job of teaching them the material. However, schools need to help many students to become test-wise, to show what they really know on standardized tests, and to get as good a score as possible.

THEORY *into* Practice

Many ethical issues are involved in helping students do well on standardized tests (Smith, 1991; Teddlie & Stringfield, 1989). For example, one way to help students score well would be to know the test items in advance and teach students the answers. Clearly, this would be cheating. A much more ethically ambiguous case arises when teachers know what subjects will be on the test and teach only material that they know will be tested. For example, if a standardized test did not assess Roman numerals, a math teacher might skip this topic to spend more time on an objective that would be tested. This practice is criticized as "teaching to the test." It could be argued that it is unfair to test students on material that they have not been taught and that instruction should therefore be closely aligned with tests (Cohen, 1987). On the other hand, a standardized test can assess only a small sample of all objectives that are taught in school. Gearing instruction toward the objectives that will be on the test, to the exclusion of all others, would produce a very narrow curriculum.

Beyond matching instructional content with test objectives, there are many ways to help students learn to do well on tests in general. Research has found that students can be taught to be test-wise and that this increases their standardized test scores (Kulik, Kulik, & Bangert, 1984; Scruggs, White, & Bennion, 1986). Students can also be taught coping strategies to deal with their anxiety about testing. These strategies can sometimes help children approach tests with more confidence and less stress (Zeidner, 1995). Questions have been raised about the effectiveness of programs that prepare students for the Scholastic Assessment Test. The consensus among researchers is now that coaching is effective for the SAT, particularly for minority and low-achieving students (B. J. Becker, 1990a; Messick, 1982).

Some ways of helping students to prepare for standardized tests follow (see Hill & Wigfield, 1984):

1. Give students practice with similar item formats. For example, if a test will use multiple-choice formats, give students practice with similar formats in routine classroom quizzes and tests. If tests use unusual formats such as verbal analogies (e.g., Big:Small::Honest: _____), give students practice with this type of item.

2. Suggest that students skip over difficult or time-consuming items and return to them later.

3. If there is no penalty for guessing on a test, suggest to students that they always fill in some answer. If there is a penalty for guessing, students should still be encouraged to guess if they can narrow down the options to two.
4. Suggest that students read all options on a multiple-choice test before choosing one. Sometimes one answer is correct but there is an even better answer.
5. Suggest to students that they use all available time. If they finish early, they should go back over their answers.

SELF-CHECK

What is the main difference between standardized and nonstandardized tests? How are standardized test results used in student selection, placement, diagnosis, and evaluation? What is a minimum competency test, and how does it hold teachers and schools accountable for what students learn?

WHAT TYPES OF STANDARDIZED TESTS ARE GIVEN?

Three kinds of standardized tests are commonly used in school settings: aptitude tests, norm-referenced achievement tests, and criterion-referenced achievement tests (Ebel & Frisbie, 1991). An **aptitude test** is designed to assess students' abilities. It is meant to predict the ability of students to learn or to perform particular types of tasks rather than to measure how much the students have already learned. The most widely used aptitude tests measure general intellectual aptitude; but many other, more specific tests measure particular aptitudes, such as mechanical or perceptual abilities or reading readiness. The SAT, for example, is meant to predict a student's aptitude for college studies. An aptitude test is successful to the degree that it predicts performance. For example, a reading readiness test given to kindergartners that did not accurately predict how well the students would read when they reached first or second grade would be of little use.

Achievement tests are used (1) to predict students' future performance in a course of study, (2) to diagnose students' difficulties, (3) to serve as formative tests of students' progress, and (4) to serve as summative tests of learning.

Norm-referenced achievement tests, discussed in Chapter 13, are assessments of a student's knowledge of a particular content area, such as mathematics, reading, or Spanish. These tests provide scores that can be compared with those of a representative group of students and are constructed to show differences among students. Typically, norm-referenced achievement tests assess some but not all of the skills that are taught in any one school. A norm-referenced achievement test cannot be too specific, because it is designed for nationwide use, even though the curricula for any given subject vary from district to district. For example, if some seventh-graders learn about base-2 arithmetic or Venn diagrams and others do not, then these topics will be unlikely to appear on a nationally standardized mathematics test.

A criterion-referenced achievement test also assesses a student's knowledge of subject matter; but rather than comparing the achievement of an individual student against national norms, it is designed to measure the degree to which the student has mastered certain well-specified skills. The information that a criterion-referenced test produces is quite specific: "Thirty-seven percent of Ontario fifth-graders can

aptitude test
A test designed to measure general abilities and to predict future performance.

achievement tests
Standardized tests measuring how much students have learned in a given context.

fill in the names of the major Western European nations on an outline map" or "Ninety-three percent of twelfth-graders at Alexander Hamilton High School know that increasing the temperature of a gas in a closed container increases the gas's pressure." Sometimes criterion-referenced test scores are used in comparisons between schools or between districts, but typically no representative norming group is used. If a group of curriculum experts decides that every fifth-grader in Ontario should be able to fill in an outline map of Western Europe, then the norm for that item is 100 percent; it is of less interest whether Ontario fifth-graders score better or worse on this item than students in other provinces. What is more important is that, overall, students improve each year on this item.

Aptitude Tests

Although aptitude tests, norm-referenced achievement tests, and criterion-referenced tests are distinct from one another in theory, there is in fact considerable overlap among them. For example, school learning definitely affects students' aptitude test scores, and a student who scores well on one type of test will usually score well on another. Many testing theorists claim that aptitude and achievement tests are so highly correlated that both should be considered achievement tests (see, e.g., Popham, 1995; Sternberg & Detterman, 1986).

The following subsections discuss the types of aptitude tests most often given in schools.

GENERAL INTELLIGENCE TESTS ● The most common kind of aptitude tests given in school are tests of **intelligence,** or general aptitude for school learning. The intelligence quotient, or IQ, is the score that is most often associated with intelligence testing, but other types of scores are also used.

Intelligence tests are designed to provide a general indication of individuals' aptitudes in many areas of intellectual functioning. Intelligence itself is seen as the ability to deal with abstractions, to learn, and to solve problems (Snyderman & Rothman, 1987; Sternberg, 1995a), and tests of intelligence focus on these skills. Intelligence tests give students a wide variety of questions to answer and problems to solve.

THE MEASUREMENT OF IQ ● The measurement of *intelligence quotient (IQ)* was introduced in the early 1900s by Alfred Binet, a French psychologist, to identify children who were unlikely to profit from regular classroom instruction. The scale that Binet developed to measure intelligence assessed a wide range of mental characteristics and skills, such as memory, knowledge, vocabulary, and problem solving. Binet tested a large number of students of various ages to establish norms (expectations) for overall performance on his tests. He then expressed IQ as a ratio of **chronological age** to **mental age** (the average test scores received by students of a particular age), multiplied by 100. For example, 6-year-olds (chronological age [CA] = 6) who scored at the average for all 6-year-olds (mental age [MA] = 6) would have an IQ of 100 (6/6 × 100 = 100). Six-year-olds who scored at a level typical of 7-year-olds (MA = 7) would have IQs of about 117 (7/6 × 100 = 117).

Over the years the mental age/chronological age comparison has been dropped, and IQ is now defined as having a mean of 100 and a standard deviation of 15 (the term *standard deviation* is defined later in this chapter). Most scores fall near the mean, with small numbers of scores extending well above and below the mean. In

intelligence
General aptitude for learning, often measured by ability to deal with abstractions and to solve problems.

chronological age
The age of an individual in years.

mental age
The average test score received by individuals of a given chronological age.

theory, about 68 percent of all individuals will have IQs within one standard deviation of the mean; that is, from 85 (one standard deviation below) to 115 (one standard deviation above).

Intelligence tests are designed to provide a general indication of an individual's aptitudes in many areas of intellectual functioning. The most widely used tests contain many different scales. Figure 14.1 shows items like those used on the Wechsler Adult Intelligence Scale (Wechsler, 1955). Each scale measures a different component of intelligence. Most often, a person who scores well on one scale will also do well on others, but this is not always so. The same person might do very well on general comprehension and similarities, less well on arithmetic reasoning, and poorly on block design, for example.

FIGURE 14.1 ● Illustrations of Items Used in Intelligence Testing Intelligence tests focus on skills such as dealing with abstractions and solving problems. This sample of items resembles those used on the Wechsler Adult Intelligence Scale. From Robert L. Thorndike and Elizabeth P. Hagen, *Measurement and Evaluation in Psychology and Education* (4th ed.), pp. 302–303. Copyright © 1986. Reprinted by permission of Prentice Hall, Upper Saddle River, New Jersey.

Verbal Subscale

1. General comprehension
   Why do people buy fire insurance?

2. Arithmetic reasoning
   If eggs cost 60 cents a dozen, what does one egg cost?

3. Similarities
   In what way are wool and cotton alike?

4. Digit span
   Listen carefully, and when I am through, say the numbers right after me.

   7-3-4-1-8-6

   Now I am going to say some more numbers, but I want you to say them backward.

   3-8-4-1-6

Performance Subscale

5. Digit-symbol substitution

6. Block design
   Using the four blocks, make one just like this:

Intelligence tests are administered either to individuals or to groups. Tests that are administered to groups, such as the Otis–Lennon Mental Ability Tests, the Lorge–Thorndike Intelligence Tests, and the California Test of Mental Maturity, are often given to large groups of students as general assessments of intellectual aptitude. These tests are not as accurate or detailed as are intelligence tests administered individually to people by trained psychologists, such as the Wechsler Intelligence Test for Children–Revised (WISC–R) or the Stanford–Binet test. For example, students who are being assessed for possible placement in special education usually take an individually administered test (most often the WISC–R), along with other tests.

IQ scores are important because they are correlated with school performance (Ceci, 1992). That is, students who have higher IQs tend, on the average, to get better grades, score higher on achievement tests, and so on. By the time a child is about age 6, IQ estimates tend to become relatively stable, and most people's IQs remain about the same into adulthood. However, some people will experience substantial changes in their estimated IQ, often because of schooling or other environmental influences (Ceci, 1991; Petty & Field, 1980).

MULTIFACTOR APTITUDE TESTS ● One other form of aptitude test that provides a breakdown of more specific skills is the **multifactor aptitude battery.** Many such tests are available, with a range of content and emphases. They include scholastic abilities tests such as the SAT; elementary and secondary school tests, such as the Differential Aptitude Test, the Cognitive Abilities Test, and the Test of Cognitive Skills; reading readiness tests, such as the Metropolitan Reading Readiness Test; and various developmental scales for preschool children. At a minimum, most of these tests provide not only overall aptitude scores but also subscores for verbal and nonverbal aptitudes. Often, subscores are even more finely divided to describe more specific abilities.

Norm-Referenced Achievement Tests

Whereas aptitude tests focus on knowledge acquired both in school and out, achievement tests focus on skills or abilities that are traditionally taught in the schools. In general, standardized achievement tests fall into one of four categories: achievement batteries, diagnostic tests, single-subject achievement measures, and criterion-referenced achievement measures. (Hopkins, 1998).

ACHIEVEMENT BATTERIES ● Standardized **achievement batteries,** such as the California Achievement Test, the Iowa Tests of Basic Skills, the Comprehensive Test of Basic Skills, the Stanford Achievement Test, and the Metropolitan Achievement Tests, are used to measure individual or group achievement in a variety of subject areas. These survey batteries include several small tests, each in a different subject area, and are usually administered to a group over a period of several days. Many of the achievement batteries that are available for use in the schools are similar in construction and content. However, because of slight differences among the tests in the instructional objectives and subject matter sampled within the subtests, it is important before selecting a particular test to examine it carefully for its match with a specific school curriculum and for its appropriateness relative to school goals. Achievement batteries usually have several forms for various age or grade levels so that achievement can be monitored over a period of several years.

CONNECTIONS

For a discussion of the use of IQ scores in the classification of learners with exceptionalities or for special-education services, see Chapter 12, page 411.

multifactor aptitude battery
A test that predicts ability to learn a variety of specific skills and types of knowledge.

achievement batteries
Standardized tests that include several subtests designed to measure knowledge of particular subjects.

DIAGNOSTIC TESTS ● **Diagnostic tests** differ from achievement batteries in that they generally focus on a specific content area and emphasize the skills that are thought to be important for mastery of that subject matter. Diagnostic tests produce much more detailed information than do other achievement tests. For example, a standardized mathematics test often produces scores for math computations, concepts, and applications, whereas a diagnostic test would give scores on more specific skills, such as adding decimals or solving two-step word problems. Diagnostic tests are available mostly for reading and mathematics and are intended to show specific areas of strength and weakness in these skills. The results can be used to guide remedial instruction or to structure learning experiences for students who are expected to learn the skill.

SUBJECT AREA ACHIEVEMENT TESTS ● Teachers make up most classroom tests for assessing skills in specific subjects. However, schools can purchase specific subject achievement tests for almost any subject. A problem with many of these tests is that unless they are tied to the particular curriculum and instructional strategies that are used in the classroom, they may not adequately represent the content that has been taught. If standardized achievement tests are considered for evaluating learning in specific areas, the content of the test should be closely examined for its match with the curriculum, instruction, and general teaching goals.

Criterion-Referenced Achievement Tests

CONNECTIONS

For more on the definitions of norm-referenced and criterion-referenced testing, see Chapter 13, page 469.

Criterion-referenced tests differ from norm-referenced standardized tests in several ways (see Shepard, 1989a). Such tests can take the form of a survey battery, a diagnostic test, or a single-subject test. In contrast to norm-referenced tests, which are designed for use by schools with varying curricula, criterion-referenced tests are often constructed around a well-defined set of objectives. For many tests, these objectives can be chosen by the school district, building administrator, or teacher to be applied in a specific situation. The items on the test are selected to match specific instructional objectives, often with three to five items measuring each objective. For this reason these tests are sometimes referred to as *objective-referenced tests.* Increasingly, criterion-referenced tests that are linked to well-specified standards (expectations of what children should know and be able to do at given ages) are used in state and district accountability programs.

A particular type of criterion-referenced test, called a *certificate of initial mastery,* requires students to complete an extended project over a period of time at a high level of quality. Several states are requiring these assessments for high school graduation (Rothman, 1995; Smith & Sherrell, 1996).

Criterion-referenced tests also differ from norm-referenced tests in that measurement on the criterion-referenced test often focuses on students' performance with regard to specific objectives rather than on the test as a whole. Therefore, the tests can indicate which objectives individual students or the class as a whole have mastered. Test results can be used to guide future instruction or remedial activities.

Finally, criterion-referenced tests differ from other achievement tests in the way in which they are scored and in how the results are interpreted. On criterion-referenced tests, it is generally the score for each objective that is important. Results could show, for example, how many students can multiply two digits by two digits or how many can write a business letter correctly. Moreover, students' scores on the total test or on specific objectives are interpreted with respect to some criterion of adequate performance independent of group performance. Examples of criterion-

diagnostic tests
Tests of specific skills used to identify students' needs and to guide instruction.

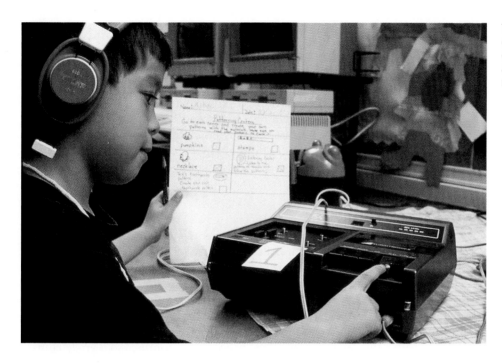

This student will later be tested on his ability to identify specific objects by name, image, sound, and word. What type of achievement test will he be taking?

referenced tests include tests for drivers and pilots, which were designed to determine who can drive or fly, not who is in the top 20 percent of drivers or pilots.

Score reports for criterion-referenced tests are frequently in the form of the number of items that the student got correct on each objective. From these data the teacher can gauge whether the student has mastered the objective.

When criterion-referenced tests are used for making decisions about mastery of a subject or topic, some procedure must be employed to determine the test score cut-off point for mastery (Kane, 1994). Most procedures for the establishment of a **cut-off score** rely on the professional judgment of teachers and other school personnel. Qualified professionals examine each item in a test and judge the probability that a student with an acceptable level of proficiency would get the item correct. They then base the cutoff score for mastery or proficiency on these probabilities.

SELF-CHECK

Define *aptitude test* and *achievement test* and describe how each is measured. What is the difference between a norm-referenced achievement test and a criterion-referenced achievement test? Give an example of an appropriate use for each type of test.

HOW ARE STANDARDIZED TESTS INTERPRETED?

After students take a standardized test, the tests are usually sent for computer scoring to the central office or the test publisher. The students' raw scores (the number correct on each subtest) are translated into one or more **derived scores,** such as percentiles, grade equivalents, or normal curve equivalents, which relate the students' scores to those of the group on which the test was normed. These statistics are described in the following sections (see Lyman, 1998).

cutoff score
The score that is designated as the minimum necessary to demonstrate mastery of a subject.

derived scores
Values computed from raw scores that relate students' performances to those of a norming group; examples are percentiles and grade equivalents.

Percentile Scores

A **percentile score,** or percentile rank (sometimes abbreviated in test reports as %ILE), indicates the percentage of students in the norming group who scored lower than a particular score. For example, if a student achieved at the median for the norming group (that is, if equal numbers of students scored better and worse than that student), the student would have a percentile rank of 50, because his or her scores exceeded those of 50 percent of the others in the norming group. If you ranked a group of 30 students from bottom to top on test scores, the 25th student from the bottom would score in the 83rd percentile (25/30 × 100 = 83.3).

Grade-Equivalent Scores

Grade-equivalent scores relate students' scores to the average scores obtained by students at a particular grade level. Let's say a norming group achieved an average raw score of 20 on a reading test at the beginning of fifth grade. This score would be established as a grade equivalent of 5.0. If a sixth-grade norming group achieved a fall test score of 30, this would be established as a grade equivalent of 6.0. Now let's say that a fifth-grader achieved a raw score of 25. This is halfway between the score for 5.0 and that for 6.0, so this student would be assigned a grade equivalent of 5.5. The number after the decimal point is referred to as "months," so a grade equivalent of 5.5 would be read "five years, five months." In theory, a student in the third month of fifth grade should have a score of 5.3 (five years, three months), and so on.

The advantage of grade equivalents is that they are easy to interpret and make some intuitive sense. For example, if an average student gains one grade equivalent each year, we call this achieving at expected levels. If we know that a student is performing 2 years below grade level (say, a ninth-grader is scoring at a level typical of seventh-graders), this gives us some understanding of how poorly the student is doing.

However, grade-equivalent scores should be interpreted as only a rough approximation. For one thing, students do not gain steadily in achievement from month to month. For another, scores that are far from the expected grade level do not mean what they appear to mean. A fourth-grader who scores at, say, 7.4 grade equivalents is by no means ready for seventh-grade work; this score just means that the fourth-grader has thoroughly mastered fourth-grade work and has scored as well as a seventh-grader would on a fourth-grade test. Obviously, the average seventh-grader knows a great deal more than what would be on a fourth-grade test, so there is no real comparison between a fourth-grader who scores at 7.4 grade equivalents and a seventh-grader who does so.

Shifting definitions of grade-level expectations can also confuse the interpretation of scores. For example, New York City school administrators were pleased during the late 1980s to report that 67 percent of students were reading at or above grade level. However, after national concern about the "Lake Wobegon Effect," wherein much more than 50 percent of students were scoring "above average" (Cannell, 1987), test makers renormed their tests. As a result, administrators in New York City could then claim that only 49 percent of their students were reading at or above grade level (Fiske, 1989).

Another common misinterpretation of grade-equivalent scores is the idea that if the gap between low-achieving and average students increases over time, the low achievers are getting worse. In fact, achievement scores become more variable (spread out) over the school years. A student who stays at the 16th percentile throughout elementary and secondary school will fall behind in grade equivalents,

percentile score
A derived score that designates what percentage of the norming group earned raw scores lower than a particular score.

grade-equivalent scores
Standard scores that relate students' raw scores to the average scores obtained by norming groups at different grade levels.

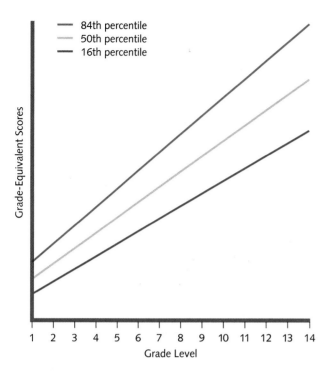

FIGURE 14.2 ● **Increasing Gap in Grade-Equivalent Scores over Years of Schooling**
A student who scores at the 16th percentile on a test in elementary school will have a corresponding grade-equivalent score that is relatively close to the score of a student in the 84th percentile. However, two students who rank correspondingly high and low as measured by percentile in secondary school would find their grade-equivalent scores relatively far apart. From J. S. Coleman and N. L. Karweit, "Information Systems and Performance Measures in Schools," *Educational Technology*, p. 97, 1972. Reprinted by permission.

as illustrated in Figure 14.2, but that student is remaining at the same point relative to agemates. When all these cautions are kept in mind, grade-equivalent scores are a useful and understandable shorthand for describing students' scores.

Standard Scores

Several kinds of scores describe test results according to their position on the normal curve. A normal curve describes a distribution of scores in which most fall near the mean, or average, with a smaller number of scores appearing the farther we go above or below the mean. A frequency graph of a **normal distribution** produces a bell-shaped curve. For example, Figure 14.3 shows a frequency distribution

normal distribution
A bell-shaped symmetrical distribution of scores in which most scores fall near the mean, progressively fewer occurring as the distance from the mean increases.

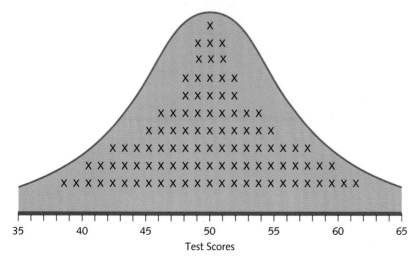

FIGURE 14.3 ● **Frequency of Scores Forming a Normal Curve**
If 100 people take a test and the score for each is marked by an x on a graph, the result could suggest a normal curve. In a normal distribution, most scores are at or near the mean (in this case, 50), and the number of scores progressively decreases farther from the mean.

from a test with a mean score of 50. Each × indicates one student who got a particular score; there are 10 ×'s at 50, so we know that 10 students got this score. Nine students got 49s and nine got 51s, and so on, and very few students made scores above 60 or below 40. Normal distributions like the one shown in Figure 14.3 are common in nature; for example, height and weight are normally distributed throughout the general population. Standardized tests are designed so that extremely few students will get every item or no item correct, so scores on them are typically normally distributed.

STANDARD DEVIATION ● One important concept related to normal distributions is the **standard deviation,** a measure of the dispersion of scores. The standard deviation is, roughly speaking, the average amount that scores differ from the mean. For example, consider these two sets of scores:

Set *A*		Set *B*
85		70
70		68
65	< Mean >	65
60		62
45		60
Standard deviation: 14.6		Standard deviation: 4.1

Note that both sets have the same mean (65) but that otherwise they are quite different, Set *A* being more spread out than Set *B*. This is reflected in the fact that Set *A* has a much larger standard deviation (14.6) than does Set *B* (4.1). The standard deviation of a set of normally distributed scores indicates how spread out the distribution will be. Furthermore, when scores or other data are normally distributed, we can predict how many scores will fall a given number of standard deviations from the mean. This is illustrated in Figure 14.4, which shows that in any normal distribution, about 34.1 percent of all scores fall between the mean and one standard deviation above the mean (+ 1 SD), and a similar number fall between the mean and one standard deviation below the mean (–1 SD).

standard deviation

A statistical measure of the degree of dispersion in a distribution of scores.

FIGURE 14.4 ● Standard Deviation
When test scores are normally distributed, knowledge of how far a given score lies from the mean in terms of standard deviations indicates what percentage of scores are higher and lower.

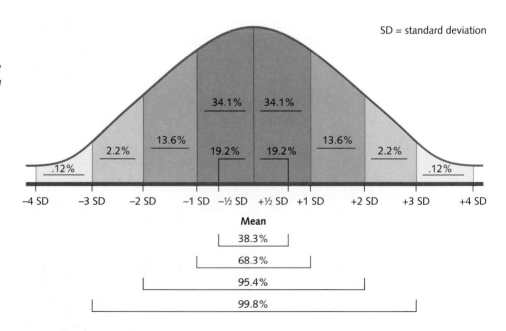

Scores on standardized tests are often reported in terms of how far they lie from the mean as measured in standard deviation units. For example, IQ scores are normed so that there is a mean of 100 and a standard deviation of 15. This means that the average person will score 100, someone scoring one standard deviation above the mean will score 115, someone scoring one standard deviation below will score 85, and so on. Therefore, about 68.2 percent of all IQ scores (that is, more than two thirds) fall between 85 (–1 SD) and 115 (+1 SD). SAT scores are also normed according to standard deviations, with the mean set at 500 and a standard deviation of 100. That puts more than two thirds of all scores between 400 and 600.

STANINES ● One standard score that is sometimes used is the **stanine score** (from the words *standard nine*). Stanines have a mean of 5 and a standard deviation of 2, so each stanine represents 0.5 standard deviation. Stanine scores are reported as whole numbers, so a person who earned a stanine score of 7 (+1 SD) actually fell somewhere between 0.75 SD and 1.25 SD above the mean.

NORMAL CURVE EQUIVALENTS ● Another form of a standard score that is often used is the **normal curve equivalent** (NCE). A normal curve equivalent can range from 1 to 99, with a mean of 50 and a standard deviation of approximately 21. NCE scores are similar to percentiles, except that intervals between NCE scores are equal (which is not the case with percentile scores). Another standard score, used more often in statistics than in reporting standardized test results, is the *z*-**score,** which sets the mean of a distribution at 0 and the standard deviation at 1. Figure 14.5 shows how a set of scores with a mean percent correct of 70 percent and a standard deviation of 5 would be represented in *z*-scores, stanines, normal curve equivalents, percentile scores, and equivalent IQ and SAT scores.

Note the difference in the figure between percentile scores and all standard scores (*z*-score, stanine, NCE, IQ, and SAT). Percentile scores are bunched up around the middle of the distribution, because most students score near the mean. This means that small changes in raw scores near the mean can produce large changes in percentiles. In contrast, changes in raw scores that are far above

stanine scores
A type of standardized score ranging from 1 to 9, having a mean of 5 and a standard deviation of 2.

normal curve equivalent
A set of standard scores ranging from 1 to 99, having a mean of 50 and a standard deviation of about 21.

z-score
A standard score having a mean of 0 and a standard deviation of 1.

SD = standard deviation

FIGURE 14.5 ●
Relationships among Various Types of Scores
Raw scores that are normally distributed can be reported in a variety of ways. Each reporting method is characterized by its mean, by the range between high and low scores, and by the standard deviation interval.

	–3 SD	–2 SD	–1 SD	Mean	+1 SD	+2 SD	+3 SD
Raw score (% correct)	55	60	65	70	75	80	85
Z-score	–3	–2	–1	0	+1	+2	+3
Stanine		1	3	5	7	9	
Normal curve equivalent	1	8	29	50	71	92	99
IQ	55	70	85	100	115	130	145
SAT	200	300	400	500	600	700	800
Percentile	1	2	16	50	84	98	99

or below the mean make a smaller difference in percentiles. For example, an increase of 5 points on the test from 70 to 75 moves a student from the 50th to the 84th percentile, an increase of 34 percentile points; but 5 more points (from 75 to 80) increases the student's percentile rank by only 14 points. At the extreme, the same 5-point increase, from 80 to 85, results in an increase of only 1 percentile point, from 98 to 99.

This characteristic of percentile ranks means that changes in percentiles should be interpreted cautiously. For example, one teacher might brag, "My average kids increased 23 percentile points [from 50 to 73], while your supposedly smart kids gained only 15 percentile points [from 84 to 99]. I really did a great job with them!" In fact, the bragging teacher's students gained only 3 points in raw score, or 0.6 standard deviation, while the other teacher's students gained 10 points in raw score, or 2 standard deviations!

THEORY into Practice

Interpreting Standardized Test Scores

This section presents a guide to interpreting test reports for one widely used standardized test of academic performance, the Terra Nova, published by CTB/McGraw-Hill (1997). Other widely used nationally standardized tests (such as the CAT, the Iowa, and the Stanford) use similar report formats.

CLASS RECORD SHEET

Figure 14.6 (on pages 516–517) shows portions of an actual Terra Nova (CTBS/5) pre–post class record sheet for children in a Title I second-grade reading class (whose names have been changed). The main information on the form is as follows.

Identification Data

Look first at the top of the form. It identifies the tests taken at the end of the previous year (pre) and at the end of the current year (post). The grade (2.7) indicates that at the time of post-testing, students were in the seventh month of second grade (April). Information at the bottom left shows testing dates, school, district, test norm, and "quarter month" (i.e., weeks since school began).

Scores

Under each column, test scores are shown in two metrics. NP refers to national percentiles; NCE, to normal curve equivalent. For example, look at the fifth child, Marvin Miller. At the end of first grade, his national percentile score in reading was 49, indicating that he scored better than 49 percent of all first-graders. By second grade, his percentile score had increased to 76. In NCEs, however, he increased from 49 to 65. The test form shows a gain of 16 NCEs; NCE scores can be added and subtracted, because they are on an equal interval scale, whereas percentile scores cannot.

Now look at the second student, Brittany Duphily. In reading, her percentile scores (and NCEs) dropped from first to second grade. Does this mean that she knows less in second grade than she did in first? Not at all. However, she did perform less well in second grade compared to other second graders. To understand this, consider a girl who is the 3rd fastest runner in the fourth grade, but a year later is the 12th fastest in the fifth grade. The girl has not slowed down, but other runners are making better progress.

Summary

At the bottom of the form is a summary of the test scores for second graders in the entire district (a class or school summary would look the same). The scores are

presented as median percentiles (the score of the middle child in the district) and the national percentile of the median, which indicates how well the district is doing among all districts. In this district, for example, the middle second-grader is scoring better than 35.3 percent of all second-graders in reading. The last set of numbers shows the mean NCEs for all second-graders and the difference between first-grade NCEs (42.5) and second-grade NCEs (41.6). The difference, a loss of 0.9 NCEs, is very small, essentially indicating that children in this district score at about the same reading level in first and second grades, in comparison to children in other districts.

INDIVIDUAL PROFILE REPORT

Like most standardized tests, the Terra Nova provides a detailed analysis of the test performance of each child. Figure 14.7 (page 518) shows an example for a third-grader, Maria Olthof (a real report, but not her real name). The form gives the following information:

Norm-Referenced Scores

At the top of the report is a list of Maria's scores on 14 scales listed six ways. The first is grade equivalent. In reading, Maria's grade equivalent is 2.0, indicating that her score is like that which would be obtained by an average child just starting second grade. Her NCE of 35 also indicates that she is performing significantly below grade level. (In general, an NCE of 50 is considered "at grade level.") Skip over scale score, which is not interpretable. Maria's *local* percentile indicates that she is reading extremely poorly in comparison to other children in her class, school, or district (however "local" was defined). A percentile of 1 is the lowest possible score.

Number correct is self-explanatory. In reading, Maria's *national* percentile indicates that she is scoring better than only 24 percent of all third-graders in the United States. "NP range" indicates the likely range of percentile scores that Maria might receive if she took the same test many times. That is, there is always a range of scores a student might get, depending on luck, inadvertent errors, testing

PRE-POST CLASS RECORD SHEET
CLASS: GRD.2 TCH 3

PRE-TEST: CTBS/5 MA
POST-TEST: CTBS/5 MA

GRADE   2.7

TITLE 1 READING

170508
170
PAGE   1

STUDENTS	FORM/LEVEL	SCORES	READING			LANGUAGE			MATHEMATICS			TOTAL SCORE ++	SCI	SOCIAL STDY	SPELL	WORD ANLYS
			READ	VOCAB	CHMPST	LANG	MECH	CMPST	MATH	COMPU	CMPST					
BEACHY JULIA M		PRE NP / POST NP	98 / 55			94 / 81			76 / 62			94 / 70				
BIRTH DATE: 5/ 4/90																
PRE GRADE: 1.7	A-11	PRE NCE / POST NCE	94 / 53			83 / 69			65 / 57			82 / 61				
POST GRADE: 2.7	A-12	DIFF	-41			-14			-8			-21				
CODES/PRE: 3916720000.....1.....																
CODES/POST: 391672.....1.....																
DUPHILY BRITTN D		PRE NP / POST NP	79 / 53			70 / 58			88 / 70			82 / 62				
BIRTH DATE: 9/25/90																
PRE GRADE: 1.7	A-11	PRE NCE / POST NCE	67 / 52			61 / 54			74 / 61			70 / 57				
POST GRADE: 2.7	A-12	DIFF	-15			-7			-13			-13				
CODES/PRE: 6613080000.....1.....																
CODES/POST: 661308.....1.....																
HARRISON ROBERT L		PRE NP / POST NP	44 / 63			30 / 34			19 / 42			28 / 46				
BIRTH DATE: 5/23/90																
PRE GRADE: 1.7	A-11	PRE NCE / POST NCE	47 / 57			39 / 41			32 / 46			37 / 48				
POST GRADE: 2.7	A-12	DIFF	10			2			14			11				
CODES/PRE: 4039710000.....1.....																
CODES/POST: 403971.....1.....																
KNOX CARLY M		PRE NP / POST NP	99 / 84			* 99 / 64			99 / 56			99 / 71				
BIRTH DATE: 7/ 9/90																
PRE GRADE: 1.7	A-11	PRE NCE / POST NCE	99 / 71			99 / 57			99 / 53			99 / 62				
POST GRADE: 2.7	A-12	DIFF	-28			-42			-46			-57				
CODES/PRE: 8441620000.....1.....																
CODES/POST: 844162.....1.....																
MILLER MARVIN R		PRE NP / POST NP	49 / 76			85 / 86			70 / 39			73 / 71				
BIRTH DATE: 5/11/90																
PRE GRADE: 1.7	A-11	PRE NCE / POST NCE	49 / 65			72 / 73			61 / 44			63 / 62				
POST GRADE: 2.7	A-12	DIFF	16			1			-17			-1				
CODES/PRE: 2905300000.....1.....																
CODES/POST: 290539.....1.....																
MOORE RICHAR J		PRE NP / POST NP	58 / 54			66 / 76			86 / 80			75 / 72				
BIRTH DATE: 8/26/90																
PRE GRADE: 1.7	A-11	PRE NCE / POST NCE	54 / 52			59 / 65			73 / 68			64 / 63				
POST GRADE: 2.7	A-12	DIFF	-2			6			-5			-1				
CODES/PRE: 352384.....1.....																
CODES/POST: 352384.....1.....																

PRE-TEST DATE: 4/14/97
QUARTER MONTH: 31
NORMS: CTBS/5 1996
PATTERN (IRT)
POST-TEST DATE: 4/22/98
QUARTER MONTH: 31
NORMS: CTBS/5 1996
PATTERN (IRT)

SCHOOL: SCHOOL 1
DISTRICT: ANY DISTRICT
CITY: ANY CITY
STATE: CA

++ TOTAL SCORE CONSISTS OF READING, LANGUAGE, MATHEMATICS

NP: NATIONAL PERCENTILE
NCE: NORMAL CURVE EQUIVALENT
DIFF: DIFFERENCE (POST-SCORE MINUS PRE-SCORE)
      DIFFERENCES ARE NOT REPORTED FOR NATIONAL PERCENTILES

*: MAXIMUM OR MINIMUM SCORE

FIGURE 14.6 ● Sample Class Record Sheet for a Standardized Test

When a class of students takes a standardized test as a pre-test and a post-test, the results may be compared by means of a form similar to the one shown here. Published by CTB/McGraw-Hill, 20 Ryan Ranch Road, Monterey, CA 93940-5703. Copyright © 1986 by McGraw-Hill, Inc. All rights reserved. Reproduced with permission of the McGraw-Hill Companies.

PRE-POST CLASS RECORD SHEET

DISTRICT: ANY DISTRICT

PRE-TEST: CTBS/5 MA
POST-TEST: CTBS/5 MA

TITLE 1 READING

GRADE 2

170508 170
PAGE 1

DISTRICT SUMMARY	SCORES	READING			LANGUAGE			MATHEMATICS			TOTAL SCORE ++	SCI	SOCIAL STDY	SPELL	WORD ANLYS
		READ	VOCAB	CMPST	LANG	MECH	CMPST	MATH	COMPU	CMPST					
	PRE MDNP	40.4			39.2			34.3			33.0				
	POST MDNP	35.3			32.5			36.3			34.0				
	PRE NPMN	36			39			36			36				
	POST NPMN	35			35			38			36				
	PRE MNCE	42.5			44.0			42.5			42.5				
	POST MNCE	41.6			42.1			43.4			42.3				
	DIFF	-0.9			-1.9			0.9			-0.2				
** NUMBER OF STUDENTS = 95		91			91			93			90				

PRE-TEST FORM/LEVEL
A-11

POST-TEST FORM/LEVEL
A-12

PRE-TEST DATE: 4/14/97
QUARTER MONTH: 31
NORMS: CTBS/5 1996
PATTERN (IRT)
POST-TEST DATE: 4/22/98
QUARTER MONTH: 31
NORMS: CTBS/5 1996
PATTERN (IRT)
CITY: ANY CITY
STATE: CA

++ TOTAL SCORE CONSISTS OF READING, LANGUAGE, MATHEMATICS

MDNP: MEDIAN NATIONAL PERCENTILE
NPMN: NATIONAL PERCENTILE OF MEAN NORMAL CURVE EQUIVALENT
MNCE: MEAN NORMAL CURVE EQUIVALENT
DIFF: DIFFERENCE (POST-SCORE MINUS PRE-SCORE)
DIFFERENCES ARE NOT REPORTED FOR NATIONAL PERCENTILES

**: SUMMARIES DO NOT INCLUDE STUDENTS WHO WERE RETAINED OR WHO SKIPPED A GRADE

CTBID: 98268627354900l-03-00078-00000?

FIGURE 14.6 (Continued)

518

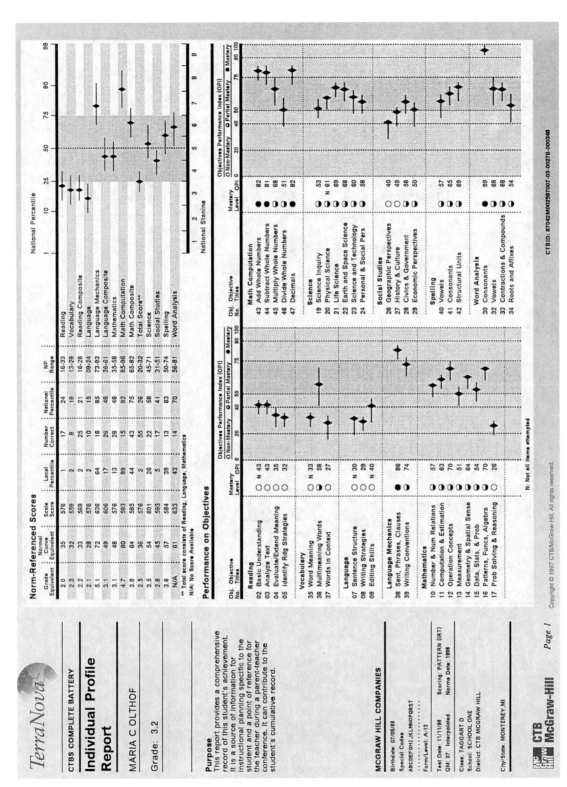

FIGURE 14.7 ● Sample Individual Test Record for a Standardized Test

Reports for individuals who take standardized tests may include overall scores and scores on specific content objectives. Published by CTB/McGraw-Hill, 20 Ryan Ranch Road, Monterey, CA 93940-5703. Copyright © 1997 by CTB/McGraw-Hill. All rights reserved. Reproduced with permission of the McGraw-Hill Companies.

conditions, motivation, and so on—all factors that could vary each time a student took a test even if his or her level of knowledge or skill stayed the same. The chart on the upper right shows this percentile range with a diamond in the center indicating the actual percentile score. The shading between the 25th and 75th percentiles indicates the "normal range"; Maria's reading score is below that range, although her own "NP range" suggests that on a good day she might score within the normal range.

Note that at the bottom of the national percentile chart is a scale indicating stanines. Recall that stanine scores range from 1 to 9, with a score of 5 indicating the national average.

Performance on Objectives

The remainder of the individual profile report breaks Maria's test down into subskills in each area. This breakdown can provide some useful information to explain overall scores. For example, look at Maria's mathematics scores. She scores very well on an "objectives performance index" in every subscale of math but one: problem solving. For Maria, this one low score could be due to her reading problems; or she may need additional work with this skill. However, subscale analyses of this kind should be taken with a grain of salt. The small number of items involved and the lack of a clear connection to the material Maria is studying mean that classroom assessments, perhaps supplemented by more fine-tuned diagnostic tests in mathematics, would give a much better indicator of Maria's strengths, weaknesses, and instructional needs.

SELF-CHECK

Describe how standardized test percentile scores, grade-equivalent scores, and standard scores are derived and interpreted.

WHAT ARE SOME ISSUES CONCERNING STANDARDIZED AND CLASSROOM TESTING?

The use of standardized tests to assess teachers, schools, and districts has increased dramatically in recent years. Most states now have statewide testing programs in which students at selected grade levels take criterion-referenced performance tests, standardized achievement tests, and/or minimum competency tests. Education departments use scores on these tests to evaluate the state's educational program as a whole and to compare the performance of individual school districts, schools, and teachers. These comparisons go under the general heading of accountability programs. Accountability is one of several issues related to uses and abuses of standardized tests. Issues concerning testing, standards, and related topics are among the most hotly debated questions in U.S. education (see Office of Technology Assessment, 1992). In recent years there have been many developments and proposals for change in testing. These are discussed in the following sections.

CASE TO CONSIDER

The Great Testing Controversy

Written by Gordon E. Greenwood, University of Florida

Jerry Natkin is beginning his seventh year of teaching English. Roscoe Carnes is beginning his fourth year as an art teacher. It is early September, and the two friends sit talking in the teachers' lounge of the only high school in a medium-sized city.

Roscoe: What's on your agenda in the English department this year, Jerry? Any new plans or projects?

Jerry: Well, it may seem early to be worrying about this, but we're determined to do something about the standardized test results in this school.

Roscoe: What's the matter with them?

Jerry: The scores are still declining. We looked back over ten years of results. On the average, last year's students scored a couple of percentage points below the kids of five years ago and even farther below the scores from ten years ago. I wonder if these kids just aren't learning.

Roscoe: Did you consider that they might be learning a lot but can't show what they know on standardized achievement tests?

Jerry: Maybe. But regardless, the issue is how to get the scores up. I think that in the English department, we should at least make sure that our courses are covering the content of the state standardized test. As I see it, with some changes in course content and classroom testing procedures, we can easily increase the school's overall average score and also our number of state finalists each year.

Roscoe: But, Jerry, that sounds like teaching to the test.

Jerry: It is. What's wrong with that?

Roscoe: Is it ethical? Should tests determine curriculum? Is doing well on standardized tests the reason kids go to school? Is testing fair to all students? Those tests contain cultural and class biases, you know. Anyway, the state exam is practically all multiple choice. If you teach to the exam, you run the risk of lowering your standards—minimums do have a way of becoming maximums. What about higher-order learning like problem solving and creative thinking?

Jerry: Higher-order thinking is always part of English, Roscoe; don't worry! But I'm convinced we can include higher-order objectives and cover the test better. Also, we need to push the kids more.

Roscoe: How?

Jerry: I'd like to involve the parents. Get them to work with their kids at home, using sample test items and such. You know, kids who score higher on tests make better grades and do better in life. We've got to coach them.

Roscoe: I'd argue with you on that. How would you coach all the kids? Would it be fair to pick only some for special treatment? And what does "doing better in life" mean? Better income? Isn't there more to life than that?

Jerry: Sure, sure. Of course achievement tests aren't everything. And they aren't perfect either. But they're there, and we need them—for feedback! How else can we as teachers know what we've accomplished? We get to see kids make measurable progress.

Roscoe: But I don't think standardized tests are a good measure of students' actual abilities or meaningful knowledge. Maybe your scores tell you something about English proficiency, but I can't measure my kids' progress that way.

Jerry: I bet you could. You could measure creativity.

Roscoe: And then teach to the creativity test? Jerry, do you really think standardized test scores should be guiding your instructional goals as an English teacher?

PROBLEM SOLVING

1. Using a problem-solving approach, address Jerry's concerns about declining test scores. How would you evaluate Jerry's plan to improve scores? Is it a good idea? Will it work? What could his department do to increase parents' involvement? How could students be coached?

2. Using a problem-solving approach, address Roscoe's concerns about overrelying on test scores. Do standardized tests lead to lower minimum standards? How could that be avoided? Where should the line be drawn—should achievement tests be used for diagnosis? For prediction? For placement? Why or why not? Can cultural and class biases be removed? How else could student achievement be measured? How else could teachers get feedback?

3. Model your solutions by adding one or more new characters and extending the dialogue in writing or role play.

Validity and Reliability

The **validity** of a test is a measure of the degree to which the test provides the type of information desired (Hopkins, 1998; Popham, 1995; Shepard, 1993a). The criteria that are used to evaluate the validity of a test vary according to the test's purpose. For example, if a test is being selected to help teachers and administrators determine which students are likely to have some difficulty with one or more aspects of instruction, the primary concern will be how the test predicts future academic performance. However, if the aim is to describe the current achievement levels of a group of students, primary interest will focus on the accuracy of that description. In short, validity deals with the relevance of a test for its intended purpose (Moss, 1992).

Because of the various roles that tests are expected to play in schools and in the education process, several types of validity may be of concern to test users. These fall into one of three basic classes: content validity, predictive validity, and construct validity.

CONTENT VALIDITY ● The most important criterion for the usefulness of a test—especially an achievement test—is whether it assesses what the user wants it to assess (Popham, 1995; Shepard, 1993a). This criterion is called **content validity.** Content validity in achievement testing is a measure of the degree of overlap between what is taught (or what should be taught) and what is tested. Content validity is determined through careful comparison of the content of a test with state or district standards or with the objectives of a course or program. For example, if a test emphasized dates and facts in history but curricula and state or local standards emphasized key ideas of history, the test could not be considered valid (Baker, 1994).

PREDICTIVE VALIDITY ● The **predictive validity** of a test is a measure of its ability to help predict future behavior. For example, if we are using a test to predict students' future school performance, one way to examine the test's validity is to relate the test scores to some measure of students' subsequent performance. If an appropriate level of correspondence exists between the test and later performance, the test can then be used to provide predictive information for students.

For example, test scores on SATs and ACTs have been shown to relate to a reasonable degree to performance in college; many college admissions officers therefore use these scores (along with high school grades and other information) in deciding which applicants to accept. Reading readiness tests and other school **readiness tests** are often used to route children into transitional first grades, extra-year kindergarten programs, and so on; this practice has come under fire in recent years, however, in large part because of the poor predictive validity of these measures (see Ellwein et al., 1991; Shepard, 1991; Wodtke, Schommer, & Brunelli, 1989).

CONSTRUCT VALIDITY ● **Construct validity** refers to the degree to which test scores relate to other scores and whether this correspondence makes sense in terms of what the test is supposed to measure (see Ebel & Frisbie, 1991). For example, consider a test of mechanical aptitude. Of course, such a test should be strongly related to a student's ability to build things. However, general intelligence (e.g., IQ) may also predict (to some degree) how well a student can build things,

validity
A measure of the degree to which a test is appropriate for its intended use.

content validity
A measure of the match between the content of a test and the content of the instruction that preceded it.

predictive validity
A measure of the ability of a test to predict future behaviors.

readiness tests
Tests to assess a student's levels of the skills and knowledge necessary for a given activity.

construct validity
The degree to which test scores reflect what the test is intended to measure.

These students will take nation-wide standardized aptitude and achievement tests this year. Will the results be equally fair to them all? Why or why not?

so it is possible that what appears to be a test of mechanical aptitude is in fact a test of general intelligence. To document the construct validity of the mechanical aptitude test, the test designer might show that the test predicts actual mechanical performance much better than does a test of general intelligence.

RELIABILITY ● Whereas validity relates to the skills and knowledge measured by a test, the **reliability** of a test relates to the accuracy with which these skills and knowledge are measured. When a test is administered, aspects related to both the test itself and the circumstances surrounding its administration could cause the results to be inaccurate. In theory, if a student were to take the same test twice, he or she should obtain the same score both times. The extent to which this would not occur is the subject of reliability. Ambiguous test items, lucky or unlucky guessing, testing experience, inconsistent motivation, and anxiety all affect test scores and could cause scores for different administrations of the same test to differ. If it could be shown that individuals received similar scores on two administrations of the same test, then some confidence could be placed in the test's reliability. If the scores were greatly inconsistent, it would be difficult to place much faith in a particular test score. Generally, the longer the test and the greater the range of items, the greater the reliability.

Test Bias

reliability
A measure of the consistency of test scores obtained from the same students at different times.

Some major criticisms of traditional multiple-choice and standardized tests relate to issues of validity and reliability. Critics argue that such tests

- Give false information about the status of learning in the nation's schools.
- Are unfair to (or biased against) some kinds of students (e.g., minority students, those with limited proficiency in English, females, and students from low-income families).

- Tend to corrupt the processes of teaching and learning, often reducing teaching to mere preparation for testing.
- Focus time, energy, and attention on the simpler skills that are easily tested and away from higher-order thinking skills and creative endeavors. (Haney & Madaus, 1989, p. 684)

One major issue in the interpretation of standardized test scores is the possibility of **test bias** against low-income or minority-group students (García & Pearson, 1994; Jones, 1988). In one sense, this is a question of test validity: A test that gave an unfair advantage to one or another category of student could not be considered valid for general use. Of greatest concern is the possibility that tests may be biased because their items assess knowledge or skills that are common to one group or culture but not another. For example, a test that includes a reading comprehension passage about a trip to the beach may be biased against students who live far from a beach or cannot afford to travel to a beach. A passage about Halloween may be unfair to Jehovah's Witnesses, who do not celebrate Halloween. It should go without saying that a test with any kind of overt cultural or gender bias should be rejected. For example, a test whose items always refer to doctors as "he" or give Hispanic names only to menial workers should not be used. Publishers of widely used tests almost always edit them in an effort to rule out cultural or gender bias, but tests should nevertheless be read carefully for possible stereotyping or other unfair elements.

SELF-CHECK

Define *validity* and *reliability*. What criticisms of standardized tests relate to issues of validity and reliability?

HOW ARE GRADES DETERMINED?

One of the most perplexing and often controversial tasks a teacher faces is grading student work (Afflerbach & Johnston, 1993; Munk & Bursuck, 1998). Is grading necessary? It is clear that some form of summative student evaluation is necessary, and grading of one kind or another is the predominant form used in most schools.

Traditional grading systems are probably less necessary in elementary school than in secondary school. According to a study conducted by Burton (1983), primary, intermediate, and secondary school teachers view the purpose of grading differently. More than half (52 percent) of the primary grade teachers in the study said that their main reason for giving grades was that the school district required them to; the evaluative and other functions of grades were not most important in their view. Furthermore, many of the primary school teachers tended to blame grading practices on the college systems. In contrast, middle school and high school teachers listed "to inform students" as the most important reason for grading. They cited letter grading as a service to students and said that teachers owed it to students as part of their education.

As for methods used to assign grades, about as many elementary school teachers used numerical scores to give overall grades in school work as depended on "their own professional judgments." Elementary teachers also listed student participation and enthusiasm as an important second criterion for grading. By comparison, about 85 percent of the middle school and high school teachers said that they assigned grades according to paper-and-pencil test results (Burton, 1983).

test bias
An undesirable characteristic of tests in which item content discriminates against certain students on the basis of socioeconomic status, race, ethnicity, or gender.

Establishing Grading Criteria

Many sets of grading criteria exist, but regardless of the level of school teachers teach in, they generally agree on the need to explain the meaning of grades they give (Burton, 1983). Grades should communicate at least the relative value of a student's work in a class. They should also help students to understand better what is expected of them and how they might improve.

Teachers and schools that use letter grades attach the following general meanings to the letters:

- A = superior; exceptional; outstanding attainment
- B = very good, but not superior; above average
- C = competent, but not remarkable work or performance; average
- D = minimum passing, but serious weaknesses are indicated; below average
- F = failure to pass; serious weaknesses demonstrated

Assigning Letter Grades

All school districts have a policy or common practice for assigning report card grades. Most use A–B–C–D–F or A–B–C–D–E letter grades, but many (particularly at the elementary school level) use various versions of outstanding–satisfactory–unsatisfactory. Some simply report percentage grades. The criteria on which grades are based vary enormously from district to district. Secondary schools usually give one grade for each subject taken, but most elementary schools and some secondary schools include ratings on effort or behavior as well as on performance.

The criteria for giving letter grades may be specified by a school administration, but grading criteria are most often set by individual teachers using very broad guidelines (Canady & Hotchkiss, 1993). In practice, few teachers could get away with giving half their students A's or with failing too many students; but between these two extremes, teachers may have considerable leeway. (See Frisbie & Waltman, 1993, for a guide to establishing grading policies.)

ABSOLUTE GRADING STANDARDS ● Grades may be given according to absolute or relative standards. Absolute grading standards might consist of preestablished percentage scores required for a given grade, as in the following example:

Grade	Percentage Correct
A	90–100 percent
B	80–89 percent
C	70–79 percent
D	60–69 percent
F	Less than 60 percent

In another form of absolute standards, called criterion-referenced grading, the teacher decides in advance what performances constitute outstanding (A), above-average (B), average (C), below-average (D), and inadequate (F) mastery of the instructional objective.

Absolute percentage standards have one important disadvantage: Student scores may depend on the difficulty of the tests they are given. For example, a student can pass a true–false test (if a passing grade is 60 percent) by knowing only 20 percent of the answers and guessing on the rest (getting 50 percent of the remaining 80 percent of the items by chance). On a difficult test on which guessing is impossible, however, 60 percent could be a respectable score. For this reason, use

TEACHERS IN ACTION

What is the best way to prepare students for standardized tests?

Richard C. Thorne Jr.
Fourth-Grade Teacher and
Assistant Principal
South Elementary School
Stoughton, Massachusetts

The best preparation for taking standardized tests is a sound program of teaching and learning all year long. All lessons should teach pupils to think logically. This will build confidence to attack unfamiliar problems. This in turn improves test performance.

Test-taking skills can be learned. Understanding how the test is structured gives the test taker an advantage. The teacher can familiarize students with the format of the test. Pupils can practice items that are similar to those that appear on the standardized test. They can also learn to deal with the type of directions given on these tests. Another way the teacher can help students be prepared for the rigors of testing week is through good home–school communication. We advise parents to encourage proper diet, exercise, and a reasonable bedtime; to avoid scheduling major family events during testing week; and to make perfect attendance the goal.

While today's educators should prepare students for standardized tests, they must not teach directly to the test. Although pressure is mounting to increase test scores, if the teacher teaches only to improve test scores, everyone involved loses. The results of these tests become meaningless. Many learning activities that are not easily measured by a standardized test will not be undertaken. Pupils will not discover their full potential. Future teachers will not be able to improve each child's pool of knowledge by using the previous year's test results to discover pupil needs. A professional educator should be able to prepare the students for the challenge of standardized tests without resorting to teaching to the test.

Louis J. Gotlib
High School Chemistry and
Third–Fifth Grade Science Teacher
South Granville High School
Creedmore, North Carolina

As a teacher, most of my experience with classroom tests comes from the State of North Carolina end-of-course (EOC) chemistry test, which all my students take each June. This test, among others, was put into place to ensure accountability on the part of the schools. The test is designed to measure how well students know the state's curriculum in chemistry. In my teaching, I feel pulled to give my students the most challenging, relevant, and enjoyable class possible to provide a solid base on which students can be successful in college chemistry classes and have my students score well on the EOC test. The difficulties come when I do not have time to teach all of the material I'd like to, an annual event. Do I cover a topic that I know will be on the test? Or should I let my students do another lab that I know they will learn more from and will find interesting?

My approach is to give students the best possible course and to cover as many topics as I can, whether or not they are on the test. I want to teach not only chemistry facts but also how chemistry affects students' lives. In addition, I am trying to help my students develop more positive attitudes toward science. Good test scores, while important, are secondary to these other goals. The EOC tests are useful in that they provide me with information on how my students did on different parts of the curriculum, which reflects on how well I did teaching the material. I can use this information to revise my course content and my teaching methods. Well-designed tests that measure higher-level thinking skills and a true understanding of a subject are a rarity. I do my students a great disservice if I let standardized tests dictate what and how I teach.

The Intentional Teacher

● **Using What You Know about Standardized Tests and Grading to Improve Teaching and Learning**

Intentional teachers know that standardized tests can provide some–albeit limited–information about how teachers, schools, and students are performing. They can interpret standardized scores and use results from standardized tests for decision making when appropriate. Intentional teachers rely upon other assessment measures to complete the complicated picture of student learning. Intentional teachers are thoughtful in the assignment of grades, selecting their grading schemes with a cogent rationale in mind.

1 What am I trying to accomplish?

Teachers do well to explore the role of standardized testing in their locale. Talk with experienced colleagues and your administrator to determine the extent to which standardized tests play a role in your professional practice. Ask about district and local expectations for your use of standardized tests.

> After a lunchtime conversation with some experienced peers, you (a first-year teacher) perceive a sense of urgency surrounding standardized testing in your district. Knowing that parents and community members are highly interested in year-end results, you take some time to reflect on your own position on standardized testing. You ask yourself, "To what extent do standardized tests measure what we value here? What information can standardized tests provide that can be useful at my school? How do we continue to teach complex thinking and still help our students prepare for tests?" You call your experienced colleagues and arrange a second lunch date to discuss your answers to tough questions such as these.

Intentional teachers choose grading schemes with an understanding of their benefits and shortcomings. When you select your grading system, consider a range of options such as absolute or relative standards, traditional grades, and mastery testing.

> You decide that the strategy you employed last year, grading on a curve, did not provide students with information about their mastery of important objectives. This year, you call the district's assessment expert to help you flesh out a criterion-referenced grading system that will give students specific information about what they have mastered and what is yet to come.

2 What are my students' relevant experiences and needs?

Teachers can use formal, standardized tests to provide information about their students' needs. Consider the use of diagnostic tests to identify learning problems and cognitive strengths.

> Mindy reads at a level that appears to be far above those of her second-grade peers. She gives sophisticated analyses of the stories she reads; and, although she is a willing learner, she sometimes appears bored with the second-grade curriculum. You call the school psychologist to learn the procedure for obtaining formal testing to determine whether special services for students who are gifted and talented would be appropriate for Mindy.

---

of absolute percentage criteria should be tempered with criterion-referenced standards. That is, a teacher might use a 60–70–80–90 percent standard in most circumstances but establish (and announce to students) tougher standards for tests that students are likely to find easy and easier standards for more difficult tests.

RELATIVE GRADING STANDARDS ● A **relative grading standard** exists whenever a teacher gives grades according to the students' rank in their class or grade. The classic form of relative grading is specifying what percentage of students will be given A's, B's, and so on. A form of this practice is called *grading on the curve,* because students are given grades on the basis of their position on a normal curve of scores.

Relative grading standards have the advantage of placing students' scores in relation to one another, without regard to the difficulty of a particular test. However, relative grading standards have serious drawbacks (see Guskey, 1994). One is that because they hold the number of A's and B's constant, students in a class of high achievers must get much higher scores to earn an A or B than students in low-achieving classes—a situation that is likely to be widely seen as unfair. Teachers often deal with this problem by giving relatively more A's and B's in high-achieving

relative grading standard
Grading on the basis of how well other students performed on the same test rather than in terms of preestablished absolute standards.

3 **What approaches and materials are available to help me challenge every student?**

Select a grading scheme that encourages all students to improve. Learning contracts are one example.

> You allow your career development students to select the grade to which they will aspire, and you help them select projects that will allow them to attain that grade. Examples of projects include "shadowing" a professional of their choice and searching the Internet for relevant information on preparing for particular careers.

Criteria for grades should be clear to students from the outset. Specify expected levels of performance. Consider, when appropriate, having students contribute to the development of grading criteria.

> You explain your grading scale to your biology students and show how each category of performance will contribute to their grade. You ask students to think about the scheme overnight. The next day you entertain a discussion of the extent to which your system will provide a valid measure of students' biology learning. Students offer a few suggestions, and you modify your scheme slightly depending upon their input.

4 **How will I know whether and when to change my strategy or modify my instruction?**

The assessments and grades that teachers use should provide information about each of their students within several domains. Ask yourself about one of your students—pick one at random—and consider how much you understand about this student's progress. Adjust your use of standardized tests, grades, and other assessment measures to provide more complete information about student learning.

Although you took a quick glance at each of your students' standardized scores from the previous year and you have your grade book, filled with letter grades, at hand, you find yourself unable to give an accurate, trustworthy picture of many students' efforts to date. To round out your understanding of student learning, you resolve to collect performance-based data through observations and attitudinal data through journal entries and interest inventories.

5 **What information will I accept as evidence that my students and I are experiencing success?**

The public is increasingly interested in maintaining teachers' and schools' accountability. Check current sources like your school's annual statements (sometimes called report cards) and newspaper reports to determine public perceptions of your success. To what extent do you consider public information a valid measure of schools' (and your!) success?

> A recent newspaper article puts your grade-level students' districtwide performance at the 48th percentile. The headline of the article is "PLEASANT CITY'S SEVENTH GRADERS SCORE WELL ON STANDARDIZED TESTS!" You sip two cups of coffee as you consider competing interpretations of the test scores.

Teachers should be careful consumers when using standardized measures. Check information related to the content, predictive, and construct validity of the tests employed in your district. Ask for information related to test bias.

> When the information booklet that accompanies the teacher's packet on the statewide test does not provide information about test bias, you call the question hot line and ask how the authors have screened for bias against students from minority groups and students acquiring English.

classes than in others. Another disadvantage of relative grading is that it creates competition among students; when one student earns an A, this diminishes the chances that others may do so. Competition can inhibit students from helping one another and can hurt social relations among classmates (Krumboltz & Yeh, 1996).

Strict grading on the curve and guidelines for numbers of A's and B's have been disappearing in recent years. For one thing, there has been a general grade inflation; more A's and B's are given now than in the past, and C is no longer the expected average grade but often indicates below-average performance. As one indication of current practices with respect to grading, Anderson (1994) summarized a national survey of eighth-graders who were asked to report their English grades since sixth grade. The results were as follows:

Mostly A's: 31 percent
Mostly B's: 38 percent
Mostly C's: 23 percent
Mostly D's: 6 percent
Mostly less than D's: 2 percent

Results were similar in mathematics, and grades were only slightly lower in high-poverty schools than in middle-class schools. It is likely that these self-reported grades are somewhat higher than what students actually received, but it is nevertheless likely that the average grade today is B, not C.

The most common approach to grading involves teachers' looking at student scores on a test, taking into account test difficulty and the overall performance of the class, and assigning grades in such a way that about the "right number" of students earn A's and B's and the "right number" fail. Teachers vary considerably in their estimates of what these right numbers should be, but schools often have unspoken norms about how many students should be given A's and how many should fail (see Fitzpatrick, 1989; Hoge & Coladarci, 1989).

CONNECTIONS

For a full description of portfolios, performance assessments, and rubrics, see Chapter 13, page 483.

Performance Grading

One of the most important limitations of traditional grades is that while they may give some indication of how students are doing in comparison to others, they provide no information about what students know and can do. A student who gets a B in English may be disappointed or may breathe a sigh of relief, depending on what she expected. However, this grade does not tell her or her parents or teachers what she can do, what she needs to do to progress, or where her strengths or weaknesses are. Furthermore, giving a single grade in each subject may reinforce the idea that students are more able or less able, or perhaps more motivated or less motivated, rather than the idea that all students are growing.

One response to these limitations that is being used in many schools at all levels is an alternative approach to grading called *performance grading*. In performance grading, teachers determine what children know and can do and then report this in a way that is easy for parents and students to understand.

Figure 14.8 (from Wiggins, 1994) shows one page of a language arts assessment keyed to fifth-grade exit standards, or expectations of what a fifth-grader should know. A parent of a student who receives a form like this could see how the student is progressing toward the kind of performance the school district has defined as essential. Note that the form does provide information on how the student is doing in comparison to other students, but that the emphasis is on growth over time.

SCORING RUBRICS FOR PERFORMANCE GRADING ● A key requirement for the use of performance grading is collection of work samples from students that indicate their level of performance on a developmental sequence. Collecting and evaluating work that students are already doing in class (such as compositions, lab reports, or projects) is called *portfolio assessment* (Herbert, 1998; Shaklee et al., 1997). An alternative is to give students tests in which they can show their abilities to apply and integrate knowledge, skills, and judgment. Most performance grading schemes use some combination of portfolios and on-demand performance tests. In either case the student performance may be evaluated against rubrics, which describe, for example, partially proficient, proficient, and advanced performance, or which indicate a student's position on a developmental sequence (as in Figure 14.8).

Other Alternative Grading Systems

Several other approaches to grading are used in conjunction with innovative instructional approaches. In *contract grading*, students negotiate a particular amount

Cherry Creek School District
Polton Community Elementary School
Fairplay Progress Report
(Language Arts Section)

Student Name _____ Grade 3 ____ 4 ____

Teacher _____ School Year ____

Performance-based graduation requirements focus on student mastery of the proficiencies. The curriculum and written progress report are geared toward preparing students for this task. A date (for example, 11/93) indicates where a student is performing on a continuum of progress based on the fifth-grade exit standards.

	Basic	Proficient	Advanced
Language Arts Proficiency 1 Listens, interpreting verbal and nonverbal cues to construct meaning.	Actively listens, demonstrates understanding, and clarifies with questions and paraphrasing.	Actively listens for purpose, demonstrates understanding, and clarifies with questions and paraphrasing.	Actively listens for purpose, demonstrates understanding, clarifies with questions and paraphrasing, classifies, analyzes, and applies information.
Language Arts Proficiency 2 Conveys meaning clearly and coherently through speech in both formal and informal situations.	Appropriately speaks to inform, explain, demonstrate, or persuade. Organizes a speech and uses vocabulary to convey a message.	Appropriately speaks to inform, explain, demonstrate, or persuade. Organizes a speech and uses vocabulary to convey a message.	Appropriately speaks to inform, explain, demonstrate, or persuade. Organizes a formal speech with details and transitions adapting subject and vocabulary. Uses eye contact, gestures, and suitable expression for an audience and topic.
Language Arts Proficiency 3 Reads to construct meaning by interacting with the text, by recognizing the different requirements of a variety of printed materials, and by using appropriate strategies to increase comprehension.	Reads varied material, comprehends at a literal level. Recalls and builds knowledge through related information. Begins to use strategies to develop fluency, adjusting rate when reading different material.	Reads varied material, comprehends literally and interpretively. Synthesizes and explores information, drawing inferences. Critiques author's intent, analyzes material for meaning and value. Applies strategies to increase fluency, adjusting rate when reading different material.	Reads varied material, comprehends and draws inferences, recalls and builds knowledge through related information. Applies strategies to increase fluency, adjusting rate when reading different material.
Language Arts Proficiency 4 Produces writing that conveys purpose and meaning, uses effective writing strategies, and incorporates the conventions of written language to communicate clearly.	Appropriately writes on assigned or self-selected topics. Clear main ideas, few details. Weak elements in the beginning, middle, end. Sentence structure lacks variety and contains errors.	Appropriately writes on assigned or self-selected topics. Clear main ideas, interesting details, clear organization, sequencing, varied sentence structure, edits to reduce errors. Appropriate voice and word choice.	Appropriately writes on assigned or self-selected topics. Connects opinions, details, and examples. Effective organization and sequencing, meaningful sentence structure, edits to eliminate most errors. Appropriate voice and word choice.

As compared to the class in the area of Language Arts, your child

Editor's Note: The teacher places a check in one box per marking period to indicate child's status in language arts.

1	2	3	Marking Periods
			Displays strong performance
			Demonstrates appropriate development
			Needs practice and support

FIGURE 14.8 ● Sample Performance Grading

From Grant Wiggins, "Toward Better Report Cards," *Educational Leadership, 52*(2), 1994, pp. 28–37. © Center on Learning, Assessment, and School Structure. Reprinted by permission of the author.

of work or level of performance that they will achieve to receive a certain grade. For example, a student might agree to complete five book reports of a given length in a marking period to receive an A. **Mastery grading,** an important part of mastery learning, involves establishing a standard of mastery, such as 80 or 90 percent correct on a test. All students who achieve that standard receive an A; students who do not achieve it the first time receive corrective instruction and then retake the test to try to achieve the mastery criterion.

CONNECTIONS

For more on mastery learning, see Chapter 9, page 301.

LETTING STUDENTS RETAKE TESTS ● Many teachers allow students to retake tests, especially if they failed the first time. This can be a good idea if it gives students an opportunity to do additional studying and master the material the class is studying. For example, a student might be given 2 days to study the content that was tested and then take an alternative form of the test. The student might then be given one letter grade lower than he or she scored on the second test, since the student had an advantage in having already seen the test. There is some danger that if students know that they can always retake tests, they may not study until after attempting the first test; but, in general, allowing students a second chance is a good way to allow students who are willing to put in extra effort to improve a poor grade.

Assigning Report Card Grades

Most schools give report cards four or six times per year; that is, every 9 or 6 weeks (Chansky, 1975). Report card grades are most often derived from some combination of the following factors (Jussim, 1991):

- Average scores on quizzes and tests
- Average scores on homework
- Average scores on seatwork
- Class participation (academic behaviors in class, answers to class questions, and so on)
- Deportment (classroom behavior, tardiness, attitude)
- Effort

One important principle in report card grading is that grades should never be a surprise to students. Students should always know how their grades will be computed, whether classwork and homework are included, and whether class participation and effort are taken into account. Being clear about standards for grading helps a teacher avert many complaints about unexpectedly low grades and, more important, lets students know exactly what they must do to improve their grades.

Another important principle is that grades should be private. There is no need for students to know one another's grades; making grades public only invites invidious comparisons among students (see Simpson, 1981). Finally, it is important to restate that grades are only one method of student evaluation. Written evaluations that add information can provide useful information to parents and students (Burton, 1983).

mastery grading
Absolute grading based on criteria for mastery.

SELF-CHECK

Describe the advantages and disadvantages of letter grades, absolute grading standards, grading on the curve, contract grading, and mastery grading.

CHAPTER SUMMARY

WHAT ARE STANDARDIZED TESTS AND HOW ARE THEY USED?

The term *standardized* describes tests that are uniform in content, administration, and scoring and therefore allow for the comparison of results across classrooms, schools, and school districts. Standardized tests such as the SAT and CTBS measure individual performance or ability against standards, or norms, that have been established for many other students in the school district, state, or nation for which each test was designed. Standardized test scores are used for selection and placement, such as grade promotion or college admission; for diagnosis and remediation; for evaluation of student proficiency or progress in content areas; and for evaluation of teaching strategies, teachers, and schools. Uses of standardized tests may be controversial, as in the cases of readiness testing of preschoolers and national testing for teacher certification.

WHAT TYPES OF STANDARDIZED TESTS ARE GIVEN?

Aptitude tests, such as tests of general intelligence and multifactor batteries, predict students' general abilities and preparation to learn. IQ tests administered to individuals or groups attempt to measure individual aptitude in the cognitive domain. Achievement tests assess student proficiency in various subject areas. Diagnostic tests focus on specific subject matter to discover strengths or weaknesses in mastery. Norm-referenced testing interprets scores in comparison with the scores of other people who took the test, and criterion-referenced testing interprets scores based on fixed performance criteria.

HOW ARE STANDARDIZED TESTS INTERPRETED?

Scores that are derived from raw scores include percentiles, the percentage of scores in the norming group that fall below a particular score; grade equivalents, the grade and month at which a particular score is thought to represent typical performance; and standard scores, the students' performance in relation to the normal distribution of scores. Standard scores include stanines (based on the standard deviation of scores), normal curve equivalents (based on a comparison of scores with the normal distribution), and z-scores (the location of scores above or below the mean).

WHAT ARE SOME ISSUES CONCERNING STANDARDIZED AND CLASSROOM TESTING?

Tests and test items must have validity, the quality of testing what is intended to be tested. Content validity means that what is tested corresponds to what has been taught. Predictive validity means that the test accurately predicts future performance. Construct validity means that the test measures precisely what it is supposed to measure. Reliability means that test results are consistent when the test is administered at different places or times. Test bias in any form compromises validity. Other issues related to standardized testing include ethics in the content of tests, student preparation for testing, the uses of test scores, and the relationship of tests to the curriculum.

HOW ARE GRADES DETERMINED?

Grading systems differ in elementary and secondary education. For example, informal assessments may be more appropriate at the elementary level, whereas letter grades become increasingly important at the secondary level. Grading standards may be absolute or relative (grading on the curve). Performance grading is a way for teachers to determine what children know and can do. A key requirement for performance grading is judicious collection of work samples from students that indicate level of performance. Another approach is to give students tests in which they can show their abilities. Other systems include contract grading and mastery grading. Report card grades typically average scores on tests, homework, seatwork, class participation, deportment, and effort.

KEY TERMS

achievement batteries   507

achievement tests   504

aptitude test   504

chronological age   505

construct validity   521

content validity   521

cutoff score   509

derived score   509

diagnostic tests   508

grade-equivalent scores   510

intelligence   505

mastery grading   530

mental age   505

minimum competency tests   502

multifactor aptitude battery   507

normal curve equivalent   513

normal distribution   511

norms   500

percentile score   510

predictive validity   521

readiness tests   521

relative grading standard   526

reliability   522

standard deviation   512

standardized tests   499

stanine score   513

test bias   523

validity   521

z-score   513

Self-Assessment

1. What are the advantages and disadvantages of minimum competency testing?

2. Which of the following types of standardized tests is designed to predict future performance?
   a. placement test
   b. achievement test
   c. aptitude test
   d. diagnostic test

3. Currently intelligence is measured as a
   a. ratio of chronological age to mental age.
   b. percentile.
   c. mean of 100 and a standard deviation of 15.
   d. percentage of items correct on an IQ test.

4. Which of the following interpretations would apply to a sixth-grade student who has scored at the mean of a standardized test?
   a. percentile = 90; stanine = 9; z = 20
   b. NCE = 50; z = 0; percentile = 50
   c. GE = 7.2; stanine = 5; NCE = 45
   d. z = 1; NCE = 60, percentile = 50

5. Two classes of math students average 75 on a test, but the students in one class have scores that are much more spread out; this means their results will have a larger
   a. mean.
   b. median.

c. standard deviation.
d. normal curve.

6. A seventh-grader has a grade-equivalent score of 9.4 on a standardized test. Which of the following interpretations can be made from these results?
   a. The student is ready for ninth-grade work.
   b. The test was too easy and should be renormed.
   c. The student has done as well on the test as an average ninth-grader.
   d. The student scored at the 9.4 percentile.

7. Which of the following terms refers to a measure of a consistency of test results over multiple applications?
   a. predictive validity
   b. content validity
   c. construct validity
   d. reliability

8. Match each type of validity with its description.
   a. construct validity
   b. predictive validity
   c. content validity

   _____ a measure of the match between the test items and instruction given

   _____ a measure of the ability of a test to forecast behaviors

   _____ a measure of the degree to which test scores reflect its intention

9. What are the major criticisms of standardized tests?

10. What are the advantages and disadvantages of absolute grading standards and relative grading standards?

REFERENCES

Abrami, P. C., Leventhal, L., & Perry, R. P. (1982). Educational seduction. *Review of Educational Research, 52,* 446–462.

Achenbach, T. M., & McConaughy, S. H. (1987). *Empirically based assessment of child and adolescent psychopathology: Practical applications.* Beverly Hills: Sage.

Achilles, C. M., Finn, J. D., & Bain, H. P. (1997/98). Using class size to reduce the equity gap. *Educational Leadership, 55*(4), 40–43.

Adams, A., Carnine, D., & Gersten, R. (1982). Instructional strategies for studying content area texts in the intermediate grades. *Reading Research Quarterly, 18,* 27–53.

Adams, G. L., & Engelmann, S. (1996). *Research on Direct Instruction: 25 years beyond DISTAR.* Seattle, WA: Educational Achievement Systems.

Adams, J. L. (1974). *Conceptual blockbusting.* San Francisco: Freeman.

Adams, M. J. (1989). Thinking skills curricula: Their promise and progress. *Educational Psychologist, 24,* 25–77.

Adams, M. J. (1990). *Beginning to read: Thinking and learning about print.* Cambridge, MA: MIT Press.

Adelman, N. E., Haslam, M. B., & Pringle, B. A. (1996). *The uses of time for teaching and learning.* Washington, DC: United States Department of Education.

Adkins, D. (1989). *Writing to read: Evaluation report: West Virginia Project for School Year 1988/89* [ERIC database document]. Clearinghouse No. CS 212218; ERIC Document Reproduction Service No. ED 3225844

Afflerbach, P. P., & Johnston, P. H. (1993). Writing language arts report cards: Eleven teachers' conflicts of knowing and communicating. *The Elementary School Journal, 94*(1), 73–86.

Airasian, P. W., & Walsh, M. E. (1997). Constructivist cautions. *Phi Delta Kappan, 78*(6), 444–449.

Alba, R. D. (1990). *Ethnic identity.* New Haven, CT: Yale University Press.

Alberto, P. A. & Troutman, A. C. (1995). *Applied behavior analysis for teachers* (4th ed.). Columbus, OH: Merrill.

Alderman, M. K. (1990). Motivation for at-risk students. *Educational Leadership, 48*(1), 27–30.

Aleman, S. R. (1990). *Attention deficit disorder.* Washington, DC: Education and Public Welfare Division of the Congressional Research Service.

Alexander, K. L., Entwisle, D. R., & Thompson, M. S. (1987). *School performance, status relations, and the structure of sentiment: Bringing the teacher back in* (Technical Report No. 9). Baltimore: Johns Hopkins University, Center for Research on Elementary and Middle Schools.

Alexander, P. A. (1992). Domain knowledge: Evolving themes and emerging concerns. *Educational Psychologist, 27,* 33–51.

Alexander, P. A. (1995). Superimposing a situation-specific and domain-specific perspective in an account of self-regulated learning. *Educational Psychologist, 30*(4), 189–194.

Alexander, P. A., & Jetton, T. L. (1996). The role of importance and interest in the processing of text. *Educational Psychology Review, 8*(1), 89–121.

Alexander, P. A., Kulikowich, J. M., & Jetton, T. L. (1994). The role of subject-matter knowledge and interest in the processing of linear and nonlinear texts. *Review of Educational Research, 64,* 201–252.

Alexander, P. A., Kulikowich, J. M., & Jetton, T. L. (1995). Interrelationship of knowledge, interest, and recall: Assessing a model of domain learning. *Journal of Educational Psychology, 87*(4), 559–575.

Alexander, P. A., & Murphy, P. K. (1994, April). *The research base for APA's learning-centered psychological principles.* Paper presented at the annual meeting of the American Educational Research Association, San Francisco.

Alfassi, M. (1998). Reading for meaning: The efficacy of reciprocal teaching in fostering reading comprehension in high school students in remedial reading classes. *American Educational Research Journal, 35*(2), 309–332.

Allen, J., Clark, F., Gallagher, P., & Scofield, F. (1982). *Classroom strategies for accommodating exceptional learners.* Minneapolis: University of Minnesota, National Support Systems Project.

Allington, R. L., & Johnston, P. (1989). Coordination, collaboration, and consistency: The redesign of compensatory and special education. In R. E. Slavin, N. L. Karweit, & N. A. Madden (Eds.), *Effective Programs for Students at Risk.* Boston: Allyn & Bacon.

Allington, R. L., & McGill-Franzen, A. (1989). School response to reading failure: Instruction for Chapter 1 and special education students in grades two, four, and eight. *Elementary School Journal, 89*(5), 529–542.

Allington, R. L., & McGill-Franzen, A. (1992). Does high-stakes testing improve school effectiveness? *ERS Spectrum, 10*(2), 3–12.

Alvermann, D. E., et al. (1985). Prior knowledge activation and the comprehension of compatible and incompatible text. *Reading Research Quarterly, 20,* 420–436.

American Association of University Women. (1992). *How schools shortchange girls.* Washington, DC: Author.

American Psychiatric Association. (1987). *Diagnostic and statistical manual of mental disorders* (3rd ed. rev.). Washington, DC: Author.

American Psychiatric Association. (1994). *Diagnostic and statistical manual of mental disorders* (4th ed.). Washington, DC: Author.

American Psychological Association. (1992). Working draft report of the APA Presidential Task Force on Psychology in Education.

American Psychological Association. (1997). *Learner-centered psychological principles: A framework for school redesign and reform.* Washington, DC: Author.

Ames, C. (1986). Effective motivation: The contribution of the learning environment. In R. S. Feldman (Ed.), *The* *social psychology of education.* Cambridge: Cambridge University Press.

Ames, C. (1992). Classrooms: Goals, structures, and student motivation. *Journal of Educational Psychology, 84,* 261–271.

Ames, C., & Ames, R. (1984). Systems of student and teacher motivation: Toward a qualitative definition. *Journal of Educational Psychology, 76,* 535–556.

Ames, C., & Archer, J. (1988). Achievement goals in the classroom: Students' learning strategies and motivation processes. *Journal of Educational Psychology, 80,* 260–267.

Ames, R., & Ames, C. (1990). *Research on motivation in education,* Vol. 3. New York: Academic Press.

Anderson, J. (1994). *What do student grades mean? Differences across schools.* Washington, DC: U.S. Department of Education, Office of Educational Research and Improvement.

Anderson, J. R. (1985). *Cognitive psychology and its implications* (2nd ed.). San Francisco: Freeman.

Anderson, J. R. (1990). *Cognitive psychology and its implications* (3rd ed.). New York: Freeman.

Anderson, J. R. (1995). *Learning and memory: An integrated approach.* New York: Wiley.

Anderson, J. R., & Bower, G. (1983). *Human associative memory.* Washington, DC: Winston.

Anderson, L. M. (1989). Learners and learning. In M. Reynolds (Ed.), *Knowledge base for beginning teachers* (pp. 85–100). New York: Pergamon.

Anderson, L. M., Blumenfeld, P., Pintrich, P. R., Clark, C. M., Marx, R. W., & Peterson, P. (1995). Educational psychology for teachers: Reforming our courses, rethinking our roles. *Educational Psychologist, 30*(3), 143–157.

Anderson, L. M., Brubaker, N. L., Alleman-Brooks, J., & Duffy, G. G. (1985). A qualitative study of seatwork in first-grade classrooms. *Elementary School Journal, 86,* 123–140.

Anderson, L. M., Evertson, C. M., & Brophy, J. E. (1979). An experimental study of effective teaching in first-grade reading groups. *Elementary School Journal, 79,* 193–223.

Anderson, L. W., & Pellicer, L. O. (1990). Synthesis of research on compensatory and remedial education. *Educational Leadership, 48*(1), 10–16.

Anderson, L. W., & Sosniak, L. A. (Eds.). (1994). *Bloom's taxonomy: A forty-year perspective.* Chicago: University of Chicago Press.

Anderson, T. H., & Armbruster, B. B. (1984). Studying. In P. D. Pearson (Ed.), *Handbook of reading research.* New York: Longman.

Andre, T. (1973). Retroactive inhibition of prose and change in physical or organizational context. *Psychological Reports, 32,* 781–782.

Andre, T., Anderson, R. C., & Watts, G. H. (1976). Item-specific interference and list discrimination in free recall. *Journal of General Psychology, 72,* 533–543.

Andrich, D., & Styles, I. (1994). Psychometric evidence of intellectual growth spurts in early adolescence. *Journal of Early Adolescence, 14*(3), 328–344.

Anglin, J. N. (1993). Vocabulary development: A morphological self-analysis. *Monographs of the Society for Research in Child Development, 58*(10), 238.

Araki, C. (1990). Dispute management in schools. *Mediation Quarterly, 8,* 51–62.

Archambault, F. X. (1989). Instructional setting and other design features of compensatory education programs. In R. E. Slavin, N. L. Karweit, & N. A. Madden (Eds.), *Effective programs for students at risk.* Boston: Allyn & Bacon.

Archibald, D., & Newmann, F. (1988). *Beyond standardized testing: Authentic academic achievement in the secondary school.* Reston, VA: NASSP Publications.

Argys, L. M., Rees, D. I., & Brewer, D. J. (1995). *The impact of ability grouping on high school student achievement: Evidence from NELS.* Washington, DC: National Center for Education Statistics, U.S. Department of Education.

Arias, M. B. (1986). The context of education for Hispanic students: An overview. *American Journal of Education, 95,* 26–57.

Armstrong, T. (1994). *Multiple intelligences in the classroom.* Alexandria, VA: Association for Supervision and Curriculum Development.

Armstrong, T. (1995). *The myth of the ADD child: 50 ways to improve your child's behavior and attention span without drugs, labels, or coercion.* New York: Dutton.

Armstrong, T. (1996). ADD: Does it really exist? *Phi Delta Kappan, 77*(6), 424–428.

Aron, I. E. (1977). Moral philosophy and moral education: A critique of Kohlberg's theory. *School Review, 85,* 197–217.

Aronson, E., Blaney, N., Stephan, C., Sikes, J., & Snapp, M. (1978). *The jigsaw classroom.* Beverly Hills: Sage.

Aronson, E. A. (1995). *The social animal.* New York: Freeman.

Aronson, J. K. (1996). How schools can recruit hard-to-reach parents. *Educational Leadership, 53*(7), 58–60.

Arter, J. A. (1990). *Using portfolios in instruction and assessment.* Portland, OR: Northwest Regional Educational Laboratory.

Arter, J. A. (1991). *Using portfolios in instruction and assessment: State of the art summary.* Portland, OR: Northwest Regional Educational Laboratory.

Asher, S. R., & Coie, J. D. (1990). *Peer rejection in childhood.* New York: Cambridge University Press.

Asher, S. R., Renshaw, P. D., & Hymel, S. (1982). Peer relations and the development of social skills. In S. G. Moore (Ed.), *The young child: Reviews of research* (Vol. 3). Washington, DC: National Association for the Education of Young Children.

Athanases, S. Z. (1994). Teachers' reports of the effects of preparing portfolios of literacy instruction. *The Elementary School Journal, 94*(4), 421–439.

Atkinson, J. W. (1958). Towards experimental analysis of human motivation in terms of motive expectancies and incentives. In J. W. Atkinson (Ed.), *Motives in fantasy, action, and society.* Princeton, NJ: Van Nostrand.

Atkinson, J. W. (1964). *An introduction to motivation.* Princeton, NJ: Van Nostrand.

Atkinson, J. W., & Birch, D. (1978). *An introduction to motivation* (2nd ed.). New York: Van Nostrand.

Atkinson, J. W., & Litwin, G. H. (1960). Achievement motive and test anxiety as motives to approach success and avoid failure. *Journal of Abnormal and Social Psychology, 60,* 52–63.

Atkinson, M. I. (1984). Computer-assisted instruction: Current state of the art. *Computers in the Schools, 1,* 91–99.

Atkinson, R. C., & Raugh, M. R. (1975). An application of the mnemonic keyword method to the acquisition of Russian vocabulary. *Journal of Experimental Psychology: Human Learning and Memory, 104,* 126–133.

Atkinson, R. C., & Shiffrin, R. M. (1968). Human memory: A proposed system and its component processes. In K. Spence & J. Spence (Eds.), *The psychology of learning and motivation,* Vol. 2. New York: Academic Press.

Atkinson, R. K., Levin, J. R., & Atkinson, L. A. (1998, April). *Mnemonic matrices for acquiring science facts and concepts: An illustration of applying through remembering.* Paper presented at the annual meeting of the American Educational Research Association, San Diego.

Atwater, E. (1996). *Adolescence.* Upper Saddle River, NJ: Prentice-Hall.

August, D., & Hakuta, K. (1997). *Improving schooling for language-minority children: A research agenda.* Washington, DC: National Research Council.

Ausubel, D. P. (1963). *The psychology of meaningful verbal learning.* New York: Grune and Stratton.

Ausubel, D. P. (1978). In defense of advance organizers: A reply to the critics. *Review of Educational Research, 48,* 251–258.

Ausubel, D. P., & Youssef, M. (1963). Role of discriminability in meaningful parallel learning. *Journal of Educational Psychology, 54,* 331–336.

Ayaduray, J., & Jacobs, G. M. (1997). Can learner strategy instruction succeed? The case of higher order questions and elaborate responses. *System, 25*(4), 561–570.

Babad, E. (1993). Pygmalion—25 years after: Interpersonal expectancies in the classroom. In P. D. Blanck (Ed.), *Interpersonal Expectations: Theory, research, and application* (pp. 125–152). Cambridge, England: Cambridge University Press.

Bacon, E. H. (1993). Guidelines for implementing a classroom reward system. In K. M. Cauley, F. Linder, & J. H. McMillan (Eds.), *Annual editions: Educational psychology 93/94.* Guilford, CT: Dushkin.

Baddeley, A. D. (1990). *Human memory: Theory and practice.* Boston: Allyn & Bacon.

Bahrick, H. P., & Hall, L. K. (1991). Lifetime maintenance of high school mathematics. *Journal of Experimental Psychology, 120,* 20–33.

Bailey, S. M. (1993). The current status of gender equality research in American schools. *Educational Psychologist, 28*(4), 321–339.

Bailey, S. M. (1995). Shortchanging girls and boys. *Educational Leadership, 53*(7), 75–79.

Baillargeon, R., DeVos, J., & Graber, M. (1989). Location memory in 8-month-old infants in a non-search AB task: Further evidence. *Cognitive Development, 4,* 345–367.

Baillargeon, R., Graber, M., DeVos, J., & Black, J. (1990). Why do young infants fail to search for hidden objects? *Cognition, 36,* 255–284.

Bainer, D. L., & Wright, D. (1998, April). *Evaluating a constructivist professional development program to improve science teaching.* Paper presented at the annual meeting of the American Educational Research Association, San Diego.

Baines, L., Baines, C., & Masterson, C. (1994). Mainstreaming: One school's reality. *Phi Delta Kappan, 76*(1), 39–40, 57–64.

Baker, E. L. (1994). Learning-based assessments of history understanding. *Educational Psychologist, 29*(2), 97–106.

Baker, E. L., & Niemi, D. (1996). School and program evaluation. In D. C. Berliner & R. C. Calfee (Eds.), *Handbook of educational psychology* (pp. 926–944). New York: Macmillan.

Baker, E. T., Wang, M. C., & Walberg, H. J. (1994/1995). The effects of inclusion on learning. *Educational Leadership, 52*(4), 33–35.

Bandalos, D. L., Yates, K., & Thorndike-Christ, T. (1995). Effects of math self-concept, perceived self-efficacy, and attributions for failure and success on test anxiety. *Journal of Educational Psychology, 87*(4), 611–623.

Bandura, A. (1965). Influence of models' reinforcement contingencies on the acquisition of imitative responses. *Journal of Personality and Social Psychology, 1,* 585–589.

Bandura, A. (1977). *Social learning theory.* Englewood Cliffs, NJ: Prentice-Hall.

Bandura, A. (1986). *Social foundations of thought and action: A social-cognitive theory.* Englewood Cliffs, NJ: Prentice-Hall.

Bandura, A. (1991). Social cognitive theory of self-regulation. *Organizational Behavior and High Performance, 50,* 248–287.

Bandura, A. (1993). Perceived self-efficacy in cognitive development and functioning. *Educational Psychologist, 28*(2), 117–148.

Bandura, A. (1997). *Self-efficacy: The exercise of control.* New York: Freeman.

Bangert-Drowns, R. L. (1993). The word processor as an instructional tool: A meta-analysis of word processing in writing instruction. *Review of Educational Research, 63*(1), 69–93.

Bangert-Drowns, R. L., Kulik, C. C., Kulik, J. A., & Morgan, M. (1991). The instructional effect of feedback in testlike events. *Review of Educational Research, 61*(2), 213–238.

Bangert-Drowns, R. L., Kulik, J. A., & Kulik, C. L. (1986, April). Effects of frequent classroom testing. Paper presented at the annual convention of the American Education Research Association, San Francisco.

Banks, C. A. M. (1993). Restructuring schools for equity: What we have learned in two decades. *Phi Delta Kappan, 75*(1), 42–49.

Banks, C. A. M. (1997). Parents and teachers: Partners in school reform. In J. A. Banks & C. A. M. Banks (Eds.), *Multicultural education: Issues and perspectives* (pp. 408–426). Boston: Allyn & Bacon.

Banks, J. A. (1993). *Multiethnic education: Theory and practice* (3rd ed.). Boston: Allyn & Bacon.

Banks, J. A. (1994). *An introduction to multicultural education.* Boston: Allyn & Bacon.

Banks, J. A. (1995a). The historical reconstruction of knowledge about race: Implications for transformative teaching. *Educational Researcher, 24*(2), 15–25.

Banks, J. A. (1995b). Historical development, dimensions, and practice. In J. A. Banks & C. A. M. Banks (Eds.), *Handbook of multicultural education.* New York: Macmillan.

Banks, J. A. (1995c). Multicultural education: Its effects on students' racial and gender role attitudes. In J. A. Banks & C. A. M. Banks (Eds.), *Handbook of multicultural education.* New York: Macmillan.

Banks, J. A. (1997a). Approaches to multicultural curriculum reform. In J. A. Banks & C. A. M. Banks (Eds.), *Multicultural education: Issues and perspectives* (pp. 229–250). Boston: Allyn & Bacon.

Banks, J. A. (1997b). Multicultural education: Characteristics and goals. In J. A. Banks & C. A. M. Banks (Eds.), *Multicultural education: Issues and perspectives* (pp. 3–31). Boston: Allyn & Bacon.

Banks, J. A., & Banks, C. A. M. (Eds.). (1995). *Handbook of research on multicultural education.* New York: Macmillan.

Barber, R. M., & Kagey, J. R. (1977). Modification of school attendance for an elementary population. *Journal of Applied Behavior Analysis, 10,* 41–48.

Baron, J., & Brown, R. V. (1991). *Teaching decision making to adolescents.* Hillsdale, NJ: Erlbaum.

Baron, R., Tom, D., & Cooper, H. (1985). Social class, race, and teacher expectations. In J. Duser (Ed.), *Teacher expectations.* Hillsdale, NJ: Erlbaum.

Baron, R. A. (1998). *Psychology* (4th ed.). Boston: Allyn & Bacon.

Barr, R. (1987). Content coverage. In M. J. Dunkin (Ed.), *International encyclopedia of teaching and teacher education.* New York: Pergamon.

Barr, R., & Dreeben, R. (1983). *How schools work.* Chicago: University of Chicago Press.

Barr, R. D., & Parrett, W. H. (1995). *Hope at last for at-risk youth.* Boston: Allyn & Bacon.

Barrish, H. H., Saunders, M., & Wolf, M. M. (1969). Good behavior game: Effects of individual contingencies for group consequences on disruptive behavior in a classroom. *Journal of Applied Behavior: Analysis, 2,* 119–124.

Barth, R. (1979). Home-based reinforcement of school behavior: A review and analysis. *Review of Educational Research, 49,* 436–458.

Baruth, L. G., & Manning, M. L. (1992). *Multicultural education of children and adolescents.* Boston: Allyn & Bacon.

Bates, J. A. (1987). Reinforcement. In M. J. Dunkin (Ed.), *The international encyclopedia of teaching and teacher education.* New York: Pergamon.

Battle, D. (1996). Language learning and use by African American children. *Topics in Language Disorders, 16,* 22–37.

Baumeister, R. F., & Leary, M. R. (1995). The need to belong: Desire for interpersonal attachments as a fundamental human motivation. *Psychological Bulletin, 117*(3), 497–529.

Baumrind, D. (1973). The development of instrumental competence through socialization. In A. Pick (Ed.), *Minnesota symposium on child psychology,* Vol. 7 (pp. 3–46). Minneapolis: University of Minnesota Press.

Bauwens, J., Hourcade, J. J., & Friend, M. (1989). Cooperative teaching: A model for general and special education integration. *Remedial and Special Education, 10*(2), 17–22.

Baxter, S. (1994). The last word on gender differences. *Psychology Today, 27*(2), 51–53.

Beady, L. L., Slavin, R. E., & Fennessey, G. M. (1981). Alternative student evaluation structures and a focused schedule of instruction in an inner-city junior high school. *Journal of Educational Psychology, 73,* 518–523.

Beane, J. (1991). Sorting out the self-esteem controversy. *Educational Leadership, 49*(1), 25–30.

Bear, G. G., Klever, A., & Proctor, W. A. (1991). Self-perceptions of nonhandicapped children and children with learning disabilities in integrated classes. *Journal of Special Education, 24,* 409–426.

Bear, G. G., & Rys, G. S. (1995). Moral reasoning, classroom behavior, and sociometric status among elementary schoolchildren. *Developmental Psychology, 30,* 633–638.

Becker, H. J. (1990a). Coaching for the scholastic aptitude test: Further synthesis and appraisal. *Review of Educational Research, 60*(3), 373–417.

Becker, H. J. (1990b, April). *Effects of computer use on mathematics achievement: Field findings from a nationwide field experiment in grade five to eight classes.* Paper presented at the annual meeting of the American Educational Research Association, Boston.

Becker, H. J. (1992). Computer-based integrated learning systems in the elementary and middle grades: A critical review and synthesis of evaluation reports. *Journal of Educational Computing Research, 8,* 1–41.

Becker, W., & Carnine, D. (1980). Direct instruction: An effective approach for educational intervention with the disadvantaged and low performers. In B. Lahey & A. Kazdin (Eds.), *Advances in child clinical psychology.* New York: Plenum.

Behrman, R. E. (1995). Long-term outcomes of early childhood programs. *The Future of Children, 5*(3), 6–221.

Behrman, R. E. (Ed.). (1996). Financing child care. *The Future of Children, 6* (2).

Behrman, R. E. (1997). Children and poverty. *The Future of Children, 7*(2), 4–160.

Bellanca, J. (1998). Teaching for intelligence: In search of best practices. *Phi Delta Kappan, 79*(9), 658–660.

Bellanca, J., & Swartz, E. (Eds.) (1993). *The challenge of detracking.* Palatine, IL: IRI/Skylight.

Benjafield, J. G. (1992). *Cognition.* Englewood Cliffs, NJ: Prentice-Hall.

Benson, P. (1997). *All kids are our kids.* San Francisco: Jossey-Bass.

Bereiter, C. (1991). Implications of connectionism for thinking about rules. *Educational Researcher, 20*(3), 10–16.

Bereiter, C., & Scardamalia, M. (1987). *The psychology of written composition.* Hillsdale, NJ: Erlbaum.

Berg, C. A., & Clough, M. (1990/1991). Hunter lesson design: The wrong one for science teaching. *Educational Leadership, 48*(4), 73–78.

Berk, L. E. (1997). *Child development* (4th ed.). Boston: Allyn & Bacon.

Berk, L. E., & Garvin, R. A. (1984). Development of private speech among low-income Appalachian children. *Developmental Psychology, 20,* 271–286.

Berko, J. (1985). The child's learning of English morphology. *Word, 14,* 150–177.

Berlyne, D. E. (1965). Curiosity and education. In J. D. Krumboltz (Ed.), *Learning and the educational process.* Chicago: Rand McNally.

Berrueta-Clement, J. R., Schweinhart, L. J., Barnett, W. S., Epstein, A. S., & Weikart, D. P. (1984). *Changed lives.* Ypsilanti, MI: High/Scope.

Beyer, B. K. (1988). *Developing a thinking skills program.* Boston: Allyn & Bacon.

Beyer, B. K. (1997). *Improving student thinking: A comprehensive approach.* Boston: Allyn & Bacon.

Biemiller, A. (1993). Lake Wobegon revisited: On diversity in education. *Educational Researcher, 22*(9), 7–12.

Biklen, D. (1990). Communication unbound: Autism and praxis. *Harvard Educational Review, 60,* 291–314.

Binder, A. (1988). Juvenile delinquency. *Annual Review of Psychology, 39,* 253–282.

Bishop, J. (1998). *Do curriculum-based external exit exam systems enhance student achievement?* Philadelphia: University of Pennsylvania, Consortium for Policy Research in Education.

Bivens, J. A., & Berk, L. E. (1990). A longitudinal study of the development of elementary school children's private speech. *Merrill-Palmer Quarterly, 36,* 121–127.

Blachman, B. A., Ball, E. W., Black, R. S., & Tangel, D. M. (1994). Kindergarten teachers develop phoneme awareness in low-income, inner-city classrooms: Does it make a difference? *Reading and Writing, 6,* 1–18.

Black, J. K. (1981). Are young children really egocentric? *Young Children, 36,* 51–55.

Black, M. M., & Krishnakumar, A. (1998). Children in low-income, urban settings. Interventions to promote mental health and well-being. *American Psychologist, 53*(6), 635–646.

Blackadar, A. R., & Nachtigal, P. (1986). *Cotapaxi/Westcliffe follow-through project: Final evaluation report.* Denver: Mid-Continental Regional Educational Laboratory.

Blasi, A. (1983). Moral cognition and moral action: A theoretical perspective. *Developmental Review, 3,* 178–210.

Block, J. H., Everson, S. T., & Guskey, T. R. (1995). *School improvement programs.* New York: Scholastic.

Block, K. K., & Peskowitz, N. B. (1990). Metacognition in spelling: Using writing and reading to self-check spelling. *Elementary School Journal, 91,* 151–164.

Bloom, B. S. (1976). *Human characteristics and school learning.* New York: McGraw-Hill.

Bloom, B. S. (1984). The 2 sigma problem: The search for methods of instruction as effective as one-to-one tutoring. *Educational Researcher, 13,* 4–16.

Bloom, B. S. (1986). Automaticity: The hands and feet of genius. *Educational Leadership, 43,* 70–77.

Bloom, B. S., Englehart, M. B., Furst, E. J., Hill, W. H., & Krathwohl, D. R. (1956). *Taxonomy of educational objectives: The classification of educational goals. Handbook 1: The cognitive domain.* New York: Longman.

Bloom, B. S., Hastings, J. T., & Madaus, G. F. (1971). *Handbook on formative and summative evaluation of student learning.* New York: McGraw-Hill.

Bloome, D., Puro, P., & Theodorou, E. (1989). Procedural displays and classroom lessons. *Curriculum Inquiry, 19*(3), 265–291.

Blume, G. W. (1984, April). *A review of research on the effects of computer programming on mathematical problem solving.* Paper presented at the annual convention of the American Educational Research Association, New Orleans.

Blumenfeld, P. C. (1992). Classroom learning and motivation: Clarity and expanding goal theory. *Journal of Educational Psychology, 84,* 272–281.

Blumenfeld, P. C., Marx, R. W., Soloway, E., & Krajcik, J. (1996). Learning with peers: From small group cooperation to collaborative communities. *Educational Researcher, 25*(8), 37–40.

Boden, M. A. (1980). *Jean Piaget.* New York: Viking Press.

Bodine, R. J., Crawford, D. K., & Schrumpf, F. (1994). *Creating the peaceable school: A comprehensive program for teaching conflict resolution.* Champaign, IL: Research Press.

Boekaerts, M. (1995). Self-regulated learning: Bridging the gap between metacognitive and metamotivational theories. *Educational Psychologist, 30*(4), 195–200.

Bogdan, R. C., & Biklen, S. K. (1982). *Qualitative research for education: An introduction to theory and methods.* Boston: Allyn & Bacon.

Borg, M. (1998). Tests of the internal/external frames of reference model with subject-specific academic self-efficacy and frame-specific academic concepts. *Journal of Educational Psychology, 90*(1), 102–110.

Borman, G. D. (1997). *A holistic model of the organization of categorical program students' total educational opportunities.* Unpublished doctoral dissertation, University of Chicago.

Borman, G. D., & D'Agostino, J. V. (1996). Title I and student achievement: A meta-analysis of federal evaluation results. *Educational Evaluation and Policy Analysis, 18*(4), 309–326.

Borman, G. D., D'Agostino, J. V., Wong, K. K., & Hedges, L. V. (1998). The longitudinal achievement of Chapter I students: Preliminary evidence from the Prospects study. *Journal of Education for Students Placed at Risk, 3*(4), 363–399.

Bornholt, L. J., Goodnow, J. J., & Cooney, G. H. (1994). Influences of gender stereotypes on adolescents' perceptions of their own achievement. *American Educational Research Journal, 31*(3), 675–692.

Bornstein, P. H. (1985). Self-instructional training: A commentary and state-of-the-art. *Journal of Applied Behavior Analysis, 18,* 69–72.

Bortnick, R. (1995). Interactive learning and hypermedia technology. In J. H. Block, S. T. Everson, & T. R. Guskey (Eds.), *School improvement programs* (pp.77–90). New York: Scholastic.

Bos, C. S., & Vaughn, S. (1988). *Strategies for teaching students with learning and behavior problems.* Boston: Allyn & Bacon.

Boutte, G. S., & McCormick, C. B. (1993). Authentic multicultural activities. In K. M. Cauley, F. Linder, & J. H. McMillan (Eds.), *Annual editions: Educational psychology 93/94.* Guilford, CT: The Dushkin Publishing Group.

Bower, G. H., Clark, M. C., Lesgold, A. M., & Winzenz, D. (1969). Hierarchical retrieval schemes in recall of categorized word lists. *Journal of Verbal Learning and Verbal Behavior, 8,* 323–343.

Bower, G. H., & Karlin, M. B. (1974). Depth of processing pictures of faces and recognition memory. *Journal of Experimental Psychology, 103,* 751–757.

Bowman, B. (1993). Early childhood education. *Review of Research in Education, 19,* 101–134.

Boykin, A. W. (1986). The triple quandary and the schooling of Afro-American children. In U. Neisser (Ed.), *The school achievement of minority children.* Hillsdale, NJ: Erlbaum.

Boykin, A. W. (1994a). Afrocultural expression and its implications for schooling. In E. Hollins et al. (Eds.), *Teaching diverse populations.* Albany: State University of New York Press.

Boykin, A. W. (1994b). Harvesting culture and talent: African American children and educational reform. In R. Rossi (Ed.), *Schools and students at risk* (pp. 116–130). New York: Teachers College Press.

Boykin, A. W. (1996, April). *A talent development approach to school reform.* Paper presented at the annual meeting of the American Educational Research Association, New York.

Braddock, J. H., & Dawkins, M. P. (1993). Ability grouping, aspirations, and attainments: Evidence from the National Educational Longitudinal Study of 1988. *Journal of Negro Education, 62*(3), 1–13.

Braddock, J. H., Dawkins, M. P., & Wilson, G. (1995). Intercultural contact and race relations among American youth. In W. D. Hawley & A. W. Jackson (Eds.), *Toward a common destiny: Improving race and ethnic relations in America.* San Francisco: Jossey-Bass.

Braddock, J. H., & Slavin, R. E. (1992). *Why ability grouping must end: Achieving excellence and equity in American education.* Baltimore: Johns Hopkins University, Center for Research on Effective Schooling for Disadvantaged Students.

Bradley, R. H., Whiteside, L., Mundfrom, D. J., Casey, P. H., Caldwell, B. M., & Barrett, K. (1994). Impact of the Infant Health and Development Program (IHDP) on the home environments of infants born prematurely and with low birthweight. *Journal of Educational Psychology, 80,* 531–541.

Bradsher, M., & Hagan, L. (1995). The kids network: Student-scientists pool resources. *Educational Leadership, 53*(2), 38–43.

Bransford, J. D. (1979). *Human cognition: Learning, understanding, and remembering.* Belmont, CA: Wadsworth.

Bransford, J. D., Burns, M. S., Delclos, V. R., & Vye, N. J. (1986). Teaching thinking: Evaluating evaluations and broadening the data base. *Educational Leadership, 44*(2), 68–70.

Bransford, J. D., & Stein, B. S. (1993). *The ideal problem solver* (2nd ed.). New York: W. H. Freeman.

Bransford, J. D., Stein, B. S., Vye, N. J., Franks, J. J., Auble, P. M., Mezynski, K. J., & Perfetto, G. A. (1982). Differences in approaches to learning: An overview. *Journal of Experimental Psychology: General, III,* 390–398.

Brehm, J. W., & Self, E. A. (1989). The intensity of motivation. *Annual Review of Psychology, 40,* 109–131.

Bretzing, B. B., & Kulhavy, R. W. (1981). Note taking and passage style. *Journal of Educational Psychology, 73,* 242–250.

Brewer, J. (1995). *Introduction to early childhood education* (2nd ed.). Boston: Allyn & Bacon.

Bridge, C. A., Compton-Hall, M., & Cantrell, S. C. (1998). Classroom writing practices revisited: The effects of statewide reform on writing instruction. *Elementary School Journal, 98*(2), 151–170.

Broden, M., Hall, R. V., Dunlap, A., & Clark, R. (1970). Effects of teacher attention and a token reinforcement system in a junior high school special education class. *Exceptional Children, 36,* 341–349.

Brooks, B. D. (1975). Contingency management as a means of reducing school truancy. *Education, 95,* 206–211.

Brooks, D. M. (1985). Beginning of the year in junior high: The first day of school. *Educational Leadership, 42,* 76–78.

Brooks, J. G., & Brooks, M. G. (1993). *The case for constructivist classrooms.* Alexandria, VA: Association for Supervision and Curriculum Development.

Brophy, J. (1981). Teacher praise: A functional analysis. *Review of Educational Research, 51,* 5–32.

Brophy, J. (1987, October). Synthesis of research on strategies for motivating students to learn. *Educational Leadership, 45,* 40–48.

Brophy, J. E. (1982, April). Fostering student learning and motivation in the elementary school classroom. Occasional Paper No. 51, East Lansing, MI: Institute for Research on Teaching.

Brophy, J. E., & Evertson, C. M. (1974). Process-product correlations in the Texas teacher effectiveness study: Final report (Research Reports No. 74-4). Austin: Research and Development Center for Teacher Education. University of Texas.

Brophy, J. E., & Evertson, C. M. (1976). *Learning from teaching: A developmental perspective.* Boston: Allyn & Bacon.

Brophy, J. E., & Evertson, C. M. (1981). *Student characteristics and teaching.* New York: Longman.

Brophy, J. E., & Good, T. L. (1974). *Teacher-student relationships: Causes and consequences.* New York: Holt, Rinehart and Winston.

Brophy, J. E., & Good, T. L. (1986). Teacher behavior and student achievement. In M. C. Wittrock (Ed.), *Handbook of research on teaching* (3rd ed.). New York: Macmillan.

Brown, A. L. (1994). The advancement of learning. *Educational Researcher, 23*(8), 4–12.

Brown, A. L., Bransford, J. D., Ferrara, R. A., & Campione, J. C. (1983). Learning, remembering, and understanding. In J. Flavell & E. M. Markman (Eds.), *Handbook of child psychology* (4th ed.) (Vol. 3, pp. 515–629). New York: Wiley.

Brown, B. B. (1990). Peer groups and peer cultures. In S. S. Feldman & G. R. Elliot (Eds.), *At the threshold: The developing adolescent* (pp. 171–196). Cambridge, MA: Harvard University Press.

Brown, D. S. (1988). Twelve middle-school teachers' planning. *Elementary School Journal, 89,* 69–88.

Brown, J. S., Collins, A., & Duguid, P. (1989). Situated cognition and the culture of learning. *Educational Research, 18,* 32–42.

Brownlee-Conyers, J., & Kraber, B. (1996). Voices from networked classrooms. *Educational Leadership, 54*(3), 34–36.

Bruner, J. S. (1966). *Toward a theory of instruction.* New York: Norton.

Bryant, D. M., Clifford, R. M., & Peisner, E. S. (1991). Best practices for beginners: Developmental appropriateness in kindergarten. *American Educational Research Journal, 28*(4), 783–803.

Burnette, J. (1987). *Adapting instructional materials for mainstreamed students.* Reston, VA: Council for Exceptional Children.

Burns, R. B. (1984). How time is used in elementary schools: The activity structure of classrooms. In L. W. Anderson (Ed.), *Time and school learning: Theory, research, and practice.* London: Croom Helm.

Burton, F. (1983). *A study of the letter grade system and its effects on the curriculum.* ERIC No. 238143.

Bussey, K. (1992). Lying and truthfulness: Children's definitions, standards, and evaluative reactions. *Child Development, 63,* 129–137.

Butler, D. L., & Winne, P. H. (1995). Feedback and self-regulated learning. *Review of Educational Research, 65*(3), 245–281.

Byrne, B., & Fielding-Barnsley, R. (1995). Evaluation of a program to teach phonemic awareness to young children: A 2- and 3-year follow-up and a new preschool trial. *Journal of Educational Psychology, 87,* 488–503.

Byrnes, J. P. (1988). Formal operations: A systematic reformulation. *Developmental Review, 8,* 66–87.

Byrnes, J. P. (1996). *Cognitive development and learning in instructional contexts.* Boston: Allyn & Bacon.

Byrnes, J. P., & Fox, N. A. (1998). The educational relevance of research in cognitive neuroscience. *Educational Psychology Review, 10*(3), 297–342.

Cairns, J. P. (1987). Behavior problems. In M. J. Dunkin (Ed.), *International encyclopedia of teaching and teacher education.* New York: Pergamon.

Calderón, M. (1994, April). *Cooperative learning as a powerful staff development tool for school renewal.* Paper presented at the annual meeting of the American Educational Research Association, New Orleans.

Calderón, M. E., Tinajero, J. V., & Hertz-Lazarowitz, R. (1992). Adapting Cooperative Integrated Reading and Composition to meet the needs of bilingual students. *Journal of Educational Issues of Language Minority Students, 10,* 79–106.

Calhoun, G., & Elliott, R. (1977). Self-concept and academic achievement of educable retarded and emotionally disturbed children. *Exceptional Children, 44,* 379–380.

Cameron, J., & Pierce, W. D. (1994). Reinforcement, reward, and intrinsic motivation: A meta-analysis. *Review of Educational Research, 64,* 363–423.

Cameron, J., & Pierce, W. D. (1996). The debate about rewards and intrinsic motivation: Protests and accusations do not alter the results. *Review of Educational Research, 66*(1), 39–51.

Campbell, F. A., & Ramey, C. T. (1994). Effects of early intervention on intellectual and academic achievement: A follow-up study of children from low-income families. *Child Development, 65,* 684–698.

Campbell, F. A., & Ramey, C. T. (1995). Cognitive and school outcomes for high-risk African American students at middle adolescence: Positive effects of early intervention. *American Educational Research Journal, 32,* 743–772.

Campbell, J. R., Donahue, P. L., Reese, C. M., & Phillips, G. W. (1996). *NAEP reading report card for the nation and the states.* Washington, DC: U.S. Department of Education.

Campbell, L., Campbell, B., & Dickinson, D. (1996). *Teaching and learning through multiple intelligences.* Boston: Allyn & Bacon.

Canady, R. L., & Hotchkiss, P. R. (1993). It's a good score! Just a bad grade. In K. M. Cauley, F. Linder, & J. H. McMillan (Eds.), *Annual Editions: Educational Psychology 93/94.* Guilford, CT: Dushkin.

Canfield, J., & Siccone, F. (1995). *101 ways to develop students' self-esteem and responsibility.* Boston: Allyn & Bacon.

Cannell, J. J. (1987). *Nationally normed elementary achievement testing in America's public schools: How all fifty states are above the national average.* Daniels, WV: Friends for Education.

Canter, L. (1989). Assertive discipline—More than names on the board and marbles in a jar. *Phi Delta Kappan, 71*(1), 41–56.

Canter, L., & Canter, M. (1976). *Assertive discipline.* Los Angeles: Lee Canter and Associates.

Canter, L., & Canter, M. (1992). *Assertive discipline: Positive behavior management for today's classroom.* Santa Monica, CA: Lee Canter & Assoc.

Capron, C., & Duyme, M. (1991). Children's IQ's and SES of biological and adoptive parents in a balanced cross-fostering study. *Cahiers de Psychologie Cognitive, II,* 323–348.

Cardelle-Elawar, M. (1990). Effects of feedback tailored to bilingual students' mathematics needs on verbal problem solving. *Elementary School Journal, 91,* 165–175.

Cardellichio, T., & Field, W. (1997). Seven strategies that encourage neural branching. *Educational Leadership, 54*(6), 33–36.

Carlsen, W. (1991). Questions in classrooms: A sociolinguistic perspective. *Review of Educational Research, 61*(2), 157–178.

Carnegie Corporation of New York (1989). *Turning points: Preparing American youth for the 21st century.* New York: Author.

Carnegie Corporation of New York. (1994). *Starting points: Meeting the needs of our youngest children.* New York: Author.

Carnegie Corporation of New York. (1996). *Years of promise: A comprehensive learning strategy for America's children.* New York: Author.

Carney, R. N., & Levin, J. R. (1998). Do mnemonic memories fade as time goes by? Here's looking anew! *Contemporary Educational Psychology, 23*(3), 276–297.

Carnine, D. (1989). Teaching complex content to learning disabled children: The role of technology. *Exceptional Children, 55,* 524–533.

Carnine, D., Grosen, B., & Silbert, J. (1995). Direct instructions to accelerate cognitive growth. In J. H. Block, S. T. Everson, & T. R. Guskey (Eds.), *School improvement programs* (pp. 129–152). New York: Scholastic.

Carpenter, T. P., & Fennema, E. (1992). Cognitively Guided Instruction: Building on the knowledge of students and teachers. *International Journal of Educational Research, 17,* 457–470.

Carpenter, T. P., Fennema, E., Fuson, K., Hiebert, J., Human, P., Murray, H., Olivier, A., & Wearne, D. (1994, April). *Teaching mathematics for learning with understanding in the primary grades.* Paper presented at the annual meeting of the American Educational Research Association, New Orleans.

Carpenter, T. P., Fennema, E., Peterson, P. L., Chiang, C. P., & Loef, M. (1989). Using knowledge of children's mathematics thinking in classroom teaching: An experimental study. *American Educational Research Journal, 26,* 499–531.

Carroll, J. B. (1963). A model of school learning. *Teachers College Record, 64,* 723–733.

Carroll, J. B. (1987). The national assessments in reading: Are we misreading the findings? *Phi Delta Kappan, 68,* 424–430.

Carroll, J. B. (1989). The Carroll model: A 25-year retrospective and prospective view. *Educational Researcher, 18,* 26–31.

Carroll, J. B. (1993). Educational psychology in the 21st century. *Educational Psychologist 28*(2), 89–95.

Carter, C. J. (1997). Why reciprocal teaching? *Educational Leadership, 54*(6), 64–68.

Carter, K., Cushing, K., Sabers, D., Stein, P., & Berliner, D. (1988). Expert-novice differences in perceiving and processing visual classroom information. *Journal of Teacher Education, 39*(3), 25–31.

Carter, L. F. (1984). The sustaining effects study of compensatory and elementary education. *Educational Researcher, 13*(7), 4–13.

Carter, R. T., & Goodwin, A. L. (1994). *Racial Identity and Education, 20,* 291–336.

Carter, T. P., & Chatfield, M. L. (1986). Effective bilingual schools: Implications for policy and practice. *American Journal of Education, 95,* 200–234.

Carver, S. M., Lehrer, R., Connell, T., & Erickson, J. (1992). Learning by hypermedia design: Issues of assessment and implementation. *Educational Psychologist, 27*(3), 385–404.

CASE. (1993). *CASE position paper on delivery of services to students with disabilities.* Washington, DC: Council for Administrators of Special Education.

Case, R. (1985). *Intellectual development: Birth to adulthood.* New York: Academic Press.

Case, R. (1992). *The mind's staircase.* Hillsdale, NJ: Erlbaum.

Case, R. (1993). Theories of learning and theories of development. *Educational Psychologist, 28*(3), 219–233.

Casto, G., & Mastropieri, M. A. (1986). The efficacy of early intervention programs: A meta-analysis. *Exceptional Children, 52,* 417–424.

Catania, A. C. (1992). *Learning* (3rd ed.). Englewood Cliffs, NJ: Prentice-Hall.

Ceci, S. J. (1991). How much does schooling influence general intelligence and its cognitive components? A reassessment of the evidence. *Developmental Psychology, 27,* 703–722.

Ceci, S. J. (1992). The new intelligence theorists: Old liberals in new guises? *Educational Researcher, 21*(6), 25–27.

Chan, C. K. K., Burtis, P. J., Scardamalia, M., & Bereiter, C. (1992). Constructive activity in learning from text. *American Educational Research Journal, 29,* 97–118.

Chance, P. (1992). The rewards of learning. *Phi Delta Kappan, 74*(3), 200–207.

Chaney, B., Burgdorf, K., & Atash, N. (1997). Influencing achievement through high school graduation requirements. *Educational Evaluation and Policy Analysis, 19*(3), 299–244.

Chansky, N. M. (1975). A critical examination of school report cards from K through 12. *Reading Improvement, 12,* 184–192.

Charles, C. M. (1989). *Building classroom discipline: From models to practice* (3rd ed.). New York: Longman.

Cheng, M., & Soudack, A. (1994). Education to promote racial and ethnocultural equity: A literature review. *ERS Spectrum, 12*(4), 28–40.

Cheung, K. C. (1995). On meaningful measurement: Issues of reliability and validity from a humanistic constructivist information-processing perspective. *Educational Research and Evaluation, 1*(1), 90–107.

Chin, C. W. T. (1998, April). *Synthesizing metacognitive interventions: What training characteristics can improve reading performance?* Paper presented at the annual meeting of the American Educational Research Association, San Diego.

Chinn, C. A., & Brewer, W. F. (1993). The role of anomalous data in knowledge acquisition. *Review of Educational Research, 63*(1), 1–49.

Chobot, R., & Garibaldi, A. (1982). In-school alternatives to suspension: A description of ten school district programs. *The Urban Review, 14,* 71–75.

Chomsky, C. (1969). *The acquisition of syntax in children from 5 to 10.* M.I.T. Press Research Monogram No. 57. Cambridge, MA: M.I.T. Press.

Christian, D. (1996). Two-way immersion education: Students learning through two languages. *The Modern Language Journal, 80,* 66–76.

Christian, D., Montone, C. L., Lindholm, K. J., & Carranza, I. (1997). *Profiles in two-way immersion education.* McHenry, IL: Center for Applied Linguistics and Delta Systems.

Christie, J. F., & Wardle, F. (1992). How much time is needed for play? *Young Children, 47*(3), 28–32.

Christof, K. J., & Kane, S. R. (1991). Relationship-building for students with autism. *Teaching Exceptional Children, 23,* 49–51.

Christoplos, F., & Renz, P. (1969). A critical examination of special education programs. *Journal of Special Education, 3,* 371–379.

Cipani, E. C. (1995). Be aware of negative reinforcement. *Teaching Exceptional Children, 27*(4), 36–40.

Cizek, G. J. (1991). Innovation or evaluation? Performance assessment in perspective. *Phi Delta Kappan, 72*(9), 695–699.

Cizek, G. J. (1993). Innovation or enervation? Performance assessment in perspective. In K. M. Cauley, F. Linder, & J. H. McMillan (Eds.), *Annual Editions: Educational Psychology 93/94.* Guilford, CT: Dushkin.

Clark, C. M., Gage, N. L., Marx, R. W., Peterson, P. L., Stayrook, N. G., & Winne, P. H. (1979). A factorial experiment on teacher structuring, soliciting, and reacting. *Journal of Educational Psychology, 71,* 534–552.

Clark, C. M., & Peterson, P. L. (1986). Teachers' thought processes. In M. C. Wittrock (Ed.), *Handbook of research on teaching* (3rd ed.). New York: Macmillan.

Clark, C. M., & Yinger, R. (1986). Teacher planning. In D. Berliner & B. Rosenshine (Eds.), *Talks to teachers* (pp. 342–365). New York: Random House.

Clark, E. E., & Ramsey, W. (1992). Making schools work: Why families matter. *The Family America, 6*(1), 1–8.

Clark, J. (1990). *Patterns of thinking: Integrating learning skills with content teaching.* Boston: Allyn & Bacon.

Clark, J. M., & Paivio, A. (1991). Dual coding theory and education. *Educational Psychology Review, 3*(3), 149–210.

Clark, R. E. (1985). Evidence for confounding in computer-based instruction studies: Analyzing the meta-analyses. *Educational Communication and Technology Journal, 33,* 249–262.

Clemens-Brower, T. J. (1997). Recruiting parents and the community. *Educational Leadership, 54*(5), 58–60.

Clements, D. H., & Battista, M. T. (1990). Constructivist learning and teaching. *Arithmetic Teacher, 38,* 34–37.

Clifford, M. M. (1984). Thoughts on a theory of constructive failure. *Educational Psychologist, 19,* 108–120.

Clifford, M. M. (1990). Students need challenge, not easy success. *Educational Leadership, 48*(1), 22–26.

Cline, Z. (1998). *Buscando su voz en dos culturas:* Finding your voice in two cultures. *Phi Delta Kappan, 79*(9), 699–705.

Cobb, N. (1995). *Adolescence.* Mountain View, CA: Mayfield.

Cobb, P. (1994). Constructivism in mathematics and science education. *Educational Researcher, 23*(7), 4.

Cochran-Smith, M. (1991). Word processing and writing in elementary classrooms: A critical review of related literature. *Review of Educational Research, 61*(1), 107–155.

Cognition and Technology Group at Vanderbilt. (1992). The Jasper series as an example of anchored instruction: Theory, program description, and assessment data. *Educational Psychologist, 27*(3), 291–315.

Cognition and Technology Group at Vanderbilt. (1996). Looking at technology in context: A framework for understanding technology and education research. In D.C. Berliner & R. C. Calfee (Eds.), *Handbook of educational psychology* (pp. 807–840). New York: Macmillan.

Cohen, E. G. (1984). Talking and working together: Status, interaction, and learning. In P. Peterson, L. C. Wilkinson, & M. Hallinan (Eds.), *The social context of instruction: Group organization and group processes.* New York: Academic Press.

Cohen, E. G. (1986). *Designing groupwork: Strategies for the heterogeneous classroom.* New York: Teachers' College Press.

Cohen, E. G. (1992, April). *Complex instruction in the middle school.* Paper presented at the annual meeting of the American Educational Research Association, San Francisco.

Cohen, E. G. (1994a). *Designing groupwork: Strategies for the heterogeneous classroom* (2nd ed.). New York: Teachers College Press.

Cohen, E. G. (1994b). Restructuring the classroom: Conditions for productive small groups. *Review of Educational Research, 64*(l), 1–35.

Cohen, E. G., & Lotan, R. A. (1995). Producing equal-status interaction in the heterogeneous classroom. *American Educational Research Journal, 32*(1), 99–120.

Cohen, R. L. (1989). Memory for action events: The power of enactment. *Educational Psychology Review, 1*(1), 57–80.

Cohen, S., & De bettencourt, L. (1983). Teaching children to be independent learners: A step-by-step strategy. *Focus on Exceptional Children, 16*(3), 1–12.

Cohen, S. A. (1987). Instructional alignment: Searching for a magic bullet. *Educational Researcher, 16,* 16–20.

Coie, J. D., Dodge, K. A., & Kupersmidt, J. (1990). Peer group behavior and social status. In S. R. Asher & J. D. Coie (Eds.), *Peer rejection in children* (pp. 17–59). New York: Cambridge University Press.

Colby, C., & Kohlberg, L. (1984). Invariant sequence and internal consistency in moral judgment stages. In W. Kurtines & J. Gewirts (Eds.), *Morality, moral behavior, and moral development.* New York: Wiley-Interscience.

Cole, D. A. (1991). Change in self-perceived competence as a function of peer and teacher evaluation. *Developmental Psychology, 27,* 682–688.

Coleman, J. (1961). *The adolescent society.* New York: Free Press.

Coley, R. L., & Chase-Lansdale, P. L. (1998). Adolescent pregnancy and parenthood. *American Psychologist, 53*(2), 152–166.

Comer, J. (1988). Educating poor minority children. *Scientific American, 259,* 42–48.

Comer, J. P. (1990). *Maggie's American dream.* New York: Plume.

Committee for Economic Development. (1995). *Connecting students to a changing world: A technology strategy for improving mathematics and science education.* New York: Author.

Commons, M. L., Richards, F. A., & Kuhn, D. (1982). Systematic and metasystematic reasoning: A case for levels of reasoning beyond Piaget's stage of formal operations. *Child Development, 53,* 1058–1069.

Conway, M. A., Cohen, G., & Stanhope, N. (1991). Very long-term memory of knowledge acquired through formal education: Twelve years of cognitive psychology. *Journal of Experimental Psychology: General, 120,* 395–409.

Cooley, W. W., & Leinhardt, G. (1980). The instructional dimensions study. *Educational Evaluation and Policy Analysis, 2,* 7–26.

Cooper, H. (1989). Synthesis of research on homework. *Educational Leadership, 47*(3), 85–91.

Cooper, H., & Derr, N. (1995). Race comparisons on need for achievement: A meta-analytic alternative to Graham's narrative review. *Review of Educational Research, 65*(4), 483–508.

Cooper, H., Lindsay, J. J., Nye, B., & Greathouse, S. (1998). Relationships among attitudes about homework, amount of homework assigned and completed, and student achievement. *Journal of Educational Psychology, 90*(1), 70–83.

Copeland, W. D. (1983, April). Classroom management and student teachers' cognitive abilities: A relationship. Paper presented at the annual convention of the American Educational Research Association, Montreal.

Cordova, D. I., & Lepper, M. R. (1996). Intrinsic motivation and the process of learning: Beneficial effects of contextualization, personalization, and choice. *Journal of Educational Psychology, 88*(4), 715–730.

Corkill, A. J. (1992). Advance organizers: Facilitators of recall. *Educational Psychology Review, 4,* 33–67.

Corno, L. (1992). Encouraging students to take responsibility for learning and performance. *Elementary School Journal, 95,* 69–84.

Corno, L. (1995). Comments on Winne: Analytic and systematic research are both needed. *Educational Psychologist, 30*(4), 201–206.

Corno, L. (1995). The principles of adaptive teaching. In A. C. Ornstein (Ed.), *Teaching: Theory into practice.* Boston: Allyn & Bacon.

Corno, L. (1996). Homework is a complicated thing. *Educational Researcher, 25*(8), 27–30.

Corno, L., & Kanfer, R. (1993). The role of volition in learning and performance. *Review of Research in Education, 19,* 301–341.

Cortés, C. E. (1995). Knowledge construction and popular culture: The media as multicultural educator. In J. A. Banks & C. A. M. Banks (Eds.), *Handbook of research on multicultural education.* New York: Macmillan.

Costenbader, V., & Reading-Brown, M. (1995). Isolation time-out used with students with emotional disturbance. *Exceptional Children, 61,* 353–363.

Council of Chief State School Officers. (1990). *School success for limited English proficient students: The challenge and state response.* Washington, DC: Author.

Craik, F. I. M. (1979). Human memory. *Annual Review of Psychology, 30,* 63–102.

Craik, F. I. M., & Lockhart, R. S. (1972). Levels of processing: A framework for memory research. *Journal of Verbal Thinking and Verbal Behavior, 11,* 671–684.

Crain, W. C. (1985). *Theories of development: Concepts and applications.* Englewood Cliffs, NJ: Prentice-Hall.

Crawford, J. (1989). Instructional activities related to achievement gain in Chapter 1 classes. In R. E. Slavin, N. L. Karweit,

& N. A. Madden (Eds.), *Effective programs for students at risk.* Boston: Allyn & Bacon.

Crévola, C. A., & Hill, P. W. (1998). Evaluation of a whole-school approach to prevention and intervention in early literacy. *Journal of Education for Students Placed at Risk, 3*(2), 133–157.

Crockenberg, S., & Litman, C. (1990). Autonomy as competence in 2-year-olds: Maternal correlates of child defiance, compliance, and self-assertion. *Developmental Psychology, 26,* 961–971.

Crocker, R. K., & Brooker, G. M. (1986). Classroom control and student outcomes in grades 2 and 5. *American Educational Research, 23,* 1–11.

Crooks, T. J. (1988). The impact of classroom evaluation practices on students. *Review of Educational Research, 58,* 438–481.

Cross, L. H., & Cross, G. M. (1980–1981). Teachers' evaluative comments and pupil perception of control. *Journal of Experimental Education, 49,* 68–71.

Cross, W. E. (1995). Oppositional identity and African American youth: Issues and prospects. In W. D. Hawley & A. W. Jackson (Eds.), *Toward a common destiny: Improving race and ethnic relations in America.* San Francisco: Jossey-Bass.

Cummins, J. (1998). Language issues and educational change. In A. Hargreaves et al. (Eds.), *International handbook of educational change* (pp. 440–459). Dordrecht, The Netherlands: Kluwer.

Cusick, P. A. (1993). Uncoiling tracking. *Educational Researcher, 22*(5), 36–37.

Czikszentmihalyi, M., & Larson, R. (1984). *Being adolescent.* New York: Basic Books.

D'Agostino, J. V., Borman, G. D., Hedges, L. V., & Wong, K. D. (1998). Longitudinal achievement and Chapter I coordination in high-poverty schools: A multilevel analysis of the Prospects data. *Journal of Education for Students Placed at Risk, 3*(4), 401–420.

Damon, W. (1983). *Social and personality development: Infancy through adolescence.* New York: Norton.

Damon, W. (1991). Putting substance into self-esteem: A focus on academic and moral values. *Educational Horizons, 70*(1), 12–18.

Damon W., & Hart, D. (1988). *Self-understanding in childhood and adolescence.* Cambridge: Cambridge University Press.

Daniels, H. (Ed.). (1995). *An Introduction to Vygotsky.* New York: Routledge.

Dansereau, D. F. (1985). Learning strategy research. In J. Segal, S. Chipman, & R. Glaser (Eds.), *Thinking and learning skills: Relating instruction to basic research,* Vol. 1. Hillsdale, NJ: Erlbaum.

Danziger, S. H., Sandefur, G., & Weinberg, D. H. (Eds.). (1994). *Confronting poverty.* Cambridge, MA: Harvard University Press.

Darder, A., Torres, R. D., & Gutierrez, H. (Eds.). (1997). *Latinos and education: A critical reader.* New York: Routledge.

Darling-Hammond, L. (1995). Inequality and access to knowledge. In J. A. Banks & C. A. M. Banks (Eds.)., *Handbook of research on multicultural education* (pp. 465–483). New York: Macmillan.

Darling-Hammond, L., Gendler, T., & Wise, A. D. (1990). *The teaching internship: Practical preparation for a licensed profession.* Santa Monica, CA: RAND.

Das, J. P. (1995). Some thoughts on two aspects of Vygotsky's work. *Educational Psychologist, 30*(2), 993–997.

Deci, E., & Ryan, R. (1985). *Intrinsic motivation and self-determination in human behavior.* New York: Plenum.

Deci, E., & Ryan, R. (1987). The support of autonomy and the control of behavior. *Journal of Personality and Social Psychology, 53,* 1024–1037.

De Lisi, R., & Staudt, J. (1980). Individual differences in college students' performance on formal operations tasks. *Journal of Applied Developmental Psychology, 1,* 201–208.

Delpit, L. (1995). Other people's children: Cultural conflict in the classroom. New York: New Press.

Delprato, D. J., & Midgley, B. D. (1992). Some fundamentals of B. F. Skinner's behaviorism. *American Psychologist, 47,* 1507–1520.

Dempster, F. N. (1989). Spacing effects and their implications for theory and practice. *Educational Psychology Review, 1,* 309–330.

Dempster, F. N. (1991). Synthesis of research on reviews and tests. *Educational Leadership, 72*(8), 71–76.

Dennis, I., & Tapsfield, P. (Eds.). (1996). *Human abilities: Their nature and measurement.* Mahwah, NJ: Erlbaum.

de Ribaupierre, A., & Rieben, L. (1995). Individual and situational variability in cognitive development. *Educational Psychologist, 30*(1), 5–14.

Derry, S. J. (1991). Strategy and expertise in solving word problems. In C. McCormick, G. Miller, & M. Pressley (Eds.), *Cognitive strategies research: From basic research to educational applications.* New York: Springer-Verlag.

Derry, S. J., & Murphy, D. A. (1986). Designing systems that train learning ability: From theory to practice. *Review of Educational Research, 56,* 1–39.

Deshler, D. D., Ellis, E. S., & Lenz, B. K. (1996). *Teaching students with learning disabilities: Strategies and methods.* (2nd ed.). Denver: Love.

DeVries, R. (1997). Piaget's social theory. *Educational Researcher, 26*(2), 4–17.

Deyhle, D., & Swisher, K. (1995). Research in American Indian and Alaskan native education: From assimilation to self-determination. In M. W. Apple (Ed.), *Review of research in education, 22* (pp. 113–194). Washington, DC: American Educational Research Association.

Dianda, M., & Flaherty, J. (1995, April). *Effects of Success for All on the reading achievement of first graders in California bilingual programs.* Paper presented at the annual meeting of the American Educational Research Association, San Francisco.

Diener, C. I., & Dweck, C. S. (1978). An analysis of learned helplessness: Continuous changes in performance, strategy, and achievement cognitions following failure. *Journal of Personality and Social Psychology, 36,* 451–462.

DiGangi, S. A., Maag, J. W., & Rutherford, R. B. (1991). Self-graphing of on-task behavior: Enhancing the reactive effects of self-monitoring on on-task and academic performance. *Learning Disabilities Quarterly, 14,* 221–230.

Dimino, J., Gersten, R., Carnine, D., & Blake, G. (1990). Story grammar: An approach for promoting at-risk secondary students' comprehension of literature. *Elementary School Journal, 91,* 19–32.

Dodd, A. W. (1996). Involving parents, avoiding gridlock. *Educational Leadership, 53*(7), 44–47.

Dolan, L. J., Kellam, S. G., Brown, C. H., Werthamer-Larsson, L., Rebok, G. W., Mayer, L. S., Laudolff, J., Turkkan, J. S., Ford, C., & Wheeler, L. (1993). The short-term impact of two classroom-based preventive interventions on aggressive and shy behaviors and poor achievement. *Journal of Applied Developmental Psychology, 4,* 317–345.

Donaldson, M. (1978). *Children's minds.* New York: Norton.

Dooling, D. J., & Lachman, R. (1971). Effects of comprehension on retention of prose. *Journal of Experimental Psychology, 8,* 216–222.

Dornbusch, S. (1994). *Off the track.* Paper presented at the annual meeting of the Society for Research on Adolescence, San Diego.

Dorr-Bremme, D. W., & Herman, J. (1986). *Assessing school achievement: A profile of classroom practices.* Los Angeles: Center for the Study of Evaluation, UCLA.

Downing, J., Coughlin, R. M., & Rich, G. (1986). Children's invented spellings in the classroom. *Elementary School Journal, 86,* 295–303.

Downs, W. R., & Rose, S. R. (1991). The relationship of adolescent peer groups to the incidence of psychosocial problems. *Adolescence, 26*(102), 377–386.

Doyle, W. (1984). How order is achieved in classrooms: An interim report. *Journal of Curriculum Studies, 16,* 259–277.

Doyle, W. (1990a). Classroom knowledge as a foundation for teaching. *Teachers College Record, 91,* 347–360.

Doyle, W. (1990b). Classroom management techniques. In O. Moles (Ed.), *Student discipline strategies.* Albany, NY: State University of New York Press.

Doyle, W., & Carter, K. (1984). Academic tasks in classrooms. *Curriculum Inquiry, 14,* 129–149.

Drabman, R., Spitalnik, R., & O'Leary, K. (1973). Teaching self-control to disruptive children. *Journal of Abnormal Psychology, 82,* 10–16.

Driscoll, M. P. (1994). *Psychology of learning for instruction.* Boston: Allyn & Bacon.

Dryfoos, J. G. (1990). *Adolescents at risk: Prevalence and prevention.* New York: Oxford University Press.

Dryfoos, J. G. (1998). *Safe passage: Making it through adolescence in a risky society.* New York: Oxford University Press.

Duell, O. K. (1994). Extended wait time and university student achievement. *American Educational Research Journal, 31*(2), 397–414.

Duffy, G. G., & Roehler, L. R. (1986). The subtleties of instructional mediation. *Educational Leadership, 43*(7), 23–27.

Dukes, R., & Seidner, C. (1978). *Learning with simulations and games.* Beverly Hills: Sage.

Duncker, K. (1945). On problem solving. *Psychological Monographs, 58* (Whole No. 270).

Dunkin, M. J., & Biddle, B. J. (1974). *A study of teaching.* New York: Holt, Rinehart and Winston.

Dunn, K., & Dunn, R. (1987). Dispelling outmoded beliefs about student learning. *Educational Leadership, 44*(6), 55–62.

Dunn, L. M. (1968). Special education for the mentally retarded—Is it justified? *Exceptional Children, 35,* 5–22.

Dunn, R., Beaudrey, J. S., & Klavas, A. (1989). Survey of research on learning styles. *Educational Leadership, 46*(6), 50–58.

DuPaul, G. J., Barkley, R. A., & McMurray, M. B. (1991). Therapeutic effects of medication on ADHD: Implications for school psychologists. *School Psychology Review, 20,* 203–219.

Durán, R. P. (1994). Cooperative learning for language-minority students. In R. DeVillar, C. Faltis, & J. Cummins (Eds.), *Cultural diversity in schools.* Albany, NY: State University of New York Press.

Durso, F. T., & Coggins, K. A. (1991). Organized instruction for the improvement of word knowledge skills. *Journal of Educational Psychology, 83,* 108–112.

Dweck, C. (1975). The role of expectations and attributions in the alleviation of learned helplessness. *Journal of Personality and Social Psychology, 31,* 674–685.

Dweck, C. S. (1986). Motivational processes affecting learning. *American Psychologist, 41,* 1040–1048.

Dyson, A. H. (1984). Teachers and young children: Missed connections in teaching/learning to write. *Language Arts, 59,* 674–680.

Eagley, A. H., & Crowley, M. (1986). Gender and helping behavior: A meta-analytic review of the social psychological literature. *Psychological Bulletin, 100,* 283–308.

Ebel, R. L., & Frisbie, D. A. (1991). *Essentials of educational measurement* (5th ed.). Englewood Cliffs, NJ: Prentice-Hall.

Eccles, J. S., Wigfield, A., Midgley, C., Reuman, D., MacIver, D., & Feldlaufer, H. (1993). Negative efforts of traditional middle schools on students' motivation. *The Elementary School Journal, 93*(5), 553–574.

Eden, G. F., Van Meter, J. W., Rumsey, J. M., Maisog, J. M., Woods, R. P., & Zeffird, T. A. (1996). Abnormal processing of visual motion in dyslexia revealed by functional brain imaging. *Nature, 382,* 66–69.

Educational Testing Service. (1995). *Performance assessment: Different needs, difficult answers.* Princeton, NJ: Author.

Educational Testing Service. (1996). *Computers in classrooms: The status of technology in U.S. schools.* Princeton, NJ: Author.

Edwards, W. (1954). The theory of decision making. *Psychology Bulletin, 51,* 380–417.

Egan, K. (1989). Memory, imagination, and learning: Connected by the story. *Phi Delta Kappan, 70,* 455–459.

Egeland, P. (1996). Pulleys, planes, and student performance. *Educational Leadership, 54*(4), 41–45.

Ehri, L. (1991). Development of the ability to read words. In R. Barr, M. Kamil, P. Mosenthal, & P. D. Pearson (Eds.), *Handbook of Reading Research* (Vol. II, pp. 383–417). New York: Longman.

Eisenberg, N., Martin, C. L., & Fabes, K. A. (1996). Gender development and gender effects. In D.C. Berliner & R. C. Calfee (Eds.), *Handbook of educational psychology* (pp. 358–398). New York: Macmillan.

Eisenberg, N., & Mussen, P. H. (1989). *The roots of prosocial behavior in children.* New York: Cambridge University Press.

Eisenberger, R., & Cameron, J. (1998). Reward, intrinsic interest, and creativity: New findings. *American Psychologist, 53*(6), 676–679.

Eisner, E. W. (1982). The contribution of painting to children's cognitive development. *Journal of Education, 164,* 227–237.

Elashoff, J. D., & Snow, R. E. (1971). *Pygmalion reconsidered.* Worthington, OH: Charles A. Jones.

Elkind, D. (1981). *The hurried child: Growing up too fast, too soon.* Reading, MA: Addison-Wesley.

Elkind, D. (1989). Developmentally appropriate practice: Philosophical and practical implications. *Phi Delta Kappan, 71*(2), 113–117.

Elkind, D. (1994). *A sympathetic understanding of the child* (3rd ed.). Boston: Allyn & Bacon.

Ellis, A. K., & Fouts, J. T. (1993). *Research on Educational Innovations.* Princeton, NJ: Eye on Education.

Ellwein, M. C., Walsh, D. J., Eads II, G. M., & Miller, A. (1991). Using readiness tests to route kindergarten students: The snarled intersection of psychometrics, policy, and practice. *Educational Evaluation and Policy Analysis, 13*(2), 159–175.

Elsmore, T. F., & McBride, S. A. (1994). An eight-alternative concurrent schedule: Foraging in a radial maze. *Journal of Applied Behavior Analysis, 28,* 236.

Emmer, E., Evertson, C., & Anderson, L. (1980). Effective classroom management at the beginning of the school year. *Elementary School Journal, 80,* 219–231.

Emmer, E. T., & Aussiker, A. (1990). School and classroom discipline programs: How well do they work? In O. C. Moles (Ed.), *Student discipline strategies.* Albany, NY: SUNY Press.

Emmer, E. T., Evertson, C. M., Clements, B. S., & Worsham, M. E. (1994). *Classroom management for secondary teachers* (3rd ed.). Boston: Allyn & Bacon.

Engle, R. W., Nations, J. K., & Cantor, J. (1990). Is "working memory capacity" just another name for word knowledge? *Journal of Educational Psychology, 82*(4), 799–804.

Englert, C. S., Raphael, T. E., Anderson, L. M., Anthony, H. M., & Stevens, D. D. (1991). Making strategies and self-talk visible: Writing instruction in regular and special education classrooms. *American Educational Research Journal, 28,* 337–372.

Ensminger, M. E., & Slusarcick, A. L. (1992). Paths to high school graduation or dropout: A longitudinal study of a first grade cohort. *Sociology of Education, 65,* 95–113.

Entwistle, D., & Hayduk, L. (1981). Academic expectations and the school achievement of young children. *Sociology of Education, 54,* 34–50.

Entwistle, D. R., & Alexander, K. L. (1992). Summer setback: Race, poverty, school composition, and mathematics achievement in the first two years of school. *American Sociological Review, 57,* 72–84.

Epstein, C. (1980). Brain growth and cognitive functioning. In *The emerging adolescent: Characteristics and implications.* Columbus, OH: NMSA.

Epstein, H. T. (1990). Stages in human mental growth. *Journal of Educational Psychology, 82*(4), 876–880.

Epstein, J. L. (1992). School and family partnerships. In M. Alkin (Ed.), *Encyclopedia of Educational Research* (pp. 1139–1151). New York: Macmillan.

Epstein, J. L. (1995). School/family/community partnerships: Caring for the children we share. *Phi Delta Kappan, 76,* 701–712.

Epstein, J. L., & Dauber, S. L. (1989). *Effects of the Teachers Involve Parents in Schoolwork (TIPS) social studies and art program on student attitudes and knowledge.* Baltimore: Johns Hopkins University, Center for Research on Elementary and Middle Schools.

Epstein, M. H., & Cullinan, D. (1992). Emotional/behavioral problems. In M. C. Alkin (Ed.), *Encyclopedia of educational research* (6th ed.) (pp. 430–432). New York: Macmillan.

Ericcson, K. A., & Kintsch, W. (1995). Long-term working memory. *Psychological Review, 102,* 211–245.

Erickson, F. (1997). Culture in society and in educational practices. In J. A. Banks & C. A. M. Banks (Eds.), *Multicultural education: Issues and perspectives* (pp. 32–60). Boston: Allyn & Bacon.

Erikson, E. H. (1963). *Childhood and society* (2nd ed.). New York: Norton.

Erikson, E. H. (1968). *Identity, youth and crisis.* New York: Norton.

Erikson, E. H. (1980). *Identity and the life cycle* (2nd ed.). New York: Norton.

Ethington, C. A. (1991). Testing a model of achievement behaviors. *American Educational Research Journal, 28,* 155–172.

Evans, T. D. (1996). Encouragement: The key to reforming the classrooms. *Educational Leadership, 54*(1), 81–85.

Everson, H., Smodlaka, I., & Tobias, S. (1994). Exploring the relationship of test anxiety and metacognition on reading test performance: A cognitive analysis. *Anxiety, Stress, and Coping, 7,* 85–96.

Everson, H., Tobias, S., Hartman, H., & Gourgey, A. (1993). Test anxiety and the curriculum: The subject matters. *Anxiety, Stress, and Coping, 6,* 1–8.

Evertson, C. M. (1982). Differences in instructional activities in higher- and lower-achieving junior high English and math classes. *Elementary School Journal, 82,* 329–350.

Evertson, C. M. (1989). Improving classroom management: A school-based program for beginning the year. *Journal of Educational Research, 83,* 82–90.

Evertson, C. M., & Emmer, E. T. (1982). Effective management at the beginning of the year in junior high classes. *Journal of Educational Psychology, 74,* 485–498.

Evertson, C. M., Emmer, E. T., & Brophy, J. E. (1980). Predictors of effective teaching in junior high mathematics classrooms. *Journal for Research in Mathematics Education, 11,* 167–178.

Evertson, C. M., Emmer, E. T., Clements, B. S., Sanford, J. P., & Worsham, M. E. (1994). *Classroom management for elementary teachers* (3rd ed.). Boston: Allyn & Bacon.

Evertson, C. M., & Harris, A. H. (1992). What we know about managing classrooms. *Educational Leadership, 49*(7), 74–78.

Evertson, C. M., & Harris, A. H. (1993). What we know about managing classrooms. In K. M. Cauley, F. Linder, & J. H. McMillan (Eds.), *Annual editions: Educational psychology 93/94.* Guilford, CT: Dushkin.

Evertson, C. M., & Randolph, C. H. (1995). Classroom management in the learning-centered classroom. In A. C. Ornstein (Ed.), *Teaching: Theory into practice.* Boston: Allyn & Bacon.

Evertson, C. M., Weade, R., Green, J., & Crawford, J. (1985). *Effective classroom management and instruction: An exploration of models.* Nashville: Vanderbilt University.

Fachin, K. (1996). Teaching Tommy: A second-grader with attention deficit hyperactivity disorder. *Phi Delta Kappan, 77,* 437–441.

Fagan, E. R., Hassler, D. M., & Szabo, M. (1981). Evaluation of questioning strategies in language arts instruction. *Research in the Teaching of English, 15,* 267–273.

Faltis, C. J., & Hudelson, S. J. (1998). *Bilingual education in elementary and secondary school communities.* Boston: Allyn & Bacon.

Fantuzzo, J. W., Davis, G. V., & Ginsburg, M. D. (1995). Effects of parent involvement in isolation or in combination with peer tutoring on student self-concept and mathematics achievement. *Journal of Educational Psychology, 87*(2), 272–281.

Fantuzzo, J. W., King, J. A., & Heller, L. R. (1992). Effects of reciprocal peer tutoring on mathematics and school adjustment: A component analysis. *Journal of Educational Psychology, 84,* 33–39.

Fantuzzo, J. W., Polite, K., & Grayson, N. (1990). An evaluation of reciprocal peer tutoring across elementary school settings. *Journal of School Psychology, 28,* 309–323.

Farlow, L. (1996). A quartet of success stories: How to make inclusion work. *Educational Leadership, 53*(5), 51–55.

Fashola, O. S., & Slavin, R. E. (1998). Effective dropout prevention and college attendance programs for students placed at risk. *Journal of Education for Students Placed at Risk, 3*(2), 159–183.

Fashola, O. S., Slavin, R. E., Calderon, M., & Durán, R. (1996). *Effective programs for Latino students in elementary and middle schools.* Baltimore: Johns Hopkins University, Center for Research on the Education of Students Placed at Risk.

Feather, N. (Ed.). (1982). *Expectations and actions.* Hillsdale, NJ: Erlbaum.

Feingold, A. (1992). Sex differences in variability in intellectual abilities: A new look at an old controversy. *Review of Educational Research, 62*(1), 61–84.

Feldhusen, J. F. (1996). How to identify and develop special talents. *Educational Leadership, 53*(5), 66–69.

Fennema, E., Carpenter, T. P., Jacobs, V. R., Franke, M. L., & Levi, L. W. (1998). A longitudinal study of gender differences in young children's mathematical thinking. *Educational Researcher, 27*(5), 6–11.

Fennema, E., Franke, M. L., Carpenter, T. P., & Carey, D. A. (1993). Using children's mathematical knowledge in instruction. *American Educational Research Journal, 30*(3), 555–583.

Fenson, L., Dale, P. S., Reznick, J. S., Bates, E., Thal, D. J., & Pethick, S. J. (1994). Variability in early communicative development. *Monographs of the Society for Research in Child Development, 59*(5), No. 242.

Feuer, M. J., & Fulton, K. (1993). The many faces of performance assessment. *Phi Delta Kappan, 74*(6), 478.

Feuerstein, R. (1980). *Instrumental enrichment: An intervention program for cognitive modifiability.* Baltimore: University Park Press.

Feuerstein, R., & Kozulin, A. (1995). The Bell Curve: Getting the facts right. *Educational Leadership, 52*(7), 71–74.

Feuerstein, R., Miller, R., Hoffman, M. B., Rand, Y., Mintzker, Y., & Jensen, M. R. (1981). Cognitive modifiability in adolescence: Cognitive structure and the effects of intervention. *Journal of Special Education, 15,* 269–287.

Fielding, L. G., Anderson, R. C., & Pearson, P. D. (1990). *How discussion questions influence children's story understanding* (Tech. Rep. No. 490). Champaign, IL: University of Illinois, Center for the Study of Reading.

Finn, J. D., & Cox, D. (1992). Participation and withdrawal among fourth-grade pupils. *American Educational Research Journal, 29*(1), 141–162.

Finn, J. D., Pannozzo, G. M., & Voelkl, K. E. (1995). Disruptive and inattentive-withdrawn behavior and achievement among fourth graders. *The Elementary School Journal, 95*(5), 421–434.

Fiordaliso, R., Lordeman, A., Filipczak, J., & Friedman, R. M. (1977). Effects of feedback on absenteeism in the junior high school. *Journal of Educational Research, 70,* 188–192.

Firestone, W. A., Mayrowetz, D., & Fairman, J. (1998). Performance-based assessment and instructional change: The effects of testing in Maine and Maryland. *Educational Evaluation and Policy Analysis, 20*(2), 95–113.

Fisher, C. W., Berliner, D. C., Filby, N. N., Marliave, R., Cahen, L. S., Dishaw, M. M., & Moore, J. E. (1978). *Teaching behaviors, academic learning time, and student achievement: Final report of Phase III-B, beginning teacher evaluation study.* (Tech. Report V-1). San Francisco: Far West Laboratory for Educational Research and Development.

Fiske, E. B. (1989, July 12). The misleading concept of "average" on reading tests changes, and more students fall below it. *New York Times.*

Fitzpatrick, A. R. (1989). Social influences in standard setting: The effects of social interaction on group judgments. *Review of Educational Research, 59*(3), 315–328.

Flanagan, C. (1993). Gender and social class: Intersecting issues in women's achievement. *Educational Psychologist, 28*(4), 357–378.

Flannery, D. J. (1997). *School violence: Risk, preventive intervention, and policy.* New York: ERIC Clearinghouse on Urban Education.

Flavell, J. H. (1985). *Cognitive development* (2nd ed.). Englewood Cliffs, NJ: Prentice-Hall.

Flavell, J. H. (1986, January). Really and truly. *Psychology Today,* 38–44.

Flavell, J. H. (1996). Piaget's legacy. *Psychological Science, 7*(4), 200–203.

Flavell, J. H., Miller, P. H., & Miller, S. A. (1993). *Cognitive development.* Englewood Cliffs, NJ: Prentice Hall.

Fletcher, J. D. (1992). Individualized systems of instruction. In M. C. Alkin (Ed.), *Encyclopedia of educational research* (6th ed.) (pp. 612–620). New York: Macmillan.

Fletcher, J. M., Shaywitz, S. E., Shankweiler, D. P., Katz, L., Liberman, I. Y., Stvebing, K. K., Francis, D. J., Fowler, A. E., & Shaywitz, B. A. (1994). Cognitive profiles of reading disability: Comparisons of discrepancy and low achievement definitions. *Journal of Educational Psychology, 86,* 6–23.

Fletcher-Flinn, C. M., & Gravatt, B. (1995). The efficacy of computer assisted instruction (CAI): A meta-analysis. *Journal of Educational Computing Research, 12*(3), 219–242.

Floden, R. E., & Klinzing, H. G. (1990). What can research on teacher thinking contribute to teacher preparation? A second opinion. *Educational Research, 19*(4), 15–20.

Florida State Department of Education. (1990). *Multicultural teaching strategies* (Tech. Report No. 9). Tallahassee: Author.

Fogarty, R. (Ed.). (1993). *The multiage classroom.* Palatine, IL: IRI/Skylight.

Foos, P. W., & Fisher, R. P. (1988). Using tests as learning opportunities. *Journal of Educational Psychology, 80,* 179–183.

Foos, P. W., Mora, J. J., & Tkacz, S. (1994). Student study techniques and the generation effect. *Journal of Educational Psychology, 86*(4), 567–576.

Ford, D. Y. (1996). *Reversing underachievement among gifted black students: Promising practices and programs.* New York: Teachers College Press.

Fordham, S. (1996). *Blacked out: Dilemmas of race, identity, and success at Capitol High.* Chicago: University of Chicago Press.

Forman, E., & McPhail, J. (1989). *What have we learned about the cognitive benefits of peer interaction? A Vygotskian critique.* Paper presented at the annual meeting of the American Educational Research Association, San Francisco.

Forsterling, F. (1985). Attribution retraining: A review. *Psychological Bulletin, 98,* 495–512.

Forsyth, D. R. (1986). An attributional analysis of students' reactions to success and failure. In R. S. Feldman (Ed.), *The social psychology of education.* Cambridge: Cambridge University Press.

Francis, D. J., Shaywitz, S. E., Shaywitz, B. A., Stuebing, K. K., & Fletcher, J. M. (1996). Developmental lag versus deficit models of reading disability: A longitudinal, individual growth curves analysis. *Journal of Educational Psychology, 88*(1), 3–17.

Frankenberger, W., & Fronzaglio, K. (1991). A review of states' criteria and procedures for identifying children with learning disabilities. *Journal of Learning Disabilities, 24,* 495–500.

Franklin, R. D., Allison, D. B., & Gorman, B. S. (Eds.). (1997). *Design and analysis of single-case research.* Mahwah, NJ: Lawrence Erlbaum Associates, Inc.

Frazier, M. K. (1995). Caution: Students on board the internet. *Educational Leadership, 53*(2), 26–27.

Frederick D. Patterson Research Institute. (1997). *The African American education data book, Volume II: Preschool through high school education.* Fairfax, VA: Author.

Frederiksen, N. (1984a). Implications of cognitive theory for instruction in problem solving. *Review of Educational Research, 54,* 363–407.

Frederiksen, N. (1984b). The real test bias: Influences of testing on teaching and learning. *American Psychologist, 39,* 193–202.

Freeman, J. M., Vining, E. P. G., & Pillas, D. J. (1991). *Seizures and epilepsy in childhood: A guide for parents.* Baltimore: Johns Hopkins University Press.

Freiberg, H. J. (1996). From tourists to citizens in the classroom. *Educational Leadership, 54*(1), 32–36.

Freiberg, H. J., Stein, T. A., & Huang, S. (1995). Effects of a classroom management intervention on student achievement in inner-city elementary schools. *Educational Research and Evaluation, 1*(1), 36–66.

French, E. G. (1956). Motivation as a variable in work partner selection. *Journal of Abnormal and Social Psychology, 55,* 96–99.

Friedman, L. (1995). The space factor in mathematics: Gender differences. *Review of Educational Research, 65*(1), 22–50.

Friend, M., & Bursuck, W. D. (1999). *Including students with special needs* (2nd ed.). Boston: Allyn & Bacon.

Frisbie, D. A., & Waltman, K. K. (1993). Developing a personal grading plan. In K. M. Cauley, F. Linder, & J. H. McMillan (Eds.), *Annual Editions: Educational Psychology 93/94.* Guilford, CT: Dushkin.

Fuchs, D., & Fuchs, L. S. (1989). Exploring effective and efficient preferral interventions: A component analysis of behavioral consultation. *School Psychology Review, 18,* 258–281.

Fuchs, D., & Fuchs, L. S. (1995). What's special about special education? *Phi Delta Kappan, 76*(7), 522–530.

Fuchs, D., & Fuchs, L. S. (1997). Peer-assisted learning strategies: Making classrooms more responsive to diversity. *American Educational Research Journal, 34*(1), 174–206.

Fuchs, D., Fuchs, L. S., Bahr, M. W., Fernstrom, P., & Stecker, P. M. (1990). Mainstream assistance teams: A scientific basis for the art of consultation. *Exceptional Children, 56,* 493–513.

Fuchs, D., Fuchs, L. S., & Fernstrom, P. (1993). A conservative approach to special education reform: Mainstreaming through transenvironmental programming and curriculum-based measurement. *American Educational Research Journal, 30,* 149–177.

Fuchs, L. S., Fuchs, D., Bentz, J., Phillips, N. B., & Hamlett, C. L. (1994). The nature of student interactions during peer tutoring with and without prior training and experience. *American Educational Research Journal, 31*(1), 75–103.

Fuchs, L. S., Fuchs, D., Hamlett, C. L., & Stecker, P. M. (1991). Effects of curriculum-based measurement and consultation on teacher planning and student achievement in mathematics operations. *American Educational Research Journal, 28*(3), 617–641.

Fuchs, L. S., Fuchs, D. Karns, K., Hamlett, C. L., Katzaroff, M., & Dutka, S. (1997). Effects of task-focused goals on low-achieving students without learning disabilities. *American Educational Research Journal, 34*(3), 513–543.

Fuerst, J. S., & Petty, R. (1996). The best use of federal funds for childhood education. *Phi Delta Kappan, 77*(10), 676–678.

Furey, P. (1986). A framework for cross-cultural analysis of teaching methods. In P. Byrd (Ed.), *Teaching across cultures in the university ESL program.* Washington, DC: National Association for Foreign Student Affairs.

Furman, W., & Buhrmester, D. (1992). Age and sex differences in perceptions of networks of personal relationships. *Child Development, 63,* 103–115.

Fuson, K. C. (1992). Research on whole number addition and subtraction. In D. Grouws (Ed.), *Handbook of research on mathematics teaching and learning* (pp. 243–275). New York: Macmillan.

Gaddy, M. L. (1998, April). *Reading and studying from highlighted text: Memory for information highlighted by others.* Paper presented at the annual meeting of the American Educational Research Association, San Diego.

Gadow, K. D. (1986). *Children on medication: Hyperactivity, learning disabilities, and mental retardation.* San Diego: College-Hill.

Gage, N. L. (1978). *The scientific basis of the art of teaching.* New York: Teachers College Press.

Gage, N. L. (1991). The obviousness of social and educational research results. *Educational Researcher, 20*(1), 10–16.

Gage, N. L. (1994). The scientific status of the behavioral sciences: The case of research on teaching. *Teaching and Teacher Education, 10*(5), 565–577.

Gage, N. L., & Berliner, D. C. (1984). *Educational psychology* (3rd ed.). Boston: Houghton Mifflin.

Gage, N. L., & Needels, M. C. (1989). Process-product research on teaching: A review of criticism. *Elementary School Journal, 89,* 253–300.

Gagné, R. (1977). *The conditions of learning* (3rd ed.). New York: Holt, Rinehart and Winston.

Gagné, R., & Briggs, L. (1979). *Principles of instructional design* (2nd ed.). New York: Holt, Rinehart and Winston.

Gall, M. (1984). Synthesis of research on teachers' questioning. *Educational Leadership, 42,* 40–47.

Gall, M., Ward, B., Berliner, D., Cahen, L., Winne, P., Glashoff, J., & Stanton, G. (1978). Effects of questioning techniques and recitation on student learning. *American Educational Research Journal, 15,* 175–199.

Gall, M. D. (1987). Discussion methods. In M. J. Dunkin (Ed.), *International encyclopedia of teaching and teacher education.* New York: Pergamon.

Gallagher, A. M., & DeLisi, R. (1994). Gender differences in scholastic aptitude test: Mathematics problem solving among high ability students. *Journal of Educational Psychology, 86*(2), 204–211.

Gallagher, J. J. (1992). Gifted persons. In M. C. Alkin (Ed.), *Encyclopedia of educational research* (6th ed.) (pp. 544–549). New York: Macmillan.

Gallagher, J. J. (1995). Education of gifted students: A civil rights issue? *Phi Delta Kappan, 76*(5), 408–410.

Gallagher, S., & Stepien, W. (1993). Problem-based learning: As authentic as it gets. *Educational Leadership, 50(7),* 25–28.

Gallini, J. K. (1991). Schema-based strategies and implications for instructional design in strategy training. In C. McCormick, G. Miller, & M. Pressley (Eds.), *Cognitive strategies research: From basic research to educational applications.* New York: Springer-Verlag.

Gamoran, A. (1984, April). Egalitarian versus elitist use of ability grouping. Paper presented at the annual convention of the American Educational Research Association, New Orleans.

Gamoran, A., Nystrand, M., Berends, M., & Le Pore, P. C. (1995). An organizational analysis of the effects of ability grouping. *American Educational Research Journal, 32,* 687–715.

Garbarino, J. (1997). Educating children in a socially toxic environment. *Educational Leadership, 54*(7), 12–16.

Garber, H. L. (1988). *The Milwaukee Project: Preventing mental retardation in children at risk.* Washington, DC: American Association on Mental Retardation.

Garcia, E. E. (1992). "Hispanic" children: Theoretical, empirical, and related policy issues. *Educational Psychology Review, 4*(1), 69–93.

Garcia, E. E. (1993). Language, culture, and education. In L. Darling-Hammond (Ed.), *Review of research in education, 19.* Washington, DC: American Educational Research Association.

Garcia, E. E. (1994, April). *The impact of linguistic and cultural diversity on America's schools: A need for new policy.* Paper presented at the annual meeting of the American Educational Research Association, New Orleans.

García, G. E., & Pearson, P. D. (1994). Assessment and diversity. In L. Darling-Hammond (Ed.), *Review of Research in Education 20.* Washington, DC: American Educational Research Association.

Garcia, J. (1993). The changing image of ethnic groups in textbooks. *Phi Delta Kappan, 75*(1), 29–35.

Gardner, H. (1991). *The unschooled mind: How children think and how schools should teach.* New York: Basic Books.

Gardner, H. (1993). *Multiple intelligences: The theory in practice.* New York: Basic Books.

Gardner, H. (1995). Reflections on multiple intelligences: Myths and messages. *Phi Delta Kappan, 77,* 200–209.

Gardner, H., & Hatch, T. (1989). Multiple intelligences go to school. *Educational Researcher, 18*(8), 6.

Gardner, M. K. (1985). Cognitive psychological approaches to instructional task analysis. In E. W. Gordon (Ed.), *Review of research in education,* Vol. 12 (pp. 157–195). Washington, DC: American Educational Research Association.

Garner, R., & Alexander, P. A. (1989). Metacognition: Answered and unanswered questions. *Educational Psychologist, 24,* 143–158.

Garnier, H. E., Stein, J. A., & Jacobs, J. K. (1997). The process of dropping out of high school: A 19-year perspective. *American Educational Research Journal, 34*(2), 395–419.

Gartner, A., & Lipsky, D. K. (1987). Beyond special education: Toward a quality system for all students. *Harvard Educational Review, 57,* 367–395.

Garvey, C. (1990). *Play* (enlarged ed.). Cambridge, MA: Harvard University Press.

Garvey, C. (1990). *Play.* Cambridge, MA: Harvard University Press.

Gay, G. (1997). Educational equality for students of color. In J. A. Banks & C. A. M. Banks (Eds.), *Multicultural education: Issues and perspectives* (pp. 195–228). Boston: Allyn & Bacon.

Gearhart, M., & Herman, J. L. (1995). *Portfolio assessment: Whose work is it?* Los Angeles: UCLA, Center for the Study of Evaluation.

Geisert, P. G., & Futrell, M. K. (1995). *Teachers, computers, and curriculum* (2nd ed.). Boston: Allyn & Bacon.

Gelman, R. (1979). Preschool thought. *American Psychologist, 34,* 900–905.

Gelman, R., & Baillargeon, R. (1983). A review of some Piagetian concepts. In J. H. Flavell & E. M. Markman (Eds.), *Handbook of child psychology. Vol. 3: Cognitive development* (4th ed.) (pp. 167–230). New York: Wiley.

Gelman, R., & Brenneman, K. (1994). Domain specificity and cultural variation are not inconsistent. In L. A. Hirschfeld & S. Gelman (Eds.), *Mapping the mind: Domain specificity in cognition and culture.* New York: Cambridge University Press.

General Accounting Office. (1994). *Limited English proficiency: A growing and costly educational challenge facing many school districts.* Washington, DC: Author.

General Accounting Office. (1995). *Early childhood centers: Services to prepare children for school often limited.* Washington, DC: Author.

George, P. (1992). *How to untrack your school.* Alexandria, VA: Association for Supervision and Curriculum Development.

George, P. (1993, March). *Examining the culture of the classroom.* Paper presented at the Comparative and International Education Society, Kingston, Jamaica.

Gergen, K. (1995). Social construction and the educational process. In L. Steffe & J. Gale (Eds.), *Constructivism in education* (pp. 17–39). Hillsdale, NJ: Erlbaum.

Gersten, R., Baker, S. K., & Marks, S. U. (1998). Strategies for teaching English-language learners. In K. R. Harris, S. Graham, & D. Deshler (Eds.), *Teaching every child every day* (pp. 208–249). Cambridge, MA: Brookline Books.

Gersten, R., & Carnine, D. (1984). Direct instruction mathematics: A longitudinal evaluation of low-income elementary students. *Elementary School Journal, 84,* 395–407.

Gersten, R., & Keating, T. (1987). Long-term benefits from direct instruction. *Educational Leadership, 44*(6), 28–31.

Gersten, R., & Woodward, J. (1995). A longitudinal study of transitional and immersion bilingual education programs in one district. *The Elementary School Journal, 95*(3), 223–239.

Giaconia, R. M., & Hedges, L. V. (1982). Identifying features of effective open education. *Review of Educational Research, 52,* 579–602.

Giangreco, M. F. (1996). What do I do now? A teacher's guide to including students with disabilities. *Educational Leadership, 53*(5), 56–57.

Gibbons, A. S., Duffin, J. R., Robertson, D. J., & Thompson, B. (1998, April). *Effects of administering feedback following extended problem solving.* Paper presented at the annual meeting of the American Educational Research Association, San Diego.

Gibbs, J. C., Arnold K. D., & Burkhart, J. F. (1984). Sex differences in the expression of moral judgment. *Child Development, 55,* 1040–1043.

Gijselaers, W. H., & Schmidt, H. G. (1995). Effects of quantity of instruction on time spent on learning and achievement. *Educational Research and Evaluation, 1*(2), 183–201.

Gilligan, C. (1982). *In a different voice: Sex differences in the expression of moral judgment.* Cambridge, MA: Harvard University Press.

Gilligan, C. (1985). *Remapping development.* Paper presented at the biennial meeting of the Society for Research in Child Development, Toronto.

Ginsburg, H. P., & Opper, S. (1988). *Piaget's theory of intellectual development* (3rd ed.). Englewood Cliffs, NJ: Prentice-Hall.

Glaser, R., & Silver, E. (1994). Assessment, testing, and instruction: Retrospect and prospect. In L. Darling-Hammond (Ed.), *Review of Research in Education 20.* Washington, DC: American Educational Research Association.

Glazer, S. M., & Burke, E. M. (1994). *An integrated approach to early literacy.* Boston: Allyn & Bacon.

Godden, D., & Baddeley, A. D. (1975). Context-dependent memory in two natural environments: On land and under water. *British Journal of Psychology, 66,* 325–331.

Gold, R. M., Reilly, A., Silberman, R., & Lehr, R. (1971). Academic achievement declines under pass-fail grading. *Journal of Experimental Education, 39,* 17–21.

Goldenberg, C. (1996). The education of language-minority students: Where are we, and where do we need to go? *Elementary School Journal, 96*(3), 353–361.

Goleman, D. (1995). *Emotional intelligence: Why it can matter more than IQ.* New York: Bantam.

Gomez, M. L., Grave, M. E., & Block, M. N. (1991). Reassessing portfolio assessment rhetoric and reality. *Language Arts, 68,* 620–628.

Good, T. (1987). Teacher expectations. In D. Berliner & B. Rosenshine (Eds.), *Talks to teachers* (pp. 159–200). New York: Random House.

Good, T., & Grouws, D. (1977). Teaching effects: A process-product study in fourth grade mathematics classes. *Journal of Teacher Education, 28,* 49–54.

Good, T., & Grouws, D. (1979). The Missouri Mathematics Effectiveness Project: An experimental study in fourth-grade classrooms. *Journal of Educational Psychology, 71,* 355–362.

Good, T., Grouws, D., & Ebmeier, H. (1983). *Active mathematics teaching.* New York: Longman.

Good, T. L., & Brophy, J. E. (1984). *Looking in classrooms* (3rd ed.). New York: Harper & Row.

Good, T. L., & Brophy, J. E. (1989). Teaching the lesson. In R. E. Slavin (Ed.), *School and classroom organization.* Hillsdale, NJ: Erlbaum.

Good, T. L., Mulryan, C., & McCaslin, M. (1992). Grouping for instruction in mathematics: A call for programmatic research on small group processes. In D. Grouws (Ed.), *Handbook of research on mathematics teaching and learning* (pp. 165–196). New York: Macmillan.

Goodlad, J. I. (1983). *A place called school.* New York: McGraw-Hill.

Goodman, G., & Poillion, M. J. (1992). ADD: Acronym for any dysfunction or difficulty. *Journal of Special Education, 26,* 37–56.

Goodman, K. S., & Goodman, Y. M. (1989). Introduction: Redefining education. In L. B. Bird (Ed.), *Becoming a whole language school: The Fair Oaks story* (pp. 3–10). Katonah, NY: Richard C. Owen.

Goodrich, H. (1996). Understanding rubrics. *Educational Leadership, 54*(4), 14–17.

Gordon, B. M. (1995). Knowledge construction, competing critical theories, and education. In J. A. Banks & C. A. M. Banks (Eds.), *Handbook of research on multicultural education.* New York: Macmillan.

Gordon, E. W. (1991). Human diversity and pluralism. *Educational Psychologist, 26*(2), 99–108.

Gordon, E. W., & Bhattacharyya, M. (1994). Race and intelligence. In R. J. Sternberg (Ed.), *Encyclopedia of human intelligence.* New York: Macmillan.

Gordon, I. (1975). *Human development: A transactional perspective.* New York: Harper & Row.

Gordon, R. L. (1997). How novice teachers can succeed with adolescents. *Educational Leadership, 54*(7), 56–58.

Gorney, B. E. (1994, April). *An integrative analysis of the content and structure of school report cards: What school systems report to the public.* Paper presented at the annual meeting of the American Educational Research Association, New Orleans.

Gottfredson, D. C., Gottfredson, G. D., & Hybl, L. G. (1993). Managing adolescent behavior: A multiyear, multischool study. *American Educational Research Journal, 30*(1), 179–215.

Gottfried, A. E. (1990). Academic intrinsic motivation in young elementary school children. *Journal of Educational Psychology, 82*(3), 525–538.

Gottlieb, J., Alter, M., & Gottlieb, B. W. (1991). Mainstreaming academically handicapped children in urban schools. In J. W. Lloyd, A. C. Repp, & N. Smith (Eds.), *The regular education initiative: Alternative perspectives on concepts, issues, and models* (pp. 95–112). Sycamore, IL: Sycamore Press.

Graham, S. (1991). A review of attribution theory in achievement contexts. *Educational Psychology Review, 3*(1), 5–39.

Graham, S. (1994). Motivation in African Americans. *Review of Educational Research, 64,* 55–117.

Graham, S. (1997). Using attribution theory to understand social and academic motivation in American youth. *Educational Psychologist, 32*(1), 21–34.

Graham, S., & Golan, S. (1991). Motivational influences on cognition: Task involvement, ego involvement, and depth of information processing. *Journal of Educational Psychology, 83*(2), 187–194.

Graham, S., MacArthur, C., & Schwartz, S. (1995). Effects of goal setting and procedural facilitation on the revising behavior and writing performance of students with writing and learning problems. *Journal of Educational Psychology, 87*(2), 230–240.

Graham, S., & Weiner, B. (1996). Theory and principles of motivation. In D.C. Berliner & R. C. Calfee (Eds.), *Handbook of educational psychology* (pp. 63–84). New York: Macmillan.

Grant, C. A., & Sleeter, C. E. (1997). Race, class, gender and disability in the classroom. In J. A. Banks & C. A. M. Banks (Eds.), *Multicultural education: Issues and perspectives* (pp. 61–85). Boston: Allyn & Bacon.

Greenblat, C. S. (1982). Games and simulations. In H. E. Mitzel (Ed.), *Encyclopedia of educational research* (pp. 713–716). New York: Free Press.

Greenbowe, T., Herron, J. D., Nurrenbern, S., Staver, J. R., & Ward, C. R. (1981). Teaching preadolescents to act as scientists: Replication and extension of an earlier study. *Journal of Educational Psychology, 73,* 705–711.

Greene, B. A., & Miller, R. B. (1996). Influence achievement: Goals, perceived ability, and cognitive engagement. *Contemporary Educational Psychology, 21*(2), 181–192.

Greene, D., & Lepper, M. R. (1974). How to turn play into work. *Psychology Today, 8,* 49–54.

Greene, R. L. (1986). Sources of recency effects in free recall. *Psychological Bulletin, 99,* 221–228.

Greenfield, P. M. (1984). Theory of the teacher in learning activities. In B. Rogoff & J. Lave (Eds.), *Everyday cognition: Its development in social context* (pp. 117–138). Cambridge, MA: Harvard University Press.

Greeno, J. G., Collins, A. M., & Resnick, L. R. (1996). Cognition and learning. In D.C. Berliner & R. C. Calfe (Eds.), *Handbook of educational psychology* (pp. 15–46). New York: Macmillan.

Greenwald, R., Hedges, L. V., & Laine, R. D. (1996). The effect of school resources on student achievement. *Review of Educational Research, 66*(3), 361–396.

Gregory, J. F. (1995). The crime of punishment: Racial and gender disparities in the use of corporal punishment in U.S. public schools. *Journal of Negro Education, 64*(4), 454–462.

Gresham, F. (1981). Social skills training with handicapped children: A review. *Review of Educational Research, 51,* 139–176.

Gresham, F. M., & MacMillan, D. L. (1997). Social competence and affective characteristics of students with mild disabilities. *Review of Educational Research, 67*(4), 377–415.

Griffin, B. W. (1996). An examination of the relationship between minimum competency test performance and dropping out of high school. *Educational Evaluation and Policy Analysis, 18*(3), 243–252.

Grolnick, W. S., Benjet, C., Kurowski, C. O., & Apostoleris, N. H. (1997). Predictors of parent involvement in children's schooling. *Journal of Educational Psychology, 89*(3), 538–548.

Gronlund, N. E. (1991). *How to write and use instructional objectives* (4th ed.). Englewood Cliffs, NJ: Prentice-Hall.

Grossman, H. (1995). *Teaching in a diverse society.* Boston: Allyn & Bacon.

Grossman H., & Grossman, S. H. (1994). *Gender issues in education.* Boston: Allyn & Bacon.

Grusec, J. E., & Goodnow, J. J. (1994). Impact of parental discipline methods on the child's internalization of values. *Developmental Psychology, 30,* 4–19.

Guilford, J. P. (1988). Some changes in the Structure-of-Intellect model. *Educational and Psychological Measurement, 48,* 1–4.

Gump, P. V. (1982). School settings and their keeping. In D. L. Duke (Ed.), *Helping teachers manage classrooms* (pp. 98–114). Alexandria, VA: Association for Supervision and Curriculum Development.

Guskey, T. R. (1990). Cooperative mastery learning strategies. *The Elementary School Journal, 91*(1), 33–42.

Guskey, T. R. (1994). Making the grade: What benefits students? *Educational Leadership, 52*(2), 14–19.

Guskey, T. R. (1995). Mastery learning. In J. H. Block, S. T. Everson, & T. R. Guskey (Eds.), *School improvement programs* (pp. 91–109) New York: Scholastic.

Gustafsson, J.-E. (1994). General intelligence. In R. J. Sternberg (Ed.), *Encyclopedia of human intelligence.* New York: Macmillan.

Guthrie, J. T., Bennett, S., & Weber, S. (1991). Processing procedural documents: A cognitive model for following written directions. *Educational Psychology Review, 3,* 249–265.

Gutiérrez, R., & Slavin, R. E. (1992). Achievement effects of the nongraded elementary school: A best evidence synthesis. *Review of Educational Research, 62*(4), 333–376.

Haertel, E. (1986, April). *Choosing and using classroom tests: Teachers' perspectives on assessment.* Paper presented at the annual meeting of the American Educational Research Association, San Francisco.

Hakuta, K., & McLaughlin, B. (1996). Bilingualism and second language learning: Seven tensions that define the research. In D.C. Berliner & R. C. Calfee (Eds.), *Handbook of educational psychology* (pp. 603–621). New York: Macmillan.

Haladyna, T. M. (1997). *Writing test items to evaluate higher order thinking.* Boston: Allyn & Bacon.

Hall, J. W. (1991). More on the utility of the keyword method. *Journal of Educational Psychology, 83*(1), 171–172.

Hall, R. H., & O'Donnell, A. M. (1992, April). *Alternative materials for learning: Cognitive and affective outcomes of learning from knowledge maps.* Paper presented at the annual meeting of the American Educational Research Association, San Francisco.

Hall, R. H., Sidio-Hall, M. A., & Saling, C. B. (1995, April). *Spatially directed post organization in learning from knowledge maps.* Paper presented at the annual meeting of the American Educational Research Association, San Francisco.

Hallahan, D. P., & Kauffman, J. M. (1991). *Exceptional children* (5th ed.). Englewood Cliffs, NJ: Prentice-Hall.

Hallahan, D. P., & Kauffman, J. M. (1997). *Exceptional learners: Introduction to special education* (7th ed.). Boston: Allyn & Bacon.

Halle, T. G., Kurtz-Coster, B., & Mahoney, J. L. (1997). Family influence on school achievement in low-income, African-American children. *Journal of Educational Psychology, 89*(3), 527–537.

Halpern, D. F. (1994). Gender differences in intellectual abilities. In R. J. Sternberg (Ed.), *Encyclopedia of human intelligence.* New York: Macmillan.

Halpern, D. F. (1995). *Thought and knowledge: An introduction to critical thinking* (3rd ed.). Hillsdale, NJ: Erlbaum.

Halpern, D. F., Hansen, C., & Riefer, D. (1990). Analogies as an aid to understanding and memory. *Journal of Educational Psychology, 82,* 298–305.

Hamaker, C. (1986). The effects of adjunct questions on prose learning. *Review of Educational Research, 56,* 212–242.

Hambleton, R. K. (1996). Advances in assessment models, methods, and practices. In D.C. Berliner & R. C. Calfee (Eds.), *Handbook of educational psychology* (pp. 899–925). New York: Macmillan.

Hamburg, D. A. (1992). *Today's children: Creating a future for a generation in crisis.* New York: Times Books.

Hamilton, R. J. (1985). A framework for the evaluation of the effectiveness of adjunct questions and objectives. *Review of Educational Research, 55,* 47–85.

Hand, B., & Treagust, D. F. (1991). Student achievement and science curriculum development using a constructive framework. *Schools, Science, and Mathematics, 91,* 172–176.

Haney, W., & Madaus, G. (1989). Searching for alternatives to standardized tests: Whys, whats, and whithers. *Phi Delta Kappan, 70*(9), 683–687.

Hanson, M. K. (1994). A conflict resolution/student mediation program: Effects on student attitudes and behaviors. *ERS Spectrum, 12*(4), 9–14.

Hanson, S. L., Morrison, D. R., & Ginsburg, A. L. (1989). The antecedents of teenage fatherhood. *Demography, 26,* 579–596.

Hardin, D. E., & McNelis, S. J. (1996). The resource center: Hub of inclusive activities. *Educational Leadership, 53*(5), 41–43.

Hardman, J. L., Drew, C., & Winston-Egan, M. (1996). *Human exceptionality: Society, school, and family* (5th ed.). Boston: Allyn & Bacon.

Hardman, M. L., Drew, C. J., Egan, M. W., & Wolf, B. (1996). *Human exceptionality: Society, school, and family* (5th ed.). Boston: Allyn & Bacon.

Hargreaves, A. (1996). Transforming knowledge: Blurring the boundaries between research, policy, and practice. *Educational Evaluation and Policy Analysis, 18*(2), 105–122.

Haring, N. G., & Liberty, K. A. (1990). Matching strategies with performance in facilitating generalization. *Focus on Exceptional Children, 22*(8), 1–16.

Harp, S. F., & Mayer, R. E. (1997). The role of interest in learning from scientific text and illustrations: On the distinction between emotional interest and cognitive interest. *Journal of Educational Psychology, 89*(1), 92–102.

Harpring, S. A. (1985, April). In-class alternatives to traditional Chapter I pullout programs. Paper presented at the annual meeting of the American Educational Research Association, Chicago.

Harris, K. R. (1990). Developing self-regulated learners: The role of private speech and self-instruction. *Educational Psychologist, 21,* 35–50.

Harris, K. R., & Alexander, P. A. (1998). Integrated, constructivist education: Challenge and reality. *Education Psychology Review, 10*(2), 155–127.

Harris, K. R., & Graham, S. (Feb. 1996). Memo to constructivists: Skills count, too. *Educational Leadership, 53*(5), 26–29.

Harris, K. R., & Pressley, M. (1992). The nature of cognitive strategy instruction: Interactive strategy construction. *Exceptional Children, 58.*

Harste, J. C., & Burke, C. L. (1980). Examining instructional assumptions: The child as informant. *Theory into Practice, 19,* 170–178.

Hart, B., & Risley, T. R. (1995). *Meaningful differences in the everyday experience of young American children.* Baltimore: Brookes.

Hart, C. H., DeWolf, D. M., Wozniak, P., & Burts, D. C. (1992). Maternal and paternal disciplinary styles: Relations with preschoolers' playground behavioral orientations and peer status. *Child Development, 63,* 879–892.

Harter, S. (1990). Self and identity development. In S. S. Feldman & G. R. Elliot (Eds.), *At the threshold: The developing adolescent* (pp. 352–387). Cambridge, MA: Harvard University Press.

Harter, S. (1993). Visions of self: Beyond the me in the mirror. In J. Jacobs (Ed.), *Developmental perspectives on the self: Nebraska symposium on motivation 1992* (pp. 99–144). Lincoln: University of Nebraska Press.

Harter, S., Whitesell, N. R., & Kowalski, P. (1992). Individual differences in the effects of educational transitions on young adolescents' perceptions of competence and motivational orientation. *American Educational Research Journal, 29,* 777–807.

Hartshorne, H., & May, M. A. (1928). *Studies in the nature of character. I: Studies in deceit.* New York: Macmillan.

Hartup, W. W. (1989). Social relationships and their developmental significance. *American Psychologist, 44,* 120–126.

Hartup, W. W. (1992). *Having friends, making friends, and keeping friends: Relationships as educational contexts.* ERIC Clearinghouse on Elementary and Early Childhood Education, EDO-PS-92-4.

Haslinger, J., Kelly, P., & O'Lara, L. (1996). Countering absenteeism, anonymity, and apathy. *Educational Leadership, 54*(1), 47–49.

Hatch, T. (1997). Getting specific about multiple intelligences. *Educational Leadership, 54*(6), 26–29.

Hattie, J., Bibbs, J., & Purdie, N. (1996). Effects of learning skills interventions on student learning: A meta-analysis. *Review of Educational Research, 66*(2), 99–136.

Hattie, J., & Marsh, H. W. (1996). The relationship between research and teaching: A meta-analysis. *Review of Educational Research, 66*(4), 507–542.

Hatzichriston, C., & Hopf, D. (1996). A multiperspective comparison of peer sociometric status groups in childhood and adolescence. *Child Development, 67,* 1085–1102.

Hawkins, J. D., Doueck, H. J., & Lishner, D. M. (1988). Changing teaching practices in mainstream classrooms to improve bonding and behavior of low achievers. *American Educational Research Journal, 25,* 31–50.

Hedges, L. V., & Friedman, L. (1993). Gender differences in variability in intellectual abilities: A reanalysis of Feingold's results. *Review of Educational Research, 63*(1), 94–105.

Hein, K. (1993). "Getting real" about HIV in adolescents. *American Journal of Public Health, 83,* 492–494.

Hembree, R. (1988). Correlates, causes, effects, and treatment of test anxiety. *Review of Educational Research, 58,* 47–77.

Hendry, G. D., & King, R. C. (1994). On theory of learning and knowledge: Educational implications of advances in neuroscience. *Science Education, 78*(3), 223–253.

Henry, S. L., & Pepper, F. C. (1990). Cognitive, social, and cultural effects on Indian learning style: Classroom implications. *Journal of Educational Issues of Language Minority Students, 7,* 85–97.

Herbert, E. A. (1998). Lessons learned about student portfolios. *Phi Delta Kappan, 79*(8), 583–585.

Herbert, E. A., & Schultz, L. (1995). The power of portfolio. *Educational Leadership, 53*(7), 70–71.

Herman, J. L., Aschbacher, P. R., & Winters, L. (1992). *A practical guide to alternative assessment.* Alexandria, VA: Association for Supervision and Curriculum Development.

Herman, J. L., & Winters, L. (1994). Portfolio research: A slim collection. *Educational Leadership, 52*(2), 48–55.

Hernandez, H. (1990). *Multicultural education: A teacher's guide to content and practice.* Columbus, OH: Merrill.

Herrnstein, R. J., & Murray, C. (1994). *The bell curve: Intelligence and class structure in American life.* New York: Free Press.

Hersen, M. (Ed.). (1986). *Pharmacological and behavioral treatment: An integrative approach.* New York: Wiley.

Hess, R. D. (1987). School-related effects of educational uses of microcomputers in kindergarten classrooms and homes. *Journal of Educational Computer Research, 3,* 269–286.

Heward, W. L., & Cavanaugh, R. A. (1997). Educational equality for students with disabilities. In J. A. Banks & C. A. M. Banks (Eds.), *Multicultural education: Issues and perspectives* (pp. 301–333). Boston: Allyn & Bacon.

Heyns, B. (1978). *Summer learning and the effects of schooling.* New York: Academic Press.

Hickey, D. T. (1997). Motivational contemporary socio-constructivist instructional perspectives. *Educational Psychologist, 32*(3), 175–193.

Hidi, S., & Anderson, V. (1986). Producing written summaries: Task demands, cognitive operations, and implications for instruction. *Review of Educational Research, 56,* 473–493.

Hiebert, E. (1983). An examination of ability groupings for reading instruction. *Reading Research Quarterly, 18,* 231–255.

Hiebert, E. H. (1996). Revisiting the question: What difference does Reading Recovery make to an age cohort? *Educational Researcher, 25*(7), 26–28.

Hiebert, J., Carpenter, T. P., Fennema, E., Fuson, K., Human, P., Murray, H., Olivier, A., & Wearne, D. (1996). Problem solving as a basis for reform in curriculum and instruction: The case of mathematics. *Educational Researcher, 25*(4), 12–21.

Hiebert, J., & Wearne, D. (1993). Instructional tasks, classroom discourse, and student learning in second grade. *American Educational Research Journal, 30,* 393–425.

Hiebert, J., Wearne, D., & Taber, S. (1991). Fourth graders' gradual construction of decimal fractions during instruction using different physical representations. *Elementary School Journal, 91,* 321–341.

Higgins, K., & Boone, R. (1990). Hypertext computer study guides and the social studies achievements of students with learning disabilities, remedial students, and regular education students. *Journal of Learning Disabilities, 23,* 529–540.

Hilgard, E. R., & Bower, G. H. (1966). *Theories of learning.* New York: Appleton-Century-Crofts.

Hill, D. (1993). Order in the classroom. In K. M. Cauley, F. Linder, & J. H. McMillan (Eds.), *Annual editions: Educational psychology 93/94.* Guilford, CT: Dushkin.

Hill, J. R. (1977). *Measurement and evaluation in the classroom.* Columbus, OH: C. E. Merrill.

Hill, K., & Wigfield, A. (1984). Test anxiety: A major educational problem and what can be done about it. *Elementary School Journal, 85,* 105–126.

Hilliard, A. G. (1991/1992). Why we must pluralize the curriculum. *Educational Leadership, 49*(4), 12–16.

Hilliard, A. G. (1992). The pitfalls and promises of special education practice. *Exceptional Children, 59,* 168–172.

Hilliard, A. G. (1994). Misunderstanding and testing intelligence. In J. I. Goodlad & P. Keating (Eds.), *Access to knowledge: The continuing agenda for our nation's schools.* New York: The College Board.

Hillocks, G. (1984). What works in teaching composition: A meta-analysis of experimental treatment studies. *American Journal of Education, 93,* 133–170.

Hirsch, B. J., & Radkin, B. D. (1987). The transition to junior high school: A longitudinal study of self-esteem, psychological symptomatology, school life, and social support. *Child Development, 58,* 1235–1243.

Hodgin, J., & Wooliscroft, C. (1997). Eric learns to read: Learning styles at work. *Educational Leadership, 54*(6), 43–45.

Hoek, D., Terwel, J., & van den Eeden, P. (1997). Effects of training in the use of social and cognitive strategies: An intervention study in secondary mathematics in co-operative groups. *Educational Research and Evaluation, 3*(4), 364–389.

Hoffer, T., & Nelson, C. (1993, April). *High school effects on coursework in science and mathematics.* Paper presented at the annual meeting of the American Educational Research Association, Chicago.

Hoffman, M. L. (1983). Affective and cognitive processes in moral internalization. In E. T. Higgins, D. N. Ruble, & W. W. Hartup (Eds.), *Social cognition and social development: A socio-cultural perspective* (pp. 236–274). New York: Cambridge University Press.

Hoffman, M. L. (1993). Affective and cognitive processes in moral internalization. In E. T. Higgins, D. Ruble, & W. Hartup (Eds.), *Social cognition and social development* (pp. 236–274). Cambridge, England: Cambridge University Press.

Hoffman, M. L., & Saltzstein, H. D. (1967). Parent discipline and the child's moral development. *Journal of Personality and Social Psychology, 5,* 45–57.

Hoffman, S. D., Foster, E. M., & Furstenberg, F. F. (1993). Reevaluating the costs of teenage childbearing. *Demography, 30,* 1–13.

Hogan, R., & Emler, N. P. (1978). Moral development. In M. E. Lamb (Ed.), *Social and personality development* (pp. 200–233). New York: Holt, Rinehart and Winston.

Hoge, R. D., & Coladarci, T. (1989). Teacher-based judgments of academic achievement: A review of literature. *Review of Educational Research, 59*(3), 297–313.

Hoge, R. D., & Renzulli, J. S. (1993). Exploring the link between giftedness and self-concept. *Review of Educational Research, 63,* 449–465.

Hohmann, C. (1990). *Young children and computers.* Ypsilanti, MI: High Scope Press.

Hokoda, A., & Fincham, F. D. (1995). Origins of children's helpless and mastery achievement patterns in the family. *Journal of Educational Psychology, 87,* 375–385.

Honig, W. (1996). *How should we teach our children to read?* Thousand Oaks, CA: Corwin.

Hooper, S., & Rieber, L. P. (1995). Teaching with technology. In A. C. Ornstein (Ed.), *Teaching: Theory into practice.* Boston: Allyn & Bacon.

Hoover-Dempsey, K. V., & Sandler, H. M. (1997). Why do parents become involved in their children's education? *Review of Educational Research, 67*(1), 3–42.

Hopkins, K. D. (1998). *Educational and psychological measurement and evaluation* (8th ed.). Boston: Allyn & Bacon.

Horgan, D. D. (1995). *Achieving gender equality: Strategies for the classroom.* Boston: Allyn & Bacon.

Howard, E. R. (1978). *School discipline desk book.* West Nyack, NY: Parker.

Howard-Rose, D., & Winne, P. H. (1993). Measuring component sets of cognitive processes in self-regulated learning. *Journal of Educational Psychology, 85*(4), 591–604.

Howes, C., & Matheson, C. C. (1992). Sequences in the development of competent play with peers: Social and social pretend play. *Developmental Psychology, 28,* 961–974.

Howes, C., & Rodning, C. (1992). Attachment security and social pretend play negotiations: Illustrative study #5. In C. Howes, O. Unger, & C. C. Matheson (Eds.), *The collaborative construction of pretend: Social pretend play functions* (pp. 89–98). Albany: State University of New York Press.

Hubbard, L., & Mehan, H. (1997, March). *Scaling up an untracking program: A co-constructivist process.* Paper presented at the annual meeting of the American Educational Research Association, Chicago.

Hu-Dehart, E. (1993). The history, development, and future of ethnic studies. *Phi Delta Kappan, 75*(1), 50–54.

Hughes, F. P. (1995). *Children, play and development* (2nd ed.). Boston: Allyn & Bacon.

Hunt, P., & Goetz, L. (1997). Research on inclusive educational programs, practices, and outcomes for students with severe disabilities. *Journal of Special Education, 31*(1), 3–29.

Hunter, M. (1982). *Mastery teaching.* El Segundo, CA: TIP Publications.

Hunter, M. (1990/1991). Hunter lesson design helps achieve the goals of science instruction. *Educational Leadership, 48*(4), 79–81.

Hunter, M. (1995). Mastery teaching. In J. H. Block, S. T. Everson, & T. R. Guskey (Eds.), *School improvement programs* (pp. 181–204). New York: Scholastic.

Hunter, M., & Barker, G. (1989). If at first . . . : Attribution theory in the classroom. *Annual editions: Educational psychology 89/90.* Guilford, CT: Duskin.

Hyde, T. S., & Jenkins, J. J. (1969). Differential effects of incidental tasks on the organization of recall of highly associated words. *Journal of Experimental Psychology, 82,* 472–481.

Hyerle, D. (1995). Thinking maps: Seeing is understanding. *Educational Leadership, 53*(4), 85–89.

Hymel, S., Bowker, A., & Woody, E. (1993). Aggressive versus withdrawn unpopular children: Variations in peer and self-perceptions in multiple domains. *Child Development, 64,* 879–896.

Inhelder, B., & Piaget, J. (1958). *The growth of logical thinking from childhood to adolescence.* New York: Basic Books.

Iran-Nejad, A., Marsh, G. E., & Clements, A. C. (1992). The figure and the ground of constructive brain functioning: Beyond explicit memory processes. *Educational Psychologist, 74,* 473–492.

Iversen, I. H. (1992). Skinner's early research: From reflexology to operant conditioning. *American Psychologist, 47,* 1318–1328.

Jagacinski, C. M., & Nicholls, J. G. (1990). Reducing effort to protect perceived ability: "They'd do it but I wouldn't." *Journal of Educational Psychology, 82,* 15–21.

Jakupcak, A. J. (1998). School programs for successful inclusion of all students. In J. W. Putnam (Ed.), *Cooperative learning and strategies for inclusion* (pp. 203–227). Baltimore: Paul H. Brookes.

James, W. (1912). *Talks to teachers on psychology: And to students on some of life's ideals.* New York: Holt.

Janzen, R. (1994). Melting pot or mosaic? *Educational Leadership, 51*(8), 9–11.

Jenkins, J. R., & Jenkins, L. M. (1987). Making peer tutoring work. *Educational Leadership, 44*(6), 64–68.

Jensen, A. R. (1980). *Bias in mental testing.* New York: Free Press.

Jenson, W., Sloane, H., & Young, K. (1988). *Applied behavior modification in education.* Englewood Cliffs, NJ: Prentice-Hall.

Jimenez, R. T., García, G. E., & Pearson, P. D. (1995). Three children, two languages, and strategic reading: Case studies in bilingual/monolingual reading. *American Educational Research Journal, 32*(1), 67–97.

Johnson, D. W., & Johnson, R. T. (1987). *Learning together and alone* (2nd ed.). Englewood Cliffs, NJ: Prentice-Hall.

Johnson, D. W., & Johnson, R. T. (1994). *Learning together and alone: Cooperative, competitive, and individualistic learning* (4th ed.). Boston: Allyn & Bacon.

Johnson, D. W., & Johnson, R. T. (1996). Conflict resolution and peer mediation programs in elementary and secondary schools: A review of the research. *Review of Educational Research, 66*(4), 459–506.

Johnson, D. W., & Johnson, R. T. (1998). Cultural diversity and cooperative learning. In J. W. Putnam (Ed.), *Cooperative learning and strategies for inclusion* (pp. 67–85). Baltimore: Paul H. Brookes.

Johnson, D. W., Johnson, R. T., Dudley, B., Ward, M., & Magnuson, D. (1995). The impact of peer mediation training on the management of school and home conflicts. *American Educational Research Journal, 32,* 829–844.

Johnson, J. E., & Hooper, F. E. (1982). Piagetian structuralism and learning: Two decades of educational application. *Contemporary Educational Psychology, 7,* 217–237.

John-Steiner, V., & Mahn, H. (1996). Sociocultural approaches to learning and development: A Vigotskian framework. *Educational Psychologist, 31* (¾), 191–206.

Johnston, P., Allington, R., & Afflerbach, P. (1985). The congruence of classroom and remedial instruction. *Elementary School Journal, 85,* 465–477.

Jones, R. L. (1988). *Psychoeducational assessment of minority group children.* Berkeley, CA: Cobb & Henry.

Jones, V. (1993). *Equity 2000: Commitment to excellence and equity.* New York: College Board.

Jones, V. F., & Jones, L. S. (1995). *Comprehensive classroom management* (4th ed.). Boston: Allyn & Bacon.

Jones, V. F., & Jones, L. S. (1998). *Comprehensive classroom management* (5th ed.). Boston: Allyn & Bacon.

Joyce, B., & Weil, M. (1996). *Models of teaching* (5th ed.). Boston: Allyn & Bacon.

Juel, C. (1991). Beginning reading. In R. Barr, M. Kamil, P. Mosenthal, & P. D. Pearson (Eds.), *Handbook of reading research* (Vol. I, pp. 759–788). New York: Longman.

Jussim, L. (1991). Grades may reflect more than performance: Comment on Wentzel (1989). *Journal of Educational Psychology, 83*(1), 153–155.

Jussim, L., & Eccles, J. (1995). Naturally occurring interpersonal expectancies. In Eisenberg (Ed.), *Social development: Review of personality and social psychology, 15* (pp. 74–108). Thousand Oaks, CA: Sage.

Juvonen, J., & Weiner, B. (1993). An attributional analysis of students' interactions: The social consequences of perceived responsibility. *Educational Psychology Review, 5,* 325–345.

Kagan, S. (1992). *Cooperative learning resources for teachers.* San Juan Capistrano, CA: Resources for Teachers.

Kagan, S., Zahn, G. L., Widaman, K. F., Schwartzwald, J., & Tyrrell, G. (1985). Classroom structural bias: Impact of cooperative and competitive classroom structures on cooperative and competitive individuals and groups. In R. E. Slavin et al. (Eds.), *Learning to cooperate, cooperating to learn.* New York: Plenum.

Kagan, S. L., & Cohen, N. E. (1997). *Not by chance: Creating an early care and education system for America's children.* New Haven, CT: The Bush Center in Child Development and Social Policy, Yale University.

Kagan, S. L., & Neuman, M. J. (1998). Lessons from three decades of transition research. *Elementary School Journal, 98*(4), 365–379.

Kahle, J., & Meece, J. (1993). Research on gender issues in the classroom. In D. Gabel (Ed.), *Handbook of research on science teaching and learning.* New York: Macmillan.

Kalichman, S. C. (1996). *Answering questions about AIDS.* Washington, DC: American Psychological Association.

Kallison, J. M. (1986). Effects of lesson organization on achievement. *American Educational Research Journal, 23,* 337–347.

Kane, M. (1994). Validating the performance standards associated with passing scores. *Review of Educational Research, 64*(3), 425–461.

Kane, M. B., & Khattri, N. (1995). Assessment reform: A work in progress. *Phi Delta Kappan, 77*(1), 30–32.

Kantor, H., & Lowe, R. (1995). Class, race, and the emergence of federal education policy: From the new deal to the great society. *Educational Researcher, 24*(3), 4–11.

Kaplan, A., & Midgley, C. (1997). The effect of achievement goals: Does level of perceived academic competence make a difference? *Contemporary Educational Psychology, 22*(4), 415–435.

Karp, S. (1998). Beyond heroes and holidays: A practical guide to K–12 anti-racist, multicultural education and staff development. *Educational Leadership, 55* (8).

Karpov, Y. V., & Bransford, J. D. (1995). L. S. Vygotsky and the doctrine of empirical and theoretical learning. *Educational Psychologist, 30,* 61–66.

Karpov, Y. V., & Haywood, H. C. (1998). Two ways to elaborate Vygotsky's concept of mediation. *American Psychologist, 53*(1), 27–36.

Karweit, N. L. (1981). Time in school. *Research in Sociology of Education and Socialization, 2,* 77–110.

Karweit, N. L. (1989b). Preschool programs for students at risk of school failure. In R. E. Slavin, N. L. Karweit, & N. A. Madden (Eds.), *Effective programs for students at risk.* Boston: Allyn & Bacon.

Karweit, N. L. (1989c). Time and learning: A review. In R. E. Slavin (Ed.), *School and classroom organization.* Hillsdale, NJ: Erlbaum.

Karweit, N. L. (1994b). Issues in kindergarten organization and curriculum. In R. E. Slavin, N. L. Karweit, & B. A. Wasik (Eds.), *Preventing early school failure.* Boston: Allyn & Bacon.

Karweit, N. L., & Slavin, R. E. (1981). Measurement and modeling choices in studies of time and learning. *American Educational Research Journal, 18,* 157–171.

Karweit, N. L., & Wasik, B. A. (1994). Extra-year kindergarten programs and transitional first grades. In R. E. Slavin, N. L. Karweit, & B. A. Wasik (Eds.), *Preventing early school failure.* Boston: Allyn & Bacon.

Kasten, W. C., & Lolli, E. M. (1998). *Implementing multiage education.* Norwood, MA: Christopher–Gordon.

Katayama, A. D., & Robinson, D. H. (1998, April). *Study effectiveness of outlines and graphic organizers: How much information should be provided for students to be successful on transfer tests?* Paper presented at the annual meeting of the American Educational Research Association, San Diego.

Katz, L. G., Evangelou, D., & Hartman, J. A. (1991). *The case for mixed-age grouping in early childhood education.* Washington, DC: National Association for the Education of Young Children.

Katz, L. G., & McClellan, D. E. (1991). *The teacher's role in the social development of young children.* ERIC Clearinghouse on Elementary and Early Childhood Education, ED 331 642.

Kauffman, J. M. (1989). *Characteristics of behavioral disorders of children and youth* (4th ed.). Columbus, OH: Merrill.

Kauffman, J. M. (1997). *Characteristics of behavioral disorders of children and youth* (6th ed.). Columbus, OH: Merrill.

Kauffman, J. M., & Burbach, H. J. (1997). On creating a climate of classroom civility. *Phi Delta Kappan, 79*(4), 320–325.

Kauffman, J. M., Lloyd, J. W., Baker, J., & Riedel, T. M. (1995). Inclusion of all students with emotional or behavioral disorder? Let's think again. *Phi Delta Kappan, 76*(7), 542–546.

Kaufman, J. J., Gottlieb, J., Agard, J. A., & Kukic, M. (1975). Mainstreaming: Toward an explication of the concept. In E. L. Meyen, G. A. Vergason, & R. J. Whelan (Eds.), *Alternatives for teaching exceptional children* (pp. 40–54). Denver: Love.

Kavale, K. A., & Reese, J. H. (1992). The character of learning disabilities: An Iowa profile. *Learning Disability Quarterly, 15,* 74–94.

Keating, P. (1994). Striving for sex equality in schools. In J. I. Goodlad & P. Keating (Eds.), *Access to knowledge: The continuing agenda for our nation's schools.* New York: The College Board.

Keith, T. Z., Reimers, T. M., Fehrmann, P. G., Pottebaum, S. M., & Aubey, L. W. (1986). Parental involvement, homework, and TV time: Direct and indirect effects on high school achievement. *Journal of Educational Psychology, 78,* 373–380.

Kellam, S. G., & Werthamer-Larsson, L. (1986). Developmental epidemiology: A basis for prevention. In M. Kessler & S. E. Goldston (Eds.), *A decade of progress in primary prevention* (pp. 154–180). Hanover, NH: University Press of New England.

Kemple, J. J. (1997). *Career academies: Communities of support for students and teachers: Further findings from a 10-site evaluation.* New York: MDRC.

Kennedy, J. H. (1990). Determinants of peer social status: Contributions of physical appearance, reputation, and behavior. *Journal of Youth and Adolescence, 19,* 233–244.

Kennedy, M. M. (1997). The connection between research and practice. *Educational Researcher, 26*(7), 4–12.

Keogh, B. K., & MacMillan, D. L. (1996). Exceptionality. In D.C. Berliner & R. C. Calfee (Eds.), *Handbook of educational psychology* (pp. 311–330). New York: Macmillan.

Kiewra, D. A. (1985). Providing the instructor's notes: An effective addition to student notetaking. *Educational Psychologist, 20,* 33–39.

Kiewra, K. A. (1991). Aids to lecture learning. *Educational Psychologist, 26,* 37–53.

Kiewra, K. A., DuBois, N. F., Christian, D., McShane, A., Meyerhoffer, M., & Roskelley, D. (1991). Note-taking functions and techniques. *Journal of Educational Psychology, 83,* 240–245.

Killen, M. (1996). *Children's autonomy, social competence, and interactions with adults and other children: Exploring connections and consequences.* San Francisco: Jossey-Bass.

Kinchla, R. A. (1992). Attention. *Annual Review of Psychology, 43,* 711–742.

King, A. (1991). Effects of training in strategic questioning on children's problem-solving performance. *Journal of Educational Psychology, 83,* 307–317.

King, A. (1992). Facilitating elaborative learning through guided student-generated questioning. *Educational Psychologist, 27,* 111–126.

King, A. (1994). Guiding knowledge construction in the classroom: Effects of teaching children how to question and how to explain. *American Educational Research Journal, 31*(2), 338–368.

King, A. (1997). Ask to think—tell why: A model of transactive peer tutoring for scaffolding higher level complex learning. *Educational Psychologist, 32*(4), 221–235.

King, A. (1998). Transactive peer tutoring: Distributing cognition and metacognition. *Educational Psychology Review, 10*(1), 57–74.

King, A., Staffieni, A., & Adelgais, A. (1998). Mutual peer tutoring: Effects of structuring tutorial interaction to scaffold peer learning. *Journal of Educational Psychology, 90*(1), 134–152.

King, N. J., & Ollendick, T. H. (1989). Children's anxiety and phobic disorders in school settings: Classification, assessment, and intervention issues. *Review of Educational Research, 59*(4), 431–470.

Kirschenbaum, H. (1992). A comprehensive model for values education and moral education. *Phi Delta Kappan, 73*(10), 771–776.

Kirst, M. W. (1990). *Accountability: Implications for state and local policymakers.* Washington, DC: U.S. Department of Education.

Klauer, K. (1984). Intentional and incidental learning with instructional texts: A meta-analysis for 1970–1980. *American Educational Research Journal, 21,* 323–339.

Klausmeier, H. J. (1992). Concept learning and concept thinking. *Educational Psychologist, 27*(3), 267–286.

Klein, S. F. (1994). Continuing the journey toward gender equity. *Educational Researcher, 23*(8), 13–21.

Klein, S. P., Jovanovic, J., Stecher, B. M., McCaffrey, D., Shavelson, R. J., Haertel, E., Solano-Flores, G., & Comfort, K. (1997). Gender and racial/ethnic differences on performance assessments in science. *Educational Evaluation and Policy Analysis, 19*(2), 83–97.

Klein, S. S., & Ortman, P. E. (1994). Continuing the journey toward gender equity. *Educational Researcher, 23*(8), 13–21.

Knapp, M. S. (1995). *Teaching for meaning in high-poverty classrooms.* New York: Teachers College Press.

Knapp, M. S., Shields, P. M., & Turnbull, B. S. (1995). Academic challenge in high-poverty classrooms. *Phi Delta Kappan, 76*(10), 770–776.

Knapp, M. S., & Woolverton, S. (1995). Social class and schooling. In J. A. Banks & C. A. M. Banks (Eds.), *Handbook of research on multicultural education.* New York: Macmillan.

Knight, C. B., Halpin, G., & Halpin, G. (1992, April). *The effects of learning environment accommodations on the achievement of second graders.* Paper presented at the annual meeting of the American Educational Research Association, San Francisco.

Koegel, R. L., & Koegel, L. K. (Eds.). (1995). *Teaching children with autism: Strategies for initiating positive interactions and improving learning opportunities.* Baltimore: Paul H. Brookes.

Kogan, N. (1994). Cognitive styles. In R. J. Sternberg (Ed.), *Encyclopedia of human intelligence.* New York: Macmillan.

Kohlberg, L. (1963). The development of children's orientations toward moral order. I: Sequence in the development of human thought. *Vita Humana, 6,* 11–33.

Kohlberg, L. (1969). Stage and sequence: The cognitive-developmental approach to socialization. In D. A. Golsin (Ed.), *Handbook of socialization theory and research* (pp. 347–380). Chicago: Rand McNally.

Kohlberg, L. (1978). Revisions in the theory and practice of moral development. In W. Damon (Ed.), *New directions for child development* (No. 2, pp. 83–87). San Francisco: Jossey-Bass.

Kohlberg, L. (1980). High school democracy and educating for a just society. In M. L. Mosher (Ed.), *Moral education: A first generation of research and development* (pp. 20–57). New York: Praeger.

Kohlberg, L. (1984). *Essays on moral development.* San Francisco: Harper & Row.

Kohn, A. (1993). Choices for children: Why and how to let students decide. *Phi Delta Kappan, 75*(1), 8–20.

Kohn, A. (1994). The truth about self-esteem. *Phi Delta Kappan, 76*(4), 272–283.

Kohn, A. (1996). By all available means: Cameron and Pierce's defense of extrinsic motivators. *Review of Educational Research, 66*(1), 1–4.

Köller, O., & Baumert, J. (1997, March). *The impact of different goal orientations on scholastic learning.* Paper presented at the annual meeting of the American Educational Research Association, Chicago.

Konig, A. (1995, March/April). *Maternal discipline and child temperament as contributors to the development of internalization in your children.* Paper presented at the biennial meetings of the Society for Research in Child Development, Indianapolis.

Koretz, D., Stecher, B., & Deibert, E. (1993). *The reliability of scores from the 1992 Vermont Portfolio Assessment Program* (Tech. Rep. No. 355). Los Angeles: UCLA, Center for the Study of Evaluation.

Kosonen, P., & Winne, P. H. (1995). Effects of teaching statistical laws of reasoning about everyday problems. *Journal of Educational Psychology, 87*(1), 33–46.

Kostelnik, M. J. (1992). Myths associated with developmentally appropriate programs. *Young Children, 47*(4), 17–23.

Kounin, J. (1970). *Discipline and group management in classrooms.* New York: Holt, Rinehart and Winston.

Kovaleski, J. F., Tucker, J. A., & Stevens, L. J. (1996). Bridging special and regular education: The Pennsylvania initiative. *Educational Leadership, 53*(5), 44–47.

Kozma, R. (1991). Learning with media. *Review of Educational Research, 61*(2), 179–211.

Kozol, J. (1991). *Savage inequalities: Children in America's schools.* New York: Crown.

Kozulin, A., & Presseisen, B. Z. (1995). Mediated learning experience and psychological tools: Vygotsky's and Feuerstein's perspectives in a study of student learning. *Educational Psychologist, 30,* 67–75.

Krashen, S., & Biber, D. (1988). *On course: Bilingual education success in California.* Sacramento: California Association for Bilingual Education.

Krechevsky, M., Hoerr, T., & Gardner, H. (1995). Complementary energies: Implementing MI theory from the laboratory and from the field. In J. Oakes & R. H. Quartz (Eds.), *Creating new educational communities.* Chicago: University of Chicago Press.

Kreitzer, A. E., & Madaus, G. F. (1994). Empirical investigations of the hierarchical structure of the taxonomy. In L. W. Anderson & L. A. Sosniak (Eds.), *Bloom's taxonomy: A forty-year perspective.* Chicago: University of Chicago Press.

Krinsky, R., & Krinsky, S. G. (1996). Pegword mnemonic instruction: Retrieval times and long-term memory performance among fifth grade children. *Contemporary Educational Psychology, 21*(2), 193–207.

Krueger, W. C. F. (1929). The effect of overlearning on retention. *Journal of Experimental Psychology, 12,* 71–128.

Krug, D., Davis, T. B., & Glover, J. A. (1990). Massed versus distributed reading: A case of forgetting helping recall? *Journal of Educational Psychology, 82,* 366–371.

Krumboltz, J. D., & Yeh, C. J. (1996). Competitive grading sabotages good teaching. *Phi Delta Kappan, 78*(4), 324–326.

Kucan, L., & Beck, I. L. (1997). Thinking aloud and reading comprehension research: Inquiry, instruction, and social interaction. *Review of Educational Research, 67*(3), 271–299.

Kuczynski, L., & Kochanska, G. (1990). Development of children's noncompliance strategies from toddlerhood to age 5. *Developmental Psychology, 26,* 398–408.

Kuhara-Kojima, K., & Hatano, G. (1991). Contribution of content knowledge and learning ability to the learning of facts. *Journal of Educational Psychology, 83*(2), 253–263.

Kulhavy, R. W., & Stock, W. A. (1989). Feedback in written instruction: The place of response certitude. *Educational Psychology Review, 1*(4), 279–308.

Kulik, C. L., Kulik, J. A., & Bangert-Drowns, R. L. (1990). Effectiveness of mastery learning programs: A meta-analysis. *Review of Educational Research, 60*(2), 265–299.

Kulik, C.-L. C., & Kulik, J. A. (1991). Effectiveness of computer-based instruction: An updated analysis. *Computers in Human Behavior, 7*(1–2), 75–94.

Kulik, J. A., & Kulik, C. L. (1988). Timing of feedback and verbal learning. *Review of Educational Research Journal, 21,* 79–97.

Kulik, J. A., & Kulik, C.-L. (1997). Ability grouping. In N. Colangelo & G. A. Davis (Eds.), *Handbook of gifted education* (2nd ed.) (pp. 230–242). Boston: Allyn & Bacon.

Kulik, J. A., Kulik, C. L., & Bangert, R. L. (1984). Effects of practice on aptitude and achievement test scores. *American Educational Research Journal, 21,* 435–447.

Kupersmidt, J. B., & Coie, J. D. (1990). Preadolescent peer status, aggression, and school adjustment as predictors of externalizing problems in adolescence. *Child Development, 61,* 1350–1362.

Kusaka, S. (1989). Awareness and solution of contradictions in the construction of length conservation schema. *Japanese Journal of Educational Psychology, 36,* 316–326.

Kutnick, P. J. (1988). *Relationships in the primary school classroom.* London: Paul Chapman.

Laboratory of Comparative Human Cognition. (1989). Kids and computers: A positive vision of the future. *Harvard Educational Review, 59,* 73–86.

Ladd, G. W., & Hart, C. H. (1992). Creating informal play opportunities: Are parents' and preschoolers' initiations related to children's competence with peers? *Developmental Psychology, 28,* 1179–1187.

Ladd, G. W., & Price, J. M. (1987). Predicting children's social and school adjustment following the transition from preschool to kindergarten. *Child Development, 59,* 986–992.

Lahaderne, H. (1968). Attitudinal and intellectual correlates of attention: A study of four sixth-grade classrooms. *Journal of Educational Psychology, 59,* 320–324.

Laird, S. (1995). Coeducational teaching: Taking girls seriously. In A. C. Ornstein (Ed.), *Teaching: Theory into practice.* Boston: Allyn & Bacon.

Lam, T. C. M. (1992). Review of practices and problems in the evaluation of bilingual education. *Review of Educational Research, 62*(2), 181–203.

Laminack, L. L. (1990). "Possibilities, Daddy, I think it says possibilities": A father's journal of the emergence of literacy. *Reading Teacher, 43,* 536–540.

Lampert, M. (1986). Knowing, doing, and teaching multiplication. *Cognition and Instruction, 3,* 305–342.

Land, M. L. (1987). Vagueness and clarity. In M. J. Dunkin (Ed.), *International encyclopedia of teaching and teacher education.* New York: Pergamon.

Langdon, H. W., & Cheng, L.-R. (1992). *Hispanic children and adults with communication disorders.* Gaithersburg, MD: Aspen.

Larrivee, B. (1985). *Effective teaching behaviors for successful mainstreaming.* New York: Longman.

Larrivee, B., & Horne, M. D. (1991). Social status: A comparison of mainstreamed students with peers of different ability levels. *Journal of Special Education, 25,* 90–101.

Larrivee, B., Semmel, M. I., & Gerber, M. M (1997). Case studies of six schools varying in effectiveness for students with learning disabilities. *Elementary School Journal, 98*(1), 27–50.

Latham, A. S. (1997a). Peer counseling: Proceed with caution. *Educational Leadership, 55*(2), 77–78.

Latham, A. S. (1997b). Responding to cultural learning styles. *Educational Leadership, 54*(7), 88–89.

Latham, A. S. (1997c). Technology and LD students: What is best practice? *Educational Leadership, 55*(3), 88.

Laupa, M. (1991). Children's reasoning about three authority attributes: Adult status, knowledge, and social position. *Developmental Psychology, 27,* 321–329.

Lave, J. (1988). *Cognition in practice.* Boston: Cambridge Press.

Lazarowitz, R. (1995). Learning science in cooperative modes in junior and senior high schools: Cognitive and affective outcomes. In J. E. Pedersen & A. D. Digby (Eds.), *Secondary schools and cooperative learning* (pp. 185–227). New York: Garland.

Learning First Alliance. (1998). *Every child reading: An action plan.* Washington, DC: Author.

Lee, S. J. (1996). *Unraveling the "model minority" stereotype: Listening to Asian American youth.* New York: Teachers College Press.

Leinhardt, G. (1993). What research on learning tells us about teaching. In K. M. Cauley, F. Linder, & J. H. McMillan (Eds.), *Annual Editions: Educational Psychology 93/94.* Guilford, CT: Dushkin.

Leinhardt, G., & Bickel, W. (1989). Instruction's the thing wherein to catch the mind that falls behind. In R. E. Slavin (Ed.), *School and classroom organization.* Hillsdale, NJ: Erlbaum.

Lepper, M. R. (1983). Extrinsic reward and intrinsic motivation: Implications for the classroom. In J. M. Levine & M. C. Wang (Eds.), *Teacher and student perceptions: Implications for learning* (pp. 281–317). Hillsdale, NJ: Erlbaum.

Lepper, M. R. (1985). Microcomputers in education. Motivational and social issues. *American Psychologist, 40,* 1–18.

Lepper, M. R. (1998). A whole much less than the sum of its parts. *American Psychologist, 53*(6), 675–676.

Lepper, M. R., Greene, D., & Nisbett, R. E. (1973). Undermining children's intrinsic interest with extrinsic rewards: A test of the overjustification hypothesis. *Journal of Personality and Social Psychology, 28,* 129–137.

Lepper, M. R., Keavney, M., & Drake, M. (1996). Intrinsic motivation and extrinsic rewards: A commentary on Cameron & Pierce's meta-analysis. *Review of Educational Research, 66*(1), 5–32.

Lerner, B. (1996). Self-esteem and excellence: The choice and the paradox. *American Educator,* Summer, 9–13, 41–42.

Lerner, J. (1997). *Learning disabilities: Theories, diagnosis, and teaching strategies.* Boston: Houghton Mifflin.

Lesgold, A. (1988). Problem solving. In R. J. Sternberg & E. E. Smith (Eds.), *The psychology of human thought* (pp. 188–213). New York: Cambridge University Press.

Lev, D. J., & Lev, D. D. (1999). *Teaching with the Internet.* Norwood, MA: Christopher–Gordon.

Levin, A. V. (1996). Common visual problems in classroom. In R. H. A. Haslam & P. J. Valletutti (Eds.), *Medical problems in the classroom: The teacher's role in diagnosis and management* (pp. 161–180). Austin, TX: Pro-Ed.

Levin, J. A., & Thurston, C. (1996). Educational electronic networks. *Educational Leadership, 54*(3), 46–50.

Levin, J. R., Shriberg, L. K., Miller, G. E., McCormick, C. B., & Levin, B. B. (1980). The keyword method as applied to elementary school children's social studies content. *Elementary School Journal, 80,* 185–191.

Levin, M. E., & Levin, J. R. (1990). Scientific mnemonics: Methods for maximizing more than memory. *American Educational Research Journal, 27,* 301–321.

Levine, C., Kohlberg, L., & Hewer, A. (1985). The current formulation of Kohlberg's theory and a response to critics. *Human Development, 28,* 94–100.

Levine, D. U., & Levine, R. F. (1996). *Society and education* (9th ed.). Boston: Allyn & Bacon.

Lewandowsky, S., & Murdock, B. B. (1989). Memory for serial order. *Psychological Review, 96,* 25–57.

Lewin, K. (1947). Group decision and social change. In T. M. Newcomb & E. L. Hartley (Eds.), *Readings in social psychology.* New York: Holt, Rinehart and Winston.

Lewis, M., & Sullivan, M. W. (Eds.). (1996). *Emotional development in atypical children.* Mahwah, NJ: Erlbaum.

Lewis, R. B. (1993). *Special education technology: Classroom applications.* Pacific Grove: CA: Brooks/Cole.

Lickona, T. (1992). *Educating for character.* New York: Bantam.

Linn, A. J. (1983). Testing and instruction: Links and distinctions. *Journal of Educational Measurement, 20,* 179–189.

Linn, R. L. (1994). Performance assessment: Policy promises and technical measurement standards. *Educational Researcher, 23*(9), 4–14.

Lloyd, J. W., Landrum, T. J., & Hallahan, D. P. (1991). Self-monitoring applications for classroom intervention. In G. Stoner, M. R. Shinn, & H. M. Walker (Eds.), *Interventions for achievement and behavioral problems* (pp. 201–213). Silver Springs, MD: National Association of School Psychologists.

Lloyd, J. W., Singh, N. N., & Repp, A. C. (Eds.). (1991). *The Regular Education Initiative: Alternative perspectives on concepts, issues, and models.* DeKalb, IL: Sycamore.

Locke, E., & Latham, G. P. (1990). *A theory of goal setting and task performance.* Englewood Cliffs, NJ: Prentice-Hall.

Lockheed, M. E. (1984). Sex segregation and male preeminence in elementary classrooms. In E. Fennema & M. J. Ayer (Eds.), *Women and education: Equity or equality?* Berkeley: McCutchan.

Loeber, R., & Stouthamer-Loeber, M. (1998). Development of juvenile aggression and violence. *American Psychologist, 53*(2), 242–259.

Lohman, D. E. (1989). Human intelligence: An introduction to advances in theory and research. *Review of Educational Research, 59*(4), 333–373.

Lohman, D. F. (1993). Teaching and testing to develop fluid abilities. *Educational Researcher, 22*(7), 12–23.

Lohman, D. F. (1995, April). *Intelligence as an outcome of schooling: Some prescriptions for developing and testing the fluidization of abilities.* Paper presented at the annual meeting of the American Educational Research Association, San Francisco.

Losey, K. M. (1995). Mexican American students and classroom interaction: An overview and critique. *Review of Educational Research, 65,* 283–318.

Lou, Y., Abrami, P. C., Spence, J. C., Poulsen, C., Chambers, B., & D'Apollonia, S. (1996). Within-class grouping: A meta-analysis. *Review of Educational Research, 66*(4), 423–458.

Loveless, T. (1998). The tracking and ability grouping debate. *Fordham Report, 2*(8), 1–27.

Lowry, R., Sleet, D., Duncan, C., Powell, K., Kolbe, L. (1995). Adolescents at risk for violence. *Educational Psychology Review, 7*(1), 7–39.

Luckasson, R., Coulter, D., Polloway, E., Reiss, S., Schalock, R., Snell, M., Spitalnik, D., & Stark, J. (1992). *Mental retardation: Definitions, classification, and systems of supports* (9th ed.). Washington, DC: American Association on Mental Retardation.

Luckasson, R., Schalock, R. L., Snell, M. E., & Spitalnik, D. M. (1996). The 1992 AAMR definition and preschool children: Response from the committee on terminology and classification. *Mental Retardation,* pp. 247–253.

Lyman, H. B. (1998). *Test scores and what they mean* (6th ed.). Boston: Allyn & Bacon.

Lyons, C. A. (1989). Reading Recovery: Preventative for mislabeling young "at-risk" learners. *Urban Education, 24,* 125–139.

Lyons, C. A., Pinnell, G. S., & DeFord, D. E. (1993). *Partners in learning: Teachers and children in reading recovery.* New York: Teachers College Press.

Lysynchuk, L. M., Pressley, M., & Vye, N. J. (1990). Reciprocal teaching improves standardized reading-comprehension performance in poor comprehenders. *Elementary School Journal, 90,* 469–484.

Ma, X., & Kishor, N. (1997). Attitude toward self, social factors, and achievement in mathematics: A meta-analytic review. *Educational Psychology Review, 9*(2), 89–120.

Maag, J. W., Rutherford, R. B., & DiGangi, S. A. (1992). Effects of self-monitoring and contingency reinforcement on on-task behavior and academic productivity of learning disabled students: A social validation study. *Psychology in the Schools, 29,* 157–172.

Mabry, L., & Stake, R. (1994). Aligning measurement with education. *Educational Researcher, 23*(2), 33–34.

MacIver, D. J., Reuman, D. A., & Main, S. R. (1995). Social structuring of the school: Studying what is, illuminating what could be. *Annual Review of Psychology, 46,* 375–400.

MacKenzie, A. A., & White, R. T. (1982). Fieldwork in geography and long-term memory. *American Educational Research Journal, 19,* 623–632.

Mackenzie, R. J. (1997). Setting limits in the classroom. *American Educator, 21* (3) 32–43.

MacLean, W. E. (1996). *Ellis' handbook of mental deficiency, psychological theory, and research.* Mahwah, NJ: Erlbaum.

MacMillan, D. L., & Forness, S. R. (1992). Mental retardation. In M. C. Alkin (Ed.), *Encyclopedia of educational research* (6th ed.). New York: Macmillan.

Madden, N. A., & Slavin, R. E. (1983a). Effects of cooperative learning on the social acceptance of mainstreamed academically handicapped students. *Journal of Special Education, 17,* 171–182.

Madden, N. A., & Slavin, R. E. (1983b). Mainstreaming students with mild academic handicaps: Academic and social outcomes. *Review of Educational Research, 53,* 519–569.

Madden, N. A., Slavin, R. E., Karweit, N. L., Dolan, L. J., & Wasik, B. A. (1993). Success for All: Longitudinal effects of a restructuring program for inner-city elementary schools. *American Educational Research Journal, 30.*

Maddox, H., & Hoole, F. (1975). Performance decrement in the lecture. *Educational Review, 28,* 17–30.

Maehr, M. L., & Anderman, E. M. (1993). Reinventing schools for early adolescents: Emphasizing task goals. *The Elementary School Journal, 93*(5), 593–610.

Maehr, M. L., & Meyer, H. A. (1997). Understanding motivation and schooling: Where we've been, where we are, and where we need to go. *Educational Psychology Review, 9*(4), 371–409.

Mager, R. F. (1975). *Preparing instructional objectives.* Belmont, CA: Fearon.

Maheady, L., Harper, G. F., & Mallette, B. (1991). Peer-mediated instruction: Review of potential applications for special education. *Reading, Writing, and Learning Disabilities, 7,* 75–102.

Mahony, M. (1997). Small victories in an inclusive classroom. *Educational Leadership, 54*(7), 59–62.

Maier, N. R. (1930). Reasoning in humans. I. On direction. *Journal of Comparative Psychology, 10,* 115–143.

Maier, S. F., Seligman, M. E. P., & Solomon, R. L. (1969). Pavlovian fear conditioning and learned helplessness. In B. A. Campbell & R. M. Church (Eds.), *Punishment and adverse behavior.* New York: Appleton-Century-Crofts.

Maker, C. J. (Ed.). (1993). *Critical issues in gifted education.* Austin, TX: Pro-Ed.

Malone, T., & Lepper, M. (1988). Making learning fun: A taxonomy of intrinsic motivation for learning. In R. Snow & M. Farr (Eds.), *Aptitude, learning, and instruction, Vol. III: Cognitive and affective process analysis.* Hillsdale, NJ: Erlbaum.

Malouf, D. B., Wizer, D. R., Pilato, V. H., & Grogan, M. M. (1990). Computer-assisted instruction with small groups of mildly handicapped students. *Journal of Special Education, 24,* 51–68.

Mamlin, N., & Harris, K. R. (1998). Elementary teachers' referral to special education in light of inclusion and prereferral: "Every child is here to learn . . . but some of these children are in real trouble." *Journal of Educational Psychology, 90*(3), 385–396.

Mandeville, G. K. (1992). Does achievement increase overtime? Another look at the South Carolina PET program. *The Elementary School Journal, 93*(2), 117–129.

Mandeville, G. K., & Rivers, J. L. (1991). The South Carolina PET study: Teachers' perceptions and student achievement. *Elementary School Journal, 91,* 377–407.

Manning, B. H. (1988). Application of cognitive behavior modification: First and third graders' self-management of classroom behaviors. *American Educational Research Journal, 25,* 193–212.

Manning, B. H. (1991). *Cognitive self-instruction of classroom processes.* Albany, NY: SUNY Press.

Manning, M. L., & Baruth, L. G. (1995). *Students at risk.* Boston: Allyn & Bacon.

Manset, G., & Semmel, M. I. (1997). Are inclusive programs for students with mild disabilities effective? A comparative review of model programs. *Journal of Special Education, 31*(2), 155–180.

Mantzicopoulos, P., & Morrison, D. (1992). Kindergarten retention: Academic and behavioral outcomes through the end of second grade. *American Educational Research Journal, 29*(1), 182–198.

Maple, S. A., & Stage, F. K. (1991). Influences on the choice of math/science major by gender and ethnicity. *American Educational Research Journal, 28*(1), 37–60.

Marcia, J. E. (1991). Identity and self-development. In R. M. Lerner, A. C. Petersen, & E. J. Brooks-Gunn (Eds.), *Encyclopedia of adolescence* (Vol. 1, pp. 527–531). New York: Garland.

Marks, H., Doane, K., & Secada, W. (1998). Support for student achievement. In F. Newmann et al. (Eds.), *Restructuring for student achievement: The impact of structure and culture in 24 schools.* San Francisco: Jossey-Bass.

Marsh, H. W. (1986). Self-serving effect (bias?) in academic attributions: Its relation to academic achievement and self-concept. *Journal of Educational Psychology, 78,* 190–200.

Marsh, H. W. (1989). Age and sex effects in multiple dimensions of self-concept: Preadolescence to early adulthood. *Journal of Educational Psychology, 81,* 417–430.

Marsh, H. W. (1993). The multidimensional structure of academic self-concept: Invariance over gender and age. *American Educational Research Journal, 30,* 841–860.

Marsh, H. W., Craven, R. G., & Debus, R. (1991). Self-concepts of young children 5 to 8 years of age: Measurement and multidimensional structure. *Journal of Educational Psychology, 83*(3), 377–392.

Marsh, H. W., & Yeung, A. S. (1997). Casual effects of academic self-concept on academic achievement: Structural equation models of longitudinal data. *Journal of Educational Psychology, 89*(1), 41–54.

Marsh, R. S., & Raywid, M. A. (1994). How to make detracking work. *Phi Delta Kappan, 76*(4), 314–317.

Martin, G., & Pear, J. (1992). *Behavior modification: What it is and how to do it* (4th ed.). Englewood Cliffs, NJ: Prentice-Hall.

Martin, G., & Pear, J. (1996). *Behavior modification: What it is and how to do it.* Englewood Cliffs, NJ: Prentice-Hall.

Martin, J. (1993). Episodic memory: A neglected phenomenon in the psychology of education. *Educational Psychologist, 28*(2), 169–183.

Martinez, M. E. (1998). What is problem solving? *Phi Delta Kappan, 70*(8), 605–609.

Marzano, R. J. (1995). Critical thinking. In J. H. Block, S. T. Everson, & T. R. Guskey (Eds.), *School improvement programs* (pp. 57–76). New York: Scholastic.

Marzano, R. J., & Costa, A. L. (1988). Question: Do standardized tests measure general cognitive skills? Answer: No. *Educational Leadership, 45*(8), 66–73.

Maslow, A. H. (1954). *Motivation and personality.* New York: Harper & Row.

Maslow, A. H. (1968). *Toward a psychology of being* (2nd ed.). New York: Van Nostrand Reinhold.

Mason, D. A. (1995). Grouping students for elementary school mathematics: A survey of principals in 12 states. *Educational Research and Evaluation, 1*(4), 318–346.

Mason, D. A., & Burns, R. B. (1997). Toward a theory of combination classes. *Educational Research and Evaluation, 3*(4), 281–304.

Mason, D. A., & Good, T. L. (1993). Effects of two-group and whole-class teaching on regrouped elementary students' mathematics achievement. *American Educational Research Journal, 30*(2), 328–360.

Massaro, D. W., & Cowan, N. (1993). Information processing models: Microscopes of the mind. *Annual Review of Psychology, 44*, 383–425.

Mastropieri, M. A., & Scruggs, T. E. (1992). Science for students with disabilities. *Review of Educational Research, 62*, 377–411.

Matheny, K. B., Aycock, D. W., & McCarthy, C. J. (1993). Stress in school-aged children and youth. *Educational Psychology Review, 5*(2), 109–134.

Matson, J. L. (Ed.). (1994). *Autism in children and adults: Etiology, assessment, and intervention.* Pacific Grove, CA: Brooks/Cole.

Mattox, B. A. (1975). *Getting it together: Dilemmas for the classroom.* San Diego, CA: Pennant Press.

Mayer, R. E. (1992). Cognition and instruction: Their historic meeting within educational psychology. *Journal of Educational Psychology, 84*, 405–412.

Mayer, R. E. (1996). Learning strategies for making sense out of expository text: The SOI model for guiding three cognitive processes in knowledge construction. *Educational Psychology Review, 8*(4), 357–371.

Mayer, R. E., & Anderson, R. B. (1991). Animations need narrations: An experimental test of dual-coding hypothesis. *Journal of Education Psychology, 83*(4), 484–490.

Mayer, R. E., & Gallini, J. K. (1990). When is an illustration worth ten thousand words? *Journal of Educational Psychology, 82*, 715–726.

Mayer, R. E., & Moreno, R. (1998). A split-attention effect in multimedia learning: Evidence for dual processing systems in working memory. *Journal of Educational Psychology, 90*(2), 312–320.

Mayer, R. E., & Wittrock, M. C. (1996). Problem-solving transfer. In D.C. Berliner & R. C. Calfee (Eds.), *Handbook of educational psychology* (pp. 47–62). New York: Macmillan.

Mazur, J. (1990). *Learning and behavior* (2nd ed.). Englewood Cliffs, NJ: Prentice-Hall.

McArdle, J. J., & Woodcock, R. W. (Eds.). (1998). *Human cognitive abilities in theory and practice.* Mahwah, NJ: Erlbaum.

McCaleb, J., & White, J. (1980). Critical dimensions in evaluating teacher clarity. *Journal of Classroom Interaction, 15*, 27–30.

McCallum, R. S., & Bracken, B. A. (1993). Interpersonal relations between school children and their peers, parents, and teachers. *Educational Psychology Review, 5*(2), 155–176.

McCarthy, B. (1997). A tale of four learners: 4 MAT's learning styles. *Educational Leadership, 54*(6), 46–51.

McClelland, D. C., & Atkinson, J. W. (1948). The projective expression of needs: II. The effect of different intensities of the hunger drive on thematic apperception. *Journal of Experimental Psychology, 38*, 643–658.

McCombs, B. L. (1984). Processes and skills underlying continuing motivation to learn: Toward a definition of motivational skills training interventions. *Educational Psychologist, 19*, 199–218.

McCormick, C. B., & Levin, J. R. (1984). A comparison of different prose-learning variations of the mnemonic keyword method. *American Educational Research Journal, 21*, 379–398.

McDaniel, M. A., & Dannelly, C. M. (1996). Learning with analogy and elaborative interrogation. *Journal of Educational Psychology, 88*(3), 508–519.

McDaniel, T. R. (1993). Practicing positive reinforcement: Ten behavior management techniques. In K. M. Cauley, F. Linder, & J. H. McMillan (Eds.), *Annual editions: Educational psychology 93/94.* Guilford, CT: Dushkin.

McInerney, V., & McInerney, D. M. (1998, April). *Metacognitive strategy training in self-questioning: The strengths of multimedia investigations of the comparative effects of two instructional approaches on self-efficacy and achievement.* Paper presented at the annual meeting of the American Educational Research Association, San Diego.

McIntyre, T. (1992). The culturally sensitive disciplinarian. *Severe Behavior Disorders Monograph, 3*, 107–115.

McKenzie, G. (1979). Effects of questions and testlike events on achievement and on-task behavior in a classroom concept learning presentation. *Journal of Educational Research, 72*, 348–350.

McKenzie, G. R., & Henry, M. (1979). Effects of testlike events on on-task behavior, test anxiety, and achievement in a classroom rule-learning task. *Journal of Educational Psychology, 71*, 370–374.

McKinney, J. D., & Speece, D. L. (1986). Academic consequences and longitudinal stability of behavioral subtypes of learning disabled children. *Journal of Educational Psychology, 78*, 365–372.

McLeskey, J., & Waldron, N. L. (1995). Inclusive elementary programs: Must they cure students with learning disabilities to be effective? *Phi Delta Kappan, 77*(4), 300–303.

McLeskey, J., & Waldron, N. L. (1996). Responses to questions teachers and administrators frequently ask about inclusive school programs. *Phi Delta Kappan, 78*(2), 150–156.

McLoyd, V. C. (1998). Socioeconomic disadvantage and child development. *American Psychologist, 53*(2), 185–204.

McPartland, J. M., Coldiron, J. R., & Braddock, J. H. (1987). *School structures and classroom practices in elementary, middle, and secondary schools* (Tech. Rep. No. 14). Baltimore: Johns Hopkins University, Center for Research on Elementary and Middle Schools.

Means, B., Olson, K., & Singh, R. (1995). Beyond the classroom: Restructuring schools with technology. *Phi Delta Kappan, 77*(1), 69–72.

Medley, D. M. (1979). The effectiveness of teachers. In P. L. Peterson & H. Walberg (Eds.), *Research on teaching: Concepts, findings, and implications* (pp. 11–27). Berkeley: McCutchan.

Meece, J. L. (1991). The classroom context and children's motivational goals. In M. Maehr & P. Pintrich (Eds.), *Advances in Motivation and Achievement* (Vol. 7, pp. 261–286). Greenwich, CT: JAI Press.

Meece, J. L., Miller, S., & Ferron, J. (1995, April). *Longitudinal changes in elementary school students' achievement goal orientations.* Paper presented at the annual meeting of the American Educational Research Association, San Francisco.

Mehlinger, H. D. (1995). *School reform in the information age.* Bloomington, IN: Indiana University, Center for Excellence in Education.

Meichenbaum, D. (1977). *Cognitive behavior modification: An integrative approach.* New York: Plenum.

Meisels, S., & Steele, D. (1991). *The early childhood portfolio collection process.* Center for Human Growth and Development. Ann Arbor: University of Michigan.

Melton, R. F. (1978). Resolution of conflicting claims concerning the effect of behavioral objectives on student learning. *Review of Educational Research, 18*, 291–302.

Menkes, J. H., & Till, K. (1990). Postnatal trauma and injuries by physical agents. In J. H. Menkes (Ed.), *Textbook of child neurology* (4th ed.) (pp. 462–496). Philadelphia: Lea & Febiger.

Mercer, C. D., King-Sears, P., & Mercer, A. R. (1990). Learning disabilities definitions and criteria used by state education departments. *Learning Disability Quarterly, 13*, 141–152.

Merrill, D. C., Reiser, B. J., Merrill, S. K., & Landes, S. (1995). Tutoring: Guided learning by doing. *Cognition and Instruction, 13*(3), 315–372.

Messerer, J., & Lerner, J. W. (1989). Word processing for learning disabled students. *Learning Disabilities Focus, 5,* 3–17.

Messick, S. (1982). Issues of effectiveness and equity in the coaching controversy: Implications for educational and testing practice. *Educational Psychologist, 17,* 67–91.

Messick, S. (1994). The interplay of evidence and consequences in the validation of performance assessments. *Educational Researcher, 23*(2), 13–23.

Metsala, J. L., Stanovich, K. E., & Brown, G. D. A. (1998). Regularity effects and the phonological deficit model of reading disabilities: A meta-analytic review. *Journal of Educational Psychology, 90*(2), 279–293.

Metz, H. H. (1990). How social class differences shape teachers' work. In J. E. Talbert & N. Bascia (Eds.), *The context of teaching in secondary schools: Teachers' realities* (pp. 40–107). New York: Teachers College Press.

Mevarech, Z. R., & Kramarski, B. (1997). Improve: A multidimensional method for teaching mathematics in heterogeneous classrooms. *American Educational Research Journal, 34*(2), 365–394.

Meyer, L., Gersten, R. M., & Gutkin, J. (1983). Direct instruction: A project follow-through success story in an inner-city school. *Elementary School Journal, 84,* 241–252.

Meyer, L. A. (1984). Long-term academic effects of the Direct Instruction Project Follow-Through. *Elementary School Journal, 84,* 380–394.

Meyer, L. A. (1987). Strategies for correcting students' wrong answers. *Elementary School Journal, 87,* 227–241.

Meyer, L. H., Harry, B., & Sapon-Shevin, M. (1997). School inclusion: Multicultural issues in special education. In J. A. Banks & C. A. M. Banks (Eds.), *Multicultural education: Issues and perspectives* (pp. 334–360). Boston: Allyn & Bacon.

Meyers, J., Gelzheiser, L., Yelich, G., Gallagher, M. (1990). Classroom, remedial and resource teachers' views of pullout programs. *Elementary School Journal, 90*(5), 531–545.

Michigan Department of Education. (1998, June 12). *Overview of career and employability skills content standards* [On-line]. Available: World Wide Web, http://cdp.mde.state.mi.us/MCF/ContentStandards/CareerEmployability/default.html.

Miller, A., & Hom, Jr., H. L. (1990). Influence of extrinsic and ego incentive value on persistence after failure and continuing motivation. *Journal of Educational Psychology, 82*(3), 539–545.

Miller, G. A. (1956). The magical number seven, plus or minus two: Some limits on our capacity for processing information. *Psychological Review, 63,* 81–97.

Miller, G. E., Levin, J. R., & Pressley, M. (1980). An adaptation of the keyword method to children's learning of verbs. *Journal of Mental Imagery, 4,* 57–61.

Miller, P. H. (1983). *Theories of developmental psychology.* San Francisco: Freeman.

Miller, P. H. (1993). *Theories of developmental psychology* (3rd ed.). New York: Freeman.

Miller, S., & Ferroggiaro, M. (1995). Class dismissed? *The American Prospect, 21,* 100–104.

Miller-Lachman, L., & Taylor, L. S. (1995). *Schools for all: Educating children in a diverse society.* New York: Delmar.

Mills, C. J., Ablard, K. E., & Stumpf, H. (1993). Gender differences in academically talented young students' mathematical reasoning: Patterns across age and subskills. *Journal of Educational Psychology, 85*(2), 340–346.

Mitchell, P., & Erickson, D. K. (1980). The education of gifted and talented children: A status report. *Exceptional Children, 45,* 12–16.

Mize, J., & Ladd, G. W. (1990a). A cognitive-social learning approach to social skills training with low-status preschool children. *Developmental Psychology, 26,* 388–397.

Mize, J., & Ladd, G. W. (1990b). Toward the development of successful social skills training for preschool children. In S. R. Asher & J. D. Coie (Eds.), *Peer rejection in childhood* (pp. 338–361). New York: Cambridge University Press.

Moats, L. C., & Lyon, R. G. (1993). Learning disabilities in the United States: Advocacy, science, and the future of the field. *Journal of Learning Disabilities, 26,* 262–294.

Monahan, B., & Tomko, S. (1996). How schools can create their own web pages. *Educational Leadership, 54*(3), 37–28.

Morgan, M. (1984). Reward-induced decrements and increments in intrinsic motivation. *Review of Educational Research, 54,* 5–30.

Morris, C. C., Bransford, J. D., & Franks, J. J. (1977). Levels of processing versus transfer appropriate processing. *Journal of Verbal Learning and Verbal Behavior, 16,* 519–533.

Morris, D., Shaw, B., & Perney, J. (1990). Helping low readers in grades 2 and 3: An after-school volunteer tutoring program. *Elementary School Journal, 91,* 133–150.

Morrison, P., & Masten, A. S. (1991). Peer reputation in middle childhood as a predictor of adaptation in adolescence: A seven-year follow-up. *Child Development, 62,* 991–1007.

Morrow, L. M. (1993). *Literacy development in the early years.* Boston: Allyn & Bacon.

Moss, P. A. (1992). Shifting conceptions of validity in educational measurement: Implications for performance assessment. *Review of Educational Research, 62*(3), 229–258.

Mullis, I., Dossey, J., Foertsch, M., Jones, L., & Gentile, C. (1991). *Trends in academic progress.* Washington, DC: National Center for Education Statistics, U.S. Department of Education.

Munk, D. D., & Bursuck, W. D. (1998). Can grades be helpful and fair? *Educational Leadership, 55*(4), 44–47.

Murphy, E., & Rhéaume, J. (1997, Summer). *Course TEN-62349, Université Laval, Québec City, Québec, Canada* [Online]. Available: World Wide Web, http://www.stemnet.nf.ca/~elmurphy/emurphy/cle2b.html.

Murphy, S. H. (1994). Closing the gender gap: What's behind the differences in test scores, and what can be done about it. In J. I. Goodlad & P. Keating (Eds.), *Access to knowledge: The continuing agenda for our nation's schools.* New York: The College Board.

Murray, H., Olivier, A., & Human, P. (1992). The development of young students' division strategies. In W. Geeslin & K. Graham (Eds.), *Proceedings of the sixteenth international conference for the psychology of mathematics instruction* (Vol. 2, pp. 152–159). Durham, New Hampshire.

Muskin, C. (1990, April). *Equity and opportunity to learn in high school U.S. history classes: Comparisons between schools and ability groups.* Paper presented at the annual meeting of the American Educational Research Association, Boston.

Nafpaktitis, M., Mayer, G. R., & Butterworth, T. (1985). Natural rates of teacher approval and disapproval and their relation to student behavior in intermediate school classrooms. *Journal of Educational Psychology, 77,* 362–367.

Nagy, P., & Griffiths, A. K. (1982). Limitations of recent research relating Piaget's theory to adolescent thought. *Review of Educational Research, 52,* 513–556.

Nash, W. R., Borman, C., & Colson, S. (1980). Career education for gifted and talented students: A senior high school model. *Exceptional Children, 46,* 404–405.

National Academy of Sciences. (1998). *The prevention of reading difficulties in young children.* Washington, DC: Author.

National Association for the Education of Young Children. (1989). *Appropriate education in the primary grades.* Washington, DC: Author.

National Association of State Boards of Education (NASBE). (1992, October). *Winners all: A call for inclusive schools.* Alexandria, VA: Author.

National Center for Education Statistics. (1988). *Digest of educational statistics.* Washington, DC: U.S. Department of Education, NCES.

National Center for Education Statistics. (1994). *The condition of education, 1994.* Washington, DC: U.S. Department of Education.

National Center for Education Statistics. (1997). *The condition of education, 1997.* Washington, DC: U.S. Department of Education, NCES.

National Education Association. (1992). *Education for all students with disabilities.* Washington, DC: Author.

National Education Commission on Time and Learning. (1994). *Prisoners of time: Schools and programs making time work for students and teachers.* Washington, DC: Author.

National Education Goals Panel. (1997). *Special early childhood report 1997.* Washington, DC: Author.

National Governors' Association. (1993). *Ability grouping and tracking: Current issues and concerns.* Washington, DC: Author.

National Information Center for Children and Youth with Disabilities. (1998). *Office of Special Education Programs' IDEA amendments of 1997 curriculum* [Internet] Available: World Wide Web, http://www.nichcy.org/Trainpkg/trainpkg.htm.

National Joint Committee on Learning Disabilities. (1988). (Letter to NJCLD member organization). Washington, DC: Author.

National PTA. (1998). *National standards for parent/family involvement programs.* Chicago: Author.

National Research Council (1995). *Losing generations: Adolescents in high-risk settings.* Hyattsville, MD: American Psychological Association.

Natriello, G. (1989). The impact of evaluation processes on students. In R. E. Slavin (Ed.), *School and classroom organization,* Hillsdale, NJ: Erlbaum.

Natriello, G., & Dornbusch, S. M. (1984). *Teacher evaluative standards and student effort.* New York: Longman.

Nattiv, A. (1994). Helping behaviors and math achievement gain of students using cooperative learning. *The Elementary School Journal, 94*(3), 285–297.

Naveh-Benjamin, M. (1991). A comparison of training programs intended for different types of test-anxious students: Further support for an information-processing model. *Journal of Educational Psychology 83,* 134–139.

Neale, D. C., Smith, D., & Johnson, V. G. (1990). Implementing conceptual change teaching in primary science. *Elementary School Journal, 91,* 109–131.

Nettles, S. M. (1991). Community involvement and disadvantaged students: A review. *Review of Educational Research, 61,* 379–406.

Neuman, S. B., & McCormick, S. (1995). *Single-subject experimental research.* Newark, DE: International Reading Association.

Neuman, S. B., & Roskos, K. (1993). Access to print for children of poverty: Differential effects of adult mediation and literacy enriched play settings on environmental and functional print tasks. *American Educational Research Journal, 30,* 95–122.

Nevin, A. (1998). Curriculum and instructional adaptations for including students with disabilities in cooperative groups. In J. W. Putnam (Ed.), *Cooperative learning and strategies for inclusion* (pp. 49–66). Baltimore: Paul H. Brookes.

Newbern, D., Dansereau, D. F., Patterson, M. E., & Wallace, D. S. (1994, April). *Toward a science of cooperation.* Paper pre-

sented at the annual meeting of the American Educational Research Association, New Orleans.

Newcomb, A. F., & Bukowski, W. M. (1984). A longitudinal study of the utility of social preference and social impact sociometric status schemes. *Child Development, 55,* 1434–1447.

Newell, A., & Simon, H. (1972). *Human problem solving.* Englewood Cliffs, NJ: Prentice-Hall.

Newman, S. B., Hagedorn, T., Celano, D., & Daly, P. (1995). Toward a collaborative approach to parent involvement in early education: A study of teenage mothers in an African-American community. *American Educational Research Journal, 32,* 801–827.

Newmann, F. M., Secada, W. G., & Wehlage, G. G. (1995). *A guide to authentic instruction and assessment: Vision, standards, and scoring.* Madison: University of Wisconsin, Wisconsin Center for Education Researcher.

Newmann, F. M., & Wehlage, G. G. (1993). Five standards of authentic instruction. *Educational Leadership, 50*(7), 8–12.

Newstead, S. E., Franklyn-Stokes, A., & Armstead, P. (1996). Individual differences in student cheating. *Journal of Educational Psychology, 88*(2), 229–241.

Nichols, P. D. (1994). A framework for developing cognitively diagnostic assessments. *Review of Educational Research, 64*(4), 575–603.

Niemiec, R. P., & Walberg, H. J. (1985). Computers and achievement in the elementary schools. *Journal of Educational Computing Research, 1,* 435–440.

Nieto, S. (1997). School reform and student achievement: A multicultural perspective. In J. A. Banks & C. A. M. Banks (Eds.), *Multicultural education: Issues and perspectives* (pp. 387–407) Boston: Allyn & Bacon.

Nitsch, K. E. (1977). Structuring decontextualized forms of knowledge. Unpublished doctoral dissertation, Vanderbilt University.

Noble, D. D. (1996). Mad rushes into the future: The overselling of educational technology. *Educational Leadership, 54*(3), 18–23.

Noddings, N. (1992). Variability: A pernicious hypothesis. *Review of Educational Research, 62,* 85–88.

Noonan, M. J., & McCormick, L. (1993). *Early intervention in natural environments.* Pacific Grove, CA: Brooks/Cole.

Norris, S. P. (1985). Synthesis of research on critical thinking. *Educational Leadership, 42,* 40–45.

Nucci, L. (1987). Synthesis of research on moral development. *Educational Leadership, 44,* 86–92.

Nurss, J. R., & Hodges, W. L. (1982). Early childhood education. In H. E. Mitzel (Ed.) *Encyclopedia of Educational Research* (5th ed.) (pp. 477–513). New York: Free Press.

Nuthall, G. (1987). Reviewing and recapitulating. In M. J. Dunkin (Ed.), *International encyclopedia of teaching and teacher education.* New York: Pergamon.

Oakes, J. (1985). *Keeping track: How schools structure inequality.* New Haven, CT: Yale University Press.

Oakes, J. (1995). Two cities: Tracking and within-school segregation. In L. Miller (Ed.), *Brown plus forty: The promise.* New York: Teachers College Press.

Oakes, J., & Guiton, G. (1995). Matchmaking: The dynamics of high school tracking decisions. *American Educational Research Journal, 32*(1), 3–33.

Oakes, J., & Lipton, M. (1994). Tracking and ability grouping: A structural barrier to access and achievement. In J. I. Goodlad & P. Keating (Eds.), *Access to knowledge: The continuing agenda for our nation's schools.* New York: The College Board.

Oakes, J., Quartz, K. H., Gong, J., Guiton, G., & Lipton, M. (1993). Creating middle schools: Technical, normative, and political considerations. *The Elementary School Journal, 93*(5), 461–480.

Oakes, J., & Wells, A. S. (1998). Detracking for high student achievement. *Educational Leadership, 55*(6), 38–41.

O'Connor, M. C. (1998). Can we trace the "efficacy of social constructivism"? In P. D. Pearson & A. Iran-Nejad (Eds.), *Review of research in education* (pp. 25–72). Washington, DC: American Educational Research Association.

Odle, S. J., & Galtelli, B. (1980). The Individualized Education Program (IEP): Foundation for appropriate and effective instruction. In J. W. Schifani, R. M. Anderson, & S. J. Odle (Eds.), *Implementing learning in the least restrictive environment.* Baltimore: University Park Press.

O'Donnell, A. M. (1996). Effects of explicit incentives on scripted and unscripted cooperation. *Journal of Educational Psychology, 88*(1), 74–86.

O'Donnell, A. M., & O'Kelly, J. (1994). Learning from peers: Beyond the rhetoric of positive results. *Educational Psychology Review, 6,* 321–349.

O'Donnell, J., Hawkins, J. D., Catalano, R. F., Abbott, R. D., & Day, L. E. (1995). Preventing school failure, drug use, and delinquency among low-income children: Long-term intervention in elementary schools. *American Journal of Orthopsychiatry, 65*(1), 87–100.

Office of Technology Assessment. (1992). *Testing in American schools: Asking the right questions.* Washington, DC: U.S. Congress, Office of Technology Assessment.

Office of Technology Assessment. (1995). *Teachers and technology: Making the connection.* Washington, DC: Author.

Ogbu, J. U. (1992). Understanding cultural diversity and learning. *Educational Researcher 21*(8), 5–14.

Ogbu, J. U. (1994). Racial stratification and education in the United States: Why inequality persists. *Teachers College Record, 96*(2), 264–298.

Okagaki, L., & Frensch, P. A. (1998). Parenting and children's school achievement: A multiethnic perspective. *American Educational Research Journal, 35*(1), 123–144.

O'Leary, K. D. (1980). Pills or skills for hyperactive children. *Journal of Applied Behavior Analysis, 13,* 191–204.

O'Leary, K. D., & O'Leary, S. G. (1972). *Classroom management: The successful use of behavior modification.* New York: Pergamon.

O'Leary, S. G. (1995). Parental discipline mistakes. *Current Directions in Psychological Science, 4*(1), 11–13.

Olson, D. R., & Pau, A. S. (1966). Emotionally loaded words and the acquisition of a sight vocabulary. *Journal of Educational Psychology, 57,* 174–178.

Olthof, T., Ferguson, T. J., & Luiten, A. (1989). Personal responsibility and antecedents of anger and blame reactions in children. *Child Development, 60,* 1326–1336.

Olweus, D. (1994). Bullying at school: Basic facts and effects of a school-based intervention program. *Journal of Child Psychology and Psychiatry, 35,* 1171–1190.

O'Neil, J. (1991). A generation adrift? *Educational Leadership, 49*(1), 4–10.

Orfield, G. (1994). The growth of segregation in America's schools. *Equity and Excellence, 29*(1), 5–8.

Osborn, A. F. (1963). *Applied imagination* (3rd ed.). New York: Scribner's.

Osborn, J. D., & Osborn, P. K. (1983). *Cognition in early childhood.* Athens, GA: Education Associates.

Osguthorpe, R. T., & Scruggs, T. E. (1986). Special education students as tutors: A review and analysis. *Remedial and Special Education, 7*(4), 15–25.

Ottenbacher, K. J., & Cooper, H. M. (1983). Drug treatment of hyperactivity in children. *Developmental Medicine and Child Neurology, 25,* 358–366.

Ovando, C. J. (1997). Language, diversity, and education. In J. A. Banks & C. A. M. Banks (Eds.), *Multicultural education:*

Issues and perspectives (pp. 272–300). Boston: Allyn & Bacon.

Overton, W. F. (1984). World views and their influence on psychological theory and research. In H. W. Reese (Ed.), *Advances in child development and behavior.* New York: Academic Press.

Owen, S. L., Froman, R. D., & Moscow, H. (1981). *Educational psychology* (2nd ed.). Boston: Little, Brown.

Owens, R. E. (1995). *Language disorders* (2nd ed.). Boston: Allyn & Bacon.

Oxley, D. (1994). Organizing schools into small units: Alternatives to homogeneous grouping. *Phi Delta Kappan, 75*(7), 521–526.

Page, R. N. (1991). *Lower track classrooms: A curricular and cultural perspective.* New York: Teachers College Press.

Pajares, F. (1996). Self-efficacy beliefs in academic settings. *Review of Educational Research, 66*(4), 543–578.

Pajares, F., & Miller, M. D. (1994). Role of self-efficacy and self-concept beliefs in mathematical problem solving: A path analysis. *Journal of Educational Psychology, 86*(2), 193–203.

Palincsar, A. S. (1986). The role of dialogue in providing scaffolded instruction. *Educational Psychologist, 21,* 73–98.

Palincsar, A. S. (1987, April). Reciprocal teaching: Field evaluations in remedial and content-area reading. Paper presented at the annual convention of the American Educational Research Association, Washington, DC.

Palincsar, A. S., Anderson, C., & David, Y. M. (1993). Pursuing scientific literacy in the middle grades through collaborative problem solving. *The Elementary School Journal, 93*(5), 643–658.

Palincsar, A. S., & Brown, A. L. (1984). Reciprocal teaching of comprehension fostering and comprehension monitoring activities. *Cognition and Instruction, 2,* 117–175.

Palincsar, A. S., Brown, A. L., & Martin, S. M. (1987). Peer interaction in reading comprehension instruction. *Educational Psychologist, 22,* 231–253.

Pallas, A. M., Entwistle, D. R., Alexander, K. L., & Stluka, M. F. (1994). Ability-group effects: Instructional, social, or institutional? *Sociology of Education, 67,* 27–46.

Palumbo, D. B. (1990). Programming language/problem-solving research: A review of relevant issues. *Review of Educational Research, 60*(1), 65–89.

Papert, S. (1980). *Mindstorms: Children, computers, and powerful ideas.* New York: Basic Books.

Paris, S., Cross, D., & Lipson, M. (1984). Informal strategies for learning: A program to improve children's reading awareness and comprehension. *Journal of Educational Psychology, 76,* 1239–1252.

Parke, B. N. (1983). Use of self-instructional materials with gifted primary aged students. *Gifted Child Quarterly, 27,* 29–34.

Parke, C. S., & Lane, S. (1996). Learning from performance assessments in math. *Educational Leadership, 54*(4), 26–29.

Parker, H. C. (1990). *C.H.A.D.D.: Children with attention deficit disorders: Parents supporting parents.* Education position paper, Plantation, FL.

Parker, J. G., & Asher, S. R. (1987). Peer relations and later adjustment: Are low-accepted children "at risk"? *Psychological Bulletin, 102,* 357–389.

Parker, W. D. (1997). An empirical typology of perfectionism in academically talented children. *American Educational Research Journal, 34*(3), 545–562.

Parkhurst, J. T., & Asher, S. R. (1992). Peer rejection in middle school: Subgroup differences in behavior, loneliness, and interpersonal concerns. *Developmental Psychology, 28,* 231–241.

Parks, C. P. (1995). Gang behavior in the schools: Reality or myth? *Educational Psychology Review, 7*(1), 41–68.

Parten, M. (1932). Social participation among preschool children. *Journal of Abnormal and Social Psychology, 27,* 243–269.

Pavan, B. N. (1992). The benefits of nongraded schools. *Educational Leadership, 50*(2), 22–25.

Pea, R. D. (1993). Learning scientific concepts through material and social activities: Conversational analysis meets conceptual change. *Educational Psychologist, 28*(3), 265–277.

Peha, J. M. (1995). How K–12 teachers are using computer networks. *Educational Leadership, 53*(2), 18–25.

Peisner-Feinberg, E., Clifford, R., Yazejian, N., Culkin, M., Howes, C., & Kagan, S. L. (1998, April). *The longitudinal effects of childcare quality: Implications for kindergarten success.* Paper presented at the annual meeting of the American Educational Research Association, San Diego.

Pellegrini, A. D., & Horvat, M. (1995). A developmental contextualist critique of attention deficit hyperactivity disorder. *Educational Researcher, 24*(1), 13–18.

Pendarvis, E., & Howley, A. (1996). Playing fair: The possibilities of gifted education. *Journal for the Education of the Gifted, 19,* 215–233.

Pepitone, E. A. (1985). Children in cooperation and competition: Antecedents and consequences of self-orientation. In R. E. Slavin, S. Sharan, S. Kagan, R. Hertz-Lazarowitz, C. Webb, & R. Schmuck (Eds.). *Learning to cooperate, cooperating to learn.* New York: Plenum.

Perfetto, G. A., Bransford, J. D., & Franks, J. J. (1983). Constraints on access in a problem solving context. *Memory and Cognition, 11,* 24–31.

Perkins, D., Jay, E., & Tishman, S. (1993). New conceptions of thinking. *Educational Psychologist, 28*(l), 1–5.

Perkins, D. N., & Salomon, G. (1988). Teaching for transfer. *Educational Leadership, 46*(1), 22–32.

Perkins, D. N., & Salomon, G. (1989). Are cognitive skills context-bound? *Educational Researcher, 18,* 16–25.

Perry, M., Vanderstoep, S. W., & Yu, S. L. (1993). Asking questions in first-grade mathematics classes: Potential influences on mathematical thought. *Journal of Educational Psychology, 85*(1), 31–40.

Persell, C. H. (1997). Social class and educational equality. In J. A. Banks & C. A. M. Banks (Eds.), *Multicultural education: Issues and perspectives* (pp. 87–107). Boston: Allyn & Bacon.

Peters, E. E., Levin, J. R., McGivern, J. E., & Pressley, M. (1985). Further comparison of representational and transformational prose-learning imagery. *Journal of Educational Psychology, 77,* 129–136.

Peterson, L. R., & Peterson, M. J. (1959). Short-term retention of individual verbal items. *Journal of Experimental Psychology, 58,* 193–198.

Petrill, S., & Thompson, L. A. (1993). The phenotypic and genetic relationships among measures of cognitive ability, temperament, and scholastic achievement. *Behavior Genetics, 23,* 511–518.

Petty, M. F., & Field, C. J. (1980). Fluctuations in mental test scores. *Educational Research, 22,* 198–202.

Peverly, S. T. (1991). Problems with the knowledge-based explanation of memory and development. *Review of Educational Research, 61*(1), 71–93.

Pfiffer, L., Rosen, L., & O'Leary, S. (1985). The efficacy of an all positive approach to classroom management. *Journal of Applied Behavior Analysis, 18,* 257–261.

Phelan, P., Yu, H. C., & Davidson, A. L. (1994). Navigating the psychosocial pressures of adolescence: The voices and experiences of high school youth. *American Educational Research Journal, 31,* 415–447.

Phillips, J. L. (1975). *The origins of intellect: Piaget's theory* (2nd ed.). San Francisco: Freeman.

Phye, G. D. (1992). Strategic transfer: A tool for academic problem solving. *Educational Psychology Review, 4,* 393–421.

Piaget, J. (1952a). *The language and thought of the child.* London: Routledge and Kegan-Paul.

Piaget, J. (1952b). *The origins of intelligence in children.* New York: Basic Books.

Piaget, J. (1964). *The moral judgment of the child.* New York: Free Press.

Piaget, J., & Garcia, R. (1986). *Toward a logic of meanings.* Geneva, Switzerland: Editions Murionde.

Piaget, J., & Inhelder, B. (1956). *The child's conception of space.* Boston: Routledge and Kegan-Paul.

Pinnell, G. S. (1989). Reading Recovery: Helping at-risk children learn to read. *Elementary School Journal, 90,* 161–182.

Pinnell, G. S. (1990). Success for low achievers through Reading Recovery. *Educational Leadership, 48*(1), 17–21.

Pinnell, G. S., DeFord, D. E., & Lyons, C. A. (1988). *Reading Recovery: Early intervention for at-risk first graders.* Arlington, VA: Educational Research Service.

Pinnell, G. S., Lyons, C., & Jones, N. (1996). Response to Hiebert: What difference does Reading Recovery make? *Educational Researcher, 25*(7), 23–25.

Pinnell, G. S., Lyons, C. A., DeFord, D. E., Bryk, A. S., & Seltzer, M. (1994). Comparing instructional models for the literacy education of high risk first graders. *Reading Research Quarterly, 29,* 8–38.

Pintrich, P. R., & Blumenfeld, P. (1985). Classroom experience and children's self-perceptions of ability, effort, and conduct. *Journal of Educational Psychology, 77,* 646–657.

Pintrich, P. R., Marx, R. W., & Boyle, R. A. (1993). Beyond cold conceptual change: The role of motivational beliefs and classroom contextual factors in the process of conceptual change. *Review of Educational Research, 63*(2), 167–199.

Plomin, R. (1989). Environment and genes: Determinants of behavior. *American Psychologist, 44*(2), 105–111.

Plumert, J. M., & Nichols-Whitehead, P. (1996). Parental scaffolding of young children's spatial communication. *Developmental Psychology, 32*(3), 523–532.

Pontecorvo, C. (1993). Social interaction in the acquisition of knowledge. *Educational Psychology Review, 5*(3), 293–310.

Pool, H., & Page, J. A. (Eds.). (1995). *Beyond tracking: Finding success in inclusive schools.* Bloomington, IN: Phi Delta Kappan Educational Foundation.

Popham, W. J. (1995). *Classroom assessment: What teachers need to know.* Boston: Allyn & Bacon.

Popham, W. J. (1997). What's wrong—and what's right—with rubrics. *Educational Leadership, 55*(2), 72–75.

Porter, A. C., & Brophy, J. E. (1988). Synthesis of research on good teaching: Insights from the work of the Institute for Research on Teaching. *Educational Leadership, 45,* 74–85.

Porter, G. L., & Stone, J. A. (1998). The inclusive school model: A framework and key strategies for success. In J. W. Putnam (Ed.), *Cooperative learning and strategies for inclusion* (pp. 229–248). Baltimore: Paul H. Brookes.

Portes, P. R. (1996). Ethnicity and culture in educational psychology. In D.C. Berliner & R. C. Calfee (Eds.), *Handbook of educational psychology* (pp. 331–357). New York: Macmillan.

Potter, E. F. (1977, April). Children's expectancy of criticism for classroom achievement efforts. Paper presented at the annual convention of the American Educational Research Association, New York.

Powell, D. R. (1995). *Enabling young children to succeed in school.* Washington, DC: American Educational Research Association.

Prawat, R. S. (1991). The value of ideas: The immersion approach to the development of thinking. *Educational Researcher, 20*(2), 3–10, 30.

Prawat, R. S. (1992). Teachers' beliefs about teaching and learning: A constructivist perspective. *American Journal of Education, 100*(3), 354–395.

Premack, D. (1965). Reinforcement theory. In D. Levine (Ed.), *Nebraska symposium on motivation.* Lincoln: University of Nebraska Press.

Pressley, M. (1991). Comparing Hall (1988) with related research on elaborative mnemonics. *Journal of Educational Psychology, 83*(1), 165–170.

Pressley, M. (1995). More about the development of self-regulation: Complex, long-term, and thoroughly social. *Educational Psychologist, 30,* 207–212.

Pressley, M., & Harris, K. R. (1990). What we really know about strategy instruction. *Educational Leadership, 48*(1), 31–34.

Pressley, M., & Harris, K. R. (1994). Increasing the quality of educational intervention research. *Educational Psychology Review, 6*(3), 191–208.

Pressley, M., Harris, K. R., & Marks, M. B. (1992). But good strategy instructors are constructivists! *Educational Psychology Review, 4,* 3–31.

Pressley, M., & Levin, J. R. (1978). Developmental constraints associated with children's use of the keyword method of foreign language vocabulary learning. *Journal of Experimental Child Psychology, 26,* 359–372.

Pressley, M., & Levin, J. R. (Eds.). (1983). *Cognitive strategy research: Educational applications.* New York: Springer-Verlag.

Pressley, M., Levin, J. R., & Delaney, H. (1982). The mnemonic keyword method. *Review of Educational Research, 52,* 61–92.

Pressley, M., Tannenbaum, R., McDaniel, M. A., & Wood, E. (1990). What happens when university students try to answer prequestions that accompany textbook material? *Contemporary Educational Psychology, 15,* 27–35.

Pressley, M., Woloshyn, V., Lysynchuk, L. M., Martin, V., Wood, E., & Willoughby, T. (1990). A primer of research on cognitive strategy instruction: The important issues and how to address them. *Educational Psychology Review, 2,* 1–58.

Pressley, M., Wood, E., Woloshyn, V. E., Martin, V., King, A., & Menke, D. (1992). Encouraging mindful use of prior knowledge: Attempting to construct explanatory answers facilitates learning. *Educational Psychologist, 27,* 91–109.

Pressley, M., & Yokoi, L. (1994). Motion for a new trial on transfer. *Educational Researcher, 23*(5), 36–38.

Pressley, M., Yokoi, L., van Meter, P., van Etten, S., & Freebern, G. (1997). Some of the reasons why preparing for exams is so hard: What can be done to make it easier? *Educational Psychology Review, 9*(1), 1–38.

Price, E. A., & Driscoll, M. P. (1997). An inquiry into the spontaneous transfer of problem-solving skill. *Contemporary Educational Psychology, 22*(4), 472–494.

Price, J. M., & Dodge, K. A. (1989). Peers' contributions to children's social adjustment. In T. J. Berndt & G. W. Ladd (Eds.), *Peer relationships in child development.* New York: Wiley.

Provenzo, E. F., Brett, A., & McCloskey, G. N. (1998). *Computers, curriculum, and cultural change.* Mahwah, NJ: Erlbaum.

Puma, M. J., Jones, C. C., Rock, D., & Fernandez, R. (1993). *Prospects: The congressionally mandated study of educational growth and opportunity.* Interim Report. Bethesda, MD: Abt Associates.

Puma, M. J., Karweit, N., Price, C., Ricciuti, A., Thompson, W., & Vaden-Kiernan, M. (1997). *Prospects: Final report on student outcomes.* Cambridge, MA: Abt Associates.

Purcell-Gates, V., McIntyre, E., & Freppon, P. A. (1995). Learning written storybook language in school: A comparison of low-SES children in skills-based and whole language classrooms. *American Educational Research Journal, 32,* 659–685.

Putnam, J. W. (Ed.). (1998a). *Cooperative learning and strategies for inclusion.* (2nd ed.). Baltimore: Paul H. Brookes.

Putnam, J. W. (1998b). The movement toward teaching and learning in inclusive classrooms. In J. W. Putnam (Ed.), *Cooperative learning and strategies for inclusion* (pp. 1–16). Baltimore: Paul H. Brookes.

Putnam, J. W. (1998c). The process of cooperative learning. In J. W. Putnam (Ed.), *Cooperative learning and strategies for inclusion* (pp. 17–48). Baltimore: Paul H. Brookes.

Qin, Z., Johnson, D. W., & Johnson, R. T. (1995). Cooperative versus competitive efforts and problem solving. *Review of Educational Research, 65,* 129–143.

Quay, H. C., & Werry, J. S. (Eds.). (1986). *Psychopathological disorders of childhood* (3rd ed.). New York: Wiley.

Raaijmakers, J. G. W., & Shiffrin, R. M. (1992). Models for recall and recognition. *Annual Review of Psychology, 43,* 205–234.

Rafoth, M. A., Leal, L., & De Fabo, L. (1993). *Strategies for learning and remembering: Study skills across the curriculum.* Washington, DC: National Education Association Professional Library.

Raison, J., Hanson, L. A., Hall, C., & Reynolds, M. C. (1995). Another school's reality. *Phi Delta Kappan, 76*(6), 480–484.

Ramey, C. T., Bryant, D. M., Wasik, B. H., Sparling, J. J., Fendt, K. H., & LaVange, L. M. (1992). Infant health and development program for low birth weight, premature infants: Program elements, family participation, and child intelligence. *Pediatrics, 3,* 454–465.

Ramey, C. T., & Ramey, S. L. (1992). *At risk does not mean doomed.* Birmingham: Civitan International Research Center, University of Alabama.

Ramey, C. T., & Ramey, S. L. (1998). Early intervention and early experience. *American Psychologist, 53*(2), 109–120.

Ramirez-Smith, C. (1995). Stopping the cycle of failure: The Comer model. *Educational Leadership, 52*(5), 14–19.

Ramsey, I., Gabbard, L., Clawson, K., Lee, L., & Henson, K. T. (1993). Questioning: An effective teaching method. In K. M. Cauley, F. Linder, J. H. McMillan (Eds.), *Annual Editions: Educational Psychology 93/94.* Guilford, CT: Dushkin.

Randhawa, B. S., Beamer, J. E., & Lundberg, I. (1993). Role of mathematics self-efficacy in the structural model of mathematics achievement. *Journal of Educational Psychology, 85*(1), 41–48.

Range, L. M. (1993). Suicide prevention: Guidelines for schools. *Educational Psychology Review, 5*(2), 135–154.

Ratner, C. (1991). *Vygotsky's sociohistorical psychology and its contemporary applications.* New York: Plenum.

Raudenbush, S. W. (1984). Magnitude of teacher expectancy effects on pupil IQ as a function of the credibility of expectancy induction: A synthesis of findings from 18 experiments. *Journal of Educational Psychology, 76,* 85–97.

Raudenbush, S. W., Rowan, B., & Cheong, Y. F. (1993). Higher order instructional goals in secondary schools: Class, teacher, and school influences. *American Educational Research Journal, 30*(3), 523–553.

Redfield, D. L., & Rousseau, E. W. (1981). A meta-analysis of experimental research on teacher questioning behavior. *Review of Educational Research, 51,* 237–245.

Reid, C., & Romanoff, B. (1997). Using multiple intelligence theory to identify gifted children. *Educational Leadership, 55*(1), 71–74.

Reimer, J., Paolitto, D. P., & Hersh, R. H. (1990). *Promoting moral growth: From Piaget to Kohlberg.* Prospect Heights, IL: Waveland Press.

Reis, S. M., & Purcell, J. H. (1993). An analysis of context elimination and strategies used by elementary classroom teachers in the curriculum compacting process. *Journal for the Education of the Gifted, 16,* 147–170.

Reiss, S., & Cellerino, M. (1983). Guiding gifted students through independent study. *Teaching Exceptional Children, 15,* 136–139.

Rekrut, M. D. (1992, April). *Teaching to learn: Cross-age tutoring to enhance strategy acquisition.* Paper presented at the annual meeting of the American Educational Research Association, San Francisco.

Renninger, K. A., Hidi, S., & Krapp, A. (Eds.). (1992). *The role of interest in learning and development.* Hillsdale, NJ: Erlbaum.

Renzulli, J. S. (1994). *Schools for talent development: A practical plan for total school improvement.* Mansfield Center, CT: Creative Learning Press.

Renzulli, J. S., & Reis, S. M. (1997). The schoolwide enrichment model: New directions for developing high-end learning. In N. Colangelo & G. A. Davis (Eds.), *Handbook of gifted education* (2nd ed.) (pp. 136–154). Boston: Allyn & Bacon.

Resnick, L. (1998, April). *From aptitude to effort: A new foundation for our schools.* Paper presented at the annual meeting of the American Educational Research Association, San Diego.

Rest, J., Edwards, L., & Thomas, S. (1997). Designing and validating a measure of moral judgment: Stage preference and stage consistency approaches. *Journal of Educational Psychology, 89*(1), 5–28.

Rest, J. R. (1983). Morality. In P. H. Mussen (Ed.), *Handbook of child psychology* (pp. 556–629). New York: Wiley.

Reynolds, A. (1995). The knowledge base for beginning teachers: Education professionals' expectations versus research findings on learning to teach. *Elementary School Journal, 95*(3), 199–221.

Reynolds, A. J. (1991). Early schooling of children at risk. *American Educational Research Journal, 28*(2), 392–422.

Reynolds, A. J. (1998). The Chicago child-parent center and expansion program: A study of extended early childhood intervention. In J. Crane (Ed.), *Social programs that work* (pp. 110–147). New York: Russell Sage Foundation.

Reynolds, A. J., & Temple, J. A. (1998). Extended early childhood intervention and school achievement: Age thirteen findings from the Chicago longitudinal study. *Child Development, 69*(1), 231–246.

Reynolds, C. R. (1992). Two key concepts in the diagnosis of learning disabilities and the habilitation of learning. *Learning Disability Quarterly, 15,* 2–12.

Reynolds, R. E. (1992). Selective attention and prose learning: Theoretical and empirical research. *Educational Psychology Review, 4,* 345–391.

Rhine, S. (1998). The role of research and teachers' knowledge base in professional development. *Educational Researcher, 27*(5), 27–31.

Rickards, J. P., Fajen, B. R., Sullivan, J. F., & Gillespie, G. (1997). Signaling, notetaking, and field independence–dependence in text comprehension and recall. *Journal of Educational Psychology, 89*(3), 508–517.

Rifkin, J. (1998). The sociology of the gene. *Phi Delta Kappan, 79*(9), 649–657.

Rivera, D. P., & Smith, D. D. (1997). *Teaching students with learning and behavior problems.* Boston: Allyn & Bacon.

Robinson, D. H., & Kiewra, K. A. (1995). Visual argument: Graphic organizers are superior to outlines in improving learning from text. *Journal of Educational Psychology, 87,* 455–467.

Robinson, D. H., & Skinner, C. H. (1996). Why graphic organizers facilitate search processes: Fewer words or computationally efficient indexing. *Contemporary Educational Psychology, 21*(2), 166–180.

Robinson, F. P. (1961). *Effective study.* New York: Harper & Row.

Roblyer, M. D., Castine, W. H., & King, F. J. (1988). *Assessing the impact of computer-based instruction.* New York: Haworth.

Roderick, M. (1994). Grade retention and school dropout: Investigating the association. *American Educational Research Journal, 31*(4), 729–759.

Roeber, E., & Dutcher, P. (1989). Michigan's innovative assessment of reading. *Educational Leadership 46*(7), 64–69.

Rogers, C., & Freiberg, H. J. (1994). *Freedom to learn* (3rd ed.). New York: Merrill.

Rogoff, B., & Chavajay, P. (1995). What's become of research on the cultural basis of cognitive development? *American Psychologist, 50,* 859–877.

Rogow, S. M. (1988). *Helping the visually impaired child with developmental problems: Effective practice in home, school, and community.* New York: Teachers College Press.

Roopnarine, J. L., Ahmeduzzaman, M., Donnely, S., Gill, P., Mennis, A., Arry, L., Dingler, K., McLaughlin, M., & Talukder, E. (1992). Social-cognitive play behaviors and playmate references in same-age and mixed-aged classrooms over a 6-month period. *American Educational Research Journal, 29,* 757–776.

Rose, T. L. (1984). Current uses of corporal punishment in American public schools. *Journal of Educational Psychology, 76,* 427–441.

Rosenbaum, J. (1980). Social implications of educational grouping. *Review of Research in Education, 8,* 361–401.

Rosenbaum, M. S., & Drabman, R. S. (1982). Self-control training in the classroom: A review and critique. *Journal of Applied Behavior Analysis, 12,* 264, 266, 467–485.

Rosenfeld, D., Folger, R., & Adelman, H. F. (1980). When rewards reflect competence: A qualification of the overjustification effect. *Journal of Personality and Social Psychology, 39,* 368–376.

Rosenfield, S. A. & Gravois, T. A. (1996). *Instructional consultation teams: Collaborating for change.* New York: Guilford.

Rosenholtz, S. J., & Simpson, C. (1984). The formation of ability conceptions: Developmental trend or social construction? *Review of Educational Research, 54,* 31–63.

Rosenshine, B., & Meister, C. (1992). The use of scaffolds for teaching higher-level cognitive strategies. *Educational Leadership, 49*(7), 26–33.

Rosenshine, B., & Meister, C. (1994). Reciprocal teaching: A review of research. *Review of Educational Research, 64,* 479–530.

Rosenshine, B., Meister, C., & Chapman, S. (1996). Teaching students to generate questions: A review of the intervention studies. *Review of Educational Research, 66*(2), 181–221.

Rosenshine, B. V. (1980). How time is spent in elementary classrooms. In C. Denham and A. Lieberman (Eds.), *Time to learn.* Washington, DC: National Institute of Education.

Rosenshine, B. V., & Stevens, R. J. (1986). Teaching functions. In M. C. Wittrock (Ed.), *Third handbook of research on teaching.* Chicago: Rand McNally.

Rosenthal, R., & Jacobson, L. (1968). *Pygmalion in the classroom.* New York: Holt, Rinehart and Winston.

Rosman, N. P. (1994). Acute head trauma. In F. A. Oski, C. D. DeAngelis, R. D. Feigin, J. A. McMillan, & J. B. Warshaw (Eds.), *Principles and practices of pediatrics* (2nd ed.) (pp. 2038–2048). Philadelphia: J. B. Lippincott.

Ross, J. A., Rolheiser, C., & Hogaboam-Gray, A. (1998, April). *Impact of self-evaluation training on mathematics achievement in a cooperative learning environment.* Paper presented at the annual meeting of the American Educational Research Association, San Diego.

Ross, S. M., Smith, L. J., Casey, J., & Slavin, R. E. (1995). Increasing the academic success of disadvantaged children: An examination of alternative early intervention programs. *American Educational Research Journal, 32,* 773–800.

Ross, S. M., Smith, L. J., Lohr, L., & McNelis, M. (1994). Math and reading instruction in tracked first grade classes. *The Elementary School Journal, 95*(2), 105–119.

Rossi, R. J., & Stringfield, S. C. (1995). What we must do for students placed at risk. *Phi Delta Kappan, 71*(1), 73–76.

Rothman, R. (1995). The certificate of initial mastery. *Educational Leadership, 52*(8), 41–45.

Rothstein, R. (1998). Bilingual education: The controversy. *Phi Delta Kappan, 79*(9), 672–678.

Rotter, J. (1954). *Social learning and clinical psychology.* Englewood Cliffs, NJ: Prentice-Hall.

Rowan, B., & Miracle, A. (1983). Systems of ability grouping and the stratification of achievement in elementary schools. *Sociology of Education, 56,* 133–144.

Rowe, M. B. (1974). Wait time and rewards as instructional variables, their influence on language, logic, and fate control. I: Wait time. *Journal of Research in Science Teaching, 11,* 81–94.

Ruble, D. N., Eisenberg, R., & Higgins, E. T. (1994). Developmental changes in achievement evaluation: Motivational implications of self-other differences. *Child Development, 65,* 1095–1110.

Ruhl, K. L., & Hughes, C. A. (1985). The nature and extent of aggression in special education settings serving behaviorally disordered students. *Behavioral Disorders, 10,* 95–104.

Ruiz, C. J. (1985). *Effects of Feuerstein instructional enrichment program on pre-college students.* Guayana, Venezuela: University of Guayana.

Rumelhart, D. E., & McClelland, J. L. (Eds.). (1986). *Parallel distributed processing: Explorations in the microstructure of cognition.* Cambridge, MA: MIT Press.

Russell, R. G., (1991, April). *A meta-analysis of word processing and attitudes and the impact on the quality of writing.* Paper presented at the annual meeting of the American Educational Research Association, Chicago.

Ryan, R., & Stiller, J. (1991). The social contexts of internalization: Parent and teacher influences on autonomy, motivation, and learning. In P. Pintrich & M. Maehr (Eds.), *Advances in Motivation and Achievement, Vol. 7* (pp. 115–149). Greenwich, CT: JAI Press.

Ryan, R. M. & Deci, E. L. (1996). When paradigms clash: Comments on Cameron and Pierce's claim that rewards do not undermine intrinsic motivation. *Review of Educational Research, 66*(1), 33–38.

Ryba, K., Selby, L., & Nolan, P. (1995). Computers empower students with special needs. *Educational Leadership, 53*(2), 82–84.

Sabers, D. S., Cushing, K. S., & Berliner, D. C. (1991). Differences among teachers in a task characterized by simultaneity, multidimensionality, and immediacy. *American Educational Research Journal, 28,* 68–87.

Sadker, M., & Sadker, D. (1985, March). Sexism in the schoolroom of the '80s. *Psychology Today, 19,* 54–57.

Sadker, M., & Sadker, D. (1994). *Failing at fairness: How America's schools cheat girls.* New York: Charles Scribner's Sons.

Sadker, M., Sadker, D., Fox, L., & Salata, M. (1994). Gender equality in the classroom. In J. I. Goodlad & P. Keating (Eds.), *Access to knowledge: The continuing agenda for our nation's schools.* New York: The College Board.

Sadker, M., Sadker, D., & Long, L. (1997). Gender and educational equality. In J. A. Banks & C. A. M. Banks (Eds.), *Multicultural education: Issues and perspectives.* (pp. 131–149). Boston: Allyn & Bacon.

Sadker, M., Sadker, D., & Steindam, S. (1989). Gender equity and educational reform. *Educational Leadership, 46*(6), 44–47.

Sadoski, M., Goetz, E. T., & Fritz, J. B. (1993). Impact of concreteness on comprehensibility, interest, and memory of text: Implications for dual coding theory and text design. *Journal of Educational Psychology, 85*(2), 291–304.

Safer, D. J. (1982). *School programs for disruptive adolescents.* Baltimore: University Park Press.

Sailor, W. (1991). Special education in the restructured school. *Remedial and Special Education, 12*(6), 8–22.

Salganik, M. W. (1980, January 27). Teachers busy teaching make city's 16 "best" schools stand out. *Baltimore Sun,* p. A4.

Salomon, G., & Perkins, D. N. (1989). Rocky roads to transfer: Rethinking mechanisms of a neglected phenomenon. *Educational Psychologist, 24,* 113–142.

Salomon, G., & Perkins, D. N. (1998). Individual and social aspects of learning. In P. D. Pearson & A. Iran-Nejad (Eds.), *Review of research in education* (pp. 1–24). Washington, DC: American Educational Research Association.

Salomon, G., Perkins, D. N., & Globerson, T. (1991). Partners in cognition: Extending human intelligence with intelligent technologies. *Educational Researchers, 20*(3), 2–9.

Sanders, M. G. (1996). Building family partnerships that last. *Educational Leadership, 54*(3), 61–66.

Sandoval, J. (1995). Teaching in subject matter areas: Science. *Annual Review of Psychology, 46,* 355–374.

Sanford, J. P., & Evertson, C. M. (1981). Classroom management in a low SES junior high: Three case studies. *Journal of Teacher Education, 32,* 34–38.

Sater, G. M., & French, D. C. (1989). A comparison of the social competencies of learning disabled and low achieving elementary-aged children. *Journal of Special Education, 23,* 29–42.

Savell, J. M., Twohig, P. T., & Rachford, D. L. (1986). Empirical status of Feuerstein's "Instrumental Enrichment" (FIE) technique as a method of teaching thinking skills. *Review of Educational Research, 56,* 381–409.

Savin-Williams, R. C., & Berndt, T. J. (1990). Friendship and peer relations. In S. S. Feldman & G. R. Elliot (Eds.), *At the threshold: The developing adolescent* (pp. 277–307). Cambridge, MA: Harvard University Press.

Scardamalia, M., & Bereiter, C. (1996). Engaging students in a knowledge society. *Educational Leadership, 54*(3), 6–10.

Scarr, S. (1998). American childcare today. *American Psychologist, 53*(2), 95–108.

Scarr, S., & McCartney, K. (1983). How people make their own environments: A theory of genotype-environmental effects. *Child Development, 54,* 424–435.

Schafer, W. E., & Olexa, C. (1971). *Tracking and opportunity.* Scranton, PA: Chandler.

Scheirer, M. A., & Kraut, R. E. (1979). Increasing educational achievement via self-concept change. *Review of Educational Research, 49*(1), 131–150.

Schickedanz, J. A. (1982). The acquisition of written language in young children. In B. Spodek (Ed.), *Handbook of research in early childhood education* (pp. 242–263). New York: Free Press.

Schickedanz, J. A., Schickedanz, D. I., Forsyth, P. D., & Forsyth, G. A. (1998). *Understanding children and adolescents* (3rd ed.). Boston: Allyn & Bacon.

Schiff, M., Duyme, M., Dumaret, A., & Tomkiewicz, S. (1982). How much could we boost scholastic achievement and IQ scores? A direct answer from a French adoption study. *Cognition, 12,* 165–196.

Schiff, M., & Lewontin, R. (1986). *Education and class: The irrelevance of IQ genetic studies.* Oxford: Clarendon Press.

Schifter, D. (1996). A constructivist perspective on teaching and learning mathematics. *Phi Delta Kappan, 77*(7), 492–499.

Schloss, P. J., & Smith, M. A. (1994). *Applied behavior analysis in the classroom.* Boston: Allyn & Bacon.

Schloss, P. J., & Smith, M. A. (1998). *Applied behavior analysis in the classroom* (2nd ed.). Boston: Allyn & Bacon.

Schmuck, R. (1997). *Practical action research for change.* Arlington Heights, IL: Skylight.

Schmuck, R. A., & Schmuck, P. A. (1997). *Group processes in the classroom.* Madison, WI: Brown & Benchmark.

Schnaiberg, L. (1998). Uncertainty follows vote on Prop. 227. *Education Week, 17*(39), 1–21.

Schneider, W. (1993). Domain-specific knowledge and memory performance in children. *Educational Psychology Review, 5,* 257–273.

Schneider, W., & Graham, D. J. (1992). Introduction to connectionist modeling in education. *Educational Psychologist, 27*(4), 513–530.

Schofield, J. W. (1995a). Promoting positive intergroup relations in school settings. In W. D. Hawley & A. W. Jackson (Eds.), *Toward a common destiny: Improving race and ethnic relations in America.* San Francisco: Jossey-Bass.

Schofield, J. W. (1995b). Review of research on school desegregation's impact on elementary and secondary school students. In J. A. Banks & C. A. M. Banks (Eds.), *Handbook of research on multicultural education.* New York: Macmillan.

Schofield, J. W. (1997). Causes and consequences of the color-blind perspective. In J. A. Banks & C. A. M. Banks (Eds.), *Multicultural education: Issues and perspectives* (pp. 251–271). Boston: Allyn & Bacon.

Schofield, J. W., Eurich-Fulcer, R., & Britt, C. L. (1994). Teachers, computer tutors, and teaching: The artificially intelligent tutor as an agent for classroom change. *American Educational Research Journal, 31*(3), 579–607.

Schraw, G., & Moshman, D. (1995). Metacognitive theories. *Educational Psychology Review, 7,* 351–371.

Schultz, G. F., & Switzky, H. N. (1990, Winter). The development of intrinsic motivation in students with learning problems: Suggestions for more effective instructional practice. *Preventing School Failure,* 14–20.

Schumaker, J. B., & Deshler, D. D. (1992). Validation of learning strategy interventions for students with learning disabilities: Results of a programmatic research effort. In B. Y. L. Wong (Ed.), *Contemporary intervention research in learning disabilities.* New York: Springer-Verlag.

Schumm, J. S., & Vaughn, S. (1992). Reflections on planning for mainstreamed students: General classroom teachers; perspectives. *Remedial and Special Education, 12*(4), 18–27.

Schunk, D. (1991). Self-efficacy and academic motivation. *Educational Psychologist, 26,* 207–231.

Schunk, D. H. (1982). Effects of effort attributional feedback on children's perceived self-efficacy and achievement. *Journal of Educational Psychology, 74,* 548–556.

Schunk, D. H. (1983). Reward contingencies, and the development of children's skills and self-efficacy. *Journal of Educational Psychology, 75,* 511–518.

Schunk, D. H. (1990). Introduction to the special section on motivation and efficacy. *Journal of Educational Psychology, 82,* 1–6.

Schunk, D. H. (1995). Inherent details of self-regulated learning include student perceptions. *Educational Psychologist, 30,* 213–216.

Schunk, D. H. (1996). Goal and self-evaluative influences during children's cognitive skill learning. *American Educational Research Journal, 33*(2), 359–382.

Schunk, D. H., & Zimmerman, B. J. (1997). Social origins of self-regulatory competence. *Educational Psychologist, 32*(4), 195–208.

Schwartz, N. H., Ellsworth, L. S., Graham, L., & Knight, B. (1998). Assessing prior knowledge to remember text: A comparison of advance organizers and maps. *Contemporary Educational Psychology, 23*(1), 65–89.

Schweinhart, L. J., Barnes, H. V., & Weikart, D. P. (1993). *Significant benefits: The High/Scope Perry preschool study through age 27.* Ypsilanti, MI: High/Scope.

Schweinhart, L. J., & Weikart, D. P. (1998). High/Scope Perry Preschool Program effects at age twenty-seven. In J. Crane (Ed.), *Social programs that work* (pp. 148–162). New York: Russell Sage Foundation.

Scott-Jones, D. (1993). Adolescent childbearing: Whose problem? What can we do? *Phi Delta Kappan, 75*(3), K1–K12.

Scruggs, T. E., & Richter, L. (1986). Tutoring learning disabled students: A critical review. *Learning Disability Quarterly, 9,* 2–14.

Scruggs, T. E., White, K. R., & Bennion, K. (1986). Teaching test-taking skills to elementary-grade students: A meta-analysis. *Elementary School Journal, 87,* 69–82.

Secada, W. G., Chavez-Chavez, R., Garcia, E., Munoz, C., Oakes, J., Santiago-Santiago, I., & Slavin, R. (1998). *No more excuses: The final report of the Hispanic dropout project.* Washington, DC: U.S. Department of Education.

Seligman, M. E. P. (1975). *Helplessness: On depression, development, and death.* San Francisco: Freeman.

Selman, R. (1980). *The growth of interpersonal understanding.* New York: Academic Press.

Selman, R. L. (1981). The child as a friendship philosopher. In S. R. Asher & J. M. Gottman (Eds.), *The development of children's friendships* (pp. 242–272). Cambridge: Cambridge University Press.

Selman, R. L., & Selman, A. P. (1979). Children's ideas about friendship: A new theory. *Psychology Today, 13,* 71–72, 74, 79–80, 114.

Semb, G. B., & Ellis, J. A. (1994). Knowledge taught in school: What is remembered? *Review of Educational Research, 24,* 253–286.

Semmel, M. I., Abernathy, T. V., Butera, G., & Lesar, S. (1991). Teacher perceptions of the regular education initiative. *Exceptional Children, 58,* 26–33.

Semmel, M. I., Gerber, M. M., & MacMillan, D. L. (1994). Twenty-five years after Dunn's article: A legacy of policy analysis research in special education. *Journal of Special Education, 27,* 481–495.

Sethi, S., Drake, M., Dialdin, D. A., & Lepper, M. R. (1995, April). *Developmental patterns of intrinsic and extrinsic motivation: A new look.* Paper presented at the annual meeting of the American Educational Research Association, San Francisco.

Shaklee, B. D., Barbour, N. E., Ambrose, R., & Hansford, S. J. (1997). *Designing and using portfolios.* Boston: Allyn & Bacon.

Shames, G. H., & Ramig, P. R. (1994). Stuttering and other disorders of fluency. In G. H. Shames, E. H. Willig, & W. A. Second (Eds.), *Human communication disorders: An introduction* (4th ed.) (pp. 336–386). New York: Merrill.

Shanahan, T. (1998). On the effectiveness and limitations of tutoring reading. In P. D. Pearson & A. Iran-Nejad (Eds.),

Review of research in education (pp. 217–234). Washington, DC: American Educational Research Association.

Shanker, A. (1994/1995). Full inclusion is neither free nor appropriate. *Educational Leadership, 52*(4), 18–21.

Sharan, S., Kussell, P., Hertz-Lazarowitz, R., Bejarano, Y., Raviv, S., & Sharan, Y. (1984). *Cooperative learning in the classroom: Research in desegregated schools.* Hillsdale, NJ: Erlbaum.

Sharan, S., & Shachar, C. (1988). *Language and learning in the cooperative classroom.* New York: Springer.

Sharan, Y., & Sharan, S. (1992). *Expanding cooperative learning through group investigation.* New York: Teachers' College Press.

Shavelson, R. J. (1987). Planning. In M. Dunkin (Ed.), *The international encyclopedia of teaching and teacher education* (pp. 483–486). New York: Pergamon.

Shavelson, R. J., Baxter, G. P., & Pine, J. (1992). Performance assessments: Political rhetoric and measurement reality. *Educational Researcher, 21*(4), 22–27.

Shaywitz, S. E., & Shaywitz, B. A. (1988). Attention deficit disorder: Current perspectives. In J. F. Kavanagh & T. J. Truss (Eds.), *Learning disabilities: Proceedings of the National Conference.* Parkton, MD: York.

Shell, D. F., Colvin, C., & Bruning, R. H. (1995). Self-efficacy, attribution, and outcome expectancy mechanisms in reading and writing achievement: Grade level and achievement-level differences. *Journal of Educational Psychology, 87,* 386–398.

Shepard, L. A. (1989a). Norm-referenced vs. criterion-referenced tests. In *Annual editions: Educational psychology 89/90* (pp. 198–203). Guilford, CT: Duskin.

Shepard, L. A. (1989b). Why we need better assessments. *Educational Leadership, 46*(7), 4–9.

Shepard, L. A. (1991). The influence of standardized tests on early childhood curriculum, teachers, and children. In B. Spodek and O. N. Saracho (Eds.), *Yearbook in early childhood education.* New York: Teachers' College Press.

Shepard, L. A. (1993a). Evaluating test validity. In L. Darling-Hammond (Ed.), *Review of Research in Education 19.* Washington, DC: American Educational Research Association.

Shepard, L. A. (1993b). The place of testing reform in educational reform: A reply to Cizek. *Educational Researcher, 22*(4), 10–13.

Shepard, L. A. (1995). Using assessment to improve learning. *Phi Delta Kappan, 52*(5), 38–43.

Shepard, L. A., & Smith, M. L. (1986). Synthesis of research on school readiness and kindergarten retention. *Educational Leadership, 44,* 78–86.

Shepard, L. A., & Smith, M. L. (Eds.). (1989). *Flunking grades: Research and policies on retention.* New York: Falmer.

Shimmerlik, S. M. (1978). Organization theory and memory for prose: A review of the literature. *Review of Educational Research, 48,* 103–120.

Shirey, L. L., & Reynolds, R. E. (1988). Effect of interest on attention and learning. *Journal of Educational Psychology, 80,* 159–166.

Shore, R. (1998). *Ready schools.* Washington, DC: National Education Goals Panel.

Shujaa, M. J. (Ed.). (1996). *Beyond desegregation.* Thousand Oaks, CA: Corwin.

Shulman, J., Lotan, R. A., & Whitcomb, J. A. (1998). *Groupwork in diverse classrooms: A cookbook for educators.* New York: Teachers College Press.

Siccone, F. (1995). *Celebrating diversity: Building self-esteem in today's multicultural classrooms.* Boston: Allyn & Bacon.

Siegler, R. S. (1988). Mechanisms of cognitive development. *Annual Review of Psychology, 40,* 353–379.

Siegler, R. S. (1991). *Children's thinking.* (2nd ed.). Englewood Cliffs, NJ: Prentice-Hall.

Sills-Briegel, T., Fisk, C., & Dunlop, V. (1996). Graduation by exhibition. *Educational Leadership, 54*(4), 66–71.

Silver, A. A., & Hagin, R. A. (1990). *Disorders of learning in childhood.* New York: Wiley.

Simmons, D. C., Fuchs, L. S., Fuchs, P., Mathes, P., & Hodge, J. P. (1995). Effects of explicit teaching and peer tutoring on the reading achievement of learning-disabled and low-performing students in regular classrooms. *The Elementary School Journal, 95*(5), 387–408.

Simmons, R. G., & Blyth, D. A. (1987). *Moving into adolescence: The impact of pubertal change and school context.* New York: Aldine de Gruyter.

Simpson, C. (1981). Classroom structure and the organization of ability. *Sociology of Education, 54,* 120–132.

Skaalvik, E. M. (1997). Self-enhancing and self-defeating ego orientation: Relations with task and avoidance orientation, achievement, self-perceptions, and anxiety. *Journal of Educational Psychology, 89*(1), 71–81.

Skinner, B. F. (1953). *Science and human behavior.* New York: Macmillan.

Skinner, B. F. (1968). *The technology of teaching.* New York: Appleton-Century-Crofts.

Slaughter, D. T., & Epps, E. (1994). The home environment and academic achievement of black American children and youth. In J. Kretovics & E. Nussel (Eds.), *Transforming urban education.* Boston: Allyn & Bacon.

Slavin, R. E. (1980). Effects of Individual Learning Expectations on student achievement. *Journal of Educational Psychology, 72,* 520–524.

Slavin, R. E. (1985). Team Assisted Individualization: A cooperative learning solution for adaptive instruction in mathematics. In M. Wang & H. Walberg (Eds.), *Adapting instruction to individual difference.* Berkeley: McCutchan.

Slavin, R. E. (1986). The Napa evaluation of Madeline Hunter's ITIP: Lessons learned. *Elementary School Journal, 87,* 165–171.

Slavin, R. E. (1987a). A theory of school and classroom organization. *Educational Psychologists, 22,* 89–108.

Slavin, R. E. (1987b). Grouping for instruction in the elementary school. *Educational Psychologist, 22,* 109–127.

Slavin, R. E. (1987c). Ability grouping and student achievement in elementary schools: A best-evidence synthesis. *Review of Educational Research, 57,* 293–336.

Slavin, R. E. (1987d). Mastery learning reconsidered. *Review of Educational Research, 57,* 175–213.

Slavin, R. E. (1987e). Cooperative learning: Where behavioral and humanistic approaches to classroom motivation meet. *Elementary School Journal, 88,* 29–37.

Slavin, R. E. (1990). Ability grouping and student achievement in secondary schools: A best-evidence synthesis. *Review of Educational Research, 60,* 471–499.

Slavin, R. E. (1992). *Research methods in education: A practical guide* (2nd ed.). Boston: Allyn & Bacon.

Slavin, R. E. (1993a). Students differ: So what? *Educational Researcher, 22*(9), 13–14.

Slavin, R. E. (1993b). Ability grouping in the middle grades: Achievement effects and alternatives. *The Elementary School Journal, 93*(5), 535–552.

Slavin, R. E. (1994a). *Using student team learning* (4th ed.). Baltimore: Johns Hopkins University, Center for Research on Elementary and Middle Schools.

Slavin, R. E. (1994b). School and classroom organization in beginning reading: Class size, aides, and instructional grouping. In R. E. Slavin, N. L. Karweit, B. A. Wasik, & N. A. Madden (Eds.), *Preventing early school failure: Research on effective strategies.* Boston: Allyn & Bacon.

Slavin, R. E. (1995a). *Cooperative learning: Theory, research, and practice* (2nd ed.). Boston: Allyn & Bacon.

Slavin, R. E. (1995b). Cooperative learning and intergroup relations. In J. Banks (Ed.), *Handbook of research on multicultural education.* New York: Macmillan.

Slavin, R. E. (1996a). Neverstreaming: Preventing learning disabilities. *Educational Leadership, 53*(5), 4–7.

Slavin, R. E. (1996b). Research on cooperative learning achievement: What we know, what we need to know. *Contemporary Educational Psychology, 21,* 43–69.

Slavin, R. E. (1997/98). Can education reduce social inequality? *Educational Leadership, 55*(4), 6–10.

Slavin, R. E., & Fashola, O. S. (1998). *Show me the evidence: Proven and promising programs for America's schools.* Thousand Oaks, CA: Corwin.

Slavin, R. E., & Karweit, N. (April 1984). Within-class ability groupings and student achievement: Two field experiments. Paper presented at the annual convention of the American Educational Research Association, New Orleans.

Slavin, R. E., & Karweit, N. (1985). Effects of whole class, ability grouped, and individualized instruction on mathematics achievement. *American Educational Research Journal 22,* 351–368.

Slavin, R. E., & Karweit, N. L. (1982, August). School organizational vs. developmental effects on attendance among young adolescents. Paper presented at the annual convention of the American Psychological Association, Washington, DC.

Slavin, R. E., Karweit, N. L., & Wasik, B. A. (1994). *Preventing early school failure: Research on effective strategies.* Boston: Allyn & Bacon.

Slavin, R. E., & Madden, N. A. (1987, April). Effective classroom programs for students at risk. Paper presented at the annual convention of the American Educational Research Association, Washington, DC.

Slavin, R. E., & Madden, N. A. (1991). Modifying Chapter 1 program improvement guidelines to reward appropriate practices. *Educational Evaluation and Policy Analysis, 13,* 369–379.

Slavin, R. E., & Madden, N. A. (1998). *Success for All/Éxito para Todos: Effects on the reading achievement of students acquiring English.* Baltimore: Johns Hopkins University, Center for Research on the Education of Students Placed at Risk.

Slavin, R. E., Madden, N. A., Dolan, L. J., & Wasik, B. A., (1996). *Every child, every school: Success for All.* Newbury Park, CA: Corwin.

Slavin, R. E., Madden, N. A., Dolan, L. J., Wasik, B. A., Ross, S., Smith, L., & Dianda, M. (1996). Success for All: A summary of research. *Journal of Education for Students Placed at Risk.*

Slavin, R. E., Madden, N. A., Dolan, L. J., Wasik, B. A., Ross, S. M., & Smith, L. J. (1994). "Whenever and wherever we choose . . . ": The replication of Success for All. *Phi Delta Kappan, 75*(8), 639–647.

Slavin, R. E., Madden, N. A., & Karweit, N. L. (Eds.). (1989). *Effective programs for students at risk.* Boston: Allyn & Bacon.

Slavin, R. E., Madden, N. A., Karweit, N. L., Dolan, L., & Wasik, B. A. (1992). *Success for All: A relentless approach to prevention and early intervention in elementary schools.* Arlington, VA: Educational Research Service.

Slavin, R. E., Madden, N. A., & Leavey, M. (1984a). Effects of Team Assisted Individualization on the mathematics achievement of academically handicapped and nonhandicapped students. *Journal of Educational Psychology, 76,* 813–819.

Slavin, R. E., Madden, N. A., & Leavey, M. B. (1984b). Effects of cooperative learning and individualized instruction on mainstreamed students. *Exceptional Children, 84,* 409–422.

Slavin, R. E., & Stevens, R. J. (1991). Cooperative learning and mainstreaming. In J. W. Lloyd, N. N. Singh, & A. C. Repp (Eds.). *The regular education initiative: Alternative perspectives on concepts, issues, and models* (pp. 177–191). Sycamore, IL: Sycamore.

Sleeter, C. E. (1995). Curriculum controversies in multicultural education. In E. Flaxman & A. H. Passow (Eds.), *Changing populations, changing schools.* Chicago: University of Chicago Press.

Smagorinsky, P., & Smith, M. W. (1992). The nature of knowledge in composition and literary understanding: The question of specificity. *Review of Educational Research, 62*(3), 279–305.

Small, M. Y., Lovett, S. B., & Scher, M. S. (1993). Pictures facilitate children's recall of unillustrated expository prose. *Journal of Educational Psychology, 85,* 520–528.

Smelter, R. W., Rasch, B. W., Fleming, J., Nazos, P., & Baranowski, S. (1996). Is attention deficit disorder becoming a desired diagnosis? *Phi Delta Kappan, 77*(6), 429–432.

Smetana, J. G., Killen, M., & Turiel, E. (1991). Children's reasoning about interpersonal and moral conflicts. *Child Development, 62,* 629–644.

Smith, C. R. (1994). *Learning disabilities: The interaction of learner, task, and setting.* Boston: Allyn & Bacon.

Smith, D. D. (1998). *Introduction to special education: Teaching in an age of challenge.* Boston: Allyn & Bacon.

Smith, D. D., & Luckasson, R. (1995). *Introduction to special education* (2nd ed.). Boston: Allyn & Bacon.

Smith, L., & Land, M. (1981). Low-interference verbal behaviors related to teacher clarity. *Journal of Classroom Interaction, 17,* 37–42.

Smith, L. J., Ross, S. M., & Casey, J. P. (1994). *Special education analyses for Success for All in four cities.* Memphis, TN: University of Memphis, Center for Research in Educational Policy.

Smith, M. L. (1991). Meanings of test preparation. *American Educational Research Journal, 28*(3), 521–542.

Smith, N., Greenlaw, M., & Scott, C. (1987). Making the literate environment equitable. *Reading Teacher, 400*–407.

Smith, R., & Sherrell, S. (1996). Mileposts on the road to a certificate of initial mastery. *Educational Leadership, 54*(4), 46–50.

Smith, T. E. C., Polloway, E. A., Patton, J. R., & Dowdy, C. A. (1998). *Teaching students with special needs in inclusive settings* (2nd ed.). Boston: Allyn & Bacon.

Snarey, J. R. (1985). Cross-cultural universality of socio-moral development: A critical review of Kohlbergian research. *Psychological Bulletin, 97,* 202–232.

Snow, R. E. (1992). Aptitude theory: Yesterday, today, and tomorrow. *Educational Psychologist, 27*(1), 5–32.

Snow, R. E., & Swanson, J. (1992). Instructional psychology: Aptitude, adaptation, and assessment. *Annual Review of Psychology, 43,* 583–626.

Snowman, J. (1984). Learning tactics and strategies. In G. Phye & T. Andre (Eds.), *Cognitive instructional psychology.* New York: Academic Press.

Snyderman, M., & Rothman, S. (1987). Survey of expert opinion on intelligence and aptitude testing. *American Psychologist, 42,* 137–144.

Solomon, D., Watson, M. S., Delucchi, K. L., Schaps, E., & Battisch, V. (1988). Enhancing children's prosocial behavior in the classroom. *American Educational Research Journal, 25,* 527–554.

Solso, R. L. (1998). *Cognitive psychology* (5th ed.). Boston: Allyn & Bacon.

Spear-Swerling, L., & Sternberg, R. J. (1998). Curing our "epidemic" of learning disabilities. *Phi Delta Kappan, 79*(5), 397–401.

Specht, L. B., & Sandling, P. K. (1991). The differential effects of experiential learning activities and traditional lecture classes in accounting. *Simulation and Games, 2,* 196–210.

Spector, J. E. (1992). Predicting progress in beginning reading: Dynamic assessment of phonemic awareness. *Journal of Educational Psychology, 84*(3), 353–363.

Sperling, G. A. (1960). The information available in brief visual presentations. *Psychological Monographs, 74,* No. 498.

Spielberger, C., & Vagg, P. (Eds.). (1995). *Test anxiety: Theory, assessment, and treatment.* Washington: DC: Taylor & Francis.

Spires, H. A., & Donley, J. (1998). Prior knowledge activation: Inducing engagement with informational texts. *Journal of Educational Psychology, 90*(2), 249–260.

Spivak, G., Marcus, J., & Swift, M. (1986). Early classroom behaviors and later misconduct. *Developmental Psychology, 22,* 124–131.

Spurlin, J. E., Dansereau, D. F., Larson, C. O., & Brooks, L. W. (1984). Cooperative learning strategies in processing descriptive text: Effects of role and activity level of the learner. *Cognition and Instruction, 1,* 451–463.

Squire, L. R., Knowlton, B., & Musen, G. (1993). The structure and organization of memory. *Annual Review of Psychology, 44,* 453–495.

Stahl, S. A., & Miller, P. D. (1989). Whole language and language experience approaches for beginning reading: A quantitative research synthesis. *Review of Educational Research, 59,* 87–116.

Stallings, J., & Krasavage, E. M. (1986). Program implementation and student achievement in a four-year Madeline Hunter follow-through project. *Elementary School Journal, 87,* 117–138.

Stallings, J. A., & Kaskowitz, D. (1974). *Follow-through classroom observation evaluation 1972–73.* Menlo Park, CA: Standard Research Institute.

Stallings, J. A., & Stipek, D. (1986). Research on early childhood and elementary school teaching programs. In M. C. Wittrock (Ed.), *Handbook of research on teaching* (3rd ed.). New York: Macmillan.

Stanley, J. C., & Benbow, C. P. (1986). Extremely young college graduates: Evidence of their success. *College and University, 58,* 361–371.

Stanovich, K. E., Siegel, L. S., & Gottard, A. (1997). Converging evidence for phonological and surface subtypes of reading disability. *Journal of Educational Psychology, 89*(10), 114–127.

Stebbins, L. B, St. Pierre, R. G., Proper, E. C., Anderson, R. B., & Cerva, T. R. (1977). Education as experimentation: A planned variation model (Vol. 4 A–D). Cambridge, MA: Abt Associates.

Steffe, L. P., & Gale, J. (Eds.). (1995). *Constructivism in education.* Hillsdale, NJ: Erlbaum.

Stein, B. S., Littlefield, J., Bransford, J. D., & Persampieri, M. (1984). Elaboration and knowledge acquisition. *Memory and Cognition, 12,* 522–529.

Stein, M. K., Leinhardt, G., & Bickel, W. (1989). Instructional issues for teaching students at risk. In R. E. Slavin, N. L. Karweit, & N. A. Madden (Eds.), *Effective programs for students at risk.* Boston: Allyn & Bacon.

Stern, D. (1996). *Active learning in students and teachers.* Paris: Organization for Economic Cooperation and Development.

Sternberg, R. (1990). *Metaphors of mind: Conceptions of the nature of intelligence.* New York: Cambridge University Press.

Sternberg, R. J. (1995). Investing in creativity: Many happy returns. *Educational Leadership, 53*(4), 80–84.

Sternberg, R. J. (1996). Myths, countermyths and truths about intelligence. *Educational Researcher, 25*(2), 11–16.

Sternberg, R. J. (1997). What does it mean to be smart? *Educational Leadership, 54*(6), 20–24.

Sternberg, R. J., & Bhana, K. (1986). Synthesis of research on the effectiveness of intellectual skills programs: Snake-oil remedies or miracle cures? *Educational Leadership, 44*(2), 60–67.

Sternberg, R. J., & Detterman, D. K. (Eds.). (1986). *What is intelligence?* Norwood, NJ: Ablex.

Stevens, R. J., Madden, N. A., Slavin, R. E., & Farnish, A. M. (1987). Cooperative Integrated Reading and Composition: Two field experiments. *Reading Research Quarterly, 22,* 433–454.

Stevens, R. J., & Slavin, R. E. (1995a). The effects of Cooperative Integrated Reading and Composition (CIRC) on academically handicapped and non-handicapped students' achievement, attitudes, and metacognition in reading and writing. *Elementary School Journal, 95*(3), 241–262.

Stevens, R. J., & Slavin, R. E. (1995b). The cooperative elementary school: Effects on students' achievement, attitudes, and social relations. *American Educational Research Journal, 32,* 321–351.

Stewart, D. A. (1992). Initiating reform in total communication programs. *Journal of Special Education, 26,* 68–84.

Stiggins, R. J. (1995). Assessment as a school improvement "innovation"? In J. H. Block, S. T. Everson, & T. R. Guskey (Eds.), *School improvement programs* (pp. 111–128). New York: Scholastic.

Stigler, S. M. (1978). Some forgotten work on memory. *Journal of Experimental Psychology: Human Learning and Memory, 4,* 1–4.

Stipek, D., Ryan, R., & Alarcon, R. (1998, April). *Practicing research and researching practice: The development and assessment of a two-way bilingual program for young children.* Paper presented at the annual meeting of the American Educational Research Association, San Diego.

Stipek, D. J. (1993). *Motivation to learn: From theory to practice* (2nd ed.). Boston: Allyn & Bacon.

Stipek, D. J. (1996). Motivation and instruction. In D.C. Berliner & R. C. Calfee (Eds.), *Handbook of educational psychology* (pp. 85–116). New York: Macmillan.

Stipek, D. J. (1998). *Motivation to learn: From theory to practice* (2nd ed.) Boston: Allyn & Bacon.

Stipek, D. J., & Ryan, R. H. (1997). Economically disadvantaged preschoolers: Ready to learn but further to go. *Developmental Psychology, 33*(4), 711–723.

Strauss, A., & Corbin, J. (1990). *The basics of qualitative research: Grouped theory research: Grounded theory procedures and techniques.* Newbury Park, CA: Sage.

Stringfield, S., Millsap, M. A., Herman, R., Yoder, N., Brigham, N., Nesselrodt, P., Schaffer, E., Karweit, N., Levin, M., & Stevens, R. J. (1997). *Special strategies studies final report.* Washington, DC: U.S. Department of Education.

Strong, R., Silver, H. F., & Robinson, A. (1995). What do students want (and what really motivates them)? *Educational Leadership, 53*(1), 8–12.

Stumpf, H., & Stanley, J. C. (1996). Gender-related differences on the College Board's advanced placement achievement tests 1982–1992. *Journal of Educational Psychology, 88*(2), 353–364.

Subotnik, R. (1997). Teaching gifted students in a multicultural society. In J. A. Banks & C. A. M. Banks (Eds.), *Multicultural education: Issues and perspectives* (pp. 361–385). Boston: Allyn & Bacon.

Suhor, C. (1989). "English Only" movement emerging as a major controversy. *Educational Leadership, 46*(6), 80–82.

Sulzby, E., & Teale, W. (1991). Emergent literacy. In R. Barr, M. L. Kamil, P. Moselthal, & P. D. Pearson (Eds.), *Handbook of reading research,* Vol. II (pp. 727–757). New York: Longman.

Sulzer-Azaroff, B., & Mayer, G. R. (1986). *Achieving educational excellence using behavioral strategies.* New York: Holt, Rinehart and Winston.

Supovitz, J. A., & Brennan, R. T. (1997). Mirror, mirror on the wall, which is the fairest test of all? An examination of the equitability of portfolio assessment relative to standardized tests. *Harvard Educational Review, 67*(3), 474–505.

Sutton, R. E. (1991). Equity and computers in the schools: A decade of research. *Review of Educational Research, 61*(4), 475–503.

Swanson, D. B., Norman, G. R., & Linn, R. L. (1995). Performance-based assessment: Lessons from the health professions. *Educational Researcher, 24*(5), 5–11, 35.

Swanson, H., O'Connor, J. E., & Cooney, J. B. (1990). An information processing analysis of expert and novice teachers' problem solving. *American Educational Research Journal, 27,* 533–556.

Swanson, H. L. (1990). Influence of metacognitive knowledge and aptitude on problem solving. *Journal of Educational Psychology, 82,* 306–314.

Swanson, M. C., Mehan, H., & Hubbard, L. (1995). The AVID classroom: Academic and social support for low-achieving students. In J. Oakes & K. H. Quartz (Eds.), *Creating new educational communities.* Chicago: University of Chicago Press.

Sweller, J., van Merrienboer, J. J. G., & Paas, F. G. W. C. (1998). Cognitive architecture and instructional design. *Educational Psychology Review, 10*(3), 251–296.

Swiatek, M. A., & Benbow, C. P. (1991). Ten-year longitudinal follow-up of ability-matched accelerated and unaccelerated gifted students. *Journal of Educational Psychology, 83*(4), 528–538.

Tamura, L. (1996). No longer strangers. *Educational Leadership, 53*(5), 23–25.

Tanner, C. K., & Decotis, J. D. (1994). The effects of a continuous-progress, non-graded program on primary school students. *ERS Spectrum, 12*(3), 41–47.

Tanner, D. (1998). The social consequences of bad research. *Phi Delta Kappan, 79*(5), 345–349.

Tanner, J. M. (1991). Adolescent growth spurt. In R. M. Lerner, A. C. Peterson, & J. Brooks-Gunn (Eds.), *Encyclopedia of adolescence* (Vol. 1, pp. 419–424). New York: Garland.

Tavris, C. (1992). *The mismeasure of woman.* New York: Simon and Schuster.

Taylor, C. (1994). Assessment for measurement or standards: The peril and promise of large-scale assessment reform. *American Educational Research Journal, 31*(2), 231–262.

Taylor, R. (1984). *Assessment of exceptional students: Educational and psychological procedures.* Englewood Cliffs, NJ: Prentice-Hall.

Teddlie, C., & Stringfield, S. (1989). Ethics and teachers: Implications of research on effective schools. *Ethics in Education, 9*(2), 12–14.

Temple, C., Nathan, R., Temple, F., & Burris, N. A. (1993). *The beginnings of writing* (3rd ed.). Boston: Allyn & Bacon.

TenBrink, T. D. (1986). Writing instructional objectives. In J. Cooper (Ed.), *Classroom teaching skills* (3rd ed.). Lexington, MA: D.C. Heath.

Tennyson, R. D., & Park, O. (1980). The teaching of concepts: A review of instructional design literature. *Review of Educational Research, 50,* 55–70.

Terman, L. M., & Oden, M. H. (1959). The gifted group in midlife. In *Genetic studies of genius,* Vol. 5. Stanford, CA: Stanford University Press.

Tetreault, M. K. T. (1997). Classrooms for diversity: Rethinking curriculum and pedagogy. In J. A. Banks & C. A. M. Banks (Eds.), *Multicultural education: Issues and perspectives* (pp. 150–170). Boston: Allyn & Bacon.

Tharp, R. G., & Gallimore, R. (1988). *Rousing minds to life.* New York: Cambridge University Press.

Thoma, S. J. (1986). Estimating gender differences in the comprehension and preference of moral issues. *Developmental Review, 6,* 165–180.

Thomas, E. L., & Robinson, H. A. (1972). *Improving reading in every class: A sourcebook for teachers.* Boston: Allyn & Bacon.

Thomas, J. W., & Rohwer, W. D. (1986). Academic studying: The role of learning strategies. *Educational Psychologist, 21,* 19–41.

Thomas, W. P., & Collier, V. P. (1998). Two languages are better than one. *Educational Leadership, 55*(4), 23–26.

Thompson, M. S., Entwisle, D. R., Alexander, K. L., & Sundius, M. J. (1992). The influence of family composition on children's conformity to the student role. *American Educational Research Journal, 29*(2), 405–424.

Thompson, T., Davidson, J. A., & Barber, J. G. (1995). Self-worth protection in achievement motivation: Performance effects and attributional behavior. *Journal of Educational Psychology, 87*(4), 598–610.

Thorkildsen, T. A. (1993). Those who can, tutor: High-ability students' conceptions of fair ways to organize learning. *Journal of Educational Psychology, 85*(1), 182–190.

Thorkildsen, T. A., & Nicholls, J. G. (1998). Fifth graders' achievement orientations and beliefs: Individual and classroom differences. *Journal of Educational Psychology, 90*(2), 179–201.

Thousand, J. S., & Villa, R. A. (1994). *Creativity and collaborative learning: A practical guide to empowering students and teachers.* Baltimore: Paul H. Brookes.

Thousand, J. S., & Villa, R. A. (1995). Inclusion: Alive and well in the Green Mountain State. *Phi Delta Kappan, 77*(4), 288–291.

Tierno, M. J. (1993). Responding to the socially motivated behaviors of early adolescents: Recommendations for classroom management. In K. M. Cauley, F. Linder, & J. H. McMillan (Eds.), *Annual editions: Educational psychology 93/94.* Guilford, CT: Dushkin.

Timpson, W. M., & Tobin, D. N. (1982). *Teaching as performing: A guide to energizing your public presentation.* Englewood Cliffs, NJ: Prentice-Hall.

Tisak, M. S., & Tisak, J. (1990). Children's conceptions of parental authority, friendship, and sibling relationships. *Merrill-Palmer Quarterly, 36,* 347–368.

Tishman, S., Perkins, D. N., & Jay, E. (1995). *The thinking classroom.* Boston: Allyn & Bacon.

Tittle, C. K. (1991). Changing models of student and teacher assessment. *Educational Psychologist, 26*(2), 157–165.

Tobias, S. (1992). The impact of test anxiety cognition in school learning. In K. A. Hagtvet & T. B. Johnsen (Eds.), *Advances in test anxiety research* (Vol. 7, pp. 18–31). Amsterdam: Swets & Zeitlinger.

Tobias, S. (1994). Interest, prior knowledge, and learning. *Review of Educational Research, 63,* 37–54.

Tobin, K. (1986). Effects of teacher wait time on discourse characteristics in mathematics and language arts classes. *American Educational Research Journal, 23,* 191–200.

Tobin, K. (1987). The role of wait time in higher cognitive level learning. *Review of Educational Research, 57,* 69–95.

Tobin, K. G., & Capie, W. (1982). Relationships between classroom process variables and middle-school science achievement. *Journal of Educational Psychology, 74,* 441–454.

Top, B. L., & Osguthorpe, R. T. (1987). Reverse-role tutoring: The effects of handicapped students tutoring regular class students. *Elementary School Journal, 87,* 413–423.

Topping, K., & Ehly, S. (Eds.). (1998). *Peer-assisted learning.* Mahwah, NJ: Erlbaum.

Torrance, E. P. (1986). Teaching creative and gifted learners. In M. C. Wittrock (Ed.), *Handbook of research on teaching* (3rd ed.). New York: Macmillan.

Trammel, D. L., Schloss, P. J., & Alper, S. (1994). Using self-recording evaluation and graphing to increase completion of homework assignments. *Journal of Learning Disabilities, 27,* 75–81.

Tredway, L. (1995). Socratic seminars: Engaging students in intellectual discourse. *Educational Leadership, 53*(1), 26–29.

Trent, S. C., Artiles, A. J., & Englert, C. S. (1998). From deficit thinking to social constructivism: A review of theory research and practice in special education. In P. D. Pearson & A. Iran-Nejad (Eds.), *Review of research in education* (pp. 277–307). Washington, DC: American Educational Research Association.

Trent, W. T. (1997). Outcomes of school desegregation: Findings from longitudinal research. *Journal of Negro Education, 66*(3), 255–257.

Tulving, E. (1993). What is episodic memory? *Current Directions in Psychological Science, 2,* 67–70.

Tulving, E., Kapur, S., Craik, F. I. M., Moscovitch, M., & Houle, S. (1994). Hemispheric encoding/retrieval asymmetry in episodic memory: Positron emission tomography findings. *Proceedings of the National Academy of Sciences, 91,* 2016–2020.

Turiel, E. (1983). *The development of social knowledge: Morality and convention.* New York: Cambridge University Press.

Turkheimer, E. (1994). Socioeconomic status and intelligence. In R. J. Sternberg (Ed.), *Encyclopedia of human intelligence.* New York: Macmillan.

Turnbull, H. R. (1991). *Free appropriate public education: The law and children with disabilities* (2nd ed.). Denver: Love.

United Cerebral Palsy Association. (1993). *Cerebral palsy: Facts and figures.* Washington, DC: Author.

Urdan, T. C., & Maehr, M. L. (1995). Beyond a two-goal theory of motivation and achievement: A case for social goals. *Review of Educational Research, 65,* 213–243.

U.S. Commission on Civil Rights. (1975). *A better chance to learn: Bilingual bicultural education.* Washington, DC: U.S. Government Printing Office.

U.S. Department of Education. (1991). *Youth indicators.* Washington, DC: Author.

U.S. Department of Education. (1993). *Reinventing Chapter I: The current Chapter I program and directions.* Washington, DC: Author.

U.S. Department of Education. (1994). *Sixteenth annual report to Congress on the implementation of the Individuals with Disabilities Education Act.* Washington, DC: Author.

U.S. Department of Education. (1996). *Eighteenth annual report to Congress on the implementation of the Individuals with Disabilities Education Act.* Washington, DC: Author.

U.S. Department of Education, Office of Special Education and Rehabilitation Services. (1998, September). *IDEA '97 general information* [Internet] Available: http://www.ed.gov/offices/OSERS/IDEA/overview.html.

U.S. Department of Health and Human Services. (1994). Washington, DC: Author.

U.S. Department of Justice. (1992). *Crime in the United States.* Washington, DC: Author.

U.S. Government Printing Office. (1993). *Statistical abstracts of the U.S.* Washington, DC: Author.

Valencia, S. W., Pearson, P. D., Peters, C. W., & Wixson, K. K. (1989). Theory and practice in statewide reading assessment: Closing the gap. *Educational Leadership, 46*(7), 57–63.

Van der Veer, R., & Valsiner, J. (1991). *Understanding Vygotsky: A quest for synthesis.* Cambridge, MA: Basil Blackwell.

Van Dyke, R., Stallings, M. A., & Colley, K. (1995). How to build an inclusive school community: A success story. *Phi Delta Kappan, 76*(6), 475–480.

Van Patten, J., Chao, C. I., & Reigeluth, C. M. (1986). A review of strategies for sequencing and synthesizing instruction. *Review of Educational Research, 56,* 437–471.

Van Riper, C., & Erickson, R. L. (1996). *Speech correction: An introduction to speech pathology and audiology* (9th ed.). Boston: Allyn & Bacon.

VanSickle, R. L. (1986, April). *A quantitative review of research on instructional simulation gaming: A twenty-year perspective.* Paper presented at the annual convention of the American Educational Research Association, San Francisco.

Van Tassel-Baska, F. S. (1989). Appropriate curriculum for gifted learners. *Educational Leadership 46*(6), 13–15.

Vasquez, J. A. (1993). Teaching to the distinctive traits of minority students. In K. M. Cauley, F. Linder, & J. H. McMillan (Eds.), *Annual editions: Educational psychology 93/94.* Guilford, CT: The Dushkin Publishing Group.

Vasta, R., & Liben, L. S. (1996). The water-level task: An intriguing puzzle. *Current Directions in Psychological Science, 5*(6), 171–177.

Veenman, S. (1995). Cognitive and noncognitive effects of multigrade and multi-age classes: A best evidence synthesis. *Review of Educational Research, 65*(4), 319–381.

Veenman, S. (1997). Combination classrooms revisited. *Educational Research and Evaluation, 3*(3), 262–276.

Vellutino, F. R. (1991). Introduction to three studies on reading acquisition: Convergent findings on theoretical foundations of code-oriented versus whole-language approaches to reading instruction. *Journal of Educational Psychology, 83,* 437–443.

Vellutino, F. R., Scanlon, D. M., Sipay, E. R., Small, S. G., Chen, R., Pratt, A., & Denckla, M. B. (1996). Cognitive profiles of difficult-to-remediate and readily remediated poor readers: Early intervention as a vehicle for distinguishing between cognitive and experimental deficits as basic causes of specific reading disability. *Journal of Educational Psychology, 88*(4), 601–638.

Verba, M. (1993). Cooperative formats in pretend play among young children. *Cognition and Instruction, 11*(3&4), 265–280.

Vernez, G. (1998). *Projected social context for education of children.* Washington, DC: RAND.

Vispoel, W. P., & Austin, J. R. (1995). Success and failure in junior high school: A critical incident approach to understanding students' attributional beliefs. *American Educational Research Journal, 32,* 277–412.

von Glaserfeld, E. (1996). Footnotes to the "many faces of constructivism." *Educational Researcher, 25*(6), 19.

Voss, J. F., & Wiley, J. (1995). Acquiring intellectual skills. *Annual Review of Psychology, 46,* 155–181.

Vygotsky, L. S. (1978). *Mind in society.* M. Cole, V. John-Steiner, S. Scribner, & E. Souberman (Eds.). Cambridge, MA: Harvard University Press.

Wadsworth, B. (1996). *Piaget's theory of cognitive and affective development* (5th ed.). New York: Longman.

Walberg, H. (1988). Synthesis of research on time and learning. *Educational Leadership, 45*(6), 76–80.

Walker, H. M., Severson, H., Stiller, B., Williams, G., Haring, N., Shinn, M., & Todis, B. (1988). Systematic screening of pupils in the elementary range for behavior disorders: Development and trial testing of a multiple rating model. *Remedial and Special Education, 9*(3), 8–14.

Walker, J. E., & Shea, T. M. (1980). *Behavior modification: A practical approach for educators* (2nd ed.). St. Louis: Mosby.

Walker, L. J. (1989). A longitudinal study of moral reasoning. *Child Development, 60,* 157–166.

Walker, L. J., DeVries, B., & Trevethan, S. D. (1987). Moral stages and moral orientations in real-life and hypothetical dilemmas. *Child Development, 58,* 842–858.

Wallace-Broscious, A., Serafica, F. C., & Osipow, S. H. (1994). Adolescent career development: Relationships to self-concept and identity status. *Journal of Research on Adolescence, 4*(1), 122–149.

Wallach, M. A., & Kogan, N. (1965). *Modes of thinking in young children: A study of the creativity-intelligence distinction.* New York: Holt, Rinehart and Winston.

Walter-Thomas, C. S. (1997). Co-teaching experiences: The benefits and problems that teachers and principals report over time. *Journal of Learning Disabilities, 30*(4), 395–407.

Wandersman, A. & Nation, M. (1998). Urban neighborhoods and mental health. Psychological contributions to understanding toxicity, resilience, and interventions. *American Psychologist, 53*(66), 647–656.

Wang, A. Y., & Thomas, M. H. (1995). Effect of keywords on long-term retention: Help or hindrance? *Journal of Educational Psychology, 87,* 468–475.

Wapner, S., & Demick, J. (Eds.). (1991). *Field dependence-independence: Cognitive style across the life span.* Hillsdale, NJ: Erlbaum.

Ward, S. L. & Overton W. F. (1990). Semantic familiarity, relevance and the development of deductive reasoning. *Developmental Psychology, 26,* 488–493.

Warger, C. L., & Pugach, M. C. (1996). Forming partnerships around curriculum. *Educational Leadership, 53*(5), 62–65.

Warrick, P. D., & Naglieri, J. A. (1993). Gender differences in planning, attention, simultaneous, and successive (PASS) cognitive processes. *Journal of Educational Psychology, 85*(4), 693–701.

Wasik, B. A. (in press). Teaching the alphabet to young children. *Young Children.*

Wasik, B. A. (in press). Volunteer tutoring programs: Do we know what works? *Phi Delta Kappan, 79*(4), 283–287.

Wasik, B. A., & Karweit, N. L. (1994). Off to a good start: Effects of birth-to-three interventions on early school success. In R. E. Slavin, N. L. Karweit, & B. A. Wasik (Eds.), *Preventing early school failure.* Boston: Allyn & Bacon.

Wasik, B. A., & Slavin, R. E. (1993). Preventing early reading failure with one-to-one tutoring: A review of five programs. *Reading Research Quarterly.*

Weade, R., & Evertson, C. M. (1988). The construction of lessons in effective and less effective classrooms. *Teaching and Teacher Education, 4,* 189–213.

Webb, N. M. (1992). Testing a theoretical model of student interaction and learning in small groups. In R. Hertz-Lazarowitz & N. Miller (Eds.), *Interaction in cooperative groups: The theoretical anatomy of group learning* (pp. 102–119). New York: Cambridge University Press.

Webb, N. M., & Farrivar, S. (1994). Promoting helping behavior in cooperative small groups in middle school mathematics. *American Educational Research Journal, 31*(2), 369–395.

Webb, N. M., & Palincsar, A. (1996). Group processes in the classroom. In D.C. Berliner & R. C. Calfee (Eds.), *Handbook of educational psychology* (pp. 841–876). New York: Macmillan.

Webb, N. M., Trooper, J. D., & Fall, R. (1995). Constructive activity and learning in collaborative small groups. *Journal of Educational Psychology, 87,* 406–423.

Webber, J., & Scheuermann, B. (1993). Managing behavior problems: Accentuate the positive . . . eliminate the negative! In K. M. Cauley, F. Linder, & J. H. McMillan (Eds.), *Annual editions: Educational psychology 93/94.* Guilford, CT: Dushkin.

Webber, J., Scheuermann, B., McCall, C., & Coleman, M. (1993). Research on self-monitoring as a behavior management technique in special education classrooms: A descriptive review. *Remedial and Special Education, 14*(2), 38–56.

Wechsler, D. (1955). *Wechsler Adult Intelligence Scale.* New York: Psychological Corporation.

Weikart, D. P. (1995). Early childhood education. In J. H. Block, S. T. Everson, & T. R. Guskey (Eds.), *School improvement programs that work* (pp. 289–312). New York: Scholastic.

Weiner, B. (1986). *An attributional theory of motivation and emotion.* New York: Springer.

Weiner, B. (1989). *Human motivation.* Hillsdale, NJ: Erlbaum.

Weiner, B. (1992). *Human motivation: Metaphors, theories, and research.* Newbury Park, CA: Sage.

Weiner, B. (1994). Integrating social and personal theories of achievement striving. *Review of Educational Research, 64,* 557–573.

Weinert, F. E., & Helmke, A. (1995). Interclassroom differences in instructional quality and interindividual differences in cognitive development. *Educational Psychologist, 30*(1), 15–20.

Weinstein, C., & Mignano, A. (1993). *Organizing the elementary school classroom: Lessons from research and practice.* New York: McGraw-Hill.

Weinstein, C., Ridley, D. S., Dahl, T., & Weber, E. S. (1988/1989). Helping students develop strategies for effective learning. *Educational Leadership, 46*(4), 17–19.

Weinstein, C. E., & McCombs, B. (Eds.). (1995). *Strategic learning: Skill, will, and self-regulation.* Hillsdale, NJ: Erlbaum.

Weinstein, R. S. (1996). High standards in a tracked system of schooling: For which students and with what educational supports? *Educational Researcher, 25*(8), 16–19.

Weinstein, R. S., Madison, S. M., & Kuklinski, M. R. (1995). Raising expectations in schooling: Obstacles and opportunities for change. *American Educational Research Journal, 32,* 121–159.

Wells, A. S. (1995). Reexamining social science research on school desegregation. *Teachers College Record, 96*(4), 681–690.

Wells, A. S., & Crain, R. L. (1994). Perpetuation theory and the long-term effects of school desegregation. *Review of Educational Research, 64*(4), 531–555.

Wells, A. S., Hirshberg, D., Lipton, M., & Oakes, J. (1995). Bounding the case within its context: A constructivist approach to studying detracking reform. *Educational Researcher, 24*(5), 18–24.

Wentzel, K. R. (1991). Relations between social competence and academic achievement in early adolescence. *Child Development, 62,* 1066–1078.

Wentzel, K. R. (1993). Does being good make the grade? Social behavior and academic competence in middle school. *Journal of Educational Psychology, 85*(2), 357–364.

Wentzel, K. R., & Asher, S. R. (1995). The academic lives of neglected, rejected, popular, and controversial children. *Child Development, 66,* 754–763.

Wentzel, K. R., & Erdley, C. A. (1993). Strategies for making friends: Relations to social behavior and peer acceptance in early adolescence. *Developmental Psychology, 29,* 819–826.

Wentzel, K. R., & Wigfield, A. (1998). Academic and social motivational influences on students' academic performance. *Educational Psychology Review, 10*(2), 155–175.

Wertsch, J. (1986, April). *Mind in context: A Vygotskian approach.* Paper presented at the annual meeting of the American Educational Research Association, San Francisco.

Wertsch, J. V. (1991). *Vygotsky and the social formation of mind.* Cambridge, MA: Harvard University Press.

West, J., Hausken, E. G., & Collins, M. (1993). *Profile of preschool children's child care and early education program participation.* Washington, DC: U.S. Department of Education.

Wheatley, G. H. (1991). Constructivist perspectives on science and mathematics learning. *Science Education, 75,* 9–21.

Wheelock, A. (1992). *Crossing the tracks: How "untracking" can save America's schools.* New York: New Press.

White, A. G., & Bailey, J. S. (1990). Reducing disruptive behaviors of elementary physical education students with sit and watch. *Journal of Applied Behavior Analysis, 3,* 353–359.

White, B. Y., & Frederiksen, J. R. (1998). Inquiry, modeling, and meta-cognition: Making science accessible to all students. *Cognition and Instruction, 16* (1) 3–118.

White, F. R. (1994). Brown revisited. *Phi Delta Kappan, 76*(1), 12–20.

White, K. J., & Kistner, J. (1992). The influence of teacher feedback on young children's peer preferences and perceptions. *Developmental Psychology, 28,* 933–940.

Whitehurst, G. J., et al. (1994). Outcomes of an emergent literacy intervention in Head Start. *Journal of Educational Psychology, 86,* 542–555.

Wiedmer, T. L. (1998). Digital portfolios: Capturing and demonstrating skills and levels of performance. *Phi Delta Kappan, 79*(8), 586–589.

Wielkiewicz, R. M. (1995). *Behavior management in the schools: Principles and procedures* (2nd ed.). Boston: Allyn & Bacon.

Wigfield, A., & Eccles, J. (1989). Test anxiety in elementary and secondary students. *Educational Psychologist, 24,* 159–183.

Wigfield, A., & Eccles, J. (1990). Test anxiety in the school setting. In M. Lewis & S. M. Miller (Eds.). *Handbook of developmental psychopathology* (pp. 237–250). New York: Plenum.

Wigfield, A., Eccles, J. S., & Pintrich, P. R. (1996). Development between the ages of 11 and 25. In D.C. Berliner & R. C. Calfee (Eds.), *Handbook of educational psychology.* New York: Macmillan.

Wigfield, A., Eccles, J. S., & Rodriguez, D. (1998). The development of children's motivation in school contexts. In P. D. Pearson & A. Iran-Nejad (Eds.), *Review of research in education* (pp. 73–118). Washington, DC: American Educational Research Association.

Wigfield, A., & Harold, R. (1992). Teacher beliefs and children's achievement self-perceptions: A developmental perspective. In D. Schunk & J. Meece (Eds.), *Student perceptions in the classroom* (pp. 95–121). Hillsdale, NJ: Erlbaum.

Wigfield, A. L. (1995, April). *Relationship of children's competence beliefs and achievement values to their performance and choice of different activities.* Paper presented at the annual meeting of the American Educational Research Association, San Francisco.

Wiggins, G. (1989). Teaching to the (authentic) test. *Educational Leadership 46*(7), 41–47.

Wiggins, G. (1991). A response to Cizek. *Phi Delta Kappan, 72*(9), 700–703.

Wiggins, G. (1993a). Creating tests worth taking. In K. M. Cauley, F. Linder, & J. H. McMillan (Eds.), *Annual Editions: Educational Psychology 93/94.* Guilford, CT: Dushkin.

Wiggins, G. (1993b). Assessment: Authenticity, context, and validity. *Phi Delta Kappan, 75*(3), 200–214.

Wiggins, G. (1993c). *Assessing student performance: Exploring the purpose and limits of testing.* San Francisco: Jossey-Bass.

Wiggins, G. (1994). Toward better report cards. *Educational Leadership, 52*(2), 28–37.

Wiggins, G. (1996). Practicing what we preach in designing authentic assessments. *Educational Leadership, 54*(4), 18–25.

Wiggins, G. (1998). *Educative assessment: Designing assessments to inform and improve student performance.* San Francisco: Jossey-Bass.

Wilcox, R. T. (1993). Rediscovering discovery learning. In K. M. Cauley, F. Linder, & J. H. McMillan (Eds.), *Annual Editions: Educational Psychology 93/94.* Guilford, CT: Dushkin.

Wilkerson, R. M., & White, K. P. (1988). Effects of the 4Mat system of instruction on students' achievement, retention, and attitudes. *Elementary School Journal, 88,* 357–368.

Williams, J. E. (1995, April). *Use of learning and study skills among students differing in self-regulated learning efficacy.* Paper presented at the annual meeting of the American Educational Research Association, San Francisco.

Willig, A. C. (1985). A meta-analysis of selected studies on the effectiveness of bilingual education. *Review of Educational Research, 55,* 269–317.

Windle, M. (1994). A study of friendship characteristic problem behaviors among middle-aged adolescents. *Child Development, 65,* 1764–1777.

Winett, R. A., & Winkler, R. C., (1972). Current behavior modification in the classroom: Be still, be quiet, be docile. *Journal of Applied Behavior Analysis, 5,* 499–504.

Winfield, L. F. (1990). School competency testing reforms and student achievement: Exploring a national perspective. *Educational Evaluation and Policy Analysis, 12,* 157–173.

Winn, W. (1991). Learning from maps and diagrams. *Educational Psychology Review, 3,* 211–247.

Winne, P. H. (1995). Inherent details in self-regulated learning. *Educational Psychologist, 30,* 172–187.

Winne, P. H. (1997). Experimenting to bootstrap self-regulated learning. *Journal of Educational Psychology, 89*(3), 397–410.

Witkin, H. A., & Goodenough, D. R. (1981). *Cognitive styles: Essence and origins.* New York: International Universities Press.

Wittrock, M. C. (1991). Generative teaching of comprehension. *Elementary School Journal, 92,* 169–184.

Wittrock, M. C., & Alesandrini, K. (1990). Generation of summaries and analogies and analytic and holistic abilities. *American Educational Research Journal, 27,* 489–502.

Wodtke, K. H., Schommer, M. A., & Brunelli, P. (1989). How standardized is school testing? An exploratory observational study of standardized group testing in kindergarten. *Educational Evaluation and Policy Analysis, 11*(3), 223–235.

Wolf, D., Bixby, J., Glenn, J., & Gardner, H. (1991). To use their minds well: New forms of student assessment. *Review of Research in Education, 17,* 31–74.

Wolfgang, C. H. (1995). *Solving discipline problems: Methods and models for today's teachers* (3rd ed.). Boston: Allyn & Bacon.

Wong, H. D., Bernstein, L., & Shevick, E. (1978). *Life science* (2nd ed.). Englewood Cliffs, NJ: Prentice-Hall.

Wong, K. K., Sunderman, G. L., & Lee, J. (1995). *When federal Title I works to improve student learning in inner-city schools: Final report on the implementation of schoolwide projects in Minneapolis and Houston.* Chicago: University of Chicago Press.

Wong, L. Y.-S. (1995). Research on teaching: Process-product research findings and the feeling of obviousness. *Journal of Educational Psychology, 87,* 504–511.

Wong-Fillmore, L., & Valadez, C. (1986). Teaching bilingual learners. In M. C. Wittrock (Ed.), *Handbook of research on teaching* (3rd ed.). New York: Macmillan.

Wood, D. J., Bruner, J. S., & Ross, G. (1976). The role of tutoring in problem solving. *Journal of Child Psychology and Psychiatry, 17,* 89–100.

Woodring, T. (1995). *Effects of peer education programs on sexual behavior, AIDS knowledge, and attitudes.* Paper presented at the annual meeting of the Eastern Psychological Association, Boston.

Woodward, J. (1994). Effects of curriculum discourse style on eighth graders' recall and problem solving in earth science. *The Elementary School Journal, 94*(3), 299–314.

Woodward, J., Carnine, D., & Gersten, R. (1988). Teaching problem solving through computer simulations. *American Educational Research Journal, 25*, 72–86.

Woodward, J., & Gersten, R. (1992). Innovative technology for secondary students with learning disabilities. *Exceptional Children, 58*, 407–421.

Woolfolk, A. E., & Brooks, D. M. (1985). Beyond words: The influence of teachers' nonverbal behaviors on students' perceptions and performances. *Elementary School Journal, 85*, 513–528.

Workman, E. A., & Katz, A. M. (1995). *Teaching behavioral self-control to students.* Austin, TX: Pro-Ed.

Worthen, B. R., & Spandel, V. (1993). Putting the standardized test debate in perspective. In K. M. Cauley, F. Linder, & J. H. McMillan (Eds.), *Annual Editions: Educational Psychology 93/94.* Guilford, CT: Dushkin.

Wright, S. C., & Taylor, D. M. (1995). Identity and the language of the classroom: Investigating the impact of heritage versus second language instruction on personal and collective self-esteem. *Journal of Educational Psychology, 87*(2), 241–252.

Wyckoff, W. L. (1973). The effect of stimulus variation on learning from lecture. *Journal of Experimental Education, 41*, 85–90.

Zahorik, J. A. (1996). Elementary and secondary teachers' reports of how they make learning interesting. *Elementary School Journal, 96*, 551–564.

Zeidner, M. (1995). Adaptive coping with test situations: A review of the literature. *Educational Psychologist, 30*(3), 123–133.

Zellermayer, M., Salomon, G., Globerson, T., & Givon, H. (1991). Enhancing writing-related metacognitions through a computerized writing partner. *American Educational Research Journal, 28*, 373–391.

Zigmond, N., Jenkins, J., Fuchs, D., Deno, S., & Fuchs, L. S. (1995). When students fail to achieve satisfactorily. *Phi Delta Kappan, 77*(4), 303–306.

Zimmerman, B. J. (1995). Self-regulation involves more than metacognition: A social cognitive perspective. *Educational Psychologist, 30*, 217–221.

Zimmerman, B. J. (1998, April). *Achieving academic excellence: The role of perceived efficacy and self-regulatory skill.* Paper presented at the annual meeting of the American Educational Research Association, San Diego.

Zimmerman, B. J., & Bandura, A. (1994). Impact of self-regulatory influences on writing course attainment. *American Educational Research Journal, 31*, 845–862.

Zimmerman, B. J., Bandura, A., & Martinez-Pons, M. (1992). Motivation for academic attainment: The role of self-efficacy beliefs and personal goal setting. *American Educational Research Journal, 29*, 663–676.

Zimmerman, B. J., & Schunk, D. H. (Eds.). (1989). *Self-regulated learning and academic achievement: Theory, research and practice.* New York: Springer.

Ziv, A. (1988). Teaching and learning with humor: Experiment and replication. *Journal of Experimental Education, 57*, 5–18.

Zohar, D. (1998). An additive model of test anxiety: Role of exam specific expectations. *Journal of Educational Psychology, 10*(2), 330–340.

Zook, K. B. (1991). Effects of analogical processes on learning and misrepresentation. *Educational Psychology Review, 3*, 41–72.

NAME INDEX

Note: Page numbers followed by *f* indicate figures; those followed by *t* indicate tables.

Abbott, R. D., 376
Abernathy, T. V., 441
Ablard, K. E., 126
Abrami, P. C., 228
Achenbach, T. M., 423
Achilles, C. M., 112
Adams, A., 206
Adams, G. L., 235
Adams, J. L., 278
Adams, M. J., 73, 133, 191, 281
Adelgais, A., 304–305
Adelman, H. F., 345
Adelman, N. E., 366, 367
Adkins, D., 75
Afflerbach, P. P., 317, 523
Agard, J. A., 430
Airasian, P. W., 268
Alarcon, R., 120
Alba, R. D., 113
Alberto, P. A., 149
Alderman, M. K., 340
Aleman, S. R., 417
Alesandrini, K., 205
Alexander, K. L., 109, 112
Alexander, P. A., 166, 202, 203, 262,
    268, 328
Alfassi, M., 265
Alleman-Brooks, J., 232, 349
Allen, J., 443
Allington, R. L., 317, 442, 448, 502
Allison, D. B., 20
Alper, S., 167
Alter, M., 397
Alvermann, D. E., 208
Ambrose, R., 484–485
Ames, C., 335, 337, 338, 338*t*, 357
Ames, R., 335
Amour, R., 82
Anderman, E. M., 337, 338, 399*t*
Anderson, C., 273
Anderson, J., 527
Anderson, J. R., 175, 177, 181, 182, 187,
    190, 197, 200, 206, 232
Anderson, L. M., 10, 32, 204, 231, 232,
    235, 349, 371, 372, 374, 375
Anderson, L. W., 318, 462
Anderson, R. B., 185
Anderson, R. C., 189, 208
Anderson, T. H., 204, 205
Anderson, V., 205
Andre, T., 189
Andrich, D., 90

Anglin, J. N., 71
Anthony, H. M., 204
Araki, C., 399
Archambault, F. X., 318
Archer, J., 338, 338*t*
Archibald, D., 489
Argys, L. M., 296
Arias, M. B., 119
Armbruster, B. B., 204, 205
Armstead, P., 59
Armstrong, T., 130, 417
Arnold, K. D., 57
Aron, I. E., 57
Aronson, E. A., 99, 271
Arter, J. A., 484, 486
Artiles, A. J., 408
Aschbacher, P. R., 469
Asher, S. R., 77, 89, 95, 96
Atash, N., 502
Athanases, S. Z., 487
Atkinson, J. W., 335, 336, 337, 340, 352,
    470
Atkinson, L. A., 196
Atkinson, M. I., 314
Atkinson, R. C., 175, 184, 196
Atkinson, R. K., 196
Atwater, E., 91, 97
Aubey, L. W., 234
August, D., 16, 75, 120, 227
Aussiker, A., 396
Austin, J. R., 332
Ausubel, D. P., 199, 208
Ayaduray, J., 209
Aycock, D. W., 96

Babad, E., 342
Bacon, E. H., 379
Baddeley, A. D., 178, 186
Bahr, M. W., 448
Bahrick, H. P., 183–184
Bailey, J. S., 151, 152*f*, 392
Bailey, S. M., 126, 127
Baillargeon, R., 40, 41
Bain, H. P., 112
Bainer, D. L., 268
Baines, C., 443
Baines, L., 443
Baker, E. L., 486, 489, 502, 521
Baker, E. T., 443
Baker, J., 441
Baker, S. K., 120
Ball, E. W., 73

Ball, M., 488
Bandalos, D. L., 343
Bandura, A., 163–166, 167, 260, 328,
    329, 333, 334, 335
Bangert, R. L., 503
Bangert-Drowns, R. L., 234, 301, 311,
    314, 466
Banjafield, J. G., 278
Banks, C. A. M., 123
Banks, J. A., 107*f,* 116, 117, 118, 122,
    123, 123*f*
Baranowski, S., 424
Barber, J. G., 332
Barber, R. M., 398
Barbour, N. E., 484–485
Barker, G., 335
Barkley, R. A., 424
Barnes, H. V., 80, 319
Barnett, W. S., 41, 80
Baron, R. A., 327, 343
Barr, R. D., 228, 316
Barrish, H. H., 20, 21*f,* 395
Barth, R., 392, 393, 466
Baruth, L. G., 123, 316
Bates, J. A., 151
Battisch, V., 86
Battista, M. T., 267
Battle, D., 421
Baumeister, R. F., 93
Baumert, J., 337
Bauwens, J., 448
Baxter, G. P., 489, 490*f*
Baxter, S., 126
Beady, L. L., 355
Beamer, J. E., 334
Beane, J., 87
Bear, G. G., 60, 415
Beaudrey, J. S., 135
Beck, I. L., 204
Becker, H. J., 313, 314, 316, 503
Becker, W., 231
Behrman, R. E., 79, 80, 110
Bellanca, J., 281, 298
Benbow, C. P., 298, 428
Bennett, S., 204
Bennion, K., 503
Benson, P., 100
Bentz, J., 304
Bereiter, C., 187, 204, 268, 313
Berends, M., 296
Berg, C. A., 219
Berk, L. E., 29, 41, 45, 91*f,* 262*f*

Berko, J., 71
Berliner, D. C., 7, 327, 374, 463
Berlyne, D. E., 348
Berndt, T. J., 95
Bernstein, L., 460t
Berrueta-Clement, J. B., 41, 80, 318, 445
Beyer, B. K., 279, 280, 284
Bhana, K., 280, 281
Bhattacharyya, M., 131
Bibbs, J., 196
Bickel, W., 319, 443, 448
Biddle, B. J., 230
Biemiller, A., 294
Biklen, D., 424
Biklen, S. K., 23
Binder, A., 397
Birch, D., 352, 470
Bishop, J., 502
Bivens, J. A., 45
Bixby, J., 469
Blachman, B. A., 73
Black, J. K., 40
Black, M. M., 110
Black, R. S., 73
Blackadar, A. R., 375
Blake, G., 203
Blaney, N., 271
Blasi, A., 60
Block, C. C., 485f
Block, J. H., 16
Block, K. K., 204
Block, M. N., 438
Bloom, B. S., 192, 301, 462, 474, 475t
Bloome, D., 373
Blume, G. W., 313
Blumenfeld, P. C., 273, 274, 335, 338
Blyth, D. A., 95
Boden, M. A., 40
Bodine, R. J., 57
Boekaerts, M., 166, 261
Bogdan, R. C., 23
Boone, R., 447
Borg, M., 86
Borman, C., 428
Borman, G. D., 318–319
Bornholt, L. J., 126
Bornstein, P. H., 166
Bos, C. S., 444
Botnick, R., 312
Boutte, G. S., 118
Bower, G. H., 143, 184, 200, 210, 212f
Bowker, A., 89
Bowman, B., 81
Boykin, A. W., 107, 110, 115, 116, 122, 316
Boyle, R. A., 337
Bracken, B. A., 88
Braddock, J. H., 116, 118, 296, 298, 299, 467
Bradley, R. H., 413
Bradsher, M., 313
Bransford, J. D., 43, 185, 186, 200, 205, 209, 240t, 256, 276
Brehm, J. W., 336
Brennan, R. T., 491

Brenneman, K., 42
Brett, A., 309
Bretzing, B. B., 204–205
Brewer, D. J., 296
Brewer, J., 83
Brewer, W. F., 32
Bridge, C. A., 489
Briggs, L., 220
Britt, C. L., 310
Broden, M., 164
Brooker, G. M., 228, 379–380
Brooks, B. D., 398
Brooks, D. M., 374, 377, 380–381
Brooks, J. G., 256, 259
Brooks, L. W., 272
Brooks, M. G., 256, 259
Brophy, J. E., 219, 231, 232, 233, 349, 353, 354, 371, 372, 375, 383
Brown, A. L., 46, 205, 264, 265
Brown, B. B., 96
Brown, D. S., 459, 464
Brown, G. D. A., 415
Brown, J. S., 256
Brownlee-Conyers, J., 313
Brubaker, N. L., 232, 349
Brunelli, P., 521
Bruner, J. S., 45, 47, 260
Bruning, R. H., 334
Bryant, D. M., 81
Bryk, A. S., 19, 306
Buhrmester, D., 95
Bukowski, W. M., 89
Burbach, H. J., 377
Burgdorf, K., 502
Burke, C. L., 76
Burke, E. M., 72
Burkhart, J. F., 57
Burnette, J., 443
Burns, M. S., 200
Burns, R. B., 299, 372
Burris, N. A., 73
Bursuck, W. D., 424, 436f, 466, 468, 523
Burtis, P. J., 204
Burton, F., 523, 524, 530
Burts, D. C., 85
Bussey, K., 58
Butera, G., 441
Butler, D. L., 165, 203
Butterworth, T., 353
Byrne, B., 73
Byrnes, J. P., 39, 41, 180, 181, 183

Cairns, J. P., 378
Calderón, M., 121
Calhoun, G., 442, 442f
Cameron, J., 19, 149, 345
Campbell, B., 130, 131, 484f
Campbell, F. A., 81, 132, 319, 413
Campbell, J. R., 108, 108t, 114t
Campbell, L., 130, 131, 484f
Campione, J. C., 205
Canady, R. L., 524
Canfield, J., 87
Cannell, J. J., 510
Canter, L., 385, 395, 396

Canter, M., 385, 395
Cantor, J., 180
Cantrell, S. C., 489
Capie, W., 231
Capron, C., 131
Cardelle-Elawar, M., 204
Cardellichio, T., 132
Carey, D. A., 203, 267
Carlsen, W., 230
Carney, R. N., 196
Carnine, D., 203, 206, 231, 235, 310, 445
Carpenter, T. P., 125, 203, 267, 268
Carranza, I., 120
Carroll, J. B., 12, 115, 291, 301
Carter, C. J., 265
Carter, K., 374, 375
Carter, L. F., 318
Carter, R. T., 113
Carter, T. P., 75
Carver, S. M., 312, 501
Cary, S., 275
Case, R., 41, 42, 441
Casey, J. P., 445
Castine, W. H., 311
Casto, G., 413
Catalano, R. F., 376
Cavanaugh, R. A., 116, 408, 415
Ceci, S. J., 132, 507
Chan, C. K. K., 204
Chance, P., 329, 345
Chaney, B., 502
Chansky, N. M., 465, 530
Chao, C. I., 210
Chapman, S., 212, 231
Charles, C. M., 372
Chase-Lansdale, P. L., 97
Chatfield, M. L., 75
Chavajay, P., 42
Cheng, L. R., 421
Cheng, M., 117
Cheong, Y. F., 296
Cheung, K. C., 486
Chiang, C. P., 267
Chin, C. W. T., 204
Chinn, C. A., 32
Chobot, R., 400
Chomsky, C., 72
Christian, D., 120
Christie, J. F., 77
Christof, K. J., 424
Christoplos, F., 429
Cipani, E. C., 147
Cizek, G. J., 489
Clark, C. M., 227, 231, 455, 464
Clark, E. E., 109
Clark, F., 443
Clark, J. M., 185, 205
Clark, M. C., 210, 212f
Clark, R., 164
Clark, R. E., 314
Clawson, K., 230
Clements, A. C., 187
Clements, B. S., 220, 376
Clements, D. H., 267

Clifford, M. M., 336, 351
Clifford, R. M., 81
Cline, Z., 119
Clough, M., 219
Cobb, N. D., 44, 91
Cobb, P., 268
Cochran-Smith, M., 311, 315
Coggins, K. A., 209
Cohen, E. G., 87, 118, 268, 273, 274, 298
Cohen, G., 183
Cohen, N. E., 79
Cohen, R. L., 194
Cohen, S. A., 444, 503
Coie, J. D., 77, 89
Coladarci, T., 528
Colby, C., 54
Coldiron, J. R., 296, 299, 467
Cole, D. A., 86
Coleman, J., 357, 511f
Coleman, M., 166
Coley, R. L., 97
Colley, K., 443
Collier, V. P., 120
Collins, A. M., 256, 257
Collins, M., 79
Colson, S., 428
Colvin, C., 334
Comer, J. P., 112, 319
Commons, M. L., 39
Compton-Hall, M., 489
Connell, T., 312, 501
Conway, E. J., 308
Conway, M. A., 183
Cooley, W. W., 303, 461, 465
Cooney, G. H., 126
Cooney, J. B., 7
Cooper, H. M., 109, 234, 343, 424
Copeland, W. D., 375
Corbin, J., 23
Cordova, D. I., 346
Corkill, A. J., 208
Corno, L., 166, 167, 208, 234, 261, 292, 298, 354
Cortés, C. E., 122
Costa, A. L., 483
Costenbader, V., 151
Coughlin, R. M., 73
Coulter, D., 412t
Cowan, N., 175
Cox, D., 370
Craik, F. I. M., 180t, 181, 184
Crain, R. L., 117
Crain, W. C., 32
Craven, R. G., 86
Crawford, J., 235, 319
Crévola, C. A., 321
Crockenberg, S., 85
Crocker, R. K., 228, 379–380
Crooks, T. J., 156, 212, 467, 468, 470
Cross, D., 204
Cross, G. M., 466
Cross, L. H., 466
Cross, W. E., 115
Crowley, M., 57

Cullinan, D., 421
Cummins, J., 121
Cushing, K. S., 7, 374
Cusick, P. A., 298
Czikszentmihalyi, M., 95

D'Agostino, J. V., 318–319
Dahl, T., 209
Damon, W., 40, 87, 95
Daniels, H., 43, 47
Dannelly, C. M., 209
Dansereau, D. F., 268, 272
Danziger, S. H., 108
Darder, A., 119–120
Darling-Hammond, L., 12, 110, 115
Das, J. P., 43
David, Y. M., 273
Davidson, A. L., 93
Davidson, J. A., 332
Davis, G. V., 304
Davis, T. B., 233
Dawkins, M. P., 118, 298
Dawson, G. C., 82
Day, L. E., 376
De Bettencourt, L., 444
Debus, R., 86
Deci, E. L., 345, 346
Decotis, J. D., 299
De Fabo, L., 205
DeFord, D. E., 19, 112, 306, 320
Deibert, E., 486
Delaney, H., 196
Delclos, V. R., 200
De Lisi, R., 41, 125, 199
Delpit, L., 116
Delprato, D. J., 145
Delucchi, K. L., 86
Demick, J., 134
Dempster, F. N., 192, 233, 234, 352, 465, 474
Dennis, I., 411
Deno, S., 443
de Ribaupierre, A., 32
Derry, S. J., 276, 281
Deshler, D. D., 416, 444
Detterman, D. K., 128, 505
DeVos, J., 40
DeVries, B., 59
DeVries, R., 32, 42
DeWolf, D. M., 85
Deyhle, D., 113
Dialdin, D. A., 149, 345
Dianda, M., 121
Dickinson, D., 130, 131, 484f
Diener, C. I., 340
DiGangi, S. A., 167
Dimino, J., 203
DiPasquale-Morello, L. J., 6
Doane, K., 342
Dodge, K. A., 89
Dolan, L. J., 320, 395
Donahue, P. L., 108, 108t
Donaldson, M., 40
Donley, J., 203
Dooling, D. J., 207

Dornbusch, S. M., 298, 467, 468
Dorr-Bremme, D. W., 472
Dossey, J., 108
Doueck, H. J., 398
Dowdy, C. A., 433
Downing, J., 73
Downs, W. R., 97
Doyle, W., 13, 374, 375, 377, 380
Drabman, R. S., 167
Drake, M., 149, 345, 346
Dreeben, R., 228
Drew, C. J., 413, 421, 447f, 449f
Driscoll, M. P., 187, 238
Dryfoos, J. G., 96, 99
Dudley, B., 399
Duffin, J. R., 349
Duffy, G. G., 232, 268, 349
Duguid, P., 256
Dukes, R., 348
Dumaret, A., 131
Duncan, C., 397
Duncker, K., 278
Dunkin, M. J., 230
Dunlap, A., 164
Dunlop, V., 489
Dunn, K., 134
Dunn, L. M., 429
Dunn, R., 134, 135
DuPaul, G. J., 424
Durán, R. P., 121
Durso, F. T., 209
Dutcher, P., 484
Dutka, S., 226
Duyme, M., 131
Dweck, C., 340
Dweck, C. S., 337, 340
Dyson, A. H., 76

Eads II, G. M., 81
Eagley, A. H., 57
Ebel, R. L., 476, 504, 521
Ebmeier, H., 15
Eccles, J. S., 90, 337, 342, 343
Eden, G. E., 191
Edison, T., 293
Edwards, L., 58
Edwards, W., 335
Egan, K., 195
Egan, M. W., 413, 447f
Egeland, P., 489
Ehly, S., 304
Ehri, L., 73
Eisenberg, N., 77, 126
Eisenberg, R., 86
Eisenberger, R., 345
Eisner, E. W., 76
Elashoff, J. D., 342
Elkind, D., 29, 41, 68, 81
Elliott, R., 442, 442f
Ellis, A. K., 16, 303
Ellis, E. S., 416
Ellis, J. A., 183, 184
Ellsworth, L. S., 208
Ellwein, M. C., 81, 521
Emler, N. P., 54, 55

Emmer, E. T., 220, 232, 372, 374, 376, 396
Engle, R. W., 180
Englehart, M. B., 462
Englemann, S., 235
Englert, C. S., 204, 408
Ensminger, M. E., 317
Entwisle, D. R., 109, 112
Epps, E., 109
Epstein, A. S., 41, 80
Epstein, H. T., 29
Epstein, M. H., 421
Erdley, C. A., 95
Ericcson, K. A., 175, 177, 180
Erickson, D. K., 427–428
Erickson, F., 106
Erickson, J., 312, 501
Erickson, R. L., 420
Erikson, E. H., 48–51, 49f, 52–54, 53t, 85
Ethington, C. A., 335
Euclid, 343–344
Eurich-Fulcer, R., 310
Evangelou, D., 83
Evans, T. D., 353
Everson, H., 343
Everson, S. T., 16
Evertson, C., 374, 375
Evertson, C. M., 220, 222, 231, 232, 233, 235, 366, 369, 370, 371, 372, 374, 375, 376, 377, 380

Fabes, K. A., 126
Fachin, K., 418
Fagan, E. R., 231
Fairman, J., 489
Fajen, B. R., 204
Fall, R., 274
Faltis, C. J., 119, 120
Fantuzzo, J. W., 268, 274, 304, 448
Fardy, Robert W., 275
Farlow, L., 441
Farnish, A. M., 203
Farrivar, S., 274
Fashola, O. S., 16, 97, 121, 319
Feather, N., 335–336
Fehrmann, P. G., 234
Feingold, A., 125, 126
Feldhusen, J. F., 428
Feldman, R. S., 202f
Fennema, E., 125, 126, 203, 267, 268
Fennessey, G. M., 355
Fenson, L., 72
Ferguson, T. J., 58
Fernandez, R., 317, 318
Fernstrom, P., 448
Ferrara, R. A., 205
Ferroggiaro, M., 108
Ferron, J., 338
Feuer, M. J., 489
Feuerstein, R., 133, 280, 281f
Field, C. J., 507
Field, W., 132
Fielding, L. G., 208
Fielding-Barnsley, R., 73

Filipczak, J., 398
Fincham, F. D., 340
Finn, J. D., 112, 370, 378
Fiordaliso, R., 398
Firestone, W. A., 489
Fisher, C. W., 232
Fisher, R. P., 474
Fisk, C., 489
Fiske, E. B., 510
Fitzpatrick, A. R., 528
Flaherty, J., 121
Flanagan, C., 126
Flannery, D. J., 423
Flavell, J. H., 30, 36, 42, 91, 182, 203
Fleming, J., 424
Fletcher, J. D., 307
Fletcher, J. M., 415
Fletcher-Flinn, C. M., 315
Floden, R. E., 10
Foertsch, M., 108
Fogarty, R., 299
Folger, R., 345
Foos, P. W., 231, 474
Ford, D. Y., 427
Fordham, S., 115
Forman, E., 46
Forness, S. R., 412
Forsyth, D. R., 332
Forsyth, G. A., 68
Forsyth, P. D., 68
Foster, E. M., 98
Fosterling, F., 341
Fouts, J. T., 16, 303
Fox, L., 127
Fox, N. A., 181, 183
Francis, D. J., 415
Franke, M. L., 125, 203, 267
Frankenberger, W., 414
Franklin, R. D., 20
Franklyn-Stokes, A., 59
Franks, J. J., 185, 200
Frazier, M. K., 313
Frederiksen, J. R., 268
Frederiksen, N., 279, 473
Freeman, J. M., 427
Freiberg, H. J., 272, 375, 376, 377
French, D. C., 415
French, E. G., 337
Frensch, P. A., 116
Freppon, P. A., 73
Freud, S., 48
Friedman, L., 125, 126
Friedman, R. M., 398
Friend, M., 424, 436f, 448
Frisbie, D. A., 476, 504, 521, 524
Fritz, J. B., 185
Froman, R. D., 36
Fronzaglio, K., 414
Fuchs, D., 226, 272, 304, 433, 441, 443, 448, 473
Fuchs, L. S., 226, 235, 272, 304, 338, 433, 441, 443, 448, 473
Fuchs, P., 235, 304
Fuerst, J. S., 80
Fulton, K., 489

Furman, W., 95
Furst, E. J., 462
Furstenberg, F. F., 98
Fuson, K. C., 267
Futrell, M. K., 309, 310

Gabbard, L., 230
Gaddy, M. L., 205
Gadow, K. D., 424
Gage, N. L., 12, 16, 233, 235, 236, 327, 463
Gagné, R., 220, 458
Gale, J., 256
Gall, M. D., 230, 231, 242
Gallagher, A. M., 125
Gallagher, J. J., 427, 428
Gallagher, M., 317
Gallagher, P., 443
Gallimore, R., 46
Gallini, J. K., 212, 227, 276
Galtelli, B., 439
Gamoran, A., 296, 342
Garbarino, J., 112
Garber, H. L., 81, 132, 320, 413, 445
Garcia, E. E., 74, 75, 117, 119, 120
García, G. E., 120, 523
Garcia, J., 119
Garcia, R., 198
Gardner, H., 129t, 129–131, 130, 257, 469
Gardner, M. K., 458
Garibaldi, A., 400
Garner, R., 203
Garnier, H. E., 97
Gartner, A., 440
Garvey, C., 72, 76, 78
Garvin, R. A., 45
Gay, G., 115, 117
Gearhart, M., 485
Geisert, P. G., 309, 310
Gelman, R., 40, 41, 42
Gelzheiser, L., 317
Gendler, T., 12
Gentile, C., 108
George, P., 298
Gerber, M. M., 429, 433
Gergen, K., 272
Gersten, R. M., 120, 203, 206, 235, 310, 447
Giaconia, R. M., 299
Giangreco, M. F., 441
Gibbons, A. S., 349
Gibbs, J. C., 57
Gijselaers, W. H., 366
Gillespie, G., 204
Gilligan, C., 57
Ginsburg, A. L., 98
Ginsburg, H. P., 30, 84
Ginsburg, M. D., 304
Givon, H., 204
Glaser, R., 500
Glazer, S. M., 72
Glenn, J., 469
Globerson, T., 204, 315
Glover, J. A., 233

Godden, D., 186
Goetz, E. T., 185
Goetz, L., 443
Golan, S., 328
Gold, R. M., 355
Goldenberg, C., 121
Goleman, D., 100
Gomez, M. L., 438
Gong, J., 298
Good, T. L., 15, 219, 220, 228, 231, 232, 233, 235, 300, 342, 371, 383
Goodenough, D. R., 134
Goodlad, J. I., 296, 297
Goodman, G., 417
Goodman, K. S., 73
Goodman, Y. M., 73
Goodnow, J. J., 77, 126
Goodrich, H., 291
Goodwin, A. L., 113
Gordon, B. M., 122
Gordon, E. W., 116, 131
Gordon, I., 88
Gorman, B. S., 20
Gorney, B. E., 502
Gotlib, L. J., 525
Gottard, A., 415
Gottfredson, D. C., 376
Gottfredson, G. D., 376
Gottfried, A. E., 344
Gottlieb, B. W., 397
Gottlieb, J., 397, 430
Gourgey, A., 343
Graber, M., 40
Graham, D. J., 187
Graham, L., 208
Graham, S., 116, 268, 328, 331, 335, 349
Grant, C. A., 118
Gravatt, B., 315
Grave, M. E., 438
Gravois, T. A., 433, 438
Grayson, N., 268
Green, J., 235
Greenblat, C. S., 348
Greenbowe, T., 41
Greene, B. A., 337
Greene, D., 18, 345
Greene, R. L., 190
Greenfield, P. M., 47
Greenlaw, M., 127
Greeno, J. G., 257
Greenwald, R., 110
Gregory, J. F., 391
Greiner, C., 44
Gresham, F. M., 415, 449
Griffin, B. W., 502
Griffiths, A. K., 40
Grogan, M. M., 445
Gronlund, N. E., 470t
Grosen, B., 235
Grossman, H., 107, 117, 118, 125, 127
Grossman, S. H., 125, 127
Grounlund, N. E., 456, 459, 462, 473, 474, 476
Grouws, D., 15, 232, 235
Gruppen, L., 384

Grusec, J. E., 77
Guilford, J. P., 129
Guiton, G., 296, 298
Gump, P. V., 373
Guskey, T. R., 16, 301, 303, 526
Gustafsson, J. E., 129
Guthrie, J. T., 204
Gutierrez, H., 119–120
Gutiérrez, R., 83, 299
Gutkin, J., 235

Haertel, E., 472
Hagan, L., 313
Hagin, R. A., 316, 445
Hakuta, K., 16, 75, 120, 121, 227
Haladyna, T. M., 476, 481
Hall, C., 443
Hall, G. S., 99
Hall, J. W., 196
Hall, L. K., 183–184
Hall, R. H., 212
Hall, R. V., 164
Hallahan, D. P., 167, 408, 425, 435
Halle, T. G., 115
Halpern, D. F., 126, 209, 283
Halpin, G., 135
Hamaker, C., 212
Hambleton, R. K., 484, 489
Hamburg, D. A., 318
Hamilton, R. J., 212, 456
Hamlett, C. L., 226, 304, 473
Hand, B., 268
Haney, W., 523
Hansen, C., 209
Hansford, S. J., 484–485
Hanson, L. A., 443
Hanson, M. K., 399
Hanson, S. L., 98
Hardin, D. E., 434
Hardman, J. L., 421, 425, 449f
Hardman, M. L., 413, 447f
Hargreaves, A., 16
Haring, N. G., 162
Harold, R., 342
Harp, S. F., 328
Harper, G. F., 268
Harpring, S. A., 318
Harris, A. H., 366, 370, 380
Harris, K. R., 19, 166, 180, 203, 268, 438
Harry, B., 415
Harshorne, H., 59
Harste, J. C., 76
Hart, B., 72
Hart, C. H., 78, 85
Hart, D., 95
Harter, S., 86, 95
Hartman, G. C., 193
Hartman, H., 343
Hartman, J. A., 83
Hartup, W. W., 88
Haslam, M. B., 366, 367
Haslinger, J., 398
Hassler, D. M., 231
Hastings, J. T., 474, 475t

Hatano, G., 180, 202
Hatch, T., 129, 129t, 130
Hattie, J., 16, 196, 203
Hatzichriston, C., 89
Hausken, E. G., 79
Hawkins, J. D., 376, 398
Haywood, H. C., 47
Hedges, L. V., 110, 126, 299, 318–319
Hein, K., 99
Heller, L. R., 274, 304, 448
Helmke, A., 235
Hembree, R., 468
Hendry, G. D., 187
Henry, M., 232
Henry, S. L., 115, 116
Henson, K. T., 230
Herbert, E. A., 484, 485, 528
Herman, J. L., 469, 472, 484, 485, 486
Hernandez, H., 123
Herrnstein, R. J., 131
Herron, J. D., 41
Hersen, M., 424
Hersh, R. H., 57
Hertz-Lazarowitz, R., 121
Hess, D., 75
Heward, W. L., 116, 408, 415
Hewer, A., 57
Heyns, B., 109
Hickey, D. T., 256
Hidi, S., 205, 344
Hiebert, E. H., 300, 320
Hiebert, J., 212, 227, 267
Higgins, E. T., 86
Higgins, K., 447
Hilgard, E. R., 143
Hill, D., 379
Hill, J. R., 477
Hill, K., 343, 468, 503
Hill, P. W., 321
Hill, W. H., 462
Hilliard, A. G., 122, 133, 411
Hillocks, G., 15, 20
Hirsch, B. J., 96
Hirshberg, D., 298
Hodge, J. P., 235, 304
Hodges, W. L., 80, 81
Hodgin, J., 134
Hoek, D., 274
Hoerr, T., 130
Hoffer, T., 298
Hoffman, M. L., 60–61, 77, 85
Hoffman, S. D., 98
Hogaboam-Gray, A., 354
Hogan, R., 54, 55
Hoge, R. D., 428, 528
Hogue, E., 488
Hohmann, C., 76
Hokada, A., 340
Hom, Jr., H. L., 345
Honig, W., 73
Hoole, F., 226
Hooper, F. E., 42
Hooper, S., 309
Hopf, D., 89
Hopkins, K. D., 474, 500, 501, 507, 521

Horgan, D. D., 127, 128
Horne, M. D., 415
Horvat, M., 417
Hoskins, G. S., 168
Hotchkiss, P. R., 524
Houle, S., 181
Hourcade, J. J., 448
Howard, E. R., 398
Howard-Rose, D., 260
Howes, C., 77, 78
Howley, A., 428
Huang, S., 375
Hubbard, L., 123, 298
Hu-Dehart, E., 118
Hudelson, S. J., 119, 120
Hughes, C. A., 423
Hughes, F. P., 77
Human, P., 267
Hunt, P., 443
Hunter, M., 219, 220, 231, 235, 335
Hybl, L. G., 376
Hyde, T. S., 185
Hyerle, D., 205
Hymel, S., 89

Inhelder, B., 35, 37, 38, 91
Iran-Nejad, A., 187
Iversen, I. H., 145

Jacobs, G. M., 209
Jacobs, J. K., 97
Jacobs, V. R., 125
Jacobson, L., 342
Jagacinski, C. M., 333
Jakupcak, A. J., 441
James, W., 200
Janzen, R., 118
Jay, E., 276, 281, 282t
Jenkins, J. J., 185
Jenkins, J. R., 304, 443
Jenkins, L. M., 304
Jensen, A. R., 131
Jenson, W., 151, 167
Jetton, T. L., 202, 328
Jimenez, R. T., 120
Johnson, D. W., 118, 242, 248, 268, 271,
    274, 357, 399
Johnson, J. E., 42
Johnson, R. T., 118, 242, 248, 268, 271,
    274, 357, 399
Johnson, V. G., 268
John-Steiner, V., 256
Johnston, P., 317, 318, 448
Johnston, P. H., 523
Jones, C. C., 317, 318
Jones, L., 108
Jones, L. S., 367, 368, 370, 380, 390f
Jones, M., 384
Jones, N., 320
Jones, R. L., 523
Jones, V. F., 367, 368, 370, 380, 390f
Joyce, B., 243
Juel, C., 73
Jussim, L., 342, 530
Juvonen, J., 332

Kagan, S. L., 79, 80, 110, 122, 268
Kagey, J. R., 398
Kahle, J., 343
Kail, R. V., 34f
Kalichman, S. C., 98
Kallison, J. M., 211, 226
Kane, M. B., 489, 509
Kane, S. R., 424
Kanfer, R., 167, 261, 354
Kantor, H., 116
Kaplan, A., 338
Kapur, S., 181
Karlin, M. B., 184
Karns, K., 226
Karp, S., 118
Karpov, Y. V., 43, 47, 256
Karweit, N. L., 81, 235, 294, 297, 300,
    318, 320, 366, 367, 367f, 511f
Kaskowitz, D., 230
Kasten, W. C., 299
Katayama, A. D., 205, 278
Katz, A. M., 166
Katz, L. G., 83, 85
Katzaroff, M., 226
Kauffman, J. M., 377, 397, 398, 408,
    423, 425, 435, 441
Kaufman, J. J., 430
Kaugman, L. R., 193
Kavale, K. A., 415
Keating, P., 127
Keating, T., 235
Keavney, M., 346
Keith, T. Z., 234
Kellam, S. G., 316
Kelly, P., 398
Kemple, J. J., 16
Kennedy, J. H., 89
Kennedy, M. M., 16
Keogh, B. K., 408
Khattri, N., 489
Kiewra, D. A., 222
Kiewra, K. A., 204, 205, 278
Killen, M., 57
Kinchla, R. A., 177
King, A., 204, 205, 230, 231, 272,
    304–305
King, F. J., 311
King, J. A., 274, 304, 448
King, N. J., 421
King, R. C., 187
King-Sears, P., 414
Kirst, M. W., 502
Kishor, N., 87
Kistner, J., 89
Klauer, K., 465
Klausmeier, H. J., 236
Klavas, A., 135
Klein, S. F., 127, 128
Klein, S. P., 491
Klein, S. S., 127
Klever, A., 415
Klinzing, H. G., 10
Knapp, M. S., 108, 109, 268, 319
Knight, B., 208
Knight, C. B., 135

Knowlton, B., 177
Kochanska, G., 85
Koegel, L. K., 424
Koegel, R. L., 424
Kogan, N., 134, 279
Kohlberg, L., 54–60, 55t, 57
Kohn, A., 87, 149, 346
Kolbe, L., 397
Köller, O., 337
Konig, A., 77
Koretz, D., 486
Kosonen, P., 241
Kostelnik, M. J., 83
Kounin, J., 370, 371, 373, 374, 375, 378,
    381
Kovaleski, J. F., 443
Kowalski, P., 96
Kozma, R., 228
Kozol, J., 23, 110, 115
Kozulin, A., 43, 133, 257
Kraber, B., 313
Krajcik, J., 273
Kramarski, B., 303
Krapp, A., 344
Krasavage, E. M., 375
Krashen, S., 75
Krathwohl, O. R., 462
Kraut, R. E., 87
Krechevsky, M., 130
Kreitzer, A. E., 462
Krinsky, R., 197
Krinsky, S. G., 197
Krishnakumar, A., 110
Krueger, W. C. F., 192
Krug, D., 233
Krumboltz, J. D., 527
Kucan, L., 204
Kucynski, L., 85
Kuhara-Kojima, K., 180, 202
Kuhn, D., 39
Kukie, M., 430
Kuklinski, M. R., 342
Kulhavy, R. W., 204–205, 350
Kulik, C. C., 466
Kulik, C. L., 151, 234, 301, 314,
    349–350, 351, 428, 468, 470, 503
Kulik, J. A., 151, 234, 301, 314,
    349–350, 351, 428, 466, 468, 470,
    503
Kulikowich, J. M., 202
Kupersmidt, J. B., 89
Kurtz-Coster, B., 115
Kusaka, S., 40
Kusayanagi, K., 308
Kutnick, P. J., 77

Lachman, R., 207
Ladd, G. W., 78, 89
Lahaderne, H., 21, 23f
Laine, R. D., 110
Laird, S., 127
Lam, T. C. M., 120
Lamb, M. E., 53f
Laminack, L. L., 72
Lampert, M., 257, 258f

Land, M. L., 227
Landes, S., 304
Landrum, T. J., 167
Langdon, H. W., 421
Larrivee, B., 231, 415, 433, 443
Larsen-Miller, L., 422
Larson, C. O., 272
Larson, R., 95
Latham, A. S., 115, 399, 445
Latham, G. P., 336
Laupa, M., 58
Lave, J., 239
Lazarowitz, R., 274
Leal, L., 205
Leary, M. R., 93
Leavey, M., 442
Lee, J., 319
Lee, L., 230
Lee, S. J., 116
Lehr, R., 355
Lehrer, R., 312, 501
Leinhardt, G., 256, 303, 319, 443, 448, 461, 465
Lenz, B. K., 416
LePore, P. C., 296
Lepper, M. R., 18, 19, 149, 345, 346, 348
Lerner, B., 87
Lerner, J., 415
Lerner, J. W., 445
Lesar, S., 441
Lesgold, A. M., 210, 212f, 279
Letts, N., 347
Lev, D. D., 313
Lev, D. J., 313
Leventhal, L., 228
Levi, L. W., 125
Levin, A. V., 425
Levin, B. B., 196
Levin, J. A., 313
Levin, J. R., 180, 196
Levin, M. E., 180
Levine, C., 57
Levine, D. U., 108
Levine, R. F., 108
Lewandowsky, S., 186
Lewin, K., 243
Lewis, M., 421, 423
Lewis, R. B., 445
Lewontin, R., 131
Liben, L. S., 91
Liberty, K. A., 162
Lickona, T., 56
Lindholm, K. J., 120
Linn, A. J., 473
Linn, R. L., 489, 491
Lipsky, D. K., 440
Lipson, M., 204
Lipton, M., 116, 298
Lishner, D. M., 398
Litman, C., 85
Littlefield, J., 209
Litwin, G. H., 340
Lloyd, J. W., 167, 433, 441
Locke, E., 336
Lockhart, R. S., 180t, 184

Lockheed, M. E., 127
Loeber, R., 423
Loef, M., 267
Lohman, D. E., 129
Lohman, D. F., 132, 133
Lohr, L., 296
Lolli, E. M., 299
Long, L., 125, 127
Lordeman, A., 398
Losey, K. M., 116, 122
Lotan, R. A., 118, 274
Lou, Y., 295, 300
Loveless, T., 294, 295
Lovett, S. B., 182
Lowe, R., 116
Lowry, R., 397
Luckasson, R., 126, 410, 411, 412, 412t, 412–413, 414, 426, 427
Luiten, A., 58
Lujan, R. E., 6
Lundberg, I., 334
Lyman, H. B., 509
Lyon, R. G., 416
Lyons, C. A., 19, 112, 306, 320, 416, 445
Lysynchuk, L. M., 265

Ma, X., 87
Maag, J. W., 167
Mabry, L., 454
McArdle, J. J., 411
MacArthur, C., 349
McCaleb, J., 227
McCall, C., 166
McCallum, R. S., 88
McCarthy, B., 134
McCarthy, C. J., 96
McCartney, K., 131
McCaslin, M., 300
McClellan, D. E., 85
McClelland, D. C., 337
McClelland, J. L., 186
McCloskey, G. N., 309
McCombs, B., 260
McCombs, B. L., 341
McConaughy, S. H., 423
McCormick, C. B., 118, 196
McCormick, L., 413
McCormick, S., 20
McDaniel, M. A., 208, 209
McDaniel, T. R., 379, 388, 389
McGill-Franzen, A., 317, 442, 502
McGivern, J. E., 196
McInerney, D. M., 204
McInerney, V., 204
McIntyre, E., 73
McIntyre, T., 117
MacIver, D. J., 87, 298
McKee, L., 422
MacKenzie, A. A., 184
McKenzie, G. R., 232
MacKenzie, R. J., 379
McKinney, J. D., 417
McLaughlin, B., 120, 121
MacLean, W. E., 411, 412
McLeskey, J., 441, 443

McLoyd, V. C., 80
MacMillan, D. L., 408, 412, 415, 429
McMurray, M. B., 424
McNelis, M., 296
McNelis, S. J., 434
McPartland, J. M., 296, 299, 467
McPhail, J., 46
Madaus, G. F., 462, 474, 475t, 523
Madden, N. A., 121, 203, 318, 320, 398, 442, 442f, 489
Maddox, H., 226
Madison, S. M., 342
Maehr, M. L., 337, 338, 339t, 346
Mager, R. F., 455, 457, 458f, 461, 464
Magnuson, D., 399
Maheady, L., 268
Mahn, H., 256
Mahoney, J. L., 115
Mahony, M., 443
Maier, N. R., 278
Maier, S. F., 340
Main, S. R., 87, 298
Maker, C. J., 429
Mallette, B., 268
Malone, T., 346
Malouf, D. B., 445
Mamlin, N., 438
Mandeville, G. K., 235
Manning, B. H., 166
Manning, M. L., 123, 316
Manset, G., 441, 443
Mantzicopoulos, P., 81
Maple, S. A., 126
Marcia, J. E., 94
Marcus, J., 316
Marks, H., 342
Marks, M. B., 203
Marks, S. U., 120
Marsh, G. E., 187
Marsh, H. W., 16, 86, 87, 95, 333
Marsh, R. S., 298
Martin, C. L., 126
Martin, G., 149, 386
Martin, J., 182
Martin, S. M., 46
Martinez, M. E., 276
Martinez-Pons, M., 334
Marx, R. W., 273, 337
Marzano, R. J., 283, 483
Maslow, A. H., 329, 330–331
Mason, D. A., 299, 300
Massaro, D. W., 175
Masten, A. S., 89
Masterson, C., 443
Mastropieri, M. A., 413, 444
Matheny, K. B., 96
Mathes, P., 235, 304
Matheson, C. C., 77
Matson, J. L., 424
Mattox, B. A., 57
Mavarech, Z. R., 303
May, M. A., 59
Mayer, R. E., 328

Mayer, G. R., 353, 391
Mayer, R. E., 5, 185, 204, 212, 239, 272, 276
Mayrowetz, D., 489
Mazur, J., 141
Means, B., 315
Medley, D. M., 233
Meece, J. L., 338, 343
Mehan, H., 123, 298
Mehlinger, H. D., 313, 315
Meichenbaum, D., 166–167
Meisels, S., 486
Meister, C., 46, 212, 231, 261
Melton, R. F., 222
Menkes, J. H., 427
Mercer, A. R., 414
Mercer, C. D., 414
Merrill, D. C., 304
Merrill, S. K., 304
Messerer, J., 445
Messick, S., 489, 503
Metsala, J. L., 415
Metz, H. H., 109
Meyer, H. A., 346
Meyer, L. A., 234, 235
Meyer, L. H., 415
Meyers, J., 317
Midgley, B. D., 145
Midgley, C., 338
Mignano, A., 368, 377
Miller, A., 81, 345
Miller, G. A., 178
Miller, G. E., 196
Miller, M. D., 334
Miller, P. D., 73
Miller, P. H., 42, 48, 165
Miller, R. B., 337
Miller, S. A., 42, 108, 338
Miller-Lachman, L., 115
Mills, C. J., 126
Milne, A. A., 36
Miracle, A., 300
Mitchell, P., 427–428
Mize, J., 89
Moats, L. C., 416
Monahan, B., 313
Montessori, M., 83
Montone, C. L., 120
Mora, J. J., 231
Moreno, R., 185
Morgan, J. V., 245
Morgan, M., 345, 466
Morris, C. C., 185
Morris, C. G., 175f
Morris, D., 305
Morris, R. C., 124
Morrison, D. R., 81, 98
Morrison, P., 89
Morrow, L. M., 74, 76
Moscovitch, M., 181
Moscow, H., 36
Moshman, D., 203
Moss, P. A., 489, 521
Mullis, I., 108, 115
Mulryan, C., 300

Munk, D. D., 466, 468, 523
Murdock, B. B., 186
Murphy, D. A., 281
Murphy, E., 272
Murphy, P. K., 262
Murphy, S. H., 126
Murray, C., 131
Murray, H., 267
Musen, G., 177
Muskin, C., 296
Mussen, P. H., 77

Nachtigal, P., 375
Nafpaktitis, M., 353
Naglieri, J. A., 126
Nagy, P., 40
Nash, W. R., 428
Nathan, R., 73
Nation, M., 112
Nations, J. K., 180
Natriello, G., 467, 468
Nattiv, A., 274
Naveh-Benjamin, M., 343
Nazos, P., 424
Neale, D. C., 268
Needels, M. C., 235, 236
Nelson, C., 298
Neuman, M. J., 79, 80
Neuman, S. B., 20, 76
Nevin, A., 442, 449
Newbern, D., 272
Newcomb, A. F., 89
Newell, A., 276
Newmann, F. M., 257, 469, 484, 489
Newstead, S. E., 59
Nicholls, J. G., 333, 338
Nichols, P. D., 501
Nichols-Whitehead, P., 46
Niemi, D., 486, 489, 502
Niemiec, R. P., 314
Nieto, S., 116, 117
Nisbett, R. E., 18
Nitsch, K. E., 240, 241
Noble, D. D., 313
Noddings, N., 126
Nolan, P., 445
Noonan, M. J., 413
Norman, G. R., 489
Norris, S. P., 284
Nucci, L., 56
Nurrenbern, S., 41
Nurss, J. R., 80, 81
Nuthall, G., 234
Nystrand, M., 296

Oakes, J., 23, 116, 296, 297, 298
O'Connor, J. E., 7
O'Connor, M. C., 256
Oden, M. H., 428
Odle, S. J., 439
O'Donnell, A. M., 212, 273, 274
O'Donnell, J., 376
Ogbu, J. U., 115, 116
Okagaki, L., 116

O'Kelly, J., 274
O'Lara, L., 398
O'Leary, K. D., 167, 391, 424
O'Leary, S. G., 150, 154, 391
Olexa, C., 296, 297
Olivier, A., 267
Ollendick, T. H., 421
Olsen, V., 124
Olson, D. R., 177
Olson, K., 315
Olthof, T., 58
Olweus, D., 89
O'Neil, J., 96
Opper, S., 30, 84
Orfield, G., 117
Ortman, P. E., 127
Osborn, A. F., 279
Osborn, J. D., 84
Osborn, P. K., 84
Osguthorpe, R. T., 305, 448
Osipow, S. H., 94
Ottenbacher, K. J., 424
Ovando, C. J., 119
Overton, W. F., 41, 198
Owen, S. L., 36
Owens, R. E., 421
Oxley, D., 298

Paas, F. G. W. C., 179
Page, J. A., 298
Page, R. N., 296
Paivio, A., 185
Pajares, F., 333, 334
Palincsar, A. S., 46, 261, 264, 264f, 265, 268, 273, 445
Pallas, A. M., 296
Palumbo, D. B., 313
Pannozzo, G. M., 378
Paolitto, D. P., 57
Papert, S., 313
Paris, S., 204
Park, O., 238
Parke, B. N., 428
Parker, H. C., 417
Parker, J. G., 96
Parker, W. D., 428
Parkhurst, J. T., 95
Parks, C. P., 398
Parrett, W. H., 316
Parten, M., 77
Patterson, M. E., 272
Patton, J. R., 433
Pau, A. S., 177
Pavan, B. N., 83, 299
Pea, R. D., 268
Pear, J., 149, 386
Pearson, P. D., 120, 208, 484, 523
Peha, J. M., 309f, 313
Peisner, E. S., 81
Peisner-Feinberg, E., 79
Pellegrini, A. D., 417
Pellicer, L. O., 318
Pendarvis, E., 428
Pepitone, E. A., 110
Pepper, F. C., 115, 116

Perfetto, G. A., 200
Perkins, D. N., 240, 241, 256, 276, 281, 282t, 315
Perney, J., 305
Perry, M., 230
Perry, R. P., 228
Persampieri, M., 209
Persell, C. H., 110, 112
Peskowitz, N. B., 204
Peters, C. W., 484
Peters, E. E., 196
Peterson, L. R., 187
Peterson, M. J., 187
Peterson, P. L., 267, 455
Petrill, S., 30
Petty, M. F., 507
Petty, R., 80
Peverly, S. T., 180
Pfiffer, L., 150
Phelan, P., 93
Phillips, G. W., 108, 108t
Phillips, J. L., 35
Phillips, N. B., 304
Phye, G. D., 238
Piaget, J., 23, 30–42, 37, 38, 52, 58, 91, 198, 256
Pierce, W. D., 19, 149, 345
Pilato, V. H., 445
Pillas, D. J., 427
Pine, J., 489, 490f
Pinnell, G. S., 19, 112, 306, 318, 320
Pintrich, P. R., 90, 335, 337
Plomin, R., 131
Plumbert, J. M., 46
Poillion, M. J., 417
Polite, K., 268
Polloway, E. A., 412t, 433
Pontecorvo, C., 259
Pool, H., 298
Popham, W. J., 469, 491, 505, 521
Porter, A. C., 219
Porter, G. L., 440
Portes, P. R., 115
Pottebaum, S. M., 234
Potter, E. F., 373
Powell, D. R., 80, 319
Powell, K., 397
Prawat, R. S., 133, 257, 281
Premack, D., 147
Presseisen, B. Z., 43, 257
Pressley, M., 19, 165, 166, 180, 196, 203, 204, 208, 212, 238, 265
Price, E. A., 238
Price, J. M., 78, 89
Pringle, B. A., 366, 367
Proctor, W. A., 415
Provenzo, E. F., 309
Pugach, M. C., 433, 448
Puma, M. J., 299, 317, 318
Purcell, J. H., 428
Purcell-Gates, V., 73
Purdie, N., 196
Puro, P., 373
Putnam, J. W., 416, 433

Qin, Z., 274
Quartz, K. H., 298
Quay, H. C., 423

Raaijmakers, J. G. W., 194
Rachford, D. L., 280
Radkin, B. D., 96
Rafoth, M. A., 205
Raison, J., 443
Ramey, C. T., 80, 81, 112, 132, 413, 445
Ramey, S. L., 80, 81, 112, 445
Ramig, P. R., 420
Ramirez-Smith, C., 319
Ramsey, I., 230
Ramsey, W., 109
Randhawa, B. S., 334
Randolph, C. H., 375
Range, L. M., 96
Raphael, T. E., 204
Rasch, B. W., 424
Ratner, C., 43
Raudenbush, S. W., 296, 342
Raugh, M. R., 196
Raywid, M. A., 298
Reading-Brown, M., 151
Redfield, D. L., 231
Rees, D. I., 296
Reese, C. M., 108, 108t
Reese, J. H., 415
Reid, C., 427
Reigeluth, C. M., 210
Reilly, A., 355
Reimer, J., 57
Reimers, T. M., 234
Reis, S. M., 428
Reiser, B. J., 304
Reiss, S., 412t
Rekrut, M. D., 305
Renninger, K. A., 344
Renshaw, P. D., 89
Renz, P., 429
Renzulli, J. S., 428
Repp, A. C., 433
Resnick, L. R., 257, 335
Rest, J. R., 58, 60
Reuman, D. A., 87, 298
Reynolds, A. J., 5, 80, 81, 112, 318
Reynolds, C. R., 177, 414
Reynolds, M. C., 443
Reynolds, R. E., 348
Rhéaume, J., 272
Rhine, S., 15
Rich, G., 73
Richards, F. A., 39
Richter, L., 448
Rickards, J. P., 204
Ridley, D. S., 209
Rieben, L., 32
Rieber, L. P., 309
Riedel, T. M., 441
Riefer, D., 209
Rifkin, J., 131
Risley, T. R., 72
Rivera, D. P., 416, 435f
Rivers, J. L., 235

Robertson, D. J., 349
Robidoux, M. P., 245
Robinson, A., 329
Robinson, D. H., 205, 278
Robinson, F. P., 206
Robinson, H. A., 206
Roblyer, M. D., 311, 314
Rock, D., 317, 318
Roderick, M., 319
Rodning, C., 78
Rodriguez, D., 337
Roeber, E., 484
Roehler, L. R., 268
Rogers, C., 272, 376
Rogoff, B., 42
Rogow, S. M., 425
Rohwer, W. D., 204
Rolheiser, C., 354
Romanoff, B., 427
Roopnarine, J. L., 77
Rose, S. R., 97
Rose, T. L., 391
Rosen, L., 150
Rosenbaum, J., 297
Rosenbaum, M. S., 167
Rosenfield, D., 345
Rosenfield, S. A., 433, 438
Rosenholtz, S. J., 87, 342
Rosenshine, B. V., 46, 212, 220, 229, 231, 232, 233, 261
Rosenthal, R., 342
Roskos, K., 76
Rosman, N. P., 427
Ross, G., 45, 47
Ross, J. A., 354
Ross, S. M., 296, 445
Rossi, R. J., 316
Rothman, R., 508
Rothman, S., 128, 505
Rothstein, R., 119
Rotter, J., 333
Rousseau, E. W., 231
Rowan, B., 296, 300
Rowe, M. B., 231, 342
Royer, J. M., 202f
Ruble, D. N., 86
Ruhl, K. L., 423
Ruiz, C. J., 280
Rumelhart, D. E., 186
Russell, R. G., 311, 314
Rutherford, R. B., 167
Ryan, R. H., 80
Ryan, R. M., 120, 345, 346
Ryba, K., 445
Rys, G. S., 60

Sabers, D. S., 7, 10, 374
Sadker, D., 125, 126, 127, 343
Sadker, M., 125, 126, 127, 128, 343
Sadoski, M., 185
Safer, D. J., 398
Sailor, W., 440
Salata, M., 127
Salganik, M. W., 368
Saling, C. B., 212

Salomon, G., 204, 240, 241, 256, 281, 315
Saltzstein, H. D., 85
Sandefur, G., 108
Sandling, P. K., 184
Sandoval, J., 268
Sanford, J. P., 220, 376, 377
Sapon-Shevin, M., 415
Sater, G. M., 415
Saunders, M., 20, 21f
Savell, J. M., 280
Savin-Williams, R. C., 95
Scardamalia, M., 204, 268, 313
Scarr, S., 79, 131
Schafer, W. E., 296, 297
Schalock, R. L., 412t, 412–413
Schaps, E., 86
Scheirer, M. A., 87
Scher, M. S., 182
Scheuermann, B., 166, 389
Schickedanz, D. I., 68
Schickedanz, J. A., 68, 70, 75
Schiff, M., 131
Schifter, D., 267
Schloss, P. J., 149, 154, 162, 167, 379, 388, 389
Schmidt, H. G., 366
Schmuck, P. A., 274
Schmuck, R. A., 9, 10, 274
Schnaiberg, L., 121
Schneider, W., 187, 202
Schofield, J. W., 117, 118, 122, 310
Schommer, M. A., 521
Schraw, G., 203
Schultz, G. F., 346
Schultz, L., 484
Schumaker, J. B., 444
Schumm, J. S., 441
Schunk, D. H., 203, 260, 261, 327, 333, 334, 337, 341
Schwartz, N. H., 208
Schwartz, S., 349
Schwartzwald, J., 110
Schweinhart, L. J., 41, 80, 319
Scofield, F., 443
Scott, C., 127
Scott-Jones, D., 97
Scruggs, T. E., 444, 448, 503
Secada, W. G., 97, 113, 121, 342, 469
Seidner, C., 348
Selby, L., 445
Self, E. A., 336
Seligman, M. E. P., 340, 341
Selman, A. P., 88
Selman, R. L., 86, 88
Seltzer, M., 19, 306
Semb, G. B., 183, 184
Semmel, M. I., 429, 433, 441, 443
Serafica, F. C., 94
Sethi, S., 149, 345
Shachar, C., 248, 274
Shaklee, B. D., 484–485, 486, 528
Shames, G. H., 420
Shanahan, T., 320
Shanker, A., 441

Sharan, S., 248, 268, 272, 273, 274
Sharan, Y., 268, 272, 273
Shavelson, R. J., 459, 464, 489, 490f
Shaw, B., 305
Shaywitz, B. A., 415, 424
Shaywitz, S. E., 415, 424
Shea, T. M., 394
Shell, D. F., 334
Shepard, L. A., 81, 319, 469, 489, 502, 508, 521
Sherrell, S., 508
Shevick, E., 460t
Shields, P. M., 319
Shiffrin, R. M., 175, 184, 194
Shimmerlik, S. M., 211
Shirey, L. L., 348
Shore,R., 79
Shriberg, L. K., 196
Shujaa, M. J., 117
Shulman, J., 274
Siccone, F., 87, 122, 123
Sidio-Hall, M. A., 212
Siegel, L. S., 415
Siegler, R. S., 42
Sikes, J., 271
Silberman, R., 355
Silbert, J., 235
Sills-Briegel, T., 489
Silver, A. A., 316, 445
Silver, E., 500
Silver, H. F., 329
Simmons, D. C., 235, 304, 305
Simmons, R. G., 95
Simon, H., 276
Simpson, C., 87, 342, 530
Singh, N. N., 433
Singh, R., 315
Skaalvik, E. M., 343
Skinner, B. F., 142, 144–145, 329, 389
Skinner, C. H., 205
Skrundz, B. M., 168
Slaughter, D. T., 109
Slavin, R. E., 16, 18, 83, 87, 97, 112, 118, 121, 122, 203, 235, 236, 268, 269, 271, 273, 274, 291, 295, 296, 297, 299, 300, 301, 303, 304, 305, 306, 307, 318, 319, 320, 321, 348, 355, 357, 367, 367f, 370, 375, 395, 398, 415, 416, 442, 442f, 445, 449, 467, 489
Sleet, D., 397
Sleeter, C. E., 118, 122, 123
Sloane, H., 151
Slusarick, A. L., 317
Smagorinsky, P., 238, 239
Small, M. Y., 182
Smelter, R. W., 424
Smetana, J. G., 57
Smith, C. R., 126
Smith, D. D., 126, 268, 412, 413, 414, 415, 416, 418, 426, 427, 435, 435f
Smith, L. J., 227, 296, 445
Smith, M. A., 149, 154, 162, 379, 388, 389
Smith, M. L., 81, 319, 445, 503

Smith, N., 127
Smith, R., 508
Smith, T. E. C., 433
Smodlaka, I., 343
Snapp, M., 271
Snarey, J. R., 56
Snell, M., 412t, 412–413
Snow, R. E., 128, 135, 310, 342
Snowman, J., 205
Snyderman, M., 128, 505
Solomon, D., 86
Solomon, R. L., 340
Soloway, E., 273
Solso, R. L., 181, 182, 187
Sosniak, L. A., 462
Soudack, A., 117
Spandel, V., 489, 502
Spear-Swerling, L., 414
Specht, L. B., 184
Spector, J. E., 47
Speece, D. L., 417
Sperling, G. A., 176, 176f
Spielberger, C., 343
Spires, H. A., 203
Spitalnik, D., 412t, 412–413
Spitalnik, R., 167
Spivak, G., 316
Spurlin, J. E., 272
Squire, L. R., 177, 181
Staffieni, A., 304–305
Stage, F. K., 126
Stahl, S. A., 73
Stake, R., 454
Stallings, J. A., 80, 230, 375
Stallings, M. A., 443
Stanhope, N., 183
Stanley, J. C., 125, 428
Stanovich, K. E., 415
Stark, J., 412t
Staudt, J., 41, 199
Staver, J. R., 41
Stebbins, L. B., 87
Stecher, B., 486
Stecker, P. M., 448, 473
Steele, D., 486
Steffe, L. P., 256
Stein, B. S., 209, 276
Stein, J. A., 97
Stein, M. K., 319
Stein, P., 374
Stein, T. A., 375
Steindam, S., 126
Stephan, C., 271
Stern, D., 273
Sternberg, R. J., 42, 128, 129, 279, 280, 281, 414, 505
Stevens, D. D., 204
Stevens, L. J., 443
Stevens, R. J., 203, 220, 229, 231, 271, 274, 442, 449
Stewart, D. A., 426
Stiggins, R. J., 489
Stigler, S. M., 190
Stiller, J., 345
Stipek, D. J., 80, 120, 337, 346

Stock, W. A., 350
Stone, J. A., 440
Stouthamer-Loeber, M., 423
Strauss, A., 23
Stringfield, S. C., 316, 319, 503
Strong, R., 329
Stuebing, K. K., 415
Stumpf, H., 125, 126
Styles, I., 90
Subotnik, R., 427
Suhor, C., 119
Sullivan, J. F., 204
Sullivan, M. W., 421, 423
Sulzby, E., 72
Sulzer-Azaroff, B., 391
Sunderman, G. L., 319
Sundius, M. J., 109
Supovitz, J. A., 491
Sutton, R. E., 315
Swanson, D. B., 489
Swanson, H. L., 7, 10, 280
Swanson, J., 310
Swanson, M. C., 123
Swartz, E., 298
Sweller, J., 179
Swiatek, M. A., 298, 428
Swift, M., 316
Swisher, K., 113
Switzky, H. N., 346
Szabo, M., 231

Tabar, S., 212
Tamura, L., 118
Tangel, D. M., 73
Tannenbaum, R., 208, 212
Tanner, C. K., 299
Tanner, D., 16
Tanner, J. M., 90
Tapsfield, P., 411
Tavris, C., 126
Taylor, C., 485, 491, 491f, 502
Taylor, D. M., 120
Taylor, L. S., 115
Taylor, R., 423
Teale, W., 72
Teddlie, C., 503
Temple, C., 73
Temple, F., 73
Temple, J. A., 80
TenBrink, T. D., 456
Tennyson, R. D., 238
Terman, L. M., 428
Terwel, J., 274
Tetreault, M. K. T., 127
Tharp, R. G., 46
Theodorou, E., 375
Thoma, S. J., 57
Thomas, E. L., 206
Thomas, J. W., 204
Thomas, M. H., 196
Thomas, S., 58
Thomas, W. P., 120
Thompson, B., 349
Thompson, G. H., 347
Thompson, L. A., 30

Thompson, M. S., 109, 112
Thompson, T., 332
Thorkildsen, T. A., 305, 338
Thorndike, E. L., 142, 143
Thorndike, R. L., 506f
Thorndike-Christ, T., 343
Thorne, R. C., Jr., 525
Thousand, J. S., 274, 443
Thurston, C., 313
Tierno, M. J., 376, 385
Till, K., 427
Timpson, W. M., 228
Tinajero, J. V., 121
Tisak, J., 58
Tisak, M. S., 58
Tishman, S., 276, 281, 282t, 283
Tittle, C. K., 469
Tkacz, S., 231
Tobias, S., 203, 343
Tobin, D. N., 228
Tobin, K. G., 231, 342
Tom, D., 343
Tomkiewicz, S., 131
Tomko, S., 313
Top, B. L., 305, 448
Topping, K., 304
Torrance, E. P., 127, 428
Torres, R. D., 119–120
Trammel, D. L., 167
Treagust, D. F., 268
Tredway, L., 230, 243
Trent, S. C., 408
Trent, W. T., 117
Trevethan, S. D., 59
Trooper, J. D., 274
Troutman, A. C., 149
Tucker, J. A., 443
Tulving, E., 181
Turiel, E., 57, 58
Turkheimer, E., 131
Turnbull, B. S., 319
Turnbull, H. R., 441
Twain, M., 46
Twohig, P. T., 280
Tyrrell, G., 110

Urdan, T. C., 338

Vagg, P., 343
Valadez, C., 120
Valencia, S. W., 484
Valsiner, J., 43
van den Eeden, P., 274
Vanderstoep, S. W., 230
Van der Veer, R., 43
Van Dyke, R., 443
van Merrienboer, J. J. G., 179
Van Patten, J., 210, 227
Van Riper, C., 420
VanSickle, R. L., 348
Van Tassel-Baska, F. S., 428
Vasquez, J. A., 115
Vasta, R., 91
Vaughn, S., 441, 444
Veeman, S., 299

Vellutino, F. R., 73, 321
Verba, M., 77
Vernez, G., 110, 112
Villa, R. A., 274, 443
Vining, E. P. G., 427
Vispoel, W. P., 332
Voelkl, K. E., 378
von Glaserfeld, E., 268
Voss, J. F., 182
Vye, N. J., 200, 265
Vygotsky, L. S., 43–47, 78, 256–257

Wadsworth, B., 30, 35f
Walberg, H. J., 314, 367, 443
Waldron, N. L., 441, 443
Walker, H. M., 423
Walker, J. E., 394
Walker, L. J., 57, 59
Wallace, D. S., 272
Wallace-Broscious, A., 94
Wallach, M. A., 279
Walsh, D. J., 81
Walsh, M. E., 268
Walter-Thomas, C. S., 448
Waltman, K. K., 524
Wanderman, A., 112
Wang, A. Y., 196
Wang, M. C., 443
Wapner, S., 134
Ward, C. R., 41
Ward, M., 399
Ward, S. L., 198
Wardle, F., 77
Warger, C. L., 433, 448
Warrick, P. D., 126
Wasik, B. A., 76, 81, 112, 304, 305, 306, 318, 320, 416
Watson, M. S., 86
Watts, G. H., 189
Weade, R., 235, 375
Wearne, D., 212, 267
Webb, N. M., 268, 273, 274
Webber, J., 166, 167, 389
Weber, E. S., 209
Weber, S., 204
Wechsler, D., 506
Wehlage, G. G., 257, 469
Weikart, D. P., 41, 79, 80, 319
Weil, M., 243
Weinberg, D. H., 108
Weiner, B., 331–332, 332t, 333, 334, 337, 340, 470
Weinert, F. E., 235
Weinstein, C. E., 209, 260, 368, 377
Weinstein, R. S., 342
Wells, A. S., 117, 296, 298
Wentzel, K. R., 89, 95, 96, 338, 378
Werry, J. S., 423
Werthamer-Larsson, L., 316
Wertsch, J. V., 45, 47
West, J., 79
Wheatley, G. H., 268
Wheelock, A., 298
Whitcomb, J. A., 274
White, A. G., 151, 152f, 392

White, B. Y., 268
White, F. R., 116
White, J., 227
White, K. J., 89
White, K. P., 135
White, K. R., 503
White, R. T., 184
Whitehurst, G. J., 73
Whitesell, N. R., 96
Wicks-Nelson, R., 34f
Widaman, K. F., 110
Wiedmer, T. L., 485
Wielkiewicz, R. M., 148, 149, 169, 328, 379
Wigfield, A. L., 90, 336, 337, 338, 343, 468, 503
Wiggins, G., 484, 487, 487f, 489, 528, 529f
Wilcox, R. T., 259
Wiley, J., 182
Wilkerson, R. M., 135
Williams, J. E., 261
Willig, A. C., 120
Wilson, G., 116, 118
Windle, M., 97
Winett, R. A., 396
Winfield, L. F., 503
Winkler, R. C., 396
Winn, W., 212

Winne, P. H., 165, 203, 241, 260
Winston-Egan, M., 421, 449f
Winters, L., 469, 486
Winzenz, D., 210, 212f
Wise, A. D., 12
Witkin, H. A., 134
Wittrock, M. C., 205, 239, 276
Wixon, K. K., 484
Wixson, K. K., 484
Wizer, D. R., 445
Wodtke, K. H., 521
Wolf, B., 413, 447f
Wolf, D., 469, 485
Wolf, M. M., 20, 21f
Wolfgang, C. H., 169, 379
Wong, H. D., 460t
Wong, K. D., 318–319
Wong, K. K., 318, 319
Wong, L. Y. S., 236
Wong-Fillmore, L., 120
Wood, D. J., 45, 47
Wood, E., 208
Woodcock, R. W., 411
Woodring, T., 99
Woodward, J., 120, 226, 310, 447
Woody, E., 89
Woolfolk, A. E., 380–381
Wooliscroft, C., 134
Woolverton, S., 108, 109

Workman, E. A., 166
Worsham, M. E., 220, 376
Worthen, B. R., 489, 502
Wozniak, P., 85
Wright, D., 268
Wright, S. C., 120
Wyckoff, W. L., 228

Yates, K., 343
Yeh, C. J., 527
Yelich, G., 317
Yeung, A. S., 87
Yinger, R., 464
Yokoi, L., 238
Young, K., 151
Youssef, M., 208
Yu, H. C., 93
Yu, S. L., 230

Zahn, G. L., 110
Zahorik, J. A., 346
Zeidner, M., 368, 503
Zellermayer, M., 204
Zigmond, N., 443
Zimmerman, B. J., 165, 166, 167, 203, 260, 261, 333, 334
Ziv, A., 228
Zohar, D., 468
Zook, K. B., 209

SUBJECT INDEX

Note: Page numbers followed by *f* indicate figures; those followed by *t* indicate tables.

Abecedarian program, 319–320, 445
Ability grouping, 294–300
  between-class, 295–298
  cross-age, 299
  dangers of, 398
  regrouping for reading and mathematics and, 299
  untracking and, 298
  within-class, 295, 299–300
Abstract material, meaning versus, 198–199
Academic achievement
  of minority-group students, 113–116, 114*t*, 115*f*
  socioeconomic status and, 107–112, 108*t*
Acceleration programs, 428
Accommodation, 31, 31*f*
Accountability, 373
  information as information for, 467
  standardized tests for, 502–503
Achievement batteries, 507
Achievement motivation, 337–343. *See also* Motivation
  anxiety and, 343
  goal orientations and, 337–340
  learned helplessness and attribution training, 340–341
  teacher expectations and, 341–343
Achievement tests, 504–505
  criterion-referenced, 469, 470*t*, 504–505, 508–509
  norm-referenced, 469, 470*t*, 504, 507–508
  principles of testing and, 473–474
Activity reinforcers, 150
ACT (American College Testing) Program, 500
Adaptation, 31*f*, 31–32
ADD (attention deficit disorder), 417
ADHD (attention deficit hyperactivity disorder), 417–419
Adolescent development, 90–100
  cognitive, 90–93, 92*t*
  physical, 90, 91*t*
  problems in, 96–99
  socioemotional, 93–96
Adult tutoring, 305–306
Advance organizers, 208
Affective objectives, 463–464
  of discussions, 242–243
African Americans, 113, 114, 115, 116–117

Aggressive behavior, 423
AIDS, during adolescence, 98–99
Alcohol abuse, during adolescence, 97
American College Testing (ACT) Program, 500
American Indians, 113, 114, 115
Analogies, 208–209
Analysis, in creative problem solving, 279–280
Antecedent stimuli, 158, 160–163
Anxiety, achievement and, 343
Applied behavior analysis, 386–397
  applications of, 392–396
  ethics of behavioral methods and, 396–397
  maintenance of misbehavior and, 386–388
  principles of, 388–392
Aptitude tests, 504, 505–507
Asian Americans, 113, 115–116
Assertive Discipline, 385
Assessment. *See also* Classroom tests; Evaluation; Test construction
  definition of, 461
  intentionality and, 492–493
  linking instructional objectives with, 461–462
  of mastery of objectives, 233–234
Assimilation, 31, 31*f*
Associative play, 77
Atkinson-Shifrin model of information processing, 175–184, 176*f*
Attention, 177
  maintaining, 228
  of peers, misbehavior to obtain, 387
  as reinforcer, 150
  of teacher, misbehavior to obtain, 386–387
Attentional phase in observational learning, 163–164
Attention deficit disorder (ADD), 417
Attention deficit hyperactivity disorder (ADHD), 417–419
Attribution theory of motivation, 331–335
Attribution training, 340–341
Authentic assessment, 469
Autism, 424
Automaticity, memory and, 191–192
Autonomous morality, 53–54
Autonomy versus doubt stage, 48–49, 49*t*

Average children, 89
Aversive stimuli, 151

Backward planning, 459, 460*t*
Bandura's theory of learning, 163–166
Baseline behavior, for applied management programs, 389
Behavioral disorders. *See* Emotional and behavioral disorders
Behavioral learning theories, 142–170
  antecedents in, 158, 160–163
  case study, 159
  consequences in, 146–152, 148*t*
  definition of, 140
  extinction in, 153–155
  maintenance and, 157–158
  of motivation, 328–329
  Pavlovian, 142, 143*f*, 144*f*
  reinforcement schedules and, 155–156, 157*t*
  shaping and, 153
  Skinnerian, 144–145
  social. *See* Social learning theories
  strengths and limitations of, 169
  of Thorndike, 143–144
Behavioral objectives. *See* Instructional objectives
Behavior content matrices, 463, 464*t*
Behavior modification, 388
  cognitive, 166–167
Between-class ability grouping, 295–298
  research on, 296–298
Bias
  gender, 127–128
  test, 522–523
Bilingual education, 74–76, 119–121
Blindness, 425–426
Bloom's taxonomy, 462–463
Brain injury, 427
Broken record strategy, for managing misbehavior, 385
Brown v. Board of Education of Topeka, 116
Buddy systems, for students with special needs, 447–448

California Achievement Tests (CATs), 497–498, 507
California Test of Mental Maturity, 507
Calling order, 231
CATs (California Achievement Tests), 497–498, 507

CBI. *See* Computer-based instruction (CBI); Conceptually Based Instruction (CBI)
CD-ROMs, 311
Centration, 34
Cerebral palsy, 426
Certificates of initial mastery, 508
CGI (Cognitively Guided Instruction), 267
Cheating, case study, 61
Child-rearing practices, socioeconomic differences in, academic achievement related to, 109
Choral responses, 231–232
Chronological age, 505
CIRC (Cooperative Integrated Reading and Composition), 271
Classical conditioning, 142, 143*f*, 144*f*
Class inclusion, 37
Classroom management, 362–402. *See also* Discipline
    case study, 379
    definition of, 365
    intentionality and, 382–383
    of misbehavior. *See* Misbehavior
    setting class rules and, 377–378
    starting out the year and, 376–377
    in student-centered classroom, 375–376
    for students with learning disabilities, 416
    time and. *See* Time
Classroom tests
    construction of. *See* Test construction
    validity and reliability of, 521–522
Coaching, of social skills, 89
Cognitive Abilities Test, 507
Cognitive ability. *See* Intelligence; Intelligence quotient (IQ)
Cognitive apprenticeship, 257
Cognitive behavior modification, 166–167
Cognitive development
    during adolescence, 90–93, 92*t*
    information-processing theories of, 42
    during middle childhood, 84
    neo-Piagetian theories of, 42
    Piaget's theory of, 30–42
    stages of, 32*t*, 32–40
    Vygotsky's theory of, 43, 45–48
Cognitive learning theories, 173–174, 175*f*
    cognitive teaching strategies and, 206–212
    definition of, 140
    information-processing. *See* Information-processing theories of learning
    metacognitive skills and, 203–204
    study strategies and, 204–206
Cognitively Guided Instruction (CGI), 267
Collaboration, for special education, 433
Communication
    clear, of teacher expectations, 349

modes of, adapting for students with special needs, 444
    of positive teacher expectations, 342–343
Communication disorders, 420–421
    alternative and augmentative devices for, 447*f*
Compensatory education, 317–319
    preschool programs, 80
    programs for, 317–318
    research on, 318–319
Completion items, 478–479
Comprehensive Test of Basic Skills, 507
Computer-based instruction (CBI), 307, 309–316
    case study, 312
    classroom applications of, 309*f*, 309–314, 310*f*
    research on, 314–316
Computer literacy, 313
Computer programming, 313
Computers
    language development and, 75–76
    for students with special needs, 445, 447, 447*f*
Concepts
    definition of, 236
    learning and teaching of, 236–238
Conceptually Based Instruction (CBI), 267
Conceptual models, 212
Concrete operational stage of development, 32*t*, 36–37, 91, 92*t*
Conditioned response, 142, 143*f*
Conditioned stimulus, 142, 143*f*
Conditioning
    classical, 142, 143*f*, 144*f*
    operant, 144–145
Conduct disorders, 423
Conflict management, 57
Connectionist models, 186–187
Consequences, 146–152, 148*t*
    immediacy of, 151–152
    judicious application of, 400
    for managing misbehavior, 385–386, 400
    punishers, 150–151
    reinforcers, 146–150
Conservation, 33–34, 34*f*
Constructivism, 32
Constructivist theories of learning, 255–268
    case study, 265
    classroom management in student-centered classrooms and, 375–376
    cooperative learning in. *See* Cooperative learning
    definition of, 256
    discovery learning in, 259–260
    historical roots of, 256–257
    Learner-Centered Psychological Principles and, 262, 263*t*
    mathematics instruction and, 267
    reading instruction and, 264*f*, 264–267

research on, 268
    scaffolding in, 257, 261–262
    science instruction and, 268
    self-regulated learning in, 260–261
    top-down processing and, 257–259, 258*f*
Construct validity, 521–522
Content
    adapting for students with special needs, 444
    case study, 237
    coverage of, 228
Content integration, 122
Content validity, 521
Context, learning in, 239–241, 240*t*
Contingencies, group, 387, 394–396
Contingent praise, 353
Continuous theory of development, 29
Contract grading, 528, 530
Control, locus of, self-efficacy and, 333–334, 334*f*
Control group, 18, 19
Controversial children, 89
Controversial topics, discussions of, 242
Conventional level of morality, 54–55, 55*t*
Cooperative Integrated Reading and Composition (CIRC), 271
Cooperative learning, 268–274
    to develop self-understanding, 272–273
    methods for, 267–272
    research on, 273–274
Cooperative play, 77
Cooperative scripting, 272
Corrective instruction, 301
Correlational studies, 20–23, 23*f*
Creative problem solving, teaching, 279–280
Criterion-referenced evaluations, 469, 470*t*, 504–505, 508–509
Critical thinking, 10, 283–285
Cross-age ability grouping, 299
Cross-age tutoring, 304
Cues, 158, 160–163
    nonverbal, for managing misbehavior, 380–381
Culture
    impact on learning and teaching, 106–107, 107*f*
    multicultural education and, 122–123
    teaching in culturally diverse schools and, 117–118
Curiosity, maintaining, 346, 348
Curriculum compacting, 428
Cut-off scores, 509

Daily report cards, 393*f*, 393–394
Databases, 311
Day-care programs, 79
Deafness, 426
Decision making, teaching as, 13–15
Deductive reasoning, 91–93, 92*t*
Deficiency needs, 330, 330*f*
Definitions, for concept teaching, 238

Delinquency, 97
  prevention of, 398–399
Demonstrations, 227–228
Derived scores, 509
Descriptive research, 23–24
Desegregation, 116–117
Development, 26–63, 66–102
  adolescent. *See* Adolescent
    development
  aspects of, 28–29
  cognitive. *See* Cognitive development
  continuous versus discontinuous,
    29
  definition of, 28
  during elementary years. *See* Middle
    childhood development
  intentional teaching and, 58–59
  issues of, 29–30
  moral. *See* Moral development
  during preschool years. *See* Early
    childhood development
Developmental assets, 99–100
Developmentally appropriate education,
  41–42
Developmentally appropriate practice,
  81–83
Diagnosis, standardized tests for, 501
Diagnostic tests, 508
Diagrams, 212
  for problem solving, 278
Differential Aptitude Test, 507
Difficult topics, discussions of, 242
Direct instruction, 220–236
  advantages and limitations of, 236
  definition of, 220
  distributed practice and review in,
    234, 234f
  independent practice in, 232–233
  intentionality and, 246–247
  learning probes in, 228–232
  lesson planning for, 221–222
  orienting students to lessons for, 222,
    223t, 224t, 225
  performance assessment and feedback
    in, 233–234
  presenting new material in,
    226–228
  research on, 235–236
  review in, 225–226
Disabilities. *See also* Learners with
    exceptionalities
  definition of, 408
Discipline, 366. *See also* Classroom man-
    agement; Misbehavior
  during middle childhood, 85
  minimizing time spent on, 370
Discontinuous theory of development,
  29
Discovery learning, in constructivist
    theories of learning, 259–260
Discrimination, 158, 160
Discussions, 242–248
  affective objectives of, 242–243
  of difficult and novel topics, 242
  small-group, 246–248

of subjective and controversial topics,
  242
whole-class, 243–244, 246
DISTAR program, 235
Distractors, in multiple-choice tests, 476
Distributed practice, 192, 234
Diversity, 104–136
  case study, 111
  cultural, 106–107, 107f
  gender, 123–128
  intellectual, 128–135
  intentionality and, 132–133
  linguistic, 119–121
  multicultural education and, 122–123
  racial and ethnic, 113–118
  socioeconomic, 107–112, 108t
Drill, computers for, 309
Dropping out, 97
Drug abuse, during adolescence, 97
Dual code theory of memory, 185

Early childhood development, 69–78
  case study, 74
  early childhood education programs
    and, 79–82, 83
  of language, 71–76
  physical, 70, 70t
  socioemotional, 76–78
Early childhood education programs,
  79–82, 83
Early intervention programs, 80–81,
  319–321
Educational psychology, definition of, 3
Education for the Handicapped Act
    (Public Law 94–142), 429–430
Effect, Law of, 143–144
Egocentrism, 35–36
Elaboration, 209
Electronic spreadsheets, 311
ELL (English language learners),
  119–121
Emergent literacy, 72, 75–76
Emotional and behavioral disorders,
  421, 423–424
  during adolescence, 96
  causes of, 421, 423
  characteristics of students with, 423
Emotional development. *See*
    Socioemotional development
Empathic distress, 60
Empowering school culture, 122–123
Enactment, learning and, 194
Engaged time, 367
  using effectively, 370–375
English as a second language (ESL),
  119–121
English language learners (ELL),
  119–121
Enrichment activities, 303
Enrichment programs, 428–429
Environment
  for creative problem solving, 279
  learning, effective. *See* Applied behav-
    ior analysis; Classroom manage-
    ment; Misbehavior; Time

Episodic memory, 181–182
Epistemic curiosity, 348
Equilibration, 31–32
Equity pedagogy, 122
ESL (English as a second language),
  119–121
Essay tests, 479–481
Ethics, of applied behavior analysis,
  396–397
Ethnic groups, definition of, 113
Ethnicity. *See also* Race and ethnicity
  definition of, 113
European Americans, 113
Evaluation, 465–492. *See also*
    Assessment; Standardized tests
  authentic, 469
  case study, 472
  criterion-referenced, 504–505,
    508–509
  definition of, 465
  formative, 302
  formative and summative, 469
  matching with goals, 469–471
  norm-referenced, 469, 470t, 504,
    507–508
  performance assessment for, 483–484,
    489–491, 490f, 491f
  portfolio assessment for, 483–487,
    485f, 528, 529f
  purposes of, 465–468
  standardized tests for, 501
  summative, 302
  test construction for. *See* Test
    construction
Examples, for concept teaching, 238
Exceptional learners. *See* Learners with
    exceptionalities
Expectancy theory, of motivation,
  335–336
Expectancy-valence model, 335–336
Expectations. *See* Teacher expectations
Experimental group, 18, 19
Experiments, 18–20
Explanations, 227
External validity, 19
Extinction, 153–155
  resistance to, 158
Extinction burst, 154
Extrinsic incentives, 344–345
Extrinsic motivation, 344–346
  enhancing, 349–352
Extrinsic reinforcers, 149

Facilitation, learning and, 190, 190t
Failure
  attributions for, 332t, 332–333
  avoiding, seeking success versus, 340
Feedback
  in creative problem solving, 280
  evaluation for, 466, 470–471
  on mastery of objectives, 233–234
  for motivation, 335, 349–352
  for students with learning disabilities,
    416
Field experiments, randomized, 19–20

Fill-in-the-blank items, 478–479
Fixed-interval schedules of reinforcement, 156, 157*t*
Fixed-ratio (FR) schedules of reinforcement, 155, 157*t*
Flashbulb memory, 181–182
Food, as reinforcer, 150
Forgetting. *See* Memory
Formal operational stage of development, 32*t*, 37–39, 38*f*, 91, 92*t*
Formative evaluations, 302, 469
FR (fixed-ratio schedules of reinforcement), 155, 157*t*
Free-recall learning, 195, 196–197
Friendships
    during adolescence, 95
    during middle childhood, 88
Full inclusion, 440–441, 443
    definition of, 440*f*
Functional fixedness, 278

Games, instructional, computers for, 310
Gender, 123–128
    cognitive differences related to, 125–126
    sex-role stereotyping and gender bias and, 126–128
General education classroom placement, for special education, 432–433
General intelligence tests, 505
Generalization, 160–163
Generativity versus self-absorption stage, 49*t*, 51
Gifted and talented students, 427–429
    characteristics of, 428
    definition of, 427–428
    education of, 428–429
Giftedness, definition of, 427–428
Goals. *See also* Instructional objectives; Learning goals
    student setting of, to maintain motivation, 348
Goal structure, incentives based on, 357–358
Good teachers, 3–10
    intentional, 7–10. *See also* Intentionality
    knowledge of subject matter, 4
    teaching skills of, 4–5
    training of, 5, 7, 8*f*
Grade-equivalent scores, 510–511, 511*f*
Grades, 523–524, 526–530. *See also* Test scores
    case study, 472
    contract grading and, 528, 530
    establishing criteria for, 524
    grading on curve and, 526–528
    as incentives, 355
    letter, assigning, 524–528
    performance grading and, 528, 529*f*
    as reinforcers, 150
    on report cards, 530
Graphs, for problem solving, 278
Gray Oral Reading Test, 498, 501
Group alerting, 373
Group comparison, evaluation for, 471

Group contingencies, 387, 394–396
Group focus
    maintaining during lessons, 373
    maintaining during seatwork, 373–374
Grouping. *See* Ability grouping
Group Investigation method, 272
Growth needs, 330, 330*f*

Handicaps. *See also* Learners with exceptionalities
    definition of, 408
Head injury, 427
Head Start program, 80
Hearing loss, 426
Helplessness, learned, 340–341
Heteronomous morality, 52–53
Hoffman's moral development theory, 60–61
Home-based reinforcement, 150, 392
Human needs, motivation and, 329–331
Hyperactivity, 424
Hypermedia, 311–312
Hypertext, 311–312
    for students with special needs, 447, 447*f*
Hypothetical conditions, cognitive development and, 39
Hypothetical-deductive reasoning, 91–93, 92*t*

IDEA 97 (Individuals with Disabilities Education Act Amendments of 1997) (Public Law 105–47), 430
IDEA (Individuals with Disabilities Education Act) (Public Law 101–476), 430–431
IDEAL problem-solving strategy, 276
Identity development, 93–94
Identity versus role confusion stage, 49*t*, 50
IEPs (Individualized Education Programs), 431, 434–435, 435*f*–437*f*, 438–439
ILE (Individual Learning Expectations), 355–357
Illustrations, 227–228
Imagery, 195, 195*f*
Immature behavior, 424
Impairments. *See also* Learners with exceptionalities
    sensory, 424–426
Incentives. *See also* Reinforcement; Reinforcers; Rewards
    based on goal structure, 357–358
    determining value of, 329
    evaluation for, 467–468, 470–471
    extrinsic, 344–345. *See also* Reinforcement; Rewards
    grades as, 355
    intrinsic, 344
    in QAIT model, 291, 293
Inclusion. *See also* Mainstreaming and inclusion
    definition of, 440*f*
    full, 440*f*, 440–441, 443

    partial, 440*f*
Income. *See also* Socioeconomic status (SES)
    differences in, academic achievement related to, 109
Incubation, in creative problem solving, 279
Independent practice, 232–233
Individualized Education Programs (IEPs), 431, 434–435, 435*f*–437*f*, 438–439
Individualized instruction, 304–316
    adult tutoring for, 305–306
    computer-based instruction for. *See* Computer-based instruction (CBI)
    intentionality and, 314–315
    peer tutoring for, 304–305
    programmed instruction for, 307
Individual Learning Expectations (ILE), 355–357
Individuals with Disabilities Education Act (IDEA) (Public Law 101–476), 430–431
Individuals with Disabilities Education Act Amendments of 1997 (IDEA 97) (Public Law 105–47), 430
Induction, in disciplining, 85
Industry versus inferiority stage, 49*t*, 50
Inert knowledge, 200
Inferred reality, 36
Information
    before discussion, 244–246
    evaluation as, 466–467
    meaningfulness of. *See* Meaningful information
    organizing, 209–212, 212*f*
    relevant, extracting in problem solving, 277
Information-processing theories of development, 42
Information-processing theories of learning, 175–187
    Atkinson-Shifrin, 175–184, 176*f*
    connectionist, 186–187
    definition of, 175
    dual code, 185
    levels-of-processing, 184–185
    long-term memory and, 180*t*, 180–184
    parallel distributed processing, 186
    sensory register and, 175–177, 176*f*
    short-term (working) memory and, 177–180
    transfer-appropriate, 185–186
Inhibition
    proactive, 189
    retroactive, 188–189
Initial-letter strategies, 197
Initiative versus guilt stage, 49*t*, 49–50
Instruction. *See also* Teaching
    adapting for mainstreaming and inclusion, 443–444
    appropriate levels of, in QAIT model, 291, 292–293
    corrective, 301
    direct. *See* Direct instruction

effective, elements of, 290–294
individualized. *See* Computer-based instruction (CBI); Individualized instruction
maintaining smoothness of, 371
programmed, 307
quality of, 291, 292
student-centered. *See* Constructivist theories of learning
using allocated time for, 367*f*, 367–370
Instructional games, computers for, 310
Instructional objectives, 454–465
  affective, 242–243, 463–464
  assessment of mastery of, 233–234
  backward planning and, 459, 460*t*
  communicating to students, 225
  linking with assessment, 461–462
  matching evaluation strategies with, 469–471
  planning courses, units, and lessons and, 459–461
  research on, 464–465
  statement of, 455, 455*t*
  stating, 221–222
  task analysis and, 457–458, 458*f*
  taxonomies of, 462–464
  writing, 456–457
Instrumental Enrichment, 280–281
Integrated learning systems, computers for, 313
Integrity versus despair stage, 49*t*, 51
Intelligence, 128–133. *See also* Cognitive development; Mental retardation
  definitions of, 128, 129*t*, 129–131, 505
  gender differences in, 125–126
  origins of, 131–133
Intelligence quotient (IQ), 128, 411, 411*f*, 505–507, 506*f*
Intelligence tests, 505–507, 506*f*
Intentionality, 7–10
  assessment and, 492–493
  behavioral learning theories and, 160–161
  cognitive theories of learning and, 210–211
  developmental theories and, 58–59, 98–99
  direct instruction and, 246–247
  diversity and, 132–133
  effective learning environments and, 382–383
  goals and, 11
  individualized instruction and, 314–315
  learners with exceptionalities and, 418–419
  motivation and, 350–351
  standardized tests and, 526–527
Interest, arousing, 346
Interference, forgetting and, 187–188
Internal validity, 19
Internet, 313–314
Interruptions, preventing, 369
Intimacy versus isolation stage, 49*t*, 50

Intrinsic incentives, 149, 344
Intrinsic motivation, 344–346, 348
  enhancing, 346, 348
Iowa Tests of Basic Skills, 507
IQ (intelligence quotient), 128, 411, 411*f*, 505–507, 506*f*

Jigsaw method, 271
Joplin Plan, 299
Judgment, suspension of, in creative problem solving, 279

Keyword method, 196
Kindergarten programs, 81
"King of Hearts method," 206–207
Knowledge
  background, importance of, 202–203
  hierarchies of, 202, 202*f*
  inert, 200
  learning how to learn and, 201
  prior, activating, 207–209
Knowledge construction, 122
Kohlberg's moral development theory, 54–60
  criticisms of, 57–60

Laboratory experiments, 19
"Lake Wobegon Effect," 510
Language development, during early childhood, 71–76
Language disorders, 420–421
Language minority, 119–121
Large muscle development, 70
Latinos, 113, 114, 115, 116, 117
Law of Effect, 143–144
Learned helplessness, 340–341
Learner-Centered Psychological Principles, 262, 263*t*
Learners with exceptionalities, 404–450
  case study, 446
  with communication disorders, 420–421
  definition of, 407–408
  with emotional and behavioral disorders, 421, 423–424
  gifted and talented, 427–429
  intentionality and, 418–419
  with learning disabilities, 413–419
  mainstreaming and inclusion of. *See* Mainstreaming and inclusion
  with mental retardation, 410–413
  with sensory, physical, and health impairments, 424–427
  special education and. *See* Special education
  types of exceptionalities and numbers of students served and, 408–410, 409*f*, 410*t*
Learning
  case study, 201
  cognitive teaching strategies and, 206–212
  of concepts, 236–238
  in context, 239–241, 240*t*
  cooperative. *See* Cooperative learning
  definition of, 140–141

discovery, 259–260
enactment and, 194
facilitation and, 190, 190*t*
free-recall, 195, 196–197
initial, transfer versus, 241
making relevant, 207–209
mastery, 301–303
mediated, in constructivist theories of learning, 257, 261–262, 262*f*
metacognitive skills and, 203–204
no-trial, 163
observational, 163–166
paired-associate, 194–196
part, 192
real-life, 236–237
rote, 199–200
self-regulated, 165–166, 260–261
serial, 195, 196–197
situated, 257
social, 256
study strategies to promote, 204–206
teaching learning-to-learn skills and, 416
transfer of, teaching for, 238–241
verbal, 194–197
vicarious, 164
Learning disabilities, 413–419
  attention deficit disorder, 417
  attention deficit hyperactivity disorder, 417–419
  characteristics of students with, 415
  identifying students with, 414–415
  teaching students with, 415–416
Learning environments
  effective. *See* Applied behavior analysis; Classroom management; Misbehavior; Time
  least restrictive, 430
Learning goals, 337
  performance goals versus, 337–338, 338*t*, 339*t*
Learning objectives. *See* Instructional objectives
Learning probes, 228–232
Learning strategies, teaching, for mainstreaming and inclusion, 444–445
Learning styles, 134–135
  aptitude-treatment interactions and, 134–135
  theories of, 134
Learning theories. *See* Behavioral learning theories; Cognitive learning theories; Constructivist theories of learning; Cooperative learning; Information-processing theories of learning; Social learning theories
Learning Together method, 271
Least restrictive environment, 430
  definition of, 440*f*
LEP (limited English proficiency), 119–121
Lesson assessments, 461
Lessons
  clarity of, 227
  emphasis in, 226–227
  engaging, 370

Lessons (continued)
    instructional objectives for, 456–461
    maintaining group focus during, 373
    pacing of, 228
    planning, 221–222, 456–461
    structure of, 226
Levels-of-processing theory, 184–185
Limited English proficiency (LEP),
    119–121
Literacy. See also Reading entries
    emergent, 72, 75–76
Loci method, 197
Locus of control, self-efficacy and,
    333–334, 334f
Logo computer language, 313
Long-term memory, 180t, 180–184
    factors enhancing, 183–184
Lorge-Thorndike Intelligence Tests, 507
Love withdrawal, in disciplining, 85

Mainstreaming. See also Mainstreaming
    and inclusion
    definition of, 430, 440f
    part-time, special-education class
      placement with, 434
Mainstreaming and inclusion, 440f,
    440–449
    adapting instruction for, 443–444
    buddy systems and peer tutoring for,
      447–448
    computers for, 445, 447, 447f
    learning strategies and metacognitive
      awareness for, 444–445
    prevention and early intervention
      and, 445
    research on, 441–443, 442f
    social integration of students with dis-
      abilities and, 448–449, 449f
    special-education teams for, 448
Maintenance of behavior, 157–158
Mapping, as study strategy, 205
Maslow's hierarchy of needs, 330,
    330f
Massed practice, 192
Mastery criterion, 301
Mastery goals. See Learning goals
Mastery grading, 530
Mastery learning, 301–303
    forms of, 301
    research on, 303
Mastery Teaching program, 235
Matching items, 479
Mathematics instruction
    constructivist theories of learning
      and, 267
    regrouping for, 299
Meaningful information, 197–203
    meaning versus abstract material and,
      198–199
    rote versus meaningful learning and,
      199–200
    schema theory and, 200–203
Means-end analysis, 276–277
Mediated learning, in constructivist
    theories of learning, 257, 261–262,
    262f

Mediation, by peers, for serious
    misbehavior, 399, 400f
Meichenbaum's theory of learning,
    166–167
Memory, 187–197
    automaticity and, 191–192
    dual code theory of, 185
    episodic, 181–182
    facilitation and, 190, 190t
    flashbulb, 181–182
    interference and, 187–188
    long-term (permanent), 180t,
      180–184
    practice and, 192, 194
    primacy and recency effects and,
      190–191
    proactive inhibition and, 189
    procedural, 182–183
    retroactive inhibition and, 188–189
    semantic, 181, 182, 183f
    short-term (working), 177–180, 179t,
      180t
    teaching strategies for, 194–197
Mental age, 505
Mental retardation, 410–413
    causes of, 411
    classifications of, 412t, 412–413
    IQ and, 411, 411f
    teaching adaptive behavioral skills
      and, 413
Mental set, establishing, 222, 223t, 224t,
    225
Metacognition, 203
Metacognitive awareness, teaching, for
    mainstreaming and inclusion,
    444–445
Metacognitive skills, learning and,
    203–204
Metropolitan Achievement Tests, 507
Metropolitan Reading Readiness Test,
    507
Middle childhood development, 83–90
    cognitive, 84
    physical, 84
    socioemotional, 84–89
Milwaukee Project, 445
Minimum competency tests, 502
Minority groups. See also Race and
    ethnicity
    definition of, 113
Misbehavior, 378–401. See also
    Discipline
    applied behavior analysis for manag-
      ing. See Applied behavior analysis
    consequences for, 385–386, 400
    identifying causes of, 397–398
    maintenance of, 386–388
    nonverbal cues for managing,
      380–381
    praising behavior incompatible with,
      381–382
    prevention of, 380, 397–401
    principle of least intervention for
      managing, 379–380, 380t
    reminders for managing, 382–383,
      385

Missouri Mathematics Program (MMP),
    235
Mnemonics, 196
Mock participation, 375
Modeling, 163–166
    of social skills, 89
Model of School Learning, 291–294,
    292f
Models, 227–228
Momentum, maintaining, 370–371
Moral development
    case study, 61
    fostering in classroom, 56–57
    Hoffman's theory of, 60–61
    Kohlberg's theory of, 54–60, 55t
    Piagetian theory of, 52–54, 53t
Moral dilemmas, 54–57, 55t
Motivation, 324–360. See also
    Achievement motivation
    attribution theory of, 331–335
    behavioral learning theory of,
      328–329
    case study, 358
    definition of, 327–328
    enhancing, 346–352
    expectancy theory of, 335–336
    extrinsic, 344–346, 349–352
    feedback for, 335
    human needs and, 329–331
    intentionality and, 350–351
    intrinsic, 344–346, 348
    rewards and, 328–329, 345–346,
      353–358
Motivational phase in observational
    learning, 164
Motor development, during early child-
    hood, 70, 70t
Multicultural education, 122–123
Multifactor aptitude batteries, 507
Multiple-choice items, 476–478
Multiple intelligences, 129t, 129–131

Native Americans, 113, 114, 115
Nature–nurture controversy, 29
NCEs (normal curve equivalents), 513f,
    513–514
Needs, motivation and, 329–331
Negative correlation, 21
Negative reinforcers, 147
Neglected children, 88–89
Neo-Piagetian theories of development,
    42
Neutral stimuli, 142
Nongraded programs, 299
Nonverbal cues, for managing misbehav-
    ior, 380–381
Normal curve, 411, 411f
Normal curve equivalents (NCEs), 513f,
    513–514
Normal distribution, 511f, 511–512
Norm-referenced evaluations, 469, 470t,
    504, 507–508
Norms, for tests, 500
Note-taking, as study strategy,
    204–205
No-trial learning, 163

Novel topics, discussions of, 242
Nursery schools, 79

Objective-referenced tests, 469, 470*t*, 504–505, 508–509
Objectives. *See* Instructional objectives
Object permanence, 33
Observational learning, 163–166
Operant conditioning, 144–145
Otis-Lennon Mental Ability Tests, 507
Outlines
    outlining as study strategy and, 205
    for problem solving, 278
Overlapping, 374–375
Overlearning, 192, 194

Pacing, of lessons, 228
Paired-associate learning, 194–196
Parallel distributed processing model, 186
Parallel play, 77
Parents
    evaluation as information to, 466–467
    involving in response to serious misbehavior, 399
Partial inclusion, definition of, 440*f*
Part learning, 192
PCMP (Problem Centered Mathematics Project), 267
Pedagogy, 4–5
Peer mediation, for serious misbehavior, 399, 400*f*
Peer relationships
    during adolescence, 95–96
    during early childhood, 76–77
    during middle childhood, 88–89
Peers, attention of, misbehavior to obtain, 387
Peer tutoring, 304–305
    for students with special needs, 447–448
Pegword method, 197
Percentile scores, 510
Perception, 176–177
Performance assessment, 483–484, 490*f*, 491*f*
    scoring rubrics for, 489–491, 528, 529*f*
Performance goals, 337
    learning goals versus, 337–338, 338*t*, 339*t*
Performance grading, 528, 529*f*
Permanent memory, 180*t*, 180–184
Perry Preschool, 445
Phonics, 73
Physical development
    during adolescence, 90, 91*t*
    during middle childhood, 84
Piagetian theories
    of cognitive development, 30–42
    of moral development, 52–54, 53*t*
Planning
    backward, 459, 460*t*
    of lessons, 221–222, 456–461
Play, 77–78

Points of view, discussions to explore, 243–244
Popular children, 88
Portfolio assessment, 483–487, 485*f*, 528, 529*f*
Positive correlation, 20–21
Positive reinforcers, 147
Postconventional level of morality, 55*t*, 55–56
Power assertion, in disciplining, 85
PQ4R method, 206
Practice
    computers for, 309
    developmentally appropriate, 81–83
    independent, 232–233
    memory and, 192, 194
Practices, enforcing, 398
Praise
    effective use of, 353–354, 354*t*
    for managing misbehavior, 381–382
    as reinforcer, 149–150
Preconventional level of morality, 54, 55*t*
Predictive validity, 521
Pregnancy, during adolescence, 97–98
Prejudice reduction, 122
Premack Principle, 147–148
Preoperational stage of development, 32*t*, 33–36, 34*f*, 35*f*
Preschoolers. *See* Early childhood development
Preschool programs, 79–82, 83
Presentation modes, to maintain motivation, 348
Presentation punishment, 151
Primacy effect, 190–191
Primary reinforcers, 146
Principles, 12
Private speech, 45
Privileges, as reinforcer, 150
Proactive facilitation, 190, 190*t*
Proactive inhibition, 189
Problem Centered Mathematics Project (PCMP), 267
Problem solving, 276–280
    creative, teaching, 279–280
    obstacles to, 278–279
    strategies for, 276–278
Problem-solving assessment, 481–483
Procedural memory, 182–183
Process–product studies, 235
Programmed instruction, 307
Prosocial behaviors, 77
Psychosocial crisis, 48
Psychosocial development, 48–51
    Eriksonian theory of, 48–51
    stages of, 48–51, 49*t*
Psychosocial theory, 48
Puberty, 90, 91*t*
Public Law 94–142, 429–430
Public Law 101–476, 430–431
Public Law 105–47, 430
Pull-out programs, 317–318
Punishers, for applied management programs, 389–392
Punishment, 150–151

QAIT model, 291–294, 292*f*
Quality of instruction, in QAIT model, 291, 292
Questions, to students during lessons, 230–232

Race and ethnicity, 113–118
    academic achievement and, 113–116, 114*t*, 115*f*
    composition of U.S. population, 113, 114*t*
    definitions of, 113
    school desegregation and, 116–117
    teaching in culturally diverse schools and, 117–118
Random assignment, 18
Randomized field experiments, 19–20
Readiness tests, 521
Readiness training, 79
Reading, learning during early childhood, 72–73
Reading instruction
    constructivist theories of learning and, 264*f*, 264–267
    regrouping for, 299
Reading Recovery program, 320
Reality, inferred, 36
Real-life learning, 236–237
Reasoning, hypothetical-deductive, 91–93, 92*t*
Recency effect, 190–191
Reciprocal teaching, 264*f*, 264–265
Recognition, as reinforcer, 150
Reflectivity, 93
Reflexes, 33
Rehearsal, 178
Reinforcement. *See also* Incentives; Reinforcers; Rewards
    of appropriate social behavior, 89
    classroom uses of, 148–149
    home-based, 150, 392
    home-based strategies for, 392
    motivation and, 328–329
    schedules of, 155–156, 157*t*, 392
Reinforcers, 146–150. *See also* Incentives; Reinforcement; Rewards
    for applied management programs, 388–389, 390*f*
Rejected children, 88
Relative grading standards, 526–528
Reliability, 522
    of tests, 474
Remembering. *See* Memory
Reminders, for managing misbehavior, 382–383, 385
Removal punishment, 151, 391–392
Report card grades, 530
Report cards, daily, 393*f*, 393–394
Reproduction phase in observational learning, 164
Research, 11–18
    application to teaching, 15
    on between-class ability grouping, 296–298
    case study, 22

Research *(continued)*
  on computer-based instruction, 314–316
  on constructivist theories of learning, 268
  on direct instruction, 235–236
  on effective programs, 15–16
  goals of, 12
  on impact of rewards on motivation, 345
  impact on educational practice, 16–18
  on instructional objectives, 464–465
  on mainstreaming and inclusion, 441–443, 442f
  on mastery learning, 303
  on peer tutoring, 304–305
  on Title I, 318–319
  value to teachers, 12–13
  on within-class ability grouping, 300
Research methods, 18–24
  correlational studies, 20–23, 23f
  descriptive, 23–24
  experiments, 18–20
Resource room placement, for special education, 433–434
Responses
  conditioned, 142, 143f
  unconditioned, 142, 143f
Retention phase in observational learning, 164
Retroactive facilitation, 190, 190t
Retroactive inhibition, 188–189
Reversibility, 34
Review, in direct instruction, 225–226
Rewards. *See also* Incentives; Reinforcement; Reinforcers
  motivation and, 328–329, 345–346
Rote learning, 199–200
Routine procedures, 369–370
Rule–example–rule pattern for explanations, 227
Rules, enforcing, 398

SAT (Scholastic Assessment Test), 500, 507
Scaffolding, 45–46
  in constructivist theories of learning, 257, 261–262, 262f
Schedules of reinforcement, 155–156
  for applied management programs, 392
Schemata, 182
Schema theory, 200–203
Schemes, 30, 31f
Scholastic Assessment Test (SAT), 500, 507
School dropouts, 97
Schools
  community factors and, 110, 112
  culturally diverse, 117–118
  desegregation of, 116–117
  enforcing attendance at, 398
  as middle-class institutions, 109–110
  standardized tests for improvement of, 501–502

Science instruction, constructivist theories of learning and, 268
Scores. *See* Grades; Test scores
Scoring rubrics, for performance assessments, 491, 491f, 528, 529f
Scripting, cooperative, 272
Seatwork, 232
  maintaining group focus during, 373–374
Secondary reinforcers, 146–147
Seizure disorders, 426–427
Self-actualization, 330–331
Self-concept, 86, 94–95
Self-contained special education, 434
Self-efficacy, locus of control and, 333–334, 334f
Self-esteem, 86–87, 94–95
Self-evaluation, of instructional effectiveness, 234, 234f
Self-praise, teaching, 354
Self-questioning strategies, 203–204
Self-regulated learners, 165–166
Self-regulated learning, in constructivist theories of learning, 260–261
Self-regulation, 43
Self-reinforcement, 149
Self-understanding, constructive methods to develop, 272–273
Semantic memory, 181, 182, 183f
Sensorimotor stage of development, 32t, 33
Sensory impairments, 424–426
Sensory registers, 175–177, 176f, 180t
Serial learning, 195, 196–197
Seriation, 36–37
SES (socioeconomic status), academic achievement and, 107–112, 108t
Sex-role stereotyping, 126–127
Shaping, 153
Short essay items, 479–481
Short-term memory, 177–180, 179t, 180t
Sign systems, 43
Simulation software, 310–311
Single-case experiments, 20, 21f
Situated learning, 257
Skinner box, 145
Small-group discussions, 246–248
Small muscle development, 70
Social comparison, 86–87
Social integration, of students with special needs, 448–449, 449f
Social learning, 256
Social learning theories, 163–167
  of Bandura, 163–166
  of Meichenbaum, 166–167
Social skill development, 89
Socioeconomic status (SES), academic achievement and, 107–112, 108t
Socioemotional development
  during adolescence, 93–96
  during early childhood, 76–78
  during middle childhood, 84–89
Software, simulation, 310–311
Solitary play, 77

Special education, 429–440, 432t
  collaboration for, 433
  definition of, 429
  general education classroom placement for, 432–433
  Individualized Education Programs for, 431, 434–435, 435f–437f, 438–439
  legislation on, 429–431
  resource room placement for, 433–434
  self-contained, 434
  special-education class placement with part-time mainstreaming for, 434
Special-education teams, for mainstreaming and inclusion, 448
Special needs students. *See* Learners with exceptionalities
Speech, private, 45
Speech disorders, 420
Spreadsheets, electronic, 311
STAD (Student Teams–Achievement Divisions), 269–271
Standard deviation, 505–506, 512f, 512–513
Standardized tests, 496–523
  case study, 520
  definition of, 499
  intentionality and, 526–527
  scores on. *See* Test scores
  teaching skills for taking, 503–504
  test bias and, 522–523
  types of, 504–509
  uses of, 500–503
  validity and reliability of, 521–522
Standard scores, 511f, 511–514
Stanford Achievement Test, 507
Stanford-Binet test, 507
Stanine scores, 513
Stem, of multiple-choice test item, 476
Stereotyping, sex-role, 126–127
Stimuli, 141
  antecedent, 158, 160–163
  aversive, 151
  conditioned, 142, 143f
  neutral, 142
  unconditioned, 142, 143f
STST (Supporting Ten-Structured Thinking), 267
Student-centered instruction. *See* Constructivist theories of learning
Students at risk, 316–321
  compensatory education programs for, 80, 317–319
  early intervention programs for, 319–321
Student Teams–Achievement Divisions (STAD), 269–271
Study strategies, 204–206
Subject area achievement tests, 508
Subjective topics, discussions of, 242
Subject matter, teachers' knowledge of, 4
Substance abuse, during adolescence, 97

Success
  attributions for, 332t, 332–333
  seeking, avoiding failure versus, 340
Success for All program, 320–321, 445
Summarizing, as study strategy, 205
Summative evaluations, 302, 469
Summer learning, socioeconomic differences in, 109
Supporting Ten-Structured Thinking (STST), 267

Table of specifications, 474–476, 475t
Talented students. See Gifted and talented students
Tangible reinforcers, 150
Task analysis, 457–458, 458f
Task goals. See Learning goals
Taxonomies, of instructional objectives, 462–464
TBI (traumatic brain injury), 427
Teacher, attention of, misbehavior to obtain, 386–387
Teacher expectations, 341–343
  clear communication to students, 349
Teacher-made tests. See Classroom tests; Test construction
Teachers
  evaluation as feedback for, 466
  good. See Good teachers
  self-evaluation of instructional effectiveness by, 234, 234f
  socioeconomic diversity of students and, 112
  value of research to, 12–13
Teaching. See also Instruction
  avoiding gender bias in, 127–128
  cognitive teaching strategies and, 206–212
  of concepts, 236–238
  of creative problem solving, 279–280
  in culturally diverse schools, 117–118
  as decision making, 13–15
  effective, research for, 15
  of good teaching, 5, 7, 8f
  reciprocal, 264f, 264–265
  of self-praise, 354
  of test-taking skills, 503–504
  of thinking skills, 280–283, 281f, 282t
  for transfer of learning, 238–241
Teaching skills, mastering, 4–5
Teaching strategies, for students with learning disabilities, 416
Teams–Games–Tournaments (TGT) method, 269
Terra Nova, interpretation of scores on, 514–515, 516f–518f, 519
Test bias, 522–523
Test construction, 472–483
  of achievement tests, 473–474
  of essay tests, 479–481

objective items and, 476–479
problem-solving items and, 481–483
table of specifications for, 474–476, 475t
Test of Cognitive Skills, 507
Tests. See also Assessment; Evaluation; Standardized tests; Test construction; Test scores
  retaking of, 530
  teaching of skills for taking, 503–504
Test scores
  cut-off, 509
  derived, 509
  grade-equivalent, 510–511, 511f
  interpretation of, 514–515, 516f–518f, 519
  percentile, 510
  standard, 511f, 511–514
  stanine, 513
  z-scores, 513
TGT (Teams–Games–Tournaments) method, 269
Theories, 12. See also specific theories
Thinking, critical, 10, 283–285
Thinking skills, 280–285
  in creative problem solving, 280
  for critical thinking, 283–285
  teaching, 280–283, 281f, 282t
Time, 366–375
  allocated for instruction, using, 367f, 367–370
  engaged, using effectively, 370–375
  lost, preventing, 368–369
  on-task, excessive, 375
  in QAIT model, 291, 293–294
Time on-task, 367, 375
Time out, 151, 391–392
Title I programs, 317–319
  research on, 318–319
Top-down processing, in constructivist theories of learning, 257–259, 258f
Tracks, 294. See also Ability grouping
Transfer-appropriate processing theory, 185–186
Transfer of learning, teaching for, 238–241
Transitions, managing, 372
Transivity, 37
Traumatic brain injury (TBI), 427
Treatments, 18
True–false items, 478
Trust versus mistrust stage, 48, 49t
Tutorial programs, computers for, 309–310, 310f
Tutoring
  adult, 305–306
  cross-age, 304

effective use of, 306–307
  peer, 304–305, 447–448

Unconditioned response, 142, 143f
Unconditioned stimulus, 142, 143f
Uncorrelated variables, 21
Underlining, as study strategy, 205
Understanding, checks for, 228–230
Units, planning instructional objectives for, 460–461
Untracking, 298

Validity, 19, 521–522
Variable-interval schedules of reinforcement, 156, 157t
Variable-ratio (VR) schedules of reinforcement, 155–156, 157t
Variables, 18
  correlated, 20–23
  uncorrelated, 21
Verbal learning, 194–197
Vicarious learning, 164
Videodiscs, 312–313
  for students with special needs, 447, 447f
Vision loss, 425–426
VR (variable-ratio) schedules of reinforcement, 155–156, 157t
Vygotskian theory of cognitive development, 43, 45–48
  applications in teaching, 46f, 46–47

Wait time, for student responses to questions, 231
Wechsler Intelligence Scale for Children-Revised (WISC-R), 507
Whites, 113
Whole-class discussions, 243–244, 246
Whole language, 73
WISC-R (Wechsler Intelligence Scale for Children-Revised), 507
Withdrawn behavior, 424
Within-class ability grouping, 295, 299–300
  research on, 300
Withitness, 374
Word processing programs, 311
  for students with special needs, 447f
Working memory, 177–180, 179t, 180t
World Wide Web, 313
Writing, learning during early childhood, 73–74
Written assignments, adapting for students with special needs, 443–444

Zone of proximal development, 45, 256–257
z-scores, 513

LINCOLN CHRISTIAN COLLEGE AND SEMINARY

Text Credits: pp. 130–131: Excerpt from *Multiple Intelligences in the the Classroom* by Thomas Armstrong, pp. 177–178, 1994, Alexandria, VA: Association for Supervision and Curriculum Development. Copyright © 1994 ASCD. Reprinted by permission. All rights reserved.

pp. 371, 373–375: Excerpts from *Discipline and Group Management in Classrooms* by Jacob S. Kounin, pp. 80, 84, 98–99, 104, copyright © 1970 by Holt, Rinehart and Winston, reprinted by permission of the publisher.

Photo Credits: **Will Hart:** pp. xxviii, 9, 10, 26, 66, 93, 97, 104, 120, 131, 134, 147, 154, 172, 185, 191, 207, 216, 248, 252, 259, 261, 277, 288, 305, 314, 324, 333, 353, 362, 399, 404, 425, 452, 480, 496; **Will Faller:** pp. 5, 60, 71, 78, 125, 188, 331, 368, 381, 391, 417, 430, 486, 509, 515, 522; **Elizabeth Crews:** p. 34; **Robert Harbison:** 45, 239, 490; **Stephen Marks:** p. 50; **Brian Smith:** pp. 138, 162, 229, 297, 320, 344, 441, 459; **Eliot Elisofon/Life Magazine:** p. 145.